북한 도시 읽기　NORTH KOREAN ATLAS

1 Edition Published May 2014
1 Edition 2nd printing Published April 2018

Edited by Dongwoo Yim · Rafael Luna
Graphics & Research Team Chong Ho Park, You Jin Lim, Green Kim
Contributing Authors
Rainer Dormels, Gianluca Spezza, David Matthew, Seoyoung Kim,
Sangjun Lee, Eunhee Cho, Dongsei Kim, Yunha Lee, Doojin Hwang,
Calvin Chua, Chongho Park, Yehre Suh, Sunggoo Yang,
Hye-Young Chung, Sejin Rubella Jo & Soobin Lee, Jungon Kim
Proofreader Christopher Guignon

Compiler DAMDI Publishing Co.
Publisher Kyeongwon Suh
Editor Yeonkyeong Choo, Jinyoun Na
Design Juneki Jeong, Cheolju Lee
Publishing office DAMDI Publishing Co.
Address 2F, 79 Samgaksan-ro, Gangbuk-gu, Seoul, 01036, Korea
Tel +82-2-900-0652
Fax +82-2-900-0657
E-mail damdi_book@naver.com
Homepage www.damdi.co.kr
facebook www.facebook.com/DAMDIPublishing

초판 발행 2014년 5월 23일
1판 2쇄 2018년 4월 20일

엮은이 임동우 · 라파엘 루나
그래픽 & 리서치 박종호, 임유진, 김그린
참여작가
라이너 도멜스, 지안루카 스페짜, 데이비트 매튜, 김서영,
이상준, 조은희, 김동세, 이윤하, 황두진,
캘빈 챠, 박종호, 서예례, 양성구,
정혜영, 조세진 & 이수빈, 김중곤
교정 크리스토퍼 기뇽

펴낸곳 도서출판 담디
펴낸이 서경원
편집 추연경, 나진연
디자인 정준기, 이철주
주소 서울특별시 강북구 삼각산로 79, 2층
전화 +82-2-900-0652
팩스 +82-2-900-0657
이메일 damdi_book@naver.com
홈페이지 www.damdi.co.kr
페이스북 www.facebook.com/DAMDIPublishing

지은이와 출판사의 허락 없이 책 내용 및 사진, 드로잉 등의 무단 복제와 전재를 금합니다.

All rights are reserved. No part of this Publication may be reproduced, transmitted
or stored in a retrieval system, photocopying, in any form or by any means,
without permission in writing from Dongwoo Yim · Rafael Luna, 17 Others and DAMDI.

정가 45,000원
ⓒ 2014 Dongwoo Yim · Rafael Luna, 17 Others and DAMDI
Printed in Korea
ISBN 978-89-6801-026-2　93340

이 도서의 국립중앙도서관 출판시도서목록(CIP)은 서지정보유통지원시스템 홈페이지(http://seoji.nl.go.kr)와
국가자료공동목록시스템(http://www.nl.go.kr/kolisnet)에서 이용하실 수 있습니다.(CIP제어번호: CIP2014015182)

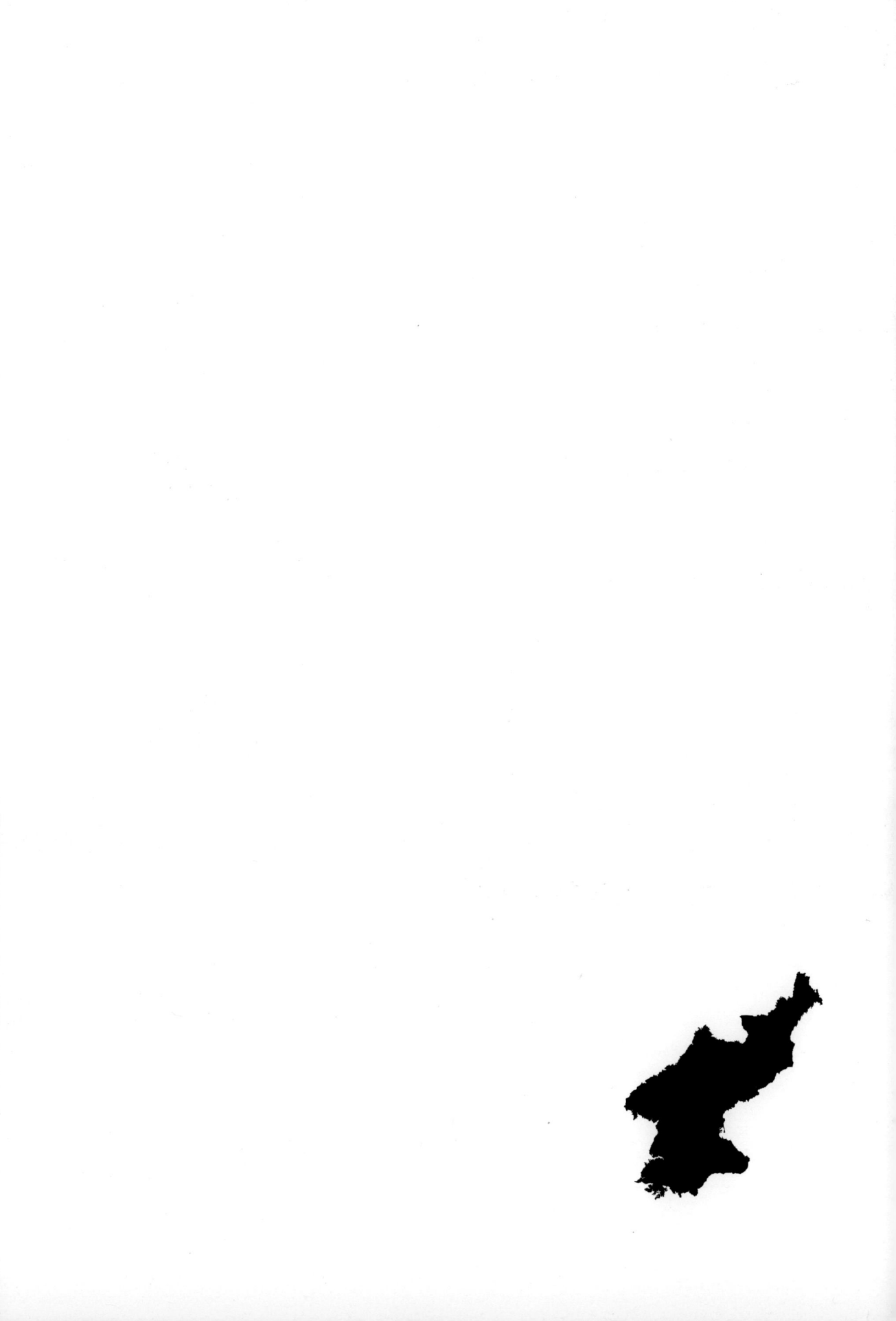

CONTENTS

00. NORTH KOREAN ATLAS _Dongwoo Yim   7

01. INTRODUCTORY ESSAYS   19
    Rainer Dormels
    Gianluca Spezza
    David Matthew
    Seoyoung Kim

02. BACKGROUND DATA   69
    Sangjun Lee
    Eunhee Cho
    Dongsei Kim
    02-1 Fact Sheets
    02-2 Geographical Facts
    02-3 Infrastructural Facts
    02-4 Industrial Geography

03. NORTH KOREAN CITIES   191
    Dongwoo Yim
    03-1 Tables of North Korean Cities
    03-2 8 Major North Korean Cities
    03-3 19 Supporting North Korean Cities

04. NORTH KOREAN TYPOLOGIES   383
    Yunha Lee
    Dongwoo Yim

05. FUTURE SCENARIOS   481
    Doojin Hwang
    Calvin Chua
    Rafael Luna
    Dongwoo Yim
    Chong Ho Park
    Yehre Suh
    Dongsei Kim
    Sungoo Yang
    Hye-Young Chung
    Sejin Rubella Jo & Soobin Lee
    Jungon Kim
    PRAUD (Dongwoo Yim+Rafael Luna)

INDEX   644

00 NORTH KOREAN ATLAS

NORTH KOREAN ATLAS

Dongwoo Yim

—

Dongwoo Yim is the author and editor of
the "North Korean Atlas," and the principal
and co-founder of architecture and research firm
PRAUD, based in Boston and Seoul. He received
a Master of Architecture in Urban Design
at Graduate School of Design (GSD),
Harvard University, and bachelor's degree
in Seoul National University.
Dongwoo is a faculty member of Rhode Island School
of Design since 2011 where he teaches seminar
and design studios. His research interest focuses on
integral urbanism and architectural typologies
that catalyze urban transformation
in various urban scales. He is the award winner
of Architectural League Prize 2013, and is the author
of "Pyongyang, and Pyongyang After"
by Hyohyung Publishing and "
I Want to be METROPOLITAN" by ORO Editions.
His works have been published
and exhibited world wide including Museum
of Modern Art New York,
International Architecture Biennale Rotterdam,
Venice Biennale and Design Center Seoul,
and he has lectured at Harvard University,
Freie Universität Berlin, Dartmouth College,
Seoul National University and Youngchoo Forum
amongst others.

Understanding North Korea

It seems that recently there has been an increasing interest in North Korea, or maybe more precisely, the way how we see North Korea has been changing. Until recently, most of the discussions related to North Korea were focused on topics such as reunification, and tasks in a post reunification period. However, after cooling down the politically hot topics, there are more lenses to see North Korea from, as ways to understand its society. Perhaps, one of the major reasons for this phenomenon is that the new generation with a more relaxed and open mind. A generation that did not experience the war, has become the major player of our society. Whatever the real reason is, the fact is that there are more variety of lenses to look from to understand North Korean society, and it means that nowadays there are more opportunities to get information about North Korea than before when things were limited and monotone.

Of course, there are discrepancies between fields. Fields such as political science, economic, and social science have had more exchange with North Korea and more government support. These fields have had quite solid and deep researches on North Korea with a fair amount of information. On the other hand, fields that get information more from direct visits and physical contacts than from documents, such as architecture and urban studies, have had less researches on North Korea as a result of having shallower information. However, as more people have a chance to visit North Korea, and as technologies like Google earth are being developed, there are increasing numbers of researches in architecture and urban field.

This phenomenon is also related to the signs of

change of North Korea. Even though we still hear many news about threats from North Korea, it is not rare to see news about how the country is being in a transition. One of the clearest example is the Masikryung Ski Resort targeting foreign tourists, which is a very unique case to have in the North Korea. Also, it is very encouraging to hear news about North Korea accepting investment from Japan on Nampo and allowing more cities to visit for foreigners. Of course, as Gianluca Spezza, research director of NK News, points out in his essay in the first chapter, expectations of neighboring countries on North Korea always have been there whenever there was a small sign of change in North Korea. He suggests to be more active to change the country from institutional level rather than waiting passively for the country to be changed. No matter if the change will last long or not, the North Korea's change is attracting the public attention, and lets us see North Korea as a country for transition and investment. Perhaps, these changes on both sides, North Korea and neighboring countries, are a reflaction to our desire to understand North Korean society.

Understanding a city

Understanding a city is a key to understanding a society. A city reflects economy, culture, and sometimes politics of the society, and the built environment is the physical result of it. In many cases, the built environment of a city contains lots of stories of the society. For instance, the Colosseum in Rome tells us so many stories of the Roman society, social structure, sports culture, and architectural tectonics of the period. Parisian boulevards represents social demand for a modern city as well as political need to show the power of the empire. Also, New York's grid system tells us the story of a society that pursues high efficiency, original Central Park shows us a conflict between classes, and tenement housing in Lower East Side tells us the story of immigrants in New York.

Therefore, reading the built environment of a city is a process of proving documents of politics, socio-economic, and culture of the society through physical form of the city. In other words, we can have clearer clues on understanding a society by reading the city, and thus, it is worth to read a city not because it has its own meaning but because it gives us different views for understanding its society.

As Rainer Dormels, professor at the Vienna University, pointed out, we conceive a city as an image. Venice has an image of being a historic city, while Hong Kong has an image of a sleepless city. Dormels argues that these images are very subjective, yet based on objective facts. The reason why we have an image of a historic city for Venice is because of the fact that it has kept most of its original urban fabric throughout the years, and the image of Hong Kong as a sleepless city is because it really has many night markets with neon signs that never turns off. Then, what kind of images do we have for North Korean cities? Are those images based on objective facts? Or are they based on framed information?

In fact, it is reasonable to have a subjective image on a city, and we can guess many objective facts through those subjective images. However, if the image making is based on rather limited source of information than various information including direct experiences, perhaps it is better to postpone to solidify the image of a city. This is why it is important to collect objective data of North Korean cities as much as possible at this moment before we have concrete preconceptions on those cities.

North Korean Atlas

It is not reasonable to say that we can understand a city through limited data. Knowing the fact that a city has one million people in population does not give us much information. However, when we start to collect data along with the initial data, it starts to mean something. If we know the area of the city, we know the density of it, and therefore, we can imagine, at least, the quality of living environment of the city. Also, if we know the numbers of institutions and factories, we can guess whether the city is an industrial town or an educational town. There are many images, rather objective images that can be made from cross-referencing important data of a city.

One of the purposes of the "North Korean Atlas" is to lay as much raw data as possible on the table. To understand North Korean cities, background data such as geography, population, infrastructure and industry data are collected as part of the first initial data. North Korea has 24 million people in about 120,000 km2 land area. Its urban population is around 60% of the population, which is a high rate considering its GDP per capita is $1,200. The urban population rate is very much related to the economic growth, just as both Korea and Japan have more than 90% of urban population. In China, the urban population recently went over 50% of the total. It is questionable to see North Korea, which has 1/5 the GDP per capita of China, has a higher urban population rate. This is because in the North Korean city structure, some rural areas are also included to the administrative boundary of urban area, which means the actual "urban" population will be less than what the statistic says. It can also be seen from the statistics of residential types in North Korea where detached single family house or attached multi-family housing type are more dominant with 80% of housing type than high-rise apartment type. There are about thirty cities in North Korea, and interestingly enough, they are very well distributed around the whole territory, excluding the mountain areas. The ten biggest cities of North Korea, in terms of population, including Pyongyang, Hamhung and Chungjin, only hold 30% of the nation's population. It means that the rest of the 70% of the population is distributed to the other twenty cities and rural areas, and it also means that North Korea does not have a high dependency rate to cities. It can also be seen from the industrial geography. In North Korean industry, aside from mining or port industries that are tied to geographical locations, many industries that have less dependency to geography, such as shoe manufacturing and textile industry, are very well distributed around the whole country. This allows for North Korea to have a more balanced development throughout mid or smaller size cities than biased development concentrated in few big cities.

The second important data of "North Korean Atlas" is, as its name tells, information of North Korean cities. Not only the basic information of a city, such as population, density and area, but also information like urbanization rate, rural rate, and geographical features. This gives us an opportunity to cross-reference for further and deeper information. For instance, the third biggest city, Chongjin, has around 92% of an urban population rate, 610,000 out of total population of 660,000. It means that unless there are new migration from outside of the city, there are less chances for Chongjin to have more urbanization, which mostly happens from having rural population migrate into an urbanized area. Whereas Kaesung has only 62% of an urban population rate, which means it has another 38% of rural population that can be potential urban population along with urbanization of the city. These are simple facts that we can assume from the current census. However, we can get more interesting pictures if we cross-reference them with geographical data. Though its 92% of urban population rate, Chongjin has only 4% of its land as urbanized area, and still has 54% of the administrative Chongjin area, excluding mountain areas, as farmland. In other words, Chongjin can grow horizontally more than ten times without changing the current density of the city. Of course, as we saw from above, the growth cannot be done only through its own population, and perhaps Chongjin needs more immigrants from outside of the city for the future growth. On the other hand, for Kaesung, which seemed to have a better chance of urbanizing its population distribution, only has 50% additional room. This means compromising its farmland over urban area, for future growth. If more radical urbanization happens in Kaesung, it has to be more vertical.

Also, a series of urban analysis in different scales, from urban structure, urban space to residential block type, shows differences and similarities of the built environment between North Korean cities. As many other socialist cities, the symbolic urban space is a very important part of the urban structure in North Korean cities; they sometimes had to squeeze into an existing urban fabric, and sometimes planned on tabula-rasa condition. As mentioned above, the size of each North Korean city is not so big, and therefore, these few symbolic urban spaces become very important marks of a city, and they are formed together with cultural facilities, monuments, or sports stadiums.

Lastly, "North Korean Atlas" collects architectural typologies of North Korea. It helps us understand the society through more daily life conditions that can be read from the different building types. Most of the times, we tend to understand architecture as "design", or in a worse case, as "real estate." If we look at an architecture deeply, however, we can read a cultural difference between societies. For instance, most of the elementary school type in South Korea has a main building oriented south with a playground, which, in fact, does not look much different from a military training field, in front. It has fences at the periphery that shows the territory, and single loaded class rooms that has the best layout to see the blackboard in front. These simple facts tell us some cultural properties of Korea. First, we can read Korean traditional architectural culture that tend to have southern front (south orientation) with natural ventilation (single loaded) and clear boundary between the lot and street (fence). From the layout of the playground and classroom, we can also read Korean educational culture that is rather indoctrinated than independent. Also, from reading how a school is injected into an apartment block and how people of the neighborhood use it, we can see what social-cultural meaning the school typology has in our society. We can read and infer more things from architectural typologies than we think.

Architectural typologies of North Korea give us the same chance. Single building type restaurants with a huge dining area gives us a clue to infer their dine-out culture. By looking at industrial facilities that are introduced in architectural magazines, which barely are introduced in our magazines, we can see how much weight they are putting onto the meaning of people's labor work and production facilities. Also, when we see what we think "consuming facilities," such as public bath, swimming pools, or hair salons, are called "service facilities," we can imagine in what perspective they provide those facilities to people. Sometimes a North Korean typology shows similarity to a South Korean one. For instance, the general layout of an apartment unit that has living room at the center with rooms surrounded and outdoor balcony can be easily found in a South Korean apartment unit. At the same time, in North Korea, it replaces the living room to a fore-room in certain regions, which shows its effort to develop various typologies based on regional characters.

In conclusion, reading a city as an architect is rather how to select and digest existing information than mining new information. This is similar to the nature of the architecture that has to digest various factors of society, such as culture, politics, economy and technology, and to be the end result of them. In general, architects draw result with subjective manner during this procedure. However, in "North Korean Atlas," it tried to lay out objective data on the table as much as possible along with essays of professionals in North Korea studies in various perspectives.

As mentioned before, the work of "North Korean Atlas" is just one of the initial steps to catalyze further and deeper researches to happen. Already there are many architects who show interests in North Korean cities. In the last chapter of the book, several architects are picturing future scenarios of North Korea regarding its change. It is similar to the atmosphere when numbers of thesis projects had addressed Dongdaemun Stadium or Sewoon Complex a decade ago. Even though, many critical discussions are still on going regarding to two projects, it is true that architects' visions and voices catalyzed the changes. Although all architectural/urban scenarios on future North Korea are "fiction" for now, I believe that we can take a role in the near future for the change of North Korea as we build up a relationship with North Korean professionals.

Lastly, I would like to note that the foundation of this publication is based on many previous studies made by professionals from various institutions, such as Ministry of Unification, Korea Research Institute for Human Settlement, Korea Institute for Industrial Economics & Trade among others. Among their profound researches, in the "North Korean Atlas," data and information that are more relevant to cities and built environments are collected for mappings and diagrams. Compiling various information was possible not only thanks to the contributors of this publication but also to the professionals who have achieved solid results in North Korea studies. One of the most frequent questions that I personally get is where do I get information of North Korea the most. As a matter of fact, there is a few country that had more study on North Korea than South Korea, and many of those studies are deep enough to use in architecture and urban studies. I believe the "North Korean Atlas" makes it easier for the future urban researches on North Korea. I would also like to thank especially to Mr. Chang Gul Cho who gave so much supports and advices on constructing new perspective on future of cities.

NORTH KOREAN ATLAS

임동우

—

임동우는 "북한 도시 읽기"의 저자이며 서울과
보스턴을 기반으로 하는 설계사무소 PRAUD의 대표이다.
그는 하버드 대학교에서 도시설계 건축학 석사,
서울대학교에서 학사를 취득하였다.
현재 그는 로드아일랜드 스쿨 오브 디자인(RISD)에
출강하고 있으며, 그의 연구는 다양한 스케일에서 도시 변화를
촉진시키는 점진적인 도시 변화와 건축 유형에 초점을 맞추고 있다.
그는 뉴욕 건축가 연맹 주관 2013년 뉴욕 젊은 건축가상 수상이며,
"평양, 그리고 평양 이후"(효형 출판)
"I Want to be METROPOLITAN"(ORO Editions)의 저자이다.
그의 작업은 뉴욕 모마, 로테르담 건축 비엔날레,
서울 디자인 센터, 베니스 비엔날레 등에 전시된 바 있으며,
하버드 대학교, 베를린 자유 대학, 다트머스 대학, 서울대학교,
영추포럼 등에서 강연한 바 있다.

북한에 대한 이해

최근 북한에 대한 관심은 전과 다르게 많이 높아진 것 같다. 아니, 정확히 이야기하자면 관심도가 높아졌다기보다는 관심의 방향이 달라졌다고 하는 것이 맞을 것이다. 예전에는 대부분의 논의가 어떻게 하면 남북한의 통일을 이룰 수 있는가, 혹은 통일 후 과제는 무엇인가 등의 질문에 초점이 맞추어져 있었다고 하면, 최근에는 오히려 그 뜨거운 감자와 같은 논의에서 한 발짝 벗어나, 북한 사회를 '이해'하려고 하는 시각에서 접근하는 경우가 많아진 것 같다. 이는 전쟁과 분단을 겪은 세대가 아니라 그 이후 세대가 사회의 주요 분야를 이끌게 되면서 자연스럽게 '차가운 머리'로 접근하게 된 것이 가장 큰 이유인 것 같다. 하지만 그 이유야 어쨌건, 이 현상을 뒤집어 놓고 생각해본다고 하면, 그 동안 북한에 대한 이해를 돕기 위한 자료나 출판물이 매우 한정되어있었고, 최근 들어서야 이들을 접할 기회가 늘어났다는 것을 의미한다.

물론 이는 분야마다 정도의 차이가 있을 것이다. 그 동안 많은 교류와 정부의 지원이 있었던 정치, 경제, 사회 분야에서는 북한에 대한 연구도 상당히 깊은 수준으로 축적되어있고 그 자료들도 상당히 방대한 것으로 안다. 반면, 문헌조사와 데이터보다는 실진적인 방문과 물리적인 접촉을 통해야 효과적인 연구를 수행할 수 있는 건축이나 도시 분야는 다른 분야에 비해 연구의 깊이나 지속성이 미진했던 것이 사실이다. 하지만 더욱 많은 사람이 북한을 직접 다녀오고 구글 어스처럼 북한의 구축환경에 대한 자료가 많이 쌓이면서, 건축과 도시 분야에서도 북한에 대한 연구가 점점 활기를 띠고 있는 점은 매우 고무적이다.

이는 현재 북한에서 일어나고 있는 변화의 조짐과도 맞물리는 부분이다. 여전히 북한의 도발과 위협에 관한 뉴스를 많이 접하고는 있지만, 동시에 북한의 변화에 관한 뉴스도 쉽게 접할 수 있게 된 것 같다. 대표적인 예가, 북한이 최근 가장 많은 노력을 기울인 원산의 마식령 스키 리조트이다. 이 리조트의 특징은 북한이 처음부터 외국인 관광객을 유치하겠다고 하는 목표를 갖고 개발했다는 점이다. 이 외에도, 남포지역에 일본의 투자를 유치한다든지 외국인 관광을 더 많은 도시에 허용을 한다든지 하는 점은 상당히 고무적인 변화다. 물론 NK news의 디렉터 Gianluca Spezza의 지적처럼 북한의 변화에 대한 주변국의 기대는 항상 있었다. 오히려 그는 북한의 변화에 차갑

게 판단하면서 북한이 완전히 변하기만을 소극적으로 기다리기보다 적극적인 자세로 북한을 변화시키기 위해서 어떠한 일을 진행해 나아가야 하는지를 제안하고 있다. 하지만 중요한 것은 북한의 이러한 변화가 대중의 관심을 이끌어내고 있다는 것이다. 이제는 북한을 단순한 호기심의 대상이나 적대적인 시각으로 보는 것이 아니라, 변화의 대상 혹은 투자의 대상 등으로 보는 시각이 많아지고 있다. 아마도 이러한 쌍방의 변화가 북한과 북한 사회를 알고 싶어하는 욕구로서 드러나는 것이 아닌가 한다.

도시를 이해한다는 것의 중요성

한 사회를 이해하는데 있어서 도시를 이해한다는 것은 매우 핵심적인 작업이다. 그 사회의 경제와 문화, 그리고 때로는 정치 시스템이 고스란히 투영된 것이 도시이고 도시의 구축환경으로 나타나기 때문이다. 때로는 그 도시의 구축 환경 하나가 수많은 이야기를 담고 있는 경우도 많다. 예를 들어, 로마 시대의 콜로세움은 당시 사회의 계급 구조, 놀이 및 스포츠 문화, 재료를 활용하고 구축하는 기술 등 많은 이야기를 전달해주고 있다. 또한, 블루바드로 대표되는 파리의 도시 구조는 도시를 근대화하기 위한 시대적 요구와 동시에 제국의 힘을 보여주기 위한 정치적 필요 등 복합적인 내용을 함축하고 있다. 뉴욕의 격자시스템은 뉴욕의 효율성을 추구하는 사회를, 센트럴 파크는 빈부의 사회적 갈등을 보여주며, 테너먼트 하우징같은 건축 유형은 뉴욕 이주민의 역사를 보여주고 있다.

따라서 도시의 구축환경을 읽어내는 작업은 당시의 정치, 경제, 사회 등의 문헌자료 등을 물리적인 실체로 증명하는 작업과도 같은 것이다. 이를 거꾸로 이야기하면, 도시를 읽는다는 것은 그 사회의 정치, 경제, 사회 등을 좀 더 명확히 이해하는 데 단서를 제공해 줄 수 있다는 것이다. 결국, 도시를 읽는다는 것은 그것 자체의 의미보다는 한 사회를 포괄적으로 이해하는 방법으로서의 가치가 있는 것이다. 비엔나 대학의 Rainer Dormels가 지적하고 있듯이 도시는 이미지로 먼저 다가온다. 베니스는 역사 속의 도시가 그대로 있는 이미지이고, 홍콩은 평생 잠들지 않는 이미지를 갖고 있다. 그에 따르면, 이러한 이미지는 매우 주관적이지만 대부분 객관적인 사실을 근거로 하고 있다. 즉 베니스가 역사 속의 도시의 이미지를 갖는 이유는 실제로 도시 대부분의 조직들이 원형 그대로 유지되고 있기 때문이며, 잠들지 않는 홍콩의 이미지는 많은 야시장과 꺼지지 않는 네온사인 때문일 것이다. 그렇다면 과연 우리는 북한 도시에 대해 어떠한 이미지를 갖고 있는가. 그리고 그 이미지들은 과연 객관적인 자료를 바탕으로 형성된 것인가 아니면 필터링 된 피상적인 정보를 바탕으로 형성된 것인가.

결국, 우리가 어떤 도시에 대해서 주관적인 이미지를 갖는 것은 당연하고, 그 주관적 이미지를 통해서 많은 객관적 사실을 유추해 낼 수 있는 것이 사실이다. 하지만 그 주관적 이미지가 직접 경험이나 다양한 정보를 바탕으로 하는 것이 아니라, 매우 제한적인 정보 소스를 바탕으로 한다고 하면, 그 이미지 형성을 보류하는 것이 좋을 것이다. 이러한 관점에서 보면 지금 시점에 북한의 도시들을 데이터와 물리적인 공간 등 객관적인 자료를 통해 보는 것이 중요한 것이다.

North Korean Atlas

물론 하나의 도시를 데이터만 갖고 이해한다는 것은 모순이다. 어떤 도시의 인구가 백만이라고 하는 자료는 우리에게 그다지 많은 사실을 알려주지는 않는다. 하지만 여러 데이터가 종합되었을 때 조금씩 의미를 갖게 된다. 이 도시의 면적을 알게 되면 밀도를 통해 이 도시가 쾌적한 환경의 도시일지 각박한 환경의 도시일지 상상해볼 수 있다. 또한, 인구 백만 도시의 학교나 공장의 수를 알면 이 도시가 교육의 도시인지 공업도시인지도 예측해볼 수 있다. 이 외에도 수많은 도시에 대한 이미지들이 주요한 데이터들의 크로스 레퍼런스를 통해 형성될 수 있다.

North Korean Atlas에서 구축하고자 하는 것은 크로스 레퍼런스가 가능한 raw data의 나열이다. 북한의 도시를 이해하기 위해서 첫째로 북한 도시의 지형과 관련된 정보, 인구와 관련된 정보, 인프라와 산업 관련된 정보 등을 배경 정보로서 축적한다. 북한은 약 2천4백만의 인구가 120,000㎢ 정도 되는 국토에 비교적 고르게 분포하고 있다. 도시에 거주하는 인구는 약 60%로서 북한의 1인당 국민소득 $1,200을 고려해보면 상당히 높은 수치이다. 왜냐하면, 약 90%의 도시인구 비율을 가진 일본이나 한국처럼 대부분 국가에서는 도시인구비율과 경제성장이 비례하기 때문이다. 중국의 경우 역시 30%에 불과하던 도시 인구비율이 최근 들어 50%를 넘어섰다. 중국의 1/5 정도의 1인당 국민소득을 지닌 북한이 더 높은 도시인구 비율을 가진 것이 의문스러울 수 있다. 하지만 이는 북한의 행정구역상 도시에는 일부 농촌 지역이 포함되기 때문에 실제 도시인구보다 행정구역상의 도시인구 비율이 높은 것으로 볼 수 있다. 이는 여전히 북한의 대표적인 주거유형이 고층 아파트와 같은 도시형 주거형식이 아니라 주택이나 연립주택과 같은 형식이 약 80%를 차지하고 있음을 알 수 있다. 북한 전체적으로 보면 약 서른 개의 도시가 분포하고 있다고 볼 수 있는데, 이 역시 매우 고르게 분포하고 있다. 평양을 비롯하여 함흥, 청진 등 북한의 10대 도시의 인구를 다 합하여도 북한 전체 인구의 30%밖에 불과하다. 즉, 기타 스무 개 도시와 농촌 지역에 나머지 지역의 70%에 해당하는 인구가 분포하고 있다는 사실은 북한의 도시 편중현상이 심하지 않다는 것을 의미한다. 이는 산업의 분포를 통해서도 알 수 있다. 북한의 산업분포를 보면, 광업이나 항만과 같이 특정 지리적 요건과 결부되지 않아도 되는 산업들, 즉 신발제조업이나 섬유산업과 같은 산업들은 대체로 국토 전반에 걸쳐 분포하고 있다. 이러한 특징이 북한으로 하여금 대도시보다는 중소도시 위주로 국토를 균형 있게 발전시킬 수 있도록 하는 요소이다.

두 번째로 축적하는 정보는 도시 별 정보이다. 도시의 가장 기본적인 정보인 인구와 밀도, 면적 등뿐만 아니라 도시화 비율, 농촌 비율, 산악지형의 비율 등의 정보는 크로스 레퍼런스를 통해 새로운 정보를 많이 제공해준다. 예를 들어, 청진의 경우 총인구 66만 명 중 약 92%인 61만 명이 도시화된 영역에 거주하고 있다. 다시 말하면 청진은 외부에서의 인구 유입이 배제된다고 하면 농촌의 인구가 도시로 유입됨으로써 발생하는 도시화가 더 이루어지기 힘들 것으로 보인다. 반면, 개성의 경우는 이 비율이 62%에 불과하다. 즉, 아직도 개성시에는 약 38%의 농촌인구가 도시화를 진행하게 할 가능 인구로 추정할 수 있다. 반면 이들 정보를 도시화 면적 비율 정보와 함께 보면 재미난 예측이 가능해진다. 즉, 청진의 경우에는 92%의 인구가 도시화된 지역에 살고 있지만, 이 면적은 전체 청진 면적의 약 4% 불과하다. 청진은 도시화가 쉽지 않은 산악지형을 제외하고도 농촌 지역 면적이 약 54%가량 되며, 이는 다시 말하면 청진은 현재 면적의 10배가 넘는 수평확장이 가능하다는 이야기가 된다. 물론 앞서 본 것처럼, 이는 청진시 인구로는 불가능하며 외부에서의 인구가 유입되어야 가능할 것으로 보인다. 반면, 인구분포 면에서 청진보다 도시화 가능성이 더 커 보였던 개성의 경우에는 도시화가 확대될 수 있는 면적이 현재 도시화 면적의 약 1.5배에 불과하다. 이는 개성의 도시화가 이루어진다고 하면 수평적인 확장보다는 수직적으로 밀도가 높아지는 방향으로 일어날 가능성이 크다는 점을 보여준다.

이외에도 도시조직 - 도시공간 - 주거단지유형으로 이어지는 도시분석은 각 도시의 구축공간의 특징과 유사성을 보여준다. 북한의 도시는 여타 사회주의 도시와 마찬가지로 상징적인 광장의 형성이 무엇보다 중요했는데, 때에 따라서 기존의 조직 위에 얹혀져야 하는 경우도 있고, 또 다른 경우에는 백지 위에 구성이 되고 이를 중심으로 도시의 다른 조직이 형성되어 나간 경우도 있다. 앞서 언급하였듯이, 북한의 각 도시는 대체로 규모가 크지 않기 때문에, 주요한 몇 개의 도로조직과 상징광장들이 그 도시 구성의 기준점이 된다. 이때에 상징적인 문화시설, 기념비 혹은 운동경기장 등 공공적인 시설을 통하여 주요 공간을 구성하는 경우가 많다.

마지막으로는 건축유형에 관한 정보를 축적한다. 건축의 유형은 조금 더 북한 주민의 삶에 밀착된 구축환경으로서 그들의 삶의 방식을 이해하는 데에 도움을 줄 것이다. 우리는 흔히 건축을 하나의 디자인으로만 보거나 아니면 반대로 단순히 부동산으로 받아들이는 경우가 있다. 하지만 하나의 건축을 자세히 들여다보면 문화적인 차이를 엿볼 수 있는 가능성도 많다. 예를 들어, 우리나라의 초등학교 시설을 생각해보면, 교사 동이 남쪽을 향해 배치되며 그 앞에는 군대의 연병장과 별반 다르지 않아 보이는 운동장과 사열대가 있으며 그 주변으로 학교의 영역을 알리는 담장이 있으며, 편복도에 형성된 각 교실은 모듈화되어있고 책상은 칠판을 보기 가장 편한 레이아웃으로 배치되어있다. 이는 몇 가지 사실을 우리에게 전달해준다. 우선 남향과 자연채광 및 자연환기를 중요시하며 담장으로 영역을 구분하던 우리나라의 전통적인 건축문화를 엿볼 수 있다. 한편, 교실의 레이아웃이나 운동장의 배치를 통해 상명하복식 (혹은 주입식)의 교육문화도 엿볼 수 있다. 또 더 넓게는 흔히 아파트 단지 내에 배치되는 이들 시설을 이용하는 주민들을 보면서, 이 건축유형이 어떠한 사회-문화적인 의미를 가지는지 읽어낼 수도 있다. 이처럼 건축유형을 살펴보면 생각보다 많은 점을 이해할 수 있게 된다.

북한의 건축유형 역시 마찬가지이다. 대규모의 식당이 단독 건축유형으로 존재하는 사실을 보고, 우리는 그들의 외식문화를 단편적으로나마 읽어볼 수 있다. 또한 우리나라에는 잘 소개되지도 않는 공장건축유형이 자주 등장하는 것을 보면서, 북한 사회가 생산시설, 혹은 노동의 장소에 얼마만큼의 무게를 두고 있는지 예측해볼 수 있다. 그리고 우리가 흔히 소비시설 혹은 근린생활시설이라고 부르는 공중목욕탕, 수영장, 미장원 등의 시설을 봉사시설로 명칭하는 것을 보면, 북한이 이러한 시설을 어떠한 관점에서 대중에게 공급을 하는지 알 수 있다. 또한, 주택의 평면을 보면 거실이 중심이 되어 방들을 구성하고 있는 형태나 발코니의 구성은 우리나라의 주택 평면에서도 볼 수 있는 요소들로서, 두 나라의 주거문화의 유사성도 발견할 수 있는 부분이다. 그 반면, 도시와는 전혀 다른 농촌형 주택유형을 개발 보급하고 때로는 거실이 제외되고 전실로 대체되는 평면을 보면서, 우리와는 다르게 지역의 특성에 따라 각기 다른 유형을 개발하고자 하는 노력을 엿볼 수도 있다.

결론적으로, 건축가로서 도시를 이해한다는 것은 새로운 정보를 생성해낸다기 보다는, 현재 있는 정보들을 어떻게 취사선택하여 소화할 것인지에 대한 문제일 것이다. 이것은 마치 도시, 혹은 건축이 사회의 여러 요소, 즉 문화, 정치, 경제, 기술 등의 요소들을 취합한 결과물로서 세상에 구축되는 것과도 같은 논리일 것이다. 일반적으로는 건축가는 이 과정에서 본인의 주관적인 가치관을 통해 결과물을 생산해 낸다. 하지만 이 책의 경우에서는 최대한 주관적인 가치관을 배제하고자 했다.

앞서 언급했듯이 이 책의 작업은 앞으로 북한, 특히 북한의 도시와 건축을 연구하고 이해하는데 있어서 끼우고 가야 할 하나의 단추에 불과하다. 이미 많은 건축가도 북한의 도시에 많은 관심을 보이고 있다. 마지막 장의 미래 시나리오에서도 볼 수 있듯이, 다양한 건축가들이 이미 북한의 변화 시나리오를 써 나아가고 있다. 이는 마치 십수 년 전에 건축과의 단골 졸업작품 주제가 세운상가와 동대문 운동장이었던 것처럼 고무적인 일이다. 동대문 운동장은 결과가 생소한 방향으로 나아갔고, 세운상가는 아직 논의가 진행 중이지만, 건축계의 지속적인 목소리가 변화를 이끌어 낼 수 있다. 아직 북한에 대한 시나리오는 상상 속의 시나리오에 불과하지만, 가까운 미래에는 우리나라의 건축가들이 북한과의 적극적인 교류를 통하여 그들의 변화에 일조 하는 시기가 오지 않을까 조심스럽게 예측해본다.

마지막으로, 이 책은 통일부, 국토연구원, 산업경제연구원 등 다양한 분야 전문가분들의 선행 연구와 도시 건축 분야 선배님들의 연구를 바탕으로 구성되었음을 밝힌다. North Korean Atlas에서는 그 동안의 선행 연구와 업적을 바탕으로, 북한의 도시와 그 구축환경을 이해할 수 있는 데에 도움이 될 만한 것들을 선별하여 시각 자료화하였다. 이는 이 책에 글과 건축 프로젝트로 직접 참여해주신 여러 국내외 전문가들뿐만 아니라, 이미 각 분야에서 북한에 대한 상당한 자료를 구축해 놓으신 전문가들의 연구 성과가 있었기에 가능한 작업이었다. 필자가 북한에 관한 연구를 하면 주변으로부터 늘 받는 질문이 자료는 미국이 많은지 한국이 많은지, 또 그 자료의 양과 깊이는 충분한지 등이다. 이 질문들에 대해서 한 가지 확실한 것은 우리나라에서만큼 북한에 대한 연구가 깊이 진행된 곳은 전 세계에 없다는 것이며, 그 자료의 깊이 역시 도시와 건축분야에서 충분히 활용할 수 있는 깊이로 진행된 부분이 분명히 있다는 것이다. 이 책은 앞으로의 북한 도시 연구의 자료에 대한 접근을 조금은 용이하게 해주지 않을까 기대한다. 그리고 이 출판과 북한 도시의 미래뿐만 아니라, 도시를 바라보는 새로운 비전과 시각을 갖는 데 많은 도움과 조언을 아끼지 않으신 한샘의 조창걸 회장님께 특별한 감사의 말씀을 전한다.

01 INTRODUCTORY ESSAYS

FACTORS OF THE IMAGE OF NORTH KOREAN CITIES[1]

Rainer Dormels

—

Rainer Dormels is Professor in Korean Studies at Vienna University, Austria. He teaches courses on the politics and regional studies of Korea as well as on Korean society and linguistics. He obtained MA in Korean linguistics from Seoul National University, PhD in Korean Studies from Hamburg University and completed his Habilitation in Korean Studies at the Ruhr University Bochum. He is author of several books and articles about linguistics, politics and geography of Korea.

It is widely known that field research on North Korean cities on site are practically impossible and special care is required for the analysis of North Korean sources. Nevertheless, those who are dealing with North Korean cities are trying to get a picture of them either consciously or unconsciously. Objective and subjective, emotionally colored, perceptions, ideas, attitudes, feelings, experiences and knowledge are connected to each city.

Merged into one whole, this is referred to by Johannsen as an image (quoted after Walter / Jessen 2006, 104). This image may have a person as the reference object, and may be shared by a group of people. An image is thus entirely subjective, but it refers to an objectively ascertainable reference object. The image of North Korean cities will especially be different for North Koreans and South Koreans, and again different for non-Koreans. Of course, only those who have engaged in some form with North Korean cities will be able to develop ideas and attitudes. The author of this essay has carried out statistical studies of the structural analysis of North Korean cities and industries, which will be published shortly. As an aid to the interpretation of these data, as well as to loosen the planned publication, I have dealt with other facts about the cities of North Korea, and in doing so, I have built an image of each city. I am of course aware that this image is based on incomplete and largely unconfirmed statements. As you might expect, most information on North Korean cities come from North Korean or South Korean sources and are, in many cases, highly politically colored. The formation of an image of a city depends on city image factors. Although the selection of these city image factors is subjective, the factors themselves have an objectively verifiable background. City image factors, which must be considered here in the case of North Korea's cities are:

- historical factors,
- natural spatial factors,
- functional spatial factors,
- socio-spatial factors.

Historical factors

In considering the North Korean system of cities, their imperialist character during, and just before, the period of Japanese rule springs immediately to mind. This period led numerous North Korean cities to the coasts. On the other hand, new cities arose after the DPRK emerged, whereby non-coastal locations were deliberately promoted. Of course, even before the influence of the Japanese on the Korean urban system, there were administrative centers in the north of the peninsula. North Korean cities can genetically be divided roughly into the above outlined groups.

Pyongyang has the image of one of the oldest cities in Korea. Vast is the literature on the history of the city, which began as the capital of the Koguryo Dynasty (37 BC -. 668) in 427. Pyongyang is the undisputed historical center of the northern half of Korea. An administrative center in the north-east of the country is and was Hamhung. Hamhung is considered the hometown of the Josŏn royal family (National Museum of Korea). Yi Sŏng-gye (1335-1408), who founded the Josŏn dynasty (1392-1910) as King Taejo (r. 1392-1398), spent his youth here and returned to this place was after he lost his office to his second son. The Hamhung Royal Villa, which Yi Sŏng-gye built at the place of his ancestral home after leaving the kingly office, was—after repeatedly being the victim of destruction—rebuilt and restored, and is now a tourist attraction for Hamhung visitors. Kaesong was the capital of Koryŏ in 919 and is referred to as a "city of geomancy." There is hardly a Korean city with more theses about its geomancy than Kaesong (see Yoon, Hong-key 2006). Haeju is also a city that has held important administrative functions for a long time. When Korea was divided into 12 Mok in 983, Haeju-mok was one of them. Other cities did not have as strong an administrative function as the above mentioned, but because the border of Korea is temporarily in the south of the present border, there were in the northern part of the country numerous military camps. Thus, the Koryŏ Kangdong Six (East of the River) Garrison Settlements were established in the reign of the Koryŏ king Kwangjong (r. 949-975) and one of these was Kuju, the current Kusŏng. The fortification of Kuju was built in 994 (Yi Ki-baek, 1984, 125), which still exists today in parts.

The modern urban development of Korea came about after the opening of Korean ports and the construction of railway lines. From 1876 to 1910, eleven ports were opened, including six that are in the area that is now part of the DPRK. Jinnampho (today, Nampho), Wonsan, Songjin (today, Kimchaek) and Chongjin were, before the First Sino-Japanese War (1894 – 1895), small fishing villages. The seaport of Taedonggang Basin, Jinnampho, was established as a military supply base for the Japanese Army (Hŏ U-gŭng 2007, 102) in the First Sino-Japanese War. Jinnampho was approved in 1897 by the Korean government as an international treaty port. The Japanese built about

6km north of the Korean village of Wonsan a concession area in a reed field, which was drained after the opening of the port. Port Wonsan was built in this part of the city and it remains the center of the city to this day. The port was opened on May 1st, 1880 for trade with Japan, and on March 11th, 1883 for international trade.

Economically, the Japanese did not benefit very much from Wonsan and the concession area, but from early on Wonsan played an important role strategically for the military. The path for a Russian advance was blocked by the construction of the Japanese concession area, and Wonsan was a base for the landing of Japanese troops during the Sino-Japanese War with Pusan and Inchŏn (Yun Jŏng-sŏp 1987, 114). As a half-way station between Vladivostok and Wonsan, Songjin (today, Kimchaek) was an important strategic point at the end of the 19th century. After the opening of the port in 1899, not only Japanese came to Songjin, other foreigners came as well, and Christianity developed here rapidly.

Chongjin was initially not more than a small fishing village, which developed leaning on a foothill within Puryong county. As this was a landing place for Japanese military equipment in the Russo-Japanese War (1904-1905), the village had about 100 houses. Chongjin opened in 1908 for international trade. During the Russo-Japanese War (1904-1905), the Japanese promoted, as a supply route for its military, a 90km long railway line from Chongjin to Hoeryong, which was completed in 1906. Chongjin was an important port for the removal of timber and other products from the forest areas of North Korea and Manchuria, and for the transport of fishery products. The Japanese had also built a large military base in 1907 in neighboring Ranam (now part of Chongjin). In this regard, the port of Chongjin had become indispensable as a place of landing for any goods (Yun Jong-sŏp, 1987, 127-128).

Sinuiju is located about 40km above the mouth of the Yalu, virtually in the northwestern-most corner of the province, directly next to the Chinese border. Sinuiju was developed in connection with the construction of a railway line by Japanese authorities, which was meant to thwart Korea from the southeast to the northwest. The most difficult problem was the question of the site for the construction of the bridge, which would cross the Yalu. A possible location was near the river crossing at the settlement, Uiju, where there was an island in the Yalu River, and delegations between the Korean and the Chinese Empire had crossed the Yalu River. Another suggestion had been to build the bridge over the Yalu River about 20 km downstream, where it meets on the Manchurian side the circle Antung (today, Dandong). In April, 1905, the latter proposal prevailed. On the flooded meadows of the Yalu River, a new city was built as planned; it was called "New Uiju," or Sinuiju.

After the devastation of the Korean War, the cities were partially rebuilt with the assistance of the states of real socialism. The most cited example in this context is the support of the German Democratic Republic in the rebuilding of the city of Hamhung. A main road in Hamhung was even named for a while after GDR President Wilhelm Pieck.

An example of a North Korean city foundation is the construction of the satellite town Phyongsong, north of the capital Pyongyang. After the Academy of Sciences found its place here, many other research institutes were built under its auspices. The main research and teaching facilities were in a special science district in the south of Phyongsong. In 1995, however, a separation of the southern part of Phyongsong followed, and this formed the Unjng-kujok of Pyongyang. Sunchŏn, which was agricultural before the Korean War is one of the areas that has been newly established as an industrial area. The change of Sunchon began immediately after the war. Based on rich limestone and coal reserves, large and small mines and factories were created. In particular, the production of cement has great significance for the city.

Sunchon is a transportation hub; the establishment of the United Vinalon Complex started during the 1980s, which attracted many people from all around, and Sunchon got the face of a large city (Chosun Ilbo 25.9.1995). Vinalon has not, for some time, produced in Sunchon. Huichon, (in case of hyphenation Hui-chon) originally an important market gateway to the plateau of Jagang Province, trading in agricultural products of the surrounding areas and high-plains region, developed rapidly after the Korean War as an important location of mechanical engineering. The largest machine tool factory and the largest precision machinery factory in North Korea are situated in this city.

Anju is an interesting city because its urbanized regions can be divided into three regions that can be assigned to each of the three groups described above genetically. The center of Anju goes back to an old fortified city. The meaning of Anju is also demonstrated by the province name, Phyonan, which is composed of the initial syllables of the cities Pyongyang and Anju. Under Japanese rule the railway line from Seoul to Sinuiju was built, which ran west of the city Anju. The "New Anju," Sinanju, developed on this railway line. The construction of the Namhŭng Youth Chemical Complex in 1974, one of the most important petrochemical factories in the western region of North Korea, in the north of the present city of Anju, marked the birth of the industrial region Anju. Around the chemical plant, new districts have been created, so that the former center of Anju, Sinanju and Namhŭng represent three city regions with different roots, which is typical for the genesis of North Korean cities.

Natural spatial factors

Nature-spatial factors for the image of cities mostly play a big role only if they are located by oceans or large rivers. Examples of port cities are mentioned in consideration of historical factors. With respect to a desired future of North Korea, South Korean journalists are already dreaming of a "miracle on the Taedong River." This river flows not only through the capital, Pyongyang, but also through Sunchon and Tokchon and is located south of the port city Nampho. Sinanju and Anju developed south of the Chŏngchŏn River, the Namhŭng area of Anju in a place north of the river. The center of northeast Korea, Hamhung, was developed where a crossing of the lower reaches of the Sŏngchŏng river was possible. To the Korean border-rivers in the north are Sinuiju, Manpho and Hyesan (at the Yalu) and Hoeryong (at the Tumen). Man-made bodies of water can also shape the image of a city. By the damming the upper reaches of the Taedong river, the Kŭmsŏng Lake in Tokchon was created in 1982, which extends east of the city center. The cityscape of Sariwon is characterized by a canal that was built after the Korean War and allowed the water of the Chaeryŏng river to flow to the city center. In 1988, a passenger-cargo wharf was built and thus the shipping route to Songnim, Nampho and Pyongyang was opened (Chosun Ilbo 12.2.1996).

Functional spatial factors

One must bear in mind, of course, that, in regards to the functional spatial factors for the image of a city, a city performs several functions. Image formative functions are mainly administrative, as the capital of a state or province, and also economic functions. It can be ascertained that many cities in North Korea specialize in a certain branch of industry. There are often one or a few factories that dominate the economic structure of a city, or are elevated to a kind of city symbol (e.g.: Huichon - Huichon Ryonha General Machinery Plant, Manpho - Aprokgang Tire Factory, Kusong - 3. April" General Factory (Kusong Machine Tool Factory), Jongju - Phyongbuk Smeltery, Anju - Namhŭng Youth Chemical Complex, Tokchon - Sŭngri Motor Complex, Songrim - Hwanghae Iron and Steel Complex, Haeju - Haeju Smeltery, Chongjin - Kim Chaek Iron and Steel Complex, Munchon - Munphyong Smeltery).

Three factories are representative for Hamhung, which are all located in Hungnam in the south of the city: the Hungnam Fertilizer Complex, the February 8 Vinalon Complex and the Ryongsong Machine Complex. The situation is similar in Nampho. The three representative factories here are located in the northeastern districts of Chollima, Taean and Kangso: Chollima Steel Complex (Chollima), Taean Heavy Machine Complex (Taean) und Kumsong Tractor Plant (Kangso). The arms industry is assumed to be in many places in North Korea. The image of the most important location for the defense industry is the intramontane city of Kanggye, the capital of Jagang Province. Sinpho is regarded as the city of the submarine industry. It is also considered a center of the fishing industry in the country, while Jongju has the reputation of an agricultural town. Products that have a direct connection to a city are the ginseng of Kaesong and Inphung spirits from Kanggye.

Of particular interest are the cities that show a special development potential after the Korean reunification, or in which current projects of economic cooperation with South Korea and other countries are realized. The city in which the most successful cooperation between North Korea and South Korea has occurred is undoubtedly Kaesong; the economic zone in Kaesong does not insignificantly contribute to the city's image as a place of cooperation between the two Korean cities. But there were also initiatives earlier by North Korea to attract investors from outside. There was much attention in December 1991 when North Korea declared Rajin and Sonbong (today, Rason) to free trade zones, but the expectations in terms of investments from abroad were not met. In recent years, however, the logistically favorable location has gained more interest of the Chinese and Russians; thus, investment in port facilities and other infrastructure projects in Rason and Chongjin have been made.

In September 2002, North Korea surprised the world by trying to establish a capitalist "Sinuiju

Special Administrative Region." It was meant to develop into an international center for finance, trade, IT industry, modern science, entertainment and tourism; but the project failed. Since 2009 it is again under consideration, whereby the DPRK gives two islands, Wihwa and Hwanggumphyong, to China to develop these areas as free trade zones. Because of its location near the capital Pyongyang Nampho, the city has always been a preferred location in North Korea for foreign or South Korean investors. The South Korean company Daewoo already in 1995, signed a joint venture agreement with the North Korean company Samchŏlli. The so founded National Industry Corporation operated as a textile plant in Nampho and exported shirts, bags and jackets to Japan and Europe (Yoon Suh-kyung 2000). Another spectacular project is the joint venture in North Korea of South Korean Pyonghwa engine, which is in the possession of the Unification Church. A contract was signed in 2000, and in 2002 a factory was completed in Nampho. In the framework of restructuring after the death of the church founder in 2012, the management of Pyonghwa engine was transferred to North Korea (Kim Sŏkjong 2013). Wonsan was already known as a tourist destination for foreigners and nationals. It was the point of departure for many for trips to the lake and Sijung in the Kumgang-san. A new "general blueprint for the Wonsan District" proposes to make Wonsan more attractive, where summer bathing in Songdowon-beach and winter skiing on Masikryong ski resort will come into existence.

Social spatial factors

An example of socio-spatial factors for the image of a city are prominent people who come from that city or live in it. In the case of North Korea, it is understood that certain political slogans are consciously localized within certain enterprises or cities. Many of the socio-spatial factors can therefore be traced back to the product of deliberate measures of the North Korean state. Even the naming of administrative regional units is often made out of political considerations. Looking only to the names of the cities, we can note two cases where personal names were used for the name of a geographical unit.

The first case is from well prior to the existence of the DPRK and refers to the old name of the city Songrim. In the 1880s, the Japanese military were looking for a landing site for the preparation of the Sino-Japanese War; it was set up in today's Songrim, which was then named after the responsible commander Watanabe Kenji: Kenji-Port (Kenjiho, in Korean Kyŏmipho). Because the last name, Watanabe, was too common, the first name was used. The second case of a personal name as a city name occurred during the Korean War. By renaming the port city on the East Sea Songjin in Kimchaek, General Kim Chaek (1903-1951), who was born in Songjin and a comrade of Kim Il Sung during the Japanese occupation in Manchuria, was honored.

Jongju was already deemed before 1945 as the home of pioneers. Born in Jongju or having attended the Christian Osan-school are (among others) the writers Yi Kwang-su (1892-1950) and Kim So-wol (1902-1934), the painter Yi Jungsŏp (1916-1956), and the philosopher Ham Sŏk-hŏn (1901-1989), also known as the "Korean Ghandi." The founder, Moon Sun Myung (1920-2012), of the Unification Church ("Moonies") was born in Jongju. Moon has subsequently traveled to the DPRK and was received in 1991 by Kim Il Sung. Moon was able to acquire two large hotels in the capital Pyongjang. Furthermore, the government allowed the Unification Church to establish a place of pilgrimage for the Moon sect in Jongju.

In North Korean sources, Hoeryong City, the birthplace and childhood home of Kim Jong Suk (1917-1949), the mother of Kim Jong Il, , is given particular importance. Sariwon, on the other hand, especially honors the Kang Kŏn (1918-1950), who fell in the Korean War. A statue was erected in 1968 in honor of him, and one of the main streets of the city, as well as a University, were named after him. To mobilize the population, several slogans carry names of cities or are locatable within cities. Mobilisation measures of the 1950 and 1960s like the Taean Work System, the Chongsanri-methode and the Chŏllima-movement have names of places that belong to the city Nampho (district Taean, Kangso and Chollima). In 1998, "the Kanggye spirit" was summoned, in 2001 the torch of Ranam was upheld and worked from 2009 with the "Huichon Speed." It is reported from the mountain province, Jagang, and the big industrial cities on the east coast, that they suffered particularly badly during the time of famine in the 1990s. The cities Kanggye and Huichon (both Jagang Province) were therefore chosen intentionally for the North Korean propaganda slogans. As the heavy industry was affected by the changes as a result of the collapse of Comecon, Hamhung was designated the "capital of the unemployed" (Bauer 2005). To the image of Chongjin as a city, which was particularly hard hit by the famine, the novel "Nothing to Envy: Real Lives in North Korea" by Barbara Demick has probably contributed too.

Depending on the viewer, the city image factors for the imagination, ideas, attitudes and feelings towards the individual North Korean cities will be different. Fortunately, there are in recent years an increasing number of scientific papers dealing with North Korean cities[2]. These studies will help to increase and consolidate the objective basis for our ideas and attitudes on North Korean cities.

북한 도시에 관한 이미지들

라이너 도멜스

―

라이너 도멜스 박사는 현재 오스트리아 빈 대학 한국학 교수이다. 이곳에서 그는 한국의 정치와 지역학 및 한국 사회와 언어학을 가르치고 있다. 도멜스 교수는 서울대학교에서 국어학으로 석사학위를 취득하였고, 함부르크 대학에서 한국학으로 박사학위를 받았으며 보훔 루르대학에서 교수자격논문을 마쳤다. 그는 한국의 언어, 정치, 지형 등과 관련한 저서와 기사의 저자이기도 하다.

북한 도시에 관한 현지 연구는 현실적으로 불가능하고 북한 자료의 분석은 조심스럽게 살펴볼 필요가 있다. 그럼에도 불구하고, 북한 도시를 다루는 사람들은 그들이 의식적이든 아니든 북한도시에 대해 무엇인가를 상상한다. 객관적이고도 주관적이며, 감정에 치우친 관점이나 생각들, 태도, 감정, 경험 그리고 지식이 각각의 도시와 연결되어있다.

이들이 하나로 합쳐지는 것을 요한센은 '이미지'라고 칭하였다. (Walter/Jessen 2006, 104 인용) 이 이미지는 개인에 의한 것일 수도 있지만, 때로는 한 무리의 사람들에 의하여 공유되기도 한다. 따라서 한 이미지는 매우 주관적이면서도, 이는 객관적으로 확인할 수 없는 참조 객체를 의미하기도 한다. 그러나 북한의 도시를 바라보는 이미지는 북한 사람과 한국 사람, 그리고 외국인들에게 모두 다르게 나타날 것이다. 물론 북한의 도시와 어떠한 방식으로든 관계를 맺고 있는 사람들만이 북한 도시에 대한 아이디어나 사고방식을 가질 수 있을 것이다. 필자는 북한 도시와 산업의 구조 분석에 관한 분석적인 연구를 진행했고, 이는 곧 출간될 예정이다. 필자는 통계를 설명하기 위해 또한 책의 흥미를 더하기 위해 도시에 대한 추가정보도 제공했으며, 그 결과 필자는 각 도시에 대한 필자만의 이미지를 구축하였다. 물론 필자가 갖고 있는 도시에 대한 이미지의 기반은 불완전한 확인되지 않은 정보를 기반으로 한다는 사실을 인지하고 있다. 북한 도시에 관한 정보의 출처는 대부분 북한 또는 한국인데, 양쪽 모두 매우 정치적으로 편향되어 있는 것이 사실이다. 한 도시에 대한 이미지를 형성하는 것은 도시의 이미지 요소들에 의해 결정된다. 이러한 도시의 이미지 요소들을 선정하는 것 자체가 주관적임에도 불구하고, 그 요소들은 객관적인 확인이 가능한 요소들이다. 북한 도시의 경우, 고려하여야 할 도시 이미지 요소들은 다음과 같다.

- 역사적 요소
- 자연 공간적 요소
- 기능 공간적 요소
- 사회 공간적 요소

역사적 요소

북한 도시의 시스템을 보면, 많은 도시를 해안가로 이끈 일제강점기와 그 직전의 제국주의 시대의 성격이 떠오른다. 반면에, 조선인민공화국이 형성된 이후에 개발된 새로운 도시들은 비 해안가 지역에 구성 되었다. 또한 일제가 한반도 도시 체계에 영향이 있기 이전에 행정적으로 중심지였던 도시들도 존재한다. 이러한 북한의 도시들은 발생적으로 위에서 언급한 세가지 그룹으로 크게 나눌 수 있다. 평양은 한반도에서 가장 오래된 도시 중 하나라는 이미지를 갖고 있다. 많은 부분이 427년부터 고구려(37BC-668)의 수도였던 역사적인 도시에 대한 문학을 통한 것이다. 평양은 이견 없이 한반도 북부의 역사적인 중심 도시였던 것이다. 동북지역의 행정중심지역은 함흥이었다. 함흥은 조선 왕조의 고향으로 알려져 있는데 (국립중앙박물관) 조선(1392-1910)을 건립한 태조 이성계(1335-1408)는 거의 어린 시절을 함흥에서 보냈으며 그의 둘째 아들에게 왕의 자리를 넘겨준 이후에 다시 이곳에 와서 시간을 보냈다. 이성계가 그의 조상들의 집터에 지은 함흥본궁은 이후 반복되는 파괴와 재건의 희생양이 되었지만, 이제는 함흥을 방문하는 방문객들의 관광지가 되었다. 개성은 919년 고려의 수도가 되었고 이는 풍수의 도시라는 의미였다. 아마도 개성만큼 풍수이론을 많이 가진 한반도의 도시는 없을 것이다. (윤홍기, 2006) 해주 역시 오랫동안 행정적으로 중요한 역할을 했다. 한반도가 983년 12개의 목으로 나뉘었을 때, 해주목이 그들 중 하나였다. 다른 도시들은 위에 언급한 도시들만큼의 중요한 의미를 지니지는 못했지만, 한반도의 경계가 지금의 경계보다 남쪽에 형성된 시기가 있었기 때문에, 한반도 북부지역에는 중요한 군사 지역이 있었다. 고려 강동 6주가 고려 시대 광종(949-975) 시대에 구성되었으며, 구주(현재 구성)가 그 중 하나였다. 현재에도 부분적으로 존재하는 구주의 토대는 994년 마련되었다. (이기백, 1984, 125)

한국 도시의 근대화는 한반도가 개항하고 철도를 건설하면서부터 시작 되었다. 1876년부터 1910년까지 11개의 항구가 개항했고, 이중 6개가 현재 북한지역에 있다. 진남포 (현재 남포), 원산, 성진 (현재 김책), 청진 등은 1차 청일전쟁 (1894-1895) 이전에는 작은 어촌에 불과했다. 대동강 하류의 항구였던 진남포는 1차 청일전쟁 직후부터 일본군의 군수기지로 개발이 되었다. (허우긍, 2007, 102) 진남포는 1897년 대한제국 정부로부터 국제 무역항으로 인가를 받게 된다. 일제는 조선인 마을에서 6km 떨어진 곳에 원산을 개발했다. 원산항은 원산의 중심에 위치하여 개발되었다. 원산항은 1880년 5월 1일에 일본과의 무역을 위하여 개항하였고 1883년 5월 11일에는 모든 교역국과의 무역을 시작했다.

경제적으로 일제는 원산이나 원산의 관할지역에서 많은 이득을 남기지는 못했다. 그러나 원산은 군사 전략적으로 매우 중요한 역할을 했다. 러시아의 확장은 청일전쟁을 통한 일제의 관할구역과 원산의 건설로 제지되었으며, 부산과 인천은 일본군의 상륙기지로 사용되었다. (윤정섭 1987, 114). 성진(현재 김책)은 19세기 말 블라디보스토크와 원산의 중간지점에 있는, 전략적으로 중요한 도시였다. 1899년 개항 이후, 많은 일본인뿐만 아니라 외국인들도 성진에 진출하였으며, 이 때문에 성진은 기독교가 빠르게 전파되었다.

청진 역시 부령군 내의 작은 언덕 변에 발달한 작은 어촌에 불과하였다. 이는 러일전쟁(1904-1905) 당시 일본군의 물자를 상륙시키기 위한 기지로 발달하였고 당시에 약 100여 채의 집이 있었다. 청진은 1908년 국제무역을 위하여 개항되었다. 러일전쟁 당시, 일본은 청진에서 회령까지 90km에 이르는 철도를 건설하였으며 이는 1906년 완성되었다. 청진은 북한과 만주 지역의 산림에서 생산되는 목재와 여타 자원들을 운반하기 위한 중요한 항구였으며 해산물 운송에도 중요한 역할을 하였다. 일제는 현재 청진의 일부인 라남을 군사기지로 1907에 건설하였다. 이러한 이유로 청진은 물류에 있어서 없어서는 안 될 중요한 항구도시로 자리잡게 되었다. (윤정섭, 1987, 127-128)

신의주는 중국과 접경한 북서지방의 압록강 하구에서 약 40km 떨어진 곳에 위치한다. 신의주는 일제의 철도건설과 함께 개발되었으며, 이는 한반도의 남동쪽과 북서쪽을 연결하는 것이었다. 이에 있어 가장 어려운 문제는 압록강을 건너는 다리를 어디에 건설할 것인가 하는 문제였다. 한가지 가능성은 압록강 위에 섬이 있었던 의주 지역에 건설하는 것이었는데, 이는 이미 중국과 조선의 사절단이 이용하던 곳이었다. 다른 안은 20km 정도 압록강의 하류로 내려가 지금의 단동 지역인 만주영역이었던 안동 지역과 만나는 곳에 다리를 설치하는 것이었다. 1905년 4월 일본은 두 번째 안으로 결정하였고, 이곳에 새로운 도시가 건설되었으며 새로움을 뜻하는 신의주가 그 명칭이 되었다.

한국전쟁 이후, 이들 도시는 부분적으로 사회주의의 이념을 바탕으로 재건되었다. 가장 인용이 많이 되는 예는 구 동독으로부터 지원을 받아 재건된 함흥이다. 함흥의 주도로는 동독의 대통령이었던 Wilhelm Pieck의 이름을 따 명명하기도 하였다.

북한 도시 토대의 한 예는 수도 평양의 북쪽에 위성도시로 건설된 평성이다. 평성 이과대학이 이곳에 자리를 잡은 이후, 많은 연구기관들이 이곳에 설립되게 된다. 주된 연구와 교사시설들은 평성 남쪽의 과학 특구 지역에 있다. 그러나 1995년 평성의 남쪽 구역은 평성에서 분리되어 평양의 은정 구역으로 편성된다.

한국전쟁 이전 농촌이었던 순천은 전쟁 후 공업도시로 재건된 도시 중 하나이다. 순천의 변화는 전쟁 직후부터 시작되었다. 풍부한 석회석과 석탄의 매장을 바탕으로 크고 작은 광산이 생겨났다. 특히, 시멘트의 생산은 이 도시에서 매우 중요한 역할을 담당하였다. 순천은 교통의 허브이자 비날론련합기업소가 1980년대에 시작된 곳이며, 이는 많은 사람을 유입시켜 순천이 도시로서의 모습을 갖게 했다. (조선일보 1995.9.25) 비날론은 현재는 더 이상 생산되지 않고 있다. 희천은 지령도에 신입하는 숭요한 곳에 위치하여, 농업지역의 생산품과 고지대 생산품의 교역을 하는 중요한 시장이었다. 이곳은 한국전쟁 이후 빠르게 기계공업 도시로 성장했다. 북한에서 가장 큰 기계공구 생산공장과 가장 큰 정밀기계 공장이 이 도시에 있다.

안주는 흥미로운 도시이다. 왜냐하면, 이 곳에서 도시화 한 지역은 세 지역으로 나뉘며, 세 지역은 서두에서 이야기한 그 세 성격을 각기 갖고 있다고도 볼 수 있다. 안주의 중심은 옛 성도시로 거슬러 올라간다. 평안도가 평양과 안주의 앞 글자로 만들어진 것을 보면 안주의 그 중요한 의미를 이해할 수 있다. 일제강점기에 서울에서 신의주를 잇는 철도가 건설되었고 이는 안주의 서쪽을 관통했다. 새로운 안주인 신안주가 이 철도를 기반으로 발달했다. 1974년 북한 서부지역에서 가장 중요한 석유화학 공장인 남흥 청년 화학공단의 건설은 공업도시로서의 안주의 탄생을 알렸다. 이 공장을 주변으로 새로운 지역이 개발되었고, 이로 인하여 안주의 구도심, 신안주, 그리고 남흥이 서로 다른 뿌리를 가진 세 개의 지역을 대표하게 되었으며, 이는 북한 도시의 전형적인 발생 타입이 되었다.

자연 공간적 요소

도시 이미지의 자연적 공간 요소는 도시들이 해안가나 큰 강에 인접해 있을 때 큰 역할을 한다. 항구도시의 예는 앞선 '역사적 요소'에서 언급되었다. 북한의 미래에 대하여 언급을 하면서 한국의 언론인들은 이미 "대동강의 기적"을 꿈꾸고 있다. 대동강은 단지 평양을 관통하는 것이 아니라 순천과 덕천을 관통하고, 항구도시인 남포의 남쪽으로 흐르고 있다. 신안주와 안주는 청천강의 남쪽에서 발달하였고, 강의 북쪽에는 남흥 지역이 발달하였다. 동북부 지역의 중심인 함흥은 송천강을 건널 수 있는 수심이 얕은 지역에 발달하였다. 한반도 북쪽의 접경지역에 있는 도시들은 신의주, 만포, 혜산 (이상 압록강 일대)과 회령(두만강 일대)이 있다. 하지만 인공적인 수로 역시 도시의 이미지를 결정한다. 대동강 상류의 합류를 통하여 덕천의 금성호가 1982년에 생겼으며, 이는 도시 중앙부의 동쪽에 위치한다. 사리원의 도시 모습은 운하에 의해서 결정된다. 이는 한국전쟁 이후 건설되었는데 채령강의 물줄기가 도심까지 올 수 있게 하기 위함이었다. 1988년 화객선이 건조되었고 이로 인해 송림, 남포, 평양을 잇는 물길이 생겨났다. (조선일보, 1996.2.12)

기능 공간적 요소

도시의 이미지에서 기능 공간적 요소는 도시가 다기능을 할 때 매우 유념해야 할 사항이다. 도시가 국가의 수도이거나 지방의 수도이면 주요한 행정기능과 경제적 기능의 이미지를 형성한다. 북한의 도시는 특정한 산업의 한 종류에 특성화되어 있다고 보아도 될 것이다. 많은 경우 하나 내지는 몇 개의 공장들이 한 도시의 경제를 지탱하고 있거나, 그러한 시설들이 도시의 상징으로 자리 잡고 있다. 예를 들어, 희천의 희천련하기계종합공장, 만포의 압록강다이어공장, 구성의 4.3 종합공장 (구성 공작기계공장), 정주의 평북정련소, 안주의 남흥 청년화학련합기업소, 덕천의 승리자동차련합기업소, 송림의 황해제철련합기업소, 해주의 해주제련소, 청진의 김책제철련합기업소, 문천의 문평제련소 등이 있다.

함흥에는 도시의 남쪽 흥남에 위치한 세 개의 대표적인 공장이 있는데, 흥남 비료련합기업소, 2.8 비닐련합기업소과 룡성기계련합기업소 등 이다. 남포의 경우도 비슷하다. 이곳의 대표적인 이 세 개의 공장들은 각각 도시의 동북쪽인 천리마, 대안, 강서 지역에 위치 한다. 천리마제강련합기업소, 대안중기계련합기업소, 그리고 금성트랙터종합공장 등이 그것이다. 북한에서의 무기공장은 많은 지역에 퍼져있는 것으로 판단된다. 그 중 가장 군수산업 도시로서의 이미지가 강한 곳은 자강도의 주도인 산맥안쪽의 강계이다. 신포는 잠수함 공업 도시로 알려져 있다. 이는 북한 어업산업의 중심으로 알려지기도 했지만, 정주는 농업도시로서 알려져 있다. 도시에 직접 연관이 있는 생산들은 개성의 인삼과 강계의 인풍술이 있다.

도시에 대한 관심은 한반도의 통일 이후의 개발 잠재성이나 혹은 한국이나 다른 국가들과의 경제 협력이 이루어지는 것을 보여주기도 한다. 물론 한국과 북한이 가장 성공적인 협력을 이룬 도시는 개성이다. 그래서 개성의 경제구역은 '한반도의 양국 협력의 장'이라고 하는 이미지를 강하게 보여준다. 하지만 이전에도 북한이 외부의 투자를 유치하기 위한 계획은 있었다. 1991년 12월 북한이 처음 나진과 선봉지역 (현재 나선)을 자유무역지구로 지정했을 때 많은 주목을 받았지만 외국 투자는 기대만큼 좋지는 못했다. 하지만 최근 들어, 이 지리적 장점을 갖춘 지역은 중국과 러시아인의 흥미를 끌었고, 나선지역과 청진의 항만시설과 다른 인프라에 대한 투자가 이루어졌다.

2002년 9월, 북한은 "신의주 특별행정구역"을 만들어 세계를 놀라게 하였다. 이 구역은 파이낸스, 무역, IT 산업, 과학, 엔터테인먼트, 그리고 관광 등을 위한 국제 지구로 개발되었어야 했다. 하지만 이 프로젝트는 실패로 돌아갔다. 2009년부터, 북한은 위화도와 황금평을 중국에 임차하면서 중국으로 하여금 이들을 자유무역지구로 개발하도록 하여, 신의주 지역을 다시금 특별지구로 개발하고자 한다. 남포의 경우, 평양에서 지리적으로 가깝다는 장점이 있기 때문에, 이는 언제나 한국이나 외국의 투자자로부터 선호지역으로 고려되었다. 한국 기업인 대우그룹은 이미 1995년에 북한 기업인 삼천리총회사와 함께 합작사업에 동의 각서를 체결하였다. 이들이 함께 세운 민족산업총회사는 남포에 섬유공장을 세우고 의류와 가방 등을 일본과 유럽에 수출하였다. (윤서경, 2000) 또 다른 중요한 남북경제협력은 통일교에 의해서 설립된 평화자동차이다. 2000년에 계약이 체결되었고 2002년에 남포에 공장이 세워졌다. 2012년 통일교 교단의 창립자가 사망하면서 평화자동차의 운영은 북한으로 이전되었다. (김석정, 2013) 원산은 이미 내국 및 외국인으로부터 관광지로서 잘 알려져 있다. 원산은 시정호수나 금강산 등으로의 관광을 위한 출발지로 인식되어왔다. 새로이 제안된 "원산지구총계획도"에 따르면 북한은 원산 송도원해수욕장과 명사십리, 갈마반도 등 해안은 여름 휴양지로, 평양-원산간 고속도로에 인접해 있는 마식령 일대는 겨울 종합레저타운으로 개발하려는 계획이다.

사회 공간적 요소

도시 이미지의 사회-공간적 요소들은 그 도시로부터 왔거나 그곳에 사는 중요한 사람들을 통해 이해된다. 북한의 경우, 어떤 특정한 정치적 슬로건은 특정 도시나 단체를 통해 지역화되곤 한다. 때문에, 많은 사회-공간적 요소는 북한이라는 국가를 이해하는데 좋은 수단이 된다. 심지어는 행정구역의 이름을 정할 때에도 정치적인 고려를 하기도 한다. 단순히 도시의 이름을 보기만 해도, 두 가지 경우에서 개인의 이름이 지역 명이 되는 것을 볼 수 있다.

첫 번째 경우는, 북한이라는 나라가 존재하기도 훨씬 이전에 생긴 도시인 송림의 경우다. 1880년, 일제는 청일전쟁을 준비하기 위하여 상륙할 곳을 찾았고, 전쟁은 지금의 송림지역에서 발발하였다. 이 이름은 전쟁의 일본군 지휘자였던 와타나베 켄지의 이름을 따 켄지포 (한국말로 교미포)라고 하였다. 와타나베라는 성은 너무 흔하였기 때문에 켄 지라고 하는 이름을 따서 만든 것이다. 두 번째 경우는 한국전쟁 중에 등장하는 개인의 이름이다. 동해안 항구 도시였던 송진은 이곳에서 태어나고 김일성이 만주에서 항일운동을 할 때 장교였던 김책 장군 (1903-1951)의 이름을 따서 김책으로 새로 명명되었다.

정주는 이미 1945년 이전에 개척자들의 고향으로 여겨졌다.

이광수(1892-1950)와 김소월(1902-1934) 등 많은 작가가 정주에서 태어났거나 오산 기독교학교에 다녔었다. 또한, 화가 이정섭(1916-1956)이나 한국의 간디라고 알려진 철학자 함석헌(1901-1989) 등은 오산학교에 재학하였다. 통일교의 설립자인 문선명(1920-2012) 역시 정주에서 태어났다. 문선명은 북한을 자주 방문하였으며 1991년에는 김일성을 만나기도 하였다. 그는 수도 평양에 두 개의 큰 호텔을 인수할 수 있었으며, 북한 정부는 통일교가 정주에 문선명의 성지순례지를 만들 수 있도록 허가해 주었다.

북한 자료에 의하면, 회령은 김정일의 모친인 김정숙(1917-1949)의 출생지로서 중요한 의미가 있다. 그녀는 이곳에서 유년시절을 보냈다. 사리원은 한국전쟁에서 사망한 강건 장군(1918-1950)을 기념한다. 1968년 그를 기리며 동상이 세워졌으며, 도시의 주도로 중 하나와 대학이 그의 이름을 따 지었다. 또한, 도시의 이름에서 기인한 슬로건들이 만들어지기도 하였다. 남포의 대안, 강서, 철리마 구역에 해당하는 이름으로부터 대안 사업체계, 청산리방법, 천리마 운동 등의 이름이 1950년대와 60년대에 등장한다. 1998년에는 "강계정신"이라는 슬로건이 있었고, 2001년 라남의 횃불, 그리고 2009년 "회천속도"가 있었다. 산맥이 주를 이루는 자강도와 동해연안의 공업도시들이 1990년대에 굉장한 기근에 시달린 것이 보고되었다. 따리시 지강도의 도시인 깅계와 회친이 북힌의 징지신진을 위힌 슬로건으로 채택된 것이다. 특히 구 공산권의 붕괴로 중공업이 타격을 입음으로써 함흥은 "실업자들의 도시"로 전락하였다 (Bauer 2005). 기근에 매우 심한 타격을 입은 청진의 도시로서의 이미지는 아마 Barbara Demick의 2010년 소설 "부러울 것이 없는 북한의 현실"이라는 소설도 한 역할을 했을 것이다.

보는 사람에 따라서 북한 도시에 대한 상상이나, 생각, 태도, 감정 등의 도시 이미지 요소들이 달라질 것이다. 하지만, 다행히 최근 들어 북한 도시들에 대한 과학적인 글들이 증가하고 있다. 이러한 연구들은 북한 도시들에 대한 우리의 생각과 태도들을 좀 더 객관성에 근거하도록 도움을 줄 것이다.

References

Bauer, Wolfgang: Die letzte Stadt der DDR. Ein Besuch in Hamhung. http://www.wolfgang-bauer.info/pages/reportagen/nordkorea/nordkorea.html

Choe Wan-gyu (et.al.) (2004): Pukhan Tosi-ŭi Hyŏngsŏng-kwa Paljŏn: Chongjin, Sinuiju, Hyesan. (The Formation and Development of North Korea's Cities: Chongjin, Sinuiju, and Hyesan). Hanul Academy.

Chosun Ilbo 25.9.1995

Demick, Barbara (2010): Nothing to Envy: Real Lives in North Korea (UK ed.). Granta Publications. ISBN 978-1-84708-141-4

Dormels, Rainer (2014 forthcomming): The North Korean Cities. Jimoondang.

Walter, Uwe-Jens/Johann Jessen (2006): Projektbericht "Die industrialisierte Stadt: Manchester, Liverpool … Berlin?". URL: home.arcor.de/postindustrielle.stadt/Pdf/Endbericht.pdf. (19.10.2013).

Hŏ U-kŭng (2007): Puhkhan Hangman-ŭi Sŏngjang-kwajŏng-kwa Kaebal Panghyang; in: Pak Sam-ok, Hŏ U-kŭng, Pak Ki-ho, Pak Su-jin (2007): Pukhan Sanop-kaebal mit Nambuk-hyŏpryŏk-pangan jirijŏk jŏpkŭn (Sam Ock Park, Woo-kung Huh, Kye-ho Park, Soo Jin Park (2007): Strategies for the Industrial Development of North Korea: A Geographical Approach.) p. 83-120. Seoul University Press.

Im Dong-u (2011): Phyŏngyang kŭrigo Phyŏngyang ihu. Hyŏhyŏng-chulphan.

Jang Se-hun (2006): Jŏnhwa-ki Pukhan Tosihwa-ŭi Chui-wa Jŏnmang. Jibang Tosi-ŭi Konggan-kuju Pyŏnhwa-rŭr jungsim-ŭro; in: Han'guk-sahoehak; Je 40jip 4ho, p. 186-222.

Kang Man-gil (1982): Merchants of Kaesong p. 89-119 In: Economic life in Korea. The Si-sa-yong-o-sa Publishers, Inc. Seoul.

Kang Sŏk-o (1984): Kaego-Sin-Han'guk-Jiri, Taehakkyo-chulphansa.

Kim Sŏk-jong (2013): Mun Sŏn-myŏng 1 Jugi aphdtun Thongilgyo•••2Se Hugye-Cheje jŏpgo gan Hakja Chongjae Jŏnsmyŏn-e. http://news.khan.co.kr/kh_news/art_print.html?artid=201308082152435. Kyonghyung News.

Kyu Yu-hwan/ Pak Hŭi-jin (2013): Pukhan-tosi Hamhŭng•Phyŏngsŏng Jaryo-haeje-jip. Sŏngin.

Lautensach, Herrman (1945): Korea. Eine Landeskunde auf Grund eigener Reisen und der Literatur.Koehler Verlag.

Maeil Kyŏngje•Han'guk-kyŏngje-yŏn'guwon•Hyŏndae-Kyŏngje-yŏn'guwon (2003): Kihoe-ŭi Ttang, Pukhan. Tagaonŭn Taedonggang-ŭi Kijŏk. Maeilkyŏngjesinmunsa.

National Museum of Korea (2010): Hamheung, The Hometown of Joseon Royal Family.

Pukhan-tosisa-yŏn'guthim (2013) : Sahoejuŭi-tosi-wa Pukan tosi-yŏn'gu-pangbop (An Introduction to the research of North Korean cities). Hanul.

Taehan thomok-hakhoe (2009): Pukhan-ŭi Tosi mit Jiyŏk-kaebal. Posŏnggak.

Yi Ki-baek (1984): A New History of Korea. Harvard University Press.

Yi Sang-jun (et.al.) (2011): Thongil Hanbando Sidae-e taebihan Pukhan juyo Kŏjŏm-ŭi Kaebal-jamjaeryŏk-kwa Jŏngchaek-kwaje 1 (Development issues of the growth centers in North Korea for preparing Korean reunification 1). KRIHS.

Yi Sang-jun (et.al.) (2012): Thongil Hanbando Sidae-e taebihan Pukhan juyo Kŏjŏm-ŭi Kaebal-jamjaeryŏk-kwa Jŏngchaek-kwaje 2 (Development issues of the growth centers in North Korea for preparing Korean reunification 2). KRIHS.

Yoon, Hong-key (2006): The culture of fengshui in Korea: an exploration of East Asian geomancy. Lexington Books, Plymouth, UK.

Yoon, Suh-kyung (2000): Dollars and Semtiments.
IRL: http://web.yonsei.kr/jgk/articles/CCG/Daewoo%20in%20NK%20NYT%20000622.doc.

Yun Jŏng-sŏp (1987): Tosi-Kyehoeksa-Kaeron. Munundang.

[1] This work was supported by the Academy of Korean Studies (KSPS) Grant funded by the Korean Government (MOE) (AKS-2011-BAA-2105).

[2] For example: Choi Wan-kyu (2004), Jang Se-hun (2006), Taehan thomok-hakhoe (2009), Im Dong-u (2011), Yi Sang-jun (et.al.) (2011; 2012), Kyu Yu-hwan/ Pak Hŭi-jin (2013), Pukhan-tosisa-yŏn'guthim (2013).

THE FUTURE OF NORTH KOREA: ICT, KNOWLEDGE GAPS AND THE ROLE OF EDUCATION*

Gianluca Spezza

—

Gianluca Spezza is the current research director at NK News, the leading website for news and analysis on North Korea and Inter-Korean affairs. He focuses his research on Education & IT in the DPRK, gender issues in North Korea, and future perspectives for the peaceful integration of the DPRK in the world context. Gianluca analyses North Korea in innovative terms. His views of the DPRK, its history and its future within the North East Asian scenario, are grounded in both social constructivism (in international relations), and DOI theories (diffusion of innovation), with emphasis placed on the role of social systems. For this reason, he researches and writes on the introduction of foreign knowledge in North Korea, the role of education in the country's future and the importance of human resources development in North Korea. He holds a Master in Humanities from the University of Torino, Italy, and recently completed his M.Soc.Sc. in Asian Studies at the University of Turku, Finland. He has lived, studied and worked in nine countries over three continents. Prior to his academic career, he has worked in East Asia as an area manager and education consultant for over five years, before taking roles in consultancy for cultural promotion and marketing within the tourism industry. A native Italian speaker, he reads and writes English, Korean and Spanish.

Introduction

Sixty years after the armistice between North and South Korea, celebrated on July 27 each year as a 'victory against invading imperialists' in the DPRK, there are many things we can speculate about the future of North Korea. Last summer, while most analysts have decided to focus on the North's military posturing and rhetoric, some media sources have shown~~n~~exposed how things can be quite different behind the façade that North Korea punctually sets up at every public occasion. Aside from revealing a more human side of the Korean People's Army, the more detailed look into the celebrations showed further proof that North Korea tends to be louder and bolder in areas where it feels threatened or inferior.

Keeping this in mind, I would recommend taking a similar approach in showing that North Korea's resistance to foreign influence is driven by a selective and reactive approach to modernization. We know that the DPRK flexes its military muscles to remind foreign observers that the country will defend its sovereignty, at any cost, but what does the leadership do in order to prevent foreign culture, which the country has been exposed to for two decades now, from causing a legitimacy crisis?

To answer in a simple manner:, we can think of the DPRK ideology as a marketing operation where, to avoid any comparison with South Korea or other countries, - a comparison that would prove embarrassing for the government, the leadership has

---

* A previous version of this article was published in two parts, on August 21 and 22, 2013, on NK News (nknews.org). The author and the editor wish to thank NK News director, Chad O'Carroll, for granting permission to publish some of the contents of this essay. The present version has been expanded, re-edited and updated with further notes, covering developments in North Korea until November 2013.

chosen to cherry-pick and re-brand every piece of outside information coming into North Korea. Through examples present in North Korean media and propaganda during the last few years we can see that the DPRK has presented both its militaristic side as well as a renewed image of the country, one 'at the forefront of scientific development', ushering a new era of prosperity for its people.

North Korea's Science And Technology 'Fever'

By looking at the latest mass games and war celebrations, we can see that new slogans such as 과학기술최첨단수준으로 (Gwahakgisul Choecheom Dansujuneuro, roughly: "Science and Technology to the Highest Level") are presented side by side with the more familiar statements dedicated to the 'final victory over US imperialists'. Another indication of this duality occurred on July 27th 2012, when a celebative video performance from the North Korean pop band, the Moranbong, aired on the DPRK's national television as the band performed the song "Bae woo ja" (배우자, literally "Let's learn"). The performance, reserved for the top elite of the country, was accompanied by futuristic imageriesimagery, while the lyrics exhorted younger North Koreans to "study hard, for the country and for the future".

This trend is quite visible on the two main media outlets of North Korea, KCNA and Rodong Sinmun, as they both feature one or two short articles, almost every week, to illustrate how scientific achievements, mainly in Science and Information and Communication Technology (ICT), are improving living standards throughout the country. Even foreign reporters in Pyongyang were pleasantly surprised to see that this year, the North Korean government had provided them with high speed Internet access for the July 27 celebrations.

Although this 'science and technology fever' is not entirely new in North Korea, this pattern, in my opinion, signals a vision of the country's future that is far more important than its display of armaments. In fact, just like anything else that is presented with fanfare in North Korean media, the push towards scientific innovation has been carefully crafted in the media to send specific signals to both domestic and international audiences. The main message, "We are ready for the future", conveys a couple of different meanings:.

First, it tells North Korean people that 21st century technology is available in North Korea, albeit generously provided by the leadership to those who are more loyal, of course. From the Red Star software, to a shift in literary production, where consumerism is seen as 'normal' or even appropriate,; North Korea has been willing to 'lift the ban' on modernity, as long as it can re-brand it with a Juche seal of approval.

Second, it makes clear that the leadership is fully aware of the increasing grassroot marketization and the growing influx of South Korean media coming from the Chinese border. T—two phenomena it can't afford to completely repress, despite clamping down on them from time to time.

The push for scientific advancement, accompanied by the rise in mobile phone usage and the recent unveiling of North Korea's own tablet PC and smartphone, is being used as a popular countermeasure to this incoming foreign culture.

In terms of propaganda, it is the same old 우리식으로 ('uri sigeuro' - our way') model, but it works very well for the DPRK: "We have our own version of all this, and we developed it without losing our identity". That's the message for both outside observers and the residents of Pyongyang, who are unfortunately the only two groups that matter in the government's view. The underlying notion is that if North Korea can have these developments in its own way, then the citizens would avoid falling for foreign temptations that they see accompanying these advancements.

However, as the more seasoned North Korea watchers know, a cross-match between political slogans and the socio-economic reality of North Korea reveals that most of what the DPRK presents as achieved results are, more often than not, just glorified expectations. Therefore, while some of the citizens of Pyongyang enjoy the occasional fast food meal or the sight of a few more skyscrapers, those in the countryside have yet to see any of the wonders promised during the Kangsong Taeguk (강성대국 - Strong and Prosperous Country) campaign.

Taking this into account, my sense is that, as North Korea tries haphazardly to show the world that its future 'is already here', we should be cautious about any developments and not give in to excessive optimism. North Korea knows the world is watching and that every little piece of novelty raises hope for reforms, but whether the country is ready for any change at all, is an entirely different story.

I have tried, in the last year, to analyse this 'science and technology' frenzy that runs through North Korean media and its educational system. What I can see from documents, reports and interviews is that our expectations of change within the country often do not match the intentions of the North Korean government, and so what we are currently doing to help North Korea may not be the best we can do for the country. There are, however, a few things that could be improved right away and it wouldn't cost too much to do them. so I will illustrate some of the main issues and then make a few proposals.

North Korea's Education Issue

I believe that one of the main obstacles on the DPRK's path to integration in the North East Asian scenario is that the country is not ready for any major change, whether we call it 'democracy' or 'globalization' or anything else, and it will not be, until we help make it so. The primary reason for this, in my view, is that the DPRK has a substantial knowledge deficiency at all levels of society, as indicated by the majority of reports and studies made on the development of education, science and technology in North Korea.

In the last decade, this issue has been partially addressed by various initiatives of educational engagement. However, these initiatives, for reasons beyond the control of foreign actors involved, are limited in scope as well as application, and are only available to a portion of the ruling elite and their children. So, for the most part, international organisations and other foreign actors who engage North Korea are providing training to the people who are already in charge, while the greater population remains ignorant of what is happening around them.

The two most common objections to such argument go more or less like this: "North Korea is not a third world country in terms of education, because it has one of the highest literacy rates in thewhole world" and "There is a steady flow of foreign culture, especially South Korean culture, which in the long run could promote grass-root change". These are valid points, but not substantial enoughlack sufficient substance.

TTrue,, North Korea has a higher degree of literacy than most countries both in Asia and the West,; however, literacy does not automatically translate into skills and knowledge, at least not in immediate terms.

The DPRK has made substantial efforts since 1945 to eradicate illiteracy, which was widespread during colonial times. By the 1970s, literacy levels in the country had greatly increased andin more recenttimesly the country has opted to participate in further educational programs, in partnership with UNESCO-UNDP, particularly a program called Education for All (EFA). The 11-year education programme established in 1977, and the more recent 12-year education programme adopted in 2012, are proudly presented in the DPRK media as proof of social development and commitment to nation-wide education.

So where is the problem? Simply put, nearly all North Koreans can read and write, but most of them do not learn anything valuable by today's standards and they haven't done so for decades now. Millions of North Koreans have little or no access to real information, modern technology and useful educational material.

The recent raise in shadow education within Pyongyang (the form of private tutoring so common in South Korea's Hagwon, where children spend hours on top of regular classroom time to prepare for exams and other competitions) has been documented in a few articles and reports and it testifies both the transformation of former literates or technicians into knowledge workers, as well as the inadequacy of current school programs in the DPRK.

Outside of the capital, people are unlikely to have experienced many of the things we take for granted.; Iit is a matter of mindset rather than literacy. Their understanding of social networks, the economy, international relations, personal finance, civil rights, politics and even health, is in fact frozen in the 1960s, at best, and conditioned by what the government dictates. To understand how and why this happened, we have to look at what the North Korean education system is and how it works.

Loyalty above Progress

The school system of North Korea was set up from the beginning with one purpose: to foster revolutionary values and produce loyal and functional North Korean citizens. Loyal, because the social system was based on absolute loyalty to the government, which for the most part, is a system still in place today. The DPRK was able to achieve this goal quite successfully until the mid-1990s crisis; therefore, for about 50 years, North Korean schools produced citizens that were perfectly functional in this system.

Functional, because they had to adapt to life in a

country that has never planned things for the long term, but rather worked on contingency. This is what national education was meant for, and this is what it did. The fact that every new generation of North Korean students could be more or less advanced in scholarly terms, was simply optional; it was welcomed, of course, but optional nonetheless. To show how the government accomplished this we can look at the structure of the education system, and the contents of North Korean education.

Even though it has presented itself to the population through different successive reincarnations of the same polity, North Korea has never steered away from the guiding principles of its ideology: the indisputable centrality of the Suryong (Leader), the principle of mass-mobilization, the faith in manpower over external circumstances, the idea of moral superiority based on ethnic Korean virtues. In the aftermath of the Korean War, the North Korean leadership directed most of its efforts towards the development of a new society within a new country, superficially inspired by Socialist principles, but ultimately aimed at creating a mechanism of self-reproduction for the regime.

In terms of structure, the DPRK has adapted education to the periodic crises and the specific tasks they called for (the post-1945 decolonization, the Korean war, the mass mobilization campaigns like the Chollima movement and so forth). The educational ladder, so to speak, was designed to resemble the social structure, where members of different social backgrounds were (more or less 'spontaneously') channelled through a specific type of school (technical, artistic, etc). Throughout the decades and various changes in this system, North Korea has always maintained a tiny group of elite schools and academies at the very top of the system. These provided access to better materials, facilities and teachers; however, their students were recruited exclusively among the highest ranks of the elite to guarantee political stability among younger generations. As for the educational contents from kindergarten onwards, studies made on North Korean school curricula up to high school level show that about 15% of classroom time is dedicated to pure political indoctrination and studying what the Kims have said and done.

This figure does not seem excessive at first glance; after taking a closer look, however, we see that this 'human remoulding' factor is present in nearly all other class subjects. A famous example comes from North Korean arithmetic books, from which children learn maths skills by solving problems that involve counting a number of dead U.S. Soldiers. There are many other similar examples. In addition, North Korea has cut back on any aspect of education that could hinder political loyalty. If a subject was compatible with the country's doctrine, economic planning and political direction then it was considered useful, otherwise it was discarded. The educational damage of such policy is evident, and this is why most university students in North Korea do not meet the criteria for admission into high-level Western institutions. By the time students reach colleges and universities it can be very hard to reverse this process. In fact, during the last decade there have been a few initiatives aimed at hosting North Korean students in Western universities for standard degree programs; however, most of them were not implemented—not because they lacked funds, or the will to cooperate on either side, but because North Korean candidates did not meet the requirements to participate in a class with local students. In brief, the current reality is that in North Korea the general population is unprepared for any radical change; or more precisely, should the status quo change abruptly, North Korea's immediate neighbours (South Korea and China) would have to cope with millions of people who have no skills to survive in a globalized world. Again, this represents a minority, and does not refer to those in Pyongyang, Kaesong and a few other cities who are slightly better off.

This is likely one of the reasons why no one really wants to change the status quo. Analysts like to point out that South Korea has turned its back to the North, that it has abandoned its northern brother, but let's be realistic: what country can afford to absorb millions of refugees, train and incorporate them into a new economic system without negatively affecting its own citizens? South Korea is doing what many others would do: buying time. The problem is, time makes North Korea's situation worse.

Knowledge Gaps and Their Wider Impact

At present the gaps in education between those in Pyongyang and those in the outer provinces have already translated into a lack of knowledge that affects many aspects of North Koreans' life. In 2010 for example, a cluster survey published by UNICEF in cooperation with the DPRK Central Bureau of Statistics showed that the knowledge of North Korean women about HIV/AIDS is dramatically low. This, in turn, greatly increases their overall vulnerability to transmitting the disease. The survey revealed that misconceptions about the nature and the transmission of HIV among North Korean women are widespread and inversely proportional to their education level. Needless to say, those who reside in Pyongyang have access to more knowledge and fare much better than female residents of external provinces. The report specified that:

Misconceptions about HIV are common and can confuse young people and hinder prevention efforts. More than two thirds of the interviewed women (69%) had heard of AIDS. However, the percentage of women who knew of both main ways of preventing HIV transmission is only 37 per cent. Only 9 per cent of women have a comprehensive knowledge about HIV transmission, although this increase to 24 per cent in Pyongyang […] The provincial differences in knowledge of prevention are quite significant. The percentage of women who know of both main ways of preventing HIV transmission increases with the woman's education level. Women in Pyongyang have very high knowledge compared to any other province. Women in Ryanggang Province have the lowest knowledge. The urban-rural difference is also significant.

The DPRK government often does nothing to improve education and prevention in what it considers 'sensitive areas'. AIDS carries a social stigma (just as it does in the South), and is difficult to address without admitting that there is a problem with sexual habits within the country, especially at its borders, all of which is definitely taboo in North Korea. If we add the fact that most of the human trafficking from the DPRK involves women from the border areas and that such trafficking has been flourishing for nearly twenty years now, it is easy to see how improving knowledge on health issues in the country's periphery could be life-saving.

In regards to the second objection, which is the flow of outside information into the DPRK: sure enough, it is there, and it has been recently documented by numerous sources, including defectors. But is that a realistic picture of North Korea as a whole?

Even if we could accept the idea that DVDs and pre-loaded USB sticks are widely circulating in the capital or in border areas, how does that address the knowledge gap for the average North Korean? South Korean dramas cannot possibly teach people what the government has neglected schools for decades. So, even if North Koreans know by now that jeans are better than vinylon uniforms, and that Girls Generation beat Moranbong anytime, it all remains irrelevant to their immediate future.

There could be a risk in overestimating this 'cultural pollution' in North Korea because pop culture and proof of material wealth from South Korea do not empower any North Korean with the skills needed to survive outside of the DPRK. They create some awareness, but then again, so do the sparkling lights of Dandong in China, just across the border. Every day, North Koreans can see how far behind they lag by simply looking across the Yalu River, yet this hasn't made them any more prepared for the future nor did it give way to any legitimacy crisis.

Let's think about this for a moment: if general assumptions about North Korea are right, then any North Korean who has witnessed the transformation of China (while North Korea remained in its shabby state) should have realized that something's very wrong with the way the country is run and therefore question the system. But this has not happened. Instead, the government retains legitimacy as it bombards citizens with tales of a future that is yet to come, while the reality remains one of a wrecked economy. This brings us to the second point: the fantasy according to which North Korea just needs to open itself to the internet and social media, to turn a page in its history. In the remainder of this article, I will explain why this proposition is probably too simplistic, and what can be gained instead from further advancing North Korea's education system.

Give them an email and they shall be free. Or shall they?

Eric Schmidt and Jared Cohen have discussed in past months—in various lectures as well as in their book, The New Digital Age—their trip to North Korea and what ICT could bring to the DPRK. Their argument is that North Korea 'will have to' turn the Internet on in order to improve its economy. It 'will have to give in' in order to obtain certain advantages; they mentioned both economic improvement, and a better society, although I am not sure whether the average North Korean would agree with Schmidt and Cohen on what such definitions entail. I also question their certainty, as some of the questions they ask about the regime sound naive to me, so I will look at just one basic fact:

North Korea has put up with a devastating famine—which it saw coming, let's not forget. Its people have been living in widespread poverty ever since. In the face of it all, in spring of 2013, it abruptly shut down for months one of the few sources of income it had, the Kaesong Industrial Zone, with nary a thought of any consequences for its shattered finances. It should be clear, therefore, that North Korea does not care much about the economy, at least not in the way we might expect. There is more. Over time, North Korea has turned extreme frugality into a social norm. The DPRK, in other words, trained its citizens to either have something 'in their own style' or live without it. To this day the leadership maintains legitimacy not by denying, but rather by openly recognizing, the material superiority of Seoul, and at the same time despising Seoul's 'moral weakness' and the loss of Korean identity to capitalism and consumerism.

This is slowly changing, but the reality remains that, in the view of the leadership, the DPRK can afford to live without 'our' Internet for the time being. Even if we were to grant to each North Korean an unfiltered email account and a tablet, what would they achieve with it? The idea of an open Internet in the DPRK, at this stage, is simple naivete. Truth be told, the way the country is structured now, it would do more harm than good for two reasons:

First, even if the current regime of international sanctions were to be removed and North Korea was willing to open the country to free information, what would the leadership ever gain from it? Schmidt and Cohen seemed genuinely convinced when they said: "North Korea is ready and they have the necessary infrastructure. All they have to do is throw the switch."
But such a proposition, given the present scenario, is the equivalent of handing a loaded gun to someone and saying, "Here. All you have to do is place it to your head and pull the trigger." It's just not going to happen. An open Internet means free flow of information, which would uncover the inconvenient truths of the leadership's failure. As Andrei Lankov eloquently put it in a recent lecture, if the North Korean people became aware of what really went on in the country since 1945, there would be only two possible outcomes for the ruling elite; they might "spend the rest of their lives working as toilet cleaners; but it's more likely that they will hang from a lamppost within a few hours." The North Korean leadership has witnessed the end of other regimes—from Berlin to Tripoli—and it will not go down as peacefully.

Second, what Schmidt and Cohen envision, according to promotional interviews for their book, is a future in which authoritarian regimes will not be able to control their citizens because the Internet will give people the possibility to exchange information; although they also believe that some governments may use technology to control citizens rather than empower them.

The bad news for a company like Google is North Korea does not need one byte of Internet to do that, because it has already implemented one of the largest social control mechanisms ever seen: the Songbun system. During the 1960s, DPRK authorities worked for over a decade to meticulously classify the entire population in every conceivable measure. Technology can only make social control easier and all the Internet could bring to the DPRK at this stage would be a digitalized version of Songbun—probably not the best gift for North Koreans.

The Alternatives

It is natural at this point to ask ourselves, "what can be done instead?" I think engagement initiatives are the way to go, and giants like Google can play an important role. But they need to address an underlying problem for the younger generation of North Koreans, which is that there will be no future for them if they remain so widely untrained. The work of NGOs and institutions interested in the future of North Korea should support the aim of making the majority of North Koreans capable of thinking that there can be a future, something that neither the leadership nor the population at large can imagine at present.

This cannot be achieved simply with top-down operations. What is really missing is a more capillary distribution of knowledge, something that would help all North Koreans adapt to the 'impact' of the increasing flow of outside information, which will occur sooner or later. Education is one of the most crucial yet overlooked issues awaiting the future of the DPRK. The final goal is to help educate North Koreans—no matter what—to prepare for emergency, and to bridge the current gap.

Education and Going the Distance

At the moment, a good number of educational engagement projects taking place in North Korea are limited to training the members of the elite—or whomever the state deems politically reliable—in the fields of economy, IT and niche sectors. There is no coordinated plan geared towards the improvement of overall knowledge standards in the DPRK. This is mainly because the North Korean government has prioritized educational developments in Pyongyang and occasionally in cities like Kaesong, just as it has done with any other form of foreign aid resources and assistance. The role of the international engagement partners should therefore focus on creating opportunities in the outer provinces, or at least balancing educational activities between the capital and the rest of the country.

I am aware of the fact that this is easier said then done. Also, some may point to the fact that North Korea doesn't like foreigners running around outside of Pyongyang, which is a valid point, but I can think of three ways around this issue. In the short term, with the implementation of distance education programs, and in the long term, with localized bridging programs and scholarships for North Koreans.

Let's start with distance education and the fundamental point of gauging whether North Koreans are interested in such programs. In recent years, after developing its own Intranet and online network, documents reveal that the DPRK has shown a keen interest for online education programs. They openly addressed this in the 2008 National Report on Adult Education:

"The government has to dynamically carry forward the work of getting distance learning under way on a higher level. [...] To this end, the government should establish regular distance learning system that can involve all members of the society on the national scale and standardize compilation of distance learning lecture plans to suit the diverse educational demands and level of the people. Besides, it has to complete communications infrastructure, support distance learning and improve and reinforce operational and management system and institutional framework of distance education so as to ensure that all members of the society study anytime anywhere".

This interest is also reported in periodic news related to the establishment (or proposed establishment) of online learning programs throughout the country. Granted, these may contain the usual discrepancies between goals and actual results, but the abundance of such reports suggests that North Korea is, at the same time, proud to show any possible achievement in this field and ready to benefit from more cooperation. Even DPRK officials participating in UNESCO-sponsored conferences in Asia have remarked on the importance of further developing online learning. This interest has also been confirmed in a few reports by the South Korean Ministry of Unification and the IFES-University of North Korean Studies in Seoul; furthermore, the development of ICT and education in the DPRK has also been discussed on South Korean blogs. Undoubtedly, online education represents a viable platform for future cooperation, for a number of reasons:

1) Distance education basically puts into practice the Education For All program goals combined with the needs for security and political stability of the DPRK. It brings in foreign knowledge at a fraction of the cost, and with minimal foreign presence in the country. More importantly, it helps reduce the gap in learning opportunities that exists today outside Pyongyang. Think about what websites such as Coursera or Khan Academy offer to the general public nowadays—it would not be too hard to set up similar services with a team of Korean and foreign experts.

2) Online learning would be particularly advantageous to North Korean authorities as it would give them the chance to obtain pre-screened, quality teaching which can be spread across the country at a controlled pace. North Korean educators could start training personnel in Pyongyang, evaluate the results and then select people from other provinces.

3) It could also give to a larger number of Western institutions, who have not set cooperation programs yet, the opportunity to establish a discreet presence within the engagement network. Preliminary meetings between DPRK professionals and foreign counterparts working on online materials could take place, for instance, in China.

Bridging the Education Gap

The second way to bring more knowledge to North Koreans is to establish bridge programs (or preparatory courses) that would give students the skills required for admission into Bachelor and Master's programs elsewhere. Generally, for similar programs, one year is enough to prepare university students for entrance exams in Western faculties. The fact that a number of European countries enjoy better relations with North Korea and have established diplomatic offices offers the possibility to monitor the development of such programs as well as the selection of candidates. For the most part, this has been limited to residents of Pyongyang.

The third thing that can and should be done is to allocate more scholarships for North Koreans. The Chevening program, run by the UK embassy in

Pyongyang, is already an important example of this. It is a model that should be imitated by other European countries with a stable presence or active relations with North Korea.

Whether one wants to look at it as a valuable educational experience, through the lens of 'soft power', or simply refer to what an expert such as James Hoare has recently expressed, the possibility for North Koreans to live and study abroad is one of the best tools for distention, because it addresses a fundamental tenet of the North Korean ideology: the notion that North Koreans are surrounded by an evil world against which they need to defend themselves. If North Koreans are welcomed into foreign institutions, as is happening over time in Canada, the UK, and Singapore, then they will be shown that there are alternatives to the current standoff. They will also learn that the western world is not limited to the US, and will inevitably bring some reflections of this back home. It is a very slow process, but needs to be fostered.

What is needed to make it work?

All of this requires political will in the first place. It will require people and institutions with a sincere interest in delivering education to North Korea, as a means to end the aid dependency, and political agenda or expectations of 'change' in North Korea must be absent. Some political circumstances (the recognition of the DPRK as a sovereign state, for instance) must change before we demand changes from North Korea. I have kept more technical details outside of this article, but I hope that at least the main point made it through: the simple exposure to foreign culture does not translate into

the power to change things from within. If that was the case, I think that a simple look across the Yalu river would be an eye-opener for all North Koreans. Since we know this is not happening, we need to accept the fact that either we make a bigger effort to help North Korea rebuild its human resources, or the country will never make it on its own. In regards to education and training (a crucial area), much needs to be done. North Koreans are not blind; one thing they know (or perceive) is that they probably do not have the knowledge (or the freedom, of course) to transform the country. In order to reinstate confidence in their workforce, the current knowledge gap needs to be thoroughly assessed and addressed. I wonder, for instance, what a test like the PISA (a comprehensive form of educational assessment run by the OECD; therefore, theoretically applicable to North Korea) could tell us about the state of knowledge in the DPRK.

In conclusion, almost every action towards positive engagement wis better than just waiting for North Korea to transform into 'a country we can talk to,' which is a highly unrealistic expectation. It is a simple matter of looking at the current situation and realizing that, if our relations with North Korea remain in terms of 'aid in exchange for regime change,' nothing will ever improve.

The 'strategic patience' approach has failed spectacularly because it was, and remains, a blatant admission of disinterest. It essentially says, "we have no clue how to solve the North Korean situation, so we'll just wait for something to happen." The underlying hope remains exactly as it was 20 years ago: maybe the new leader in Pyongyang will not last that long. But doing nothing about North Korea does not keep the problem at bay, it only allows it to fester. It widens the gap, and at the same time, it wastes the social capital that has managed to survive extreme conditions and deserves a fairer chance. The idea of 'preserving the status quo' is a dangerous illusion because, at the current rate of technological and social development in South Korea and China, every year that passes leaves North Korea further behind, which in turn increases the cost of any possible rescue. The more we wait, the less we will be motivated to do later.

북한의 미래:
ICT, 지식의 편차와 교육의 역할*

지안루카 스페짜

―

지안루카 스페짜는 현재 남북한 관련 뉴스와 정보 등을 중점적으로 다루는 NK News의 리서치 디렉터(Research Director)이다. 그는 북한 교육과 IT, 성 문제, 그리고 북한의 세계로의 평화적인 편입에 관한 전망에 대하여 연구하고 있다. 그의 동북아 시나리오 상에서 북한의 역사 및 미래에 관한 관점은 사회 시스템의 역할을 강조하는 사회 구성주의와 혁신의 확산 이론 등에 근거하고 있다. 따라서 그는 북한내에서의 외부 지식과 북한 미래를 위한 교육의 역할, 그리고 북한 내 인적자원 개발의 중요성을 강조한다. 스페짜는 이탈리아 토리노 대학에서 인류학 석사를, 필란드의 투르크 대학에서 아시아학 사회과학 석사과정을 수료하였다. 그는 3개 대륙에 거쳐 9개 국가에서 학업과 일을 하였다. 그는 지역 매니저와 교육 컨설턴트로 아시아 지역에서 5년 이상 일하였고, 이후 관광산업에서 문화 홍보와 마케팅분야 컨설팅 일을 담당하였다. 그는 이탈리아어를 포함해 한국어, 영어, 스페인어에 능통하다.

서론

매해 7월 27일 북한에서 제국주의자들의 침략에 대한 승리를 기념하는 한국전쟁의 휴전이 된 지 60년이 지난 지금, 북한의 미래에 대해서 예측해볼 수 있는 많은 일이 일어나고 있다. 많은 분석가들이 북한의 군사적인 태도와 도발에 주목하고 있던 지난여름, 몇몇 미디어는 북한이 매번 때가 되면 조성하는 대외적인 태도의 이면에서는 얼마나 다른 일들이 벌어질 수 있는지에 대해서 보여주었다. 이들은 북한 인민군의 인간적인 면을 드러내는 것 외에도, 북한이 그들 스스로 위협을 느끼거나 부족하다고 느끼는 부분에 대해서 더 요란스럽고 거친 입장을 취하는 것을 보여주었다.

이를 염두에 두었을 때, 필자는 외국의 영향에 대한 북한의 저항은 근대화를 다루는 데 있어서 선택적이고 특정 반응을 일으키는 데에 기인하는 것으로 본다. 우리는 어떠한 희생을 치르더라도 북한이 그들의 정권 유지를 위해 군사력을 이용할 것이라는 것을 알고 있다. 반면 20여 년 이상 외국 문화와 접하면서 그들 정권이 위기에 봉착하지 않기 위해 북한의 정권은 지금 어떠한 것을 하고 있는가?

간단히 생각해보면, 북한정부는 한국이나 다른 나라들과의 비교를 피하기 위해 북한에 들어오는 정보를 취사선택하고 재해석하는 마케팅 전략을 취한다. 지난 몇 년간의 북한 미디어나 선전을 보면, 우리는 북한이 군사적인 부분뿐만 아니라, 인민들을 위한 새로운 번영을 추구하는 과학적인 개발의 선봉에 있다고 하는 북한의 새로운 이미지를 보여주고 있다는 것을 알게 된다.

북한의 과학과 기술의 열병

북한의 최근 매스게임과 군사기념행사 등을 보면, "과학기술 최첨단수준으로"와 같은 새로운 슬로건이 그 동안 흔하게 보였던 "미 제국주의에 대한 승리"와 나란히 게재되는 것을 볼 수 있다. 이러한 현상은 2012년 7월 27일, 북한의 대중 밴드

* 이 글의 바탕이 된 글은 2013년 8월 21일과 23일 두번에 걸쳐서 NK News (nknews.org)에 게재되었다. 필자는 NK News 디렉터인 Chad O'Carroll에게 이 글을 출판할 수 있는 허락을 해준 것에 대하여 감사드리고자 한다. 이 글은 더 폭넓게 2013년 11월까지의 북한 상황을 다루고 있다.

인 모란봉이 북한의 공공 텔레비전에 나와 "배우자"라는 노래를 부르는 것을 볼 때도 확인할 수 있었다. 북한의 엘리트층들을 위한 이 공연은 북한의 젊은 인민들에게 조국과 조국의 미래를 위하여 열심히 공부하여야 한다는 가사를 담고 있는 노래와 함께 미래의 이미지를 함께 선보였다.

물론 이 "과학과 기술의 열병"이 북한에서 완전히 새로운 것은 아니지만, 필자의 의견으로는 이러한 경향이 국가의 군사력을 보여주는 것보다 미래에 대한 비전이 훨씬 중요하다는 것을 보여준다고 생각한다. 실제로, 북한 미디어에서 다루고 있는 여타의 내용과 마찬가지로, 과학혁명을 위한 노력은 국내뿐만 아니라 국외의 시청자들에게 특정한 신호를 전달하기 위하여 매우 조심스럽게 포장되었다. 주요한 메시지인 "우리는 미래를 위한 준비가 되었다"는 몇 가지의 뜻을 내포하고 있다.

첫째로 이것은 비록 특정계층을 위하여 제공된 것일지라도, 현재 북한 주민들에게 북한에서는 이미 21세기의 기술이 사용 가능하다고 말해주고 있다. 붉은 별 소프트웨어에서부터 문학을 생산해내는 것까지 소비가 이루어져야 하는 부분에서 북한은 그것이 주체사상을 통해 포장된다고만 하면 현대화에 대한 금지를 해제해 줄 용의가 있는 것으로 보인다.

둘째로, 북한의 정권은 중국과의 국경지대를 통해서 들어오는 증가하는 한국의 미디어와 풀 뿌리 시장경제가 확산되고 있음을 정확히 인식하고 있다. 두 현상은 종종 규제되고는 있지만, 완벽히 통제할 수 없는 현실이다.

최근 휴대전화 사용자의 증가와 공개된 북한의 태블릿 PC와 스마트 폰을 통해 알 수 있는 현재 북한의 과학 발전을 위한 노력은 외국 문화의 유입에 대응하는 조치로 사용되고 있다.

체제선전에 서는 여전히 구시대에서 사용하던 '우리 식으로'라는 모델을 사용하고 있기는 하지만, 이는 북한에서 매우 잘 활용된다. "우리는 우리의 정체성을 잃지 않으면서도 이 모든 것들을 우리식대로 갖추고 있다." 이는 북한의 관심에 있는 유일한 두 그룹인 밖에서 북한을 바라보는 외부인들과 평양 주민을 위한 메시지였던 것이다. 이것이 함축하고 있는 논점은, 만약 북한이 그들 스스로 이들을 만들어 낼 수 있다고 하면, 북한 주민들이 외국의 진보한 기술에 현혹되지 않을 것이라는 점이다.

그러나 경험 많은 북한의 전문가들이 알고 있듯, 정치적인 슬로건과 사회경제적인 현실의 접합은 북한이 선전하는 결과물이 단순히 선전화된 기대에 불과하다는 것을 보여줄 뿐이다. 결국, 평양의 주민들이 패스트푸드나 몇몇 고층건물들을 즐기고 있을 때 여전히 지방에 사는 사람들은 "강성대국"캠페인에서 선전한 것들을 전혀 볼 수 없는 현실이다.

이러한 점들을 고려해보았을 때, 필자의 의견으로는 북한이 미래가 이미 도래하였다고 전 세계를 향하여 외칠 때 우리는 개발에 조심히 접근해야 하며 과도한 낙관론을 견지해야 한다. 북한은 전 세계가 자신들을 주시하고 있다는 사실을 알고 있으며, 아주 작은 시도도 개혁을 위한 희망을 고무시킨다는 것을 알고 있다. 하지만 북한이 진짜로 변화의 준비가 되어있는가는 완전히 다른 이야기이다.

지난해 필자는 현재 북한의 미디어와 교육제도에서 다루고 있는 '과학과 기술'이라는 흐름에 대해서 분석해보고자 했다. 필자가 문헌과 리포트, 인터뷰 등을 통해서 알게 된 사실은 우리가 기대하는 북한의 변화가 북한 정부 자체의 의도와는 같지 않다는 것이며, 결국 우리가 현재 북한을 위해 도움을 주고 있는 부분들이 막상 북한을 위해 가장 좋은 방법은 아닐 수도 있다는 것이다. 하지만 여전히 많은 비용을 들이지 않고도 개선할 방안들이 몇 가지가 있고, 여기서 몇 가지 중요한 사안을 짚고 제안해보고자 한다.

북한의 교육사안

북한의 변화를 동북아시아 사나리오에 편입시키는 데에 가장 걸림돌이 되는 것 중에 하나는 북한이 근본적인 변화를 위한 준비는 되어있지 않다는 점이다. 우리가 그것을 '민주주의'로 부르건 '세계화'로 부르건 간에 우리가 그들을 바꾸기 전까지는 바뀌지 않을 것이라는 점이다. 필자의 의견으로는 이것의 주된 이유는, 북한의 교육, 과학, 기술 등에 대한 주요한 연구와 보고서가 지적하고 있듯이 북한은 사회 전반에 거쳐서 지식의 편차가 심하다는 것이다.

지난 십여 년간, 이러한 문제는 다양한 교육계획에서 부분적으로 다루어져 왔다. 그러나 이러한 계획들은 외국인이 참여하고 있다는 부분에서 그 범위와 적용이 제한적일 수밖에 없었고, 단지 일부의 엘리트와 그들의 자녀들에게만 적용되곤 했다. 따라서 많은 경우 북한과 연관된 국제기관들과 외국인 활동가들이 소수 계층을 교육하고 있지만, 여전히 대부분의 북한 주민들은 그들 주변에 무엇이 일어나고 있는지 인지하지 못하고 있다.

이러한 의견에 대한 두 가지 가장 흔한 비판은 다음과 같다. 첫째로 "북한은 전세계에서 가장 낮은 문맹률을 갖고 있기 때문에 교육 면에 있어서는 제3세계가 아니다"는 주장과 둘째로 "한국 등의 외국 문화가 점진적으로 흘러 들어오고 있으며 이는 장기적으로 봤을 때 풀 뿌리 변화를 이끌어낼 수 있을 것이다"고 하는 점이다. 이들은 일리 있는 주장이긴 하지만 충분하지는 못하다.

실제로 북한이 여타 아시아 국가나 서방국가들보다 문맹률이 낮은 것은 사실이다. 하지만 글을 읽고 쓸 줄 안다는 사실 자체가 곧 기술이나 지식을 습득할 수 있다는 의미는 아니다.

북한은 1945년부터 일제강점기에 만연해 있던 문맹률을 낮추기 위한 노력을 지속했다. 1970년대에는 문맹률이 상당히 낮아졌고, 더 최근에는 북한은 UNESCO-UNDP 와 연계한 EFA(모두를 위한 교육)이라고 불리는 교육 프로그램에 참여하기도 하였다. 11년제 교육시스템이 1977년 도입되었으며, 최근 2012년에는 12년제 교육프로그램을 도입하면서 북한은 이를 범국가적인 교육과 사회개선의 증거로서 홍보하였다.

그렇다면 무엇이 문제인가? 대부분의 북한 주민들은 읽고 쓸 수는 있지만, 대부분의 경우 그들은 현대의 기준에 맞는 것들을 지난 수십 년간 배우지 못하고 있다는 점이다. 수백만의 북한주민들은 제대로 된 정보와 현대 기술, 유용한 교육 자료에 대한 접근이 거의 없는 편이다.

최근 들어 평양에 한국의 학원과 같은 사설 교육시스템이 음성적으로 발생하고 있다고 보고되고 있는데, 이는 현재 북한의 붕괴한 학교 프로그램뿐만 아니라 기존의 식자층이나 기술자들이 지식 노동계층으로 전환되고 있음을 증명해 주는 것이다.

수도 이외의 지역에서 인민들은 우리가 당연시하는 것들을 경험하기가 쉽지 않은 듯하다. 이는 글을 읽고 쓸 줄 아는 문제라기보다는 태도에 관한 문제이다. 그들의 사회 네트워크, 경제, 국제관계, 개인 경제, 시민의 권리, 정치와 건강 등의 문제에 대한 이해는 거의 1960년대에 머물러 있으며 이는 북한 정부에 의해서 차단되고 있다.

진보에 우선하는 신뢰

이것이 왜 그리고 어떻게 일어났는가를 알기 위해서 우리는 북한의 교육 시스템이 어떠하고 어떻게 운영되는지를 알아야 한다. 북한의 교육시스템은 시작 당시부터 단 하나의 목표만을 갖고 있었다. 이는 혁명의 가치를 조장하고 북한 주민들의 충성을 이끌어 내는 것이었다. 북한의 사회는 정부에 대한 절대적인 신뢰를 바탕으로 하고 있기 때문에, 신뢰라는 것은 현재에도 유지되고 있는 시스템이다. 북한은 1990년대 중반 위기가 오기 전까지는 이 목표를 잘 실천해 갈 수 있었다. 즉, 약 50여 년간 북한의 학교들은 이 시스템에서 완벽하게 기능하는 주민들을 길러낼 수 있었다.

그들은 장기적인 계획보다는 그때그때 상황에 따라 바뀌는 나라의 생활에 적용되어야 했기 때문에, 기능이라는 것은 북한의 교육이 목적한 바이고 그들이 이룬 것이다. 북한학생의 새로운 세대가 학술적인 의미에서 좀 더 낫다고 하는 사실은 부수적인 옵션에 불과하다. 이는 물론 환영 받을 일이지만 전적으로 부가적인 부분이다. 북한 정부가 이를 성취했는가를 보기 위해서는 우리는 북한 교육 시스템의 구조와 그 내용을 살펴보아야 한다.

북한이 그들의 주민들에게 같은 조직의 서로 다른 세습적인 윤회를 보여주었음에도 불구하고, 북한은 그들의 사상을 전달하는 기본원칙에서 벗어난 적은 없었다. 반론의 여지가 없는 절대적인 수령이나, 대중동원의 원칙, 외부환경을 극복하는 인간에 대한 믿음, 한민족의 가치에 근거하는 도덕적인 우월성에 대한 가치 등이 그들이 전달하고자 하는 사상이었다. 한국전쟁 이후 북한의 정권은 새로운 국가에 새로운 사회를 건설하는 것에 모든 노력을 기울였으며, 이는 표면적으로는 사회주의 원칙에 영향을 받은 것이지만, 궁극적으로 이것이 추구하고자 했던 것은 그들의 정권을 위한 체계를 만드는 데에 있었다.

구조적인 면에서, 북한의 교육은 위기가 있을 때나 1945년 이후 탈 식민지화, 한국전쟁, 혹은 천리마 운동, 등 대중동원 캠페인과 같은 특정한 목적을 위해서 적용되어왔다. 교육의 사다리는 서로 다른 배경을 가진 사회 구성원들이 자연스럽게 기술이나 예술 등의 특정 타입의 학교를 거치는 것과 비슷하게 디자인되었다. 시대를 거치고 시스템상에서의 많은 변화를 겪으면서도 북한은 늘 극소수의 엘리트 학교와 아카데미를 가장 상위의 시스템으로 유지했다. 이들은 수준 높은 자료와 환경, 그리고 선생님들을 보유하였지만, 그 학생들은 젊은 세대에서 정치적인 안정을 확보하기 위하여 고위간부 등의 엘리트층에서만 선발되었다. 교육 내용 면에 있어서는, 유치원에서부터 고등학교 레벨까지의 교과과정에 대해 진행된 연구에 의하면, 약 15%의 시간이 김일성 부자의 교시와 정치적인 교화에 할당되는 것으로 나타났다.

이 수치는 처음에는 굉장한 것처럼 보이지는 않지만, 이를 자세히 들여다보면 거의 모든 교과목에서 '인간을 재구성'하는 요소들이 존재하고 있음을 알게 된다. 유명한 예로서, 북한에서의 산수 과목에서 아이들은 사망한 미군의 숫자를 세는 것이 포함된 문제를 풀면서 산수를 배운다. 게다가, 북한에서는 정치적인 충성을 해할 수 있는 것은 어떤 것이라도 철저히 차단을 한다. 만약에 어떠한 주제가 북한의 체제나 계획경제, 또는 정치적인 방향과 양립할 수 있으면 유용하다고 보고, 그렇지 않으면 바로 외면 한다. 이러한 정책은 교육에 해를 입일 수 밖에 없으며, 이러한 부분 때문에 대부분의 북한 대학생들이 상위레벨의 서양교육기관의 입학 기준에 미달하는 것이다. 학생들이 대학 수준까지 교육을 받았을 때에는 이미 그 고정관념을 깨기가 힘든 것이다. 실제로, 십여 년 전부터 북한의 학생들을 서방세계의 대학들의 정규 학위과정에서 교육받을 수 있도록 하는 프로그램들이 몇몇 계획되었다. 하지만 이 계획은 실패로 돌아갔는데, 이유는 펀드가 부족하다든지 북한과 서양의 대학들이 협조하기 싫어서가 아니라, 북한의 학생들이 그 대학들에 와서 공부할 수 있는 수준이 갖추어져 있지 않아서였다. 간단히 말해, 일반적인 북한의 주민들은 어떠한 급진적인 변화에도 준비되어있지 않은 상황이며, 더 정확히 이야기하면, 현재 상황이 갑자기 바뀐다고 하면, 북한의 인접국인 한국이나 중국에서는 세계화에 살아남기 위한 능력이 전혀 없는 수백만의 북한 주민들에 대한 적절한 대처를 해야 한다. 앞서 설명했지만, 이는 평양이나 개성, 혹은 몇몇의 좀 더 나은 상황의 도시들에 있는 사람들에 해당하는 것이 아니라, 마이너 계층에 대한 문제다.

아마도 이러한 점 때문에 아무도 현재 상황을 변화시키고자 하는 생각이 없는 것인지도 모른다. 전문가들은 한국이 북한을 등지고 포기했다고 이야기하기를 좋아한다. 하지만 좀 더 현실적으로 생각해 보자. 과연 어떤 나라가 그들 국민들에게 부정적인 영향을 끼치지 않는 범위 내에서 수백만의 난민을 구제하고 새로운 경제시스템으로 유입시키는 훈련을 시킬 수 있는가. 한국은 다른 많은 국가가 그러는 것처럼 시간을 벌고 있다. 단지 문제는, 시간이 흐를수록 북한의 상황은 더 안 좋게 가고 있다는 것이다.

지식의 편차와 그 영향

현재 평양인민과 지방인민들의 교육수준의 차이는 북한 생활의 많은 부분에 영향을 미치는 지식의 부족현상으로 나타나고 있다. 예를 들어 2010년, 유니세프가 북한의 통계청과 함께 조사한 바에 따르면 HIV/AIDS에 대해 알고 있는 북한의 여성 비율은 현저히 낮았다. 이러한 사실은 그들을 전반적으로 취약하게 한다. 조사를 보면, HIV의 전염에 대해서 북한의 여성들은 상당한 오해를 하고 있으며, 이 잘못된 지식은 교육 수준에 반비례하여 널리 퍼져있는 것으로 나타났다. 물론, 평양에 거주하는 여성들은 다른 지역의 여성들보다 훨씬 더 쉽게 정보에 접근할 수 있다. 보고서는 다음과 같이 서술하고 있다.

"HIV에 대한 오해는 젊은 사람들을 혼동시킬 수 있고 예방의 노력을 저해할 수 있다. 인터뷰한 여성의 2/3에 해당하는 69%의 여성이 에이즈에 대하여 들어봤다고 한다. 하지만 HIV 전염을 예방할 수 있는 두 가지 주요한 방법을 알고 있는 여성은 37%에 불과하였다. 단지 9%에 해당하는 여성만 HIV 전염에 대해서 상세히 알고 있었으며, 이 수치는 평양지역에서는 24%까지 증가하였다. […] 예방지식에 관한 지역 편차는 꽤 컸다. HIV전염을 예방하는 방법을 알고 있는 비율은 교육 수준이 높아질수록 증가했다. 평양의 여성들은 다른 지역의 여성들보다 훨씬 높은 수준의 교육을 하고 있으며, 랴강도의 여성이 가장 낮은 교육 수준을 받고 있다. 도시와 농촌의 격차 역시 매우 큰 것으로 나타났다."

북한 정부는 '민감한 영역'이라고 간주하는 것들에 대해서는 이들에 대한 교육과 예방을 증대시키고자 하는 노력을 전혀 기울이지 않는다. 한국에서 그러한 것처럼 북한에서도 에이즈를 사회적인 수치로 간주한다. 그리고 이러한 문제는 북한에서 터부시되는 내용인 사회 내, 특히 국경 지역에서 성생활과 관련된 문제가 있다는 것을 인정하지 않으면 해결되기 힘든 문제들이다. 우리가 북한에서의 인신매매가 대부분 국경 지역의 여성을 대상으로 이루어지고 있고 지난 20여 년간 인신매매가 지속해서 증가하고 있다는 사실을 염두에 둔다면, 국경 지역에서의 건강에 대한 지식을 함양시키는 것이 생명을 구하는 일이 될 수도 있음을 알게 된다.

북한에 유입되고 있는 외부의 정보와 관련한 두 번째 비판에 대해서 살펴보자. 물론 탈북자들을 포함한 많은 자료 등을 통해 북한에 외부의 정보가 유입되고 있다는 것은 잘 알고 있다. 하지만 그것이 북한 전체에 관한 현실이라고 볼 수 있는가?

우리가 DVD나 자료로 가득 찬 USB 메모리 스틱이 평양이나 국경지대에서 널리 유통되고 있다는 사실을 인정하더라도, 그것이 일반적인 북한 주민이 가진 정보의 격차에 어떤 영향을 미치는가? 한국의 드라마가 지난 수십 년간 학교에서 무시되어 온 것들을 가르칠 수는 없는 격이다.따라서 북한 사람들이 지금에 와서 청바지가 비닐 유니폼보다 좋다는 사실을 안다고 한들, 또한 소녀시대가 모란봉(북한의 악단)보다 낫다고 하는 사실을 안다고 한들 이들 모두는 당장 미래와는 무관해 보인다.

북한의 '문화인구'를 과대평가하는 것에는 위험이 따른다. 왜냐하면, 한국의 대중문화와 물질적인 풍요는 북한 주민이 북한 밖에서 살아남기 위한 능력을 키워주는데 아무런 도움을 주지 않기 때문이다. 물론 그것들은 새로운 사실에 대해 인식을 하게 해주지만, 이런 역할은 신의주 맞은편에 있는 중국의 단둥도 한다. 매일같이 북한의 주민은 압록강 너머를 보면서 그들이 얼마나 시대에 뒤쳐져 있는지를 확인할 수 있지만, 이것이 그들로 하여금 미래를 위해 더 나은 준비를 하게 하거나 체제의 위기를 가져오지는 않았다.

이 부분을 조금 더 생각해보자. 만약 북한에 대한 일반적인 가정이 옳다고 하면, 북한이 여전히 가난한 나라로 있는 동안 중국의 변화를 목격한 북한 사람은 북한에 무엇이 잘못되어도 잘못된 것이 있다고 깨달았을 것이고 그 시스템에 대해 문제점을 제기했을 것이다. 하지만 이러한 일은 일어나지 않았다. 대신 (여전히 실상은 경제난에 허덕이고 있지만) 북한 정부는 아직 오지 않은 미래에 대한 희망을 보여줌으로써 정권을 지켰다. 이것이 우리에게 두 번째 중요한 점을 보여준다. 북한이 새로운 역사로 나아가기 위해선 인터넷과 소셜 미디어를 개방해야 한다는 점에 대한 환상이다.

인민들에게 이 메일을 주어라. 그러면 그들이 자유로울 것이다. 과연?

Eric Schimidt 와 Jared Cohen 은 지난 몇 달 동안 많은 강연과 책 (The New Digital Age)을 통해 그들의 방북과 ICT가 북한에 가져올 수 있는 미래에 대해서 논의했다. 그들의 주장은 북한이 그들의 경제를 성장시키기 위해서는 인터넷을 개방해야 한다는 것이었다. 북한은 더 큰 이득을 얻기 위해 작은 것을 포기해야 한다고 수상했나. 평균의 북인 주민이 슈미드니 고헨이 이야기하는 정의에 동의할지는 모르지만, 이들은 경제 성장과 더 나은 사회를 위하여 작은 것을 포기해야 한다고 주장했다. 그들의 북한 정권에 대한 질문들이 너무 순진해 보이기 때문에 그들의 확신이 무엇을 근거로 하는지는 불분명해 보인다. 몇 가지 기본적인 사항들만 짚어보도록 하자.

우리가 잊지 말아야 할 것은 북한이 극심한 기근을 겪었다는 것이다. 북한 주민들은 만연한 가난에 시달렸으며, 2013년 북한정부는 그들의 주 수입원 중에 하나였던 개성공단을 경제의 부작용에 대한 아무런 생각 없이 몇 달간 차단까지 했다. 다시 말하면, 북한은 경제를 우리가 생각하는 방식대로 생각하지 않는다는 것이다. 또한, 북한은 세월을 거치면서 극단적인 절약 정신이 일반화되었다. 다시 말하면, 북한은 주민들로 하여금 '그들 방식대로' 갖거나, 아니면 그냥 없이 살도록 하였다. 현재까지, 북한 정권은 서울의 물질적인 우월성을 부인하기보다는 그것을 보여주면서도 얼마나 한국사람들이 자본주의와 소비주의에 정체성을 잃었는지 '도덕적인 취약성'을 보여줌으로써 그들 정권 체제를 유지하였다.

물론 이 모든 것들이 조금씩 변하고 있다. 하지만 현실은, 북한 정권에서는 서방세계의 인터넷이 없이도 북한은 살아남을 수 있다고 생각한다는 것이다. 게다가, 만약 우리가 북한 개개인이 모두 필터링 되지 않은 이 메일과 태블릿을 가질 수 있게 해준다고 한들, 그들이 그것을 통해 무엇을 얻을 것인가? 북한 내에서의 오픈 인터넷에 대한 생각은 지금 수준에서는 매우 순진한 생각이다. 진실을 알 필요가 있다. 두 가지 이유에서 오픈 인터넷은 장점보다는 단점이 많을 것이다.

첫째로, 현재의 검열이 사라지고 북한이 정보에 대한 접근을 모두 허용한다고 했을 때, 북한의 정권이 이를 통해 무엇을 얻을 것인가? 슈미트와 코헨이 "북한은 준비되었고, 이를 위한 인프라가 깔렸다. 이제 스위치만 올리면 된다"고 말했을 때 그들은 매우 확신에 차 있었던 것 같고, 필자 역시 그들이 진심이었다고 생각한다.

하지만 이는 마치 장전이 된 총을 누군가에게 겨누고 "너는 단지 이것을 너의 머리에 겨누고 방아쇠를 당기기만 하면 된다"라고 말하는 것과 마찬가지이다. 이것은 절대 일어나지 않을 것이다. 오픈 인터넷은 자유로운 정보의 이동을 의미하고, 이는 북한 정권의 실패에 대한 진실이 드러난다는 것을 의미한다. 그리고 Andrei Lankov가 그의 최근 강연에서 언급하였듯, 만약 북한의 주민들이 1945년 이후로 진짜 어떠한 일들이 일어났는가를 알게 된다면, 아마도 지배계층에게는 두 가지 경우의 결과만 낳을 것이다. 낙관적인 입장은, 아마도 그들은 "남은 삶을 여생을 화장실 청소부로 지내거나, 몇 시간 내로 그들 스스로 목을 매달 것이다." 북한의 정권은 베를린이나 트리폴리 등을 통하여 다른 공산 정권이 평화적으로 무너지지 않았다는 것을 너무나도 잘 알고 있다.

둘째로, 슈미트와 코헨이 그들의 책에 관한 인터뷰에서 언급한 점은, 이들 스스로 어떤 정권들의 경우에는 기술이 시민들에게 힘을 실어주기 위함이 아닌 그들을 통제하기 위한 수단으로 쓰이는 것을 알고 있음에도 불구하고, 인터넷이 정보교류를 가능하게 하기 때문에 독재 정권이 시민을 제어하는 것은 불가능할 것이라고 가정한다.

구글에는 안 좋은 소식이지만, 북한은 이미 가장 방대한 사회 통제 시스템인 성분조직을 갖추고 있기 때문에 인터넷이 전혀 필요 없다고 하는 점이다. 1960년대에, 북한은 모든 측정 가능한 면에서 인구 전체를 체계적으로 계급화하는 작업을 10여 년간 진행했다. 기술은 사회 통제를 더 쉽게끔 할 뿐이고, 인터넷은 아마도 북한이 북한 주민들에게는 좋을 것이 없는 전자화된 성분 조직을 갖도록 할 뿐이다.

대안

이 시점에서 우리 스스로 "그러면 무엇을 해야 하는가?"라고 질문해보는 것이 당연하다. 아마도 조약체결과 같은 것이 한 방법일 것이고, 구글은 여기에 있어서 매우 중요한 역할을 할 수도 있다. 그러나 이것들은 북한의 젊은 세대가 안고 있는 문제점들을 직시하여야 한다. 왜냐하면, 이들이 제대로 훈련 받지 못한 상황이 해결되지 않고서는 미래가 보장되지 않기 때문이다. 북한의 미래에 관심이 있는 NGO나 여타 기관들은 대다수의 북한 주민이 현재의 북한 정권이나 대다수 사람들이 상상하지 못하고 있는 미래가 올 수 있다는 것을 알게 해야 한다.

이것은 상명하복의 원리로 이루어질 수 없다. 북한에서 현재 가장 필요한 것은 모세혈관처럼 퍼지는 지식이다. 이것은 조만간 있을 것으로 보이는 바깥세상의 정보를 모든 북한 주민이 접하도록 해줄 것이다. 교육이 북한의 미래를 준비하기 위한 이슈들에서 가장 중요하지만 간과되고 있는 부분이다. 최종적인 목표는 어떠한 상황에서도 북한의 주민들을 변화에 대비하고 현재의 간극을 줄일 수 있도록 교육하는 것이다.

교육과 원격교육

현재 북한지역에서 이루어지고 있는 교육 관련 사업들은 경제나 IT 혹은 다른 주요분야의 엘리트나 정치적으로 신뢰할 만한 사람들을 훈련하는 데에 한정되고 있다. 현재로서는 북한의 전반적인 지식수준을 향상하기 위해 정리된 계획이 없다. 이것은 아마도 북한 정권이 외국의 원조품을 분배할 때와 마찬가지로 평양이나 개성과 같은 지역에만 교육의 우선권을 두기 때문일 것이다. 국제협력 파트너들은 외곽지역에 기회를 만들어내거나, 적어도 평양과 평양 이외의 지역 간의 교육의 격차를 줄이는 데에 노력을 기울여야 할 것이다.

물론 이것은 실천해내는 것이 어렵다. 또한, 누군가는 북한에서 외국사람들이 평양 이외의 지역에서 돌아다니는 것을 싫어한다고 말할지도 모른다. 이 모두 옳은 지적이다. 하지만 이 부분에 있어서 세 가지 단계가 있다. 단기적으로는 원격교육 프로그램의 도입이고, 장기적으로는 지역화된 연계프로그램과 북한 주민들을 위한 장학금제도이다.

북한주민이 관심이 있는지 알아보기 위한 근본적인 사항들과 원격교육부터 시작하면 될 것이다. 최근 들어, 북한 내의 인트라넷과 온라인 네트워크를 구축한 이후의 보고서를 보면 북한은 원격교육에 상당한 관심을 보이고 있고, 2008년 성인교육에 대한 보고서에서 공개적으로 그 관심을 드러내고 있다.

"정부는 원격교육을 더 높은 수준으로 이루는 것에 박차를 가해야 한다. […] 이를 위해, 정부는 범국가 차원에서 모든 인민이 포함될 수 있는 원격교육시스템을 구축하여야 하며, 다양한 계층의 인민들과 교육의 필요에 적합하도록 원격교육 강의 계획을 표준화하여야 한다. 동시에 모든 인민이 언제 어디서든 학습을 할 수 있도록 통신망 구축을 완성하고 원격교육을 지원하며 원격교육의 제도와 운영을 강화하고 개발해야 한다."

이는 북한의 모든 지역에서 구축되고 있는 온라인 교육과 관련한 뉴스를 통해서도 드러났다. 물론 대부분 그렇듯이 이 부분에서도 목표와 현실의 간극이 드러나겠지만, 이러한 뉴스는 북한이 이 부분에 대한 성과에 대해 자랑스러워 하며 좀 더 많은 협력을 통해 이익을 얻을 준비가 되어있다는 것을 보여준다. 온라인교육을 앞으로 더 발전시키는 것에 대한 중요성은 유네스코에서 주체한 아시아에서 있었던 한 콘퍼런스에서 발표한 북한의 관리에 의해서도 드러났다. 북한의 이에 대한 관심은 한국의 통일부 보고서나 북한학 대학원의 보고서를 통해서도 나타났다.

게다가 북한에서의 ICT나 교육의 개발은 한국의 블로그에서 항상 거론되는 주제이다. 의심할 여지 없이 온라인교육은 몇 가지 이유에서 미래협력을 위한 중요한 플랫폼이 될 것이다.

1) 원격교육은 북한의 정치적 안정과 보안에 대한 필요를 지키면서 동시에 모든 인민을 위한 교육 프로그램의 목표를 달성할 수 있다. 원격교육은 북한 내에 최소한의 외국인을 두면서 외국 지식을 적은 비용을 들여 실천할 수 있다. 더 중요한 점은, 현재 평양 이외의 지역에 존재하는 교육 기회의 격차를 줄일 수 있다는 것이다. 요즘 Coursera나 KhanAcademy가 일반인들에게 어떠한 정보를 제공해주는지 생각해보라. 한국과 외국 전문가들이 이와 비슷한 서비스를 만들어 내는 것이 그다지 힘든 일은 아닐 것이다.

2) 원격교육은 북한 정권으로 하여금 국가 전반에 걸쳐 제어된 속도로 퍼져 나갈 수 있는 미리 검열된 교육을 할 기회를 갖게 하는 장점이 있다. 북한의 교육자들은 평양에서 개인을 훈련하고, 결과를 평가하여 다른 지방에 보낼 사람들을 선별할 수 있을 것이다.

3) 북한과 아직 교류 프로그램들이 있지는 않지만 원격교육은 교육 프로그램들을 만들 가능성이 있는 서양의 교육기관들로 하여금 교류를 위한 신중한 관계를 맺어나갈 수 있도록 해줄 것이다. 예를 들어 온라인 자료들로 협업하는 북한의 신문가들과 해외의 전문가들이 중국 같은 곳에서 미팅을 할 수도 있다.

교육간극 좁히기

북한 주민들에게 더 많은 정보를 제공하기 위한 두 번째 방법은 북한의 학생들이 외국에서 학사나 석사 프로그램에 들어갈 수 있는 수준이 되게 하는 프로그램들을 만드는 것이다. 일반적으로, 비슷한 전공인 경우에는 대학생이 서양의 입학시험을 준비하기 위해서는 1년이면 충분하다. 많은 유럽의 국가들이 북한과 더 나은 관계를 갖는 것들을 좋아하고 외교 부서들을 설립하기도 한다는 사실은, 현재에는 평양에만 한정되어있는 프로그램 개발이나 학생선정의 선별에 대한 가능성을 보여주기도 한다.

세 번째로 생각해볼 수 있는 것은 북한 학생들에 대한 더 많은 장학금을 유치하는 것이다. 평양의 영국 대사관에서 운영되고 있는 Chevening 프로그램은 더할 나위 없이 중요한 사례이다. 이는 북한과 지속적이거나 적극적인 관계를 맺고 있는 다른 유럽의 국가들이 참고해야 할 모델이다.

이것을 가치 있는 교육의 경험으로 보고자 하든, James Hoare가 언급한 '소프트 파워'의 입장으로 보고자 하든, 북한 사람으로서 외국에 나가 공부하고 산다는 것은 시야를 넓히기 위한 가장 좋은 방법이다. 왜냐하면, 그것 자체가 북한은 적들에 둘러싸여 있고 그들 스스로 방어할 수 있어야 한다는 북한의 사고방식을 근본적으로 질문하게 할 것이기 때문이다. 만약 북한 학생이 캐나다나 영국, 혹은 싱가포르에서 그 동안 그래 왔듯이 외국 학교에서 환영 받는다고 하면, 그들은 현재 상황에 대한 대안이 있다는 것을 알게 될 것이다. 그리고 그들은 서방세계라고 하는 것이 단순히 미국만 있는 것이 아니라는 것을 깨닫게 될 것이며, 필연적으로 그들의 경험을 본국으로 전달하게 될 것이다. 이것은 매우 느린 방식이지만 반드시 지향되어야 할 점이다.

우선과제

이 모든 것들은 물론 정치적인 의지가 우선해야 한다. 이것은 사람들과 학교기관들로 하여금 북한 내의 정치적 아젠다나 변화의 기대감 없이도 원조받는 현재 상황을 끝낼 수 있는 수단으로서 북한에 교육을 도입하는 것에 대한 관심을 이끌어 낼 수 있다. 물론 북한의 변화를 원한다고 하면 북한을 전제 왕권 국가로 인식한다든지 하는 정치적인 상황을 먼저 바꾸어야 한다. 이는 북한의 변화에 의한 결과물로서가 아니라 우선 해결되어야 할 부분이다. 필자는 좀 더 세부적인 사항은 이 글에서 배제했다. 하지만 적어도 이 글이 주요한 부분을 지적해내고 있다고 본다. 외국 문화에 대한 단순한 노출이 그 내부의 변화를 이끌어내지는 않는다. 다시 말하지만, 그게 일어날 수 있는 사항이라고 하면, 압록강 너머의 상황이 이미 모든 북한 주민들로 하여금 눈을 뜨게 했었을 것이다. 우리는 이미 이것이 일어나지 않는 상황이라는 것을 알기 때문에 우리는 우리가 북한의 인재를 양성시키기 위한 눈에 띄는 노력을 기울여야지, 그렇지 않으면 북한은 그 스스로 변하지는 않을 것이다. 교육과 훈련에서 너무 많은 것들이 이루어져야 한다. 북한 사람들은 시각장애인이 아니다. 만약에 그들이 인지는 하고 있지만, 북한을 다른 무언가로 바꿀 수 있지 못하고 있는 것이라고 하면 아마도 그것은 정보(물론 자유도 해당한다)의 부족일 것이다. 그리고 그들의 힘을 얻어내기 위해서는 현재의 지식간극에 대한 부분이 해결되어야만 한다. OECD에서 운영되고 있는 교육 평가제도인 PISA와 같은 테스트가 북한의 교육수준에 대해 어떤 결과를 보여줄 것인지 궁금해지는 부분이기도 하다.

결론적으로, 거의 모든 긍정적인 협력들이 그냥 앉아서 북한이 (거의 일어날 일 없을 것으로 보이는) 스스로 '대화할 수 있는 상대'로 바뀌기만을 기다리는 것보다는 나을 것이다. 이것은 현재 우리와 북한이 갖고 있는 '정권의 변화를 담보로 하는 원조'라는 생각에서 벗어나지 못하면 아무것도 개선되지 않을 것이다.

'전략적인 침묵' 방식은 볼만하게 실패하였다. 왜냐하면 이것은 단순히 "우리는 북한에 대한 어떠한 해결책도 모르겠으니 그냥 어떤 일이 일어날 때까지 기다리겠다"고 이야기 하는 노골적인 무시에 불과했고, 이에 깔린 희망은 20년 전이나 지금이나 별반 다를 바 없으며 현재의 북한 리더에 대한 변화의 희망도 그다지 오래가지 않을 것이기 때문이다. 하지만 북한에 대해 어떠한 것도 안 한다는 것이 문제를 덮어두지는 못한다. 오히려 이것은 문제를 더 곪게 할 것이다. 왜냐하면 그것은 간극을 더 극대화 시킴과 동시에 더 나은 기회를 가질 수 있고 더 극악한 상황에서 생존할 수 있었던 사회적 자본을 낭비하는 것이기 때문이다. 또한 '현재 상황을 유지하는 것' 역시 위험한 발상이다. 왜냐하면, 현재 한국과 중국에서 일어나고 있는 기술과 사회 진보의 속도는 매해 북한을 상대적으로 더 많이 뒤처지게 만들 것이고, 이는 결국 후에 회생 비용만을 증가시킬 것이기 때문이다. 많이 기다릴수록 동기를 더 잃게 될 것이다.

"WHY AND HOW NORTH KOREA COULD EXPERIENCE ECONOMIC LIBERALIZATION IN THE COMING YEARS"

David Matthew

—

David Matthew graduated with a Master's Degree in Public Policy from the University of Edinburgh in 2013. He is interested in East Asian comparative politics and economics, and works in the information technology industry in Washington D.C.

In a June 20, 2012 interview with the Washington, D.C.-based Korean Economic Institute, scholar Andrei Lankov argued that North Korea is not in a position to follow the path of economic reform witnessed in countries like China due to the onerous presence of South Korea. As he put it, "In China, reforms are possible because there is no South China." But this notion that China was able to undertake economic reforms in a cultural or geographic vacuum does not seem well-supported by evidence.

What we do know is that when Deng Xiaoping started instituting economic reforms in China in 1978, the various countries with high populations of ethnic Chinese in the region – Singapore, Hong Kong, and Taiwan among others – had per capita GDPs as high as 15 times that of mainland China. At the same time there was a sizable Chinese diaspora around the world, numbering as many as 50,000,000 people – many of whom we might imagine would have been in contact with family and friends on the mainland about outside levels of prosperity and opportunity. All of which is to say that an economically opened China, where the citizens often still live below the prosperity of ethnic Chinese elsewhere in the world or even in nearby Asian nations, is not experiencing the type of dramatic revolution that many like Lankov forecast for an economically opened North Korea.

The method of China's reform could be valuable for the DPRK, not least of all because China has the organizational capacity to help achieve it in North Korea. Deng started reforms with what was referred to as the Household-responsibility system that partially privatized agriculture and provided people with ownership of plots of land. This initiative increased agricultural output dramatically and was popular enough to be adopted by 93 percent of the agriculture-based production teams by 1983. This model has short term attractiveness in regard to boosting North Korea's food supply and making the country less reliant on foreign food aid, but it is also a good place to start economic liberalization because rural communities are the least likely to reach a critical mass of revolution and the most likely to be in the dark about outside prosperity differences.

Information Flows and the Nexus of Revolution

Of course information flows are capable of subverting regimes by virtue of connecting people both within a state and between states. Additionally, information can travel faster and farther than ever before in human history, and North Korea possesses the physical infrastructure to facilitate such movement. But while this might be the source of a large existential problem for the Kim regime, the government has demonstrated before its ability to circumscribe the amount and type of information that permeates its borders. There is no reason to suspect that economic liberalization would equally demand full or even partial openness. China is a clear example of a country that thrives on market principles but has restricted access to information. The Great Firewall of China being one example, but the quick scrub job by the online censors of the 2012 Bo Xilai scandal is one too. There are plenty of other instances where regimes maintain tight control of information in conjunction with high levels of economic competitiveness and growth, such as Bahrain and Vietnam.

Even within the implausible context of everyone in North Korea becoming fully informed about the disparity in prosperity between themselves and the rest of the world, it would not necessarily indicate the undoing of the government. On the contrary, it might be sold to citizens as further evidence not only of the immoral culture of consumption that drives the West, but also of the past and continuing efforts of North Korea's enemies to deprive the country of goods and resources. As North Korean defector Sohn Jung-hoon noted in a 2012 Reuters post, "[The] regime won't stop brainwashing and saying that poverty is because of our enemies."

Additionally, the notion that rebellion would more easily foment, or would be guaranteed to foment, at the point where North Koreans are fully informed about the disadvantaged position of their country is disputable. The Arab Spring was a pan-cultural idea that captivated and moved forward the spirit of an entire geographic region. While this is assuredly true, the number of countries that witnessed regime change as a result of popular uprising comprises a tiny margin of the whole. In very poor Sudan, where per capita GDP is around $2,600, protests were minimal and the Arab Spring was largely absent. This, despite the fact that the Sudanese are primarily ethnically Arabic like their neighbors in Egypt, a full magnitude poorer than their neighbors in Egypt, and reasonably aware of their relative poverty and lack of democratic process. While it is not accurate to use another part of the world as analogous to the Korean situation, the landscape in the wake of Middle Eastern upheaval provides some clarity about the reasons and incentives for outright revolution in the twenty-first century.

As it stands now though, many in North Korea are increasingly aware of South Korea's wealth and material success. A number of recent reports, mostly stemming from a 2012 InterMedia study conducted by Nate Kretchum and Jane Kim, indicate that "a substantial, consistently measurable portion of the population has direct access to outside media". Much of this has come through the highly fictionalized accounts of life found in South Korea's televised dramas, but North Koreans also access foreign media through illegal file sharing, news reports and films. Whether or not citizens in the DPRK take the depictions of life south of the border at face value is difficult to ascertain, but this foreign media inflow does not appear to be pushing the country toward revolution. B.R. Myers and others have well-documented the cultural superiority that North Koreans are indoctrinated with by the state. It may be the case that this sense of cultural superiority can carry the country through a transition from an autarky to a developmental state with little conflict.

How Liberalization Could Look

It is possible that North Korea could reform its economic engine relatively quickly. As Orascom figured out when implementing North Korea's mobile network, the absence of many technologies and logistics frameworks means that upgrading the country to a high level of quality is not as difficult as it would be in, say, the United States or Western Europe where pre-existing redundancies slow down adoption and change. As China and East Asia's other developmental states have shown, rapid economic growth can paper over weaknesses of governance or a lack of freedoms. From a development standpoint, North Korea may well be in a fortuitous geographic location. Undoubtedly China and South Korea are interested in developing its economy and stabilizing the country, but it is also neighbors with Russia and Japan. In other words, it is surrounded by some of the largest exporters of both raw and manufactured goods in the world, as well as some of the largest markets.

The opening of trade financing opportunities and FDI could additionally see the government operate from a position of strength in terms of offering more welfare options for citizens in exchange for steady control over the population. While some countries would surely not go along with this set of circumstances unless there were promises for political reform alongside proposed economic reform, it is highly unlikely that its potential primary investment and trade partners – Russia and China in particular – would ask for these same conditions.

With the North Korean population constantly on the verge of famine due to poor resource allocation and the systemic inefficiency of the Korean economic model, Pyongyang has almost always relied on aid from other countries. After the collapse of the Soviet Union this was largely achieved through regional belligerence. But if recent incidents under Kim Jong-un are anything to go by, the current government may not be as deft at pulling the levers of global economic manipulation as the previous one. The next time talks of providing aid are conducted, the United States and others will be even more wary that Pyongyang will immediately renege on the agreement. If Kim Jong-un cannot effectively harass and cajole the United States and others into providing aid, his government may find that it has little other option but to liberalize the economy.

"왜 그리고 어떻게 북한은 앞으로 경제의 자유화를 겪게 될 것인가"

데이비트 매튜

―

데이비드 매튜는 2013년 에딘버그 대학에서
공공 정책학 석사학위를 취득하였다.
그는 동아시아 비교 정치학과 경제학에
관심을 갖고 있으며, 현재는 미국 워싱턴DC에서
IT 분야에서 활동 중이다.

2012년 6월 20일, 워싱턴을 기반으로 하는 한국경제연구소와의 인터뷰에서 안드레이 란코프(Andrei Lankov)는 현재 북한은 부담스러운 한국의 존재로 인하여 중국과 같은 나라에서 행해진 경제구조의 변화를 취할 것 같지는 않다고 주장하였다. 그는 "중국에는 남 중국이라는 존재가 없었기 때문에 구조변화가 가능하였다."고 했다. 하지만 중국이 문화적·지리적 공백기에 경제구조 변화를 이루었다는 것은 그다지 명백하게 증명되지 않는 듯 하다.

우리가 아는 사실은, 덩샤오핑이 1978년 중국의 경제개혁을 시작했을 때, 싱가포르, 홍콩, 또는 대만과 같은 중국계가 다수였던 다양한 국가들이 중국 본토보다 1인당 GDP가 15배 정도 높았다는 것이다. 또한, 당시에는 중국 본토에 있는 가족이나 친구들에게 바깥세상의 번영과 기회에 대해서 말해줄 수 있었던 중국 교포들만 전 세계에 약 5천만 가량이 있었다. 이러한 사실이 말해주는 것은 중국은 아직도 대부분의 국민이 다른 중국계 교포나 인근 아시아 국가의 국민들 보다 낮은 수준에 살고 있고 경제개방을 통해 란코프와 같은 사람들이 북한의 경제개방과 관련하여 예측한 급진적인 혁명과는 전혀 다른 삶을 살았다는 것이다.

중국의 경제개혁 방식은 북한입장에서는 가치 있을지 모른다. 특히 중국이 북한이 경제개혁을 이룰 수 있도록 도와줄 수 있는 능력을 지녔기 때문이다. 덩샤오핑의 경제개혁은 농업지역의 부분적인 사유화를 인정하고 사람들에게 땅을 나누어주는 가정연산승포책임제를 통해 시작되었다. 이는 눈에 띄는 생산량의 증가를 가져왔고, 1983년까지 93%에 해당하는 농촌 지역이 이 시스템을 도입하기에 이르렀다. 이 모델은 북한의 농업생산량을 높이고 북한이 외국에 식량을 의존하는 비율을 줄이는데 단기적인 효과가 있다. 하지만 지방정부의 대규모 변혁이 일어날 가능성이 가장 적은 동시에 외부와의 경제수준 차이에 가장 둔감할 수 있기 때문에 이는 경제 자유화를 위한 좋은 출발점일 수도 있다.

정보의 전달과 변혁의 결합

정보는 물론 국가 내는 물론 국가 간의 사람들을 연결함으로써 체제를 전복시킬 수 있는 힘이 있다. 또한, 정보는 인류 역사상 가장 빠르게 퍼져나가고, 동시에 북한은 이러한 현상을 받아들일 수 있는 인프라를 갖추고 있다. 이것이 북한 정권의 존재를 위협하는 상황이기는 하지만, 북한은 자신들이 받아들이는 정보의 종류와 양에 대하여 충분히 통제 가능하다는 것을 보여주었다. 경제의 자유화가 전체적 혹은 부분적인 정보의 개방을 동일하게 요구할 것이라고 믿을 이유는 없다. 중국의 경우 완전한 시장 경제 원칙에 돌아가면서도 동시에 정보에의 접근을 제한하고 있는 매우 명확한 사례국가이다. 정보차단 수단인 Great Firewall of China 도 한 예이고, 2012년 있었던 BoXilai 스캔들도 중국이 정보를 통제하고 있는 예이다. 중국뿐만 아니라, 바레인이나 베트남처럼 경제의 경쟁력과 성장은 유지하면서도 정부의 정보에 대한 통제는 유지하고 있는 나라들은 얼마든지 있다.

북한의 주민들이 그들 자신과 그 외 다른 세상 사람들 간의 빈부격차에 대해 완벽하게 알고 있을지라도, 그것이 북한 정부의 전복을 갖고 온다는 보장은 없다. 오히려 이러한 사실은 북한 정부에 의해서 북한 주민들에게 서방세계의 비도덕적인 소비문화뿐만 아니라 그들의 적국이 북한의 자원을 수탈해간다는 것을 증명해주는 자료로서 이용될 것이다. 탈북자 손정훈이 2012년 로이터 통신과의 인터뷰에서 말한 것처럼, "북한 체제는 북한의 가난이 그들의 적국 때문이라고 이야기하고 세뇌하는 작업을 멈추지는 않을 것이다."

게다가, 반동분자는 북한 주민이 그들의 불공평한 위치를 확실히 알았을 때 더 쉽게 분란을 조장할 것이라는 생각은 반론의 여지가 없다. 아랍의 봄(The Arab Spring)은 범 지리적인 지역의 정신을 사로잡고 움직인 범 문화적인 아이디어였다. 이것이 확실한 사실이지만, 군중의 봉기로 인한 체제의 교체를 목격한 많은 나라는 아주 작은 부분을 타협한다. 1인당 국민소득이 $2,600에 불과한 수단의 경우, 시민들의 시위는 매우 적었고 아랍의 봄은 거의 존재하지 않았다. 수단인들이 그들의 이웃국가인 이집트인들처럼 아랍인이고, 이집트인보다 가난했으며 그들의 가난과 척박한 민주주의에 대해서 알고 있었음에도 불구하고 말이다. 물론 지구 반대편 국가의 예를 북한의 상황에 대입한다는 것은 정확하지는 않지만, 중동지역의 새로운 바람은 21세기 혁명의 이유와 대가에 대해서 말해주고 있다.

이제는 많은 북한 사람들이 한국의 부와 경제적 성공에 대해 알고 있다. Nate Kretchum과 Jane Kim에 의해 실시된 2012년 인터미디어 연구에서 그들은 "측정 가능한 상당수의 북한 주민이 외부의 미디어에 접근할 수 있다"고 이야기한다. 이들 중 대부분은 한국의 TV 드라마를 통해 접근하는 것이지만, 북한 주민들은 불법파일 공유라든지 뉴스 리포트 또는 영화 등을 통한 외국의 미디어에 접근할 수 있기도 하다. 북한의 주민들이 한국의 생활상을 확인하는 것이 힘들든 아니든 간에, 이러한 외국 미디어의 유입이 북한을 변혁으로 이끌고 가지는 않는 듯이 보인다. B. R. Myers 등은 북한 주민이 국가에 의하여 세뇌 당하는 문화적 우월성에 대하여 잘 짚어 냈다. 이러한 문화적 우월감은 아마도 순조롭게 북한을 자급자족 경제에서 개발국가로 변환해 나아가는 데 도움을 줄지도 모른다.

자유화가 어떻게 보여질 것인가

북한이 생각보다 빠르게 경제개혁을 이룰 가능성은 충분해 보인다. 오라스콤이 북한에 무선통신망을 깔 때에 발견한 것처럼, 많은 기술과 복잡한 실행 계획이 없다는 것은 그 나라를 높은 수준으로 끌어올리는 것이 기존의 과잉 기술이 새로운 변화를 받아들이는 데에 장애가 된 미국이나 서유럽국가보다 쉬울 수 있다는 것을 의미한다. 중국이나 여타 동아시아의 개발 국가들이 보여준 것처럼 빠른 경제성장은 자유의 어제와 관리의 부재를 덮을 수 있다. 개발의 입장에서 본다면, 북한은 지리적으로 운이 좋은 곳에 위치해있다. 의심할 여지없이 중국과 한국은 북한의 경제를 개발하고 이를 안정시키는 데에 관심이 있다. 또한, 북한은 러시아와 일본과도 인접하고 있다. 다시 말하면, 북한은 전세계에서 가장 큰 원자재 및 제조품 수출국과 인접하고 있으며, 가장 큰 시장에 둘러싸여 있는 것이다.

무역의 기회를 개방하고 외국인 투자를 받아들인다는 것은 정부 입장에서 보면 국민들을 안정적으로 통치하기 위하여 국민들에게 좀 더 많은 부를 안겨줄 수 있는 위치에 있다는 것을 의미한다. 물론 어떤 나라들의 경우에는 경제개혁과 더불어 정치개혁이 수반되어야만 한다는 약속이 있을 때에만 이 이러한 상황을 받아들이기도 하지만, 북한의 주된 투자와 무역상대국이 될 것으로 예상하는 중국과 러시아가 북한에 이러한 조건을 내걸 것으로 보이지는 않는다.

북한의 비효율적인 경제모델과 자원활용의 문제점으로 평양 주민들은 지속적으로 기근을 걱정해야 했고, 결국 매번 외국으로부터의 원조에 의존할 수밖에 없는 처지에 이르렀다. 구 소련의 붕괴 이후 이러한 전략은 매번 지역의 위기감을 조성함으로써 얻어낼 수 있었다. 하지만, 최근 김정은 체제를 기준으로 보자면, 현 정권은 이전의 정권만큼 세계 경제의 변화를 당겨올 만큼 재빠르지는 못한 것 같다. 새로운 원조를 위한 회담이 계획되어있지만, 미국을 비롯한 주변국들의 평양이 조약을 깰 것에 대한 걱정은 증가할 것이다. 만약, 북한 정권이 미국과 주변국들에서 지원을 해주도록 회유하지 못한다면, 아마도 그들은 경제 자유화를 하는 것 이외에는 별다른 방법이 없을 것으로 보인다.

ON THE SYSTEMATIC PREPARATION FOR CULTURAL EXCHANGES IN THE KOREAN PENINSULA, WITH GERMANY AS THE CASE STUDY

Seoyoung Kim

—

Seoyoung Kim is curator, former artistic director and senior curator at the Die Neue Aktionsgalerie in Berlin, and TF director in Shanghai. She currently works as a research project's coordinator of the Art History Institute, dept. East Asian Art History at the Freie Universität Berlin. She graduated with a Bachelor's degree of Fine Arts, Bachelor's degree of Art History in dept. History and Cultural Studies, and Master's degree (ongoing) of Art History in global context. She has received grants for international exchanges and collaborations from Arts Council Korea with which she is developing her curatorial project: "A Radical Place". Currently she has received a grant for the research on the "Analyze the status of international collaboration regarding cultural exchange with the Korean peninsula". Her recent edited and co-edited publications include: A Radical Place. Berlin explore, A Radical Place. Reference Book, Comprehensive Dictionary of Artists, and What's going on in... Gwangju and Busan? Two major biennials in South Korea..

Awareness of the problems about cultural exchange in Germany's unification process

The division of the Korean peninsula, which fragmented the Korean people, occurred when the U.S. and USSR formed a political polarization structure after the Second World War, which in turn triggered the establishment of separate administrations in the North and South. Of course, the Korean War played a critical role in the division, but the world was being reconfigured into the Cold War hegemony amidst the conflict between liberalism and socialism under the U.S. and the USSR's reinforced division strategy. This dual-node ideology resulted in the spatial division of the Korean Peninsula. Germany suffered a similar fate, divided into the more liberalist West- and socialist East Germany at the time. However, while Germany's case bears notable similarity to that of Korea's in terms of the political climate that germinated the division, the methods in which the degree of tension and conflict were dealt with differed in the two cases. Germany recognized the division more as the result of culture-triggered Cold War in Europe rather than a rupture among its own people, and maintained its emphasis on politics that highlight interrelations with other countries. Unlike Korea, which was culturally divided after having experienced a civil war, East and West Germany maintained cultural exchanges with the surrounding countries. Although spatial division persisted, there were cultural allegiances within the two Germanys, and as well as movements aimed at cultural unification with adjacent countries such as France, Czech, Switzerland and Poland (e.g. Baden-Wüttemberg-Schweiz-Elsaß or Saar-Lothringen-Luxemburg-Rheinland-Pfalz). Pre-reunification Germany's continuous cultural interaction with neighboring countries may have been influenced by political alliances, but there is also the possibility that both East and West were clearly aware of the need for systematized, government-driven discussions and procedures for reinstating national identity despite the division. Different societies coming together and sharing history and culture is the basic condition for symbiosis in a postmodern society. Germany's reunification in 1990 was made possible by social changes that occurred through such continuous, long-term cultural exchanges.

However, despite such efforts, the cultural differences in East and West due to disparate social systems served as an obstacle in the social unification process of the East being incorporated into the West. The cause may be attributed more to individual disappointments (GLASER, Hermann, p.9) that happened when the East faced the indifference of the West, rather than differences in political ideology. As shown in Germany's case, changes in the South's understanding of the North require the establishment of a systematic preparation process for cultural exchange on a national level. Existing researches on the two Koreas' exchange within Germany were largely based on comprehension and cognition of the political situations and economic changes that occurred during Germany's reunification. Also, Korea's unification policy, while sharing the need for cultural exchange, shows differing attitudes towards the sustainability of cultural exchange within the peninsula according to political situations. Therefore, an analysis of studies on cultural exchanges within Germany, focusing on the cultural exchange politics of Germany as a once-divided nation, may be productive for Korea's reunification process. Such study may provide ways to understand cultural exchange politics in divided nations within new contexts, and also make connections to the value of potential and sustainable cultural exchanges in the Korean Peninsula. This study will be focusing, therefore, on international cultural collaboration and systematic support seen in the reunification process of Germany, and long-term measures for sustainable cultural exchange based on Korea's current conditions.

Looking at North Korea through Culture, History, and Cultural Exchange in the Korean Peninsula

Cultural exchange within the Korean peninsula goes beyond artistic creation or activities. In 1981, UNESCO defined cultural exchange, which was a central concept in the regulation it announced (Act on UNESCO Activities, 1981), takes on the form of collaboration based on mankind's ethical and intellectual cooperation that enhances mutual understanding among different cultures and countries. In this light, the subject of intra-peninsular cultural exchange in Korea can be expanded from civil subjects to the global village as a whole. Therefore, for the two Koreas to collaborate, there is a need for cultural planning in relation to human resources in order to ensure a long-term, sustainable interaction rather than promoting national ideology. Such plans should invite all constituents of the human society in general. Through such participations, intra-peninsula cultural exchange in Korea will be able to expand and become further vitalized. Also, the implementation of a system that could be overseen and accepted by the global community, the tensions between the two Koreas may see a true sense of relief. Systematic reorganization and the collaborative effort of the government as well as the legal sector are crucial in this process.

I studied methodology focusing on cultural assets regarding intra-peninsular cultural exchange in Korea in collaboration with Professor Dr. Jeonghee Lee-Kalisch (East Asian Art History, Art History Institute in Freie Universität Berlin), and planned the International Workshop on the "Protection and Preservation of Cultural Heritage on the Korean Peninsula" for the Asian Art Museum, Berlin National Museums, Prussian Cultural Heritage Foundation in Germany on the subject of "Protecting and Preserving North Korea's Cultural Assets." The objective was to raise awareness of the propriety and need for studying North Korea's cultural assets among cultural policy experts in Germany and international organizations in Europe, as well as specialists in related fields. Recently, the global community has been developing various levels and types of networks centered on Europe, promoting activities such as restoring cultural properties damaged by threats of war as in Egypt or Afghanistan in relation to the protection of cultural assets around the world and expanding their influence over decisions being made in cultural policy sectors while improving the overall system. I became aware of the fact that the National Museums in Berlin (Staatliche Museen zu Berlin)'s Rathgen Research Laboratory (Rathgen-Forschungslabor) has restored a 1,500-years old Goguryeo (Koguryo) ancient tomb mural from 6th Century B.C. in the process of collecting cases of cultural asset restoration conducted through such forms of international cooperation. Germany has been providing continuous and systematized cultural support to North Korea, including preservation and management of cultural assets, scholarly exchange, and fostering educational institutions and developing human resources based on international relationships. Agencies and institutions that take on such roles or the kinds of support provided widely vary, from public foundations such as the German Academic Exchange Service (DAAD: Deutscher Akademischer Austausch Dienst) or the Goethe Institut to civil party organizations (foundations) such as Hans-Seidel Stiftung, Friedrich-Naumann-Stiftung, and Friedrich-Ebert-Stiftung. It has been reported that a German government organization is preparing a project for resuming the restoration of the historical sites in Gaesung (Kaesong). Such efforts may be seen as admirable accomplishments, given that the systematic infrastructure in North Korea is lacking in many ways. Up till now, North Korea has been more favorable and open towards cultural support from Europe in contrast to their conflicted relationship with the U.S. As noted above, if we are to attempt a systematic planning for cultural assets with regards to the intra-peninsular cultural exchange in Korea, a scholarly consideration of collaborative methodology in conjunction with Europeans international organizations will be a potential trajectory. As Korea's division persists, the differences in North and South Korea's stance will face continuous obstacles without the assistance of international collaboration. Also, considering how the interests of neighboring countries such as China and Japan regarding intra-peninsular cultural exchange fall short to the desired level, discussions and collaborations with international organizations will offer alternative approaches to resolving problems in the two Koreas' cultural interaction. Moreover, such approaches will enable sustainable relationships regardless of the political situations in the peninsula. For instance, the recent political tension originating from the Gaesung (Kaesong) Complex issue has been ameliorated when the historic monuments and sites in Gaesung (Kaesong) North Korea was acknowledged as a world heritage by UNESCO.

However, if one is to attempt a systematic planning of intra-peninsular cultural exchange from the perspective of cultural assets, there is a need to clearly highlight the fact that cultural properties in both Koreas are to be shared uniformly regardless of nationality. The cultural assets in North Korea should be preserved by the North Korean government, and the surrounding countries including Korea should be guaranteed of their right and position to participate through an international collaboration system. Also, as the scope of cultural assets includes not only relics and historical sites but also natural environments in the urban environment such as roads, protection of cultural properties should be conducted from the stance of history and culture that covers the entirety of the spatial range. At times, protecting cultural assets can be narrowly defined as restoring traces of lost history such as rebuilding ruins. Such tendencies may limit the range of cultural asset protection to an act of historicity, but the fundamental principle of protecting cultural properties includes intangible assets (Prof. Dr. SIMON, Stephan), and must be seen as changing the overall space of life in our lived experience. With such principles as the guiding posts, North Korea's urban space may be recognized as cultural heritage in our historical purview, and we will be able to gradually overcome the sense of regional disjuncture originating from the national division. In addition, as cases of cultural asset protection can be collected across fields such as art, architecture, language, and environment, an interdisciplinary research will be able to maximize our comprehension of North Korea's history and culture.

Future Visions of Intra-Peninsular Cultural Exchange in Korea

It is time for us to seek concrete ways to approach the issue of establishing a consensus regarding intra-peninsular cultural exchange in collaboration with the global community and neighboring countries, in connection to the task of peacefully reuniting the two Koreas. Noting the fact that European countries' interest in Korea's cultural exchange is mainly focused on North Korea's history and culture, we must first build an international collaboration system (international cultural governance), observe the situation in North Korea in relation to cultural assets through the given system and even attempt indirect management. Promoting an East Asia-wide environment for cultural exchange in Korea based on the precedent of Germany where systematic vitalization of cultural exchange was based on relationships with nearby countries will ensure the stability of this plan. As North Korea cannot neglect China due to its geopolitical station, there is a need to consider the regional context of East Asia in order to understand the history of the Korean peninsula.

Therefore, from our perspective, such cultural exchanges must be based on Korea's historical contexts and problems as a universal value, and such exchanges must become systematic preparations and processes for unification and cultural re-fusion concerning the entire peninsula from a long-term perspective. The political role of nearby ally countries arising from Korea's division must not become the condition of cultural exchange; an approach that completely differs from the existing relations must be applied in order to comprehend and establish future visions of Korea's cultural exchange. As mentioned above, in order to approach intra-peninsular cultural exchange in Korea from the perspective of cultural assets, scholarly research must precede in order to protect and preserve North Korea's cultural assets in collaboration of Europe's international world heritage preservation organizations or cultural asset restoration specialists. Especially, there is a need to reorganize and reestablish systems concerning the preservation of North Korea's urban space from historical and cultural stances, and such efforts will hopefully vitalize cultural exchange in the Korean peninsula in connection to Korea's unification policies.

한반도 문화교류의 제도적 준비에 대하여 독일 사례를 중심으로

김서영

—

김서영(1985, 서울)은 현재 베를린자유대학 미술사학연구소 동아시아 미술사 연구 프로젝트 코디네이터이며, 베를린 Die Neue Aktionsgalerie 아트 디렉터 (artistic director) 및 수석 큐레이터 (senior curator), TF 디렉터 (TF director), Shanghai (상하이)를 역임했다. 베를린, 본, 런던, 상하이, 도쿄, 서울, 마드리드, 브뤼셀, 리스본에서 다수의 프로젝트와 전시의 기획을 담당했다. 베를린 자유대학 문화 역사학 동아시아 미술사학 학사, 미술사학 석사(과정)를 거쳤다. 문화체육관광부와 (재)예술경영지원센터에서 한국 미술의 국제화를 선도할 글로벌 큐레이터 양성 목표로 시행하는 조사.연구지원(2013)으로 〈한반도(남북) 문화교류 국제협력현황분석〉 주제를 연구하고 있다. 그밖에 한국문화예술위원회의 국제문화예술교류 (2012~2013), 차세대예술인력집중육성 (2011~2012) 지원을 받아 베를린 거점으로 한 A Radical Place 국제 교류 프로젝트를 책임·기획했다. 최근 주재한 출판 및 발행물은 A Radical Place (2013, Seoul, Mediabus, ver.2 / 2011, Frankfurt am Main, MVB, ver.1); German Comprehensive Dictionary of Artists, International Artists Database (2012-2013, Munich, De Gruyter); What's going on in... Gwangju and Busan? Two major biennials in South Korea (2013, Madrid, art.es); East People Power (2012, Leipzig) 등이 있다.

독일 통합 과정에서 문화교류의 문제의식

한반도 분단은 제2차 세계대전 이후 미국과 구 소련에 의한 이원적 정치대립 구도가 남과 북에 구축되고, 서로 각각의 단독정부가 수립하면서 한민족이 분열된 현상이다. 물론 한국전쟁이 중요한 계기가 되었지만 비슷한 시기에 미·소의 분할체계 강화로 세계는 자유주의와 사회주의와의 대립 속에서 냉전 체계의 지배질서로 재편성되었고, 이러한 이원적 이데올로기는 한반도의 분단이라는 공간적 분할로 형성되었다. 당시 독일도 한반도와 마찬가지로 자유주의 진영인 서독과 사회주의 진영인 동독체제로 분열되었다. 그러나 독일은 한반도의 분단과 정치적 대립 상황에선 유사한 점이 많지만, 그 긴장의 정도와 갈등을 대처하는 방식에선 많은 차이점을 보였다. 왜냐하면, 독일은 처음부터 분단국가를 민족의 단절로 보지 않고 유럽의 문화적 냉전의 대립으로 인식하였고, 다른 국가와의 상호 관계를 중시하는 정책 노선을 고수하였기 때문이다. 민족 전쟁을 체험하고 문화적으로 단절된 한반도와는 다르게 동·서독은 각각 주변국과 함께 지속해서 문화를 교류해왔다. 비록 공간적으로 국가는 분열되었지만 동서독 내부의 문화적 연대 과정도 있었고 체코, 폴란드, 스위스 및 프랑스[1]와 같이 각각의 국경에 인접한 지역과 문화적으로 통합하려는 움직임이 있었다. 이처럼 통일 전 독일이 주변의 국가와 문화적으로 활발히 교류하는 모습은 정치적 동맹이 작용했겠지만 분단 상황임에도 정체성 회복이라는 국가 차원의 제도화된 논의와 과정의 필요성을 절감하고 있었다고 생각한다. 서로 다른 사회가 만나 역사와 문화를 함께 경험하는 것은 탈근대적 사회 통합에서 요구하는 기본적인 상생 조건이다. 1990년 독일의 재통일 과정도 그러한 장기적이고 지속적인 문화 교류를 통하여 일어난 사회 변화 속에서 가능했다.

그러나 이런 노력에도 불구하고 동·서독의 서로 다른 체제에 따른 문화적 차이는 동독이 서독으로 편입되는 사회 통합의 과정에서 장애 요소로 작용하였다. 그 원인은 정치적 이념의 차이보다도 동독 사회에 무관심한 서독 사회가 서로 만나서 생기는 개개인의 심리적인 실망감 때문이라고 볼 수 있다.[2] 이처럼 독일의 사례에서 보는 바와 같이, 한반도 분단 문제에서도 북한에 대한 인식 변화는 국가 차원의 문화교류에 대한 제도적 준비와 과정의 수립이 필요하다. 그 동안 독일에서 한반도 교류에 관한 기존 연구는 독일 재통일의 정치적 상황과 경제적 변화에 대한 이해와 인지를 기반으로 하였다. 또한, 우리나라의 통일 정책은 독일 통합 과정에서 문화 교류에 대한 인식을 공유하면서도 한반도의 지속 가능한 문화 교류에 대해서는 정치적 상황에 따라 상반된 입장을 보여주었다고 할 수 있다. 따라서 독일에서 최근까지 진행된 문화교류에 연구 결과를 분석해 본다면, 분단국가로서 독일의 문화 교류 지원 정책은 한반도의 재통일 과정에서 많은 성과가 있을 것으로 파악된다. 이것은 분단국가에서의 문화교류 정책을 새로운 맥락에서 이해할 수 있는 단서를 제공하고, 또한 오늘날 계획 가능한 지속적인 한반도 문화교류에 대한 가치와도 연계해서 보여줄 수 있기 때문이다. 이러한 논의에 대하여 필자는 독일 통합 과정에서 국제적인 문화교류 협력 및 제도적 활성화와 관련한 한반도 실제적 현실을 고려한 지속 가능한 문화교류의 장기적 대안 중심으로 전개하고자 한다.

문화와 역사를 통해 바라보는 북한, 그리고 한반도 문화 교류

한반도 문화 교류는 예술적 창작이나 활동에 국한되는 것은 아니다. 1981년, 유네스코(UNESCO)가 발표한 법령[3]의 핵심적 내용이 되는 문화교류의 정의는 국가 및 문화간 상호 이해를 증진시키고 인류사회의 지적, 도덕적 연대에 기초한 협력의 형상이다. 이런 점에서 한반도 문화 교류의 주체는 국가 구성원 뿐만 아니라 인류 공동체, 국제 공동체 전체로 확대될 수 있다. 따라서 한반도 협력에는 국가 이데올로기의 선전 효과를 노리는 것보다 장기간 지속적으로 교류할 수 있도록 인적 지원과 관련한 문화적 기획이 필요하다. 이러한 기획에는 인류공동체 구성원 모두가 참여할 수 있어야 한다. 참여를 통해 한반도 문화 교류는 더 확대되고 활성될 수 있을 것이며, 나아가 국제사회, 국제 공동체 모두가 관심 있게 지켜볼 수 있는 제도가 정착된다면 이것은 진정한 의미의 한반도 긴장 완화를 만들어 낼 수 있을 것이다. 이 과정에서 무엇보다 중요한 것은 제도적인 정비이며 정부와 법학계 모두의 공동 노력이 필요하다.

필자는 독일 베를린자유대 미술사학 연구소의 동아시아 미술사 이정희 교수와 함께 한반도 문화 교류 문제에 관한 문화재 측면에서 방법을 연구하였으며 "북한의 문화재 보호와 보존"을 주제로 독일 프로이센 문화재 재단의 베를린 동아시아국립박물관에서 국제 전문가 회의[4]를 기획하였다. 한반도 문화 교류 문제에 대해 공감할 수 있는 독일과 유럽의 국제전문기구의 문화정책 전문가들과 연계 분야 전문가들을 대상으로 북한 문화재 연구의 타당성 및 필요성 인식을 재고하기 위한 것이다. 최근 국제 사회에서는 세계 문화재 보호와 관련하여, 아프가니스탄과 이집트의 사례처럼 전쟁 위협으로 손실된 문화재의 복원과 같은, 유럽을 중심으로 한 다양한 수준과 성격의 네트워크를 발전시켜 문화 정책의 의사 결정에 그들의 영향력을 확대하거나 제도화하는 수준을 높이고 있다. 필자는 이와 같은 국제협력체계를 통한 문화재 복원 사례에 대해 자료를 확보하는 과정에서 베를린 국립박물관 연합의 라트겐 연구소(Rathgen-Forschungslabor)가 유네스코의 지원으로 1,500년의 세월을 견뎌낸 6세기 고구려 고분 벽화를 복원한 사실을 접하게 되었다. 독일은 통일 이전부터 국제 관계에 기반을 두고 문화재 보존 관리뿐만 아니라 학술교류, 교육기관 및 인재의 양성 등 한반도의 북한에 대해 꾸준히 체계적인 문화적 지원을 해오고 있다. 여기에는 독일의 학술교류처 (DAAD), 괴테 인스티튜트(Goethe Institut)와 같은 공공 재단에서부터 한스-자이델(Hans-Seidel Stiftung), 프리드리히-나우만(Friedrich-Naumann-Stiftung), 프리드리히-에베르트(Friedrich-Ebert-Stiftung) 재단과 같이 민간 정당 기구 등 교류 지원의 기관이나 지원 종류가 다양하다. 최근에는 독일 정부기관이 중단되었던 개성의 역사 지구 복원을 제기하는 사업을 준비 및 추진 중인 것으로 알려졌다. 이는 북한의 제도적 인프라가 미비한 실정에서 실로 놀라운 업적으로 보인다. 그 동안 북한은 미국과 대립했던 관례에 비하여 유럽 기반의 문화 지원에 대해서는 우호적인 입장을 일관했다. 앞에서 기술한 바와 같이, 우리가 한반도 문화교류 문제에 대해 문화재 측면에서 제도적 기획을 시도한다면, 북한의 문화재 보호와 보존 방법을 위해 유럽의 국제적인 기관과 함께 어떤 방법으로 참여할지 학술적으로 고려해 볼 수 있을 것이다. 한반도의 분단이 오랫동안 지속되면서 이와 같은 국제 협력에 의하지 않고는 남북한의 문화적 입장 차이가 해소되기 힘들 것이다. 그리고 우리나라가 한반도 문화 교류에 대해 여전히 중국, 일본 등 주변 국가와 이해관계가 부족한 것을 고려한다면, 국제적인 기구의 합의를 통해서 한반도 문화 교류의 문제들을 해결하기 위한 여러 가지 대안을 찾을 수 있을 것이다. 또한, 이것은 한반도 정치 상황과 무관하게 지속적인 교류를 가능토록 하여 줄 것이다. 최근의 예를 들면, 북한과 개성 공단 문제로 정치적으로 대립했던 상황이 북한 개성 역사 유적지구가 유네스코 세계문화유산으로 등재되면서, 이것으로 인하여 한반도 긴장도 완화되고 개성공단의 정치적 대립도 해결된 것으로 여겨 진다.

그러나 한반도 문화 교류를 문화재 측면에서 제도적 기획을 시도한다면 분단 상황과 상관없이 남북한 문화재는 우리 모두의 문화재라는 점을 명확히 해야 한다. 북한 지역의 문화재는 기본적으로 북한이 주도하여 보호 관리해야 하고, 한국을 포함한 주변의 국가는 국제협력체계로서 참여할 명분과 지위를 보장받아야 한다. 또한, 문화재의 범위는 유물, 유적뿐만 아니라 도시, 도로(길) 등의 자연환경을 모두 포함하기 때문에 문화재 보호는 공간적 범위 전체를 함께 보며 역사와 문화적 보존 차원에서 접근해야 한다. 간혹 문화재 보호가 폐허가 된 도시를 재건하는 것처럼 대부분 소실된 역사의 흔적을 복원하는 보존 작업으로만 한정되어 의미가 축소 전달되는 경우도 있다. 그래서 문화재 보호가 역사적으로만 접근한다고 보일 수 있겠지만, 문화재 보호의 근본 원리는 무형적인(intangible)것을 모두 포함하는 것으로[5], 현실에서 살아있는 삶의 공간 전체를 변화시키는 것에 가깝다고 할 수 있다. 우리가 한반도의 북한을 바라볼 때도 이런 원칙들이 전제된다면 북한의 도시 공간은 문화유산으로서 역사 속에서 인정될 수 있을 것이며, 더불어 우리는 국가 분열로 인해 생긴 지역 단절감을 조금씩 극복할 수 있을 것이다. 그밖에, 문화재 보존의 실례는 예술, 도시, 건축, 언어, 환경 등 다양한 분야의 조합을 모두 활용할 수 있으므로 분야별 연구 결과가 동반될 수 있다면, 우리의 북한에 대한 문화와 역사의 이해가 극대화될 것으로 보인다.

미래 한반도 문화교류의 모습

이제 우리는 한반도의 문화교류를 이러한 국제 및 주변 국가와의 합의를 구축하는 문제와 어떻게 접근하고 해결할 것인지 한반도 평화 · 통일 문제와 연결하여 구체적 계획을 모색해야 할 것이다. 한반도 문화교류에 대한 유럽의 관심은 주로 북한 문화와 역사에 연관된 것을 고려하여 우리는 그 문제를 해결하기 위한 국제협력체계(국제 문화 거버넌스)를 만드는 데 먼저 집중하고, 그 후 그 국제협력체계를 통하여 문화재와 관련한 북한의 상황을 관찰하면서 간접적 관리까지 시도할 수 있을 것이다. 무엇보다 분단 독일에서 문화 교류의 제도적 활성화가 주변의 국가와의 관계를 기반으로 한 사실을 참고하여 한반도의 문화교류를 동아시아 차원의 문화교류가 되도록 접근하고 해결하면 더 안정적일 것이다. 한반도의 북한이 지리적 입지에서 중국의 존재를 무시할 수 없는 것과 같이 한반도 역사를 이해할 때에는 항상 동아시아의 지역적 맥락을 고려하여 분석되어야 한다.

따라서 우리의 입장에서 이러한 문화 교류는, 먼저 보편적 가치로 접근한 한반도의 역사적 문제의식을 기반으로 하여야 하고, 나아가 그 교류는 장기적으로 봤을 때 한반도 공동체 차원의 문화적 재결합과 통합의 제도적인 준비와 과정이 되어야 한다. 여기에 한반도 분단으로 인한 주변 동맹국의 정치적 역할이 문화 교류의 조건으로 직접 작용해서는 안 되며, 미래 한반도 문화교류가 놓인 국제적 조건은 기존 입장과는 전혀 다른 접근이 요구될 것이다. 앞서 밝힌 대로, 한반도 문화교류를 문화재 측면에서 접근한다면 북한의 문화재 보호와 보존을 위해 유럽의 국제적인 세계 문화유산 보호 기관이나 문화재 복원 전문가와 함께 학술적인 연구들이 먼저 이루어져야 할 것이다. 특히 북한 도시 공간보존과 관련해서 역사와 문화적 관점의 제도 정비가 필요하며, 이러한 내용이 발전 돼서 앞으로 한반도 통일 정책과 연결하여 한반도 문화교류가 활성화될 수 있길 바란다.

References

1 Baden-Wüttemberg-Schweiz-Elsaß or Saar-Lothringen-Luxemburg-Rheinland-Pfalz

2 GLASER, Hermann, p.9

3 Act on UNESCO Activities, 1981

4 Protection and Preservation of Cultural Heritage on the Korean Peninsula

5 Prof. Dr. SIMON, Stephan

02 BACKGROUND DATA
1. FACT SHEETS
2. GEOGRAPHICAL FACTS
3. INFRASTRUCTURAL FACTS
4. INDUSTRIAL GEOGRAPHY

POLICY ISSUES FOR THE FUTURE OF THE KOREAN PENINSULA AND ITS SPATIAL DEVELOPMENT

Sangjun Lee

—

Sang-Jun Lee, Ph D, is the senior research fellow and the head of Center for the Korean Peninsula & Northeast Asian Studies at Korea Research Institute for Human Settlements (KRIHS). He received the Doctor of Engineering in Urban & Regional Planning Technical University at Berlin in Germany, and the Master's degree in Architectural Engineering at Yonsei University in Korea. He has presented in various international conferences, and his articles were published world widely. His active experiences include the visiting fellow at National Institute for Research Advancement in Japan and Federal Office for Building and Regional Planning in Germany.

Introduction

A rapid change in the political situation of Northeast Asia raises up the need to actively discuss about a future vision of the Korean peninsula, and a development strategy for the coexistence between North and South Korea. In this article, I want to propose the vision for an integrated Korean Peninsula, and policy issues of spatial development in North Korea based on a phased economic unification between North and South Korea. Even though both countries keep different political systems, I contrived the task for vision and spatial development on the assumption that they have a unified market system in the future.

Potential of the Korean Peninsula

The most powerful factor that the Korean Peninsula offers is its political and economic potential due to its geography on the Eastern end of the Asian continent. Its geographical position strategically positions the peninsula as a gateway and crossroads for economic cooperation in east Asia. Its centrality between the continental and coastal neighbors places it in the middle of the the West Sea Rim and the East Sea Rim, consisting of a population of 640 million, and a market of 7 trillion dollars per year. South Korea's investment on human capital has allowed it to advance its development on information technology at a much faster speed than its competitors. This increases its chances of becoming a leader in economic cooperation in Northeast Asia. This position can also be secured with the construction of the transcontinental railway giving Korea the potential for having a larger distribution network, and cooperating in the energy production process for the region.

The weakest factor of the Korean Peninsula is the security issue that occurred because of the confrontation between the two Koreas. According to the yearly report 'Global Peace Index (GPI)', in the rank of 'peaceful nation' South Korea and North Korea rank in33th and 131st respectively among 144 countries. The economic potential of the Korean Peninsula is being consumed by the military tension between the two countries. The conflict between the peninsula and the surrounding countries can also be conceptualized as a weakness of historical and cultural aspects.

According to the survey from the Korean Research Institute of Human Settlement in 2009, the future outlook of Korean Peninsula is anticipated as a positive one. In response to the survey about the future outlook of the Korean Peninsula in 2030, 83.1% answered "mostly positive," 5.1% "very positive," 7.6% "Pessimistic." The survey focused on factors of relationship between South and North Korea, international relations, world economic order, and proliferation of local economic integration, which are factors that are expected to create a positive influence in the Korean Peninsula. It is expected that the future Korean Peninsula will have two different states but one integrated economic zone. The survey says, 44.9% of people pictured 2030 of Korean Peninsula as two independent states with one economic market, and 29.7% of people pictured close economic relationship between two states.

As opposed to "positive future", "standstill conditional future" means that both South-North Korea relationship and international relationship will continue in similar manner. If North Korea refuses to adopt market-economic system and political and economical conflicts restrict the economic cooperation, the future of Northeast Asia and the Korean Peninsula will not be much different from the present condition. It means that 60 years of standstill condition since the independence may last even longer than we expect.

The survey says the most influential restrictions to developing the future Korean Peninsula are South and North Korea division (36.2%) and enlarging power of neighboring nations (18.4%).

In this kind of conditions, it is important to utilize given changes actively and to make visions and strategies that respond to the challenges. Raising up the needs for cooperation in political, diplomatic, security and economical fields will give us, both South and North Korea, a new opportunity, because the Korean Peninsula is the area that clearly reflects interests between nations in Northeast Asia.

Vision of the Korean Peninsula

The future of the Korean Peninsula will be strongly influenced by the two previously mentioned variables, the relationship between the two Koreas and the relationship between the Korean Peninsula to other countries. Consequently, two optimistic visions can be introduced. The first is Korea as a "Network Hub" where Korea becomes the networking center, leading the interchange of ideas and by means of its geo-economic and geopolitical potential. This vision can be represented as a socioeconomic barrier free Korean Peninsula, and a peaceful nuclear free Korean Peninsula. A "barrier free Korean Peninsula" would mean that there would be no restrictions of interchange of ideas and contents within the peninsula and abroad. A "Peaceful nuclear free Korean Peninsula" would mean that it would be an interacting space free from military conflict usually categorized as a nuclear threat.

Networking would imply not only the formation of links but also the structuring of a socioeconomic and military framework that offers security and efficiency in the process of interchange. In order to become a regional leader, this framework must have global competitiveness. In the case that the Korean Peninsula maintains its status quo for a considerable period, it can begin the process of bridging its network to other countries.

Spatial Structure of an integrated Korean Peninsula

In order for the Korean Peninsula to become a hub for collaborative networking within the foundation of "Global competitiveness," it must first conceive a comprehensive management strategy in order to improve land management from an economic development point of view. It must reinforce the internal integrity within the Korean Peninsula and reinforce the international networking.

Spatial Structure for the integrity reinforcement in the Korean Peninsula

The reinforcement of industrial and infrastructural integrity between the two Koreas is a significant step in order for the peninsula to become a single economic block. For this to occur, a cluster of industrial collaboration and energy must be form along the east and west corridors. It should establish a regional industrial cluster and promote a long term connection between North and South Korea. From the south, it will require to form clusters in areas like Seamankum Project Area, Gunsan Free Economic Zone, Yellow Sea Free Economic Zone (Pyongtaek, Danjin, and Seosan), and Incheon Free Economic Zone. From the North Korean side, it must aim at consolidating industrial links promoting living and basic industry in Haeju, Pyongyang, Nampo, and Sinuiju. The eastern corridors will need to establish an energy industrial cluster. In South Korea, Busan-Jinhae Free Economic Zone, and Ulsan Industrial District will need to foster a central cluster for shipbuilding, fine chemistry, and green vehicle. Pohang should focus as a central cluster for renewable energy, new materials, and metals industry. Cities like Hamhung, Sinpo, Chungjin, Rason in North Korea should establish a distribution system between north and south. In the aspect of infrastructure it will also be necessary to study the supply chain between North and South Korea. To reinforce the integrity between North and South Korea, it will be necessary to develop metropolitan clusters.

Spatial structure for the national networking reinforcement in the Korean Peninsula

To activate the vision of a positive future, the Korean Peninsula must propel its spatial development by shifting a promotion of "close land" to "open land." It must acknowledge an openness of exchange and collaboration beyond the physical domain. There must be an efficient strategy of outreach to the rest of the world. This could be done by means of collaborative points (interface cities), and collaborative line (city alliance).

Interface city should be developed in existing metropolitan areas not as the concept of special districts providing merely freedom of economic activity, but as the international exchange and unification of culture and economy, which is able to exchange without any restriction between the companies and people from diverse nations. This could act as a plug-in that connects diverse layers of culture and knowledge. Cities containing the potential to become interface cities are Mokpo, and Saemankum in South Korea; Pyongyang, Nampo, Wonsan Sinuiju, and Rason in North Korea. Mokpo and Saemankum could harness the collaboration and exchange between the Korean Peninsula and Shenzen and Shanghai in China. Pyongyang and Nampo could collaborate with Beijing-Tianjin. Wonsan and Hamhung could be ports of interchange. Sinuiju could be the point of collaboration between the Korean Peninsula and China. Rason and Chongjin could create a synergy effect by connecting high-speed traffic networks and comprehensive energy supply chains with surrounding countries.

For these cities to perform their role, there must be alliances with major cities from neighboring countries. This means increasing the level of exchange beyond that of a twin city in order to create cultural exchange and an intelligence industry. It would be necessary to promote construction of joint events such as international expos, human resource exchange among the regional higher learning institutions, and enduring the exchange of human resources among the companies in relevant cities. Some of the necessary links are in the pan-yellow sea territory between Mokpo, Incheon, Nampo, Tianjin, and Weihai. Another link would be between Busan, Pohang, Ulsan, Sokcho, Wonsan, Rason, Nakhodka, Vladivostok, and Niigata.

At the regional level of Northeast Asia, it is necessary to consider a progressive access, which promotes the link of exchange system in a movable territory within five hours, and then expand the link to the movable territory within one day.

For the establishment of a one-day business zone, it is necessary to create the exchange network by land, sea, and air in the interface city. This can reinforce the exchange link of 3 major economic blocks in China (Pearl river delta, Changjang delta, and Bohai sea economic blocs) and industrial belt in southern and western coast in the Korean Peninsula. It is necessary to aim at constructing the East Sea Rim which can develop a North Pole route and attempt to be a liaison for high value products exchange with Russian Fas East and Japan in the long term.

Issues of North Korean development according to reconstructing Korean Peninsula.

Some of possible proposals are noted below that are based on the future Korean Peninsula's spatial structure above.

<u>Medium term issue</u>
This phase requires the industrial infrastructure development in and around the North Korean western area and the contiguous area between North and South Korea. Among the infrastructures needed to be developed, partial modernization of necessary road sections and electrical infrastructure should be considered to expedite transportation of goods. The aspect of having an integral

economy in North and South Korea, it will be necessary to promote primarily industrial infrastructure development, which connects our metropolitan area with Pyongyang-Nampo in North Korea (Lee, Sang Jun with others in 2011). It is necessary for the area including Sinuiju in North Korea and Dandong in China to be developed exploring their fullest usage of geoeconomic potential for the Korean Peninsula. From this perspective, it is necessary for China, North Korea, and us to promote collaborative development of road, railway, and industrial districts in and around Sinuiju and Dandong. In this phase it is necessary to keep the current condition of the railway and road network, especially the railway between Seoul and Sinuiju, as well as a road renovation plan.

Long term issue

For a long term, it is necessary to promote a comprehensive development of industrial infrastructure in and around the western and eastern corridors of North Korea. Progressive development is necessary to expand the ripple effect from the growth of the major cities along the western and eastern corridors.(Lee, Sang jun with others in 2012). The reorganization plan of the existing manufacturing areas is necessary in the long term. It is also necessary for this phase the construction of a new traffic network connecting the Korean Peninsula with the Northeast area of China through a high-speed transportation system. It is necessary to construct the high speed railway in Gyeongui Line axis and promote new highway construction in Gyeongwon-Tonghae Line. It is necessary to promote the facility modernization, which matches the international criteria for a seaport and airport. In this phase there is also earnest promotion of traffic network collaboration between the Korean Peninsula and international traffic network.

Conclusion

The establishment of the Korean Peninsula's spatial structure and development of North Korea will make or break the vision of the Korean Peninsula. In this perspective, I want to finish this article with the review of our policy issues.

First, in order to lead the collaboration of surrounding countries, it is necessary to define the new concept of a 'Korean Peninsula Initiative'. This concept will be established with the base of intimate relationship between North and South Korea. Through the collaborative relationship with China and Russia, which North Korea currently maintains and collaborative relationship with America and Japan, which South Korea maintains, a 'Korean Peninsula Initiative' will be promoted. Especially, it will be an essential task for the Korean Peninsula to establish the collaborative network with China, which is emerging as a powerful nation in the world.

Second, North and South Korea should lead the liberalization to promote the commerce network for obtaining the position as facilitators of economic exchange in Northeast Aisa. The position will be acquired through an integration between economy and culture. It is necessary for North and South Korea to lead the formation of a new 'Asian cultural and economic block' which promotes the exchange and collaboration of international societies and supports mutual harmony of diversity. North and South Korea should secure the leading position of cultural exchange from the current condition of post-nationalism, post-ideology, post-hegemonism, post-territorialism. In order to secure such position, it is necessary for a 'cultural Korean stream' and an 'economic Korean stream' to achieve the cultural and economic balance among China, Japan, and Russia.

Future Korean Peninsula should overcome many restrictions to perform the central function of exchange and collaboration in Northeast Aisa. We have a task of persuading the interest group, which is passive about opening and also the task of improving the collaboration with North Korea which is still pessimistic. Afterward, our way to lead the cooperation with North Korea will make or break the vision and strategy of the Korean Peninsula. It is primary thing for us to persuade North Korea by proposing the prosperity through the aim, which we will achieve together. It is difficult to receive the admission of the Korean Peninsula's function from China, Japan, Russia, and America which are outwardly competing with each other. We should consider what kind of the potential benefits will come to the Korean Peninsula and neighbor countries as it becomes the center of networking.

한반도의 미래와 북한국토 공간개발의 과제

이상준

―

이상준 박사는 국토연구원 한반도, 동북아시아 연구 센터 장이며 선임 연구위원이다. 그는 독일 베를린 공대에서 도시 및 지역 계획학 박사학위를 취득하였으며, 연세대학교에서 건축공학 석사학위를 취득하였다. 이 박사는 많은 국제 컨퍼런스에서 발표한 경험이 있으며, 그의 기사 역시 전세계적으로 출판되었다. 그는 일본 종합연구개발기구와 베를린 Federal Office for Building and Regional Planning의 객원 연구원이었다.

서문

급변하는 동북아의 상황은 한반도차원의 미래 비전과 남북 상생의 발전 전략에 대한 본격적 논의의 필요성을 제기하고 있다. 한반도의 비전에 따라 지금부터 무엇을 남북이 해야 할 것인지도 보다 분명해질 것이다. 이 글에서는 단계적인 남북경제 통합을 전제로 새로운 한반도의 비전과 북한 공간개발의 과제를 제시하고자 한다. 이 글에서는 미래 남북한이 별도의 정치체제를 유지하지만, 경제적으로는 하나의 시장경제권이 형성되는 상황을 전제로 비전과 공간개발의 과제를 모색하였다.

한반도의 잠재력

한반도의 최대 강점은 유라시아대륙 동쪽 끝에 위치한 반도로서의 지정학적, 지경학적 입지잠재력이라 할 수 있다. 한반도는 동북아 경제권의 전략적 관문이자 십자로에 위치한다. 대륙과 해양의 교차점에서 교류의 중심으로서 한반도는 환 황해경제권과 환 동해경제권을 양 날개로 구성되는 인구 6억 4,000만 명, 연 7조 달러의 동북아시장 한가운데에 위치한다. 특히 한국은 세계에서 가장 빠른 정보기술 성장 속도를 보이고 있으며, 고급 인적자원도 풍부해서 동북아 교류의 거점으로서 발전할 수 있는 잠재력이 있다. 대륙철도(TKR-TSR)연결, 아시아 고속도로 건설, 항만 및 공항연계, 극동 러시아 천연가스 연결 등을 통해 한반도가 동북아 물류 및 에너지협력의 거점으로 발전할 수 있는 잠재력이 있다.

반면에 한반도의 최대 약점은 남북대치에 따른 안보의 불안정성이다. '세계평화지수(GPI)' 연례 보고서에 따르면, '평화로운 나라' 순위에서 조사대상 144개국 가운데 남한은 33위, 북한은 131위에 머물고 있다. 남북분단과 군사안보적 긴장상황은 반도로서의 지경학적 잠재력을 잠식하고 있는 것을 의미한다. 그리고 역사, 문화 측면에서 남북한과 주변국 간의 갈등 요인들도 약점을 지적될 수 있다.

국토연구원이 2009년에 실시한 전문가 설문조사 결과 한반도 미래 전망은 대체로 낙관적일 것으로 예상되고 있다. 2030년 한반도의 미래 전망에 대해서 '대체로 낙관적 83.1%', '아주 낙관적 5.1%', '비관적 7.6%' 등으로 응답했다(이상준외 2009). 전문가들은 남북관계와 국제관계, 세계 경제질서, 지역 경제통합의 확산 등이 한반도의 미래에 대체로 긍정적 영향을 미칠 것으로 전망하고 있다. 미래 남북한은 정치적으로는 별도의 국가이나 실질적인 경제통합을 이룩하게 될 것으로 예상된다. 설문결과 2030년 남북한 관계는 정치적으로 독립적이나 경제적으로 하나의 시장 통합 상태(44.9%) 또는 긴밀한 경제적 협력관계(29.7%)로 예상되었다.

'낙관적 미래'와 대치되는 '현상유지적 상황의 미래'란 남북관계와 국제관계의 양 측면에서 현재와 비슷한 상황이 전개되는 것을 의미한다. 만약 북한이 적극적 개방을 거부하고 역내 국가간 정치·외교적 갈등이 경제협력의 발전을 제약하게 될 경우 동북아 및 한반도의 미래는 현재와 크게 달라질 것이 없을 것이다. 해방 이후 지난 60년 동안의 한반도를 지배했던 '현상유지적' 환경이 상당기간 지속될 가능성도 배제할 수 없다.

설문결과 한반도 미래 발전에 남북분단(36.2%)과 주변국의 세력확대 경쟁(18.4%)이 가장 중요한 제약요인으로 작용할 것으로 전망되었다.

이러한 전망에서는 기회를 적극적으로 활용하고 도전에 대응하는 비전과 전략이 필요하다. 정치·외교·안보·경제적 측면에서 다자간 협력의 필요성이 제기되고 여건이 성숙하고 있다는 것은 우리 남북한에 새로운 기회가 될 수 있다. 동아시아에서 다자간 이해관계가 가장 뚜렷하게 드러나고 있는 지역이 바로 한반도이기 때문이다.

한반도의 비전

앞으로 한반도의 미래 상황은 남북관계와 주변국 간의 국제관계라는 두 가지 변수가 큰 영향을 미칠 것으로 예상된다. 따라서 이 글에서는 남북관계와 주변국 간의 국제관계라는 변수를 중심으로 낙관적인 미래와 현상유지적 미래에 따른 두 가지 비전을 상정해 보았다.

최선의 한반도 비전은 '글로벌 경쟁력을 기반으로 동아시아 교류와 융합을 선도하는 네트워크 허브 코리아(Network Hub Korea)'이다. 한반도의 지정학적, 지경학적 잠재력을 활용하여 상생과 공영을 위한 동아시아의 교류와 융합을 선도하는 네트워킹의 중심으로서의 비전이 타당한 것으로 판단된다. '네트워킹의 중심지역으로서 한반도'의 비전은 '사회경제적 장벽이 없는(barrier free) 자유 한반도'와 '핵이 없는(nuclear free) 평화 한반도'로 표현할 수 있다. '장벽이 없는 자유 한반도'는 교류와 협력의 물리적, 비물리적 제약요소를 제거함으로써 어떠한 형식과 내용의 교류도 가능할 수 있도록 국제사회와 연결된(networked) 한반도를 의미한다. '핵이 없는 평화 한반도'는 핵무기로 상징되는 군사적 갈등과 혼란으로부터 해방된 평화로운 교류공간으로서의 한반도를 의미한다.

여기에서 네트워킹은 한반도가 단순한 연결지대가 아닌 교류와 협력이 체계적이고도 효율적으로 이루어질 수 있는 사회경제적, 군사 안보적 연계망 형성을 의미한다. 네트워크의 선도지역이 되기 위해서는 먼저 그러한 내부 역량을 확보하는 것이 중요하며 이러한 측면에서 글로벌 경쟁력을 갖춘 제도와 인프라가 필요하다. 반면에 현상유지적 상황이 앞으로 상당기간 지속될 전망에 기초한 차선의 비전은 남북을 주변국간의 교류와 협력을 촉진하는 동아시아의 '가교(bridge)'로 설정하는 것이다. 미래 상황이 크게 개선되지 못할 경우 한반도가 동아시아 교류와 융합을 선도하기는 어렵다고 할지라도 국가 간 교류와 협력의 촉진자 역할을 할 수 있는 '가교'로서의 역할은 가능할 것이다.

미래 한반도의 공간구조

이 글에서는 낙관적 미래전망에 기초한 비전을 중심으로 한반도의 발전을 위한 공간구조를 검토하였다. 한반도가 '글로벌 경쟁력'을 기반으로 아시아 교류와 융합을 선도하는 네트워킹(collaborative Networking)의 중심(Hub)이 되기 위해서는 한반도의 종합적인 경영전략이 필요하다. '경제개발의 대상'으로서의 한반도라는 공간에서 종합적인 '경영' 대상으로서 국토관리의 개념적 진화가 필요한 것이다.

이 글에서는 한반도 비전 실현을 위한 공간구조의 기본 구도

구축을 위해 다음과 같이 두 가지 방향을 제시하고자 한다.

한반도 내부의 통합성 강화를 위한 공간구조
한반도가 동아시아 교류와 융합의 중심적 역할을 하기 위해서는 한반도가 하나의 경제권을 형성하고 교류에 장애가 없어야 한다. 한반도가 하나의 경제권을 형성하는 데 있어서 중요한 것은 남북 간 산업과 인프라의 통합성이 강화되어야 한다. 이러한 측면에서 다음과 같은 과제가 검토될 필요가 있다. 첫째, 한반도 서해안과 동해안 축을 따라 산업과 에너지 협력클러스터를 구축하는 것이 필요하다. 이를 위해서는 일차적으로 남북한 각 지역에 지역 산업클러스터를 구축한 후 장기적으로 남북한 연계를 추진하는 것이 필요하다. 남측의 새만금·군산 경제자유구역, 황해경제자유구역(평택, 당진) 및 서산, 인천경제자유구역 등을 신성장 산업 클러스터로 육성하는 것이 필요하다. 북측의 해주, 평양-남포, 신의주는 북한의 생활 관련 산업, 기간산업육성 거점으로 추진한 후 서해안의 남북한 산업거점 지역 간 산업연계 강화를 통해 동반성장을 도모하는 것이 필요하다. 한반도 동해안 지역에는 에너지산업 클러스터를 구축하는 것이 필요하다. 남측의 부산·진해 경제자유구역, 울산 산업단지는 조선, 정밀화학, 그린 카, 포항은 신 재생 에너지 및 철강 신소재 등 중심의 클러스터로 육성하는 것이 필요하다. 북측의 함흥, 신포, 청진, 나선 등은 원자력·신 재생 에너지 등 에너지 산업과 기간산업 클러스터로 육성한 후 남북한 간 에너지산업 연계를 통한 분업체제를 구축하는 것이 필요하다. 둘째, 인프라 측면에서는 남북 간의 통합 물류망을 구축하는 것이 필요하다. 한반도 고속간선교통망과 국가 성장 동력형 산업단지가 연계되는 결절점을 중심으로, 단계적으로 통합 물류망 구축을 추진할 필요가 있다. 셋째, 남북간 통합성 강화 측면에서 한반도차원의 신(新)경기만 광역도시클러스터 육성도 추진할 필요가 있다.

한반도의 국제네트워킹 강화를 위한 공간구조
한반도가 미래의 비전을 실현해 가기 위해서는 '닫힌 영토, 폐쇄적 영토'에서 '열린 영토' 개념으로의 한반도 공간 발전을 추진해 가는 것이 중요하다. 국토의 개념이 물리적 영역을 넘어 교류와 협력의 '열린 공간'으로서 새롭게 인식될 필요가 있는 것이다. 그리고 주변국의 잠재력을 적극적으로 활용하는 전략적 인식과 자세 필요하다.

한반도가 동아시아 교류와 융합의 중심이 되기 위해서는 한반도와 외부를 효율적으로 연결하기 위한 전략을 개발하는 것이 필요하다. 이를 위한 핵심과제로서 이 글에서는 '협력 점(interface cities 공유거점도시)'과 '협력 선(city alliance 도시연대 및 동북아 물류네트워크 구축)'을 제시하고자 한다.

한반도가 네트워크의 허브가 되기 위해서는 교류를 위한 '공유거점도시(interface city)'를 개발하고 주변국 도시들과 연계망(city alliance)을 구축하는 것이 필요하다. 공유거점도시는 기존 대도시의 일부나 특구 등의 형식으로 조성하는 것이 가능할 것이다. 공유거점도시는 단순히 경제활동의 자유만을 부여하는 특구개념이 아니라 다양한 국적의 사람과 기업이 서로 제약 없이 교류할 수 있는 문화와 경제의 국제교류·융합 거점으로서 개발하는 것이 필요하다. 특히 공유거점도시 간에 역사문화, 경제교류, 기술 및 인적자원개발 등 다양한 주제를 중심으로 문화지식 네트워크를 구축하는 것이 중요하다. 한마디로 공유거점도시는 다양한 수준의 문화와 지식이 서로 접속될 수 있는 '멀티 콘센트' 또는 '멀티 플러그'와 같은 역할을 하는 것이 필요한 것이다. 한반도에서 이러한 공유거점도시로서 잠재력을 가지는 지역은 남측의 목포, 새만금, 북측의 평양-남포, 원산, 신의주, 나선 등이 될 수 있을 것이다. 목포와 새만금은 한반도와 중국 심천, 상해지역과의 교류협력 거점으로서, 평양-남포는 베이징-텐진권 교류협력의 관문역할을 할 수 있을 것이다. 원산-함흥은 환 동해권 교류협력의 거점으로서, 신의주는 한반도와 동북 3성, 몽골 연결의 북서부 대륙협력거점지대로 역할을 할 수 있을 것이다. 나선-청진은 한반도와 극동 러시아, 중국 동북 3성 연결의 북동부 대륙협력거점지대로서 육성하는 것이 필요할 것이다. 이러한 한반도 공유거점도시들은 주변국 주요 도시들과 초고속교통망 및 통합 물류망을 통해 상호 연계됨으로써 시너지 효과를 창출할 수 있을 것이다. 공유거점도시들이 제 역할을 하기 위해서는 주변국의 주요 도시들과 시티 얼라이언스(city alliance)를 구축하는 것이 필요하다. city alliance는 기존의 자매도시 수준의 교류에서 지식산업과 문화교류의 수준을 한 단계 업그레이드하는 것을 의미한다. 공동 Expo 등 국제행사의 공동추진, 지역대학들을 중심으로 항상적인 인적교류를 추진하고 해당 도시 간 기업 및 인적 교류에 대한 인센티브 제공을 통해 이러한 연대 구축을 촉진할 필요가 있다. 공유거점도시(interface city)와 동북아시아 주요 개방 도시들을 연계하는 도시간 국제협력 네트워크 구축은 다음과 같이 추진할 필요가 있다. 환 서해권에서는 목포-인천-남포-텐진-웨이하이, 환 동해권에서 부산포항-울산-속초-원산-나선-나홋트카-블라디보스톡-니이가타를 연계하는 시티 얼라이언스(City Alliance)를 추진할 필요가 있다. 특히 북한의 남포, 신의주, 원산, 나선은 시티 얼라이언스(city alliance)의 핵심적인 신 교류거점 도시로 육성할 수 있도록 남북협력 및 국제협력을 추진할 필요가 있다.

한반도의 국제네트워킹 강화를 위해서는 동북아차원의 통합적 물류네트워크 구축을 추진하는 것이 필요하다. 동북아차원의 물류네트워크 구축 측면에서 우선 5시간 이내 이동가능지역간 물류체계 연계를 추진한 후 1일 이동 가능지역까지의 물류체계 연계를 추진하는 단계적 접근을 고려할 필요가 있다.

1일 비즈니스 권역 수립을 위해 중단기적으로 중국 3대 경제권(주장·창장·환 보하이만 경제권)과 한반도 남·서해안 산업벨트의 물류연계를 강화할 수 있는 육·해·공 통합형 물류네트워크를 공유거점도시에 조성할 필요가 있다. 장기적으로 북극항로 개발 및 극동 러시아·일본과의 고부가가치 물류연계를 꾀할 수 있는 환 동해 물류 네트워크 구축을 도모할 필요가 있다.

미래 한반도의 공간구조에 따른 북한 개발의 과제

앞에서 제기된 미래 한반도의 공간구조를 중심으로 북한 개발의 과제를 간략히 제시해보면 다음과 같다.

<u>중단기 과제</u>
이 단계에는 공간적으로는 남북접경지역과 북한 서부지역을 중심으로 한 산업인프라의 개발이 필요할 것으로 판단된다. 인프라 가운데에는 신속한 물자수송에 필요한 도로부문과 전력부문의 부분적인 현대화가 필요할 것으로 판단된다. 남북경제의 통합 측면에서는 우리의 수도권과 북한의 평양-남포 지역을 연결하는 산업인프라의 개발이 먼저 추진될 필요가 있을 것이다(이상준 외 2011). 북서부의 신의주와 중국의 단동 지역을 포괄하는 지대는 한반도의 지경학적 잠재력을 최대한 활용할 수 있도록 개발을 추진하는 것이 필요하다. 이러한 측면에서

우리와 중국, 북한이 신의주와 단동을 중심으로 도로, 철도, 산업단지 등의 공동개발을 추진하는 것도 중단기에 추진할 필요가 있을 것이다. 이 단계에는 남북 간에 이미 연결된 철도와 도로망의 정상운영을 유지하고 단절된 나머지 철도 및 도로의 연결을 추진하는 것이 필요하다. 특히 서울~신의주 간의 철도와 도로 개보수는 교통부문의 가장 중요한 과제가 될 것이다.

<u>장기 과제</u>
장기적으로는 북한 서부 축과 동부 축을 중심으로 산업인프라의 본격적인 종합개발이 추진될 필요가 있을 것이다. 서부 축과 동북축의 주요 거점도시들의 개발을 중심으로 개발의 파급효과를 주변에 확산시키는 단계적 개발이 필요하다(이상준 외 2012). 장기적으로는 북한의 기존 산업시설의 실태조사를 통해 정비가 필요한 공업지대를 파악하여 단계적인 정비를 추진하는 것이 필요할 것이다. 장기적으로는 기존 공업지대 재정비가 진행될 필요가 있다. 이 단계에서는 중국 동북지역과 남북한을 고속으로 연결하는 새로운 교통망의 건설도 필요할 것이다. 경의선 축에 고속철도를 건설하고 경원-동해선에 새로운 고속도로 건설을 추진할 필요가 있다. 항만과 공항의 경우 국제적인 기준에 맞는 시설 현대화가 본격 추진될 필요가 있을 것이다. 또한, 한반도와 대륙 간의 아시아하이웨이 통합운영 등 국제교통망과의 남북한 교통망 통합도 이 단계에 본격 추진될 수 있을 것이다.

결론

한반도의 비전과 이것을 실현하기 위한 한반도 공간구조의 구축 및 북한 개발은 우리와 북한 그리고 주변국들의 협력 여하에 따라 성패가 좌우될 것이다. 이러한 측면에서 우리의 정책과제를 살펴보면서 이 글을 마무리하고자 한다.

첫째, 주변국의 협력을 이끌어내기 위해서는 새로운 개념의 '한반도 이니셔티브(Initiative)' 추진이 필요하다. 이것은 남북의 긴밀한 협력을 기반으로 가능하다. 북한이 갖고 있는 중국, 러시아와의 협력관계, 그리고 우리가 갖고 있는 미국, 일본과의 협력관계를 적절히 활용하는 전략이 필요하며, 이를 통해 '한반도 이니셔티브(Initiative)' 추진이 가능할 것이다. 특히 강

국으로 부상하는 중국과의 협력네트워크 구축이 한반도가 네트워킹의 중심 역할을 하는데 핵심적인 과제가 될 것이다.

둘째, 아시아경제교류 촉진자(facilitators)로서의 위상을 확보하기 위해서는 교역과 투자의 역내 네트워킹(networking)을 촉진할 수 있도록 남북이 먼저 개방화를 선도해 갈 필요가 있다. 이것은 경제와 문화의 융합을 통해 가능할 것이다. 국제사회의 교류와 협력을 촉진하고 다양성의 상호 조화를 지향하는 '신(新)아시아문화경제권' 형성을 남북이 선도해 갈 필요가 있다. 미래 탈 민족주의, 탈 이데올로기, 탈 패권주의, 탈 영토주의의 흐름 속에서 문화교류의 주도적 역할을 확보해 갈 필요가 있는 것이다. 이를 위해서는 '문화적 한류'와 '경제적 한류'가 중국, 일본, 러시아의 문화 및 경제와 조화와 균형을 이룩하는 것이 필요하다.

미래 한반도가 동아시아 교류와 융합의 중심 역할을 하기 위해서는 여러 제약 요인을 극복해야 할 것이다. 우리 내부적으로는 개방에 소극적인 이해집단을 설득해야 하는 과제가 있고, 여전히 폐쇄적인 북한과의 협력을 심화시켜 가야 하는 과제가 있다. 한반도의 비전과 전략은 결국 우리가 어떻게 북한의 협력을 이끌어 낼 것인가에 그 성패가 달려있기도 하다. 북한에 우리가 함께 도달할 목표와 그것을 통한 번영의 과실을 설득시키는 것이 최우선 과제이다. 대외적으로는 주도권 경쟁을 벌이고 있는 중국과 일본 그리고 러시아와 미국으로부터 한반도의 역할을 인정받는 것이 어려운 과제가 될 것이다. 따라서 한반도가 네트워킹의 중심이 됨으로써 그들에게 돌아갈 이익이 무엇인지에 대해서도 우리가 심도 있게 고민해야 할 것이다.

References

Lee, Sang Jun (other). 2009. The vision of the Korean Peninsula and territorial networking strategies. Korea Research Institute for Human Settlements.

Lee, Sang Jun (other). 2011. Unified North Korea against age potential and policy challenges in the development of key points (I). Korea Research Institute for Human Settlements.

Lee, Sang Jun (other). 2012. Unified North Korea against age potential and policy challenges in the development of key points (II). Korea Research Institute for Human Settlements.

SYMBOLIC SPACE AND NATIONAL RITUAL OF NORTH KOREA

Eunhee Cho

—

Eunhee Cho, PhD, is a professor in Soongsil University, and received PhD in Sociology from Ewha Womans University. She started to have her interest in North Korean society when she first read the article 17 years ago about a North Korean defector returned back to the North Korea. She has been researching on North Korean society, especially symbolism and ceremonial event of North Korea, and recently she expands her interest to the transition and new generations of North Korea.

Introduction

North Korea has been emphasizing on 'ideological arming' whenever the nation is at a state of crisis. At the time of severe financial difficulty and food shortage in the mid 1990's, North Korea named the period as the second "march of hardship," which alludes to the period of "March of hardship" that Kim Il-Sung went through in the 1930's during the anti-Japanese partisan movement to overcome the crisis by emphasizing on ideological arming. The main objective of ideological arming, which North Korea emphasizes is originating from anti-Japanese 'revolutionary tradition', the history of Kim Il-Sung's armed struggle against Japanese imperialism. Like this, regardless of which society, including North Korea, the man in power constantly makes an effort to maintain its system and justify its regime by mobilizing various ways like ideology and idea besides using physical force. Police force or military is utilized to reinforce the regime's justification as a method of physical compulsion for short term use, but other methods are utilized for long term use besides this compulsion force; history and ideology are especially considered to be the typical method. Historical description that utilizes collective memory, creation of regime's ideology and its reinforcement are frequently used by each regime and through political symbolism these immaterial factors get more solidified and reinforced.

In this essay, we will look at how North Korean regime has been excavating meaningful history and constructing symbolic places in efforts to elicit a voluntary agreement from North Korean residents. Specifically we will be looking at; first, theoretical arguments on political symbol and use of space; second, a history of constructing North

Korea's politically symbolic space. Third, the ritual that takes place in North Korea's political symbolic space. It is to analyze what process does theoretical ideology, a method utilized by the regime to consolidate justification, goes through to be able to allow North Koreans to see and experience it.

Political symbol and space

Military and police power is a system that is frequently chosen by men in power to exercise political power. Its results are instantly and directly exercised thus members cannot easily resist these physical forces. But as Merriam points out, if political power depends only on the power of force, its authority cannot be sustained. She explains its reason that "power is not strong enough to sustain itself against events caused by sense of rivalry and dissatisfaction".[1] Therefore, men in power actively use agreement mechanism other than exertion of force such as physical power to elicit justification of its regime from people. In other words, regime's stability is something that gets symbolically accelerated by its people's prosaic motivation or by appealing for conventional sanctity[2], therefore no matter what system, it will prepare a basis for establishment of its existence and appeal for physical, emotional, ideological motivation. Power system constantly tries to build faith in its regime's legitimacy and to promote the faith.[3]

To do this political power actively utilizes ideology that supports their legitimacy. The concrete method is to unify government and regime and to use formality and symbol, which forms a deep consensus between people's common interest, and typically these ritual and symbol can be a factor for government and regime to be positively evaluated.[4] Especially ritual and symbol that are conducted for strengthening the justification of political power should be consisted of tradition or authentic idea that are accepted by society at large, in other words, should be consisted of ideology. Because ideology takes effect when it is expressed as concrete means such as ritual, ceremony, regime's physical symbol.[5] Also, justification of regime is a process that continuously progress, not something that gets completed at any moment. Though obtained to some degree, men in power should not accept his justification as granted as it can be depleted quickly.[6] Even though regime is stabilized and survived for a long time, the member should constantly update on public opinion. Specifically, ideology that supports legitimacy of political power only functions when doctrine is constantly injected, its atmosphere and emotion are created, and when these are confirmed as beliefs. Cohen saw regime's legitimacy is achieved through symbol and ritual and it can only be maintained through repetitive reconfirm process.

"People are usually absorbed in their everyday private matter and immersed in their direct and practical profits, so they should be led out of their self-centered interest on a regular basis, and the basic principles of political group in the regime should be regularly reconfirmed. The more the ideology expresses elements of the political group, ritual also need to be performed more frequently. This corresponds to all the political organization. However, the systematic use of physical force is impossible so it is especially the case if the use of ritual and moral mechanism increases and one group is organized in atypical way."[7]

Thus, men in power continue to make effort for consolidation of their political power and social integration. Ideology for creation of regime's legitimacy is abstract so to obtain voluntary consent from members the insubstantial ideology is concretely expressed as symbols and through this experience members build trust on the regime. As Cohen said justification of regime is maintained through constant repetition of ideology so the political power holds many specific activities and repeated rituals like commemoration ceremony in symbolic spaces to involve as many members as possible.

To summarize, one political group may work and maintained for a short time by physical force but it maintains its stability and durability mainly through symbols operated by political power. So, no matter which society or political power, they make their abstract concepts like social or political value, principles, or rules into a variety of symbols to maintain their legitimacy. People understand existence of such idea through symbol and apply these concepts to their daily lives. North Korea creates ideology like 'revolutionary tradition' for justification of its regime and should have created symbolic space with actual political function. Process of creating North Korea's political symbolic space will be looked at and also through analysis of rituals in the space its political factors will be analyzed.

Construction of politically symbolic space of North Korea

Politically symbolic space
It is after the war in 1953 where the politically symbolic space starts to form in North Korea. It started at the time when North Korea sent out a research committee to Kim Il-Sung's Anti-Japanese partisan revolutionary battle field.[8] 'Anti-Japanese partisan revolutionary battle field' is Mt. Baekdu region including Manchu area and refers to the place where Kim Il-Sung had armed struggle against Japan from the 1930's until the liberation in 1945. From 1956, North Korea calls history of this period as 'revolutionary tradition'. Since then North Korea emphasizes their politic, ideology, military and every part of its nation's organization are rooted in 'revolutionary tradition' of anti-Japanese movement.[9] Before the war, Kim Il-Sung's partisan group, Yeon Ahn group, Soviet group, and communists of domestic party coexisted in the party. But after the war in 1953 the authority has been concentrated on Kim Il-Sung as communists of domestic party including Heon-Yeong Park, and key figures of Yeon-Ahn party and Soviet party are purged.

To fulfill their desire for postwar recovery and consolidation of Kim Il-Sung's authority, in 1953 North Korea restores the historical truths of the 'Bocheonbo battle' the greatest accomplishment of partisan army and constructs Bocheonbo area in Mt. Baekdu region as a symbolic space of armed struggle through historical excavation. In the wake of the sectarian incident in August, 1956, the Soviet party and Yeon-Ahn party are purged eliminating all the opposition forces toward Kim Il-Sung and since then Kim Il-Sung's history of armed struggle against Japan is crystallized as 'revolutionary tradition'.[10] In North Korea only Kim Il-Sung's anti-Japanese partisan history is recognized and all others are eliminated. During the 1960's and 70's, places that are related to Kim Il-Sung's armed struggle against Japan are constructed as revolutionary battle fields.

Modern nations excavate and create their national greatness, history and ideology to consolidate the nation's justification and to flaunt these they actively utilizes art or symbolic tools. Especially large-scale national symbolic icons and buildings are preserved for a long period of time, thus have an impact on multiple generations. Therefore these have greater effect than any other artistic tools. In that sense, creation of a historical place in relation to a nation's legitimacy is a key tool for political socialization. The Bocheonbo area in Mt. Baekdu region as a start, North Korea regularizes excavation of anti-Japan partisan history and in these areas monuments and statues are erected to be completed as a symbolic places. In North Korea these type of places are called revolutionary battle fields and revolutionary historical sites. According to <Table 1> a revolutionary battle field refers to 'a place where the revolutionary army fought against opposite forces' and revolutionary historical site refers to 'a place where a revolutionary activity and achievements of struggle are imbued'; these two terms include all of Kim Il-Sung's achievements during the period of armed struggle against Japan.

North Korea grants importance and meaning on creating revolutionary battle fields and revolutionary historic sites, thus in this area, revolutionary historic objects and revolutionary historic places are organized, and with it revolutionary historic monuments, statues, great monuments, revolutionary museums and revolutionary historic centers are also constructed. In a conversation titled with 'let's organize Yanggang-do as a solid base of educating revolutionary tradition" in 1968, Kim Jung-Il says, "organizing a revolutionary battle field and a revolutionary historic site is a very important business to maintain and honor Kim Il-Sung's great achievements accomplished during armed struggle against Japan and to educate party members and workers with our party's revolutionary tradition.",[13] emphasizing importance of constructing a revolutionary historic site and a revolutionary battle field. Also, in this conversation Kim Jung-Il proposes guidelines on the construction of revolutionary battle fields and revolutionary historic sites.

<Table 2> concretely explains the objectives, principles, important matters, construction method, administration of preservation, and plan on use of space for revolutionary battle fields and revolutionary historic sites. In particular, the part of the plan on use of space mentions about party members and workers visiting a revolutionary battle field and a revolutionary historic site; it is clear that these symbolic spaces are actively utilized for 'revolutionary tradition' education.

Revolutionary historic sites and revolutionary battle fields are a symbolic spaces that strengthen

Modern North Korean dictionary[11]	Revolution ary historic site	A place where revolutionary activity and achievements by the leader or a superior revolutionist are imbued
	Revolutionary battle field	A place where revolutionary army fought against enemies

<Table 1> Definition of North Korea's revolutionary historic site and revolutionary battle field

Construction objective	Educate party member and workers with revolutionary tradition
Construction principle	Construct with Kim Il-Sung's revolutionary activity site as a base
Important matter	Guarantee purity of Kim Il-Sung's achievement on revolutionary tradition
Construction method	Excavate investigation on ruins and artifacts in relation with revolutionary activity
Preservation of revolutionary ruins and remains	Preserve revolutionary ruins and relics the way it originally was without damage, discoloration or corruption
Plan on use of space	Party member and workers' site visit to revolutionary historic site and revolutionary battle field

<Table 2> Construction principle on North Korea's revolutionary battle field and historic site[14]

and maintain the legitimacy of North Korea's 'revolutionary tradition,' which becomes regularized when Kim Jung-Il starts political activities in the 1960's, and continues to expand even into the 2000's.[15]

History of the composition of symbolic spaces
North Korea excavated and restored the history of Kim Il-Sung's armed struggle against Japan after the war, and these excavation sites became symbolic spaces of 'revolutionary tradition'. Since then almost every area where Kim Il-Sung had an armed struggle against Japan has become a revolutionary battle field and a revolutionary historic site. Typical revolutionary battle fields are: Bocheonbo revolutionary battle field in 1950's, Mt. Baekdu region Musan district revolutionary battle field in 1960's, Wangjae Mountain conference-related revolutionary battle field and entire Mt. Baekdu area including Samjiyeon revolutionary battle field in 1970's, great Mt. Baekdu Milyoung and Kim Jung-Il-related revolutionary battle field in 1980. Construction of these symbolic spaces reflects a political change of North Korea. Revolutionary battle field excavation business[16], started in 1953, is more briskly propelled after a sectarian incident in August, 1956. In 1958, museums throughout North Korea start research study and collection business on modern history sector, and particularly visiting the battle field of armed struggle against Japan as well as liberation war-related site and collection business are actively propelled.[17] Also, to excavate revolutionary tradition, literary artists like Wun-Kyung Han, Chun-Chu Lim and Hyuk Gho are summoned for academic exploration and collection business on historic site and battle field where raid activities occurred in the past in Manchuria[18], thus actualizing anti-Japan revolution struggle.

Bocheonbo revolutionary battle field in 1953 as a start these movements have expanded. Revolutionary battle field and revolutionary historic sites are constructed in consideration of residents' site visit and exploration that except for Pyonyang, usually these spaces are concentrated in Mt. Baekdu jungle area, Duman River and Aprok river coast area, Hamkyung South, North Province, Yanggang-do, and Jagang-do area.[19]

<Table 3> summarizes the status of revolutionary tradition-related political symbolic spaces created

Period	Revolutionary battle field/historic site(historical event)	space	year	sculpture
1953~	Bocheonbo revolutionary battle field	Bocheonbo battle-related area	55	Bocheonbo revolutionary museum
	(Bocheonbo battle-related	Area where order for the battle is made		Kim Il-Sung statue in Bocheonbo
	Feb. 1936-Jan. 1937	Gushimool-dong revolutionary battle field	58	Bocheonbo battle field memorial museum
			67	Bocheonbo victory monument
			77	Revolutionary historic monument, Gonjangdukhunshi monument
1960~	Baekdu region	5th Muldong	69	Kim Il-Sung Statue
	Musan district revolutionary battle field	Cheongbong, Geonchang, Baegaebong	71	Musan district battle victory monument
	(Entire Baekdu region	Samjiyeon, Baekdu region, Mupo	72	Baekdu Mountain monument
	Musan district battle-related	Shinsa-dong revolutionary battle field		
	1939 April-May)	Daehongdan revolutionary battle field		
1974~	Wangjae Mountain revolutionary historic site	Wangjae Mountain conference site	75	Kim Il-Sung Statue
	(Wangjae Mountain Conference-related	Wangjae Mountain revolutionary historic site		Wangjae Mountain great monument
	1933 Mar-May)	Takamgol revolutionary historic site		
		Ryuda Island revolutionary historic site		
	1976~1979 Samjiyeon revolutionary battle field		79	Samjiyeon great monument, revolutionary historic center
				Samjiyeon pond Kim Il-Sung statue
				Cheongbong monument
				Shinsa-dong revolutionary battle field monument
	1976 Jangja Mountain revolutionary historic site (Kim Jung-Il)			
	1979 Eoeun revolutionary historic site (Kim Jung-Il)			
1980~	1980 Bonghwa revolutionary historic site (Kim Hyung-Jik)		04	Bonghwa-ri revolutionary historic center
	1986 Kwangjeong revolutionary historic site (Kim Hyung-Jik)			
	1987 Baekdu Milyoung(Kim Jung-Il)			
	1990 Hongwon revolutionary historic site (Kim Hyung-Kwon)			
	1994 Doodan revolutionary historic site (Kim Hyung-Jik)			
	1997 Chaho revolutionary historic site (Kim Jung-suk)			

<Table 3> Status of the composition of political symbolic space in North Korea[20]

in North Korea. 1953 Bocheonbo revolutionary battle field as the start, 1955 Bocheonbo revolutionary museum and Kim Il-Sung statue, 1958 Bocheonbo battle field memorial museum, 1967 Bocheonbo victory monument, 1977 revolutionary monument, and Gonjangduk monument are constructed. Within the Mt. Baekdu region, Bocheonbo area is the most symbolic historical place for armed struggle against Japan, and is the key space to consolidate justification of Kim Il-Sung's regime.

From 1960 until 1964 construction of revolutionary battle fields is actively carried out in Yanggang-do region including Mt. Baekdu region and entire Northern border in Northern Hamgyong province. Content in "Chosun Chungangnyeongam" from 1961 to 1965 says billeting place, campsite, and roads are newly built in Yanggang-do region and border on northern Hamgyong province, and construction of a cultural recreational facility is actively at work. Also, it mentions that as the region's ruins and monuments are repaired and restored, the revolutionary battle field is restored to its original shape.[21] All of Mt. Baekdu region has been created as a revolutionary battle field called "street museum".

If you see <Table 3> you can find the entire Mt. Baekdu region like Samjiyeon, Mt. Baekdu region, Mupo billeting place, 5th Muldong, Cheongbong, Geonchang, Baegaebong billeting place are restored since 1961. Meanwhile Yanggang-do Bureau of the People's Committee of revolutionary battle field and Bureau of 5 districts (Hyesan, Bocheonbo, Leemyeongsu, Samjiyeon, Daehongdan) are created[22] and through this research on revolutionary battle field and maintenance business in the Mt. Baekdu region are actively proceeded.

However, in 1964 when Kim Jung-Il becomes the secretary of the Party Central Committee, from 1964 to 1966 in "Chosun Chungangnyeongam" subject of creating revolutionary battle fields and historic sites. Gapsan party, used to be in charge of the culture of ideology sector, asserted diversification of revolutionary tradition and at 15th party meeting on May 1967 they are purged. Amid all the political factions been purged, except Kim Il-Sung's partisan party, Kim Il-Sung's monolithic ideology system is established throughout North Korean society after 1967.

In 1967 Bochenobo victory monument is constructed in Bocheonbo, and in 1969 30th anniversary Musan district battle victory Kim Il-Sung statue is built. Also in the same year, construction of the Musan district battle victory monument is started and completed in 1971, and in 1972 a monument is built in Mt. Baekdu region. In 1979 Samjiyeon monument, Kim Il-Sung statue, and monuments are built to celebrate 40th anniversary of the victory in Musan district battle. So starting from 1967 and as Kim Jung-Il becomes a Political Committee member of Party Central Committee in March 1974, creation of the symbolic space is further expanded.

As Kim Jung-Il emerges as the successor, there is a change in creation of symbolic space like revolutionary battle fields and revolutionary historic sites. Before the focus had been on excavation of revolutionary battle fields, the actual battle site during Kim Il-Sung's armed struggle against Japan, but in 1970's every area with a trace of Kim Il-Sung's are excavated as revolutionary historic sites. Also, places related to Kim Il-Sung's family, Kim Hyung-Jik, Kim Hyung-Kwon, and Kim Jung-Suk, and

Kim Jung-Il-related revolutionary historic site like revolutionary historic site are built. These symbolic spaces are systematically organized by the nation to allow North Koreans to always visit and march.

Symbolic space and national ritual

What role does the symbolic spaces created throughout North Korea play for the nation, especially revolutionary battle field and revolutionary historic site that are around Mt. Baekdu region? In order to arm party members and workers with revolutionary spirit, North Korea emphasizes on education of 'revolutionary tradition', and particularly the education method through revolutionary historic sites and revolutionary battle fields is considered to be the most important. Since revolutionary battle fields and revolutionary historic sites vividly show Kim Il-Sung and Kim Jung-Il's 'revolutionary struggle history' with real background, this method tends to have a great influence on the people. In North Korea the government actively utilizes this method as an important means to foster party members, workers and new generations as communists.[23] Most of all they emphasize 'education through the Mt. Baekdu region milyoung and Mt. Baekdu region revolutionary battle field' In North Korea they provide a specific way of constructing revolutionary historic sites and revolutionary battle fields.

"When we construct great monuments, our party decides on a scale first to form it well around our great leader Kim Il-Sung's statue, illustrate the right time period, situate it in a place where revolutionary historic sites are concentrated; our party proposes new and creative ways and carefully guides people to strictly experiment them." [24]

From 1959 North Korea organized broad scale

Year	Construction of revolutionary battle field / revolutionary historic site	Year	Organization of exploration march
1953~	Bocheonbo revolutionary battle field	1959	\<revolutionary battle field race
1960~	Baekdu region Musan district revolutionary battle field	1967	\<revolutionary battle field race\> connection to revolutionary tradition
1974~75	Wangjae Mountain revolutionary historic site	1973 1974 1975	\<Cheonligil of learning relay race\> \<Cheonligil of learning\> exploration march \<Cheonligil of liberation\> exploration march
1976~79	Samjiyeon revolutionary battle field (Completion of Baekdu region street museum)	1982	\<Baekdu region revolutionary battle field\> revolutionary exploration march
1976 1979 1987	Jangjae Mountain revolutionary historic site (Pyongyang, Kim Jung-Il) Eoeun revolutionary historic site (Pyongyang, Kim Jung-Il) Baekdu region Milyoung Gaeyoung (Baekdu region, Kim Jung-Il)	1986	\<Jeongilbong\>, \<Baekdu region Milyoung\> Exploration march(Baekdu region revolutionary battle field site visit) \<Jangjae Mountain revolutionary historic site\> exploration march(\<Baekdu revolutionary battle field\> to celebrate 30th anniversary of pioneering)
		1997	\<Baekdu Milyoung hometown\>Exploration march (Baekdu region revolutionary battle field site visit)

\<Table 4\> Organization of exploration march on revolutionary battle field and revolutionary historic site [25]

event the exploration march trips at revolutionary battle field and revolutionary historic site to systematically involve many people. Especially at first it is organized for party member and students but later gradually all the residents became the subject.

We can see from <Table 4> theBocheonbo revolutionary battle field as a start, Mt. Baekdu region Musan district revolutionary battle field is constructed in 1960's and as symbolic spaces start to form around revolutionary battle fields, <revolutionary battle field race> type of national event that is programmed to experience the trace of Kim Il-Sung's revolutionary achievements of anti-Japan partisan is created with students as a main subject. It is first mentioned in Nodong newspaper on February 5th 1959 that youth and students exploration team has visited the battle field.[26] Academic exploration business after the change in title to <collective race to revolutionary battle field> since 1960, the event <revolutionary battle field race> is organized nationally to allow ordinary people to personally visit and experience Kim Il-Sung's revolutionary achievements of anti-Japan period. During this period Kim Il-Sung's armed struggle against Japan is emphasized and focuses on'Pyongyang, Bocheonbo, and Mt. Baekdu region'. Since 1968 <Revolutionary battle field race> is closely tied to education of revolutionary tradition.[27] Year 1968 is a period where purge of Gapsan party who was in charge or idea sector is finished; it is a period where Kim Il-Sung has monopolistic political power and at last Kim Il-Sung's anti-Japan revolutionary tradition alone is accepted as North Korea's 'revolutionary tradition'. In this sense, national ritual like <revolutionary battle field race> is created to involve residents and promote social integration. 1974 as the starting point for excavation and creation of revolutionary battle fields and revolutionary historic sites becomes a large-scale project. Exploration marches like <Chunligil of learning> and <Chunligil of liberation> starts from 1973 and it is to commemorate and experience Kim Il-Sung's trip between Mangyeongdae in Pyongyang and Popyeong in Yanggang-do when he was 11 years old (1923) and 13 years old (1925). It is a national ritual event administered to students at the time of appointment of Kim Jung-Il as successor and importance of educating 'revolutionary tradition' is confirmed towards new generation.

At the same time Kim Jung-Il the successor excavates the Wangjae Mountain revolutionary historic site as a symbolic space and in 1979 completes the entire Mt. Baekdu region as a "street museum" constructing the Samjiyeon revolutionary battle field as a grand large-scale site as well. After Kim Jung-Il is publicly announced as successor at the 6th party congress with his accomplishment in completing symbolic spaces, this type of exploration march is organized and settled as a national event. < Mt. Baekdu region revolutionary battle field> exploration march is the nation's official event that continues until now since the beginning of the exploration march and organization of < Mt. Baekdu region youth exploration march troop> in July, 1982. However, North Korea explains < Mt. Baekdu region revolutionary battle field> exploration march starts under Kim Jung-Il's supervision when sects are having a bad influence on the idea business. Officially appeared in 1980 as a successor, Kim Jung-Il describes < Mt. Baekdu region revolutionary battle field>, an exploration march organized with new meaning and form in 1982, as an organization formed to deal with political conditions in 1956; it emphasizes that 'revolutionary tradition' begins from Kim Jung-Il and he is the one who inherits 'Mt. Baekdu blood'.

"<4,00km Mt. Baekdu region revolutionary battle field exploration march road>: 26 years ago glorious Party Central guide the first exploration march troop coming from Bocheonbo through Samjiyeon to climb the Baekdu Mountain. Thus, 400 km exploration march road to Baekdu Mountain is open for the first time in this complex, and a harsh period where anti-party counter revolutionary sects viciously tries to destroy out party's glorious revolutionary tradition. Since then, youths, students and workers all around the nation, oversee compatriots, and foreign friends who visited our country, visited the Mt. Baekdu region revolutionary battle field along the roads pioneered by our party. Party Central changed Yanggangdo area into one street museum for educating on revolutionary tradition. Glorious Party Central also builds a logical exploration system for Mt. Baekdu region revolutionary battle field, systematize it, and even takes a measure to guarantee that the nation will bear the entire physical and financial expense." [28]

At the end of 1970's Kim Jung-Il related revolutionary historic sites like Jangja Mountain revolutionary historic site and Eoeun revolutionary historic site, and restoration of the Mt. Baekdu Milyoung started in 1982 is completed in 1987. Mt. Baekdu Milyoung is a place where Kim Il-Sung had armed struggle against Japan and is claimed to be the birthplace of Kim Jung-Il. Thus, Mt. Baekdu Milyoung is indeed the place that justifies Kim Il-Sung's 'Mt.Baekdu blood'. <Table 4> shows that at the time of constructing Mt. Baekdu Milyoung in 1986, an exploration march is organized at a larger scale than before to celebrate the 30th anniversary of pioneering < Mt.Baekdu region revolutionary battle field>. From this period < Mt. Baekdu revolutionary battle field> explora-

Period	1950's-60's	1970's	1980's	1990's
Major political event	1953 ceasefire 1956 August Sectarian incidents	1974 Kim Jung-Il is appointed as successor (domestic)	1980 Kim Jung-Il is appointed as successor (foreign)	1994 death of Kim Il-Sung
<Chunligil of learning > <Chunligil of liberation>		73 ▬▬▬▬▬▬▬▬▬▬▬▬▬▬▬▬▬▬		
<Baekdu region revolutionary battle field>		59 <revolutionary battle field race> ▬▬▬▬▬▬▬▬▬▬▬▬	82<Baekdu region revolutionary battle field> ▬▬▬▬▬▬▬▬▬▬▬▬	
<Baekdu Milyoung, Jangja Mountain, Eoeun revolutionary historic site>			86 ▬▬▬▬▬▬▬▬▬▬▬▬	

<Table 5> Peiord and characteristic of national exploration march

tion march includes < Mt. Baekdu Milyoung> and <Jungilbong> which symbolizes Kim Jung-Il.

According to <Table 5>, during 1950's and 1960's North Korea focuses on creating symbolic space in Mt. Baekdu region and starts to systematize and grow in scale from 1970's when Kim Jung-Il appears. After Kim Jung-Il is appointed as official successor in 1980, national ritual events, like exploration march, take place in symbolic spaces of anti-Japan revolutionary tradition around Mt. Bekdu region. < Mt. Baekdu region revolutionary battle field> exploration march takes place on national holidays and anniversaries that North Korea regards as important, such as Kim Il-Sung and Kim Jung-Il's birthday and Bocheonbo battle anniversary; it is mandatory that party members and students are to join exploration march according to nation's plan all year round. North Korea has found its nation's origin from Kim Il-Sung's armed struggle against Japan since 1950's to consolidate Kim Il-Sung's regime, and creates places around the Mt. Baekdu region where Kim Il-Sung's armed struggle against Japan took place as a symbolic space of 'revolutionary tradition'. Since then, national events take place at these symbolic spaces in the Mt. Baekdu region and North Koreans pay site visit to symbolic spaces according to nation's plan. This type of use and utilization of symbol and national ritual is being employed regardless of the regime and particularly in North Korea the creation of symbolic spaces has been well utilized in the 1970's, and after the 1980's. Utilization of symbolic space of 'revolutionary tradition' strengthens justification of establishing North Korean regime and at the same time has an emphasis on 'Mt. Baekdu blood'; it consolidate Kim Il-Sung's regime and furthermore serves a function of consolidating hereditary succession from Kim Il-Sung to Kim Il-Sung and now to Kim Jung-Eun.

Conclusion

Political power seeks various ways to draw not only physical force, but also agreements to consolidate their justification of political power. This means if you rely only on force the power cannot be sustained for a long time. For this reason, men in power employs rituals and symbols to arouse a consensus towards a regime from the people.

North Korea constructs symbolic space by choosing 'revolutionary tradition' of Kim Il-Sung's armed struggle against Japan to strengthen and justify Kim Il-Sung's power after war, and utilizes rituals to educate the people. From 1960 to 1970, the entire area of Mt. Baekdu region and Pyongyang area is constructed as a revolutionary battle field and revolutionary historic site to be sanctified, and during the 1980's after the official announcement of Kim Jung-Il as the successor, national ritual the exploration march to symbolic spaces is organized and continues until today.

In North Korea history of Kim Il-Sung's armed struggle against Japan from 1930 to 1945 becomes the sole history to support legitimacy of North Korean regime and becomes ideology as 'revolutionary tradition'. Revolutionary tradition not only consolidates justification of regime, but as its meaning expands and reinforces through symbolic space and national ritual it also acts as ideology that strengthens legitimacy of North Korea's hereditary system.

북한의 상징적 공간과 국가의례

조은희

―

조은희는 현재 숭실대학교 교수로 재직하고 있으며, 이화여자대학교에서 사회학 박사학위를 취득하였다. 조은희는 17년전 국내입국 탈북자가 재입북했다는 기사를 보고 난 이후 북한사회에 대한 관심을 갖기 시작하였다. 이후 북한사회에 대한 연구를 지속하였고, 특히 북한의 상징과 의례에 대해 관심을 갖고 현재까지 연구를 지속해 오고 있다. 최근에는 북한사회의 변동과 새로운 세대에 대해 관심을 갖고 있다.

서론

북한은 국가적 위기상황에 처할 때마다 '사상적 무장'에 대해 거듭 강조해 왔다. 1990년대 중반 극심한 경제난과 식량난을 겪었을 당시 북한은 1930년대 김일성의 항일빨치산 활동 당시 겪었던 '고난의 행군' 시기에 빗대어 제2의 '고난의 행군'으로 명명했고 이를 극복하기 위한 사상적인 무장을 강조하였다. 또한 북한에서 강조하는 사상적 무장의 핵심은 김일성의 항일무장투쟁의 역사인 항일의 '혁명전통'으로부터 비롯된다고 할 수 있다. 이처럼 북한을 포함한 그 어떤 사회를 막론하고 권력자들은 체제유지와 정권의 정당성 강화를 위해 물리적 강제력 외에 이데올로기, 사상 등 여러 방법을 동원하는 등 부단히 노력한다고 볼 수 있다. 정권의 정당성 강화를 위해서는 경찰력과 군대 같이 단기적으로는 물리적 강제에 의한 방법을 활용하기도 하지만 장기적으로는 이러한 강제력 외에 여러 방법들을 활용하는데 특히 역사와 이데올로기의 활용은 그 대표적인 방법이라고 할 수 있다. 집단적 기억을 활용한 역사의 서술, 정권의 이데올로기의 창출과 그것의 강화는 각 정권에 의해 많이 사용되는데 이러한 것들은 실체가 없는 것으로 정치적인 상징을 통해서 더욱 구체화되고 강화된다.

본 논문에서는 북한 정권이 정권에 대한 북한 주민들의 자발적 동의를 이끌어 내기 위해 의미 있는 역사를 발굴하고, 상징적 공간을 조성한 역사를 살펴보고자 한다. 그리고 이와 더불어 상징적 공간의 정치적 기능을 강화하기 위해 행해지는 국가의 의례 또한 분석해 보고자 한다. 구체적으로 첫째, 정치적 상징과 공간의 활용에 대한 이론적 논의를 살펴보고, 둘째, 북한의 정치적 상징 공간의 조성 역사를 살펴보고자 한다. 셋째, 북한의 중요 정치적 상징 공간에서 행해지는 의례에 대해 살펴봄으로써 북한의 상징공간의 정치적 기능에 대해 분석해 보고자 한다. 이러한 분석과정을 통해 정치 권력자들이 정권의 정당성 강화를 위해 활용하는 추상적 이데올로기가 어떠한 과정을 거쳐 주민들에게 보여 지고 체험되는지에 대해 분석하고자 한다.

정치적 상징과 공간

군대와 경찰력은 권력자들이 정치권력을 행사하는데 있어서 가장 쉽게 선택하는 제도이다. 군대와 경찰력의 결과는 즉각적이고 직접적으로 행사되는 것으로 이러한 물리력에는 구성원들이 쉽게 대항할 수 없기 때문이다. 하지만 메리암(Merriam)이 지적하는 것처럼 정치권력이 폭력에만 의존한다면 권력은 지탱될 수 없다. 그 이유로 그는 "힘이란 경쟁심과 불만족으로 인하여 일어나는 사건에 대항하여 자신을 지탱할 만큼 강하지 않기 때문"이라고 설명한다.[1] 때문에 권력자들은 사람들로부터 정권의 정당성을 끌어내기 위하여 폭력과 같은 강제력 행사 외에 동의의 기제를 적극 활용한다는 것이다. 즉 정권의 안정성은 국민들의 세속적인 동기나 관습상의 신성함에 호소함으로써 상징적으로 촉진 되는 것으로[2], 모든 권력체제는 자체의 존속을 위해 근거를 마련하고 물질적이나 감정적, 이상적인 동기에 호소한다고 한다. 뿐만 아니라 모두 그 조직의 '정당성'에 믿음을 쌓게 하고 믿음을 촉진시키려고 부단히 노력을 하게 되어 있다고 한다.[3]

이를 위하여 정치권력은 그들의 정당성을 뒷받침하는 이데올로기를 적극 활용한다. 그 구체적인 방법으로는 정부와 정권을 일체화 시키고 사람들 사이의 공통 관심사에 깊은 공감대를 불러일으키는 의례와 상징을 사용하는 것이 일반적인데, 이러한 의례와 상징은 정부와 정권이 긍정적으로 평가 받게 되는 요인이 될 수 있다.[4] 특히 정치권력의 정당성 강화를 위해 수행되는 상징과 의례는 사회 전반적으로 받아들여지는 전통이나 정통이념, 즉 이데올로기로 구성되어야 한다. 왜냐하면 이데올로기는 의례, 의식, 정권의 물질적 상징과 같은 구체적인 수단으로 표현되어 사람들에게 전달되어야 그 효력을 발휘할 수 있기 때문이다.[5] 또한 메리암은 권력의 정당성은 어느 순간 완성되는 것이 아니고 진행하고 있는 과정이라고 한다. 때문에 권력자들은 어느 정도의 정당성을 확보하였다고 하더라도 급속히 고갈되어질 수 있기 때문에 결코 자신의 정당성을 당연한 것으로 받아들여서는 안 된다.[6] 비록 정권이 오래되고 안정화되었다고 하더라도 구성원 입장에서 정당성에 대한 여론을 끊임없이, 그리고 새롭게 해야 한다는 것이다. 구체적으로 정치권력의 정당성을 뒷받침하는 이데올로기는 끊임없는 교리의 주입과 그것에 대한 분위기 및 감정의 조성, 그리고 신념으로 확인될 때, 비로서 그 기능을 다한다. 코헨(Cohen)은 정권의 정당성은 상징과 의례를 통해 성취되는 것이며 이것이 반복적인 재확인 과정을 통해서만 유지된다고 보았다.

"인간은 보통 그들 일상의 개인적인 문제에, 그리고 직접적이고 실리적인 그들의 이익에 몰두하므로, 그들은 자기중심적인 관심 영역 바깥으로 정기적으로 이끌어 내져야 하며, 정치집단 조직의 기본적인 원리에 의해 신념이나 지지를 정기적으로 재확인시켜야 한다. 이데올로기가 표출하는 정치조직의 요소들이 많으면 많을수록, 의식(의례)을 빈번히 행할 필요도 더욱 커진다. 이것은 정치조직의 모든 경우에 해당한다. 그러나 조직화된 물리적 강제력의 체계적인 사용이 불가능해서 제의적, 도덕적 메카니즘의 사용이 증가되는 경우 그리고 하나의 집단이 비정형적으로 조직되는 경우에는 특히 그러하다."[7]

이처럼 권력자들은 그들의 정치권력에 대한 정당성 강화와 사회통합을 위하여 계속 노력하고 있다. 정권의 정당성 창출을 위한 이데올로기는 추상적인 것으로, 구성원들의 자발적인 동의를 구하기 위해서는 실체가 없는 이데올로기가 구체적인 표현수단의 상징으로 구체화되었고 구성원들은 그 상징에 대한 경험을 통하여 정권에 대한 신뢰를 쌓아가게 되는 것이다. 코헨이 언급한 것처럼 정치권력의 정당성은 이데올로기의 끊임없는 반복을 통해 유지되기 때문에 정치권력은 의미 있는 상징적 공간에서의 여러 구체적인 활동, 예를 들면 기념식과 같은 반복된 의례를 개최하여 많은 구성원들을 참여시키고자 한다.

정리하면 한 정치집단이 얼마 동안은 단순히 물리적인 힘에 의해서 움직이고 유지될지 모르나 그 안정성과 지속성은 주로 그 정치권력에 의해 조작되는 상징을 통해서 유지된다고 볼 수 있다. 때문에 어떠한 사회 또는 정치권력이든 간에 그들의 정당성을 유지하기 위해서는 사회적 또는 정치적 가치, 이념, 규율 등의 추상적인 개념들을 다양한 싱징들로 만들어 낸다. 그리고 사람들은 상징을 통해 그러한 개념의 존재를 알고 이해하며 그 개념들을 그들의 일상생활에 적용하게 된다. 북한은 정치권력의 정당성 강화를 위하여 '혁명전통'과 같은 이데올로기를 만들었고 이와 관련된 상징공간을 만들어 실제 정치적으로 기능하게 했을 것이다. 이에 북한의 정치적 상징공간의 조성 과정을 살펴보고 또한 그 공간에서 이루어지는 의례 분석을 통해 표출되는 정치적 요소들이 무엇인지 파악해 볼 것이다.

북한의 정치적 상징공간의 조성

정치적 상징 공간

북한에서 정치적 상징공간이 조성되기 시작한 것은 1953년 전쟁 직후이다. 당시 북한이 김일성의 항일빨치산 투쟁전적지로 조사단을 파견하면서부터라고 할 수 있다.[8] '항일빨치산 투쟁전적지'라고 하면 만주지역을 포함한 백두산 지역을 말하는 것으로 1930년대부터 1945년 해방까지 김일성이 항일무장투쟁을 벌였던 공간을 지칭하는 것이다. 북한은 이 시기 역사를 1956년부터 '혁명전통'으로 언급[9]하였다. 이후 북한에서는 정치, 사상, 군사 등 국가구성의 모든 부분의 기원을 항일의 '혁명전통'에서 비롯되었다고 강조했다. 전쟁 전 북한은 당내에 김일성의 빨치산파 외에 연안파, 소련파, 국내파 공산주의자들이 공존했다. 하지만 1953년 전쟁을 계기로 박헌영을 비롯한 국내파 공산주의자들과 연안파와 소련파의 핵심인물의 숙청을 계기로 김일성을 중심으로 권력이 집중되었다.

1953년, 북한은 전후 복구에 대한 열망과 함께 김일성 권력을 공고히 하기 위해 김일성 빨치산부대의 가장 큰 공적으로 알려져 있는 '보천보 전투'와 관련된 역사적 사실을 복원했고 백두산의 보천보 지역 역사발굴을 통해 항일무장투쟁의 상징적 공간으로 만들었다. 1956년 8월 종파사건을 계기로 소련파와 연안파 모두 숙청되면서 김일성 권력에 도전할 수 있는 세력이 모두 제거되었고 이후 김일성의 항일무장투쟁역사가 '혁명전통'으로 확고해 졌다.[10] 북한에서는 김일성의 항일빨치산 역사만이 인정되었고, 그 외의 역사는 배제되었다. 이후 1960-70년에 걸쳐 김일성의 항일무장투쟁관련 공간은 혁명전적지로 조성되었다.

근대국가는 국가의 정당성을 강화하고자 그들의 민족적 위대성, 역사, 이데올로기를 발굴·창조하여 이것을 과시하기 위하여 예술 및 상징적 도구를 적극적으로 활용했다. 특히 대규모의 국가적 상징물이나 건축물들은 장기간 보존되기 때문에 세대에 걸쳐 영향을 주었다. 때문에 다른 예술적 도구보다 효과가 크다고 할 수 있다. 그런 의미에서 국가의 정통성과 관련된 역사적으로 의미 있는 공간의 조성은 핵심적인 정치사회화 도구라고 할 수 있다.

북한은 1953년 백두산 보천보 지역을 시작으로 김일성의 항일빨치산 역사 발굴을 본격화하였고, 그 공간에는 기념탑, 동상, 기념비 등 조형물을 세워 상징적 공간을 완성하였다. 북한에서는 이러한 공간을 혁명전적지, 혁명사적지로 지칭한다. 〈표 1〉에 의하면 혁명전적지는 '혁명군대가 적들과 맞서 싸운 전투가 진행된 장소'를 말하고 혁명사적지는 '혁명 활동과 투쟁업적이 깃들어 있는 장소'를 지칭하는 것으로 김일성의 항일무장투쟁시기 모든 업적을 망라하는 것이라 하겠다.

북한은 혁명전적지와 혁명사적지를 만들어내는 것에 대해 그 의미와 중요성을 부여하여, 이 장소에 혁명사적물, 혁명사적장소 등을 꾸렸으며 혁명사적기념비, 동상, 대기념비, 혁명박물관, 혁명사적관 등을 함께 세웠다. 김정일은 1968년 '량강도를 혁명전통교양의 거점으로 튼튼히 꾸리자'라는 제목의 담화에서 "혁명전적지와 혁명사적지를 꾸리는 것은 수령님께서 항일무장투쟁시기에 이룩하신 위대한 혁명업적을 고수하고 길이 빛내며 당원들과 근로자들을 우리 당의 혁명전통으로 교양하기 위한 매우 중요한 사업입니다."[13]라며 혁명사적지와 혁명전적지 건설의 중요성을 강조하였다. 또한 이 글에서 김정일은 혁명전적지와 혁명사적지를 건설하는 데에 가이드라인을 제시하였다.

다음의 〈표 2〉를 보면, 혁명전적지와 혁명사적지 건설의 목적, 원칙, 중요사항, 건설방법, 보존관리 및 공간활용 계획에 대해 구체적으로 밝히고 있다. 특히 공간활용계획을 보면 당원과 근

「현대조선말사전」[11]	혁명 사적지	수령 또는 탁월한 혁명가의 혁명 활동과 투쟁업적이 깃들어 있는 장소
	혁명 전적지	혁명군대가 적들과 맞서 싸운 전투가 진행된 자취가 깃들어 있는 장소

〈표 1〉 북한의 혁명사적지와 혁명전적지에 대한 정의

건설목적	당원 및 근로자들의 혁명전통 교양
건설원칙	김일성의 혁명활동 사적을 기본으로 하여 건설
건설시 중요사항	김일성이 이룩한 혁명전통 순결성 보장
건설방법	혁명활동의 내용을 담은 유적 및 유물 발굴 조사
혁명유적 및 유물의 보존관리	혁명유적 및 유물이 손상, 퇴색, 변질됨이 없이 본래의 모습 그대로 보존
공간활용계획	당원 및 근로자들의 혁명사적지 및 혁명전적지 답사

〈표 2〉 북한의 혁명전적지 사적지 건설 원칙[14]

로자들의 혁명전적지와 혁명사적지 답사에 대해 언급하고 있어 '혁명전통' 교육에 상징적 공간이 적극 활용되고 있음을 확인할 수 있다.

혁명사적지와 혁명전적지는 북한 '혁명전통'의 정당성을 강화하고 유지해 나가는 상징적 공간으로 김정일이 당내 정치 활동을 시작한 1960년대를 전후로 건설이 본격화되었고 2000년대 들어서도 지속적인 확장 및 신설이 이루어지고 있다.[15]

상징공간의 조성 역사
북한은 전쟁 직후인 1953년부터 김일성의 항일무장투쟁과 관련된 역사 복원 발굴하였고, 이렇게 발굴된 혁명전적지와 혁명사적지는 '혁명전통'의 상징적 공간이 되었다. 이후 북한은 백두산 전역, 그리고 김일성의 항일무장투쟁당시 활동했던 거의 모든 지역이 혁명전적지와 혁명사적지로 되었다. 대표적으로는 1950년대는 보천보 혁명전적지, 1960년대에는 백두산 일대 무산지구전투 관련 혁명전적지, 1970년대 왕재산 회의 관련 혁명사적지와 삼지연혁명전적지를 포함한 백두산 전역, 1980년대 백두산 밀영과 김정일 관련 혁명전적지로 정리해 볼 수 있다. 이러한 상징 공간의 조성은 북한의 정치변화가 반영되어있다. 1953년 시작된 혁명전적지 발굴사업은[16] 1956년 8월 종파사건 이후 더욱 활발히 추진되었다. 1958년에는 북한 전역의 박물관에서는 현대사 부문에 관한 조사연구 및 수집사업을 시작하였고 특히 항일무장투쟁 전적지와 조국해방전쟁관련 지역의 답사와 수집사업이 적극 추진되었다.[17] 또한 혁명전통을 발굴하기 위하여 한운경, 임춘추, 고혁 등의 문인들을 불러 과거 만주에서 유격활동을 하던 사적지와 전적지에 대해 학술답사 및 수집사업을 진행[18]하여 항일혁명투쟁을 사실화 하였다.

1953년 보천보 혁명전적지를 시작으로 이후 점차 확대되어갔다. 혁명전적지와 혁명사적지는 주민들의 답사 및 참관을 고려하여 지어지기 때문에 평양시를 제외하고는 주로 백두산 밀림지대, 두만강 및 압록강 연안일대, 함경남북도, 량강도, 자강도 지역에 집중되었다.[19]

〈표 3〉은 북한에 조성된 혁명전통과 관련된 정치적 상징 공간 조성 현황을 정리한 것이다. 1953년 보천보혁명전적지는 역사 발굴을 시작하여 1955년 보천보혁명박물관과 김일성 동상 건립, 1958년 보천보전적지기념박물관, 1967년 보천보승리기념탑, 1977년 혁명사적비, 곤장덕 헌시비가 건립되었다. 보천보 지역은 백두산 중에서도 김일성의 항일무장투쟁의 가장 상징적인 역사로 김일성 정권의 정당성을 강화하는데 있어서 가장 핵심적인 공간이다.

1960년부터 1964년까지는 백두산을 포함한 량강도 지방과 함경북도 북부국경일대의 혁명전적지 건설이 활발히 이루어진다. 「조선중앙년감」 1961년부터 1965년까지의 내용을 살펴보면, 량강도 지방과 함경북도 북부국경일대의 혁명전적지들에는 숙소, 야영소, 답사도로 등이 새로 건설되고, 문화후생시설들의 건설공사가 활발히 이루어지는 것을 알 수 있다. 또한 그 일대 유적 및 기념물들을 보수하고 정비하면서 혁명전적지를 원상대로 복원하였다고 언급하고 있다.[21] 백두산 일대는 북

시기	혁명전적지 · 사적지 (역사적 사건)	공간	년도	조형물
1953~	보천보혁명전적지 (보천보 전투 관련 36년2월–37년1월)	보천보전투 관련 지역	55	보천보혁명박물관
		전투명령을 내린 곳		보천보에 김일성 동상
		구시물동 혁명전적지	58	보천보전적지기념박물관
			67	보천보승리기념탑
			77	혁명사적비, 곤장덕헌시비
1960~	백두산 일대 무산지구혁명전적지 (백두산 일대 무산지구전투 관련 39년4월–5월)	5호물동	69	김일성동상
		청봉 · 건창 · 배게봉	71	무산지구전투승리기념탑
		삼지연 · 백두산 · 무포	72	백두산사적비
		신사동 혁명전적지		
		대홍단 혁명전적지		
1974~	왕재산혁명사적지 (왕재산회의 관련 33년3월–5월)	왕재산 회의장소	75	김일성동상
		왕재산 혁명사적지		왕재산 대기념비
		타막골 혁명사적지		
		류다섬 혁명사적지		
	76–79삼지연혁명전적지 76–79삼지연혁명전적지 76–79삼지연혁명전적지 76–79삼지연혁명전적지		79	삼지연 대기념비, 혁명사적관
				삼지연못가 김일성 동상
				청봉헌시비
				신사동혁명전적지 사적비
	76장자산혁명사적지(김정일)			
	79어은혁명사적지(김정일)			
1980~	80봉화혁명사적지(김형직)		04	봉화리 혁명사적관
	86광정혁명사적지(김형직)			
	87백두산 밀영(김정일)			
	90홍원혁명사적지(김형권)			
	94두단혁명사적지(김형직)			
	97차호혁명사적지(김정숙)			

〈표 3〉 북한 정치적 상징공간 조성 현황 [20]

한에서 "대로천 박물관"이라고 지칭할 정도로 모두 혁명전적지로 조성되었다.

실제 〈표 3〉을 보면 1961년부터 삼지연, 백두산, 무포숙영지, 5호물동, 청봉, 건창, 배게봉 숙영지 등 백두산 일대 공간들이 대거 복원되었음을 확인할 수 있다. 그 사이 1963년에는 량강도 인민위원회 혁명전적지 관리국과 5개의 지구 관리소(혜산, 보천보, 리명수, 삼지연, 대홍단)가 생겼으며[22] 이를 통해 백두산과 북부국경일대의 혁명전적지의 연구와 정비 사업이 활발히 진행되었다.

그러나 1964년 김정일이 당중앙위원회 조직지도부 비서로 당 활동을 시작한 후 1964년부터 1966년까지의 「조선중앙년감」에서는 혁명전적지와 사적지 조성에 대한 언급이 자제되었다. 사상문화분야를 담당하던 갑산파가 혁명전통의 다원화를 주장했고, 결국 1967년 5월 제4기 15차 전원회의에서 이들은 숙청되었다. 이렇게 김일성의 빨치산파 외에 모든 정치적 파벌들이 숙청된 가운데 1967년 이후 북한사회 전역에는 마침내 김일성의 유일사상체계가 확립되었다.

1967년에는 보천보에 보천보 승리기념탑이 세워지고, 1969년에는 무산지구 전투승리 30돐 기념 김일성 동상이 들어서게 되었다. 또한 같은 해 무산지구전투승리 기념탑이 준공되어 1971년 완공되었고, 1972년에는 백두산에 사적비가 세워졌다. 1979년에는 무산지구전투승리 40돌을 기념하면서 삼지연에 대기념비, 김일성 동상, 헌시비 등이 대거 만들어졌다. 이렇게 1967년을 기점으로 1974년 3월에는 김정일이 당 중앙위원회 정치위원회 위원으로 되면서 상징공간 조성은 더욱 확장되었다.

그러나 김정일이 후계자로 등장하면서 혁명전적지와 혁명사적지와 같은 상징공간의 조성에 변화가 있었다. 그 이전에는 김일성의 항일무장투쟁과정에서 실제 전투가 있었던 공간, 즉 혁명전적지 발굴 중심이었다면 1970년대에는 그 외 김일성이 활동한 흔적이 있는 지역은 모두 혁명사적지로 발굴되었다. 또한 김일성 뿐 아니라 김일성의 가족, 즉 김형직, 김형권, 김정숙과 관련된 공간과 장자선, 어은 혁명사적지와 같은 김정일 관련 혁명사적지도 조성되었다. 1987년 김정일의 출생 장소로 주장되는 백두산 밀영이 개영되었다. 백두산 혁명전적지와 사적지는 1960-70년대 김정일의 등장으로 규모가 커지고 체계화되어 완성되었다. 이렇게 조성된 상징공간은 북한주민들이 항상 방문하고 답사행군 할 수 있도록 국가가 조직적으로 행가를 조직하고 있다.

상징적 공간과 국가의례

그렇다면 이렇게 북한전역에 걸쳐 조성된 상징적 공간, 특히 백두산을 중심으로 한 혁명전적지와 혁명사적지들은 어떠한 역할을 하는 것일까? 북한에서는 당원과 근로자들을 혁명정신으로 무장시키는데 가장 중요한 것은 '혁명전통'교양이라 강조하는데 그 중에서도 혁명전적지와 혁명사적지를 통한 교양 방법이 가장 중요하다고 한다. 혁명전적지와 혁명사적지는 김일성과 김정일의 '혁명투쟁역사'를 생동하게 그리고 실물을 전시하여 보여주기 때문에 매우 감화력이 크다는 것이다. 때문에 북한에서는 당원과 근로자, 새로운 세대들을 공산주의자로 육성하는데 중요한 수단으로 이를 적극 활용하고 있다.[23] 그 중에서 가장 중요한 것은 '백두산 밀영을 비롯한 백두산 혁명전적지를 통한 교양'이라고 강조한다. 북한에서는 혁명사적지와 혁명전적지를 만드는데 구체적인 방법도 제시하고 있다.

"우리당은 혁명전적지와 사적지들에 대기념비를 세울 때에는 먼저 위대한 수령 김일성동지의 동상을 중심으로 하여 잘 형성되도록 그 규모를 바로 정하고 형상에서 시대적 배경을 옳게 살리며 혁명 사적이 집중 되여 있는 곳에 모시도록 하는 새롭고도 독창적인 방침들을 제시하며 그것을 철저히 관철하도록 세심히 이끌어 주었다."[24]

북한에서는 1959년부터 혁명전적지와 혁명사적지에 국가의 대대적인 행사인 답사행군대를 조직하여 많은 사람들을 조직적으로 참여하게 하였다. 특히 처음에는 당원들과 학생들을 대상으로 많이 조직되었는데 이후 점차 모든 주민들이 대상이 되었다.

〈표 4〉를 살펴보면 보천보혁명전적지를 시작으로 1960년대 백두산일대 무산지구혁명전적지가 조성되기 시작하였고 혁명전적지를 중심으로 상징공간이 조성되면서 1959년부터 〈혁명전적지 달리기〉형식으로 학생들을 중심으로 김일성의 항일빨

년도	혁명전적지/혁명사적지 조성	년도	답사행군 조직
1953 ~	보천보혁명전적지	1959	〈혁명전적지 달리기〉
1960 ~	백두산일대 무산지구혁명전적지	1967	〈혁명전적지 달리기〉 혁명전통과 연결
1974 ~75	왕재산혁명사적지	1973 1974 1975	〈배움의 천리길 이어달리기〉 〈배움의 천리길〉답사행군 〈광복의 천리길〉답사행군
1976 ~79	삼지연혁명전적지(백두산 대로천박물관 완성)	1982	〈백두산혁명전적지〉답사행군
1976 1979 1987	장자산혁명사적지(평양, 김정일) 어은혁명사적지(평양, 김정일) 백두산 밀영 개영(백두산, 김정일)	1986	〈정일봉〉, 〈백두산밀영〉답사행군(백두산혁명전적지 답사) 〈장자산혁명사적지〉답사행군(〈백두산혁명전적지〉 개척 30돐을 기념)
		1997	〈백두산밀영 고향집〉답사행군(백두산혁명전적지 답사)

〈표 4〉 혁명전적지와 혁명사적지에 대한 답사행군 조직 [25]

치산 혁명업적을 따라 체험하게 하는 국가적 행사를 만들어 냈다. 1959년 2월 5일자 노동신문에서는 청년학생답사대가 전적지를 답사했음을 처음 언급했다.[26] 또한 1960년부터 〈혁명전적지에로의 집단적 달리기〉로 명칭이 바뀌어 학술답사 사업이 진행된 이후부터는 〈혁명전적지 달리기〉라는 행사를 국가적으로 조직해 일반인들에게 김일성의 항일혁명업적을 직접 참관하고 체험하게 했다. 이 시기에는 김일성의 항일무장투쟁을 강조하면서 '평양, 보천보, 백두산'에 집중하였다. 1968년부터는 〈혁명전적지 달리기〉를 혁명전통교양과 밀접히 결부하여 진행한다.[27] 1968년은 사상부문을 담당하고 있었던 갑산파의 숙청이 마무리된 시기로 김일성의 정치권력이 독점적으로 행사되던 때로 비로소 김일성의 항일혁명전통만이 북한의 '혁명전통'으로 인정되었다. 그런 의미에서 〈혁명전적지 달리기〉라는 국가의례를 만들어 주민들을 참여를 유도 사회적 통합을 도모했다고 볼 수 있다. 1974년을 기점으로 혁명전적지와 혁명사적지 발굴과 조성이 전면화되었고 또한 대규모화 되었다. 1973년부터 시작된 〈배움의 천리길〉답사행군과 〈광복의 천리길〉답사행군은 김일성이 각각 11세(1923년)과 13세(1925년)이 되던 해에 평양의 만경대와 량강도의 포평까지 14일이 걸려 오간 것을 기념하여 이를 체험하는 공간이라고 할 수 있다. 이것은 학생들을 대상으로 진행된 국가적 의례 행사로 당시 김정일이 후계자로 결정되던 시기 새로운 세대에 대한 '혁명전통' 교양의 중요성을 확인한 것이다.

같은 시기 후계자로 지명된 김정일은 왕재산혁명사적지를 상징공간으로 발굴해 내는 것은 물론 1979년 삼지연혁명전적지를 대규모로 웅장하게 조성하면서 백두산 전역을 "대로천 박물관"으로 조성·완성하였다. 상징적 공간의 완성으로 1980년 6차 당대회에서 김정일이 후계자로 공식화된 이후에는 지금과 같은 형식의 답사행군을 조직하여 국가행사로 정착되게 하였다. 〈백두산혁명전적지〉 답사행군은 1982년 7월 〈백두산청년답사행군대〉가 조직되어 답사행군이 시작된 이래 현재까지도 진행되는 국가공식 의례행사이다. 하지만 북한은 〈백두산혁명전적지〉 답사행군은 1956년 8월 종파들이 사상 사업에서 나쁜 영향을 끼치고 있을 때 김정일 주도하에 처음으로 시작되었다고 설명하고 있다. 1980년 후계자로 공식 등장한 김정일이 1982년이라는 시점에서 새로운 의미와 형식으로 조직되는 〈백두산혁명전적지〉답사행군을 1956년의 정치적 상황에 대처하기 위해 조직한 것으로 설명하며, '혁명전통'은 김정일에 의한 것이며 김정일은 '백두의 혈통' 이어받은 존재라는 것을 강조한 것이라 할 수 있다.

"〈1천여리 백두산혁명전적지 답사 행군 길〉: 영광스러운 당중앙에서는 26년전 보천보로부터 삼지연을 거쳐 백두산마루에 오르는 첫 답사행군대오를 무어주고 이끌어 주었다. 이리하여 백두산에로의 1천여리 답사 행군 길은 반당 반혁명종파분자들이 우리 당의 빛나는 혁명전통을 말살하려고 악랄하게 날뛰던 전후의 어렵고 복잡한 시기에 우리당에 의하여 처음으로 열렸다. 그때부터 전국각지의 근로자들과 청소년학생들, 해외동포들과 우리나라를 방문한 외국의 벗들이 우리 당에 의하여 개척된 길을 따라 백두산혁명전적지를 답사하였다. 당중앙에서 그 후 량강도 일대를 하나의 혁명전통교양의 대로천 박물관으로 전변시켰다. 영광스러운 당중앙에서는 또한 백두산혁명전적지에 대한 정연한 답사체계를 세우고 그것을 조직화하며 근로자들의 답사 길과 일체적 물질적 및 재정적 부담까지 국가가 전적으로 책임지고 보장하도록 하는 조치까지 취해주셨다."[28]

1970년대 말에는 장자산 혁명사적지, 어은 혁명사적지 등 김정일과 관련된 혁명사적지들이 조성되었고 1982년부터 복원하기 시작한 백두산 밀영은 1987년 완성되었다. 백두산 밀영은 김일성이 항일무장투쟁 활동을 하였던 지역이고 그곳에서 1942년 김정일이 태어났다고 주장되는 공간이다. 때문에 백두산 밀영은 김일성의 '백두의 혈통'을 정당화하는 공간이라 할 수 있다. 〈표 4〉를 보면 1986년 백두산 밀영을 조성하고 있을 당시 〈백두산혁명전적지〉 개척 30돌 기념 답사행군을 조직, 그 이전과 비교하여 대대적으로 조직하였다. 이 시기부터 〈백두산혁명전적지〉 답사행군은 김정일을 상징하는 공간인 〈백두산밀영〉, 〈정일봉〉을 포함하여 진행되었다.

〈표 5〉를 보면 1950년대와 60년대에는 백두산 지역의 상징적 공간을 조성하는 데에 집중했고 1970년대 김정일의 등장과 함께 대규모로 그리고 체계적으로 조성되기 시작했다. 이후 1980년 김정일이 공식적인 후계자로 된 이후 백두산을 중심으로 한 항일혁명전통의 상징공간에서는 답사행군과 같은 국가의례행사가 진행되고 있다. 〈백두산혁명전적지〉 답사행군은 김일성의 생일, 김정일의 생일, 보천보전투기념일 등 북한에서 중요시하는 국경일과 기념일에 진행되는 것은 물론 당원들과 학생들은 1년 내내 국가의 계획에 의하여 답사행군을 하게 되어있다. 이처럼 북한은 김일성 체제의 정당성을 강화하기 위하여 1950년대부터 김일성의 항일무장투쟁의 전통으로부터 그 기원을 찾았고, 백두산을 중심으로 김일성의 항일무장투쟁이 진행되었던 공간을 '혁명전통'의 상징공간으로 조성했다. 이후 백두산의 상징공간에서는 국가의 의도가 포함된 국가적 행사들이 진행되고 주민들은 국가의 계획에 의하여 상징적 공간을 방문 및 답사하게 된다. 이러한 상징과 국가적 의례와 활용은 어떠한 체제를 막론하고 활용되는 것으로 북한에서는 특히

연대	1950~60년대	1970년대	1980년대	1990년대
주요 정치적 사건	53 휴전 56 8월 종파사건	74 김정일 후계자 지정 (대내)	80 김정일 후계자 지정 (대외)	94 김일성 사망
〈배움의 천리길〉 〈광복의 천리길〉		73		
〈백두산 혁명전적지〉	59 〈혁명전적지달리기〉		82〈백두산혁명전적지〉	
〈백두산밀영·장자산·어은 혁명사적지〉			86	

〈표 5〉 국가 답사행군의 시기와 특징

1970년대까지 상징적 공간조성을, 1980년대부터는 의례를 적극적으로 활용하여 1980년대 이후 현재까지 잘 활용되고 있다고 보아야 한다.

'혁명전통'의 상징적 공간의 활용은 북한 정권 수립의 정당성을 강화하는 것과 동시에 '백두의 혈통'을 강조하게 되면서 김일성 정권의 정당성 강화와 더 나아가 김일성-김정일-김정은으로 이어지는 세습의 정당성까지 강화하는 기능을 강화하고 있다.

결론

정치권력은 자신의 권력 정당성을 강화하기 위하여 물리적 강제력 뿐 아니라 동의를 이끌어 낼 수 있는 여러 방법들을 모색한다. 즉 정치권력이 폭력에만 의존한다면 권력을 오래 지탱할 수 없기 때문이다. 때문에 정치권력들은 정권에 대한 사람들의 공감대를 불러일으키기 위해 의례와 상징을 활용한다.

북한은 1950년대 전쟁 직후 김일성의 권력을 강화하고 정당화하기 위하여 김일성의 항일무장투쟁의 '혁명전통'을 선택하여 상징공간을 조성했고, 의례를 활용해 사람들을 교양하고자 했다. 1960-70년대 북한의 백두산 전지역과 평양지역은 혁명전적지, 혁명사적지로 조성되어 성역화 되었고, 1980년대 김정일의 공식적인 후계자 선정이후 그 상징적 공간에서는 답사행군이라는 국가의례가 조직되어 지금 현재까지도 지속되고 있다. '혁명전통'과 관련된 상징공간과 그 공간에서 행해지는 국가의례에 사람들이 참가하게 되면서 의식적이든 무의식적이든간에 정치권력에 대해 긍정적인 느낌을 갖게 되어, 믿음을 촉진하게 되는 것이다.

북한에서는 1930년부터 1945년간 진행되었던 김일성의 항일무장투쟁의 역사가 북한 정권의 정당성을 뒷받침하는 유일한 역사가 되었고 '혁명전통'으로 이데올로기화 되었다. 혁명전통은 체제의 정당성을 강화하는 것은 물론 공간 상징과 국가적 의례를 통해 의미가 확장되고 강화되면서 현재 북한의 세습체제에 대한 정당성을 강화하는 이데올로기로 작용하고 있다.

References

Cohen, Abner, Two-dimensional man:An essay on the anthropology of power and symbolism in complex society, Berkeley : University of California Press, 1974.

Easton, David, A systems analysis of political life, Chicago:University of Chicago Press, 1979

Max Weber(tr. by A. M. Henderson and Talcott Parsons), The theory of social and economic organization, Glencoe : Free Press, 1947.

Merriam, Charles Edward, Political Power, Collier Book, New York, 1964.

국토통일원 조사연구실, 「조선노동당대회 자료집」Ⅰ Ⅱ, 1988.

김신원(1996), "북한의 국토 및 지역개발에 의한 조경공간 형성에 관한 연구", 경희대학교 조경학과 박사논문.

김정일, "량강도를 혁명전통교양의 거점으로 튼튼히 꾸리자(량강도 책임일군 및 항일혁명투사들과 한 담화 1968년 7월 21일)", 「김정일 선집」제1권, 조선로동당출판사, 1992.

북한사회과학원 언어학연구소, 「현대조선말사전」,1988.

신복룡 옮김, 「정치 권력론」, 선인, 2006.

윤승용 옮김, 「이차원적 인간」, 한벗, 1982.

이용필 역, 「정치생활의 체계분석」, 법문사, 1988

조은희, "북한 혁명전통의 상징화 연구", 이화여자대학교 박사학위논문, 2007.

"김일성 원수 항일 빨찌산 투쟁의 전적지 청년 학생 답사대 현지로 출발", 「로동신문」, 1959년 2월 5일자.

"김일성원수 항일빨찌산 투쟁 전적지 조사단 현지로 향발", 「로동신문」, 1953년 9월 3일자.

"혁명전통 연구와 전투력량강화로 2.8절을 맞는 방선용사들", 「로동신문」, 1956년 2월 2일자.

「조선중앙년감」 1953년-2009년.

1 Merriam, Charles Edward, Political Power, Collier Book, New York, 1964., 신복룡 옮김, 「정치 권력론」, 선인, 2006, p159.
2 Max Weber(tr. by A. M. Henderson and Talcott Parsons), The theory of social and economic organization, Glencoe : Free Press, 1947, p125.
3 위의 책, p325.
4 위의 책, p277.
5 Easton, David, A systems analysis of political life, Chicago:University of Chicago Press, 1979(이용필 역, 「정치생활의 체계분석」, 법문사, 1988).p309; Cohen explains this as "power is an abstract object which can only be seen through symbolic system and proposal.", Cohen, Abner, Two-dimensional man:An essay on the anthropology of power and symbolism in complex society, Berkeley : University of California Press, 1974., 윤승용 옮김, 「이차원적 인간」, 한벗, 1982, pp137-138.
6 Easton(이용필, 1988), pp306-308.
7 Cohen expresses it as ritual but in this thesis it is expressed as rite. Cohen(윤승용, 1982), pp137-138.
8 「로동신문」, 1953년 9월 3일자, "Kim Il-Sung departures to the research site of Anti-Japanese Partisan Revolutionary battle field.".
9 「로동신문」, 1956년 2월 2일자, "방선용사 greets February 8th Day with research on revoulutionary tradition and reinforcement of fighting efficacy".
10 To look at North Korea's 당대회 자료집, the regulation on nature of 조선로동당 is mentioned as a 'successor of 조선인민's revolutionary tradition' at 3rd party convention on April, 1956 and as a 'direct successor of glorious revolutionary tradition of Anti-Japanese armed struggle' at 4th party convention in 1961, which shows that since 1956 'revolutionary tradition' has been settled as North Korea's core ideology. 국토통일원 조사연구실, 「조선노동당대회 자료집」Ⅰ Ⅱ, 1988.
11 북한사회과학원 언어학연구소(1988), 「현대조선말사전」.
13 북한사회과학원 언어학연구소(1988), 「현대조선말사전」.
15 김정일, "량강도를 혁명전통교양의 거점으로 튼튼히 꾸리자(량강도 책임일군 및 항일혁명투사들과 한 담화 1968년 7월 21일)", 「김정일 선집」제1권(조선로동당출판사, 1992), p380.
16 위의 글, p375-389 내용 발췌 정리.
17 "The 1st stage of construction is completed in October for greater management of Revolutionary battle field in Baekdu Mountain region and to have it as our treasure forever; the 2nd stage of construction is being actively carried out to permanently preserve the sites and relics of battle field and historical site and to guarantee instructors a better living condition." 조선로동당출판사, 「조선중앙년감 2001」(2002).
18 「로동신문」, 1953년 9월 3일자 1면, "Kim Il-Sung departures to the site of Anti-Japanese Partisan Revolutionary battle field."It is the first time that sending research group to battle field is mentioned in 로동신문. According to 2003 4th issue「력사과학」, it describes that excavation business on Anti-Japanese Revolutionary battle field and historical site progresses in August, 1946 and research group is sent to Northeastern region of China, but the excavation business on Anti-Japanese Revolutionary battle field does not only mean that of Kim Il-Sung's achievement.
19 조선중앙통신사(1959), 「조선중앙년감」1959년, p225.
20 위의 책, p220.
21 김신원(1996), "Research on development of landscape space by North Korea's terrirory and regional development", 경희대학교 조경학과 박사논문.
22 「조선중앙년감 1953년-2009년」에서 발췌 정리
23 조선중앙통신사(1961,1962,1963,1964), 「조선중앙년감」1961년, pp227-228, 1962년, p279, 1963년, p247, 1964년, p217, 1965년, p183.
24 조선중앙통신사(1965), 「조선중앙년감」1965년, p183.
25 과학, 백과사전출판사, 「백과전서」제5권(1984), p660.
26 조선중앙통신사, 「조선중앙년감」1983년(1983), p258.
27 「조선중앙년감 1953년-2009년」에서 발췌 정리.
28 "Kim Il-Sung departures to Youths and Students research site of Anti-Japanese Partisan Revolution battle field", 「로동신문」2nd Page, February 5th ,1959.
29 "Through 〈Revolutionary Battle Field Race〉, be armed as Kim Il-Sung's true revolutionary soldier and train one's mind and body strongly", 조선중앙통신사, 「조선중앙년감」1969년(1969), p293.
30 조선중앙통신사, 「조선중앙년감」1983년, p258.

1 Merriam, Charles Edward, Political Power, Collier Book, New York, 1964., 신복룡 옮김, 「정치 권력론」, 선인, 2006, p159.
2 Max Weber(tr. by A. M. Henderson and Talcott Parsons), The theory of social and economic organization, Glencoe : Free Press, 1947, p125.

3 위의 책, p325.
4 위의 책, p277.
5 Easton, David, A systems analysis of political life, Chicago:University of Chicago Press, 1979(이용필 역, 『정치생활의 체계분석』, 법문사, 1988). p309; 코헨은 이것에 대해 "권위는 오로지 상징체계와 제의를 통해서만 볼 수 있는 추상물이다."라고 설명한다. Cohen, Abner, Two-dimensional man:An essay on the anthropology of power and symbolism in complex society, Berkeley : University of California Press, 1974., 윤승용 옮김, 『이차원적 인간』, 한벗, 1982, pp137-138.
6 Easton(이용필, 1988), pp306-308.
7 코헨은 의식으로 표현하지만, 본 논문에서는 의례로 표기한다. Cohen(윤승용, 1982), pp137-138.
8 『로동신문』, 1953년 9월 3일자, "김일성원수 항일빨찌산 투쟁 전적지 조사단 현지로 향발".
9 『로동신문』, 1956년 2월 2일자, "혁명전통 연구와 전투력량강화로 2.8절을 맞는 방선용사들".
10 북한의 당대회 자료집을 살펴보면, 조선로동당의 성격에 대한 규정이 1956년 4월 3차 당대회에서 조선로동당은 '조선인민의 혁명적 전통의 계승자'로 1961년 4차 당대회에서는 '항일무장투쟁의 영광스러운 혁명전통의 직접적 인 계승자' 로 언급되어 1956년부터 '혁명전통'이 북한의 핵심이념으로 자리 잡았음을 알 수 있다. 국토통일원 조사연구실, 『조선노동당대회 자료집』Ⅰ·Ⅱ, 1988.
11 북한사회과학원 언어학연구소(1988), 『현대조선말사전』.
13 북한사회과학원 언어학연구소(1988), 『현대조선말사전』.
15 김정일, "량강도를 혁명전통교양의 거점으로 튼튼히 꾸리자(량강도 책임일군 및 항일혁명투사들과 한 담화 1968년 7월 21일)", 『김정일 선집』 제1권(조선로동당출판사, 1992), p380.
16 위의 글, p375-389 내용 발췌 정리.
17 "10월 백두산지구 혁명전적지를 우리 혁명의 만년재보로 더 훌륭히 꾸리기 위한 제1단계건설이 완공, 전적지, 사적지들의 혁명사적물과 유적유물들을 영구보존하고 강사들의 생활조건을 더 잘 보장해주기 위한 제2단계공사가 적극 추진되고 있다." 조선로동당출판사, 『조선중앙년감 2001』(2002).
18 『로동신문』, 1953년 9월 3일자 1면, "김일성원수 항일 빨찌산 투쟁전적지 조사단 현지로 출발". 전적지에 대한 조사단 파견이 로동신문에서 처음 언급되어 진다. 2003년 4호『력사과학』에 의하면 1946년 8월 항일혁명전적지와 사적지들에 대한 발굴사업이 진행되었고 답사단을 중국동북지방에 파견하였다고 서술되어지고 있지만, 그때의 항일혁명전적지에 대한 발굴사업은 '김일성의 업적'만을 의미하지 않는 것이다.
19 조선중앙통신사(1959), 『조선중앙년감』 1959년, p225.
20 위의 책, p220.
21 김신원(1996), "북한의 국토 및 지역개발에 의한 조경공간 형성에 관한 연구", 경희대학교 조경학과 박사논문.
22 『조선중앙년감 1953년-2009년』에서 발췌 정리
23 조선중앙통신사(1961,1962,1963,1964), 『조선중앙년감』1961년, pp227-228. 1962년, p279. 1963년, p247. 1964년, p217. 1965년, p183.
24 조선중앙통신사(1965), 『조선중앙년감』1965년, p183.
25 과학, 백과사전출판사, 『백과전서』제5권(1984), p660.
26 조선중앙통신사, 『조선중앙년감』1983년(1983), p258.
27 『조선중앙년감 1953년-2009년』에서 발췌 정리.
28 "김일성 원수 항일 빨찌산 투쟁의 전적지 청년 학생 답사대 현지로 출발", 『로동신문』1959년 2월 5일자 2면.
29 "〈혁명전적지달리기〉를 통하여 수령의 참된 혁명전사로 무장하여 몸과 마음을 튼튼히 단련", 조선중앙통신사, 『조선중앙년감』1969년(1969), p293.
30 조선중앙통신사, 『조선중앙년감』1983년, p258.

A WHITE PAPER ON THE DEMILITARIZED ZONE: SOME FACTS AND QUESTIONS FOR THE FUTURE

Dongsei Kim

—

Dongsei Kim is a registered architect and urbanist. He is an adjunct assistant professor at Columbia University, GSAPP and principal of axu studio. He received his MDesS with distinction from Harvard University, MsAUD from Columbia University, and a B.Arch (Hons) from Victoria University of Wellington. Dongsei's research focuses on how extreme border conditions and their territories can inform fundamental spatial negotiation processes such as "inclusion and exclusion," and how "us and them" are defined in urbanism. He has practiced in New York, Wellington, and Seoul. He has also extensively taught architecture and urbanism with leading universities in Australia, Canada, New Zealand, US, and Korea.

In the late 19th century, long before the Japanese colonial period (1910-1945) the 38th parallel line was proposed as a delimiting line for then expanding Russian and Japanese imperialists' influence over the Korean peninsula. This precedes the Korean Demilitarized Zone (DMZ) by almost half a century, which was later established with the Armistice Agreement on July 27, 1953 following the Korean War. Growing ideological schism in Korea after its independence from Japanese colonization in 1945 coupled with global geopolitical tensions instigated the Korean War in 1950, which is considered as one of the first proxy wars between the superpowers (Kim 2011, 33).

This ideological contestation between the communist powers of China and the Soviet Union, on the one hand, and the Free World led by the U.S. on the other hand, left behind a relic approximately 250-km (148-miles) long and 4-km (2.5-mile) wide military infrastructure called the Demilitarized Zone (DMZ). The area agreed in the Armistice Agreement in 1953 was 992-km2 (245,129 acres). This area accounts for about 0.5% of the Korean peninsula. It is about twice the size of Seoul and one-third of Pyongyang, the capital cities of two Koreas. Its land area is comparable to Berlin that is 892-km2 and Singapore city-state at 716.1-km2. To this day the Military Demarcation Line (MDL) runs through the center of the DMZ and separates the communist North and the capitalist South. Under a temporary armistice, the two Koreas are technically still at war after more than 60 years since the war broke out (NASA's Earth Observatory 2003).

" 1. A Military Demarcation Line shall be fixed and both sides shall withdraw two (2) kilometers

A White Paper on The Demilitarized Zone: Some Facts and Questions for the Future | Dongsei Kim

Image 01. An aerial view, the Korean Demilitarized Zone (DMZ) highlighted in red.

from this line so as to establish a Demilitarized Zone between the opposing forces. A Demilitarized Zone shall be established as a buffer zone to prevent the occurrence of incidents which might lead to a resumption of hostilities." (United Nations Command 1953, 237)

Given the DMZ's past 60 years of relative refuge from human interventions, it has supposedly become one of the most bio-diverse areas in Korea, perhaps in the world. Starting in the early 2000s, many calls and proposals have been made to conserve and preserve the area as an international peace park. The DMZ has claimed to be home to endangered Asian cranes, black-faced spoonbills, angora goats, Amur leopards, and bears (NASA's Earth Observatory 2003). For many years or-

Image 03. Omnipresent land mine warning sign near the DMZ.
© 2011 Dongsei Kim.

ganizations such as the DMZ Forum have been working towards proclaiming the DMZ a UNESCO World Heritage Site (Kim 2011, 33). In September 2013, the South Korean government allocated US $37.3 million for a call to establish a Peace Park in the DMZ in their 2014 budget (Yonhap News Agency 2013).

Nevertheless, the DMZ is not free from other depredations. The "Landmines and Human Security: International Politics and War's Hidden Legacy" book points out the life threatening 2.2 million estimated land mines scattered within, and around the DMZ (Ohe 2004, 227). In 2003, United Nations Environment Programme's report and NASA Landsat 7 satellite exposed multiple burn scars in the DMZ linked to military surveillance, a procedure the two Koreas agreed to end in 2001 (NASA's Earth Observatory 2003). Adding to this, Green Korea United, a South Korean nongovernmental organization (NGO) released a report in July 2013, claiming that the agreed 992-km2 footprint of the DMZ in the Armistice Agreement is now close to half. Standing at 570-km2 this is almost 43% less than the original footprint, undermined by the constant military transgressions and territorial contestations nudging into the buffer

Image02. Scattered military Guard Posts (GPs) and Scenrity fences near the east coast hills near the DMZ on the South Korean side.
© 2011 Dongsei Kim.

zone (Green Korea 2013, 25).

Moreover, with the proliferating economic transactions such as the DMZ "security tourisms," and urbanization pressure triggered by future Peace Park speculations, these territories are more than ever under pressure for change. In this context, beyond the existing history, heavy military fortifications, security concerns, and ecologically themed tourism and other moneymaking ventures, what more can the DMZ become of? What can it do? Can it be a more productive landscape, such as harnessing energy? Or can it be a site of cultural production that brings added value to North and South Korea at the same time? Alike, if the DMZ were to embrace the anticipated pressures, how would a new hybrid urbanization model foster a synergistic relationship between the two Koreas? Or to put it differently: what does the DMZ desire to be? Or what should it not be? Ultimately, an extensive and rigorous imaginative visualizations and mappings, thus deeper and refreshed understanding of the DMZ and its environment can evoke new inventive thoughts to envision the DMZ's alternative future. This could further inspire an array of exciting potentials and explorations that is facilitative to DMZ's metamorphosis from an impenetrable barrier to an agile asset.

Image 04. The infamous Joint Security Area (JSA) looking towards North Korea from the South. © 2011 Dongsei Kim.

비무장지대 백서(白書):
몇 가지 사실들과 미래를 위한 질문들

김동세

—

김동세는 건축가이자 어바니스트(Urbanist)이며, 미국 컬럼비아 대학 겸임 조교수이고 axu studio 소장이다. 그는 하버드 대학교에서 디자인 석사 최우수 학위로 졸업을 하였으며, 컬럼비아 대학에서 도시설계 건축학 석사를, 뉴질랜드 웰링턴의 빅토리아 대학에서 건축학 학사를 취득하였다. 그의 연구는 극단적인 경계부와 그들의 영역이 어떻게 "포용과 배제"와 같은 근본적인 공간적 타협 과정에 영향을 미칠 수 있는지, 또한 "우리와 그들"이 어바니즘에서 어떻게 정의되는지 주목하고 있다. 그는 뉴욕과 웰링턴, 그리고 서울에서 실무를 익혔으며, 호주, 캐나다, 뉴질랜드, 미국, 한국 등 여러 국가의 유수 대학에서 강의를 하였다.

일제 강점기(1910–1945) 이전인 19세기 후반, 38선은 한반도에 러시아와 일본 제국주의의 영향을 제한하기 위해 제안되었다. 이 선은 반세기가 지난 1953년 7월 27일, 한국전쟁의 정전협정과 함께 확립된 한국 비무장지대(DMZ)의 토대가 된다. 초강대국 사이의 첫 대리전이라 간주되는 한국전쟁은 1945년 해방 이후 이념적 분열의 확산과 세계적 지정학적 긴장으로 1950년 발발했다. (Kim 2011, 33).

중국과 소련의 공산주의 세력과 미국의 자유진영의 이념적 논쟁은 길이 250㎞, 4㎞ 너비의 비무장지대(DMZ)라는 군사 시설을 남겼다. 정전 협정에서 합의한 992㎢ 넓이는 한반도 면적의 0.5%이며 남한의 수도 서울의 3배, 북한의 수도 평양의 3분의 1이나 되는 면적이다. 이는 면적 892㎢인 베를린과 716.1㎢ 인 도시국가 싱가폴과 견줄만하다. 오늘날까지 군사분계선 (MDL)은 비무장지대의 중앙을 지나며 사회주의 북한과 자본주의 남한을 나누고 있다. 엄밀히 따지면 남한과 북한은 정전 협정 아래 전쟁 발발 60년이 지난 지금까지 전쟁 중에 있다. (NASA's Earth Observatory 2003).

"1. 한 개의 군사분계선을 확정하고 쌍방이 이 선으로 부터 각기 (2) 키로 메터 후퇴함으로써 적대 군대간에 한 개의 비무장지대를 설정한다. 한 개의 비무장지대를 설정하여 이를 완충지대로 함으로써 적대행위의 재발을 초래할 수 있는 사건의 발생을 방지한다. (제 1조, 제 1항. 군사분계선과 비무장지대, 정전협정 제 1 권 협전문)"

지난 60년 동안 인간의 개입이 거의 없던 비무장지대는 한반도에서, 어쩌면 세계에서, 생태적으로 가장 다양한 생태 지역이라고 여겨진다. 2000년대 초반부터 이 지역을 국제적인 평화 공원으로 만들어 아끼고 보호하기 위한 많은 요청과 제안이 여러 번 있었다. 현재 비무장지대는 멸종 위기에 처한 두루미, 저어새, 앙고라염소, 아무르표범과 곰의 서식지로 알려져 있다. DMZ 포럼과 같은 단체들은 비무장지대를 유네스코 세계유산으로 등재하기 위해 수년간 노력했다. 그리고 2013년 9월 남한정부는 2014년 예산에 비무장지대 평화 공원 설립 제안을 위해 (한화) 402억 원을 배정하였다. (연합뉴스 2013).

그러나 비무장지대는 다른 위협들로부터 자유롭지 못하다. '지

Image 05. MILITARY Guard Post (GP) and fences at Kosung, South Korea, near the DMZ. © 2011 Dongsei Kim.

뢰와 인간안보: 국제 정치와 전쟁의 숨겨진 유산'은 생명을 위협하는 2백 2십만 개의 지뢰가 비무장지대 안과 주위에 흩어져있다고 추정 하고 있다 (Ohe 2004, 227). 그리고 2003년에는 국제 연합 환경 계획의 보고와 나사 랜드샛 7 위성이 남한과 북한이 2001년 중단하기로 한 다수의 군사적 목적 [시계(視界), 사계(射界) 확보] 산불이나 맞불 작전들의 화상 반흔의 흔적을 드러냈다. (NASA's Earth Observatory 2003). 또한 지난 2013년 7월 남한의 민간인단체 (NGO)인 녹색연합은 정전 협정에서 합의했던 992㎢ 비무장지대 면적이 현재 그 절반에 가깝다고 주장하는 보고서를 발표했다. 45% 줄어든이 50㎢ 면적은 비무장지대 완충지대 내에서 지속적인 군사 침범과 영역경합으로 인해 줄어든 결과다. (녹색연합 2013, 25).

더욱이 비무장지대는 "보안관광"과 같은 급증하는 경제교류와 앞으로 평화 공원 조성 과정에서 촉발할 도시화의 압박으로 인해 이 지역은 그 어느 때보다 큰 변화의 요구를 받고 있다. 이러한 문맥에서, 현 비무장지대는, 그동안 존재해온 역사, 그 많은 군사 방어시설, 보안 문제와 생태학 테마의 관광 그리고 다른 돈벌이 사업 등을 넘어선 그 이상의 무엇이 될 수 있는가? 이 비무장지대는 무엇을 할 수 있는가? 이 곳이 에너지를 생산한다든지, 조금 더 생산적인 땅이 될 수는 없는가? 아니면 남한과 북한에 동시에 부가 가치를 가져오는 문화 생산의 장이 될 수는 없는가? 이런 맥락에서, 비무장지대가 예상된 도시화의 압력을 수용한다고 가정하면, 새로운 혼성적 (하이브리드) 도시화의 모델이 한반도의 시너지적 관계를 어떻게 발전 시킬 수 있을까? 다르게 말하자면: 비무장지대는 무엇이 되기를 열망하는가? 혹은 무엇이 되지 말아야 하는가? 궁극적으로, 광범위하고 철저한 창의적 시각화와 지도 제작은, 비무장지대와 그 주변에 대한 대안적 미래를 그릴 수 있는 새로운 창의적인 생각 및 이를 불러일으킬 수 있는 새롭고 깊은 이해들을 가능하게 할 것이다. 그리고 이러한 노력들은 비무장지대를 꿰뚫을 수 없는 장벽에서 민첩한 자산의 변형을 촉진하는 다수의 흥미로운 가능성과 탐사를 한층 고무할 수 있을 것이다.

Background Data

Image 06. Railway, road connections, and barriers near the DMZ viewed from Koseong Unification Observation Platform, South Korea.
© 2011 Dongsei Kim.

References

Green Korea. 2013. "2013 Green Korea DMZ Area Report (2013년 녹색연합 DMZ 공간조사 보고서)." July 23. Seoul: Green Korea. Accessed August 29. http://www.greenkorea.org/wp/wp-content/uploads/2013/07/녹색연합-DMZ-공간조사-보고서.pdf

Kim, Dongsei. 2011. "Demilitarized Zone: Redrawing the Border between North and South Korea Beyond Tourism. 3rd Edition." Cambridge, MA: Blurb.

Kim, Dongsei. 2013. "Borders as Urbanism: Redrawing the Demilitarized Zone (DMZ) between Democratic People's Republic of Korea and Republic of Korea." Landscape Architecture Frontiers. Vol.1 (2) April. 150–157.

NASA's Earth Observatory. 2003. "Korean Demilitarized Zone." Images of the Day. July 28. Accessed December 01 2013. http://earthobservatory.nasa.gov/IOTD/view.php?id=3660

Ohe J. A. 2004. "Are Landmines Still Needed to Defend South Korea? A Mine Use Case Study." In "Landmines and Human Security: International Politics and War's Hidden Legacy." Edited by Matthew, Richard A. McDonald, Bryan, and Rutherford, Ken. New York: State University of New York Press.

Yonhap News Agency. 2013. "S. Korea sets aside 40.2 billion won for DMZ peace park project." "GlobalPost-International News". September 26. Accessed November 14, 2013. http://www.globalpost.com/dispatch/news/yonhap-news-agency/130926/s-korea-sets-aside-402-billion-won-dmz-peace-park-project

United Nations Command. 1953. "Military Armistice in Korea and Temporary Supplementary Agreement, Signed at Panmunjom, Korea, July 27, 1953, Entered into Force July 27, 1953." Vol. 5197; 2782. Washington: U.S. Govt.

Image Credit & References

Image 01.
Caption: Page 105 correoicow
Sources: Original satellite image: Jesse Allen, NASA's Earth Observatory, Goddard Space Flight Center. 2003. "Korean Demilitarized Zone." Images of the Day. July 28. Accessed December 01 2013. ⟨http://eoimages.gsfc.nasa.gov/images/imagerecords/3000/3660/landsat_dmz_korea_lrg.jpg⟩

Modified map: Kim, Dongsei. 2011. "Demilitarized Zone: Redrawing the Border between North and South Korea Beyond Tourism." 3rd Edition. Cambridge, MA: Blurb. pp.11.

Image 02.
Caption: Page 106
Sources: 2011 Dongsei Kim.

Image 03.
Caption: Page 106
Sources: 2011 Dongsei Kim.

Image 04.
Caption: Page 107
Sources: 2011 Dongsei Kim.

Image 05.
Caption: Page 109
Sources: 2011 Dongsei Kim.

Image 06.
Caption: Page 110
Sources: 2011 Dongsei Kim.

02 BACKGROUND DATA
1. FACT SHEETS
2. GEOGRAPHICAL FACTS
3. INFRASTRUCTURAL FACTS
4. INDUSTRIAL GEOGRAPHY

Background Data

HISTORY TIMELINE

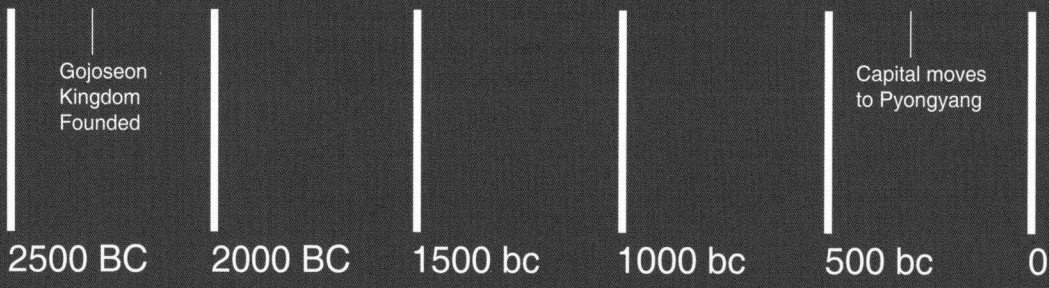

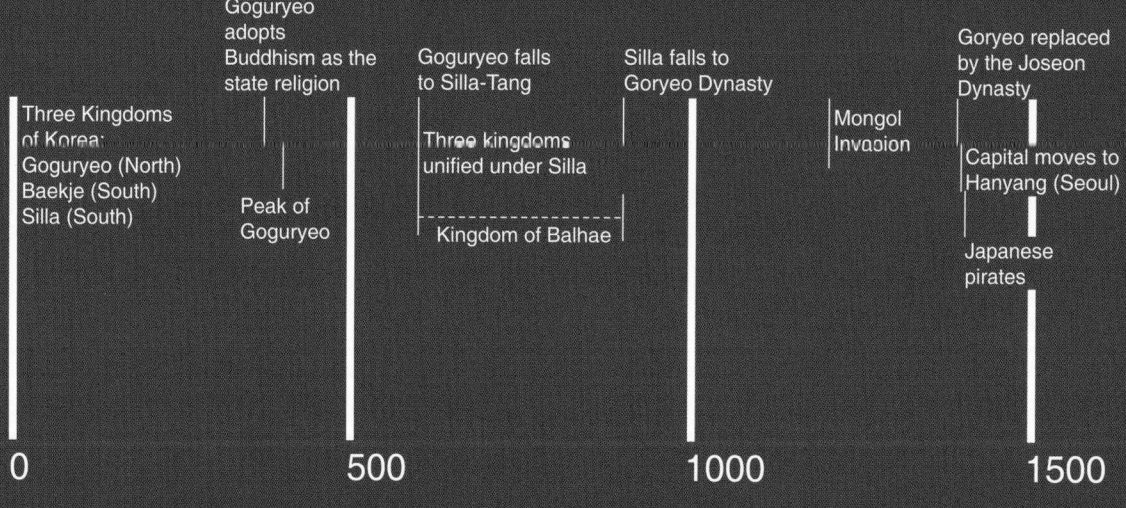

Fact Sheets   115

```
|
|  Japan attempts                              Trade treaty
|  to conquer Korea                            with Japan
|                                              |
|     | War with the                           | Trade treaty
|     | Manchus                                | with USA
|                                         Sino-Japanese
|                                         War
|                                         End of Joseon
|                                         dependency on   Joseon
|                                         China           renamed
|                                                         Korean
|                                                         Empire
|                                                         |
1500                                                    1900
```

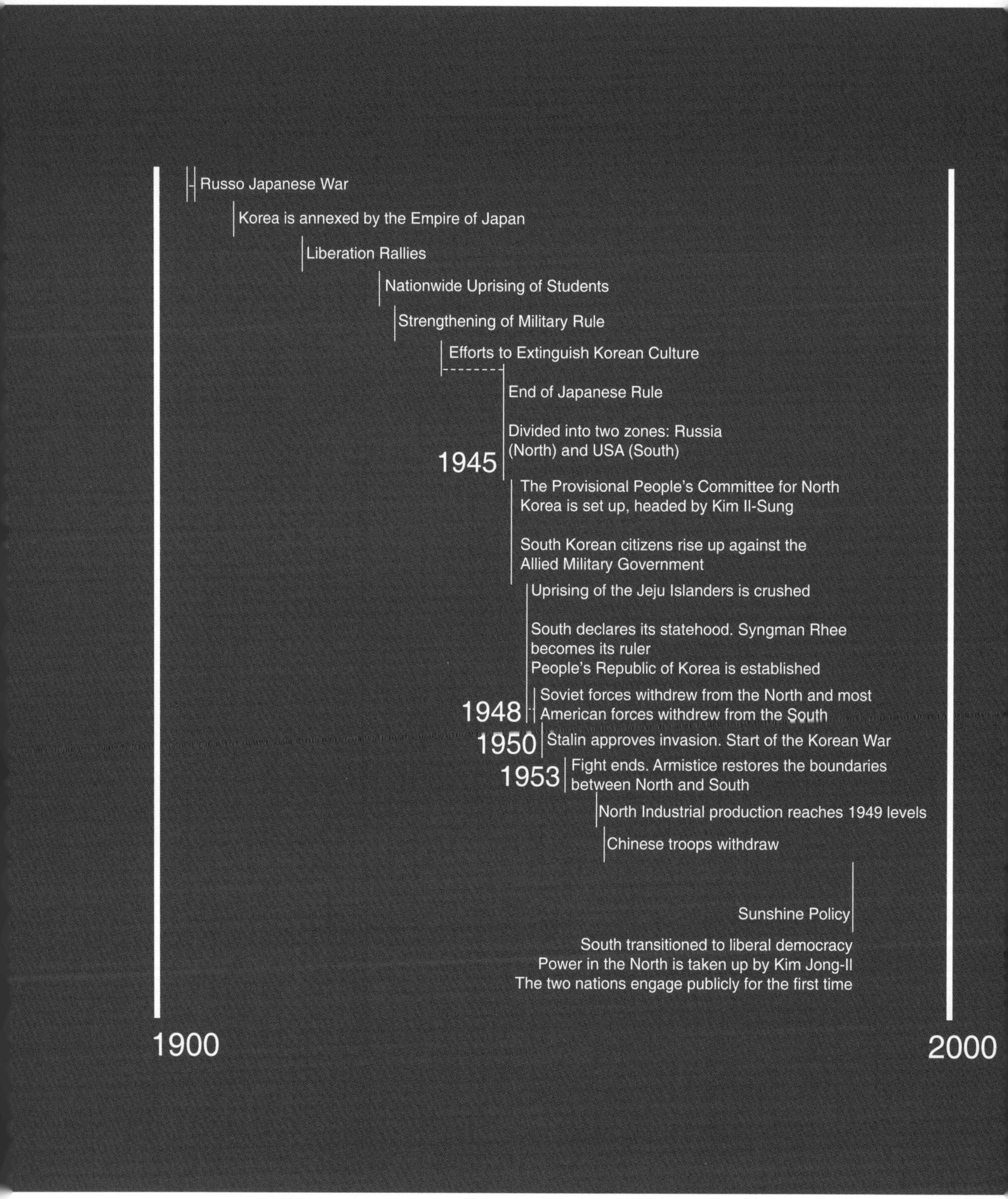

Background Data

- Russo Japanese War
- Korea is annexed by the Empire of Japan
- Liberation Rallies
- Nationwide Uprising of Students
- Strengthening of Military Rule
- Efforts to Extinguish Korean Culture
- End of Japanese Rule
- Divided into two zones: Russia (North) and USA (South)

1945

- The Provisional People's Committee for North Korea is set up, headed by Kim Il-Sung
- South Korean citizens rise up against the Allied Military Government
- Uprising of the Jeju Islanders is crushed
- South declares its statehood. Syngman Rhee becomes its ruler
- People's Republic of Korea is established
- Soviet forces withdrew from the North and most American forces withdrew from the South

1948

1950 — Stalin approves invasion. Start of the Korean War

1953 — Fight ends. Armistice restores the boundaries between North and South

- North Industrial production reaches 1949 levels
- Chinese troops withdraw

- Sunshine Policy
- South transitioned to liberal democracy
- Power in the North is taken up by Kim Jong-Il
- The two nations engage publicly for the first time

1900 **2000**

Fact Sheets

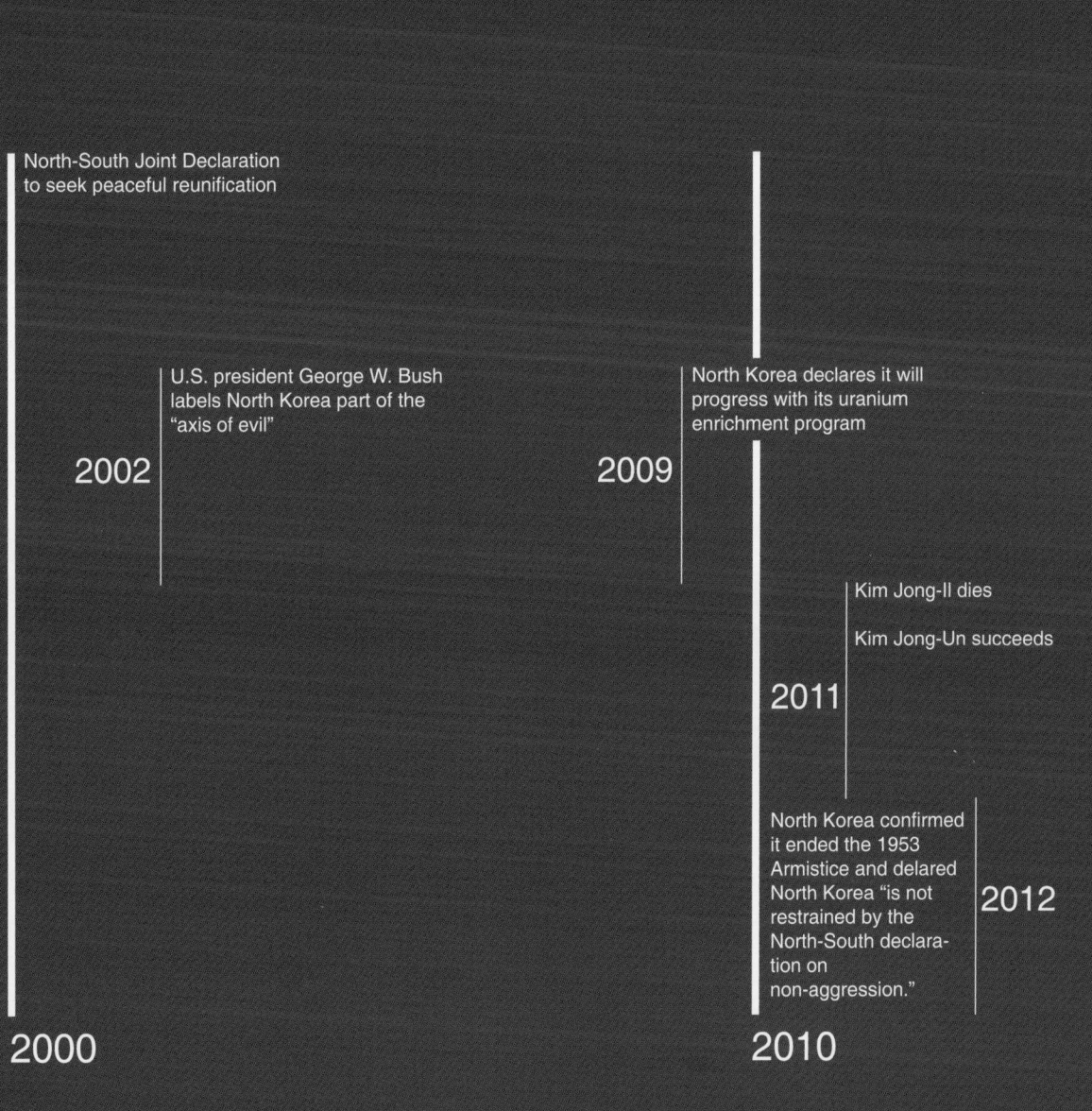

- 2000 — North-South Joint Declaration to seek peaceful reunification
- 2002 — U.S. president George W. Bush labels North Korea part of the "axis of evil"
- 2009 — North Korea declares it will progress with its uranium enrichment program
- 2011 — Kim Jong-Il dies / Kim Jong-Un succeeds
- 2012 — North Korea confirmed it ended the 1953 Armistice and delared North Korea "is not restrained by the North-South declaration on non-aggression."

Background Data

GOGURYEO DYNASTY (BC 37 - 668) 고구려 시대

220 - The Han Dynasty comes to an end with establishment of the Three Kingdoms in ancient China.
395 - Roman Emperor Theodosius I dies, causing the Roman Empire to split permanently.
570 - Birth of Mohammad, founder of Islam.
618 - Tang Dynasty of China initiated by Li Yuan.

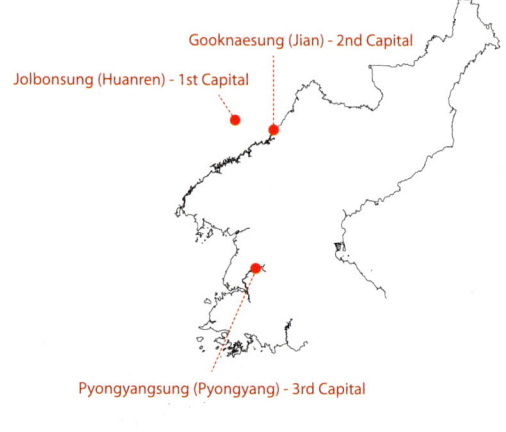

Gooknaesung (Jian) - 2nd Capital
Jolbonsung (Huanren) - 1st Capital
Pyongyangsung (Pyongyang) - 3rd Capital

MAJOR CITIES

UNIFIED SILLA DYNASTY (668 - 935) 통일신라 시대

726 - Byzantine Emperor Leo III the Isaurian destroys the icon of Christ above the Chalke Gate in the capital city of Constantinople, beginning the first phase of the Byzantine Iconoclasm.
805 to 820 - Tang Dynasty was under the rule of Emperor Xianzong of Tang.

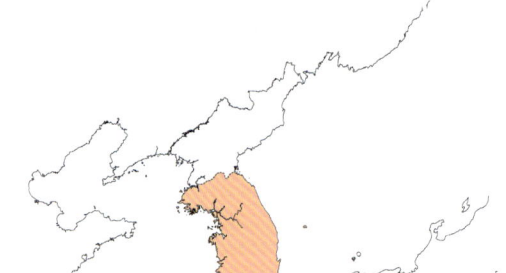

Janggujin (An-ak) - Trade city
Song-ak (Kaesong)

MAJOR CITIES

Fact Sheets

GORYEO DAYNASTY (918 - 1392) 고려 시대

927 - Kingdom of England becomes a unified state.
1099 - the Siege of Jerusalem by European Crusaders.
1347 - The Black Death, on its march across Asia to Europe, reaches Constantinople.

Uiju (Sinuiju) - Trade city
Pyongyang - West Capital
Song-ak (Kaesong) - Main Capital

MAJOR CITIES

JOSEON DYNASTY (1392 - 1897) 조선 시대

1453 - Constantinople falls to the Ottoman Turks, ending the Byzantine Empire and beginning the Ottoman Empire.
1492 - Christopher Columbus landed in the Americas from Spain.
1804 - Napoleon crowns himself Emperor of the French.

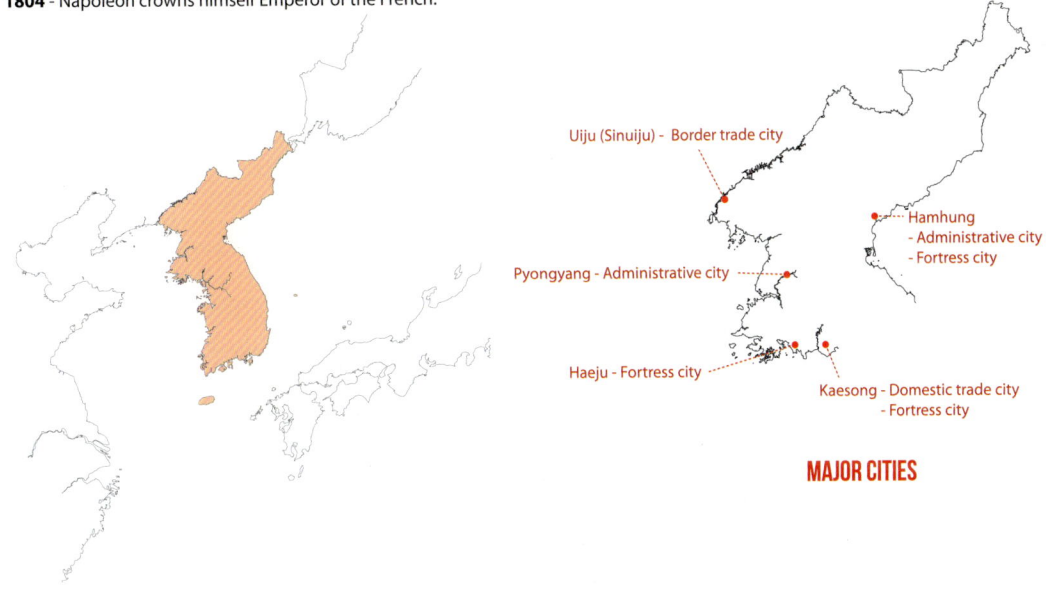

Uiju (Sinuiju) - Border trade city
Hamhung
 - Administrative city
 - Fortress city
Pyongyang - Administrative city
Haeju - Fortress city
Kaesong - Domestic trade city
 - Fortress city

MAJOR CITIES

Background Data

120

MAJOR CITIES FROM GOGURYEO TO JOSEON
(BC 37-668)   (1392-1897)

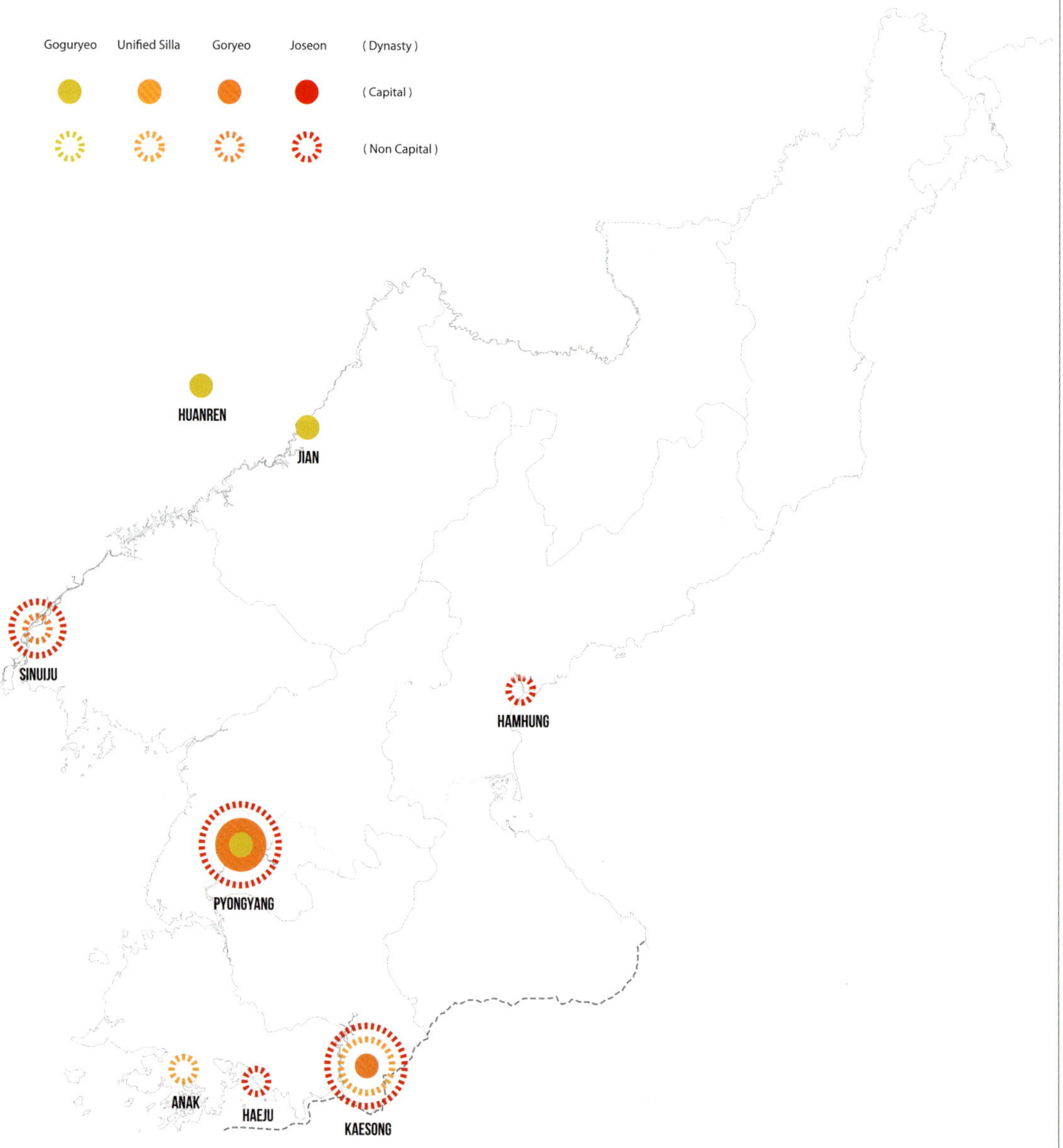

Goguryeo   Unified Silla   Goryeo   Joseon   (Dynasty)

● ● ● ● (Capital)

○ ○ ○ ○ (Non Capital)

HUANREN

JIAN

SINUIJU

HAMHUNG

PYONGYANG

ANAK   HAEJU   KAESONG

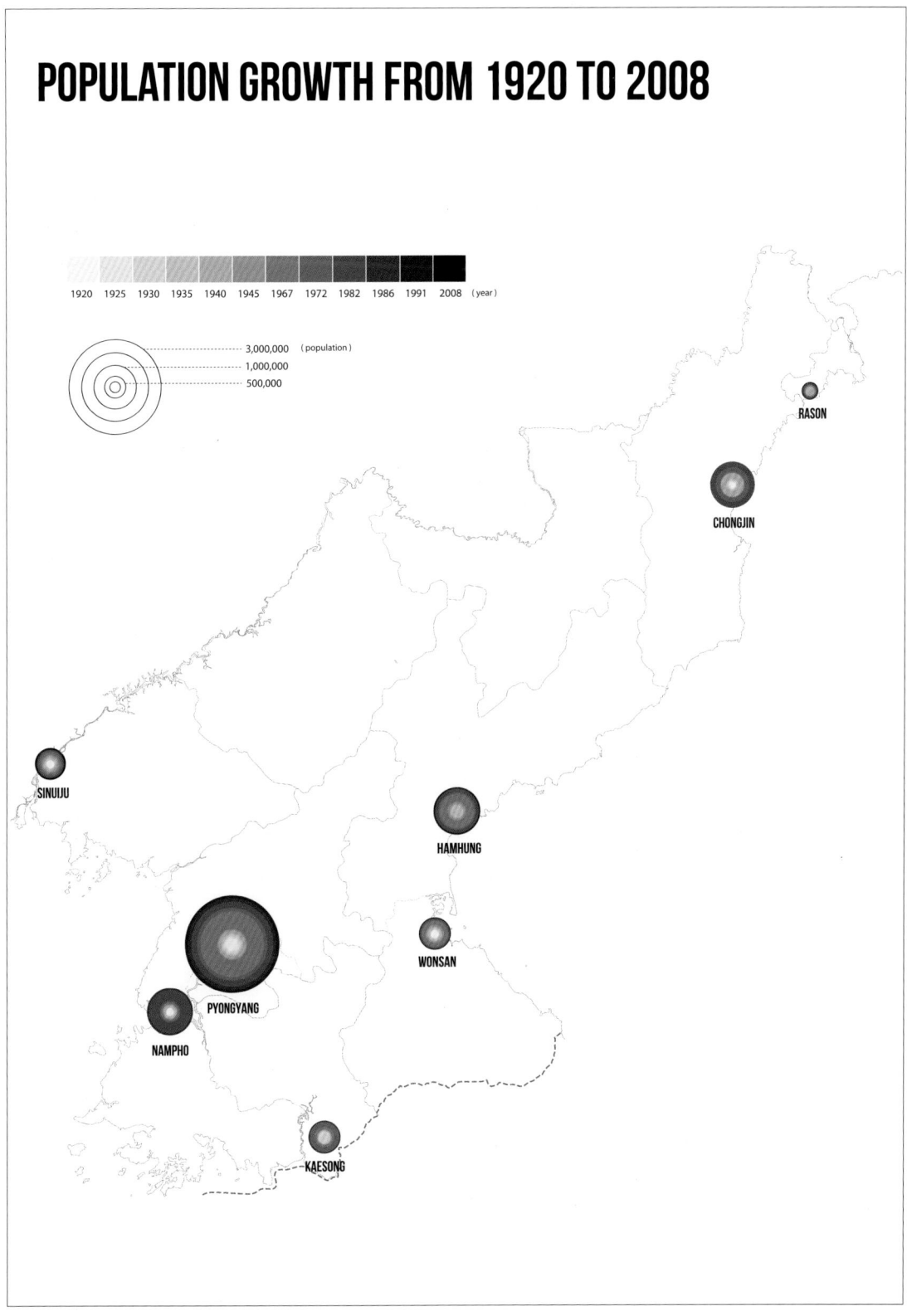

Background Data

120,540 KM²
TOTAL AREA

4.9 %
WATER

42,100 KM²
FLAT LAND AREA

1,377 KM
NORTH BORDER

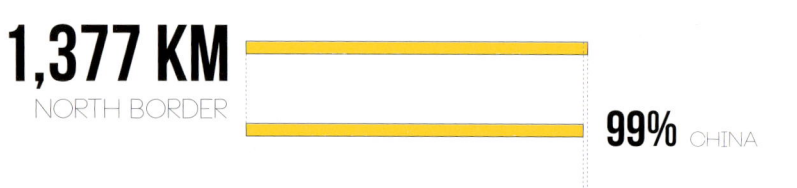

99% CHINA

1% RUSSIA

250 KM
SOUTH BORDER

100% SOUTH KOREA

2,495 KM
COASTLINE

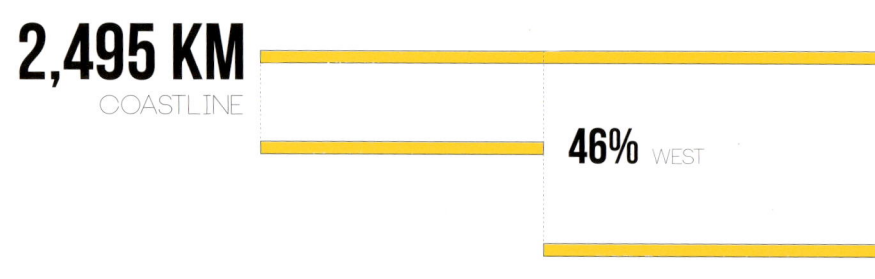

46% WEST

54% EAST

COOL CONTINENTAL
CLIMATE

💧 26 %
FALLS IN JULY

919 MM
AVERAGE RAINFALL

-13 °C, 27 °C
TEMPERATURE RANGE

2,744 M
ALTITUDE

37° 46' N - 42° 59' N
LATITUDE

124° 09' E - 130° 41' E
LONGITUDE

* Source: CIA World Factbook

Background Data

24,052,231
TOTAL POPULATION

60.6%
RESIDE IN URBAN AREAS

39.4%
RESIDE IN RURAL AREAS

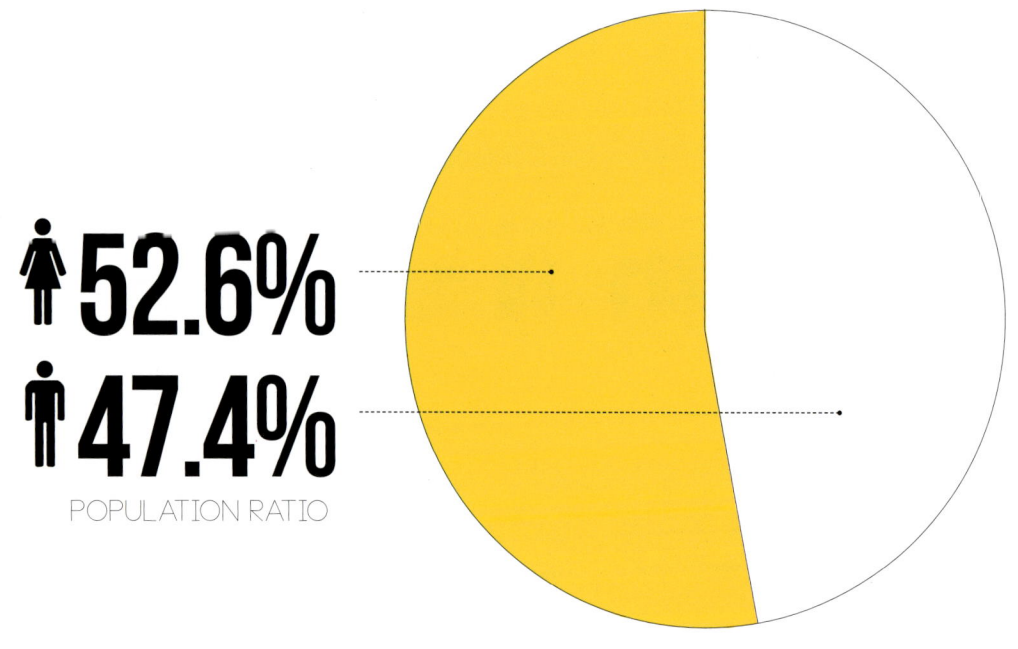

♀ 52.6%
♂ 47.4%
POPULATION RATIO

* Source: Central Bureau of Statics, DPR Korea 2009. National report <DPR KOREA 2008 Population Census>.

Fact Sheets

HOUSE	**73.5%** OF HOUSEHOLDS 50-75 SQ M	**1.9%** OF HOUSEHOLDS OVER 100 SQ M
WATER	**85%** HOUSEHOLDS WITH PIPED WATER	**2.7%** HOUSEHOLDS USE PUBLIC TAP
TOILETS	**58.3%** HOUSEHOLDS USE PRIVATE FLUSH TOILET	**34.7%** HOUSEHOLDS USE PRIVATE PIN LATRINE
HEAT	**47.1%** HOUSEHOLDS HEAT WITH COAL BOILER	**4.5%** HOUSEHOLDS HAVE CENTRAL HEAT
COOKING FUEL	**46.9%** HOUSEHOLDS USE WOOD	**1.34%** HOUSEHOLDS USE ELECTRIC

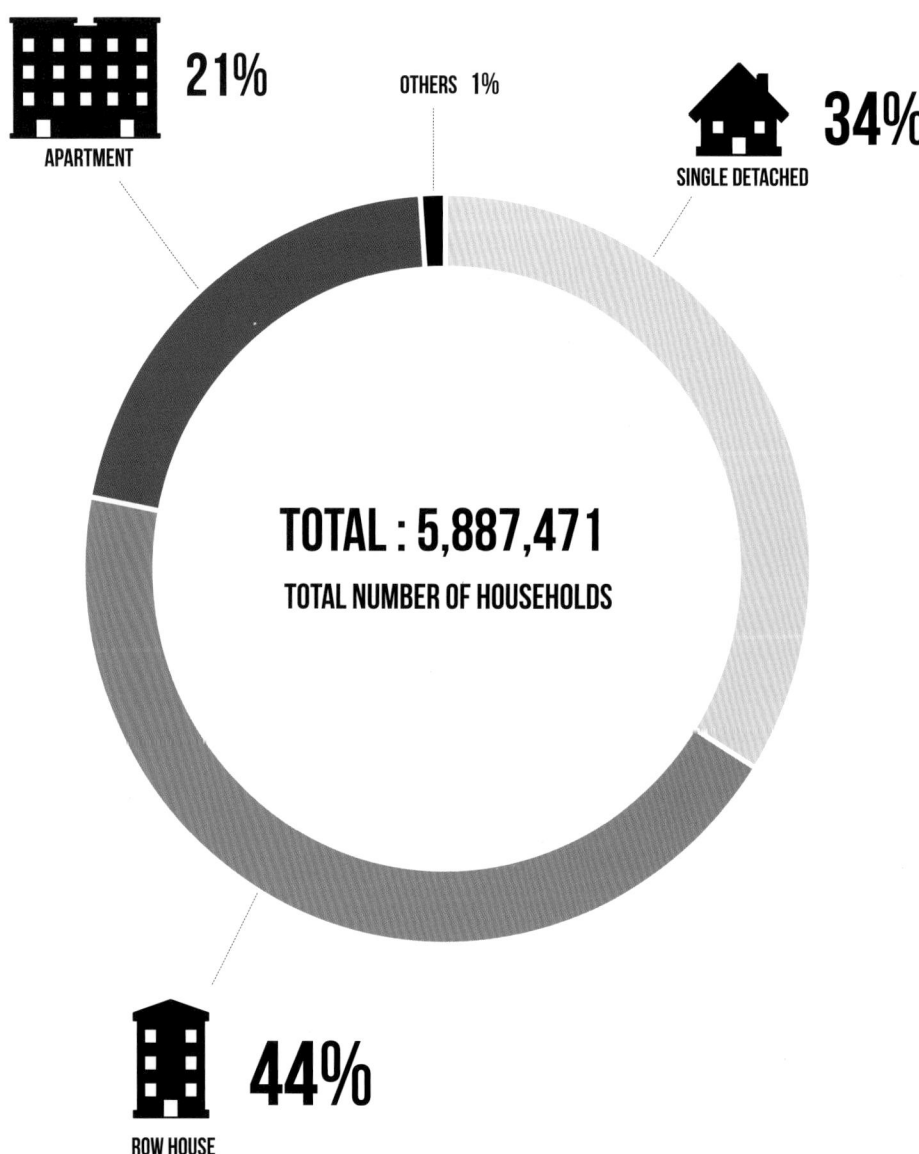

Fact Sheets

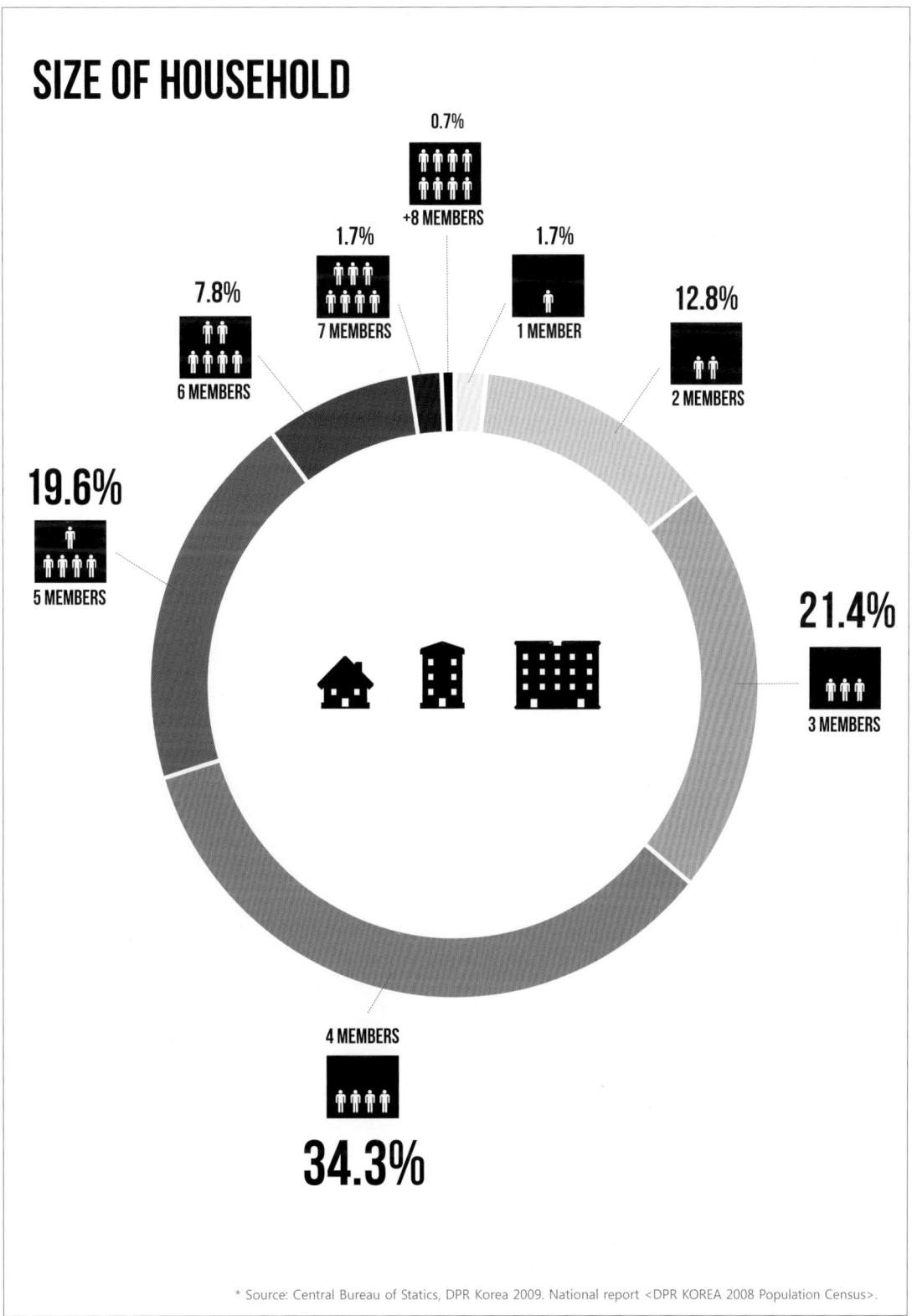

* Source: Central Bureau of Statics, DPR Korea 2009. National report <DPR KOREA 2008 Population Census>.

Background Data

LEVEL OF EDUCATION

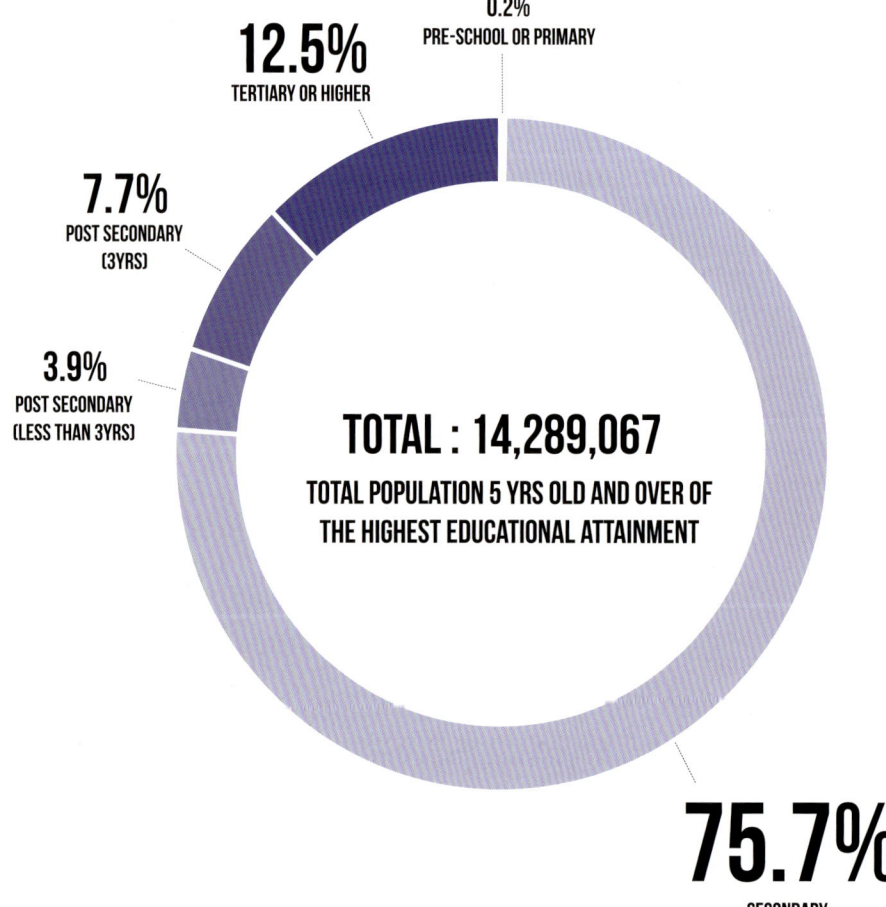

0.2% PRE-SCHOOL OR PRIMARY
12.5% TERTIARY OR HIGHER
7.7% POST SECONDARY (3YRS)
3.9% POST SECONDARY (LESS THAN 3YRS)
75.7% SECONDARY

TOTAL : 14,289,067
TOTAL POPULATION 5 YRS OLD AND OVER OF THE HIGHEST EDUCATIONAL ATTAINMENT

* Source: Central Bureau of Statics, DPR Korea 2009. National report <DPR KOREA 2008 Population Census>.

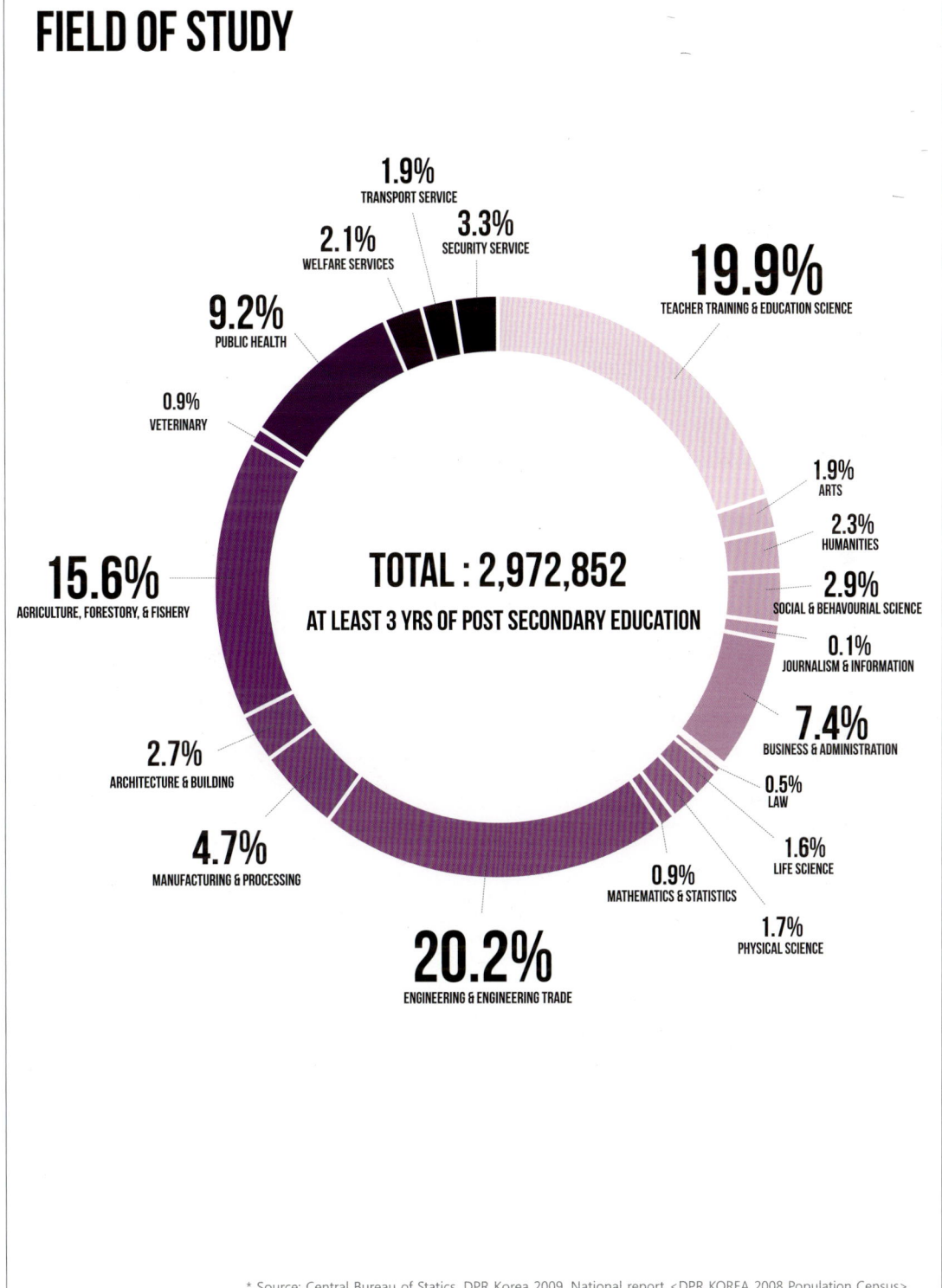

Background Data

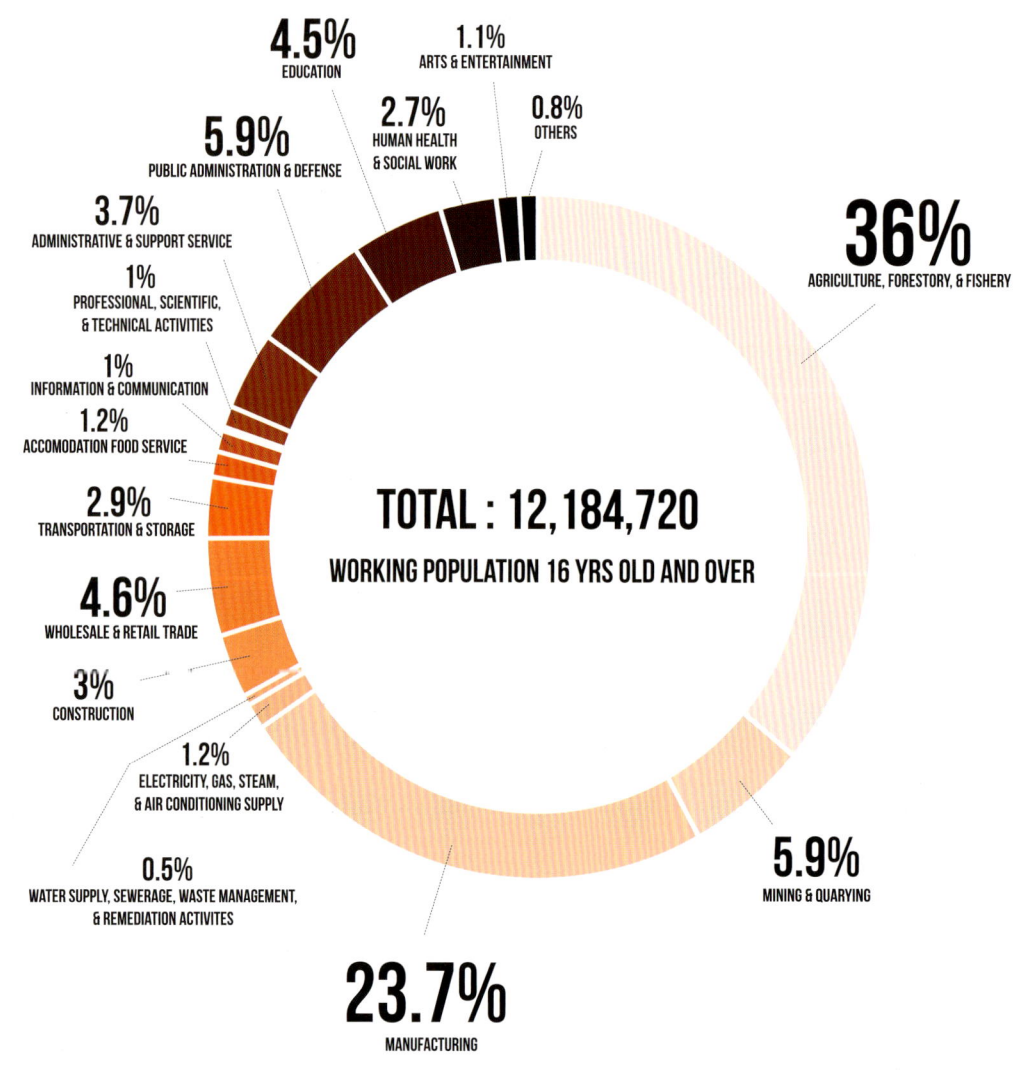

* Source: Central Bureau of Statics, DPR Korea 2009. National report <DPR KOREA 2008 Population Census>.

GROUP OF OCCUPATION

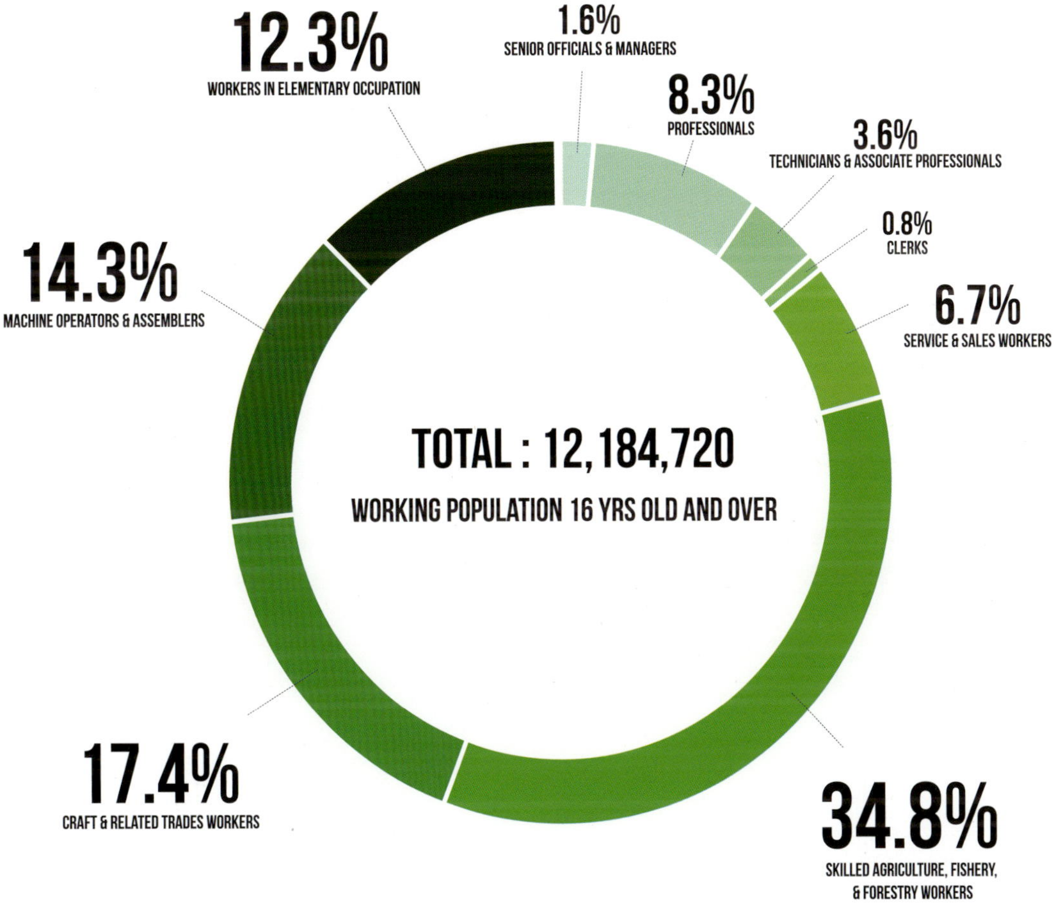

12.3% WORKERS IN ELEMENTARY OCCUPATION
1.6% SENIOR OFFICIALS & MANAGERS
8.3% PROFESSIONALS
3.6% TECHNICIANS & ASSOCIATE PROFESSIONALS
0.8% CLERKS
6.7% SERVICE & SALES WORKERS
14.3% MACHINE OPERATORS & ASSEMBLERS
17.4% CRAFT & RELATED TRADES WORKERS
34.8% SKILLED AGRICULTURE, FISHERY, & FORESTRY WORKERS

TOTAL : 12,184,720
WORKING POPULATION 16 YRS OLD AND OVER

* Source: Central Bureau of Statics, DPR Korea 2009. National report <DPR KOREA 2008 Population Census>.

02 BACKGROUND DATA
1. FACT SHEETS
2. GEOGRAPHICAL FACTS
3. INFRASTRUCTURAL FACTS
4. INDUSTRIAL GEOGRAPHY

Background Data

Korean Peninsula always has been considered as a strategic point since the 19th century as it is located between the Pacific, which in other words the American Force, and Asia. During the Cold War period, North Korea was the eastern bumper of the communist block, especially for China and the Soviet Union, that directly faced the capitalist countries, while South Korea was also the frontal country of the "West". This strategical situation has not changed much even after the communist block collapsed. And at the moment, the world is giving attentions to North Korea how it will change, and its change, for sure, will transform the whole landscape of the East Asia, which includes China, Japan, South Korea, and even Russia and the United States.

한반도는 미대륙 세력으로 비유될 수 있는 태평양과 아시아의 사이에 위치해있는 이유로인하여 19세기 이후 지금까지 전략적으로 매우 중요한 곳으로 평가되어왔다. 냉전시기에 북한은 공산권, 특히 중국과 구소련의 동쪽 범퍼와 같은 역할을 하였고, 이는 자본주의 세력에 직접 맞닿아 있는 곳이었다. 반면 한국은 "서방세계"의 서쪽 관문이었다. 이러한 전략적인 상황은 공산권이 붕괴된 이후로도 많이 변하지 않았으며, 지금 이 순간에도 전 세계는 북한이 어떻게 변할 것인가 주목하고 있다. 이 변화는 중국, 일본, 한국은 물론 러시아와 미국을 포함하는 동아시아 지형에 큰 영향을 미칠 것으로 보인다.

Background Data

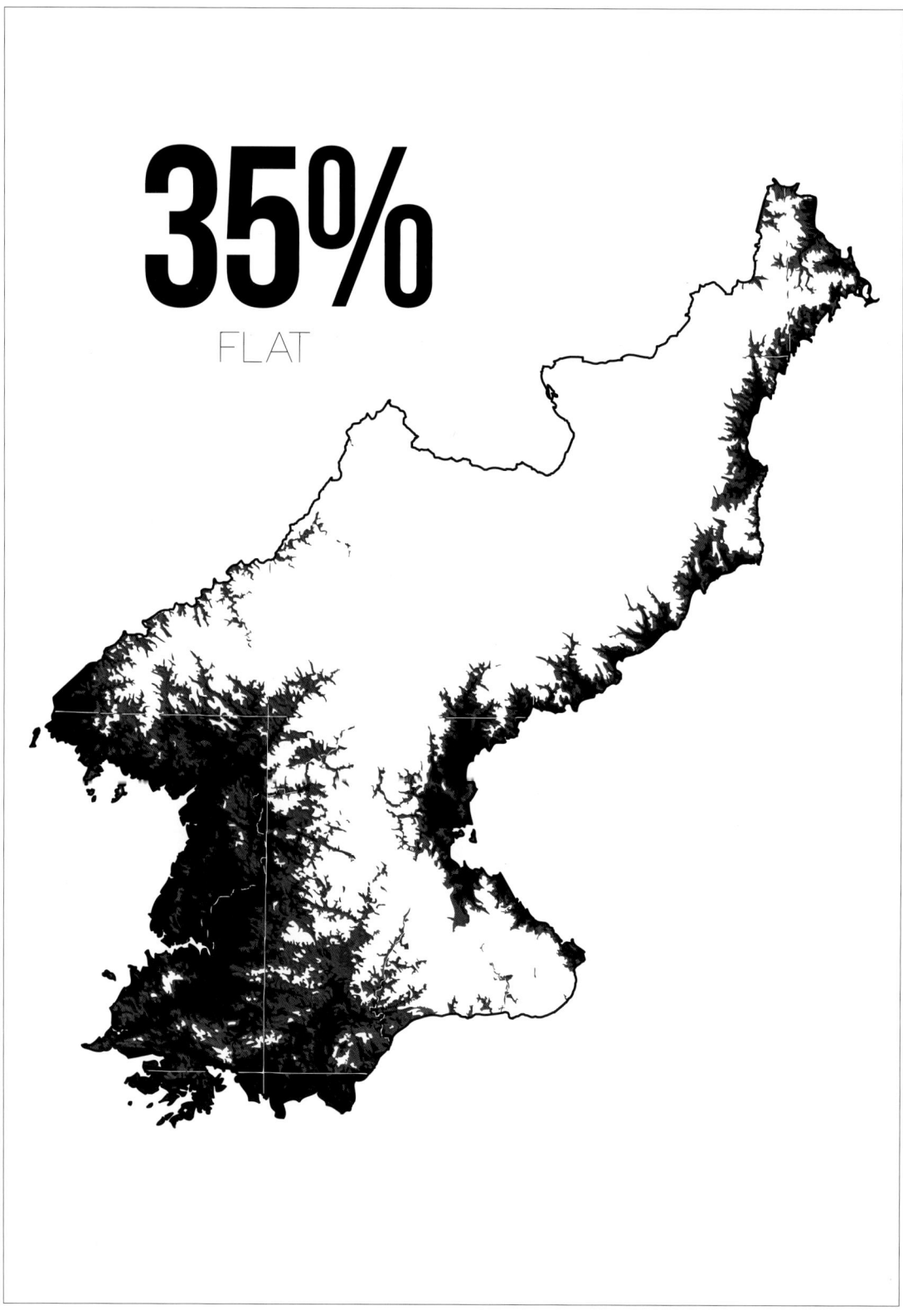

35%
FLAT

Geographical Facts

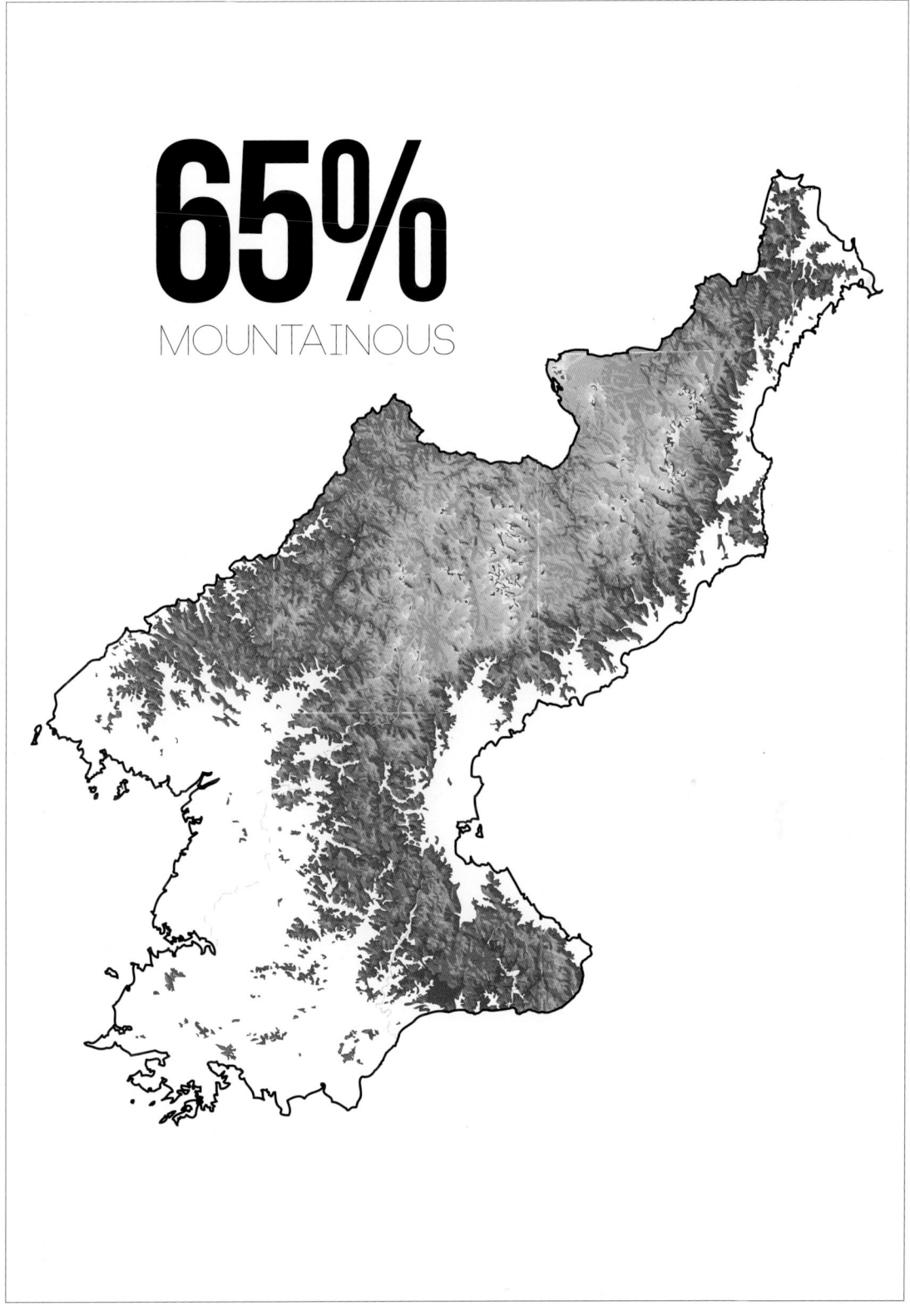

65%
MOUNTAINOUS

GEOGRAPHICAL SECTION

Geographical Facts

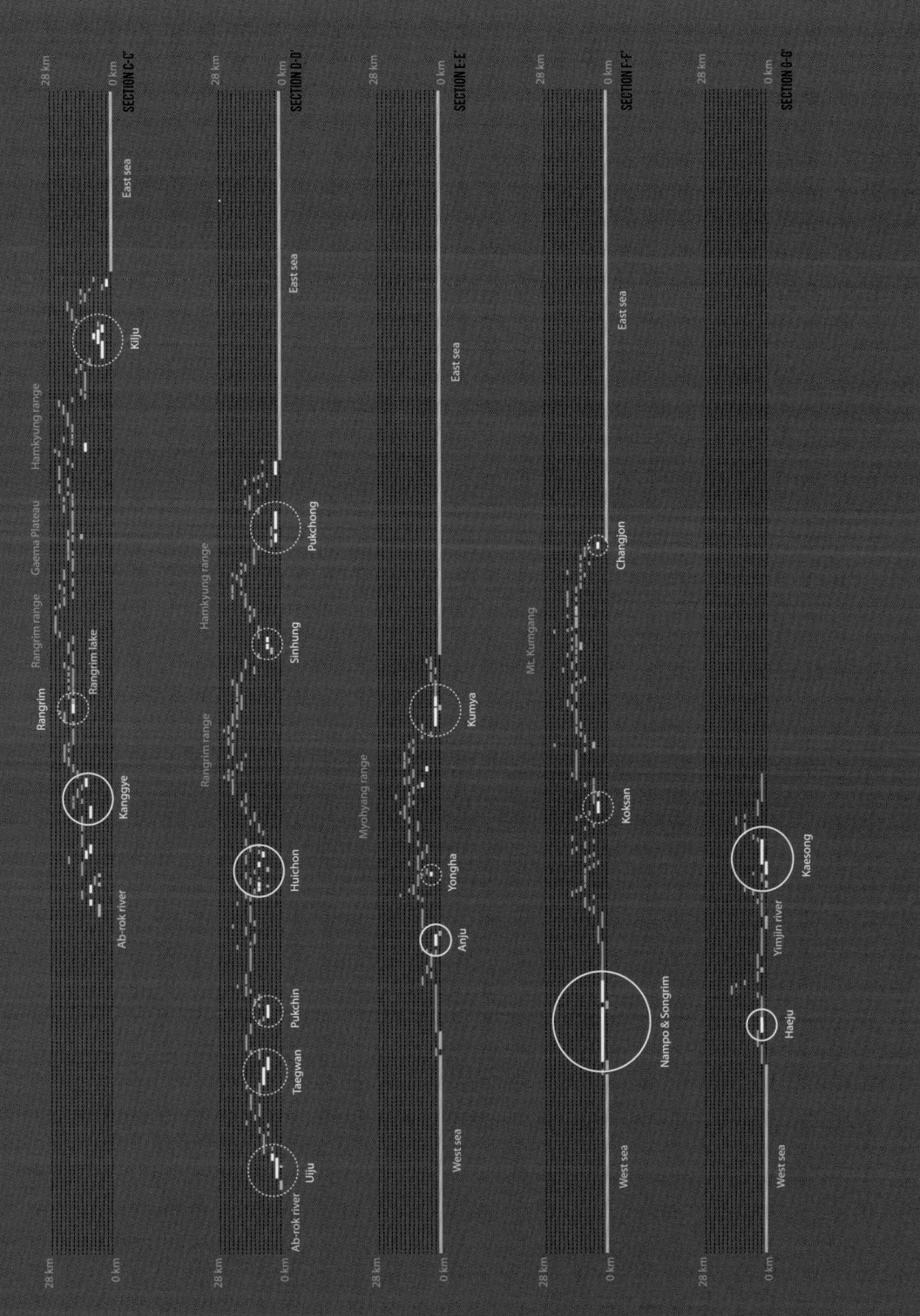

BORDER CONDITIONS

Geographical Facts

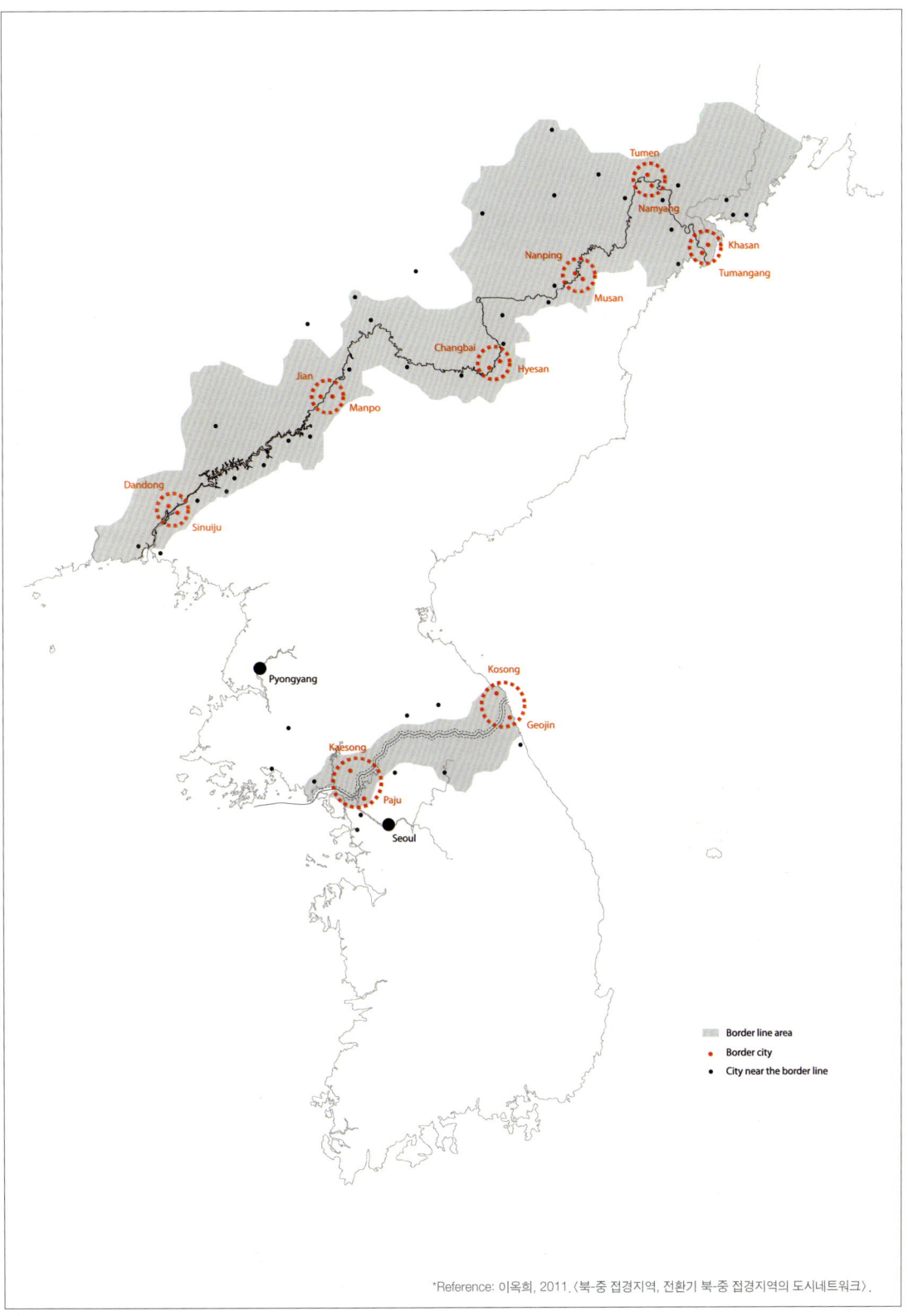

NORTHERN BORDER (NK-CHINA, NK-RUSSIA)

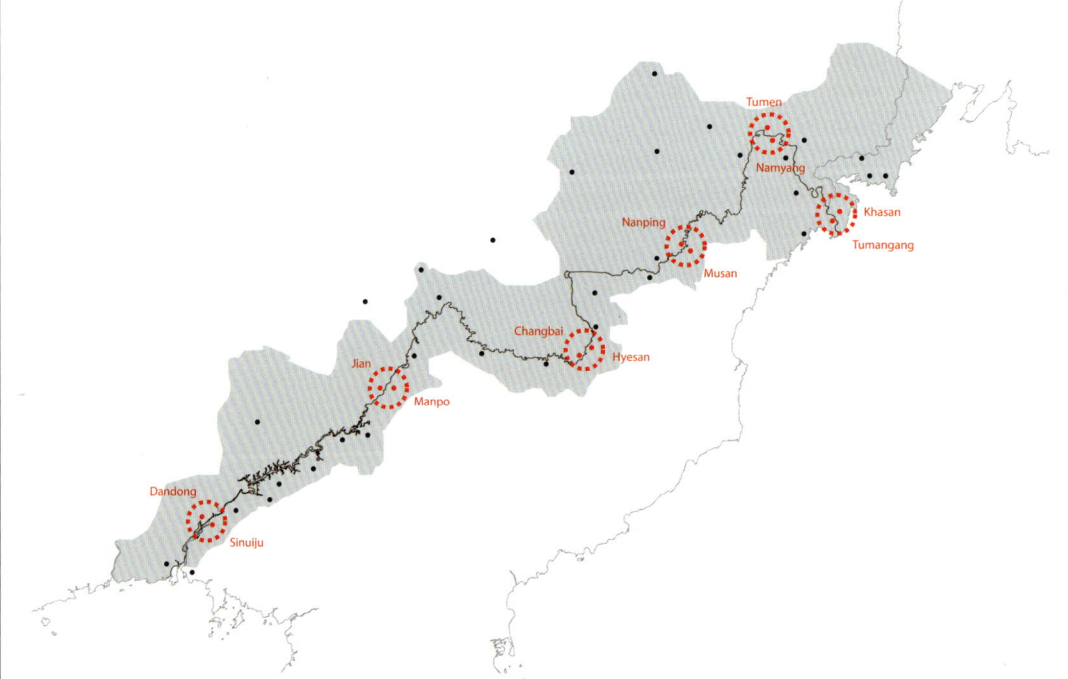

13 VEHICLE ROAD

4 RAILROAD

4 DAM

Geographical Facts

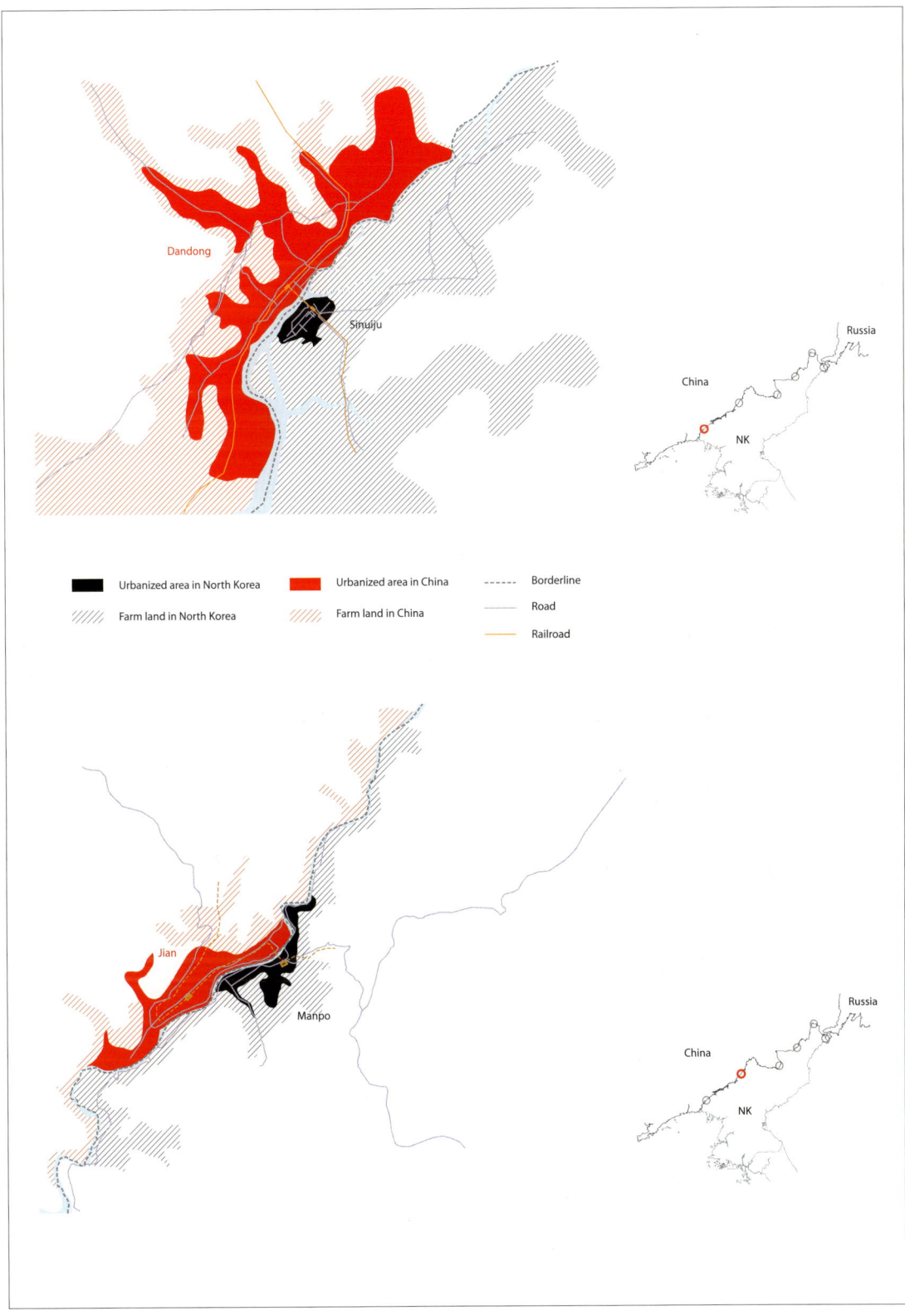

Background Data

144

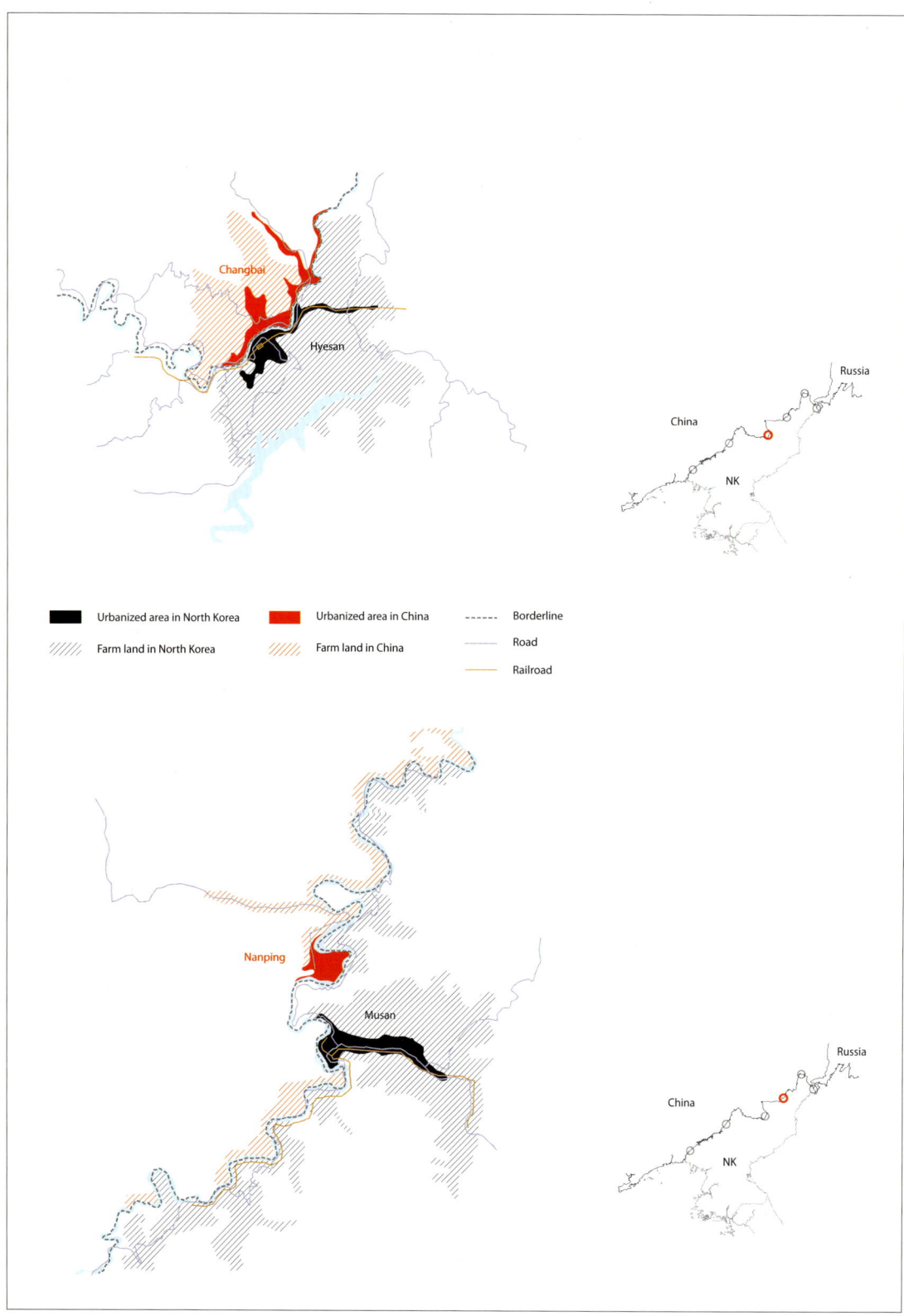

Geographical Facts

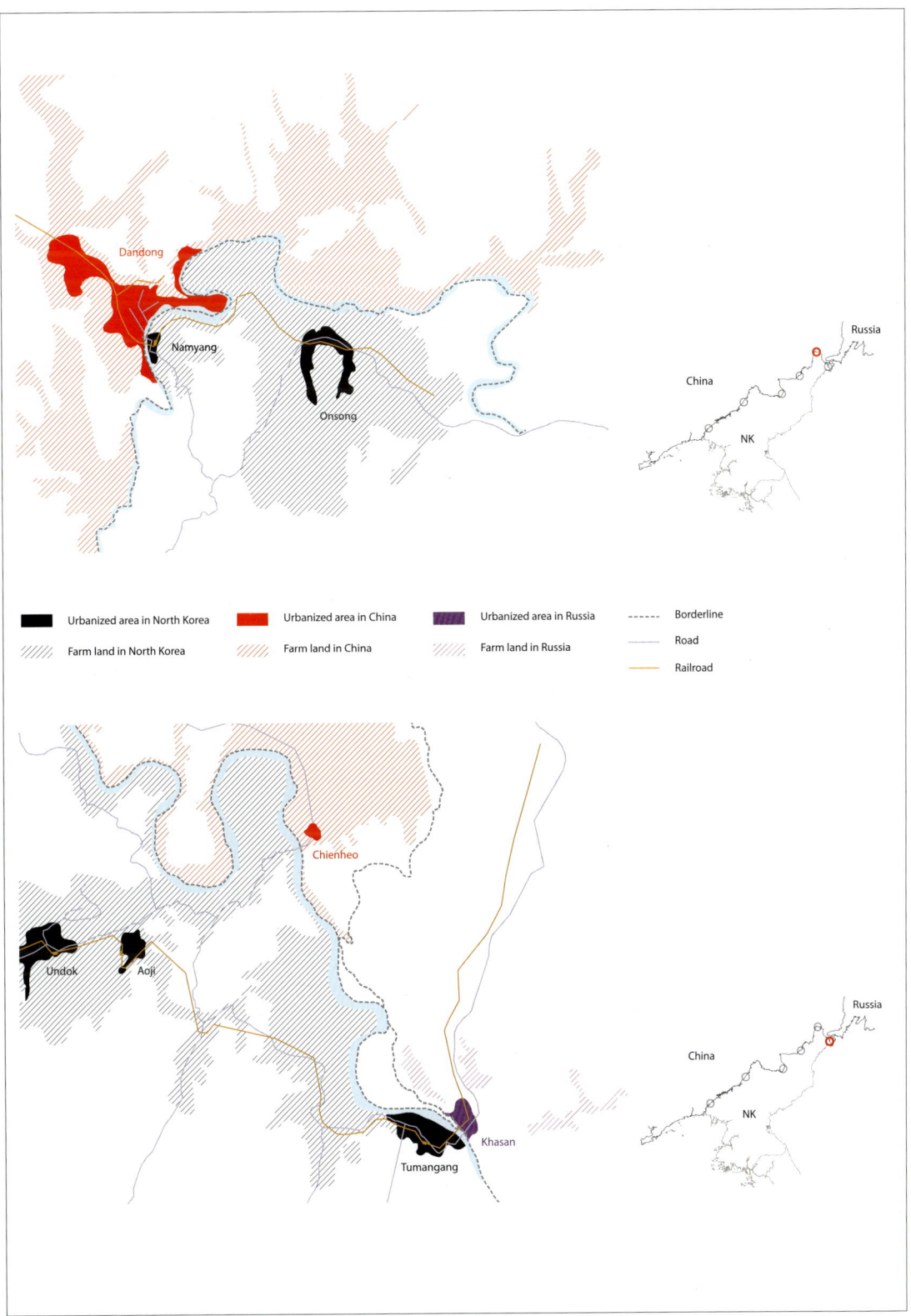

Background Data

SOUTHERN BORDER (DMZ: NORTH KOREA-SOUTH KOREA)

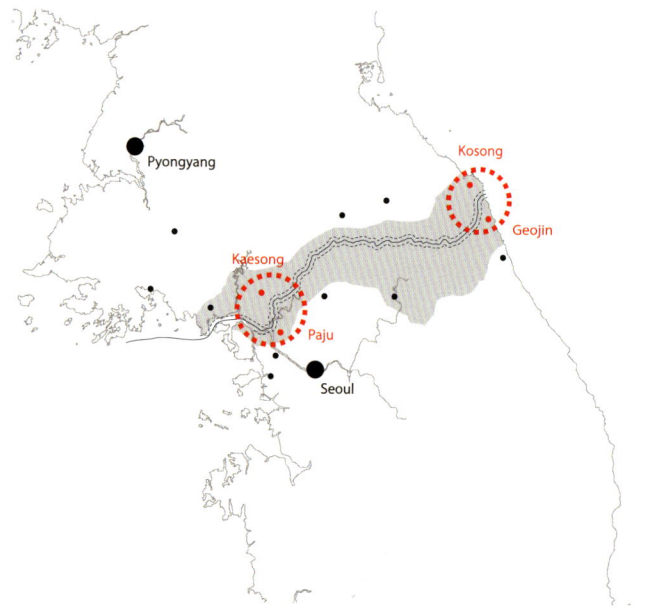

2 VEHICLE ROAD   **2** RAILROAD   **0** DAM

Geographical Facts

Background Data

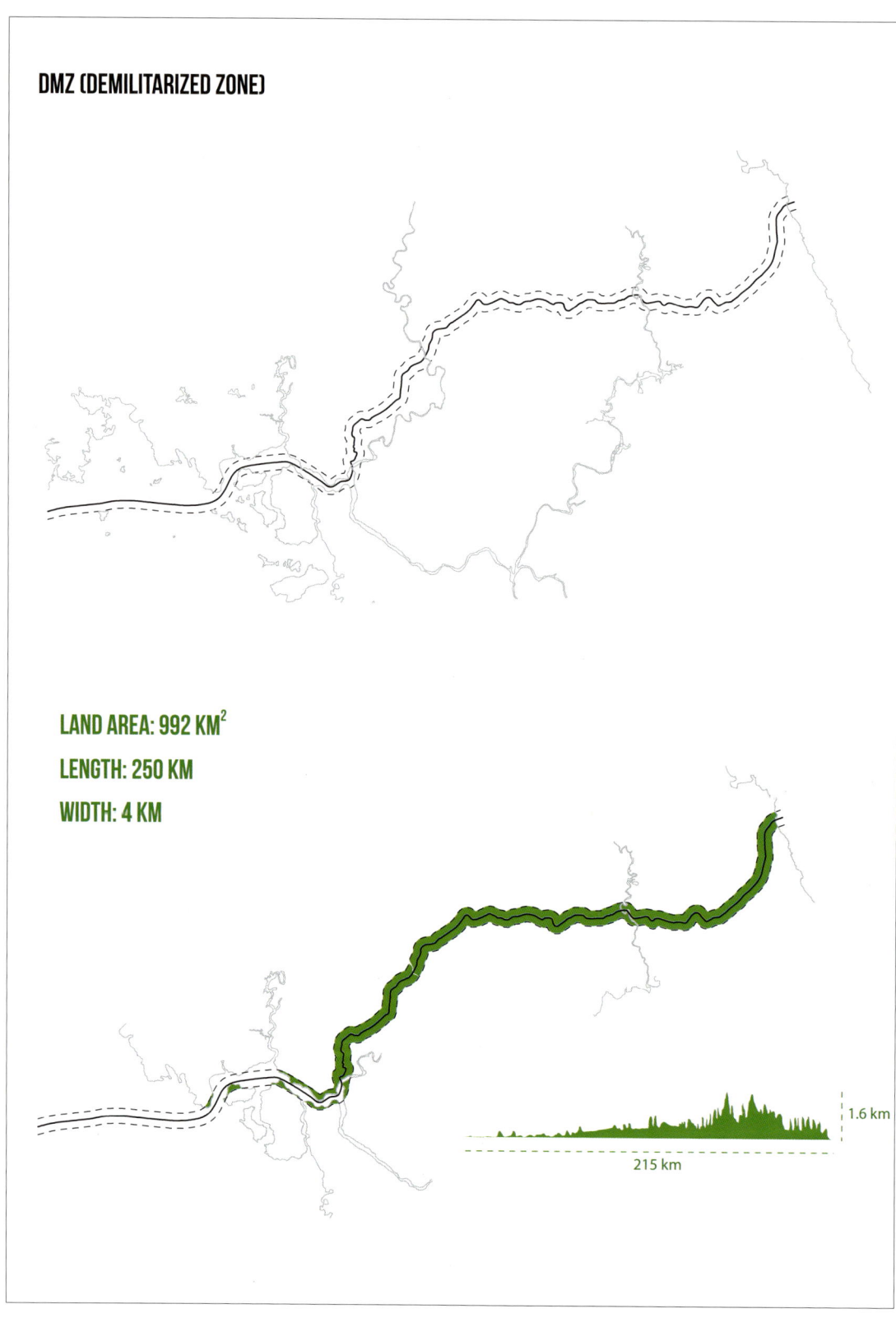

DMZ (DEMILITARIZED ZONE)

LAND AREA: 992 KM²
LENGTH: 250 KM
WIDTH: 4 KM

1.6 km
215 km

Geographical Facts

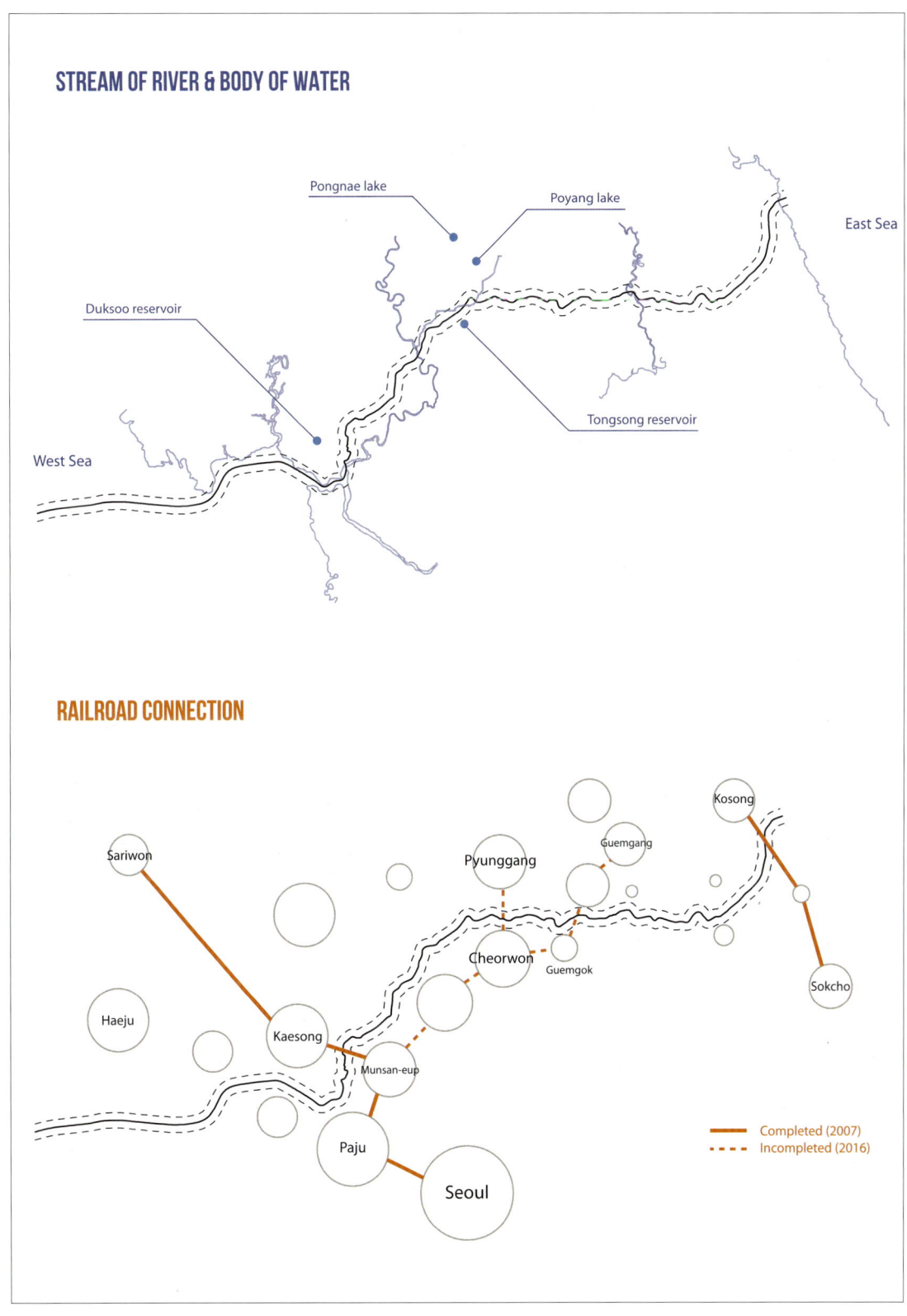

02 BACKGROUND DATA
1. FACT SHEETS
2. GEOGRAPHICAL FACTS
3. INFRASTRUCTURAL FACTS
4. INDUSTRIAL GEOGRAPHY

Background Data

RAIL (INTERNATIONAL)

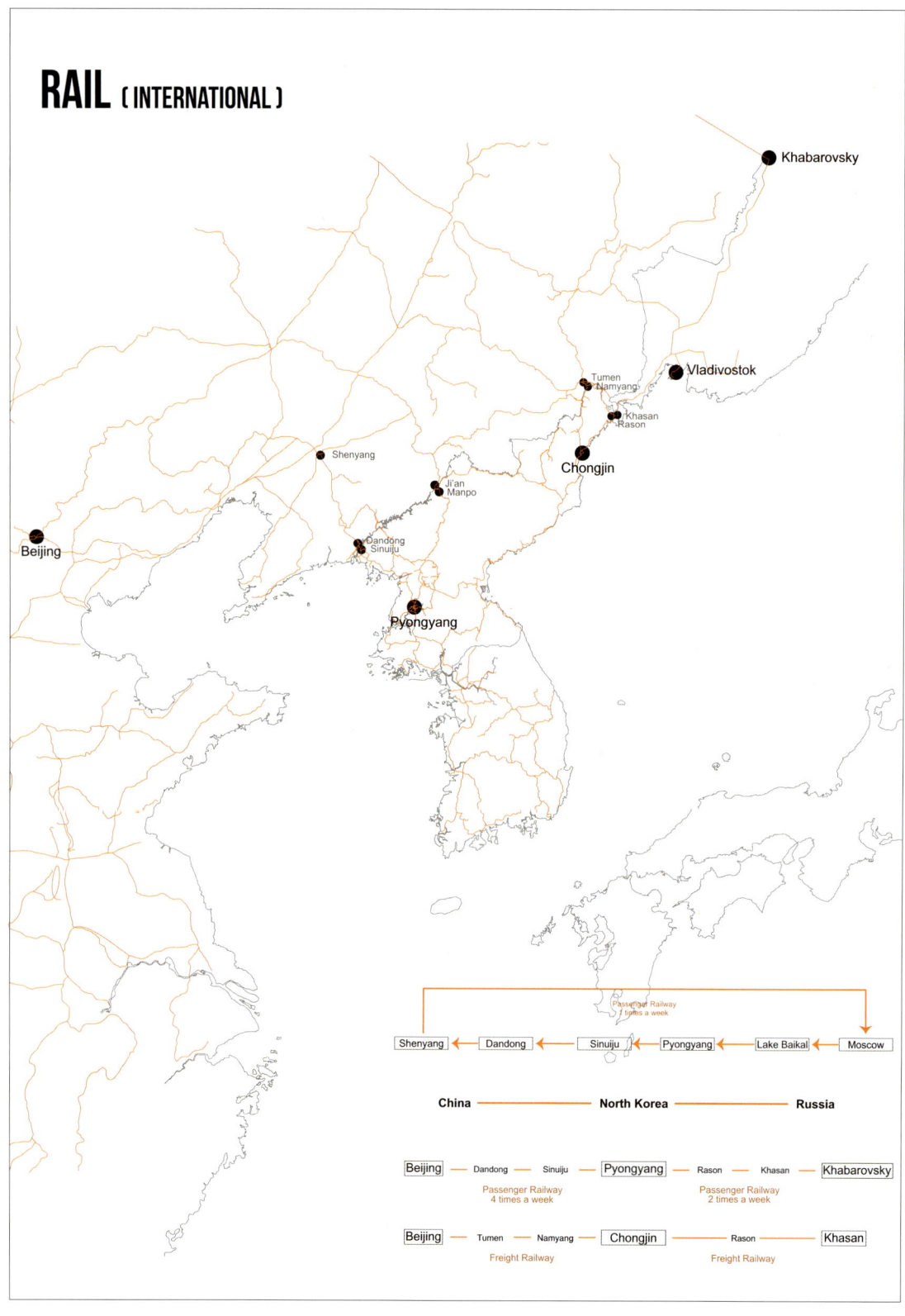

Infrastructural Facts

153

RAIL (DOMESTIC)

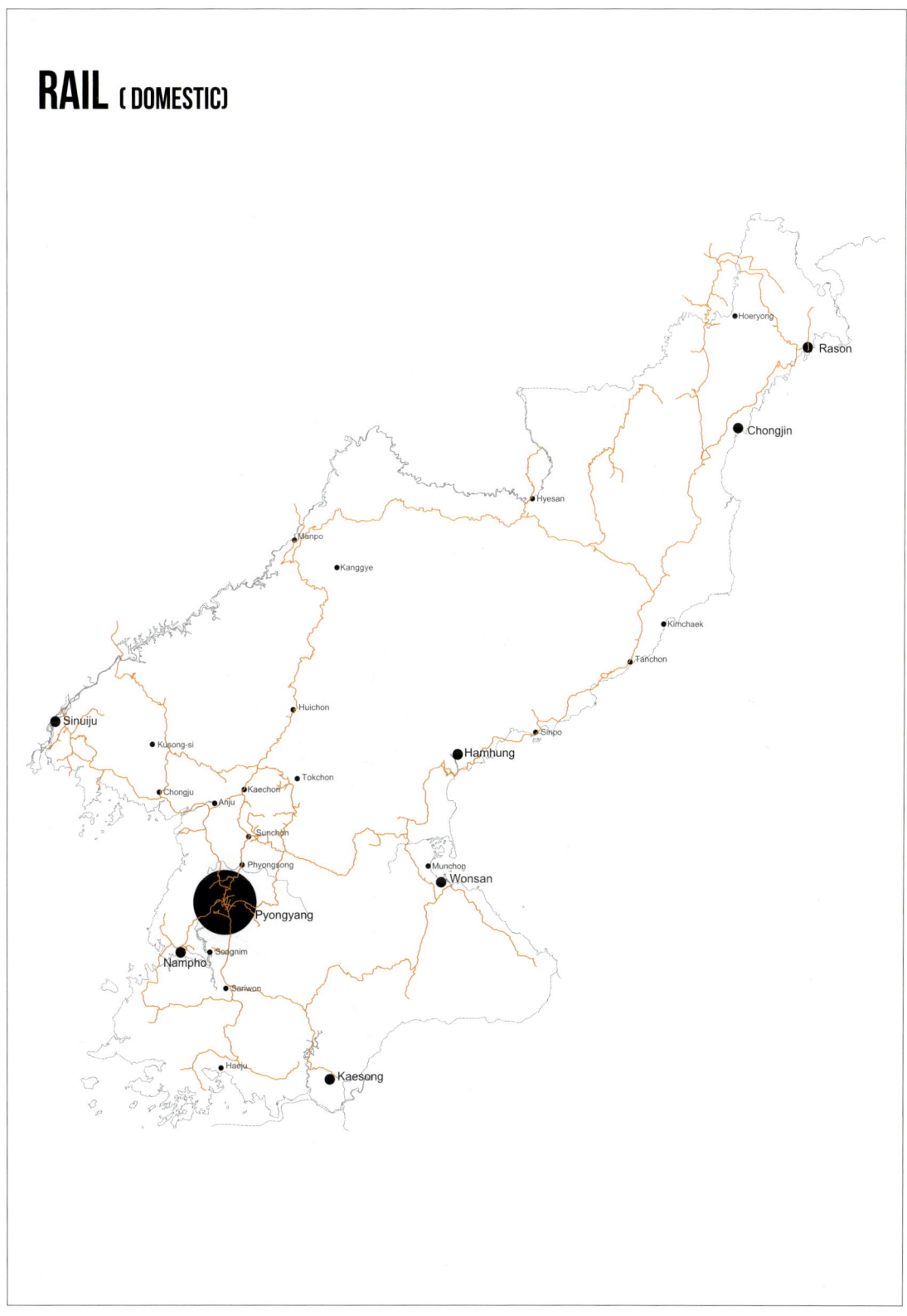

Background Data

ROAD (INTERNATIONAL)

Infrastructural Facts

ROAD (DOMESTIC)

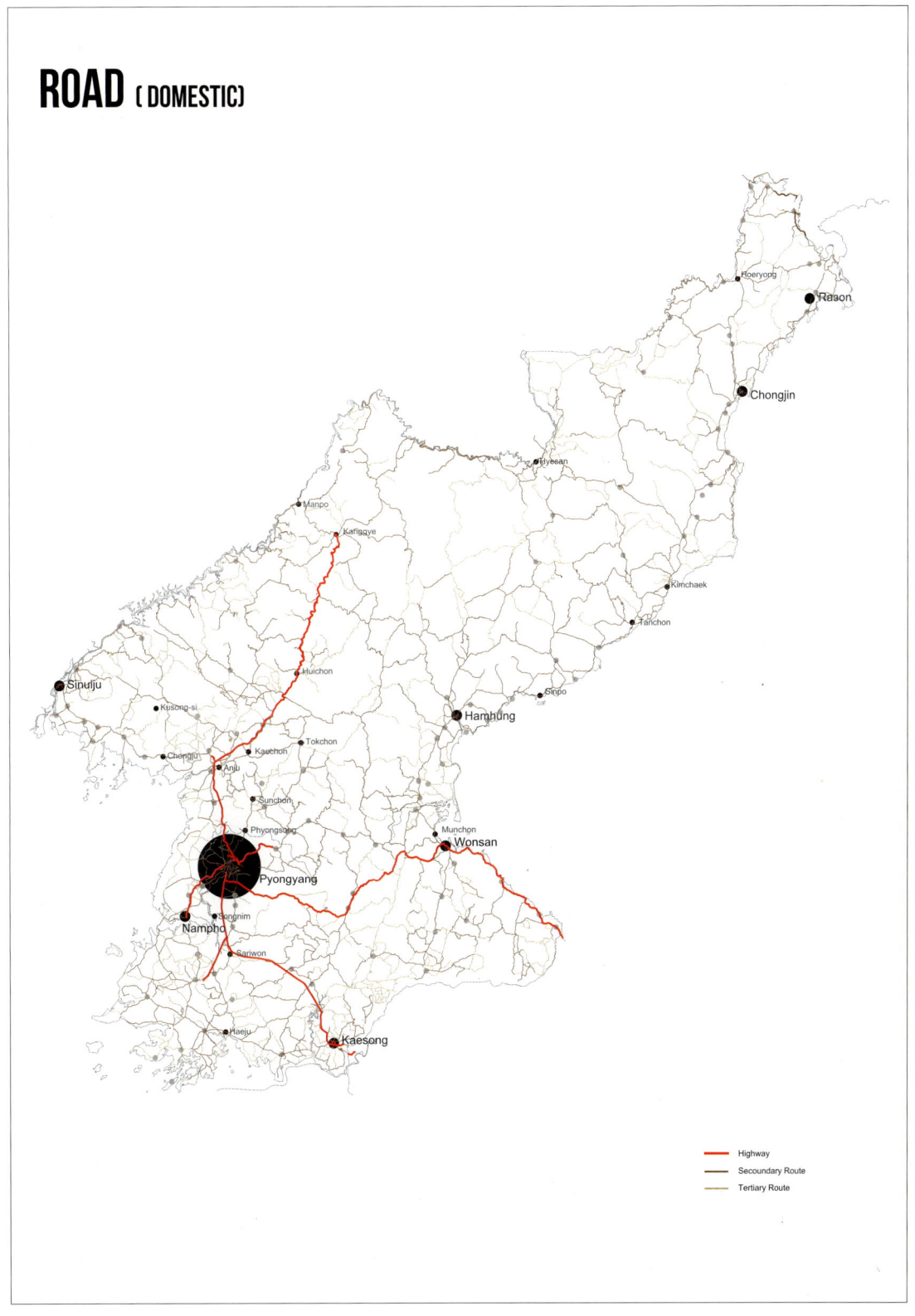

Infrastructural Facts

AIRLINE (DOMESTIC)

Background Data

158

PORT

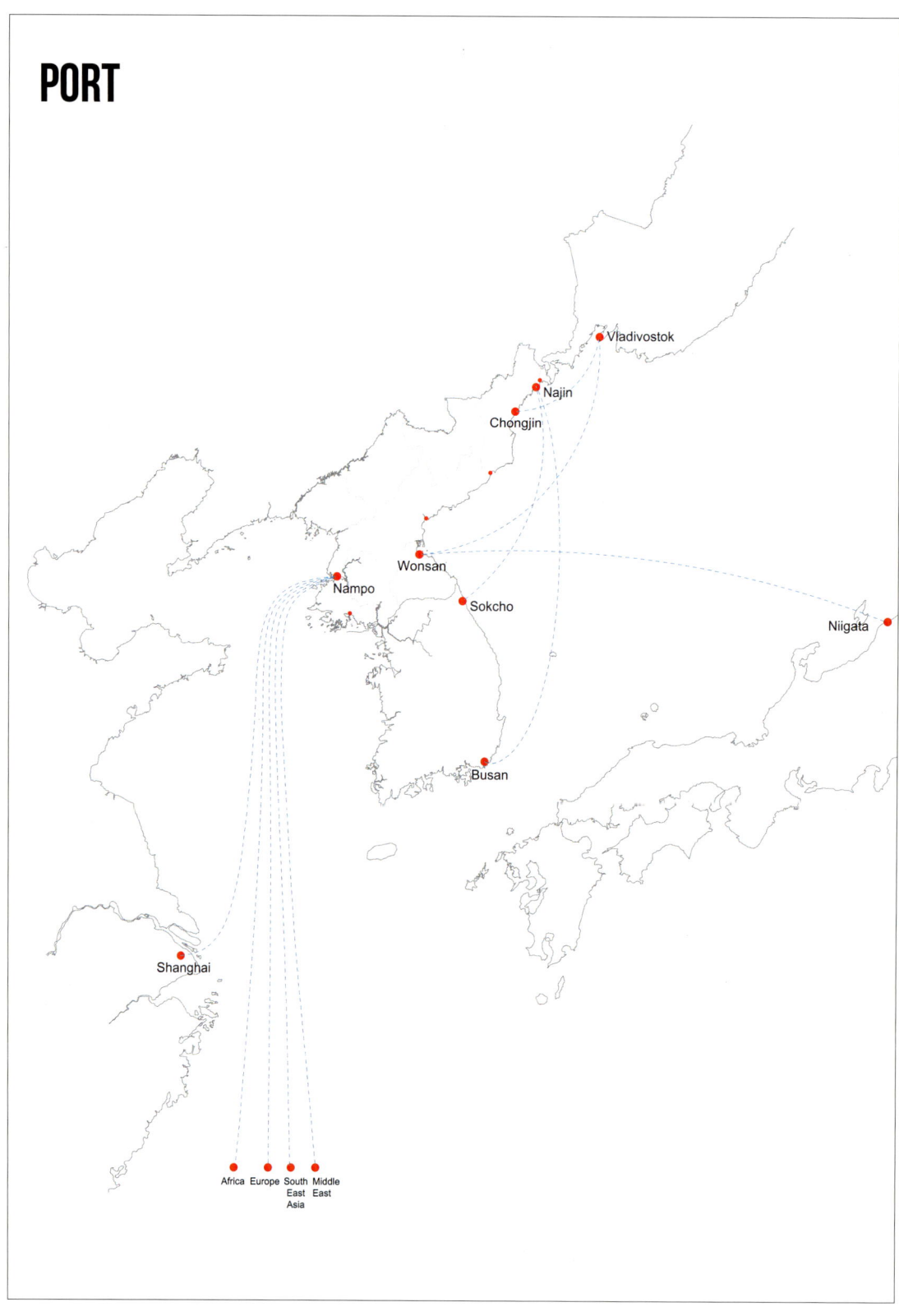

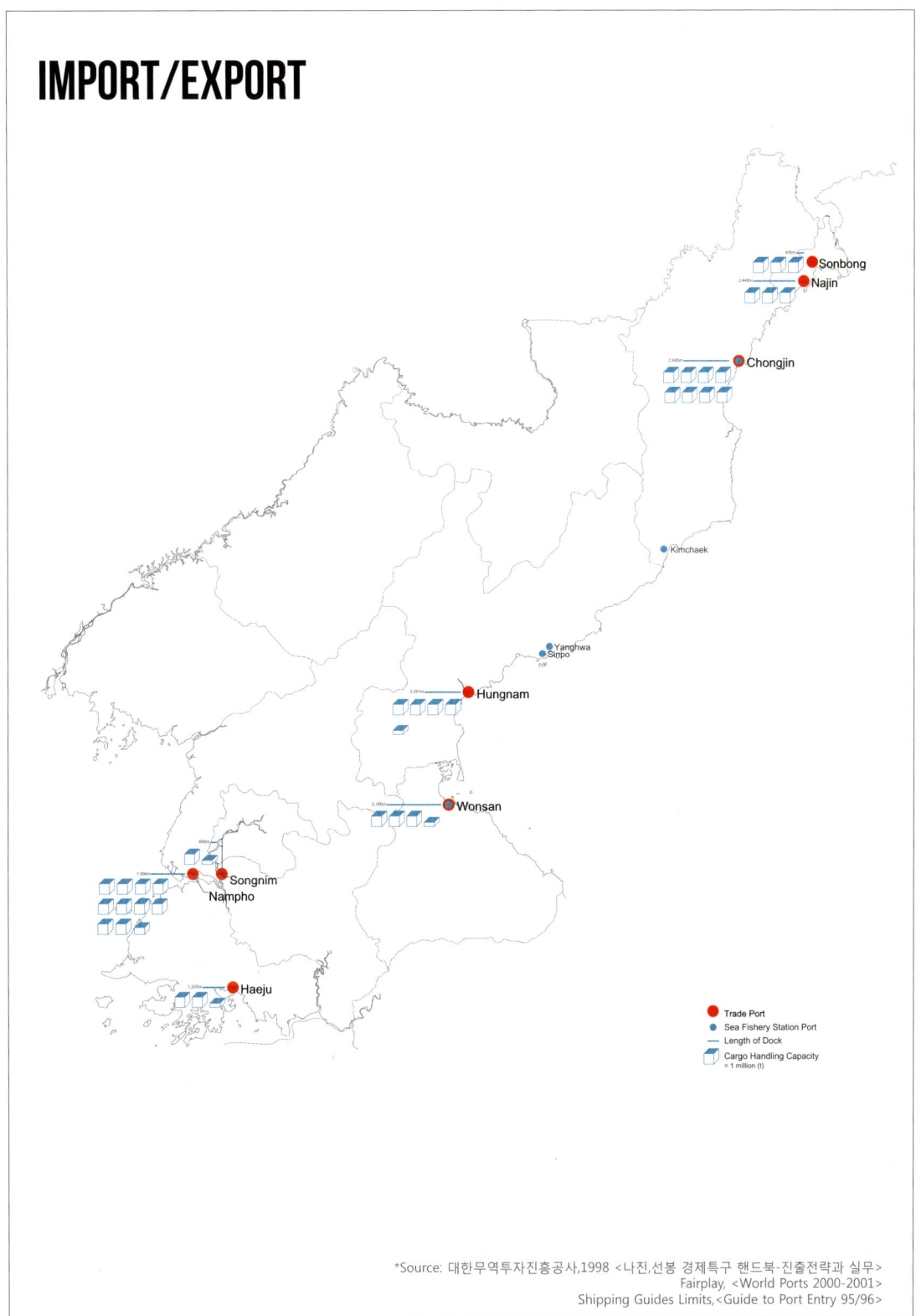

02 BACKGROUND DATA
1. FACT SHEETS
2. GEOGRAPHICAL FACTS
3. INFRASTRUCTURAL FACTS
4. INDUSTRIAL GEOGRAPHY

ECONOMIC SITUATIONS

Industrial Geography

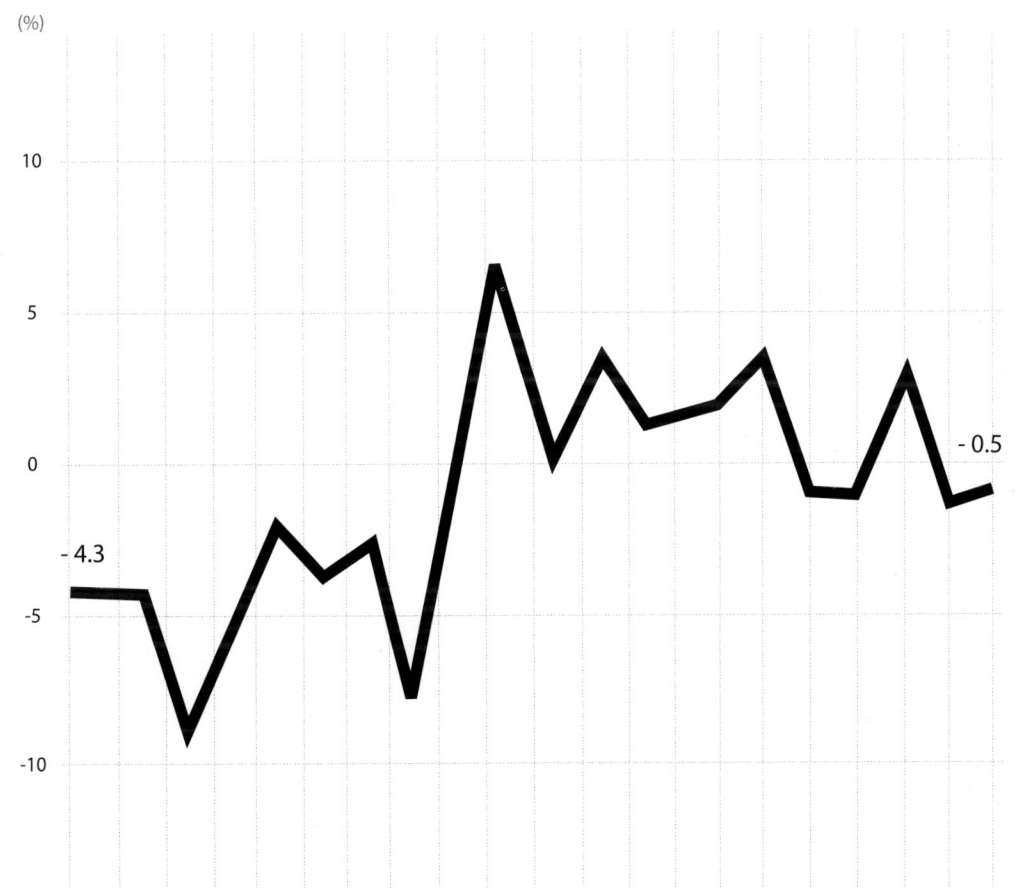

TRENDS IN GDP GROWTH

* Source: Bank of Korea (BOK), Economic report <Understanding North Korea 2012>.

GOVERNMENT BUDGET

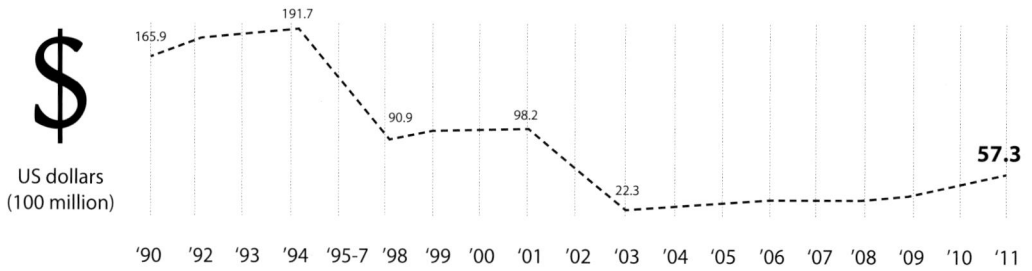

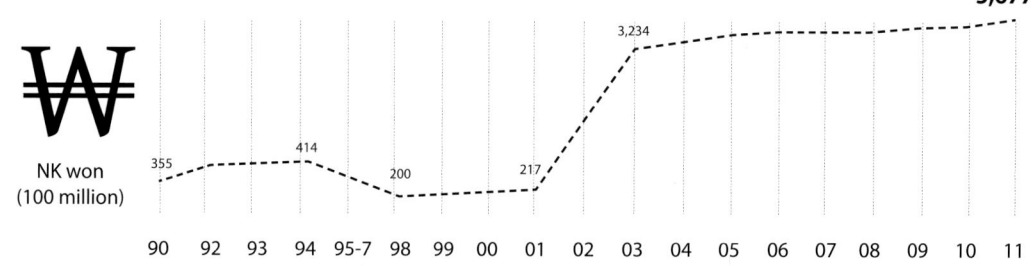

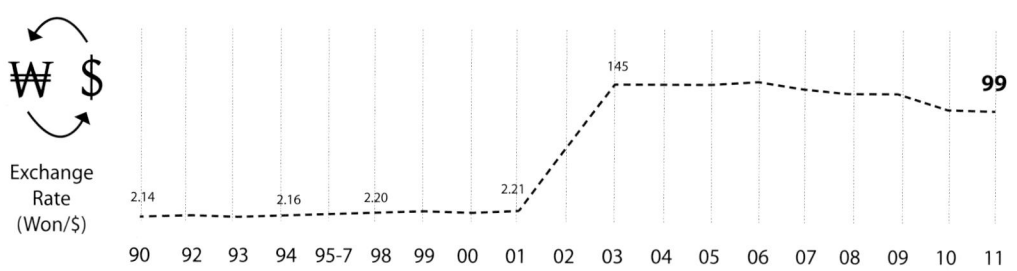

* Source: Bank of Korea (BOK), Economic report <Understanding North Korea 2012>.

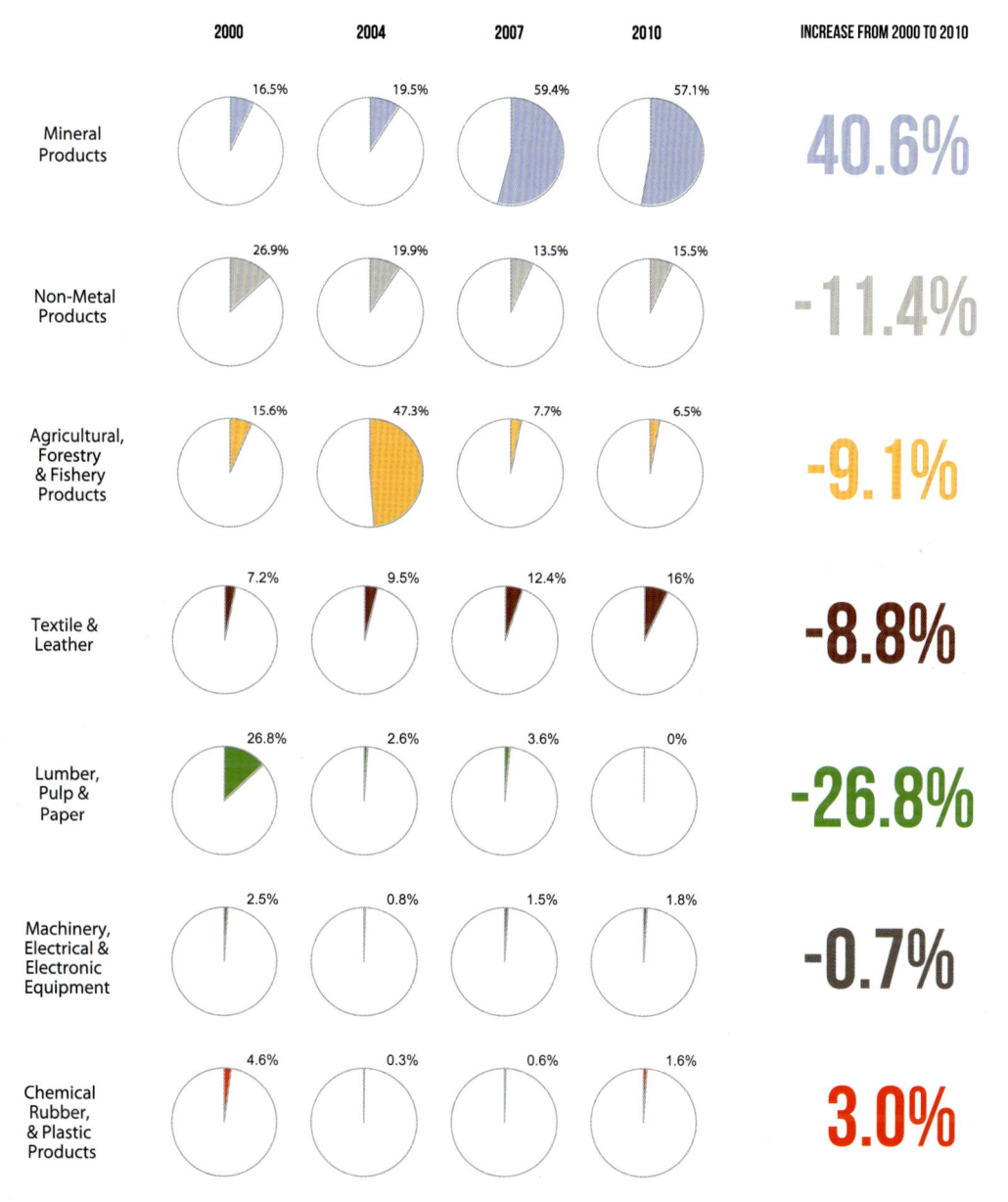

TRENDS IN ENERGY SUPPLY

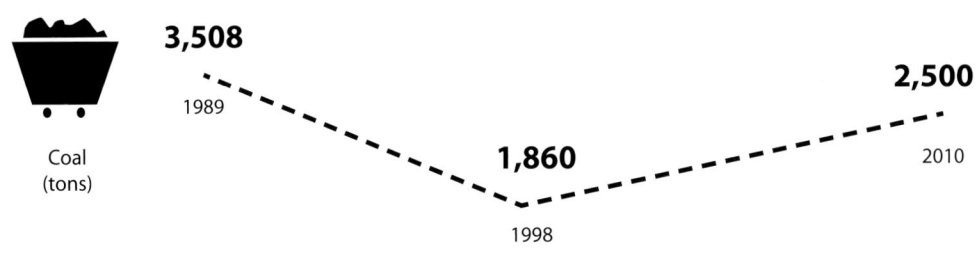

Coal (tons)
- 3,508 (1989)
- 1,860 (1998)
- 2,500 (2010)

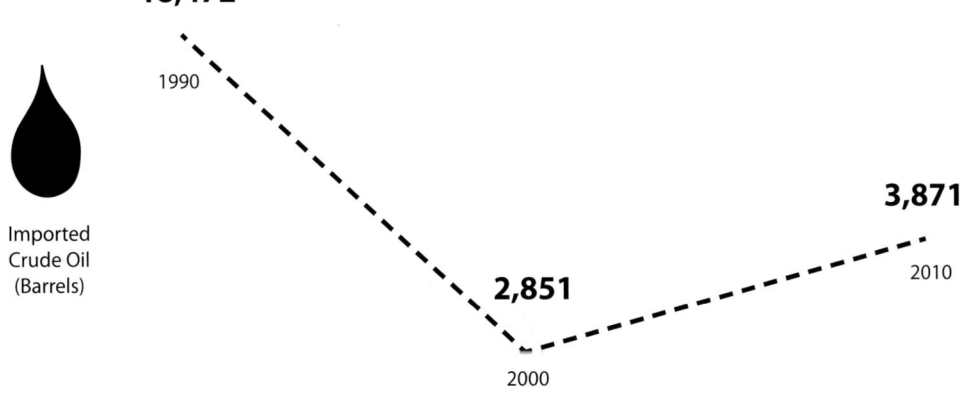

Imported Crude Oil (Barrels)
- 18,472 (1990)
- 2,851 (2000)
- 3,871 (2010)

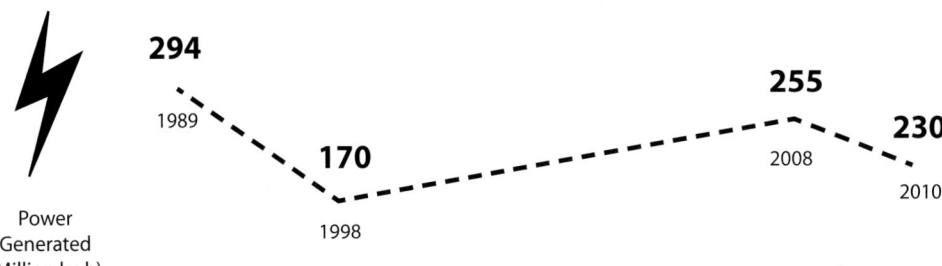

Power Generated (Million kwh)
- 294 (1989)
- 170 (1998)
- 255 (2008)
- 230 (2010)

*Source: National Statics Bureau, <Key Statics on North Korea>, each year.

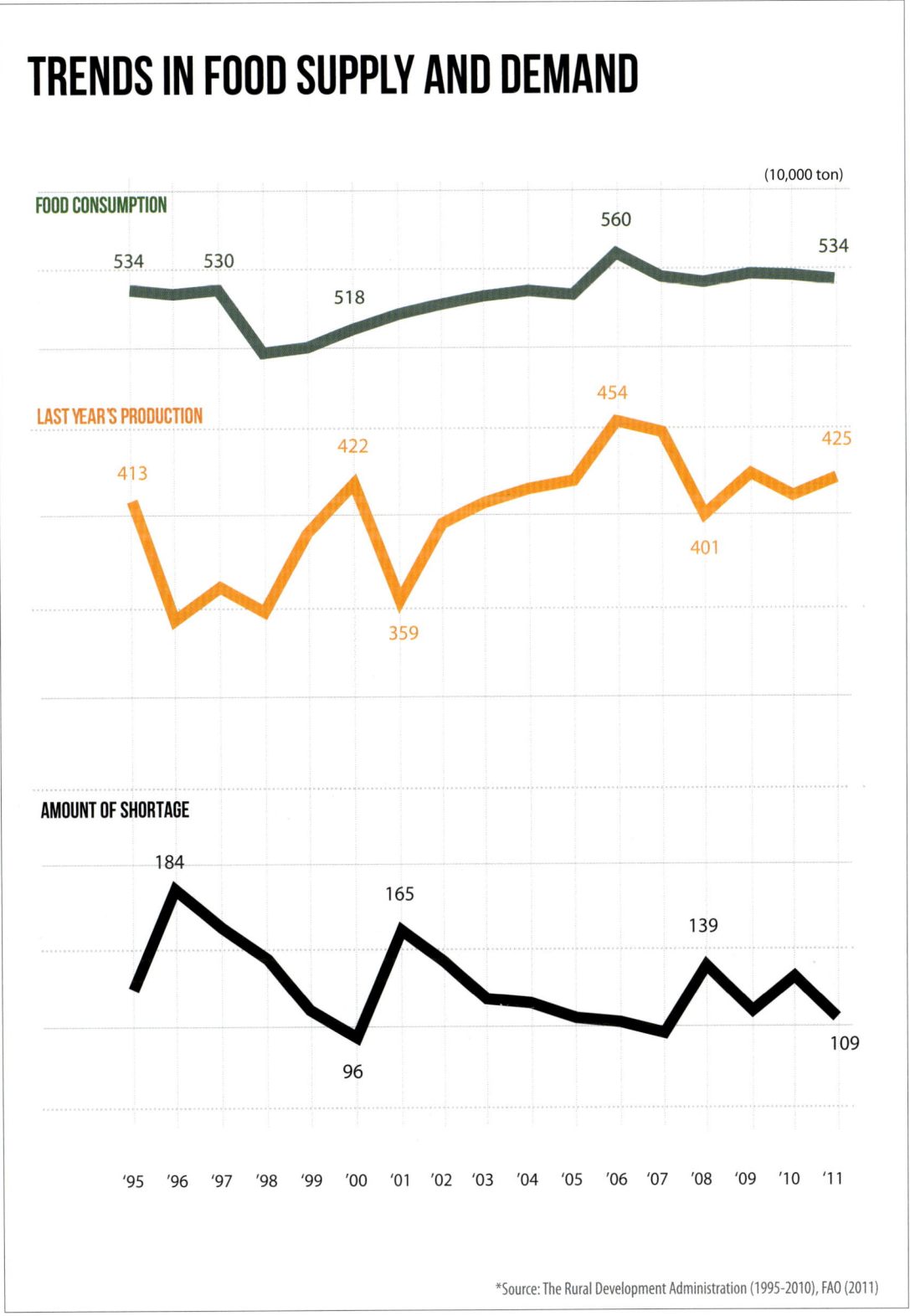

INTER-KOREAN EXCHANGES (PEOPLE AND GOOD)

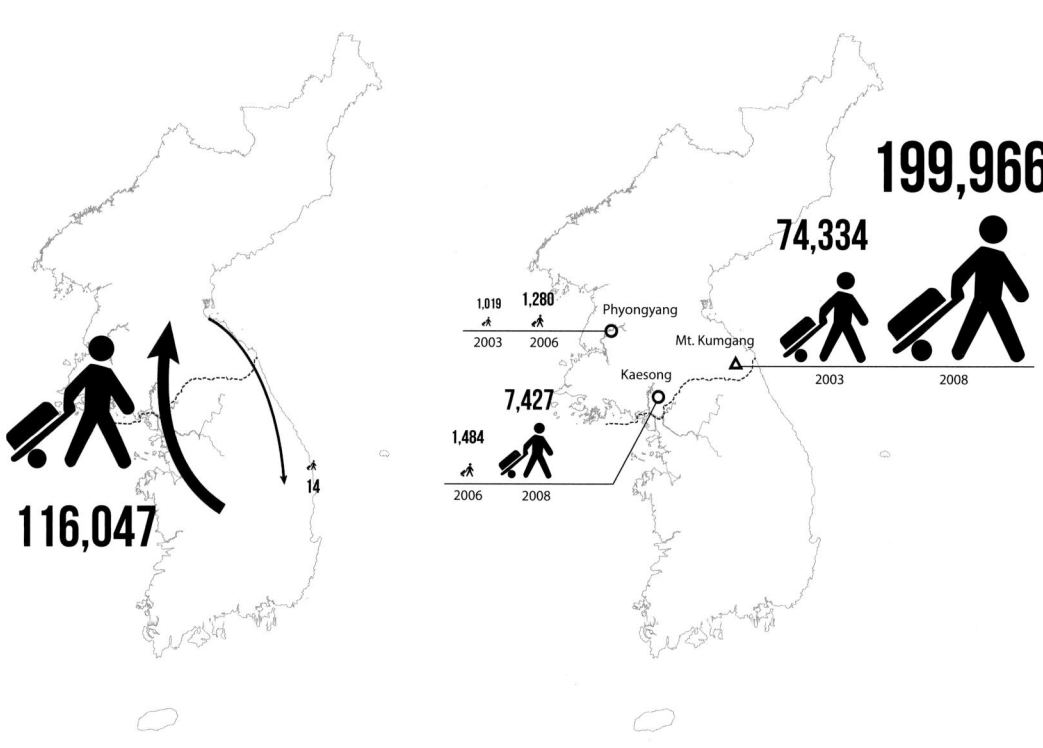

CROSS-BORDER TRAVELERS

3 MAJOR TOURISM SITES

Industrial Geography

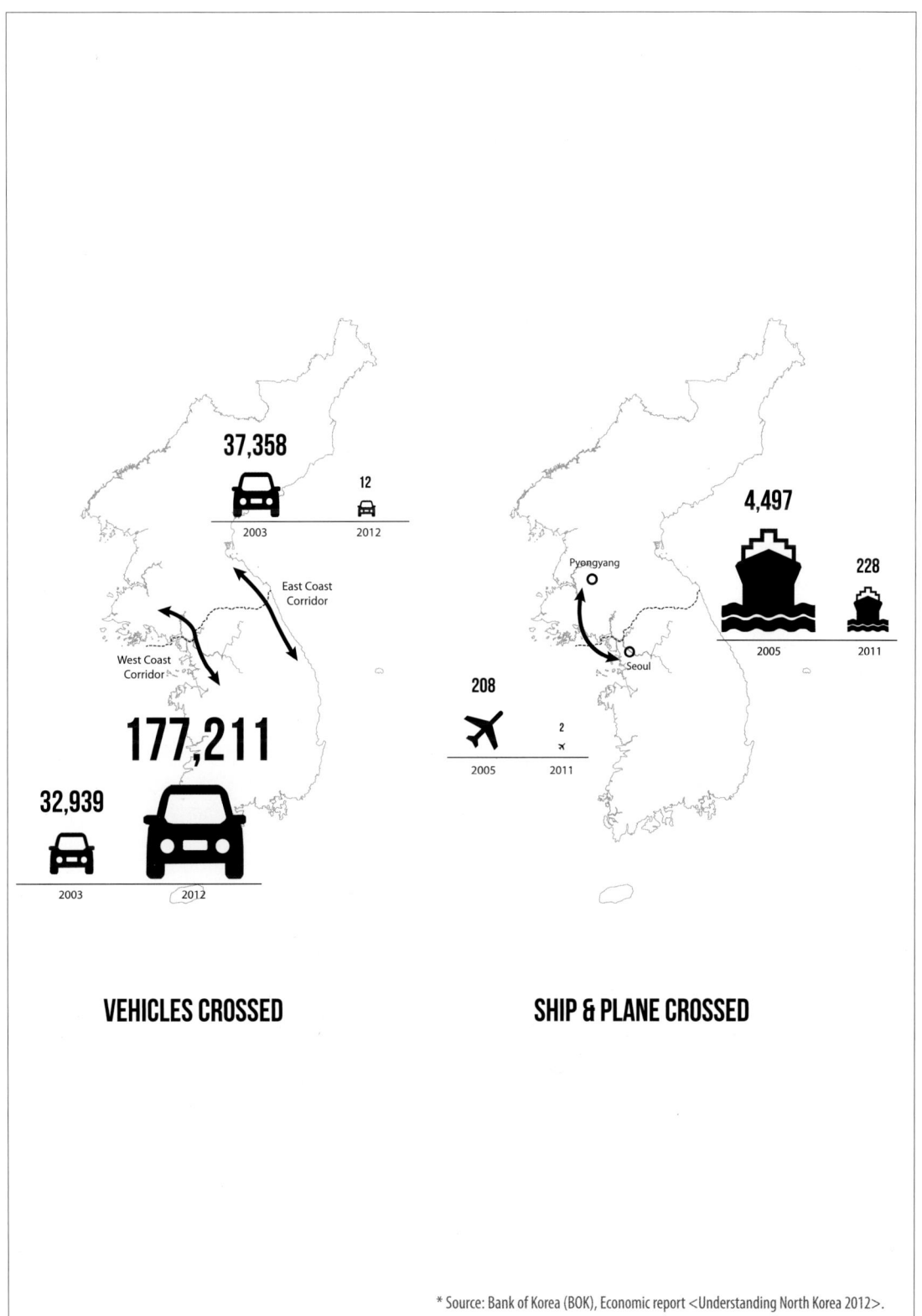

* Source: Bank of Korea (BOK), Economic report <Understanding North Korea 2012>.

Background Data

KAESONG INDUSTRIAL COMPLEX

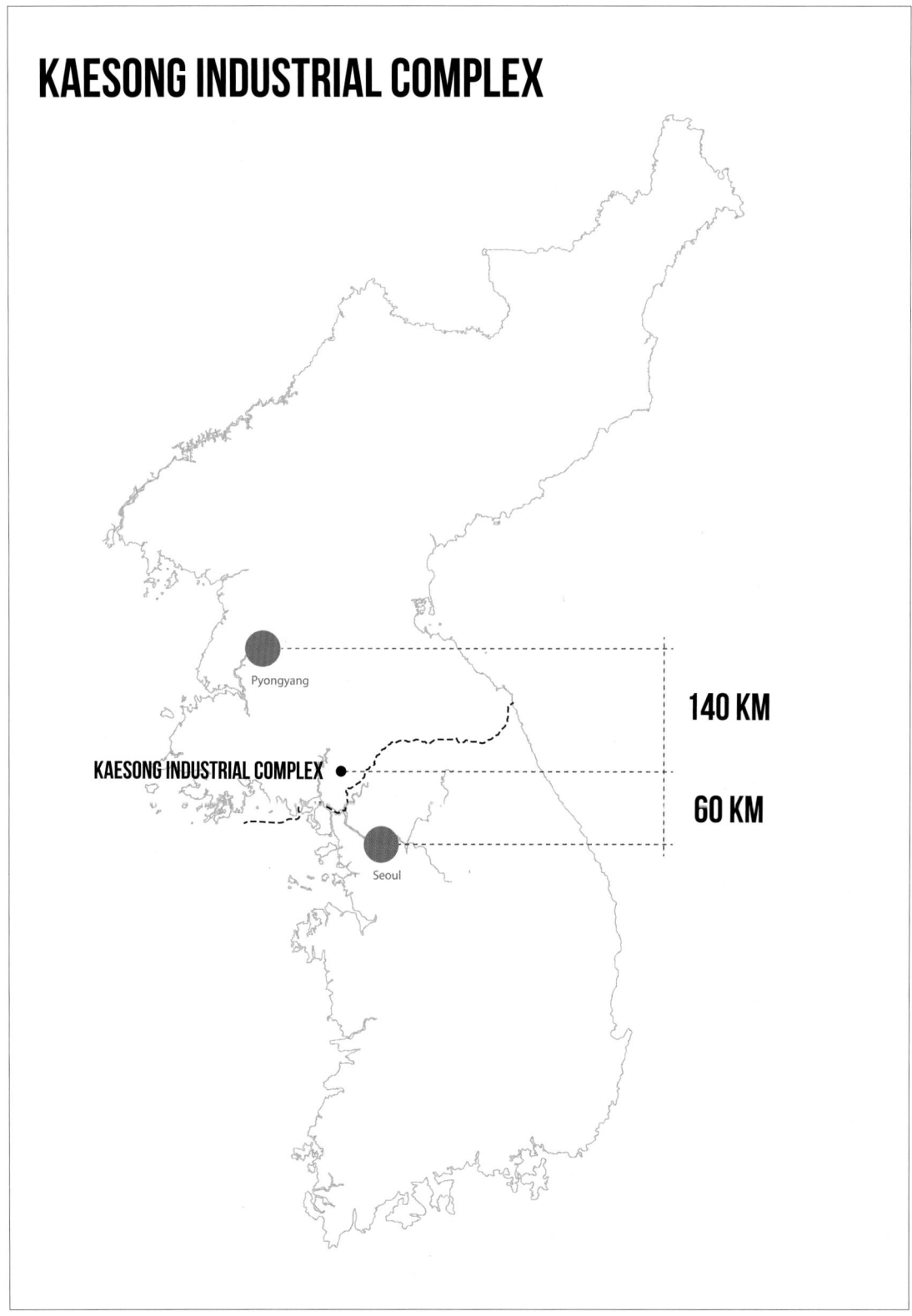

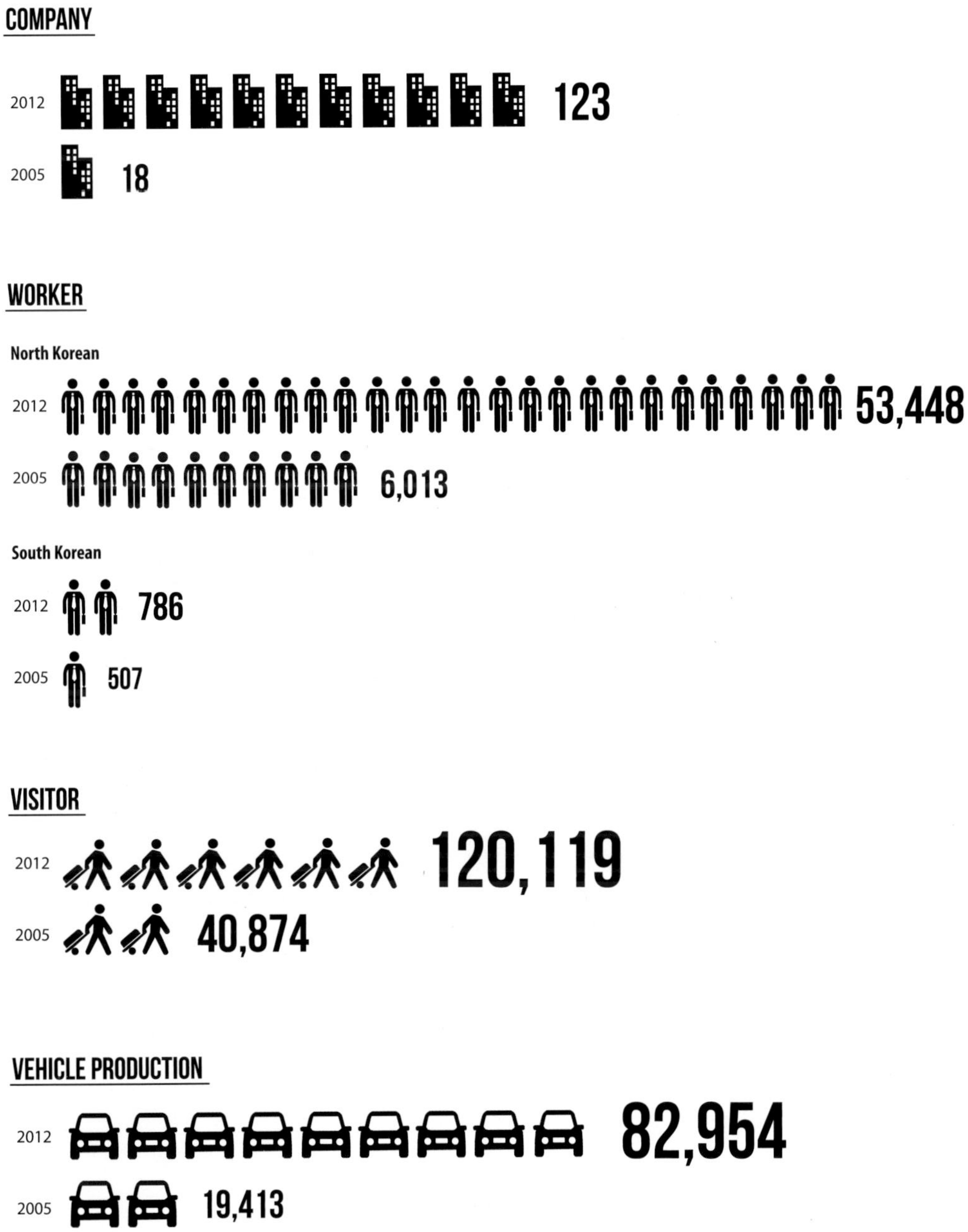

Industrial Geography

COMPANY

2012 123
2005 18

WORKER

North Korean

2012 53,448
2005 6,013

South Korean

2012 786
2005 507

VISITOR

2012 120,119
2005 40,874

VEHICLE PRODUCTION

2012 82,954
2005 19,413

* Source: Bank of Korea (BOK), Economic report <Understanding North Korea 2012>.

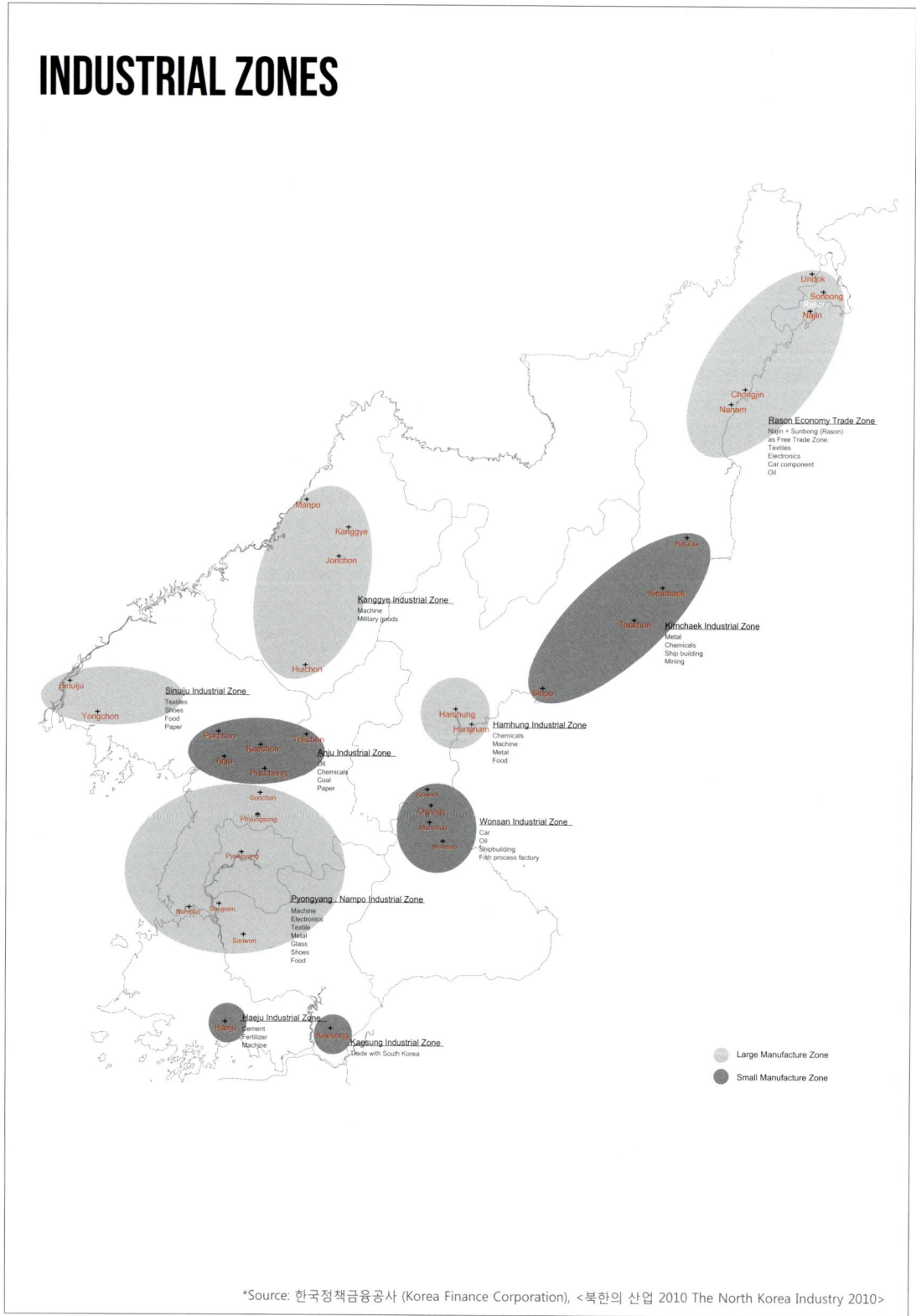

Industrial Geography

IMPORT / EXPORT

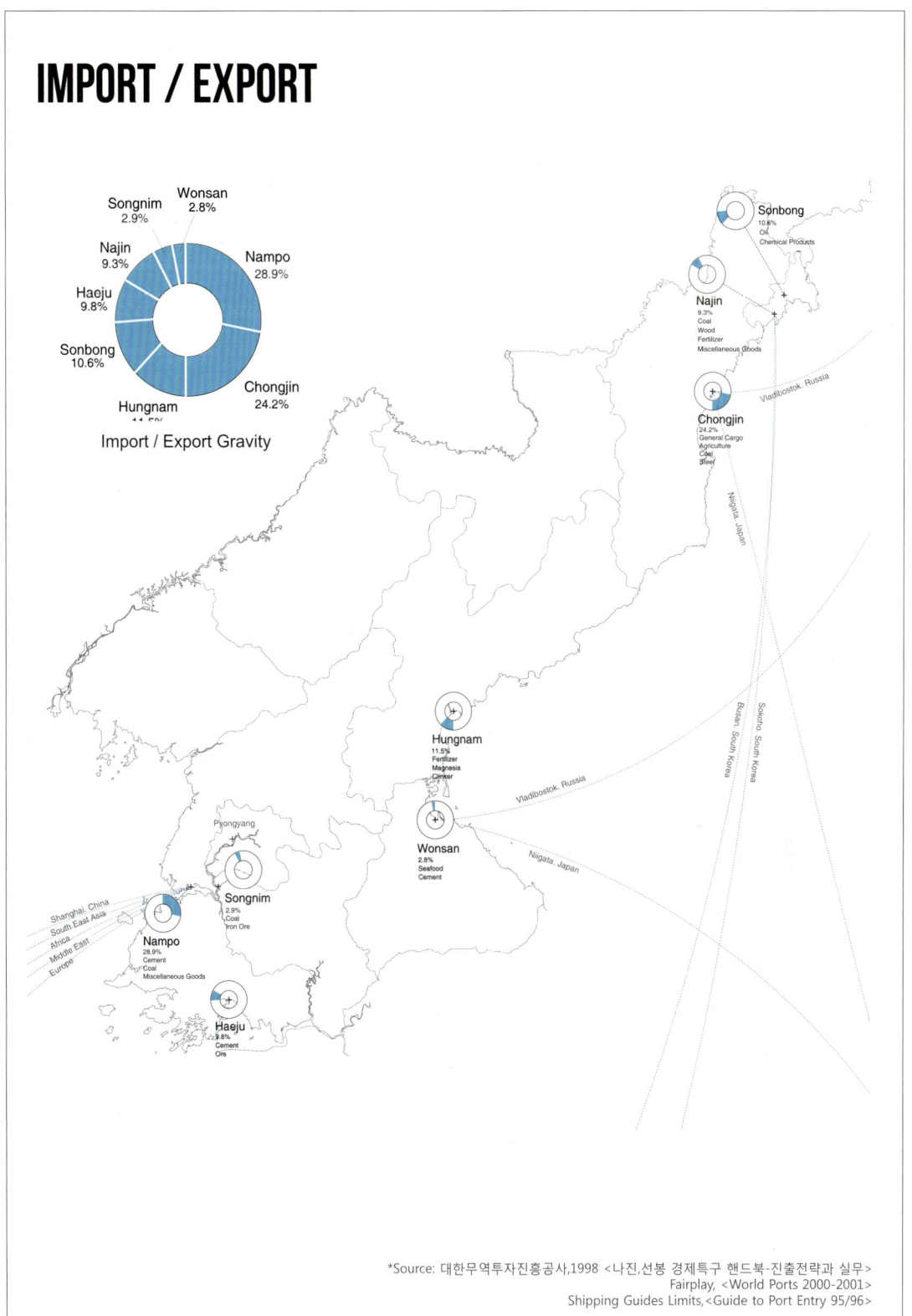

*Source: 대한무역투자진흥공사,1998 <나진,선봉 경제특구 핸드북-진출전략과 실무>
Fairplay, <World Ports 2000-2001>
Shipping Guides Limits, <Guide to Port Entry 95/96>

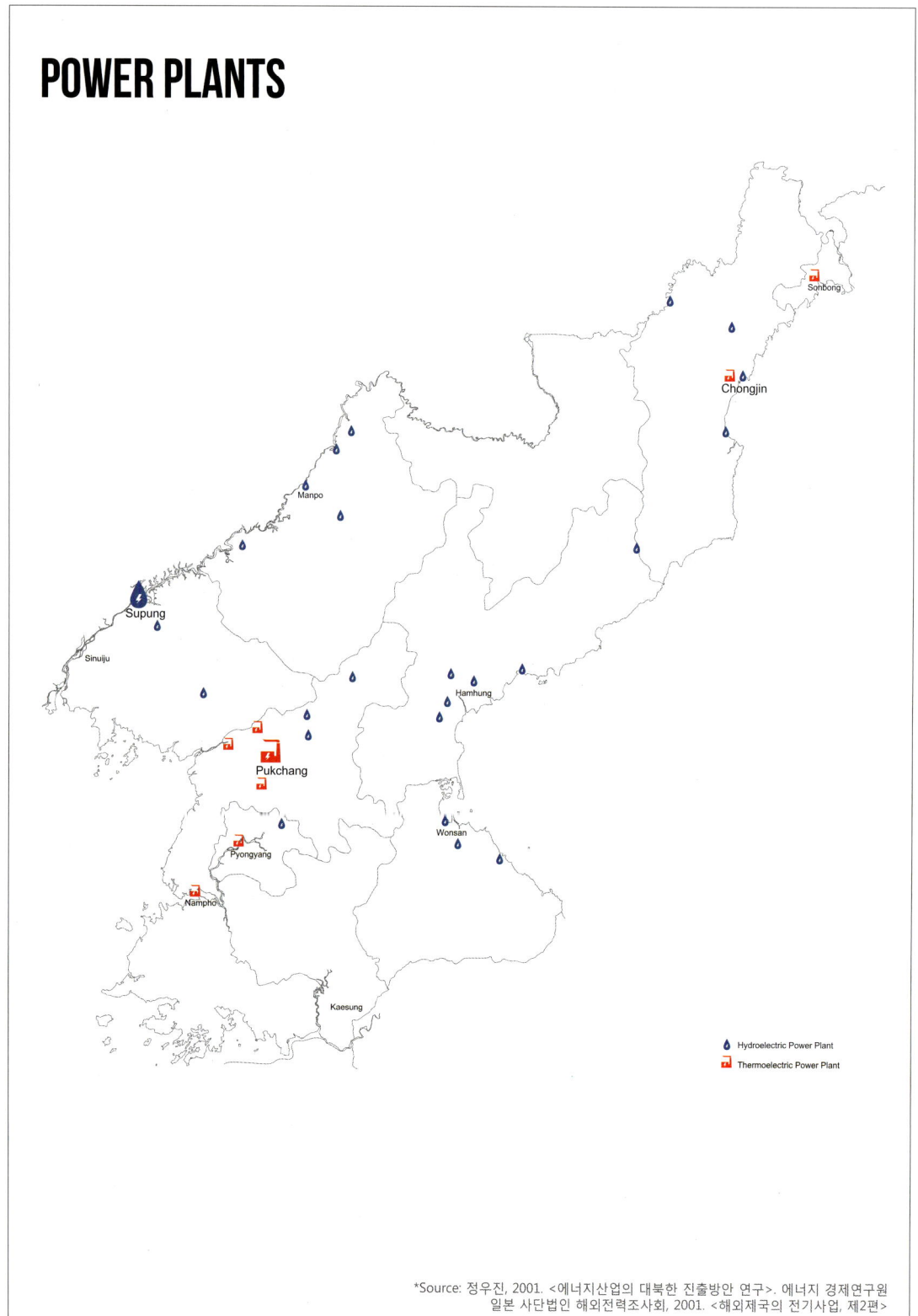

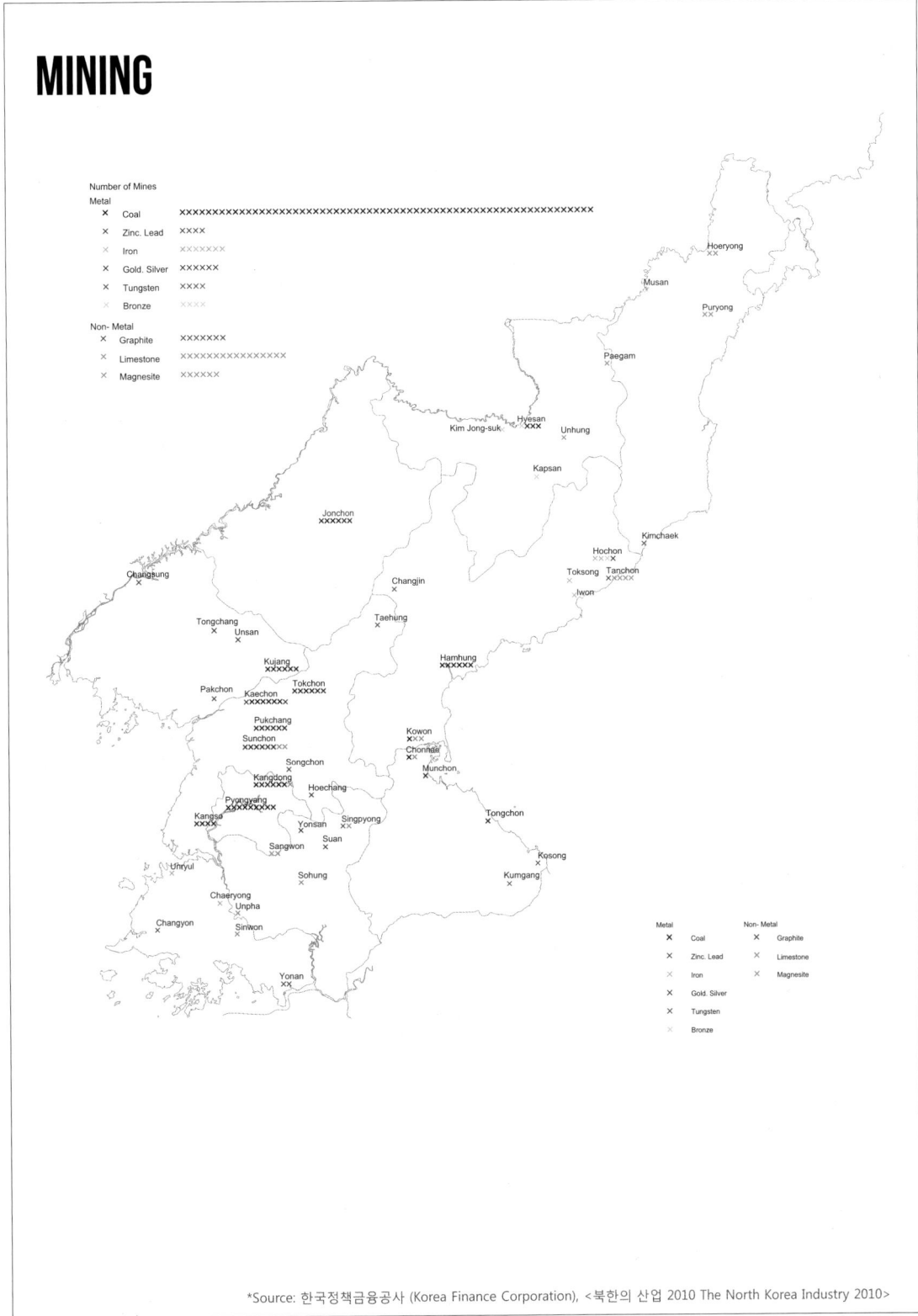

Background Data

STEEL MANUFACTURING

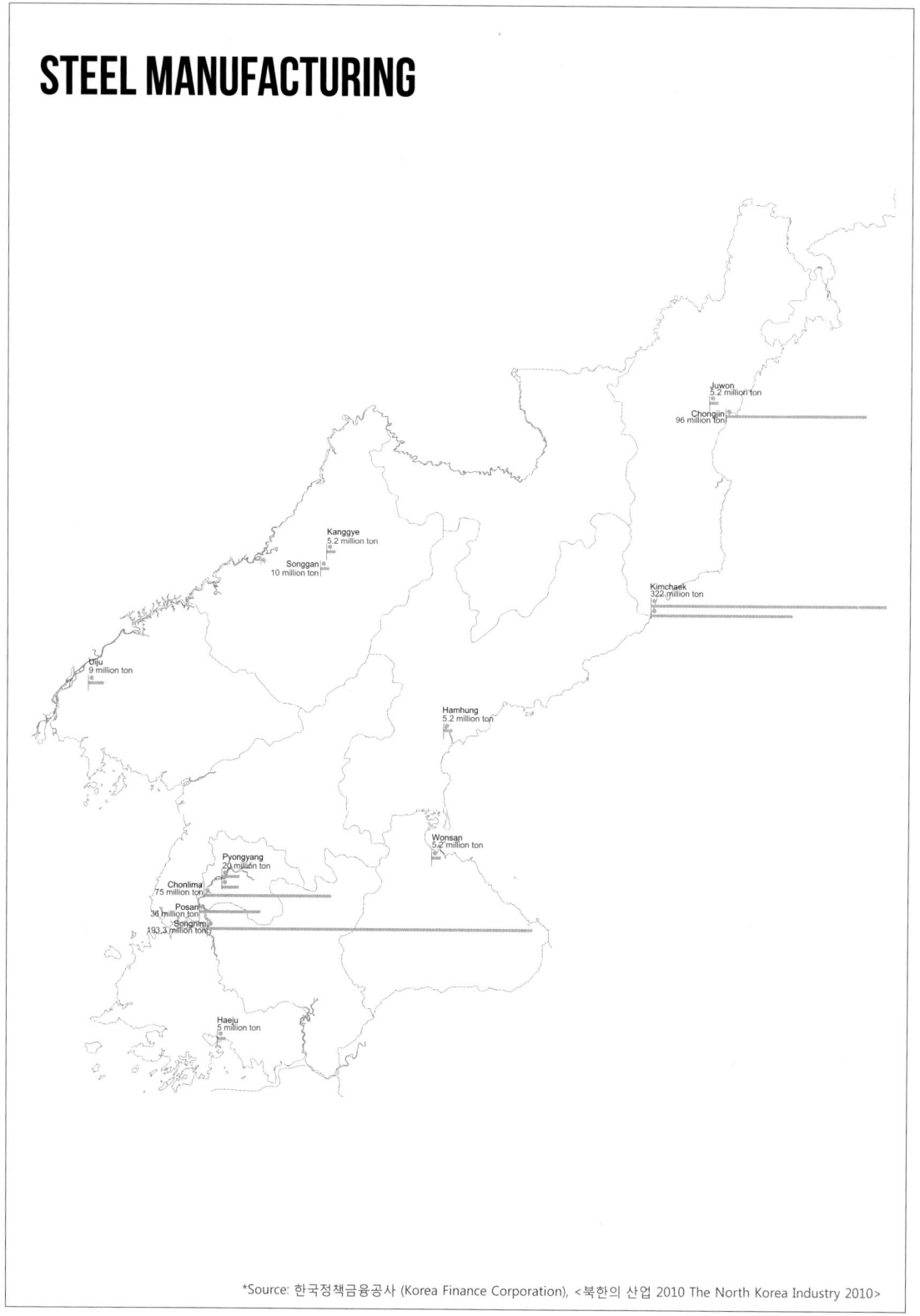

*Source: 한국정책금융공사 (Korea Finance Corporation), <북한의 산업 2010 The North Korea Industry 2010>

Industrial Geography

NON FERROUS MANUFACTURING

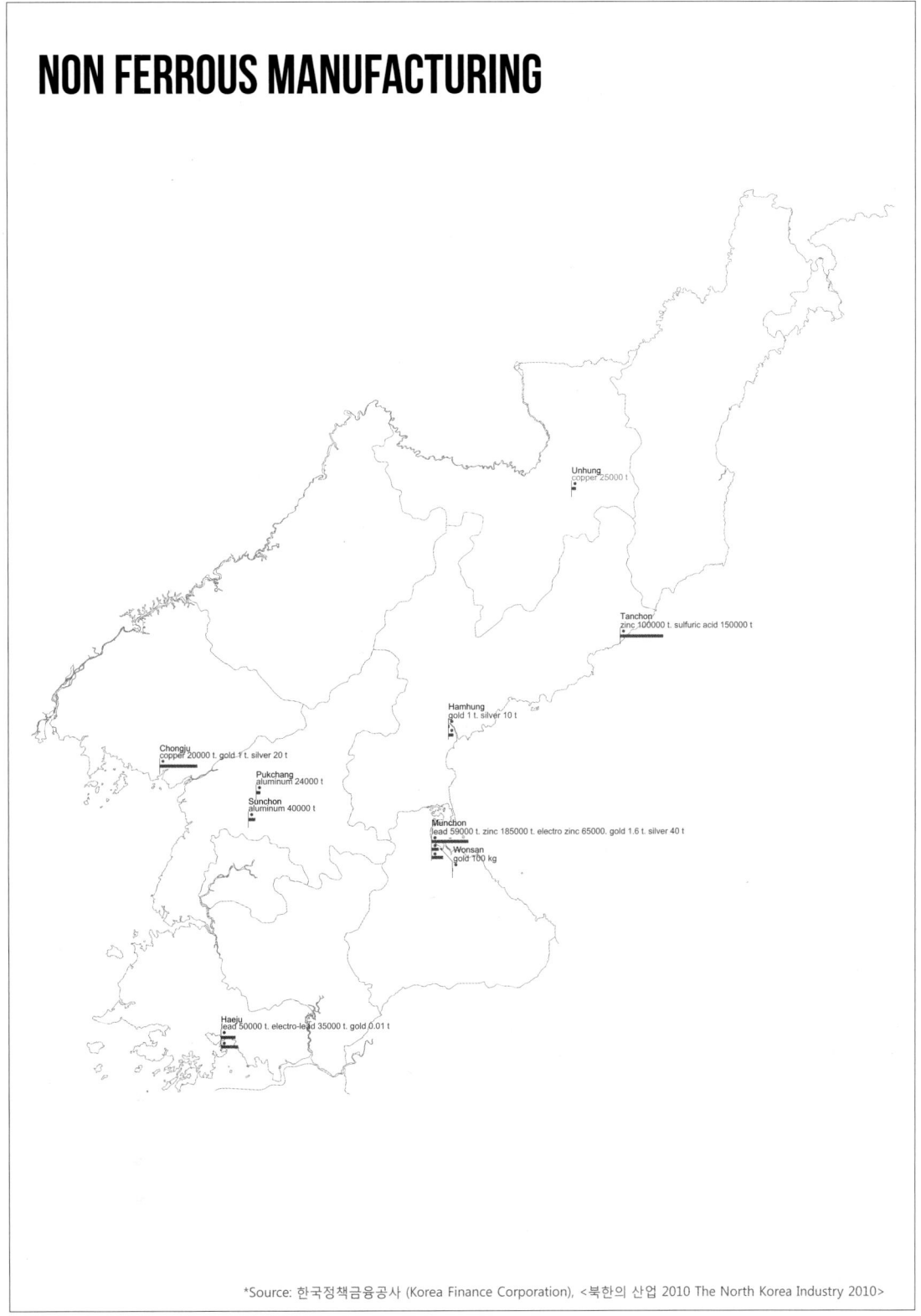

*Source: 한국정책금융공사 (Korea Finance Corporation), <북한의 산업 2010 The North Korea Industry 2010>

Background Data 178

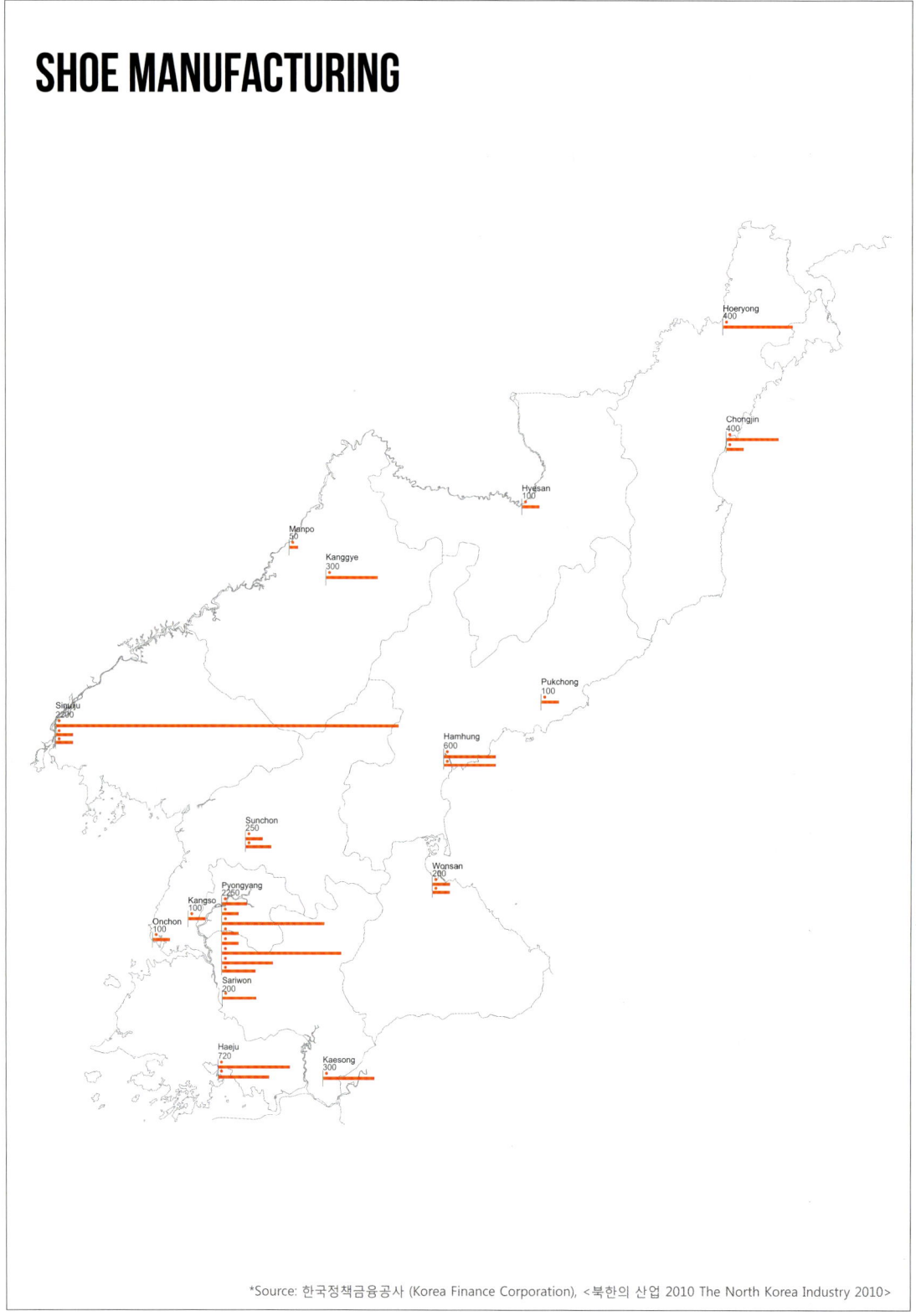

SHOE MANUFACTURING

*Source: 한국정책금융공사 (Korea Finance Corporation), <북한의 산업 2010 The North Korea Industry 2010>

Industrial Geography

TEXTILE MANUFACTURING

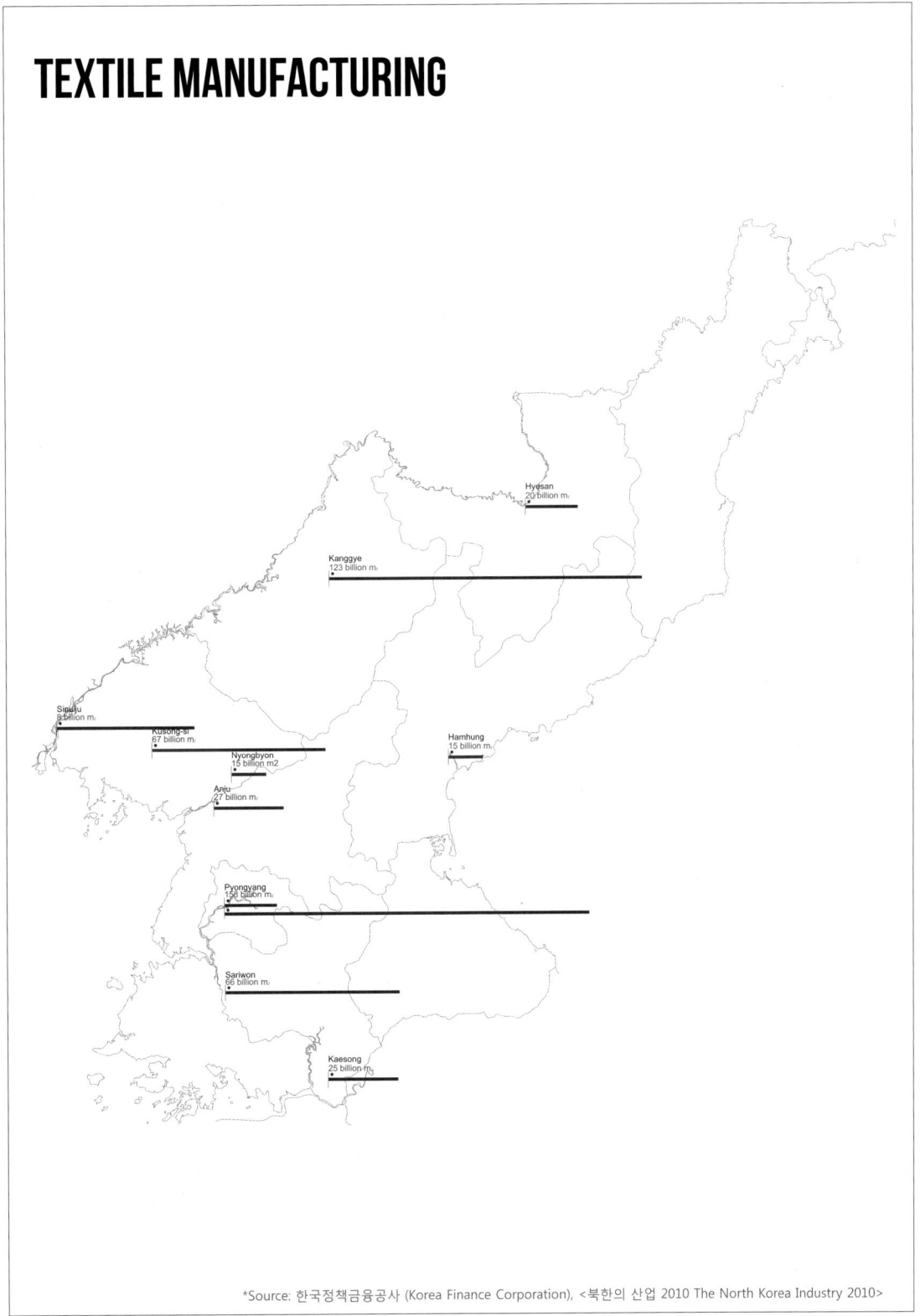

*Source: 한국정책금융공사 (Korea Finance Corporation), <북한의 산업 2010 The North Korea Industry 2010>

Background Data

CAR MANUFACTURING

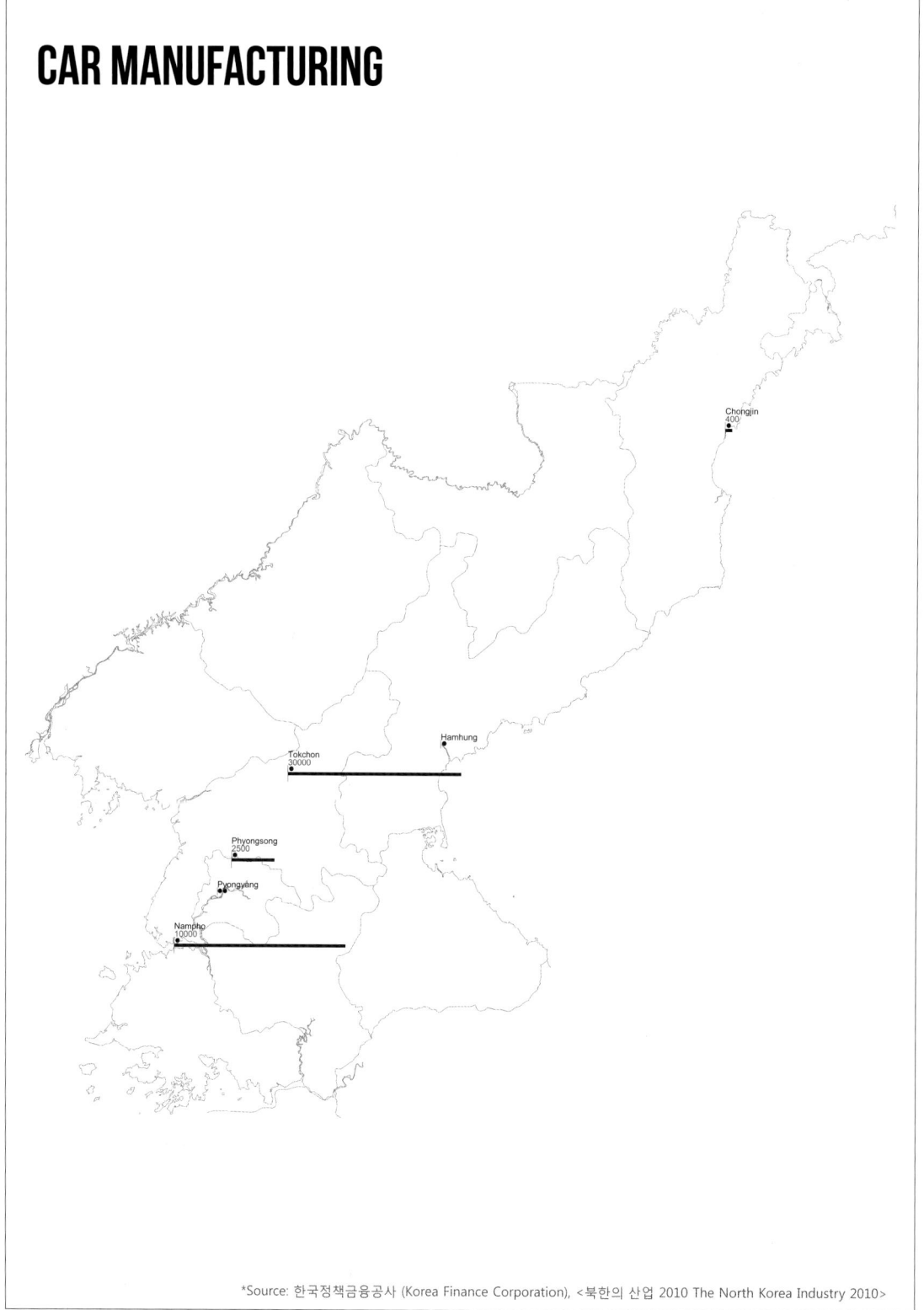

*Source: 한국정책금융공사 (Korea Finance Corporation), <북한의 산업 2010 The North Korea Industry 2010>

Industrial Geography

SHIP BUILDING

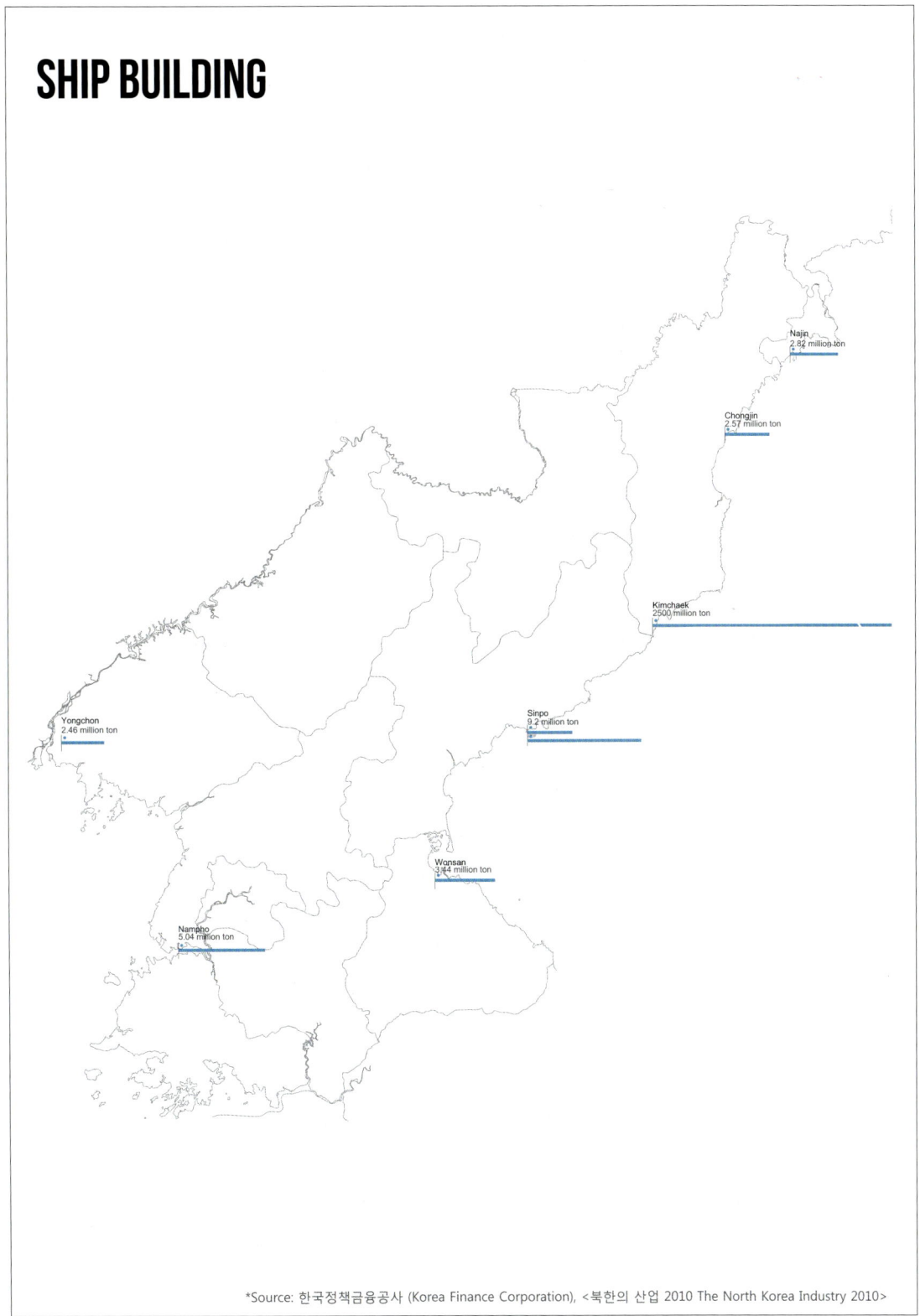

*Source: 한국정책금융공사 (Korea Finance Corporation), <북한의 산업 2010 The North Korea Industry 2010>

Background Data

ELECTRONICS MANUFACTURING

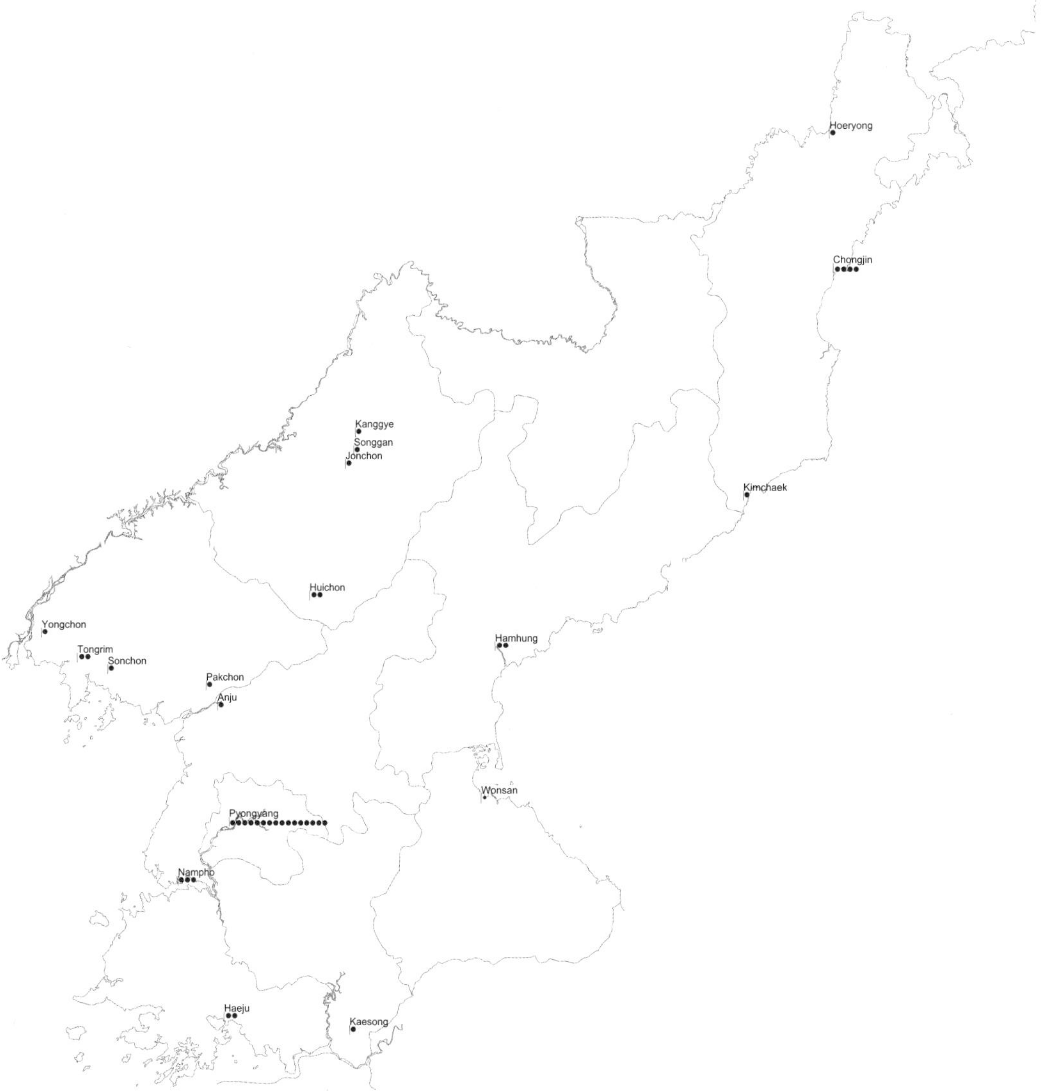

Locations marked on map:
- Hoeryong
- Chongjin
- Kanggye
- Songgan
- Jonchon
- Kimchaek
- Huichon
- Hamhung
- Yongchon
- Tongrim
- Sonchon
- Pakchon
- Anju
- Pyongyang
- Wonsan
- Nampho
- Haeju
- Kaesong

*Source: 한국정책금융공사 (Korea Finance Corporation), <북한의 산업 2010 The North Korea Industry 2010>

Industrial Geography

MACHINE MANUFACTURING

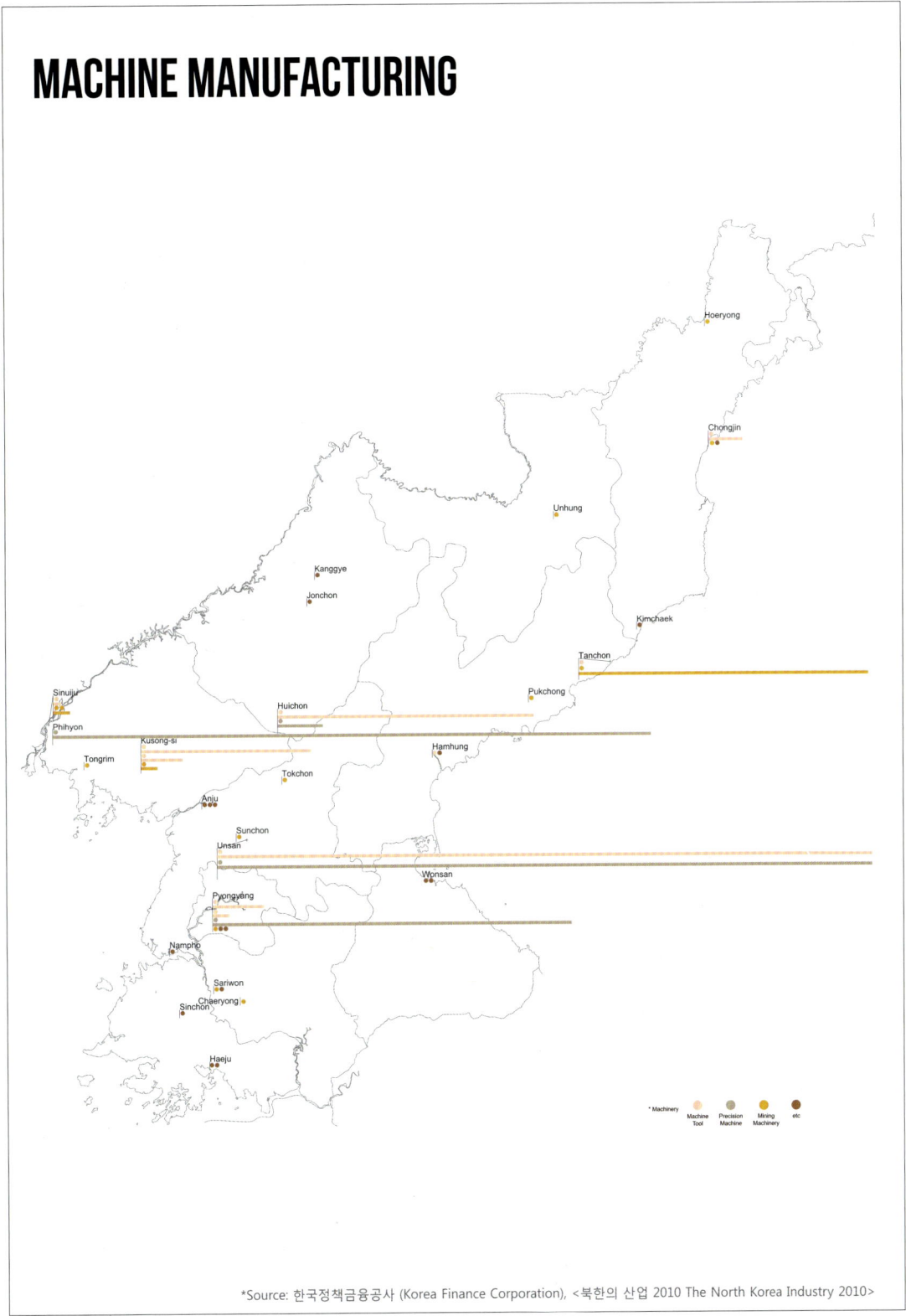

*Source: 한국정책금융공사 (Korea Finance Corporation), <북한의 산업 2010 The North Korea Industry 2010>

Background Data

184

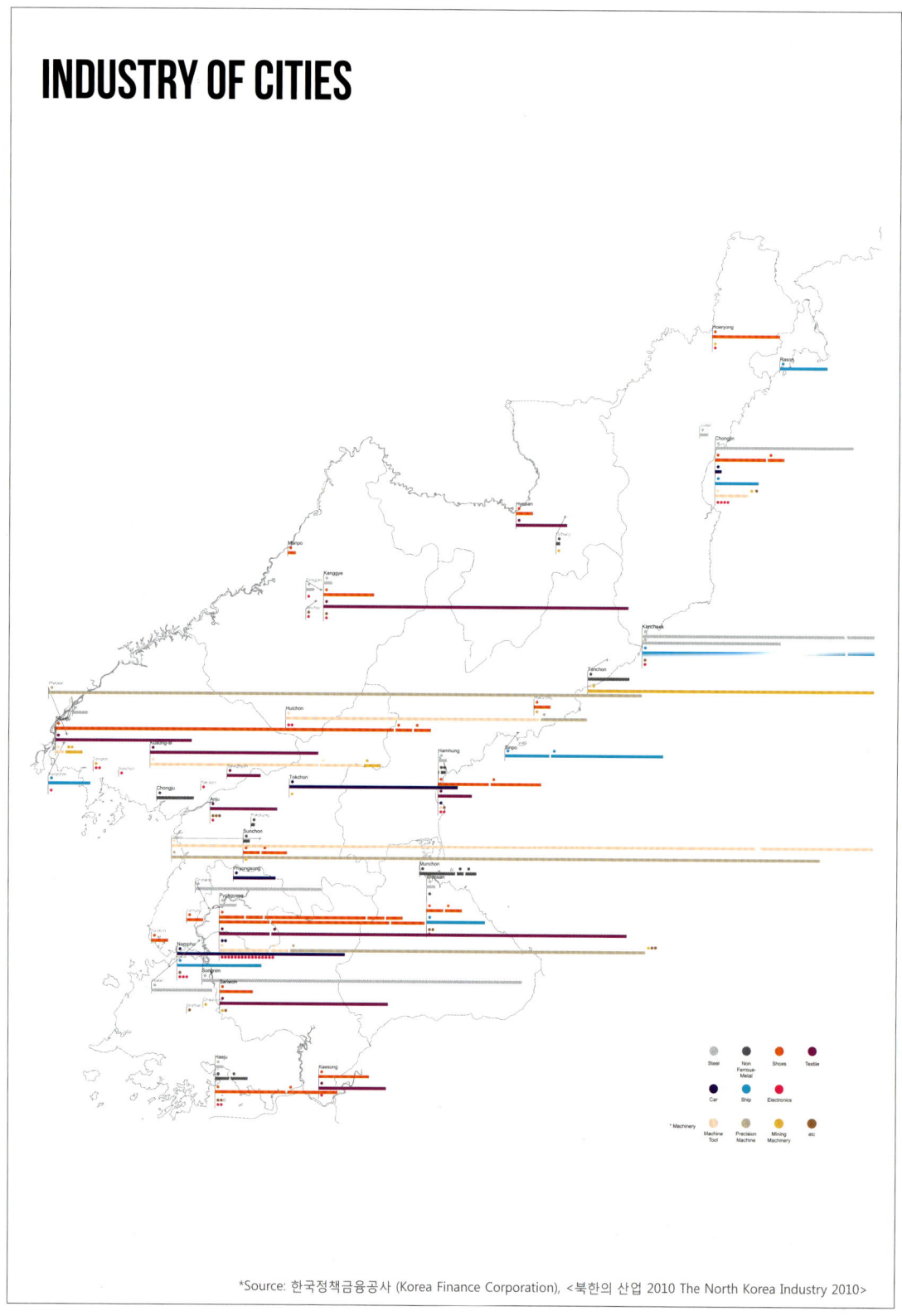

*Source: 한국정책금융공사 (Korea Finance Corporation), <북한의 산업 2010 The North Korea Industry 2010>

Industrial Geography

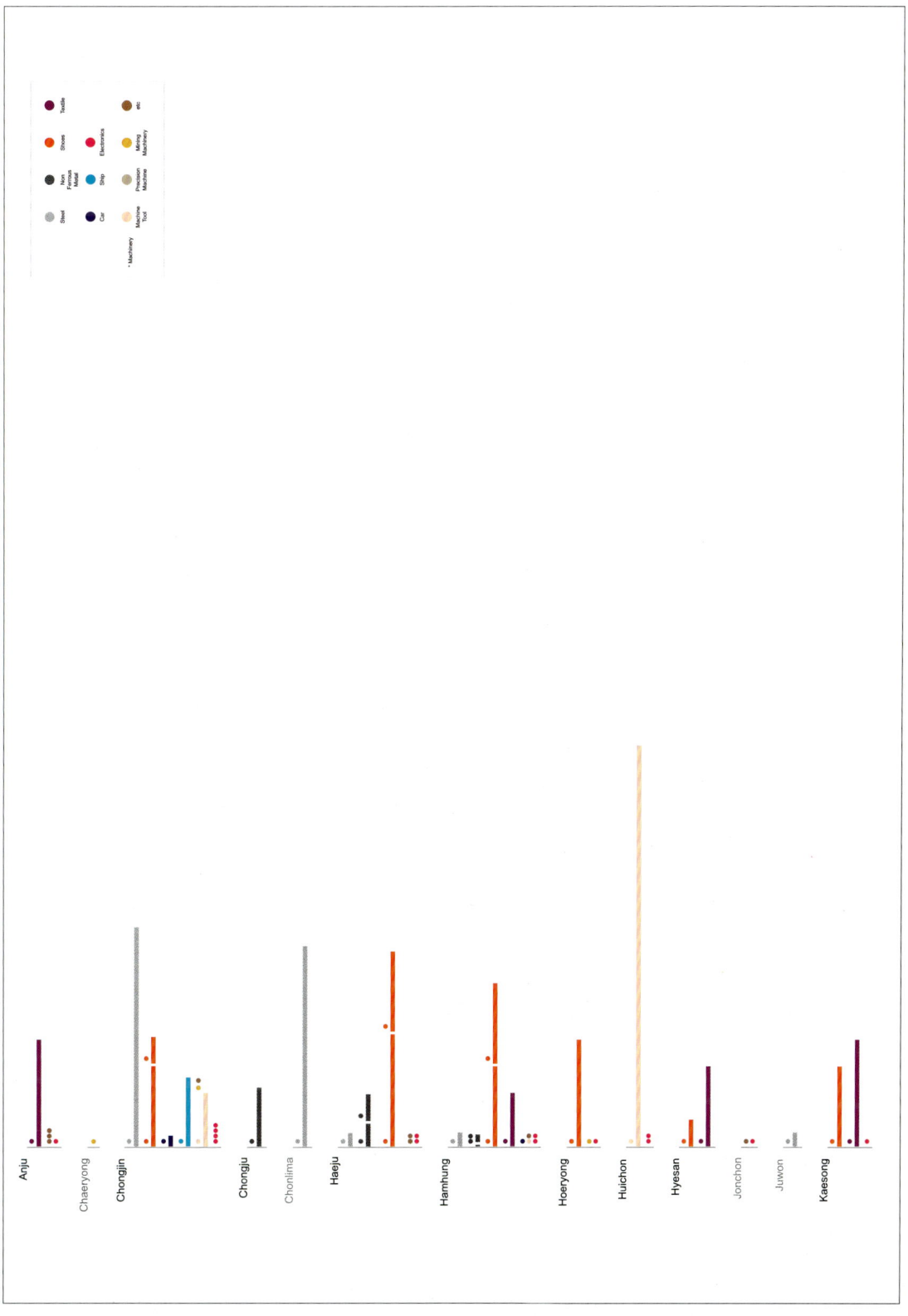

Background Data

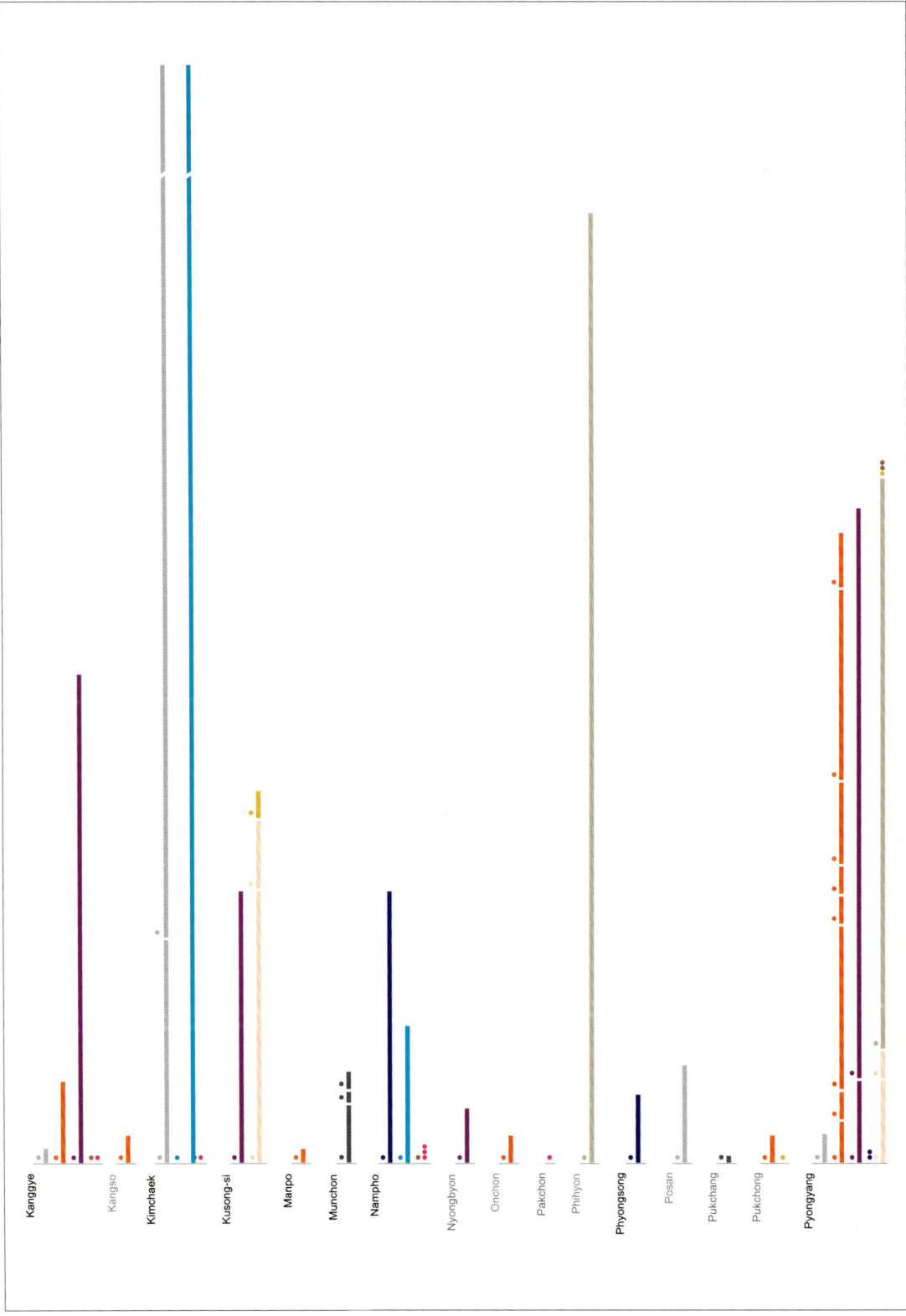

Industrial Geography

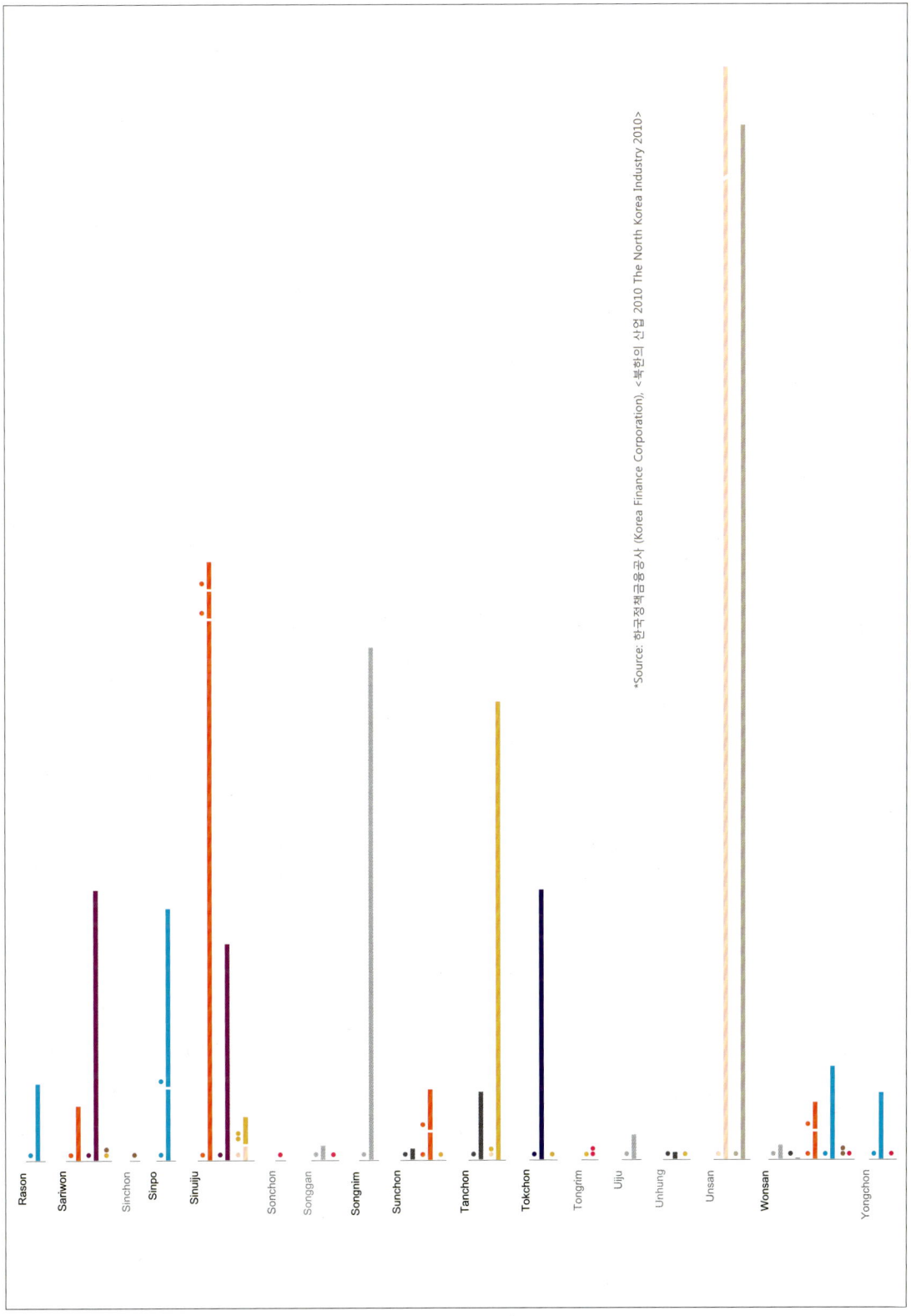

Background Data

MAJOR INDUSTRIAL CITIES

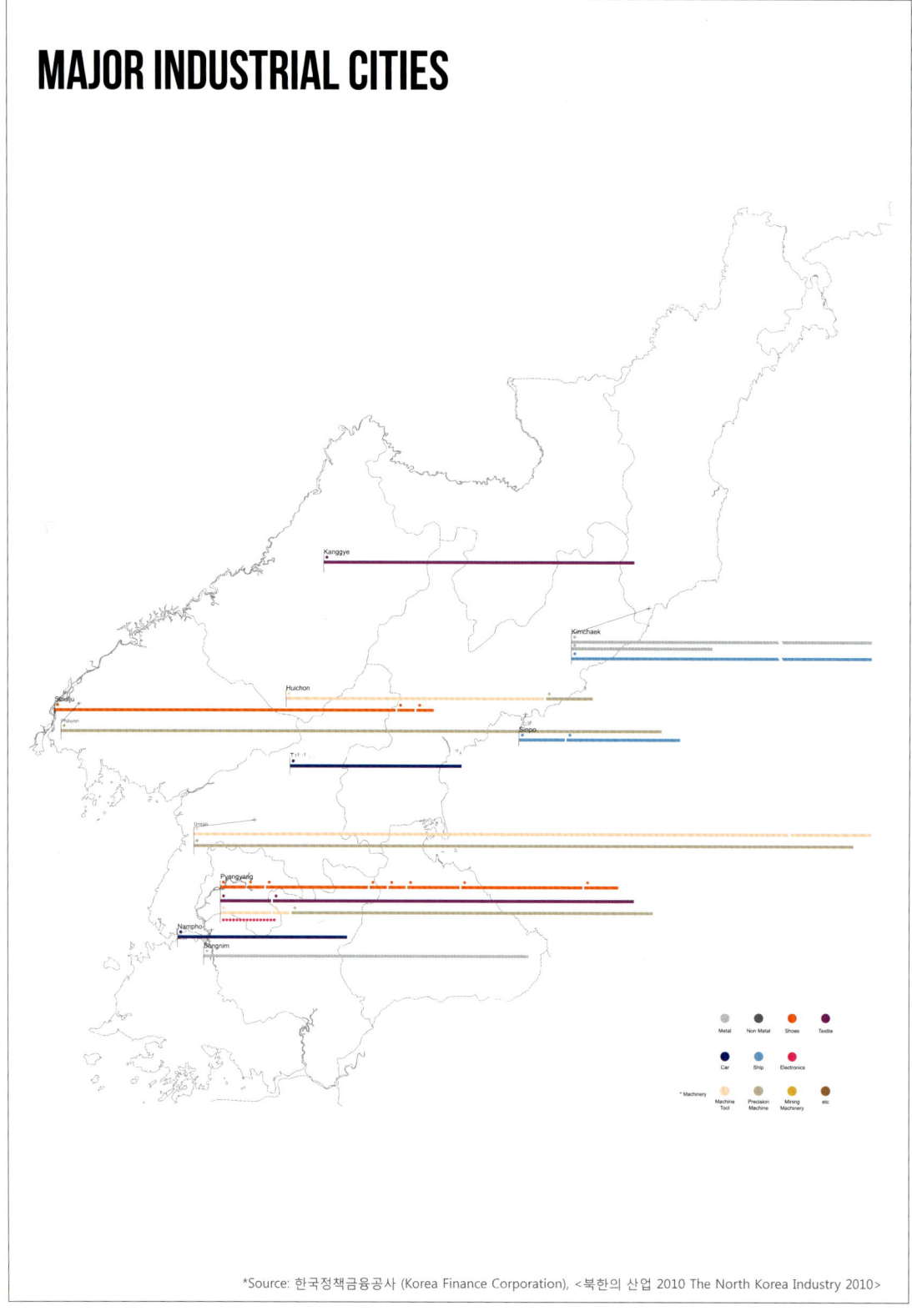

*Source: 한국정책금융공사 (Korea Finance Corporation), <북한의 산업 2010 The North Korea Industry 2010>

Industrial Geography

INDUSTRY OF 8 MAJOR CITIES

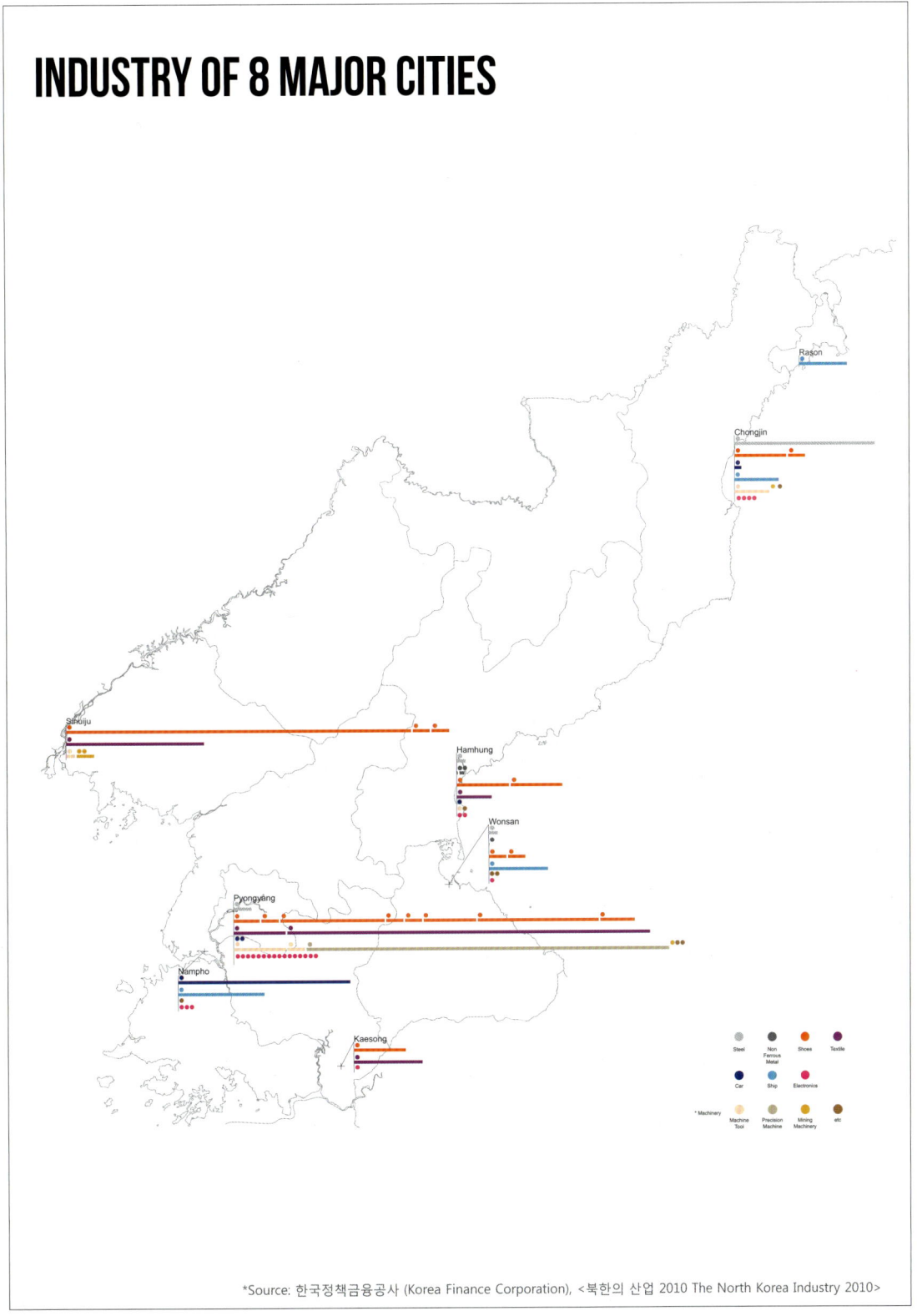

*Source: 한국정책금융공사 (Korea Finance Corporation), <북한의 산업 2010 The North Korea Industry 2010>

03 NORTH KOREAN CITIES
1. TABLES OF NORTH KOREAN CITIES
2. 8 MAJOR NORTH KOREAN CITIES
3. 19 SUPPORTING NORTH KOREAN CITIES

LEARNING FROM THE SOCIALIST CITY

Dongwoo Yim

—

Dongwoo Yim is the author and editor of
the "North Korean Atlas," and the principal
and co-founder of architecture and research firm
PRAUD, based in Boston and Seoul. He received
a Master of Architecture in Urban Design
at Graduate School of Design (GSD),
Harvard University, and bachelor's degree
in Seoul National University.
Dongwoo is a faculty member of Rhode Island School
of Design since 2011 where he teaches seminar
and design studios. His research interest focuses on
integral urbanism and architectural typologies
that catalyze urban transformation
in various urban scales. He is the award winner
of Architectural League Prize 2013, and is the author
of "Pyongyang, and Pyongyang After"
by Hyohyung Publishing and "
I Want to be METROPOLITAN" by ORO Editions.
His works have been published
and exhibited world wide including Museum
of Modern Art New York,
International Architecture Biennale Rotterdam,
Venice Biennale and Design Center Seoul,
and he has lectured at Harvard University,
Freie Universität Berlin, Dartmouth College,
Seoul National University and Youngchoo Forum
amongst others.

Generalized concept of socialism

It seems "socialism" is not an unfamiliar word or concept in Korean society anymore. When many discussions arise these days in areas such as welfare, medicare, and educational policies, it is not hard to find policies that adopted socialist ideals. Of course, there still are many people who cannot tell the difference between socialism and communism, and among them, there are people who still think socialism is an evil. However, it is true that in general, our society has grown up to absorb some of socialist's ideas and has become more flexible. Then, what would this mean for a city? How will the change of a society that absorbs more socialist ideals influence a city that is a built form of thoughts and demand of the society? Are our cities transforming towards cities with socialist features as the society is adopting more socialist's ideals? Or are they transforming independently from the change of the society?

Before answering these questions, we should first ask ourselves, "Is there a socialist city?" It is quite a tricky question to answer, even among the professionals, because it is not easy to find an actual realized example of a socialist city, although there is a clear strategy on how to make a "socialist city." Perhaps, a more clear reason is that a socialist city, which is based on the idea of socialist urban planning strategy, does not look that different from a, so called, capitalist city. And we will know why there is no clear cut between a socialist city and a capitalist city once we understand the background of how a socialist urban planning strategy emerged.

Birth of the Socialist City

As we all know, socialism was born based on experiences of Karl Marx and Friedrich Engels when they were young. In his early twenties, in the mid-nineteenth century, Engels visited Manchester, which had a radical speed of growth since the Industrial Revolution. The trip was suggested by his parents to let him learn the mill industry and its management, but as he experienced workers' living conditions in the back alleys, he stood by the workers instead of being a manager. Manchester already had wide streets that can have carriages on both sides, and middle class housings were standing along those streets. For Engels, who only used wide streets, it was a shock to see the reality of back alleys in a block. It was too tight to walk around, there was no light coming in, nor sewage system, and the workers were living with rats. He made a goal in his mind that he will change that situation, and when he met Marx shortly after, all his experiences were resolved into the idea of socialism.

Therefore, from the beginning of socialism, there was an idea that socialists need to fix the urban problems that were caused by urbanization. In other words, socialists needed a clear strategy to solve the problems, and as a result, socialist urban planning theory emerged. However, this is also why we cannot find a clear difference between a socialist city and a capitalist city.

As the Industrial Revolution progressed in the 19th century, fast urbanization was happening in many European cities. They were expanding with unprecedented speed, and the urban population and density kept on increasing. As there were always new jobs in cities, rural population migrated to the urban area, and as a new transportation system was developed, cities could expand more horizontally with less confinement. Therefore, it was inevitable to not have problems caused by urbanization, and the socialist movement was one of many movements focused in solving them. As we know, a city is like a living organ, so when there is a wounded part, it also transforms itself for self-healing as a respond to social demand to solve the problem. In other words, cities have been developed to deal with their own urbanization problems, and they are changing at the moment and will change in the future as well. Therefore, for us, who see socialist city as a problem solver, it is not easy to clearly tell the difference between the two.

Characters of the Socialist City

No matter whether it now has some similarities to other non-socialist cities, in the beginning, it was clear that socialists had to deal with urbanization problems through a clear urban planning strategy. There had been many discussions and arguments during the development of socialist urban planning strategy, and until now it is not easy to say what is a socialist city in one sentence. Though various theories, it is clear that the master plan for Moscow, Russia, which is the heart of socialist revolution, became the model for other socialist cities. The 1935 Master Plan for Moscow, basically has Ebenezer Howard's Garden city movement concept as its background layer. As mentioned above, in the last nineteenth century, there were many problems cause by urbanization, and many professionals tried to suggest solutions in various ways. Garden city movement was one of them. Even though it was not only the socialist urban planning that adopted a Garden city concept, there are important socialist urban planning features that were driven by the concept.

What are the common grounds between the Garden city movement and socialist urban planning? Garden city movement emerged to break radical expansion of a city. Howard thought that it was not the city itself, but the way of expansion of the city that caused urban problems by not having capacity to hold an increased population. Therefore, instead of radial expansion from the center, he suggested a new way of expansion of the city that constructs networks of small towns. This was welcomed by socialists because there was common ground with socialism that tried to abolish the difference between urban and rural area. In socialism, industrialized city is just a plunder that exploits working class from the country. In other words, the class conflict between bourgeois and proletarian in a city is a conflict between urban and rural. Therefore, in a socialist city, although it had to admit the existence of city, it tried to have as least gap as possible with the rural area. And the fact that it was suggesting limited size of a city, which in fact can reduce the gap between urban and rural, was the main reason why socialists adopted the Garden city movement concept as their background logic.

Another important concept in the movement that allowed socialists to adopt it is the concept of "garden" of course. In that period, density in an urban condition was extremely increasing with unprecedented speed, and therefore, securing green space was a very important issue. Even in "Ville Contemporaine" or "Plan Voisin", Le Corbusier was trying to secure as much green space as possible. In the Garden city movement, Howard gives a stronger role to the green space in a city. The limited size of a city, mentioned above, is realized not just by policy, but also by physical networks of green space. And therefore, Garden city, by nature, has more green space than any other plans, and at the desire of socialist activists to provide more leisure space for the workers can easily dissolved into the concept. In that period, as we can tell from the history of the Central Park of New York, green spaces were not for everybody. You have to fit a dress code to get in to the park, and you have to behave properly to use the park. So for the socialists, real public park was needed to provide resting place for workers, and the Garden city movement met their criteria.

North Korean City

These concepts were implemented to North Korean cities as well. Among others, there are two main characters in a North Korean city; limited size in scale, which means there is less discrepancies between cities, and sustainable unit system. Pyongyang, the capital of North Korea, of course, is the biggest city in the country. It has around 3 million people, which is about 13% of the whole North Korean population, and is the only city in North Korea that has more than a million population. The second and third biggest cities are located on the east coast of the country, which are Hamhung (760,000) and Chungjin (660,000). Asides from these three big cities, which are still relatively small compared to other Asian cities, another 14 cities have similar size with 200,000~300,000 population, and the rest 10 cities have about 100,000 population. This is a very well distributed structure for population in over all the country, considering the facts that proper Seoul has 25% of the nation's population, Metropolitan Seoul has 50%, and the five biggest cities in South Korea holds more than 50% of the total population. As mentioned above, this is mainly because it is avoided to have densely urbanized city in socialists urban planning strategy. And therefore, instead of concentrating population in few cities, they rather distributed people to many cities so that the whole country could be developed more equally. This fact also shows why the second and third biggest cities in North Korea are located on the east coast, while Pyongyang is on the west.

The second character is the self-sustainable unit system. There is a bit of discrepancy between what we call "city" and what North Koreans call "city." As mentioned above, the population of Pyongyang is 1/3 of Seoul. But the area is more than 2,500 km², which is more than 4 times the area of Seoul. Some articles say North Korean authority changed administrative boundary of the city because Pyongyang wanted to compete against Seoul in size. But in fact, this is not the case. There is a certain logic in North Korea to structure a city; creating a self-sustainable unit. They conceive a city to be not just an area where people live and consume, but also where production occurs, and therefore, it becomes a self-sustaining unit. In this case, production means products from both manufacturing and agricultural industries. In a North Korean city, urban area is composed of residential with industrial area, and the rural area is where agriculture happens. The North Korean city is always composed with both, urban and rural areas. Within this structure there is another level of urban area within rural area, and another level of rural area within urban area. As a result, in any scale of urban or rural area, there is urban function as well as rural function.

These two main characteristics of North Korean cities were possible because they were based on the concept of socialist urban planning strategy that tries to abolish the difference between urban and rural area. For them, rural area is not the area that urban area should encroach over, but rather the area that has to coexist, and not only the area for agricultural product, but also the area that functions as buffer zone that limits expansion of urban area. Of course, this self-sustaining city unit brings inefficiency in some parts that perhaps could be resolved if certain industries were concentrated in few areas. However, this may not be what North Korea, the country which tried to realize spatial equilibrium throughout the territory, wanted to achieve.

Learning from the Socialist City

In short, the goal that a socialist city is trying to achieve, and the structure that a North Korean city has are somewhat different from what we see from our capitalist cities. Of course, having differences does not always mean it has an advantage, and we cannot adopt another city model without any filtering process even if we had urban problems to solve. Socialist urban planning strategy disregards the private sector, leaving all construction of new building stock to be done by public authorities. This condition desaturates identities and the variety of developments of a city making the city less responsive to social and market demands. Also, as there are so many repetitive facilities and industries among North Korean cities, expenses caused from the inefficiency are unpredictable. Although there are all these disadvantages, there are also essential factors of a socialist city to be learned.

First, we can learn the urban-rural coexistence model. Recently, many developed cities, including Seoul, with the concept of "urban farming", have started to put efforts on how we can produce food ingredients, and consume them in a city. Sometimes, it has achieved this by developing new distributing systems, which is a passive way, and sometimes through using urban pocket spaces or roof surfaces of buildings. MVRDV even had the proposal of a "Pig Farm" within a building. No matter what the methodology to realize urban-rural coexistence is, the concept was already there in socialist urban planning strategy, and somewhat realized in socialist cities. Although the way how it was realized was rather two dimensional than three dimensional, the life pattern of a city that coexist with rural function gives us a clue how our cities will change and what new demand we will have regarding to "urban farming." Because agricultural area is not just an area for farming, but also an urban structure, or buffer zone, that restricts urban expansion and prevents some urban problems, it can be considered as a precaution of urbanization.

Secondly, we must address the concept of "spatial equality" in a city. Of course, it is still arguable whether it was well realized in a socialist city or not, the concept "spatial equality" is worth to develop. In a socialist city, it tried to achieve the equilibrium not only between urban and rural, but also within a city. Theoretically, there should not be a specific area that has more cultural facilities with more parks than the other. Also, there should not be a designated area for all industries so that a certain district has poor living environment. These facilities and functions should be well distributed throughout a city so that it can minimize the spatial inequality, which is why the concept "microdistrict," emerged, where production facilities as well as educational and service facilities coexist with housing. We sometimes take it for granted to have "good/or rich neighborhood" and "bad/or poor neighborhood". Of course, each neighborhood should have its own identity, but if the identity is based on inequality, perhaps we should rethink how we can restructure a city.

In conclusion, our society, similar to European societies, is becoming a mature society by adopting some features of socialism. Without a doubt, Korea is more developed now than anytime before in history, and the society is more open to a variety of ideas, including socialist features. Perhaps, it is time to think about how our cities should respond to these changes. A city has been, is, and will be transforming, responding to change of social demand, paradigms, technology and so on, and it means that we should see how our society has been developed so far when we think of the future of our cities. Therefore, what we need to address is not how we can show our superiority over a socialist city, but how we can adopt some advantages of a socialist city to our city.

사회주의 도시의 교훈

임동우

—

임동우는 "북한 도시 읽기"의 저자이며 서울과
보스턴을 기반으로 하는 설계사무소 PRAUD의 대표이다.
그는 하버드 대학교에서 도시설계 건축학 석사,
서울대학교에서 학사를 취득하였다.
현재 그는 로드아일랜드 스쿨 오브 디자인(RISD)에
출강하고 있으며, 그의 연구는 다양한 스케일에서 도시 변화를
촉진시키는 점진적인 도시 변화와 건축 유형에 초점을 맞추고 있다.
그는 뉴욕 건축가 연맹 주관 2013년 뉴욕 젊은 건축가상 수상자이며,
"평양, 그리고 평양 이후"(효형 출판)
"I Want to be METROPOLITAN"(ORO Editions)의 저자이다.
그의 작업은 뉴욕 모마, 로테르담 건축 비엔날레,
서울 디자인 센터, 베니스 비엔날레 등에 전시된 바 있으며,
하버드 대학교, 베를린 자유 대학, 다트머스 대학, 서울대학교,
영추포럼 등에서 강연한 바 있다.

'사회주의'의 보편화

최근 들어 우리 사회에서 '사회주의'라는 말은 더 이상 낯선 말이 아니다. 복지 정책, 의료 정책, 교육 정책 등 사회 다방면에 걸친 다양한 논의가 진행되는 가운데 '사회주의'의 아이디어를 채용한 정책들도 상당수 눈에 띄고 그에 관한 논쟁도 활발해졌기 때문이다. 물론 아직도 이 사회에는 사회주의를 공산주의와 혼동하는 사람들도 있고, 여전히 사회주의는 '나쁜 것'으로 규정하는 부류들도 있다. 하지만 전반적으로 우리나라 사회가 사회주의라는 개념에 좀 더 융통성을 갖고 바라보고 있는 것은 확실하다. 그렇다면 이러한 현상은 도시에 어떠한 의미가 있을까. 한 사회가 사회주의의 개념과 생각들을 더 수용한다는 사실이 구성원의 욕구와 생각들을 반영한 구축환경인 도시에 어떠한 의미를 가져올 수 있을까. 우리 사회가 사회주의 개념을 예전보다 더 많이 받아들이고 있으니, 우리의 도시 역시 사회주의 개념을 받아들인 도시로 변화하고 있는 것인가. 아니면 정책과 보편적 사고의 변화와 관계 없이 우리의 도시는 독자적으로 변화하고 있는 것일까?

이 질문에 답하기에 앞서 우리가 전제해서 보아야 할 문제는, 과연 사회주의 도시라고 하는 것이 존재 하는가 하는 질문이다. 이 문제에 대해서는 사실 전문가들 사이에서도 의견이 분분했다. 이유는 간단하다. 사회주의 운동가들 사이에서 도시는 어떻게 구성되어야 한다고 하는 명백한 도시 구성의 원리가 있었지만 실제로 그 도시의 구성원리가 완벽히 구현된 도시를 찾아보기 힘들었기 때문이다. 하지만 더 중요한 이유는 사회주의 도시의 구성원리, 즉 사회주의 도시 계획론에서 말하는 사회주의 도시의 모습이라는 것이 우리가 현재 알고 있는 자본주의 도시, 혹은 비 사회주의 도시의 모습과 아주 큰 차이를 보이지 않고 있기 때문이다. 아마도 이는 사회주의 도시 계획론 혹은 사회주의 이념의 발생 배경을 살펴보면 쉽게 이해가 되지 않을까 한다.

사회주의 도시의 발생

사회주의는 우리가 잘 알고 있듯이 두 젊은 청년 카를 마르크스와 프리드리히 엥겔스가 주축이 되어 주창한 사회 이념이다.

이 중 엥겔스는 그의 나이 20대 초반, 19세기 중반에 당시 산업혁명 이후 급속도로 성장한 영국의 맨체스터를 방문한다. 이는 그의 부모님이 그로 하여금 가족이 운영하고 있는 방직공장에 가서 공장의 운영과 관련한 일을 배우게 하려고 보낸 것인데, 아이러니 하게도 엥겔스는 경영자 수업을 한 것이 아니라 맨체스터의 뒷골목에서 자신이 평소에는 보지 못하던 노동자들의 생활환경을 접하게 되면서 노동자의 입장에 서게 된다. 당시 멘체스터의 주요 도로는 폭이 넓어 마차가 양방향으로 다닐 수 있었고 흔히 말하는 중산층이 사는 집들이 구성되어 있었다. 늘 큰길로만 다니던 엥겔스는 어느 날 뒷골목으로 들어가 보게 되는데 그곳은 평소에 그가 알던 멘체스터의 모습이 아니었다. 사람들이 오다니기 힘들 정도로 비좁은 골목은 햇빛이 들지 않았으며, 처리되지 않은 오수로 뒤덮여 있었고 쥐들이 들끓고 있었고 그 환경에서 노동자들이 밀집되어 살고 있었다. 이후 그는 이러한 도시환경을 개선해야겠다는 목표가 생겼고, 직후 마르크스를 만나면서 이러한 생각은 사회주의 이념에 고스란히 녹아 들었다.

결국, 사회주의라고 하는 이념의 발생 배경에는 산업화로 인한 급격한 도시화, 그리고 그 도시화가 낳는 수많은 부작용을 구조적으로 해결을 해보겠다고 하는 의지가 포함되어있었다. 다시 말하면, 사회주의 운동가들에게는 도시화로 인한 문제를 해결하기 위한 체계적인 도시계획이 필요했던 것이고 이는 곧 사회주의 도시계획 이론으로 발전하게 된 것이다. 하지만 결국 이 지점에서 우리가 사회주의 도시와 비사회주의 도시와의 차이점을 크게 찾아내지 못했다.

물론 19세기 유럽의 주요 도시들에서 산업화가 진행됨에 따라 곳곳에서 도시화가 급격히 이루어졌다. 즉, 이전까지는 없었던 속도로 도시가 팽창하기 시작했고 밀도가 높아졌으며 인구는 계속 유입되었다. 새로운 일자리가 계속 생겨났으므로 농촌의 인구는 일자리를 찾아 계속해서 도시로 유입되었고, 교통수단의 발달로 도시는 전에 없던 크기로 팽창할 수 있었다. 때문에 앞서 말한 도시화의 부작용이 생겨났고, 사회주의 운동도 부분적으로는 이를 타개하기 위한 운동이었다. 하지만 우리가 알고 있듯이, 도시라고 하는 것은 하나의 생명체와 같아서, 아픈 곳이 생기면 스스로 치유하는 힘도 가지고 있다. 물론 도시가 실제 살아 움직이며 재생한다는 말이 아니라, 사회 구성원들의 욕구와 생각들을 반영하며 마치 생명체처럼 끊임없이 변화할 수밖에 없는 존재라는 것이다. 따라서 도시화로 인한 문제들이 점점 많이 노출되면 그것을 타개하기 위한 사회 구성원들의 요구가 생겨나고, 결국 도시는 그것을 해결하는 방향으로 변화하게 된다. 즉, 사회주의 도시계획이론을 따르지 않더라도 도시는 그 동안 (비록 그 속도가 느릴지언정) 점차 도시화의 문제점을 해결해 나아가는 방향으로 발전했고, 그 변화한, 또 현재도 변화하고 있는 도시를 지금 이 시점에서 바라보는 우리에게는 특별히 사회주의 도시의 특성이 무엇인지 체감하기는 쉽지 않다.

사회주의 도시의 특성

하지만 앞서 언급하였듯이 사회주의 이념에서는 도시화로 인한 문제를 해결하기 위해서 철저한 도시계획을 바탕으로 문제점을 해결해 나아가야 한다는 것이 당면한 과제였다. 사회주의 도시 계획론에 대한 논의는 사회주의 운동가들 사이에서도 많은 시도와 토론이 있었다. 결국, 하나로 정리된 이론보다는 사회주의 혁명의 핵심이었던 러시아의 모스크바를 위한 마스터플랜이 제정되면서 그것이 이후 사회주의 도시계획 이론을 설명하는 바탕이 되었다. 1935년에 작성된 모스크바 마스터플랜은 기본적으로 에바네저 하워드의 정원의 도시 개념은 그 밑바탕에 깔고 있다. 당시 유럽의 많은 도시는 도시화로 인하여 많은 부작용을 낳고 있었고, 따라서 많은 전문가는 이를 해결하기 위한 새로운 도시 이론을 제시하기에 이르렀다. 하워드의 정원의 도시 역시 이러한 맥락에서 나온 개념이다. 결국, 사회주의 도시계획에서 차용하고 있는 정원의 도시 개념 역시 사회주의 이념을 바탕으로 하고 있기 보다는 도시화로 인한 문제점을 해결하고자 하는 당면 과제를 바탕으로 하고 있다는 점에서 앞서 언급한 "과연 사회주의 도시는 존재하는가"라고 하는 질문은 여전히 논쟁거리일 수밖에 없다.

하지만 우리는 정원의 도시와 사회주의 이념이 갖는 공통분모에 좀 더 집중해 볼 필요가 있다. 정원의 도시는 기본적으로 하나의 도시가 비대해지는 것을 막고자 하는 데서 기본 개념이 시작된다. 하워드는 도시화의 문제점이 '도시'에 있기보다는 비대해지는 도시가 늘어난 인구를 적합한 환경에서 수용하지 못 하는 데에 있다고 보고, 도시의 성장은 도심에서 확장하는 형식이 아니라 일정 규모의 여러 도시가 하나의 도시 네트워크를 구성하는 방식으로 도시의 성장을 계획하고 있다. 이 지점에서 사회주의 이념이 강조하고 있는 도시와 농촌의 구분을 없애자고 하는 개념과 접점이 생기는 것이다. 즉, 사회주의에서 산업화가 발달한 도시는 농촌의 노동력을 착취하는 수탈자일 뿐이다. 때문에 도시 내의 부르주아와 프롤레타리아 계급간의 갈등 구조의 근본은 결국 도시와 농촌의 차별인 것이다. 따라서 사회주의에서는 도시는 인정하되 도시와 농촌의 격차를 최소화하는 것이 중요한 과제였는데, 하워드의 정원의 도시는 그 점에 대한 해결책을 제시하고 있었다. 다시 말하면, 도시의 규모가 일정 규모로 제한된다고 하면 그만큼 농촌과의 격차를 최소화할 수 있음을 의미하는 것이다.

정원의 도시 개념에서 사회주의 운동가들이 택할 수밖에 없던 또 다른 중요한 개념은, 그 이름에서도 알 수 있듯이 '정원'이라는 개념이다. 당시 도시의 밀도는 이전에 비하여 놀라운 속도로 높아지고 있었고, 따라서 '녹지'의 확보는 중요한 도시계획의 화두가 되었다. 르코르뷔지에의 3백만의 도시, 혹은 브아종 계획안 등도 결국 어떠한 도시계획을 제안해야 현재의 도시보다 더 많은 녹지공간을 확보할 수 있는지에 대한 고찰을 그 바탕에 깔고 있는 것이다. 정원의 도시에서의 정원은 브아종 계획에서보다 훨씬 더 큰 규모의 녹지 역할에 대해 이야기하고 있다. 즉, 앞서 이야기한 도시 규모의 제한은 단순히 정책적으로만 제한되는 것이 아니라 도시간에 녹지영역을 두어 물리적인 구조로서 도시의 확장을 제한하고 있다. 따라서 정원의 도시에서는 다른 도시에 비하여 구조적으로 녹지면적이 많을 수 밖에 없는데, 사회주의 운동가들에게는 이 부분이 자신들이 구현하고자 하는 노동자들에게 이상적인 생활환경을 주고자 하는 부분과 상응하는 것이었다. 당시만 하더라도, 도시 속의 녹지 공원이라고 하는 것은 특정 계층을 위한 휴식 공간이었다. 뉴욕의 센트럴 파크만 하더라도 초기에는 아무나 사용할 수 있는 공간이 아니었다. 그곳에 들어가기 위하여는 특정한 드레스 코드를 맞춰야 했으며 공원 안에서의 활동에 대해서 제한되었다. 결국, 사회주의자들에게는 모든 노동자에게 휴식처가 될 수 있는 도심 속의 공원이 필요했고 따라서 정원 속의 도시 개념은 이들이 택하기에 가장 알맞은 개념이었다.

북한의 도시

이러한 개념은 북한의 도시들에도 그대로 적용되었다. 북한의 도시를 살펴보면 크게 두 가지 특성을 지니고 있다. 첫째로는 각각의 도시가 그다지 크지 않다는 것이고 (이는 다른 말로 하면 도시 간 규모 차이가 크지 않다는 것이다), 둘째로는 도시는 하나의 자생구조로 구성되어있다는 점이다. 북한에서 가장 규모가 큰 도시는 물론 평양이다. 평양은 인구 약 3백만의 도시로서 북한 인구의 약 13%를 담당하고 있다. 평양은 북한에서 유일하게 인구 백만이 넘는 도시이다. 인구수로 2위와 3위는 함흥과 청진으로 모두 동해안에 위치하며 각각 76만 명과 66만 명의 인구를 지니고 있다. 이 외의 14개 상위 도시들은 모두 인구수가 20~30만 명으로 비슷한 규모이며, 나머지 10여 개 도시도 인구수 10만 명으로 많은 차이를 보이지는 않는다. 이는 행정구역 서울에만 전체 인구의 25%가량이 집중되고, 서울을 포함한 수도권 도시에 50%, 상위 5개 도시에 전체 인구 50%가 집중되는 한국의 경우와 비교해 보면 많은 차이를 지닌다. 이는 앞서 설명하였듯이, 사회주의 도시계획에서는 도시화하는 경향을 지양하고자 했기 때문이다. 따라서 소수의 도시에 인구를 집중시키기 보다는 자유로운 인구 이동을 제한함으로써 전반적인 도시에 골고루 인구를 분포시켜 국토가 균형 있게 발전되도록 했다. 이는 2, 3위 도시인 함흥과 청진이 평양이 위치한 서해안 쪽이 아니라 동해안에 있는 점과도 일맥상통하는 부분이다.

또한, 북한의 도시는 단순히 우리가 이야기하는 '도시'라고 볼 수는 없다는 점이 특징이다. 앞서 본 바와 같이 평양의 인구는 서울 인구의 1/3에 불과하다. 하지만 그 면적은 서울의 4배인 2,500㎢가 넘는다. 일부의 글에서는 이것을 두고 평양이 서울과 면적 경쟁에서 우월한 위치를 점하고자 행정구역을 재편한 것이라고 해석하는 경우가 있다. 하지만 이는 북한의 도시 구성원리에 대한 이해가 부족해서 나온 해석이 아닐까 한다. 북한에서는 하나의 도시가 자생구조를 갖추는 것을 매우 중요하게 생각한다. 따라서 북한의 도시는 단순히 도시민들의 생활권이나 소비시설만이 있는 것이 아니라 생산영역도 함께 존재하여 하나의 자생 단위를 이루고 있다. 이때 생산영역이란 제조업 등의 공업지역만을 의미하는 것이 아니라 농업생산도 함께 포함하는 개념이다. 북한에서는 생활권과 공업지역을 도시영역으로 규정하고 농업생산지역을 농촌영역으로 보고 있으며, 북한의 도시는 언제나 도시영역과 농촌영역이 공존하고 있는 특징이 있다. 또한, 여기서 재미있는 사실은 한 농촌영역 내에서도 다른 스케일의 도시영역이 존재한다는 사실이다. 결국, 어떠한 규모의 도시영역, 농촌영역이던지 간에 언제나 도시영역은 농촌 기능을 포함하고, 농촌영역은 도시 기능을 포함하고 있다.

이처럼 가장 큰 북한 도시의 두 가지 특징은 모두 정원도시 개념과 일맥상통하며, 이는 도시와 농촌 간의 구분을 최대한 없애고자 했던 사회주의 도시계획이론을 바탕으로 하고 있었기 때문에 가능했던 구성이었다. 즉, 농촌이라고 하는 것은 도시가 잠식해 나아가야 할 대상이 아니라 함께 공존해야 할 대상이었으며, 단순히 농산물이 생산되는 영역이 아니라 도시화를 억제하는 완충 역할을 하는 영역이었다. 물론 이러한 개념은 비효율적인 국토의 이용을 가져오기도 한다. 특정 도시나 지방에 공업을 특화시킨다면 더 효율적인 국토개발이 가능했을 수도 있다. 하지만 이는 효율성이나 생산성보다는 국토 전반에 걸친 '공간의 평등'을 꾀하고자 했던 북한의 이데올로기가 더 크게 작용한 것으로 보인다.

사회주의 도시론이 우리에게 주는 의미

아주 간단하게 살펴보긴 하였지만, 사회주의 도시론이 추구하는 도시의 모습, 혹은 북한 도시가 갖는 구성상의 특징은 우리가 흔히 알고 있는 도시의 모습과는 사뭇 다르다. 하지만 이 다르다고 하는 점이 그대로 그것의 장점이 되거나, 우리의 도시가 문제가 있다고 해서 다른 도시 모델을 아무런 필터링 없이 받아들여도 된다는 말은 아니다. 사회주의 도시론은 개인 섹터의 투자나 개발은 배제되고 공공 섹터에서 모든 것을 담당한다. 이는 우리가 잘 알고 있듯이 개별의 정체성이나 요구사항을 민첩하게 수용하지 못한 채로 도시가 구성되어 나아간다는 문제점을 낳는다. 또한 북한의 도시에서처럼 모든 것이 균등하게 분포되어 각각의 도시에 비슷한 시설과 용도가 분포하고 있다면, 비효율적인 비용도 엄청날 것이다. 하지만 우리가 이 모델에서 배울 점은 분명히 있다.

첫째로 '도시와 농촌이 공생하는 모델'을 배울 수 있다. 최근 들어 서울을 포함한 많은 선진 도시들에서 '도시농업'이라는 개념을 통해, 어떻게 하면 도시 내에서 농산물을 생산하고 소비할 것인가에 대한 노력이 생겨나고 있다. 어떤 경우에는 단순히 유통망 개선을 통하여 소극적으로 대처하는 경우도 있고, 또 어떤 경우에는 건물의 옥상이나 도시의 자투리 땅에서 간단한 농작이 가능하도록 하여 이곳의 농산물들이 바로 도시 내에서 소비되도록 하는 등의 적극적인 노력을 하는 경우도 있다. 심지어는 MVRDV처럼 돼지농장건물을 아이디어로 내놓는 경우까지 있다. 하지만 방법론적인 부분을 떠나 개념상으로 도시와 농촌의 공존은 이미 사회주의 도시론에서 나왔으며 실천되었다. 물론 이들은 단순히 도시와 농촌이 평면상으로 공존하게 함으로써 그 개념을 현실화했지만, 그들의 생활 방식을 통하여 좀 더 적극적으로 도시와 농촌이 공존한다는 것이 과연 어떠한 새로운 도시 생활, 혹은 도시 풍경이 생겨날지 생각해보는 것도 중요할 것이다. 왜냐하면, 앞서 언급했듯이 사회주의 도시에서의 농경지는 단순한 농산물이 생산되는 영역이 아니라, 확장되는 도시화로 인한 문제를 예방해주는 완충공간이고, 이는 도시화 문제의 해결책으로서 도입될 수도 있기 때문이다.

둘째로 '공간의 평등'에 대한 개념은 우리가 반드시 생각해보아야 할 이슈가 아닌가 한다. 이 공간의 평등이 실제 사회주의 도시, 혹은 북한의 도시에서 현실화되었는가 하는 부분은 논쟁이 될만한 소재이긴 하지만, 중요한 것은 오히려 그 개념이다. 사회주의 도시에서는 도시와 농촌의 평등을 추구하기도 했지만, 도시 내에서의 공간의 평등을 이루고자 하는 개념도 있었다. 따라서 적어도 개념적으로는, 어떤 특정한 지역에 가야만 더 많은 문화시설이 있고, 더 좋은 공원이 있는 것이 아니다. 또한, 특정 지역에만 공장 지역이 몰려있어 그곳은 살기 열악한 지역이 되는 것도 아니다. 이러한 기능들을 도시 내에서 비교적 균등하게 분포시킴으로써 공간의 불평등을 최소화시키고자 했다. 따라서 생산시설이 주거와 함께 구성되며 여타 교육 및 봉사시설 등이 함께 구성되는 마이크로 디스트릭트 개념이 나오게 된 것이며, 공원 및 광장, 그리고 문화시설 등도 고르게 분포되어야 한다고 본 것이다. 우리는 언젠가부터 너무나도 당연히 '좋은 동네 (혹은 잘사는 동네)', '나쁜 동네 (혹은 못사는 동네)'가 있는 것을 당연시했던 것 같다. 물론 동네, 혹은 지역별로 개성은 존중되어야 한다. 하지만 그 개성이라고 하는 것이 공간의 불평등에서 나온다고 한다면, 다시 생각해보아야 할 문제이다. 기능의 고른 분포를 통해 공간의 평등을 실천할 수 있다면 우리의 도시가 훨씬 성숙해지지 않을까 생각한다.

결론적으로, 우리 사회는 현재 여타 유럽의 선진국들처럼 사회주의에서 근원을 찾을 수 있는 개념들을 조금씩 도입함으로써 발전하고 있다. 분명히 지금 한국 사회는 이전 사회보다 물질적으로 풍요롭고, 더 많은 사회주의 개념의 차용은 사회를 더욱 성숙시키고 있다. 아마도 이제는 이러한 변화의 결과물로서 도시의 변화된 모습을 상상해볼 시기라고 볼 수 있을 것이다. 도시는 사회의 요구, 패러다임의 변화, 기술의 진보 등으로 늘 변화해 왔으며 현재도 변화를 거듭하고 있다. 그렇다고 하면, 현재 우리가 미래의 도시를 계획할 때에는 현재 사회의 요구가 어떻게 변화하고 있는지를 보면 되는 것이다. 결국, 우리가 풀어야 할 숙제는 어떻게 하면 우리의 도시가 사회주의 도시보다 우월한가 보여주는 것이 아니라, 사회주의 도시 모델을 어떻게 우리의 도시에 맞는 모습으로 도입할 것인가 이다.

CONCEPT OF CITY DIVISIONS

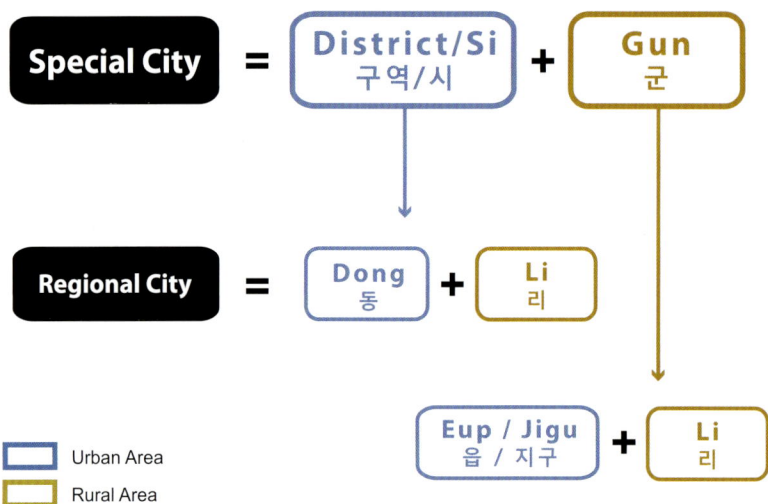

*Source: 김병로, <북한지역개발 현황과 과제 발표자료> 중

The basic concept of structuring a North Korean city is making it as one single cell that can sustain itself without depending on other cities. It is important to have function of production within a city. In this case, the production is not limited to the manufacturing production but also includes the agricultural area. Therefore, a North Korean city is always composed with both urban/industrial area and rural/agricultural area. The concept met well with the idea of socialist urban planning, which tried to abolish the difference between urban and rural area. So by providing administrative boundary of urban area that includes rural, there is not much difference between them. Also, the idea of urban-rural combination is kept in rural area as well. It means that even in a rural area, there are parts that has a character of "urban", which is for consumption and manufacturing.

북한의 도시 구조를 구성하는 가장 기본적인 개념은, 하나의 도시를 다른 도시에 의존하지 않고 자생할 수 있는 독립적인 세포구조를 갖추도록 하는 것이다. 따라서 도시 내에 소비시설 뿐만 아니라 생산시설을 갖추게 하는 것이 중요하다. 이 경우에 있어서 생산시설이란 단순히 제조업을 의미하는 것이 아니라 농업생산도 포함하는 개념이다. 따라서 북한의 도시는 항상 도시/상공업지대와 농촌/농업지대로 구성되어있다. 이 개념은 사회주의 도시계획이론과도 잘 맞아떨어지는데, 이는 도시와 농촌의 구분을 없애고자 하는 개념이었다. 결국 도시의 행정구역내에 농촌의 영역을 포함시킴으로서 도시와 농촌사이의 차이는 줄어들게 되는 것이다. 또한 도시-농촌 조합은 농촌에서도 잘 반영된다. 즉, 농촌 영역내에서도 다시금 "도시"의 영역이 존재하여 소비와 제조를 담당하는 영역이 존재하는 것이다.

ADMINISTRATIVE DIVISIONS

North Hamgyong
1 Special City (Rason) + 3Si
+ 7District + 12Gun

Ryanggang
1Si + 11Gun

Jagang
3Si + 15Gun

North Pyongan
1 Special District (Shinuiju) +
3Si + 22Gun

South Hamgyong
3Si + 7District + 1Gu
+ 1Jigu + 15Gun

South Pyongan
1 Special City (Nampo) +
5Si + 1 Gu + 2 Jigu + 19Gun

Pyongyang Special City
14District + 2Gun

Kangwon
2Si + 15Gun

South Hwanghae
1Si + 19Gun

North Hwanghae
1 Special City (Kaesung) +
2Si + 16Gun

DISTRICT(SI) / GUN (4 SPECIAL CITIES)
구역(시) / 군

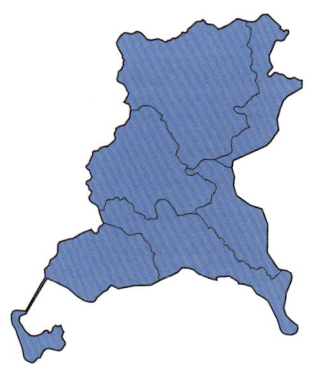

NAMPO

6 District

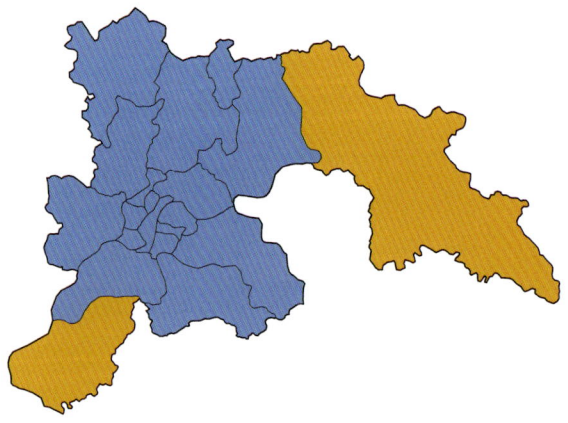

PYONGYANG

14 District + 2 Gun

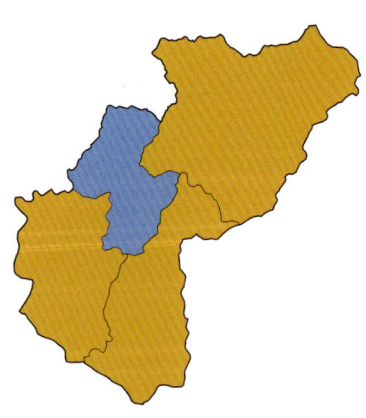

KAESONG

1 Si + 3 Gun

RASON

1 District + 1 Gun

DONG / JIGU / LI (4 SPECIAL CITIES)
동 / 지구 / 리

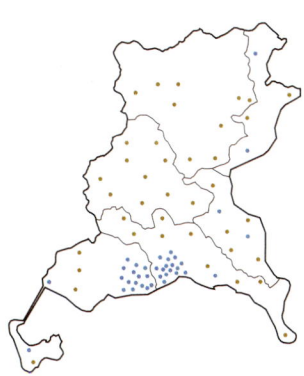

NAMPO

32 Dong + 41 Li

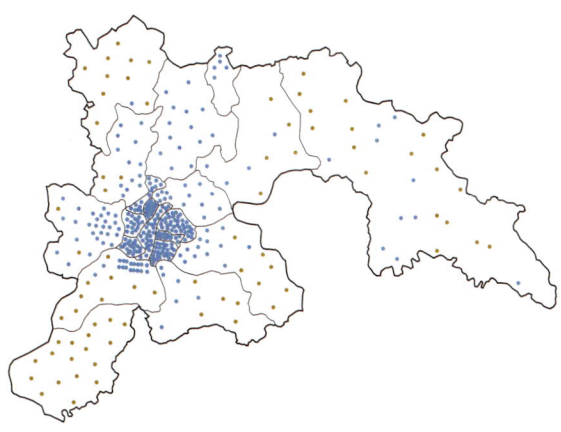

PYONGYANG

249 Dong + 10 Jigu + 74 Li

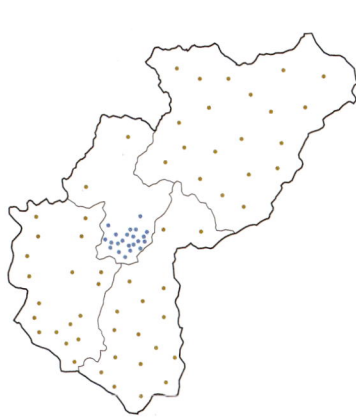

KAESONG

21 Dong + 57 Li

RASON

10 Dong + 1 Jigu + 14 Li

03 NORTH KOREAN CITIES
1. TABLES OF NORTH KOREAN CITIES
2. 8 MAJOR NORTH KOREAN CITIES
3. 19 SUPPORTING NORTH KOREAN CITIES

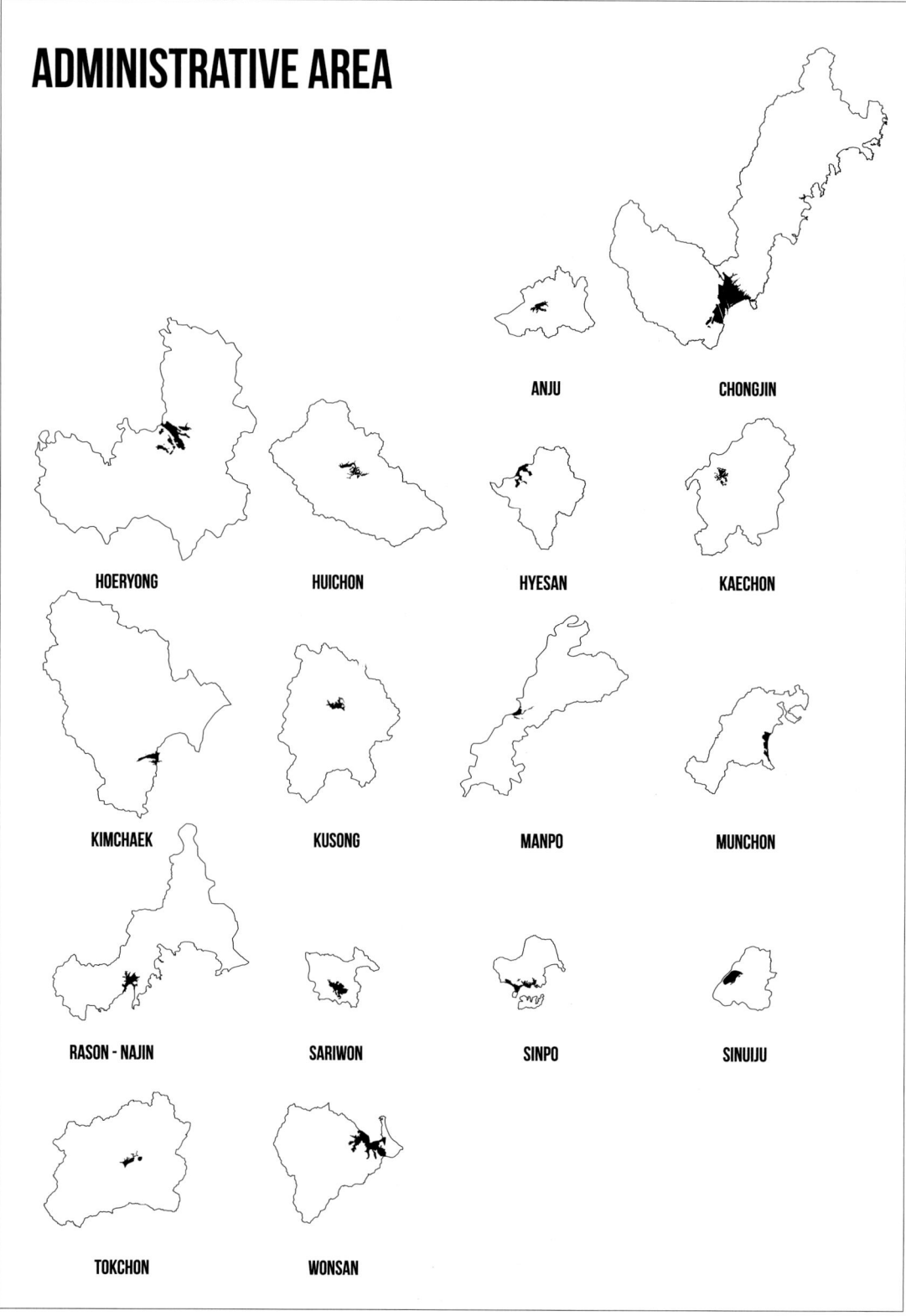

Tables of North Korean Cities

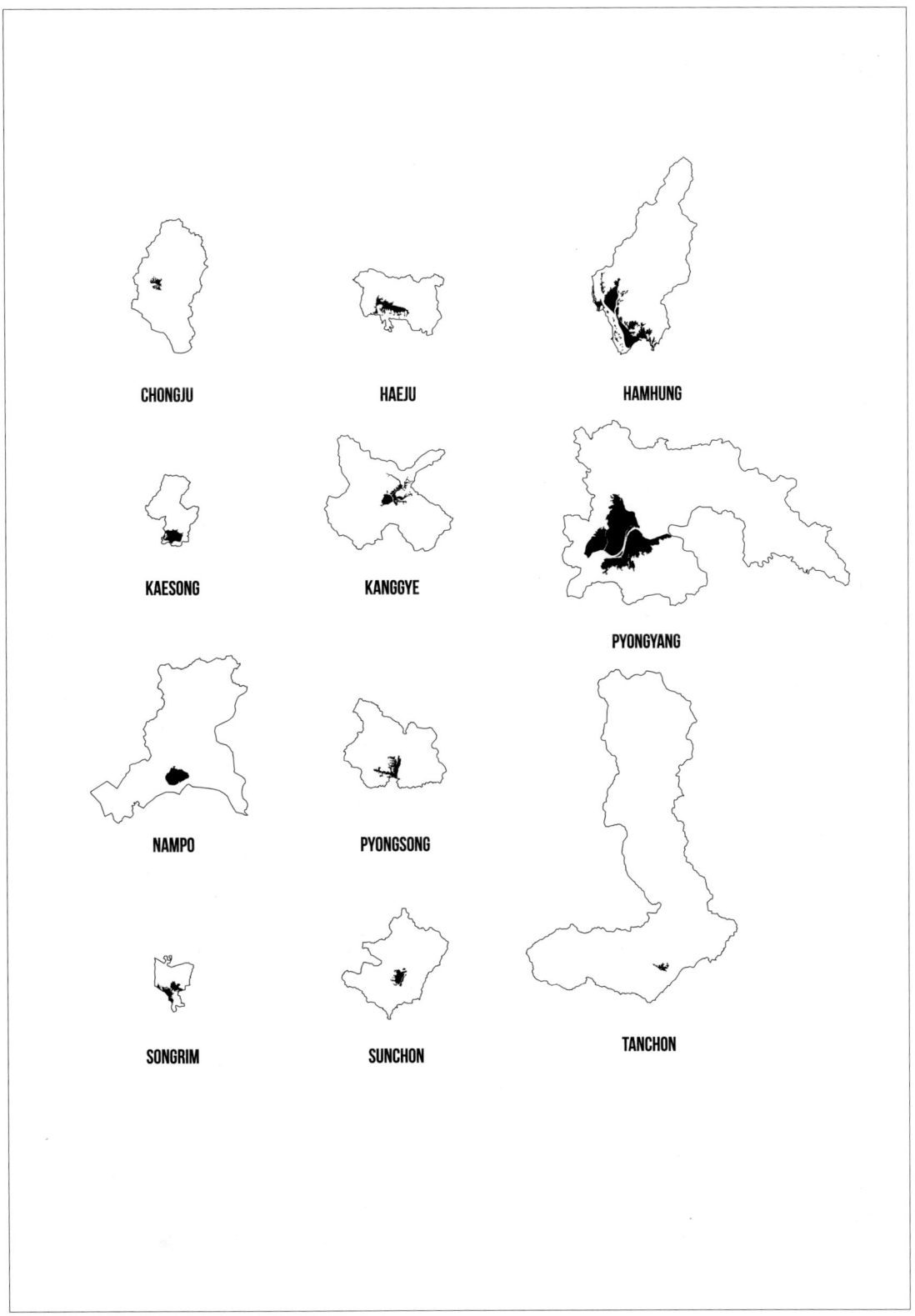

Tables of North Korean Cities

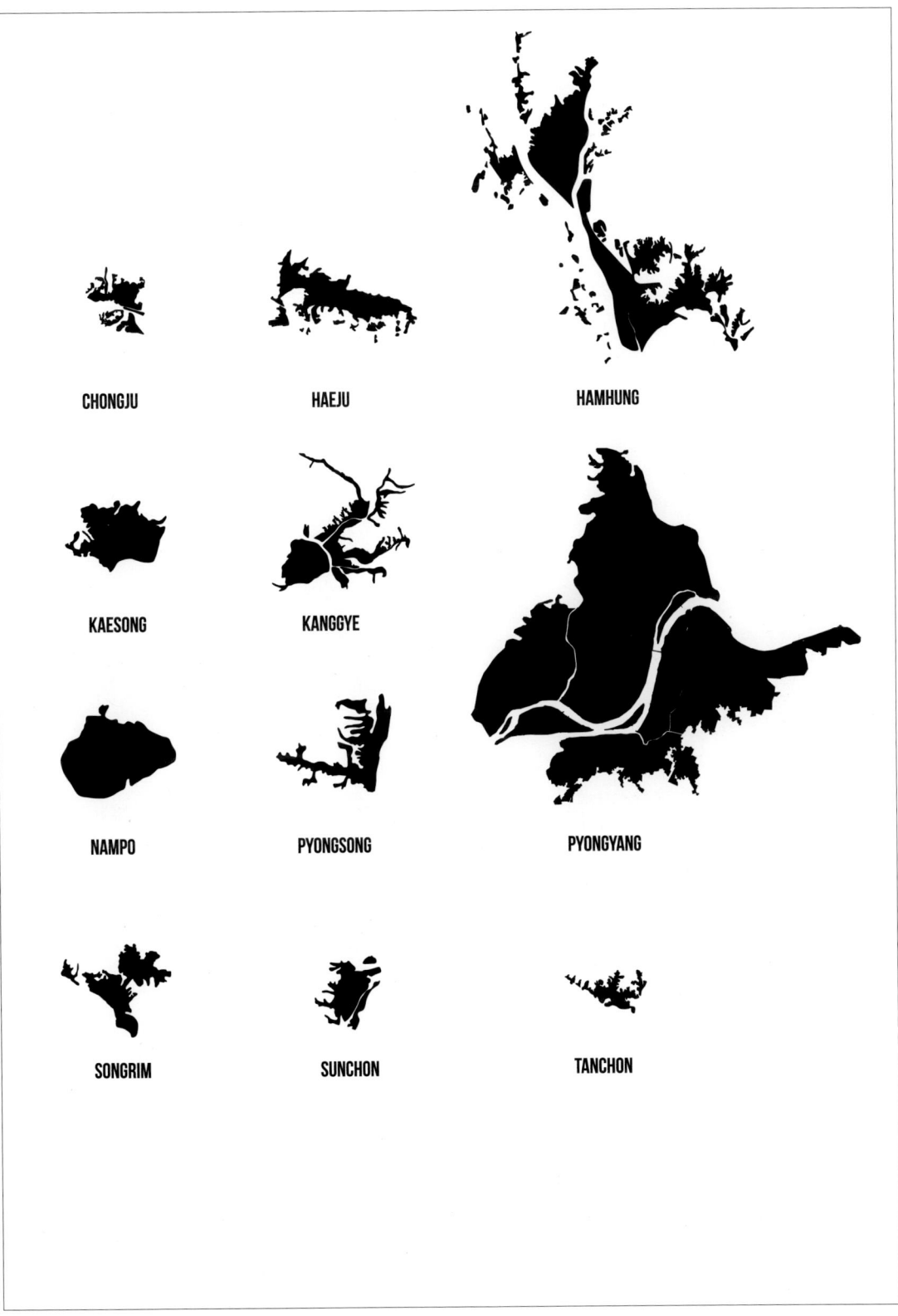

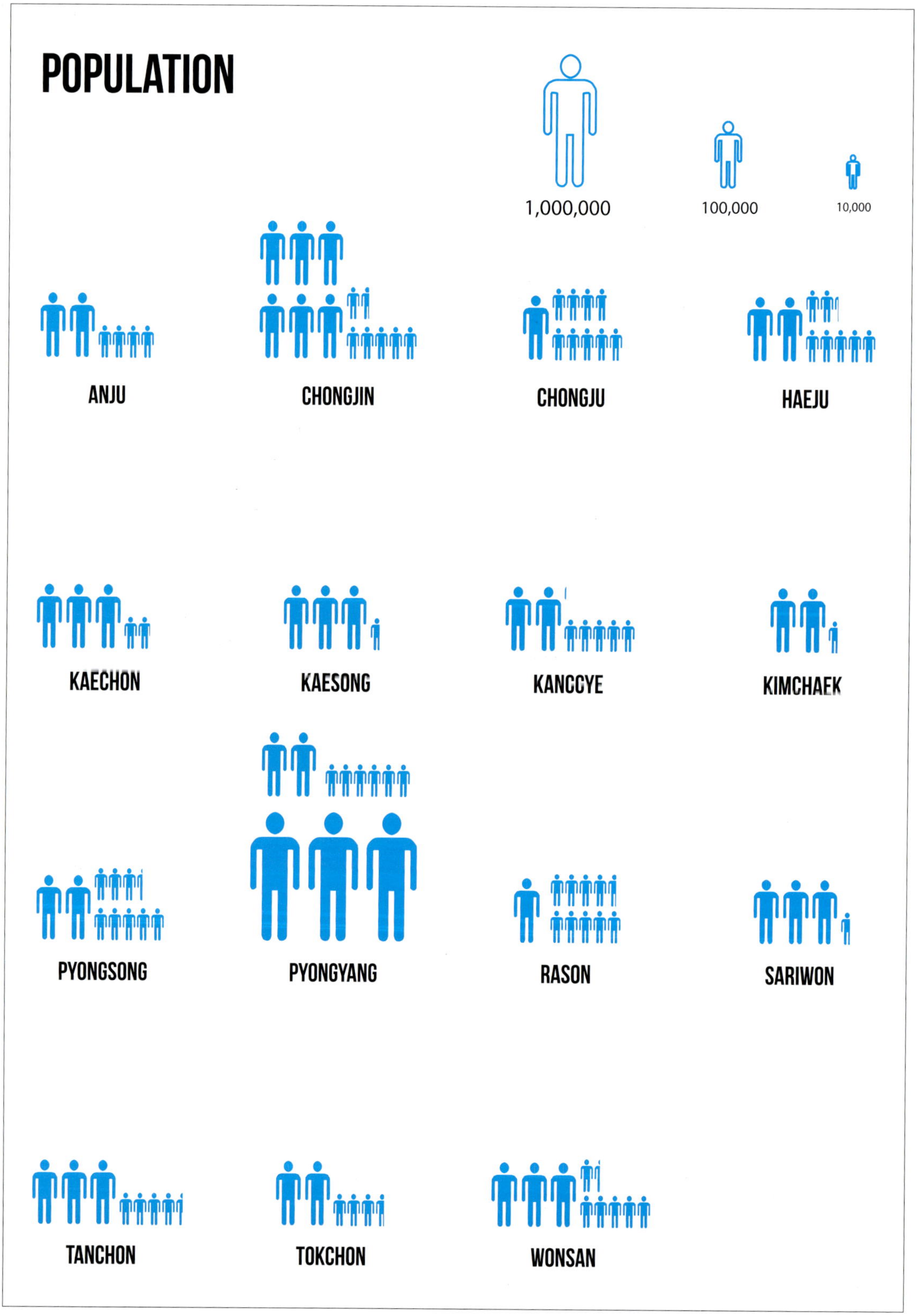

POPULATION

| | 1,000,000 | 100,000 | 10,000 |

ANJU

CHONGJIN

CHONGJU

HAEJU

KAECHON

KAESONG

KANGGYE

KIMCHAEK

PYONGSONG

PYONGYANG

RASON

SARIWON

TANCHON

TOKCHON

WONSAN

Tables of North Korean Cities

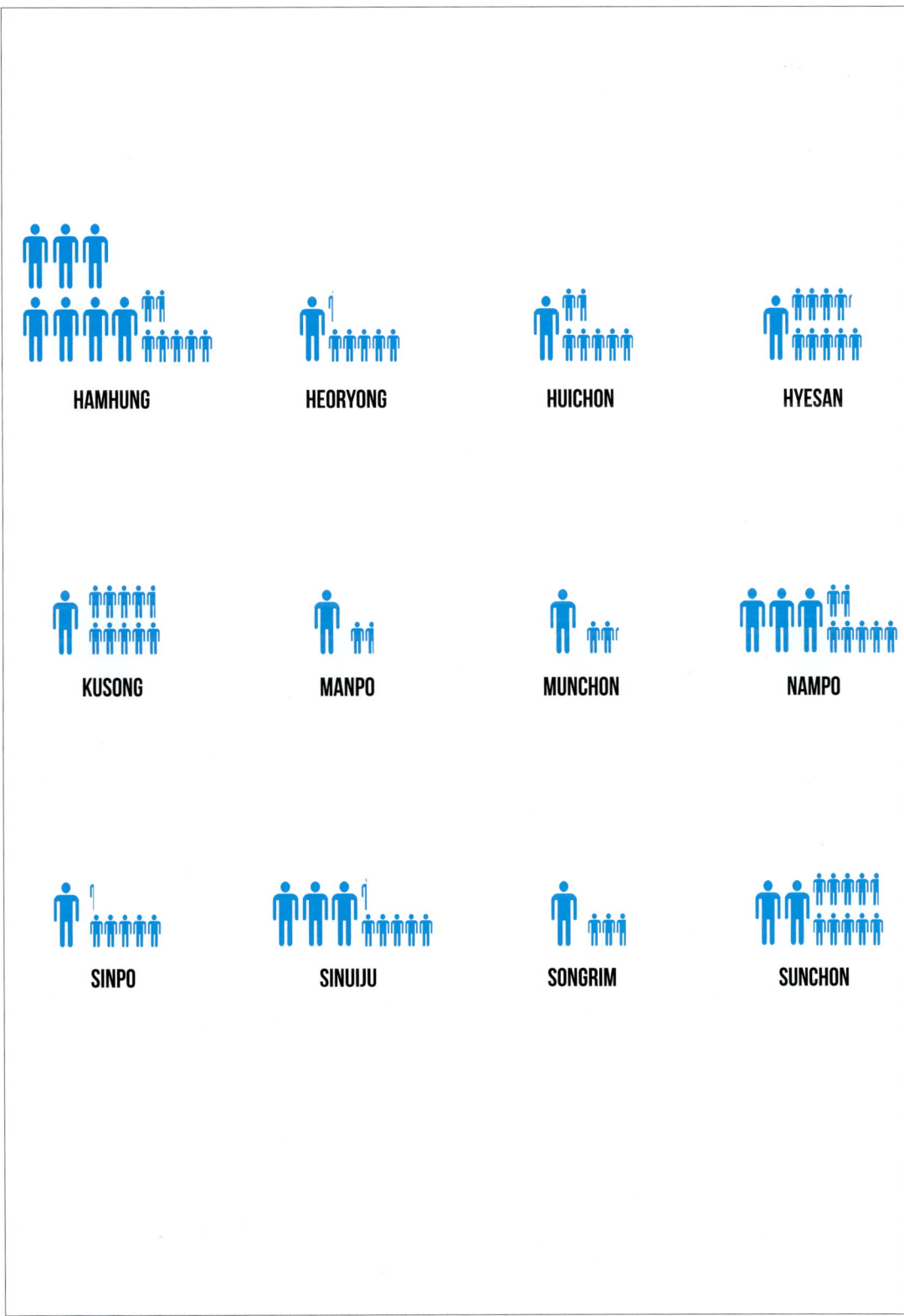

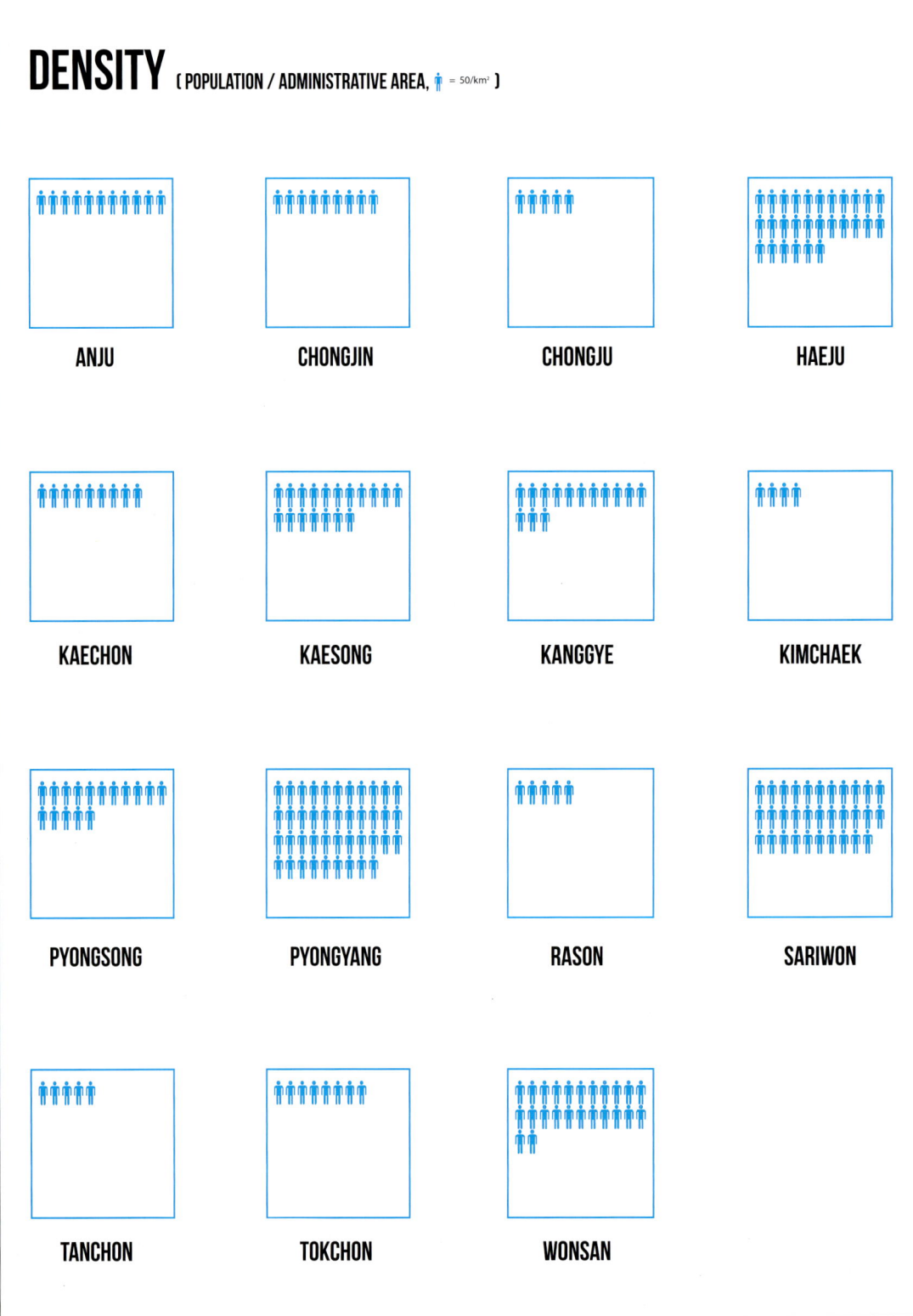

Tables of North Korean Cities

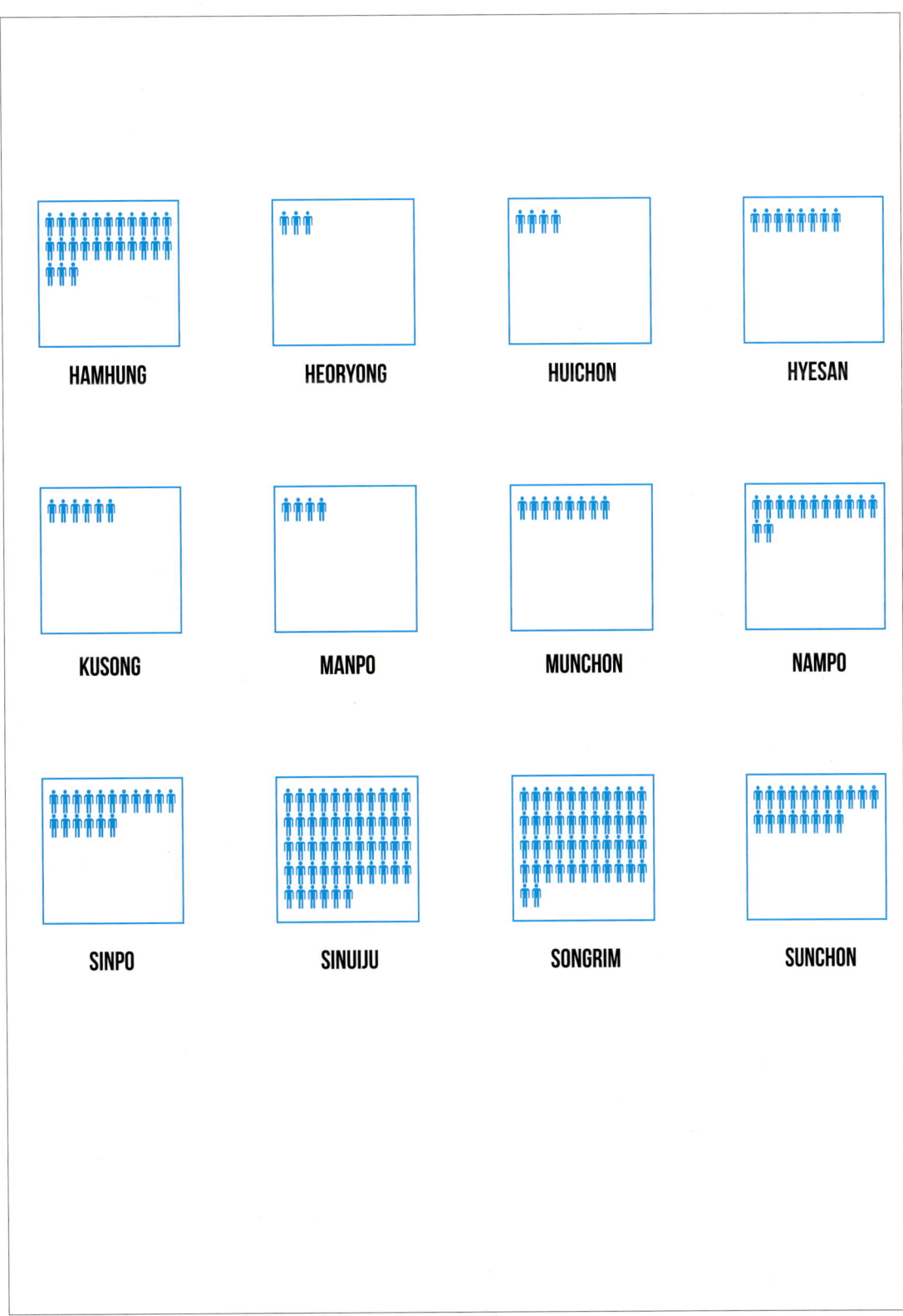

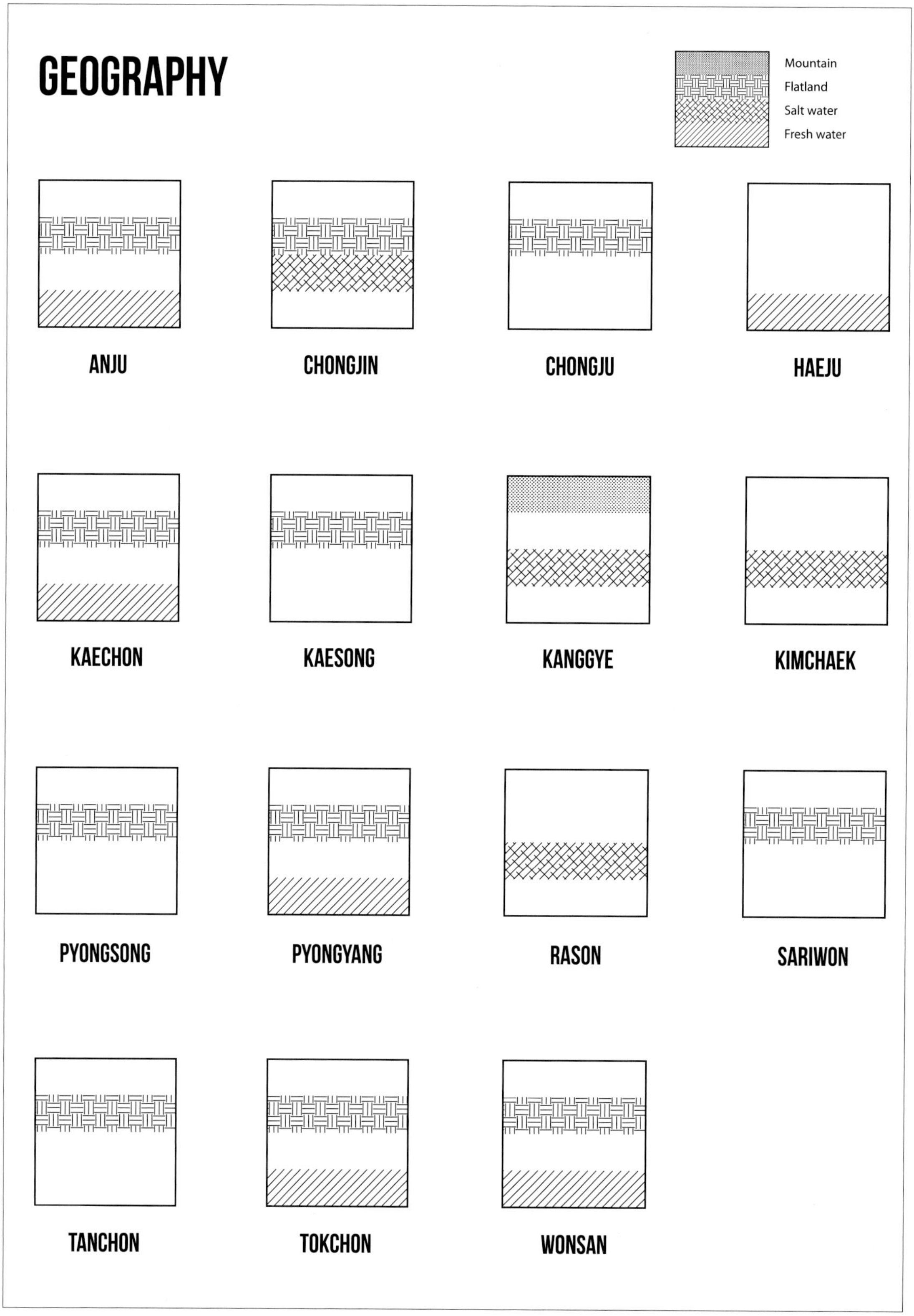

GEOGRAPHY

Mountain
Flatland
Salt water
Fresh water

ANJU

CHONGJIN

CHONGJU

HAEJU

KAECHON

KAESONG

KANGGYE

KIMCHAEK

PYONGSONG

PYONGYANG

RASON

SARIWON

TANCHON

TOKCHON

WONSAN

Tables of North Korean Cities

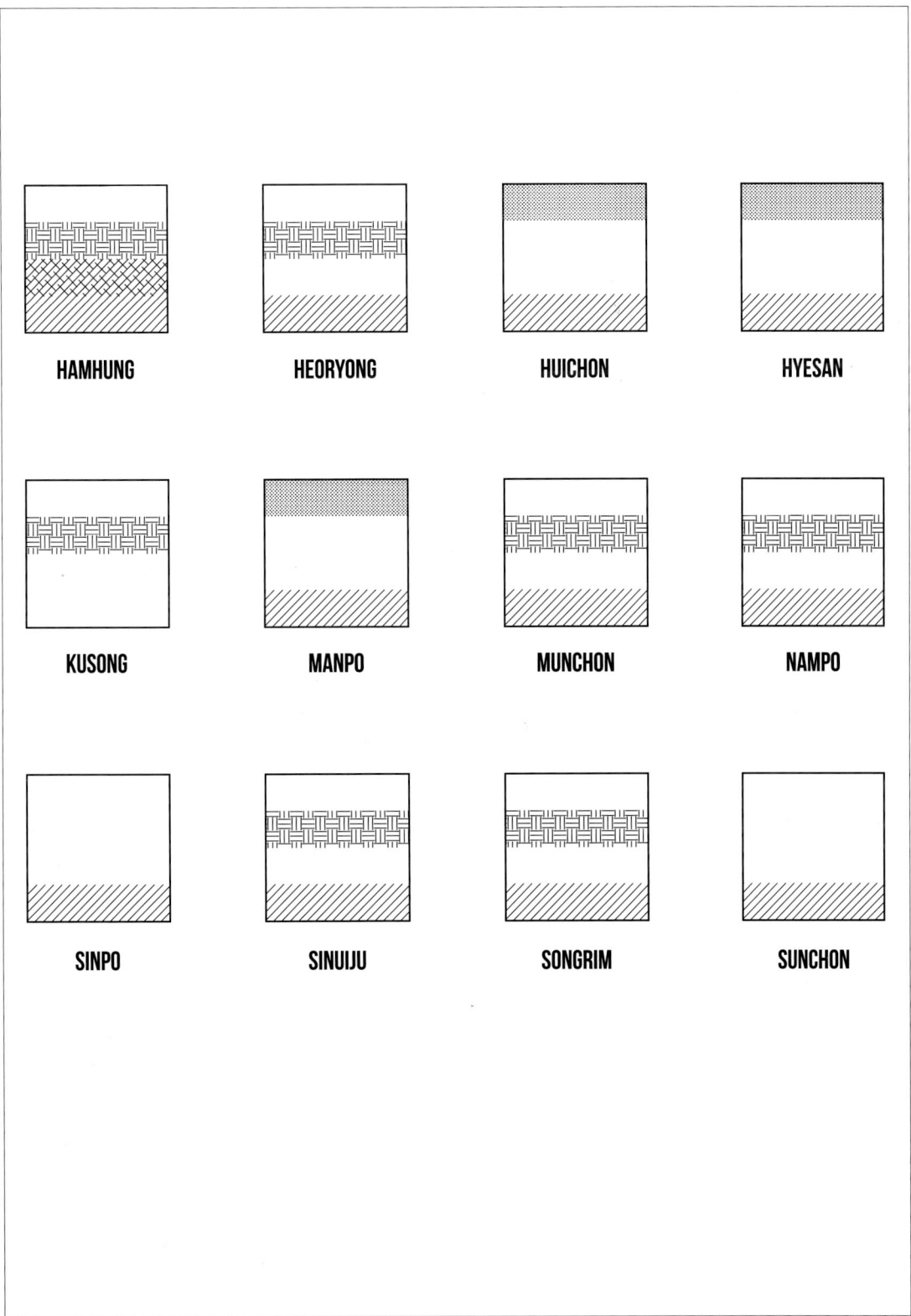

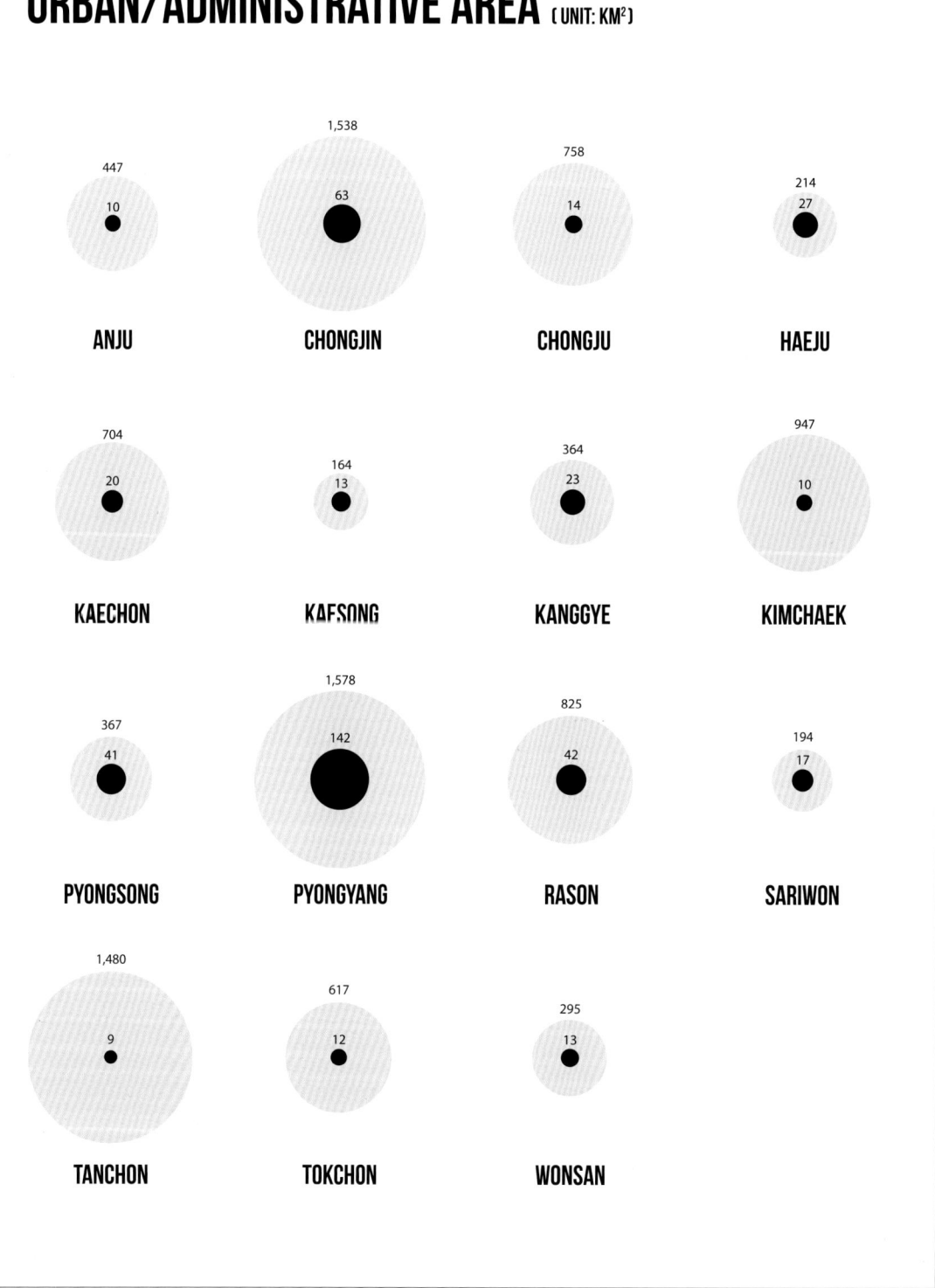

Tables of North Korean Cities

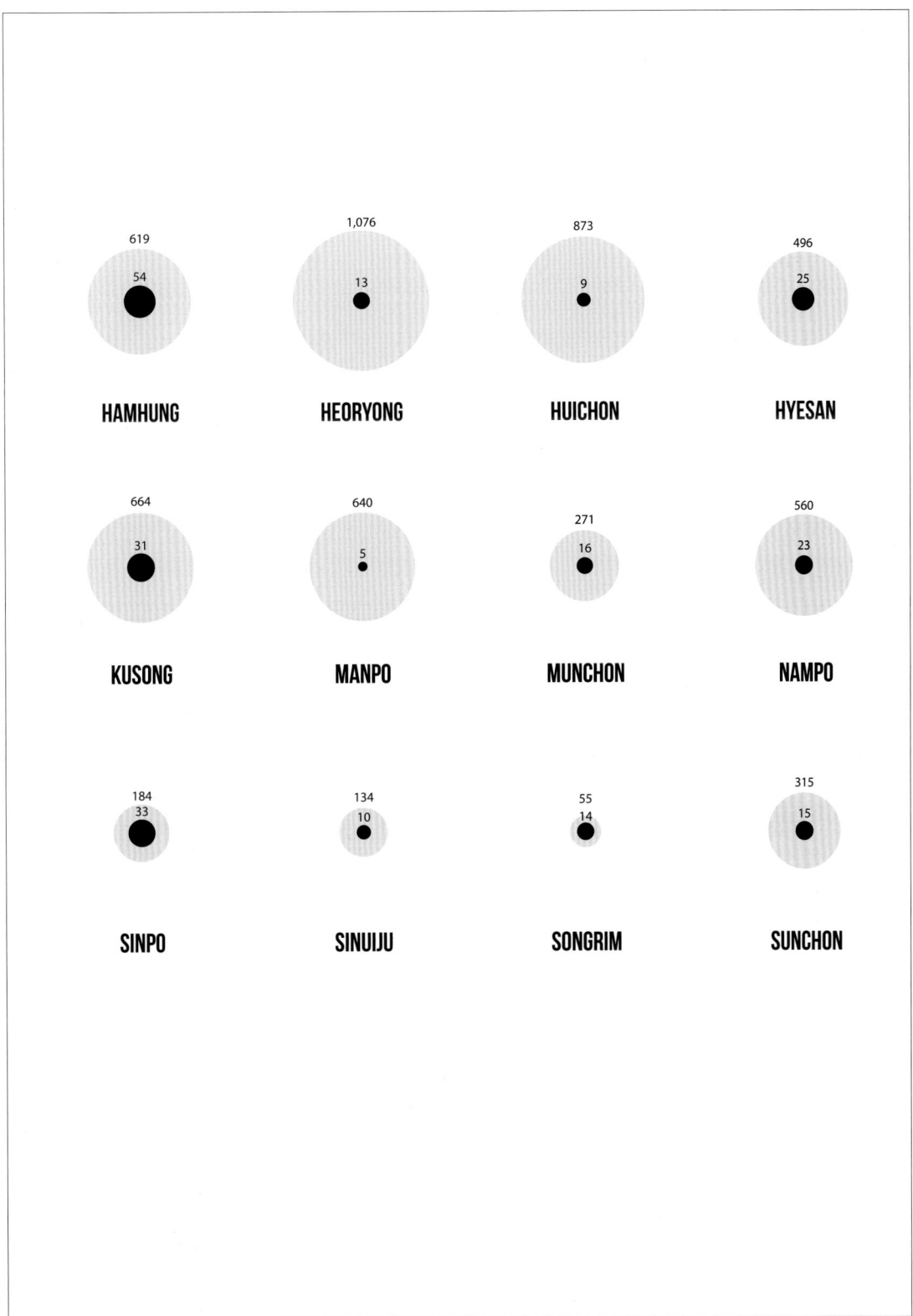

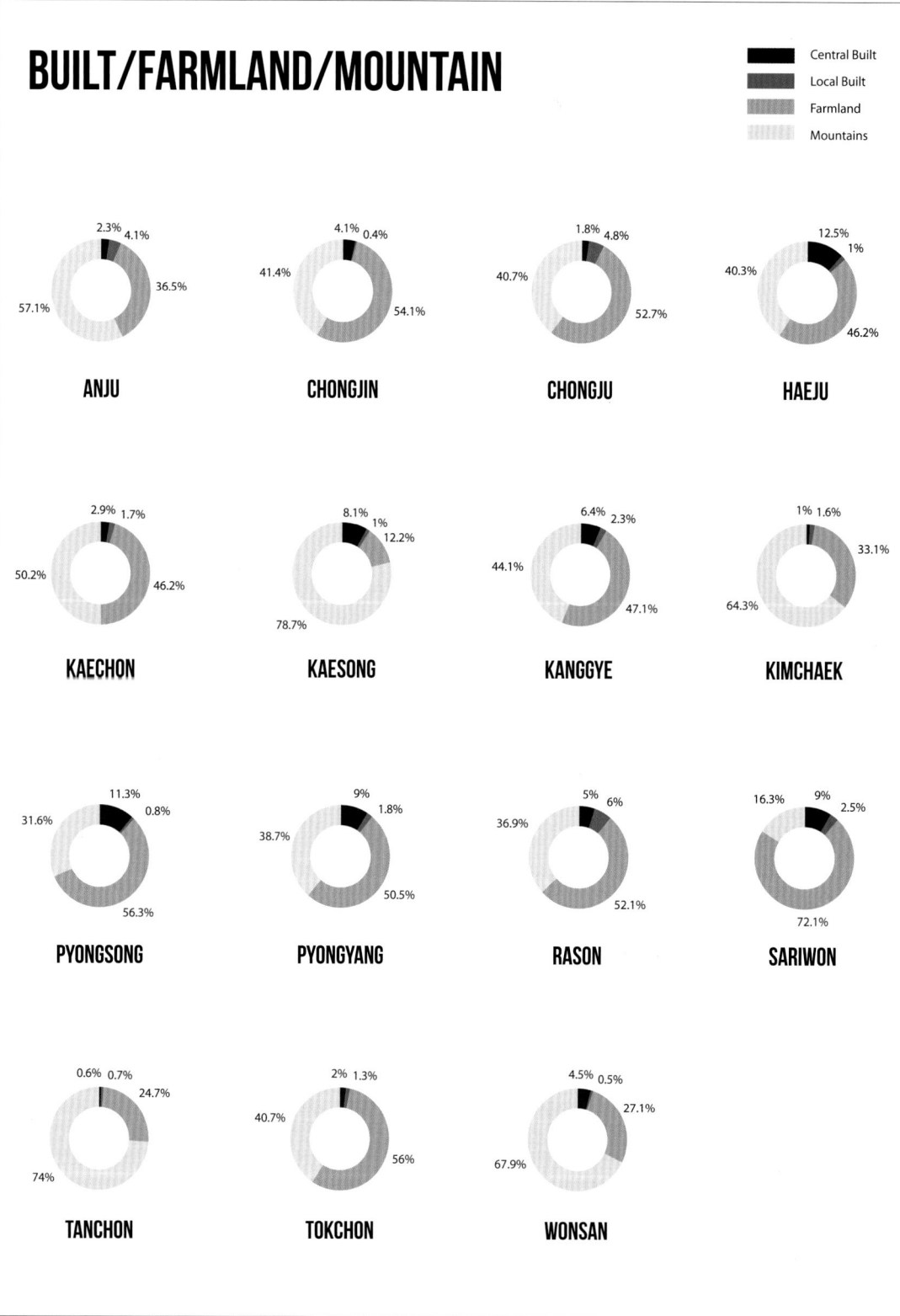

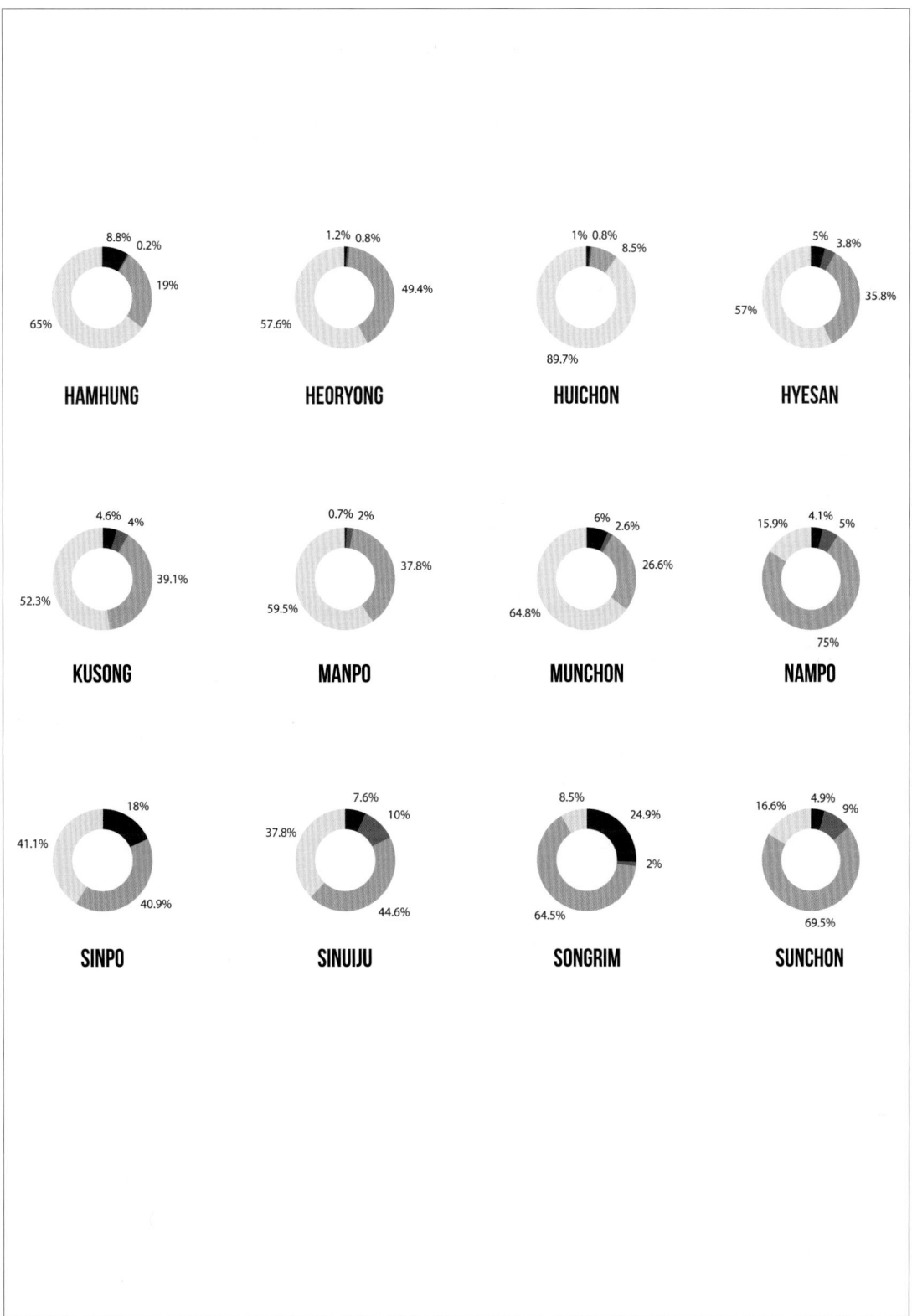

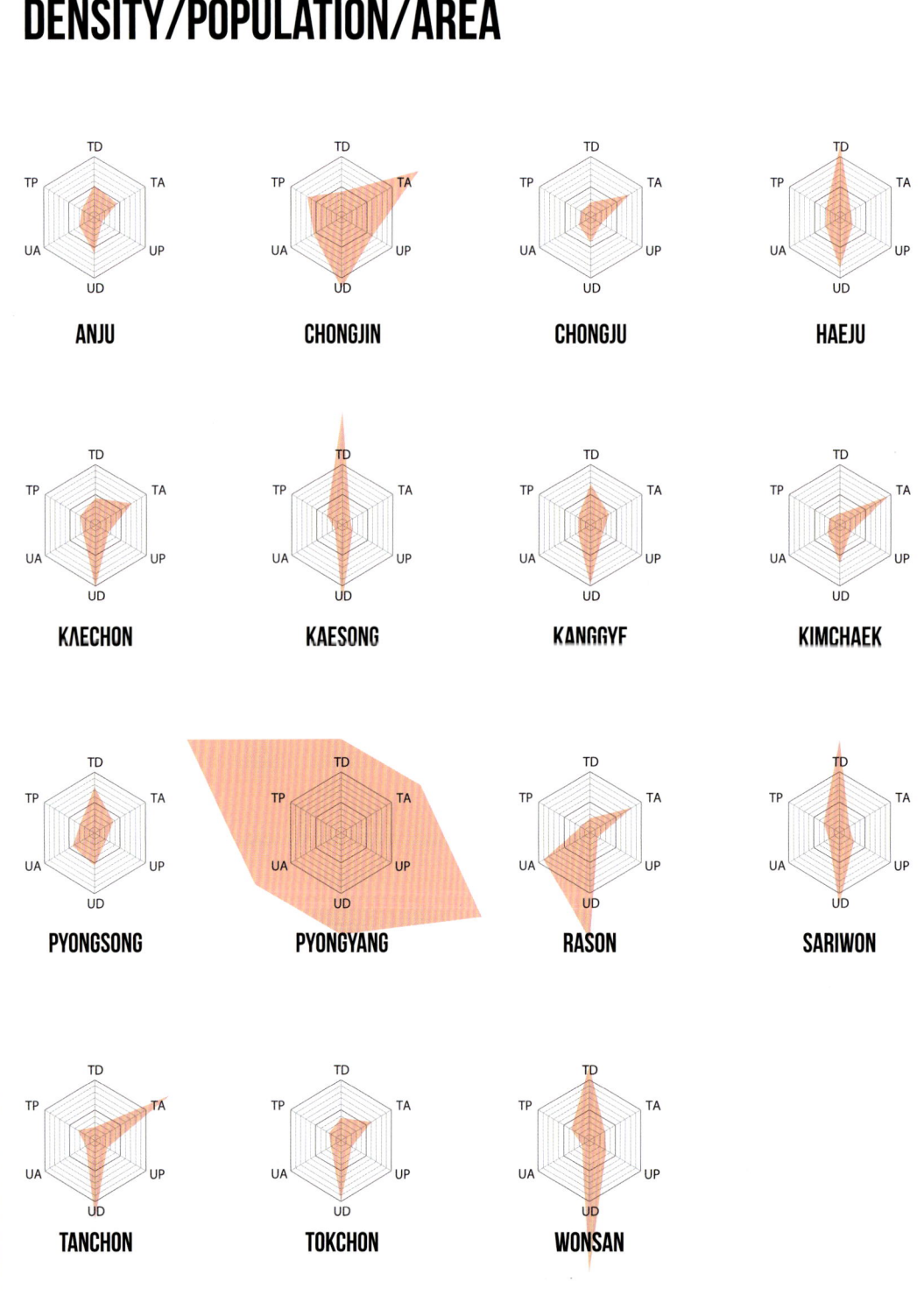

Tables of North Korean Cities

TD - Total density (1000 / km2)   UD - Urban density (10,000 / km2)
TP - Total population (1,000,000) UP - Urban population (1,000,000)
TA - Total area (1,000 km2)   UA - Urban area (100 km2)

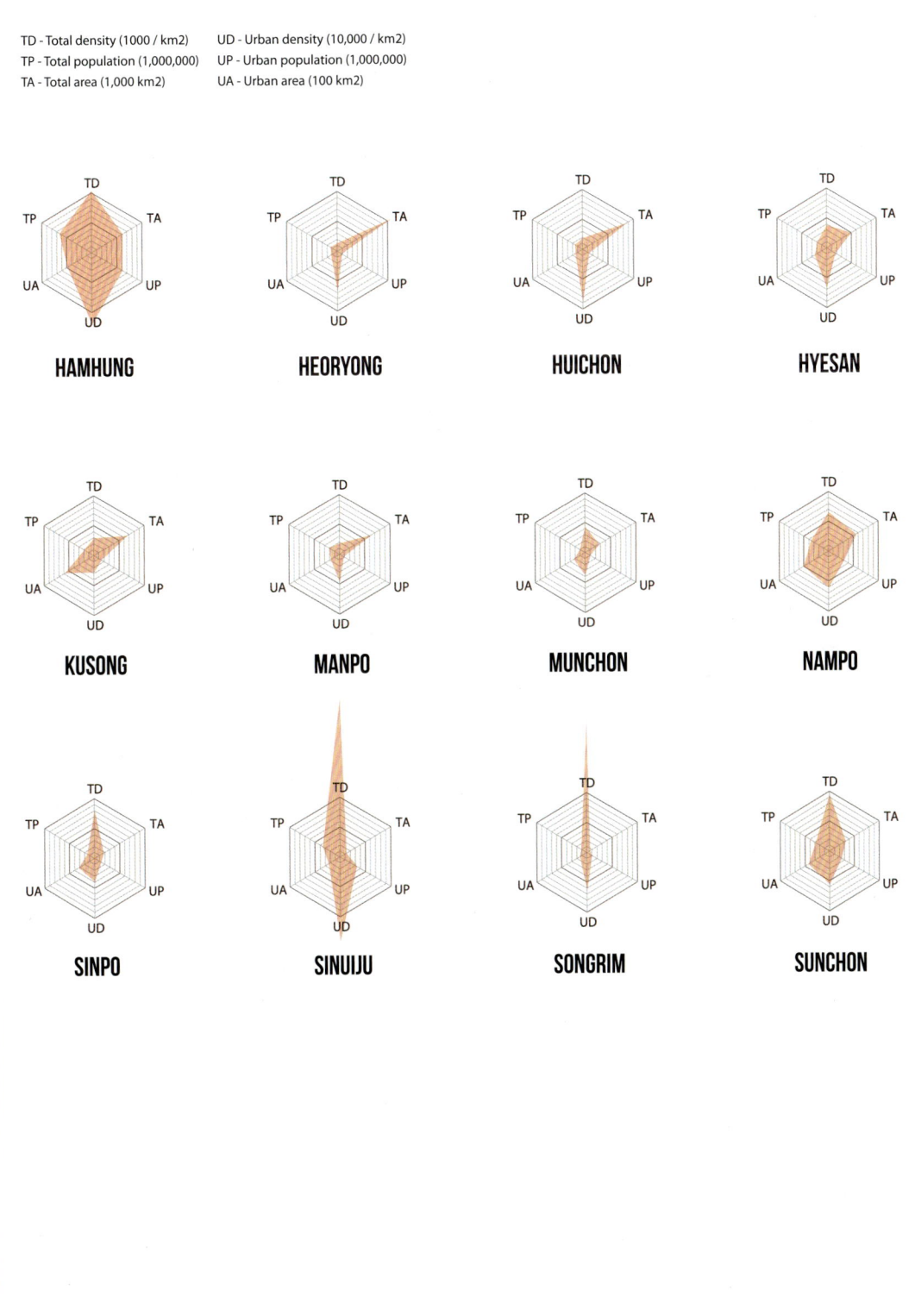

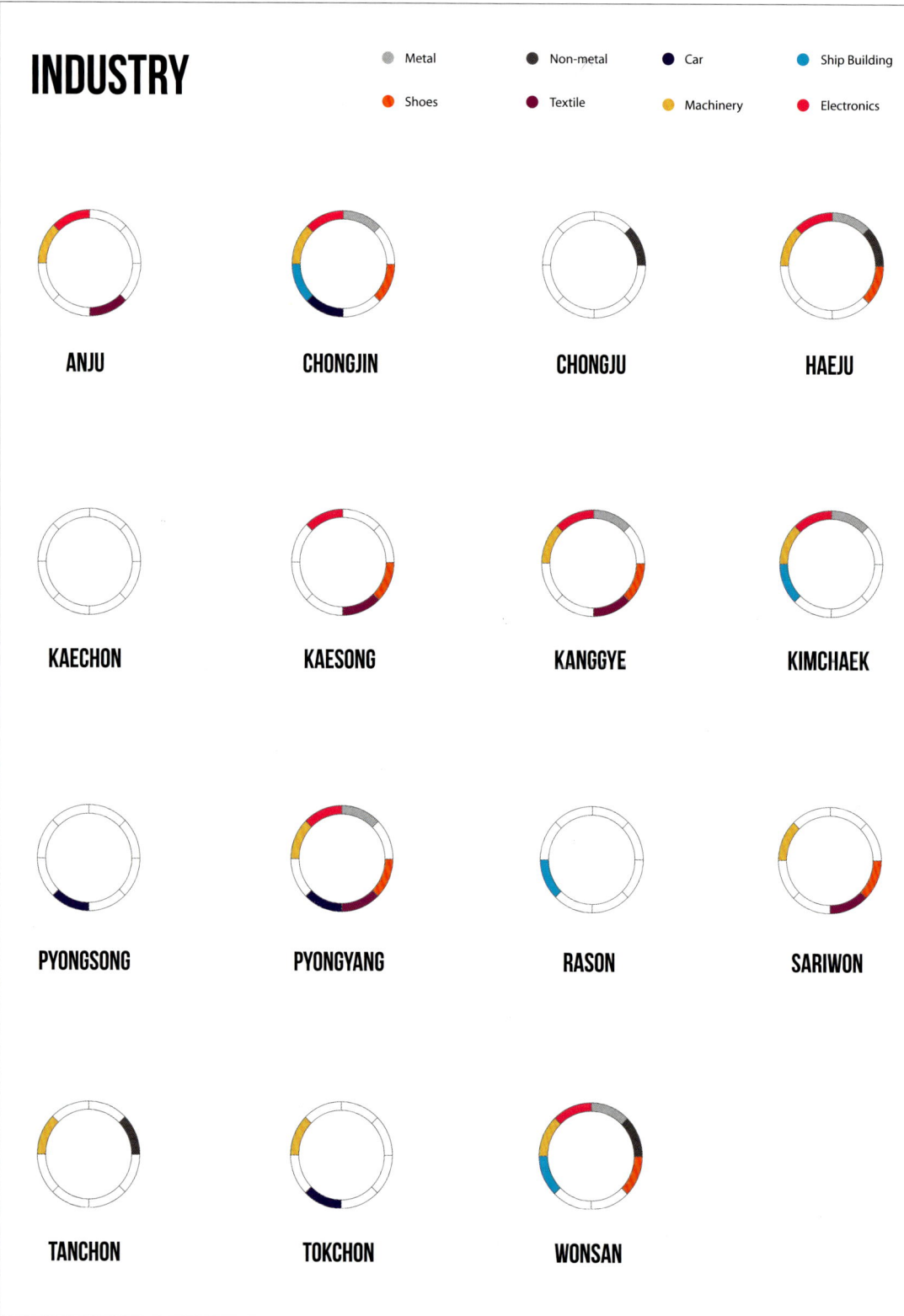

Tables of North Korean Cities

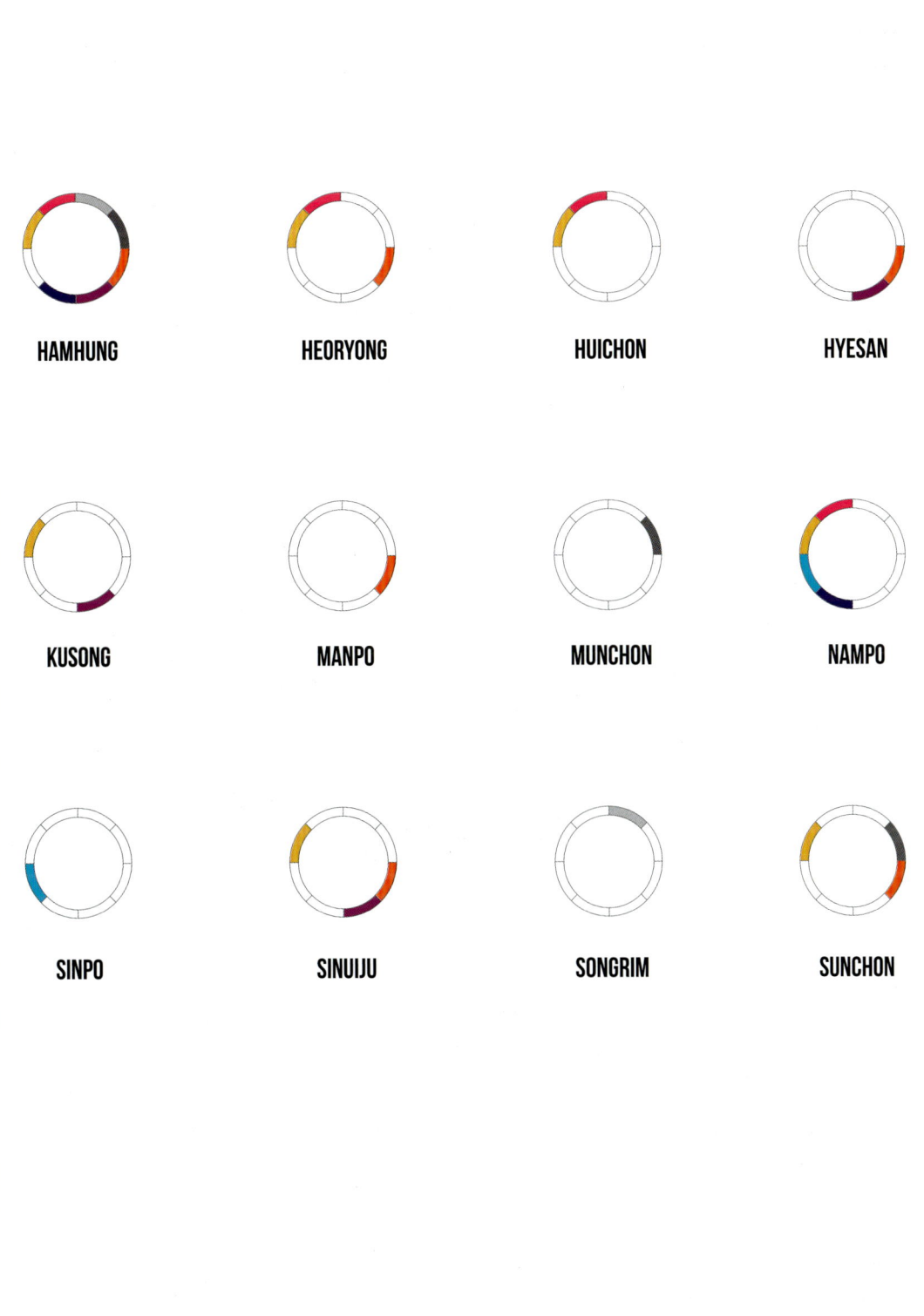

03 NORTH KOREAN CITIES
1. TABLES OF NORTH KOREAN CITIES
2. 8 MAJOR NORTH KOREAN CITIES
3. 19 SUPPORTING NORTH KOREAN CITIES

8 MAJOR CITIES 8개 주요 도시

- ✈ **MAJOR AIRPORT** 주요 공항 — MAP
- 🚢 **SEAPORT** 항구 — PORT
- 🏭 **FACTORY** 공장 — FAC
- 🏛 **THEATER / PUBLIC HALL** 극장 / 공공 회관 — CUL
- ✈ **LOCAL AIRPORT** 지역 공항 — LAP
- 🚆 **TRAIN STATION** 지하철 역 — RAIL
- 🏢 **COMPANY** 산업체 — CO
- 🏥 **HOSPITAL** 병원 — HOSP
- ✈ **AIRFIELD** 비행장 — AF
- 🏫 **INSTITUTION** 교육기관 — EDU
- 🏟 **STADIUM / SPORTS FACILITIES** 경기장 / 운동 시설 — SPOR

* The number of key factors in each city is calculated by the base of the major or identifiable buildings indicated in *Encyclopedia of North Korean Geography and Culture*.

* Source: *Encyclopedia of North Korean Geography and Culture*.

POPULATION 인구
Inhabitants 거주자
% Urban % 도시
% Rural % 농촌
% Male % 남
% Female % 여

POPULATION DENSITY 인구 밀도
Inhabitants 거주자
Administrative Area (km^2) 행정 구역 (km^2)
Population Density (inhabitants/km^2) 인구 밀도 (거주자 수 / km^2)

URBAN DENSITY 도시 인구 밀도
Inhabitants 거주자
Urban Area (km^2), Central built 시가지 (km^2)
Population Density (inhabitants/km^2) 도시 인구 밀도 (거주자 수 / km^2)

* Source: National report *DPR Korea 2008 population census*.

GEOGRAPHY 지리
% Built (Central+ Local) % 시가지
% Farmland % 농촌지
% Mountains % 산악지

* The percentage of each geographical elements in each city.

POTENTIAL GROWTH 잠재 성장률
Urbanized Area (km^2) 시가지 면적
% Area Increase 면적 증가율
Urban Population 도시 인구
% Population Increase 인구 증가율
Max. Population (million) 최대 가능 인구

* Urbanized Area = Farmland+Built Area
Urban Population = Rural+Urban Population
Max. Population = (Urban Density) x (Built + Farmland Area)

CENSUS HEXAGRAM

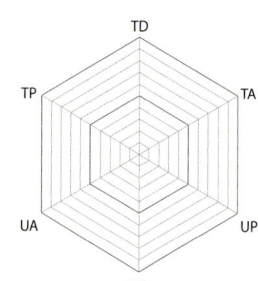

* The profile composed of 6 census data shapes hexagonal relationship as an analyzing system for defining the characterization of individual city.

TD - Total density (1000 / km^2)
TP - Total population (1,000,000)
TA - Total area (1,000 km^2)
UD - Urban density (10,000 / km^2)
UP - Urban population (1,000,000)
UA - Urban area (100 km^2)

GEOGRAPHICAL CIRCLE

- Central Built
- Local Built
- Farmland
- Mountains

INDUSTRIAL CIRCLE

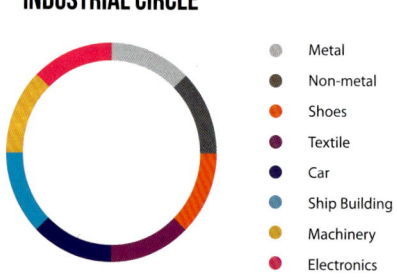

- Metal
- Non-metal
- Shoes
- Textile
- Car
- Ship Building
- Machinery
- Electronics

8 Major north korean cities

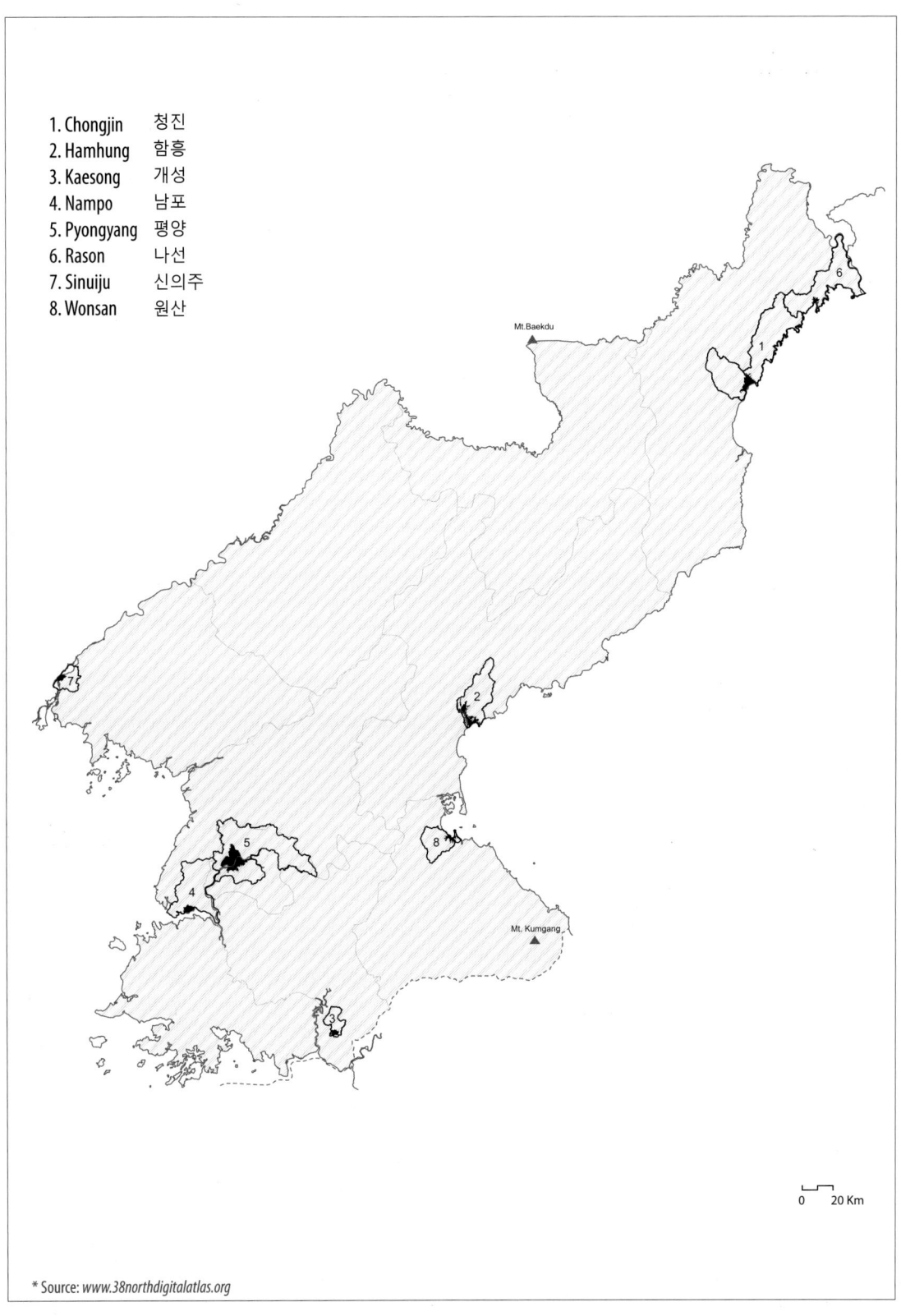

1. Chongjin 청진
2. Hamhung 함흥
3. Kaesong 개성
4. Nampo 남포
5. Pyongyang 평양
6. Rason 나선
7. Sinuiju 신의주
8. Wonsan 원산

* Source: www.38northdigitalatlas.org

8 MAJOR CITIES

ANJU CHONGJIN

HOERYONG HUICHON HYESAN KAECHON

KIMCHAEK KUSONG MANPO MUNCHON

RASON - NAJIN SARIWON SINPO SINUIJU

TOKCHON WONSAN

8 Major north korean cities

CHONGJIN 청진
NORTH HAMGYONG PROVINCE

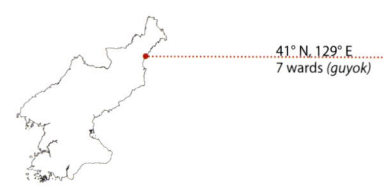

41° N, 129° E
7 wards (guyok)

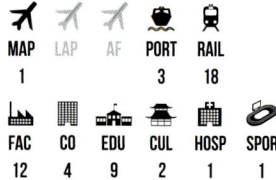

MAP	LAP	AF	PORT	RAIL
1			3	18

FAC	CO	EDU	CUL	HOSP	SPOR
12	4	9	2	1	1

POPULATION
Inhabitants	**667,929**
% Urban	92.1
% Rural	7.9
% Male	47.6
% Female	52.4

POPULATION DENSITY
Inhabitants	667,929
Administrative Area (km²)	1,538
Population Density (inhabitants/km²)	**434**

URBAN DENSITY
Inhabitants	614,892
Urban Area (km²)	63
Population Density (inhabitants/km²)	**9,760**

GEOGRAPHY
% Built (Central+ Local)	4.5
% Farmland	54.1
% Mountains	41.4

POTENTIAL GROWTH
Urbanized Area (km²)	901
% Area Increase	1,429
Urban Population	667,929
% Population Increase	1,317
Max. Population (million)	8.8

CENSUS HEXAGRAM

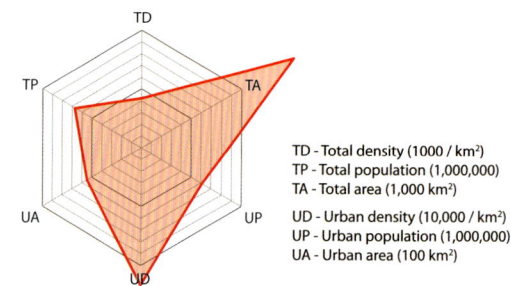

TD - Total density (1000 / km²)
TP - Total population (1,000,000)
TA - Total area (1,000 km²)
UD - Urban density (10,000 / km²)
UP - Urban population (1,000,000)
UA - Urban area (100 km²)

GEOGRAPHICAL CIRCLE

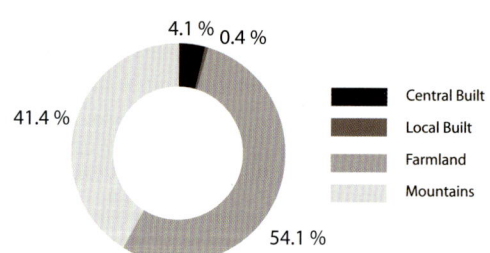

- Central Built 0.4 %
- Local Built 4.1 %
- Farmland 54.1 %
- Mountains 41.4 %

INDUSTRIAL CIRCLE

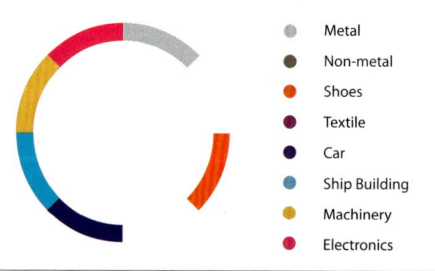

- Metal
- Non-metal
- Shoes
- Textile
- Car
- Ship Building
- Machinery
- Electronics

8 Major north korean cities | Chongjin 233

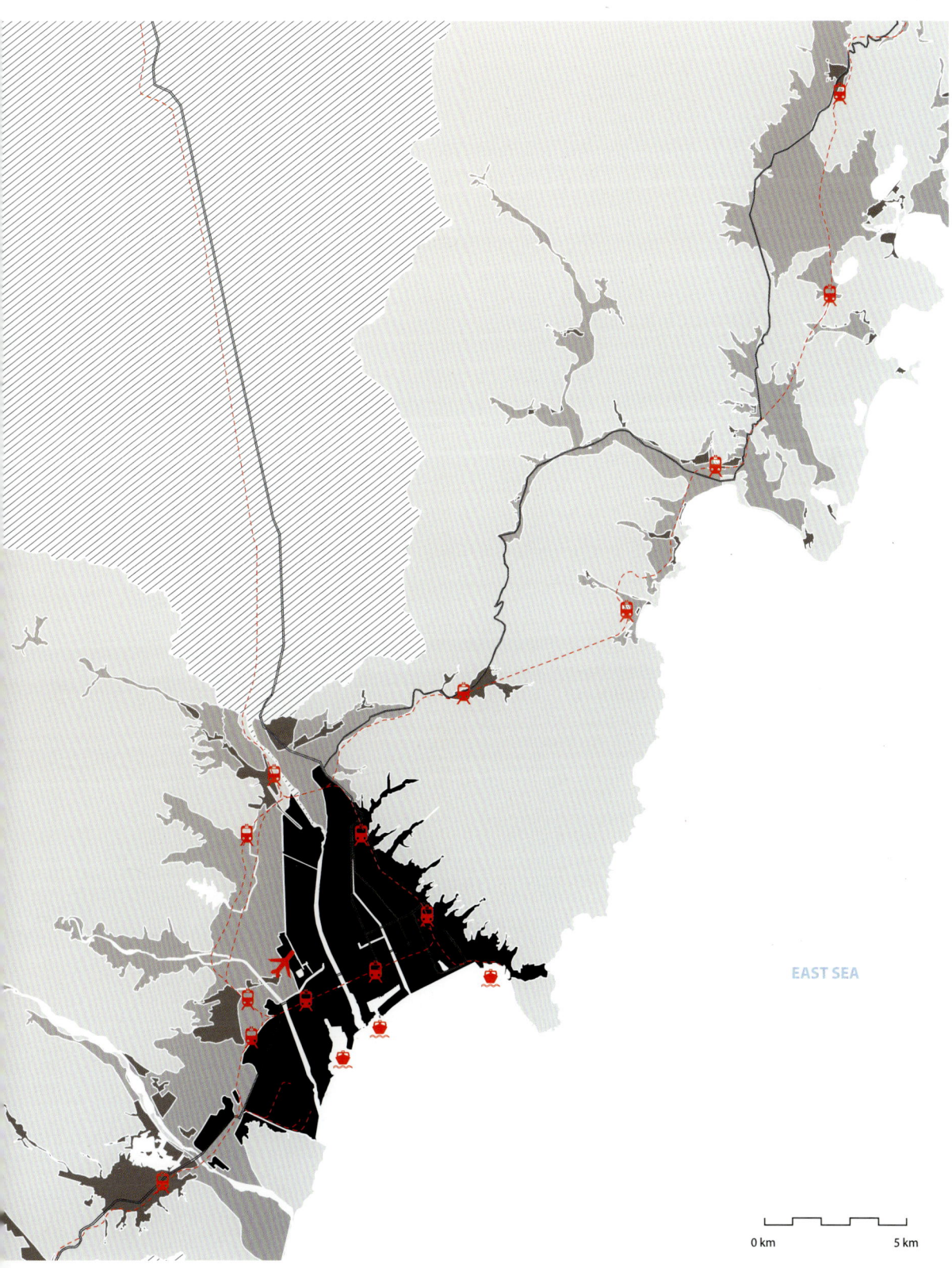

EAST SEA

0 km 5 km

North Korean Cities

8 Major north korean cities | Chongjin

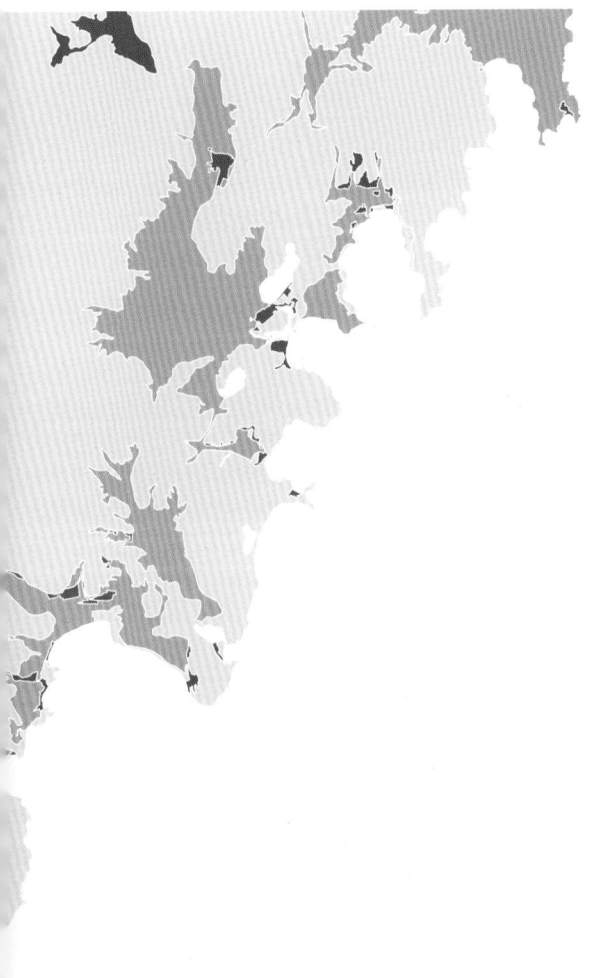

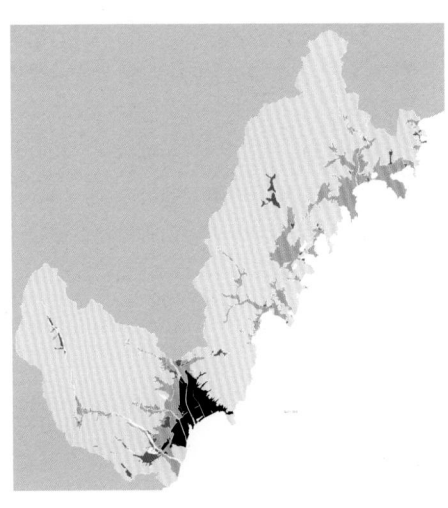

EAST SEA

North Korean Cities

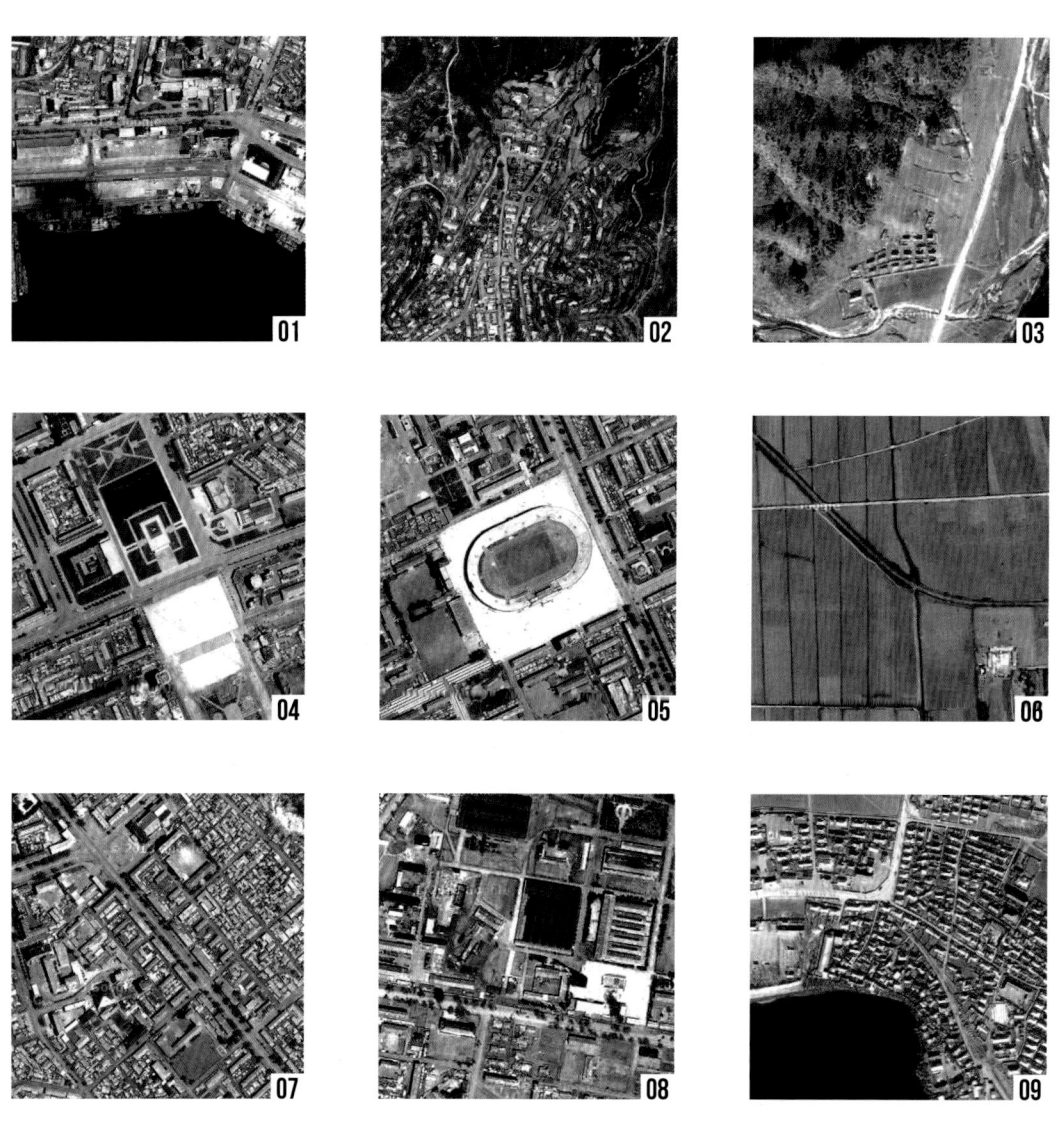

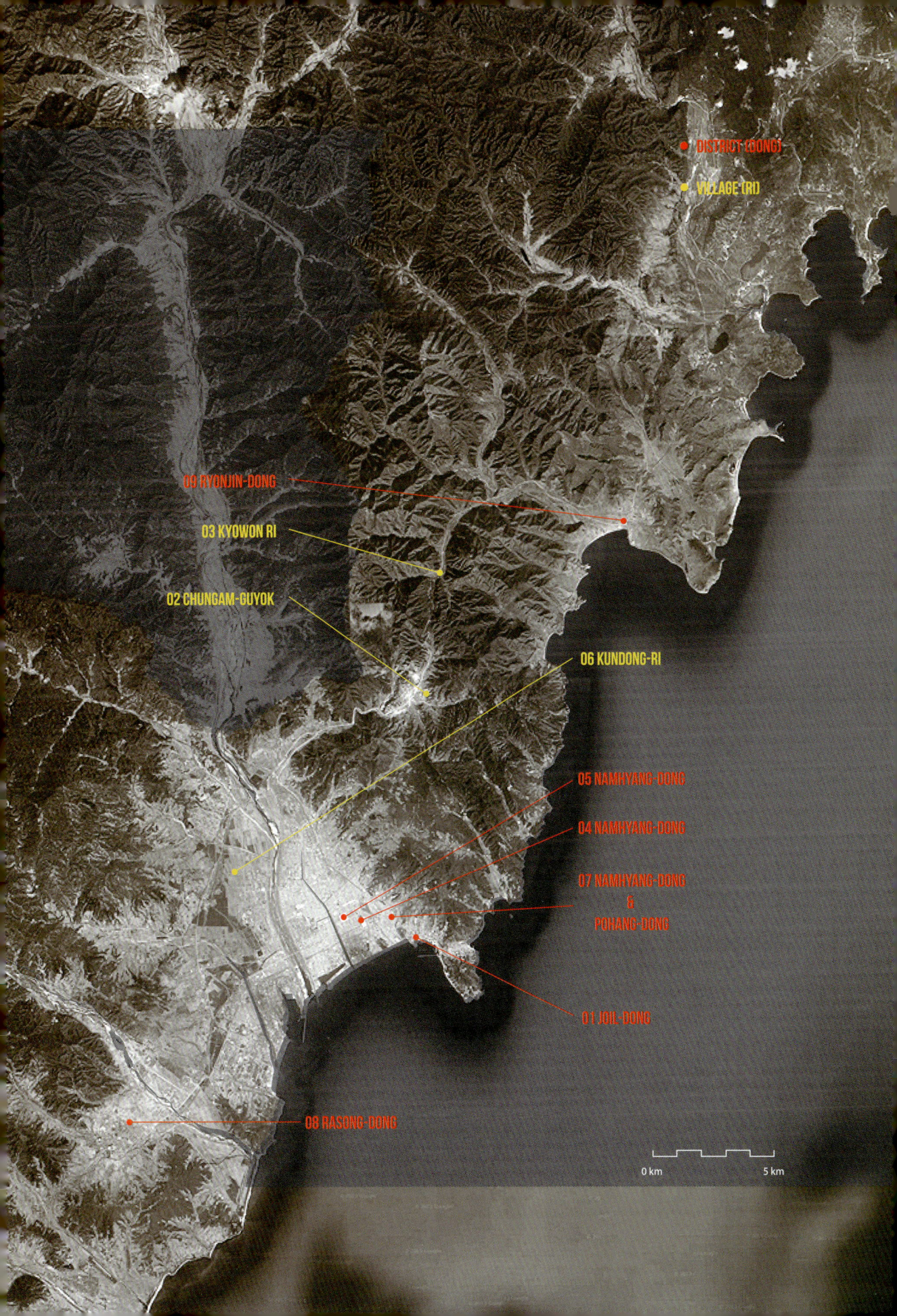

MAJOR CITY STRUCTURE - CHONGJIN
주요 도시 구조 – 청진

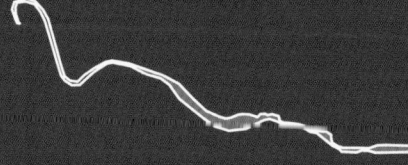

Chongjin is the third biggest city in North Korea in terms of population. It was first developed as city scale right before the Japanese colonial period, and prior to that, it was just a small fishing town. When the Russia-Japan war started in 1904, Japan used the city as a landing port for the military. Ever since, it became one of the most important strategic city in the East coast of North Korea. Currently, it has very well developed industries, especially of steels and fibers, as well as shipyards.

청진은 인구면에 있어서 북한에서 3번째로 큰 도시이다. 청진은 일제시대 직전에 도시스케일로 성장하기 시작했으며, 그 이전에는 작은 어촌 마을에 불과하였다. 1904년 러일전쟁이 발발하였을 때, 일본은 청진을 상륙기지로 사용하였으며, 이때 이후로 줄곧 청진은 북한 동해안 연안에서 가장 중요한 도시 중의 하나였다. 현재 청진은 철강산업과 섬유산업이 발달하였으며, 조선소 역시 발달하였다.

8 Major north korean cities | Chongjin

North Korean Cities

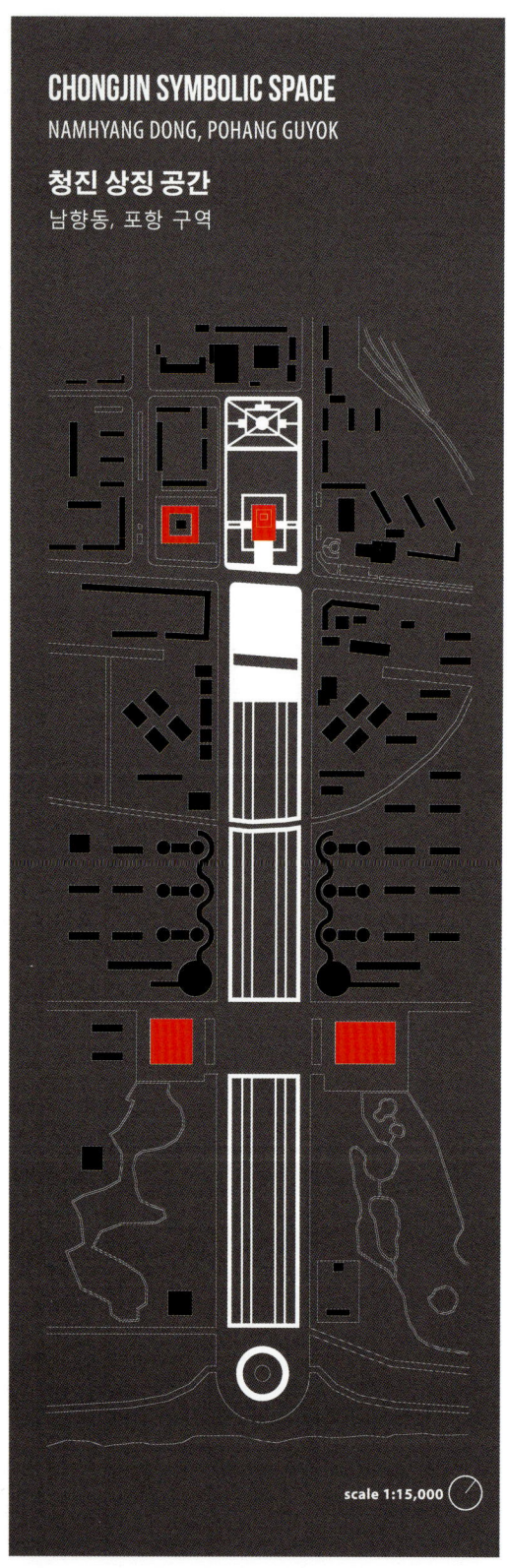

CHONGJIN SYMBOLIC SPACE
NAMHYANG DONG, POHANG GUYOK

청진 상징 공간
남향동, 포항 구역

scale 1:15,000

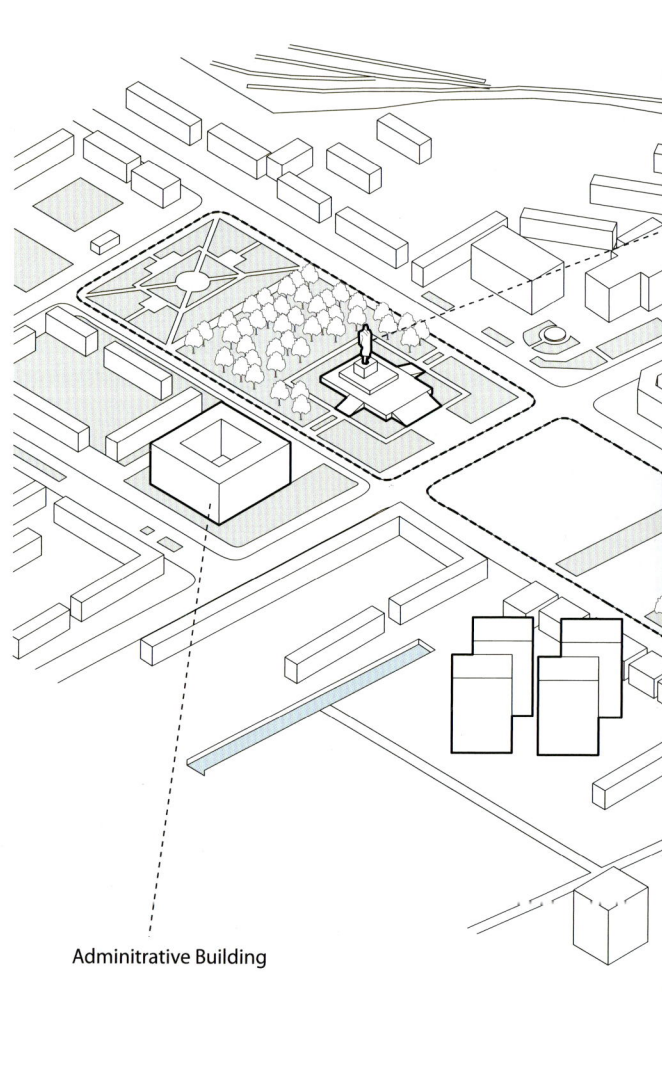

Adminitrative Building

Theater
(under construction)

8 Major north korean cities | Chongjin 241

* This master plan is organized with the major or identifiable buildings indicated in *Chongjin's 5year Redevelopment Plan* from the source of *www.nknews.org*.

Kim Il Sung Statue

High-rise Residential (under construction)

Residential and Commercial Block (under construction)

Cultural Hall (under construction)

0 50m 100m

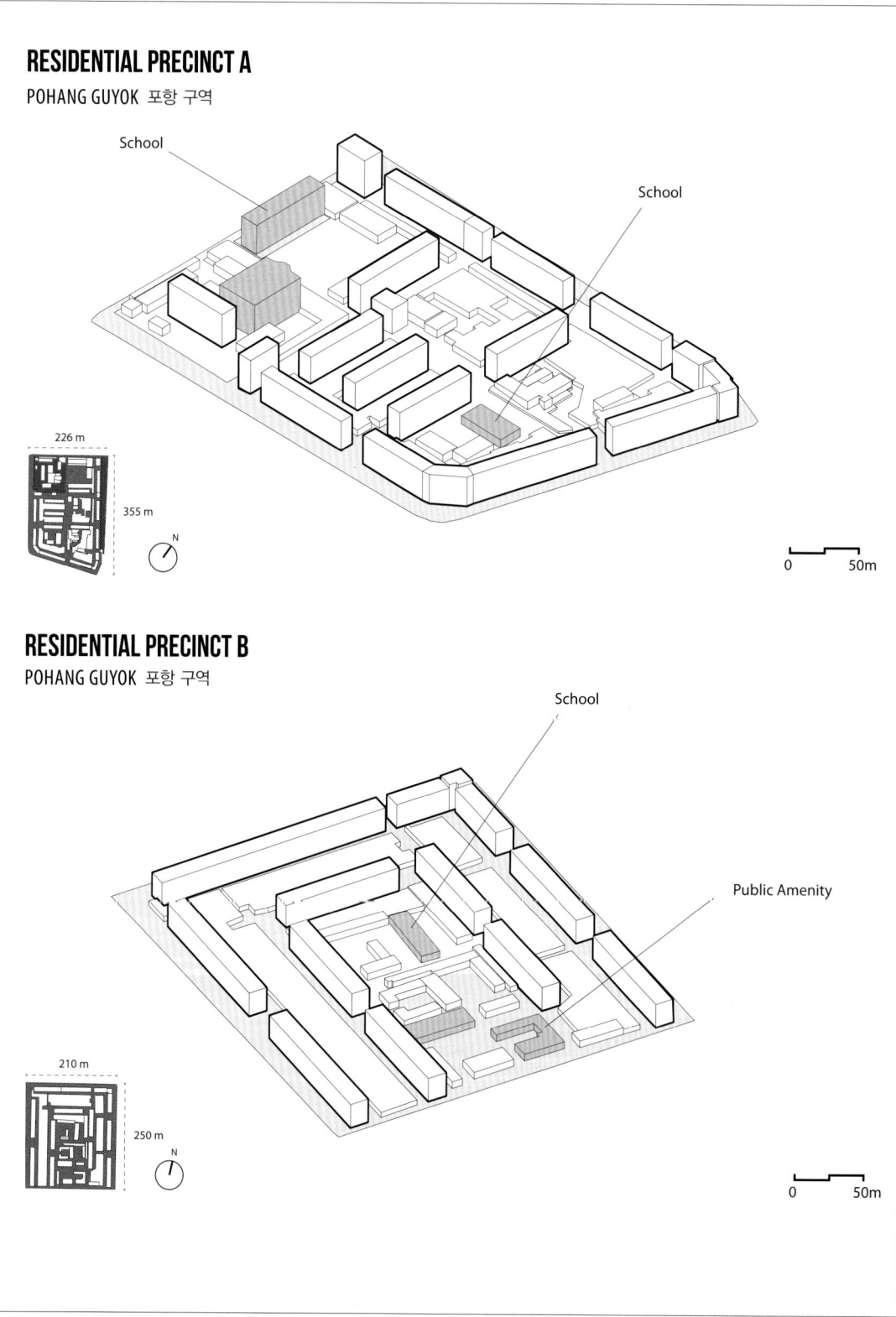

8 Major north korean cities | Chongjin

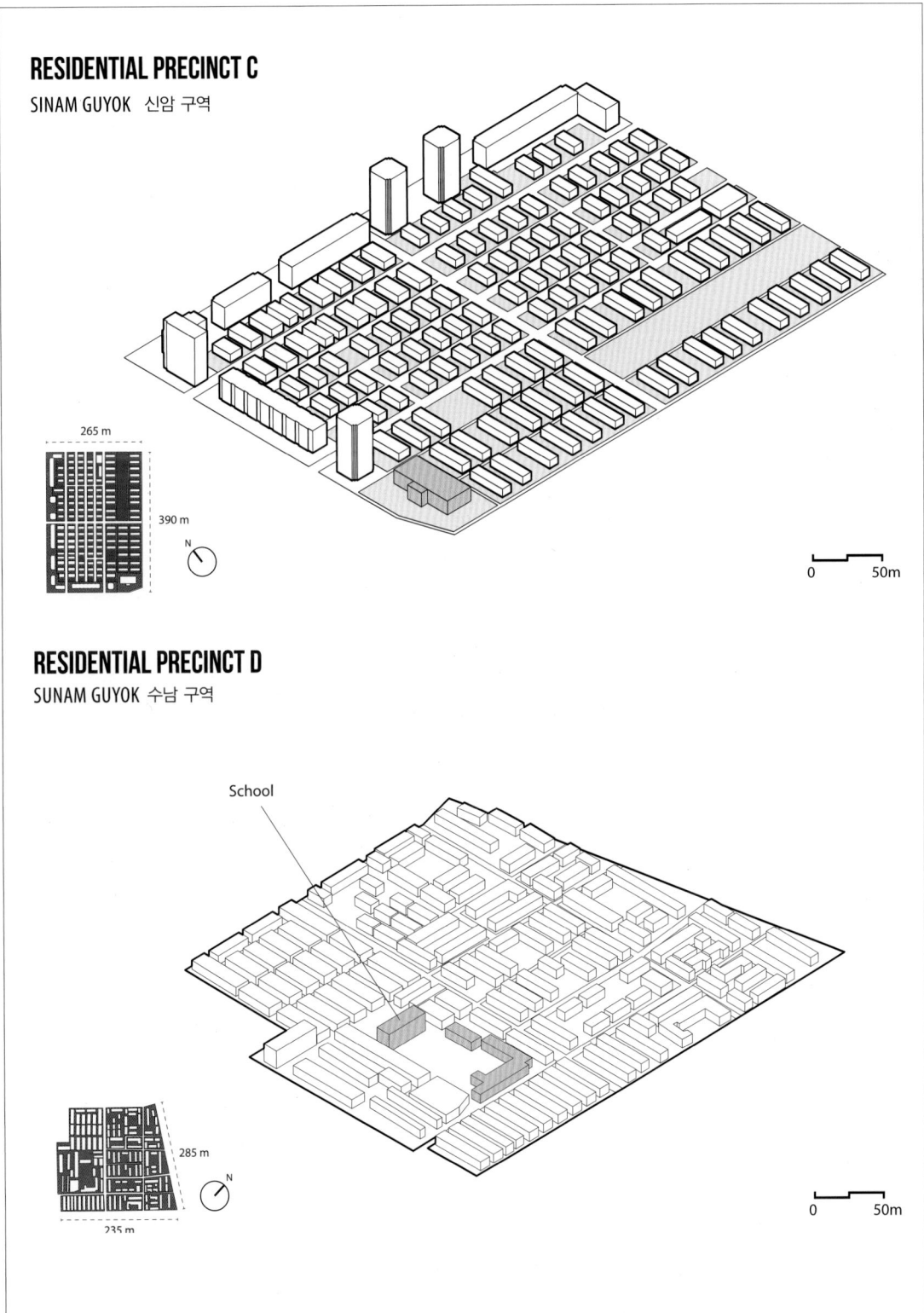

RESIDENTIAL PRECINCT C
SINAM GUYOK 신암 구역

RESIDENTIAL PRECINCT D
SUNAM GUYOK 수남 구역

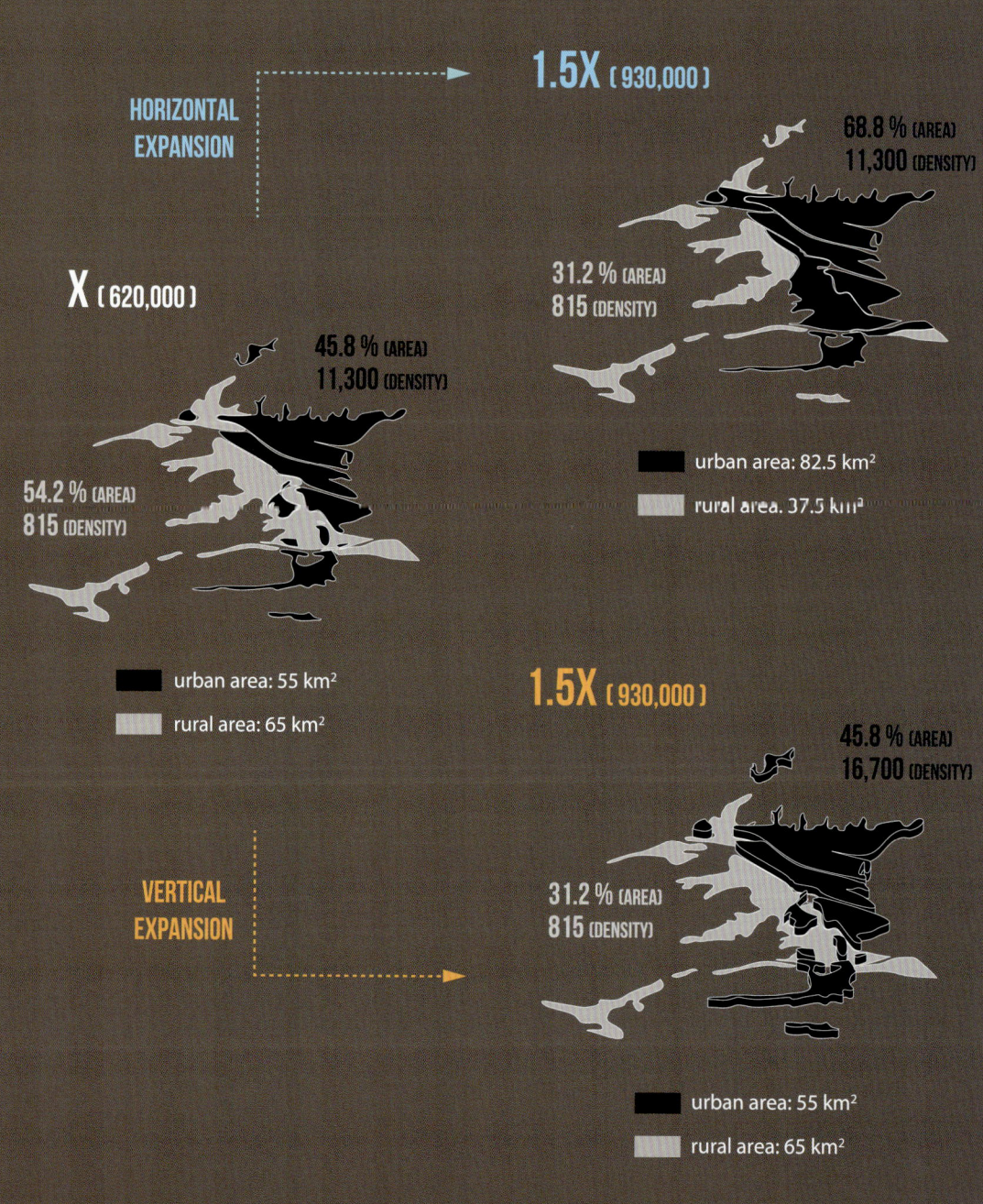

8 Major north korean cities | Chongjin

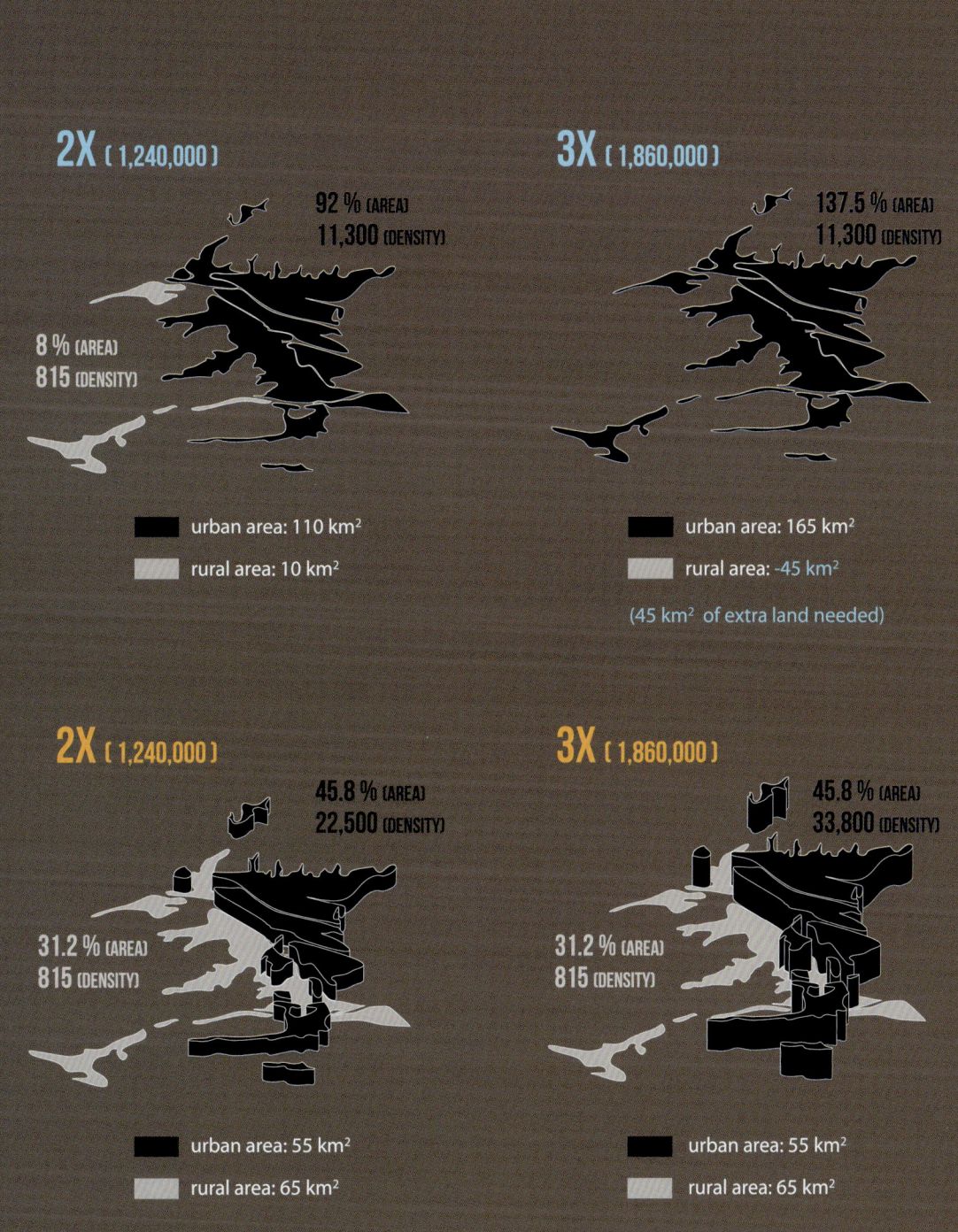

HAMHUNG 함흥
SOUTH HAMGYONG PROVINCE

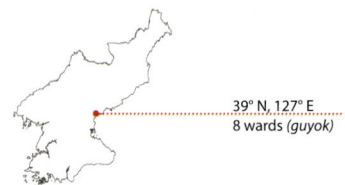

39° N, 127° E
8 wards *(guyok)*

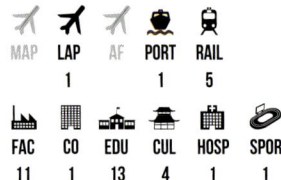

MAP | LAP | AF | PORT | RAIL
  | 1 | | 1 | 5
FAC | CO | EDU | CUL | HOSP | SPOR
 11 | 1 | 13 | 4 | 1 | 1

POPULATION
Inhabitants	768,551
% Urban	91.9
% Rural	8.1
% Male	47.5
% Female	52.5

POPULATION DENSITY
Inhabitants	768,551
Administrative Area (km²)	618.5
Population Density (inhabitants/km²)	**1,243**

URBAN DENSITY
Inhabitants	706,298
Urban Area (km²)	54.4
Population Density (inhabitants/km²)	**12,983**

GEOGRAPHY
% Built	9
% Farmland	19
% Mountains	65

POTENTIAL GROWTH
Urbanized Area (km²)	173
% Area Increase	211
Urban Population	768,551
% Population Increase	292
Max. Population (million)	2.3

CENSUS HEXAGRAM

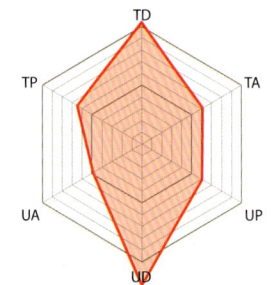

TD - Total density (1000 / km²)
TP - Total population (1,000,000)
TA - Total area (1,000 km²)
UD - Urban density (10,000 / km²)
UP - Urban population (1,000,000)
UA - Urban area (100 km²)

GEOGRAPHICAL CIRCLE

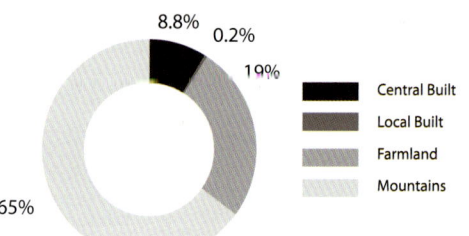

8.8% 0.2% 19% 65%

- Central Built
- Local Built
- Farmland
- Mountains

INDUSTRIAL CIRCLE

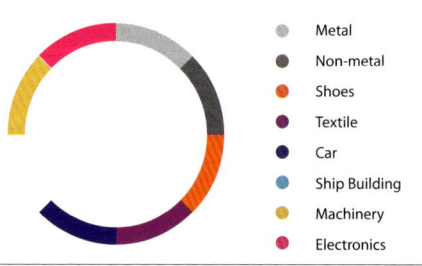

- Metal
- Non-metal
- Shoes
- Textile
- Car
- Ship Building
- Machinery
- Electronics

8 Major north korean cities | Hamhung 247

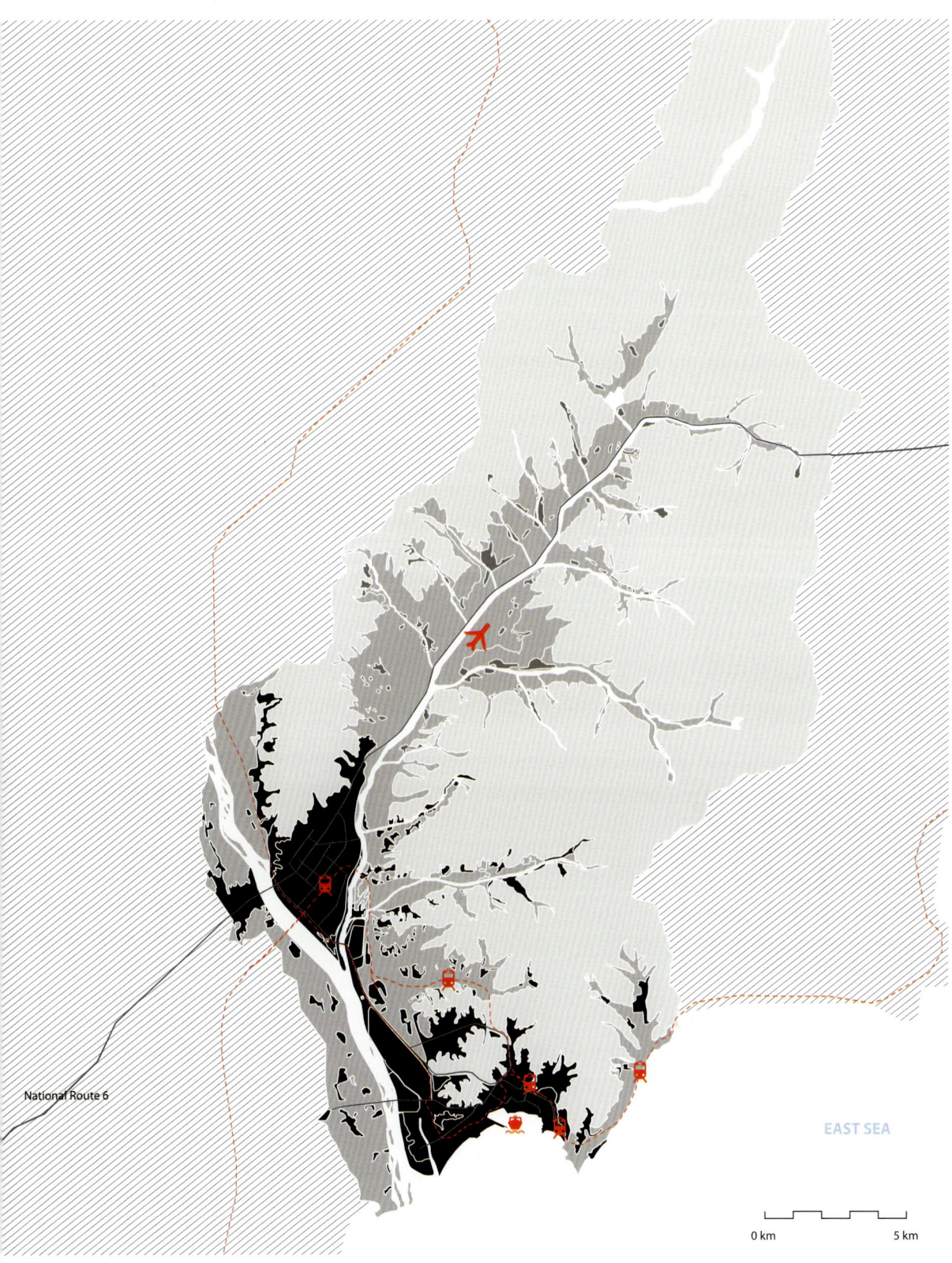

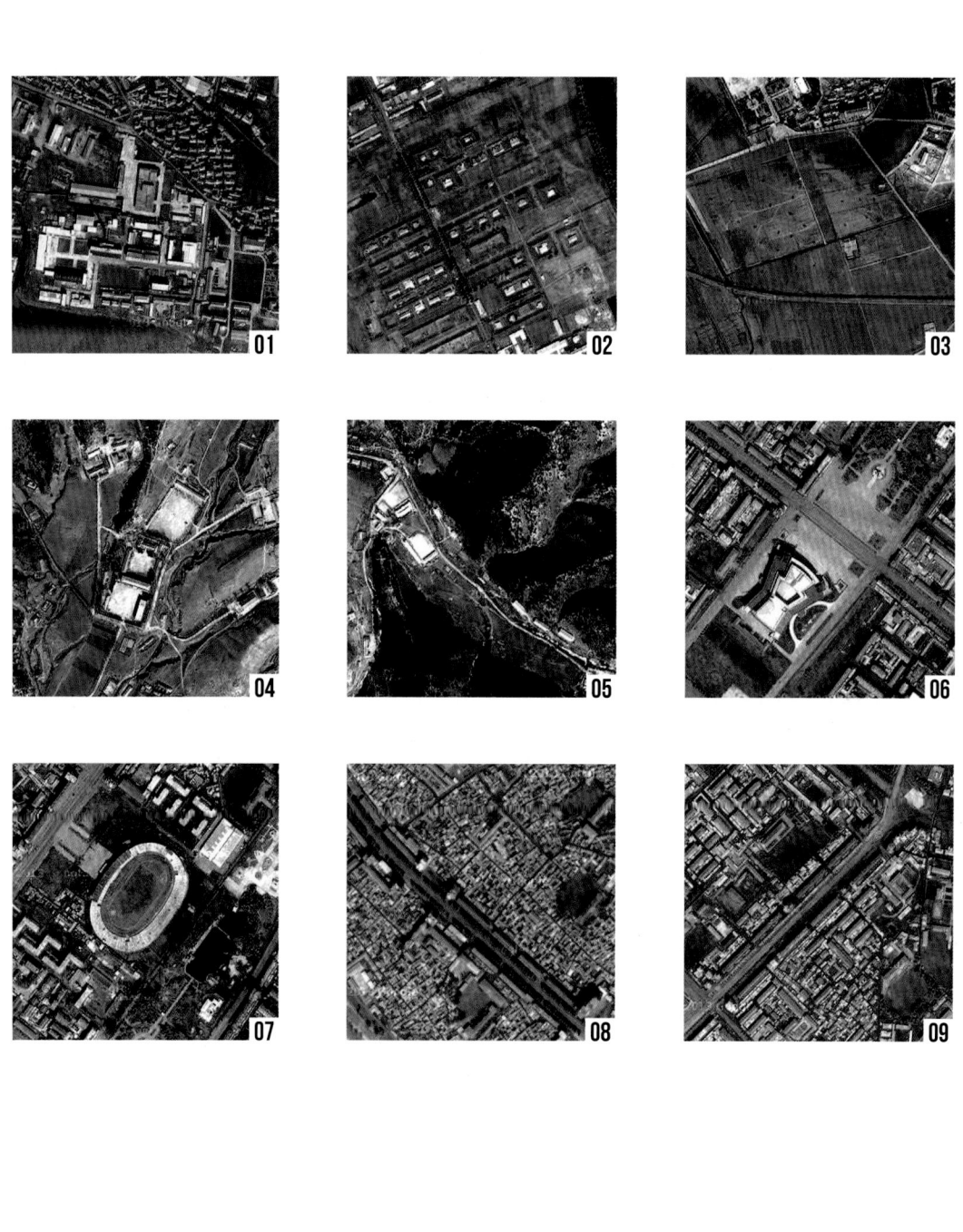

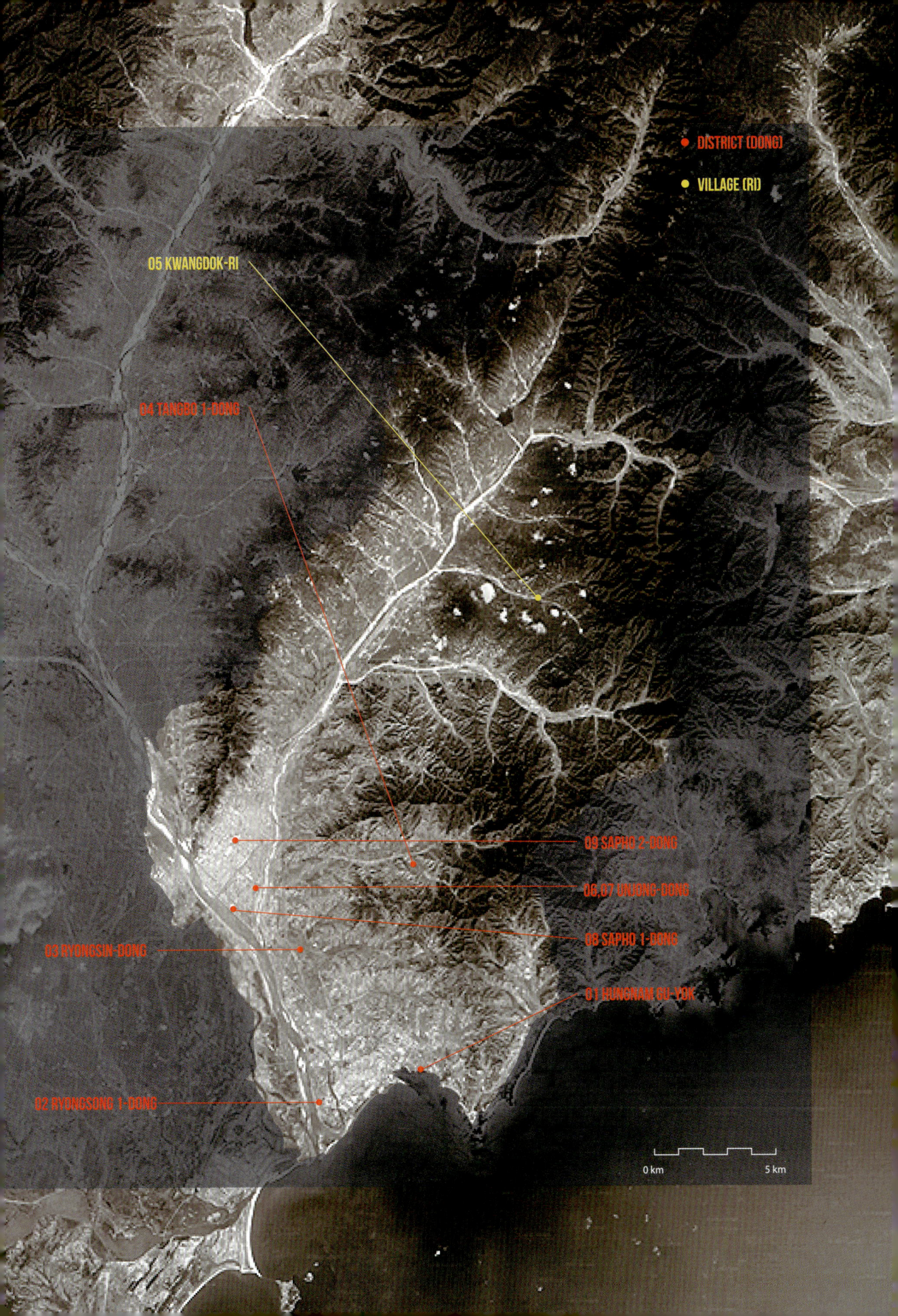

MAJOR CITY STRUCTURE - HAMHUNG
주요 도시 구조 - 함흥

Hamhung College of Medicine

Hamhung Stadium

Kim Il Sung Statue

Yongseong Plant Machinery Association

Sapo Market

Hamhung was known as the home town of Yi Sung-ke who founded Joseon Dynasty in 1392, and it still is know as a destination for heritage tourism. The whole structure of the city was heavily destroyed during the Korean War, and was reconstructed with the help of East Germany. Now, it has the second biggest population in the nation, and is the important city for the nation's chemical industry.

함흥은 1392년 조선왕조를 건국한 이성계의 고향으로 알려져 있으며, 현재까지 이를 이용한 관광이 이루어지고 있다. 함흥의 도시 조직은 한국전쟁때 대부분 소실되었으며, 이는 주로 동독의 지원으로 재건이 되었다. 현재 함흥은 북한내 인구면에서 두 번째로 큰 도시이며, 북한의 주요 화학산업들이 분포하고 있다.

Huichon Street Market

8 Major north korean cities | Hamhung

North Korean Cities

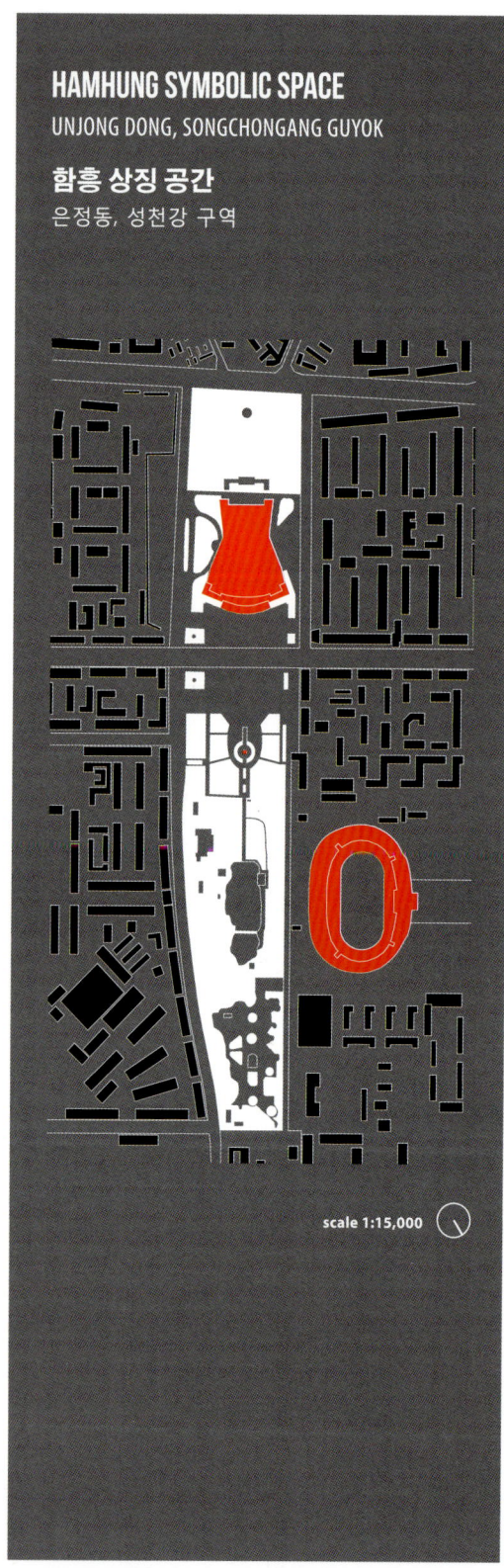

HAMHUNG SYMBOLIC SPACE
UNJONG DONG, SONGCHONGANG GUYOK

함흥 상징 공간
은정동, 성천강 구역

scale 1:15,000

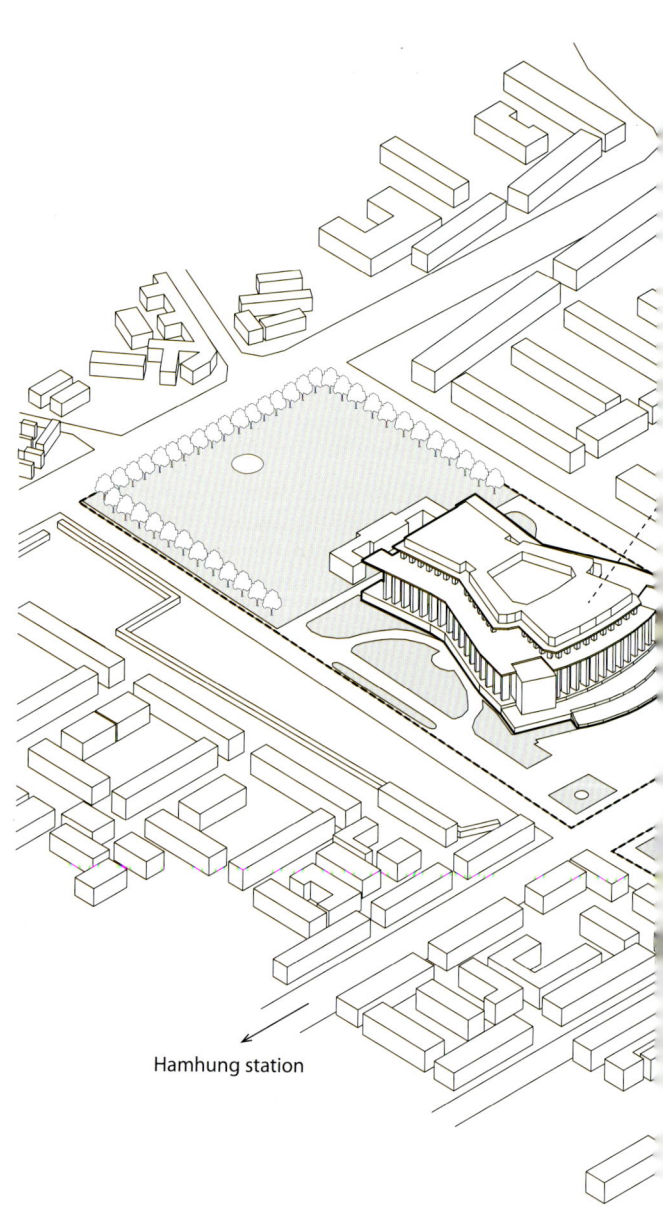

Hamhung station

8 Major north korean cities | Hamhung

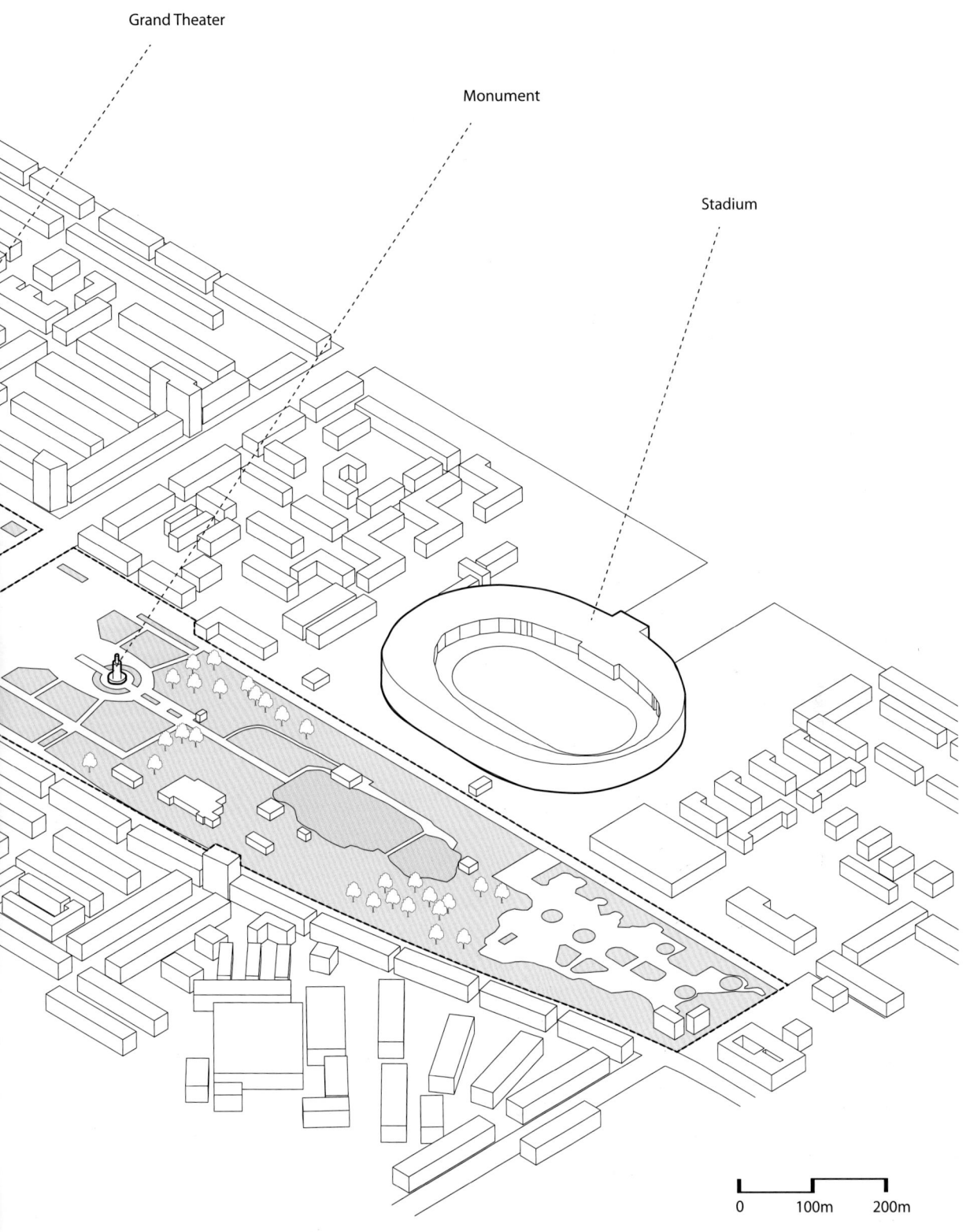

PRECINCT TYPE A
SONGCHONGANG GUYOK 성천강 구역

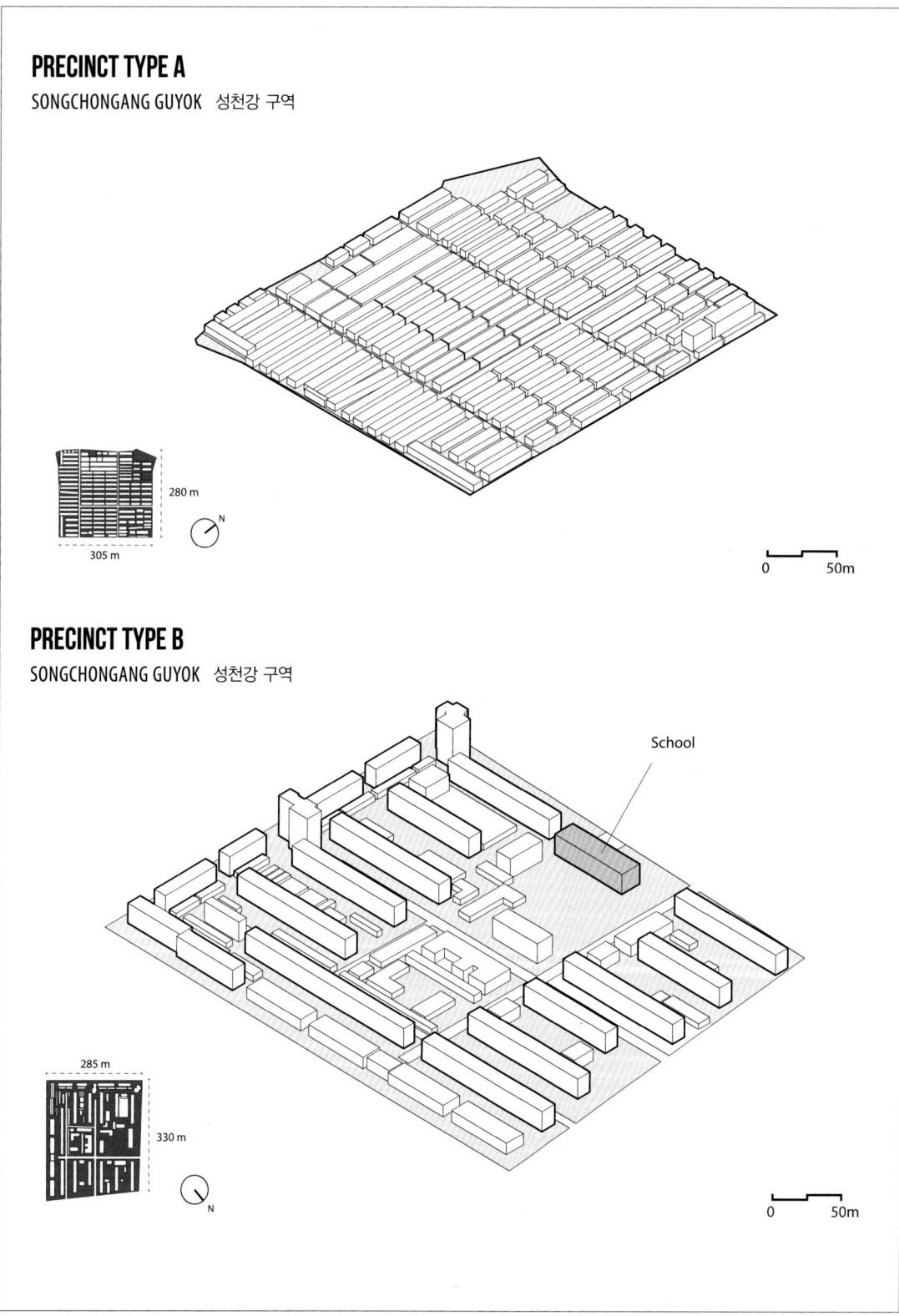

280 m
305 m

PRECINCT TYPE B
SONGCHONGANG GUYOK 성천강 구역

School

285 m
330 m

8 Major north korean cities | Hamhung 255

PRECINCT TYPE C
HOESANG GUYOK 회상 구역

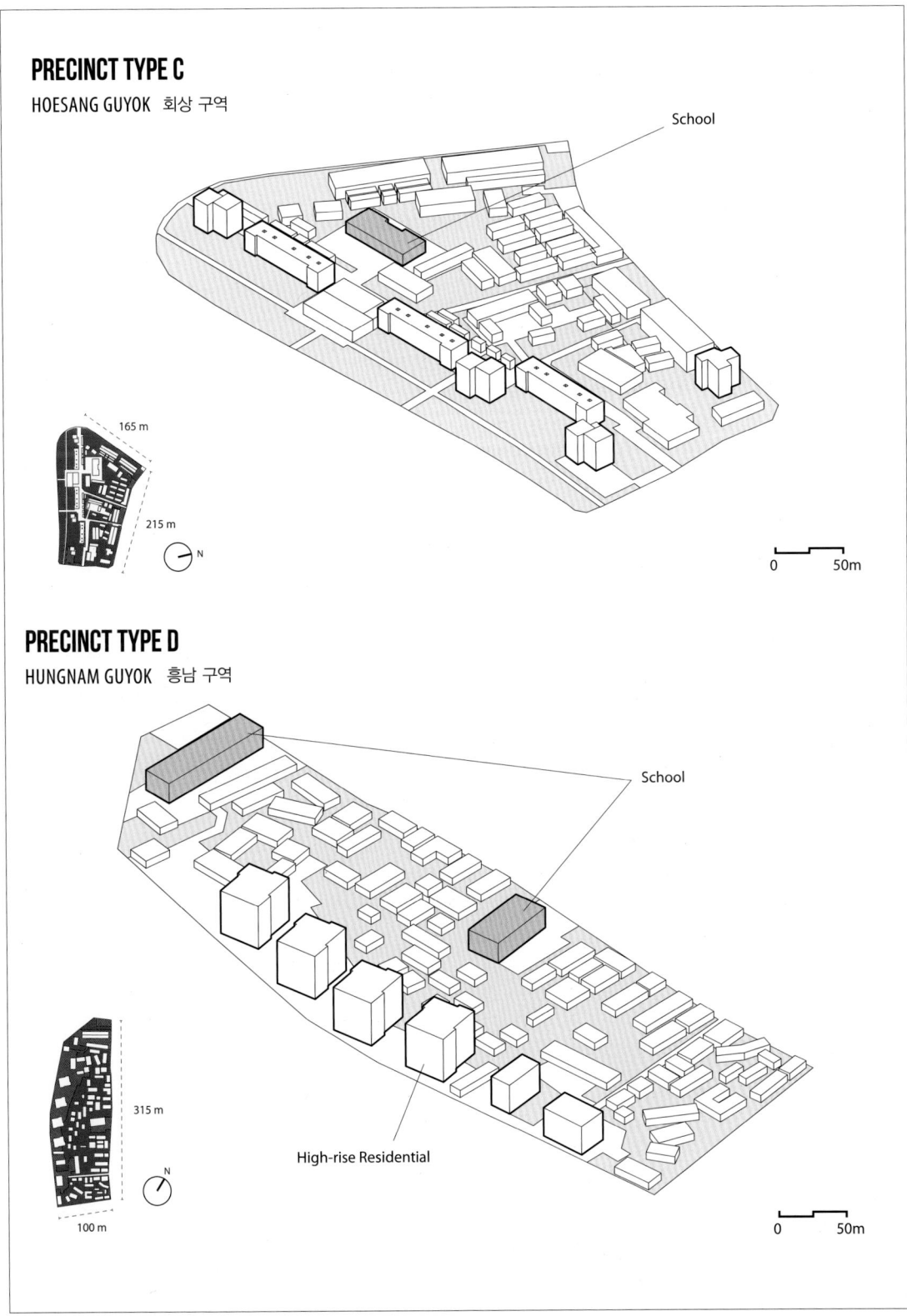

PRECINCT TYPE D
HUNGNAM GUYOK 흥남 구역

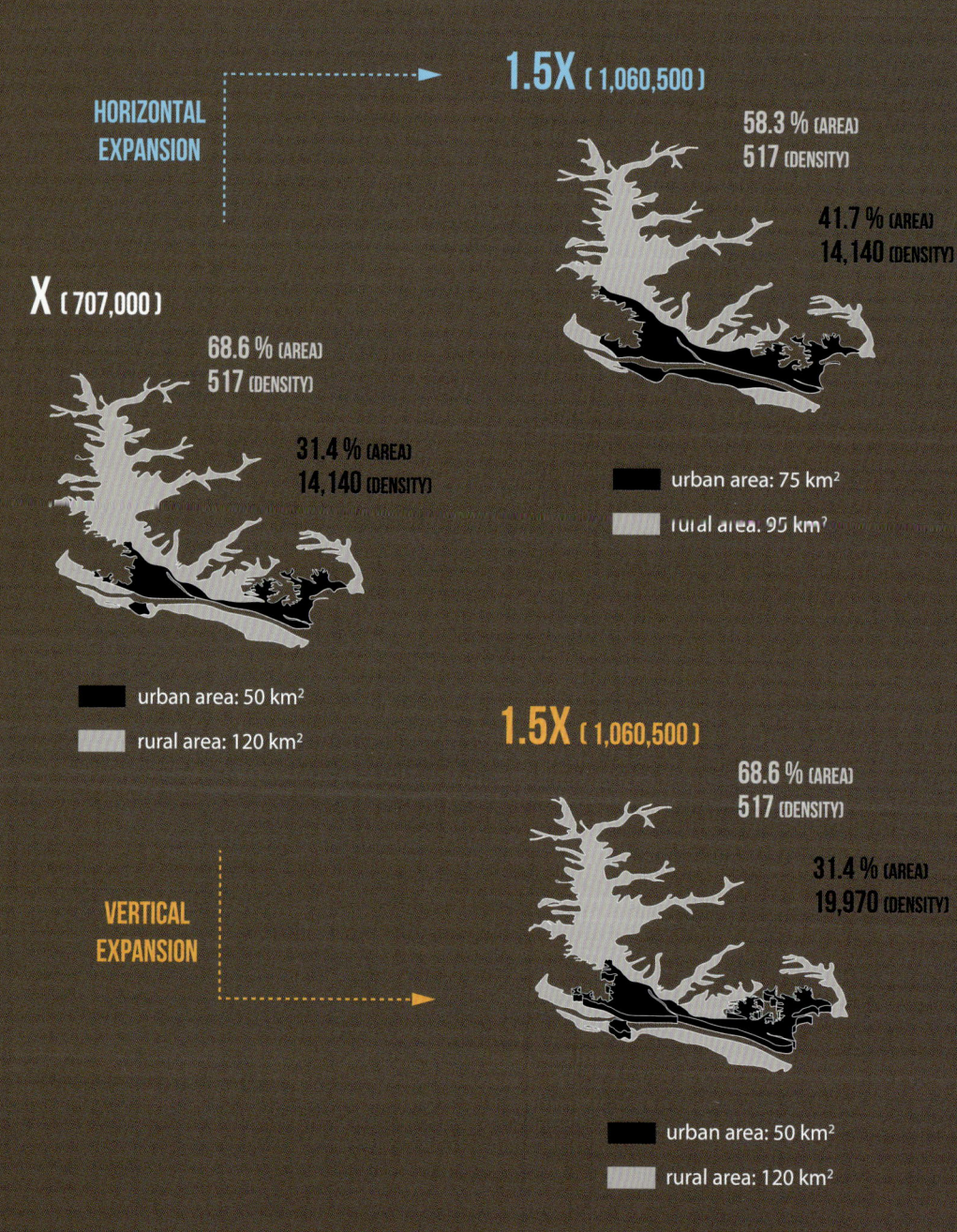

8 Major north korean cities | Hamhung

2X (1,414,000)

41.8 % (AREA)
517 (DENSITY)

58.2 % (AREA)
14,140 (DENSITY)

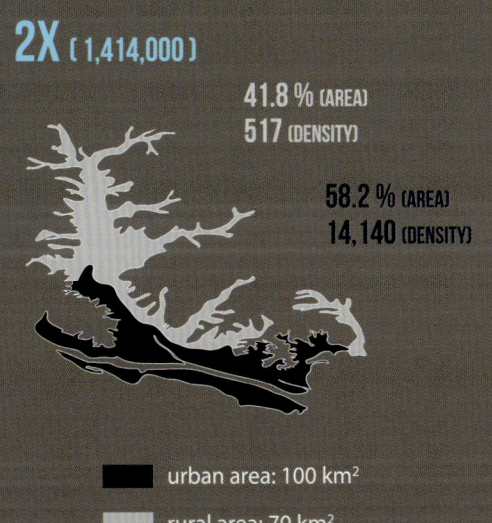

■ urban area: 100 km²
▨ rural area: 70 km²

3X (2,121,000)

11.8 % (AREA)
517 (DENSITY)

88.2 % (AREA)
14,140 (DENSITY)

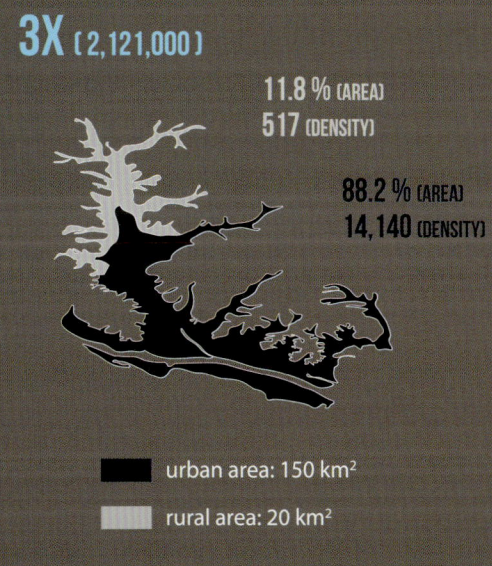

■ urban area: 150 km²
▨ rural area: 20 km²

2X (1,414,000)

68.6 % (AREA)
517 (DENSITY)

31.4 % (AREA)
27,040 (DENSITY)

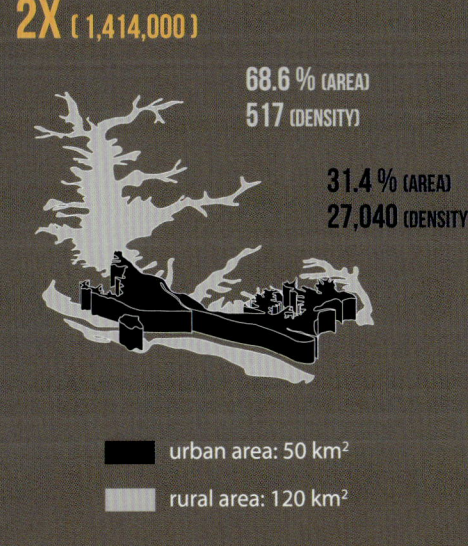

■ urban area: 50 km²
▨ rural area: 120 km²

3X (2,121,000)

68.6 % (AREA)
517 (DENSITY)

31.4 % (AREA)
41,180 (DENSITY)

■ urban area: 50 km²
▨ rural area: 120 km²

KAESONG 개성
NORTH HWANGHAE PROVINCE

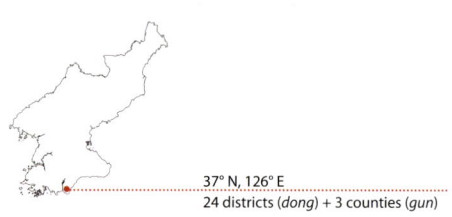

37° N, 126° E
24 districts (*dong*) + 3 counties (*gun*)

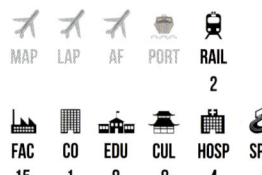

MAP	LAP	AF	PORT	RAIL
				2

FAC	CO	EDU	CUL	HOSP	SPOR
15	1	8	8	4	3

POPULATION
Inhabitants	**308,440**
% Urban	62.4
% Rural	37.6
% Male	47.4
% Female	52.6

POPULATION DENSITY
Inhabitants	308,440
Administrative Area (km²)	164
Population Density (inhabitants/km²)	**1,881**

URBAN DENSITY
Inhabitants	192,578
Urban Area (km²)	13.3
Population Density (inhabitants/km²)	**14,480**

GEOGRAPHY
% Built	9.1
% Farmland	12.2
% Mountains	78.7

POTENTIAL GROWTH
Urbanized Area (km²)	34.9
% Area Increase	163
Urban Population	308,440
% Population Increase	164
Max. Population (million)	0.5

CENSUS HEXAGRAM

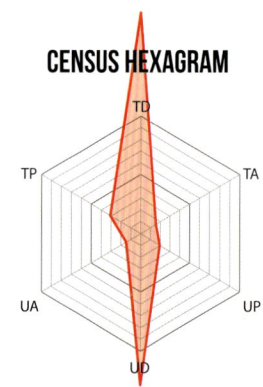

TD - Total density (1000 / km²)
TP - Total population (1,000,000)
TA - Total area (1,000 km²)
UD - Urban density (10,000 / km²)
UP - Urban population (1,000,000)
UA - Urban area (100 km²)

GEOGRAPHICAL CIRCLE

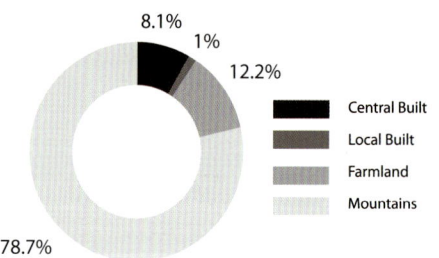

- Central Built — 8.1%
- Local Built — 1%
- Farmland — 12.2%
- Mountains — 78.7%

INDUSTRIAL CIRCLE

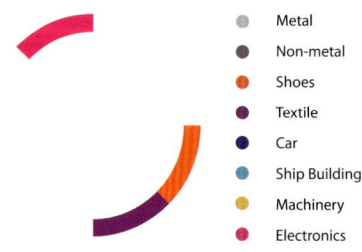

- Metal
- Non-metal
- Shoes
- Textile
- Car
- Ship Building
- Machinery
- Electronics

8 Major north korean cities | Kaesong

North Korean Cities

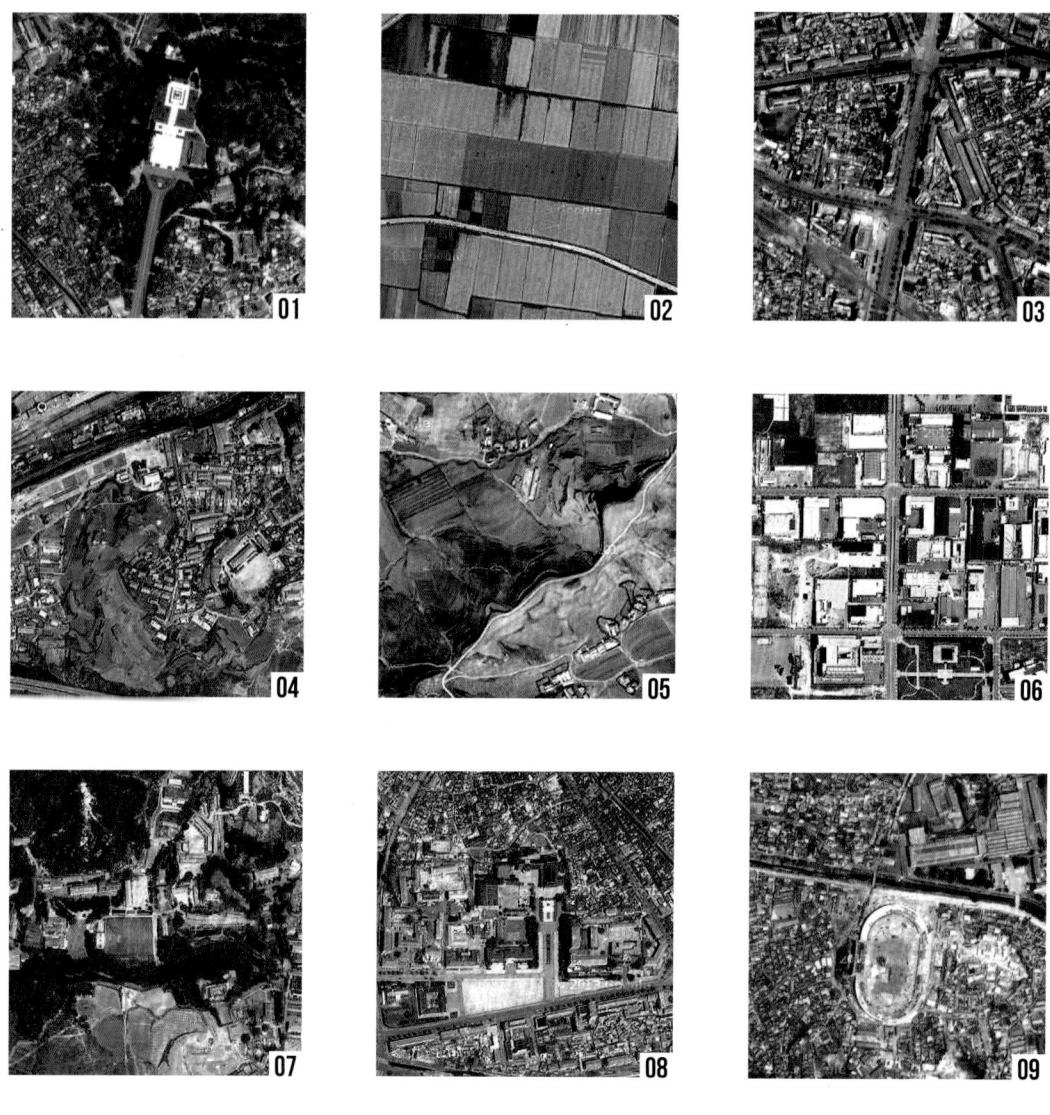

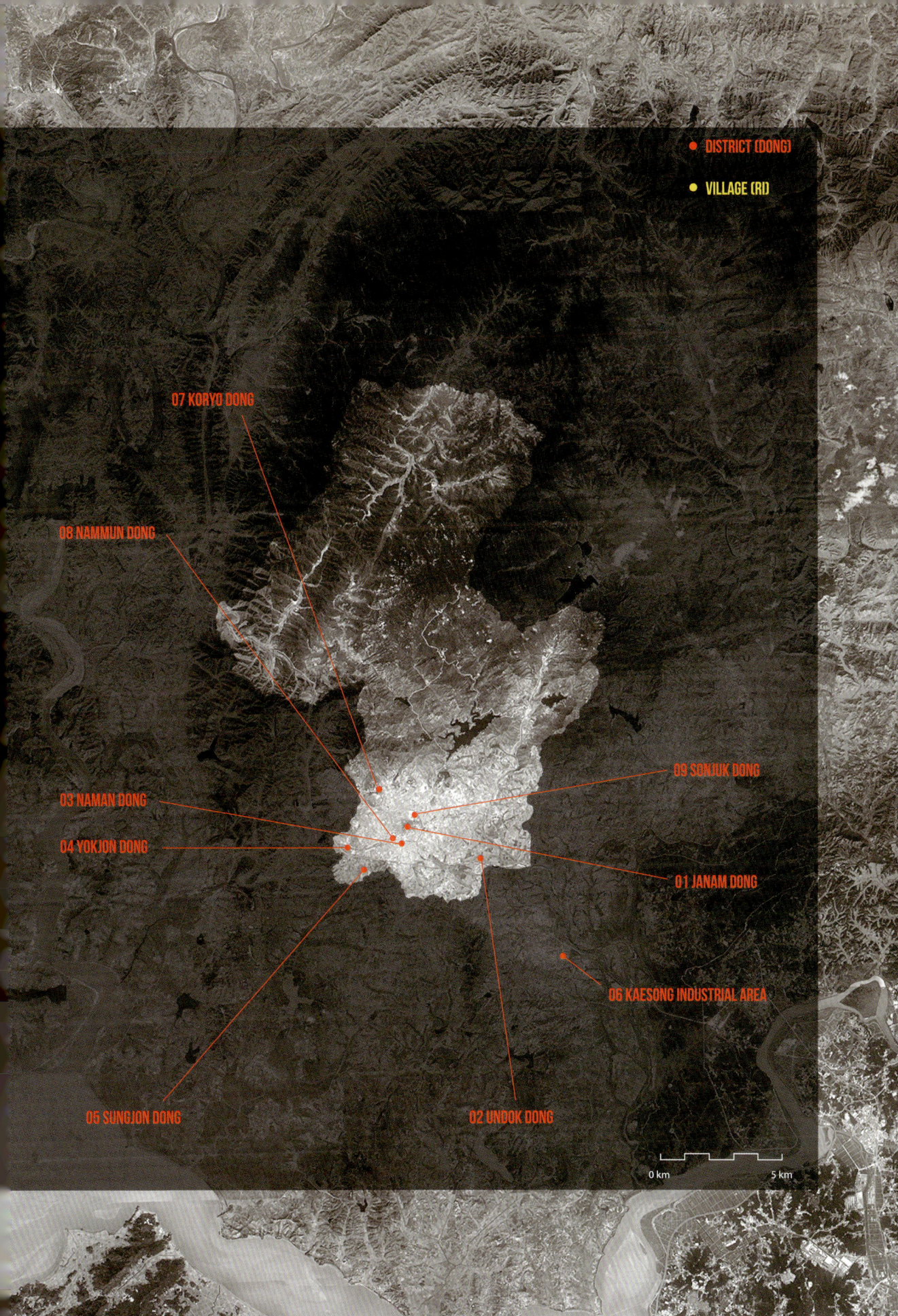

MAJOR CITY STRUCTURE - KAESONG
주요 도시 구조 - 개성

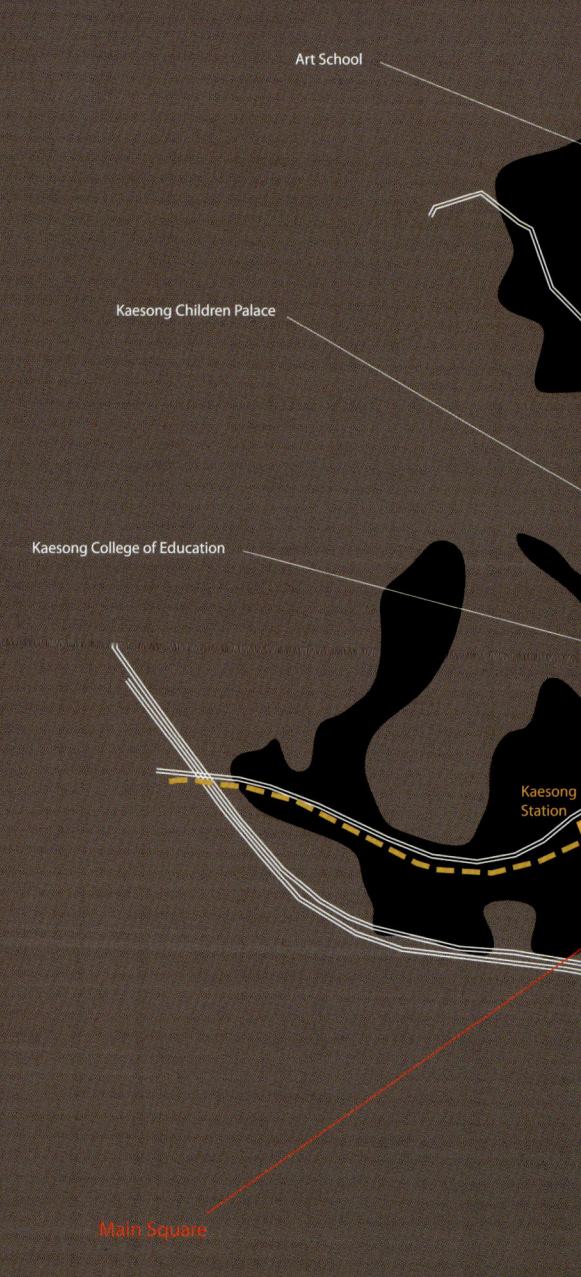

As it used to be in the South Korean territory before the Korean War broke out in 1950, Kaesong is one of the cities that has the least damage from the bombing. Therefore, it still has an old city fabric with Korean traditional type housings. Even though they are not well used these days, they are well kept until now at least. Currently, it is designated as a special city for the economic corporation between South Korea and North Korea.

한국전쟁 이전에 남한에 속해 있었던 개성은, 전쟁 중 폭격의 피해가 가장 적었던 도시 중에 하나이다. 따라서, 개성에는 역사적인 도시의 모습이 남아있으며 전통 가옥도 잘 보존되어있다. 이들이 잘 사용되고 있지는 않지만, 적어도 그 모습을 유지하고는 있다. 현재 개성은 남북한 경제협력을 위한 특별지구로 지정되어있다.

8 Major north korean cities | Kaesong

North Korean Cities 264

KAESONG SYMBOLIC SPACE
PUKAN DONG & NAMMUN DONG, KAESONG CITY

개성 상징 공간
북안동 & 남문동, 개성시

scale 1:15,000

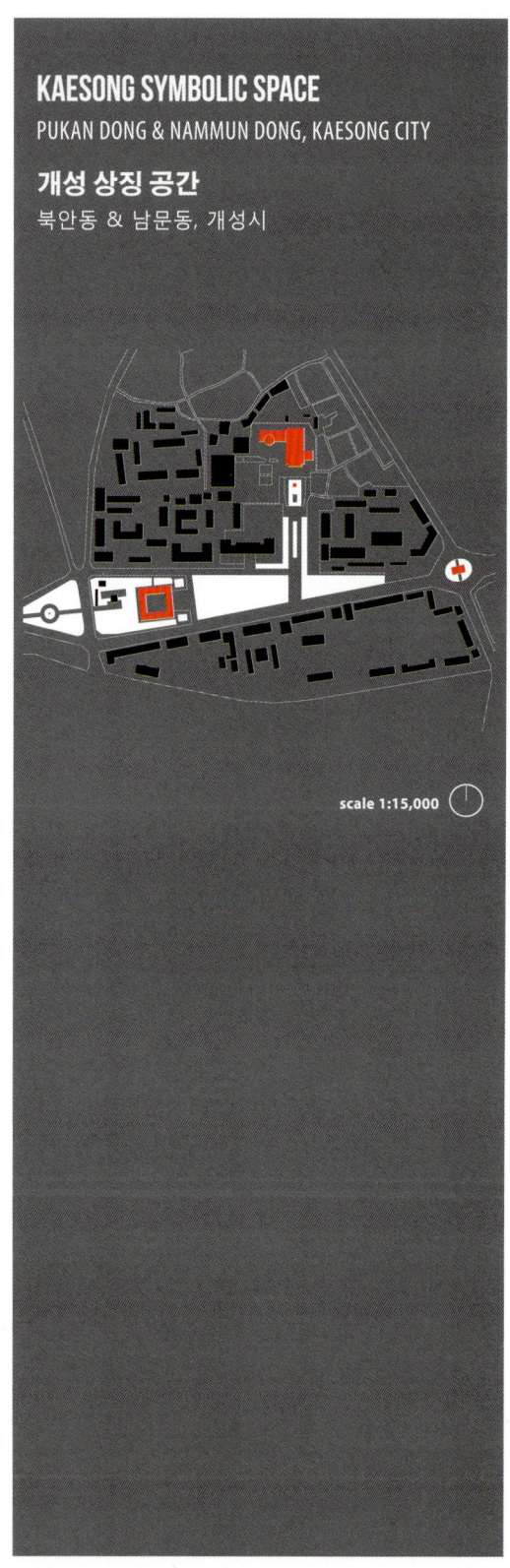

Kaesong Children's Palace

Indoor Gymnasium

Monument

8 Major north korean cities | Kaesong

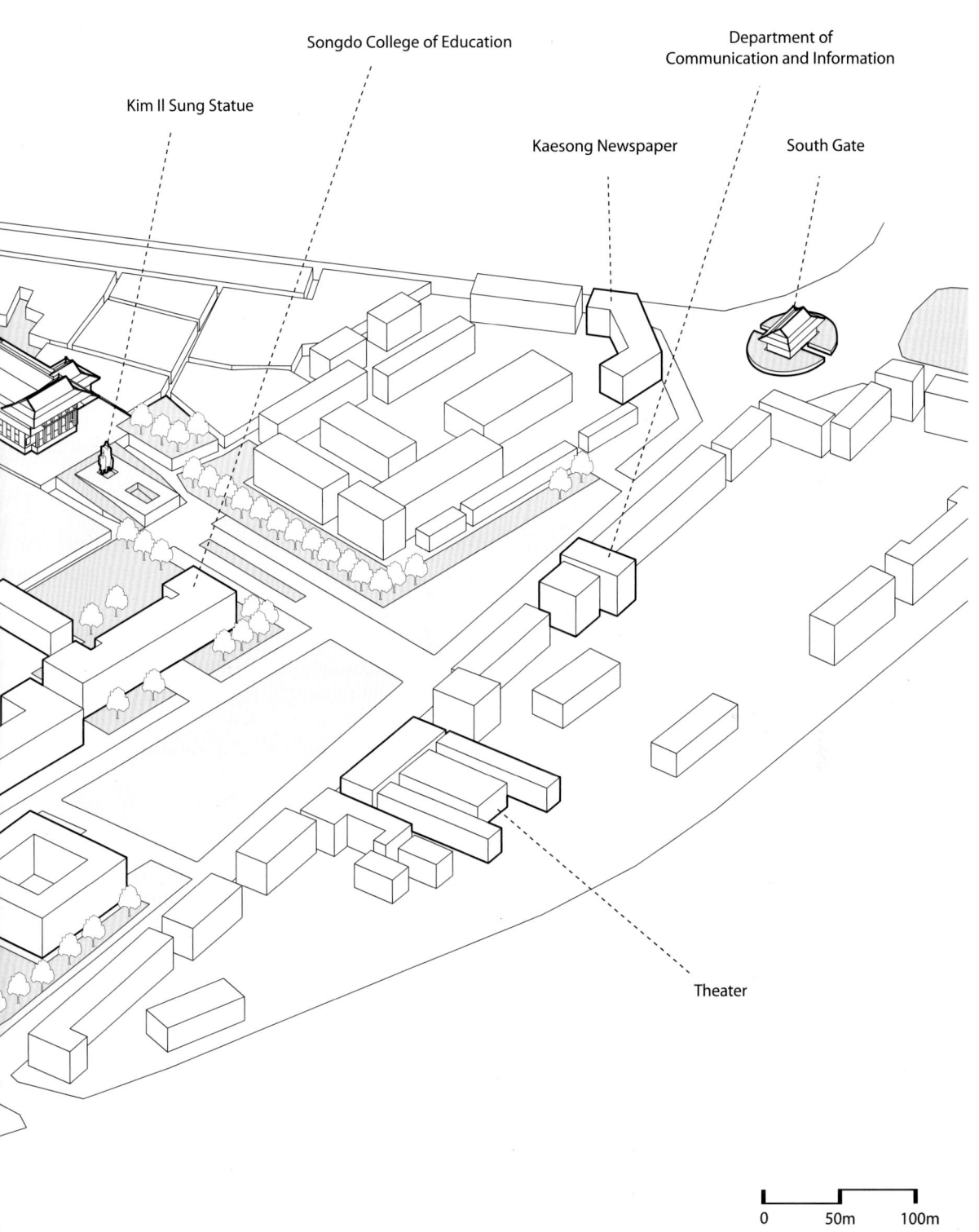

PRECINCT TYPE A
JANAM DONG 자남동

PRECINCT TYPE B
PUSAN DONG 부산동

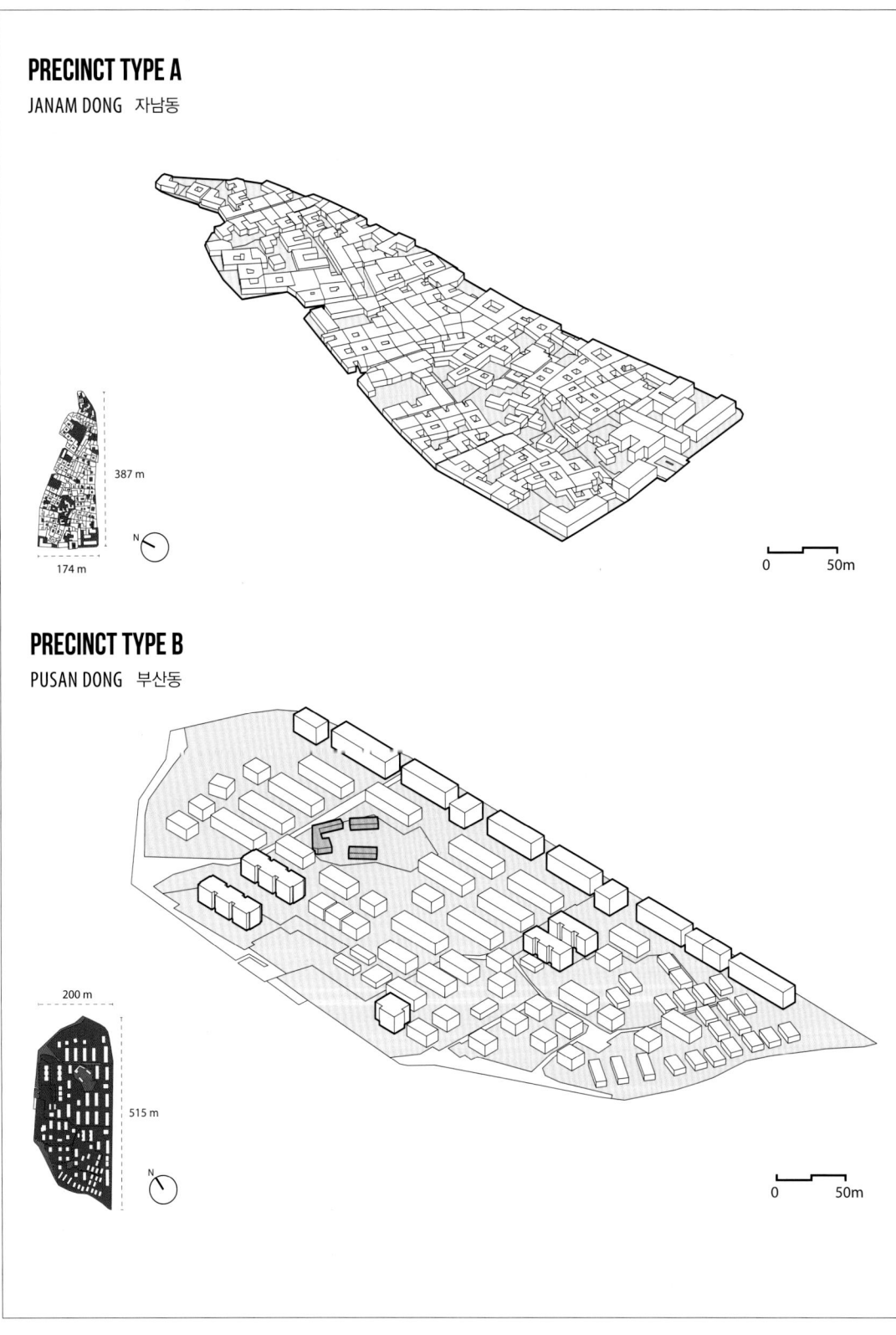

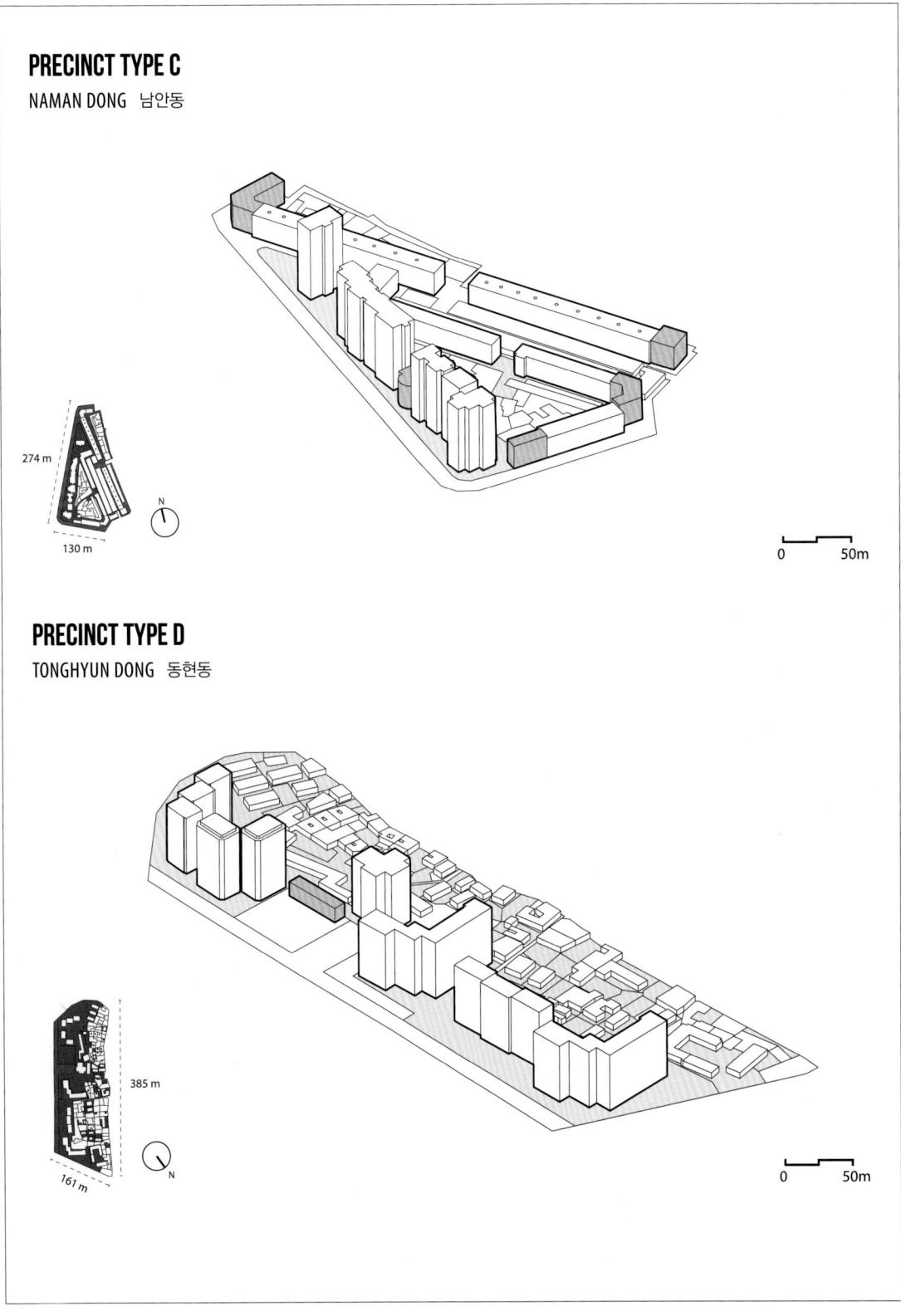

PRECINCT TYPE C
NAMAN DONG 남안동

274 m
130 m

PRECINCT TYPE D
TONGHYUN DONG 동현동

385 m
161 m

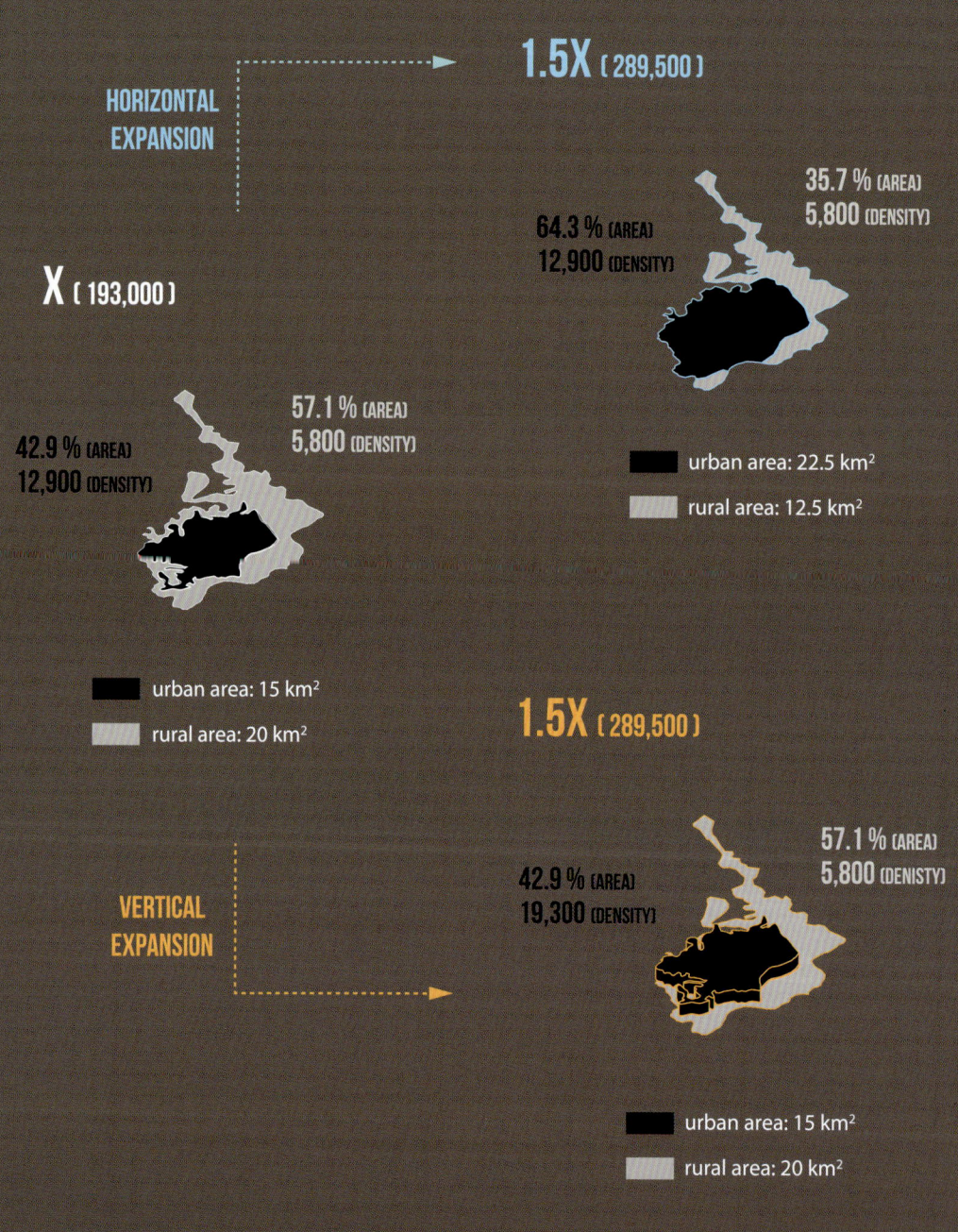

8 Major north korean cities | Kaesong

2X (386,000)

85.7 % (AREA)
12,900 (DENSITY)

14.3 % (AREA)
5,800 (DENSITY)

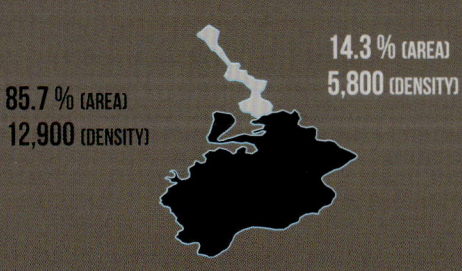

▪ urban area: 30 km²
▪ rural area: 5 km²

3X (579,000)

128.6 % (AREA)
12,900 (DENSITY)

-28.6 % (AREA)
0 (DENSITY)

▪ urban area: 45 km²
▪ rural area: -10 km²

2X (386,000)

42.9 % (AREA)
25,700 (DENSITY)

57.1 % (AREA)
5,800 (DENSITY)

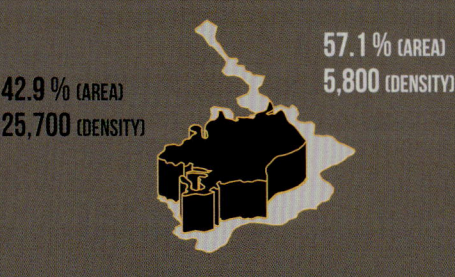

▪ urban area: 15 km²
▪ rural area: 20 km²

3X (579,000)

42.9 % (AREA)
38,600 (DENSITY)

57.1 % (AREA)
5,800 (DENSITY)

▪ urban area: 15 km²
▪ rural area: 20 km²

NAMPO 남포
SOUTH PHYONGAN PROVINCE

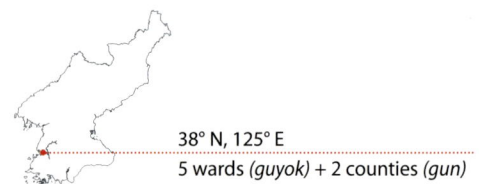

38° N, 125° E
5 wards *(guyok)* + 2 counties *(gun)*

MAP	LAP	AF	PORT	RAIL
			3	8

FAC	CO	EDU	CUL	HOSP	SPOR
24	8	16	16	4	2

POPULATION
Inhabitants	**366,815**
% Urban	84.7
% Rural	15.3
% Male	48.2
% Female	51.8

POPULATION DENSITY
Inhabitants	366,815
Administrative Area (km²)	560
Population Density (inhabitants/km²)	**655**

URBAN DENSITY
Inhabitants	310,864
Urban Area (km²)	23
Population Density (inhabitants/km²)	**13,516**

GEOGRAPHY
% Built	9.1
% Farmland	75
% Mountains	15.9

POTENTIAL GROWTH
Urbanized Area (km²)	471
% Area Increase	2,048
Urban Population	667,929
% Population Increase	953
Max. Population (million)	6.4

CENSUS HEXAGRAM

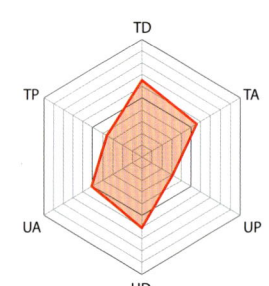

TD - Total density (1000 / km²)
TP - Total population (1,000,000)
TA - Total area (1,000 km²)
UD - Urban density (10,000 / km²)
UP - Urban population (1,000,000)
UA - Urban area (100 km²)

GEOGRAPHICAL CIRCLE

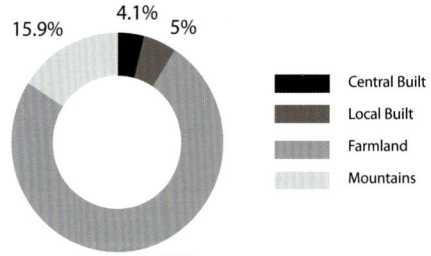

4.1% Central Built
5% Local Built
75% Farmland
15.9% Mountains

INDUSTRIAL CIRCLE

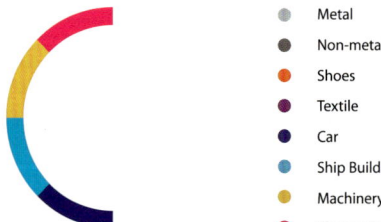

- Metal
- Non-metal
- Shoes
- Textile
- Car
- Ship Building
- Machinery
- Electronics

8 Major north korean cities | Nampo

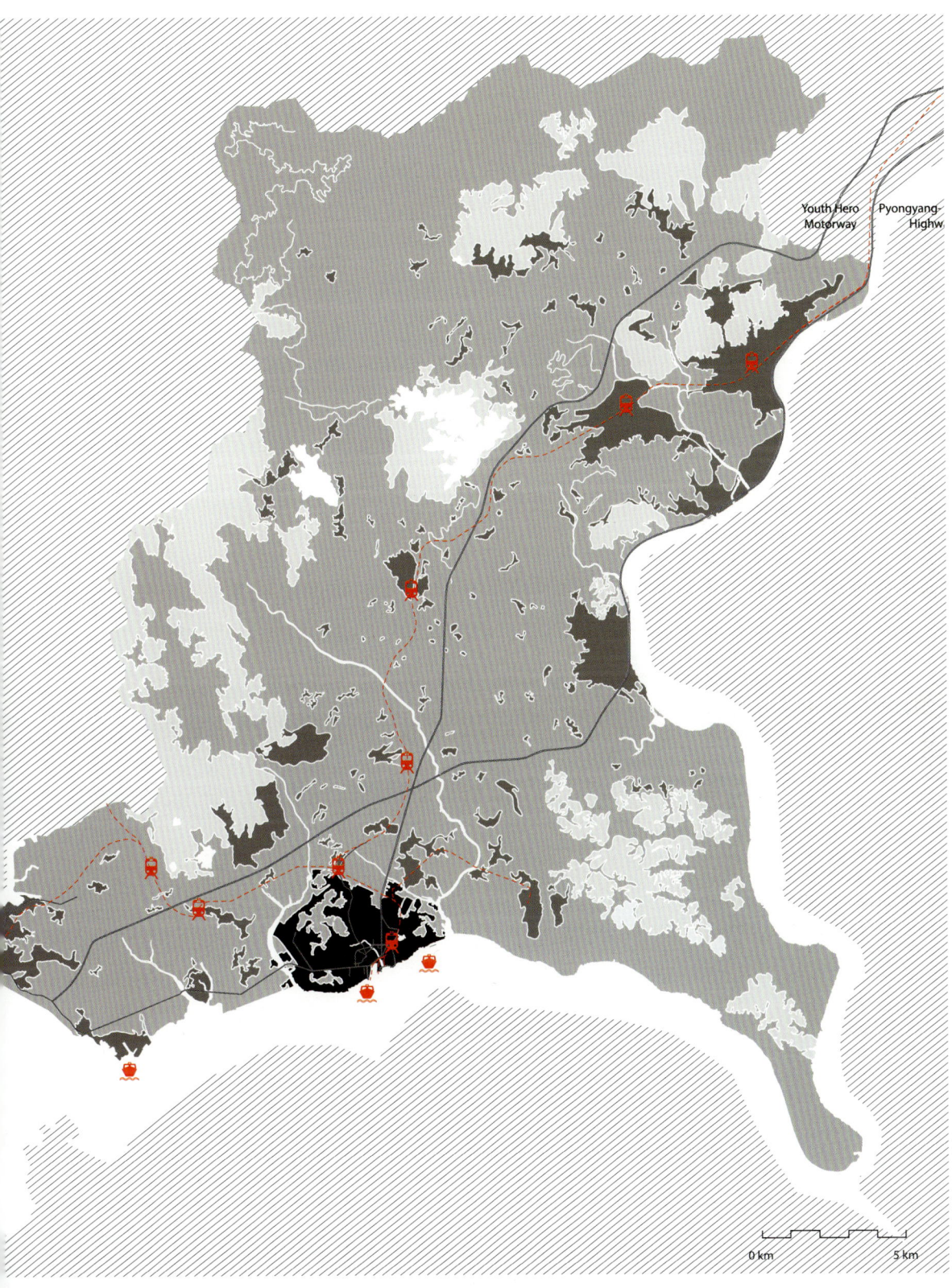

North Korean Cities

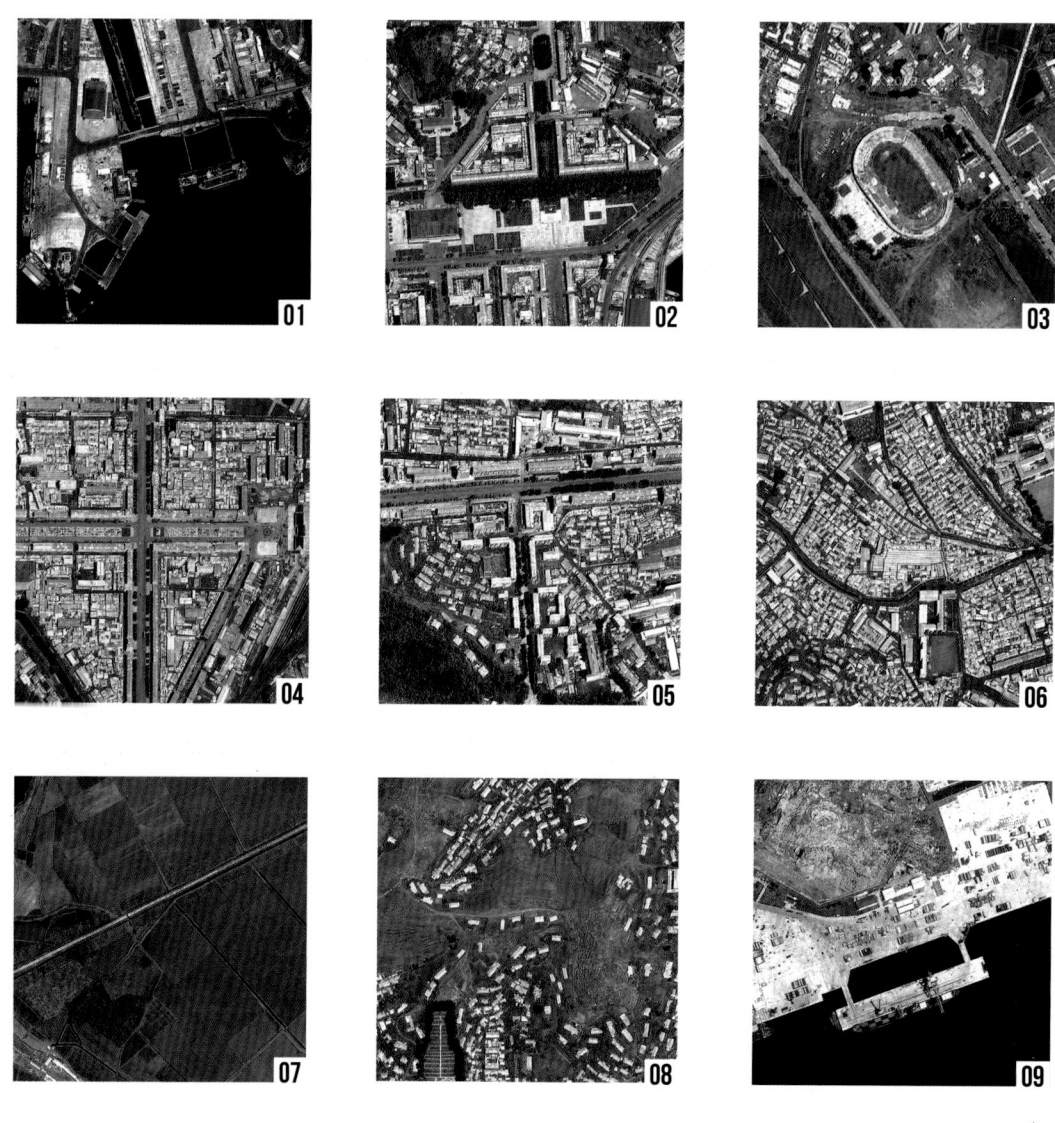

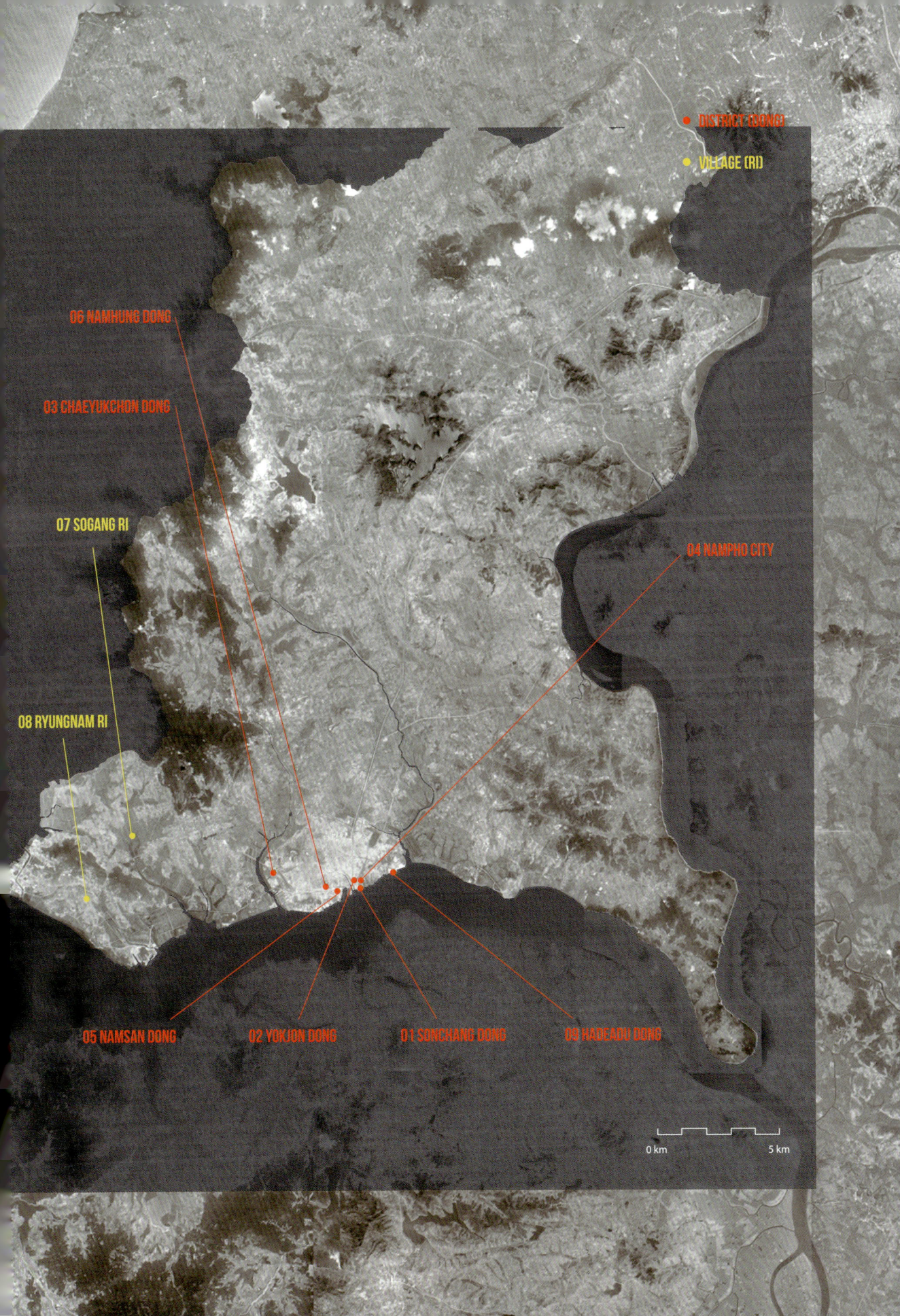

MAJOR CITY STRUCTURE - NAMPO
주요 도시 구조 - 남포

As many of port cities in North Korea, Nampo also started to have city scale development when Japanese military used it as a landing port during the Sino-Japanese war in the late 19th century. Ever since, the city had taken an important role in trades during the colonial period. As it is located at the river mouth of Daedong River, which is connected to the capital Pyongyang, it still takes an important role with its West Sea Barrage that controls the level of the river.

여타 북한의 많은 항구도시들 처럼, 남포 역시 일본군이 19세기 후반 청일전쟁 당시 상륙기지로 사용하면서 도시의 모습을 갖추기 시작하였다. 이후 남포는 일제시대 동안 한반도의 대표 무역항으로서 중요한 역할을 하였다. 평양과도 연결되어있는 대동강 하류에 위치한 남포는 서해갑문으로 강의 수위를 조절하며 현재도 중요한 역할을 수행하고 있다.

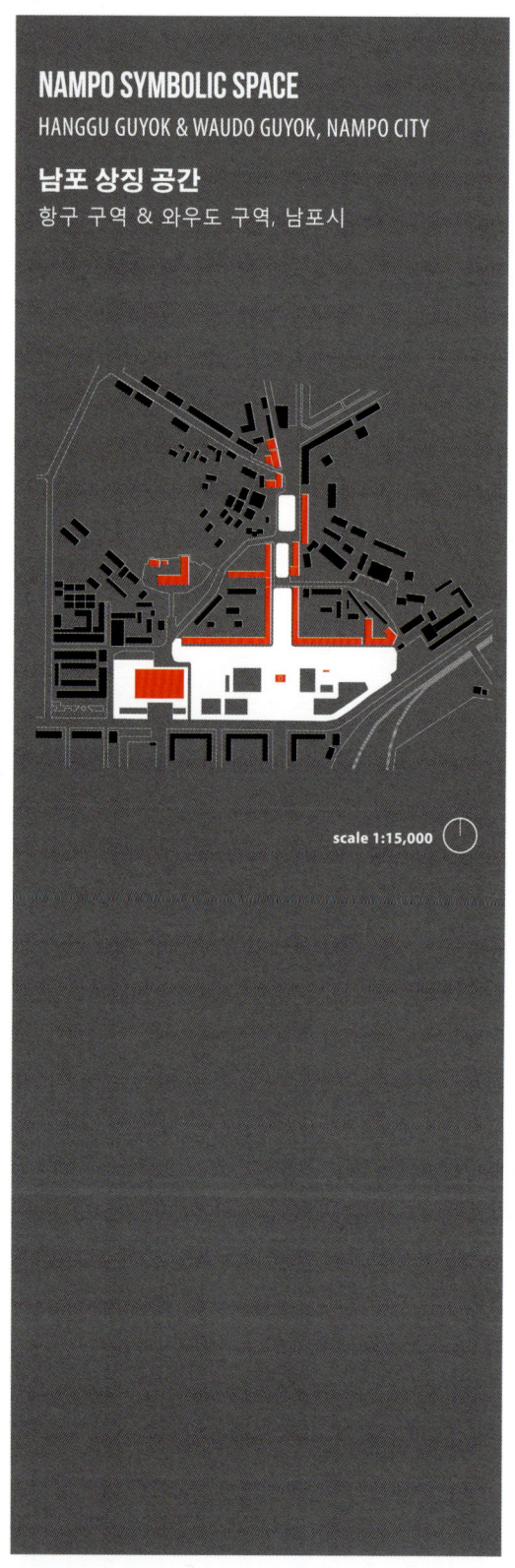
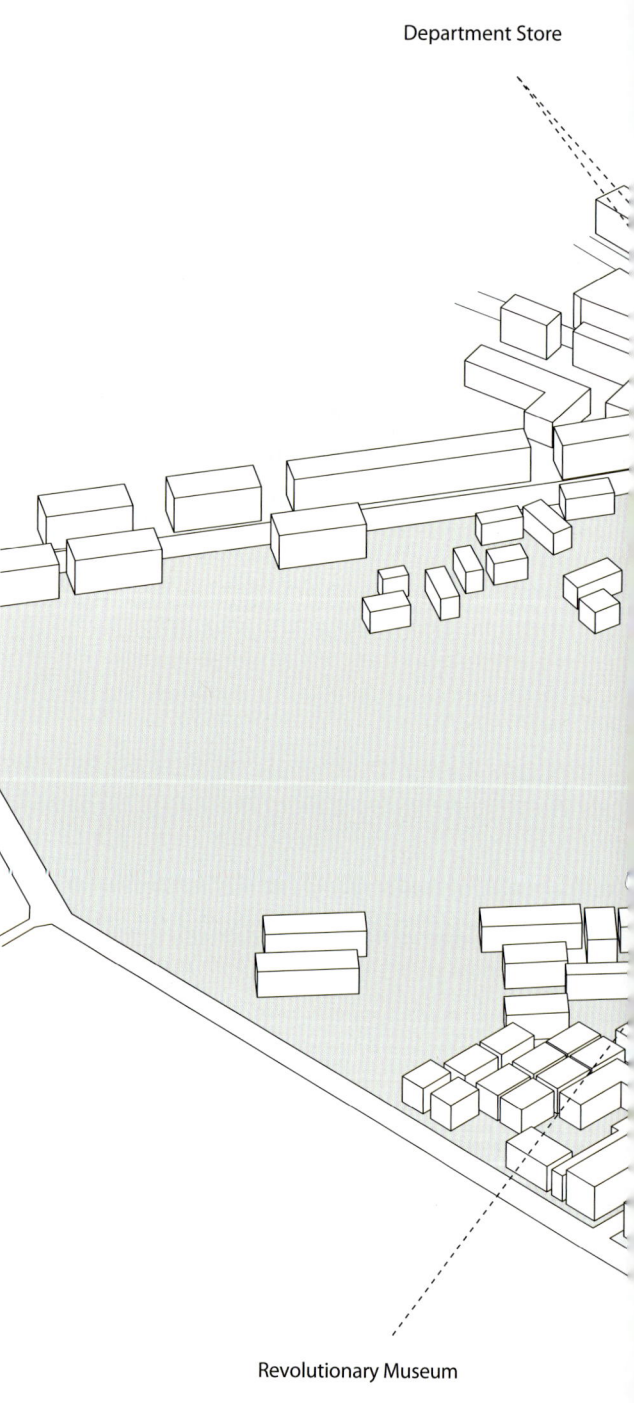

NAMPO SYMBOLIC SPACE
HANGGU GUYOK & WAUDO GUYOK, NAMPO CITY

남포 상징 공간
항구 구역 & 와우도 구역, 남포시

scale 1:15,000

Department Store

Revolutionary Museum

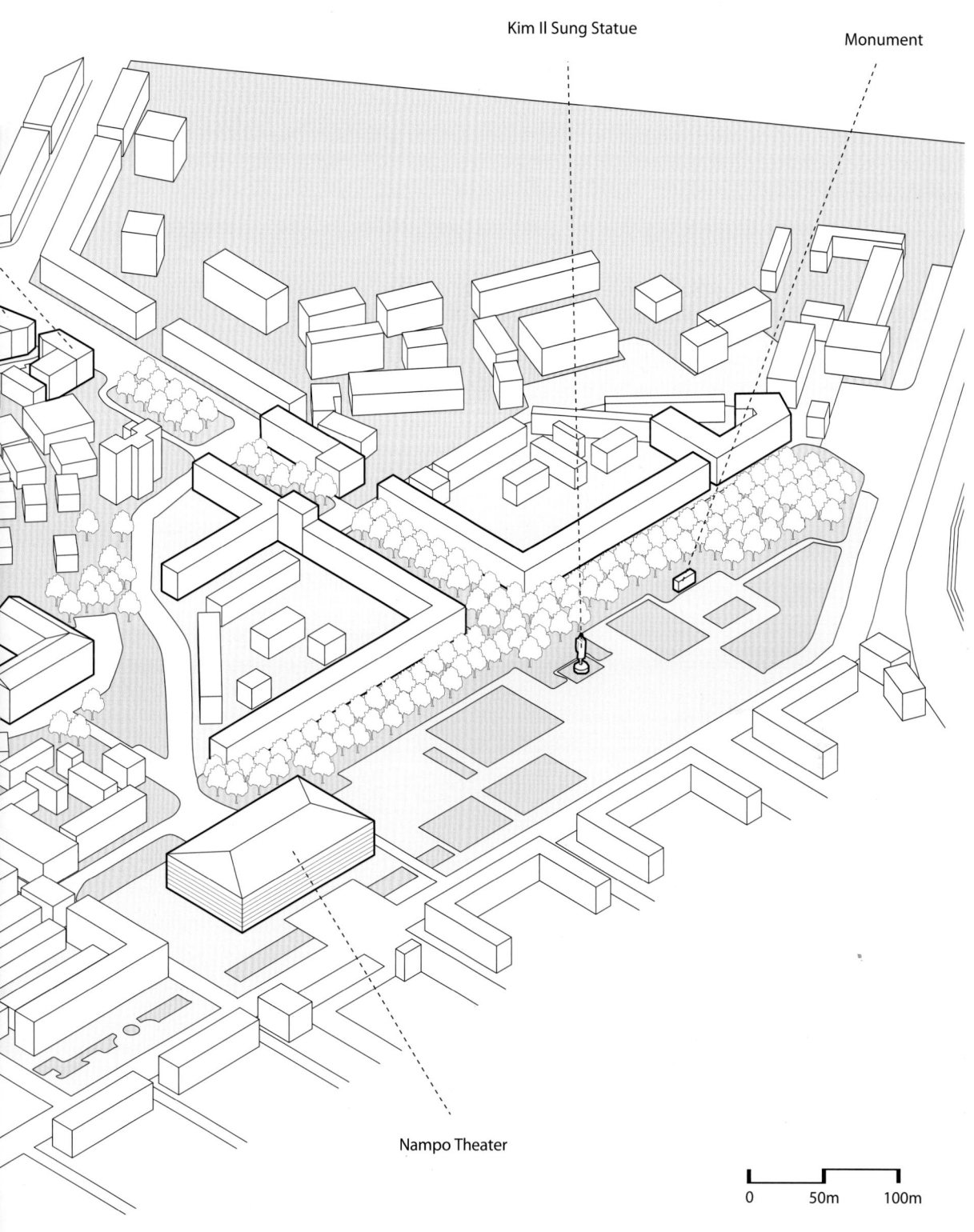

North Korean Cities

PRECINCT TYPE A
YOKJON DONG 역전동

PRECINCT TYPE B
MUNHWA DONG 문화동

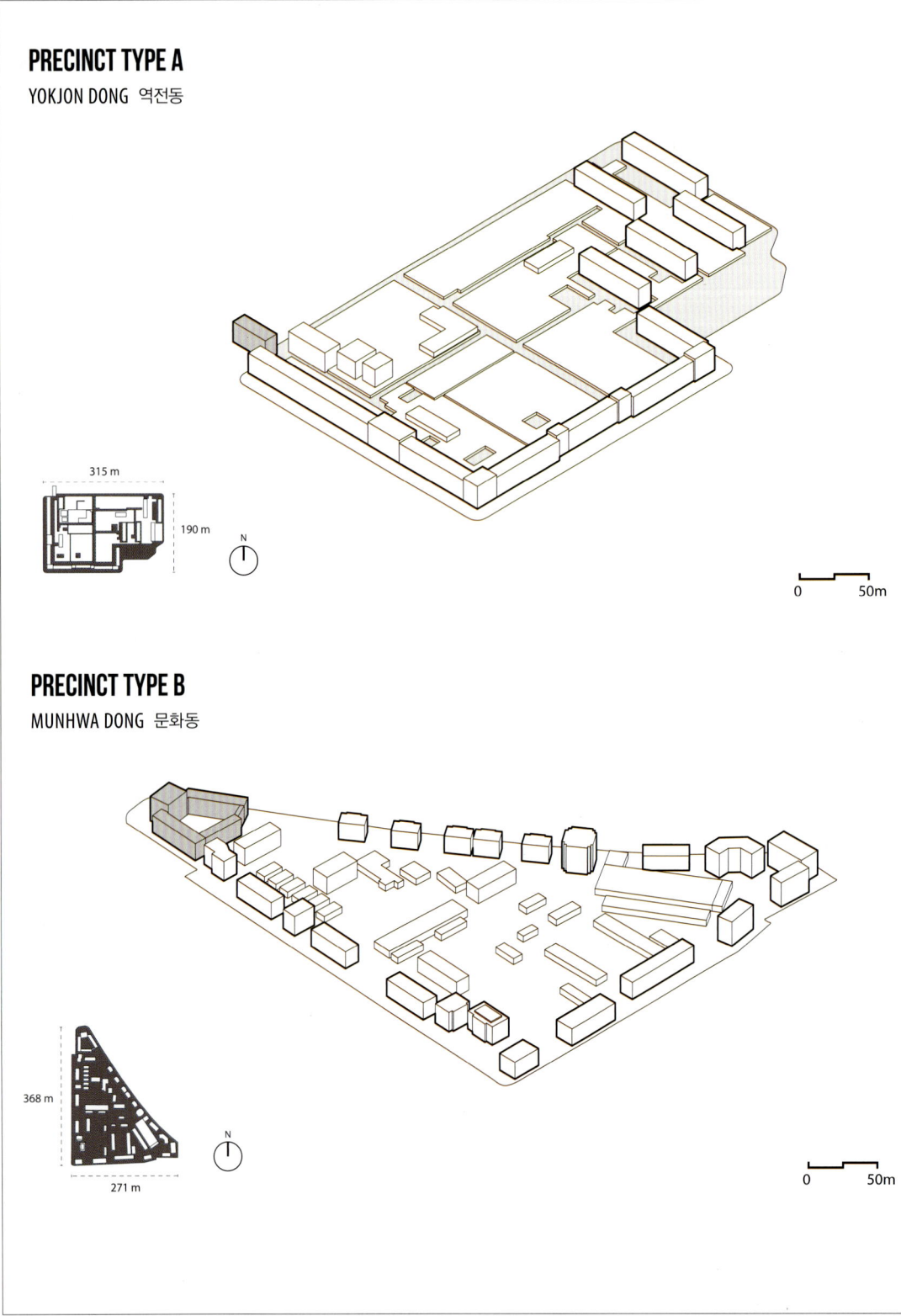

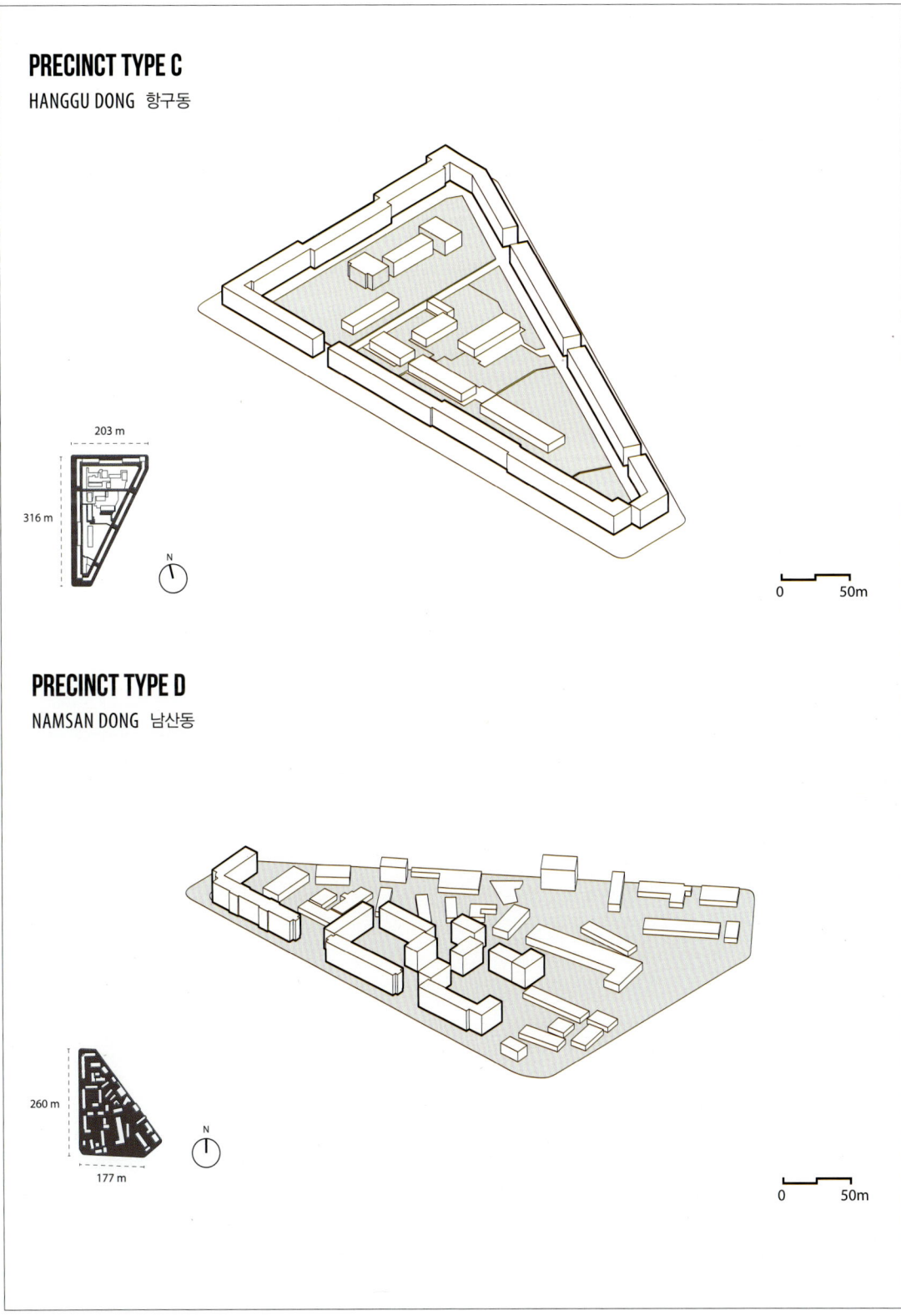

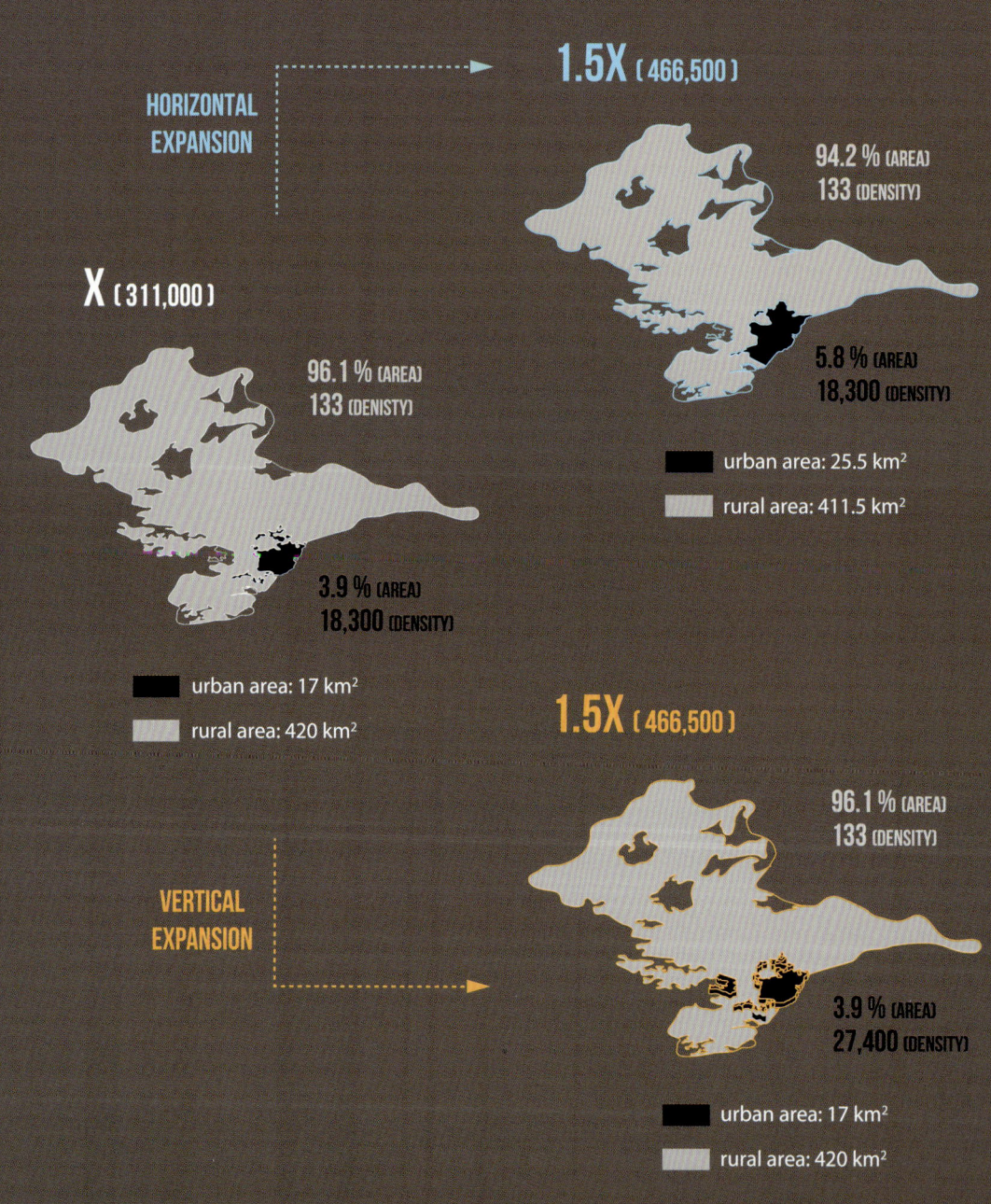

8 Major north korean cities | Nampo

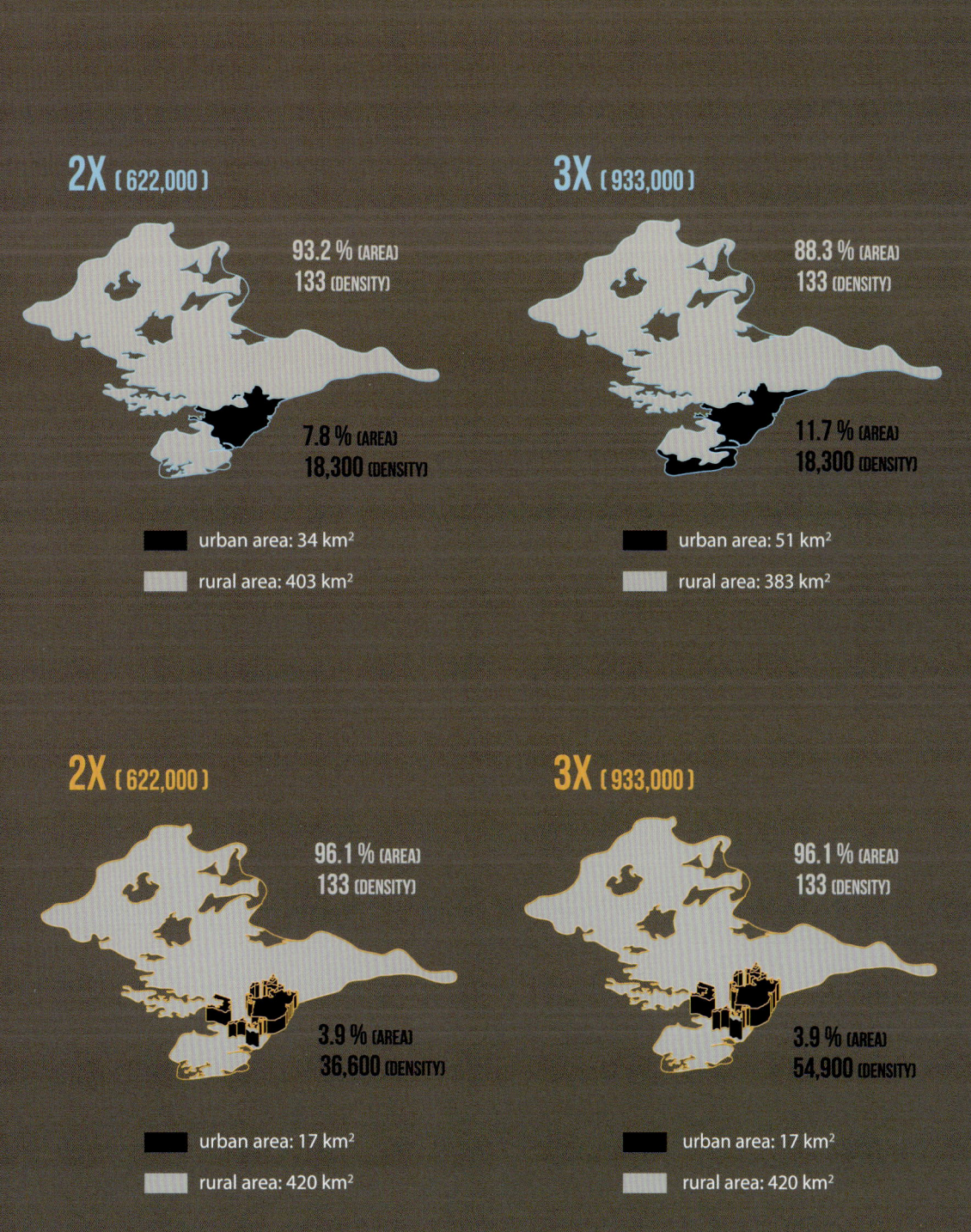

PYONGYANG 평양
PYONGYANG PROVINCE

39° N, 125° E
18 wards (*guyok*) + 2 counties (*gun*)

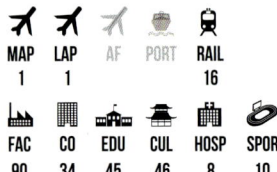

MAP	LAP	AF	PORT	RAIL
1	1			16

FAC	CO	EDU	CUL	HOSP	SPOR
90	34	45	46	8	10

POPULATION
Inhabitants	**3,255,288**
% Urban	86.7
% Rural	13.3
% Male	47.6
% Female	52.4

POPULATION DENSITY
Inhabitants	3,255,288
Administrative Area (km²)	1,578
Population Density (inhabitants/km²)	**2,063**

URBAN DENSITY
Inhabitants	2,823,414
Urban Area (km²)	142
Population Density (inhabitants/km²)	**19,883**

GEOGRAPHY
% Built	10.8
% Farmland	38.7
% Mountains	50.5

POTENTIAL GROWTH
Urbanized Area (km²)	781
% Area Increase	550
Urban Population	667,929
% Population Increase	2,325
Max. Population (million)	15.5

CENSUS HEXAGRAM
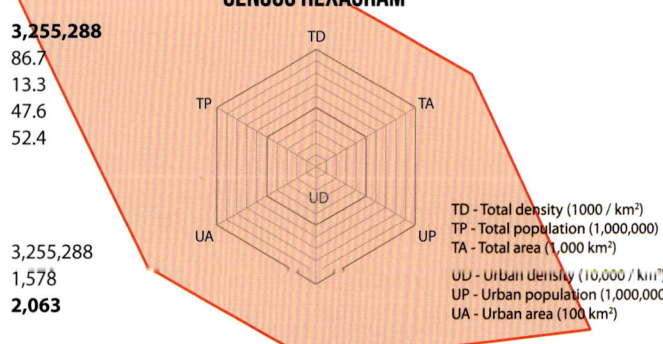

TD - Total density (1000 / km²)
TP - Total population (1,000,000)
TA - Total area (1,000 km²)
UD - Urban density (10,000 / km²)
UP - Urban population (1,000,000)
UA - Urban area (100 km²)

GEOGRAPHICAL CIRCLE
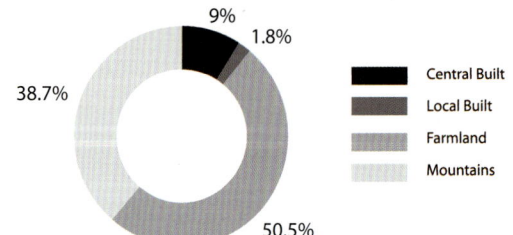

- Central Built — 1.8%
- Local Built — 9%
- Farmland — 38.7%
- Mountains — 50.5%

INDUSTRIAL CIRCLE
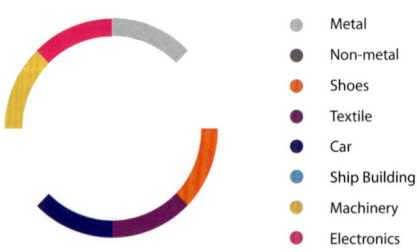

- Metal
- Non-metal
- Shoes
- Textile
- Car
- Ship Building
- Machinery
- Electronics

8 Major north korean cities | Pyongyang

Youth Hero Motorway

North Korean Cities

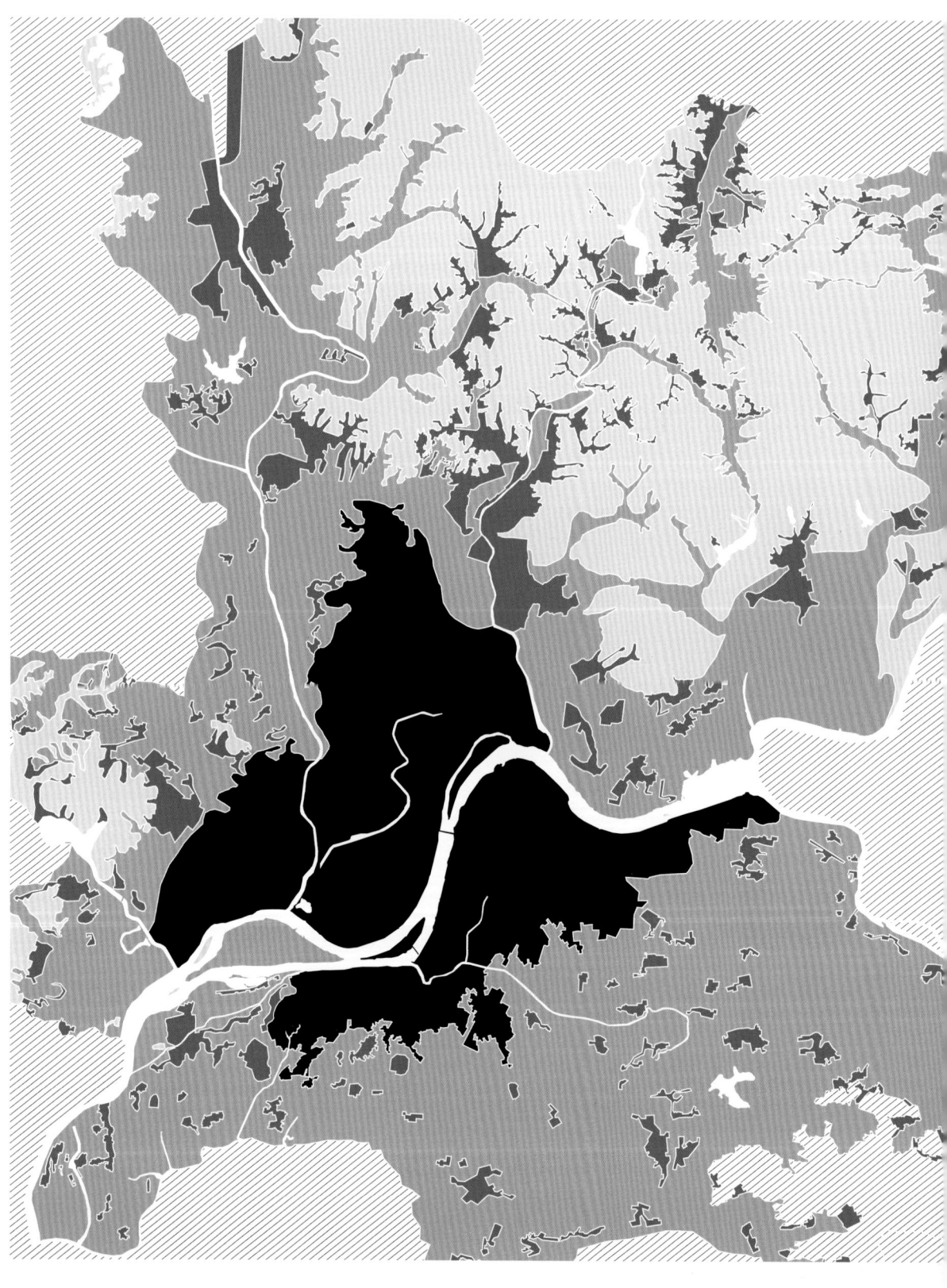

8 Major north korean cities | Pyongyang

North Korean Cities

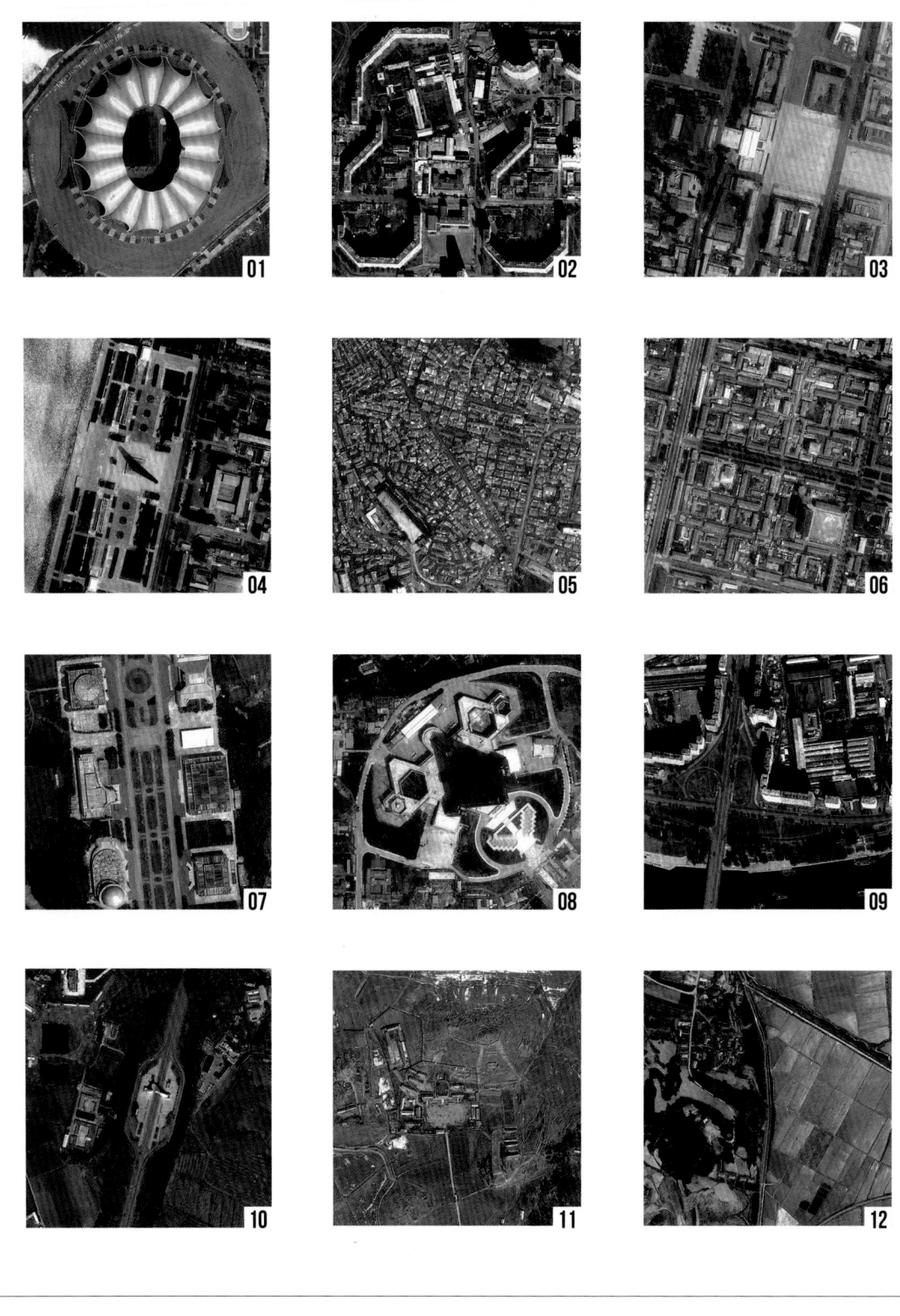

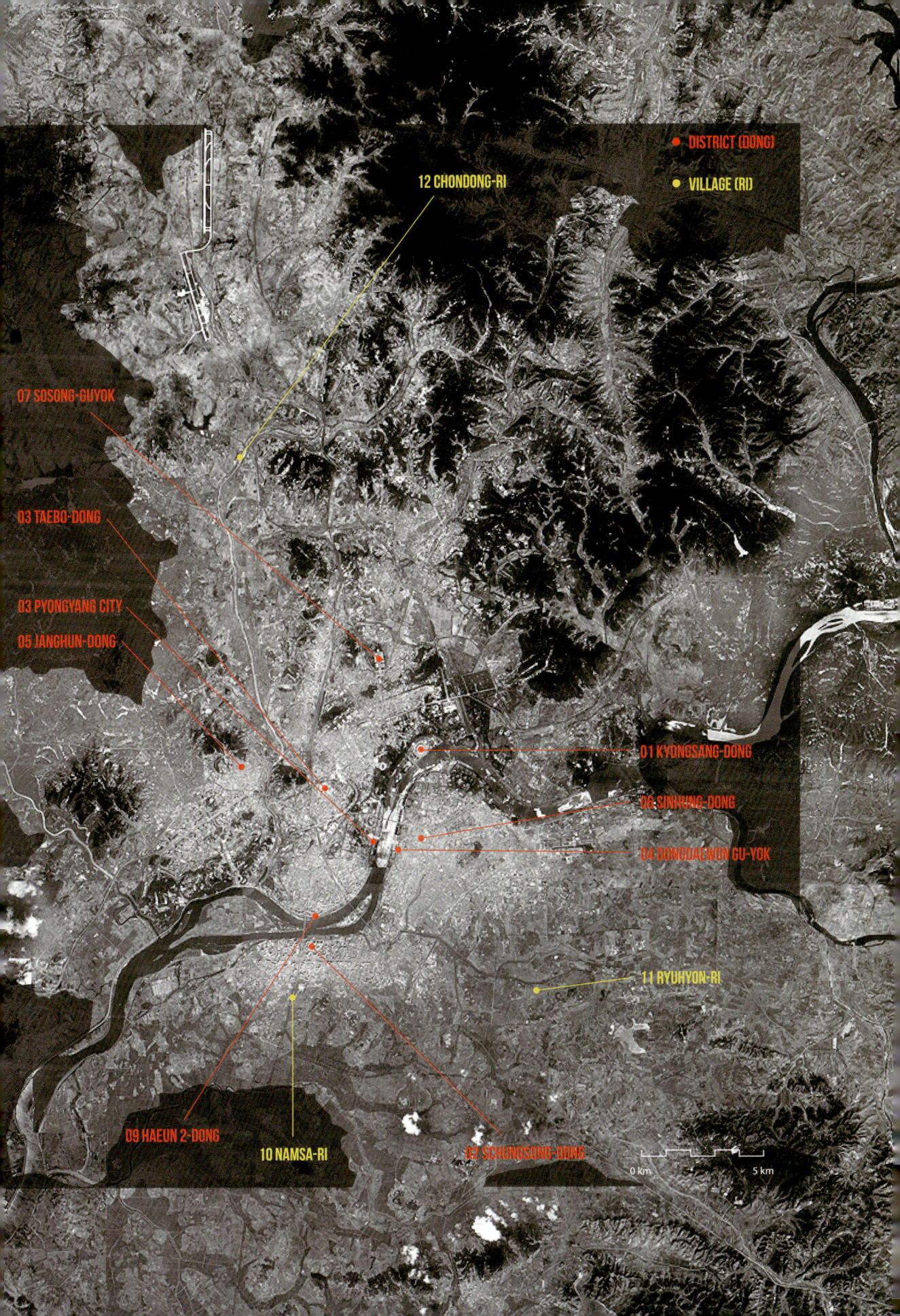

MAJOR CITY STRUCTURE - PYONGYANG
주요 도시 구조 - 평양

Pyongyang is the only city in North Korea that has more than a million people. It has about 3 million people in the city, which is around 13% of the total population of North Korea. Even though the whole city structure was reset during the Korean War, Kim Il Sung decided to keep the city as the nation's capital, and built an ideal socialist city on top of the ruins. As it is considered as the face of the country, it has numbers of symbolic spaces as well as monumental buildings as part of its propaganda.

평양은 북한의 도시에서 유일하게 백만이 넘는 인구를 가진 도시이다. 평양은 3백만정도의 인구를 갖고 있으며 이는 북한 전체 인구에 약 13%에 해당하는 수치이다. 한국전쟁 당시 대부분의 도시조직이 소멸되었음에도 불구하고, 김일성은 평양을 북한의 수도로서 재건되길 원했고, 결국 전쟁의 잔해 위에 이상적인 사회주의 도시가 건설되었다. 평양은 북한의 얼굴로 간주되기 때문에, 수많은 상징적인 공간과 건물들이 북한의 선전의 일부로 존재하고 있다.

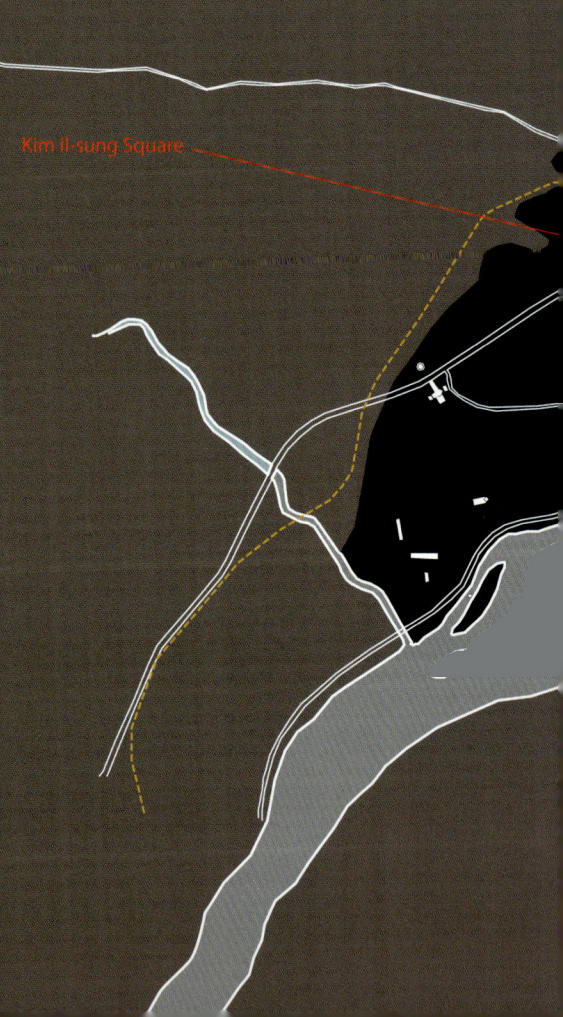

Liberation War Monument

Ryugyung Hotel

Kim Il-sung Square

North Korean Cities

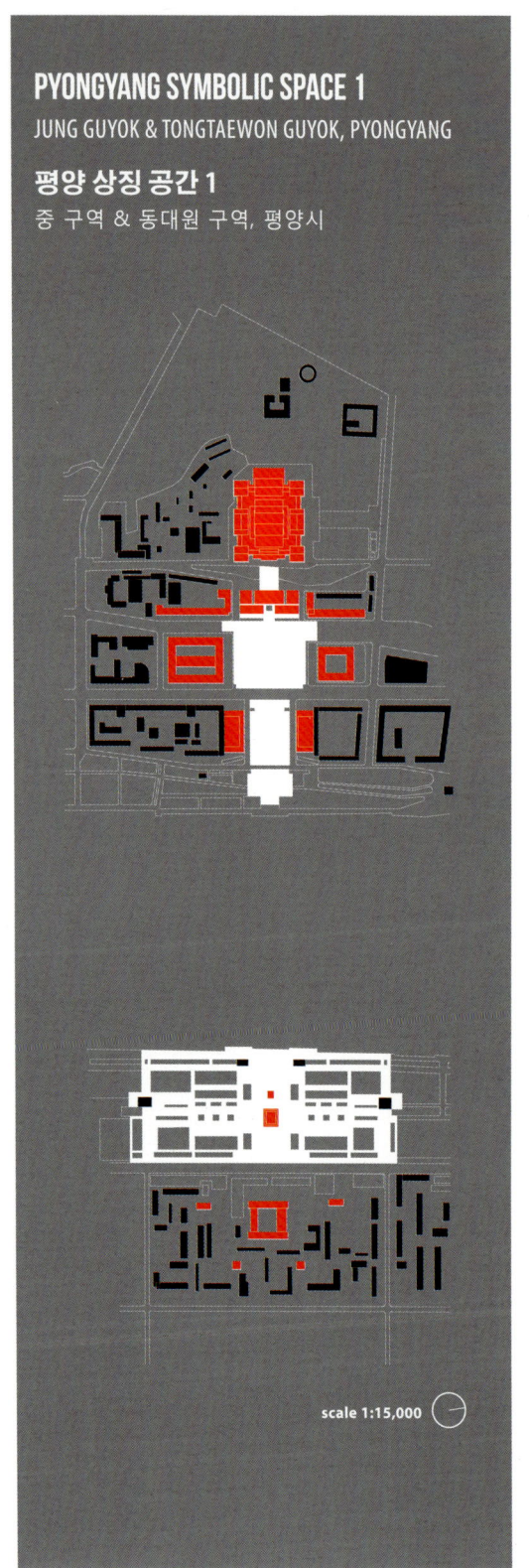

PYONGYANG SYMBOLIC SPACE 1
JUNG GUYOK & TONGTAEWON GUYOK, PYONGYANG

평양 상징 공간 1
중 구역 & 동대원 구역, 평양시

scale 1:15,000

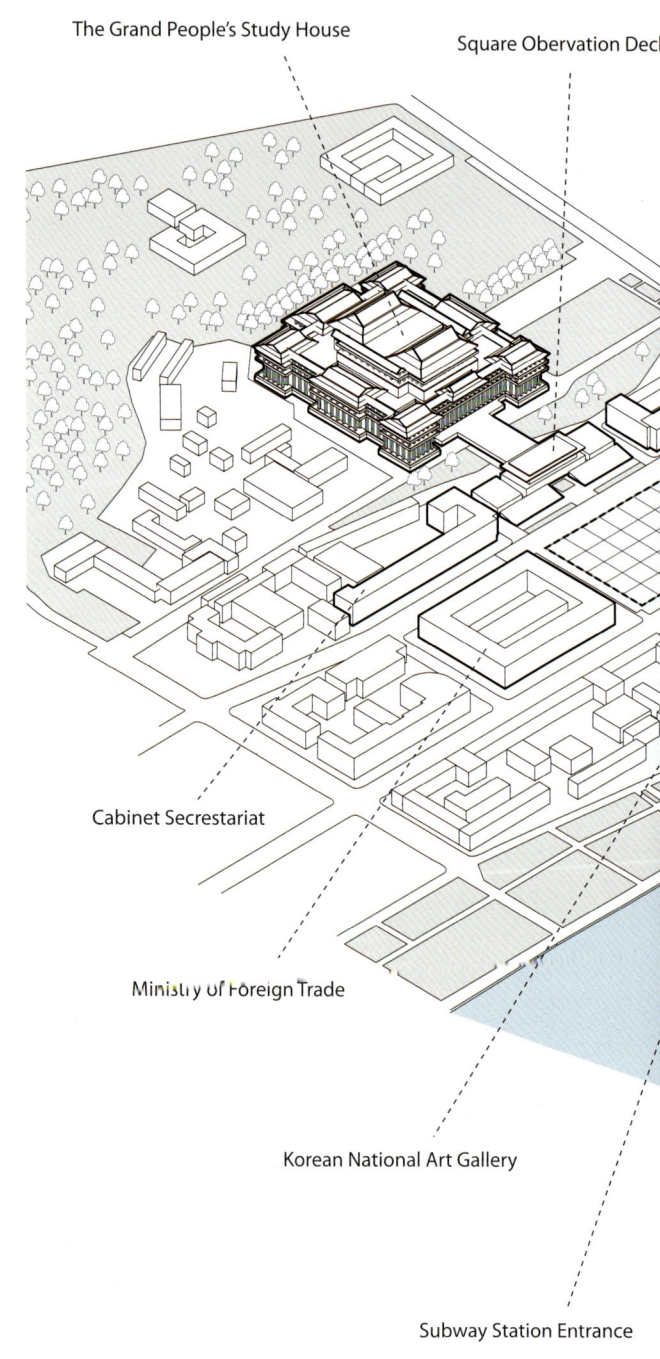

- The Grand People's Study House
- Square Obervation Deck
- Cabinet Secrestariat
- Ministry of Foreign Trade
- Korean National Art Gallery
- Subway Station Entrance

8 Major north korean cities | Pyongyang

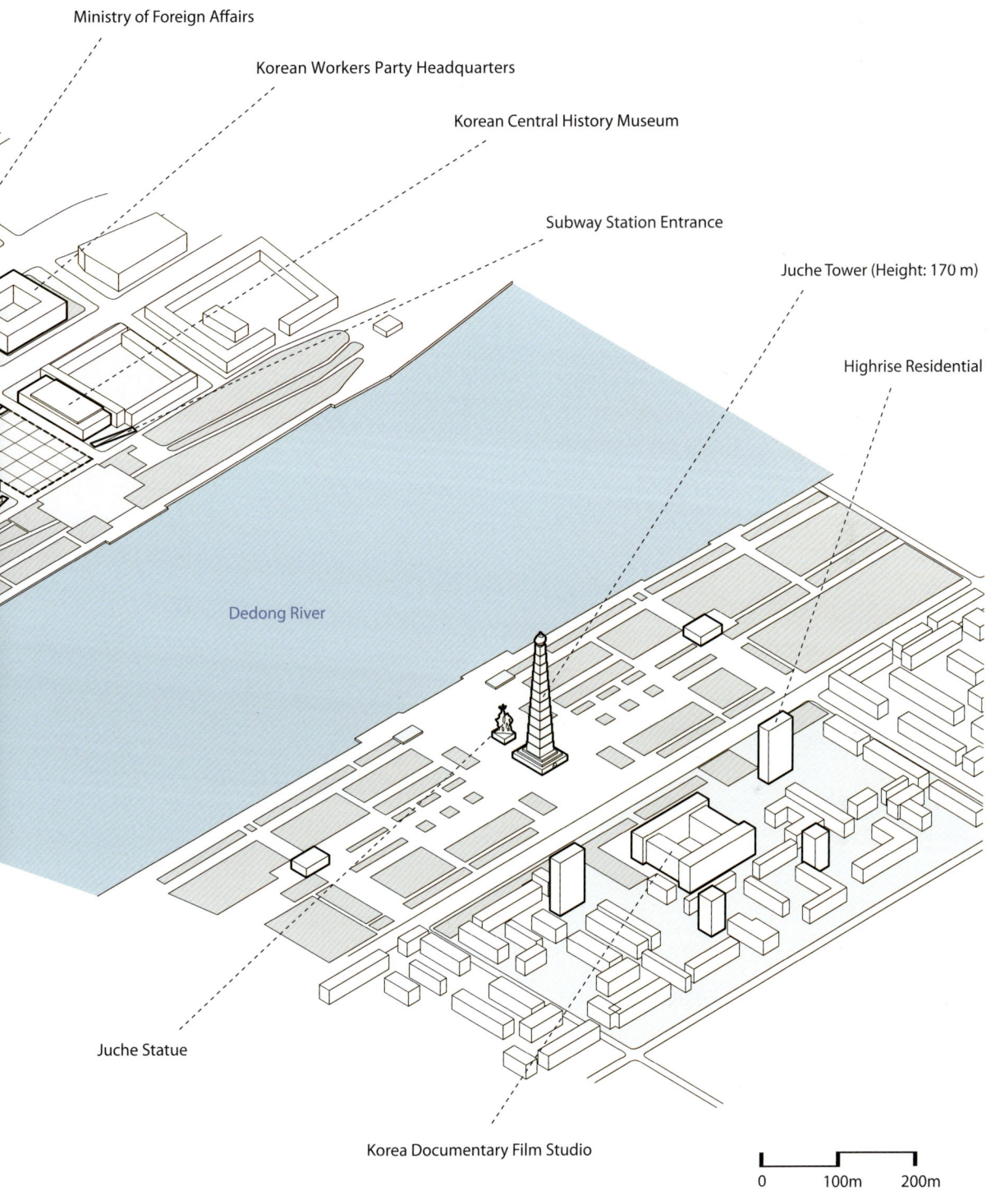

North Korean Cities

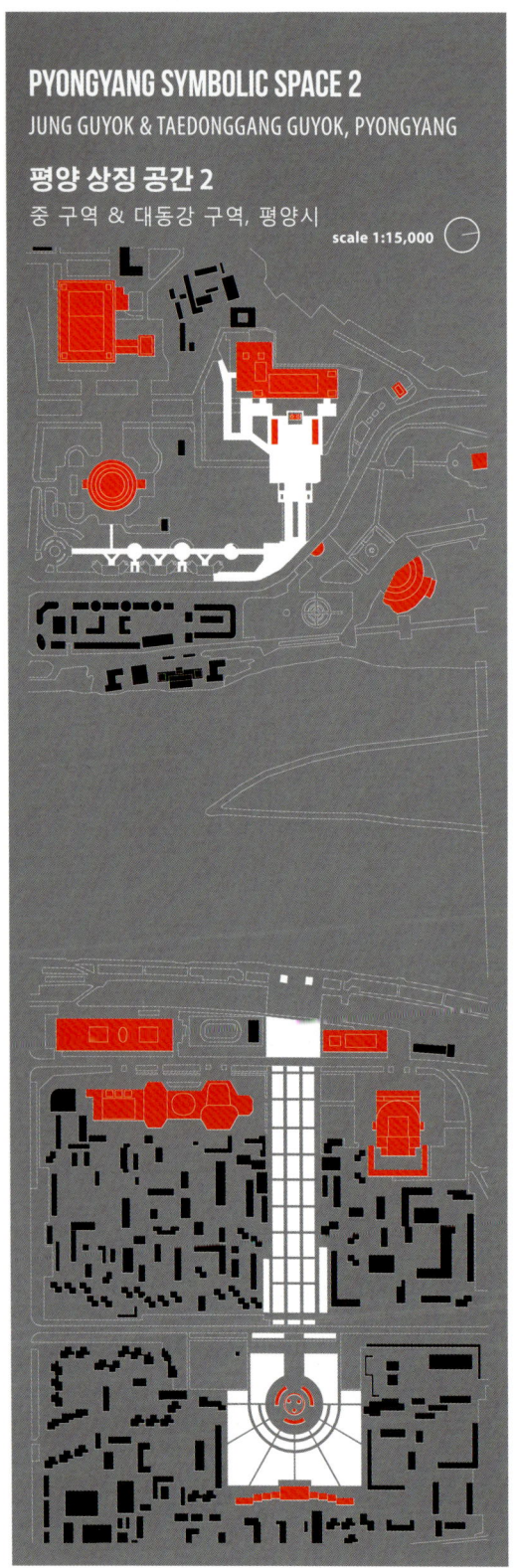

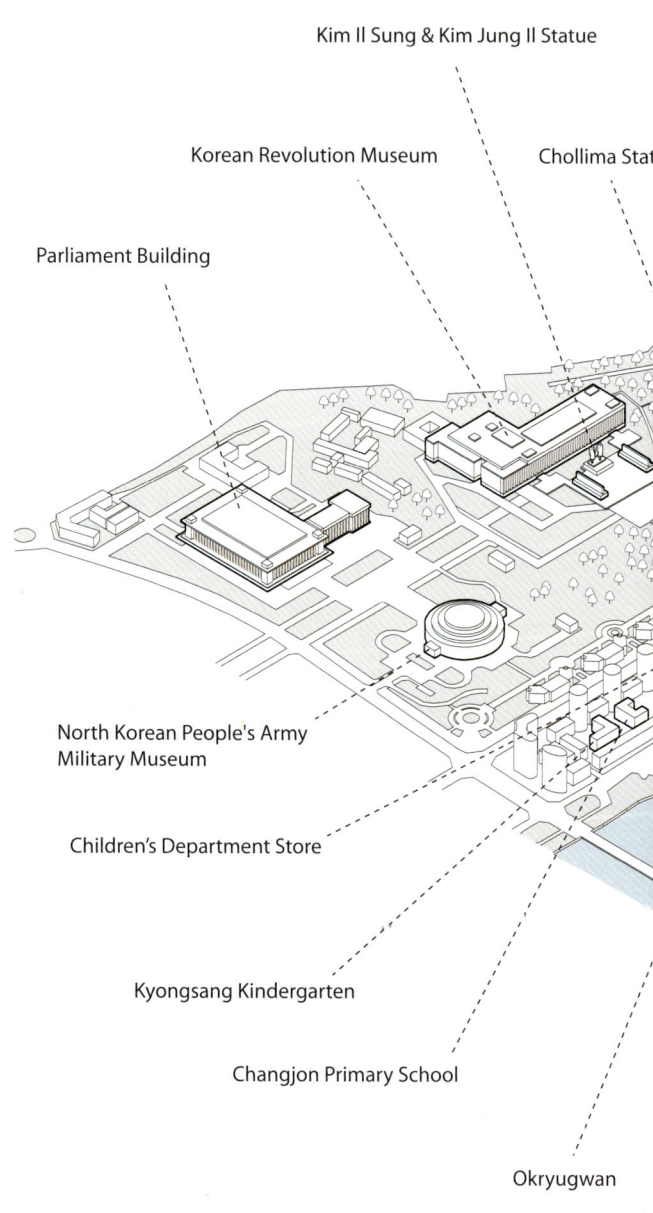

Kim Il Sung & Kim Jung Il Statue
Korean Revolution Museum
Chollima Statue
Parliament Building
North Korean People's Army Military Museum
Children's Department Store
Kyongsang Kindergarten
Changjon Primary School
Okryugwan

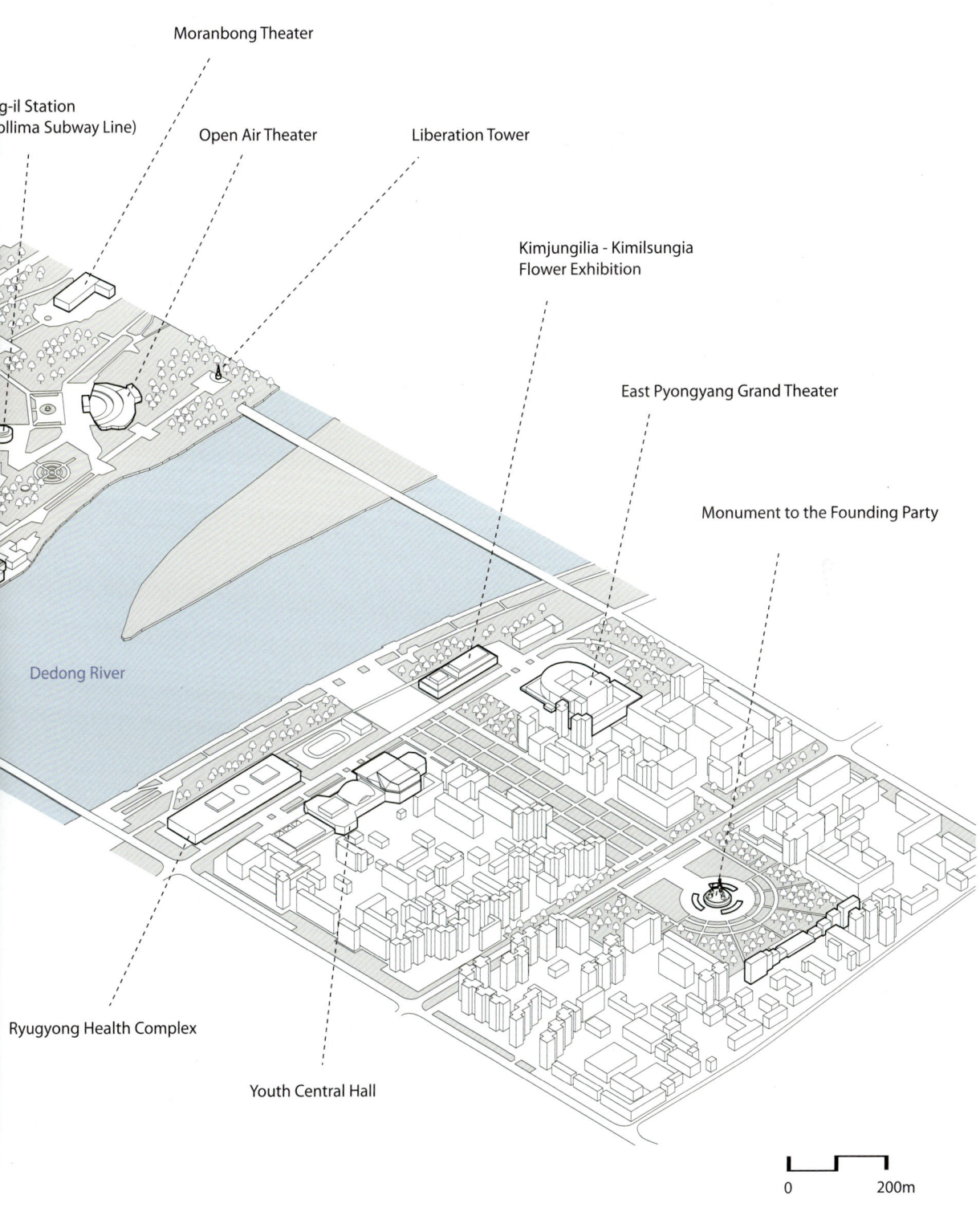

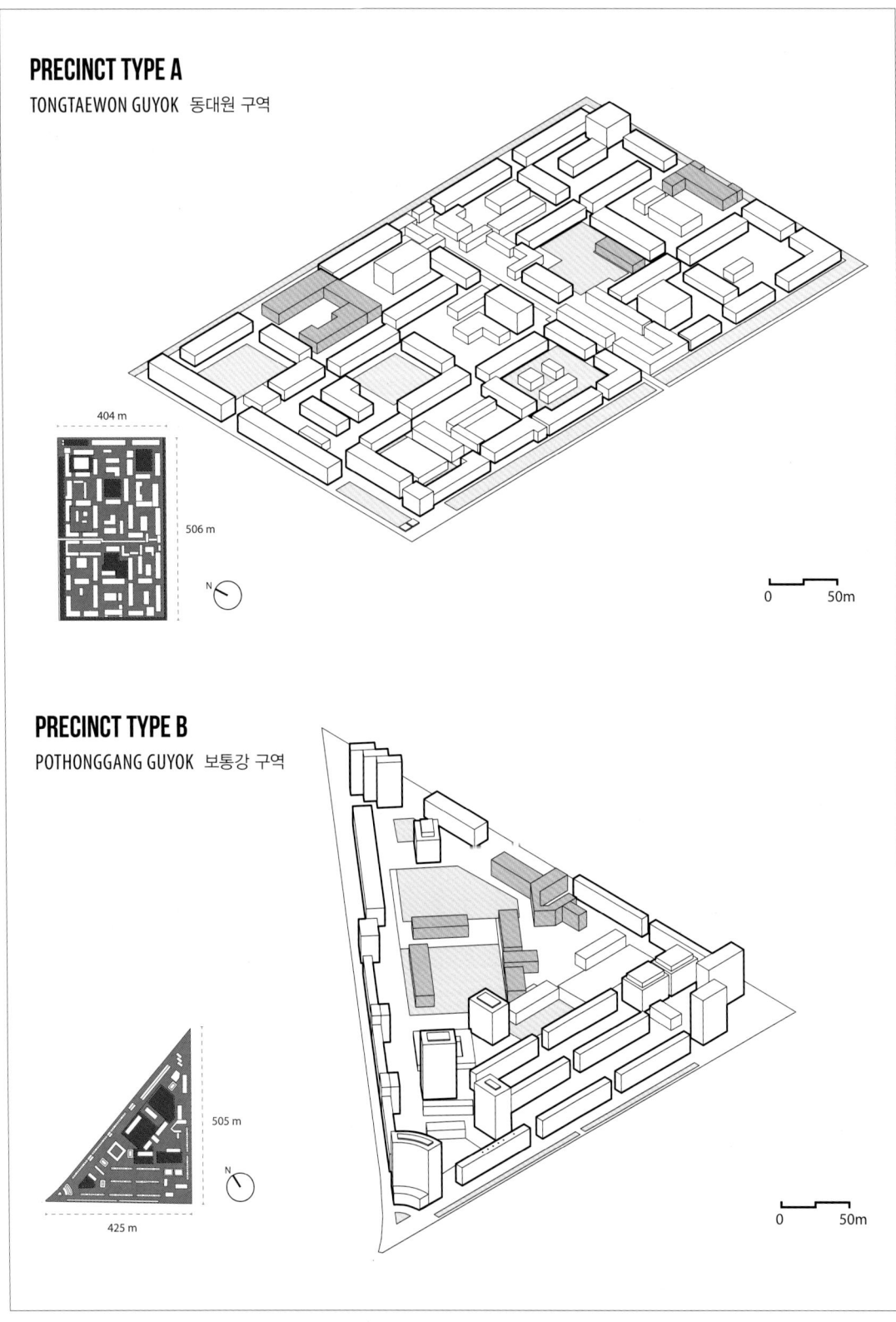

PRECINCT TYPE A
TONGTAEWON GUYOK 동대원 구역

PRECINCT TYPE B
POTHONGGANG GUYOK 보통강 구역

8 Major north korean cities | Pyongyang

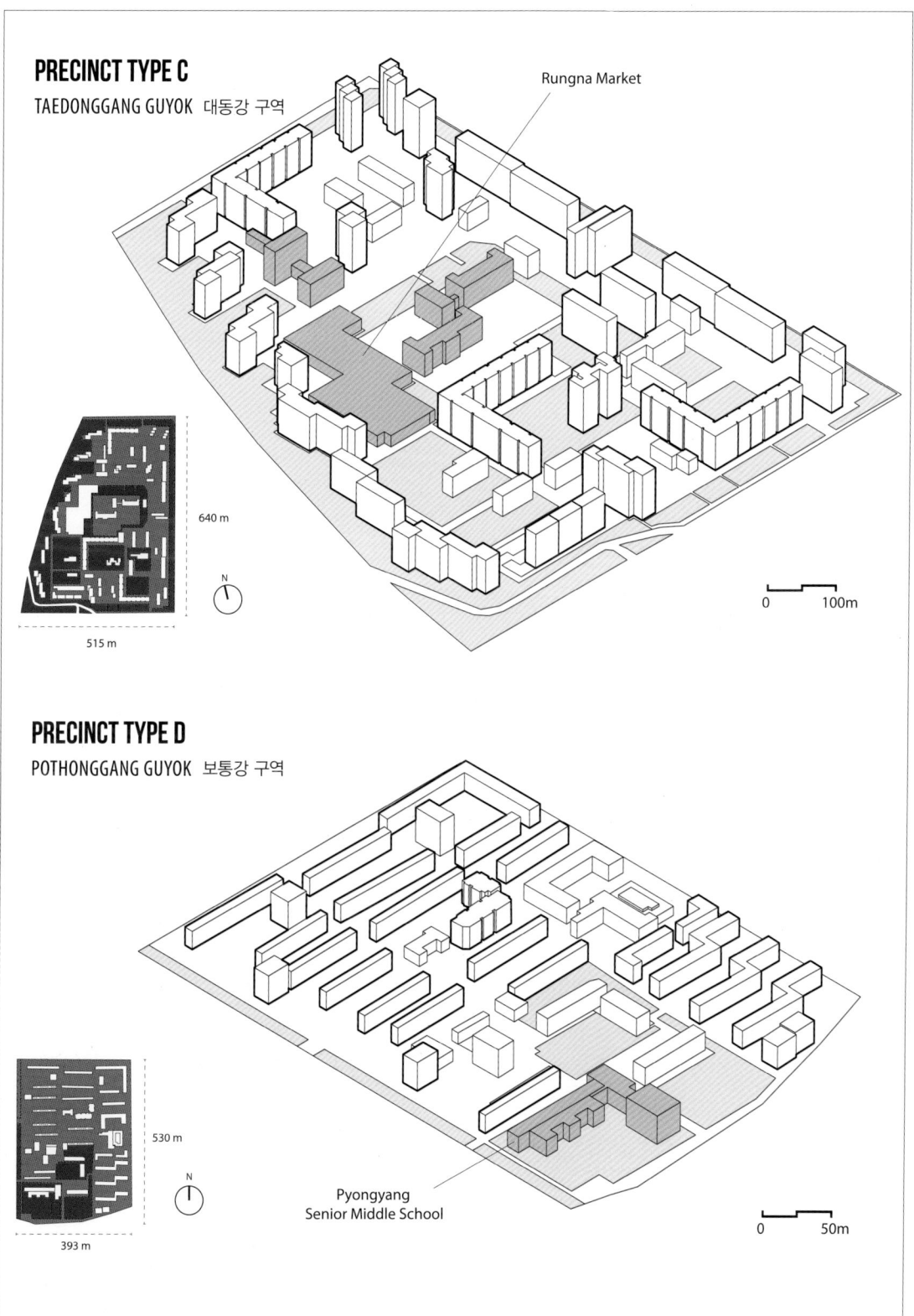

PRECINCT TYPE C
TAEDONGGANG GUYOK 대동강 구역

Rungna Market

PRECINCT TYPE D
POTHONGGANG GUYOK 보통강 구역

Pyongyang Senior Middle School

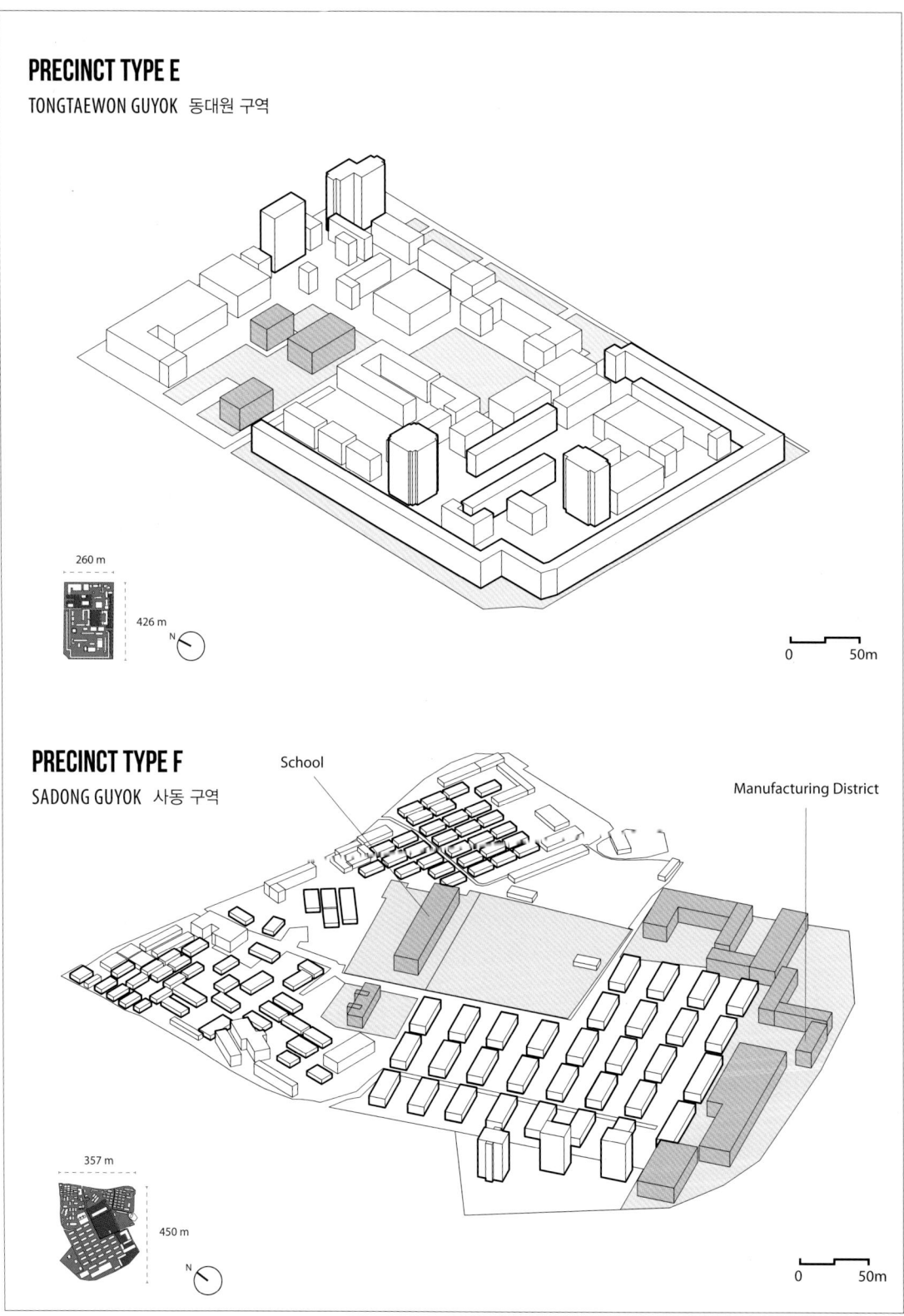

8 Major north korean cities | Pyongyang

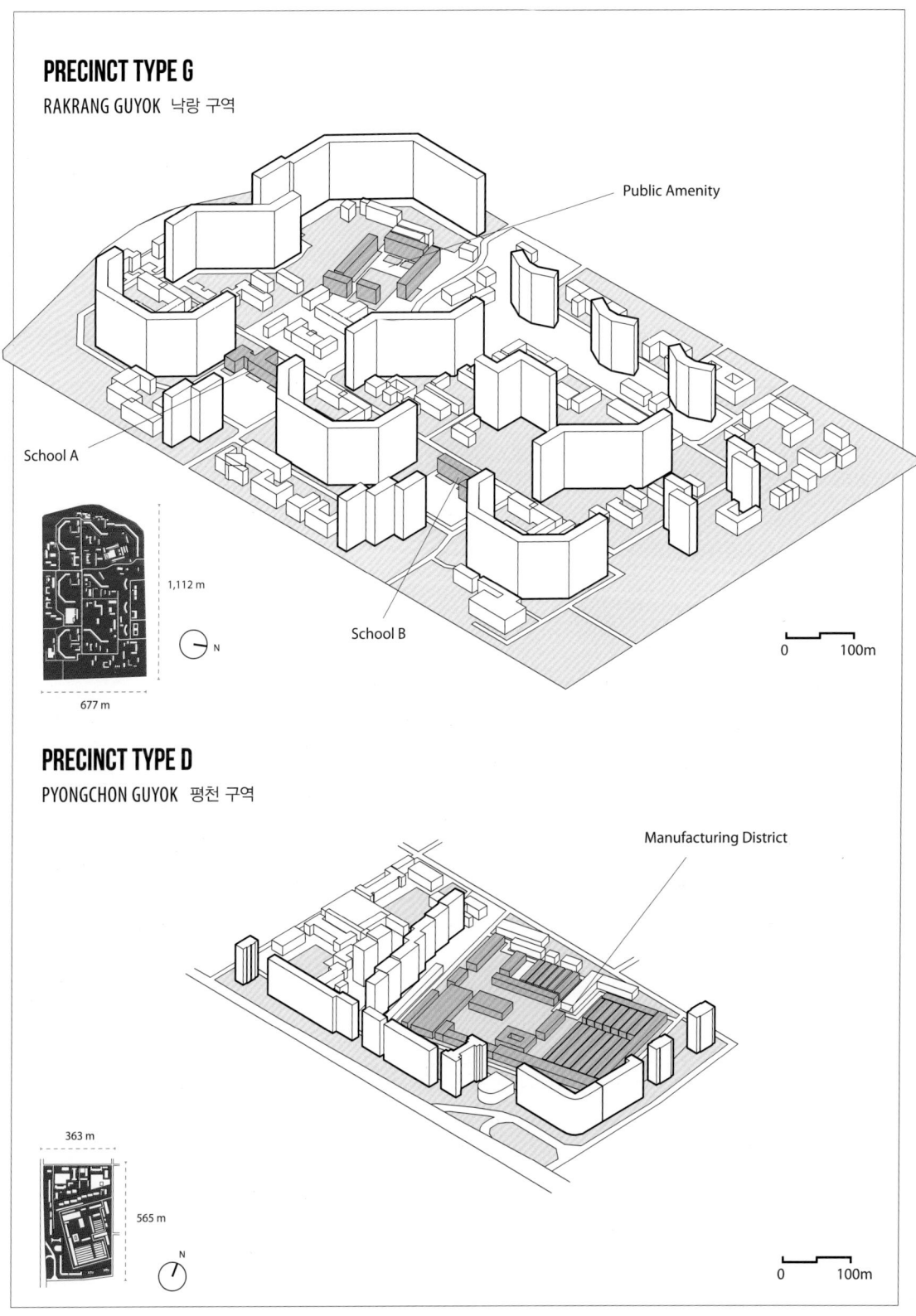

PRECINCT TYPE G
RAKRANG GUYOK 낙랑 구역

PRECINCT TYPE D
PYONGCHON GUYOK 평천 구역

POSSIBLE URBAN GROWTH - PYONGYANG (X= URBAN POPULATION: 2,823,000)
도시 성장 잠재력 분석 - 평양

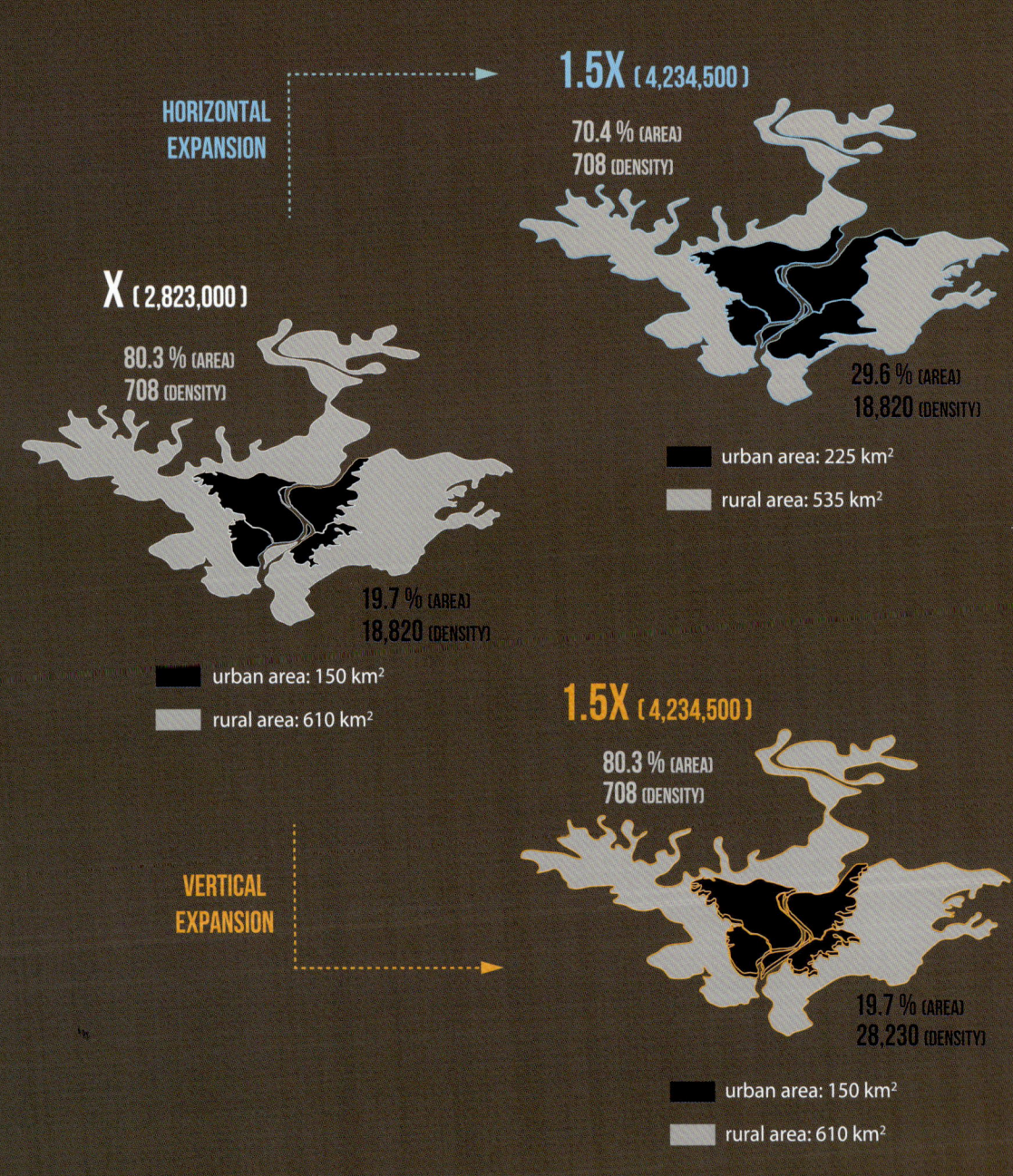

8 Major north korean cities | Pyongyang

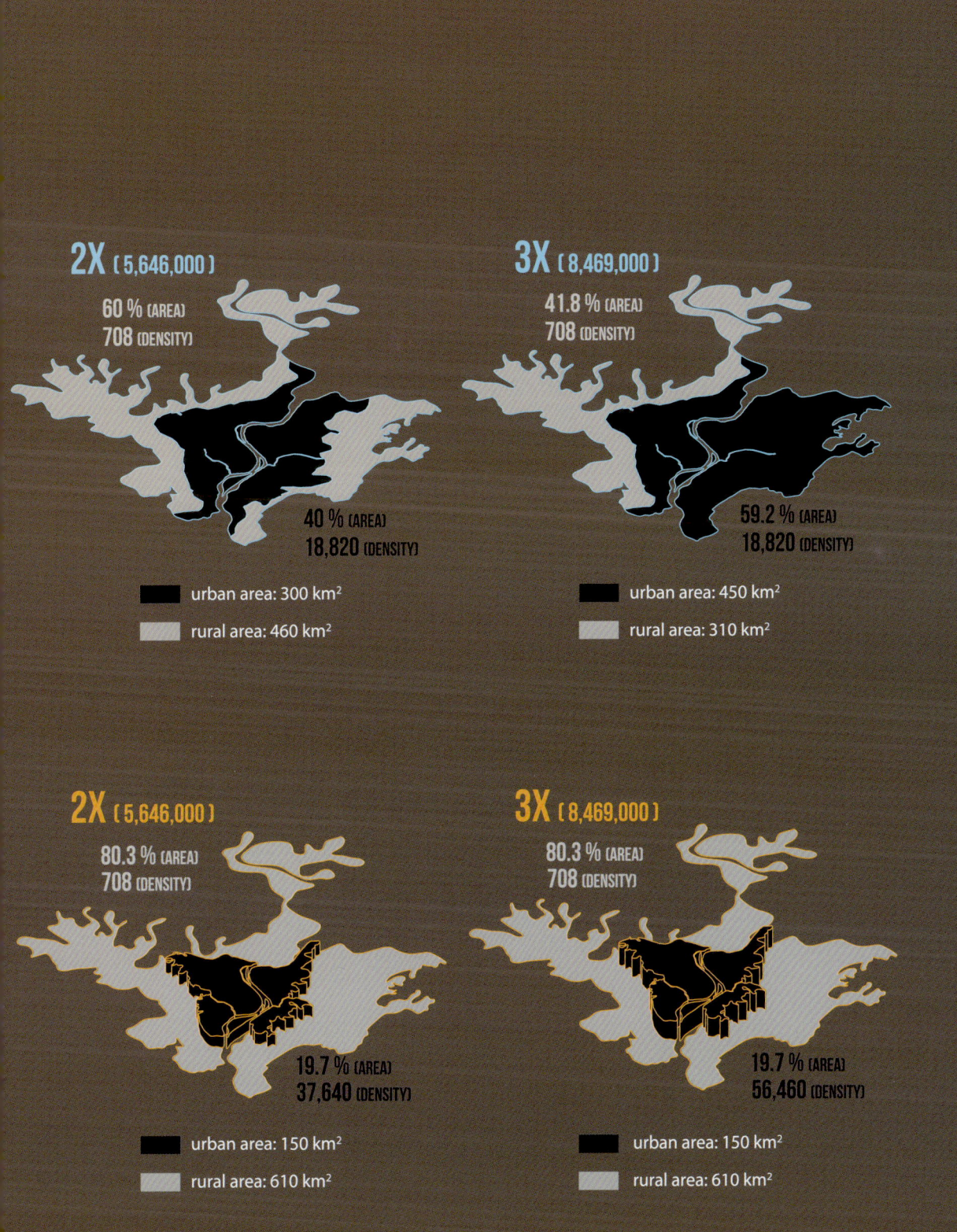

RASON 라선
NORTH HAMGYONG PROVINCE

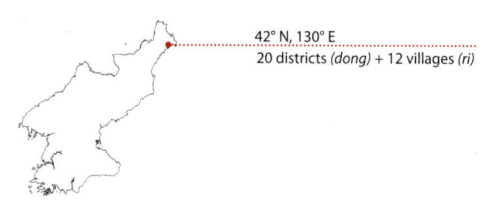

42° N, 130° E
20 districts *(dong)* + 12 villages *(ri)*

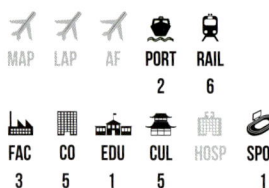

MAP	LAP	AF	PORT	RAIL
			2	6

FAC	CO	EDU	CUL	HOSP	SPOR
3	5	1	5		1

POPULATION
Inhabitants	**196,964**
% Urban	80.4
% Rural	19.6
% Male	47.2
% Female	52.8

POPULATION DENSITY
Inhabitants	196,964
Administrative Area (km²)	825
Population Density (inhabitants/km²)	**239**

URBAN DENSITY
Inhabitants	158,337
Urban Area (km²)	42
Population Density (inhabitants/km²)	**3,748**

GEOGRAPHY
% Built	11
% Farmland	52.1
% Mountains	36.9

POTENTIAL GROWTH
Urbanized Area (km²)	521
% Area Increase	1,240
Urban Population	196,964
% Population Increase	991
Max. Population (million)	1.9

CENSUS HEXAGRAM

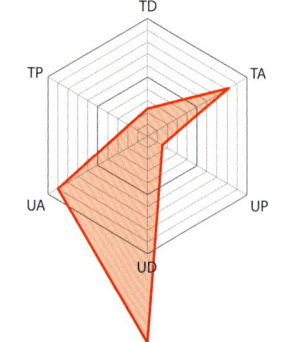

TD - Total density (1000 / km²)
TP - Total population (1,000,000)
TA - Total area (1,000 km²)

UD - Urban density (10,000 / km²)
UP - Urban population (1,000,000)
UA - Urban area (100 km²)

GEOGRAPHICAL CIRCLE

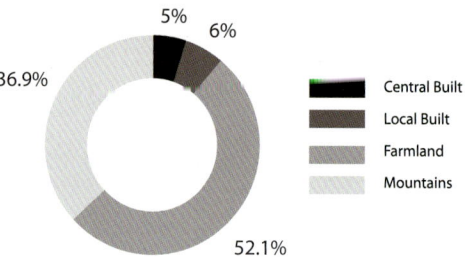

- Central Built — 5%
- Local Built — 6%
- Farmland — 52.1%
- Mountains — 36.9%

INDUSTRIAL CIRCLE

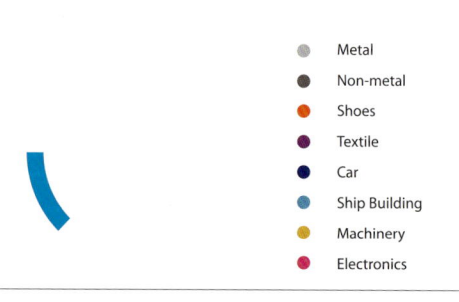

- Metal
- Non-metal
- Shoes
- Textile
- Car
- Ship Building
- Machinery
- Electronics

8 Major north korean cities | Rason

8 Major north korean cities | Rason

North Korean Cities

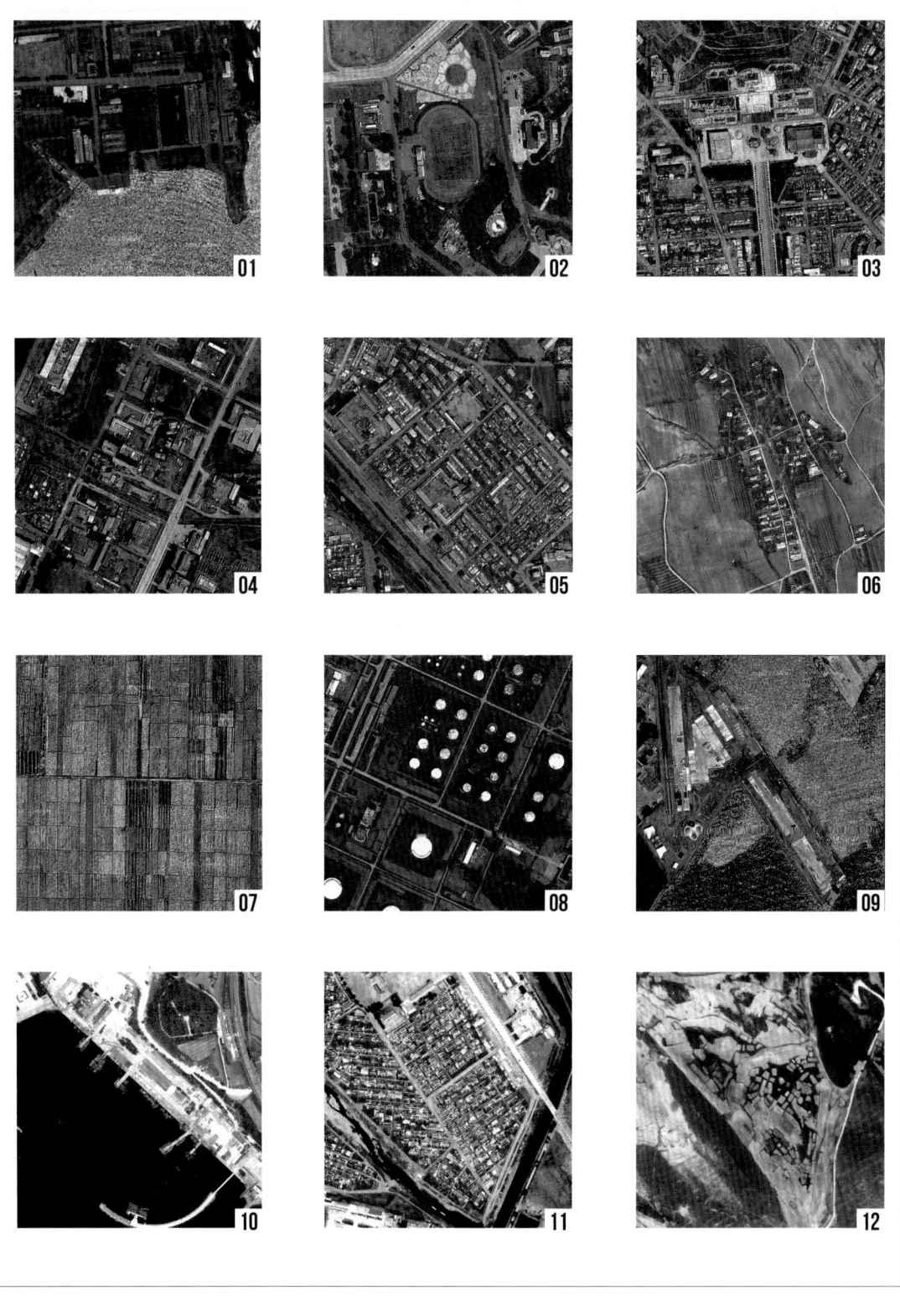

MAJOR CITY STRUCTURE - RASON
주요 도시 구조 - 라선

Hospit

Monument A

School A

Monument C

The name Rason, Ra+Son, is the combination of Najin (or Rajin) area, which is the urban area, and Sonbong area, which is the rural area. For its close location to both Russia and China, Rason is designated as special economy zone to attract foreign investment from those two countries. As it has a very good harbor to the East Sea (Pacific), Rason always has been the strategic spot that both China and Russia wanted to occupy.

라선이라는 이름은, 라+선으로서 도시지역인 라진시와 농업지역인 선봉지구를 행정구역상에서 합친데에서 유래하였다. 라선은 중국과 러시아 모두와 인접해 있음으로 해서, 특별경제구역으로 지정되었고 외국인의 투자를 유도하고 있다. 라선은 역사적으로 태평양으로 진출할 수 있는 항구를 갖고 있기 때문에, 항상 중국과 러시아가 점령하고자 했던 전략적인 지역이었다.

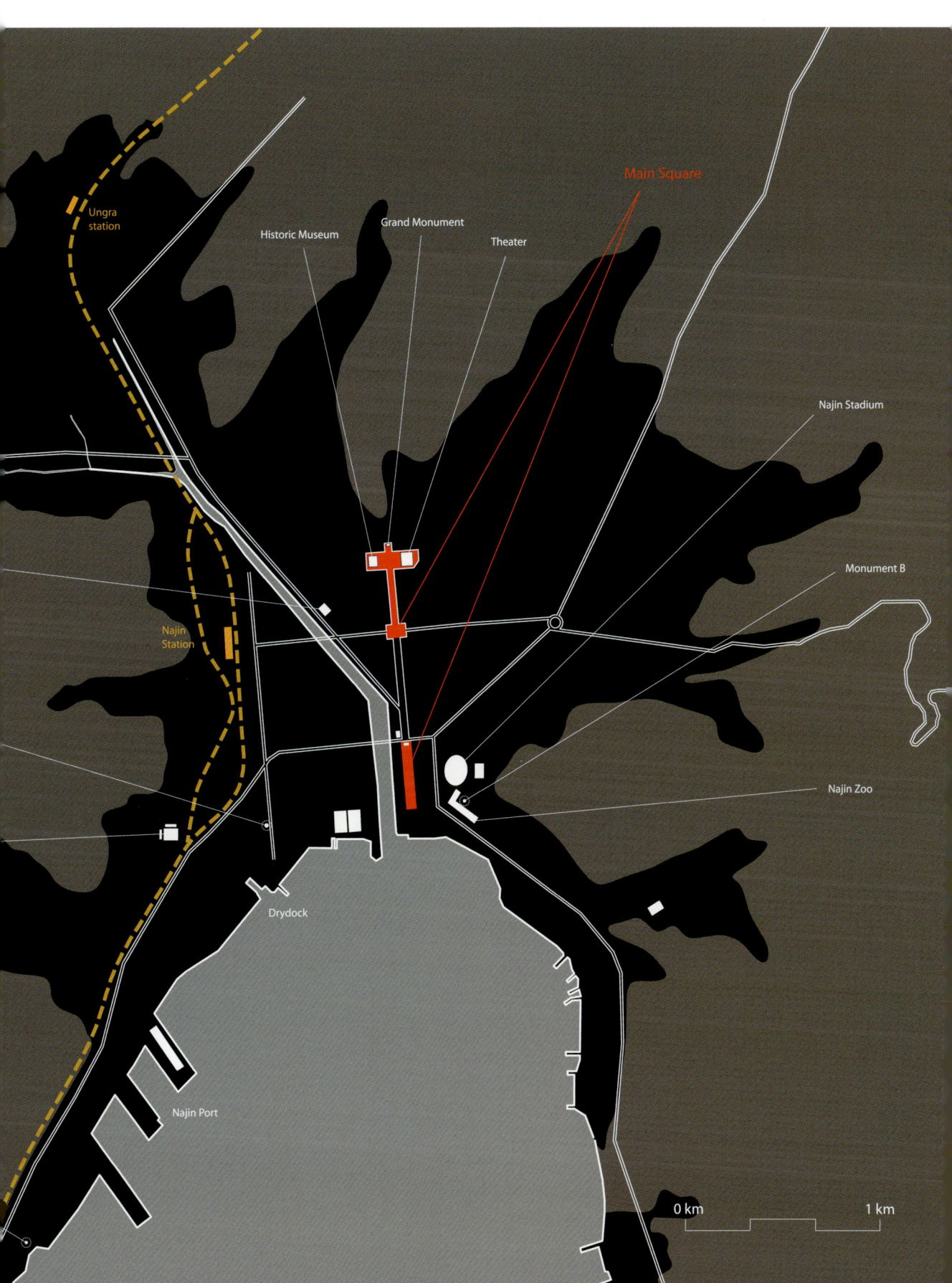

NAJIN SYMBOLIC SPACE
NAJIN CITY, RASON
나진 상징 공간
나진시, 라선 특구

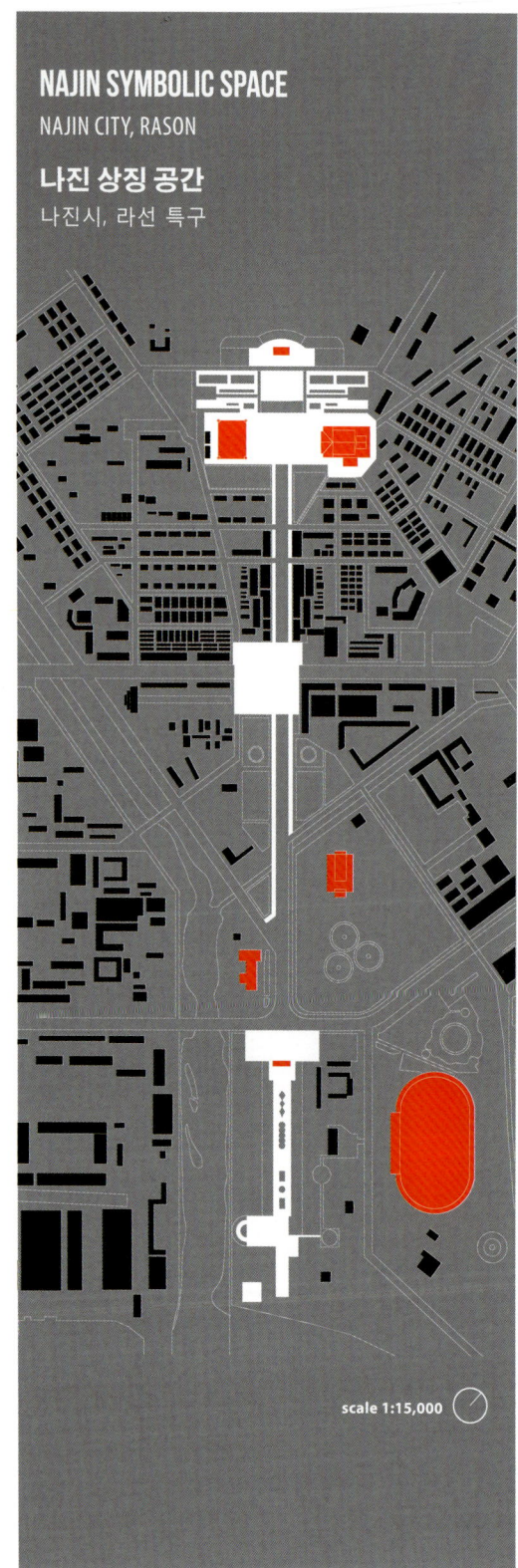

scale 1:15,000

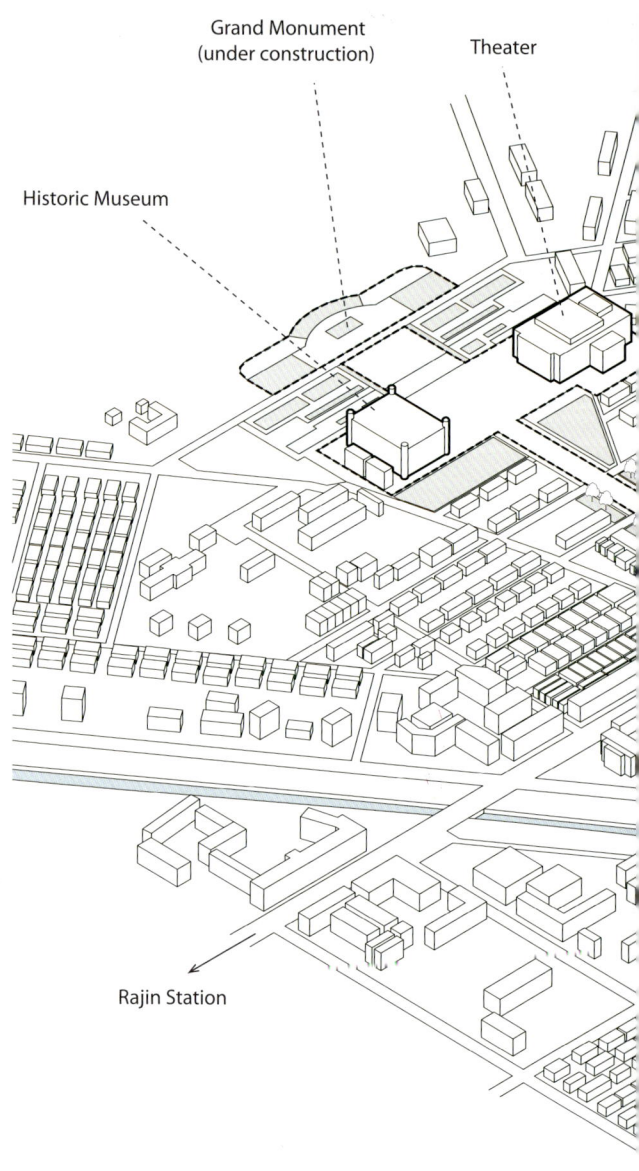

Historic Museum
Grand Monument (under construction)
Theater
Rajin Station

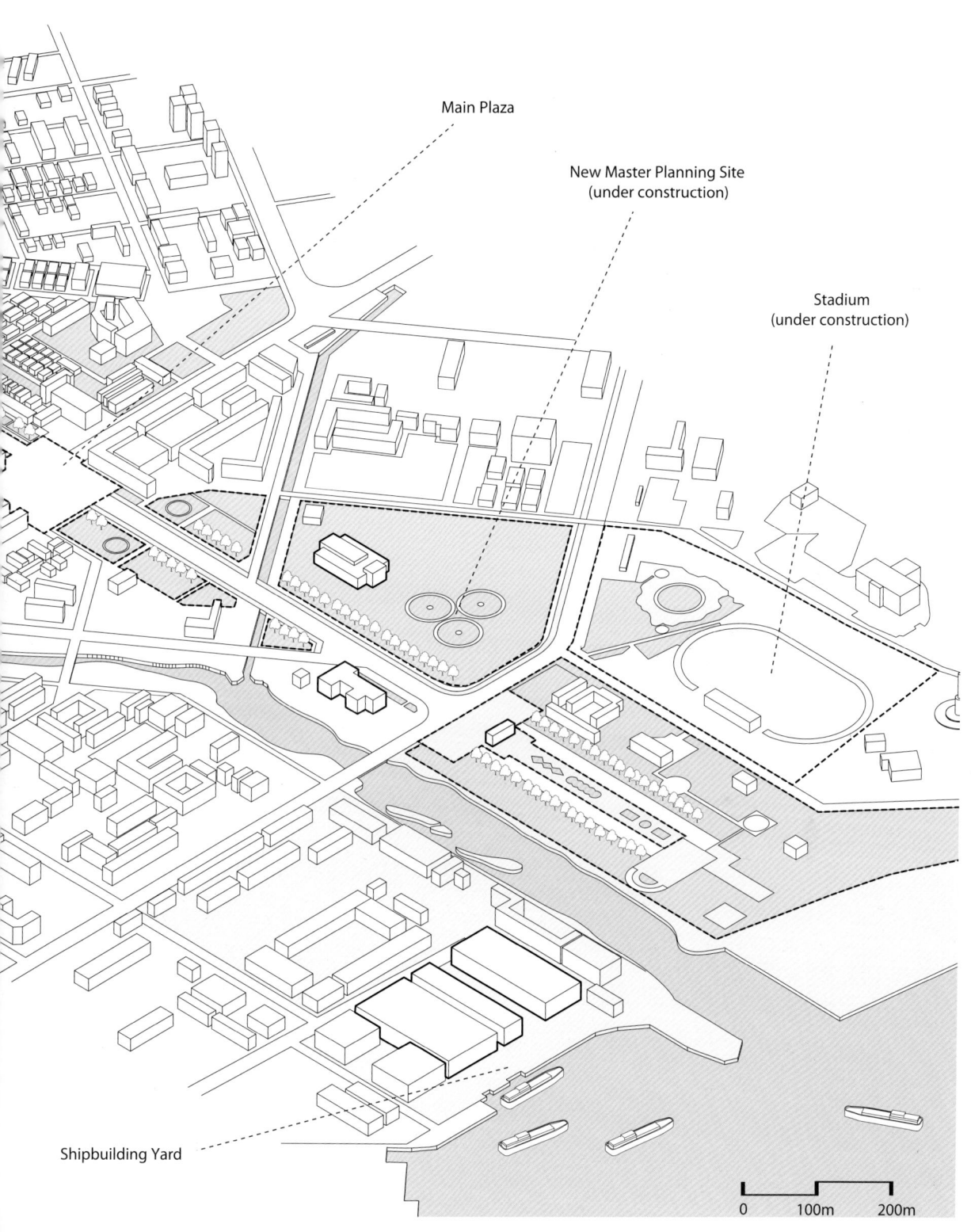

North Korean Cities

PRECINCT TYPE A
NAJIN CITY 나진시

PRECINCT TYPE B
CHONGGYE DONG 청계동

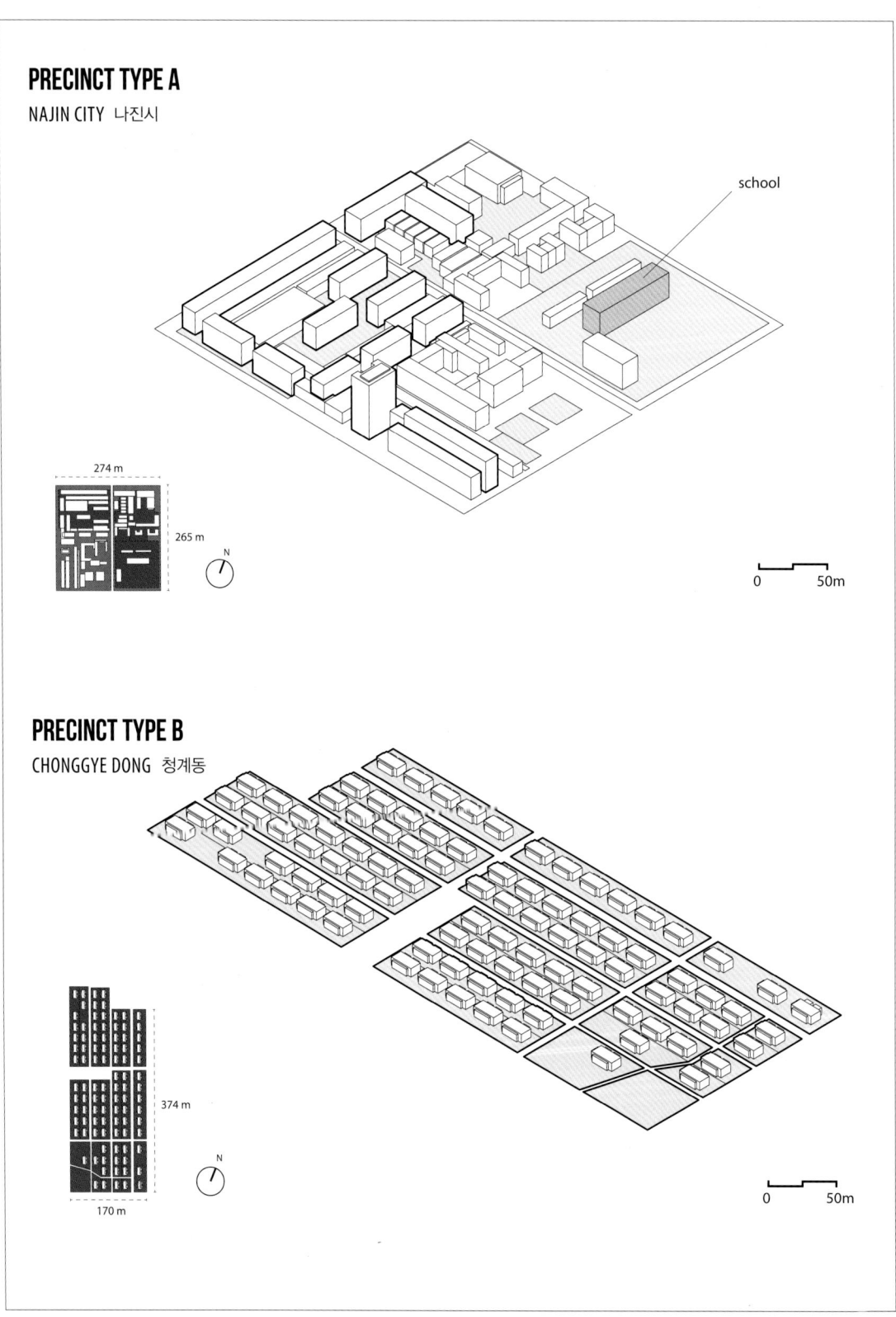

PRECINCT TYPE C
NAJIN CITY 나진시

110 m
288 m

0   50m

PRECINCT TYPE D
NAJIN CITY 나진시

256 m
35 m

0   50m

North Korean Cities

POSSIBLE URBAN GROWTH - RASON (X = URBAN POPULATION: 237,000)
도시 성장 잠재력 분석 - 라선 특구 (나진 시 + 선봉 구)

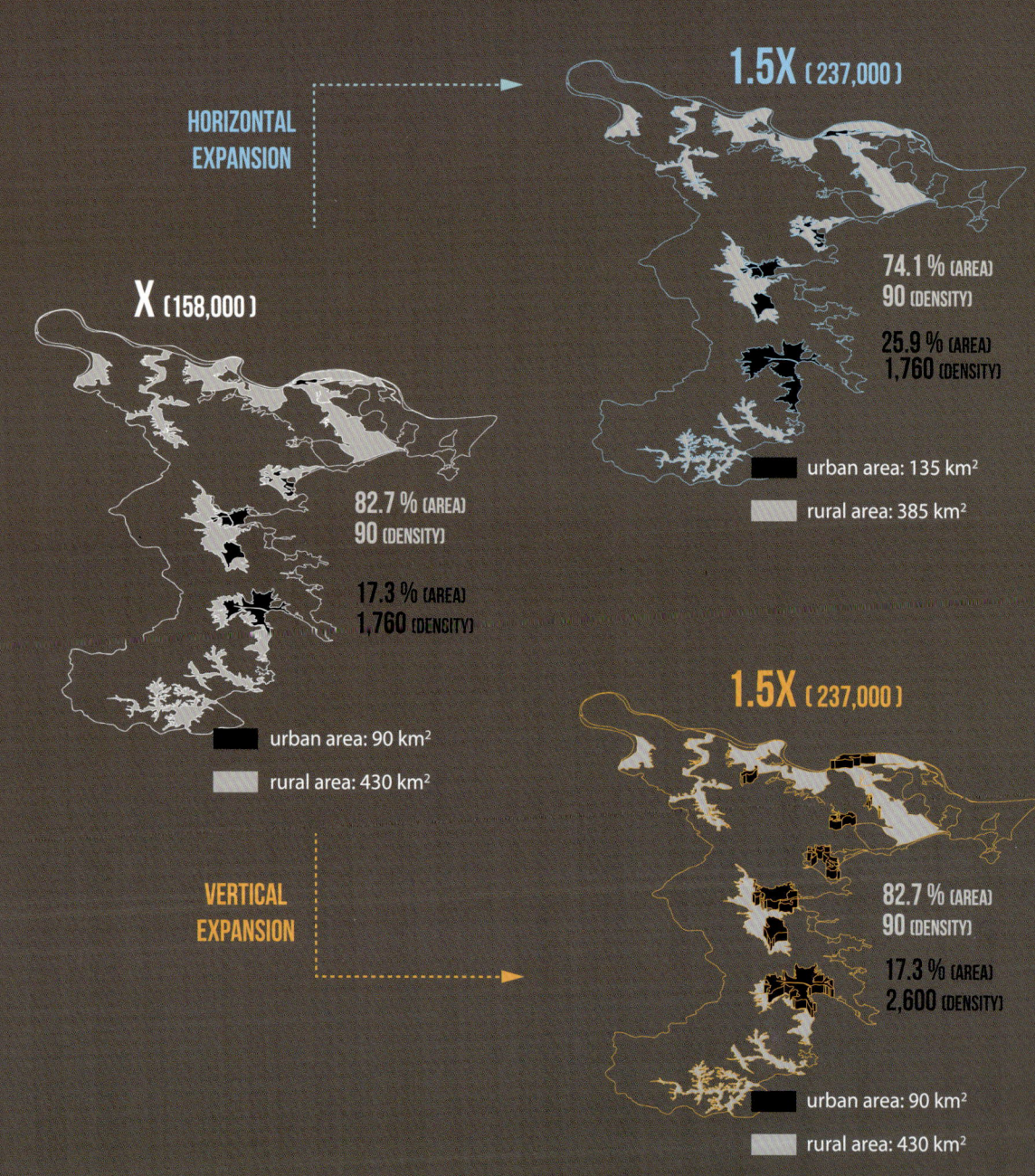

8 Major north korean cities | Rason

SINUIJU 신의주
NORTH PHYONGAN PROVINCE

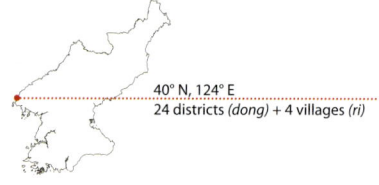
40° N, 124° E
24 districts (*dong*) + 4 villages (*ri*)

MAP	LAP	AF	PORT	RAIL
	1	1		6

FAC	CO	EDU	CUL	HOSP	SPOR
28	2	12	3		1

POPULATION
Inhabitants	359,341
% Urban	93
% Rural	7
% Male	47.3
% Female	52.7

POPULATION DENSITY
Inhabitants	359,341
Administrative Area (km²)	134.4
Population Density (inhabitants/km²)	**2,673**

URBAN DENSITY
Inhabitants	334,031
Urban Area (km²)	10.2
Population Density (inhabitants/km²)	**32,748**

GEOGRAPHY
% Built	17.6
% Farmland	44.6
% Mountains	37.8

POTENTIAL GROWTH
Urbanized Area (km²)	82.2
% Area Increase	806
Urban Population	359,341
% Population Increase	749
Max. Population (million)	2.7

CENSUS HEXAGRAM

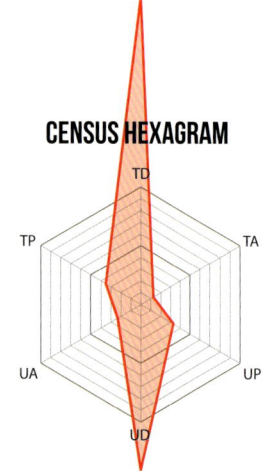

TD - Total density (1000 / km²)
TP - Total population (1,000,000)
TA - Total area (1,000 km²)
UD - Urban density (10,000 / km²)
UP - Urban population (1,000,000)
UA - Urban area (100 km²)

GEOGRAPHICAL CIRCLE

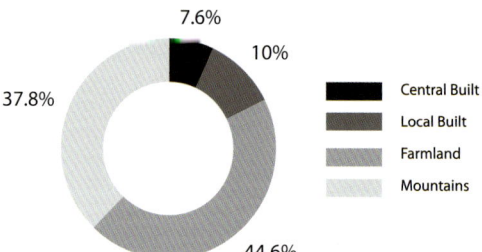

7.6%
10%
37.8%
44.6%

- Central Built
- Local Built
- Farmland
- Mountains

INDUSTRIAL CIRCLE

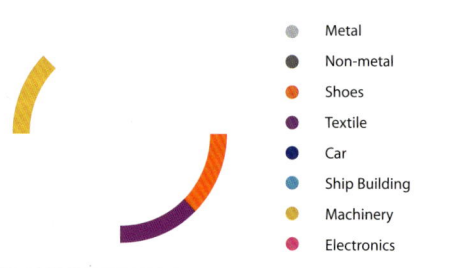

- Metal
- Non-metal
- Shoes
- Textile
- Car
- Ship Building
- Machinery
- Electronics

8 Major north korean cities | Sinuiju

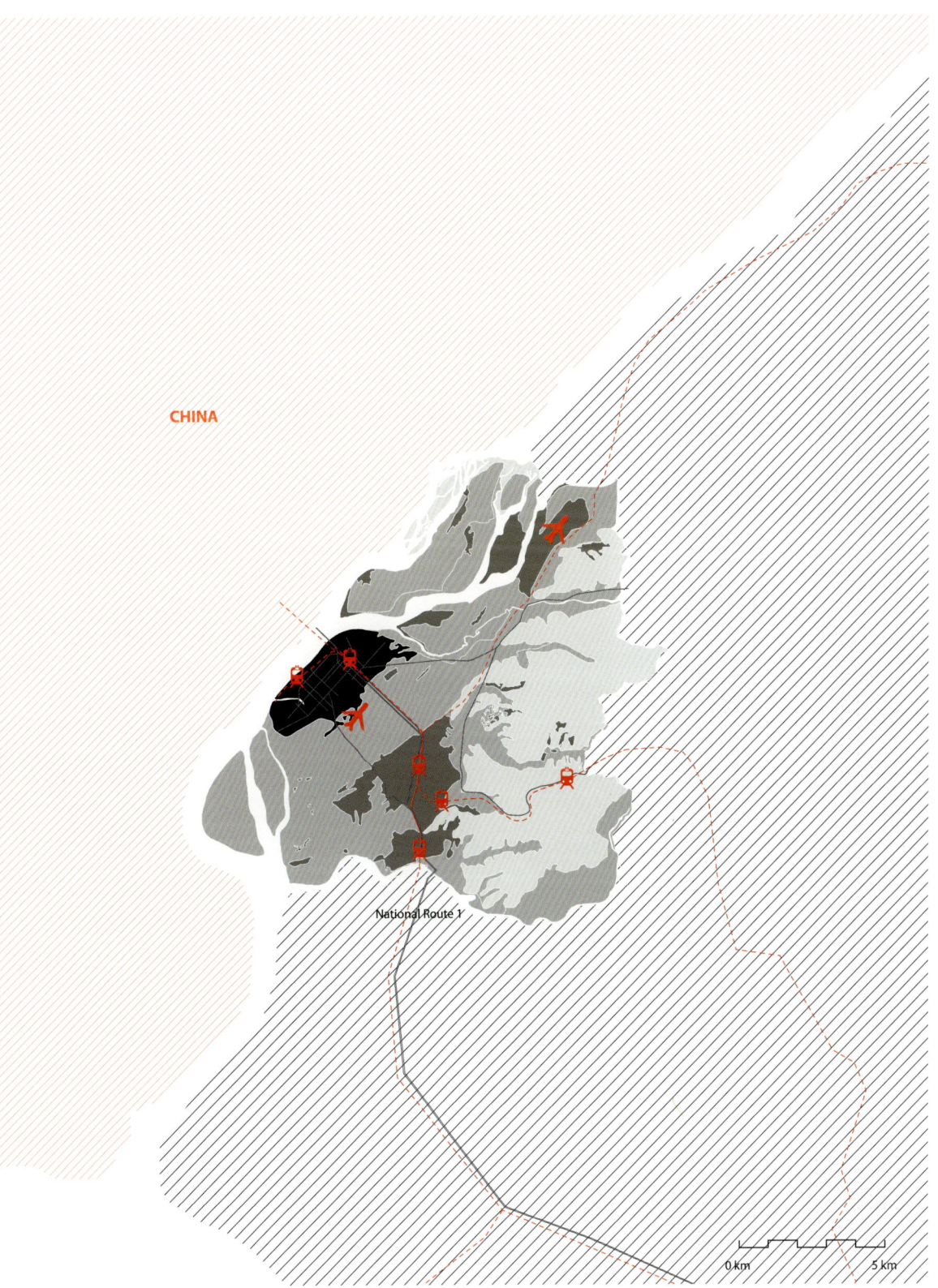

CHINA

National Route 1

0 km   5 km

North Korean Cities

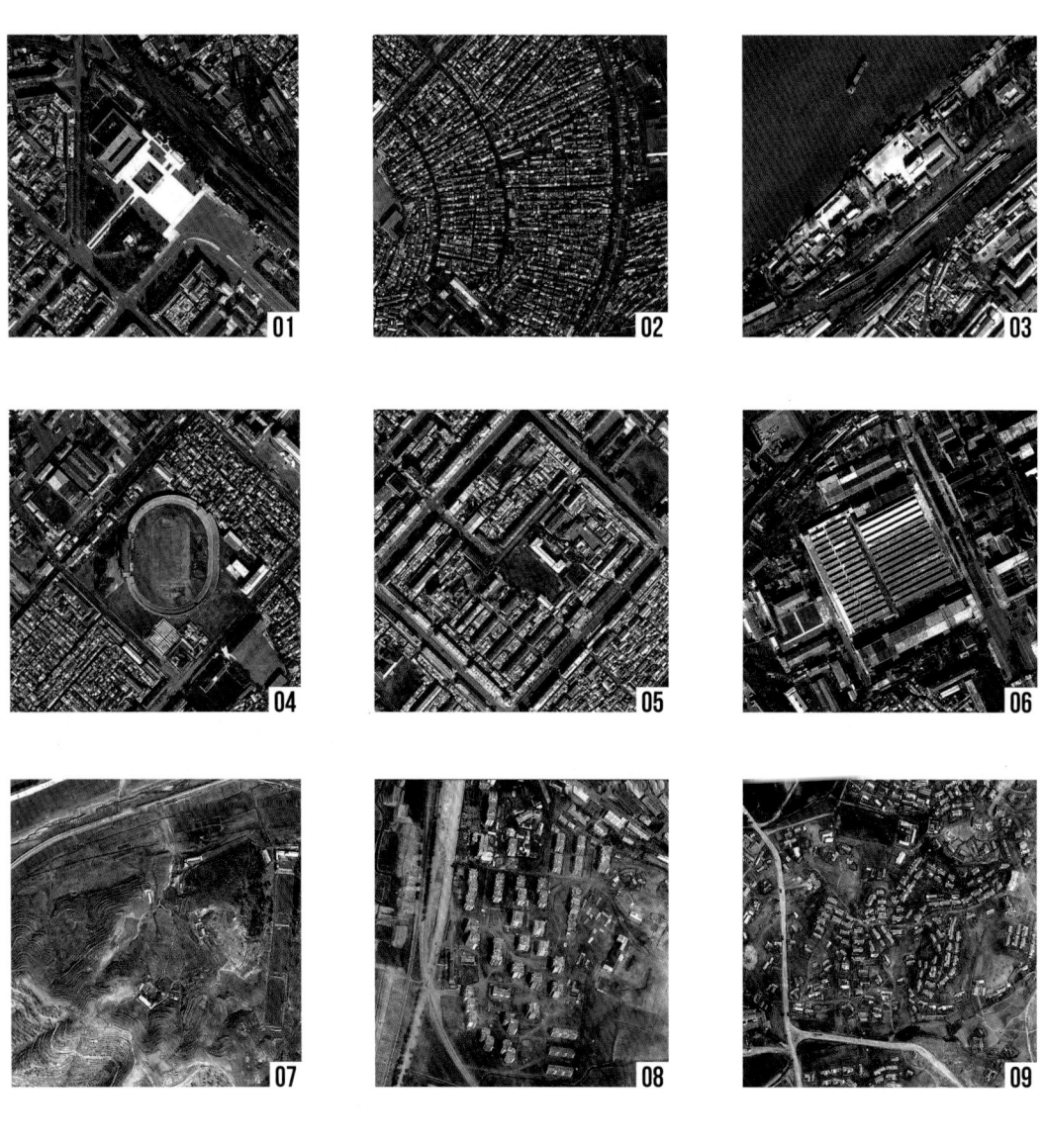

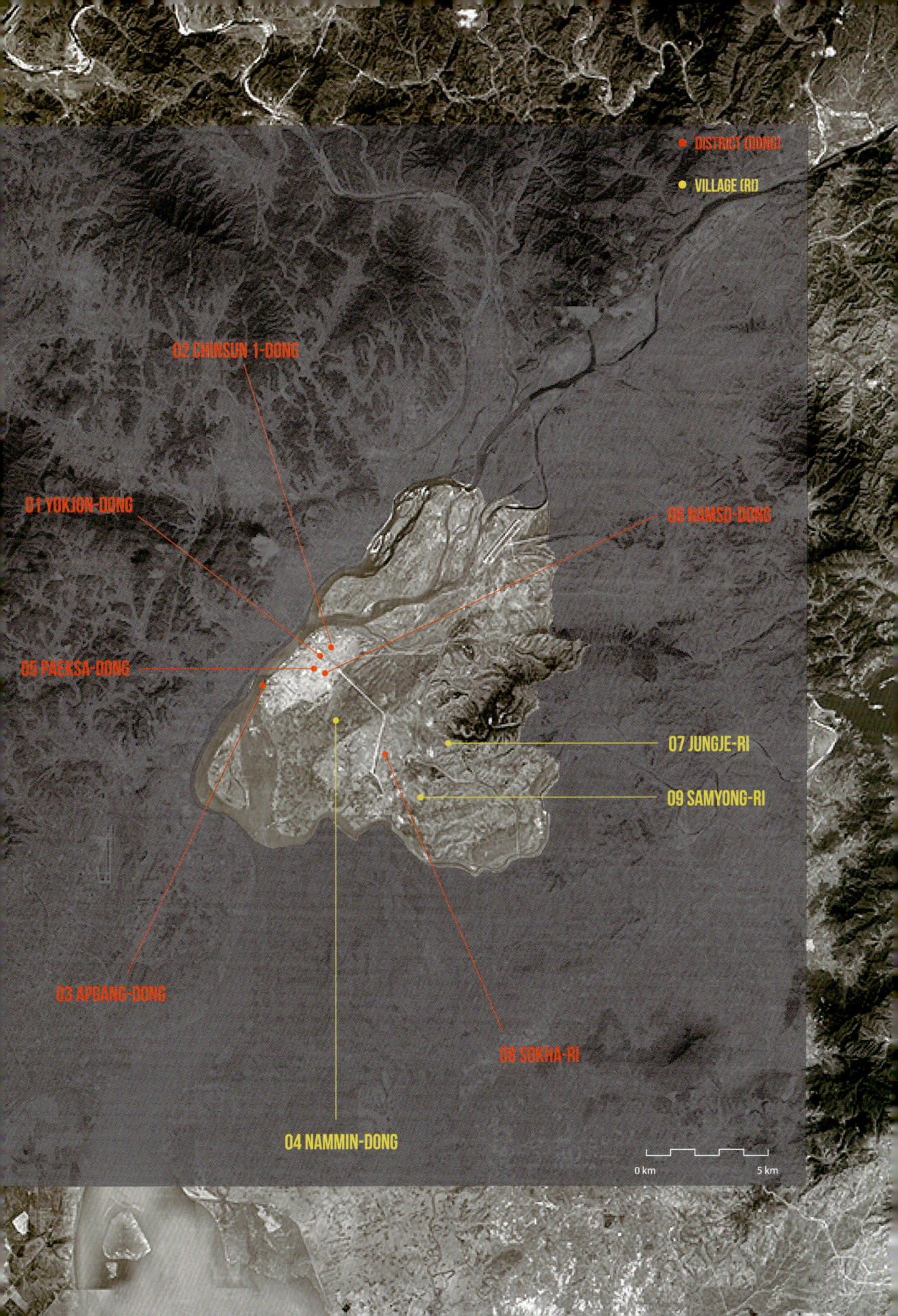

MAJOR CITY STRUCTURE - SINUIJU
주요 도시 구조 - 신의주

Main Square

Sinuiju College of Education

Temple

High school

Naval Base

Sinuiju was developed as a port city at the river mouth of Aprok River and a gateway between China and the Korean Peninsula during the Japanese colonial period. It was mainly developed along with the rail way that extends through the whole Asia continent. As the border city to Dandong, China, Sinuiju was established as a Special Administrative Region in 2002 to adopt some market economic system to the city.

신의주는 일제시대에 압록강 하구의 항구도시이자, 중국과 한반도의 경계도시로서 발달을 하였다. 이는 아시아 대륙을 관통하는 철도로 연결되는 철도망 상에 개발된 것이다. 중국 단둥에 인접한 도시인 신의주는 2002년 특별행정지구로 지정이 됨으로서 더 적극적으로 자유경제시스템을 도입하고자 하고 있는 상황이다.

8 Major north korean cities | Sinuiju

SINUIJU SYMBOLIC SPACE
YOKJUN DONG & NAMSAN DONG, SINUIJU

신의주 상징 공간
역전동 & 남산동, 신의주 시

scale 1:15,000

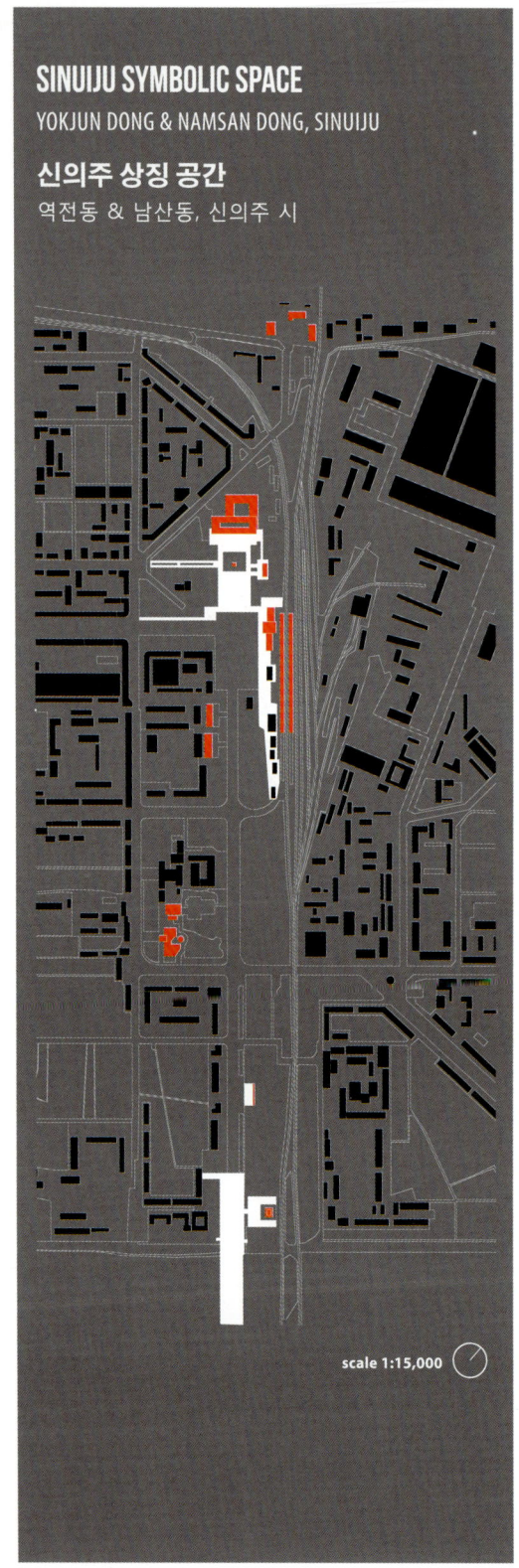

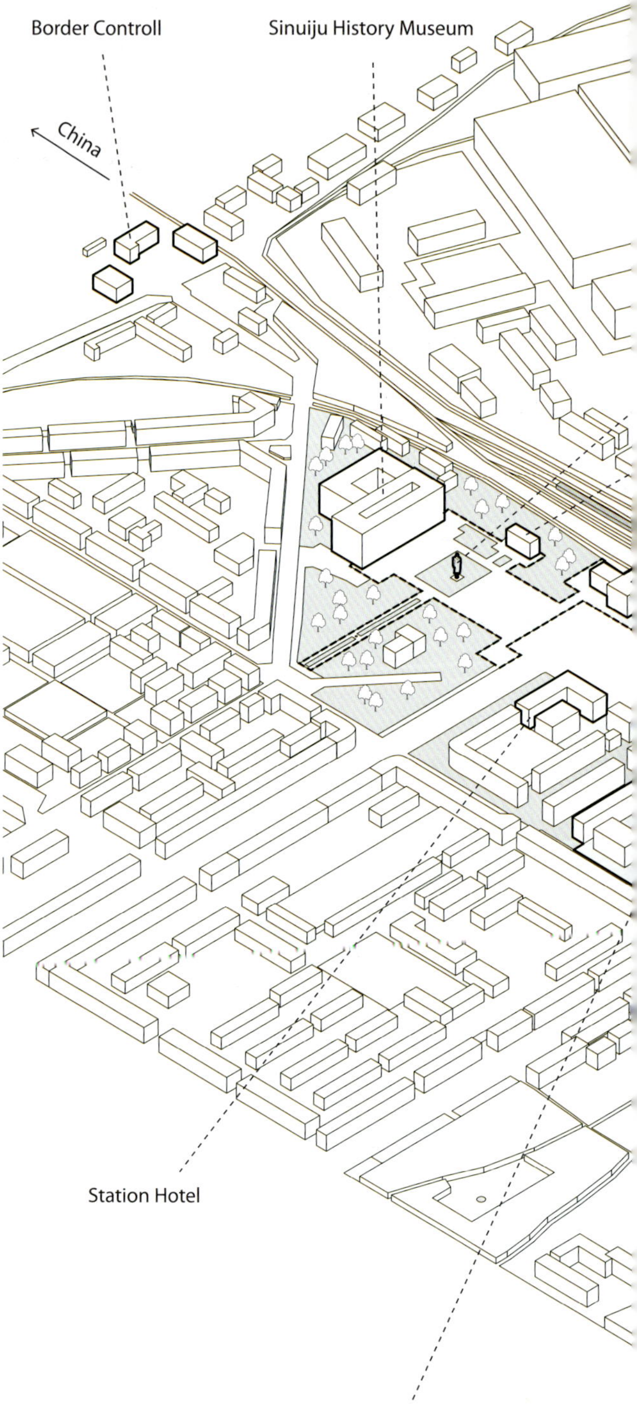

Border Controll

Sinuiju History Museum

China

Station Hotel

Dong Senior Middle School

8 Major north korean cities | Sinuiju

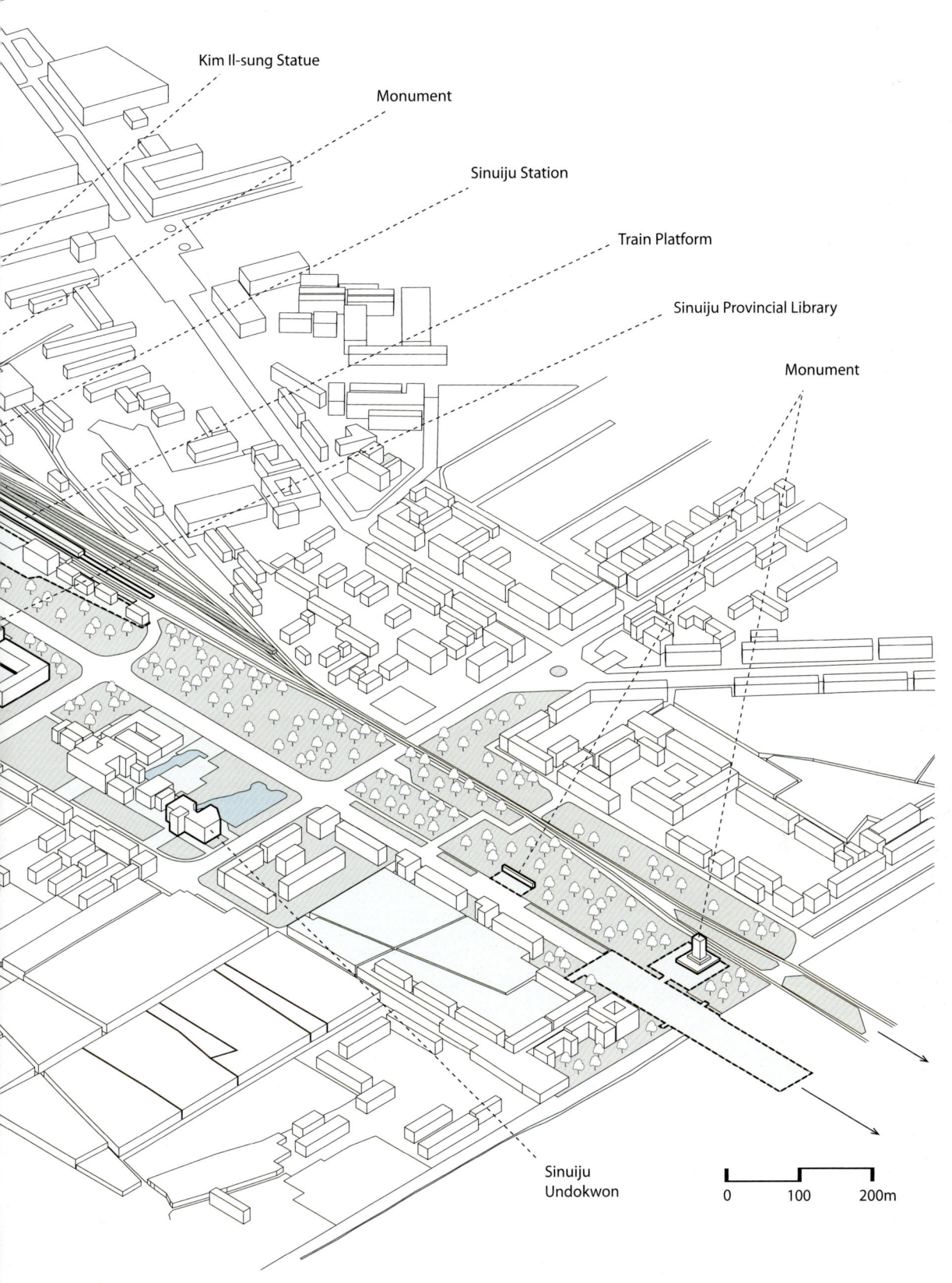

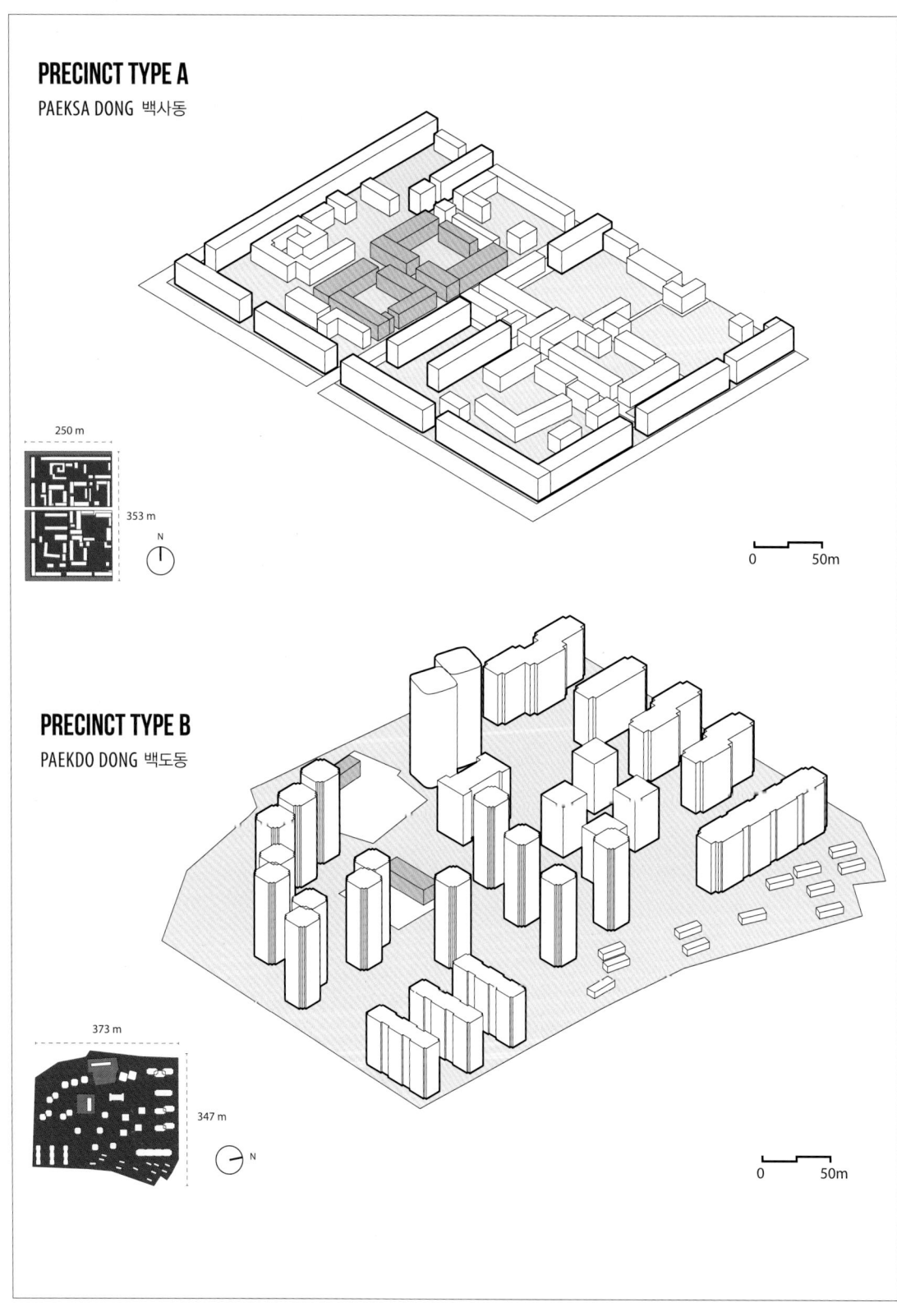

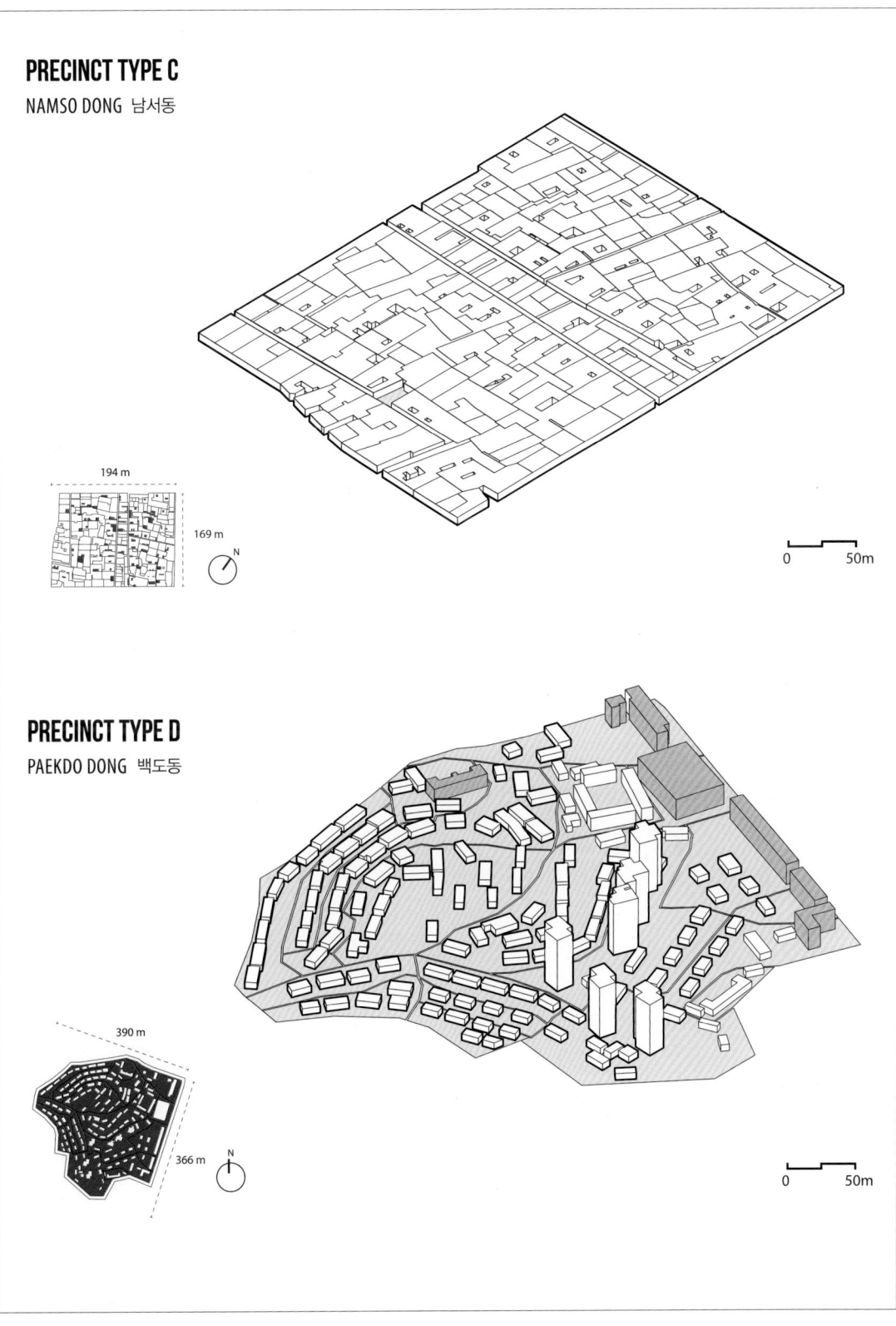

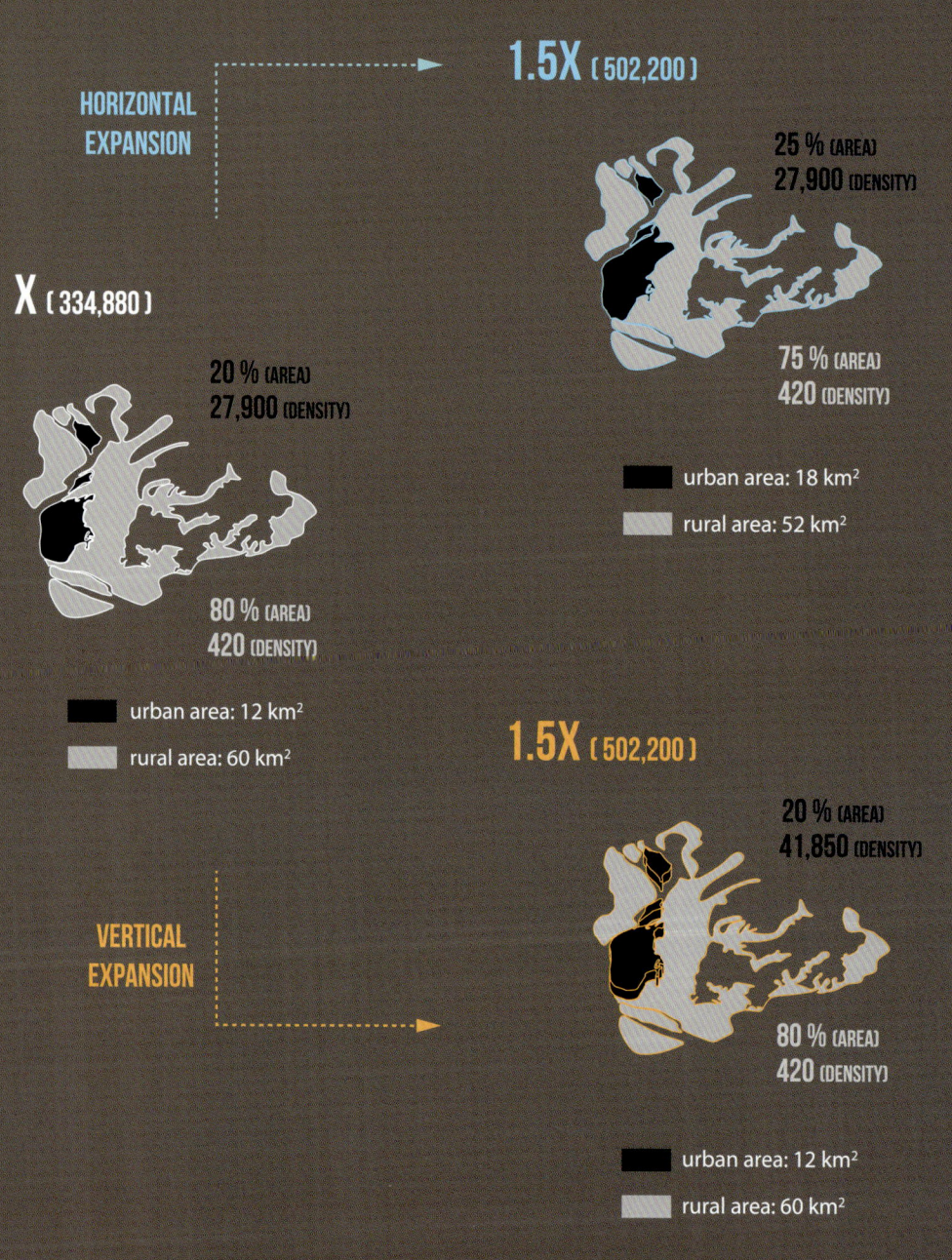

2X (669,600)

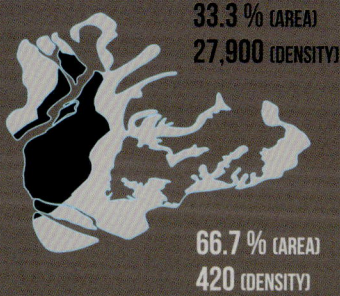

33.3 % (AREA)
27,900 (DENSITY)

66.7 % (AREA)
420 (DENSITY)

■ urban area: 24 km²
▫ rural area: 48 km²

3X (1,004,400)

50 % (AREA)
27,900 (DENSITY)

50 % (AREA)
420 (DENSITY)

■ urban area: 36 km²
▫ rural area: 36 km²

2X (669,600)

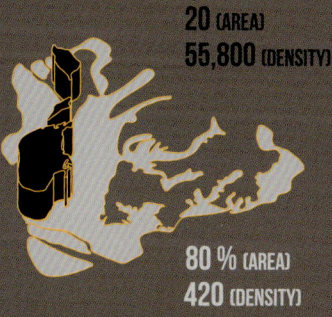

20 (AREA)
55,800 (DENSITY)

80 % (AREA)
420 (DENSITY)

■ urban area: 12 km²
▫ rural area: 60 km²

3X (1,004,400)

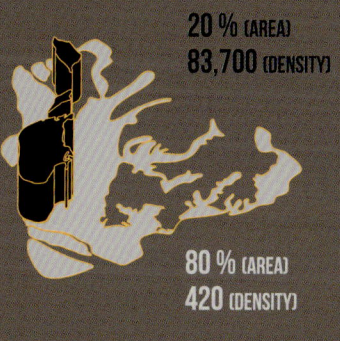

20 % (AREA)
83,700 (DENSITY)

80 % (AREA)
420 (DENSITY)

■ urban area: 12 km²
▫ rural area: 60 km²

WONSAN 원산
KANGWON PROVINCE

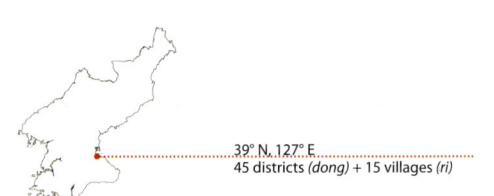

39° N, 127° E
45 districts (dong) + 15 villages (ri)

MAP	LAP	AF	PORT	RAIL
	1	2		2

FAC	CO	EDU	CUL	HOSP	SPOR
12	4	9	5	1	1

POPULATION
Inhabitants	**363,127**
% Urban	90.5
% Rural	9.5
% Male	47.4
% Female	52.6

POPULATION DENSITY
Inhabitants	363,127
Administrative Area (km²)	295
Population Density (inhabitants/km²)	**1,231**

URBAN DENSITY
Inhabitants	328,467
Urban Area (km²)	13
Population Density (inhabitants/km²)	**25,266**

GEOGRAPHY
% Built	5
% Farmland	27.1
% Mountains	67.9

POTENTIAL GROWTH
Urbanized Area (km²)	94.7
% Area Increase	720
Urban Population	363,127
% Population Increase	659
Max. Population (million)	2.4

CENSUS HEXAGRAM

TD - Total density (1000 / km²)
TP - Total population (1,000,000)
TA - Total area (1,000 km²)
UD - Urban density (10,000 / km²)
UP - Urban population (1,000,000)
UA - Urban area (100 km²)

GEOGRAPHICAL CIRCLE

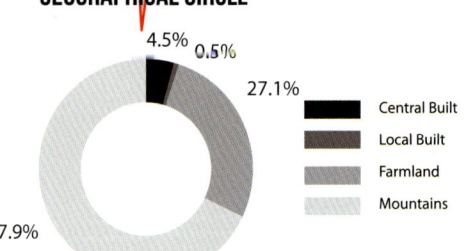

4.5% 0.5% 27.1% 67.9%

- Central Built
- Local Built
- Farmland
- Mountains

INDUSTRIAL CIRCLE

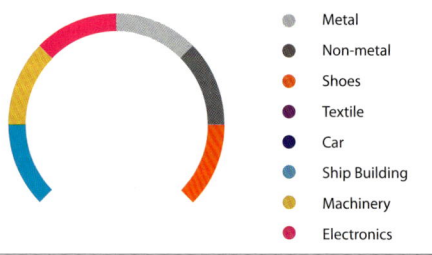

- Metal
- Non-metal
- Shoes
- Textile
- Car
- Ship Building
- Machinery
- Electronics

8 Major north korean cities | Wonsan

North Korean Cities

8 Major north korean cities | Wonsan

EAST SEA

North Korean Cities

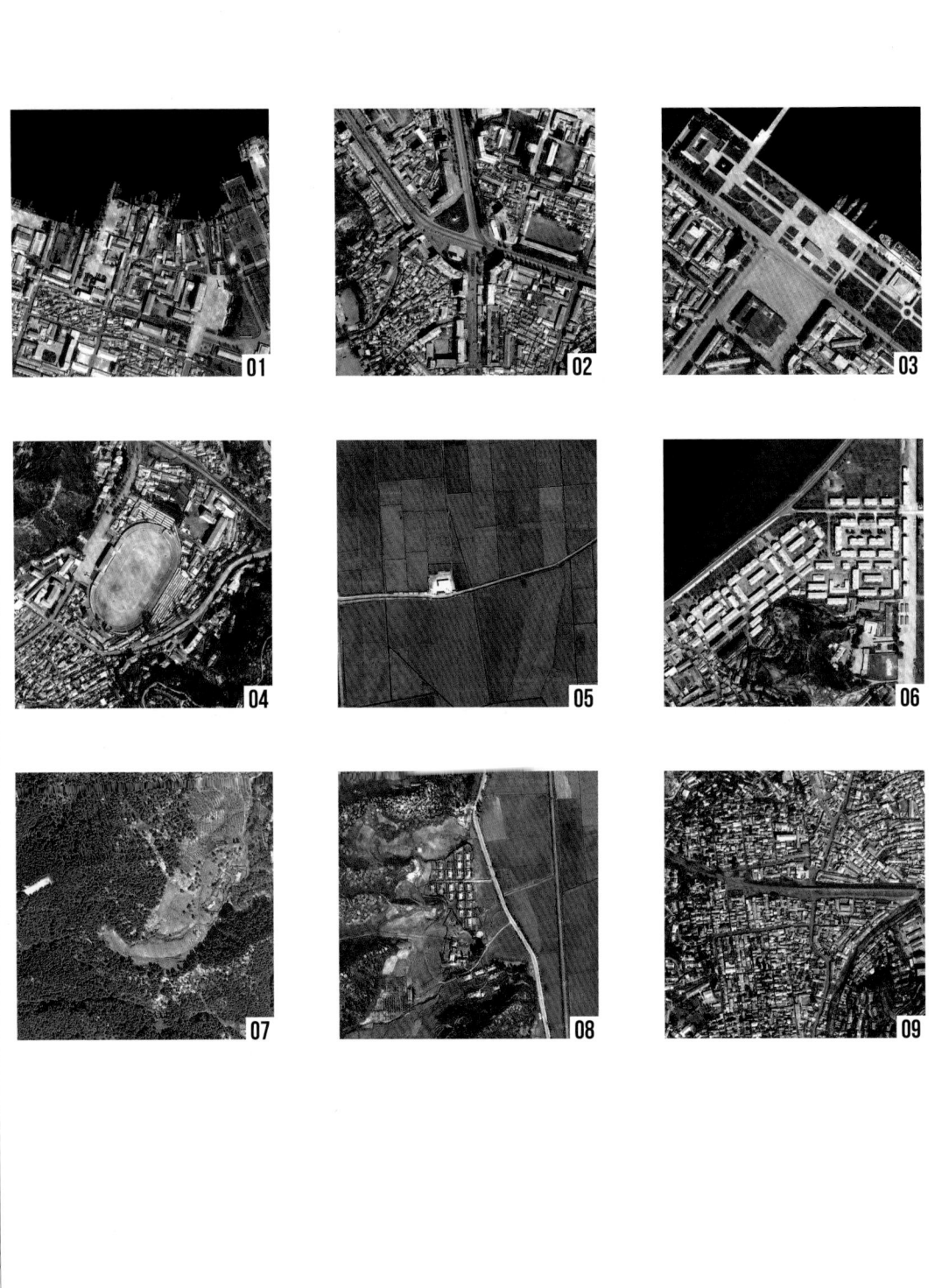

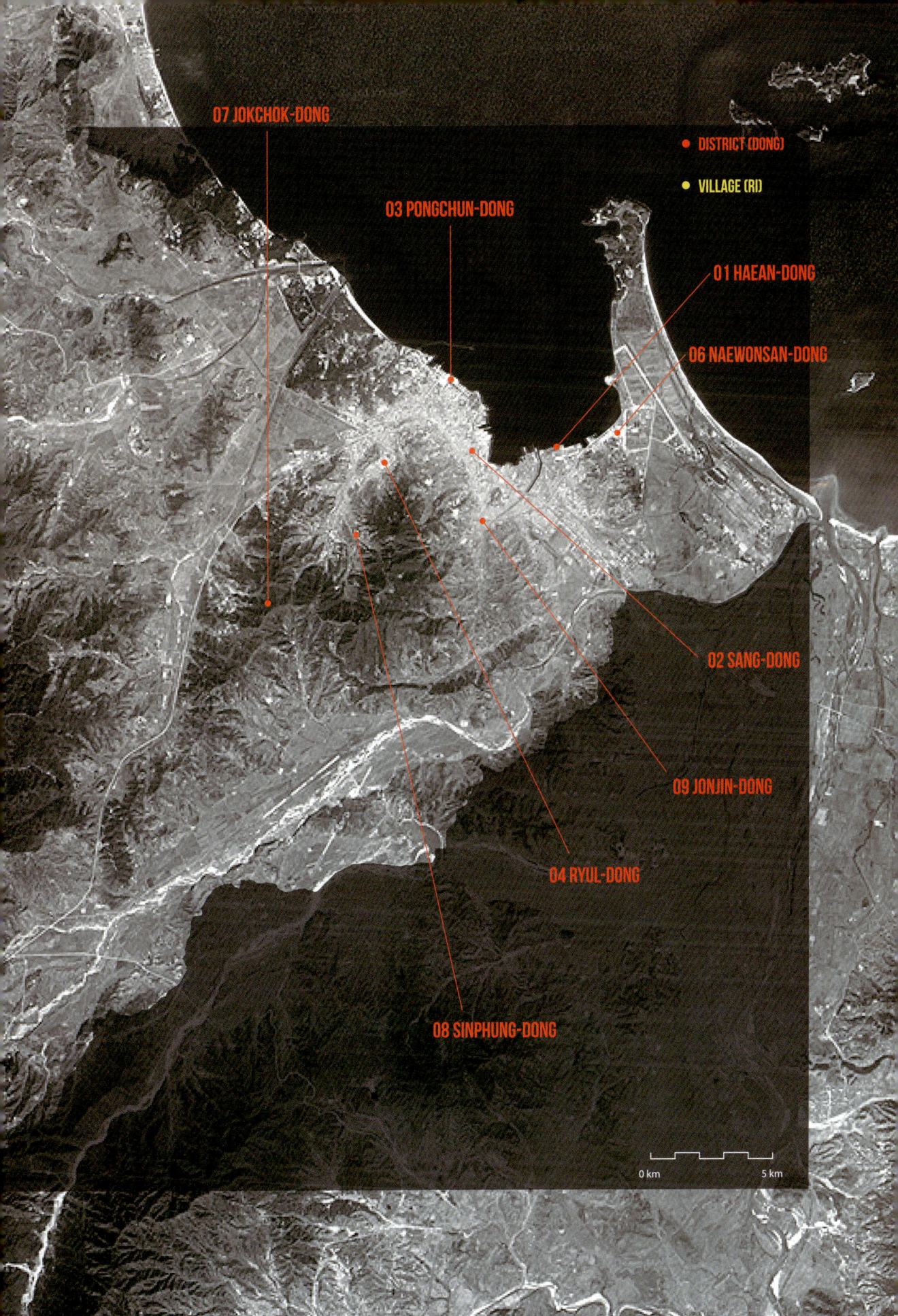

MAJOR CITY STRUCTURE - WONSAN
주요 도시 구조 - 원산

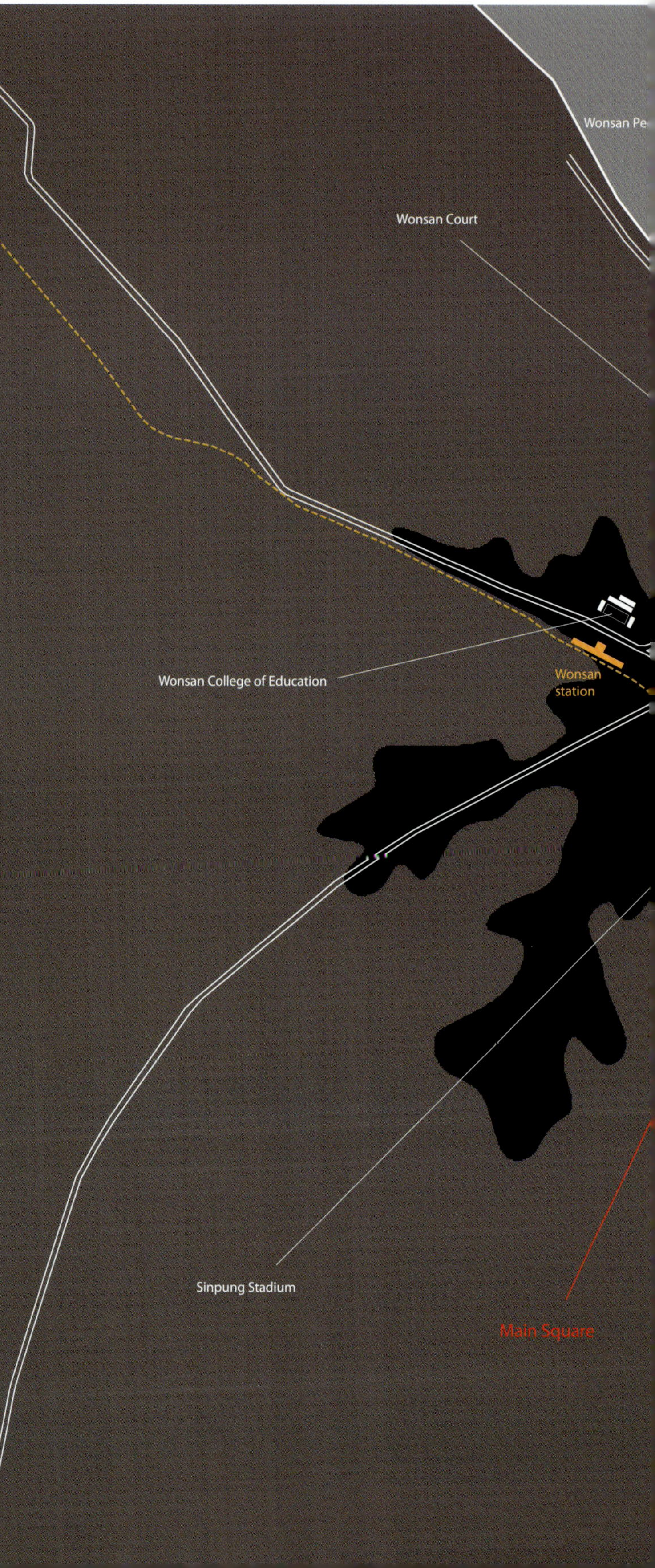

Wonsan is one of the most important port city in the east coast of the North Korea that opens the country to the Pacific. It started to have a major development since 1880 when the Japanese military forced it to open its port for the trade. Currently, Wonsan, which is now a Special Tourism Region, is one of the hottest spot in the nation. Along with new ski and resort, Kim Jung Un regime is putting lots of investment to the city to make it as a touristic destination not only for domestics but also for internationals.

원산은 태평양으로의 길을 열어줌으로서 북한 동해안의 매우 중요한 도시 중에 하나이다. 원산은 1880년 일본군이 무역을 위해 항구를 개항하게 함으로서 주요한 개발이 이루어지기 시작하였다. 현재 관광특구로 지정된 원산은 북한 내에서 가장 주목받고 있는 지역 중에 하나이다. 해안리조트 및 스키리조트 등과 함께, 김정은 정권은 원산에 북한주민 뿐만아니라 외국인 관광객을 유치하기 위하여 많은 투자를 하고 있다.

North Korean Cities 334

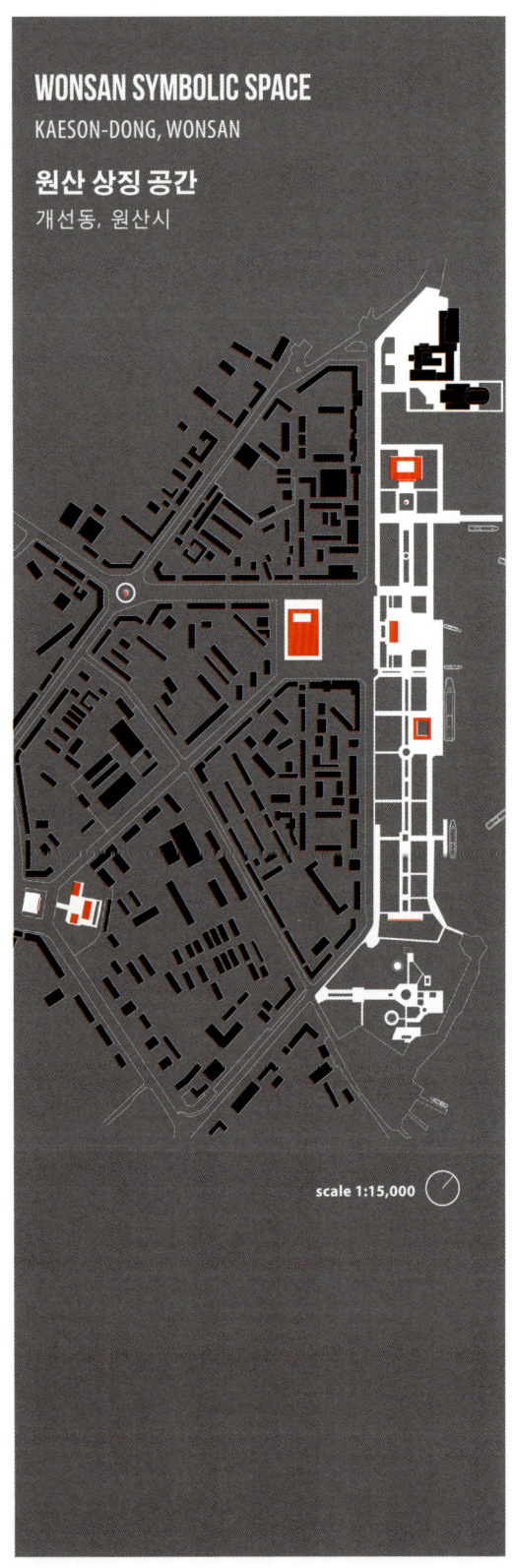

WONSAN SYMBOLIC SPACE
KAESON-DONG, WONSAN

원산 상징 공간
개선동, 원산시

scale 1:15,000

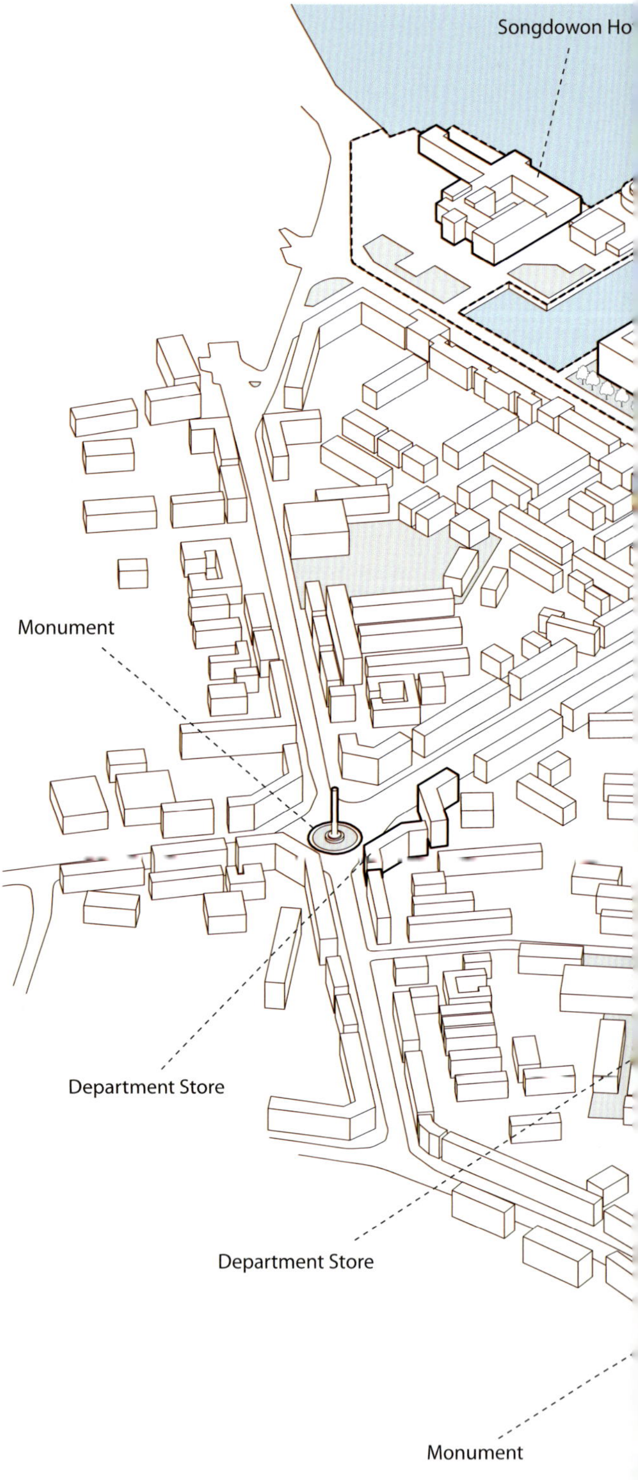

Songdowon Ho
Monument
Department Store
Department Store
Monument

8 Major north korean cities | Wonsan

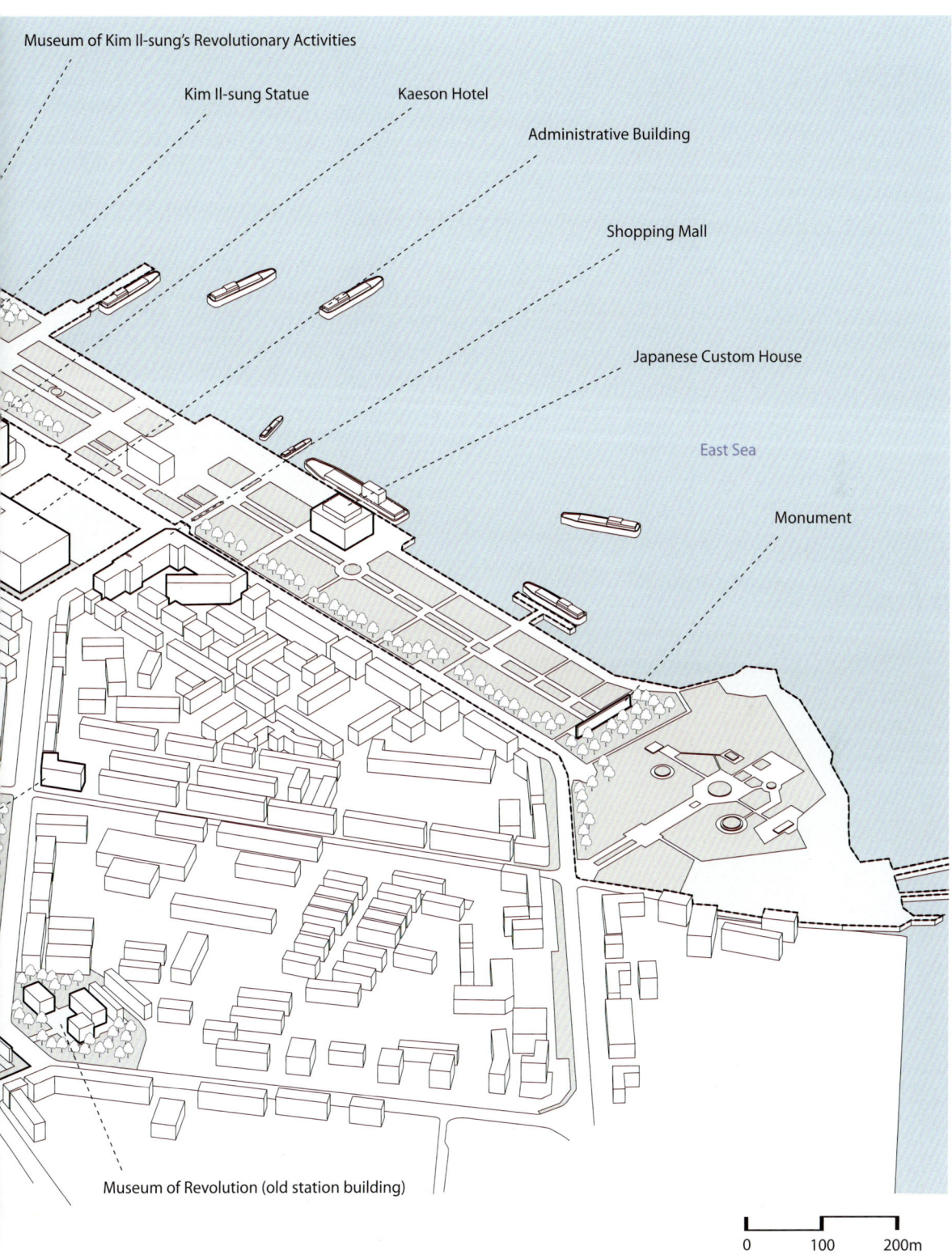

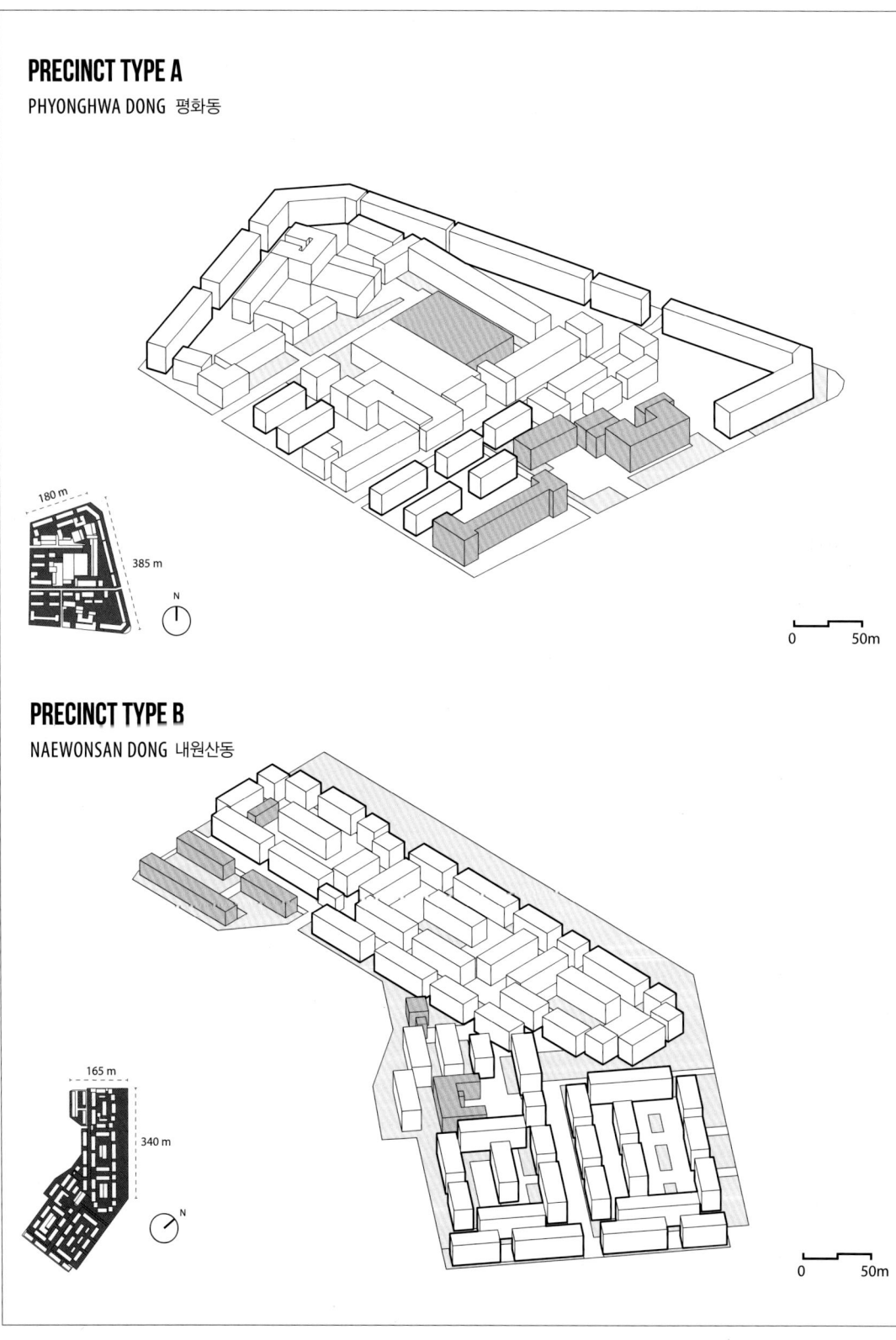

PRECINCT TYPE C
PANGHASAN DONG 방하산동

PRECINCT TYPE D
TOKSONG DONG 덕성동

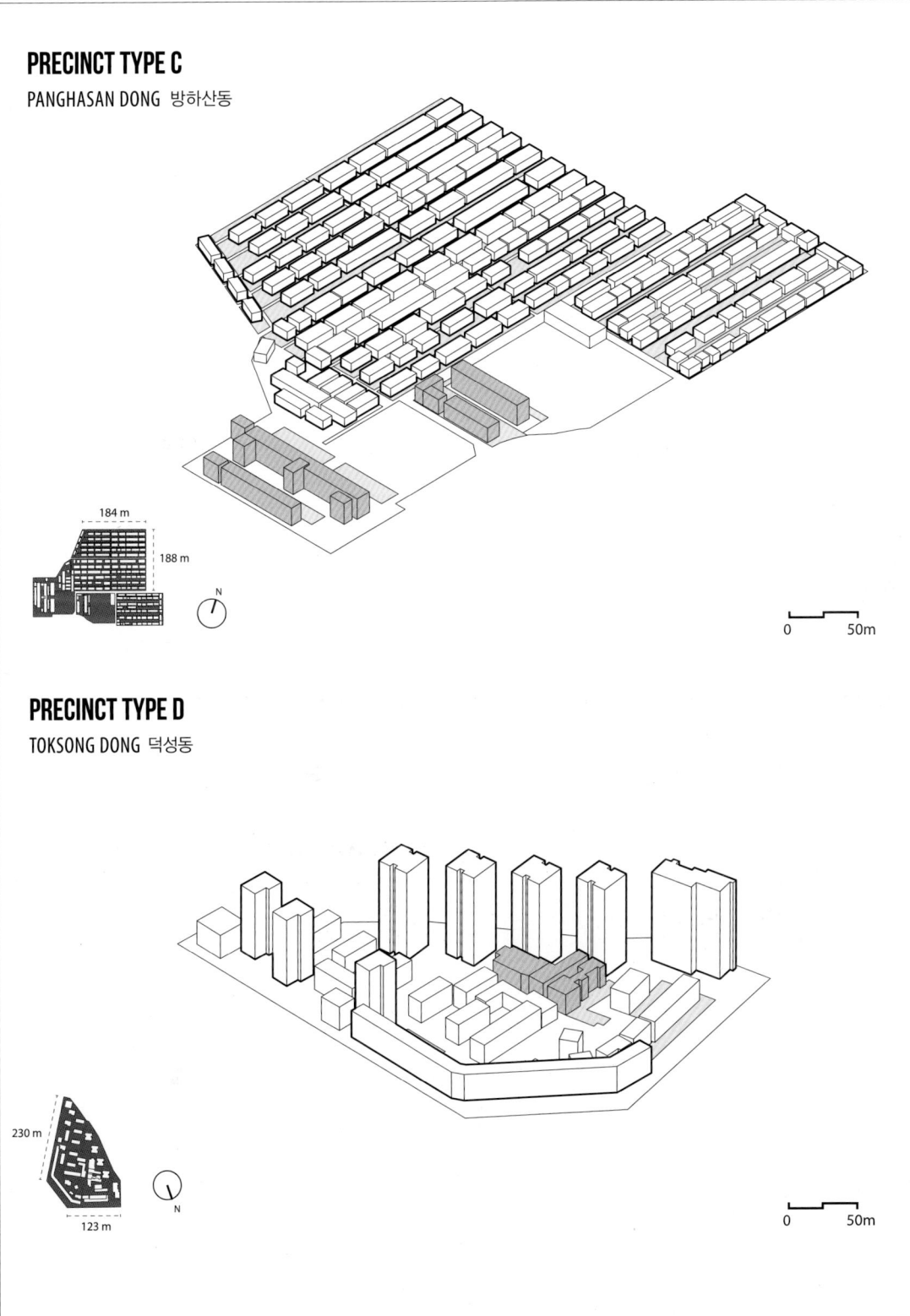

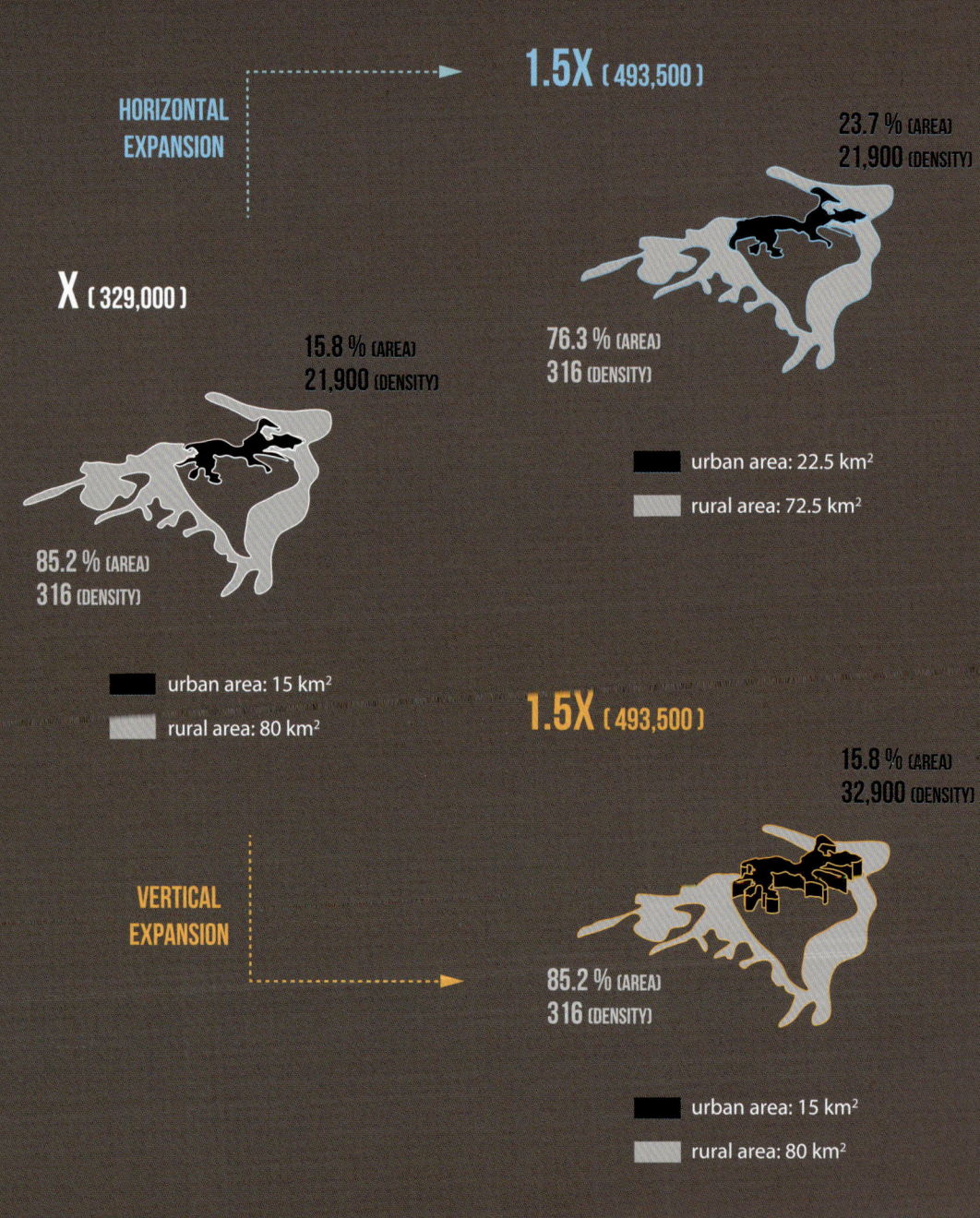

8 Major north korean cities | Wonsan

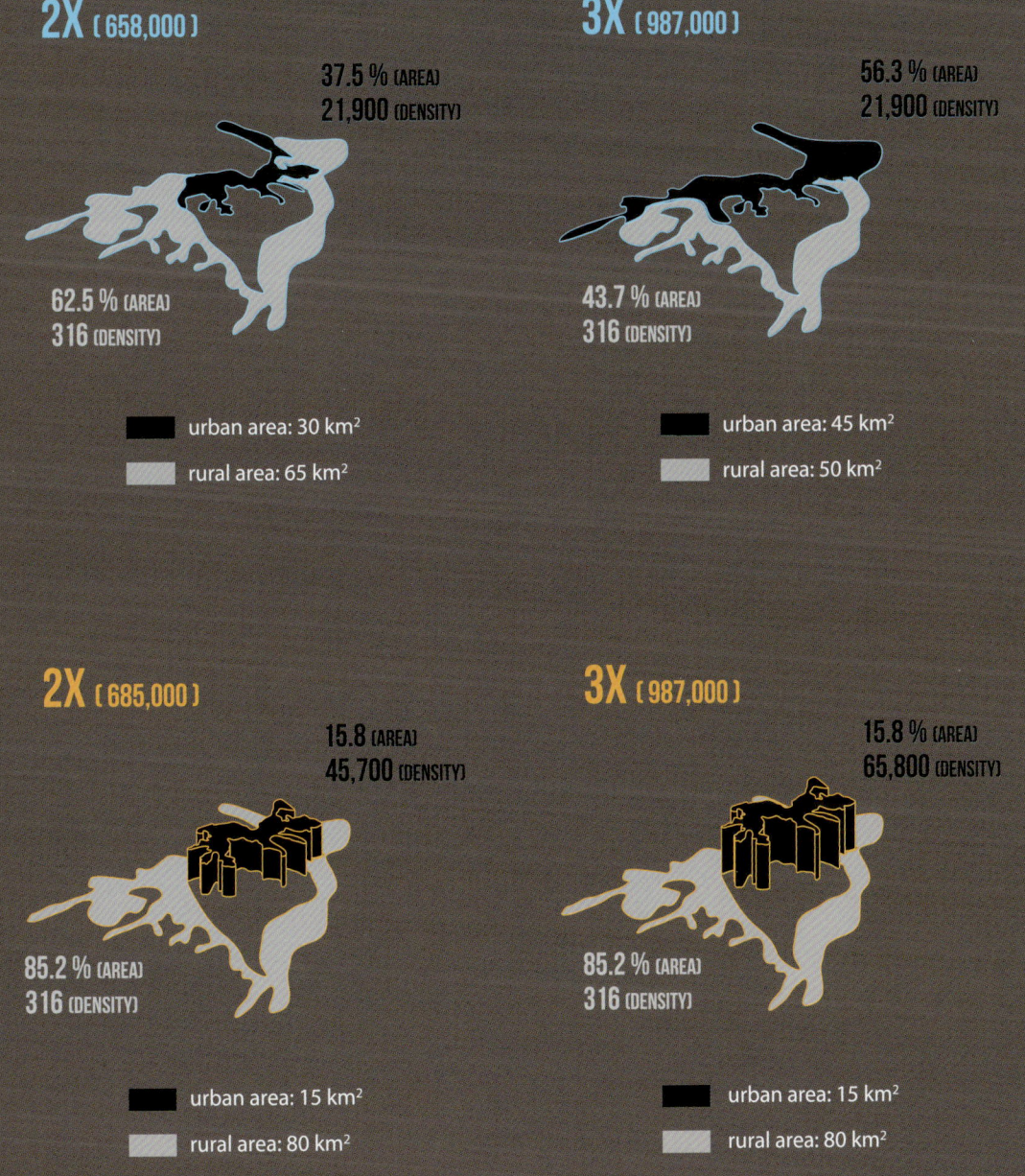

03 NORTH KOREAN CITIES
1. TABLES OF NORTH KOREAN CITIES
2. 8 MAJOR NORTH KOREAN CITIES
3. 19 SUPPORTING NORTH KOREAN CITIES

19 SUPPORTING CITIES 19개 보조 도시

✈ - MAJOR AIRPORT
MAP 주요 공항

🚢 - SEAPORT
PORT 항구

🏭 - FACTORY
FAC 공장

🏛 - THEATER / PUBLIC HALL
CUL 극장 / 공공 회관

* The number of key factors in each city is calculated by the base of the major or identifiable buildings indicated in *Encyclopedia of North Korean Geography and Culture*.

✈ - LOCAL AIRPORT
LAP 지역 공항

🚆 - TRAIN STATION
RAIL 지하철 역

🏢 - COMPANY
CO 산업체

🏥 - HOSPITAL
HOSP 병원

✈ - AIRFIELD
AF 비행장

🏫 - INSTITUTION
EDU 교육기관

🏟 - STADIUM / SPORTS FACILITIES
SPOR 경기장 / 운동 시설

* Source: *Encyclopedia of North Korean Geography and Culture*.

POPULATION 인구
Inhabitants 거주자
% Urban % 도시
% Rural % 농촌
% Male % 남
% Female % 여

POPULATION DENSITY 인구 밀도
Inhabitants 거주자
Administrative Area (km^2) 행정 구역 (km^2)
Population Density (inhabitants/km^2) 인구 밀도 (거주자 수 / km^2)

URBAN DENSITY 도시 인구 밀도
Inhabitants 거주자
Urban Area (km^2) 시가지 (km^2)
Population Density (inhabitants/km^2) 도시 인구 밀도 (거주자 수 / km^2)

* Source: National report *DPR Korea 2008 population census*.

GEOGRAPHY 지리
% Built (Central + Local) % 시가지
% Farmland % 농촌지
% Mountains % 산악지

* The percentage of each geographical elements in each city.

POTENTIAL GROWTH 잠재 성장률
Urbanized Area (km^2) 시가지 면적
% Area Increase 면적 증가율
Urban Population 도시 인구
% Population Increase 인구 증가율
Max. Population (million) 최대 가능 인구

* Urbanized Area = Farmland+Built Area
Urban Population = Rural+Urban Population
Max. Population = (Urban Density) x (Built + Farmland Area)

CENSUS HEXAGRAM

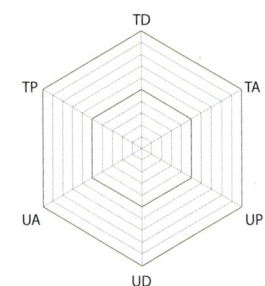

* The profile composed of 6 census data shapes hexagonal relationship as an analyzing system for defining the characterization of individual city.

TD - Total density (1000 / km^2)
TP - Total population (1,000,000)
TA - Total area (1,000 km^2)
UD - Urban density (10,000 / km^2)
UP - Urban population (1,000,000)
UA - Urban area (100 km^2)

GEOGRAPHICAL CIRCLE

- Central Built
- Local Built
- Farmland
- Mountains

INDUSTRIAL CIRCLE

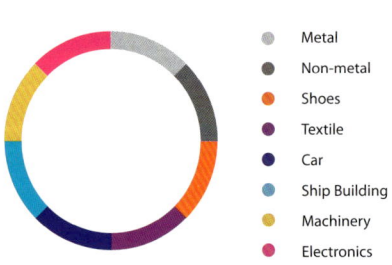

- Metal
- Non-metal
- Shoes
- Textile
- Car
- Ship Building
- Machinery
- Electronics

19 Supporting north korean cities

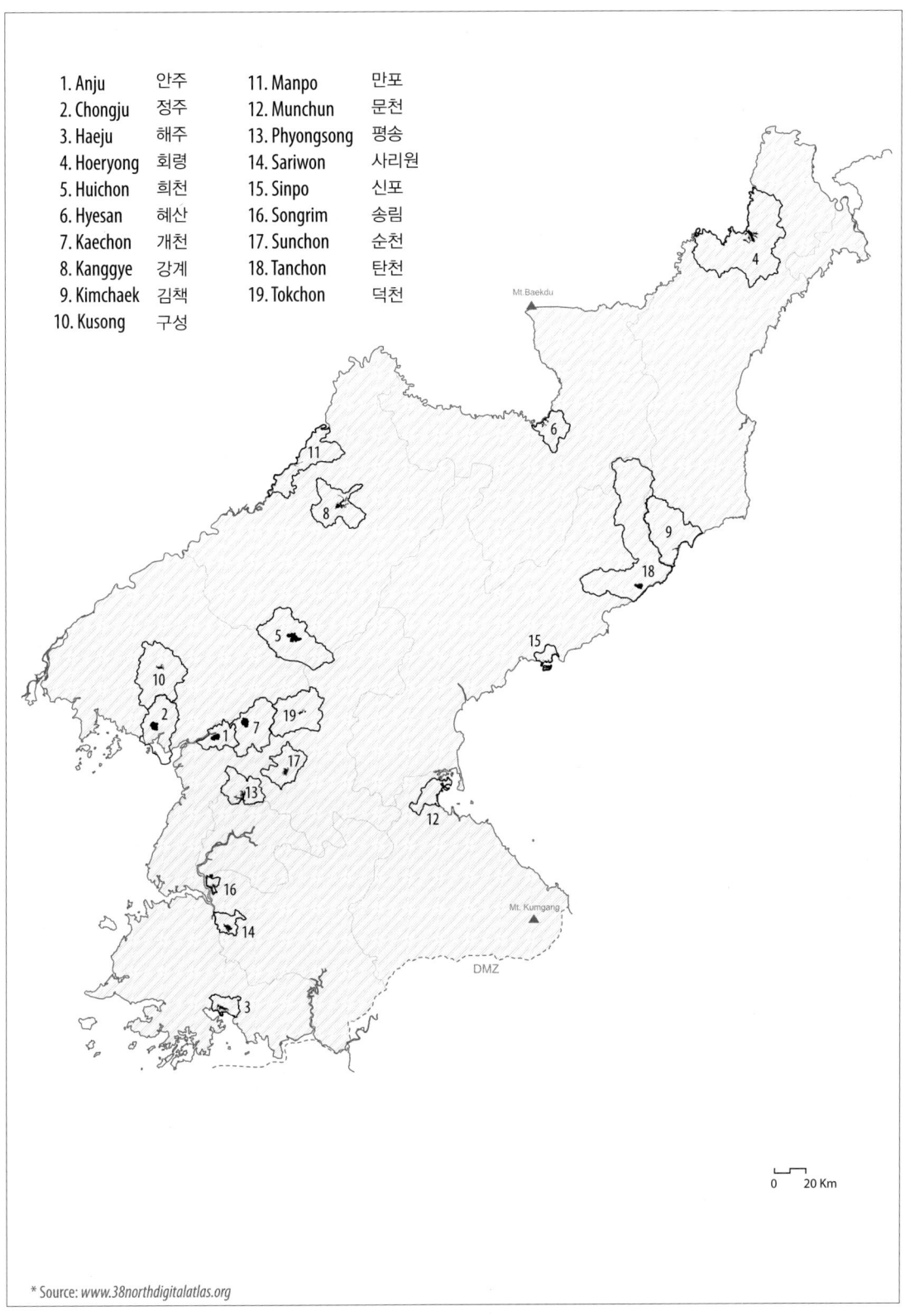

* Source: www.38northdigitalatlas.org

ANJU 안주
SOUTH PHYONGAN PROVINCE

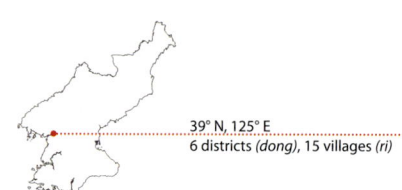

39° N, 125° E
6 districts (dong), 15 villages (ri)

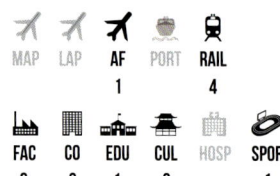

MAP	LAP	AF	PORT	RAIL
		1		4

FAC	CO	EDU	CUL	HOSP	SPOR
6	3	1	2		1

POPULATION
Inhabitants	**240,117**
% Urban	69.8
% Rural	30.2
% Male	47.3
% Female	52.7

POPULATION DENSITY
Inhabitants	240,117
Administrative Area (km²)	446.8
Population Density (inhabitants/km²)	**537**

URBAN DENSITY
Inhabitants	167,646
Urban Area (km²)	10.3
Population Density (inhabitants/km²)	**16,276**

GEOGRAPHY
% Built	6.4
% Farmland	36.5
% Mountains	57.1

POTENTIAL GROWTH
Urbanized Area (km²)	192
% Area Increase	1,860
Urban Population	240,117
% Population Increase	1,301
Max. Population (million)	3.1

CENSUS HEXAGRAM

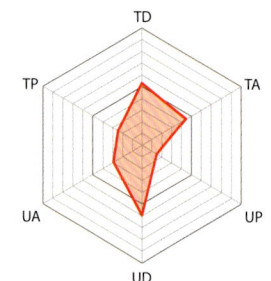

TD - Total density (1000 / km²)
TP - Total population (1,000,000)
TA - Total area (1,000 km²)
UD - Urban density (10,000 / km²)
UP - Urban population (1,000,000)
UA - Urban area (100 km²)

GEOGRAPHICAL CIRCLE

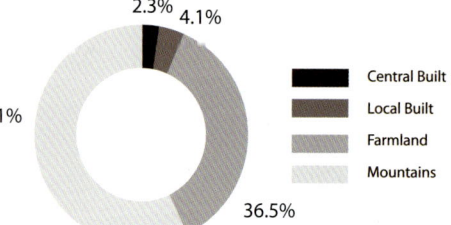

- Central Built — 2.3%
- Local Built — 4.1%
- Farmland — 36.5%
- Mountains — 57.1%

INDUSTRIAL CIRCLE

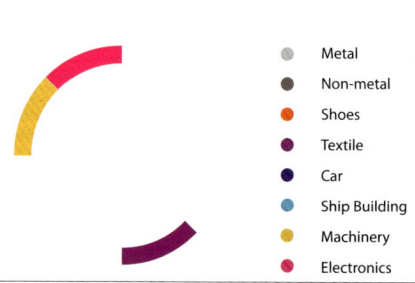

- Metal
- Non-metal
- Shoes
- Textile
- Car
- Ship Building
- Machinery
- Electronics

19 Supporting north korean cities | Anju

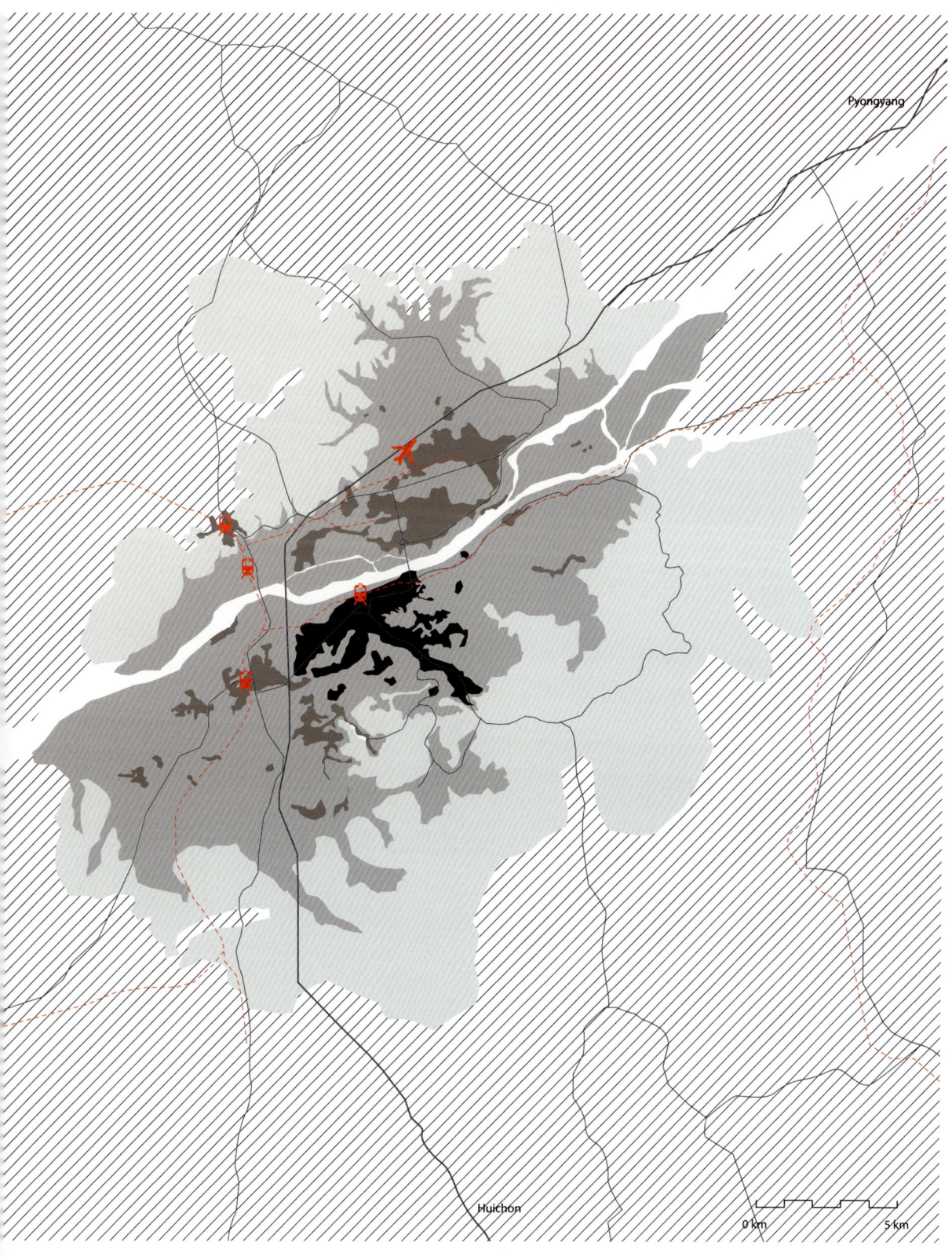

CHONGJU 정주
NORTH PHYONGAN PROVINCE

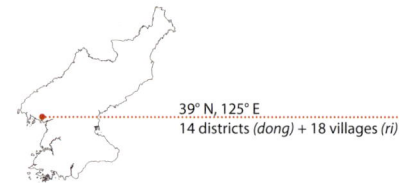

39° N, 125° E
14 districts *(dong)* + 18 villages *(ri)*

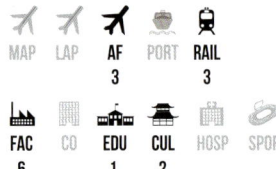

| MAP | LAP | AF 3 | PORT | RAIL 3 |
| FAC 6 | CO | EDU 1 | CUL 2 | HOSP | SPOR |

POPULATION
Inhabitants	**189,742**
% Urban	54.1
% Rural	45.9
% Male	47.2
% Female	52.8

POPULATION DENSITY
Inhabitants	189,742
Administrative Area (km²)	758
Population Density (inhabitants/km²)	**250**

URBAN DENSITY
Inhabitants	102,659
Urban Area (km²)	13.6
Population Density (inhabitants/km²)	**7,548**

GEOGRAPHY
% Built	6.6
% Farmland	52.7
% Mountains	40.7

POTENTIAL GROWTH
Urbanized Area (km²)	449
% Area Increase	3,301
Urban Population	189,742
% Population Increase	1786
Max. Population (million)	3.4

CENSUS HEXAGRAM

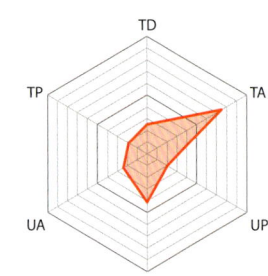

TD - Total density (1000 / km²)
TP - Total population (1,000,000)
TA - Total area (1,000 km²)
UD - Urban density (10,000 / km²)
UP - Urban population (1,000,000)
UA - Urban area (100 km²)

GEOGRAPHICAL CIRCLE

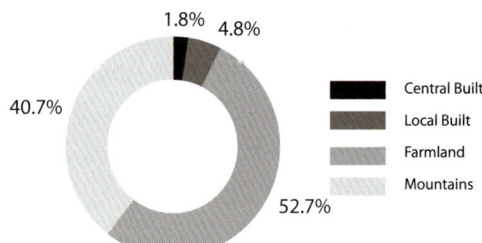

- Central Built 1.8%
- Local Built 4.8%
- Farmland 52.7%
- Mountains 40.7%

INDUSTRIAL CIRCLE

- Metal
- Non-metal
- Shoes
- Textile
- Car
- Ship Building
- Machinery
- Electronics

19 Supporting north korean cities | Chongju

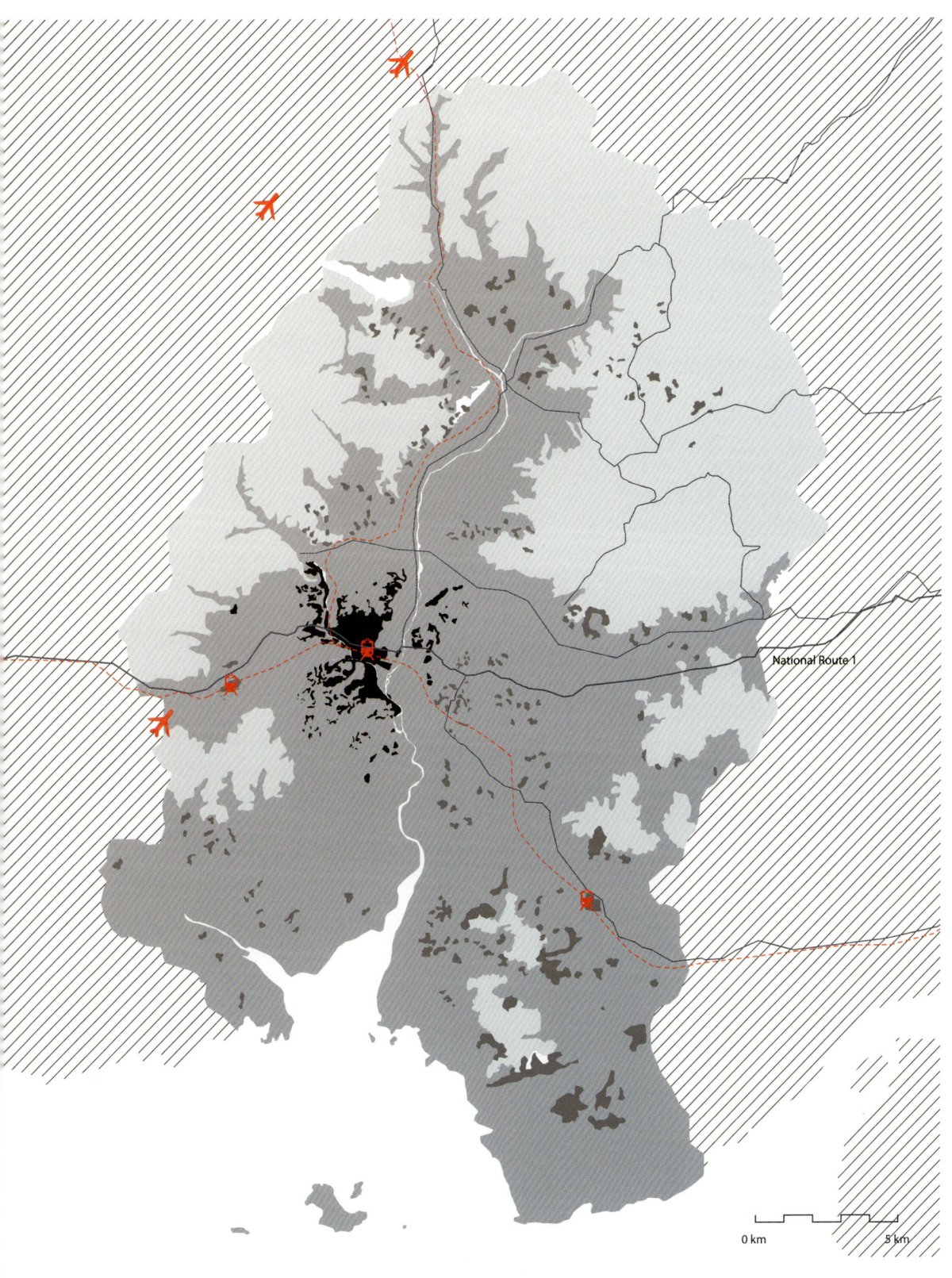

HAEJU 해주
SOUTH HWANGHAE PROVINCE

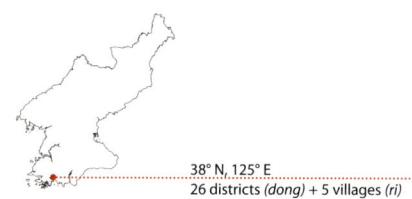

38° N, 125° E
26 districts (dong) + 5 villages (ri)

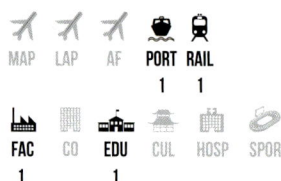

MAP	LAP	AF	PORT	RAIL
			1	1

FAC	CO	EDU	CUL	HOSP	SPOR
1		1			

POPULATION
Inhabitants	**273,300**
% Urban	88.4
% Rural	11.6
% Male	48.1
% Female	51.9

POPULATION DENSITY
Inhabitants	273,300
Administrative Area (km²)	214
Population Density (inhabitants/km²)	**1,277**

URBAN DENSITY
Inhabitants	241,599
Urban Area (km²)	26.7
Population Density (inhabitants/km²)	**9,049**

GEOGRAPHY
% Built	13.5
% Farmland	46.2
% Mountains	40.3

POTENTIAL GROWTH
Urbanized Area (km²)	128
% Area Increase	479
Urban Population	273,300
% Population Increase	424
Max. Population (million)	1.2

CENSUS HEXAGRAM

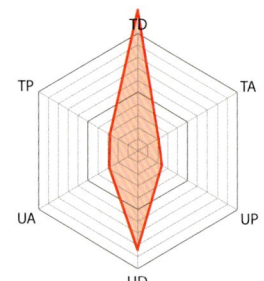

TD - Total density (1000 / km²)
TP - Total population (1,000,000)
TA - Total area (1,000 km²)
UD - Urban density (10,000 / km²)
UP - Urban population (1,000,000)
UA - Urban area (100 km²)

GEOGRAPHICAL CIRCLE

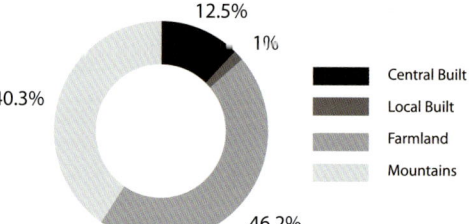

- Central Built — 1%
- Local Built — 12.5%
- Farmland — 46.2%
- Mountains — 40.3%

INDUSTRIAL CIRCLE

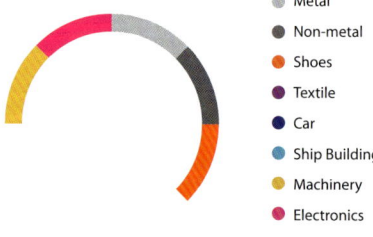

- Metal
- Non-metal
- Shoes
- Textile
- Car
- Ship Building
- Machinery
- Electronics

19 Supporting north korean cities | Haeju

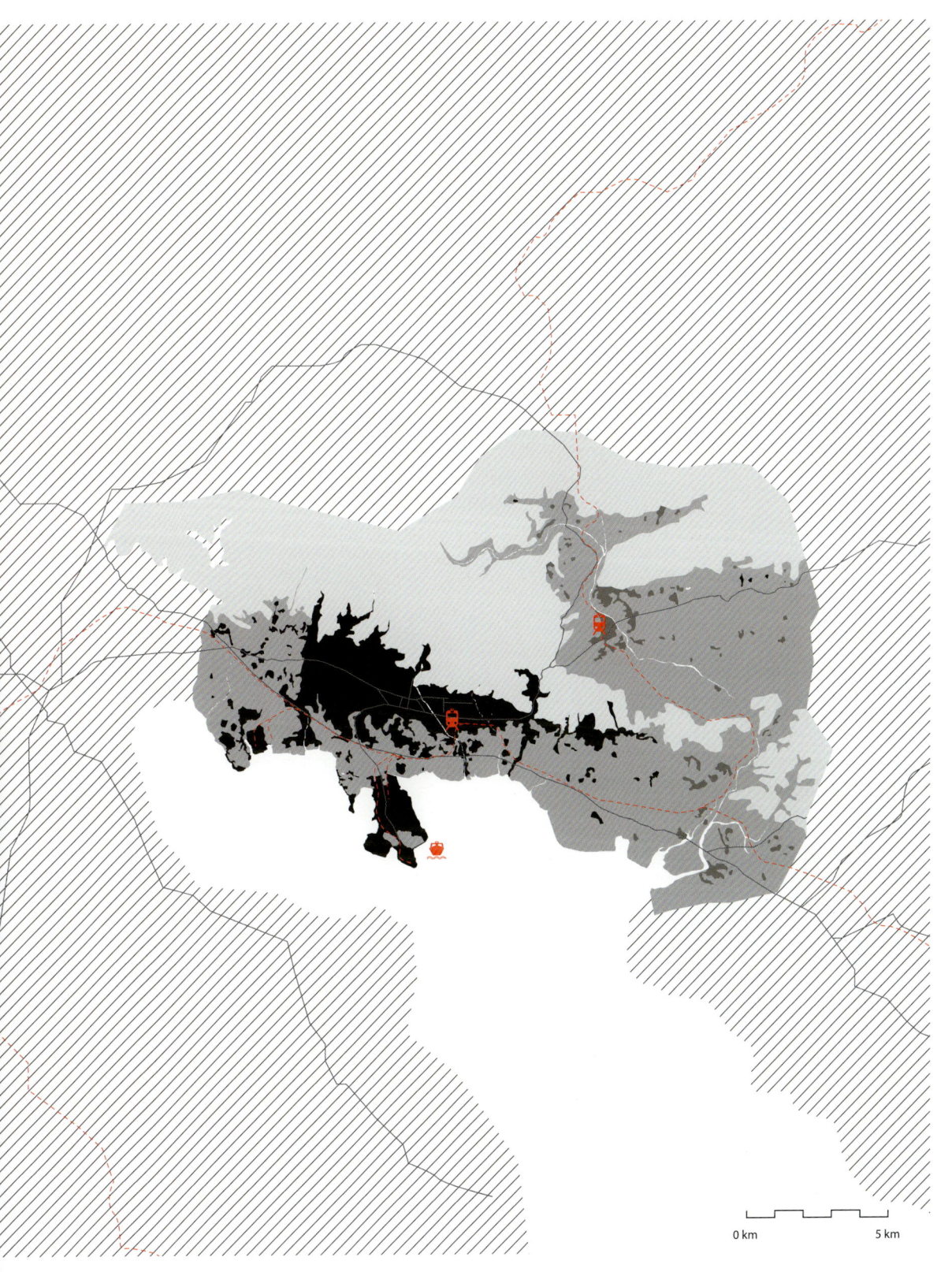

HEORYONG 회령
NORTH HAMGYONG PROVINCE

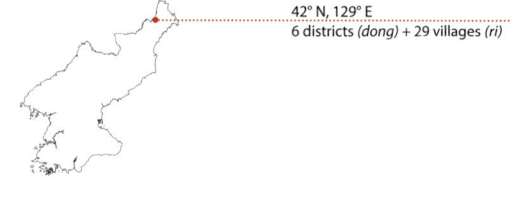

42° N, 129° E
6 districts (dong) + 29 villages (ri)

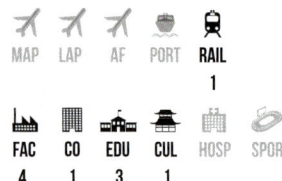

MAP	LAP	AF	PORT	RAIL
				1

FAC	CO	EDU	CUL	HOSP	SPOR
4	1	3	1		

POPULATION
Inhabitants	**153,532**
% Urban	60.2
% Rural	39.8
% Male	47.1
% Female	52.9

POPULATION DENSITY
Inhabitants	153,532
Administrative Area (km²)	1,076
Population Density (inhabitants/km²)	**142.7**

URBAN DENSITY
Inhabitants	92,494
Urban Area (km²)	12.9
Population Density (inhabitants/km²)	**7,170**

GEOGRAPHY
% Built	2.0
% Farmland	40.4
% Mountains	57.6

POTENTIAL GROWTH
Urbanized Area (km²)	456
% Area Increase	3,535
Urban Population	153,532
% Population Increase	2,130
Max. Population (million)	3.3

CENSUS HEXAGRAM

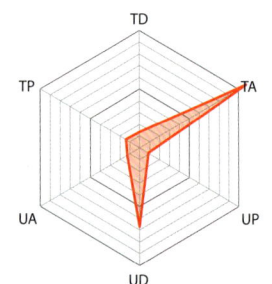

TD - Total density (1000 / km²)
TP - Total population (1,000,000)
TA - Total area (1,000 km²)
UD - Urban density (10,000 / km²)
UP - Urban population (1,000,000)
UA - Urban area (100 km²)

GEOGRAPHICAL CIRCLE

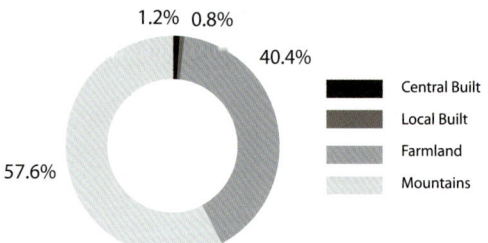

1.2% 0.8% 40.4% 57.6%

- Central Built
- Local Built
- Farmland
- Mountains

INDUSTRIAL CIRCLE

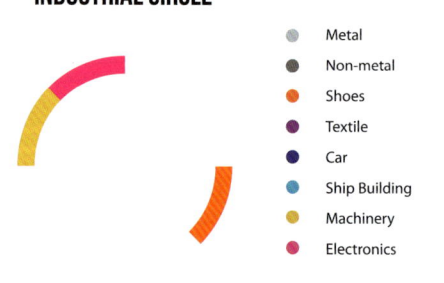

- Metal
- Non-metal
- Shoes
- Textile
- Car
- Ship Building
- Machinery
- Electronics

19 Supporting north korean cities | Heoryong

China

0 km 5 km

HUICHON 희천
JAGANG PROVINCE

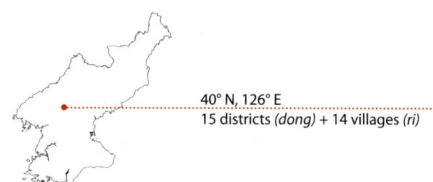

40° N, 126° E
15 districts *(dong)* + 14 villages *(ri)*

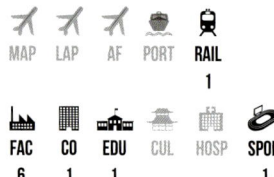

MAP	LAP	AF	PORT	RAIL
				1

FAC	CO	EDU	CUL	HOSP	SPOR
6	1	1			1

POPULATION
Inhabitants	**168,180**
% Urban	80.9
% Rural	19.1
% Male	47.4
% Female	52.6

POPULATION DENSITY
Inhabitants	168,180
Administrative Area (km²)	873.4
Population Density (inhabitants/km²)	**192.6**

URBAN DENSITY
Inhabitants	136,093
Urban Area (km²)	8.7
Population Density (inhabitants/km²)	**15,643**

GEOGRAPHY
% Built	1.8
% Farmland	8.5
% Mountains	89.7

POTENTIAL GROWTH
Urbanized Area (km²)	90
% Area Increase	1,034
Urban Population	168,180
% Population Increase	837
Max. Population (million)	1.4

CENSUS HEXAGRAM

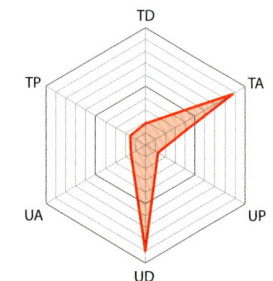

TD - Total density (1000 / km²)
TP - Total population (1,000,000)
TA - Total area (1,000 km²)
UD - Urban density (10,000 / km²)
UP - Urban population (1,000,000)
UA - Urban area (100 km²)

GEOGRAPHICAL CIRCLE

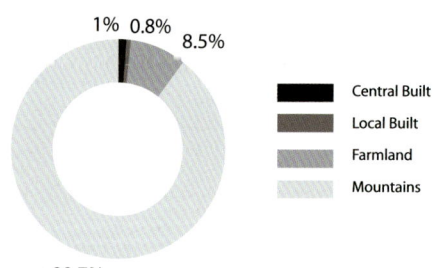

- Central Built — 1%
- Local Built — 0.8%
- Farmland — 8.5%
- Mountains — 89.7%

INDUSTRIAL CIRCLE

- Metal
- Non-metal
- Shoes
- Textile
- Car
- Ship Building
- Machinery
- Electronics

19 Supporting north korean cities | Huichon

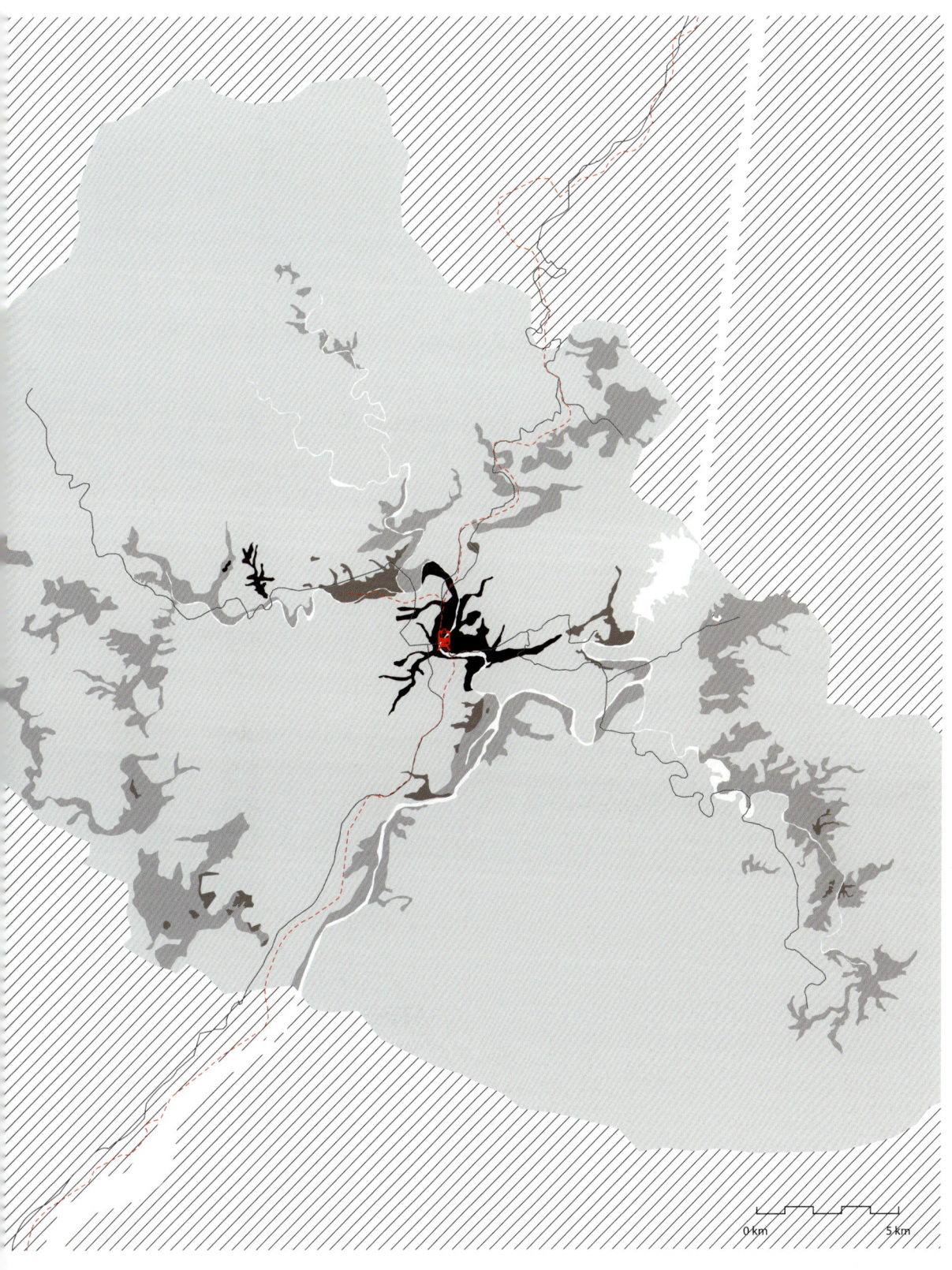

HYESAN 혜산
RYANGGANG PROVINCE

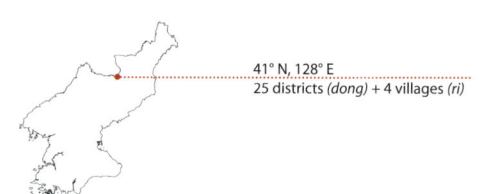

41° N, 128° E
25 districts *(dong)* + 4 villages *(ri)*

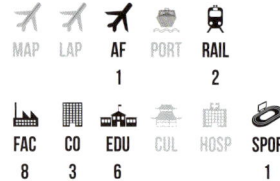

MAP	LAP	AF	PORT	RAIL
		1		2

FAC	CO	EDU	CUL	HOSP	SPOR
8	3	6			1

POPULATION
Inhabitants	**192,680**
% Urban	90.3
% Rural	9.7
% Male	47.4
% Female	52.6

POPULATION DENSITY
Inhabitants	192,680
Administrative Area (km²)	495.6
Population Density (inhabitants/km²)	**388.8**

URBAN DENSITY
Inhabitants	174,015
Urban Area (km²)	24.7
Population Density (inhabitants/km²)	**7,045**

GEOGRAPHY
% Built	8.2
% Farmland	35.8
% Mountains	57

POTENTIAL GROWTH
Urbanized Area (km²)	213.3
% Area Increase	864
Urban Population	192,680
% Population Increase	780
Max. Population (million)	1.5

CENSUS HEXAGRAM

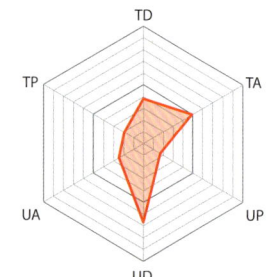

TD - Total density (1000 / km²)
TP - Total population (1,000,000)
TA - Total area (1,000 km²)
UD - Urban density (10,000 / km²)
UP - Urban population (1,000,000)
UA - Urban area (100 km²)

GEOGRAPHICAL CIRCLE

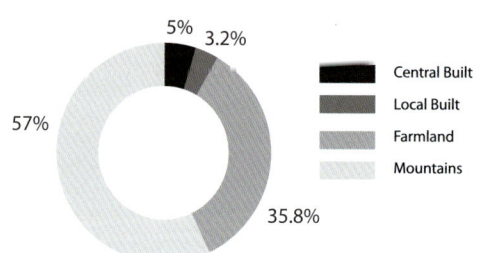

- Central Built — 3.2%
- Local Built — 5%
- Farmland — 35.8%
- Mountains — 57%

INDUSTRIAL CIRCLE

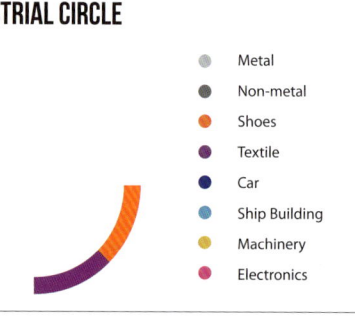

- Metal
- Non-metal
- Shoes
- Textile
- Car
- Ship Building
- Machinery
- Electronics

19 Supporting north korean cities | Hyesan

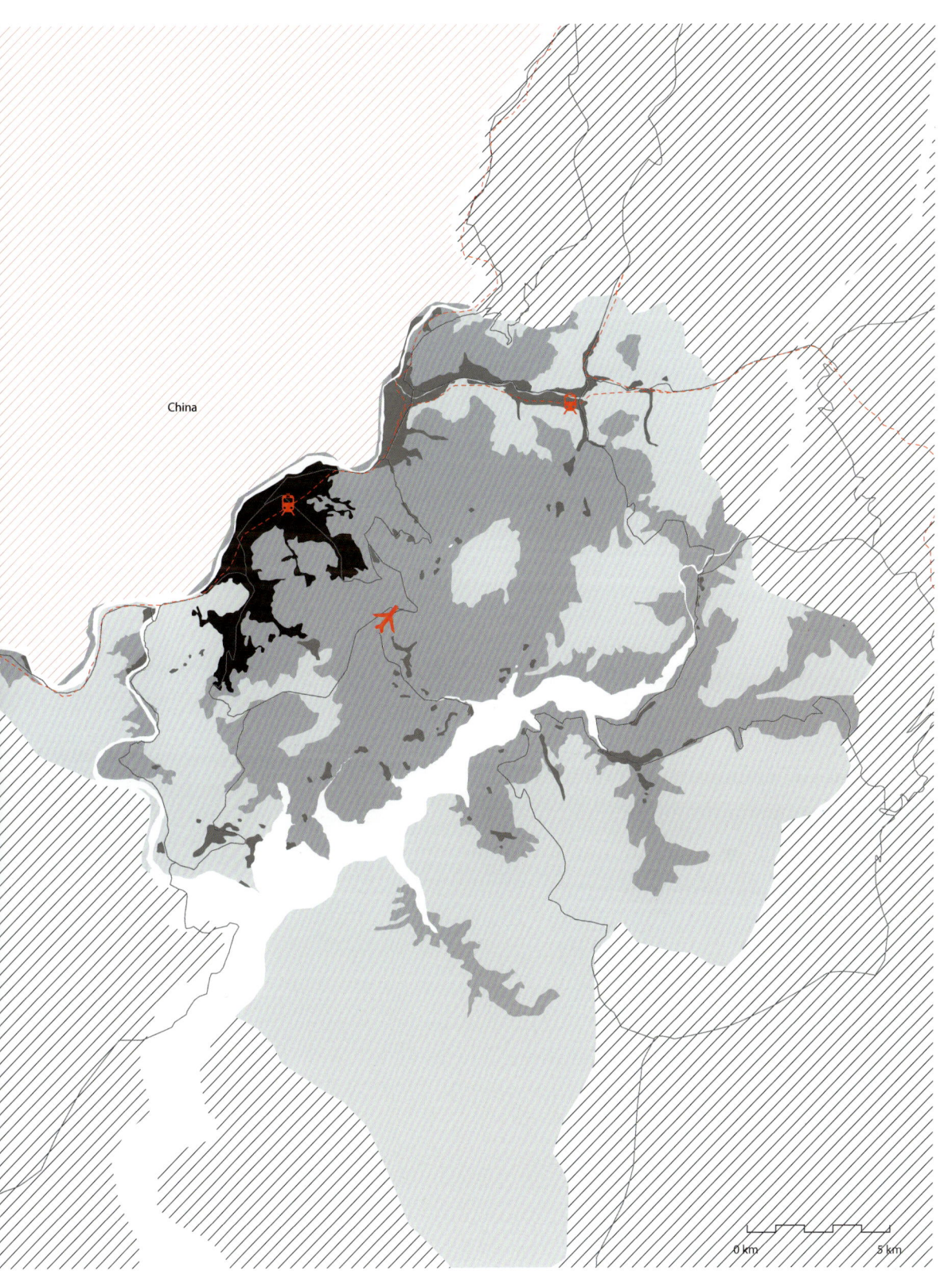

China

0 km   5 km

KAECHON 개천
SOUTH PHYONGAN PROVINCE

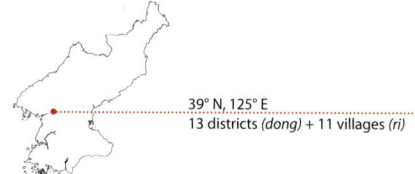

39° N, 125° E
13 districts (*dong*) + 11 villages (*ri*)

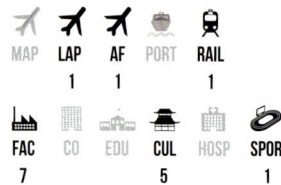

MAP	LAP	AF	PORT	RAIL
	1	1		1

FAC	CO	EDU	CUL	HOSP	SPOR
7			5		1

POPULATION
Inhabitants	**319,554**
% Urban	82.1
% Rural	17.9
% Male	47.3
% Female	52.7

POPULATION DENSITY
Inhabitants	319,554
Administrative Area (km²)	704.1
Population Density (inhabitants/km²)	**453.8**

URBAN DENSITY
Inhabitants	262,389
Urban Area (km²)	20.4
Population Density (inhabitants/km²)	**12,862**

GEOGRAPHY
% Built	4.6
% Farmland	46.2
% Mountains	50.2

POTENTIAL GROWTH
Urbanized Area (km²)	350.6
% Area Increase	1,719
Urban Population	319,554
% Population Increase	1,411
Max. Population (million)	4.5

CENSUS HEXAGRAM

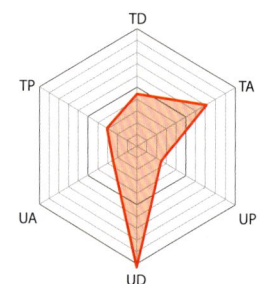

TD - Total density (1000 / km²)
TP - Total population (1,000,000)
TA - Total area (1,000 km²)
UD - Urban density (10,000 / km²)
UP - Urban population (1,000,000)
UA - Urban area (100 km²)

GEOGRAPHICAL CIRCLE

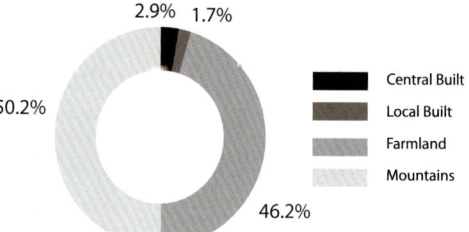

- Central Built — 1.7%
- Local Built — 2.9%
- Farmland — 46.2%
- Mountains — 50.2%

INDUSTRIAL CIRCLE

- Metal
- Non-metal
- Shoes
- Textile
- Car
- Ship Building
- Machinery
- Electronics

19 Supporting north korean cities | Kaechon

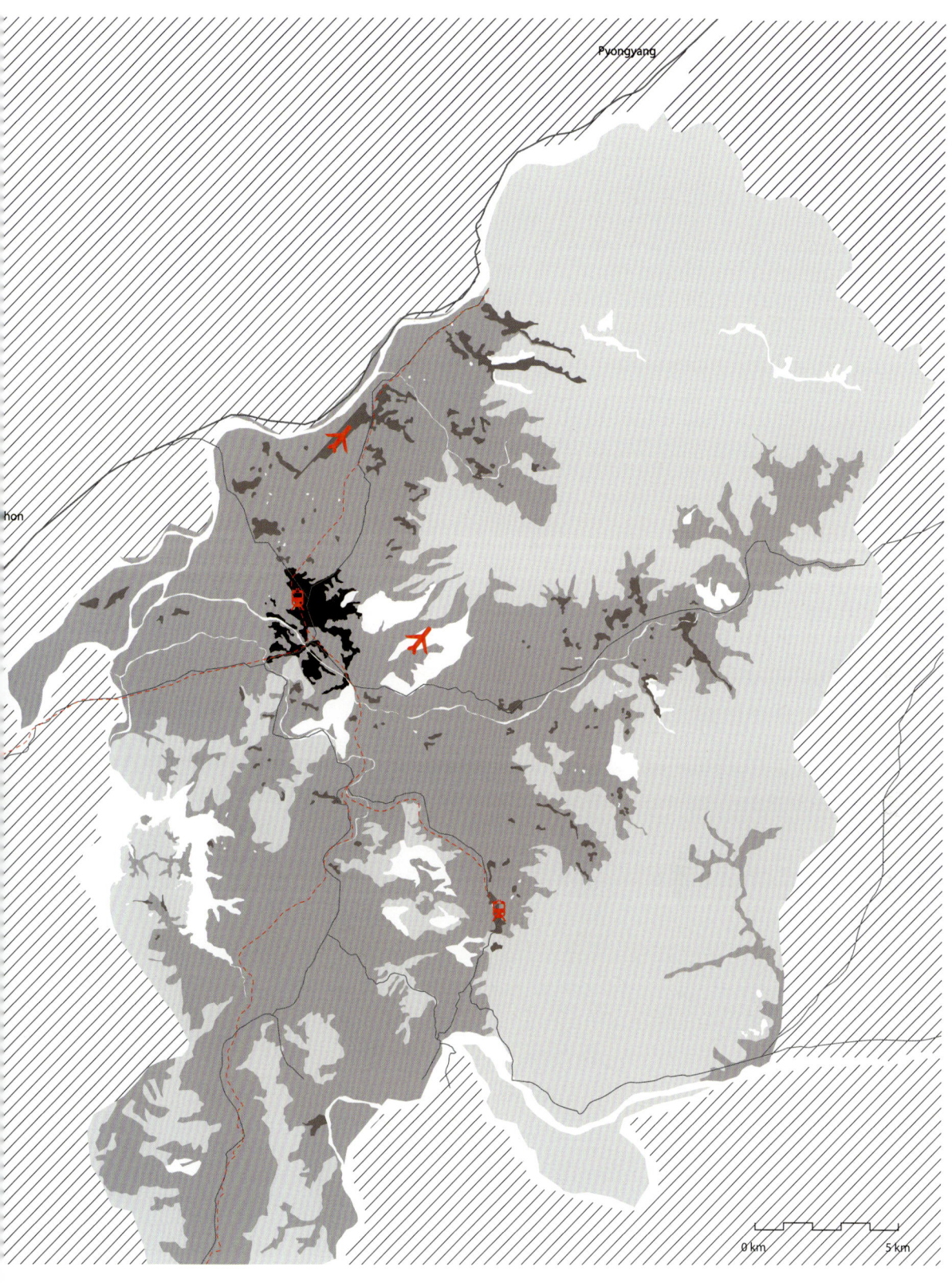

KANGGYE 강계
JAGANG PROVINCE

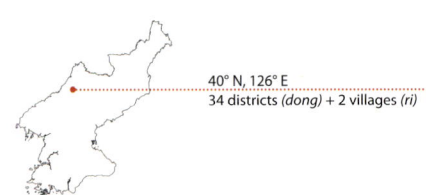
40° N, 126° E
34 districts (*dong*) + 2 villages (*ri*)

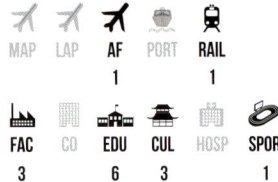

MAP	LAP	AF	PORT	RAIL
		1		1
FAC	CO	EDU	CUL	SPOR
3		6	3	1

POPULATION
Inhabitants	**251,971**
% Urban	100
% Rural	0
% Male	47.7
% Female	52.3

POPULATION DENSITY
Inhabitants	251,971
Administrative Area (km²)	363.8
Population Density (inhabitants/km²)	**692.6**

URBAN DENSITY
Inhabitants	251,971
Urban Area (km²)	23.3
Population Density (inhabitants/km²)	**10,814**

GEOGRAPHY
% Built	8.7
% Farmland	47.1
% Mountains	44.1

POTENTIAL GROWTH
Urbanized Area (km²)	203
% Area Increase	871
Urban Population	251,971
% Population Increase	871
Max. Population (million)	2.2

CENSUS HEXAGRAM
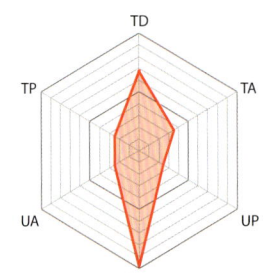

TD - Total density (1000 / km²)
TP - Total population (1,000,000)
TA - Total area (1,000 km²)
UD - Urban density (10,000 / km²)
UP - Urban population (1,000,000)
UA - Urban area (100 km²)

GEOGRAPHICAL CIRCLE
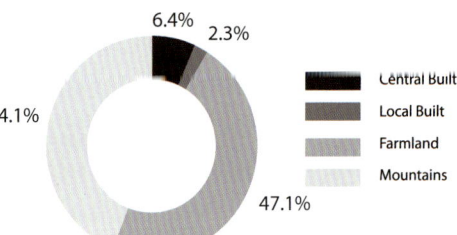

- Central Built — 2.3%
- Local Built — 6.4%
- Farmland — 47.1%
- Mountains — 44.1%

INDUSTRIAL CIRCLE
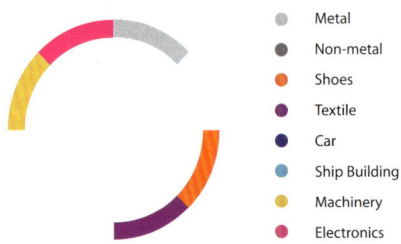

- Metal
- Non-metal
- Shoes
- Textile
- Car
- Ship Building
- Machinery
- Electronics

19 Supporting north korean cities | Kanggye

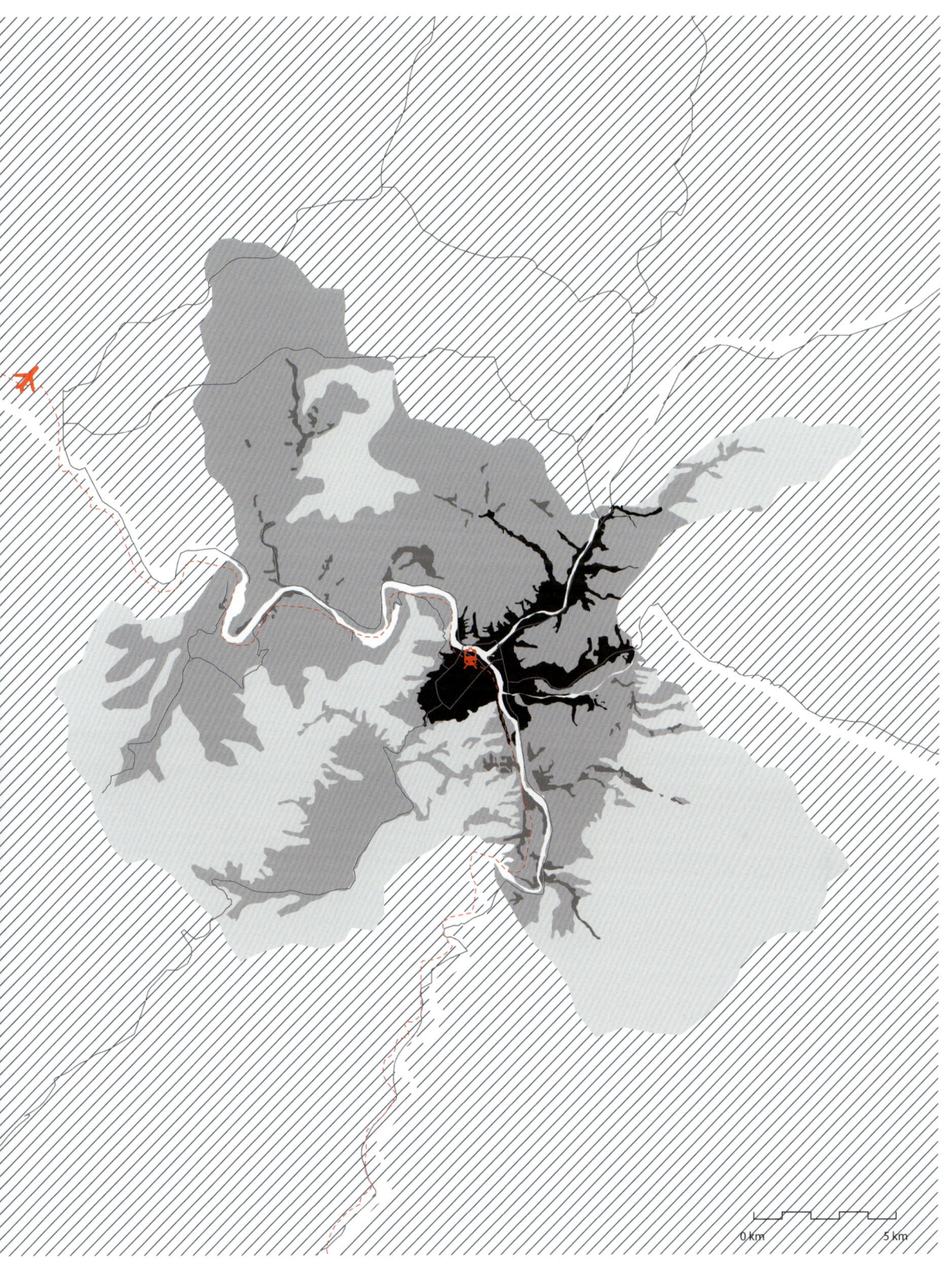

KIMCHAEK 김책
NORTH HAMGYONG PROVINCE

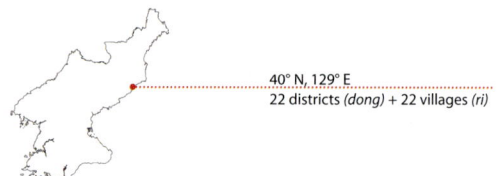

40° N, 129° E
22 districts *(dong)* + 22 villages *(ri)*

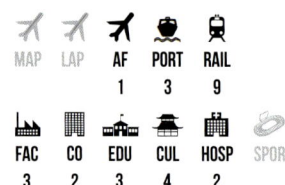

MAP	LAP	AF	PORT	RAIL
		1	3	9

FAC	CO	EDU	CUL	HOSP	SPOR
3	2	3	4	2	

POPULATION
Inhabitants	**207,299**
% Urban	74.9
% Rural	25.1
% Male	47.1
% Female	52.9

POPULATION DENSITY
Inhabitants	207,299
Administrative Area (km²)	947
Population Density (inhabitants/km²)	**218.9**

URBAN DENSITY
Inhabitants	155,284
Urban Area (km²)	9.5
Population Density (inhabitants/km²)	**16,346**

GEOGRAPHY
% Built	2.6
% Farmland	33.1
% Mountains	64.3

POTENTIAL GROWTH
Urbanized Area (km²)	338
% Area Increase	3,558
Urban Population	207,299
% Population Increase	2,665
Max. Population (million)	5.5

CENSUS HEXAGRAM

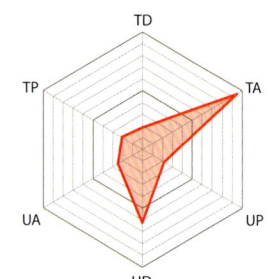

TD - Total density (1000 / km²)
TP - Total population (1,000,000)
TA - Total area (1,000 km²)
UD - Urban density (10,000 / km²)
UP - Urban population (1,000,000)
UA - Urban area (100 km²)

GEOGRAPHICAL CIRCLE

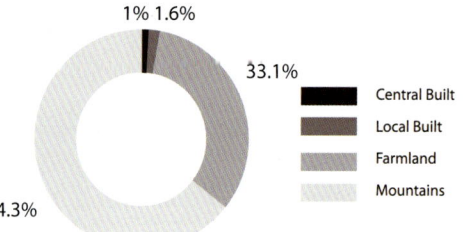

1% — Central Built
1.6% — Local Built
33.1% — Farmland
64.3% — Mountains

INDUSTRIAL CIRCLE

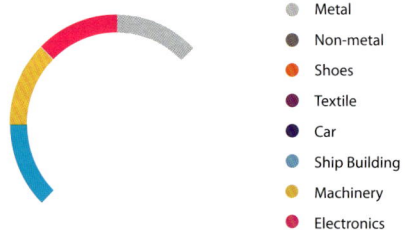

- Metal
- Non-metal
- Shoes
- Textile
- Car
- Ship Building
- Machinery
- Electronics

19 Supporting north korean cities | Kimchaek

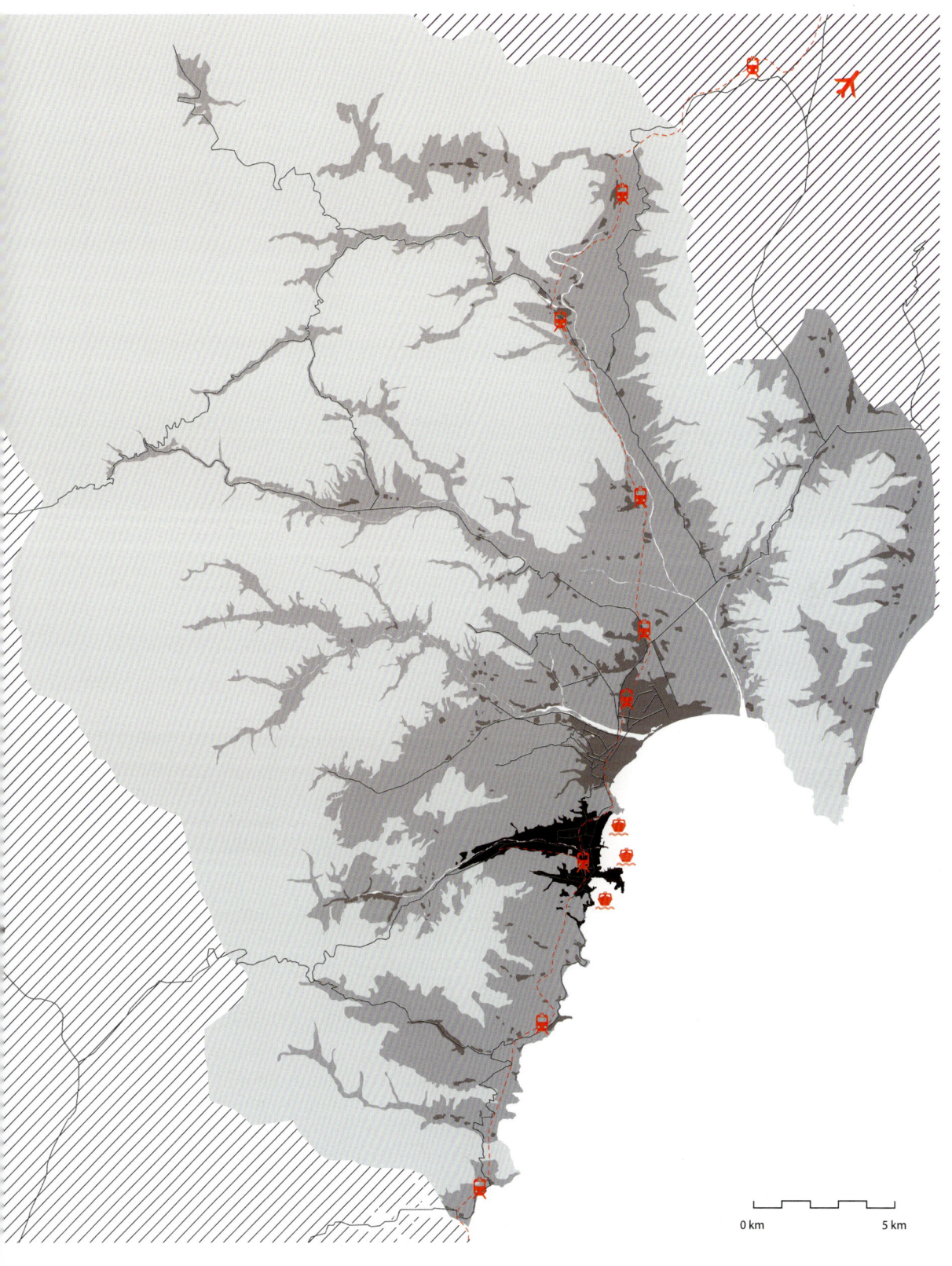

KUSONG 구성
NORTH PHYONGAN PROVINCE

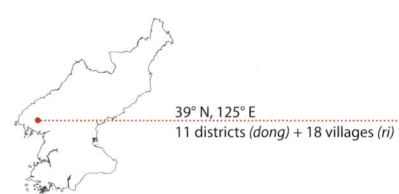

39° N, 125° E
11 districts *(dong)* + 18 villages *(ri)*

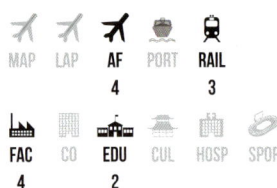

MAP	LAP	AF 4	PORT	RAIL 3
FAC 4	CO	EDU 2	CUL	HOSP	SPOR

POPULATION
Inhabitants	**196,515**
% Urban	80
% Rural	20
% Male	47.4
% Female	52.6

POPULATION DENSITY
Inhabitants	196,515
Administrative Area (km²)	664
Population Density (inhabitants/km²)	**296**

URBAN DENSITY
Inhabitants	155,181
Urban Area (km²)	30.5
Population Density (inhabitants/km²)	**5,088**

GEOGRAPHY
% Built	8.6
% Farmland	39.1
% Mountains	52.3

POTENTIAL GROWTH
Urbanized Area (km²)	317.3
% Area Increase	1,040
Urban Population	196,515
% Population Increase	822
Max. Population (million)	1.6

CENSUS HEXAGRAM

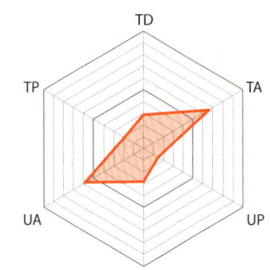

TD - Total density (1000 / km²)
TP - Total population (1,000,000)
TA - Total area (1,000 km²)

UD - Urban density (10,000 / km²)
UP - Urban population (1,000,000)
UA - Urban area (100 km²)

GEOGRAPHICAL CIRCLE

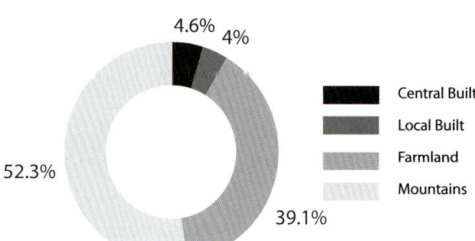

4.6% Central Built
4% Local Built
39.1% Farmland
52.3% Mountains

INDUSTRIAL CIRCLE

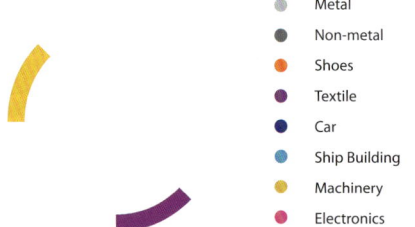

- Metal
- Non-metal
- Shoes
- Textile
- Car
- Ship Building
- Machinery
- Electronics

19 Supporting north korean cities | Kusong

MANPO 만포
JAGANG PROVINCE

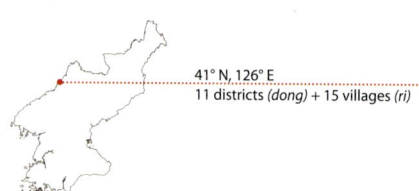
41° N, 126° E
11 districts (dong) + 15 villages (ri)

MAP　LAP　AF　PORT　RAIL
　　　　　　　　　　　2

FAC　CO　EDU　CUL　HOSP　SPOR
5

POPULATION
Inhabitants	**116,760**
% Urban	70.8
% Rural	29.2
% Male	47.4
% Female	52.6

POPULATION DENSITY
Inhabitants	116,760
Administrative Area (km²)	640
Population Density (inhabitants/km²)	**182**

URBAN DENSITY
Inhabitants	82,631
Urban Area (km²)	4.8
Population Density (inhabitants/km²)	**17,214**

GEOGRAPHY
% Built	2.7
% Farmland	37.8
% Mountains	59.5

POTENTIAL GROWTH
Urbanized Area (km²)	259.2
% Area Increase	5,400
Urban Population	116,760
% Population Increase	3,841
Max. Population (million)	4.5

CENSUS HEXAGRAM

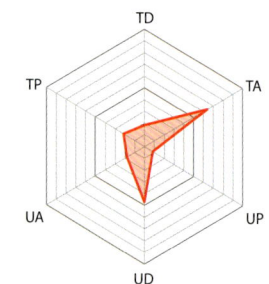

TD - Total density (1000 / km²)
TP - Total population (1,000,000)
TA - Total area (1,000 km²)
UD - Urban density (10,000 / km²)
UP - Urban population (1,000,000)
UA - Urban area (100 km²)

GEOGRAPHICAL CIRCLE

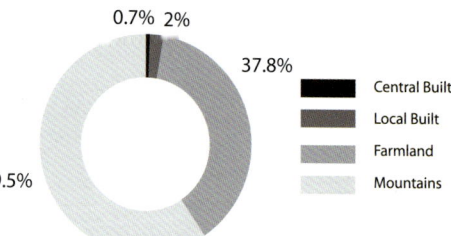

0.7% 2% 37.8% 59.5%

- Central Built
- Local Built
- Farmland
- Mountains

INDUSTRIAL CIRCLE

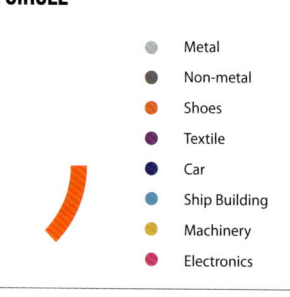

- Metal
- Non-metal
- Shoes
- Textile
- Car
- Ship Building
- Machinery
- Electronics

19 Supporting north korean cities | Manpo

MUNCHON 문천
KANGWON PROVINCE

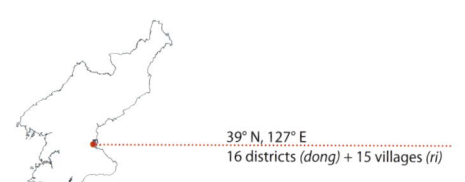

39° N, 127° E
16 districts *(dong)* + 15 villages *(ri)*

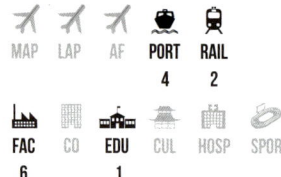

MAP	LAP	AF	PORT 4	RAIL 2
FAC 6	CO	EDU 1	CUL	HOSP	SPOR

POPULATION
Inhabitants	**122,934**
% Urban	75.3
% Rural	24.7
% Male	46.4
% Female	53.6

POPULATION DENSITY
Inhabitants	122,934
Administrative Area (km²)	270.8
Population Density (inhabitants/km²)	**454**

URBAN DENSITY
Inhabitants	92,525
Urban Area (km²)	16.2
Population Density (inhabitants/km²)	**5,711**

GEOGRAPHY
% Built	8.6
% Farmland	26.6
% Mountains	64.8

POTENTIAL GROWTH
Urbanized Area (km²)	95.3
% Area Increase	588
Urban Population	122,934
% Population Increase	443
Max. Population (million)	0.5

CENSUS HEXAGRAM

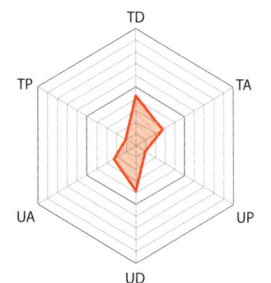

TD - Total density (1000 / km²)
TP - Total population (1,000,000)
TA - Total area (1,000 km²)
UD - Urban density (10,000 / km²)
UP - Urban population (1,000,000)
UA - Urban area (100 km²)

GEOGRAPHICAL CIRCLE

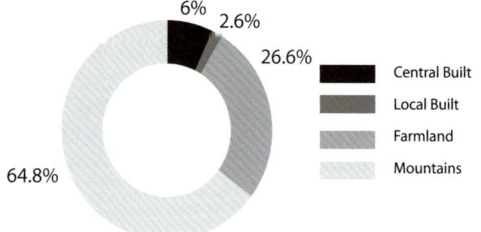

6% 2.6% 26.6% 64.8%

- Central Built
- Local Built
- Farmland
- Mountains

INDUSTRIAL CIRCLE

- Metal
- Non-metal
- Shoes
- Textile
- Car
- Ship Building
- Machinery
- Electronics

19 Supporting north korean cities | Munchon

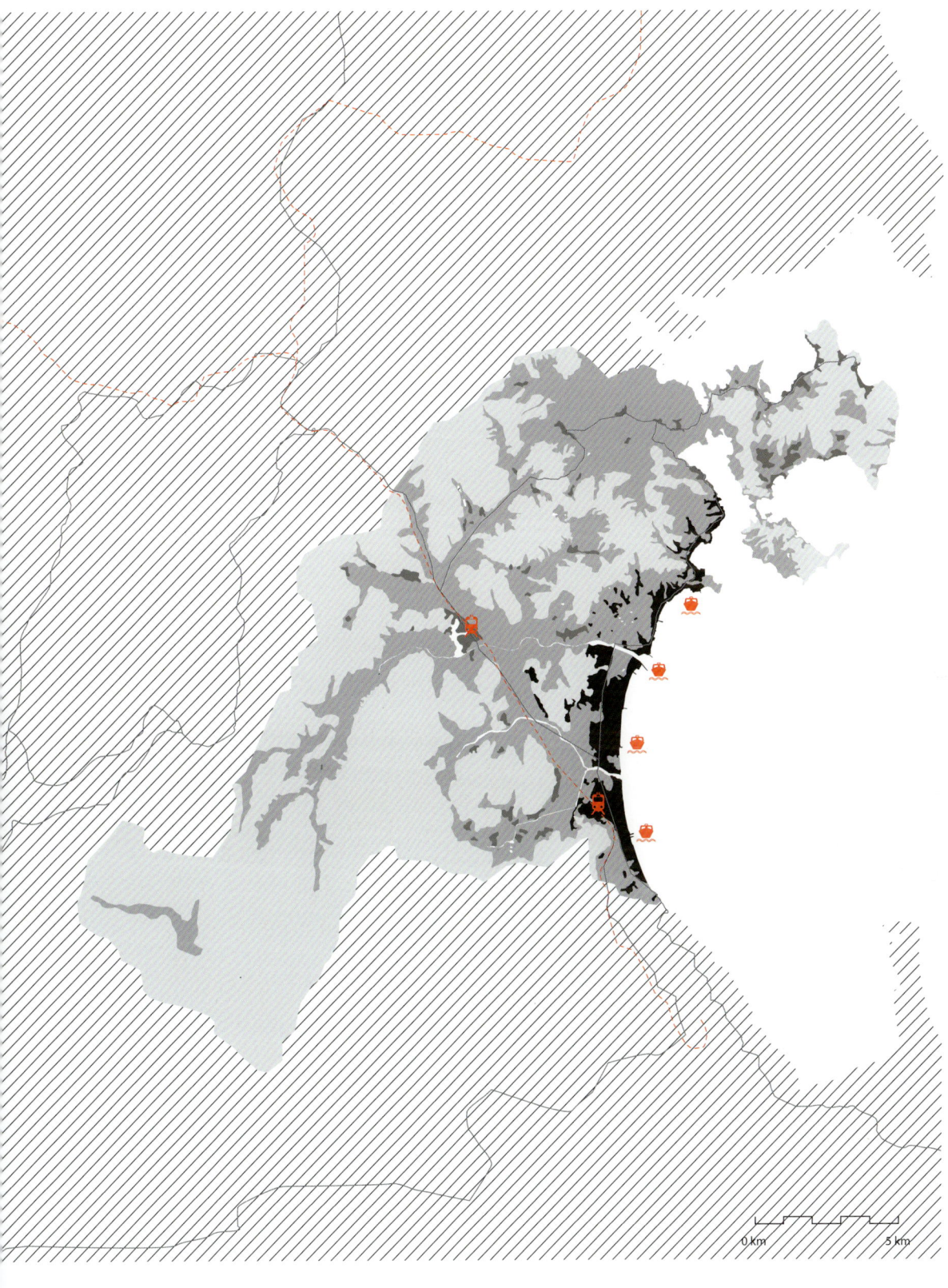

PHYONGSONG 평성
SOUTH PHYONGAN PROVINCE

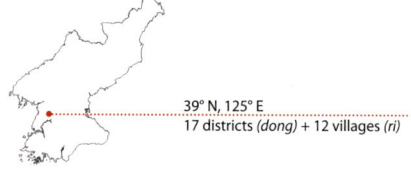

39° N, 125° E
17 districts *(dong)* + 12 villages *(ri)*

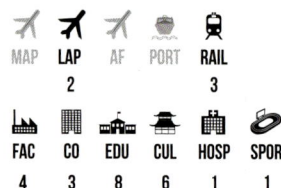

MAP	LAP	AF	PORT	RAIL
	2			3

FAC	CO	EDU	CUL	HOSP	SPOR
4	3	8	6	1	1

POPULATION
Inhabitants	**284,386**
% Urban	83.2
% Rural	16.8
% Male	48.8
% Female	51.2

POPULATION DENSITY
Inhabitants	284,286
Administrative Area (km²)	366.5
Population Density (inhabitants/km²)	**775.6**

URBAN DENSITY
Inhabitants	236,586
Urban Area (km²)	41.4
Population Density (inhabitants/km²)	**5,715**

GEOGRAPHY
% Built	12.1
% Farmland	56.3
% Mountains	31.6

POTENTIAL GROWTH
Urbanized Area (km²)	250.6
% Area Increase	606
Urban Population	284,386
% Population Increase	504
Max. Population (million)	1.4

CENSUS HEXAGRAM

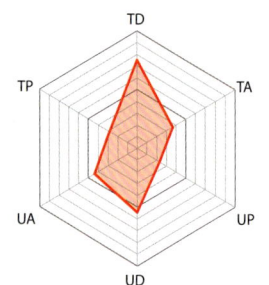

TD - Total density (1000 / km²)
TP - Total population (1,000,000)
TA - Total area (1,000 km²)
UD - Urban density (10,000 / km²)
UP - Urban population (1,000,000)
UA - Urban area (100 km²)

GEOGRAPHICAL CIRCLE

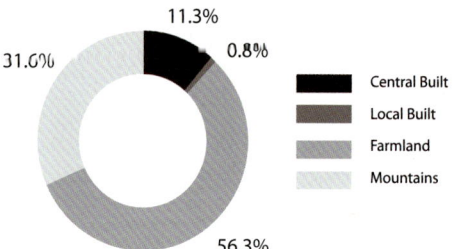

- Central Built
- Local Built
- Farmland
- Mountains

INDUSTRIAL CIRCLE

- Metal
- Non-metal
- Shoes
- Textile
- Car
- Ship Building
- Machinery
- Electronics

19 Supporting north korean cities | Phyongsong

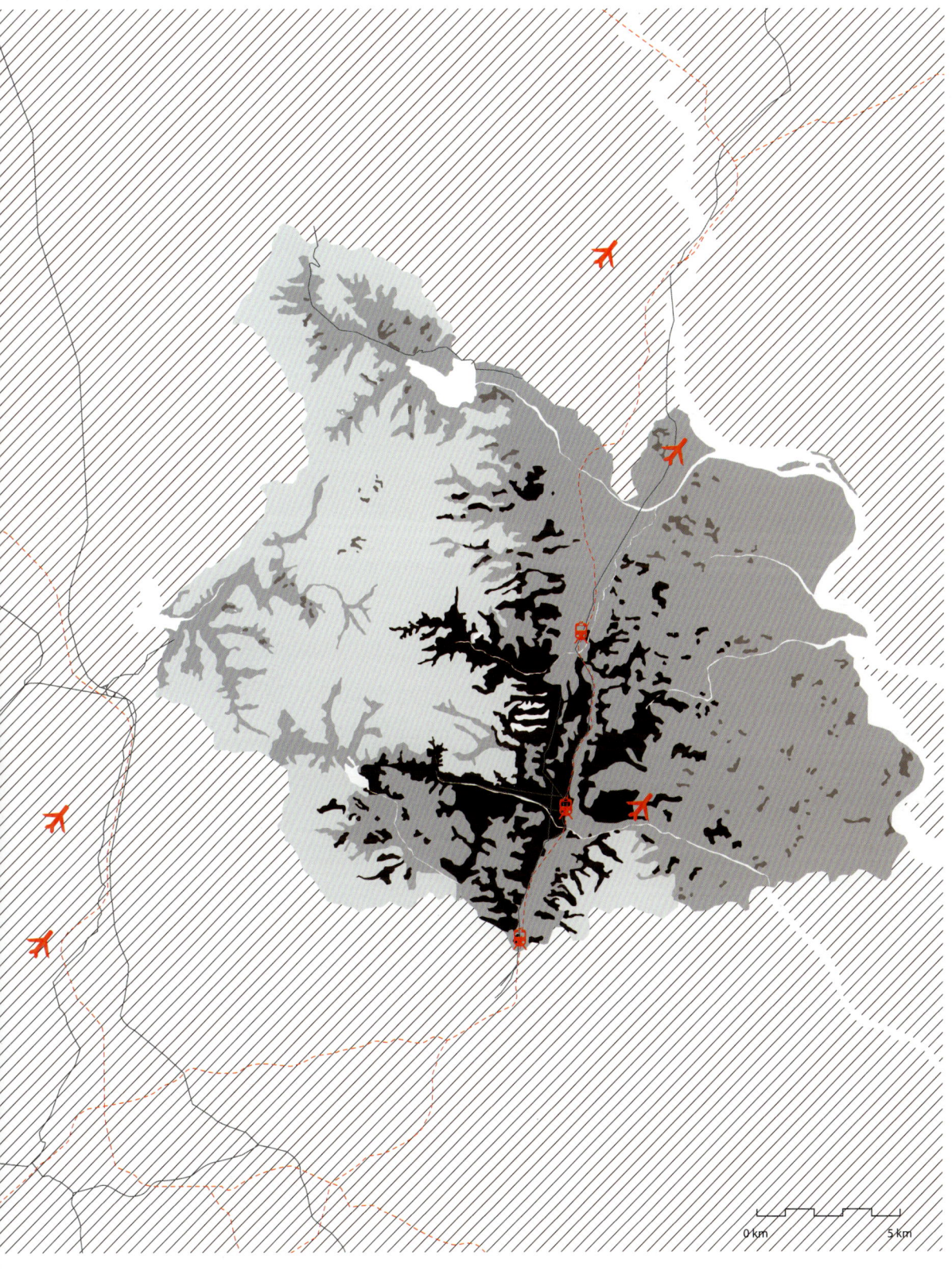

SARIWON 사리원
NORTH HWANGHAE PROVINCE

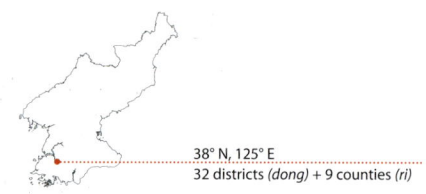

38° N, 125° E
32 districts *(dong)* + 9 counties *(ri)*

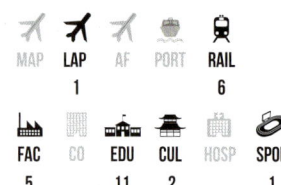

MAP	LAP	AF	PORT	RAIL
	1			6
FAC	CO	EDU	CUL	HOSP	SPOR
5		11	2		1

POPULATION
Inhabitants	**307,764**
% Urban	88.2
% Rural	11.8
% Male	47.8
% Female	52.2

POPULATION DENSITY
Inhabitants	307,764
Administrative Area (km²)	194
Population Density (inhabitants/km²)	**1,586**

URBAN DENSITY
Inhabitants	271,434
Urban Area (km²)	17.4
Population Density (inhabitants/km²)	**15,546**

GEOGRAPHY
% Built	11.5
% Farmland	72.1
% Mountains	16.3

POTENTIAL GROWTH
Urbanized Area (km²)	162.1
% Area Increase	929
Urban Population	307,764
% Population Increase	819
Max. Population (million)	2.5

CENSUS HEXAGRAM

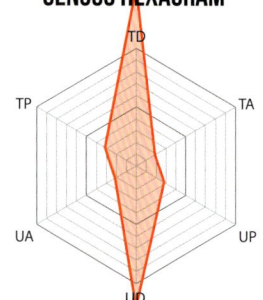

TD - Total density (1000 / km²)
TP - Total population (1,000,000)
TA - Total area (1,000 km²)
UD - Urban density (10,000 / km²)
UP - Urban population (1,000,000)
UA - Urban area (100 km²)

GEOGRAPHICAL CIRCLE

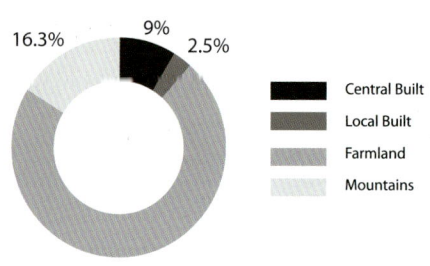

- Central Built
- Local Built
- Farmland
- Mountains

INDUSTRIAL CIRCLE

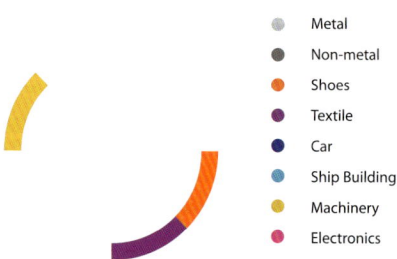

- Metal
- Non-metal
- Shoes
- Textile
- Car
- Ship Building
- Machinery
- Electronics

19 Supporting north korean cities | Sariwon

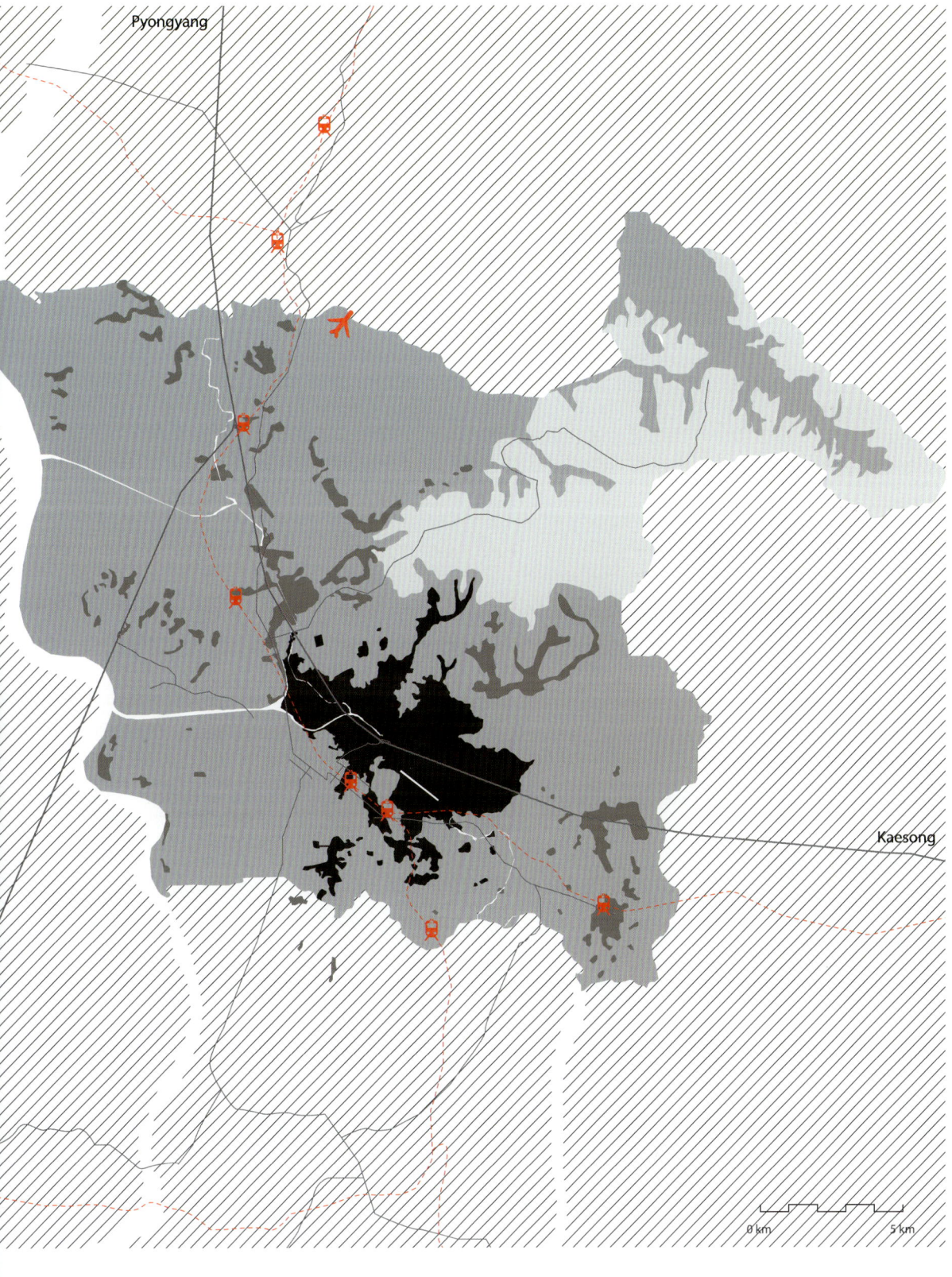

SINPO 신포
SOUTH HAMGYUNG PROVINCE

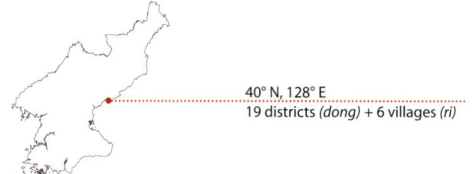

40° N, 128° E
19 districts *(dong)* + 6 villages *(ri)*

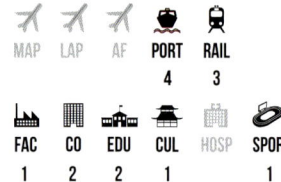

			PORT	RAIL
MAP	LAP	AF	4	3

FAC	CO	EDU	CUL	HOSP	SPOR
1	2	2	1		1

POPULATION
Inhabitants	**152,759**
% Urban	85.7
% Rural	14.4
% Male	48.1
% Female	51.9

POPULATION DENSITY
Inhabitants	152,759
Administrative Area (km²)	183.6
Population Density (inhabitants/km²)	**832**

URBAN DENSITY
Inhabitants	130,951
Urban Area (km²)	33
Population Density (inhabitants/km²)	**3,968**

GEOGRAPHY
% Built	18.0
% Farmland	40.9
% Mountains	41.1

POTENTIAL GROWTH
Urbanized Area (km²)	108.4
% Area Increase	328
Urban Population	152,759
% Population Increase	282
Max. Population (million)	0.4

CENSUS HEXAGRAM

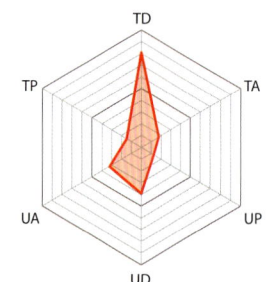

TD - Total density (1000 / km²)
TP - Total population (1,000,000)
TA - Total area (1,000 km²)
UD - Urban density (10,000 / km²)
UP - Urban population (1,000,000)
UA - Urban area (100 km²)

GEOGRAPHICAL CIRCLE

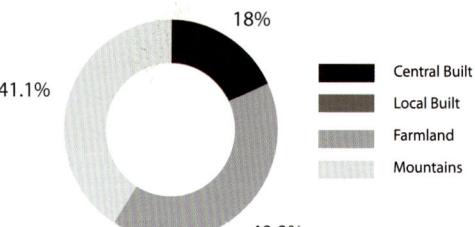

- Central Built — 18%
- Local Built
- Farmland — 40.9%
- Mountains — 41.1%

INDUSTRIAL CIRCLE

- Metal
- Non-metal
- Shoes
- Textile
- Car
- Ship Building
- Machinery
- Electronics

19 Supporting north korean cities | Sinpo

SONGRIM 송림
NORTH HWANGHAE PROVINCE

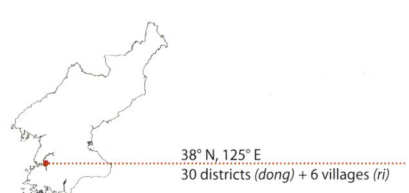

38° N, 125° E
30 districts (dong) + 6 villages (ri)

MAP LAP AF PORT **RAIL**
                      3

FAC **CO** **EDU** HOSP SPOR
     3   **2**   **1**

POPULATION
Inhabitants	**128,831**
% Urban	74.4
% Rural	25.6
% Male	47.1
% Female	52.9

POPULATION DENSITY
Inhabitants	128,831
Administrative Area (km²)	55
Population Density (inhabitants/km²)	**2,342**

URBAN DENSITY
Inhabitants	95,878
Urban Area (km²)	13.7
Population Density (inhabitants/km²)	**6,998**

GEOGRAPHY
% Built	26.9
% Farmland	64.5
% Mountains	8.5

POTENTIAL GROWTH
Urbanized Area (km²)	50.3
% Area Increase	367
Urban Population	128,831
% Population Increase	273
Max. Population (million)	0.3

CENSUS HEXAGRAM

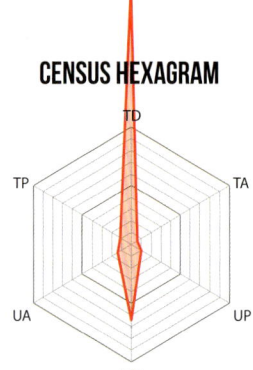

TD - Total density (1000 / km²)
TP - Total population (1,000,000)
TA - Total area (1,000 km²)
UD - Urban density (10,000 / km²)
UP - Urban population (1,000,000)
UA - Urban area (100 km²)

GEOGRAPHICAL CIRCLE

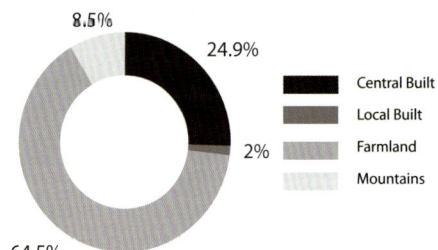

- Central Built — 24.9%
- Local Built — 2%
- Farmland — 64.5%
- Mountains — 8.5%

INDUSTRIAL CIRCLE

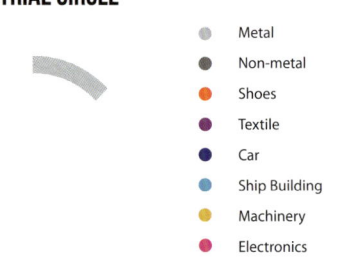

- Metal
- Non-metal
- Shoes
- Textile
- Car
- Ship Building
- Machinery
- Electronics

19 Supporting north korean cities | Songrim

SUNCHON 순천
SOUTH PHYONGAN PROVINCE

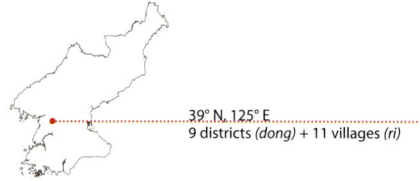

39° N, 125° E
9 districts (dong) + 11 villages (ri)

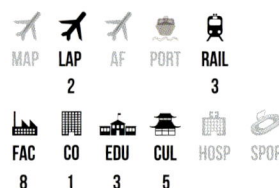

| MAP | LAP 2 | AF | PORT | RAIL 3 |
| FAC 8 | CO 1 | EDU 3 | CUL 5 | HOSP | SPOR |

POPULATION
Inhabitants	**297,317**
% Urban	84.3
% Rural	15.7
% Male	47.7
% Female	52.3

POPULATION DENSITY
Inhabitants	297,317
Administrative Area (km²)	315.3
Population Density (inhabitants/km²)	**943**

URBAN DENSITY
Inhabitants	250,738
Urban Area (km²)	15.4
Population Density (inhabitants/km²)	**16,282**

GEOGRAPHY
% Built	13.9
% Farmland	69.5
% Mountains	16.6

POTENTIAL GROWTH
Urbanized Area (km²)	262.9
% Area Increase	1,708
Urban Population	297,317
% Population Increase	1,440
Max. Population (million)	4.3

CENSUS HEXAGRAM

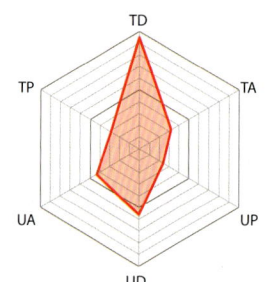

TD - Total density (1000 / km²)
TP - Total population (1,000,000)
TA - Total area (1,000 km²)
UD - Urban density (10,000 / km²)
UP - Urban population (1,000,000)
UA - Urban area (100 km²)

GEOGRAPHICAL CIRCLE

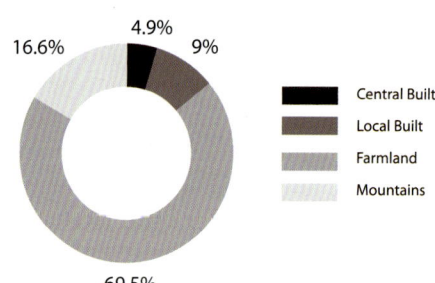

4.9% Central Built
9% Local Built
69.5% Farmland
16.6% Mountains

INDUSTRIAL CIRCLE

- Metal
- Non-metal
- Shoes
- Textile
- Car
- Ship Building
- Machinery
- Electronics

19 Supporting north korean cities | Sunchon

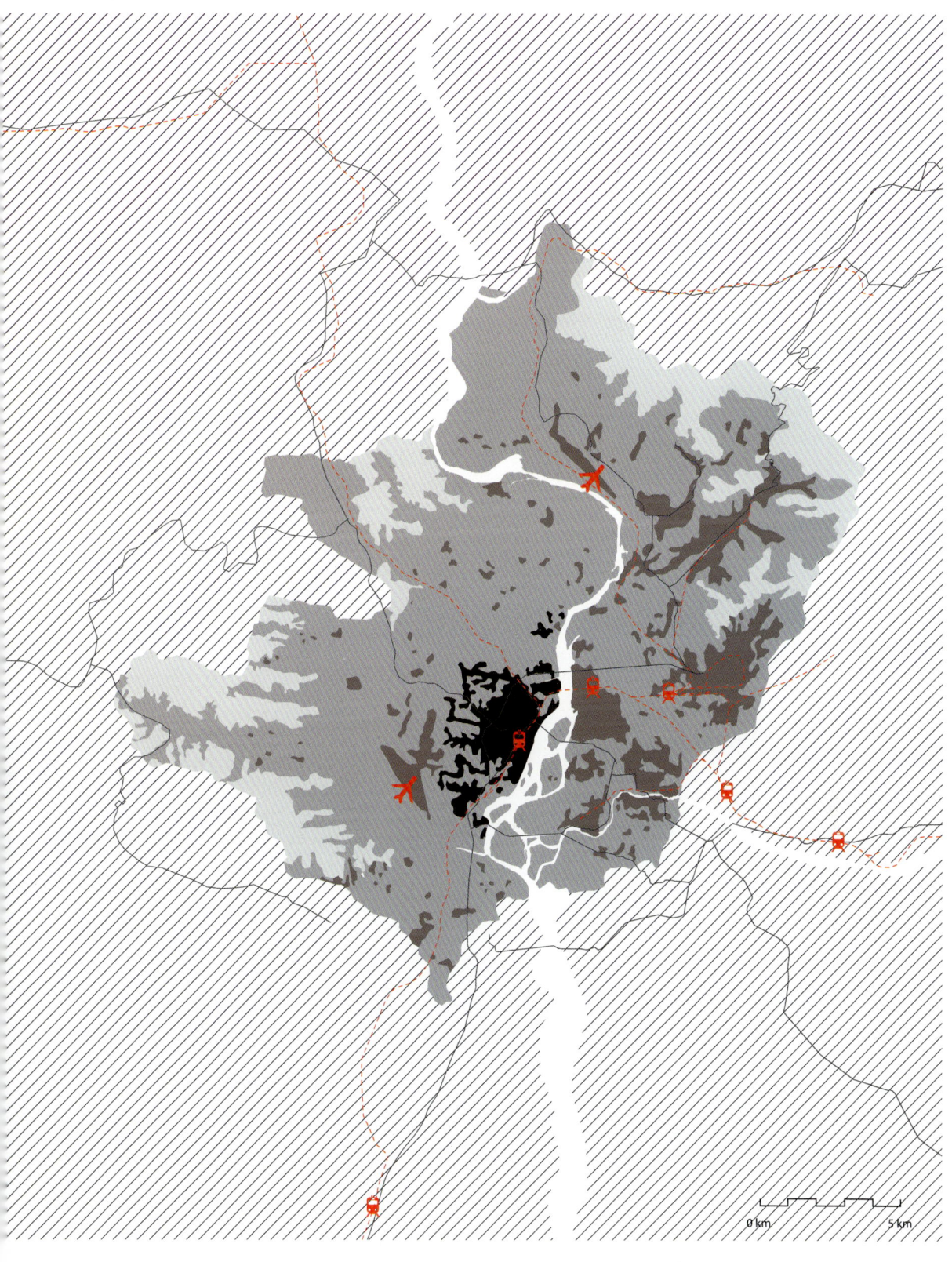

TANCHON 탄천
SOUTH HAMGYONG PROVINCE

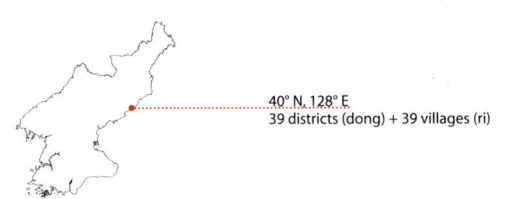

40° N, 128° E
39 districts (dong) + 39 villages (ri)

MAP	LAP	AF	PORT	RAIL
				6
FAC	CO	EDU	CUL	HOSP	SPOR
8	1	3	5		

POPULATION
Inhabitants	**345,875**
% Urban	69.6
% Rural	30.4
% Male	47
% Female	53

POPULATION DENSITY
Inhabitants	345,875
Administrative Area (km²)	1,480
Population Density (inhabitants/km²)	**234**

URBAN DENSITY
Inhabitants	240,873
Urban Area (km²)	8.8
Population Density (inhabitants/km²)	**27,125**

GEOGRAPHY
% Built	1.3
% Farmland	24.7
% Mountains	74

POTENTIAL GROWTH
Urbanized Area (km²)	384.8
% Area Increase	1,429
Urban Population	345,875
% Population Increase	3,018
Max. Population (million)	10.4

CENSUS HEXAGRAM

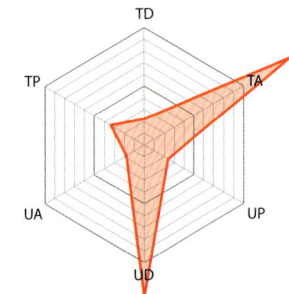

TD - Total density (1000 / km²)
TP - Total population (1,000,000)
TA - Total area (1,000 km²)
UD - Urban density (10,000 / km²)
UP - Urban population (1,000,000)
UA - Urban area (100 km²)

GEOGRAPHICAL CIRCLE

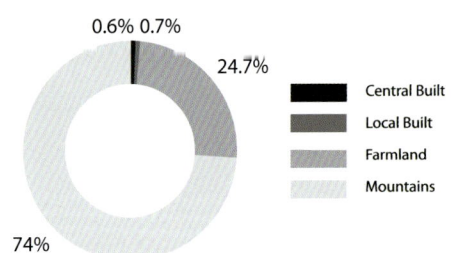

- Central Built 0.6%
- Local Built 0.7%
- Farmland 24.7%
- Mountains 74%

INDUSTRIAL CIRCLE

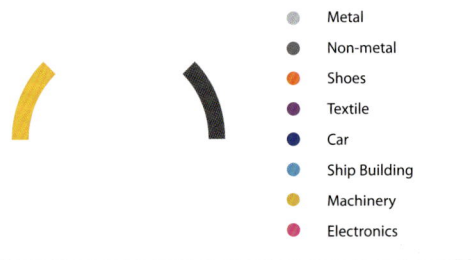

- Metal
- Non-metal
- Shoes
- Textile
- Car
- Ship Building
- Machinery
- Electronics

TOKCHON 덕천
SOUTH PHYONGAN PROVINCE

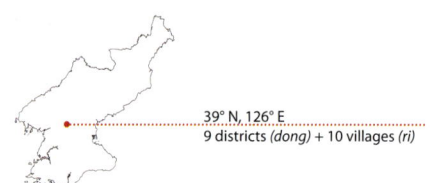

39° N, 126° E
9 districts *(dong)* + 10 villages *(ri)*

MAP	LAP	AF	PORT	RAIL
				8

FAC	CO	EDU	CUL	HOSP	SPOR
2	3	2	1		3

POPULATION
Inhabitants	**237,133**
% Urban	88.8
% Rural	11.2
% Male	47.4
% Female	52.6

CENSUS HEXAGRAM

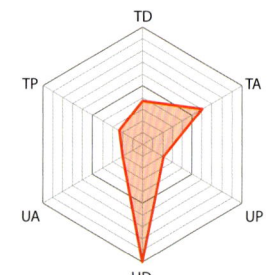

TD - Total density (1000 / km²)
TP - Total population (1,000,000)
TA - Total area (1,000 km²)
UD - Urban density (10,000 / km²)
UP - Urban population (1,000,000)
UA - Urban area (100 km²)

POPULATION DENSITY
Inhabitants	237,133
Administrative Area (km²)	617.1
Population Density (inhabitants/km²)	**384**

URBAN DENSITY
Inhabitants	210,571
Urban Area (km²)	12.3
Population Density (inhabitants/km²)	**17,120**

GEOGRAPHICAL CIRCLE

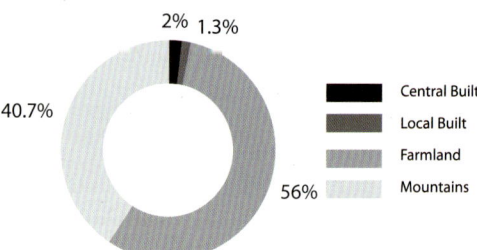

- Central Built — 2%
- Local Built — 1.3%
- Farmland — 56%
- Mountains — 40.7%

GEOGRAPHY
% Built	3.3
% Farmland	56
% Mountains	40.7

POTENTIAL GROWTH
Urbanized Area (km²)	365.9
% Area Increase	1,429
Urban Population	237,133
% Population Increase	2,642
Max. Population (million)	6.3

INDUSTRIAL CIRCLE

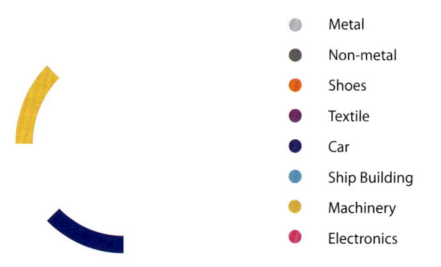

- Metal
- Non-metal
- Shoes
- Textile
- Car
- Ship Building
- Machinery
- Electronics

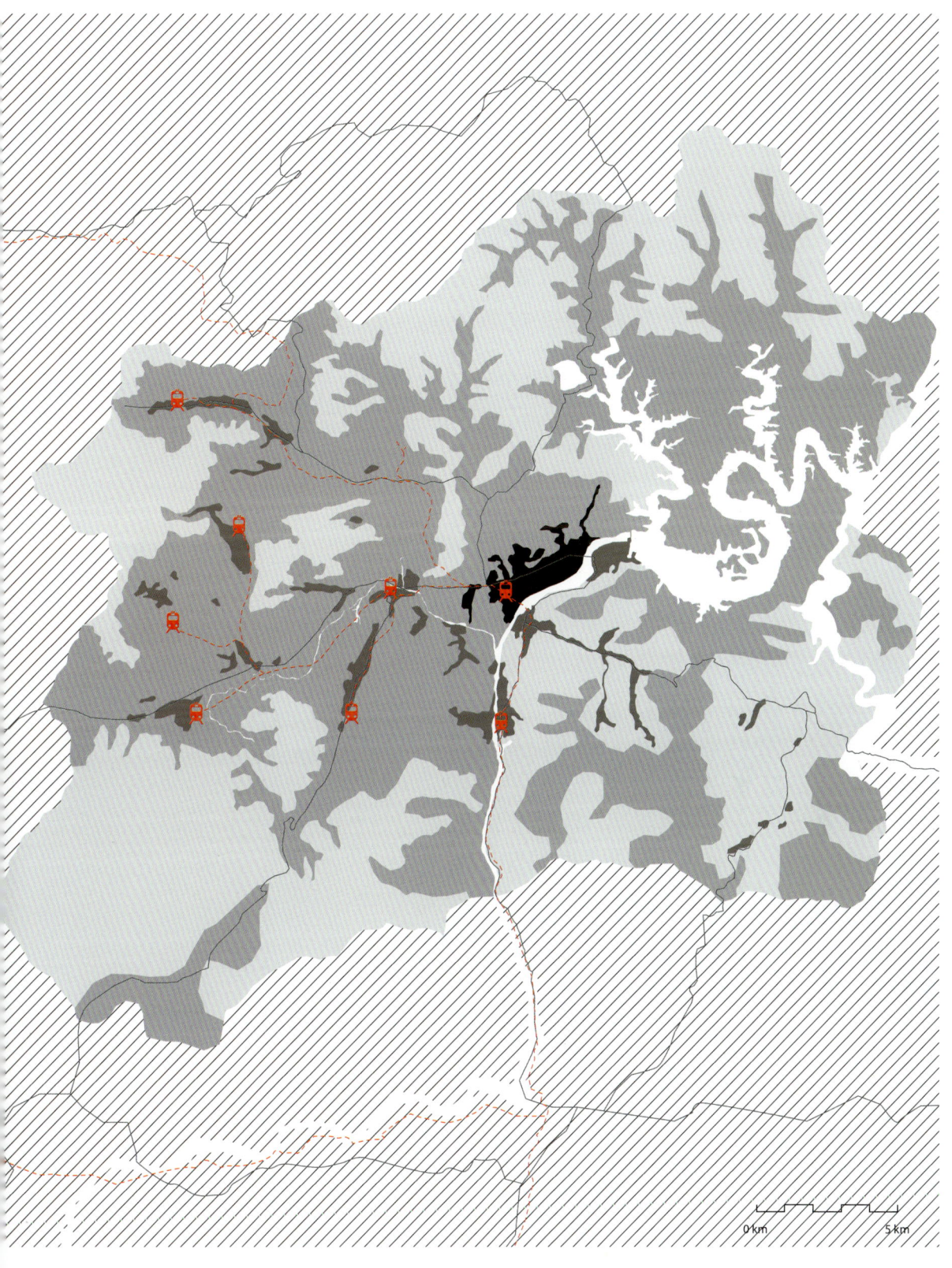

04 NORTH KOREAN TYPOLOGIES

HOW WAS NORTH KOREAN ARCHITECTURE BORN IN THE KIM JUNG IL ERA?

Yunha Lee

—

Yunha Lee is a poet, architect and principal of NoDD Architecture Design Group.
He pursues ecology and eco-friendly architecture through researches, projects and lectures, and currently is teaching at Hong Ik University.
He has published series articles in journal <Minjok 21>, and was involved in the program of KBS <Nam-buk-ui-chang (Window between North and South korea)>.
His publication, among others, includes <Nine Architects, Nine Figure> and thesis <Research on North Korean Architecture during the post Kim Jung Il regime>
Also, his built projects include <Cho-Tae-Il Literature Museum>, <Ha-Nul Garden>, <Bi-Ung-Sa>, and <Se-Jin-Dang>.

Introduction

In any period of history, it is difficult to define a major stream of architecture only by looking at a single ruling period, under one specific ruling authority. The styles and ideologies reiterate from an accumulation of past architecture. However, a planned economy under Centralism facilitates the will and aesthetic point of view of an entity in power to be reflected on the construction industry. Critic G. Bernard Shaw describes the relationship between architecture and power by stating "architecture is the most powerful weapon for the politicians." For North Korea, Kim Jung-Il's regime has been the most dynamic from a perspective that his period sees the completion of current architectural topology of North Korea, and it is valuable enough to look closely at the background of this period.

Kim Jung-Il influences the architecture field through publishing books like "Theory on Creative Architecture" and local guidance. He applies his comprohensive knowledge on architecture, and his past experience in Sun-jeon-sun-dong-bu (municipal authority of controlling ideology)I in this period, and his instructions in the concern of architecturetakes over Kim Il-Sung's views for the countrie's architecture. One of the representative instructions states "architecture is also art--therefore architectural creation must be non-repetitive"; evidence of Kim Jung-Il's encouragement to use architecture from a planning stage.

In order to truly become the head or leader of a country, one needs to be approved of his/ her leadership. Kim Il-Sung took the head through leadership shown in Anti-Japan Revolution, anti-imperialism struggle, and internal political line struggle, but for Kim Jung-Il getting 'approved for extensive leadership' has been his Achilles heel. Because Kim Jung-Il did not have a solid achievement as a successor, he had to be qualified as a leader through loyalty to his father-the predecessor of power, and needed to retain legitimacy of power succession through idolization of himself. Hence for Kim Jung-Il, architecture in a planned economy, where national budget and system of public mobilization is advantageous, became an important stepping stone to retain political leadership.

Background history on the period's architecture

My first impression of Pyongyang is that buildings are well laid out according to an intentional design standard of urban planning. Like a stage setting in a theater, buildings have been exhibited for long under the conduction of a producer revealing the city's identity. But after a little study on building placement, arrangement method and form, I could see transitions resulted in need of the times. Rather than savoring individual buildings, it is more interesting to trace intentions of a decision maker of that period. This is the reason why I am curious about the background of the architecture in Kim Il-Sung's regime.

The reason for naming it "Kim Jung-Il Period" is that although it shares the general context of Kim Il-Sung's, during this period Kim Jung-Il's acted greatly on architecture, and there is a distinction in the context of the architecture business and architecture form as well. The range of the period is set from early 1970's when Kim Jung-Il grooms for his upcoming position in power until late 1980's where large architecture contracts take place. Due to collapse of Eastern Europe Socialism and Soviet Union From 1990's most of architecture businesses see no more progression. This period should be observed from its political and economical aspect, its social phenomenon, as well as its architectural advancement in order to analyze the background history.

System's dignity through competition between South and North Korea

South and North Korea compete by window dressing their architecture. Since the beginning of Kim Jung-Il's regime, conflicting ideology between South and North Korea has been riddled with battles over superiority of their own political structure. They especially seek to take the superior position by competitively announcing and constructing demonstrative architecture. On one hand, this is interpreted as a development policy mainly focused on civil engineering, and construction that resulted from the desire of keeping strength in the regime. On the other hand, it is a byproduct of the competitive system between South and North Korea. This phenomenon not only includes civil engineering and construction policy at a national level, but also concentrated in Seoul and Pyongyang, the capital city and a key base of its regime. In this process architecture is used as a demonstrative tool for the regime thus resulting in a 'size of architecture' to be altered and used as a symbol of national power.

The construction of Pyongyang's subway, which opened on September, 1973, is a symbol of the regime's pride in construction. Pyongyang starts construction in 1961 with a 7-year plan, and opens a year ahead of South Korea. Construction of the subway is propagated as a symbol of national power, encompassing high-tech excavation technique, and electric vehicle aside from an enormous construction budget. In Seoul, '5.16 Square',contrast with 'Kim Il-Sung Square' in the middle of Pyongyang, is constructed to hold mass meetings, or government events to gather and unite its people. Again in Pyongyang, Juche Idea Tower gets built across from Daedong River near Kim Il-Sung Square to propagate Regime's superiority. In Seoul, several projects like Yeoido development, take lead on a development boom like large scale Gangnam apartment complexes including Jamsil area, and redevelopment of Saejong Street in downtown and area near Chunggae stream. As Pyongyang proceeds with their development projects at Seungri Street area, Gaesunmun Street area, Dongpyongyang district, it now becomes a full-scale construction competition.

When South Korea sees rapid urbanization under high economic growth and gets incorporated in world economic order while the capital city Seoul continues to expand, North Korea proceeds development plans to make Pyongyang a model city of Socialism. While a major company in Seoul constructs '63 Building' in Yeoido, Seoul and advertise they have built the tallest building in Asia, Pyongyang plans to build 105-floor 'Ryukyung Hotel,' which will be the tallest building in the world. While Seoul boasts about completion of the premier 'Shilla Hotel', Pyongyang builds the upscale 'Korea Hotel' with materials imported from Japan. Competition between South and North reached its peak with the 'Seoul Olympic Games' in 1988 and 'the 13th World Festival of Youth and Students' in Pyongyang in 1989. While South Korea proudly builds all sorts of sports facilities to host the Olympics in Seoul, North Korea builds the world's largest '5.1 Stadium' that holds 150 thousand people and other facilities to host the 13th World Festival of Youth and Students in Pyongyang. After the event, large scale new town developments start in the suburbs of Seoul , while Pyongyang also starts large scale urban development. Since there is no exchange in architecture between South and North, experts do not know about this phenomenon, but architecture has been used as a tool to compete with each other.

During the Kim Jung-Il Period a series of architecture and urban developments are propagated and came into action alternating in the lead between South and North up until the so called 'march of hardship', and therefore it is seen as an effort to acquire the system's superior position and propaganda of regime.

Idolization through monument construction

For Kim Jung-Il, the son and successor of the man in power, it is necessary to have an image of a devoted son and a loyal successor. He needs to build a foundation as the legitimate 'Bakdu blood'. For this, he needs to highlight the meaning of Kim Jung Il's trace in Anti-Japan Movement and Socialism Revolution in the present. This leads to a great monumental architecture endeavor and the so called 'Immortal monument architecture' gets built.

During and after the 1970's, monuments of unprecedented scale are constructed; 'Musan district victory in a battle monument' in 1971, 'Mansudae Great monument' on Mansudae Hill in Pyongyang on April, 1972, in 1975 a great monument is constructed at Wangje mountain for 30th anniversary of the Labor Party, and in 1979 a great monument is constructed at Samjiyon for 40th anniversary of Musan district victory in a battle. Also, on April, 1982, 'Juche Idea Tower' and 'Triumph Tower' are built in Pyongyang. Kim Il-Sung uses the socialist method of constructing monuments in order to promote his accomplishments and achievements during the Anti-Japan Revolution Period and propagate the Juche idea. Hence this undertaking is a foundation for Kim Il-Sung's dictatorship as well as a service that accelerates, and consolidates the idolization of him. Therefore, these constructions have the fundamental principle of being revolutionary monuments that 'contribute to arm people as ones who serve the ruler unconditionally'. When creating a monument, the form should project Kim Il-Sung's figure.

The characteristics of the monuments could be in scale and artistry in the Juche idea. 'Wangjae mountain revolution historic site' is constructed in a site that is 1,487,610m2, which includes 'Wangjae mountain conference site' and a series of battle fields. The area where 'Wangjae mountain great monument', 'Wangjae mountain revolution museum' are 158,678 m2 and height of signal fire tower is 55m. The height of 'Juche Idea Tower' being 170m and 'Pyongyang Triumph Gate' 60m, it is proudly being said that these are taller than the "Arc de Triomphe" in Paris.

There are two main types of monuments; one is an architectural form like 'Juche Idea Tower' and 'Triumph Gate', the other is a statue-form like 'Mansudae Monument', 'Samjiyon Monument' and 'Wangjae mountain Monument' that project Kim Il-Sung's figure.

Juche Idea Tower is a type of architectural form that is highlighting architectural characteristic of a stone tower and a traditional fortress gatehouse. Monuments differ in arrangements; around Kim Il-Sung Statue are statue-types, signal fire tower and flags; In 'Mansudae Monument' flags and statue-types are located in the front of the statue; and in 'Wangjae mountain Monument' signal fire tower is built at the back of the statue and also sculptures and historical landmark sign; also in 'Samjiyon Monument', having the statue in the middle, statue-types and signal fire tower are located on the left and right. All these monuments and statues relate to historical sites associated with Kim Il-Sung.

Huge influence on the Succession system establishment

In 1972 when North Korea revises their Socialist Constitution, they regulate three revolutions and form a three revolutionary team to be dispatched at each administrative agency. According to Professor Choi Wan-Gyu, the three revolutionary team movement has an external objective of converting executives for ideology struggle, but actually there lies a true objective of constructing a succession-system of Kim Jung-Il. In architecture and construction, having three revolutionary teams as the center, hauls the business with a leading and concentrated mind. Construction business widely proceeded during the 'revolution period of complete victory of Socialism' to build a revolutionary battlefield and a revolutionary historic site. In North Korea's case, aside from military expenditure, the construction rush of political propaganda heavily influenced productive investment in the 1980's. This is what North Korea Economist Yang Mun-su calls the large-scale unproductive construction.

In this period architecture business sponsors Kim Il-Sung, and Kim Jung-Il directly leads architecture. With Kim Il-Sung's 70th birthday ahead Kim Jung-Il constructs extensive monumental architecture in the capital city Pyongyang as 'gifts of loyalty'. To declare completion of constructing socialism and victory of Juche Idea the world's largest 'Juche Idea Tower', 'Triumph Gate', 'Grand People's Study House' and 'Kim Il-Sung Stadium' are constructed. Moreover, to compete with Seoul Olympic in 1988, with the 13th World Festival of Youth and Students ahead, about 260 related facilities are built over a period of three years. It is called "reconstructing the capital"(수도대건설). According to North Korean authority's announcement, 4.7 billion dollars was invested in these constructions. This enormous amount adds up to be 22.6% of official statistic of North Korea's GDP in 1992.

According to Cho Hyun-Sik's estimate, within 60 large constructions constructed from 1980 to 1996 about 18 of them are monumental architecture that are pure propaganda for political purpose and construction expenses sum up to $10 billion dollars. Yang Mun-Su states that "it is not difficult to imagine how these large-scale unproductive constructions that require heavy labor, capital, equipment, and material exert a bad influence on 'productive investment'; especially it comes to an attention that these constructions are concentrated in 1980's when the economy of North Korea gets worse than before". Yang Mun-Su concerns about negative influences on economy resulted from competition on system and political subordination.

And from late 1970's or early 1980's agriculture and industrial production start to slow down and as a result the government takes action by intensifying a forced saving. National finance of North Korea shows unprecedented form of forcing sacrifice from workers and farmers to barely maintain a certain level of accumulation rate to unproductively invest on the construction of monumental architecture for political propaganda.

Juche architecture

A formative period of the succession system from 1974 to 1980 is a period that gives shape to the Juche Idea, which will retain the identity of North Korean Socialism. Also it is a period to seek 'our own socialism' and argue out 'socialistic realism' through 'ethnicity realization' to retain relative identity with other socialist countries. It is a strategic choice to overcome Marxism-Leninism and form a society of absolute dictatorship through Kim Il-Sung. Therefore, revolution and ethnic aspects intensify also in the literary art field.

In this period, formal side of early socialistic realism of North Korea starts to change into Juche realism. Hence, from 1970's, the form of absolute dictatorship resulted from a reorganization of political power and a new generation, Juche Idea and Juche ethnic structure accomplish consolidation. Juche realism, literary art power, serves to assist in Kim Il-Sung and Kim Jung-Il's heritage as a propaganda instigating power, and becomes a political tool. Full-scale Juche realism and Juche architecture has begun from the mid 1970's. Nationalistic form of development can be seen in the context of Socialistic realism from 1970's in North Korea. After passing through mid-late 1960's where ethnic architecture argument has regularized and reaching 1970's, the principle of 'creating architecture in our own way' is set.

Formerly a political idea, now settled as a literary art of Juche realism, Juche architecture with a context of nationalism been knitted into it comes to dominate the center of the capital city Pyongyang to a full-scale. This opens the new period of North Korean architecture. North Korea tries to retain its own identity different than other socialist countries by differentiating an architectural style from 'Russian neo-classical style,' which is accepted uncritically during Stalin's Period. It is Kim Il-Sung's numerous political efforts to escape from political subordination of Soviet Union's.

Socialistic realism is still a root of North Korea's artistic aesthetic. But during this period a concept of 'Juche architecture' is actively introduced, thus enabling to escape from the architecture aesthetic of the Soviet Union, and build architecture with an ethnic originality. 'Juche architecture' is a combination of socialistic architecture and ethnic aesthetic. Kim Jung-Il defines the principles of 'Juche architecture' in his collected writings [Theory on Architecture and Art] by stating "architecture creation should include ethnic form and socialistic content; this is the main characteristic of Juche architecture where it reveals ethnic style and socialistic content."

This architectural style is in need of research on nationalism in order to overcome another expression of authoritarian architecture. Socialistic realism is chosen as the basic literary theory during the process of establishing the country, but in 1967 it becomes a target of "ban-jong-pa-tu-jaeng" (political struggle against the opposition). Thus, from the late 1960's traditional socialistic realism gets modified from North Korea's literary policy. According to North Korea's culture critic Lee Woo-Young, after the late 1960's, a tendency to emphasize revolution and ethnicity became the basic trait of Kim Jung Il's literary policy. From the 1970's, 'Juche architecture theory,' which have Juche literary theory as a base, will soar.

There is an argument on the nationalism style over 'Pyongyang Station' built in modern style of North Korea in the 1950's. After liberation, it falls under Soviet Union's orbit at the hands of Russian architects and students that studied abroad; entering 1960, a new architecture theory is in need to overcome this. At this point, the discussion on Juche architecture becomes serious. 'Grand People's Study Hall' in the middle of Pyongyang is evaluated as a monumental masterpiece that very well embodies ethnic style and socialistic content. It is considered as an architectural example that expresses ethnicity of Juche architecture.

"At the beginning the design stage of the Grand People's Study Hall, our Great Leader has said it is better to have a traditional style. At that moment, workers and architects promote a view that since the building will be located in the core of the city, it should be designed in a modern style so that the core could be struck with awe." Kim Jung-Il, [Theory on Architecture and Art], p.36

Through these progressions, the 'Grand People's

Study Hall' is built in a form that uses the nationalistic aesthetic 'traditional Chosun architecture style'. The main characteristic of Juche architecture is 'socialistic realism architectural style 'seasoned with 'ethnic characteristic,' but in the 1960's when the Juche Idea became mainstream, Juche architecture still is unable to find its place. However, entering the 1970's, the start of monumental architecture construction and Grand People's Study Hall establishes an opportunity to give shape to a 'nationalistic style and socialistic content'.

To summarize, since North Korea uncritically accepted the architectural style of the Soviet Union after the liberation, theory on socialist architecture passes through a perdio of uncertainty between the 1950's and 1960's and finally gave shape in new forms. Still, it is being restricted in its application in a big frame of socialistic realism and 'ethnic style' is limited to symbolic monumental architecture.

Sultanism aspect appears in architecture

Though one person's absolute power and individual idolization idea, passing on power in the family in absolute dictatorship are originated from North Korea's distinct characteristic, it also shows characteristics of the Sultan system in context of a typical system of methodology comparing socialism. J. Lintz sees totalitarianism combined with Sultanism elements in North Korea. Especially passing on power from father to son is a characteristic of the Sultanism system, and during this period it extensively occurred in the architecture field. Change in the government system is achieved through formalizing a Succession system. Previous socialistic systems start to reveal characteristics of the Sultanism system after trasnforming to Kim Il-Sung's absolute dictatorship. Kim Il-Sung exercised his power on law and ideology without interruption from executives of important organization. Compulsory standards and relationships to government official administrative agencies are endlessly intensified monumentally, a result from individual's dogmatic decisions with no need for explanations. After all, this tendency of Sultanism appears as a form of passing of power from father to son.

In the late 1960's and early 1970's Kim Jung-Il directly takes lead on the literary arts, and conducts his father's idolization project as a priority. Also, he initiates a society remodeling for Juche Idea consistent in the Juche revolutionary world view and revolutionary leader. For 'all parts of the society to be under Juche Idea', Kim Jung-Il advocates things that the literary art field should serve, and reenact 'imperishable classical masterpieces' that Kim Il-Sung personally created during the Anti-Japan revolution struggle period. It is an expression of loyalty to his father.

The 1970's is a period that Kim Jung-Il completes his succession system. Under Kim Il-Sung's sponsorship, being called the 'Center of Party' Kim Jung-Il takes the lead on the literary art field. In this period Kim Jung-Il gets recognized for his ability by elders in the party through 'the 1st literary art revolution' and officially approved as a successor, and through the 'three revolution team movement" intensifies his political space and foundation of power.

It is an unprecedented example where the son and successor supervises the literary art field and leads his father's idolization, even for a socialist country. This is where a characteristic of a Sultanism society is revealed, especially for monumental architecture, which is needed to retain legitimacy by spatially preserving tradition of the Anti-Japan revolution struggle, and by shaping main districts in Pyongyang. These serve as phenomenal idols to visually express 'be loyal from father to son'.

With this background, architecture unfolds in two directions. One has an aspect of shaping Kim Il-Sung's achievements in the present through monumental architecture like the 'Triumph Gate', and the 'Juche Idea Tower.' The other is proceeded in a direction to sanctify places and traces of Anti-Japan revolution struggle by constructing revolutionary historic sites like the 'tomb of revolutionary patriot' and 'Wangjae mountain revolution historic site'. The fact that these architecture projects reveal strong characteristics of the Sultanism system, is a testimony of the background and occurances at the time of construction. . The background of the Juche Idea Tower and Triumph Gate are constructed to express the Juche Idea for Kim Il-Sun'gs 70th birthday. The 'Tomb of revolutionary patriot' is built in 1975 and is newly renovated and expanded in 1985 on the 40th anniversary of the Party. The Revolution historic site construction is done on the 30th anniversary of the Party and the 40th anniversary of battle victory in Musan district, North Korea's biggest anniversary. During this period sites like 'Wangjae mountain revolution historic site', historical sites of 'Chunligil of Learning', 'Chunligil of Independence', 'Bonghwa revolution historic site', 'Eunha revolution historic site', 'Yongpo revolution historic site', 'Yeonpoong revolution historic site', 'Gunja revolution historic site', 'Hyangha revolution historic site', 'Hoiryung revolution historic site', 'Eunyool revolution historic site', 'Chungsu revolution historic site', 'Chunggang revolution historic site', Hongwon revolution historic site' get rebuilt or extensively reorganized. After the 1970's these large-scale monumental architecture projects see a completion under the lead of Kim Jung-Il.

Speed Battle is Kim Jung-Il's style of mass movement

The system of mobilization, a mass movement route in North Korea, is an extremely important component in architecture that requires intensive heavy labor. In architecture Kim Jung-Il-wise mass movement is being formed. They proudly announced Nakwon Street in Pyongyang be constructed in a short period of time; 'builders in Nakwon Street says new record, new miracle are continuously created that it only takes 6-months to complete the grand Nakwon Street, which includes modern apartments housing 3,000 families, various public buildings, roads and bridges while regular official construction plan will take a number of years'.

'Speed battle' has been utilized as a key material to maximize productivity and it appears in every field as the most generalized form of mass movement. Entering the 1970's after Kim Jung-Il appeared, one of the representative movements that appeared is the 'three revolutions team movement'. To initiate the three revolution in areas of Idea, Technology, and Cultural Revolution, Kim Jung-Il impose 'three revolutions team'. Three revolution is founded in 1972 when it is regulated in the Socialist Constitution. Formation of mass movement under mass route is a business method of speed battle started on February, 1974. Especially, mass movements like the '70 day Battle (Speed)' and 'Speed of Loyalty' which lasted for 70 days starting on October 1974. Cha Mun-Suk says there is an intention to tie a level of idea education with productivity of labor. As a result, at the building site where labor is concentrated, achievements on reaching goals and speed of loyalty are positively reflected 'The three revolutions winning red flag movement' that is offered on November, 1975 is 'a People's mass movement which will push construction of socialism by widening an idea revolution, technology revolution, and culture revolution'. This movement spreads for a month on December, 1975 in places like 'Gumduk Mine', 'Chungsanli collective farm', 'Daean electricity factory', 'Kim Il-Sung University', 'and Chosun Art Movie Studio' throughout every part and field of People's economy and has extended to be the whole country's mass movement besides architecture. It is said that there are "Effort Heroes" in the construction field who exceeded the scheduled amount of work at an inadequate working environment without equipment and technology.

On October, 1979, "follow hidden heroes movement" occurs; "Follow Oh Jeung-Heup, Kim Hyuk the military hero movement" is one of the main movements. Since then "New standard new record creating movement" on September 1981, "Follow 26-ho-sun-ban loyalty and model expectation creating movement" on June 1982, and "1980's speed creating movement" on July 1982 continuously operated. In 1980's these speed battle movements continue. But these movements execute plans ahead, thus resulting in chaos the nation's long year plans, lowered the will to work, and caused demoralization in workers. It lead to a decrease in the productivity rate, and is raised as a cause for hardship to the nation's economy and lives of North Koreans.

North Korea's effort-competing movement has heightened its competitive intensity while changing its forms and gradually becomes compulsive and political rather than voluntary and creative participation. As effort-competing continues less of short-time achievement is seen. After all, aspect of Kim Jung-Il's new speed battle does not gain a great outcome, but it cannot be denied that large-scale architecture projects are made possible due to these movements.

Replace authority in architecture through (반당반종파) struggle

In architecture, struggles against the anti-party / opposition (반당반종파) can also be seen. It is predictable that there could be the opposition on large-scale construction. "Yunhwansun Street," an old name for "Changhwang Street," is defined as an outcome of sin that old cultism (종파분자) cased on construction field, also criticizes the anti-party and anti-revolution group (반당반혁명종파분자) that they disregard the Party's construction policy and designed apartments in an incongruous way. Thus the newly constructed "Changgwang Street" boldly erases existing framework and becomes a modern street. Residences on "Yunhwansun Street" used to be a 2-3 storied brick houses but now high-rise apartments fill the place.

Changgwang Street regards previous Yunhwansun Street as an old thing and orders new guidelines. This is where Juche construction can be seen in the architecture field. In Kim Il-Sung Instruction "the construction of Yunhwansun Street should be the starting point of bringing new revolution in the construction field of our country... in all aspects from planning to construction of Yunhwansun Street it should be a turning point, a historical opportunity that will initiate fast growth and revolution by boldly breaking existing framework and old standards". From this point it is clear that architecture imposes Juche Ideals, and proceeds as a continuous struggle against the opposition.

Before the struggle against Sectarian counter-revolutionary anti-party struggle(반당반혁명종파투쟁) at Yunhwansun Street, there has been a precedent in the construction field in the 1950's. Kim Il-Sung instructs to "disclose Counter-revolutionary sect molecule anti-party(반당반혁명종파분자)'s moves at Power of the Party Central Committee Meeting(당중앙위원회 전원회의)on October 1957 and thoroughly erect Juche in the construction field" and keep purging the opposition force in architecture. In 1967, through Literary art (반종파) struggle, (구카프계열 문학예술인)CAP nine literature-based artists are purged and judging from the fact that Kim Il-Sung's personal connection settles within literary art field, background of Juche architecture in architecture and art field is forged. Lee Woo-Young defines the result of progressive intensification and materialization of ethnicity after Sectarian strife(종파투쟁) in 1967 is Juche realism.

This period is a moment where a gloomy atmosphere under new attempts in building the economy and frustration, crosses with the hope and worries on the official declaration of Kim Jung-Il's succession system and his regime. Kim Jung-Il is to show his ability and talent as a leader to his father and his people.

In this process, Kim Jung-Il attempts to demonstrate his ability to seize the public through large-scale architecture projects by utilizing his previous experience at Propaganda seondongbu(선전선동부). Kim Jung-Il is in need to show his loyalty to his father on the occasion of Kim Il-Sung's 70th birthday in 1982, and he attempts to complete a leadership system by successfully conducting the 13th World Festival of Youth and Students in 1989.

Kim Jung-Il says absolute authority of the Party is "a system to realize the leader's Idea and leadership in all parts of the society and also a leadership system that will lead us to victory and progress out revolution under the will of our leader". This remark is the oath of fidelity to his father that he will accept his father's idea and guidance, which implies succession of the power.

Political situation at the time has been gaining power,but the economy and internal foundation are still in a gloomy state. Condition of social overhead capitals like roads and railroads are bad and worn out machines in need to be replaced and expanded. As a successor Kim Jung-Il is to challenge a tough situation. He has to reorganize and expand the socialism system inherited under limited goods and technology. The only method that he could take is rehashing concentrated and rapid mass movement, which has been utilized up until now. Thus, Kim Jung-Il utilizes his previous experience in Propaganda St. East(선전성동부) and his comprehensive knowledge on architecture. In this period of architecture, Kim Il-Sung's instructions gradually disappear and Kim Il-Sung's instructions replace them. One of the representative instructions say, "Architecture is one of art; therefore architecture creation must be non-repetitive". it is an evidence of how Kim Jung-Il encourages and takes care of architecture from planning stage.

Large-scale architecture at that time appears in a form to reinforce Kim Jung-Il's power. He pulls through this period of economic hardship, and builds up his power with a public mobilization movement for construction.

Conclusion

Basis of North Korean architecture is still 'socialistic content'. In this period the idea of Juche architecture acquires an 'ethnic style' that is extensively realized in public architecture. Beyond stiffness of the idea, a new experiment on style proceeds within various desire of expression in creative art. Architectural achievements of this period are considered to be a valid standard to understand architecture in North Korea and Pyongyang until now. It will also be the touchstone of experiment to predict the future of North Korean architecture.

Above all, North Korean architecture goes through many changes according to the political change during the period of succession, from 1976 to 1980. It is seen as a result of political situation having an influence on architecture. It will be summarized as follows.

First, it appears as an aspect of competition between South and North Korea, and architecture serves to carry their system's dignity. Externally, the issue of differentiating its identity from Soviet Union rears up to escape from political and cultural subordination. Thus, a different architectural style from 'Russian neo-classical style' of early North Korean architecture is in need. Internally, architecture proceeds competitively between South and North Korean politicians in the aspects of keeping the regime's security by propagating their own system's superiority.

Secondly, through construction of 'imperishable great monument' North Korea flaunts their revolutionary tradition and it is utilized as a way of educating the idea to be loyal to predecessor. Here, architecture with Sultanism aspects appear through passing on power from father to son and idolization from consecrating absolute power.

Thirdly, Kim Jung-Il utilizes these architecture projects as a significant achievement to accomplish consolidation as a succession. He imposes Juche architecture as a new value, retains crowd mobilization mass movement system, and centralize his power through Anti-party anti-sectarian strife(반당반종파투쟁).

Kim Jung-Il's architecture business can be understood solely with the fact that he spearheads and leads the unprecedented architecture in North Korea. In South Korea many architecture projects are achieved during the same period with different aspects so it will be meaningful to compare them. And since this writing mainly describes political and social backgrounds there are some stiff inferences. This is an interpretation from outside North Korea and there will be people who have a different view. In reality there is insufficient research on North Korean architecture and I regrettably admit limitation of the writing by an architect. I anticipate for more exchange of North Korean architecture and it is the reason why I write this essay..

김정일 시대의
북한건축은
어떻게 탄생하였나?

이윤하

―

이윤하는 시인이며 건축가이자 건축사사무소 노둣돌 대표이다. 생태주의 및 친환경을 주제로 연구, 작품활동 및 강연을 하고 있으며, 홍익대학교 건축학과에서 설계를 가르치고 있다. 〈민족21〉 등에서 북한건축에 대해 연재를 하였으며, KBS 〈남북의 창〉 특집 기획에 참여하였다. 주요 저서에는 〈아홉 건축가 아홉 무늬〉 등 다수, 관련 논문에는 〈김정일 후계체제 구축기의 북한건축 특성연구〉가 있으며 주요 작품에는 〈조태일 문학관〉, 〈하늘뜨락〉, 〈비웅사〉, 〈세진당〉 등 다수가 있다.

서문

어느 시대라도 건축의 큰 흐름을 특정 권력가의 재임기간을 한정해서 규정하기는 쉬운 일이 아니다. 그 양식과 주된 사상이 과거의 건축적 축적 위에서 중첩되어 나타나기 때문이다. 그러나 계획경제 하의 중앙집권적 체제 아래서는 그 시대의 권력자의 의지와 미학적 관점이 그대로 건축사업에 반영되어 표현되기가 쉽다. 비평가인 G. 버나드 쇼는 '건축은 정치인이 가진 가장 강력한 미학적 무기'라고 하면서 건축과 권력자의 관계를 서술하고 있다. 그리고 북한 건축에 있어서 김정일 시대의 건축은 그 어느 시기보다 역동적이었으며 지금의 북한 건축지형을 완성했다는 측면에서 그 배경을 자세히 살펴 볼 만한 가치가 충분하다. 특히 김정일위원장은 〈건축예술론〉의 저작물을 내놓고 현지지도 등으로 건축부문에 많은 영향을 끼친다. 김정일위원장은 젊은 시절의 선전선동부의 경력과 건축에 관한 해박한 지식을 활용한다. 이 시기는 건축사업에 있어 김일성 교시가 점점 사라지고 김정일 교시로 건축사업이 이루어지는 시기이다. 대표적인 교시 중에는 "건축도 하나의 예술입니다. 그러므로 건축창작도 반드시 비반복적 이어야 합니다."라는 것이 있는데 실제로 건축사업을 기획부터 직접 챙기고 독려한 흔적을 찾아 볼 수 있다.

어느 한 국가의 수반이 되거나 지도자가 되려면 그 사회에서 지도력을 인정받아야 정체성을 획득할 수 있다. 김일성주석은 항일혁명과 반제국주의 투쟁을 통한 지도력과 내부적인 노선투쟁을 통해 수령에 반열에 올랐지만, '지도력의 폭넓은 인정'을 받아야 한다는 측면은 김정일위원장에게는 취약한 아킬레스건이었다. 뚜렷한 후계자로서의 업적을 마련하지 못한 그는 아버지인 선임 권력자의 충성심과 지도력을 동시에 검증 받아야 했으며, 우상화를 통한 후계세습의 당위성을 확보해야 했을 것이다. 이에 막대한 국가예산과 대중동원체계가 유리한 계획경제체제 내에서의 건축사업은 정치적 지도력 확보의 중요한 발판이 되었다.

이 시기 건축사업의 몇 가지 배경에 대하여

평양을 방문하여 첫 번째 느낀 점은 의도된 도시계획에 따라 건축물이 연극무대의 장치처럼 잘 연출되어 있다는 것이다. 거대한 연출자의 지휘에 따라 오랜 시간 동안 전시된 건물들이 도시의 정체성을 드러내고 있었다. 그러나 건축물의 위치와 배치기법, 형태에 관하여 조금 공부하고 난 다음에는 켜켜이 쌓여진 시간의 층위와 시대적 상황에 따라 변화한 모습을 찾아낼 수 있었다. 이러한 시간의 켜를 들추어 보고 그 시대의 디시즌 메이커(decision maker)의 의도를 들추어 보는 것이 개개의 건축물을 감상하는 것보다 더 흥미로운 일이라 생각된다. 이것이 김정일 시대의 건축 배경이 궁금한 이유이다.

굳이 '김정일 시대'라고 이름 붙인 것은 이전의 김일성 시대와는 조금은 맥락을 함께하지만 김정일위원장의 건축적 의지가 크게 작용하고 있고, 건축사업 내용과 건축형태에 있어서도 차별성이 나타나기 때문이다. 이 시기는 김정일위원장이 후계구도를 형성하는 1970년대 초반부터 규모가 있는 건축사업이 벌어진 1980년대 후반까지로 한정하여 살펴보았다. 1990년대에 들어와서 동구사회주의와 소비에트의 실험이 몰락으로 인해 더 이상 이렇다 할 건축사업이 진행되지 못했기 때문이다. 이 시대는 정치, 경제적으로 주목해야 할 시대이며 건축물은 어떤 배경과 정당성을 확보하며 건축사업이 진행되었냐는 것에 초점을 맞춰야 한다. 이에 몇 가지 이 시대에 나타난 사회적 현상으로 그 배경을 살펴보기로 한다.

남북한 경쟁을 통한 체제위신적 양상이 보인다

남북한의 건축물에는 보여주기 식 경쟁이 엿보인다. 김정일 정권 초기부터 남북한의 이데올로기적 대립은 서로의 체제 우위에 대한 대결로 점철되었다. 특히 대외과시용 건축물을 통해 체제우위를 선점하고자 건축물들을 경쟁적으로 건설하고 발표하게 했다. 이는 정권 안위적 차원에서 벌어진 토건 위주의 개발정책이자 남북한의 묵시적 경쟁체제의 산물로 해석된다. 이러한 현상은 전국토적 차원에서 벌어진 토건정책뿐만 아니라, 서로의 정권적 차원의 거점이 되고 있는 수도인 서울과 평양을 중심으로 집중되었다. 이러한 과정에서 건축물들이 체제 과시용으로 이용되면서 '건축물의 규모'가 국력의 상징으로 변질되었다.

무엇보다도 체제경쟁적 자존심이 걸린 북한의 건설사업은 1973년 9월에 개통된 평양의 지하철이다. 남한보다 앞서서 1961년 인민경제7개년 계획 기간 중에 건설하기 시작했고 1년 정도 먼저 개통하였다. 지하철 공사는 막대한 건설비용뿐만 아니라, 첨단의 굴착 시공기술과 전동차 관련 중공업 기술이 망라된 국력의 상징으로 선전되었다. 또한 서울에서는 평양 한복판에 있는 대표적으로 '김일성 광장'과 대비되는 '5.16광장'을 조성하여 군중집회 및 정권차원의 기념행사를 개최하며 국민들을 결집해 나갔으며, 평양에서는 김일성 광장을 중심으로 대동강 맞은편에 주체사상 탑을 건설하여 체제의 우월성을 선전해 나갔다. 또한 서울에서는 개발 붐을 주도한 여의도 개발, 잠실을 비롯한 대규모 강남 아파트단지, 도심의 세종로 및 청계천 주변 재개발 등이 있었고, 평양에서는 서해 갑문, 김일성 광장을 중심으로 한 승리거리 일대, 개선문거리, 동 평양지구 개발 등이 진행되면서 본격적인 건설 경쟁 체제가 되었다.

고도의 경제성장을 배경으로 도시화가 급격하게 이루어지면서 남한이 세계 경제질서에 편입되기 시작하고, 수도 서울이 비대해지고 있을 때, 북한에서는 평양을 사회주의 모범 도시로 만들기 위한 개발 계획이 진행되었다. 자본을 앞세운 서울의 대기업이 서울 여의도에 '63빌딩'을 세워 동양 최대의 고층 빌딩을 만들었다고 선전할 때, 평양에서는 철근 콘크리트로 세계 최고층인 105층 규모의 '유경 호텔'을 계획하고 있었다. 또한 세계에 자랑할 만한 최고급 '신라호텔'을 서울에 만들었다고 자랑할 때, 평양에서도 모든 자재를 일본에서 수입하여 최고급 '고려호텔'을 건립하였다. 무엇보다도 남북 경쟁의 절정은 1988년의 '서울 올림픽'과 1989년 평양에서 열린 '제13차 세계청년학생축전'을 들 수 있다. 남한이 서울에 올림픽을 유치하고 각종 스포츠 시설물을 자랑 삼아 건립할 때, 북한은 평양에서 제13차 세계청년학생축전을 유치하였고, 이 축전을 위하여 15만 명을 수용하는 세계 최대 규모의 '5·1경기장'과 각종 체육관을 건립하였다. 그 후 비대해진 서울 근교에 대규모 신도시 개발을 이루었고, 이때 북한 역시 평양 근교에 대규모 도시 개발을 진행하였다. 남북이 건축적으로 교류를 하지 않아 전문가조차도 잘 모르고 있었지만 건축물을 또 하나의 경쟁 도구로 활용한 것이다.

결국 김정일 시대는 이른바 '고난의 행군' 이전까지 이러한 일련의 건축 및 도시개발사업들은 남북한이 앞서거니 뒤서거니 실행되고 선전되었으며, 결국은 체제의 우월적 지위 선점과 정권의 선전물로 비춰지게 된다.

기념비 건축을 통한 우상화를 진행하였다.

김일성의 아들이면서 후계자 김정일위원장은 아버지 권력자에게 지극한 효심과 충성스런 후계자 이미지가 절실했던 시기이다. 선임자의 업적을 칭송하며 이른바 '백두 혈통'의 적자로서의 반석이 필요했다. 이를 위해 선대의 항일운동과 사회주의 혁명의 자취에 현재적 의미를 부각해야 했다. 이는 기념비적 건축사업으로 이어지고 이른바 '불멸의 대 기념비 건축'들이 건립되기에 이른다.

1970년대와 그 이후에 이르러 전례 없는 규모와 폭을 가지는 대 기념비들이 건립되었다. 과정을 살펴보면, 1971년에 '무산지구전투승리기념탑', 1972년 4월 평양 만수대 언덕에 '만수대 대 기념비', 1975년에는 노동당 창건 30돌을 맞아 왕재산에 대 기념비가 세워졌고, 1979년에 무산지구전투승리 40돌이 되어 삼지연에 대 기념비가 건립되었다. 또한 1982년 4월에는 평양에 '주체사상 탑'과 '개선문'이 건설되었다. 사회주의 국가에서 많이 사용하는 기념비 창조사업은 김일성의 업적과 항일투쟁시기의 성과, 주체사상 등의 업적을 선전하는 데 유효한 수단으로 사용된다. 이러한 기념비 창조사업은 결국 김일성 일인 지배체제의 기반이 되며 우상화를 가속화 및 공고화하는 데 복무하고 있다. 그래서 이 기념비들은 '혁명적 수령관으로 무장시키는 데 이바지'하는 혁명적 기념비가 되어야 한다는 창작의 근본원칙을 지니고 있다. 또한 대 기념비 창조에서 김일성 영상을 형상에서 기본으로 삼으며 중심으로 해야 한다고 밝히고 있다. 김일성의 혁명역사를 내용으로 하는 창작사업에서 혁명사적에 대한 역사주의적 원칙을 견지하면서 건축구조물의 규모를 대담하고 '통이 크게' 하며 북한식대로 형성할 것 등의 원칙을 내세우고 있다.

기념비들의 특징은 규모의 방대성과 주체식 사상 예술성을 들 수 있다. '왕재산 혁명사적지'는 '왕재산 회의장소'를 비롯한 일련의 혁명전적지를 포괄하여 무려 450정보의 넓은 부지에 건설되었다. '왕재산 대 기념비', '왕재산 혁명박물관'이 있는 구역만도 그 면적이 16정보이며 거기에 세운 봉화 탑의 높이는 66m이다. '주체사상 탑'의 높이는 170m이며, '평양개선문'은 높이가 60m나 되어 원전이 파리 개선문 보다 훨씬 높다고 자랑한다.

이 시기에 건립된 기념비들은 유형별로 보면 크게 두 가지로 나눌 수 있다. 하나는 '주체사상 탑'이나 '개선문'과 같은 건축적 형태로 이루어진 기념비들이고 다른 하나는 '만수대 기념비', '삼지연 기념비'나 '왕재산 기념비'와 같은 수령의 동상을 중심에 둔 조각상 형태의 기념비로 볼 수 있다.

건축 조형적 형태를 위주로 한 주체 사상탑은 층층으로 쌓아 올린 돌탑의 양식상 특징을 살린 것이며, 전통적인 성문루의 건축적 특징을 살려 형성한 것이라고 한다. 김일성 동상을 중심으로 형성한 유형의 기념비들은 조각상, 봉화탑, 깃발 등으로 이루어져 있다. '만수대 기념비'에서는 깃발과 조각상들을 동상 앞 양쪽에 배치하였고, '왕재산 기념비'에서는 동상을 중심으로 그 뒤에 봉화탑을 세우고 또 그 뒤에 조각군상과 사적비를 배치 한 형식이고, 삼지연 기념비에서는 동상을 중심으로 한 좌우와 그 앞에 조각상과 봉화탑을 전개하는 등 모두 서로 다르게 형성되어있다. 그리고 기념비의 동상들은 김일성의 사적에 관한 내용으로 만들어졌다.

후계체제 구축에 영향이 컸다.

1972년 북한은 사회주의 헌법을 개정하면서 3대혁명을 규정하고 전위대인 3대혁명소조를 조직하여 각 기관에 파견한다. 최완규 교수에 따르면 3대혁명소조운동은 표면적으로는 당정책 관철을 명분으로 간부들을 개조하기 위한 사상투쟁에 목적이 있었지만, 실질적으로는 김정일 후계체제 구축에 목적이 있었다. 이에 건축·건설사업에서도 김정일의 전위대로서 3대혁명소조를 중심으로 주도적이고 전일적으로 견인해 나갔다. '사회주의 완전승리를 위한 투쟁시기'에 혁명역사와 투쟁업적이 깃들어 있는 혁명사적지와 혁명전적지를 건설하는 사업이 널리 진행되었다. 북한의 경우, 축적의 이용 면에서 투자, 즉 생산적 투자에 큰 영향을 준 요인으로서 군사지출의 뒤를 잇는 것이 1980년대에 집중적으로 이루어졌던 정치선전 목적의 기념비적 건조물의 건설 러시, 즉 대규모 비생산적 건설이라고 북한 경제학자 양문수가 말하고 있다.

이 시기에 건축사업에서는 김일성을 후원하고 김정일이 직접 건축을 진두지휘하였다. 김정일은 1982년 4월 김일성의 70세 생일을 앞두고 '충성의 선물'이라고 칭하며 수도 평양에 대대적인 기념비적 건축물을 건립한다. 사회주의건설의 완성과 주체사상의 승리를 선언하기 위하여 세계 제일규모를 자랑하는 '주체 사상탑', '개선문', '인민 대 학습당', '김일성 경기장' 등의 건축물을 세우기에 이른다. 더욱이 1988년도 서울올림픽에 맞서기 위하여 1989년에 평양에서 제13회 세계청년학생제전을 개최하기 앞두고 약 3년간에 걸쳐 260여 개의 관련시설이 건설되었다. 이를 이른바 '수도 대건설'이라고 한다. 북한당국의 발표로는 이들의 건설에 47억 달러라는 거액의 돈이 투입되었다고 한다. 이것은 1992년의 북한의 GDP 공식통계의 22.6%에 달하는 막대한 금액이다.

조현식의 추산에 의하면, 1980-96년 동안 북한에 건설된 60건의 대형공사 중 순수한 정치선전 목적의 기념비적 건조물은 18건으로 그 공사비는 100억 달러 정도였다고 한다. 양문수는 "대량의 노동, 자본, 설비, 자재를 필요로 하는 이러한 대규모의 비생산적 건설이 이른바 '생산적 투자'에 어떠한 악영향을 주었을까는 상상하기 어렵지 않다. 특히 이러한 건설들이 북한 경제의 경제상황이 종전보다 나빠진 1980년대에 집중적으로 이루어졌다는 점에 주목할 필요가 있다"고 하면서 체제경쟁과 정치적 종속성에 대한 경제의 악영향을 우려하고 있다. 그리고 1970년대 후반 혹은 1980년대 전반부터 농업과 공업 생산이 둔화되기 시작하면서, 이에 대해 국가는 강제저축을 한층 더 강화하는 방향으로 대응했다. 노동자, 농민에게 일방적으로 희생을 강요함으로써 어느 정도 높은 수준의 축적율을 간신히 유지할 수 있었던 북한의 재정은, 기념비적 건축물에 비생산적으로 투자되어 체제 선전용으로 전용되는 찾아보기 힘든 형태를 보이고 있다.

주체건축이 태동 되었다

1974년부터 1980년에 이르는 후계체제 형성기는 북한 사회주의의 정체성 확보를 위해 주체사상을 구체화하는 시기였다. 또한 여타 사회주의 국가와의 상대적 독자성을 확보하기 위해 '우리식 사회주의'를 모색하고 '민족성 구현'을 논쟁으로 '사회주의적 사실주의'에 수정을 가하는 시기이기도 했다. 이는 마르크스·레닌주의를 극복하고 김일성의 혁명적 수령관을 통해 일인 유일지배체제의 사회를 형성하기 위한 전략적 선택이었다. 이에 문학예술분야에서도 혁명성과 민족성의 경향이 강화되었다.

이 시기에는 초기 북한의 사회주의적 사실주의의 형식적 측면이 주체사실주의로 변화하기 시작했다. 이에 1970년대부터는 명실상부하게 새롭게 등장한 세대와 재편된 정치세력에 의한 유일지배체제의 형식과 주체사상, 주체 문화 구조가 공고히 되었다. 이렇게 성장한 주체 사실주의 문학 예술 세력이 주체 사상의 전위대로 복무하면서 김일성과 김정일 부자의 세습에 선전선동세력의 역할을 하고 정치 세력화하게 된다. 주체 사실주의와 주체건축은 1970년 중반부터 본격적으로 전개되었다. 1970년대에 북한에서 이야기 하는, 사회주의적 사실주의 내용에 민족주의적 형식의 맹아가 보인다는 것이다. 민족주의 건축 논쟁이 본격화되었던 60년대 중후반을 지나 70년대에 이르러 '건축을 우리 식으로 창조'하자는 원칙을 세우게 되었던 것이다.

정치적으로 등장했던 주체사상이 주체사실주의의 문학예술 이념으로 자리잡으면서, 민족주의적 내용이 접합된 주체건축이 70년대 이후에 본격적으로 북한의 수도 평양의 중심부를 장악하게 된다. 이로써 북한건축은 새로운 전기가 마련되었다. 스탈린 시기 소련에서 무비판적으로 수용된 '러시아 신고전주의' 건축 양식과 차별화를 시도함으로써 여타 사회주의 국가와 다른 독자적인 정체성을 확보하고자 했다. 이는 국제사회의 역학관계에서 맹방인 소련의 정치예속에서 벗어나려고 한 김일성의 여러 정치적 시도와 무관하지 않다는 것을 발견할 수 있다.

사회주의적 사실주의는 여전히 북한의 예술적 미학의 근간이다. 그러나 이 시기에는 '주체 건축'의 개념이 적극적으로 도입되면서 소비에트 건축미학의 영향권에서 탈피하여 민족적 독창성을 주요 내용으로 설계된다는 것이 큰 특징이다. '주체 건축'은 사회주의적인 건축과 민족적 미학의 결합이다. 김정일위원장은 저작집 『건축예술론』을 통해 "건축창조에 민족적 형식에 사회주의적 내용을 담아야 한다. 형식에서 민족적이고 내용이 사회주의적인 여기에 주체건축의 중요한 특징이 있다."라며 '주체건축'의 개념을 정의하고 있다.

이러한 건축양식은 또 다른 권위주의적 건축의 표현으로, 이를 극복하기 위한 민족주의적인 건축양식의 연구가 필요했던 것으로 귀결된다. 북한의 건국과정에서도 사회주의적 사실주의는 기본 문예이론으로 채택되었으나 1967년의 반종파 투쟁의 대상이 되었다. 이에 1960년대 후반부터 전통주의적인 사회주의적 사실주의는 북한 문예정책에서 수정이 가해진다. 북한 문화비평가 이우영에 따르면, 혁명성과 민족성을 강조하는 경향은 1960년대 후반 이후 김정일 문예정책의 기본적인 특성이 되었다. 따라서 1970년부터는 본격적인 주체적 문예 이론을 기반으로 하는 '주체 건축론'이 대두되었다고 보아야 할 것이다.

1950년대에 북한의 현대건축으로 지어진 '평양역사'를 놓고 민족주의 양식 논쟁이 있었다. 해방 후 러시아건축가와 유학파에 의해 소련의 영향권 아래에 놓여졌는데, 이를 극복하기 위해 1960년에 들어와서 새로운 건축사상이 필요했다. 이러한 상황 속에서 주체 건축에 대한 논의가 본격화 된다. 평양시 중심부에 자리잡고 있는 '인민 대 학습당'은 민족적 형식에 사회주의적 내용을 훌륭히 담은 기념비적 작품으로 평가 받는다. 이는 주체건축의 민족성을 잘 표현한 건축의 사례로 꼽힌다.

"위대한 수령님께서는 인민 대학습당을 건설하기 위하여 설계를 시작하던 초기에 건물형식을 조선식으로 하는 것이 좋을 것 같다고 하시었다. 그때 일부 일군들과 건축가들은 인민대학습당이 수도의 중심부에서도 중심에 놓이는 건물이기 때문에 현대식으로 크게 건설하여야 중심부가 눌리지 않고 살아날 수 있다고 하면서 조선식으로 건설하지 말고 현대식으로 건설하자고 하였다." 김정일, 『건축예술론』, p.36

이러한 과정을 거쳐 '인민대학습당'은 '조선식 건축형식'인 민족주의적 미학이 결합된 형태로 건설되었다. 이른바 '사회주의적 사실주의 건축양식'에 '민족적 특성'을 가미한 것이 주체건축의 가장 큰 특징이라 볼 수 있지만, 주체사상이 전면화 되던 60년대에도 여전히 주체건축은 제 자리를 구축하지 못했다. 하지만 70년대에 접어들면서 대대적인 기념비 건축이 건설되고, 인민대학습당 등을 통해 '민족주의적 형식에 사회주의적 내용'이 구체화되는 계기를 마련하게 되었다.

요약하면, 북한이 해방 이후 소련의 건축적 양식을 무비판적으로 도입한 이래, 사회주의 건축이념은 50, 60년대의 회의기 및 모색기를 거치고 70년대에 새로운 형식으로 구체화된 것이다. 그러나 여전히 사회주의적 사실주의의 큰 틀 속에서 제한적으로 적용되고 있으며, '민족적 형식'은 특히 상징성이 강한 기념비적 건축에 국한되어 있는 것을 발견할 수 있다.

술탄주의적 건축 경향이 나타난다.

유일지배체제에서 일인의 절대권력과 개인 숭배사상, 부자 세습은 북한의 특수성에서 비롯되었지만, 일반적인 비교사회주의 체제의 맥락 속에서 술탄체제의 특성을 함께 보여주고 있다. J. 린츠는 북한에서 술탄주의적 요소가 조합된 전체주의가 나타난다고 보고 있다. 여기서 특히 주목할 것은 부자권력세습이라는 술탄주의적 체제 특성이 이 시기 건축사업에서도 대대적으로 일어난다는 것이다.

후계구도의 정식화를 통하여 통치체제의 변화가 이루어졌다. 이전의 사회주의적 체제는 김일성유일지배체계로 전환되면서 술탄체제의 성격이 나타나기 시작한다. 김일성주석은 통치자인 자신의 판단에 방해되는 것 없이, 그리고 법률이나 이데올로기 또는 중요한 조직의 위원회에 얽매임 없이 그의 권력을 행사한다. 강제적 규범과 관료 행정기관의 관계는 이데올로기적 규정으로 뒷받침할 필요를 느끼지 못하는 통치자의 개인적 독단적 결정들에 의해 끊임없이 유일적으로 강화되어 간다. 이러한 술탄체제적 경향은 급기야 부자세습의 형태로 나타나고 술탄주의적 체제를 완성하기에 이르는 것이다.

1960년대 말과 1970년대 초 김정일위원장은 직접 문학예술사업을 주도하며 아버지의 우상화 작업을 선두에서 지휘한다. 그리고 주체의 혁명적 세계관과 혁명적 수령관에 일관된 주체 사상화를 위한 사회 개조에 착수한다. '온 사회의 주체사상화'를 위해 문학예술분야가 전면에서 복무해야 할 것을 제창하고, 항일혁명투쟁시기에 김일성주석이 직접 창작했다는 이른바 '불후의 고전적 명작'들을 재현해 간다. 아버지 수령에 대한 세습 후계자의 충성심의 발로인 것이다.

1970년대는 김정일위원장의 후계구도를 완성해 나가는 시기이다. 김일성주석의 후원 아래 '당중앙'이라는 호칭으로 불리며 문학예술계를 주도적으로 지휘해나간다. 오양열은 이 시기의 김정일은 이른바 '제1의 문학예술혁명'을 통해 당 원로들로부터 능력을 인정받아 후계자로 공인되고, 3대 혁명소조운동을 통해 자신의 정치적 공간과 권력 기반을 강화해 나간다.

이러한 세습 후계자로서의 아들이 문학예술분야를 지도하며 아버지의 우상화를 주도한 예는 사회주의 국가에서도 보기 드문 상황이다. 여기에서 술탄주의적 사회의 특징이 발견된다. 특히 이 시기에 활발하게 전개되었던 기념비적 건축사업에서 잘 나타나고 있다. 기념비적 건축사업은 항일혁명투쟁의 전통을 공간적으로 길이 보존하여 정통성을 확보하는 데 필요하였으며, 평양의 주요 지구에 대규모로 조형적으로 형상화함으로써 가시권내에서 '대를 이어 충성하자'는 현상적 우상물이었던 것이다.

이러한 배경에서 진행된 건축사업은 두 가지 방향으로 전개되었다. 하나는 '개선문', '주체 사상탑'과 같이 대기념비 건축 사업을 통해 김일성주석의 업적을 현재적으로 형상화하는 성향을 띠며, 다른 하나는 '혁명 열사능', '왕재산 혁명사적지' 등과 같이 혁명혁명사적지 건설로 항일혁명투쟁의 흔적과 장소를 신성화하는 방향으로 진행되었다. 이러한 건축사업이 술탄주의적 체제성격을 강하게 드러낸다는 점에서 이 건축물과 건축사업들의 건립배경과 건립시기에 주목할 필요가 있다. 주체사상탑과 개선문의 건립배경은 주석탄생 70돌 기념으로 주체사상의 기념비적 형상화를 위하여 건립되었다. '혁명 열사릉'은 1975년에 건설된 것인데 1985년 당창건 40돌을 계기로 새롭게 개건확장하였다. 혁명사적지 건설은 북한 최대의 기념일인 당창건 30돌, 무산지구전투승리 40돌을 계기로 시작되었다. 이 시기 '왕재산 혁명사적지', '배움의 천리길'과 '광복의 천리길' 혁명사적지, '봉화혁명사적지', '은하혁명사적지', '용포혁명사적지', '연풍혁명사적지', '군자혁명사적지', '향하 혁명사적지', '회령 혁명사적지', '은율 혁명사적지', '청수혁명사적지', '중강 혁명사적지', '홍원 혁명사적지'들이 새로 건설되거나 대대적으로 정비되었다. 70년대 이후 이러한 대규모적이고 대 기념비적 건축사업은 김위원장의 발기와 건설 주도에 의해 완성되었다.

김정일식 대중운동의 속도전이다

북한의 대중운동노선인 군중동원체제는 노동력이 집중적으로 투여되는 건축사업에서는 대단히 중요한 구성 요소이다. 건축사업에서도 김정일 식 대중운동이 결합되고 있다. 평양의 낙원거리는 당 창건 30돌을 맞으며 짧은 기간에 세운 거리라고 자랑한다. '낙원거리의 건설자들은 새 기록, 새 기적을 연이어 창조하여 일반 건설공정계획으로서는 몇 년이 걸려야 할 3,000세대의 현대적인 살림집을 비롯하여 각종 공공건물, 도로와 다리들을 종합적으로 갖춘 웅장한 낙원거리를 불과 6개월이라는 짧은 기간에' 완성하여 세웠다고 한다.

생산성을 극대화하기 위한 중요한 기제로서 활용되었던 '속도전'은 대중운동의 가장 일반화된 형태로 모든 분야에서 나타나고 있다. 또한 1970년대에 들어서서 김정일의 등장으로 대표적으로 등장한 것은 '3대 혁명소조 운동'이다. 이른바 사상, 기술, 문화혁명의 3대혁명을 추진하기 위해서 '3대혁명소조'를 내세웠다. 3대혁명은 1972년 사회주의 헌법에 규정되면서 설립되었으며 군중 노선 하에 발기된 대중운동은 1974년 2월부터 개시된 속도전적인 사업방식이다. 특히 1974년 10월부터 70일 동안 추진된 '70일 전투(속도)'와 '충성의 속도'와 같은 대중 운동들에 대하여 차석은 사상 교양의 수준을 생산성, 즉 노동의 성과와 연관지으려는 의도를 갖고 있다고 한다. 이에 노동집중적인 건축현장에서의 목표달성과 충성의 속도는 일정부분 성과가 긍정적으로 반영되었다. 이 시기의 대중운동은 건축사업에서도 같은 방법으로 동원되었다. 특히 국가의 주요 건설사업에 노동력을 동원할 목적으로 청년층을 중심으로 조직된 '속도전 청년돌격대'가 있다. 사회주의 대건설을 구상하고 실현하기 위하여 '더 많은, 더 잘, 더 빨리 건설하자'는 기치로 조직된 청년 전위집단이 건축현장에 투입되어 이 많은 건설사업에 동원되고 건설속도를 높여나갔던 것이다. 이 돌격대는 엄격한 규율과 노동의 군사화를 잘 보여주면서 건축현장에서의 일사분란한 조직력으로 건설현장을 주도해 나갔다. 1975년 11월에 제시된 '3대 혁명 붉은 기 쟁취 운동'도 북한에서는 '사상혁명, 기술혁명, 문화혁명을 힘있게 벌려 사회주의 건설을 다그치기 위한 인민적 대중 운동'이라고 한다. 이 운동은 1975년 12월 한 달 동안 '검덕광산', '청산리 협동농장', '대안전기공장', '김일성종합대학', '조선예술영화촬영소' 등 인민경제

모든 부문과 단위로 확산되어 건설사업 뿐만 아니라 전 군중적 대중운동으로 확대되어 갔다. 건설분야에서도 열악한 노동환경에서 장비와 기계도 없이 손으로 노동을 하여 목표량을 초과달성한 건설노동자들에게 '로력영웅'이 나오기도 하였다한다.

1979년 10월에는 '숨은 영웅 따라 배우기 운동'이 일어났으며 군인 영웅인 '오증흡, 김혁을 따라 배우기 운동'이 대표적이다. 이후에도 지속적으로 1981년 9월에 '새 기준 새 기록 창조운동', 1982년 6월에 '26호 선반 따라 배우는 충성의 모범 기대 창조 운동', 1982년 7월에 '80년대 속도 창조 운동' 등이 실시되었다. 1980년대에도 이러한 군중적 대중노선은 속도전적 운동은 지속되었다. 하지만 속도전적 대중 운동의 전개는 계획을 앞당겨 시행함으로써 국가의 장기 계획화의 혼란 상태를 가중시키며 노동의욕의 감소와 사기저하로 이어진다. 이는 결국 생산량 감소로 이어지고 국가경제와 주민생활을 어렵게 하는 원인으로 대두하게 된다.

북한의 노력경쟁운동은 그 형태를 바꾸어가면서 경쟁의 강도를 높여 갔고 점차 자발적이고 창의적인 참여보다는 강제성을 띠었으며 정치색이 더욱 강조되었다. 노력경쟁이 반복되면서 단기적으로 별 성과가 나타나지 않았다. 결국은 김정일식 새로운 속도전의 양상도 크게 성과를 거두지 못했지만, 이러한 운동으로 인해 대규모 건축사업들이 가능했다는 것은 부정할 수 없다.

반당반종파 투쟁을 통한 건축권력를 교체하였다

건축 작품에서 반당반종파와의 투쟁도 엿보인다. 대규모 건설에 대한 반대파가 있었으리라는 예측이 가능한 대목이다. '창광거리'는 이전의 '윤환선거리'를 낡은 종파분자들이 건설분야에 끼친 죄악의 산물이라고 규정하고 반당반혁명종파분자들은 당의 건설방침을 외면하며 주민들의 생활감정과 실정에 맞지도 않는 살림집설계에 의하여 촌스럽게 윤환선 거리를 꾸며놓았다고 비판하기에 이른다. 이에 새로 건설한 '창광 거리'는 기존 틀과 낡은 방법을 대담하게 없애고 새로운 방식으로 건설된 현대적인 거리라고 한다. '윤환선 거리'의 집들은 보통 2-3층의 벽돌집이었는데 이것을 고층형으로 새롭게 건설하였다.

창광 거리는 이전의 윤환선 거리를 낡은 것으로 치부하고 새로운 지침을 내린다. 건축에서의 새로운 주체적 건설을 엿볼 수 있는 대목이다. 김일성 교시에서 "이번 윤환선 거리건설은 1980년대에 들어오면서 우리나라 건설부분에서 새로운 변혁을 가져오는 시발점으로 되게 하여야 하겠습니다. ... 윤환선 거리 건설을 설계로부터 시공에 이르기까지 모든 면에서 기존 틀과 낡은 기준을 대담하게 깨고 도시건설에서 비약과 변혁을 일으키는 전환점으로, 역사적인 계기로 되게 하여야 하겠습니다." 이를 통해 알 수 있는 것은 이러한 건축사업도 주체사상을 내세우며, 반당파 반종파와의 투쟁의 연장선에서 진행되었다는 것이다.

윤환선 거리의 반당반혁명종파투쟁 이전에도, 이미 1950년대에도, 이미 건설부문에서도 이러한 선례가 있었다. 김일성주석은 "당중앙위원회 1957년 10월전원회의에서 반당반혁명종파분자들의 책동을 낱낱이 폭로분쇄하시고 건설부문에서 주체를 철저히 세울데 대하여"를 통해 지시하면서 건축사업 부문에서 반대파들을 숙청해나갔다. 1967년의 문화예술계 반종파 투쟁을 통하여 구카프 계열의 문학예술인은 제거되고 문학예술분야에서도 김일성 중심의 인맥이 자리잡게 되었음을 미루어 보아 건축예술에도 주체건축의 배경이 구축되었음을 알 수 있다. 이를 이우영은, 1967년의 종파투쟁 이후 민족성은 점진적으로 강화, 구체화되었고 이의 결과가 주체사실주의라고 정의한다.

이 시기는 70년대의 경제건설 분야의 새로운 시도와 좌절을 통해 암울한 분위기에서도 김정일의 후계체제 공식 선언으로 김정일 체제에 대한 우려와 희망이 교차되던 시기였다. 김정일은 명실상부한 지도자로서 능력과 자질을 수령과 인민들에서 보여 주어야 했다.

이러한 과정 속에서 김정일위원장은 선전 선동부에 있었던 전력을 활용하여 대규모 건축사업을 통해 대중장악력을 발휘하고자 하였다. 1982년 김일성 탄생 70년 기념에 즈음해 아버지에 대한 충성심을 보일 필요가 있었고, 1989년 세계청년축전을 성공적으로 수행함으로써 지도자체제를 완성하고자 했다.

김정일위원장은 당의 유일적 지도체제는 "수령의 사상과 령도를 전당과 온 사회에 철저히 구현하기 위한 체제이고 수령의 의

도대로 우리 혁명을 진전시키고 승리로 이끌기 위한 지도체제이며 수령이 개척하신 혁명위업을 대를 이어 끝까지 완성하기 위한 지도체제"라고 했다. 이러한 발언은 아버지인 수령의 사상과 영도를 받겠다는 충성서약이며 아버지 수령의 의도대로 대를 이어 받들겠다는 지도체계의 승계를 의미하는 말로 볼 수 있다.

당시 정치적 상황으로는 권력을 잡아 나가고 있었지만, 경제적 여건이나 내부 기반은 암담했다. 도로나 철도와 같은 부족한 사회간접자본은 여건이 좋지 않았고, 노후해진 기계설비는 교체, 확충해야 했다. 후계자로서는 녹록치 않은 상황에 도전해야 했다. 제한된 재화와 기술로 이어받은 사회주의 제도를 정비, 확대해 나가야 했다. 그가 선택할 수 있는 유일한 방식은 지금까지 활용해 왔던 집중적이고 신속한 대중운동의 재탕이었다. 이에 이전의 선전선동부의 경력과 건축에 관한 해박한 지식을 활용한다. 이 시기는 건축사업에 있어 김일성 교시가 점점 사라지고 김정일 교시로 건축사업이 이루어진다. 대표적인 교시 중에는 "건축도 하나의 예술입니다. 그러므로 건축창작도 반드시 비반복적이어야 합니다."라는 것이 있는데 건축사업을 직접 챙기고 독려한 흔적을 찾아 볼 수 있다. 건축사업에서도 김정일 식 속도전은 대중운동의 지도체계로 활용되고 있다. 1980년대 대표적인 노동동원운동에 속하는 '80년대 속도창조운동'은 김일성 탄생 70주년 기념을 위한 사업에 이바지한다. 또한 이 속도운동을 통해 '주체 사상탑', '개선문' 건립, '김일성 동상', '인민 대학습당', '창광 거리', '평양 산원'과 '빙상관', '남포 갑문', '태천 발전소', '북부철길' 등이 건설되었다. '80년대 속도 창조운동'과 유사한 '200일 전투'는 1988년 2월 20일부터 그해 9월 9일 정원 창립 40주년까지의 200일 노력동원운동이다. 이를 김귀옥은 세계 청년 축전을 앞두고 건축물을 앞당겨 완공하기 위한 의도도 담겨 있던 것으로 보인다고 평한다.

이로써 당시 벌여진 대규모의 방대한 건축사업은 김정일의 권력 강화에 복무하는 형태로 나타난다. 건축 자체의 상징성도 그러하지만 경제적 시련기를 건설을 위한 대중 동원운동으로 헤쳐 나가면서 권력을 강화해 나갔던 것이다.

결론

북한의 건축은 여전히 '사회주의적 내용'이 근간이 되고 있으며, 이 시기에 공공적 성격의 건축물에서 본격적으로 실현한 '민족주의 형식'이 더해진 주체건축의 이념이 상징화되는 형태로 전개되고 있다. 그러나 이념의 경직성 너머에는 순수창작예술의 다양한 표현 욕구 사이에 새로운 형식실험이 진행되고 있다. 이 시기의 건축의 성과는 지금까지 북한과 평양의 건축을 이해하는 데 유효한 기준이 되고 있으며, 미래의 북한건축을 예측하는 면에서도 이 시기의 건축은 연구의 시금석으로 삼을 수 있다.

우선, 1976년에서 1980년대까지의 북한건축은 후계 구축기의 정치변화에 따라 많은 변화가 나타났음을 알 수 있다. 이는 정치적 상황이 건축에 미친 영향의 결과로 볼 수 있는데, 요약해 보면 다음과 같은 건축적 특성을 밝혀낼 수 있었다.

첫째로는 체제위신적 건축과 남북한의 경쟁 양상으로 나타난다. 대외적으로는 소련과의 정체성 차별화가 대두되었으며 정치적, 문화적 예속을 벗어나기 위한 시기였다. 따라서 초기 북한건축의 '러시아 신고전주의' 건축양식에서 변화된 주체적 건축양식의 대두가 필요했다. 대내적으로는 남북한의 위정자들이 전권안위 차원에서 건축사업이 체제 우월성을 선전하는 대외과시용으로, 경쟁적으로 진행되었다.

둘째로는 '불멸의 대 기념비' 건축을 통해 혁명전통을 과시하고, 이를 선임 권력자에게 충성을 다하는 사상교양의 수단으로 활용되었다. 여기에서 부자세습과 우상화라는 절대권력의 신성화를 통한 술탄주의적 경향의 건축이 나타나기에 이른다.

셋째로는 김정일위원장이 이러한 일련의 건축사업을 후계를 공고화하기 위한 중요한 업적으로 활용하고 있다는 점이다. 주체주의 건축을 새로운 기치로 내세우고, 군중동원적 대중운동체계를 확립하고, 반당 반종파 투쟁을 통하여 권력을 집중화해 나간다.

이 시기에 북한에서는 전례 없는 건축사업이 이루어졌고 이를 김정일위원장이 진두지휘하며 사업을 이끌었다는 사실만으로도 김정일 식 건축사업의 독특한 방식으로 이해 할 수 있다. 그리고 이 시기는 남에서도 많은 건축사업이 이루어졌는데 서로 다른 양상으로 전개되었기에 비교해 보는 것도 의미가 있다. 그리고 이 글이 정치 사회적 배경을 위주로 서술하다보니 다소 경직된 추론이 나오기도 한다. 이는 외부에서 보는 북한건축의 해석이며, 견해를 달리하는 사람들도 있으리라 본다. 그러나 안타깝게도 북한건축에 대한 연구가 미흡한 현실에서 한 건축가가 쓸 수 있는 한계를 인정하면서, 앞으로 북한 건축에 대한 교류가 더 있으면 하는 기대가 이 글을 쓰게 된 이유이기도 하다.

---

* This article is based on the author's thesis "A Study on the Feature of North Korean Architecture During the Kim Jong-Il Succession System Building Period," and part of it is revised and edited.

TYPOLOGICAL STUDIES ON NORTH KOREAN ARCHITECTURE

Dongwoo Yim

—

Dongwoo Yim is the author and editor of the "North Korean Atlas," and the principal and co-founder of architecture and research firm PRAUD, based in Boston and Seoul. He received a Master of Architecture in Urban Design at Graduate School of Design (GSD), Harvard University, and bachelor's degree in Seoul National University.
Dongwoo is a faculty member of Rhode Island School of Design since 2011 where he teaches seminar and design studios. His research interest focuses on integral urbanism and architectural typologies that catalyze urban transformation in various urban scales. He is the award winner of Architectural League Prize 2013, and is the author of "Pyohgyang, and Pyongyang After" by Hyohyung Publishing and "I Want to be METROPOLITAN" by ORO Editions. His works have been published and exhibited world wide including Museum of Modern Art New York, International Architecture Biennale Rotterdam, Venice Biennale and Design Center Seoul, and he has lectured at Harvard University, Freie Universität Berlin, Dartmouth College, Seoul National University and Youngchoo Forum amongst others.

Just as in many other fields, architectural information in North Korea is very limited. Although architecture can be best understood through direct experience, the fact that access to the primary source material was limited meant our view towards North Korean architecture was fragmented. Therefore, the most common path we took, in an effort to understand North Korean architecture, was through "style." Architectural style is a very important method in differentiating one architecture from another and in explaining the culture and society of the period. We can read the religious values of the Middle Ages through Gothic churches, and humanistic values through Renaissance architecture. This is not so different in the Modern era—when no style became a style—or even in the post-modernist period, and it holds true not just for Western architecture but also for Eastern architecture. We differentiate periods and regions by understanding styles of roofs or pillars.

However, there are critical perspectives that say style in architecture is meaningless now. Perhaps many reasons can be stated for such a claim, but one of the main reasons is that modern architecture is being developed through pursuing rational functions in architecture rather than through style. Increasing the variety of programs in architecture makes it almost impossible to implement one style to many different architectures; therefore, even though we still can understand culture through architectural style, we should start looking into architectural typologies to understand socioeconomic or sociocultural aspects of a society. In fact, this idea has a thread of connection to a recent movement in South Korea that attempts to understand Koreans' dwelling patterns and life styles through typologies of apartments and other residential types.

Therefore, it should be said that there are various ways of seeing North Korean architecture. Of course, it helps considerably to have an initial understanding of the categorization of North Korean architecture by style, such as Realism, Traditionalism, Monumentalism and so on. At the same time, however, there is a clear limitation in understanding North Korean culture and architecture only through style. Other than architecture that clearly displays a specific style with symbolic gestures for certain programs, we have put less effort on understanding average (everyday) architectural types such as housing, factories, or schools. Just as we have for many other societies, perhaps we need to look at not only symbolic architecture but also average architecture to understand North Korea's society and culture. While we can read South Korean society through buildings like the National Museum of Korea, the President's House, and Seoul City Hall—all of which have very distinguishing architectural styles—we can understand the society at a deeper level by looking into apartments, multiplex housing, offices, and neighborhood service facilities. Although these projects may not be masterpieces, but rather spontaneous projects by demand, they are very important subjects that show the society, culture, and lifestyles of Korea.

Properties of NK Architecture

Before getting into the typology of North Korean architecture, we should understand the system of it first. Its most unique feature is that all the facilities are planned and provided by the public sector, the government. Although some private developments can be witnessed, as the control system has loosened recently, major buildings in the country are all provided by the public sector. The system brings two interesting menus to the table: 1) development of typology, and 2) architectural program. In a system where the public sector provides all the buildings, there tends to be mass production and, therefore, developing architectural typology becomes important. This is especially so in residential developments that need modular systems for massive production and reasonable supply. Of course, it also happens in areas where there needs to be massive supply, such as residential apartments in South Korea or even suburban housing in the United States. In the case of North Korea, however, where there is no real estate market, architectural typologies are developed more to have rationality than to give individual character to the building. Therefore, there is more effort to develop reasonable solutions in plan types and symbolic gestures in forms.

North Korean residential types, especially mid- and high-rise types, were not so different from the South Korean ones until the 1990s when a massive amount of apartment supply was generated. They had to be both mass produced and have a reasonable cost of construction. Few changes were made to give identity to the apartments besides the individual unit plan. This was an ironic situation in South Korea because, in most free economic markets, residences need more variety to satisfy a number of different tastes and demands. Perhaps this can be used as a barometer to understand South Korean society. Coming back to North Korean residential, the biggest difference between it and South Korean residential is the formative approach. Until 2000, the goal of most South Korean developers was to maximize FAR while following the regulations of footprint area, diagonal lines, right-to-sunlight and so on, which led to little option in form. However, in North Korea, there was no such kind of FAR to meet and, therefore, they could pursue formal approaches as they wanted. These forms are driven by the concept that cityscape should be carefully sculpted by architecture and composed to give the aesthetics of the city. Although the formal approach was possible because of the government's authority, it is also true that a lack of market-economy logic let the city explore it more freely. In other words, residential typologies in North Korea are developed not only to achieve rational plans but also to experiment co-relationships to the cityscape.

The second important way to understand North Korean architecture is through architectural program. When we see what type of architectural projects are introduced to the public, including residential projects, we can see how the society's perspective is different from ours—in this case, South Korea's. In the magazine Chosun Architecture—the most outstanding architectural magazine in North Korea—there are specific types of architecture that the magazine gives attention to, and two of the most interesting programs are factories and restaurants. Of course, it is not impossible to find these type of projects in South Korean magazines, but they are featured surprisingly often in Chosun Architecture. Along with these programs, library, sports facilities and educational facilities are some of the favorite architecture that the magazine features. This is mainly because the idea of socialism, that the nation should take care of people's eating and education, is positioned as a backbone of North Korean ideology. Additionally, the idea that all people must be workers, lets the country put effort into developing typologies for factories; the idea that the people need to rest after work lets it develop sports facilities. They may not be as interesting as symbolic architecture that shows North Korean style, but Chosun Architecture puts a lot of weight on "daily life" buildings. This, of course, is in contrast to South Korean architectural magazines that mostly feature high-end cultural facilities, private houses, or office buildings that are "architecturally" interesting. This tells us a cultural difference between the two Koreas: one focuses on concept and the perfection of an architecture, while the other focuses primarily on meaning of the program and how it represents the nation's ideology.

Understanding North Korean architecture does not just mean that we will see architecture through an architectural perspective, it should also be understood as part of the reading of North Korean cities. Just as reading a city is to understand the culture and values of the society, reading architecture is to understand lifestyles and paradigms of the society through the typologies of built form. There should be a slightly different approach to understanding the society through architecture. It is true that some architectural styles in symbolic buildings reflect values of North Korean society; we can read North Korea's pride in traditional culture through the People's Study House, and their sense of superiority through Mankyungdae Children Palace. However, above all, we should really look into the everyday architecture to understand the society better. It is not just to understand the technical aspects of architecture, such as construction methods, materials and design process, but to look into how the society works and what the life in the society is like. For instance, by looking into service facilities, we can see how the society provides sanitation buildings, such as public baths, hair salons or barbershops, to the public. By looking at restaurants that are provided in rather big and singular buildings rather than small scale spaces, we can make assumptions about their eating culture. We can also read their efforts on sustainable energy by looking into rural house typology proposals that have solar panels and wind turbines, although it remains unknown whether they have been realized or not.

In conclusion, just as we try to read North Korean cities objectively through the built environment, we should also have a neutral perspective when we see their architecture. Often are there some examples of architecture, such as the People's Study House or Ryukyung Hotel, that show the unreasonable authority of North Korea, but in fact, South Korea also has its share. Therefore, at the moment when we do not have a full understanding of North Korean architecture, we should put as much data as possible on the table and analyze their typologies rather than try to confirm our preconceptions on North Korea through extraordinary buildings. Also, the time for competition has passed. We no longer have to show off our superior achievement in architecture by pointing out crude details and outdated facilities in North Korean architecture, we now have to understand the architecture and society of North Korea not through photos that only show the look but through drawings that show inner workings of the architecture.

북한건축과 유형

임동우

—

임동우는 "북한 도시 읽기"의 저자이며 서울과
보스턴을 기반으로 하는 설계사무소 PRAUD의 대표이다.
그는 하버드 대학교에서 도시설계 건축학 석사,
서울대학교에서 학사를 취득하였다.
현재 그는 로드아일랜드 스쿨 오브 디자인(RISD)에
출강하고 있으며, 그의 연구는 다양한 스케일에서 도시 변화를
촉진시키는 점진적인 도시 변화와 건축 유형에 초점을 맞추고 있다.
그는 뉴욕 건축가 연맹 주관 2013년 뉴욕 젊은 건축가상 수상자이며,
"평양, 그리고 평양 이후"(효형 출판)
"I Want to be METROPOLITAN"(ORO Editions)의 저자이다.
그의 작업은 뉴욕 모마, 로테르담 건축 비엔날레,
서울 디자인 센터, 베니스 비엔날레 등에 전시된 바 있으며,
하버드 대학교, 베를린 자유 대학, 다트머스 대학, 서울대학교,
영추포럼 등에서 강연한 바 있다.

북한과 관련된 다른 정보와 마찬가지로 북한의 건축에 대한 정보는 매우 제한적이었다. 특히, 직접 경험하고 봄으로써 알 수 있는 건축의 경우에는 원천 자료에의 접근이 쉽지 않다는 사실은 우리가 북한의 건축을 보는 데 단편적인 시각을 가질 수밖에 없게 했다. 그 동안 우리가 북한의 건축을 바라볼 때, 가장 흔하게 취했던 방식이 북한 건축을 양식적으로 접근하는 것이었다. 건축에서의 양식이란, 한 건축을 규정하고 다른 건축과 구분 짓는 데에 가장 중요한 방법 중 하나이며, 한 시대와 문화를 설명하는 데에도 매우 중요하게 쓰인다. 우리는 고딕 건축양식의 교회들을 보며 중세의 종교적 가치관을 읽어내고, 르네상스 양식을 보며 당시의 인본주의 철학을 읽는다. 이는 현대건축의 뿌리가 되고 무양식이 양식이 된 모더니즘을 비롯하여 이후 나타난 포스트 모더니즘 시대에도 해당하는 사항이다. 이는 비단 서양 건축에만 해당되는 이야기가 아니다. 한국건축을 보면서도 지붕의 양식, 기둥의 양식 등을 통하여 한 시대를 다른 시대와 구분하기도 하며, 한 지역을 다른 지역과 구분하기도 한다.

하지만, 이제는 건축에서의 양식 논쟁은 끝났다고 보는 시각도 많다. 이유는 다양하지만, 가장 큰 이유는 아무래도 근래의 건축은 양식보다는 건축의 합리적인 기능을 추구하는 쪽으로 발달하고 있고, 건축 프로그램 또한 다양성은 하나의 양식이 모든 건축에 적용되기 힘든 구조를 갖추었기 때문이다. 다시 말하면, 여전히 양식으로서 설명할 수 있는 건축 문화적인 부분이 존재하지만, 그 외에도 유형적인 접근을 통하여 양식으로서 설명하기 힘든 사회-경제적, 혹은 사회-문화적인 부분도 존재한다. 이는 최근 한국의 건축계에서도 아파트 유형, 주택 유형 등을 통해서 한국인들의 주거 패턴과 삶을 이해하고자 하는 노력하는 부분과 일맥상통한다.

따라서 북한 건축을 바라보는 시각도 좀 더 다양해질 필요가 있다. 물론 그 동안 북한 건축을 사실주의, 전통주의, 조형주의 등의 양식으로 접근한 시각은 우리에게 낯설었던 북한의 건축을 이해하는 데에 큰 도움을 주었다. 하지만 그와 동시에, 양식만으로는 북한의 건축, 혹은 북한의 문화를 폭넓게 이해하는 데에는 한계가 있었다. 다시 말하면, 건축의 양식이 도드라지게 나타나는 특정 프로그램의 건축이나 상징성을 갖는 건축을 제외한, 좀 더 일상적인 건축인 주거시설, 공장시설, 교육시설 등과 같은 건축을 이해하고자 하는 노력은 부족했던 것이 사실이

다. 하지만 모든 사회가 그렇듯, 북한에서도 상징적인 건축물뿐만 아니라 이러한 일상의 건축을 이해할 때 그 사회를 조금이나마 이해할 수 있지 않을까 싶다. 즉, 한국의 사회를 건축을 통해서 이해할 때에는 국립박물관, 청와대, 서울시청 등과 같은 독립적인 건축의 양식을 통해서 이해할 수도 있지만, 오히려 한국의 아파트, 다세대 주택, 근린상가시설, 오피스텔 등을 통해서 사회의 더 많은 것을 이해할 수도 있다. 이들 건축은 기존의 관점으로는 소위 말하는 '작품'이 되기 쉽지 않은, 자연 발생적인 건축에 가깝지만, 오히려 한국의 사회와 문화, 그리고 삶의 방식을 이해하기 위하여는 더할 나위 없는 좋은 소재이다.

북한 건축의 특징

유형적인 관점에서 북한의 건축을 바라보기에 앞서 북한 건축이 갖는 시스템적인 특징을 알아보면, 우선 북한 건축은 정부가 모든 시설을 공급한다는 점이 특이하다. 물론 최근 들어 북한의 경제체제가 조금씩 바뀌고 국가의 통제가 느슨해 지면서, 민간 차원에서의 건설도 이루어지고는 있긴 하지만, 아직까지 주된 북한 건축물의 공급은 국가 주도하에 이루어지고 있다. 이러한 조건이 갖는 가장 큰 두 가지 특징은 '유형(타이폴로지)의 개발'과 '건축 프로그램'이다. 즉, 국가 주도하에 건축 공급이 이루어지는 북한에서는 대량공급이라는 것은 항상 중요하게 적용되는 요소이다. 특히 주거시설의 경우 대량공급 시스템을 통하여 건축의 모듈화를 이루면 합리적인 공급을 할 수 있기 때문에, 이를 위한 '유형의 개발'을 중요하게 생각한다. 이는 자본주의 사회에서도 우리나라의 아파트나 미국 서브어반(suburban)의 주택같이 대량으로 공급되는 주거의 경우에는 이러한 유형개발에 역점을 두는 경우가 많다. 하지만 부동산 매매가 이루어지지 않는 사회인 북한의 주거 유형 개발의 경우, 주관적이고 개별성을 강조하는 유형보다는 객관적이고 합리성을 중심에 두는 유형을 개발하는 경우가 많다. 따라서 주거의 경우, 합리적인 평면을 갖추기 위해 '유형의 개발'이 많이 이루어지며, 외형적인 부분에서는 미적인 부분보다는 조형성을 강조하는 개발이 이루어지고 있다.

사실 개별성 보다는 대량 공급에 초점이 맞춰진 한국의 아파트, 특히 1990년대까지 대량으로 공급된 아파트의 경우와 비교해 보면, 이들과 북한의 살림집, 특히 중·고층 살림집들은 대동소이하다. 이들은 모두 합리적인 공급가격을 제시할 수 있어야 했고 대량 복제가 가능해야 했으며 대부분의 차별성은 개별 평면에서만 이루어졌다. 이는 자율적인 시장의 다양한 입맛에 따라 주택이 공급되는 대부분의 자본주의 국가에서는 나타나지 않는 아이러니한 현상인데, 이 또한 우리나라 사회와 문화를 이해하는 실마리가 되지 않을까 한다. 이러한 한국의 아파트와 다르게 북한의 살림집이 갖는 가장 큰 특징은 아마도 조형성에 있을 것이다. 즉, 2000년대 이전의 한국의 아파트는 건폐율, 사선제한, 일조권 등 많은 제한 조건 속에서 최대한의 용적률을 뽑아내는 것이 목적이다 보니, 오히려 천편일률적으로 공급되는 부분이 많았다. 하지만 북한의 중·고층 살림집들의 경우에는 최대한의 용적률을 맞춰야 한다는 부담이 없었기 때문에 오히려 조형성을 강조할 수 있었다. 이는 단순히 이형의 조형성을 추구한다는 차원이 아니라, 거리에서 보았을 때 중·고층 살림집의 어떠한 조합과 배치가 더 나은 조형성을 갖는지를 고민한 것이다. 물론 조형성을 추구할 수 있는 가장 큰 이유는 국가 체제의 특수성 때문이기도 하지만, 건물이 최대 용적률을 맞춰야 한다는 시장의 논리가 없기 때문이기도 하다. 이러한 부분에서 북한의 주거시설, 즉 살림집들은 단순한 합리성을 강조한 것만이 아닌, 다양한 실험적인 유형을 근간으로 형성된 것이다.

한편, 북한 건축을 이해하는 데에 있어서 또 다른 특징인 주요 '건축 프로그램'을 관심 있게 살펴볼 필요가 있다. 주거시설도 마찬가지지만, 어떠한 용도의 건축물의 유형이나 작품이 주로 소개되는지 살펴보면 북한사회가 우리와 어떻게 다른지 바라볼 수 있다. 우리에게도 잘 알려진 북한의 〈조선건축〉이라고 하는 대표적 건축잡지를 살펴보면, 북한이 주로 소개하고 있는 건축 프로그램 중 눈에 띄는 몇 가지가 있는데, 그것은 바로 공장과 식당 건축이다. 물론 이러한 용도의 건축이 우리나라의 건축잡지에 게재되지 않는 것은 아니지만 〈조선건축〉에서는 어렵지 않게 찾아볼 수 있는 건축이다. 이들과 함께 도서관, 체육시설, 교육시설 등도 많이 등장하는 데, 이유는 사회주의를 바탕으로 하는 북한에서는 국가가 국민의 먹거리와 교육을 담당해야 한다는 주된 철학이 반영되기 때문이다. 또한 모든 인민은 노동자라고 하는 가치관은 그들로 하여금 공장건축에 대해서도 중요하게 생각하게 하였고, 인민들이 노동 후 레저를 즐길 수 있어야 한다는 시각은 체육시설의 보급으로 이어졌다. 흔히 생각했을 때 '건축적'으로 북한 건축 양식을 설명할 수 있는 여타 '상징성'을 지닌 건축물보다는 상대적으로 흥미롭지 않을 수 있는 이러한 건축시설들에 대해서 〈조선건축〉은 꽤 비중 있게 다루는 편이다. 이는 '건축적'인 흥미를 끌 수 있는 호화 문화시설이나 고급주택, 혹은 오피스 건축이 주로 소개되는 국내외의 잡지와는 조금은 다른 구성으로 볼 수 있다. 즉, 북한에서 바라보는 건축은 얼마나 건축적 완성도가 있느냐 하는 문제라기보다는, 어떠한 건축이 인민들에게 필요하고 그들의 가치관을 담고 있느냐 하는 문제에 가깝다고 볼 수 있다.

북한의 건축을 바라본다는 것은 단순히 한 건축을 건축적인 시각으로만 분석해보고자 하는 것이 아닐 것이다. 이 역시 북한의 도시를 읽는 것의 한 부분이다. 도시를 읽고자 하는 이유가 그 사회의 문화와 가치관 등을 알기 위함인 것처럼, 건축을 보는 것 역시 그 사회의 생활과 패러다임을 건축이라는 물리적인 유형을 통해 읽어내고자 함이다. 그러기 위해서는 북한의 건축에 접근하는 데에 그 동안 해온 방식과 조금 다른 시각의 접근이 필요하다. 북한의 주요 상징 건축물을 통해서 설명 가능한 북한의 건축 양식 역시 북한 사회의 가치관을 어느 정도 반영하는 것은 사실이다. 우리는 인민 대학습당 등에서 나타나는 북한의 민족주의 건축 양식을 통해서 그들이 전통 건축에 두는 무게감을 짐작할 수 있다. 또한, 만경대 소년학생 궁전 등 상징주의 양식 건축을 통해 그들이 추구하고자 하는 집단적 우월의식을 엿볼 수도 있다. 하지만 무엇보다도 건축을 통해 그들 사회를 이해하기 위해서는 조금 더 일상적인 건축을 들여다볼 필요가 있다. 이는 단순히 북한건축에서 주되게 쓰이는 건축 재료라든지, 공법, 설계기법 등의 건축 전문적인 부분을 보고자 하는 차원을 넘어, 북한이라는 사회가 어떻게 움직이고 삶의 방식이 어떠한지를 읽어내기 위함이다. 즉, 예를 들어, 봉사시설 건축의 프로그램 혹은 규모 등을 통해 인민들을 위해 제공하는 대중목욕탕, 이발소, 미용실 등의 주민위생 (이들은 소비시설이라기보다는 위생시설로 보는 편이 맞을듯하다)을 얼마나 체계적으로 공급하는 사회인지 살펴볼 수 있고, 소규모가 아닌 대규모 위주로 공급되는 식당시설을 통해 이들의 외식문화를 엿볼 수 있는 것이다. 또한, 지방에 공급되는 태양열 전지판과 풍력발전기가 있는 주택유형의 제안을 통해 (실제 실현되었는지는 미지수임에도 불구하고) 그들이 신 재생 에너지 등을 새로운 주택에 적용하고자 했던 노력을 읽어낼 수 있는 것이다.

결론적으로, 우리가 물리적인 공간을 통해서 최대한 북한 도시를 객관적으로 보고자 하는 것처럼, 북한 건축을 바라볼 때에도 이를 최대한 중립적인 자세로 이해하고자 해야 할 것이다. 간혹, 북한의 인민대학습당이라던지 류경호텔과 같은 상징적인 건축을 북한 정권의 비합리적인 우월의식의 표출로 바라보는 경우가 있는데, 우리나라 역시 이러한 상징성을 가진 건물들은 얼마든지 많다. 결국 아직 북한 건축에 대한 이해가 부족한 이 시점에서는 일부의 건축을 통해 우리가 기존에 갖고 있던 북한 사회에 대한 선입견을 갖기 보다는, 오히려 최대한 많은 자료들을 테이블 위에 올려놓고 유형분석을 하는 노력이 필요한 때 이다. 지금은 그들의 낙후된 공법과 투박한 건축 디테일, 노후화된 시설들을 지적하며 상대적 우위에 있는 우리나라 건축의 우월함을 자랑할 때는 아니다. 이제는 사진에서 보이는 북한 건축의 겉모습이 아니라, 도면에서 보이는 북한 건축과 북한 사회의 모습을 이해할 때이다.

North Korean Typologies 412

CHRONOLOGY OF ARCHITECTURAL TYPOLOGY

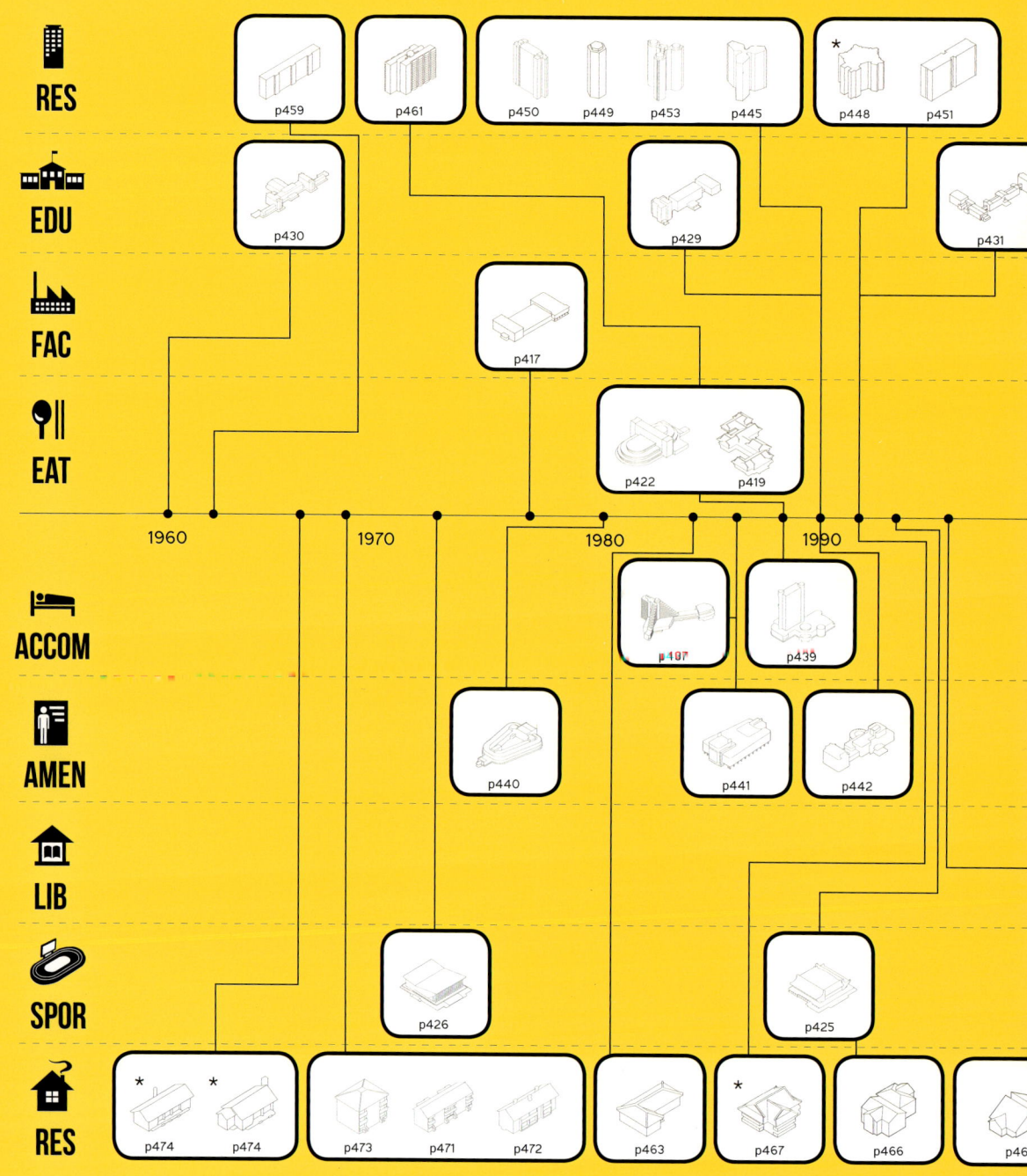

Architectural Typology

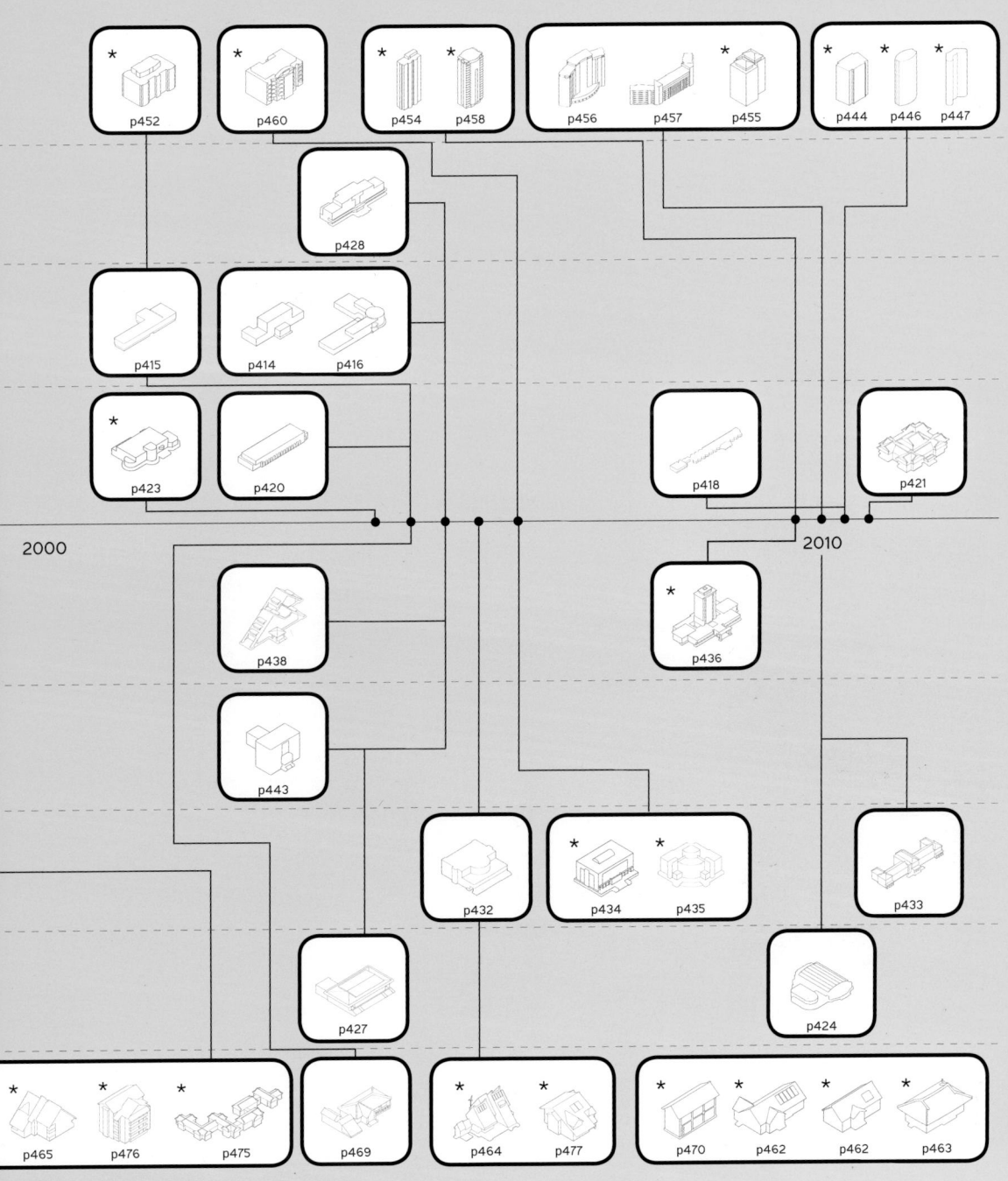

★ 계획안 (Proposal)　★★ 별도 표기외 출처 조선건축 (ref. Chosun Architecture unless noted)

RASON BASIC FOOD FACTORY

라선기초식품공장

Program : Factory
Location : Rason-Si
Building Area : 884.3m²
Gross Area : 3,000m²
Built Year : 2005

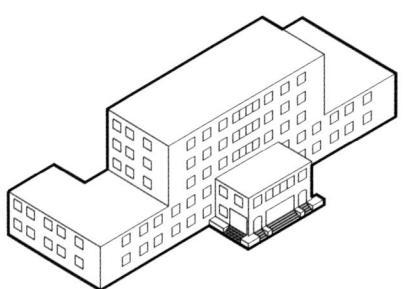

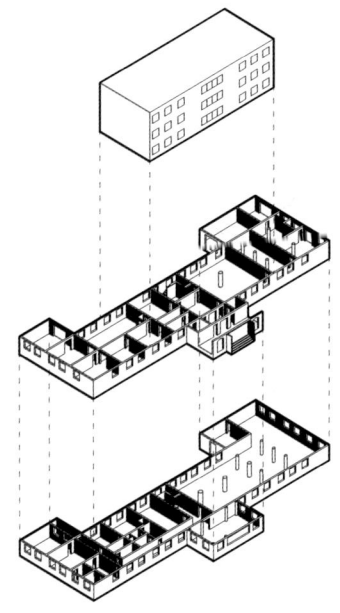

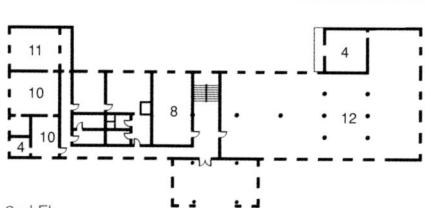

2nd Floor

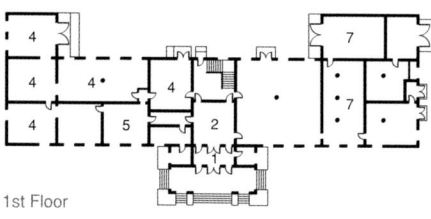

1st Floor

1 Entrance
2 Product Display Room
3 Sterilization Room
4 Storage
5 Salt Dissolusion Room
6 Storage
7 Product Withdrawal Room
8 Purified Salt Dry Grinding
9 Room
10 Incubation Room
11 Laboratory
12 Prototype making Room
   Fermentation Room

Architectural Typology

RAKWON CLOTHES FACTORY
락원피복공장

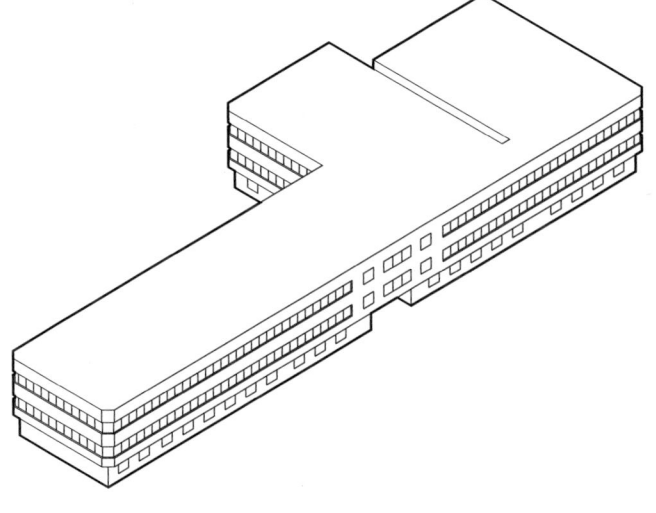

Program : Factory
Location : Pyongyang-Si
Building Area : 1,500m²
Gross Area : 3,000m²
Magazine Year : 2004

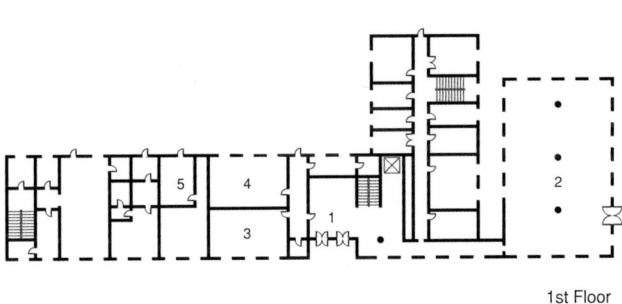

1st Floor

1 Entrance
2 Work Space
3 Interview Room
4 Preparation Room
5 Dining Room

RAJIN BREAD FACTORY
라진빵공장

Program : Factory
Location : Rason-Si
Building Area : 1,370m²
Gross Area : 2,500m²
Magazine Year : 2005

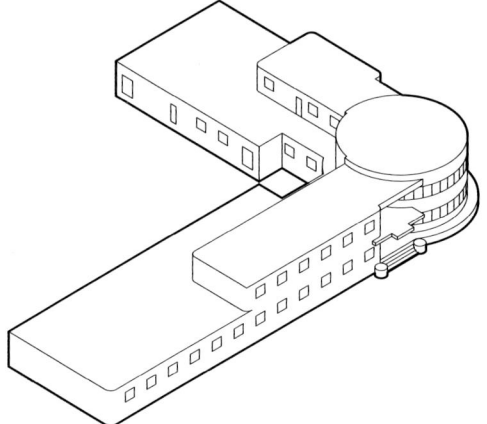

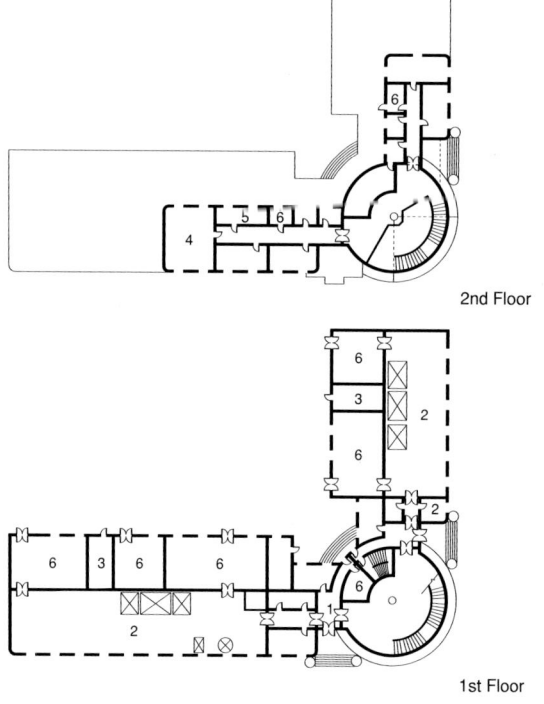

2nd Floor

1st Floor

1 Entrance
2 Bread Making Room
3 Fire Box
4 Dining Room
5 Kitchen
6 Storage

PYONGYANG FLOUR PROCESSING FACTORY

평양밀가루종합가공공장

Program : Factory
Location : Pyongyang-Si
Building Area : 5,673.94m²
Built Year : 1978

Standard Floor

1 Product Storage
2 Dough Molding Room
3 Dry Room
4 Packing Room

DAEDONGGANG BEER PUB
대동강맥주집

Program : Eatery
Location : Pyongyang-Si
Building Area : 1.937.3m²
Capacity : 1,000 Seats
Built Year : 1987
Renovated : 2010

1 Entrance
2 Drinking Hall
3 Beer Counter

TONGILGWAN

통일관

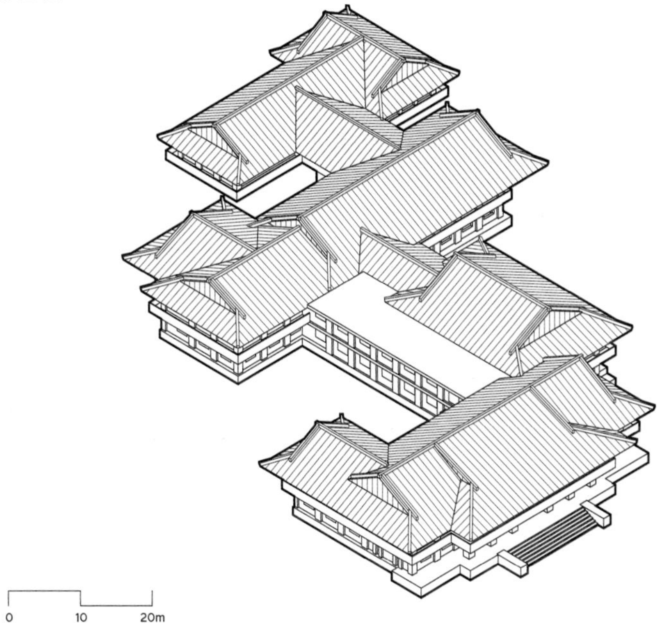

Program : Eatery
Location : Kaesong-Si
Building Area : 1,550m²
Gross Area : 3,100m²
Capacity : 500 Seats
Magazine Year : 1989

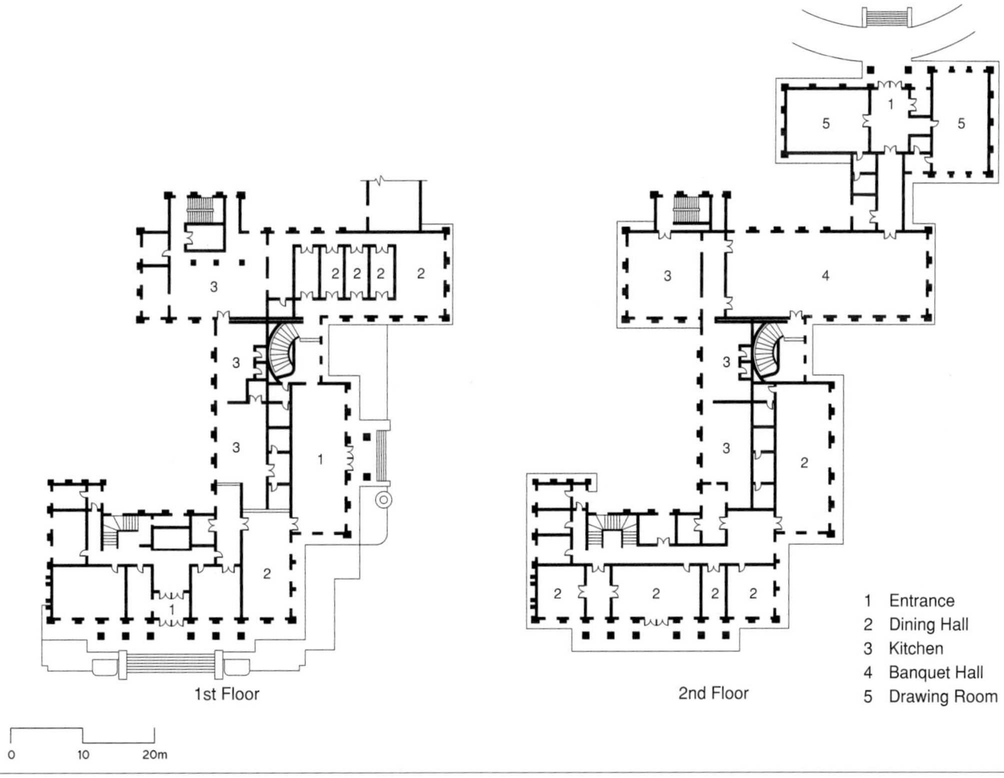

1st Floor

2nd Floor

1 Entrance
2 Dining Hall
3 Kitchen
4 Banquet Hall
5 Drawing Room

JINDALAE RESTAURANT

진달래식당

Program : Eatery
Location : Pyongyang-Si
Building Area : 900m²
Gross Area : 1,400m²
Magazine Year : 2005

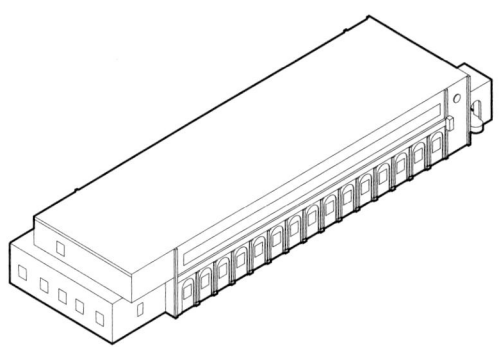

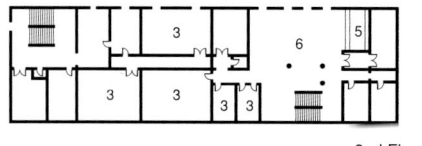

2nd Floor

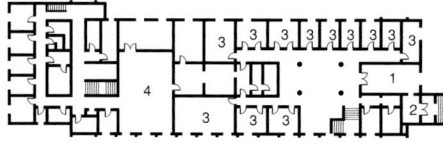

1st Floor

1 Entrance Hall
2 Ante-chamber
3 Dining Room
4 Kitchen
5 Counter
6 Dining Hall

HOERYONGGWAN

회령관

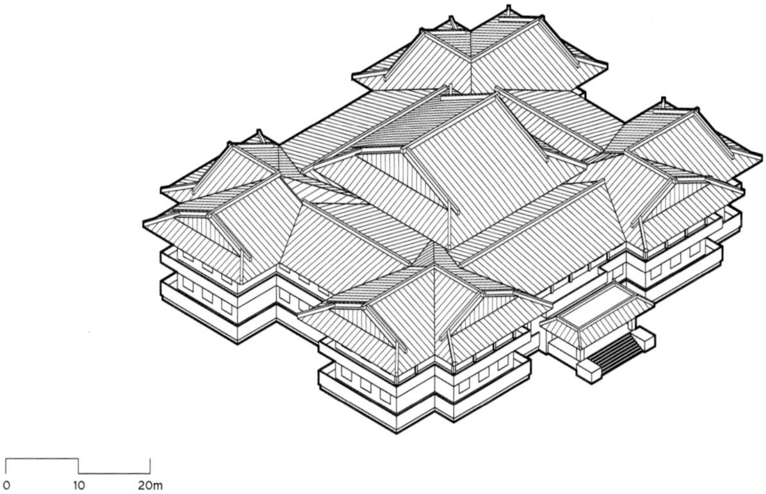

Program : Eatery
Location : Hoeryong-Si
Building Area : 2,100m²
Gross Area : 4,200m²
Capacity : 500 Seats
Magazine Year : 2012

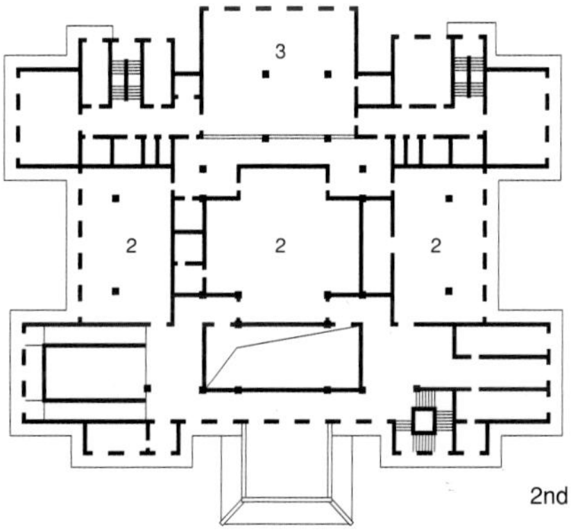

2nd Floor

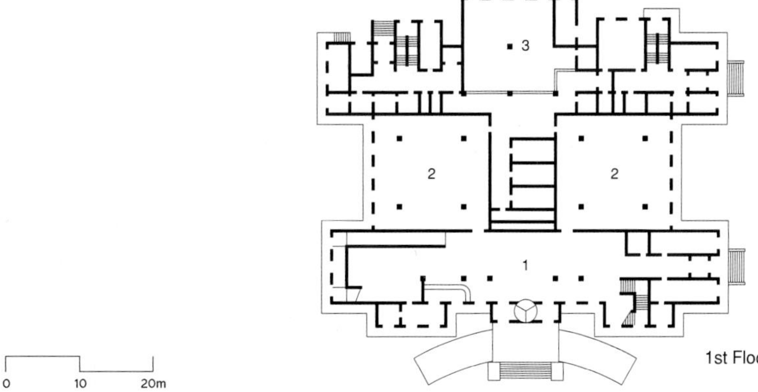

1st Floor

1 Entrance Hall
2 Dining Room
3 Kitchen

HYANGMALLU RESTAURANT

향만루식당

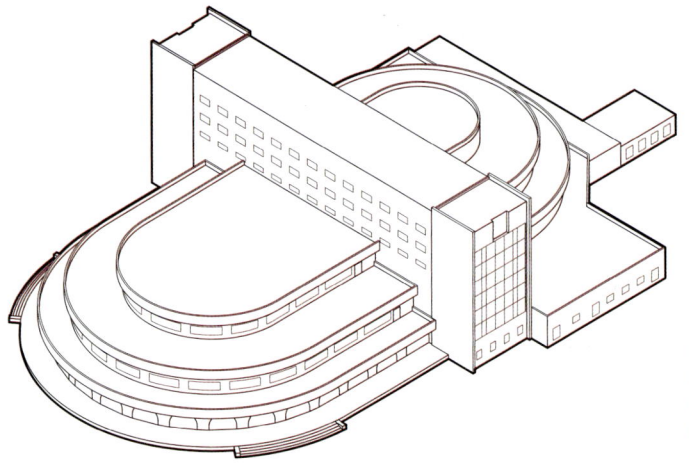

Program : Eatery
Location : Pyongyang-Si
Building Area : 5,653m²
Built Year : 1989

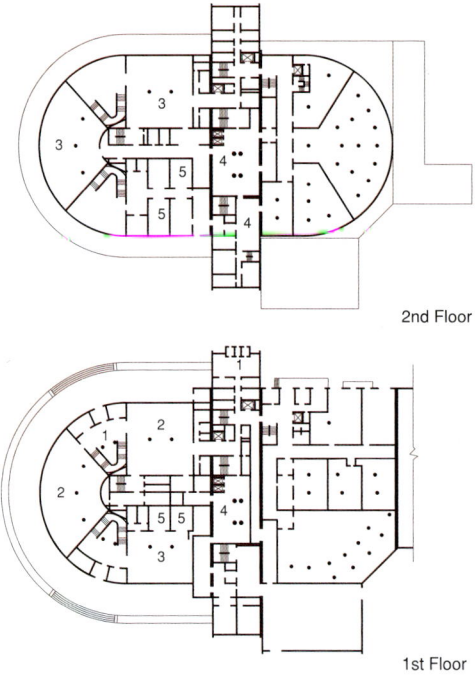

2nd Floor

1st Floor

1 Entrance Hall
2 Shop
3 Dining Room
4 Kitchen
5 Small Dining Room

RYONGCHEON NOODLE RESTAURANT

롱천국수집

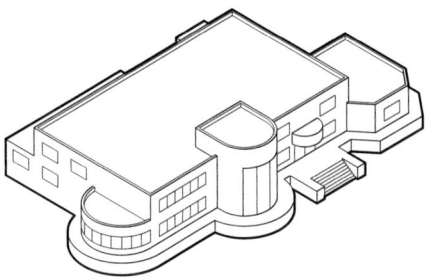

Program : Eatery
Proposal for Ryongcheon-Gun
Building Area : 380m²
Gross Area : 660m²
Magazine Year : 2004

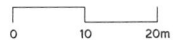

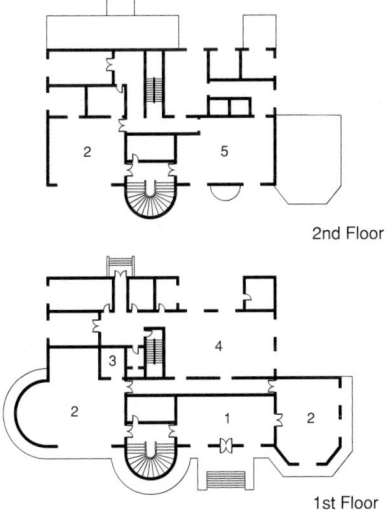

1 Entrance Hall
2 Dining Hall
3 Family Dining Room
4 Kitchen
5 Arcade

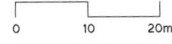

KIM IL-SUNG UNIVERSITY SWIMMING COMPLEX
김일성종합대학 수영장

Program : Sports Facility
Location : Pyongyang-Si
Building Area : 884.3m²
Gross Area : 3,000m²
Magazine Year : 2010

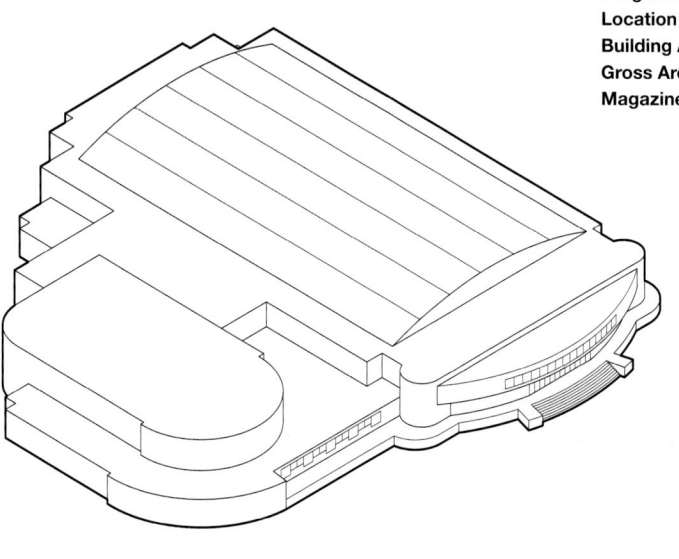

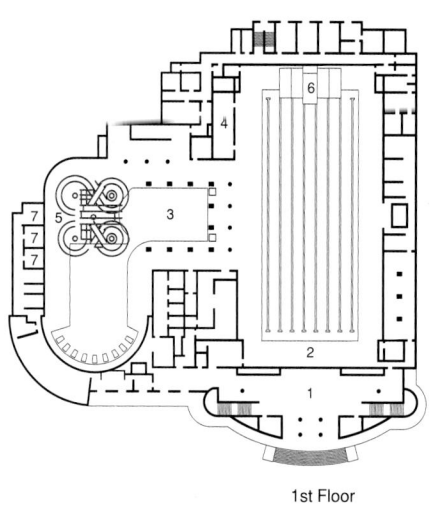

1st Floor

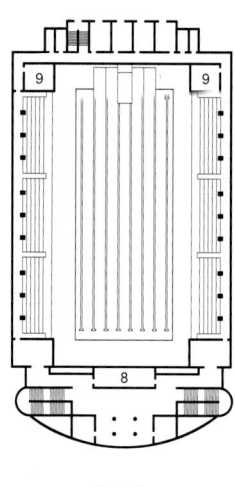

2nd Floor

1 Entrance Hall
2 Swimming Pool
3 Water Park
4 Therapy Room
5 Water Slide
6 Diving Board
7 Sauna
8 Drink Stand
9 Stand

Architectural Typology

TAEWOKNDO PALACE
태권도전당

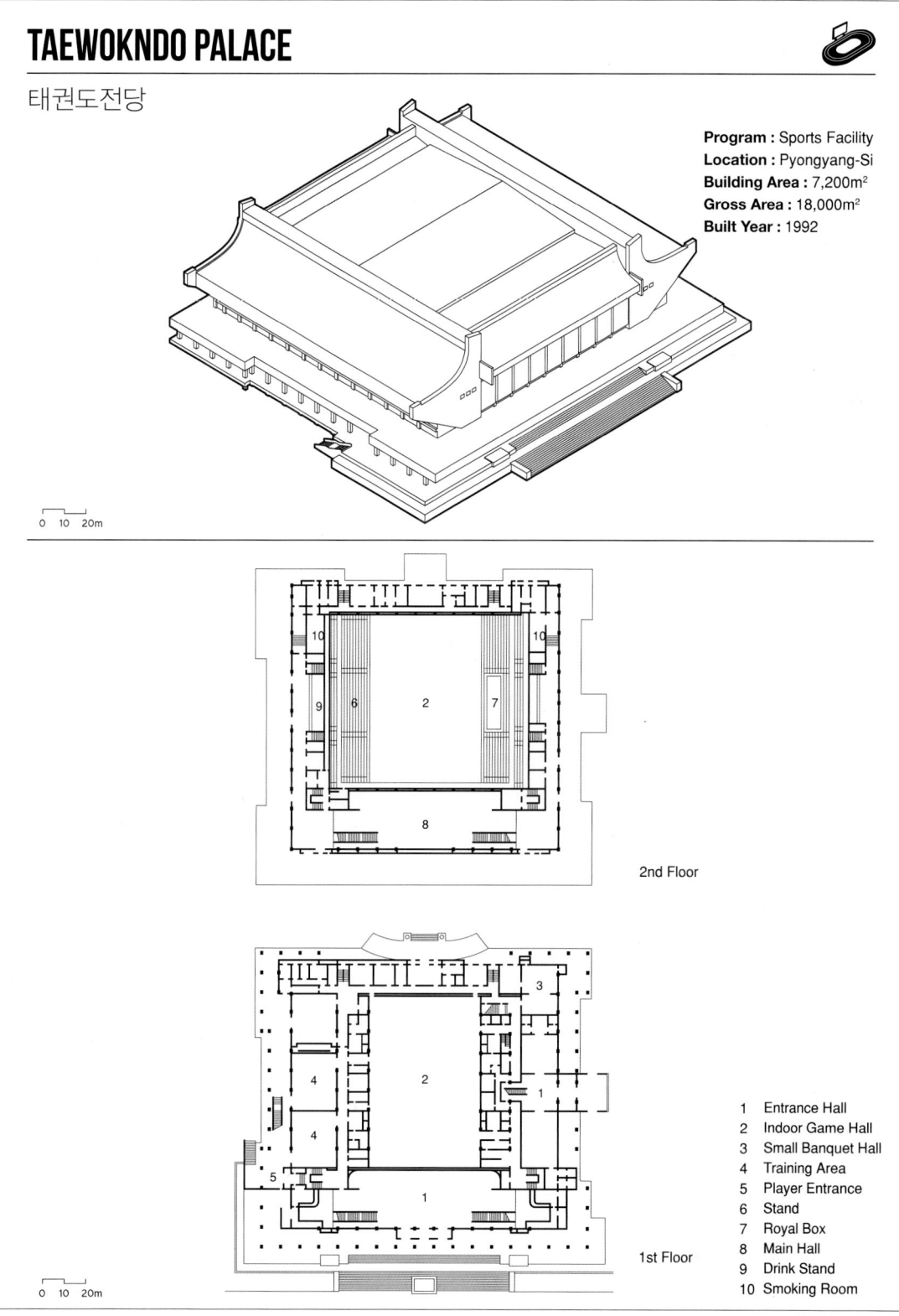

Program : Sports Facility
Location : Pyongyang-Si
Building Area : 7,200m²
Gross Area : 18,000m²
Built Year : 1992

2nd Floor

1st Floor

1 Entrance Hall
2 Indoor Game Hall
3 Small Banquet Hall
4 Training Area
5 Player Entrance
6 Stand
7 Royal Box
8 Main Hall
9 Drink Stand
10 Smoking Room

PYONGYANG SPORTS CENTER

평양체육관

Program : Sports Facility
Location : Pyongyang-Si
Building Area : 20,000m²
Gross Area : 70,000m²
Built Year : 1973

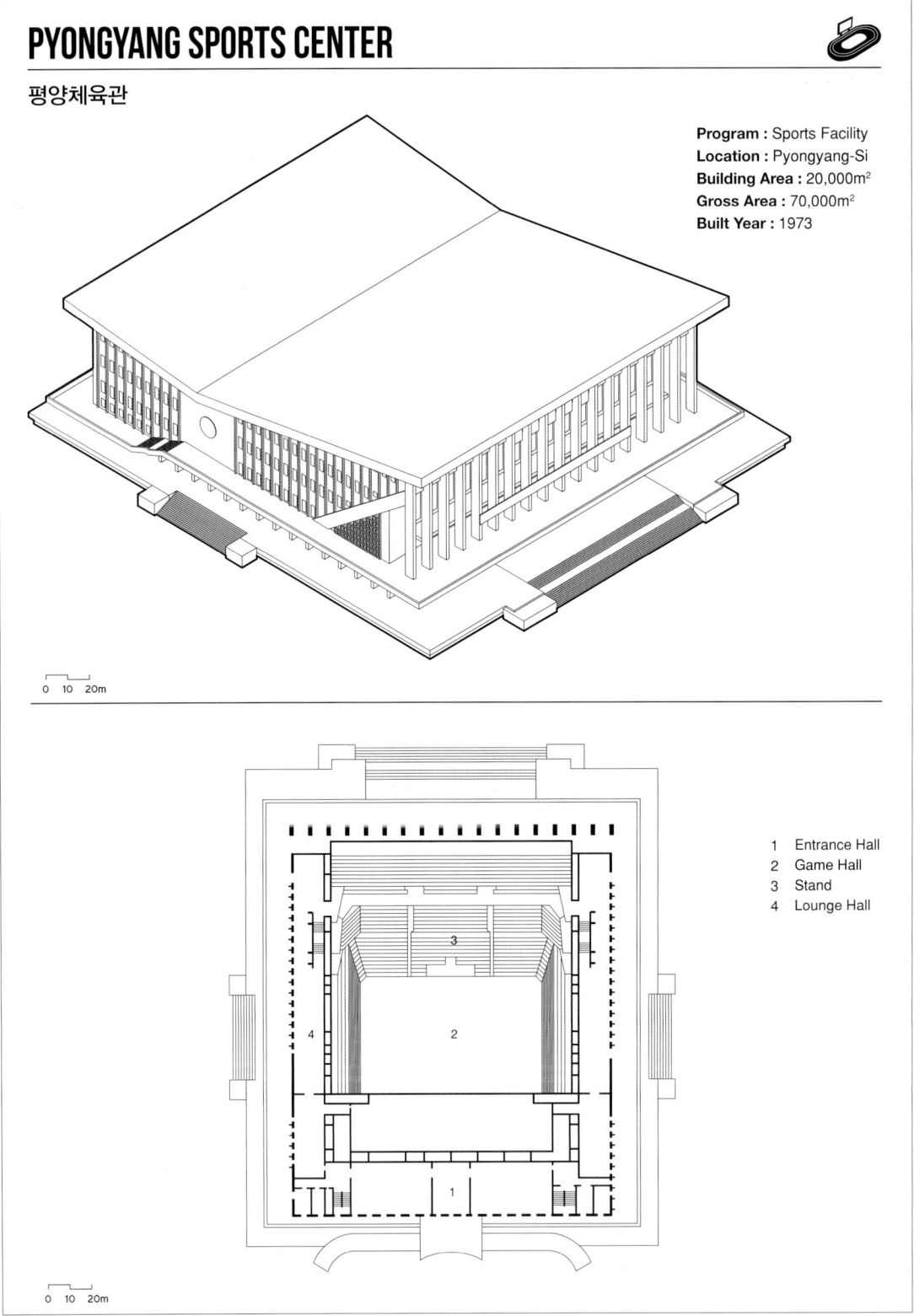

1 Entrance Hall
2 Game Hall
3 Stand
4 Lounge Hall

Architectural Typology   427

KIM CHAEK UNIVERSITY OF TECHNOLOGY SPORTS CENTER
김책공업종합대학 체육관

Program : Sports Facility
Location : Pyongyang-Si
Building Area : 6,184.3m²
Built Year : 2006

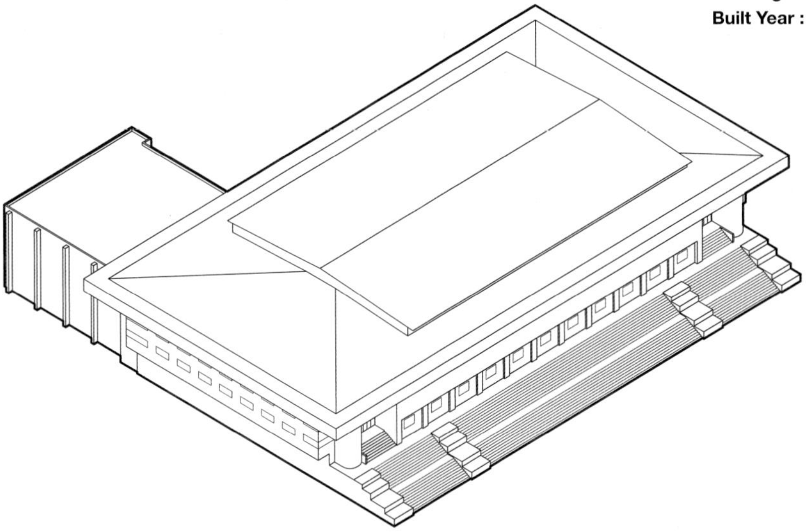

0 10 20m

1 Game Hall
2 Stage
3 Boxing / Ping Pong Training Area
4 Basketball Training Area

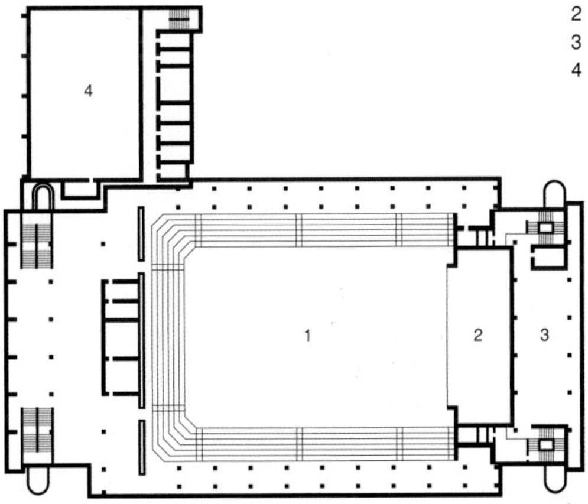

2nd Floor

0 10 20m

RAJIN KINDERGARTEN
라진유치원

Program : Institution
Location : Rason-Si
Building Area : 650m²
Gross Area : 2,175.3m²
Magazine Year : 2005

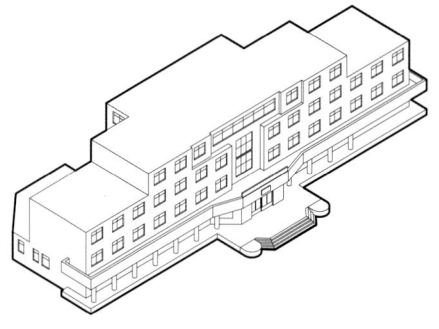

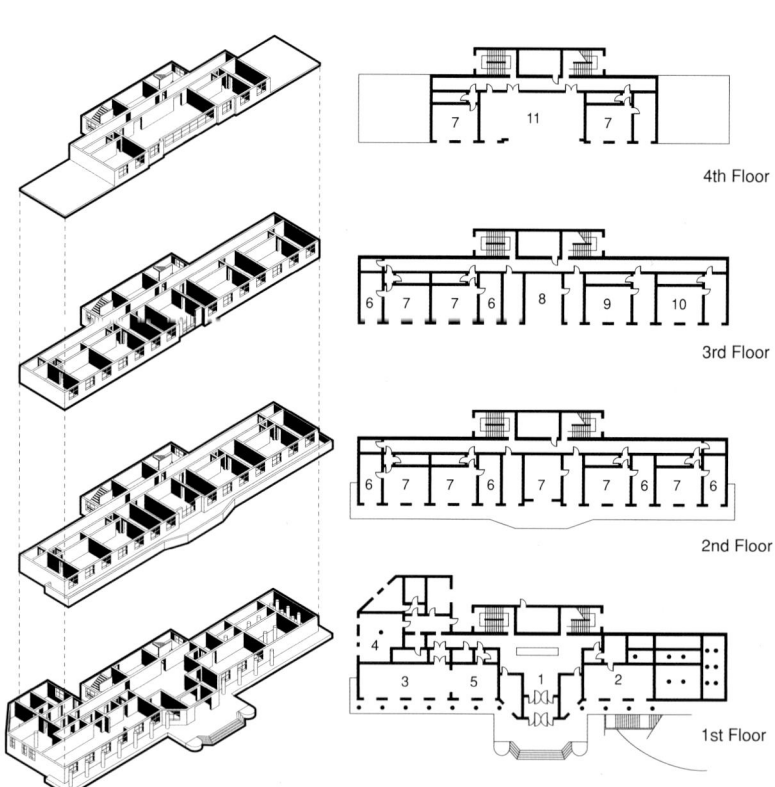

4th Floor
3rd Floor
2nd Floor
1st Floor

1 Entrance Hall
2 Swimming Pool
3 Dining Room
4 Kitchen
5 Principal's Office
6 Sleeping Room
7 Educational Room
8 Great Father Kim Il-Sung Educational Room
9 Father Kim Jung-Il Educational Room
10 Mother Kim Jung-Suk Educational Room
11 Play Room

Architectural Typology

KAESEONG 1ST MID-HIGH SCHOOL
개성제1고등중학교

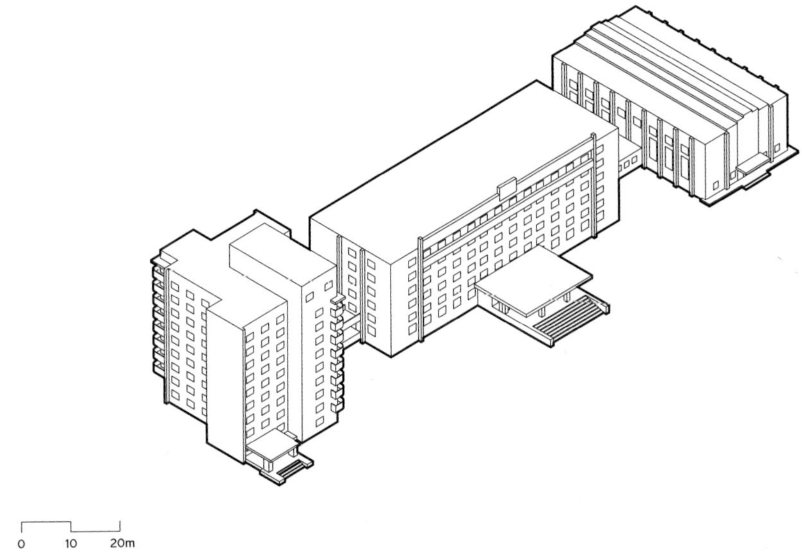

Program : Institution
Location : Kaesong-Si
Building Area: 9,000m²
Site Area : 35,000m²
Magazine Year : 1990

1 Entrance
2 Classroom
3 Gymnasium
4 Sleeping
5 Study Room
6 Laboratory

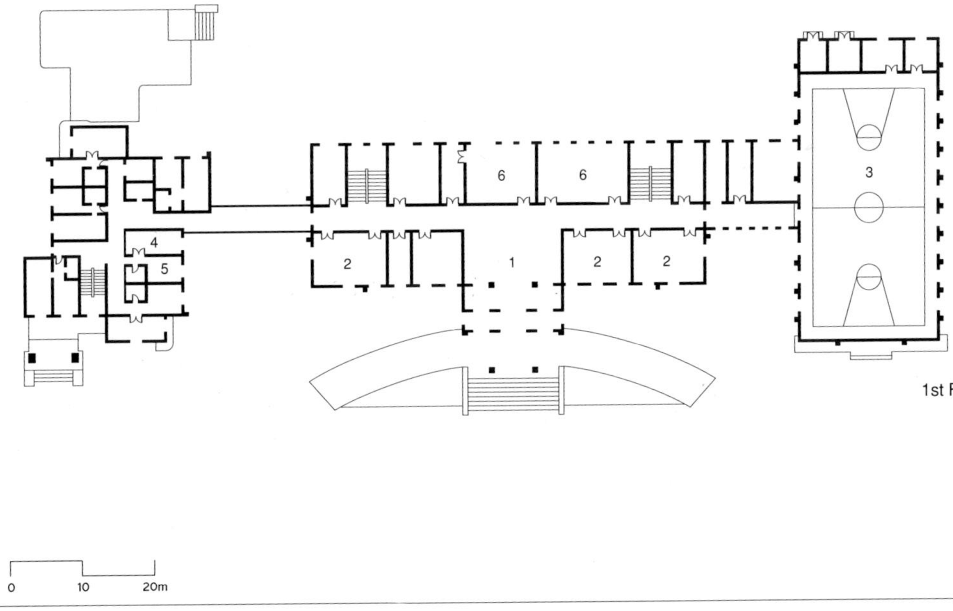

1st Floor

North Korean Typologies 430

KIM JUNG-SUK UNIVERSITY
김정숙사범대학

Program : Institution
Location : Hyesan-Si
Building Area : 7,850m²
Built Year : 1961

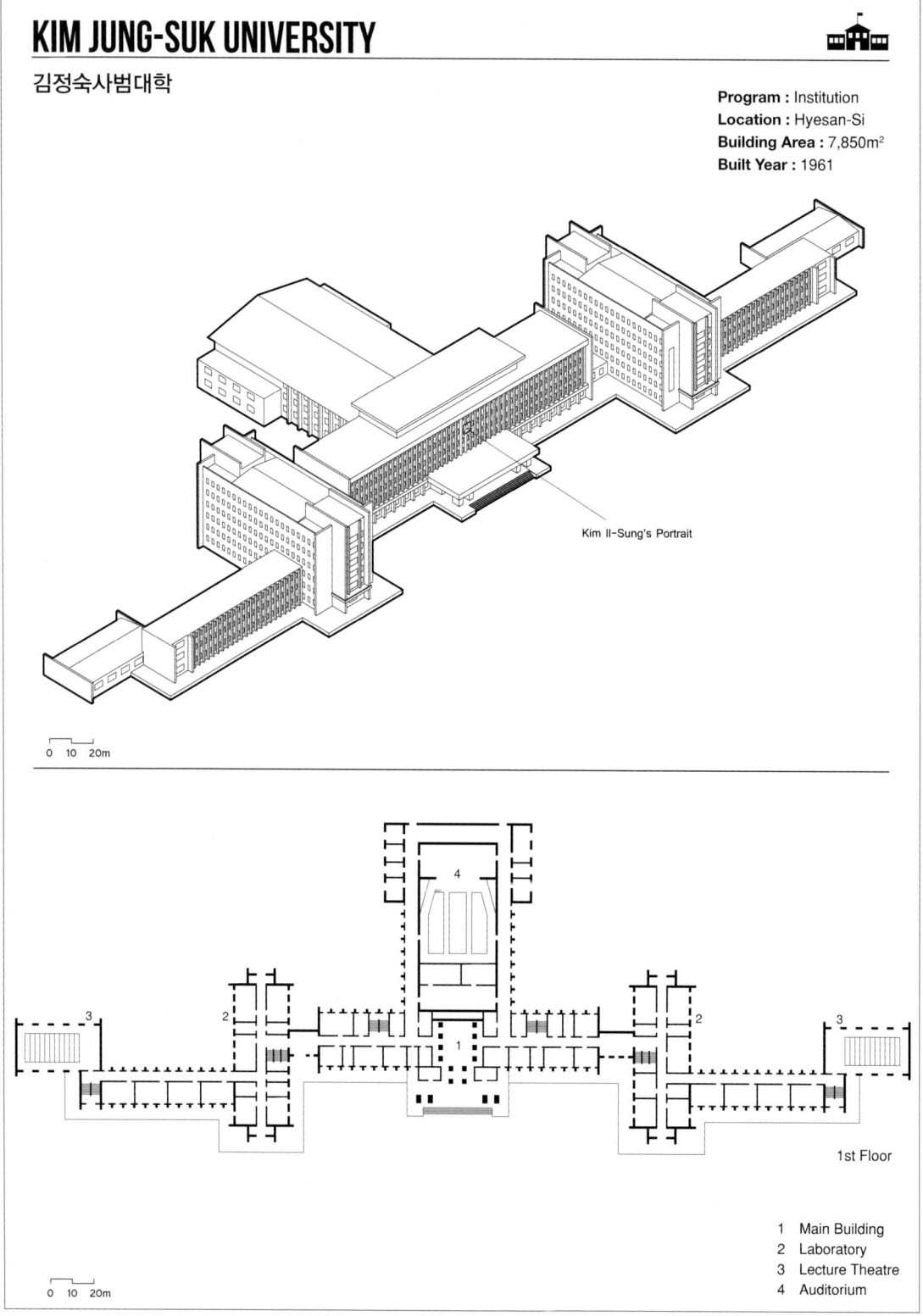

Kim Il-Sung's Portrait

1st Floor

1 Main Building
2 Laboratory
3 Lecture Theatre
4 Auditorium

CHANGDUK SCHOOL

창덕학교

Program : Institution
Location : Pyongyang-Si
Building Area: 3,804m²
Magazine Year : 1991

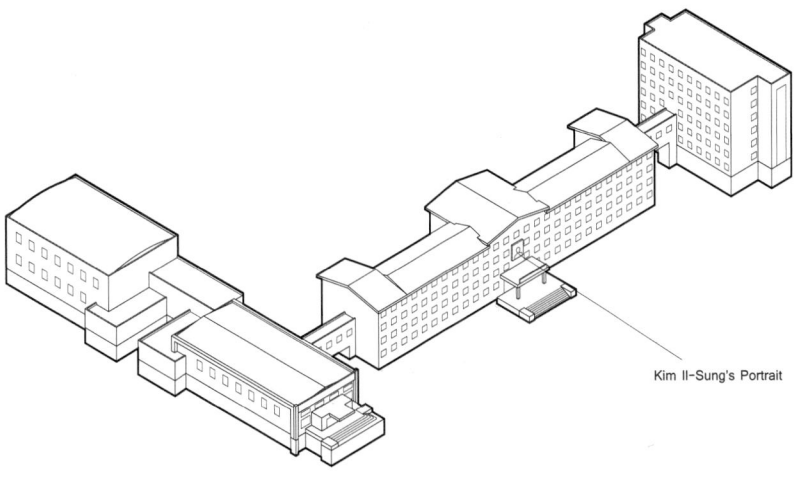

Kim Il-Sung's Portrait

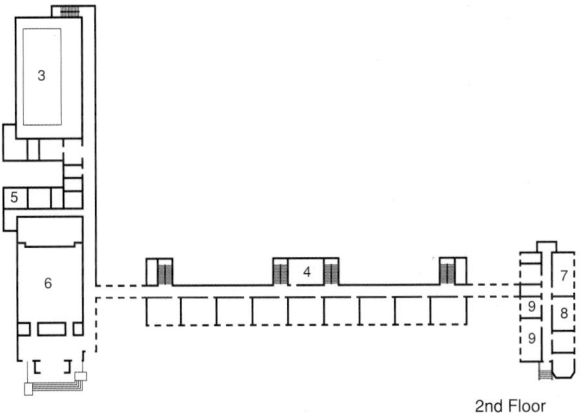

2nd Floor

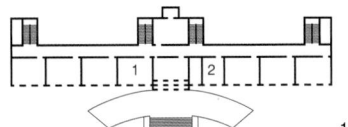

1st Floor

1 Classroom
2 Principal's Office
3 Swimming Pool
4 Sewing Practice Room
5 Music Room
6 Auditorium
7 Automobile Laboratory
8 Physics Laboratory
9 Circle Room

KIM CHAEK UNIVERSITY OF TECHNOLOGY DIGITAL LIBRARY
김책공업종합대학 전자도서관

Program : Library
Location : Pyongyang-Si
Building Area : 4,000m²
Gross Area : 16,000m²
Built Year : 2006

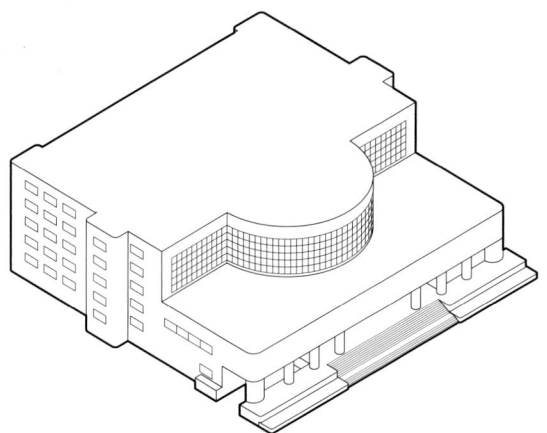

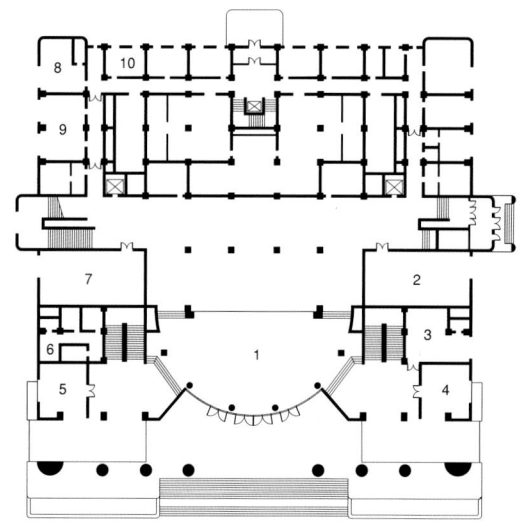

1st Floor

1 Main Hall
2 Discussion Digital Reading Room
3 Scholarship Exchange Discussion Room
4 Scholarship Reading Room
5 International Exchange Room
6 International Communication Room
7 Professor/Doctor Digital Reading Room
8 Kitchen
9 Dining Room
10 Data Compiling Room

KIM IL-SUNG UNIVERSITY DIGITAL LIBRARY
김일성종합대학 전자도서관

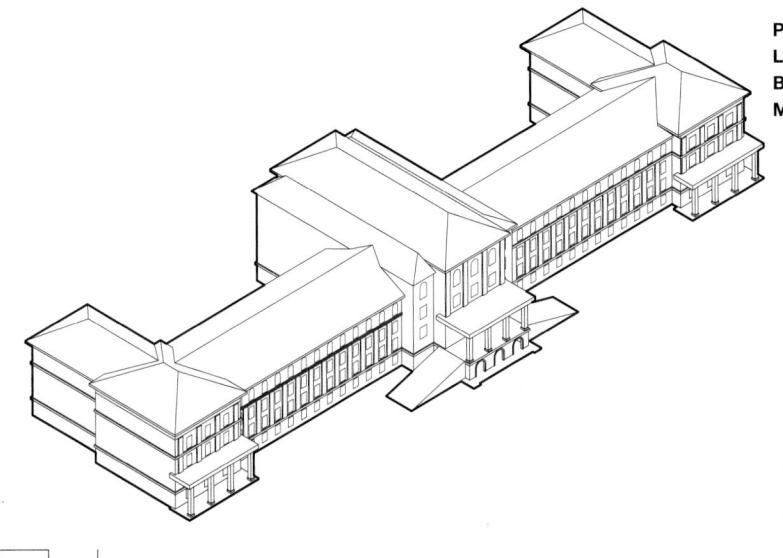

Program : Library
Location : Pyongyang-Si
Building Area: 3,360.27m²
Magazine Year : 2010

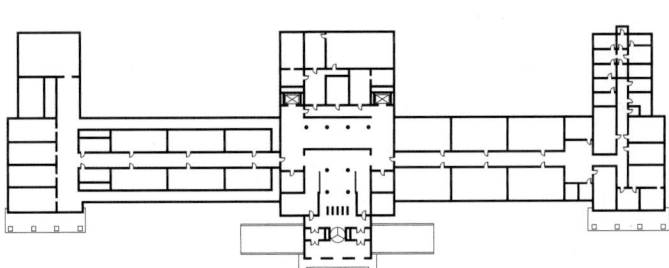

JIHYANG-2

지향-2

Program : Library
Proposal
Building Area : 1,225.3m^2
Gross Area : 4,901.2m^2
Magazine Year : 2007

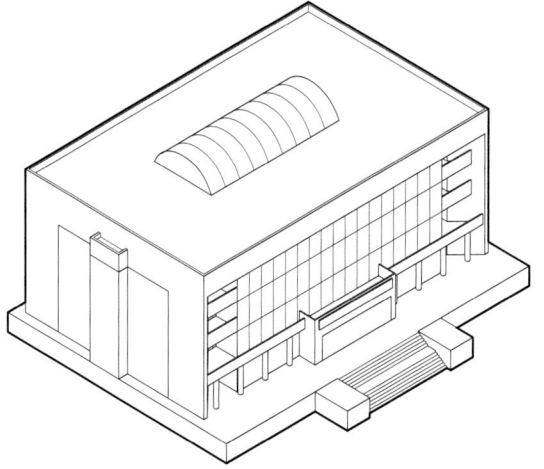

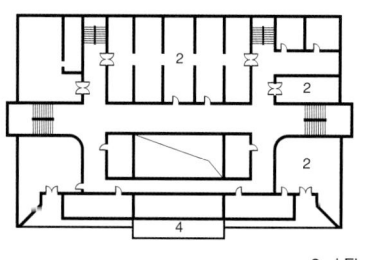

2nd Floor

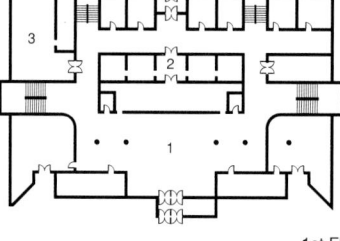

1st Floor

1 Entrance Hall
2 Library
3 Auditorium
4 Balcony

TAMGOO

탐구

Program : Library
Proposal
Building Area: 872.19m²
Gross Area : 2,616.57m²
Magazine Year : 2007

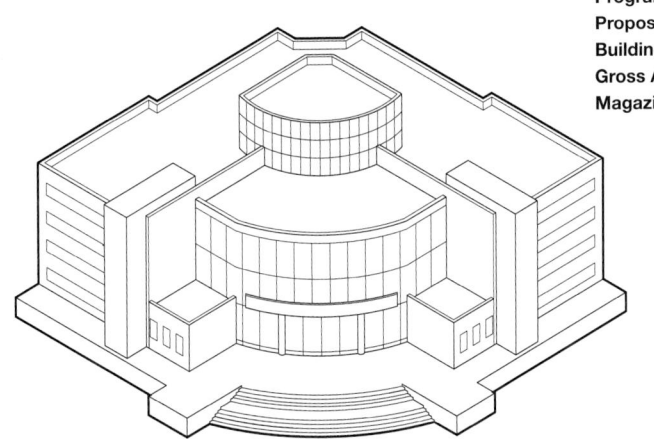

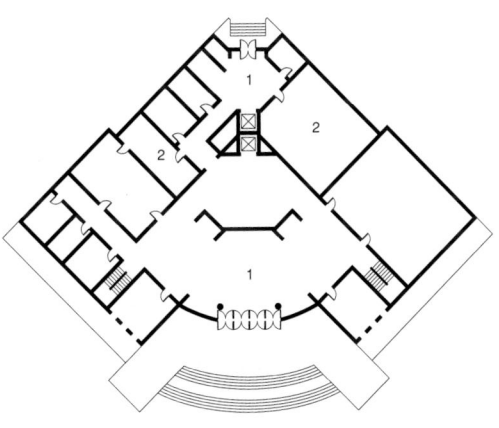

1st Floor

1 Entrance Hall
2 Library

North Korean Typologies

436

SEOKTAP HOTEL
석탑호텔

Program : Accomodation
Proposal
Building Area : 9,700m²
Gross Area : 38,000m²
Magazine Year : 2008

0 10 20m

2nd Floor

1st Floor

1 Entrance Hall
2 Souvenir Shop
3 Regional Product Shop
4 Grocery Shop
5 Bathroom
6 Regular Dining Room
7 Public Dining Room
8 Kitchen
9 Storage
10 Changing Room
11 Shower Room
12 Water Park
13 Movie Theater
14 Inner Courtyard

HYANGSAN HOTEL

향산호텔

Program : Accomodation
Location : Hyangsan-Gun
Building Area: 4,420.6m²
Built Year : 1986

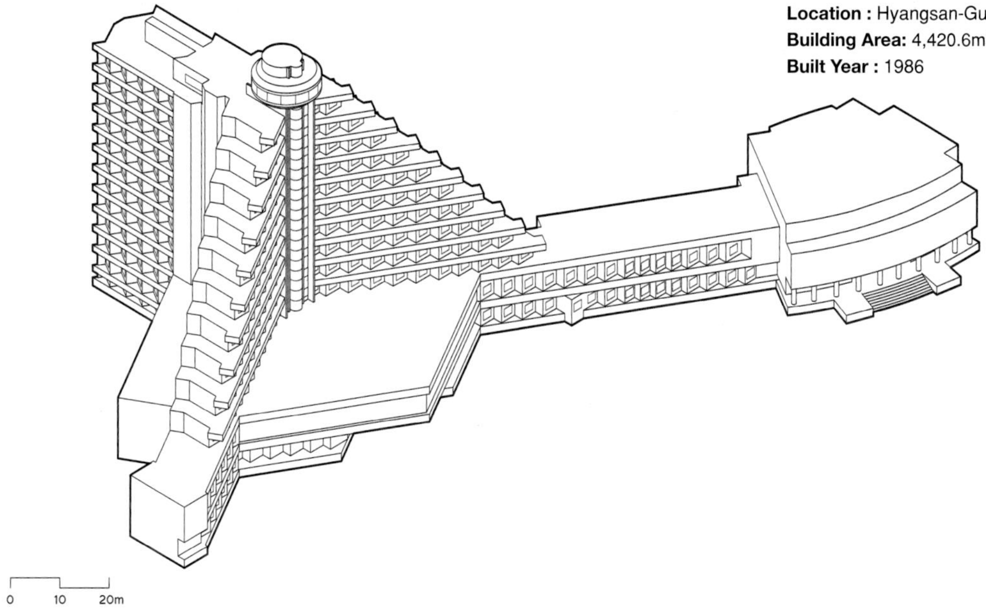

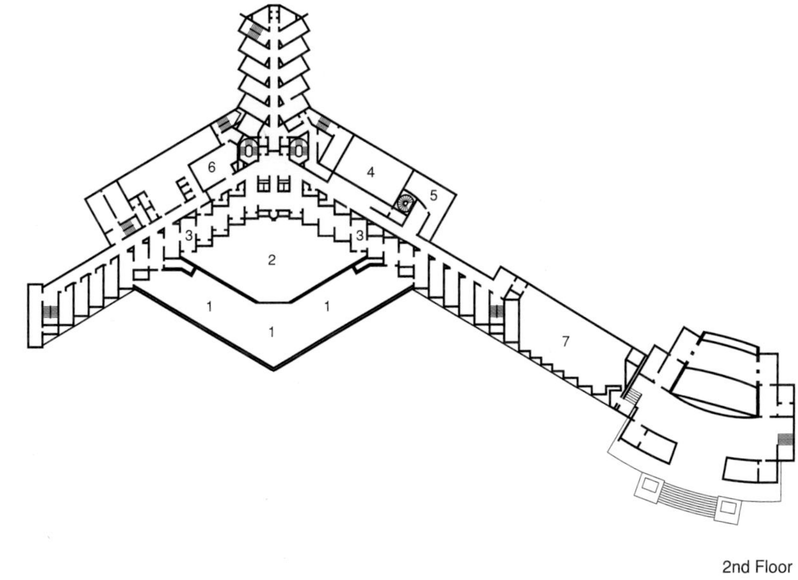

2nd Floor

1 Banquet Hall
2 Void
3 Balcony Dining Room
4 Small Theater
5 Shop
6 Small Dining Room
7 Arcade

SAMJIYON 1 INN

삼지연1려관

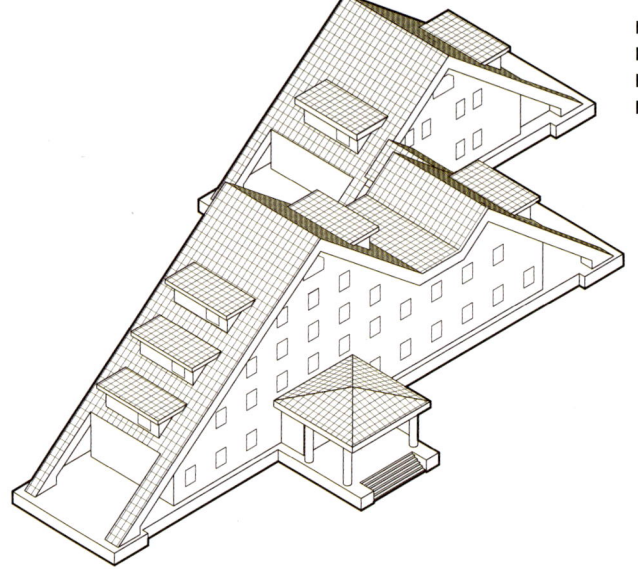

Program : Accomodation
Location : Samjiyon-Gun
Building Area : 706.4m²
Magazine Year : 2005

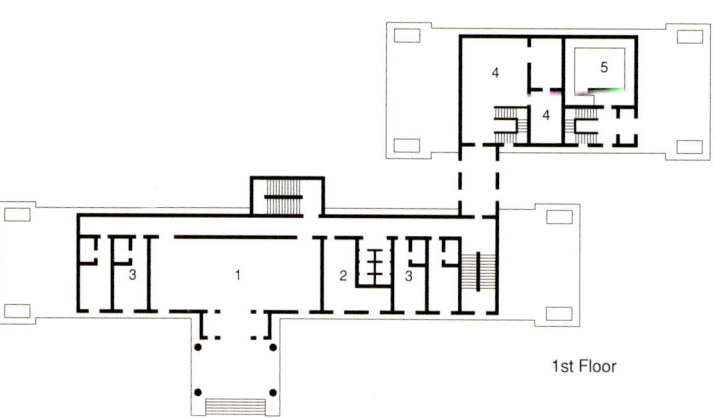

1st Floor

1 Entrance Hall
2 Office
3 Guest Room
4 Dining Hall
5 Kitchen

CHONGNYON HOTEL

청년호텔

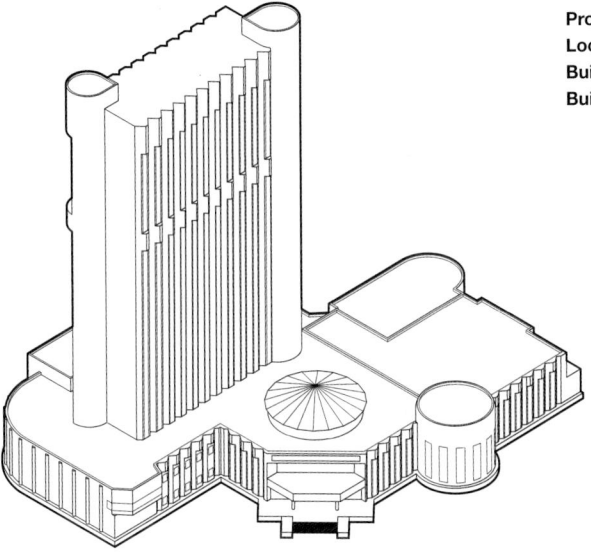

Program : Accomodation
Location : Pyongyang-Si
Building Area: 6,015.59m²
Built Year : 1989

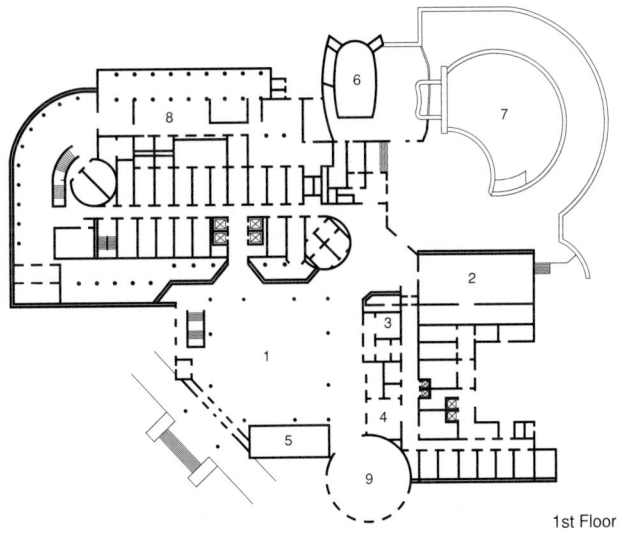

1st Floor

1 Main Hall
2 Dining Room
3 Floor-sitting style Chosun Restaurant
4 Western-style Chosun Restaurant
5 Cafe

6 Indoor Swimming Pool
7 Outdoor Swimming Pool
8 Ball Room
9 Circular Dining Room

MUNSUWON

문수원

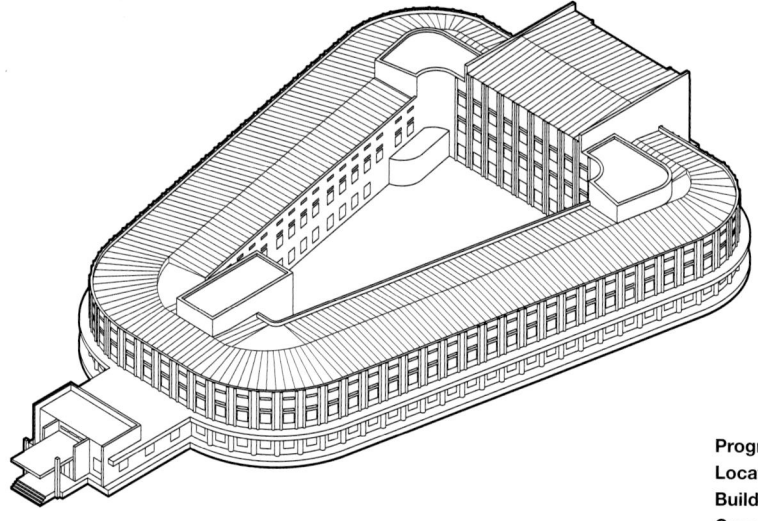

Program : Public Amenity
Location : Pyongyang-Si
Building Area : 3,500m²
Gross Area : 7,000m²
Capacity : 500
Built Year : 1982

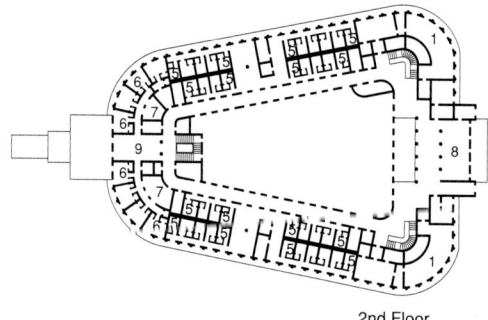

2nd Floor

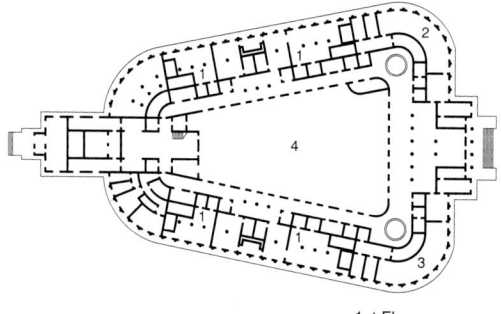

1st Floor

1 Public Bath
2 Barbershop
3 Beauty Parlor
4 Courtyard
5 Individual Bath
6 Family Bath
7 Massage Therapy
8 Room
9 Drinnk Stand
　Gymnasium

Architectural Typology

PYONGYANG 1ST DEPARTMENT STORE
평양제1백화점

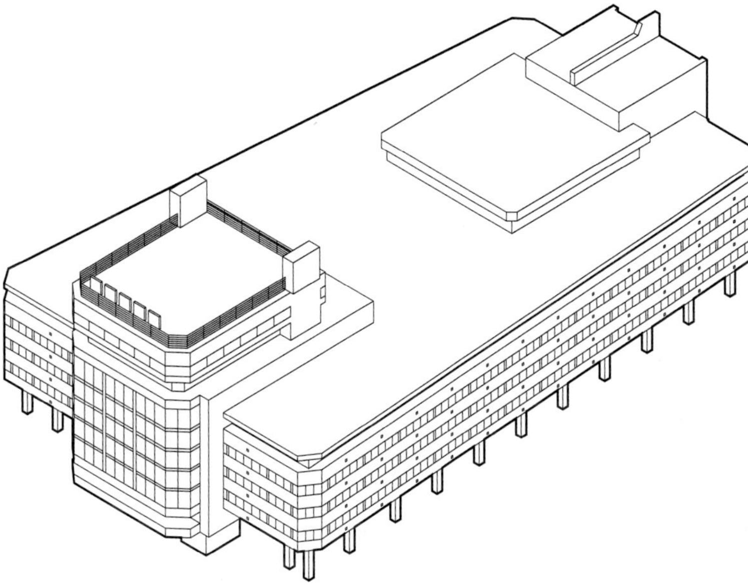

Program : Public Amenity
Location : Pyongyang-Si
Building Area: 5,000m²
Gross Area : 40,000m²
Built Year : 1980's

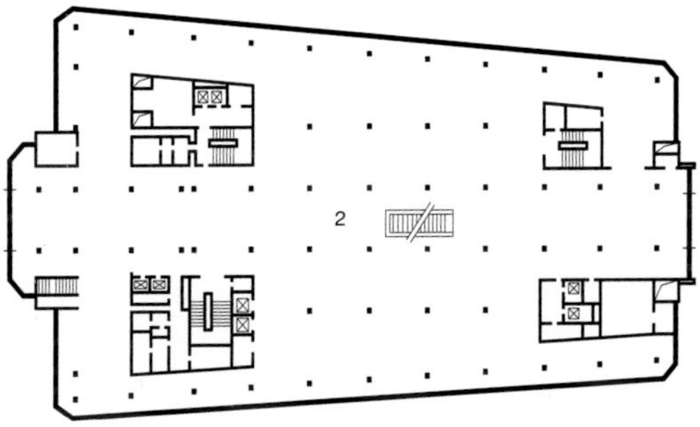

2nd Floor

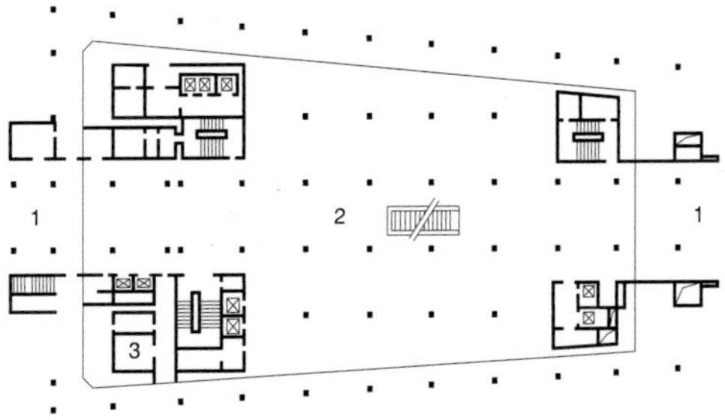

1st Floor

1 Entrance
2 Shopping Hall
3 Children's Care Room

EUNDUKWON

은덕원

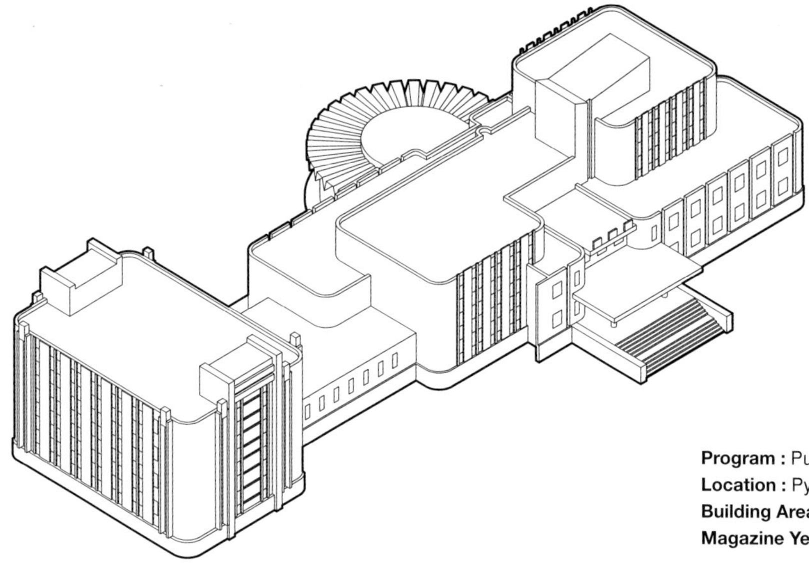

Program : Public Amenity
Location : Pyongyang-Si
Building Area : 1,400m²
Magazine Year : 1990

0 10 20m

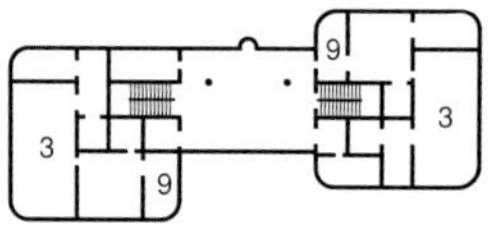

3rd Floor

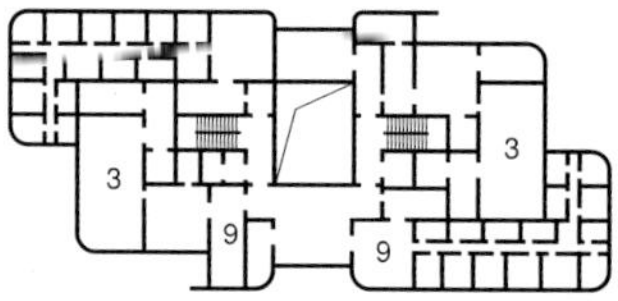

2nd Floor

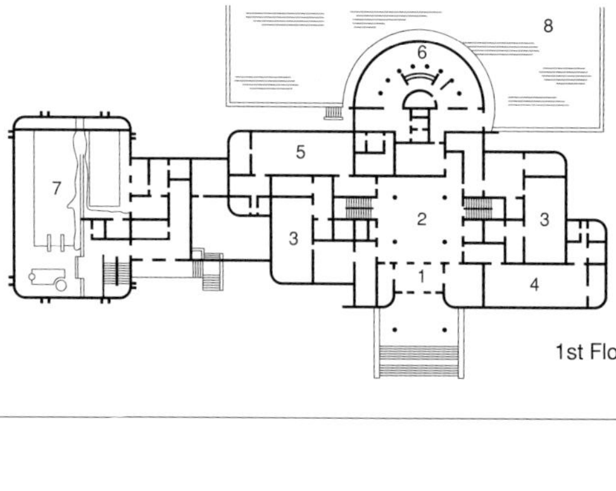

1st Floor

1 Entrance
2 Main Hall
3 Public Bath
4 Barber Shop
5 Beauty Parlor
6 Cafe
7 Children's Pool
8 Artificial Pond and Fountatin
9 Massage Room

0 10 20m

Architectural Typology

RASON-SI STORE
라선시직매점

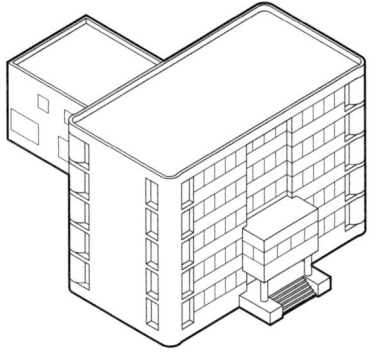

Program : Public Amenity
Location : Rason-Si
Building Area: 511m²
Gross Area : 2,055m²
Magazine Year : 2005

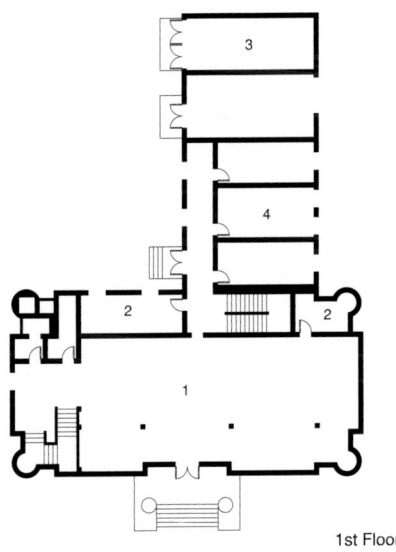

1st Floor

1 Shopping Hall
2 Storage
3 Garage
4 Office

URBAN RESIDENCE PROPOSAL

도시 살림집

Program : Urban Residence
Proposal for Pyongyang-Si
Building Area : 6,080m²
Gross Area : 94,240m²
Unit Area : 98.2m²
Number of Family : 992
Number of Floors : 10~18
Magazine Year : 2011

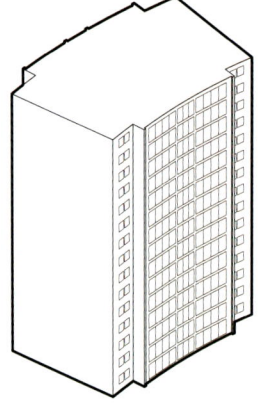

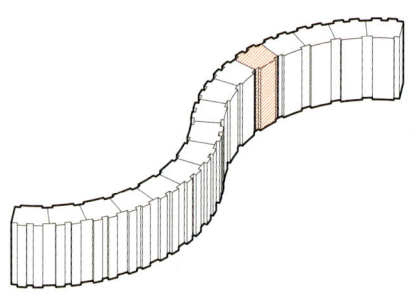

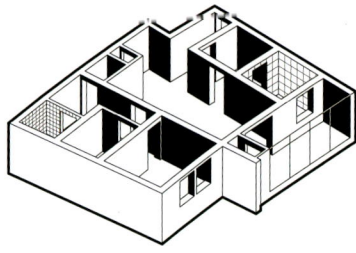

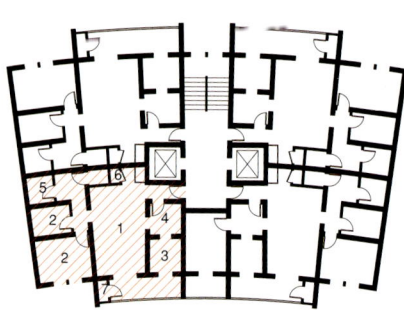

1 Living Room
2 Room
3 Kitchen
4 Dining Room
5 Bathroom
6 Storage
7 Kimchi Storage

Architectural Typology

TYPE WINDMILL
바람개비형 살림집

Program : Urban Residence
Location : Pyongyang-Si
Building Area : 1,395.7m²
Gross Area : 36,288.2m²
Unit Area : 101.4m²
Number of Family : 312
Number of Floors : 26
Magazine Year : 1990

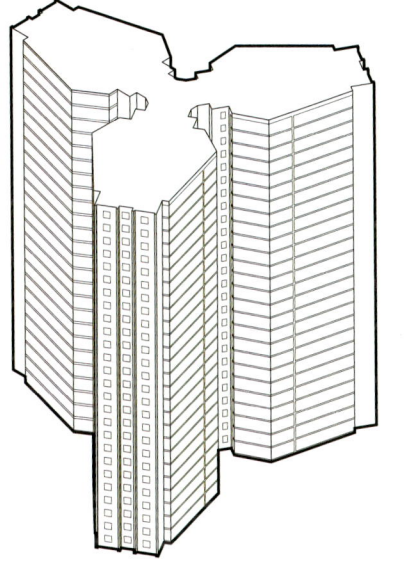

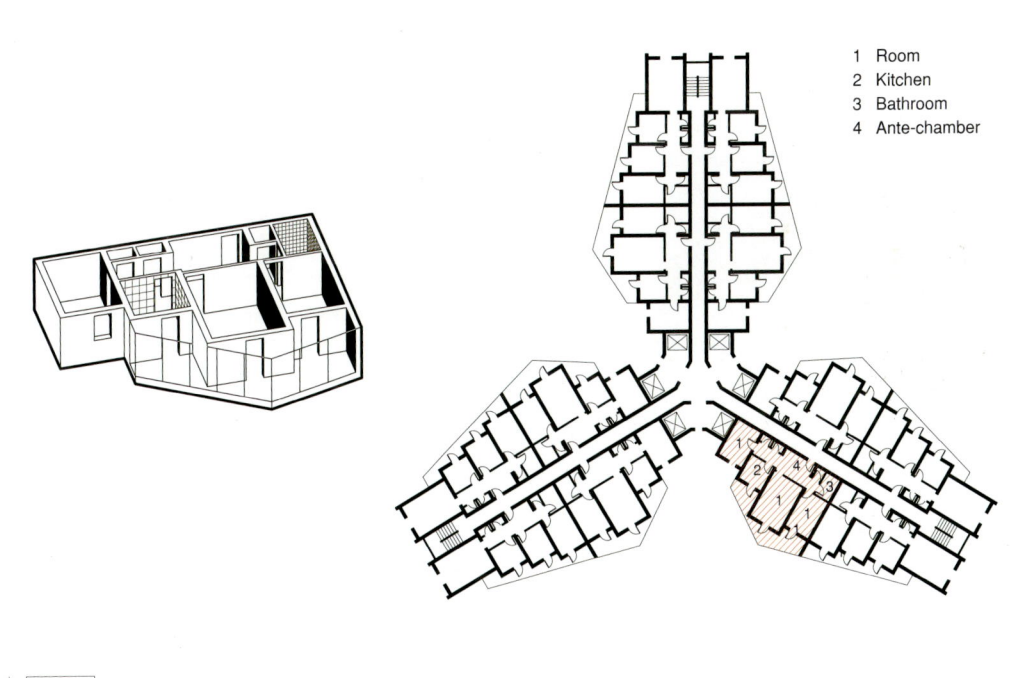

1 Room
2 Kitchen
3 Bathroom
4 Ante-chamber

URBAN RESIDENCE PROPOSAL
도시 살림집

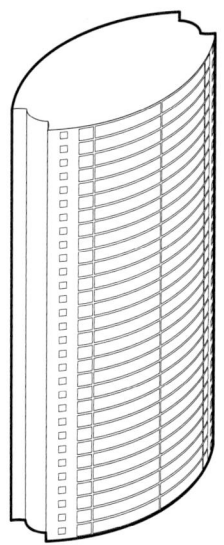

Program : Urban Residence
Proposal for Pyongyang-Si
Building Area : 640m²
Gross Area : 19,200m²
Unit Area : 106.67m²
Number of Family : 180
Number of Floors : 30
Magazine Year : 2011

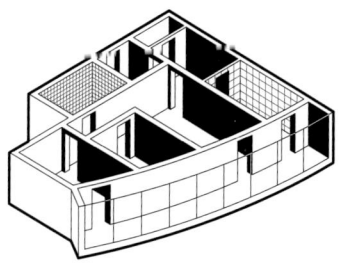

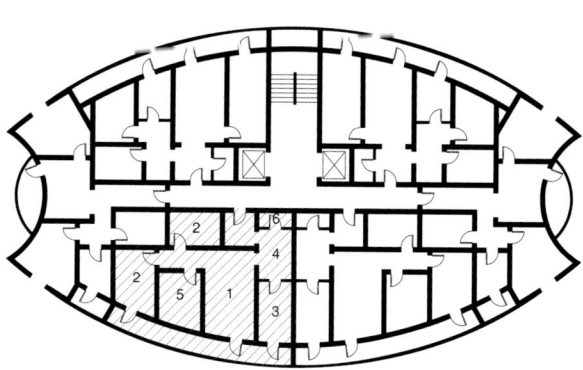

1 Living Room
2 Room
3 Kitchen
4 Dining Room
5 Bathroom
6 Storage

URBAN RESIDENCE PROPOSAL
도시 살림집

Program : Urban Residence
Proposal for Pyongyang-Si
Building Area : 1,120m²
Site Area : 50,400m²
Unit Area : 112m²
Number of Family : 450
Number of Floors : 45
Magazine Year : 2011

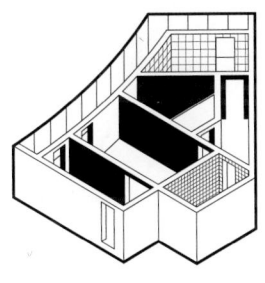

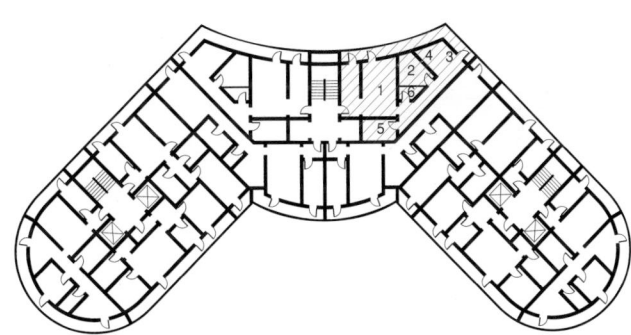

1 Living Room
2 Room
3 Kitchen
4 Dining Room
5 Bathroom
6 Storage

YONGHAEGONG RESIDENCE

용해공 살림집

Program : Urban Residence
Proposal for Chunlima-Gun
Building Area : 2,476.2m²
Gross Area : 15,480m²
Unit Area : 68m²
Number of Family : 140
Number of Floors : 6~8
Magazine Year : 1991

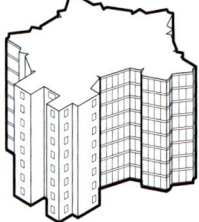
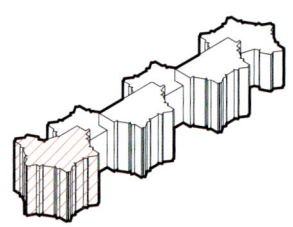

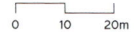

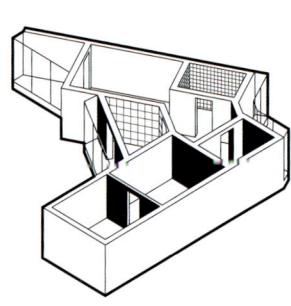
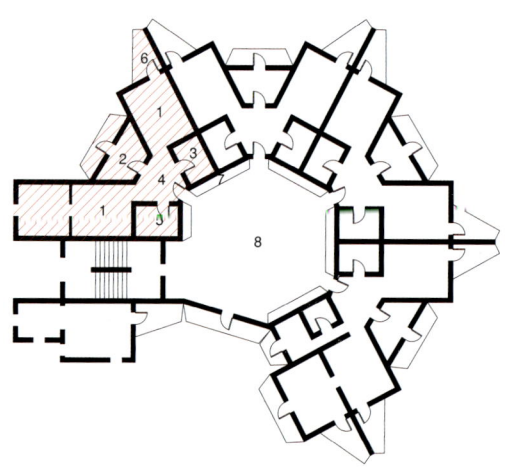

1 Room
2 Kitchen
3 Bathroom
4 Ante-chamber
5 Storage
6 Balcony
7 Flower Stand
8 Communal Lounge

TYPE HEXAGON

6각형 살림집

Program : Urban Residence
Location : Pyongyang-Si
Building Area : 463.8m²
Gross Area : 138,484m²
Unit Area : 96m²
Number of Family : 112
Number of Floors : 28
Magazine Year : 1990

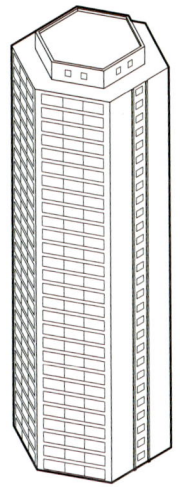

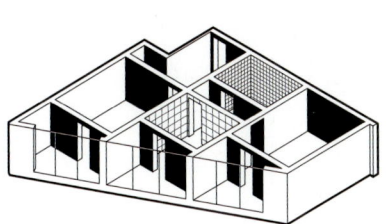

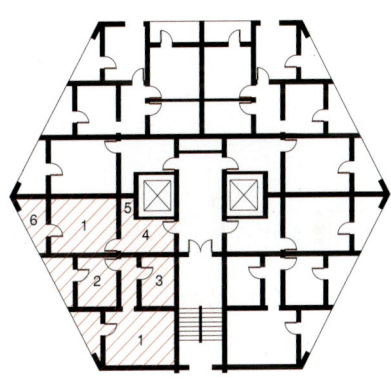

1 Room
2 Kitchen
3 Bathroom
4 Ante-chamber
5 Storage
6 Balcony

BUKSAE DISTRICT RESIDENCE BLOCK 44

북새지구 살림집 44호동

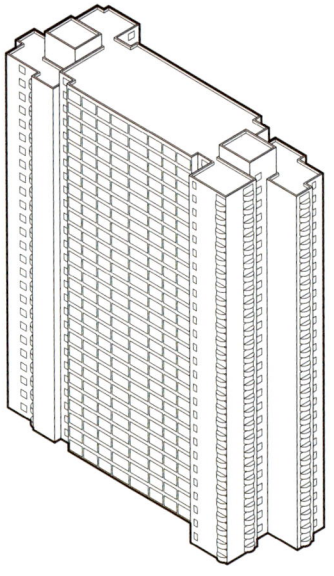

Program : Urban Residence
Location : Pyongyang-Si
Building Area : 974.6m²
Gross Area : 25,339.6m²
Unit Area : 108.66m²
Number of Family : 200
Number of Floors : 25
Magazine Year : 1990

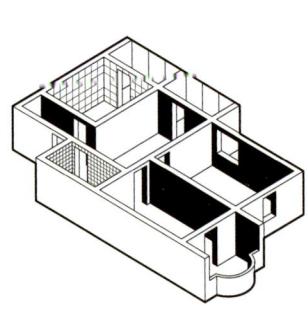

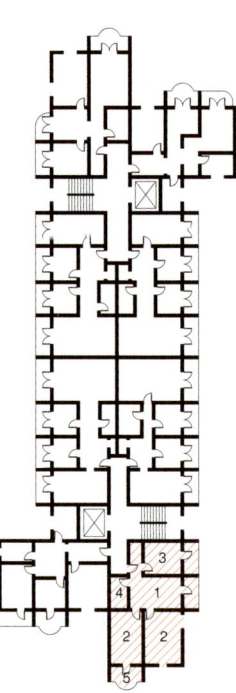

1 Living Room
2 Room
3 Kitchen
4 Bathroom
5 Balcony

Architectural Typology

BONGHWA STREET RESIDENCE
봉화거리 살림집

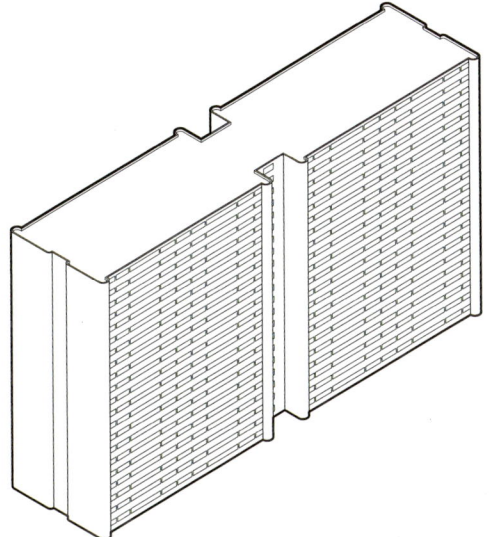

Program : Urban Residence
Location : Pyongyang-Si
Building Area : 2,224m²
Gross Area : 57,824m²
Unit Area : 256.95m²
Number of Family : 208
Number of Floors : 26
Magazine Year : 1991

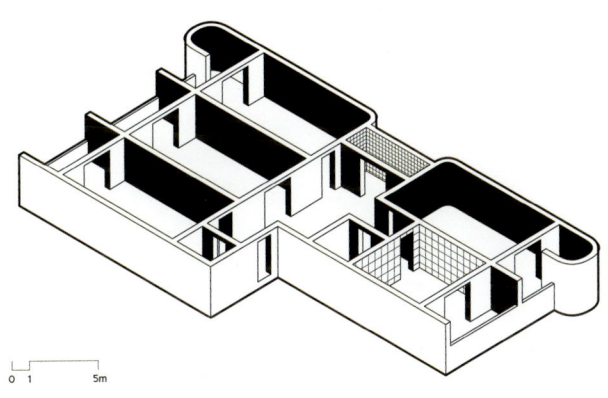

1   Room
2   Kitchen
3   Bathroom
4   Ante-chamber
5   Drawing Room

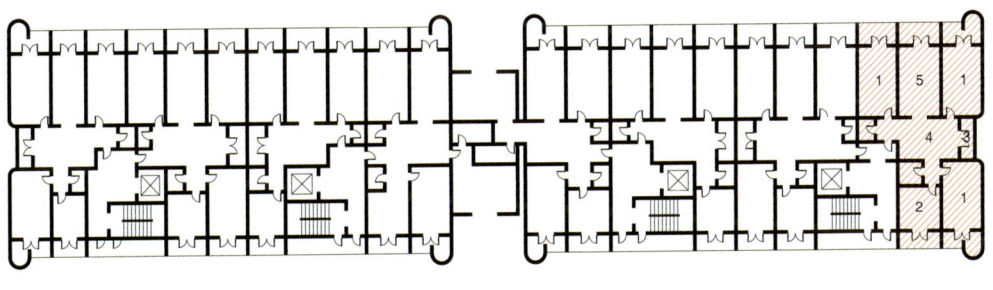

HANA-1

하나-1

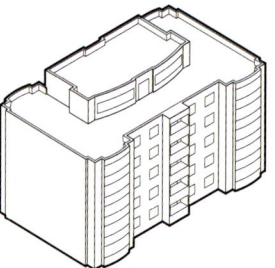

Program : Urban Residence Proposal
Building Area : 349.5m²
Gross Area : 1,747.5m²
Unit Area : 168.1m² / 181.4m²
Number of Family : varies
Number of Floors : 5
Magazine Year : 2004

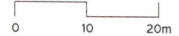

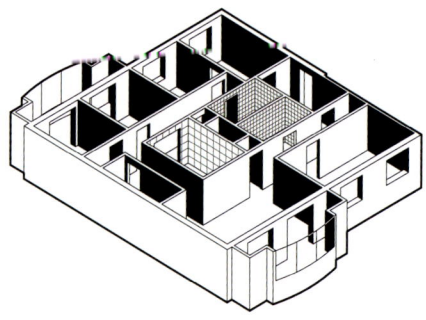

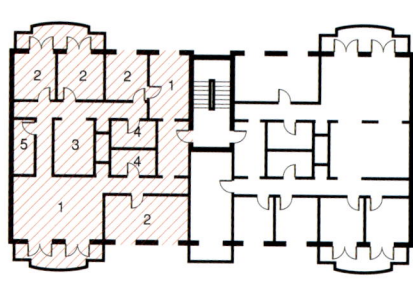

1 Living Room
2 Room
3 Kitchen
4 Bathroom
5 Storage

TYPE Y

Y형 살림집

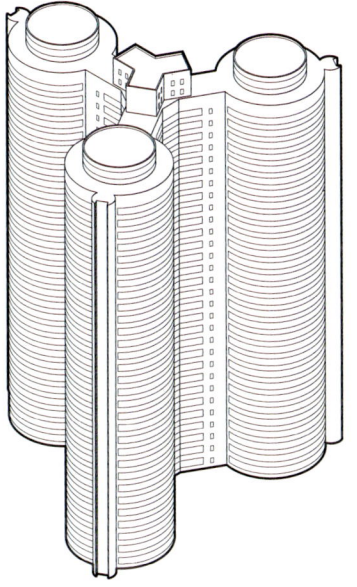

Program : Urban Residence
Location : Pyongyang-Si
Building Area : 1,889.3m²
Gross Area : 56,679m²
Unit Area : 98m²
Number of Family : 450
Number of Floors : 30
Magazine Year : 1990

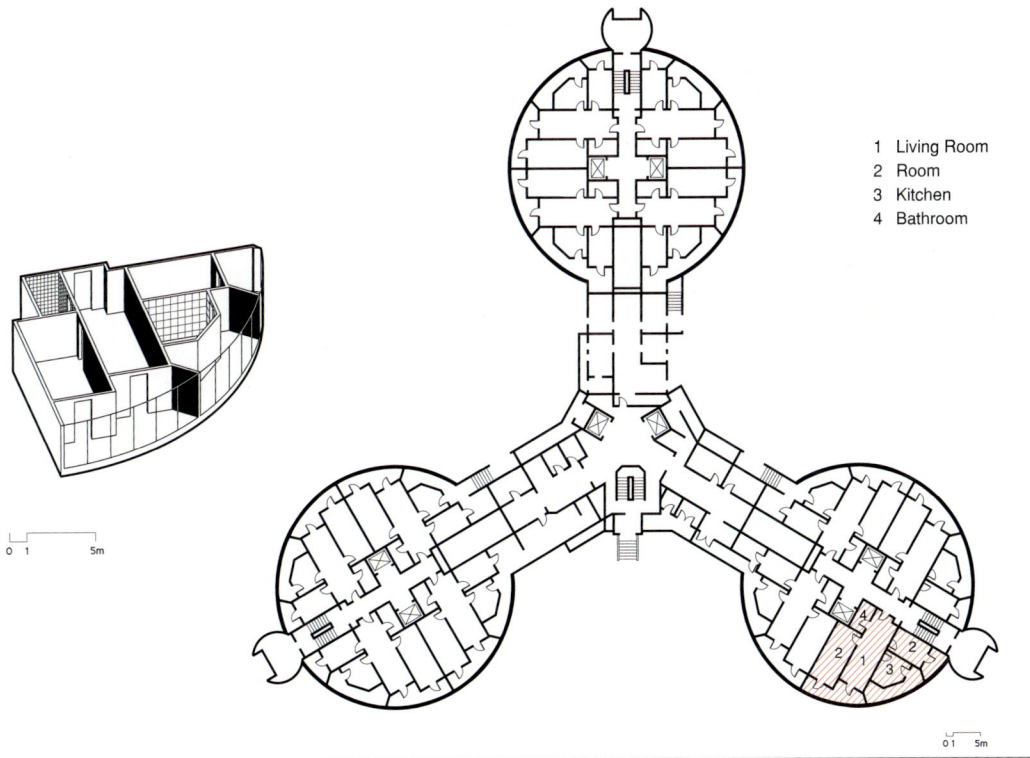

1 Living Room
2 Room
3 Kitchen
4 Bathroom

GWANGMYONG

광명

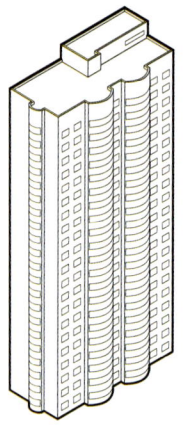

Program : Urban Residence
Proposal
Building Area : 326.9m²
Gross Area : 6,864.9m²
Unit Area : 159.9m²
Number of Family : 42
Number of Floors : 21
Magazine Year : 2009

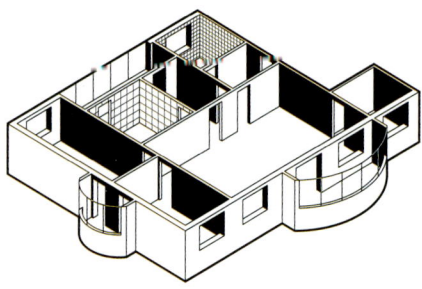

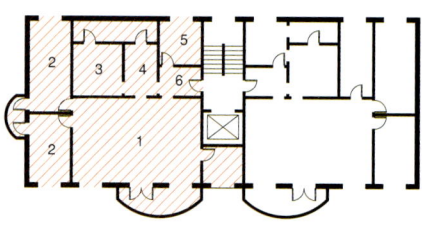

1 Living Room
2 Room
3 Kitchen
4 Dining Room
5 Bathroom
6 Ante-chamber

Architectural Typology

MORAN 46TH SECTION RESIDENCE BLOCK 25
모란 46호 구획 살림집 25호동

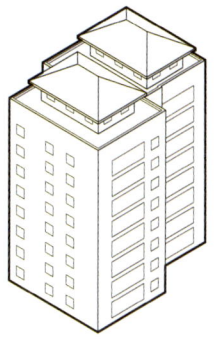

Program : Urban Residence
Proposal for Pyongyang-Si
Building Area : 280.67m²
Gross Area : 2,245.36m²
Unit Area : 135.65m²
Number of Family : 8
Number of Floors : 16
Magazine Year : 2010

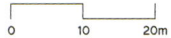

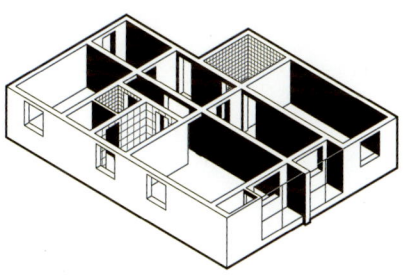

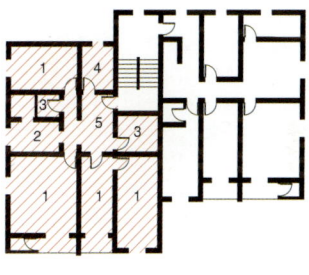

1   Room
2   Kitchen
3   Bathroom
4   Storage
5   Ante-chamber

MANSUDAE STREET RESIDENCE BLOCK 4-7

만수대거리 살림집 4–7호동

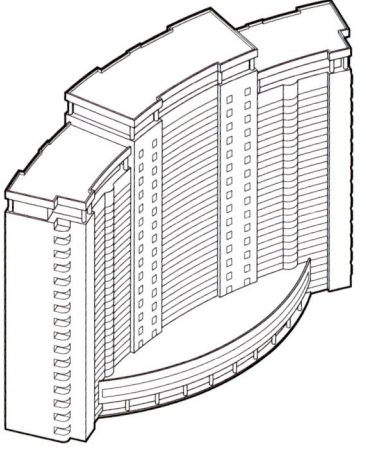

Program : Urban Residence
Locatoin : Pyongyang-Si
Building Area : 930m²
Gross Area : 14,190m²
Unit Area : 84m²/124m²/148m²
Number of Family : 232
Number of Floors : 84
Magazine Year : 2010

1 Living Room
2 Room
3 Kitchen
4 Bathroom
5 Ante-chamber

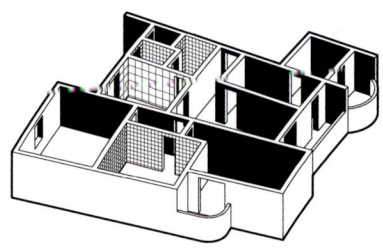

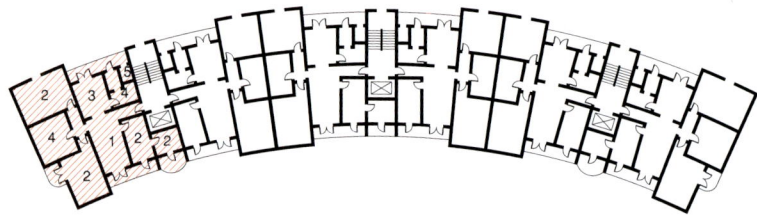

Architectural Typology

MANSUDAE STREET RESIDENCE BLOCK 1-1
만수대거리 살림집 1-1호동

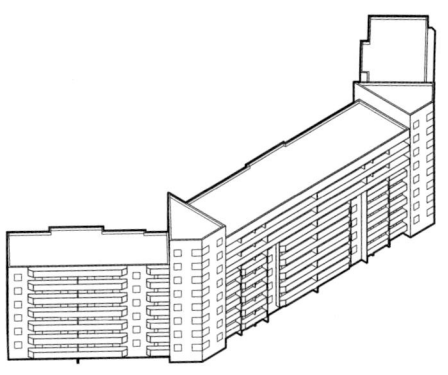

Program : Urban Residence
Location : Pyongyang-Si
Building Area : 4,088.3m²
Gross Area : 29,067.3m²
Unit Area : 122.6m²/120.8m²/98m²
Number of Family : 68
Number of Floors : 6~8
Magazine Year : 2010

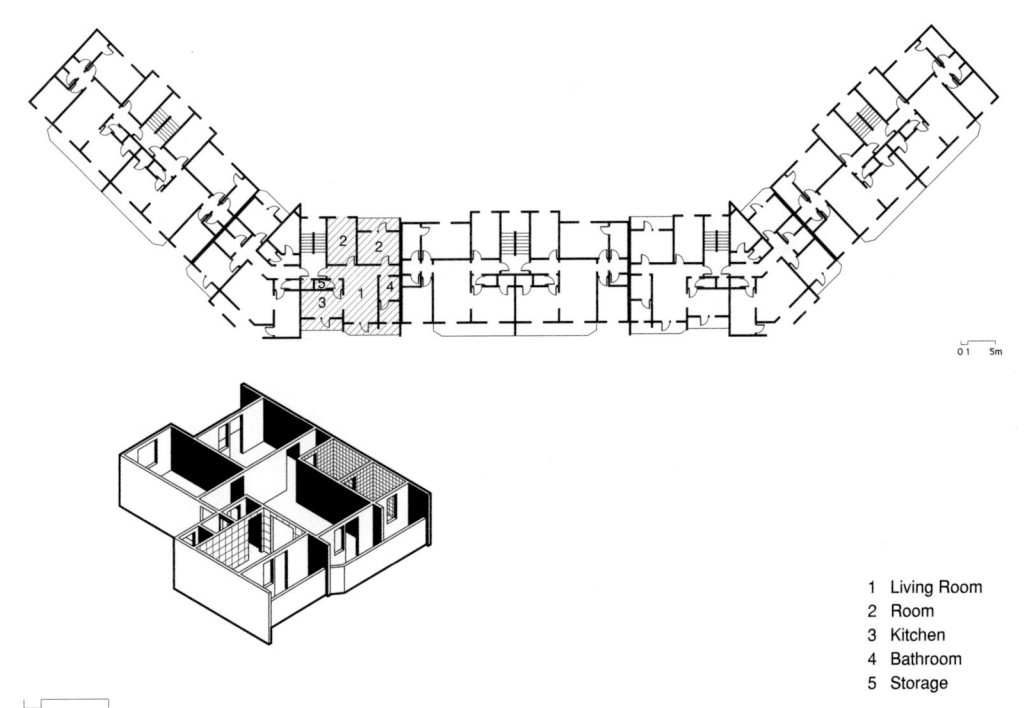

1 Living Room
2 Room
3 Kitchen
4 Bathroom
5 Storage

YORAM-3

요람-3

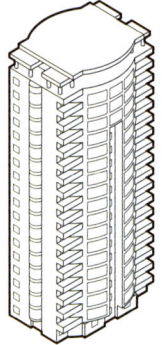

Program : Urban Residence Proposal
Building Area : 238.8m²
Gross Area : 4,298.27m²
Unit Area : 122m²/135m²
Number of Family : 36
Number of Floors : 18
Magazine Year : 2009

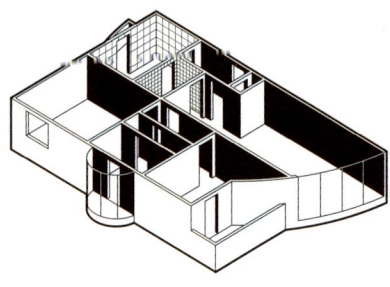

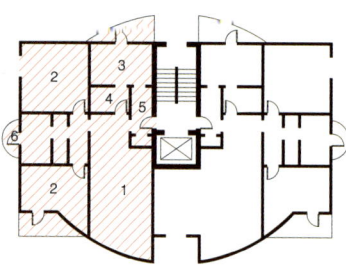

1 Living Room
2 Room
3 Kitchen
4 Bathroom
5 Ante-chamber
6 Solarium

PYONGYANG RESIDENCE STANDARD TYPE IN 1962

1962년 평양시 표준살림집

Program : Urban Residence
Location : Pyongyang-Si
Building Area : 761.49m²
Unit Area : 48.94m²
Number of Family : 14/floor
Number of Floors : Mid-rise
Built Year : 1962
Reference : Chosun Architecture History III

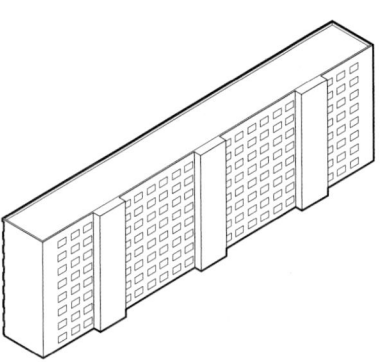

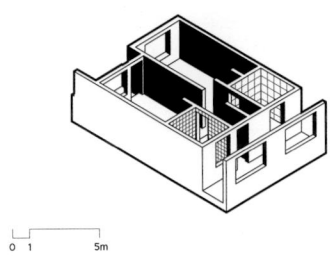

1 Room
2 Kitchen
3 Bathroom

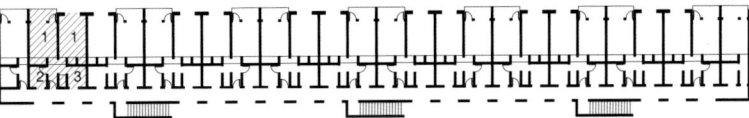

CHULZZUK

철쭉

Program : Urban Residence
Proposal
Building Area : 499.25m²
Gross Area : 2,995.5m²
Unit Area : 121.68m²/140.20m²
Number of Family : 12
Number of Floors : 6
Magazine Year : 2007

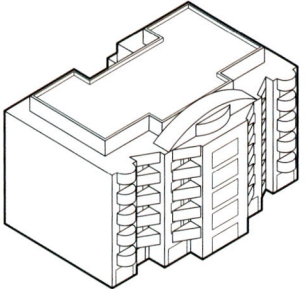

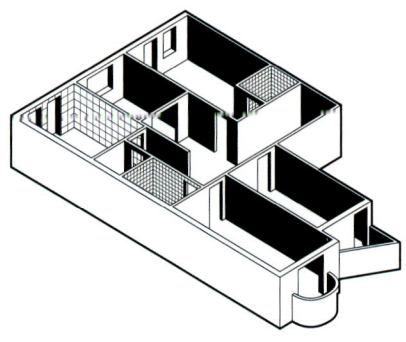

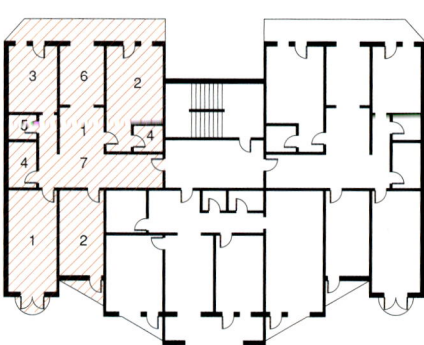

1 Drawing Room
2 Room
3 Kitchen
4 Bathroom
5 Storage
6 Study
7 Hallway

TYPE SHEARED

어김형 살림집

Program : Urban Residence
Location : Pyongyang-Si
Building Area : 1,475m²
Gross Area : 22,125m²
Unit Area : 100.82m²
Number of Family : 150
Number of Floors : 15
Built Year : 1980's
Reference : Chosun Architecture History III

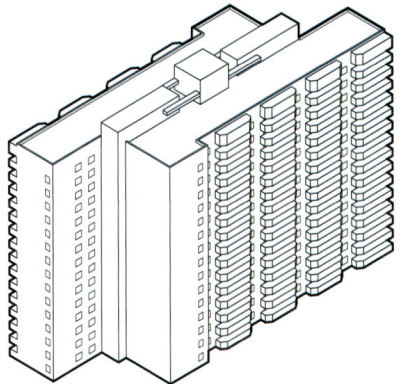

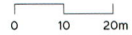

1 Living Room
2 Room
3 Kitchen
4 Bathroom
5 Ante-chamber

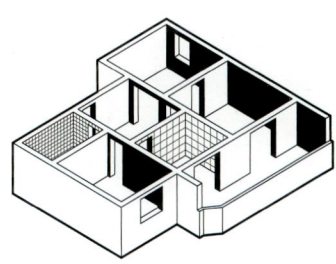

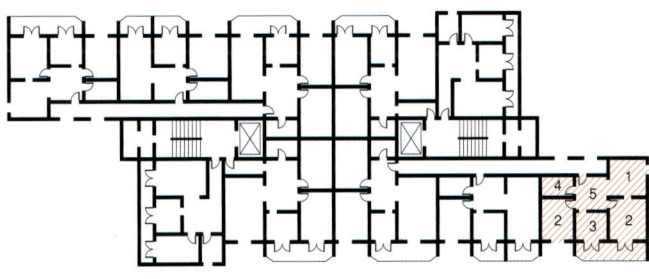

MUREUNGDOWON

무릉도원

Program : Rural Residence Proposal
Building Area : 61.1m²
Magazine Year : 2007

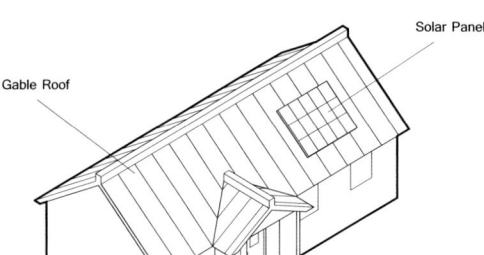

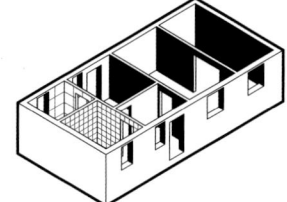

1 Living Room
2 Room
3 Kitchen
4 Dining Room
5 Bathroom

JONGDARI

종다리

Program : Rural Residence Proposal
Building Area : 100m²
Magazine Year : 2007

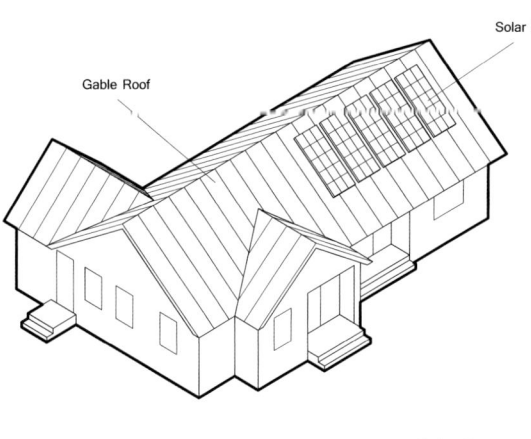

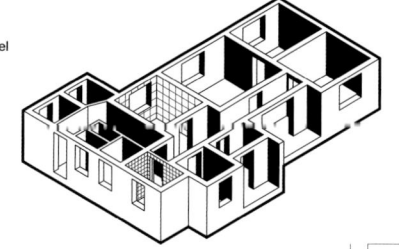

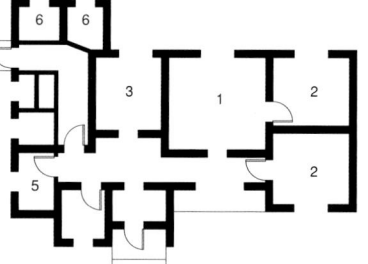

1 Living Room
2 Room
3 Kitchen
4 Dining Room
5 Bathroom
6 Storage

Architectural Typology

JONGDARI

종다리

Program : Rural Residence
Proposal
Building Area : 100m²
Magazine Year : 2007

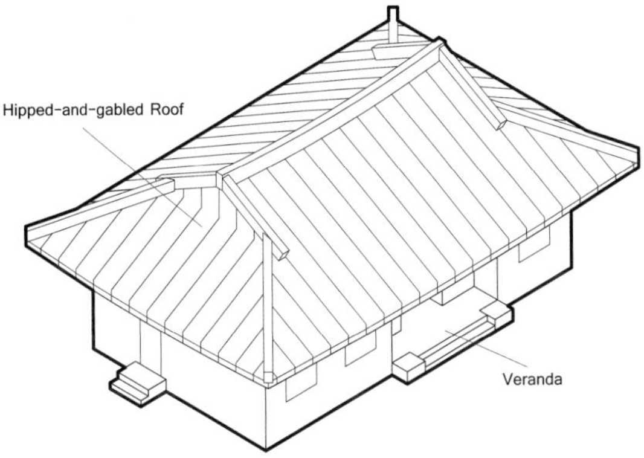

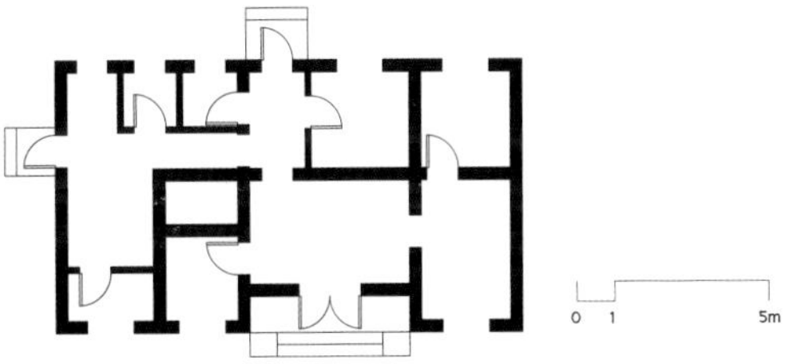

Hipped-and-gabled Roof

Veranda

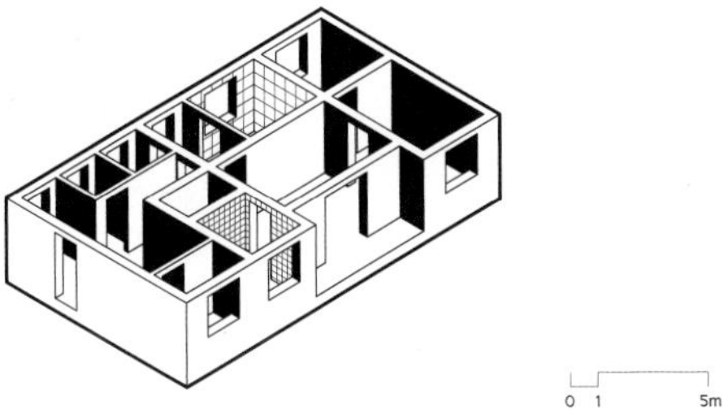

1 Living Room
2 Room
3 Kitchen
4 Dining Room
5 Bathroom

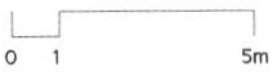

SOMEGOL RESIDENCE

소매골 살림집

Program : Rural Residence
Location : Pyongyang-Si
Building Area : 90m²
Built Year : 1985

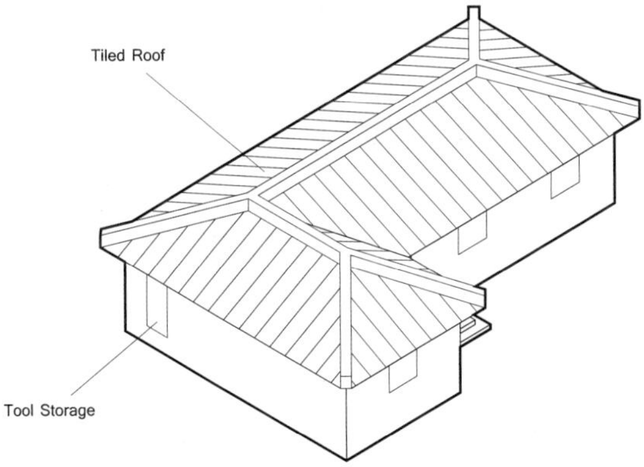

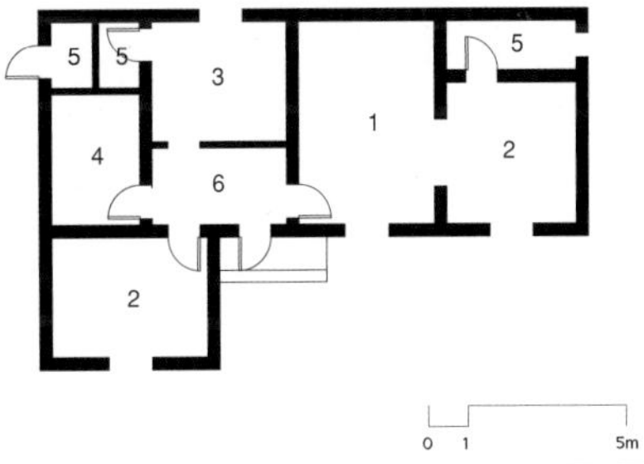

Tiled Roof

Tool Storage

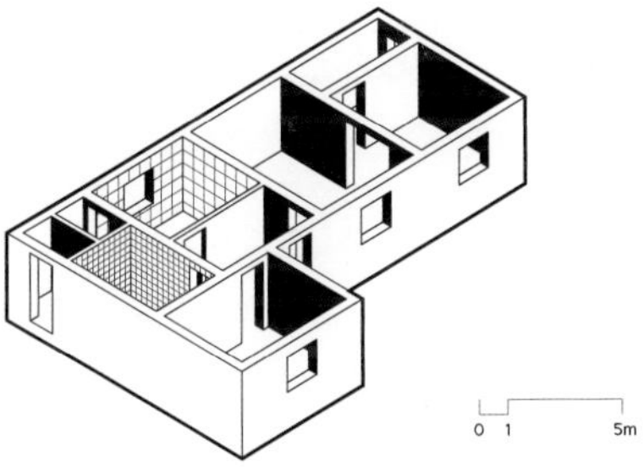

1 Living Room
2 Room
3 Kitchen
4 Bathroom
6 Storage
7 Ante-chamber

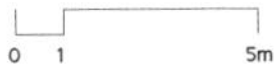

BUKBYUN
북변

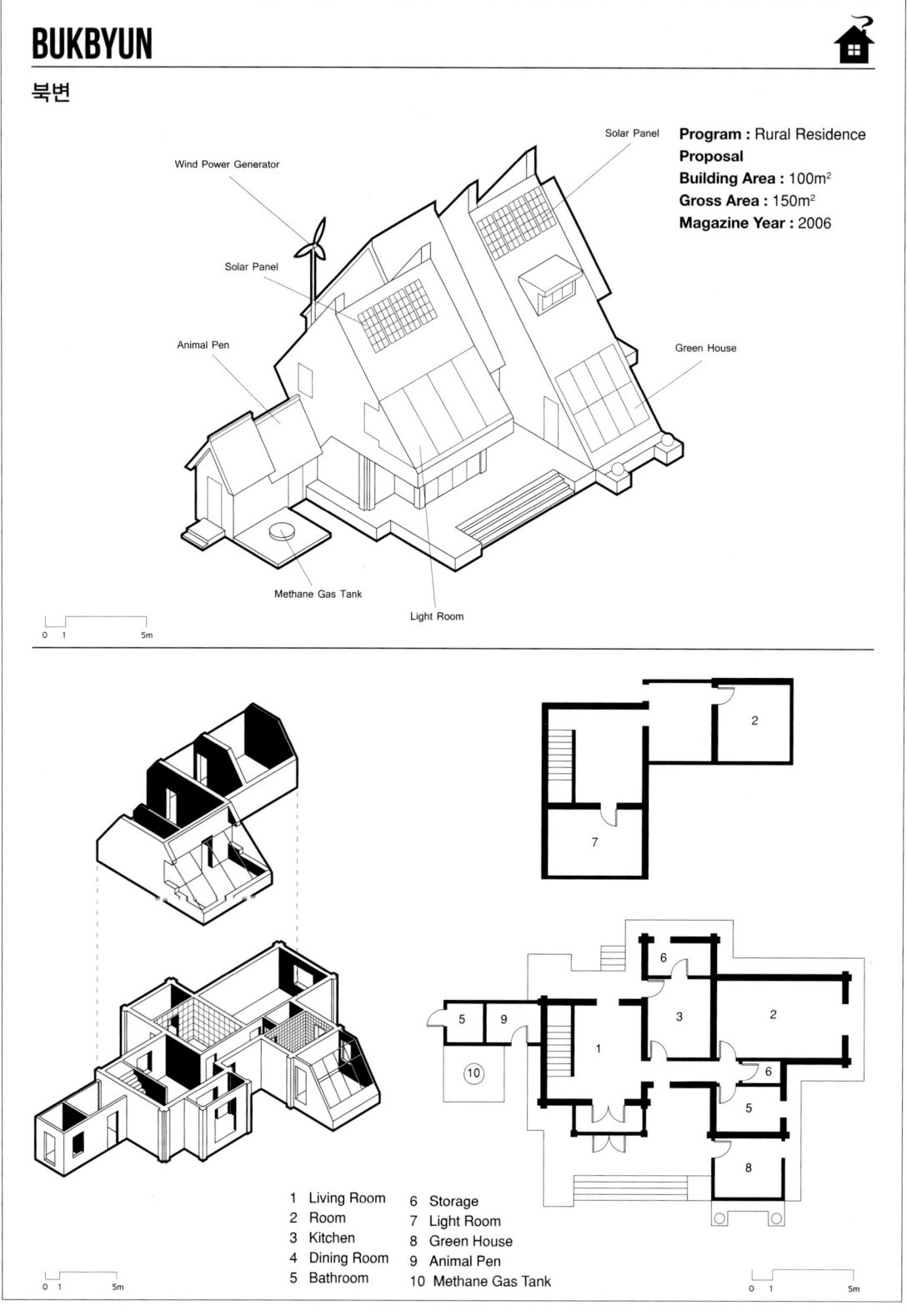

Program: Rural Residence Proposal
Building Area: 100m²
Gross Area: 150m²
Magazine Year: 2006

1. Living Room
2. Room
3. Kitchen
4. Dining Room
5. Bathroom
6. Storage
7. Light Room
8. Green House
9. Animal Pen
10. Methane Gas Tank

Architectural Typology

SAMJIYON-EUP RESIDENCE
삼지연읍 살림집

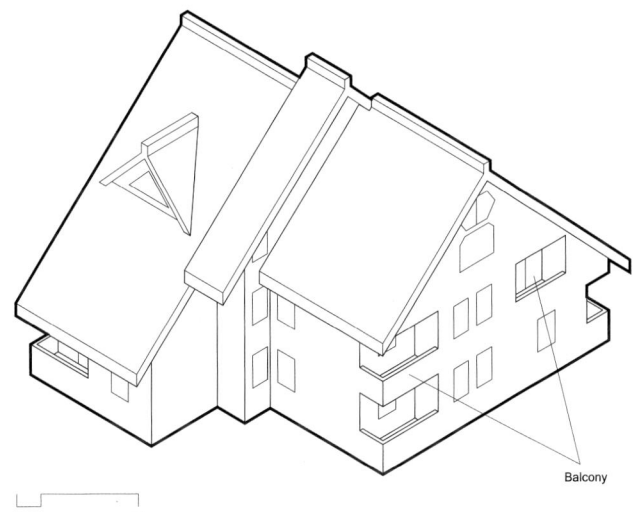

Program : Rural Residence
Proposal for Samjiyon-Gun
Building Area : 138m²
Gross Area : 326.6m²
Unit Area : 69m²
Number of Family : 5
Number of Floors : 3
Magazine Year : 1993

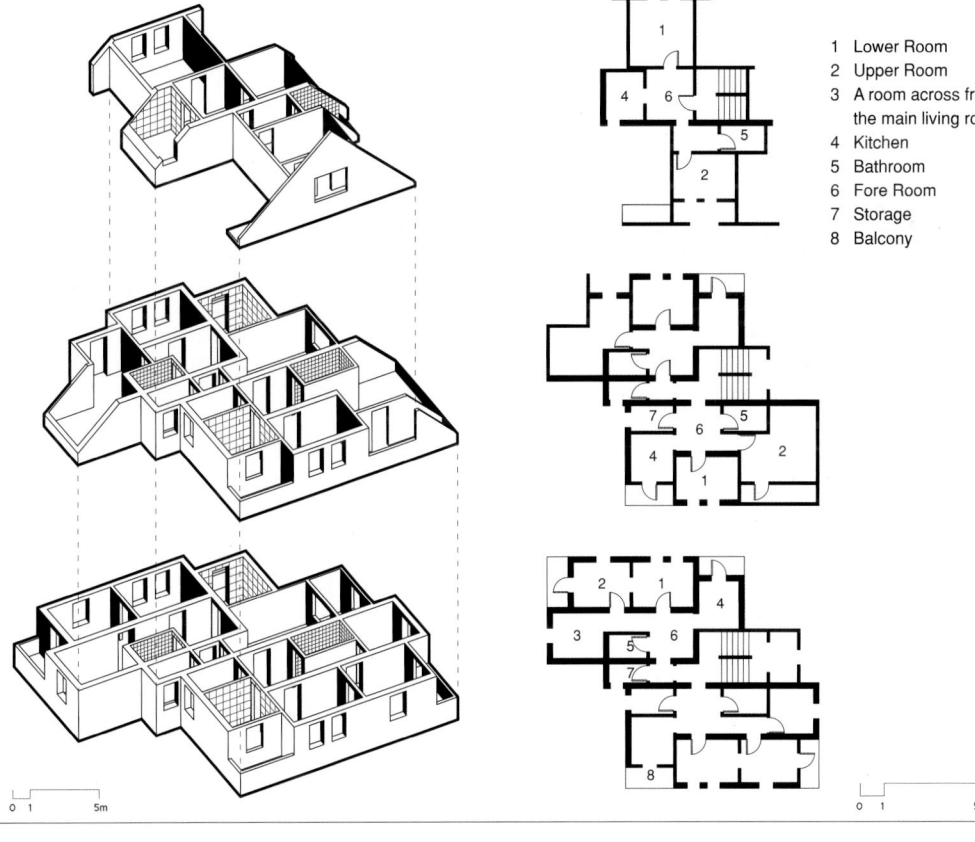

1. Lower Room
2. Upper Room
3. A room across from the main living room
4. Kitchen
5. Bathroom
6. Fore Room
7. Storage
8. Balcony

RYONGJEON-RI RESIDENCE

룡전리 살림집

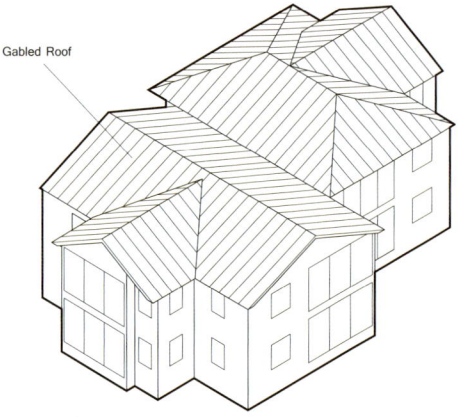

Gabled Roof

Program : Rural Residence
Location : Pukchon-Gun
Building Area : 233.56m²
Unit Area : 97.12m²
Number of Family : 4
Number of Floors : 2
Magazine Year : 1992

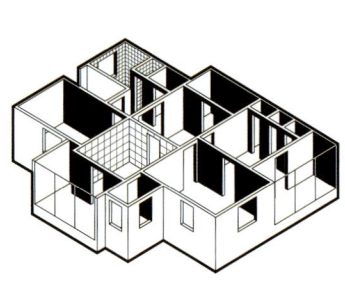

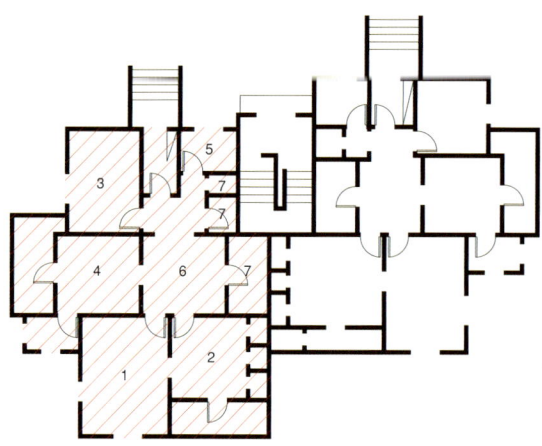

1 Lower Room
2 Upper Room
3 A room across from the living room
4 Kitchen
5 Bathroom
6 Fore Room
7 Storage

SUNGAN-DONG TRADITIONAL STYLE RESIDENCE

성안동 조선식 살림집

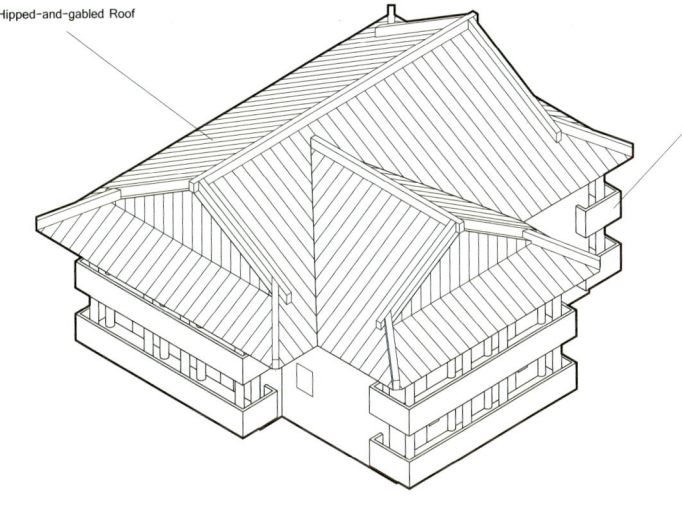

Program : Rural Residence
Proposal for Guseong-Si
Building Area : 226.17m²
Unit Area : 75.39m²
Number of Family : 6
Number of Floors : 2
Magazine Year : 1991

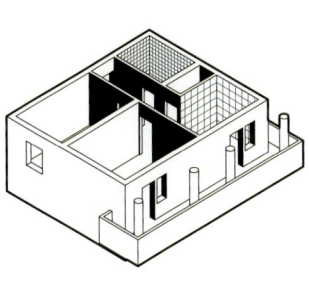

1 Room
2 Kitchen
3 Bathroom
4 Storage

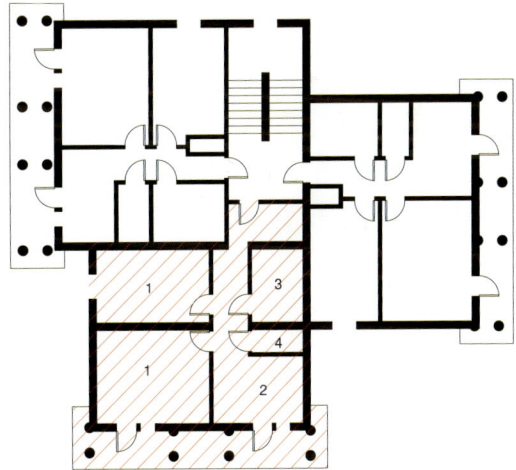

COLD CLIMATE REGION RESIDENCE

추운지대 살림집

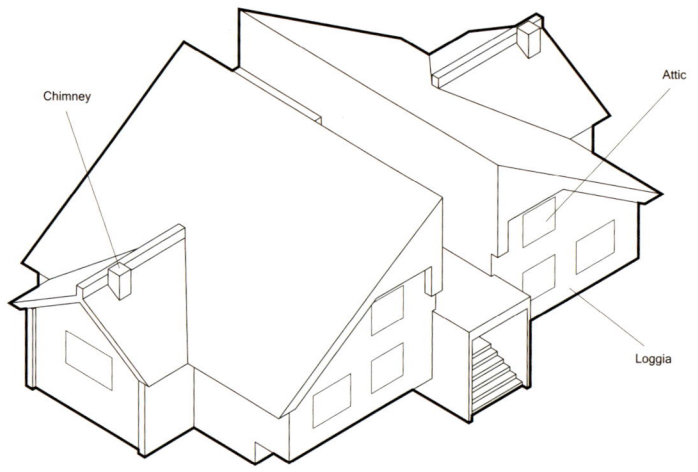

Program : Rural Residence Proposal
Building Area : 206m²
Gross Area : 412m²
Unit Area : 103m²
Number of Family : 2
Number of Floors : 2
Magazine Year : 1993

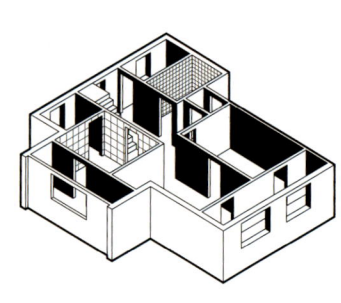

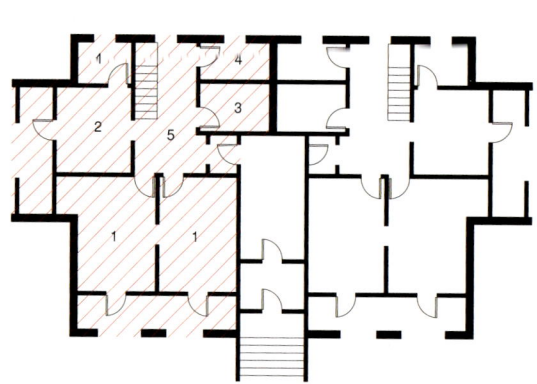

1 Room
2 Kitchen
3 Bathroom
4 Storage
5 Ante-chamber

Architectural Typology

DONGNAM TOWN RESIDENCE

동남마을 살림집

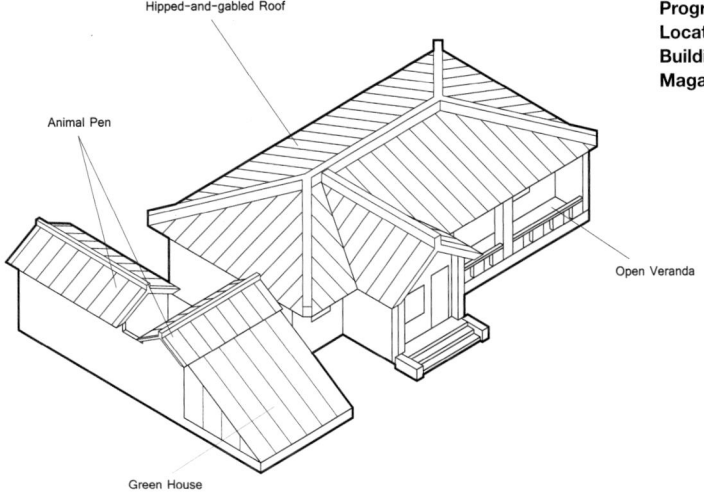

Program : Rural Residence
Location : Pakchon-Gun
Building Area : 130m²
Magazine Year : 2004

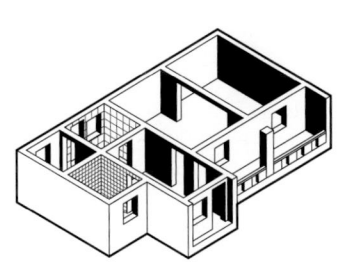

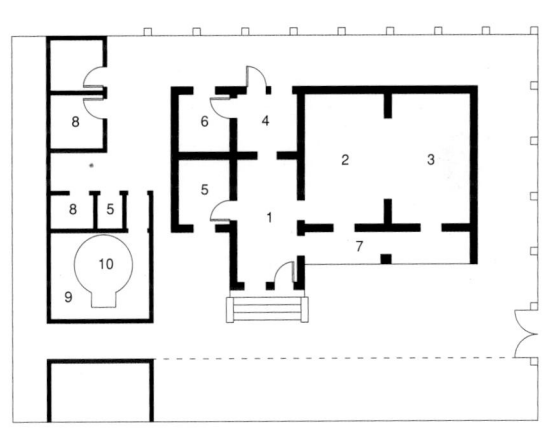

1 Living Room
2 Lower Room
3 Upper Room
4 Kitchen
5 Bathroom

6 Storage
7 Open Veranda
8 Domestic Animal Pen
9 Green House
10 Methane Gas Tank

2-STORY 1 FAMILY RESIDENCE
2층 1세대 살림집

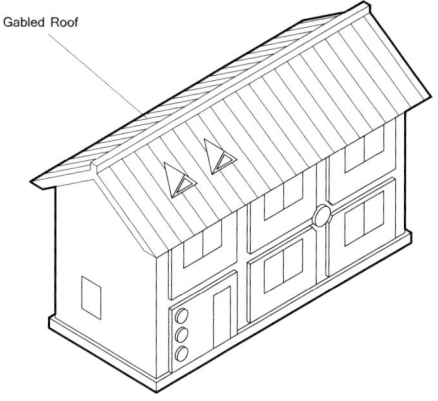

Program : Rural Residence
Proposal
Building Area : 52.62m²
Magazine Year : 2007

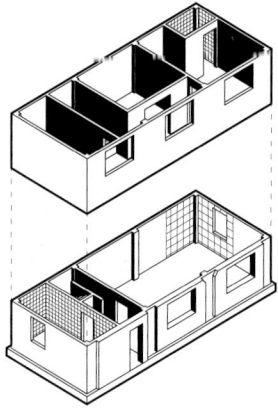

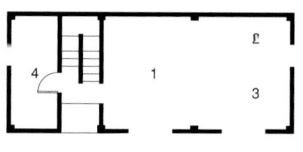

2nd Floor

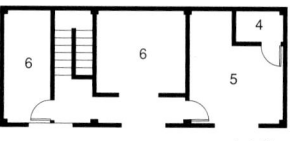

1st Floor

1 Living Room
2 Kitchen
3 Dining Room
4 Bathroom
5 Master Bedroom
6 Bedroom

CHANGDONG-RI RESIDENCE
창동리 살림집

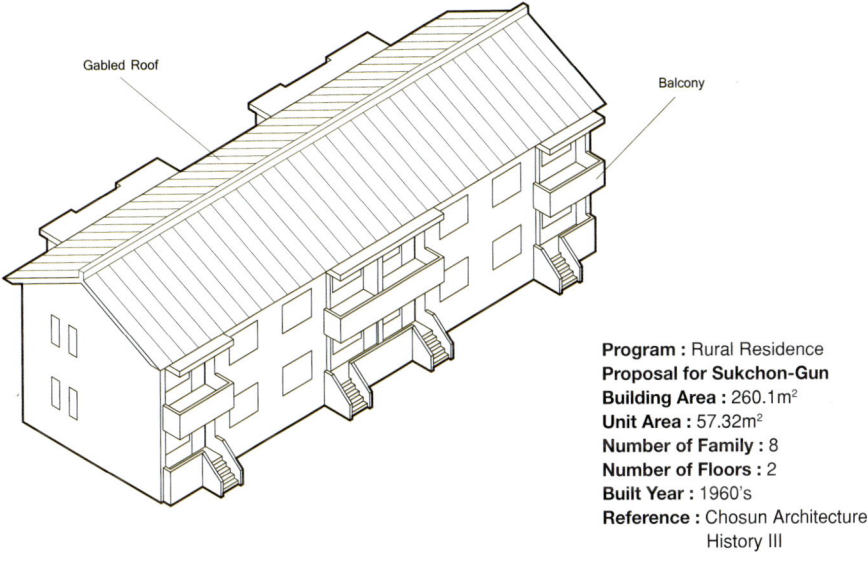

Program : Rural Residence
Proposal for Sukchon-Gun
Building Area : 260.1m²
Unit Area : 57.32m²
Number of Family : 8
Number of Floors : 2
Built Year : 1960's
Reference : Chosun Architecture History III

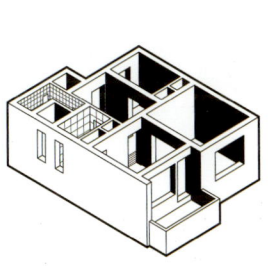

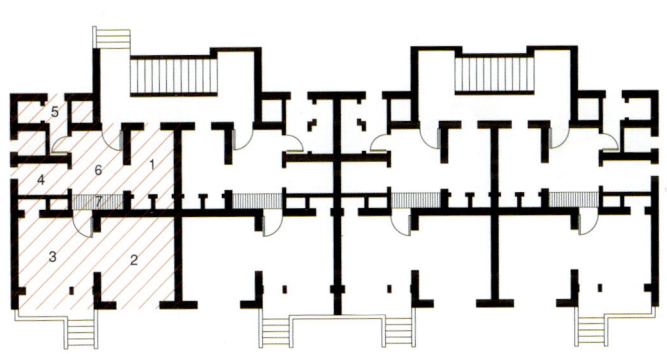

1 Living Room
2 Floor Panel Heating Room
3 Wooden Floor Room
4 Kitchen
5 Bathroom
6 Fore Room
7 Wooden Floor

RURAL RESIDENCE PROPOSAL

농촌살림집

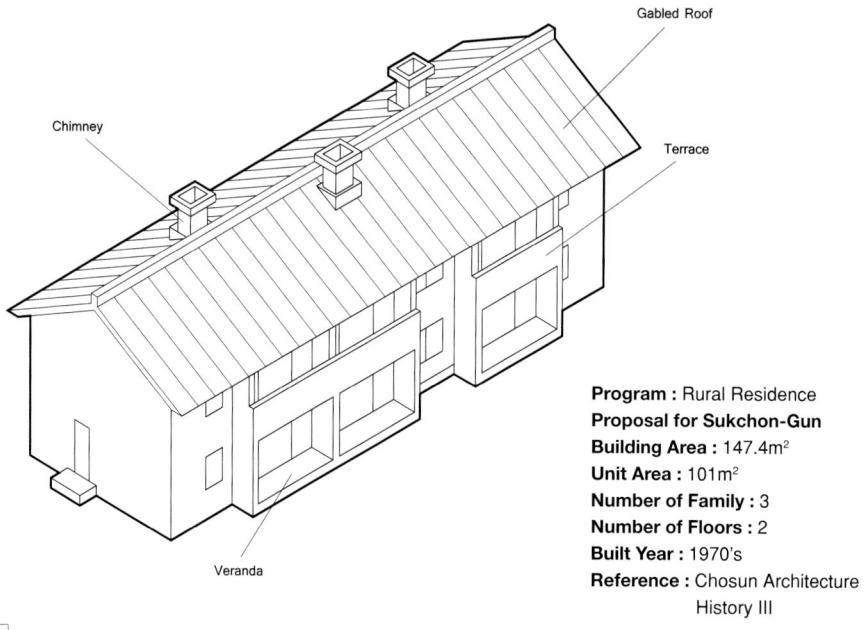

Program : Rural Residence Proposal for Sukchon-Gun
Building Area : 147.4m²
Unit Area : 101m²
Number of Family : 3
Number of Floors : 2
Built Year : 1970's
Reference : Chosun Architecture History III

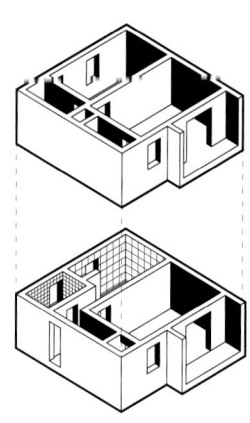

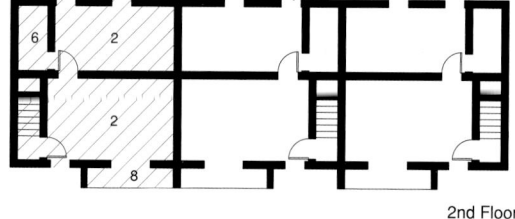

2nd Floor

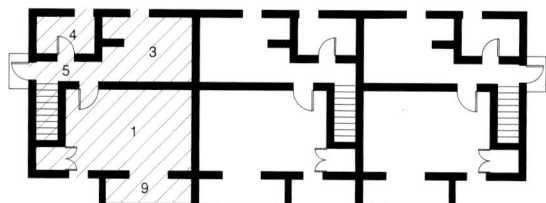

1st Floor

1. Lower Room
2. Upper Room
3. Kitchen
4. Bathroom
5. Fore Room
6. Storage
7. Veranda
8. Terrace

Architectural Typology

CHANGDONG-RI RESIDENCE
창동리 살림집

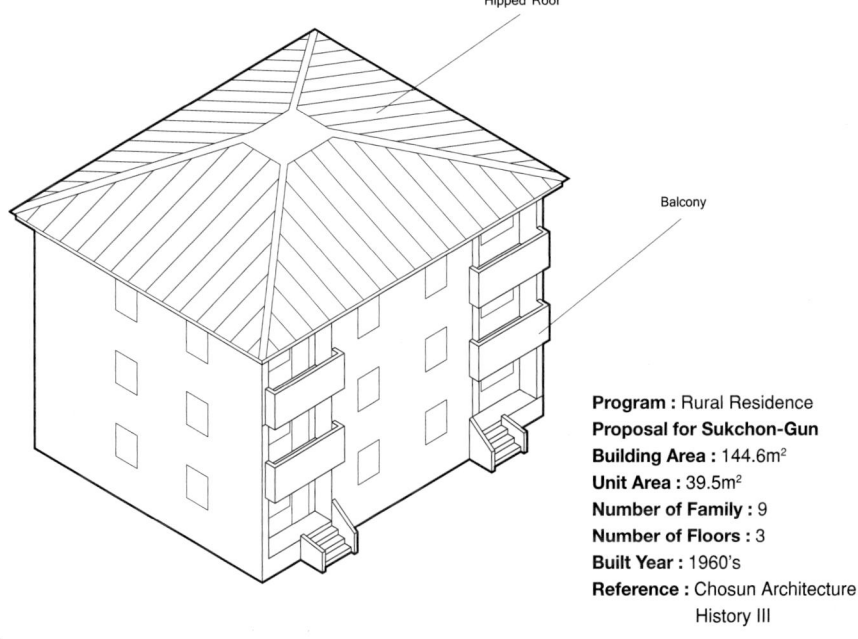

Program : Rural Residence
Proposal for Sukchon-Gun
Building Area : 144.6m²
Unit Area : 39.5m²
Number of Family : 9
Number of Floors : 3
Built Year : 1960's
Reference : Chosun Architecture History III

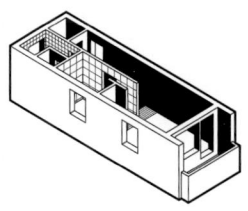
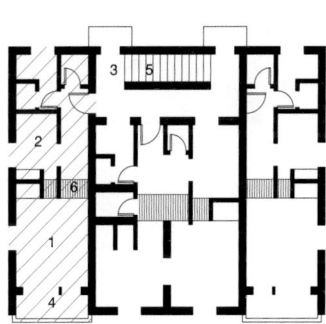

1 Floor Panel Heating Room
2 Kitchen
3 Bathroom
4 Loggia
5 Storage
6 Wooden Floor

1967 RURAL RESIDENCE STANDARD TYPE

1967년 농촌주택 표준설계

Program : Rural Residence Proposal
Building Area : 47.25m²
Year : 1967
Reference : North Korean Architecture and Cities, Our Other Half

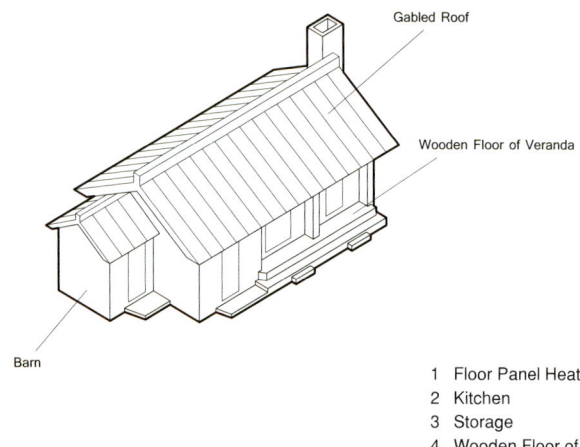
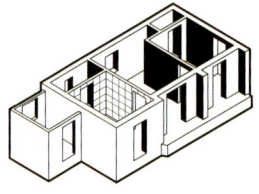
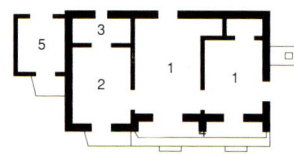

1 Floor Panel Heating Room
2 Kitchen
3 Storage
4 Wooden Floor of Veranda
5 Barn

1967 RURAL RESIDENCE STANDARD TYPE

1967년 농촌주택 표준설계

Program : Rural Residence Proposal
Building Area : 59.4m²
Unit Area : 33.75m² / 25.65m²
Number of Family : 2
Year : 1967
Reference : North Korean Architecture and Cities, Our Other Half

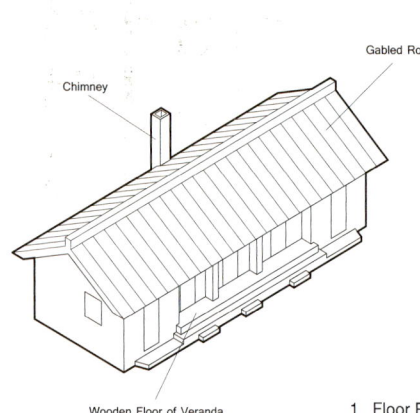
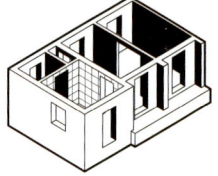
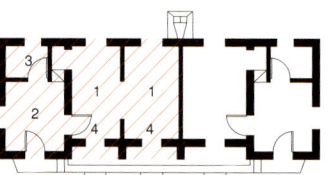

1 Floor Panel Heating Room
2 Kitchen
3 Storage
4 Wooden Floor of Veranda

HYANGSAN-EUP TRADITIONIAL STYLE RESIDENCE

향산읍 조선식 살림집

Program : Rural Residence
Proposal for Hyangsan-Gun
Building Area : 3457.4m²
Unit Area : 98.1m²
Number of Family : 110
Number of Floors : 3~4
Magazine Year : 1993

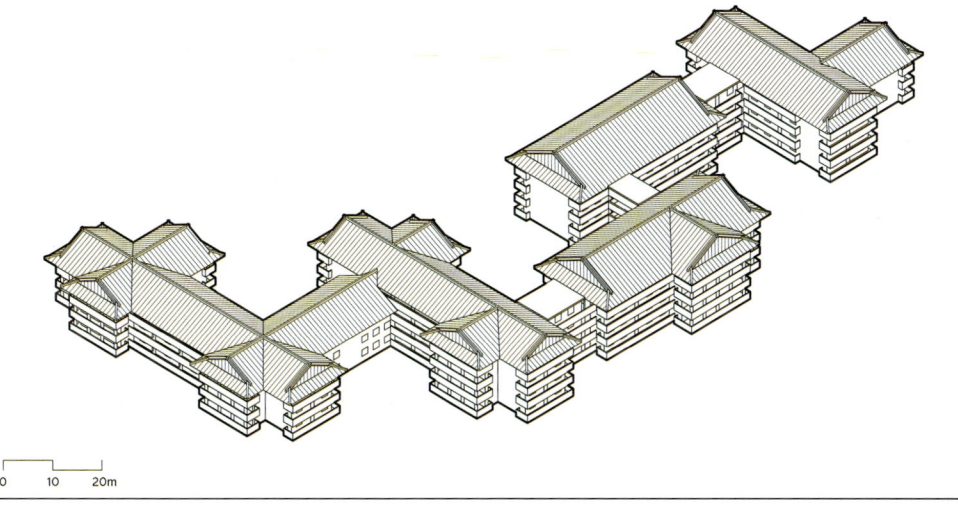

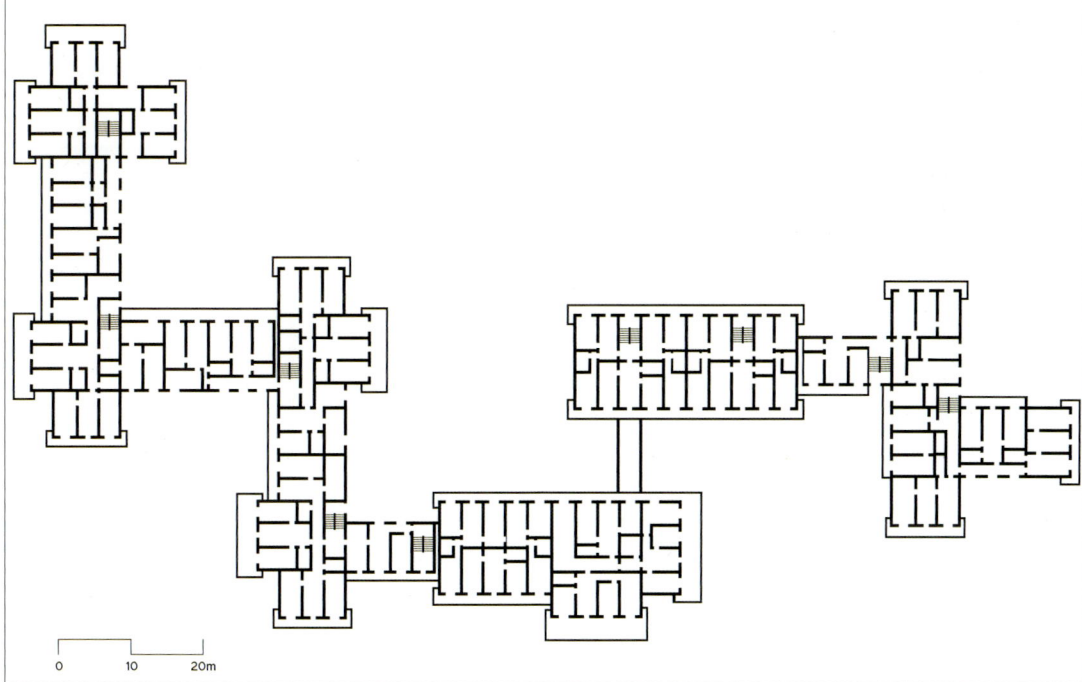

SAMJIYON-EUP RESIDENCE

삼지연읍 살림집

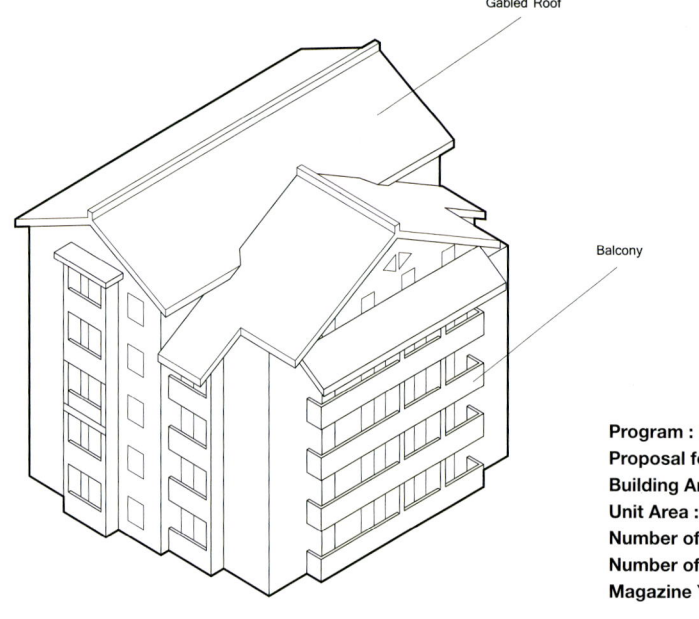

Program : Rural Residence
Proposal for Samjiyon-Gun
Building Area : 261.2m²
Unit Area : 58.9m²
Number of Family : 19
Number of Floors : 5
Magazine Year : 1993

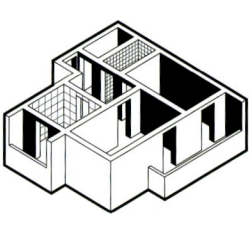
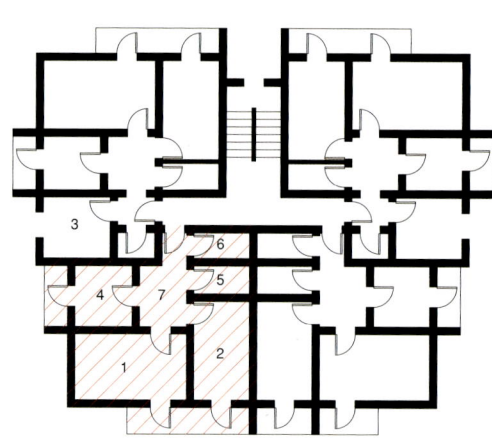

1. Lower Room
2. Upper Kitchen
3. A room across from the main living room
4. Kitchen
5. Bathroom
6. Storage
7. Ante-chamber
8. Balcony

Architectural Typology

EUNJEONG
은정

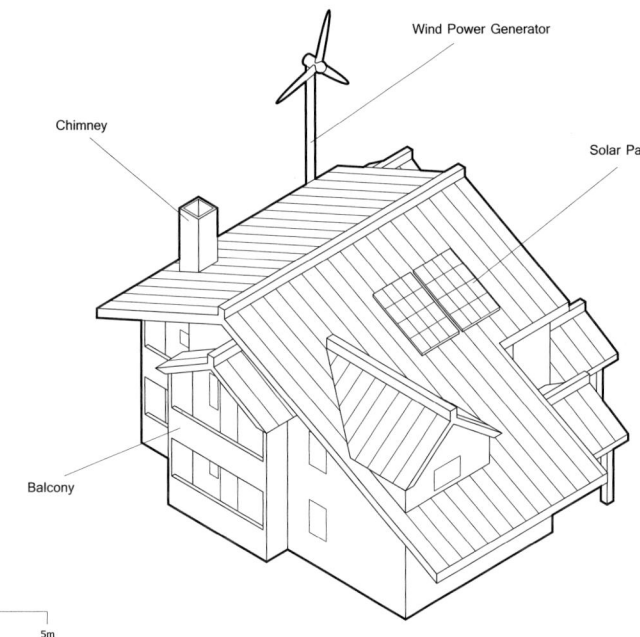

Program : Rural Residence
Proposal
Building Area : 129.8 m²
Magazine Year : 2006

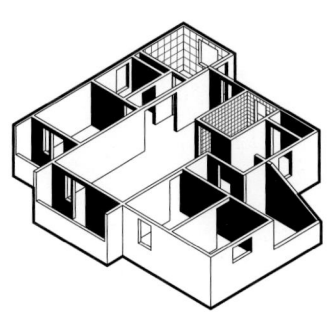

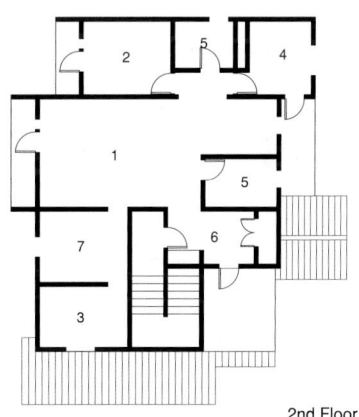

2nd Floor

1 Living Room
2 Master Bedroom
3 Children's Room
4 Kitchen
5 Bathroom
6 Ante-chamber
7 Play Room

DICTIONARY

English 영어	North Korean 조선어	Korean 한국어
A room across from the main living room	건너방	건넌방
Ante-chamber	전실, 앞칸	전실
Arcade	오락실	오락실
Artificial Pond and Fountain	인공분수못	인공호수와 분수
Attic	다락방	다락방
Auditorium	강당	강당
Automobile Laboratory	자동차 연구실	자동차 연구실
Balcony	로대	노대
Ball Room	무도장	무도장
Banquet Hall	연회장	연회실
Barbershop	리발실	이발소
Bathroom	위생실	화장실
Beauty Parlor	미용실	미용실
Changing Room	탈의실	탈의실
Children's Care Room	탁아실	탁아실
Children's Room	아이방, 어린이방	아동실
Circle Room	소조실	서클실
Circular Dining Room	원형식당	원형식당
Communal Lounge	공동휴식홀	공용라운지
Detached House	헛간	거느림채, 헛간
Dining Hall	식사홀	식사홀
Dining Room	식사실	식사실
Diving Board	조약대	다이빙대
Domestic Animal Pen	집짐승우리	가축우리
Drawing Room	응접실	응접실
Dry Room	건조실	건조실
Educational Room	교양실, 교육실	교실
Entrance	현관홀	현관
Family Bath	가족욕실	가족욕실
Firebox	화실	연소실, 연실
Floor-sitting Style Chosun Restaurant	좌식조선료리식당	좌식 조선 식당
Floor Panel Heating Room	온돌방	온돌방
Flower Stand	화분대	화단
Gabled Roof	배집지붕	배집지붕
Green House	온실	온실
Grocery Shop	식료품상점	식료품상점
Hallway	복도	복도
Hipped-and-gabled Roof	합각지붕	합각지붕
Inner Corridor	퇴마루	퇴마루
Inner Courtyard	내정	안뜰
Interview Room	면담실	면담실

* 출처 : 남북과학기술용어집 [건축공학], 한국과학기술단체총연합회

Architectural Typology

English 영어	North Korean 조선어	Korean 한국어
Kimchi Storage	김치고	김치저장고
Laboratory	실습실	실습실
Light Room	광실	광실
Loggia	로지	노지 / 개랑
Lower Room	아래방	아래방
Main Hall	중심홀	메인홀
Methane Gas Tank	메탄가스탕크	메탄가스탱크
Music Room	악기연습실	음악실
Open Veranda	퇴마루	퇴마루
Packing Room	포장실	포장실
Preparation Room	준비실	준비실
Principal's Office	원장실, 교장실	원장실, 교장실
Product Storage	제품창고	제품창고
Public Bath	대중욕실	공중목욕탕
Royal Box	주석단	귀빈석
Sauna	한증칸	사우나
Service Amenity	봉사건물	편의시설
Sewing Practice Room	재봉실습실	재봉실습실
Shop	상점	상점
Sleeping Room	잠실	수면실
Small Banquet Hall	소연회장	소연회장
Small Dining Room	작은식당	작은식당
Smoking Room	담배피우는칸	흡연실
Solarium	일광욕실	일광욕실
Souvenir Shop	기념품상점	기념품점
Study	서재	서재
Study Room	학습실	학습실
Terrace	내민대	테라스
Therapy Room	치료체육실	물리치료실
Training Area	훈련장	훈련장
Upper Room	웃방	웃방
Veranda	툇마루	베란다
Void	관통홀	보이드
Water Park	물놀이장	워터파크
Water Slide	물미끄럼대	워터슬라이드
Western-style Chosun Restaurant	입식조선료리식당	입식 조선 요리식당
Wooden Floor of Veranda	퇴마루, 퇴	퇴마루
Work Space	작업장	작업실

*참고문헌: 이왕기, 《북한건축 또 하나의 우리 모습》, 서울포럼, 2000 / 리화선, 《조선건축사 III》, 발언, 1993
**자료내 면적표는 참고도면을 바탕으로 한 바, 실제와 다를 수 있음.

05 FUTURE SCENARIOS

NORTH KOREA: AN AESTHETIC PROJECT

Doojin Hwang

—

Architect Doojin Hwang was born in Seoul in 1963. With both parents having originated from North Korea, he has a strong sense of identity about himself being a second generation of displaced Koreans. He studied architecture at Seoul National University and Yale School of Architecture; in 2000, he started his own practice and has since produced a wide range of projects. Geometry, porosity, mixed-use and tradition are a few of his keywords.

Introduction

To me, North Korea is an aesthetic project. As I write this, I imagine a certain situation in the future, in which incidents involving ROKS Cheonan, Yeonpyeong Island and nuclear bombs are things of the past. In short, my interest in North Korea as an architect is how to create an ideal human habitat on the Korean peninsular. It can only be done aided by lessons from all the trials and errors in different ways of nation building practiced in both Koreas. Compared to the over-built South Korea, the under-developed North Korea with its smaller population offers more room for new experiments, and the result will bring winds of change to the South as well. The awakened awareness for new types of collective life will gradually change the way we build and live on the Korean peninsular. Yes, this indeed is an aesthetic project.

Two incidents contributed to the conception of these ideas on my part. The one is Byeokcho Hong, Myeonghee's book 'Im, Ggeokjeong' which I read a few years ago. The various men and women in the story traveled extensively, visiting every little corner of the peninsula. I believe the author did it on purpose. He contributed this novel to a newspaper for 10 years from 1928, when Japan, having colonized Korea, knew no limits in expansion and any hopes for Korea's liberation grew dimmer in proportion. Hong tried to tell a story about various places, sceneries and people on the Korean peninsula. The concept of the Korean peninsula as "a small but complete world" ran through this epic novel. For its relatively small size, the Korean peninsula is yet endowed with various micro-climates and habitats, due to its long north-south orientation. Add to this numerous mountains and rivers, fields and seas; you get a kaleidoscope of natural habitats. Hong was trying to tell his fellow Koreans not to lose hope for this land of remarkable beauty and diversity.

The other incident was a piece of painting. Years ago, I saw in a North Korean art exhibition a painting titled, "Into the Woods" ('Surimeuro'). It was a traditional landscape painting in ink, yet the depicted scenery was quite different; there were neither gentle, sloping hills, nor weeping willows, nor pine trees. Instead the painting had two horses pulling a cart full of wood, seen through a forest of birch tress in a rugged, snow-covered mountain valley. The painter's name was Choi, Changho, a North Korean cultural hero associated with the Mansoodae Art Production in Pyeongyang. To me, it was a rude awakening: this too was Korea. The concept of 'the Korean peninsula as, "a small but complete world" jumped to me once again. The coconut tree-lined, tropical seasides of Jeju Island or South Sea area, or the tundra forest thick with birch trees in Choi's ink painting are equally as Korean as the Hahoe or Yangdong villages surrounded by a large number of twisted and bent pine trees. We have a right to enjoy all the diversities this land has to offer. The chance shall come again.

Then what is an ideal human habitat on the Korean peninsula? Some look towards the premodern farming villages for answers. However, with urbanization being an undeniable current fact, this no longer makes sense. It is imperative that we have an urban perspective. Also, the Korean peninsula is not an exception when it comes to global concerns such as environment, quality of life and cultural diversity. The regional uniqueness of nature, culture and history of the Korean peninsula will produce a set of worthy objectives only when mixed with these universal values. In light of this view, the following is the list of proposals regarding North Korea; in short, it is about small, compact and mixed-use cities.

Small, compact and mixed-use cities

<u>Maintenance of the Current Urban Footprint</u>
Following the principles of socialist urban planning, North Korea has suppressed the urban explosion, with an intention to minimize the gap between cities and the countrysides.. This has resulted in the country lacking metropolises, except for Pyongyang with the population of 2.5 million. Hamheung and Cheongjin, the 2nd and the 3rd in population, have only 0.77 million and 0.67 million respectively. Even with relatively smaller overall population in North Korea, the numbers seems odd, especially when compared to South Korea, where metropolises with several million in population are the norm.. The future development in North Korea will definitely bring a huge increase in population.

There are two solutions to this problem; cities can either choose to grow horizontally or vertically. The latter has more potential in the future than the former; density, after all, is what makes a city work.. Density increases the efficiency in urban infrastructures such as telecommunication and transportation, decreasing the traveling distance within the city. Urban horizontal sprawl on the other hand is a cause for many urban problems, as many metropolises in the world testify. Nature is hard to access; any investment in infrastructure in low density area will turn out to be inefficient; due to long travel distances, more time and energy will be needed. Seoul is a good example for this problem. According to Professor Kim, Sunghong, the average number of floors in Seoul's buildings is mere 2.5. What this means is that, if the number goes up to 4 or 5, the entire habitat footprint of Seoul can be reduced in half. At the same time this also shows that cities do not really need skyscrapers to achieve sufficient density, as in the case of many European cities.

• Mixed-use, Pedestrian-friendly Cities to Minimize Journey-to-work Distance
Another keyword for future cities is 'mixed-use'. Under the current system of horizontal zoning plan, mass movements among various places within a city are inevitable. This not only puts an enormous burden on infrastructures and causes excessive energy consumption, but also degrades the lives of individuals. The best measure for any society to improve the quality of life of its members is to reduce the distance and time for daily commuting. The most preferable solution is to create cities where daily lives take place within walking distance. In short, minimizing commuting distances is on the priorities for future cities. Unfortunately, it is practically impossible to achieve this in the current cities in South Korea. It is interesting to note that in North Korea the concept of minimizing commuting distances has been given a priority in urban planning.

The futures cities will need more mixed-use approaches than ever. A single-use building, tall or low, no loner makes urban sense. ('Shiruddeok', named after a Korean rice cake with identical layers); on the other hand, a growing number of mixed-use buildings ('Mujigaeddeok', or 'rainbow cake', a different type of Korean rice cake with layers of different colors) will decrease the average commuting distance. This is the very first step in creating both pro-human and pro-environment cities. ('Shiruddeok' Buildings vs. 'Mujigaeddeok' Buildings)

• Environmental Concerns on the Korean Peninsula
What is the Korean peninsula like then? Even global warming has not really changed the overall weather system in this part of the world; Korea still has 4 distinctive seasons, the sun follows different tracks in the sky depending on times of the year, the summer is hot and humid and the winter is cold and dry. In addition, there are 3 surrounding bodies of water (being a peninsula), a network of rivers and lakes, mountains and hills that dominated the landscape, not extensive but fertile agricultural fields, and finally all that is produced by this diversity. These are the things that make the Korean peninsula one of the most blessed pieces of land in the world. Cities designed and built with a good understanding of these values will turn out to be good places for living as well.

The pre-modern times had these values well respected. The advent of the modern times however made them obsolete; the cities with an ever growing population had to be built with imported theories and methodologies totally unrelated to the concerns for the existing environment. The resulting inefficiency was to be dealt with unlimited consumption of energy; the lack of beauty on

Image 1. Shiruddeok(Left), Mujigaeddeok or Rainbow cake(Right)

the other hand was to be tolerated in the name of economic progress. To stop such a vicious cycle, we need to see what was given to us in the first place. The relatively under-developed North Korea offers such opportunities. We should understand the concept of wind paths, water systems and sun's directions. We should also be wise to avoid building too close to hill slopes, utilizing flat areas as efficiently as possible. Setting limits to urban sprawl, we can create cities with sufficient density with 4- or 5-story buildings; the infrastructure will need to be integrated with mixed-use buildings as well. Buildings with gardens and courtyard on the roof will allow the residents to enjoy the same kind of views our ancestors had on the ground in the old days. The lack of sense of spaciousness caused by high density can be effectively alleviated by introducing the concept of highly porous architecture with balconies, pilotis and other covered outdoor spaces within buildings' mass.

Cities like this do not threaten the nature; their citizens will take care of daily business either on foot or using public transportation. The overall energy consumption will follow a highly efficient pattern; the unpolluted nature is just outside the city boundary. We have never experienced cities like this; it takes just one example for us to realize what it means to live in such cities. As a result the cities on the Korean peninsula will start to change.

Conclusion

The Project North Korea is neither isolated nor unique. It will be less so, once the current political gridlock is done and gotten over with. We need to be more concerned with the universal requirements of human habitat and the basic conditions of the natural environment on the Korean peninsula. The future North Korea should not be subject to mythical understanding or a specially devised approach. The two competing systems of the two Koreas have both failed, in that the South has literally transformed the entire landscape into industrial production base for the greater cause of economic development and the North, having isolated itself from the rest of the world, has lost its momentum of healthy social and economical progress. Between these two, we see more future values in the North simply because it is less developed. The key to the project North Korea is how to create the new and better value set, based on lessons from two types of failures. It is also an effort to find answers for how a large number of people can live in a beautiful and harmonious environment. Therefore, this after all, is an aesthetical project. (Architect Doojin Hwang was born in Seoul in 1963. With both parents having originated from North Korea, he grew up with a strong sense of identity about himself being a second generation of displaced Koreans. He studied architecture at Seoul National University and Yale School of Architecture; in 2000, he started his own practice and has since produced a wide range of projects. Geometry, porosity, mixed-use and tradition are his keywords.)

북한이라는 미학적 과제

황두진

—

건축가 황두진은 1963년 서울에서 태어났다.
아버지 고향은 평양, 어머니 고향은 원산으로
그는 실향민 2세대라는 정체성을 가지고 살아왔다.
서울대학교와 예일대학교에서 수학하였고
2000년 자신의 사무실을 개업한 이후에
기하학, 다공성, 복합, 전통 등의 키워드를 중심으로
다양한 작업을 진행해오고 있다.

서문

나에게 북한은 미학적 과제다. 나는 천안함, 연평도 그리고 핵무기 같은 사건들이 모두 과거지사가 된, 미래의 어떤 상황을 상상하며 이 글을 쓴다. 결론부터 이야기하자면 건축가로서 '한반도의 이상적 정주환경의 창조'야말로 북한에 대한 나의 기대다. 그것은 지금까지 한반도의 남과 북에서 이루어진 서로 다른 방식의 건설과 개발이 겪은 시행착오에 대한 반성에 기초한다. 이미 국토의 대부분이 난 개발된 한반도 남쪽 지역보다 상대적으로 인구밀도도 낮고 개발도 덜 이루어진 한반도 북쪽 지역이 앞으로 새로운 시도를 수용하기에 더 적합하다. 그리고 그 결과는 궁극적으로 남쪽 지역에도 변화의 바람을 가져올 것이다. 따라서 '아, 우리가 이 땅에서 이렇게 살 수 있었구나'라는 즐거운 깨달음을 통해 한반도 전체를 서서히 변화시켜 나가자는 것이다. 그렇다. 이것은 궁극의 미학적 과제다.

이러한 생각을 하게 된 데에는 두 가지 계기가 있었다. 하나는 몇 년 전 벽초 홍명희의 '임꺽정'을 통독한 일이다. 이 대하소설에 등장하는 수 많은 인물들은 제주도에서 개마고원까지, 그야말로 한반도의 구석구석을 누빈다. 나는 이것이 명백한 저자의 의도라고 생각한다. 이 소설이 신문에 연재된 것은 1928년 이후 10년 간, 일본은 갈수록 승승장구하고 해방은 그만큼 요원하던 시절이었다. 저자는 이 소설을 통해서 한반도 내에 존재하는 다양한 장소와 경관, 그리고 사람들에 대한 이야기를 담아내려 했다. '작지만 완전한 세계로서의 한반도'라는 개념이 이 대하소설을 관통한다. 면적은 작지만 동서 보다는 남북으로 긴 국토의 형상 때문에 한반도 안에는 갖가지 미세기후와 식생이 존재한다. 이는 수 많은 산과 강, 들판과 바다와 결합하여 실로 다양한 상황을 만들어 낸다. 나는 홍명희가 이 소설을 통해 아름답고 다채로운 땅에 대한 희망을 잃지 말자고 동포들을 설득하려 한 것이라고 믿는다.

또 다른 계기는 한 폭의 그림이었다. 몇 년 전 북한 관련 전시회에서 '수림으로'란 제목이 붙은 그림을 하나 보았다. 분명 수묵으로 그린 산수화지만 그 풍광이 이전까지 봐왔던 어떤 전통 산수화와도 달랐다. 그 배경은 완만하고 부드러운 산세가 아니었고 휘휘 늘어진 수양버들이나 소나무도 등장하지 않았다. 그 대신 험하고 깊은 산 속, 빽빽한 자작나무 숲 사이로 나무를 잔뜩 실은 수레를 끌고 가는 두 마리의 말이 등장하고 있었다. 작가의 이름은 최창호. 평양 만수대창작단에 소속된 공훈화가의 작품이었다. 이 때 나는 '이것도 한반도'임을 깨달았다. '작지만 완전한 소우주로서의 한반도'라는 개념을 다시 한 번 확인하는 순간이었다. 열대의 야자수가 우거진 제주도와 남해안의 해안가나 최창호의 그림에서와 같은 툰드라의 자작나무 숲은 소나무가 운치 있게 휘휘 구부러진 하회나 양동 못지 않게 모두 한반도의 풍광인 것이다. 우리에게는 이러한 이 땅의 다양성을 모두 누리고 살아갈 권리가 있다. 그리고 그 기회는 다시 올 것이다.

그렇다면 '한반도의 이상적인 정주환경'이란 무엇일까? 근대 이전의 농촌의 모습에서 이와 관련된 해답이 있다고 믿는 사람들도 있지만, 도시화를 기정 사실로 인정하지 않을 수 없는 현재의 상황으로 보아 이것은 더 이상 보편적인 설득력을 갖지 못한다. 따라서 우리는 일단 도시적 관점을 염두에 두지 않을 수 없다. 또한 당연한 이야기지만 지구적 환경문제, 삶의 질, 문화적 다양성과 같은 인류 공통의 과제들은 한반도라고 예외가 아니다. 이러한 보편성이 한반도의 자연적, 문화적, 역사적 특성과 결합할 때 비로소 추구할 가치가 있는 실천적 체계가 만들어진다. 이러한 생각을 바탕으로 한반도 북쪽지역과 관련하여 다음과 같은 접근 방식을 제안한다. 이것은 간단히 말해서 작고, 밀도가 높으며, 복합적인 도시에 관한 이야기다.

작고, 밀도가 높으며, 복합적인 도시

도시 정주면적(footprint)의 유지
북한은 사회주의적 도시계획의 원칙에 따라 도농 간의 격차를 줄이기 위해 대도시의 성장을 억제해 온 것으로 알려져 있다. 이에 따라 인구가 250만명인 평양을 제외하고는 대도시가 없다. 제2, 제3의 도시인 함흥이나 청진의 인구가 각각 77만, 67만에 불과하다. 인구가 수백만 명에 달하는 대도시가 즐비한 남한의 입장에서 보면 상대적으로 적은 북한의 인구에도 불구하고 이것은 매우 특이한 현상으로 보인다. 단 앞으로 경제발전이 가속되는 경우 상당한 인구의 증가는 피할 수 없다고 할 것이다.

이에 대한 도시적 대응 방식은 크게 두 가지다. 하나는 도시권역을 평면적으로 확대시켜가는 것이고, 또 다른 하나는 밀도를 높이는 것이다. 나는 여기서 후자의 방식이 훨씬 더 큰 미래적 가치를 갖는다고 생각한다. 어차피 적절한 밀도는 도시로서는 꼭 갖추어야 할 엔진과도 같은 것이다. 그만큼 도로, 통신 등의 인프라 효율도 좋아지며 도시 내 이동거리도 짧아진다. 도시 안은 고밀도지만 조금만 벗어나면 바로 자연을 접할 수 있는 이점도 있다. 반대로 도시가 수평적으로 지나치게 성장하는 경우, 전세계 대도시에서 보듯이 수 많은 문제들을 야기한다. 자연은 그 만큼 멀어지고 평균 밀도 이하의 지역에 대한 인프라 투자는 효율이 그만큼 떨어진다. 시민들의 공간 이동 거리가 멀어짐에 따라 시간과 에너지의 사용도 급증한다. 서울은 이러한 폐단의 대표적인 예다. 김성홍 교수의 연구에 의하면 수 많은 고층건물에도 불구하고 서울의 평균 건물 층수는 2.5에 불과하다. 이것은 적어도 4, 5층 정도의 평균밀도만 가져도 서울의 전체 정주면적을 지금의 절반 이상으로 줄일 수 있다는 것을 의미한다. 동시에 이것은 고층건물에 의지하지 않고도 한 도시가 필요로 하는 밀도는 얼마든지 만들어낼 수 있다는 것을 보여준다. 저층건물을 위주로 하면서도 세계적인 도시경쟁력을 보여주는 유럽의 도시들이 그 살아있는 예다.

● 복합개발을 통한 직주 근접 및 보행자 중심의 도시 조성
미래 도시의 또 다른 키워드는 '복합'이다. 현재와 같은 수평적 용도구역 체계에서는 한 지역에서 다른 지역으로의 대량 이동은 필연적이다. 하지만 이것은 인프라에 과도한 영향을 주고 과도한 에너지 소비를 유발하고 무엇보다 개인의 삶을 피폐하게 만든다. 한 사회가 그 구성원의 삶의 질을 향상시키기 위해서 할 수 있는 가장 근본적인 조치의 하나는 출퇴근 시간을 줄여주는 것이다. 가장 바람직하게는 대부분의 일상생활을 걸어 다니며 해결할 수 있는 도시를 만드는 것이다. 즉 직주 근접은 앞으로의 도시들이 해결해야 할 최우선적 과제다. 불행하게도 현재까지 남한의 도시에서는 개인이 아무리 이러한 삶을 원해도 도시구조상 거의 불가능에 가깝다. 이와 반대로 북한이 직주 근접을 도시계획의 중요한 개념으로 보고 이를 실천해온 것은 매우 흥미롭다.

앞으로의 도시에는 복합의 개념을 과감하게 도입할 필요가 있다. 저층이건 고층이건 전 층의 용도가 단일한 건물은 근본적으로 더 이상 도시적이지 않다. (나는 이것을 '시루떡'이라고

부른다.) 반대로 한 건물 내에 서로 다른 기능이 수직적으로 배치되는 복합건물이 늘어나면 (나는 이것을 '무지개떡'이라고 부른다.) 그 도시 내 직주 근접지수의 평균은 비약적으로 증가하게 된다. 이것은 가장 인간적이며 동시에 친환경적인 도시환경을 만드는 첫 걸음이다. 〈Image 1. 참조〉

• 한반도 환경에 대한 고려
한반도란 어떤 곳인가? 지구 온난화 등으로 기후 패턴이 이전과 달라졌다고는 하지만 여전히 4계절이 있고 태양의 고도가 철마다 바뀌며 여름은 덥고 습하며 겨울은 춥고 건조하다. 거기에 3면을 둘러싸고 있는 바다와 풍부하게 발달된 강과 호수, 국토의 대부분을 차지하는 산과 언덕, 면적은 넓지 않지만 퇴적작용에 의해 잘 발달된 평야, 그리고 이 다양한 환경이 생산해 내는 각종 물산 등을 고려하면 사실상 전세계적으로도 가장 축복받은 땅 중 하나임에 틀림 없다. 이런 요소들만 잘 이해하고 도시를 만들어도 충분히 살아가기에 좋은 환경을 만들 수 있다.

인구도 많지 않고 농업을 위주로 했던 전근대 시대에는 이러한 가치들이 비교적 잘 지켜졌다. 그러나 근대 이후 이러한 태도는 거의 사라졌고, 우리의 도시는 폭발적으로 증가하는 인구를 수용하는 과정에서 주어진 환경과는 거의 상관 없는 이론과 방식에 의해 만들어졌다. 그 결과로 만들어진 온갖 비효율은 에너지를 무한히 소비함으로써 메꿔졌고, 또 다른 결과물인 미적 결핍은 경제발전이라는 미명하에 그냥 무시하면 되는 것이었다. 이제 이러한 악순환을 중단시킬 때가 되었고 이를 위해서 우리는 다시 한 번 근본적으로 주어진 조건들에 눈을 돌릴 필요가 있다.

상대적으로 덜 개발된 북한이 바로 그 기회를 제공한다. 우리는 도시를 만드는 과정에서 우선 바람 길과 물길을 이해하고 태양의 방향을 고려하며 인근 산과 언덕의 3부 이상을 넘어가지 않는 범위 내에서 가용면적을 확보하는 지혜를 가져야 한다. 무리하게 대도시로 성장시키지 않는 범위 내에서 4, 5층 정도의 평균 층수를 가지는 상대적 고밀도의 도시를 만들고, 인프라와 건물이 서로 복합적으로 결합하며 각각의 건물은 수직적으로 복합 용도를 가져야 한다. 각 건물의 옥상에는 마당이 조성되어 전근대 시절 조상들이 땅에서 누리던 경관을 4, 5층 높이에서 즐기게 될 것이다. 높은 밀도에서 오는 압박감은 건물에 발코니, 필로티 등을 많이 도입하여 소위 다공성의 건축 (highly porous architecture)을 만드는 것으로 완화할 수 있다.

이런 도시는 자연을 위협하지 않을 것이며 시민들은 일상생활의 대부분을 걸어서, 혹은 효율적인 대중교통 수단을 통해 해결할 것이다. 도시 전체의 에너지 소비는 매우 효율적인 패턴을 보일 것이고, 조금만 도시를 벗어나면 오염되지 않은 자연이 기다리고 있을 것이다. 우리는 지금까지 이런 도시를 경험해본 적이 없다. 그러니 한번이라도 이런 도시가 만들어지면 '아, 이런 것이었구나'라고 깨닫게 될 것이다. 그리고 그 가치에 대한 믿음은 한반도의 정주환경을 장기간에 걸쳐 보다 바람직한 것으로 바꿀 수 있다.

결론

결국 북한이라는 과제는 절대로 고립되거나 특수한 것은 아니다. 현재와 같은 정치적 대립의 관계가 어느 정도 정리되고 난 이후의 북한은 더더구나 그렇다. 우리는 인간의 정주환경이 갖는 보편성, 그리고 한반도라는 환경이 갖는 기본적 조건 등에 보다 관심을 가질 필요가 있다. 미래의 북한을 어떤 신비한 지역으로 보거나, 어떤 특수한 방식에 의해서만 다룰 수 있는 대상으로 볼 필요는 없다. 다만, 그 동안 경제발전이라는 지상의 과제를 위해 국토를 오직 산업생산기지로만 이해하고 다뤄온 남한의 시행착오와, 경직된 체제 속에서 사회의 건강한 발전을 억압해 왔던 북한의 또 다른 시행착오를 통해 얻는 교훈을 바탕으로 한 새로운 시도들을 적용하는데 있어서, 과개발된 한반도 남쪽 지역보다는 상대적으로 덜 개발된 한반도 북쪽 지역이 더 많은 가능성을 갖고 있다고 보여질 뿐이다. 두 개의 실패 사례를 통해 얻은 학습효과를 바탕으로 더 나은 새로운 가치를 만들어내야 하는 것, 그것이 북한이라는 과제의 핵심이다. 이것은 경제적, 산업적 논리를 넘어 다수의 인간이 과연 얼마나 아름다운 환경에서 살 수 있는가라는 궁극적인 질문에 대한 답을 구하는 과정이기도 하다. 그래서 결국 이것은 미학적 과제다.

LESSONS FOR THE FUTURE X-O-POLIS: NEW MARKET CITIES

Rafael Luna

—

Rafael received a Master of Architecture from Massachusetts Institute of Technology. He has professional experiences in many countries such as Japan, UK, France, and the US. His background in many countries and cultures influenced on his research that focuses on hybrid architectural typologies in dense urban settings. He is the award winner of Architectural League Prize 2013, and is a faculty member of Rhode Island School of Design where he conducts a studio "Metropolitan Hybrids," and co-author of "I Want to be METROPOLITAN" and "North Korea Atlas." His projects include "Casa Periscopio" in El Salvador and "Leaning House" in S.Korea amongst others, and works had been exhibited in many places around the world, including Museum of Modern Art in New York, Parsons the New School for Design in New York and Venice Biennale.

NBA Hall of Famer Dennis Rodman's recent visits in 2013 to North Korea has generated a flurry of news, as well as questions, about the future of the so-called hermit kingdom. Interest was piqued especially when Rodman brought back sentiments of good faith from Kim Jung Un, implying a future where North Korea might open its market. If we allow ourselves to ignore the news of nuclear weapons that usually inundate the media, we can start to imagine the possibilities an untapped market like North Korea might offer as a test ground for new development and urban theory. The focus on nuclear weapons has been the major economic strategy so far, but by opening its market, new soft factors (industries) can be introduced along with new hard factors (urbanity) generating case studies for new city typologies that could be used as models for other emerging markets. The big question is how can North Korea improve its GDP by means of urban strategies rather than nuclear weapon development? In a recent article in The Guardian, there is a passage that reads, "Many economists outside the country argue that if it is serious about improving its economy, North Korea should implement market reforms, build its energy and agricultural sectors and improve international relations by focusing less on nuclear weapons and ballistic missiles." (Talmadge, Eric) Although these may be necessary strategies for improving its economy, they are soft factors (similar to software for a computer). And just as there is software, there should be hardware, urban strategies. How should these cities reform their industries as well as their built environment?

The article in The Guardian was critical of the opening of Masik Pass Ski Resort in Wonsan, North Korea. The massive endeavor to create a luxury ski resort, which can only be used by 0.02% of the population, is criticized as being a playground for the elite, designed on a whim. However, when looked at from the bigger perspective of North Korea opening its doors, Masik Pass could be viewed as an urban strategy for introducing new industry into the country by generating a new typology of city. How can North Korea have its own Aspen or Bern? A year ago, one could only visit Pyongyang on certain designated times of the year, now tourism has opened to new cities and the time frames keep expanding in an effort to promote the tourism industry. So, maybe Masik Pass can only be used by 0.02% of DPRK's population currently; however, if Wonsan introduces this new industry and creates typologies for a ski city, it has the potential to generate new construction, new jobs, and immigration from other countries, raising Wonsan's GDP. This should be the focus of study for the new future X-o-polis of the world: how introducing new urban strategies can also help introduce new industry.

When countries like China, Vietnam, and Cambodia opened their markets, it seemed that there was no clear model of how to operate amidst the urban growth under these new conditions. Many Western models of urbanism were adopted and many of the same urban mistakes were made. We constantly seek new markets and new territories to explore new urban models and typologies in the hopes that we can create better cities. Some of the newer proposals for the 21st century future city include Plan IT Valley in Portugal, Masdar City in the United Arab Emirates, Konza Techno City in Kenya, and Songdo in South Korea, in addition to lesser known Chinese smart pilot cities. A lot of these proposals assume the possibility of starting from zero, but the potential for tapping into a new market is the ability to create new models and typologies by adapting existing conditions, not by ignoring them—as would be the case in transforming Wonsan into a ski city. We usually hear about developing countries in Latin America, Africa, and South East Asia as having market potential, but North Korea opening its market could usher in the most dramatic change. When we start hearing about changes in the global scene from countries like North Korea, it raises the question: What could these new models be and what would come from merging existing socialist structures with a market economy? This presents the possibility of testing out new urban models for density, transportation, energy production, food production, waste management, construction technologies, water production, material research, information technology, and even education integrated into the built environment.

Since "history repeats itself," it would be important to understand the nature of formation of the modern city and its connection to industry to hypothesize how future industries could also shape future cities. Many historians attribute the initial growth of the urban condition to the first industrial revolution in England, which happened somewhere between the mid 1700s to the early half of the 1800s (historians debate the exact dates). With the new technologies that were being developed, the way that people lived changed dramatically in every aspect. Growth in industries within city limits produced jobs that attracted more people. The population of England alone doubled within the first fifty years of the 1800s, and it doubled again in the next fifty. Within the 19th century, it rose rapidly from nearly 8 million people to more than 30 million. This greatly impacted living conditions. Factories took over the urban landscape, and shanty towns started appearing as the rural population migrated into the city, leading to poor living conditions with no proper system for sewage and sanitation, clean water and disease control. The factory became the first new architectural typology associated with the industrialization of the city. Housing was second to the factory when it came to building stock inside the city. This Industrial City model of mechanizing an industry within a city was then adopted from England to the rest of continental Europe, followed by the rest of the world, especially in America and Japan. The city became a machine for mass production.

Belgium was the first to follow England, importing the English engineering and technologies in order to bring new industry to its cities. By adopting the industrial city model, Belgium became the second largest industrial world power. Germany was next to follow. The German Ruhr Valley was nicknamed "Little England" for its resemblance to the English industrial model. Aside from just adopting the model like Belgium did, Germany invested in education and research in the chemical industry, making it the leading world power in chemical technologies. Sweden was another European country to follow, but it started its revolution within the agricultural industry by commercializing the farming industry and producing smaller industries in the countryside, which benefited a larger section of the population. Because of the limits on the transportation of information at that time, European countries with closer proximity to England benefited first. As information started traveling further out, the industrial process started emerging in colonies and emerging markets of the time.

In the American continent, New England was the first point of connection to the trade of information with England, and as such, it became the birthplace of the American Industrial Revolution. Cities along New England's rivers started growing, due to the new mill industry.

From this brief historical oversimplification we can learn a few key points about the growth of cities that may be self-evident now but are still important to identify in order to lay the framework for the pairing of soft factors to hard factors. The first point to mention is that new industry equals new jobs, which generate new migration into the city. This migration into the city also forces a demand on new living conditions, which speaks to idealizing housing typologies for the working masses, as well as how the city should define its edge condition between rural and urban areas as it expands.

This condition was true in the 1800s, as it is true today, and we have seen this condition repeated over and over. For example, Boston was the primary city for the British Empire before the 1800s; as New York became accessible to the West through the Erie Canal, and a faster connection to Europe due to the new clipper ships, New York saw a growth in industry and commerce, bringing an increase in its population of immigrants looking for new opportunities and surpassing Boston. As New York City started to grow dramatically in population, quickly surpassing London as the biggest city in the world, the city saw demand for housing as well as space for its industries to grow. A new architectural typology was developed thanks to improvements in building technology (steel framing, and safety mechanisms for elevators). The skyscraper became the new typology which allowed square footage to be multiplied vertically, providing more area in a limited city.

The skyscraper provided an architectural solution to the lack of space, but sometimes new typologies are luxuries not available to everyone; this results in shantytowns as poor rural immigrants flood the city. Shantytowns, like those that sprang up around English cities at the turn of the 19th century, also exist today in developing cities around the world. The Brazilian favelas are quite notorious in Latin America. Although these shantytowns present a problem for cities in terms of security and sanitation, they also indicate a desire to move to that particular city in search of opportunity. In his book, "The Triumph of the City," Harvard Economist Edward Glaeser explains how these shantytowns are actually indicators of the potential for a better life that the city represents for a rural population. These shantytowns provide a sense of opportunity and ambition for success in the city, one that does not exist in a rural condition. Shantytowns do present a problem however, a physical problem of an urban architectural nature that has become a modern concern for developing cities, and is sometimes neglected in "future city" plans, as is the case for the Masdar proposal. Planned as the most sustainable city in the world, Masdar integrates low-rise density in a limited footprint, built for the highest standards of living. This means that people with lower means cannot afford to occupy the city. Instead, a secondary city for workers outside of the confinements of Masdar has been built. And although Masdar may be the most sustainable built environment as a singular object, the objective of a sustainable city should be for the entire city to operate efficiently, not just a limited area for the ones privileged enough to afford it. So, when planning the success of a city, one should take into consideration the growth in population that may occur from migration of rural to the urban and the diversity of population with varying income levels that that may bring.

As a socialist country, the DPRK has more clear demarcations of rural and urban areas (built vs farmland vs nature) than capitalist countries. This allows us to calculate the rural population and the urban population and indicate potential growth within a single city. Because of rules and regulations imposed on migration, there would not be drastic movement between cities, rather the shift would occur within the city's own rural to urban population. This allows us to calculate the potential built growth of a city in relation to a desired density, for which new typologies of housing would have to be developed, which lays down a very clear set of design parameters for proposing new housing stock that anticipates the population growth and avoids shantytowns. This can also form an urban strategy for shaping the city and defining boundaries. Could these new housing typologies for the masses be what defines a demarcation, as fortification walls did for the medieval city, and periphery ring roads try to do for the modern city? A similar study was proposed by Steven Holl for the "Edge of a City" project in Phoenix, where the boundary between city and nature was demarcated by a ring of hybrid megastructures. The clear boundaries in cities like Sinuiju would demand these hybrid typologies between mass housing, infrastructure like ring roads, and even urban farming.

A second historical reference point is that of expenditure on human capital: investing in human capital and education further innovates the industry giving that city an edge over the others. As the industry evolves and becomes more specialized, so should its urban fabric. As we now know, cities that did not diversify their industry or invest on human capital ended up declining, as was the case with Manchester, the first industrial city, also nicknamed "Cottonopolis." The once thriving metropolis lost its rank as the leading world textile manufacturer as its single industry started dying out in England and shifted to other cities with cheaper labor or better technologies. We see the same condition now, more than 100 years after the Second Industrial Revolution, in cities like Detroit, where Glaeser explains, "Traditionally, single-industry cities, like Detroit and Manchester, haven't done well in the long run because their industrial monocultures discourage the growth of new ideas and companies" (Glaeser, 33). Detroit failed to develop the capacity to expand their knowledge on an industry that they dominated. It shifted from an idea-making city where the most innovative thinkers of the time pondered on the future of transportation, to a factory city that depended on unskilled labor.

Silicon Valley has been able to survive despite its monoculture in the IT industry. This is because it has been able to invest on human capital, attracting very bright young professionals, venture capitalists, start-ups, and big high-tech companies, yet the city itself lacks the urban fabric that would identify it as an "IT City." Silicon Valley was actually started as a series of office parks, with low density, and a car oriented grid. It's low density and monoculture, has created a real estate market that prices out less skilled people. In that sense, Silicon Valley has become the largest IT office park in the world, not a city. Joi Ito described this condition in an interview with the Boston Globe and Wired Magazine when he became the director for the MIT Media Lab:

"Entrepreneurs in Silicon Valley may be international, but they're not good at thinking globally. Silicon Valley has no culture. Have you ever tried to get food in Palo Alto? I don't think Silicon Valley spends a lot of energy on art, culture, and the humanities. When you're building 3Com and [data] switches, all you need is people who sit and focus on bits. But as we get to the World-Wide Web and think about how does social media impact politics, how does it affect fashion, how do we bring museums online — that is much more New York, Boston, and Washington, D.C. There are hopefully some regional advantages." (Kirsner)

Silicon Valley hasn't been able to adapt its urban fabric as a smart city, just as Detroit wasn't able to become a test lab for new models of transportation within the city. This is despite the fact that the transportation industry has been one of the biggest factors in urban grid modifications, which should have been obvious for Detroit. For example, when horses and carriages were the main means of transportation, streets needed to be the dimensions of a carriage. Then the motorized car transformed the dimensions to that of two cars side by side. As cars got faster and more available, streets expanded. We see this evolution of streets getting wider and wider, yet all new transportation models point to smaller and more efficient means of micro-transport and public transport within the city, such as the "City-Car," developed at the

MIT Media Lab, bike-sharing programs, light rail, and even the Segway. Streets that were once too wide could develop slender housing typologies as medians as micro transportation takes over. We still do not know an exact strategy for how existing urban fabric can be drastically modified with other industries, but we can envision new typologies emerging within the allowable new in-between condition for cities, and adapting existing building stock to create new hybrid typologies.

The last point is Proximity, which allows for a rapid propagation of ideas. Proximity is immediately associated with density. New models for urban density, through clusters (the micro-district, multi-urban cores, border cities); and architectural density, through diversity in Typology, avoid a monoculture. As mentioned in the previous point, Silicon Valley is a condition that is trying to be repeated in other places around the world, but some of these proposals fail to see that innovation clusters cannot be created from scratch. Even Silicon Valley has a history tied back to the founding of Stanford University. Kendall Square in Cambridge, MA, has become the densest concentration of start-ups in the world, attracting the second most venture capital funding outside of Silicon Valley. Described in a recent article entitled "The Next Silicon Valley" in the September/ October volume of the MIT Technology Review,

...founders of 450 companies crowd into nine floors, many in common rooms...On a heat map of innovation, the place is glowing red. Sharing same elevator banks are venture capital firms that collectively manage $8.7 billion...Kendall has become what economist call a cluster, a concentration of interconnected companies that both compete and collaborate... (Regalado, 84)

Kendall Square was also not built from scratch but happened because of several variables, including its proximity to MIT, which has a large concentration of PhDs and MDs, making it remarkably easy to start a company. Governments around the world want to reproduce this process by proposing "innovation clusters" and investing millions in new cities. As mentioned in the same Tech Review article, "The problem for governments is that they often try to define where and when innovation will occur."

These clusters happen organically. In the case of Kendall, it makes sense for pharmaceutical companies to be near MIT to benefit from the human capital, forming a bio-tech cluster. For North Korea, there already exist a model for socialist clustering in the form of the micro-district. This model allows for a whole city block to act independently from other neighborhoods, providing work, manufacturing, education, and housing within it, like a city within a city. Demarcations of parcels for real estate are non-existant since the government owns the land. If the market were to open, creating a system of parcels would be the first step. The challenge is to develop a new capitalist form of micro-district that would allow for diversity in typologies within a housing block that still provides new forms of manufacturing, education facilities, cultural facilities, office buildings on top of retail podiums that define inner pedestrian streets, recreational centers, parks, and high-rises as density boosters.

There is also proximity at a regional scale. Cities like Boston, Philadelphia, Washington DC and

New York thrive on the proximity factor because of their higher density and their proximity to each other. This allows resources of human capital to be shared within a region. This is another density condition at a city level that is a potential for North Korean border cities. These cities share a border with Chinese cities that provide trade between the two countries. Cities like Sinuiju, Mampo, and even the Rason Special Area could become special economic zones for trade that grow as twin cities between two countries. New typologies would emerge that support the infrastructure of connecting these sister cities. Contemporary versions of Ponte Vecchio could emerge as a diplomatic trade zone of international commerce, not only increasing trade between the two but potentially increasing tourism as well.

In conclusion, cities should be treated as an adaptable living organism, not as a finished mechanized product. With this said, new market opportunities allow for urban architectural explorations that seek to introduce new industries, new typologies, and new spatial configurations. This can only be done by the adaptation of an already existing framework. Injecting new models into these cities would allow for unforeseen results that would have never been possible from a tabula rasa condition. New markets like North Korea could benefit from retrofitting its cities in order to experiment on how to grow its GDP through urban interventions. Let's not disregard Masik Pass as a whim, as it could be just the starting point for a new North Korean X-o-Polis.

LESSONS FOR
THE FUTURE X-O-POLIS:
NEW MARKET CITIES

라파엘 루나

—

라파엘은 보스턴과 서울을 기반으로 하는
설계사무소 PRAUD 공동대표이다. 그는 MIT에서
건축학 석사학위를 취득하였으며 일본, 영국,
프랑스, 미국 등 여러 문화의 다양한 국가에서 실무를 익혔다.
그는 이러한 다양한 경험을 바탕으로 고밀도 도시에서의
하이브리드 건축에 대해 연구를 진행한다.
그는 2013 뉴욕 젊은 건축상 수상자이며, 현재 로드아일랜드
스쿨오브디자인 (RISD)에서 설계 스튜디오
"메트로폴리탄 하이브리드"를 가르치고 있다.
그는 "I Want to be METROPOLITAN"과
"North Korea Atlas"의 공동저자이기도 하다.
그의 대표작은 엘 살바도르의 "카사 페리스코피오"와
한국의 "리닝 하우스(수헌정)"을 포함하며,
그의 작품은 뉴욕 모마, 뉴욕 파슨스 대학, 베니스 비엔날레에서
전시되기도 하였다.

2013년, NBA 명예의 전당에 입성한 데니스 로드맨의 북한 방문은 은둔 국가의 미래와 관련한 질문과 뉴스들을 야기했다. 특히나 그가 김정은이 근시일 내에 북한의 시장을 개방할 것이라고 암시하는 소식을 가지고 돌아온 것이 가장 큰 촉매 역할을 했다. 만약 우리가 미디어에 범람하고 있는 핵무기와 관련한 정보들을 잠시 차치한다면, 북한과 같은 미개발 시장을 새로운 발전과 도시 이론의 시험장이라는 가능성으로 상상할 수 있을 것이다. 현재까지 북한의 주된 경제 전략은 핵무기였으나 시장개방을 통해 새로운 소프트요인과 하드요인(도시생활)의 도입은 신흥 시장의 사례연구로 사용이 가능한 새로운 도시 유형학에 대한 사례 연구를 제시할 수 있다. 여기서 중요한 점은 북한의 핵무기 개발이 아니라 그들이 도시 전략을 이용하여 어떻게 GDP를 개선할 수 있는가하는 것이다. 가디언지의 기사 중 한 부분에서 "해외 경제학자들은 북한이 그들의 경제 상황을 개선하는 문제에 있어서 진지한 태도를 갖고 있다면, 핵무기와 탄도 미사일에의 투자를 줄이고 시장 개혁, 에너지와 농업 부문의 신장 그리고 국제 관계의 개선에 힘써야 한다고 주장한다"고 보도했다. 이는 경제를 개선하는데 있어서는 필요한 전략일지도 모르겠으나 위와 같은 요소들은 소프트요인이며 따라서 소프트웨어가 존재하는 것처럼 도시 전략으로서의 하드웨어도 존재해야만 한다. 그렇다면 이와 같은 도시들이 어떻게 산업과 건조 환경을 재구성할 것인가?

최근 가디언지는 북한의 원산에 위치한 마식령 스키장의 개장에 대한 비평을 실었다. 오직 인구의 0.02%밖에는 사용할 수 없는 스키 리조트를 만들겠다는 거대한 시도는 한눈에도 엘리트를 위한 유희공간을 만든다는 것처럼 보였기에 비판을 면치 못했다. 하지만 시장의 개방이라는 관점에서 마식령을 조명한다면 이는 새로운 도시 유형학의 생성을 통해 국가에 새로운 산업을 소개하는 도시 전략이 될 수 있다. 북한이 어떻게 그만의 아스펜과 베른을 가질 수 있는가? 일 년 전에는 연중 오직 지정된 날에만 평양을 방문할 수 있었지만 현재 관광업은 두 개의 도시를 새롭게 더 개방하였으며 기간의 연장과 관광산업을 홍보하려는 노력이 계속되고 있다. 따라서 비록 현재는 다소 폐쇄적이지만 원산의 새로운 산업과 도시 유형이 소개된다면 다른 지역으로부터 원산으로의 이주를 촉진할 수 있는 새로운 도시개발과 직업이 발생할 것이며 이로부터 원산의 GDP를 신장시킬 수 있는 가능성을 모색할 수 있을 것이다. 그러므로

앞으로의 X-O-Polis 연구의 초점은 이와같은 종류의 것이 되어야 할 것이다.

증국, 베트남, 캄보디아 등의 국가들은 새로운 조건 하에서의 도시 성장을 위한 모델을 갖지 못한 채 시장을 개방했다. 따라서 여러 종류의 서양 어버니즘 모델들이 차용되었으며 비슷한 실수들이 발생했다. 보다 나은 도시의 건설이라는 희망을 통해 새로운 도시 모델과 유형의 탐사를 위해 새로운 시장과 지역의 모색이 지속되고 있다. 중국의 소규모 실험도시, 포르투갈의 플랜 IT 밸리, 아랍 에미레이트의 마스다 시티, 케냐의 테크노 시티, 그리고 한국의 송도 등은 21세기의 미래 도시를 표방하고 있다. 이들 계획안의 가능성은 영점에서 시작하지만 새로운 시장에 접근하는 잠재력은 기존의 상태를 조정하여 새로운 모델과 유형을 생성하는 가능성을 제공한다. 이와 같은 현상을 뒷받침할 사례로서 원산의 스키 도시를 들 수 있다. 현재까지 시장 가능성의 문제는 라틴아메리카, 아프리카, 남-동아시아 등의 개발도상국에서 시작하였으나 이제부터는 북한의 시장개방이 가장 극적인 변화를 야기할 것이다. 이로부터 변화를 겪고 있는 북한을 위한, 그리고 북한과 비슷한 상황에 처한 국가들을 위한 새로운 모델은 무엇이 될 수 있을 것인가? 또한 북한의 사회적 구조를 시장 경제와 융합한다면 어떠한 현상이 발생할 것인가?하는 질문들이 제기된다. 이러한 상황과 질문들을 실제로 밀도, 교통수단, 에너지 생성, 식량 생산, 폐기물 관리, 건설 기술, 물 생산, 재료 연구, 정보 기술 그리고 심지어 건조 환경에 통합된 교육을 새로운 도시 모델을 실현할 수 있는 가능성을 선사한다.

"역사는 반복된다" 그러므로 미래 산업이 어떻게 미래 도시를 형성하는지 가설을 세우기 위해 현대 도시 생성의 섭리와 산업과의 관계를 이해하는 것이 중요하다. 많은 역사가들은 도시 조건의 초기 성장을 1700년대 중반에서 1800년 초반 사이(역사가들은 확실한 년도를 논쟁 중이다) 일어난 영국의 첫 산업혁명의 결과로 본다. 모든 면에서 사람들의 생활 방식이 발달하고 있던 새로운 기술로 급격히 변화했다. 도시 내의 산업 성장은 더 많은 사람을 끌어들이는 일자리를 생성했다. 1800년대의 처음 50년 안에 단독으로 영국의 인구는 두 배로 늘었고, 그 다음 50년 동안 또 다시 두 배가 되었다. 19세기에 8백만 명에서 3천만 명 이상으로 급격히 상승했다. 이것은 생활 조건에 큰 영향을 미쳤다. 공장이 도시 경관을 차지했으며 농촌 인구가 도시로 이동하며 빈민가가 나타나기 시작했고 그와 함께 제대로 된 하수시설과 위생시설, 깨끗한 물과 질병 예방이 없는 열악한 생활 여건을 가지고 왔다. 공장은 도시의 산업화와 관련된 첫 건축적 타이폴로지가 되었다. 주택은 공장에 이어 도시 내에서 주식 구축에 관한 두 번째 타이폴로지였다. 이런 도시 내 산업을 기계화하는 산업 도시 모델은 영국에서부터 나머지 유럽 대륙, 그 후 미국과 일본에서 차용되었다. 도시는 대량 생산의 기계가 되었다.

벨기에는 자국의 도시들에 새로운 산업을 가져 오기 위하여 영국의 엔지니어링 및 기술을 수입하여 영국을 첫 번째로 따랐다. 산업 도시 모델을 차용함으로써 벨기에는 두 번째로 큰 산업 강대국이 되었다. 그리고 독일이 그 뒤를 따랐다. 독일의 루르 계곡은 영국의 산업 모델과의 유사성으로 "작은 영국"이라는 별명이 붙었다. 벨기에가 단순히 모델을 차용했던 것과 별개로 독일은 화학 산업의 교육 및 연구에 투자하여 화학 기술 분야를 이끄는 세계 최고가 되었다. 스웨덴은 영국을 따른 또 다른 유럽 국가였는데, 농업을 상업화하고 더 많은 인구에 이득이 되는 소규모 산업을 시골지역에 만들어 농공업 내에서 혁명을 시작하였다. 그 시대의 정보운송의 한계로 인해 영국에 근접한 유럽 도시들이 먼저 편익을 얻었다. 정보다 더 멀리 퍼지기 시작하면서 당시의 식민지와 신흥 시장에 산업 공정이 나타나기 시작했다. 미국 대륙에서는 뉴 잉글랜드가 영국과의 정보 교환이 첫 연결지점이었고 그렇게 미국 산업 혁명이 발생지가 되었다. 뉴 잉글랜드 강을 걸친 도시들은 새로운 제분 공업으로 인해 성장하기 시작했다.

이 짧고 단순한 역사에서 우리는 이제 자명할지 모르, 그러나 소프트 요인과 하드 요인의 페어링을 위한 사전 준비를 위해 짚고 넘어가는 것이 여전히 중요한, 도시의 성장에 관한 몇 가지 주요 포인트를 배울 수 있다. 첫 번째 포인트를 들자면 새로운 산업은 이 도시로의 새로운 이주를 발생시키는 새로운 직업이라는 점이다. 이 도시로의 새로운 이주는 또한 새로운 생활 조건을 요구한다. 이는 노동자를 위한 주택 타이폴로지를 이상화하고 도시가 농촌과 도회지 사이의 주변 조건을 어떻게 정의해야 하는지에 대해 말한다.

이러한 상태는 1800년대와 같이 현재도 사실이며 우리는 이러한 상태가 계속해서 반복되어 온 것을 보았다. 예를 들면, 보스턴은 1800년대 전 대영 제국의 주된 도시였다. 뉴욕이 이리 운하를 통해 서부로 접근이 가능해지고, 새로운 쾌속 범선으로 인해 유럽으로 보다 빠르게 연결이 되자 뉴욕은 산업과 상업의 성장을 보았고 그것은 새로운 기회를 찾는 이민자 수의 증가를 가져왔으며, 보스턴을 넘어섰다. 뉴욕의 인구가 급격히 늘어나기 시작하면서 세계에서 가장 큰 도시로서 런던을 빠르게 넘어섰고, 이 도시는 주택과 산업의 성장을 위한 공간의 요구를 보았다. 새로운 건축 타이폴로지는 새로운 건설 기술(철골, 그리고 엘리베이터의 안전메커니즘)의 향상 덕분에 발달되었다. 마천루는 면적이 수직으로 증식할 수 있게 하는 새로운 타이폴로지가 되었고 제한된 도시에 더 많은 면적을 제공하였다.

마천루는 공간 부족에 건축학적 솔루션을 제공하였으나 때때로 이런 새로운 타이폴로지들은 모두에게 유효한 호사가 아니었으며 가난한 시골 이민자들이 도시로 물밀듯이 밀려들어오며 빈민가를 낳았다. 19세기의 전환기에 영국 도시들 주위에 갑자기 생겨난 빈민가는 오늘날에도 세계의 개발도상국에 존재한다. 브라질의 "파벨라스"는 라틴 아메리카에서 상당히 악명 높다. 이런 빈민가들이 안전과 위생 측면에서 도시의 문제점을 드러내지만 이것은 또한 기회를 찾아 특정한 도시로 이주하는 사람들의 욕망을 나타낸다. 하버드 경제학자 에드워드 글레이저는 그의 저서 "도시의 승리"에서 도시가 가지고 있는 이런 빈민가들이 사실 농촌 인구를 위한 더 나은 삶의 가능성의 지표라는 것을 설명한다. 이런 빈민가들이 사실은 지방 조건에서는 존재하지 않는 기회와 도시에서의 성공의 야망을 제공한다. 그렇지만 빈민가는 문제를 드러내기는 한다. 현대 개발중인 도시들의 우려가 된 도시 건축 특성의 물리적인 문제, 그리고 마스다르 계획안의 경우처럼 때때로 "미래 도시" 계획에서 도외시된다. 세계에서 가장 지속 가능한 도시로 계획되어, 이 도시는 높은 생활 수준을 위해 만들어진 제한된 면적안에 저층 밀도를 통합한다. 이것은 낮은 수입을 가진 사람들이 도시 거주를 감당할 수 없고 마스다르의 국한된 장소 밖의 노동자를 위해 이차적인 도시를 만들어야 한다는 뜻이다. 그리고 마스다르가 단일 개체로서 가장 지속 가능한 건조 환경일지라도 지속 가능한 도시의 목적은 단지 여유 있는 운 좋은 사람들을 위한 한정된 장소가 아니라 도시 전체가 효율적으로 작동하는 것이

되어야한다. 그러므로 도시의 성공을 예견할 때 농촌에서 도시로 발생할 수 있는 인구 증가와 그것이 가져올 수 있는 다양한 소득 수준을 가진 인구의 다양성이 고려되어야 한다.

사회주의 국가로서 북한은 자본주의 국가에 비해 더 명확한 농촌과 도시 지역의 경계(건조 vs 농지 vs 열린 자연)를 가지고 있다. 이것은 우리가 농촌 인구와 도시 인구를 산출할 수 있도록 하고 단일 도시내의 잠재 성장을 나타낸다. 이주의 규칙과 규정으로 인해 도시간의 급격한 이주는 없고 도내의 농촌에서 도시로 인구 이동이 발생한다. 이것은 또한 어떠한 새로운 주택 타이폴로지가 개발되어야 할지를 위해 도시의 잠재적 built growth를 요구된 밀도에 비교하여 산출할 수 있도록 한다. 이것은 인구 증가를 예상하는 새로운 주택 재고의 제안과 빈민가 방지를 위한 아주 명확한 설계 파라미터를 내놓는다. 또한 이것은 경계를 정의하고 도시를 형성하는 도시 전략을 구성할 수 있다. 이런 노동자를 위한 새로운 주택 타이폴로지가 중세 시대에서 방어 성벽이 그랬던 것처럼, 그리고 현대 도시에서 가장자리의 외곽 순환 도로가 그런 것처럼 경계를 정의하는 것이 될 수 있는가? 스티븐 홀이 피닉스에서 계획한 "도시의 가장자리" 프로젝트에 비슷한 연구가 있는데 도시와 자연의 경계가 하이브리드 메가스트럭처 링에 의해 표시되어 있다. 신의주 같은 도시의 명확한 경계는 이런 대중 주택, 순환 도로와 같은 기반 구조, 그리고 또한 도시 농장 사이의 하이브리드 타이폴로지를 요구한다.

두 번째 역사 참고 포인트는 인적 자본의 지출이다. 인적 자본의 투자와 교육은 산업을 훨씬 더 혁신하고 그 도시에 다른 도시를 뛰어넘는 edge를 준다. 산업이 발달하고 더욱 전문화된다면 도시구조 역시 그렇게 되어야 한다. 우리가 알고 있듯이 산업을 다양하게 하지 않고 인적 자본에 투자하지 않은 도시들은 결국 소멸되었다. "코튼폴리스"라고 별명이 붙은 첫 산업 도시 맨체스터의 경우가 그랬다. 한때 번창했던 대도시는 영국에서 단일 사업이 자취를 감추면서부터, 그리고 저임금 노동과 더 나은 기술을 가진 다른 도시들로 옮겨지며 세계 최고의 섬유 제조 업체의 지위를 잃었다. 그리고 다시 우리는 제2차 산업 혁명이 100년 넘게 지난 지금 같은 상황을 디트로이트 같은 도시들에서 다시 본다. 글레이저가 설명하기를, "전통적으로 디트로이트나 맨체스터같은 단일 산업 도시들은 산업의 단

일 문화가 새로운 아이디어와 회사의 성장을 막기 때문에 장기적으로는 잘 되지 못했다." (Glaeser, p33) 디트로이트는 그들이 지배하는 산업에 대한 지식을 확장할 수 있는 능력을 개발하는데 실패했다. 교통의 미래를 숙고하는 당대의 가장 혁신적인 사상가들이 이아이디어를 만드는 도시에서 비숙련 노동에 의존하는 공장 도시로 변했다.

"실리콘 밸리는 IT산업의 단일 문화에도 불구하고 살아남을 수 있었다. 이것은 인적 자본에 투자를 해서 아주 명석한 젊은 전문가, 벤처 투자가, 신생 기업, 그리고 큰 첨단 기술 기업을 끌어들였기 때문이다. 그러나 도시 자체는 그것을 "IT 도시"라고 정의할 수 있을만한 도시 조직이 부족하다. 실리콘 벨리는 사실 저밀도와 자동차 중심의 그리드로 일련의 복합 상업지구로서 시작했다. 저밀도와 단일 재배는 덜 숙련된 사람에게 터무니없는 가격을 매기는 특정 부동산 시장을 만들었다. 그런 의미에서, 실리콘 벨리는 도시가 아닌 세계에서 가장 큰 IT 복합 상업지구가 되었다. 조이 이토가 MIT 미디어 랩의 디렉터가 되었을 때 보스톤 글로브와 와이어드 매거진과 한 초기 인터뷰에서 이런 상태를 설명한다."

"실리콘 밸리의 사업가는 국제적일수는 있으나 글로벌하게 생각하는데 능숙하지 않다. 실리콘 밸리에는 문화가 없다. 당신은 팔로 알토에서 음식을 구하려 한 적이 있는가? 내 생각에 실리콘 밸리는 예술, 문화 그리고 인류에 많은 에너지를 쓰고 있는것 같지 않다. 당신이 3Com과 [data] 스위치를 만들고 있을때, 오직 당신에게 필요한 것은 앉아서 비트에 집중할 사람이다. 하지만 월드와이드 웹에서 어떻게 소셜 미디어가 정치에 영향을 주는지, 패션에 영향을 주는지, 뮤지엄을 온라인에 어떻게 가지고 갈건지를 생각한다면-뉴욕, 보스톤, 그리고 워싱턴 D.C. 를 넘어 그곳에 지역적 장점이 있기를 희망한다."

교통 산업이 도시 그리드 수정의 가장 큰 요소였음에도 불구하고 디트로이트가 도시 내 새로운 교통의 모델을 위한 실험 장소가 되지 못했던 것처럼 실리콘 밸리는 스마트 도시로서의 도시 조직을 적응시키지 못하고 있다. 예를 들어 말과 마차가 교통의 주요 수단이었을 때 도로는 마차의 폭이 되어야 했다. 그리고 동력화된 자동차가 그 폭을 두 대의 차가 나란히 서있는 것으로 바꿨다. 자동차가 더 빨라지고, 더 구하기 쉬우며 도로가 확장되었다. 그리하여 우리는 도로의 진화가 점점 더 넓어지는 것을 보았지만, 모든 새로운 교통 모델은 마이크로-수송의 더 작고 더 효율적인 수단과 MIT 미디어 랩에서 개발한 "city-car", 자전거 공유 프로그램, 경철도, 그리고 개발 시기의 세그웨이같은 도시내 대중교통을 제안한다. 지나치게 넓은 도로는 마이크로 교통이 대체하며 슬림한 주택 타이폴로지를 중간 값으로 해서 개발할 수 있다. 우리는 여전히 기존의 도시 조직이 어떻게 다른 산업과 함께 과감하게 수정될 수 있는지에 대한 정확한 전략을 모른다. 하지만 우리는 허용 범위 안에서 도시의 새로운 중간 상태에서 나타나는 새로운 타이폴로지를 그릴 수 있고, 기존의 건물 재고를 개조하여 새로운 하이브리드 타이폴로지를 만들 수 있다.

마지막 포인트는 빠른 증식을 가능하게 하는 근접성이다. 근접성은 밀도와 직접적으로 연관된다. 클러스터(마이크로 지역, 멀티 도시 코어, 국경 도시)를 통한 도시 밀도의 새로운 모델, 그리고 타이폴로지의 다양성을 통한 건축 밀도는 단일 문화를 피할 수 있다. 앞에서 언급한 바와 같이 실리콘 밸리는 세계 다른 곳에서 반복하려고 하는 상태이지만, 이러한 제안 중 일부는 혁신 클러스터를 처음부터 만들어낼 수 없다는 것을 보지 못한다. 심지어 실리콘 밸리는 스탠포드 대학을 설립하는 것에서부터 역사가 시작한다. 매사추세츠 주의 캠브릿지에 있는 캔달 스퀘어는 실리콘 밸리의 외부에서 두 번째로 많은 벤처 캐피탈 펀딩은 끝어든이는 세계에서 한업이 가장 밀도있는 곳집이 되었다. MIT 테크놀로지 리뷰의 9/10월호에 있는 "차세대 실리콘 밸리"라는 제목의 최근 기사가 설명하길,

"…450개 회사의 설립자들은 9개 층 안으로 밀려 들어왔고, 대부분 휴게실에 있었다…혁신의 열지도 위에 이 장소는 붉게 빛났다. 엘리베이터를 함께 타는 것은 공동으로 8억 7천 달러를 관리하는 벤처 캐피탈 회사였다…캔달은 경제학자가 부르는 클러스터, 경쟁하고 협력하는 상호 연결된 회사의 결집이 되었다…"

캔달 스퀘어 역시 처음부터 건설된 것이 아니었지만 박사 학위와 의학 박사가 집중되어있어 회사의 창설을 놀랄 만큼 쉽게 만드는 MIT와의 근접성을 포함한 여러 변수로부터 생겨났다. 세계의 정부는 "혁신 클러스터"를 제안하고 새로운 도시들에

수백만 달러를 투자하여 이 과정을 재현하고 싶어한다. 같은 테크 리뷰 기사에서 언급한 바와 같이 "정부의 문제는 그들이 종종 혁신이 언제 어디서 일어날지 정의하려고 하는 것이다."

이런 클러스터는 유기적으로 생겨난다. 켄달의 경우 약학 회사가 인적 수혜를 위해 MIT 가까이에 위치하여 바이오 테크 클러스터를 형성하는 것은 이해된다. 북한의 경우 이미 마이크로 디스트릭트의 형태로 사회주의적 클러스터화 모델이 존재한다. 이 모델은 도시 블럭 전체가 다른 이웃 지역으로부터 독립적으로 작동할 수 있게 하며 마치 도시 안의 도시처럼 그 안에서 작업, 제조, 교육, 그리고 주택을 제공한다. 정부가 토지를 소유하므로 부동산의 구획 경계는 존재하지 않는다. 시장이 개방을 한다면, 구획 시스템을 구축하는 것이 첫걸음이 될 것이다. 도전은 새로운 양상의 제조, 교육 시설, 문화 시설, 내부 보행자가로를 정의하는 리테일 포디움 위의 오피스 건물, 오락 센터, 공원, 그리고 밀도 부스터 고층 건물을 계속해서 제공하는 주택 블록 내 타이폴로지의 다양화를 가능하게 하는 새로운 자본주의 형태의 마이크로 지역을 개발하는 것이다.

지역적인 규모의 근접성도 있다. 보스턴, 필라델피아, 워싱턴 D.C.와 뉴욕같은 도시들은 근접성 요소로부터 번창하는데 이것은 다른 미국 도시들보다 높은 밀도와 그들 서로의 근접성 때문이며 이것은 지역 안에서 인적 자본의 자원을 공유할 수 있도록 한다. 이것은 북한 경계 도시의 잠재적인 도시 수준의 다른 밀도 상태이다. 이 도시들은 중국 도시들과 경계를 공유하며 두 나라 사이의 무역을 제공한다. 신의주와 라선은 무역을 위한 경제 특구가 되어 두 나라 사이의 쌍둥이 도시로 성장할 수 있을 것이다. 이 자매 도시를 연결하는 기반 시설을 지원하는 새로운 타이폴로지가 등장할 것이다. 현대 버전의 폰테 베키오가 국제 상거래의 외교 무역 지역으로 부상할 수 있고, 두 나라 간의 무역을 증가시키는 것 뿐만 아니라 관광업도 잠재적으로 증가시킬 것이다.

끝으로 도시는 완성품의 기계화된 생산물이 아니라 적응하는 생물로서 취급되어야 할 것이다. 이렇게 말한다면, 새로운 시장 기회는 새로운 산업, 새로운 타이폴로지, 그리고 새로운 공간 구성을 도입하려 하는 도시 건축의 탐구를 가능하게 해야한다. 이것은 기존의 틀을 조정함으로써 수행될 수 있다. 이 도시들에 새로운 모델을 주입하는 것이 타뷸라 라자에서 불가능했을, 예상치 못한 결과를 가능하게 했다. 북한같은 새로운 시장은 도시의 개입을 통해 어떻게 GDP를 성장시킬 수 있을지에 대한 실험을 하기 위해 도시를 개조하여 이득을 취할 수 있을 것이다. 마식령을 변덕이라고 무시하지 말아야 할 것이다. 새로운 북한의 x-o-polis를 위한 출발점이 될 수 있기 때문이다.

References

Talmadge, Eric. "North Korea's Luxury Ski Resort Opens for Business." Theguardian.com. Guardian News and Media, 08 Oct. 2013. Web. 16 Dec. 2013. 〈http://www.theguardian.com/world/2013/oct/07/north-korea-ski-resort-masik-pass〉.

Glaeser, Edward L. Triumph of the City: How Our Greatest Invention Makes Us Richer, Smarter, Greener, Healthier, and Happier. New York: Penguin, 2011. Print.

Kirsner, Scott. "Media Lab Director Joi Ito Talks about the Valley's Weaknesses, Open Technologies, Global Opportunities, and Whether the Lab Is 'selling Itself Too Cheap'" Boston.com. N.p., 10 Jan. 2012. Web. 16 Sept. 2013. 〈www.boston.com/business/technology/innoeco/2012/01/media_lab_director_talks_about.html〉.

Regalado, Antonio. "The Next Silicon Valley." MIT Technology Review 116.5 (2013): 84-86. Print.

MINI METROPOLIS PYONGYANG

Dongwoo Yim

—

Dongwoo Yim is the author and editor of
the "North Korean Atlas," and the principal
and co-founder of architecture and research firm
PRAUD, based in Boston and Seoul. He received
a Master of Architecture in Urban Design
at Graduate School of Design (GSD),
Harvard University, and bachelor's degree
in Seoul National University.
Dongwoo is a faculty member of Rhode Island School
of Design since 2011 where he teaches seminar
and design studios. His research interest focuses on
integral urbanism and architectural typologies
that catalyze urban transformation
in various urban scales. He is the award winner
of Architectural League Prize 2013, and is the author
of "Pyongyang, and Pyongyang After"
by Hyohyung Publishing and "
I Want to be METROPOLITAN" by ORO Editions.
His works have been published
and exhibited world wide including Museum
of Modern Art New York,
International Architecture Biennale Rotterdam,
Venice Biennale and Design Center Seoul,
and he has lectured at Harvard University,
Freie Universität Berlin, Dartmouth College,
Seoul National University and Youngchoo Forum
amongst others.

Pyongyang on the table

There has been much discussion on urban structure and architecture in Pyongyang throughout various periods of Korean architectural scholarship. Despite the limitation of data and materials, a variety of discussion has occurred, at times spontaneous and at times constant. The reason why discussion on Pyongyang or North Korea these days is interesting is that, unlike in the past, they focus on the future of Pyongyang rather than the current condition of the city. Past discussions mostly focused on what built environment we knew of in the city, based on the limited sources of data. However, even though there is still a lack of resources, the conversation these days focuses on how North Korean architecture and its cities will transform in the near future. It is extremely important to see the future of the city in a more constructive way, because no matter whether we, as South Koreans, have enough data or not, Pyongyang will change, and is, in fact, already changing. Thus, South Korean architects should focus on finding their roles in the transition of Pyongyang and on putting effort into professional exchange with the North Korean architectural field. At the moment, when Pyongyang has not really gotten into the momentum of transformation yet, perhaps one of the most important challenges we face is having a clear perspective on how to structure the future of Pyongyang, because it will influence not only the actual urban structure of Pyongyang but also the relationship between North Korean cities.

MINI Metropolis, a new perspective on city

Rem Koolhaas contended that urbanism has died. This does not mean that there is no reason to have architects' perspectives on the city but rather that anything can be viewed as urbanism. We are already living in cities that are different than the ones when the word "urbanism" first came to be. More than 50% of the world's population live in cities and, by 2050, more than 75% of the population will make up the urban population. This does not only mean that the current cities will become expanded and denser but it also means that new types of cities will emerge in the world. In other words, there will be more cities that cannot be explained by historical concepts of the city or metropolis. The frame of "urbanism" is very much outdated in understanding the full gradation of present and future cities. Arjen van Susteren picked one hundred metropolises and analyzed them in the book "Metropolitan World Atlas;" however, it seems it is not so easy to put cities like Seattle or Sydney together with cities like New York or Tokyo. This means we need a more precise taxonomic concept that can differentiate one metropolis from another metropolis; MINI Metropolis is one of the concepts that groups cities like Boston, Seattle and Copenhagen together. These cities have less density and population but have stable growth with high a quality of living. We believe Pyongyang as well as other North Korean cities can be restructured in the future using the perspective of the MINI Metropolis.

In the 1927 film, "Metropolis," by Fritz Lang, the ultimate end of growth of a city is described as a megalopolis such as New York. Of course, not all-cities are megalopolises, nor should they be, but there are numerous cities, especially in developing countries, that look like they are running with the goal of being a megalopolis. Neither Seoul, which has one of the fastest urban booms in history, nor many recent Chinese cities, are exceptions to that race. And, after all, mid or small scale cities seem like they are the losers in such a race. Those second-tier cities have a low quality of built environment and insensible, sometimes negative, growth. This is mostly because they once had a goal of becoming a megalopolis like New York. In a MINI Metropolis, you find a high quality built environment, gradual growth, and stable industries, all of which you barely see in a second-tier city. And unlike a second-tier city, a MINI Metropolis has a unique identity, is more sustainable, and is more independent from other megalopolises. Compared to a megalopolis, a MINI Metropolis has the advantage of having less urban problems and more flexibility. For instance, bio-technology industries have grown dramatically in Boston since 2000 with close relationships to major institutions of the city; now the city has become the world's biggest bio-technology cluster. This is not easily found in a megalopolis such as New York or London, because they are less flexible and, therefore, can not so easily adopt new types of industries or systems. Thus, flexibility and high quality built environment are very strong advantages of a MINI Metropolis, and it can easily become a model for a small/or mid size city.

MINI Metropolis Pyongyang

Can Pyongyang become a MINI Metropolis? Prior to answering this question, perhaps it is important to ask whether Pyongyang should become a MINI Metropolis. One of the primary factors of socialist urban planning is to abolish the difference between urban and rural areas. It is based on socialism's fundamental thought that city bourgeoisie exploit labor from rural areas, and thus, in a socialist city, the size of the city is very much limited in order to not have an overgrown city that causes urban strife. North Korea followed this very concept. Even though Pyongyang is five times bigger than Seoul, it only has a population of 2.5 million, which is just 10% of the whole population of the nation, whereas Seoul has 10 million people in the city—25% of the nation's population—and 20 million people in metropolitan Seoul, which is half of the South Korean population. In other words, Pyongyang is already closer to a MINI Metropolis than a megalopolis. Considering the total population of the country, which is 25 million, its economic scale, and its close distance to one of the super megalopolises, Seoul, it is not easy to foresee Pyongyang becoming a megalopolis.

What approach then should we take to make Pyongyang a MINI Metropolis? Although it is true that much of Pyongyang's infrastructure is very old, it is also true that the city has better infrastructure than another city of similar economic condition. This is because of North Korea's stable growth until the late 1980s, and its desire to make Pyongyang an international city. The current built environment of Pyongyang gives enough reason to appreciate the existing urban fabric and improve upon it instead of developing an ad-hoc master plan for the city. There are two scales of approach to respect the urban fabric of the city and keep its identity: urban scale and architectural scale.

In the 1953 Master Plan that architect Kim Jung-Hee proposed, Pyongyang was planned as a multi-core (or multi-district) city. Based on the socialist urban planning strategy, this was to control radical expansion of the city and to provide enough green space within the city. In the master plan, each district is structured with a centralized square, and main roads run between districts. Of course, this multi-core idea is not fully implemented to the current urban structure of Pyongyang, but it still keeps the big idea. Multi-core is one of the most outstanding features of MINI Metropolis and, therefore, we can easily link Pyongyang's development path to the MINI Metropolis.

The biggest difference between a second-tier city and a MINI Metropolis is the multi-core system. This mostly occurs in big metropolises; instead of having one single center, it has various cores for each feature, such as, finance, education, commercial, cultural, and so on. In a MINI Metropolis, though its small in scale, we can see a multi-core system easily. It helps to define a city in various ways rather than in a singular way, and allows a city to be recognized as a 'metropolis' rather than just a city. For instance, in Seoul, the character of Jongro is different from Gangnam, and the atmosphere of Youido is different from Shinchon. That being said, multi-core systems distribute enormous urban functions to many different districts and form various characters in the city. It allows a city to grow more evenly rather than being centralized. In other words, Pyongyang may realize its original idea of spatial equality through a multi-core system of the MINI Metropolis. The satellite districts that were planned in the 1953 Master Plan can be developed as cores for programs that have not been vibrant in communist society; such as the finance and commercial programs.

The next scale we should consider is, of course,

the architectural scale. There are many side effects when a city is developed too quickly based on a master plan. For sure, a master plan is needed to develop a city in more strategic way; however, it has to be transformed in a more autonomous way throughout time, rather than in a controlled way in too short a period of time. A city like Pyongyang that has an existing infrastructure, given a perspective of Integral Urbanism, especially needs smaller scale projects that can catalyze incremental transformation of the city, not a mammoth development plan. There are two levels in architectural scale that can lead urban transformation; one is catalyzing developments through a key project, and the other is introducing new typology that can reform the city fabric into a city. A key project, according to Joan Busquets, is an iconic project that has an ability to catalyze transformation of urban space around it. In fact, there are many iconic projects in Pyongyang that can eventually become Key Projects; however, as they are mostly built as symbolic gestures to show the regime's propaganda, they have little connection to the surrounding fabric. Therefore, the question for future Pyongyang is not what to build as a key project, but how to transform existing iconic buildings into a key building that can open the potential of the surrounding district. For instance, Ryukyung Hotel has recently restarted construction and finished the exterior envelop which has been abandoned for more than a decade. Even when construction is done, it will mostly likely remain an island in the city. However, if the surrounding district is reformed regarding the function of Ryukyung Hotel, as happened in the relationship between COEX hotel & conventions in Seoul, there is a possibility that the hotel can become a catalyst for the city. Another way to transform the urban structure is the proposal of a new architectural typology. Urban structure can be differentiated by many factors and architectural typology is one that forms urban space through co-relationship with urban fabric. In the case of Pyongyang, the most demanding area that needs a new typology is the residential area. There are many residential typologies in the city currently; however, most of them are very much outdated, and more importantly, they are incompatible with a market economy. Most residential blocks in Pyongyang are following the system of a micro-district, which is a concept of socialist residential block planning that pairs residential development with production and service facilities. As we witnessed in many other former socialist cities, there will be more demand on new types of housing as North Korea opens its market, and it seems it is becoming less desirable to have residential units next to production facilities. Therefore, in the near future, there should be new residential typologies that reflect new demands of the public in Pyongyang; they will not only transform the urban structure of the city but also change the socioeconomics of the city. While it should respond to the amount of residential demand, it also should keep former micro-districts' features that have the advantage of live-work relationships, as well as community units.

Future of Pyongyang

It seems that North Korea is perpetually unstable in terms of politics. However, when we look into the history of marketization of former socialist countries, North Korea's transformation is inevitable. Even so, it may be hard to compare the market scale of Pyongyang directly to that of Chinese cities when they opened their market.

It is not reasonable for Pyongyang to take the model of a Chinese city just because it is similarly a former socialist city. We have witnessed, and still see, the side effects of Chinese development models which are fast and radical. This does not mean that we should plan to retrofit Pyongyang, as is, so that socialist features of the city remain. Instead, at the moment when the gears of transformation have not yet turned in earnest yet, it is very important to open up the discussion of what paradigm is appropriate for the future of Pyongyang. This will give Korean architects a chance to collaborate with North Koreans as well. Indeed, we will have a clear role in the Korean Peninsula only when we can foresee what is needed for the future of Pyongyang and can propose a new paradigm for the city. And for this, there should be more dynamic open discussions on Pyongyang as well as for other North Korean cities.

미니메트로폴리스 평양

임동우

—

임동우는 "북한 도시 읽기"의 저자이며 서울과
보스턴을 기반으로 하는 설계사무소 PRAUD의 대표이다.
그는 하버드 대학교에서 도시설계 건축학 석사,
서울대학교에서 학사를 취득하였다.
현재 그는 로드아일랜드 스쿨 오브 디자인(RISD)에
출강하고 있으며, 그의 연구는 다양한 스케일에서 도시 변화를
촉진시키는 점진적인 도시 변화와 건축 유형에 초점을 맞추고 있다.
그는 뉴욕 건축가 연맹 주관 2013년 뉴욕 젊은 건축가상 수상자이며,
"평양, 그리고 평양 이후"(효형 출판),
"I Want to be METROPOLITAN"(ORO Editions)의 저자이다.
그의 작업은 뉴욕 모마, 로테르담 건축 비엔날레,
서울 디자인 센터, 베니스 비엔날레 등에 전시된 바 있으며,
하버드 대학교, 베를린 자유 대학, 다트머스 대학, 서울대학교,
영추포럼 등에서 강연한 바 있다.

평양에 대한 논의

평양의 도시와 건축에 대한 한국 건축계의 논의는 시대를 거쳐서 이어온 것으로 알고 있다. 물론 자료와 접근성에 제약이 따랐지만, 그 동안 때로는 산발적으로 때로는 지속해서 다양한 논의들이 있었다. 하지만 최근 한국의 건축계에서 주목하고 있는 북한 혹은 평양에 대한 논의가 흥미로운 점은, 그 논의가 '미래'의 평양에 주목하고 있기 때문이다. 그 동안의 논의는 한정된 자료를 갖고 우리가 모르고 있는 평양의 '실상'에 주목했다면, 근래에는 그보다는 평양을 중심으로 하는 북한의 도시와 건축이 앞으로 어떠한 방향으로 나아갈지에 주목하는 경향이 있다. 물론 아직도 그 토대를 뒷받침해줄 만한 자료들이 충분치 않은 것은 사실이다. 하지만 우리가 인지해야 할 사실은 우리 손안의 자료 유무를 떠나 평양은 변화할 것이고 (혹은 이미 변화하고 있고), 따라서 한국의 건축계는 평양에 대한 논의에서 한국 건축가의 역할과 북한과의 교류 가능성에 더 초점을 맞출 필요가 있다. 그리고 지금, 평양이 아직 본격적인 변화에 들어서지는 않은 이 시점에서 아마도 가장 중요한 화두는 어떠한 패러다임으로 평양을 비롯한 북한의 도시들의 미래를 구상할 것인가 이다. 이 패러다임은 평양의 도시 공간을 구성할 때는 물론 북한 내의 도시들이 서로 간에 어떠한 역학적인 관계를 갖고 형성·발전할 수 있을 것인가 구상을 하는 데에도 매우 중요하리라 본다.

미니 메트로폴리스, 새로운 패러다임

렘 콜하스는 어바니즘은 죽었다고 선언했다. 이는 도시에 대한 건축가의 패러다임이 존재할 이유가 없다는 의미가 아니라, 이미 건축계에서 이루어지는 모든 도시에 대한 논의가 '어바니즘'의 범주 안에 포함된다는 의미이다. 우리는 이미 '어바니즘'이라는 단어가 생성될 당시의 규정된 도시에 살고 있지 않다. 현재 세계 인구의 50%가 '도시'에 살고 있고 2050년경에는 전 세계 인구의 75%가 도시인구가 될 것이라는 예측이 있다. 이는 그만큼 기존의 도시가 비대해진다는 의미도 되지만, 동시에 새로운 도시, 혹은 새로운 개념의 도시가 계속해서 출현했고 또 할 것이라는 의미이다. 즉, 100여 년 전에 생겨난 도시, 혹은 메트로폴리스라는 개념으로는 더는 이 수 많은 도시의 개

성을 담아내기 힘들고 당시의 '어바니즘'이라는 틀로는 현재 다양한 개념의 도시를 설명할 수 없다. Arjen van Susteren은 Metropolitan World Atlas 에서 전 세계 100여 개의 '메트로폴리스'들을 선택 및 분석하고 있다. 하지만 우리가 인지하고 있듯이 뉴욕, 도쿄와 같은 도시를 시애틀, 시드니 같은 도시와 같은 범주에서 바라본다는 것은 어딘가 무리가 있어 보인다. 즉, 메가폴리스(Megapolis ; 거대도시) 라는 개념을 통해 뉴욕과 도쿄 같은 도시를 구분 지어 인식하듯이 현대 도시는 좀 더 세분화된 개념이 필요하다. 그리고 필자는 보스턴, 시애틀, 코펜하겐과 같이 인구수와 밀도는 높지 않지만 지속해서 저속 성장을 이어가고 있고 상대적으로 높은 수준의 구축환경을 갖추고 있는 도시들을 Mini Metropolis 라는 개념을 써서 새로이 규정하려고 한다. 그리고 평양을 비롯한 북한의 도시들은 이 미니 메트로폴리스라는 패러다임을 바탕으로 재구성될 수 있지 않을까 한다.

영화 Metropolis (Fritz Lang의 1927년 작)를 보면 마치 도시 발달의 종착점은 현재 뉴욕과 같은 메가폴리스로 묘사되어있다. 물론 모든 도시가 메가폴리스도 아니고 또 그렇게 될 수도 없지만, 실제로 새로이 발달하는 많은 수의 도시들은 마치 메가폴리스가 되기 위해 달려가는 경주마 같다. 지난 50여년간 빠른 속도로 성장해온 서울도 예외일 수 없고, 현재 산업화를 이루고 있는 수많은 중국의 도시들도 마찬가지이다. 그리고 마치 중소규모의 도시들은 그 경주에서 낙오한 듯 덜 성숙한 모습으로 남아있다. 이들 2류 도시(Second Tier City)들의 구축환경은 낙후되었고 인구는 계속해서 빠져나가고 성장은 멈춘 듯 보인다. 이는 애당초 이들 규모의 도시가 성장 모델로 삼은 도시들이 대도시들이기 때문이다. 하지만 미니 메트로폴리스에서는 이러한 2류 도시에서 볼 수 없는 점진적 성장과 높은 수준의 구축환경 그리고 도시를 지탱하는 안정된 산업 구조를 볼 수 있다. 이들은 2류 도시들과는 다르게 도시의 개성이 분명히 드러나고 다른 대도시에 종속되기보다는 자생능력을 갖춘 도시들이다. 또한, 이러한 미니 메트로폴리스의 장점은 도시의 과밀화로 인한 문제가 적고 개발의 유연성이 있다는 점이다. 일례로, 미국의 보스턴은 2000년대 이후부터 성장하기 시작한 BT (Bio-Technology) 산업이 주변의 학교와 연계하기 시작하면서, 현재는 세계에서 가장 발달한 BT 산업도시로 경쟁력을 갖추고 있다. 이러한 새로운 산업과 시대에 적절히 반응하는 유연성은 기존의 뉴욕이나 런던과 같은 대도시 보다는 미니 메트로폴리스에서 강점으로 나타난다. 따라서 이러한 유연성과 높은 수준의 구축환경을 지닌 미니 메트로폴리스는 중규모 도시의 성장모델로서 충분히 가능성이 있어 보인다.

미니 메트로폴리스 평양

그렇다면 평양은 앞으로 새로운 미니 메트로폴리스로서 성장할 수 있을 것인가? 그에 앞서 평양을 여타 대도시가 아니라 미니 메트로폴리스로서 성장시키는 것이 맞는 것인가 생각해 볼 필요가 있다. 사회주의 도시계획의 가장 큰 특징 중 하나가 도시와 농촌 간의 격차를 없애는 것이었다. 이는 급격한 도시화로 인해 농촌에서 도시로 흡수된 노동자들의 삶이 각박해지는 것을 목격하고 사회주의의 기틀을 마련한 마르크스와 엥겔스의 경험 및 분석에 근거하는 것이었다. 따라서 사회주의에서는 도시의 성장을 어느정도 규제하는 것을 원칙으로 하였고, 북한 역시 이 원칙을 받아들여 도시를 구성했다. 결과적으로, 면적 상으로는 서울보다 5배나 큰 평양은 북한 전체 인구의 10% 정도만을 담당하는 250만 정도의 중규모 도시로 성장했다. 이는 전체 인구의 20% 이상을 담당하는 1천만 도시 서울에 비교하면 굉장히 낮은 수치이다. (서울의 수도권까지 따지면 그 수치는 40% 이상으로 올라간다) 다시 말하면, 평양의 도시 규모 자체는 메가폴리스보다는 이미 미니 메트로폴리스에 가깝다. 또한 미래의 평양을 생각할 때에는, 인구 2천5백만 국가에서 예상되는 경제규모와 대표적인 메가폴리스 중에 하나인 서울과 불과 250km 정도 밖에 떨어져 있지 않은 것을 감안하지 않을 수 없다. 결국, 여러 환경적 요소들과 좀더 유연하고 점진적인 성장을 고려한다면 평양은 대도시 모델보다는 미니 메트로폴리스 모델로의 성장이 적합해 보인다.

미니 메트로폴리스가 미래의 평양을 위한 새로운 패러다임이라 했을 때 어떠한 접근이 필요할까? 현재 평양의 인프라들은 많이 낙후 된 것이 사실이지만 북한과 비슷한 소득 수준의 다른 국가 도시와 비슷한 수준일 것으로 생각하는 것은 큰 오해다. 평양, 특히 평양의 도심지 경우에는 인프라가 잘 정비되어 있는데 이는 1980년대 초반까지만 해도 평양을 국제적인 도시로 성장시키고자 했던 계획이 있었던 것을 생각해보면 이해가 된다. 이는 평양의 마스터플랜을 백지상태에서 계획하기 보다는 기존에 있는 도시 조직과 인프라를 살려 어떻게 재구성할 것인가에 초점을 맞추어 계획해야 하는 타당한 이유를 제시한다. 또한, 도시에 대한 기억을 축적한다는 의미에서도 기존의 도시 조직을 최대한 존중하는 계획이 있어야 할 것이며, 이를 위해서는 평양의 새로운 방향을 두 단계의 스케일로 고려하는 것이 필요하다; 첫 번째는 도시공간 스케일이고 둘째는 건축 스케일에서의 제안이다.

평양 도시구조의 기본 틀을 제시한 김정희의 1953년 평양 마스터플랜에 따르면 평양은 다핵화로 구성된 도시이다. 이는 도시의 무분별한 확장을 제어하고 도시에 녹지 영역을 확장하기 위한 사회주의 도시계획 이론을 바탕으로 한 것인데, 평양 마스터플랜에서의 다핵화는 상징광장을 중심으로 주변의 방사형 조직이 지역을 형성하고 다시 대로를 통해 지역 간이 연결된다. 물론 이 다핵화가 현재 평양에 모두 실현된 것은 아니지만 영역에 따라서는 다핵화의 기본 틀을 유지하고 있다. 다핵화는 미니 메트로폴리스의 큰 특징 중 하나이기 때문에 이는 평양이 미니 메트로폴리스로 성장할 수 있는 발판을 제공한다.

앞서 언급한 2류 도시들과 미니 메트로폴리스의 가장 큰 차이점 중 하나가 이 다핵화, 혹은 Multi-Core 구조이다. 대도시에서 흔히 나타나는 이 구조는 하나의 도시가 하나의 '중심', 혹은 다운타운(downtown)에 의존해 확장되는 것이 아니라 경제, 교육, 소비, 문화 등 여러 종류의 '중심'이 혼재되는 구조인데, 미니 메트로폴리스에서는 이러한 특징이 작은 규모로나마 나타난다. 즉, 도시의 성격이 하나로 규정되기 보다는 다핵화로 인하여 다양하게 규정되고 이는 한 도시가 City 보다는 Metropolitan 으로 인식되기 위한 매우 중요한 요소 중 하나이다. 서울에서 종로와 강남의 성격이 다르고 여의도와 신촌의 성격이 다르듯 다핵화 구조는 도시의 거대한 기능을 분산시킬 뿐 아니라 도시에 나타나는 다양한 성격을 각기 다른 영역에 담아낼 수 있는 중요한 요소이다. 또한, 다핵화는 도시가 하나의 중심부에 의존하지 않고 다양한 영역으로 확대하여 도시가 균형적으로 발달할 수 있도록 하는 장점을 지닌다. 다시 말하면, 평양이 원래 추구하고자 했던 도시 공간의 평등화를 다른 방식으로 실현할 수 있다. 예를 들면, 1953 마스터플랜 상에서 상징광장을 중심으로 계획되었던 위성지역들은 각각 시장의 개방과 함께 도입될 수 밖에 없는 새로운 기능, 즉 사회주의 국가에서는 보기 힘들던 금융과 상업 등의 새로운 도시기능들을 담당하며 미니 메트로폴리스 평양을 구성할 수 있을 것이다.

다음 단계는 역시 건축 스케일에서 고민해 보아야 할 문제들이다. 도시를 도시계획에 근거하여 급속하게 성장시키는 것은 많은 부작용을 낳는다. 커다란 밑그림을 위한 도시계획은 필요하지만, 그것이 실현되는 과정은 인위적이기보다는 자율적이어야 한다. 특히나 평양과 같이 나름의 도시 조직과 인프라가 있는 경우에는 대규모 개발계획보다는 작은 규모의 개발을 통하여 다른 개발을 점진적으로 촉진하는 이른바 Integral Urbanism의 시각으로 접근할 필요가 있다. 건축 스케일에서 도시 조직의 변화를 이끌어 내는 방법은 두 가지 정도로 정리할 수 있는데, 하나는 Key Project를 통하여 주변부의 개발을 촉진하는 것이고 다른 하나는 Typology의 개발로 도시 조직을 새롭게 구성하는 것이다. Joan Busquets 가 규정하는 핵심 프로젝트(Key Project)는 그 규모와 프로그램만으로도 도시의 상징적인 프로젝트(iconic project)가 될 수 있지만, 그것에 더하여 주변부 도시조직을 재구성하는 데에 촉진제 역할을 할 수 있는 프로젝트들을 말한다. 사실 문화시설을 비롯한 공공시설 확충에 집중하는 사회주의 도시의 특성상 현재 평양의 조직을 보면 상징 프로젝트는 물론 Key Project가 될 수 있는 프로젝트는 많이 있다. 문제는 이들이 인위적으로 상징성만을 위해 계획되다 보니 주변 도시조직과의 연계성이 떨어진다는 것이다. 결국 미래의 과제는 얼마나 새로운 상징적 건축물을 만들어 내느냐라기보다는, 현재 평양 내에서 Key Project가 될 잠재성을 지닌 프로젝트와 그 주변부가 어떠한 연계성을 갖게끔 할 것인가 하는 문제이다. 한 예로, 이미 류경호텔은 외장공사가 마무리되었고 내장공사의 마무리를 기다리고 있기는 하지만 이것이 완성되더라도 류경호텔은 여전히 도심 속의 외딴섬으로 남을 가능성이 크다. 하지만 마치 서울 코엑스의 호텔 및 컨벤션 센터가 주변의 업무지구를 형성하는데 촉진제 역할을 한 것처럼, 류경호텔과의 연계성을 고려한 주변조직이 재구성된다면 류경호텔 역시 그 주변부를 새로운 (기존 사회주의 도시에서는 찾아볼 수 없는 형태인) 업무지구 형성을 위한 촉진제 역할을 할 수 있을 것이다.

건축 스케일에서 평양의 도시 조직을 재구성하기 위한 또 하나의 방안은 새로운 타이폴로지의 제안이다. 같은 격자 체계 내에서도 다른 타이폴로지로 인하여 도시 조직의 공간 구성이 달라질 수 있는 것처럼, 타이폴로지는 도시 조직 체계와 상호 작용을 통해 도시 공간을 구성한다. 현재 평양에서 새로운 타이폴로지에 대한 스터디가 가장 절실한 부분은 역시 주거영역이다. 평양에는 현재 다양한 주거형식이 존재하는데, 문제는 주거의 대부분이 노후화되었고 더욱 중요한 것은 이들이 새로운 '시장'의 요구와 상충한다는 것이다. 평양의 주거는 사회주의 도시계획이론에서 내세우고 있는 마이크로 디스트릭트 (북한에서의 소구역 계획)를 근간으로 하고 있는데, 이는 주거와 생산시설, 그리고 부대시설을 함께 묶어 단지를 계획하는 개념이다. 헌데 우리가 기존 사회주의 국가들에서 목격했듯이, 북한의 시장이 점차 개방이 되면 시장경제를 경험한 많은 사람들이 새로운 주거형식을 요구할 것이고, 주거환경적인 측면에서 볼 때 기존의 생산시설과 함께 묶여 있는 주거시설은 더는 선호하는 형식이 아닐 것이다. 따라서 가까운 미래의 평양에는 앞으로 대중의 새로운 욕구를 반영할 수 있는 새로운 타이폴로지의 소구역 계획이 나와야 하며 이는 새로운 사회의 변화를 반영하는 것은 물론 도시의 물리적인 환경을 바꾸는 데 지대한 영향을 끼칠 것이다. 또한, 이는 단순히 양적 수요를 충족시켜주는 차원이 아니라, 직주 근접 및 커뮤니티 등 기존의 소구역 계획이 가진 장점을 최대한 살리면서 새로운 주거형식에 대한 수요를 충족시키는 방향으로 나아가야 할 것이다.

평양의 미래

북한의 정치 상황을 보면 늘 불안정해 보인다. 하지만 기존의 다른 사회주의 국가들의 개방화 역사를 보면, 그것이 급진적이었든 점진적이었든, 북한의 변화는 필연적으로 보인다. 하지만 평양을 비롯한 북한의 경제 규모는 아무리 시장경제가 바로 도입이 되더라도 중국과 직접 비교하기는 힘든 규모일 것이다. 다시 말하면 북한의 도시화 모델 역시 단순히 '사회주의 도시의 자본주의화'라는 이유만으로 인접국인 중국의 도시를 모델로 삼는다는 것은 어딘가 무리가 있어 보인다. 게다가 우리는 중국의 급속한 계획적 도시 성장 정책과 도시화의 부작용들을 이미 목격했다. 또한, 통일 한반도를 미리 가정하여 평양을 이상적인 사회주의 도시의 모습만을 간직한 박제 도시로 만든다는 것도 자연스러운 도시 성장을 위한 구상같지 않아 보인다. 이러한 상황 가운데 북한의 대표 도시로 성장할 평양이 어떠한 모델을 취해야 하는지 논의하는 것은 매우 중요하고 시의적절해 보인다. 지금 어떠한 패러다임으로 평양을 바라보는가에 따라서 앞으로 평양이 어떠한 성장 모델을 갖고 발전할 것인지 구상하고 예측할 수 있을 것이며, 나아가 한국의 건축계가 북한과 교류할 수 있는 계기를 마련해줄 것이다. 즉, 우리가 북한의 변화를 미리 진단하고 평양을 위한 새로운 패러다임을 제안할 수 있을 때 비로소 한국 건축계의 역할이 분명해질 것이다. 이를 위해서는 평양을 비롯한 북한의 도시에 대해 더욱더 다양한 패러다임이 제안되고 그에 대한 논의가 활발해져야 하는 것이 아닌가 한다.

POP-UP PYONGYANG, THE IMPORTANCE OF SMALL-SCALE INTERVENTIONS OVER LARGE-SCALE PROJECTS IN NORTH KOREA

Calvin Chua

—

Calvin Chua is a registered architect and urban designer trained at the Architectural Association in UK. In addition to his professional experience in London, Singapore and Shanghai, Calvin writes on topics of urban development in emerging economies for various architectural journals and magazines and has taught workshops at the Architectural Association and Istanbul Bilgi University. Calvin is also a founding member of Choson Exchange, a non-profit organization focusing on economic policy, business and legal training for young North Koreans. He has conducted workshops on the importance of urban design and infrastructural planning to planners, policy makers and industry experts in North Korea.

Just as economic outlook in North Korea began to look rosy after a month of news coverage on the creation new Special Economic Zones across the country, a dramatic political purge is currently taking place. While the larger impact of such a political event on the SEZ development is still yet to be seen, it nonetheless reveals the intrinsic uncertain political condition (both internal and external) investors have to deal with when investing in these large infrastructure and construction projects. Such precarious conditions have led to intermittent developments in Rason SEZ and Kaesong Industrial Complex over the years. Even the seemingly promising tourism zone in Wonsan is not spared. Less than two months after releasing shiny concept images of a new international airport in Wonsan, investors halted their $200 million project, citing "political instability issues".

However, apart from precarious political conditions which is a given context when operating in North Korea, perhaps the biggest fundamental problem facing the leaders, planners and policy makers is asking the right questions, selecting the right project to pursue and setting feasible targets to follow through to fruition. These fundamental issues became evident during a recently concluded workshop on developing tourism zones in Wonsan. The site visits and interaction with various participants provided some insights into their obsession with big projects and the difficulties in achieving them.

Anecdotes and Observations

During our journey to the provinces, we were brought to two tourist attractions that recently opened, a beach resort along the Kalma Peninsula in Wonsan and the Sinphyong Kumgang Scenic Beauty Resort. After enduring a 4-hour journey on an uneven road from Pyongyang to Wonsan, we headed straight for the Kalma Peninsula, where our bus stopped right in front of what appeared to be a series of beachfront villas spaced 60m apart and fronting a long pristine coastline. However, upon closer inspection and further explanation by the guides, these villa-like buildings were in fact toilets and showering facilities, with the capacity to accommodate possibly around 100 users in each building.

Perhaps, the local planners are preparing the ground for 1 million visitors a year – their target number for the beach resort – but it still does not explain why locate all the ancillary services in a location with the best view, instead of capitalising on the visitors' experience with private residential units or food and entertainment facilities along the beachfront. Such an unusual planning of facilities became apparent during the workshop with local officials and planners. Instead of having an engaging discussion on latest trends in tourism products, services and experience, discussions were focused on technical questions on physical infrastructure.

"What is the typical global average for the number of toilets per person per resort?"

"What is the typical global average for the amount of electricity and water consumption per person per resort?"

"Where should we site a power generator plant for our resort?"

These questions reveal several issues. First, there

A series of beachfront villas containing ancillary services in Wonsan (Photo by: Calvin Chua)

is a lack of basic technical knowledge in delivering a large-scale project. Second, no extensive market research or feasibility studies have been carried out for the sites. Third, their perception of luxury is relatively dated and the concept of visitors' experience seem to be absent from their planning dictionary, where their idea of delivering a tourist resort is simply the provision of basic facilities and amenities. For a country that has frequent power cuts and lack of running hot water in hotels, perhaps the concept of 'experience' (in a positive way) is a level of sophistication, which they cannot afford to invest in at the moment. However, to achieve their goal of developing Wonsan into a tourist destination to an acceptable level for the average tourists, local planners and officials have to step up the game.

Already, North Korea is not blessed with the best climate, where its seas are cold for more than half a year. In order to tap on the landscape asset of a bay and a peninsula (the key geographical ingredients for a beach resort), planners in Wonsan need to think beyond basic service; or else, their grand

A 15-bed hotel at the entrance of Sinphyong Kumgang Scenic Beauty Resort (Photo by: Calvin Chua)

plans for the 8km long coastline from from Songdowon Beach in the West to Myongsasipri Beach in the East will just be a string of resorts with giant 'shower villas'.

Again, the lack of understanding of 'experience' can also be witnessed in other resorts. Unlike the resort name, the perceived beauty of the landscape in Sinphyong Kumgang Scenic Beauty Resort does not correspond with the visitors' experience. With only a 15-bed hotel located at the entrance of the resort and a guided nature trail in a bus, visitors can hardly immerse themselves within the landscape, which is supposed to be the raison d'être of the resort. As such, a trip to the resort at most warrant a lunch visit, rather than a week long retreat. However, the problem with the planners is not only their lack of understanding in executing quality projects but their focus on quantity of projects in order to fulfill their grand targets.

Brought by the local official to the top of a border with a view of the site, I assumed the local official would ask for advice on improving the quality and experience of a tourist in the resort; but instead, he started asking for my opinions on designing a golf course within the hilly landscape.

For a start, developing and maintaining golf courses is an expensive infrastructural investment given the climate and terrain in Sinphyong, where proper irrigation system has to be provided, earth has to be moved and leveled, etc. More importantly, what this encounter reveals is the obsession in accumulating large-scale projects, without solid technical understanding of delivering them to a reasonable standard and quality. Perhaps, the local officials' performance is judged by the amount of projects executed rather than the quality, but as we have witnessed, such a mindset will only lead to mediocre outcomes.

What do all this mean?

It is common for leaders (across all political systems) to desire for grande projets, not only as a tool to leave traces of their legacy, but also as a genuine belief that these projects will improve the economy and social life of its people. However, history has informed us that the reality of these projects - evident in various new cities across Asia – often do not match up to the original intended visions. North Korea is no exception. However, when compared to other global examples, North Korea's problems are perhaps more exacerbated. Its precarious political scene, unfavourable geography and climate, coupled with the lack of technical understanding in the product they are developing will only lead to mediocre results. Such fundamental entrenched problems do not only exist within their grand plans for tourism but in other major projects too. Even though the industries are different but the system's fundaments and approach are similar.

However, when compared to other industries, where the results at most remain as numbers and figures, these problems are most evident within the tourism and service sector, as visitors to North Korea can immediately see, feel and experience the discrepancy between their visions and reality through the relatively modest services and physical infrastructure provided. Therefore, without fundamentally changing the way the regime operates, these projects can only remain at best expensive white elephants.

Pop-Ups: The Small and the Temporary

Apart from delivering basic infrastructure, such as smooth roads, constant electricity and water supply, leaders in North Korea need to rethink whether large-scale physical projects, especially for the tourism and service sector, are the only way to achieve their grand visions. Instead of looking at fulfilling big quantitative targets, perhaps it is time they look towards small-scale quality interventions within the existing city as a possible alternative. and complementing larger prjs. These small projects could include short-term pop-up spaces that could host restaurants, cafes and exhibitions, common elements within the developed world but currently absent in North Korea.

Being smaller in scale, these interventions will be less costly in the initial investment, less susceptible to political changes and the results can be evaluated within a shorter time frame. More importantly, it exposes the locals to the concept of 'experience' that is crucial for the tourism and service sector and encourages locals to be more entrepreneurial and collaborative between different disciplines and organisations. These pop-ups could be local and foreign joint collaboration between restaurant and event managers, with designers and builders fulfilling the spatial requirements through refurbishing an existing interior space or creating a temporary pavilion. In addition, events and exhibitions that are normally held in specific locations can be introduced to these pop-up spaces. The collaboration between local and foreign experts in various fields could be achieved through a series of workshops while these pop-up spaces could last for a couple of weeks to a month. Such collaboration with foreign experts in various fields is pivotal in ensuring some level of success of success in the pop-ups, through the

Reusing disused and run-down site within the city
(Photo by: Calvin Chua)

Strategic insertion of housing blocks, monuments and public spaces
(Photo by: Calvin Chua)

gradual training of the locals and exposing them to these ideas of service and experience.

There could be three potential effects through these collaborations. First, it encourages collaboration between discipline and organisations, which is currently lacking in the system, especially within the construction industry, where there are multiple organisations with overlapping functions. Second, it encourages entrepreneurship amongst the locals, which will in turn train their senses in developing an understanding of quality visitor's experience for the tourism industry. Third, the potential success of training the locals through an incremental way can be rolled out to other cities or adapted in existing tourist resorts.

Pyongyang as a Ground for Experimentation

On an urban scale, the city of Pyongyang could become the fertile ground for these pop-ups to take place. Compared to other provinces, Pyongyang has better infrastructure and resources to start with. In addition, there are several disused and run-down sites within the city that can host these pop-ups, which hopefully in turn can be the catalyst for urban regeneration in the city.

This logic of strategic urban insertion, like the pop-up spaces, is not a new concept for Pyongyang. While is it a common reading of Pyongyang as a city that was conceived and choreographed at its entirety from the inception of the state; but in reality, despite having an overall masterplan, the city was developed over the years through a series of strategic experimentation with various types of housing and strategic insertion of public spaces within the city. Razed to the ground after the end of Korean War, Pyongyang was built from scratch based on the urban model of the Superblock. Measuring 200m x 200m, various types of housing models, ranging from the perimeter block fronting the wide boulevard to the high-rise towers and the sporadic low-rise building, were test on this blank canvas. Public spaces on the other hand have been choreographed and strategically inserted into the existing urban fabric, to form a well-distributed sequences of civic buildings and plazas – including monuments, sport halls, theatres and museums.

Perhaps, the main difference between the pop-ups and the experimenting of housing types and insertion key public spaces is the scale of execution. Pop-ups and small-scale developments can be developed within each neighborhood block without affecting the overall logic of the urban landscape. The existing low-rise buildings behind the rows of residential towers can be altered to accommodate different small-scale private businesses, such as convenience stalls and restaurants, or provide civic amenities and parks. In this way, each neighborhood block can develop its own unique identity while preserving the overall monumental image of the city. In addition, by concentrating development within a small area, planners can test out their ideas not only in terms of services but also possible new technologies – such as natural energy sources - that accompany these small-scale projects. Planners can tap on the gridded configuration of the neighborhood blocks, which allow new technologies to be tested out incrementally within each neighborhood block before efficiently rolling out to different other blocks and eventually other cities.

In conclusion, given the ever-precarious political environment in North Korea, it is perhaps time to reevaluate models of development. As visionary as the plans to roll out large number of SEZs may sound, their eventual reality as witnessed from existing examples, are likely to achieve only mediocre results if there are no fundamental changes to the way the regime operates at all levels. Instead of going for large-scale projects, small-scale interventions may offer an alternative way to kick-start changes in the country.

팝업 평양, 북한의 대규모 프로젝트에서 소규모 중재의 중요성

캘빈 촤

―

캘빈 촤는 영국의 AA스쿨에서 수학하였으며 어반 디자이너(Urban Designer)이자 건축가이다. 그는 런던, 싱가포르, 상하이 등에서 실무를 익혔으며, 이 외에도 경제성장이 진행되는 도시들의 도시개발에 대한 주제로 다양한 건축 잡지 및 저널에 기고했다. 그는 AA 스쿨과 이스탄불의 Bilgi University 등에서 워크샵 등을 가르쳤다. 캘빈은 북한의 젊은이들을 위한 경제 정책, 비지니스 그리고 법률 교육 등에 활동의 중점을 두는 "조선교류"의 창립멤버이다. 그는 북한의 도시계획가, 정책 입안가 및 여러 전문가들과 함께 도시계획과 인프라망 계획에 관한 워크샵을 개최하기도 하였다.

새로운 경제 특구를 만들면서 북한 경제 전망에 장미빛을 예고했던 뉴스가 있은 지 한 달이 지난 지금 극적인 정치 숙청작업이 일어나고 있다. 경제 특구 지역 개발 중 이와 같은 정치적 사건이 가져올 더 큰 영향이 아직 확실치 않은 반면, 내부와 외부의 투자자들에게는 큰 기반시설과 건설 프로젝트의 투자에 있어서 고려해야 할 본질적으로 불확실한 정치적 상황이 노출되어있다. 이러한 불안정한 상황은 몇 년 동안 라선 경제 특구와 개성 공단의 간헐적인 개발을 야기시켰다. 심지어 전망이 있어 보이는 원산의 관광지역 개발에는 할애되지도 않았다. 원산에 새로운 국제 항공의 빛나는 영상들이 공개되고 두 달이 안되어서 투자자들은 "정치적 불안정성의 이슈"를 이유로 그들의 2억 달러 프로젝트를 중단했다.

그러나 북한에서 작업할 때 주어진 배경이라 할 수 있는 불안정한 정치적인 상황에서 벗어나 지도자들, 설계자들, 그리고 정치가들은 올바른 질문을 하고 올바른 프로젝트를 선택하며 성과를 내기 위해 실현 가능한 목표를 설정한다. 이 근본적인 이슈들은 최근 원산에서 '조선교류'(Choson Exchange)가 조직한 개발 진행 중인 관광지역에서 있었던 워크샵에서 확연히 들어났다. 현장 답사와 다양한 참가자들과의 상호교류는 그들의 큰 규모 사업에 대한 집착과 이를 성취하는데 있어서 어려움에 대한 인지를 제공해준다.

이야기와 관찰

여행 중에 우리는 최근 개장된 원산 갈마 반도에 위치한 해변 리조트와 신평 금강 리조트를 관광 대상으로 관심있게 보게 되었다. 평양에서 원산까지 비평탄한 도로를 4시간 동안 참아오며 우리는 갈마 반도에 다다랐다. 우리의 버스는 해변가 마을에서 60m정도 떨진 곳에서 멈추었고 우리는 곧 길고 깨끗한 해안 면을 마주하게 되었다. 그러나 가이드의 계속되는 설명 속에서 더 가까이 관찰했을 때 빌라처럼 보인 건물들은 사실 100인 이상의 사용자가 있는 화장실과 샤워 시설이었다. 아마 지역 설계자들은 해안 리조트의 목표수치인 연간 백만의 관광객을 대비할 것으로 보인다. 그러나 관광객들이 머물 수 있는 개인 주택이나 먹고 즐길 수 있는 음식점과 오락시설들 대신에 왜 보조 서비스시설들이 가장 좋은 전망에 위치하고 있는 지에 대해서 여전히 설명하지 않고 있다.

이와 같이 시설 및 공간에 대한 익숙하지 않은 계획은 유일한 실수처럼 보인다. 하지만 이것은 지방 공무원들과 설계자들과의 워크샵 기간 동안 명확해졌다. 비록 우리가 관광 상품, 서비스와 경험에 대한 최신유행을 논하기를 희망한다 할지라도 우리는 그 대신 물리적인 기반시설에 대한 매우 기술적인 문제들을 안고 있다.

"한 리조트에 일인당 변기의 수에 대한 국제적인 평균 수치는 몇인가?"
"한 리조트에 일인당 전력과 물 소비량에 대한 국제적인 평균 수치는 몇인가?"
"리조트에 발전기는 어디에 위치해야 하는가?"

이러한 질문은 심각한 이슈를 보여주고 있다. 첫째로, 큰 규모의 프로젝트를 이끄는 기본적인 기술지식의 부족이다. 둘째로, 어떠한 시장조사나 실현 가능성 연구도 현장으로부터 끌어내지 못하고 있다. 셋째로, 그들의 사치에 대한 인지는 구시대적이며, 관광객들의 경험에 대한 개념은 그들의 계획 일지에서 사라졌다. 빈번한 정전과 부족한 온수공급을 겪고 있는 나라로서 '경험'의 개념은 지금 그들이 투자할 여력이 안되는 성숙도이다. 그러나 그들이 원산을 관광객들이 받아드릴 수 있는 수준의 관광지로 발달시키는 목표를 이루기 위해서는 지방의 도시계획가들과 공무원들이 사업을 진보시켜야 한다.

이미 북한은 일년의 반 이상 동안 바다가 찬 곳으로, 좋은 기후의 축복을 받지 못했다. 만과 반도(해안 리조트의 주요 지형적 구성요소)의 지형적 자산을 건드리기 위해서 원산 도시계획가들이 기본적인 서비스 이상을 생각할 필요가 있다. 또는 그들의 서쪽 송도원 해안부터 동쪽 명사십리 해안까지 이르는 8km 길이의 해안선에 대한 웅장한 계획들은 단지 거대 '샤워 빌라'를 갖춘 일련의 리조트가 될 것이다.

또한 '경험'에 대한 이해부족은 다른 리조트에서도 찾아볼 수 있다. 리조트의 이름과 달리 신평 금강 절경 리조트는 방문자들의 경험에 상응하지 않는다. 리조트와 버스에서 안내원이 인솔하는 자연탐방 오솔길 입구에 위치한, 15개의 침실이 있는 단 하나의 호텔에서 방문객들은 리조트의 존재이유로 가정되는 경치에 빠지기 어렵다. 이리하여 리조트 여행은 일주일 단위의 휴식이 아닌, 기껏해야 점심시간 방문정도를 보장한다. 그러나 북한 계획가들의 문제는 질 좋은 프로젝트를 실행하는 것에 대한 이해 부족뿐만 아니라 그들의 웅대한 비전을 충족하기 위한 프로젝트의 양적인 측면에 초점을 맞추는 것(거의 집착에 가까운) 또한 문제다.

지역 공무원이 전경으로 둘러싸인 가장자리의 윗부분을 보여줬을 때 나는 관광객들이 리조트에서의 경험과 질을 향상시키는 것에 대해 지역공무원은 조언을 구할거라 생각했다. 하지만 그 대신 그는 언덕이 많은 지형을 골프장으로 만들자는 사안에 나의 의견을 물었다.

시작의 단계로, 골프 코스를 개발하고 유지하는 것은 적절한 관개체제를 갖추고 지면을 움직이거나 기울여야 하는 등 신평의 기후와 지형에 주어지는 값 비싼 공공 기반 시설에 대한 투자이다. 하지만 심각하게도 이는 합리적인 기준과 질을 가져다 주는 확실한 기술적 이해 없이 그들의 큰 규모 프로젝트들을 축적하는 것에 대한 집착을 보인다. 아마도 지역 공무원의 수행능력을 프로젝트의 질 대신 실행된 양으로 판단되기 때문이다. 그러나 우리가 목격했듯이 이러한 마음가짐은 썩 좋지 않은 결과물들을 이끌 뿐이다.

이 모든 것이 무슨 의미가 있는가?

지도자들(모든 정치 체제를 아울러)이 grande projects에 대해 열망하는 것은 흔한 일이다. 그들의 흔적을 남기는 도구로서뿐만 아니라 자신들이 추진한 이러한 프로젝트들이 국민의 경제와 사회생활을 개선시킬 것이란 진정한 믿음 때문이다. 그러나 역사가 우리에게 알려준 이러한 프로젝트들의 현실은(최근 올림픽 경기들부터 아시아의 다양한 새로운 도시들까지) 본래 의도한 비전과 맞지 않는 경우가 많다. 북한도 예외는 아니다. 그러나 다른 세계적인 예들과 비교해봤을 때, 북한의 문제점들은 아마 좀 더 과장된 것 같다. 그들이 발전시키려는 생산물에 대한 기술적인 이해 부족과 함께 불안정한 정치적인 배경, 좋지 않은 지형과 기후는 평범한 수준의 결과물을 이끌 뿐일 것이다.

이러한 기본적인 문제들은 단지 그들의 관광산업에 대한 큰 계획안에서만 존재하는 것이 아니라 다른 주요 사업들에서도 존재한다.

그러나 그 결과들이 기껏해야 숫자로 남을 다른 산업들과 비교했을 때, 관광객들이 상대적으로 무난한 서비스와 물리적인 기반시설을 통한 그들의 비전과 현실 사이의 괴리를 보고 느끼고 경험할 수 있듯이 이 문제들은 관광산업과 서비스 분야에서 가장 두드러진다. 그러므로 근본적으로 운영방식을 바꾸지 않는다면 이 사업들은 기껏해야 돈 많이 드는 흰 코끼리밖에 되지 않는다.

팝업: 작은 것과 일시적인 것

평탄한 도로, 지속적인 전력, 그리고 급수와 같은 기본 기반시설의 제공을 멀리한 채 북한의 지도자들은 특히 관광과 서비스 분야를 위한 대규모 사업이 그들의 중대한 비전을 성취할 수 있는 유일한 방법인지에 대해 다시 생각해봐야 한다. 많은 양의 목표들을 성취하는 것을 바라보는 대신에 지금은 대안 가능성으로서 기존의 도시 안에 작은 규모의 질적인 개선을 향해 바라봐야 할 시기인 것 같다.

이 작은 규모의 프로젝트들은 선진화 국가들에서 흔히 볼 수 있는, 하지만 북한에서는 부재한 식당, 카페 및 전시관과 같은 요소들을 갖출 수 있는 단기간 팝업 공간(pop-up space)이 될 수 있다. 규모적으로 더 작아서인 이러한 개입들은 초기 투자의 측면에서 덜 비쌀 것이고, 정치적인 변화를 덜 수용할 것이며, 그 결과는 더 짧은 시간의 틀 안에서 평가될 수 있다. 더 중요하게는 관광 서비스분야에서 중요한 '경험'의 개념을 지역에 드러내고 서로 다른 규칙들과 조합들 사이에 더욱 기업가적이고 협동적일 수 있게 한다. 이러한 팝업들(pop-ups)은 기존의 실내공간을 재단장하거나 임시로 정자를 만들면서 공간적인 필수 요소들을 충족시키는 설계자 및 건설자들과 식당과 이벤트 매니저 간의 지역적이면서 대외적인 공동작업이 될 수 있다. 게다가 특정 지역에 열리는 이벤트와 전시들은 팝업공간으로 소개될 수 있다. 이러한 팝업(pop-up)공간들이 몇 주에서 한 달 정도의 기간 동안 지속될 수 있는 동안 지역에서의 점진적인 교육과 서비스와 경험의 아이디어를 드러냄으로써 일련의 워크샵을 통한, 다양한 분야의 국내와 국외 전문가들의 합동작업을 이룰 수 있다. 이와 같은 다양한 분야의 해외 전문가들과의 작업은 팝업(pop-up)공간의 일정 수준의 성공을 보장하는 중추가 된다.

이 합동작업들을 통해 세가지 잠재적인 효과를 얻을 수 있다. 첫째, 기능이 겹치는 여러 단체들이 존재하는 건설 산업 안에 결핍한 규율과 단체 사이의 결합을 북돋을 수 있다. 둘째, 관광산업에서 관광객 경험의 질 이해를 발전시키는 감각을 기를 수 있는 지역들간의 기업가 정신을 야기할 수 있다. 셋째, 증대하는 방법을 통해 지역 교육의 잠재적인 성공이 다른 도시들에서 나타나거나 현존하는 리조트들에서 채택될 수 있다.

실험의 땅으로서의 평양

도시적 규모에서 평양은 팝업공간(pop-ups)이 발생하기 좋은 지역이 될 수 있다. 다른 도시들과 비교했을 때, 평양은 더 좋은 기반시설과 자원을 갖추고 있다. 게다가 점차적으로 도시 재개발의 촉매재가 될 수 있는 이러한 팝업공간(pop-ups)들을 열 수 있을 것으로 보이는, 그럼에도 사용되지 않거나 개발이 멈춘 여러 장소들이 도시 안에 존재한다.

이러한 도시 안에 팝업공간과 같은 전략적인 삽입의 논리는 평양의 새로운 개념은 아니다. 평양을 도시의 시초에서 완선한 형태로 인식하고 연출된 도시로 읽는 것이 흔한 반면 평양은 다양한 형태의 가정집과 공공공간의 주입과 함께 일련의 전략적인 실험을 통해 수년간 발전했다. 한국전쟁 이후 완전히 파괴된 평양은 슈퍼 블럭(Superblock)의 도시유형에 기반을 두고 처음부터 건설되기 시작했다. 넓은 대로를 앞에 둔 테두리 블럭에서 고층 타워와 분산된 저층 건물까지 이르는 200m x 200m크기의 다양한 형태의 가정집 유형들은 이러한 흰 도화지와 다름 없는 평양 땅에 시도된 것이다. 그리고 다른 한편으로는 잘 분배된 시민을 위한 건물들과 기념탑, 체육관, 극장, 그리고 박물관을 포함한 광장을 형성하기 위해 공공공간들을 기존의 도시구조 안에 전략적으로 주입하고 연출해왔다.

아마도, 팝업공간의 도입과 가정집 및 주요 공공공간들의 실험적 주입의 주된 차이점은 실행 규모라고 할 수 있다. 팝업공간과 소규모 개발은 도시 전경의 전반적인 논리에 영향을 주지 않으면서 각 이웃 블록 안에 이루어질 수 있다. 초고층 주거형 건물 아래 기존 저층 건물들은 편의점 과 식당과 같은 소규모 개인 사업 들여오거나 시민 봉사시설과 공원들을 제공하는 것으로 대체할 수 있다. 이러한 방법으로 각 이웃 블록은 도시의 전반적인 기념비적 이미지를 보존하면서 고유의 독특한 정체성을 형성할 수 있다. 또한 작은 지역 안에 개발을 집중하면서 계획가들은 서비스 측면에서 뿐만아니라 소규모 프로젝트를 동반하는 천연 에너지 자원과 같은 잠재적인 새로운 기술들의 측면에서 그들의 아이디어를 시험해 볼 수 있다. 결론적으로는 다른 블록들과 다른 도시들에 효과적으로 나타내기 전에 계획가들은 새로운 기술을 허용하는 이웃 블록의 구조 배열을 손볼 수 있다.

결론적으로, 항상 불안정한 정치 환경 속에서 현재 북한의 개발 유형을 재 평가할 시기가 온 것 같다. 만약 개발 영역이 모든 수준에서 작동하는 방법으로 어떠한 근본적인 변화가 없다면 현재 많은 수의 경제 특구 지역(Special Economic Zones)을 출시하는 계획만큼 현존 사례들을 바탕으로 한 선각적인 그들의 궁극점은 단순히 평범한 결과를 얻을 것으로 보인다. 따라서 대규모 프로젝트를 실행하는 대신에 소규모 개발을 국가 변화의 시발점이 되는 대안책으로 제공해야 할 것이다.

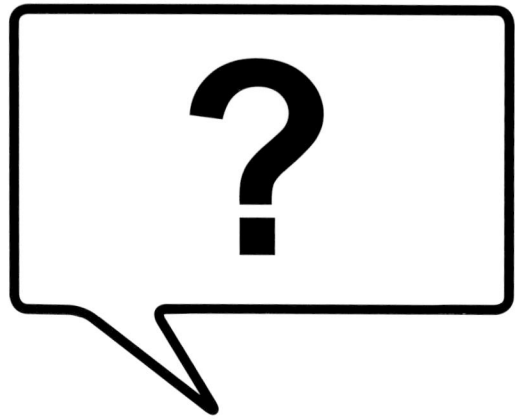

North Korea has an image problem in the global stage. The epistemological questions surrounding North Korea as an outsider is an intriguing and an important one. How does one acquire *facts* about North Korea, and assemble them into *knowledge*? What *is* available and what is *not*? Why? However, things are rarely about merely what they appear to be, but one needs to understand what they *do*, and how and what they eventually *affect*.

New technology such as *Google Earth*, has enabled many of us to see what North Korea looks like, something that was not available to the public even a decade ago. In this ubiquitously connected world, North Korea maintains to be exceptionally secretive, and behind closed doors, intensifying the curiosity and misinterpretations from others. This is a collection of *"quotes"* from my ongoing research on North Korea. This is precisely how the contested ground where North Korea is cultivated ultimately *experienced*, *perceived*, thus understood as *reality* for many.

세계의 무대에서 북한의 이미지는 문제가 있다. 제3자로서 북한에 관한 인식론적인 질문들은 흥미로우면서도 중요한 부분이다. 우리는 북한에 대한 사실들을 어떻게 수집하며, 그들을 지식으로서 취합하는가? 무엇이 수집 가능하며 무엇이 불가능한가? 또 그러한 것이 왜 수집 가능하며 불가능한가? 대부분의 실체는 보이는 것만이 다가 아니며, 우리는 그것들이 어떠한 역할을 하고 어떠한 영향을 미치는지 이해해야 한다.

구글어스와 같은 새로운 기술은 불과 십여년 전만 해도 불가능했던 북한의 모습을 볼 수 있게 해 준다. 현재 실시간으로 연결되어있는 세상에서도, 북한은 매우 예외적으로 폐쇄적이며 호기심을 강하게 불러 일으키고 외부로부터의 오해를 사기도 한다. 다음은 본인이 진행하고 있는 북한에 관한 연구에서 발췌한 인용문들이다. 이것은 북한에 대한 이미지 형성과정이 논쟁의 장소 속에서 어떻게 "경험"되고, "인식"되고, 결과적으로 많은 사람들에게 "사실"이 되어가는 지를 보여준다.

WHAT DO THEY SAY? REALITY IS WHAT WE PERCEIVE IT TO BE

DONGSEI KIM

"No country in the world is as isolated as North Korea. The totalitarian regime uses strict control of the media to keep its people in ignorance. Listening to a foreign-based radio station can land you in a concentration camp."
1. Reporters Without Borders

"For decades North Korea has been one of the **world's most secretive societies**. It is one of the few countries still under nominally communist rule."
2. BBC, "North Korea country profile"

"Travel by U.S. citizens to North Korea is not routine, and U.S. citizens crossing into North Korea without proper documentation, **even accidently, have been subject to arrest and long-term detention**"
9. Travel Warning, U.S. DEPARTMENT OF STATE, Bureau of Consular Affairs

"**The scariest place on Earth**"
3. "Bill Clinton, after touring the no man's land in 1993."

Bill Clinton b.1946
42nd President of the US
1993.01 - 2001.01

"But this is **one of the most despotic regimes and Kim Jong Il is one of the worst men on Earth.** Isn't that a fair assessment?"
8. CNN, The Situation Room with Blitzer

"**I am absolutely convinced that the North Koreans are absolutely sincere.** There's really no reason -- no reason for them to cheat or do anything to violate this very forward agreement."
7. CNN, The Situation Room with Blitzer

Wolf Blitzer b.1948
CNN The Situation Room anchor
2005 -

Ted Turner b.1938
Founder of CNN & TBS
Forbes 2013 Net Worth $2.1 billion

WHAT DO THEY SAY? REALITY IS WHAT WE PERCEIVE IT TO BE | Dongsei Kim

> "**Let the whole place go to shit,** that's the best thing that could happen,"... "aid that could prop up [North Korea's] failing infrastructure should be withheld to **bring an end to the regime's tyranny.**"
>
> 12. The SMH, Alexander Downer told the commander of United States and United Nations forces in South Korea at a meeting in Canberra in February 2005.

Hon. Alexander Downer, b.1951
Former Foreign Minister of Australia
1996.03 - 2007.12

> "But on the occasion of Kim Jong Il's death, I said that it is our hope that the new leadership will choose to **guide their nation onto the path of peace** by living up to its obligations. **Today's announcement represents a modest first step in the right direction.**"
>
> 15. The NY Times, Secretary of State Hillary Rodham Clinton on NK agreeing to freeze nuclear work

> "**We urge** North Korea to **demonstrate a change in behavior.**"
>
> 5. Hillary Clinton at ASEAN Summit meeting July, 2011

Hillary R. Clinton b.1947
67th US Secretary of State
2009.01 - 2013.02

> "With growing interaction among countries, it is inevitable that they encounter frictions here and there. What is important is that **they should resolve differences through dialogue,** consultation and peaceful negotiations in the larger interest of the sound growth of their relations."
>
> 19. The Diplomat, Xi Jinpinh during his keynote address to the Boao Forum, April 2013

Xi Jinping b.1953
7th President of the
People's Republic of China
2013.03 -

> "**Waitresses are some of the friendliest people** you will meet in North Korea, often they are keen to practice their English with the visitors and **they are usually not too shy to pose for pictures also.**"
>
> 20. Koryo Tours

> "**He's my friend for life.** I don't care what you guys think about him. I don't give a shit what people around the world think about him," he said. **"He's my friend,** and you saw it on the pictures, **he's my friend."**
>
> 17. Rodman on on Kim Jong Un, USA TODAY

> "About the relationship, no one man can do anything. **Do not hate people,** life is not about that. **I love him, he is an awesome guy.**"
>
> 18. Rodman on on Kim Jong Un, China Daily

Dennis K. Rodman b.1961
Retired NBA basketball player
1986-2006

"Pyongyang is definitely one of the **world's strangest capitals**, often wrapped in a thick mist and dominated by the immeasurably sinister and humungous pyramid of the unfinished Ryugyong Hotel."

4. Lonley Planet, "Introducing Pyongyang"

"visiting North Korea was a **little spooky,** but after working with them nearly 25 years...they are **not people with horns and tails, they are human beings**..."

16. Former US government official

"End horror of North Korean political prison camps"

13. Amnesty International

"In order to get off the list, the **'axis of evil'** list, then the North Korean leader is going to have to make certain decisions...**I can't predict the North Korean leader's decision making.**" 10. Reuters

George W. Bush b.1946
43rd President of the US
2001.01 - 2009.10

"North Korea's continued pursuit of nuclear weapons will only lead to more isolation and less security. **But there is another path available to North Korea.**"

6. Obama in a visit to South Korea, November 2010

Barack H. Obama b.1961
44th and 45th President of the US
2009.01 -

"He's the 29-year-old ruler of North Korea, **the world's least known, most dangerous country.**" ... "**North Korea is a cocktail of poisonous elements:** autocratic, repressive, isolated and poor. It is a place where not even an iota of freedom is imaginable. Its regime is **dangerous not only to its people but also to the rest of the world.**"

14. Time Magazine

"**Some people are having to eat manure** when they cannot get rice or corn,' said one refugee, 68-year-old Kim Yeong. The United Nations World Food Program says North Korea faces its **worst food shortage in a decade, with 6 million people at risk** and the regime is unwilling to spend its dwindling hard currency reserves on buying food for its population of 24 million."

11. The Sydney Mornign Herald

References

1 Reporters Without Borders, http://en.rsf.org/report-north-korea,58.html Retrived 2011.07.23

2 BBC, "North Korea Profile," http://news.bbc.co.uk/2/hi/country_profiles/1131421.stm Retrived 2011.07.23

3 The Huffington Post, "Clinton, Gates DMZ Visit: Unprecedented Trip To Demilitarized Zone Dividing Koreas" Matthew Lee. http://www.huffingtonpost.com 2011.07.20 Retrived 2011.07.23

4 Lonely Planet, "Introducing Pyongyang" http://www.lonelyplanet.com/north-korea/pyongyang 2009.02.17 Retrived 2011.07.23

5 Washington Post, "Clinton issues challenges on N.Korea, South China Sea," http://www.washingtonpost.com/world/asia-pacific/clinton-issues-challenges-on-n-korea-south-china-sea/2011/07/23glQA7805UI_story.html 2011.07.23

6 Guardian, "Barack Obama warns North Korea it faces deeper isolation" http://www.guardian.co.uk/world/2010/nov/11/obama-north-korea-nuclear-weapons 2010.11.11

7 & 8 CNN, The Situation Room with Blitzer, Megan McCormack "Turner: Give North Korea a Break," http://newsbusters.org/node/1324 2005.09.20

9 U.S. Department of State, Bureau of Consular Aairs, "Travel Warning," http://www.travel.state.gov/travel/cis_pa_tw/tw/tw_5137.html 2010.08.27

10 Reuters, " Bush says North Korea still "axis of evil" member," Jeremy Pelofsky, http://www.reuters.com/article/2008/08/06/us-bush-axis-idUSN0634840020080806 2008.08.06

11 The Sydney Morning Herald, "Refugees flee famine ravaging North Koea," Peter Foster, http://www.smh.com.au/world/refugees-flee-famine-ravaging-north-korea-20110717-1hk2a.html 2011.07.18

12 The Sydney Morning Herald, "Downer wanted collapse, Philip Dorling, http://www.theage.com.au/national/downer-wanted-collapse-20101221-194i8.html 2010.12.22

13 Amnesty International, "End horror of North Korean political prison camps" http://www.amnesty.org/en/appeals-for-action/north-korean-political-prison-camps 2011.05.04

14 Time Magazine, " Meet Kim Jong Un" Bill Powell, http://www.time.com/time/magazine/article/0,9171,2106986,00.html#ixzz1noHC4YJa 2012.02.27

15 The New York Times, "North Korea Agrees to Curb Nuclear Work; U.S. Oers Aid" Steven L. Myers and Choe Sang Hun, http://www.nytimes.com/2012/03/01/world/asia/us-says-north-korea-agrees-tocurb-nuclear-work.html 2012.02.29

16 Former U.S government official's comment at an "off the record" talk at Harvard University, Cambridge, MA, USA. Early 2012.

17 USA Today, "Dennis Rodman hangs out with North Korean dictator again." http://www.usatoday.com/story/news/world/2013/09/06/dennis-rodman-kim-jong-un-north-korea-pyongyang/2778507/ 2013.09.03

18 China Daily, "DPRK top leader meets visiting Rodman" Xinhua, http://europe.chinadaily.com.cn/world/2013-09/07/content_16951695.htm 2013.09.07

19 The Diplomat, "Did Xi Jinping Really Rebuke North Korea?" Zachary Keck, http://thediplomat.com/the-editor/2013/04/10/did-xi-jinping-really-rebuke-north-korea/ 2013.04.10 Retrived 2013.10.05

20 Koryo Tours , Caption from a website that organizes foreigners to tour Norht Korea as a group. http://www.koryogroup.com/dprk_galleries_people.php Retrived 2013.10.05

FUTURE SCENARIOS

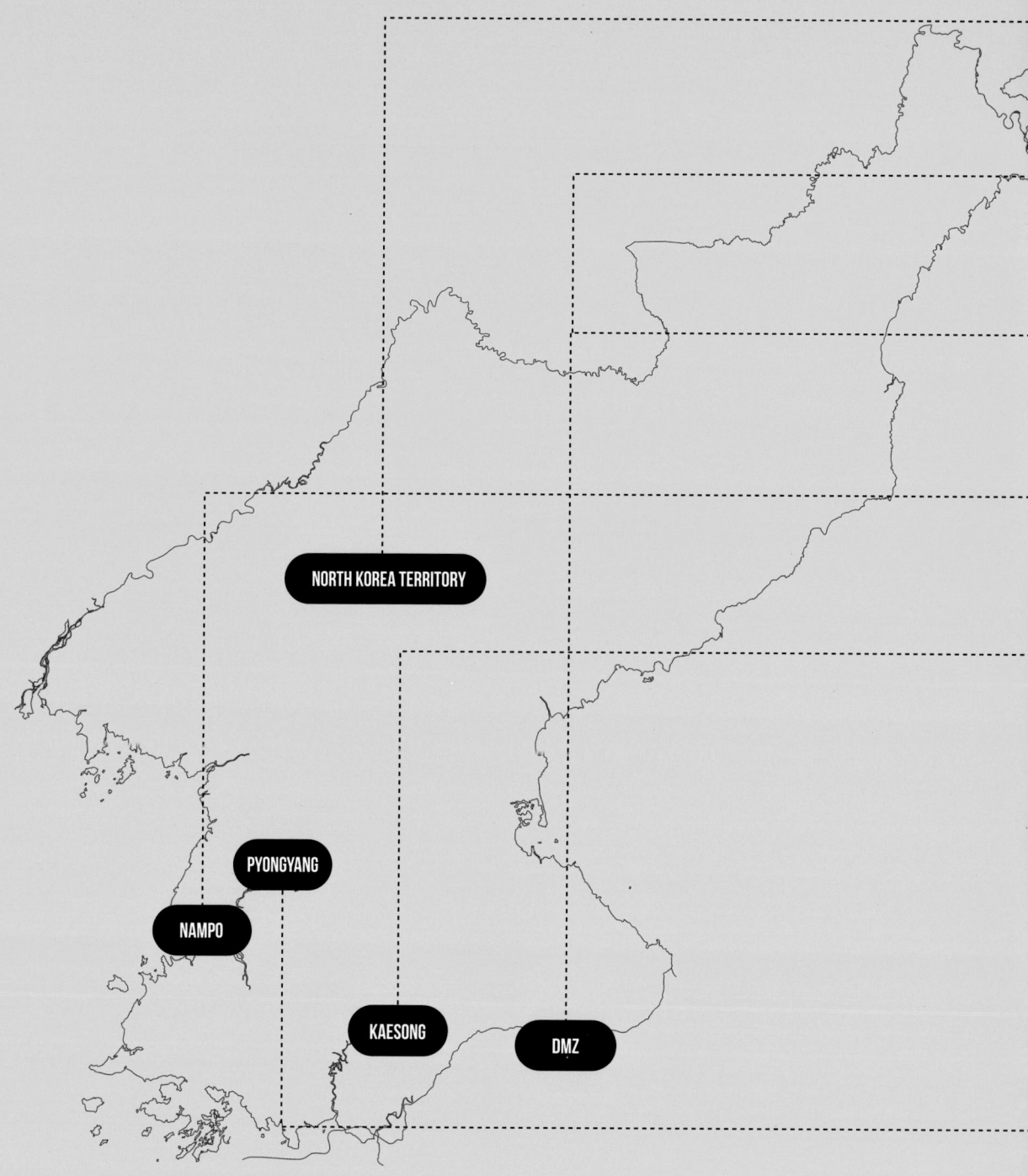

Future Scenarios

CHONG HO PARK
FUTURE INDUSTRIES OF NORTH KOREA

YEHRE SUH
RESILIENT SPATIAL SCENARIOS FOR TRANSBOUNDARY ZONE

DONGSEI KIM
DECONSTRUCTING THE DMZ FOR THE IMAGINARY

SUNG GOO YANG
DAEDONG RIVER PARK

HYE YOUNG CHUNG
KAESONG BORDER STATION

SEJIN RUBELLA JO & SOOBIN LEE
LIVING IN THE BORDERLESS

JUNGON KIM
PERSONAL AND COLLECTIVE MEMORY

PRAUD DONGWOO YIM + RAFAEL LUNA
NEW MICRO DISTRICT

FUTURE INDUSTRIES OF NORTH KOREA

Chong Ho Park

—

Chong Ho Park is an architectural designer and researcher at PRAUD. He currently takes charge in study of urban typologies in major North Korean cities as a member for the publication of "North Korean Atlas" and participates with the exhibition of its materials for 2014 Venice Biennale and Berlin DNA. He received his Bachelor of Architecture from Rhode Island School of Design (RISD) where he pursued his thesis on "Trace of old protective wall in Seoul." He also proceeds with the research of the methodology about architectural preservation within border condition in urban infrastructure.

Introduction

The industrial development of North Korea is a significant task to have a balanced growth in the Korean Peninsula. We long for the unication of two Koreas. However, we simultaneously have a fear about breaking the status quo. To resolve such contradictory perspective towards the Korean re-unification, it is necessary to discuss the practical level of development which North Korea needs to have, and define the specific plan for industrial development in individual cities across North Korea. Although the reality of its unstable political status is the chronic problem, which should be solved for North Korea to step up to the next level, this essay will narrate future scenarios imagined by the potential of North Korea's industries, which have not received much attention.

Development of Existing Industries

The first phase is to improve the industrial infrastructure from the level of the existing industries. Through the long-term industrial development plan, North Korea will be expected to create a considerable economic value from the contact with a larger industrial market. In this perspective, the research encourages the discussion on potential types of industries to boost North Korea's industrial growth and competitiveness based on the current status of North Korea's industries. The future scenario plan based on the existing industry development categorizes the types of industry with the following list.

- Textile / Fashion
- Healthcare / Pharmaceutical / Medical tourism

- Agronomy

Kusong and Kanggye are the cities of textile industries. Those cities have potential of growth if they introduce the modernized industrial infrastructure and capitalistic market. The way to actualize the potential is to contrive the specific plan based on specific cases from other global cities. Lyon's textile industry and Milan's fashion industry are the exemplary cities of successful cases. Lyon's TECHTERA project, the innovation cluster for textile and flexible materials, is the innovative contribution to keep its textile industry prosper and make it expand to wider ranges such as research, education, and business. In the case of Milan, Fashion events based on the strong production allows Milan to have historic expansion of its role as a city of fashion and city of designer from the textile production center. The economic revenue of Fashion week in Milan is approximately 35.6 million dollars (10% of GDP).

Hamhung is the second largest city of North Korea and has a great educational infrastructure in healthcare and medicine. By using the well-established educational facilities, Hamhung can be expected to have healthcare/ pharmaceutical / medical tourism industry. The sequence of industrial connection among education, business, and tourism, is clear and has a strong linkage to achieve diverse dimensional development. The case of the medical industry in Boston will be an exemplary case for Hamhung. Medical education is a prosperous segment of Boston's economy and essential factors to cluster 63 bio-tech companies and 13 relative research centers which contribute currently 125 million dollars economic revenue (2.5% of GDP). In Hamhung, the existing medical institutions such as Hamhung University of Pharmacy, Hamhung University of Chemistry, and Hamhung University of Medicine are great potential to expand as the essential role for economic benefits as Boston has. Furthermore, Hamhung will step up to medical tourist city as Kuala Lumpur did. Medical tourism in Kuala Lumpur started after 1997 Asian Finance Crisis. The city currently creates approximately 60 million dollars economic revenue from the medical tourism industry.

Agriculture is the most prevailed and basic industry in North Korea, but limits to the function as means of living in general. Among many cities in North Korea, Sariwon is the city that has the largest proportion of farmland (72.1% of whole administrative area). In terms of industrial development, such large portion of farmland will be utilized as diverse types of industrial purpose. Campinas, the 10th richest city in Brazil, is the exemplary city of successful agronomy industry. Its major industrial segments are composed of EMBRAPA (Agriculture Farming Enterprise), IAC (Agronomy Institute), and ITAL (Food Technology). The economic revenue from agronomy industry is 25% of Brazil GDP.

Injecting New Industries

The second phase is to inject new types of industries into the cities, where do not have any specialized industry. Except for several major cities, most of North Korean cities do not posses specialized industries that have economic competitiveness among the cities. The major cities which posses comparatively thriving industries even can not be compared with many advanced global cities in terms of their scale. In this situation, besides the effort to improve the existing industries, we can expect a huge leap of economic development from the injection of new attractive industries on the following list.

- Casino
- Theme park / Recreation
- Global organization

Casino industry is a very tempting industry. Las Vegas and Macao are remarkable exemplary cities which shows the great economic benefit from the injection of this industry. It is not too much to say that a certain industry makes a city. In the case of Las Vegas, the capacities of the casino industry composed of 122 casinos, 355 accommodations, and approximately 40,000,000 tourists, with a revenue of 9.5 billion dollars, 24% of Las Vegas's GDP.

Theme parks and Recreational Industries are also considered as promising industries for the improvement of North Korean economic status. The cities along the east coast line have potential to attract tourists by theme parks and recreational programs, as the Kumgangsan area has induced a number of tourists from South Korea, the extension of similar programs in the east coast line has possibility to have great sequence of tourism especially Theme park / Recreation.

As the agenda under the investigation by Paju city government, the world peace park and global organization in the DMZ (demilitarized zone) has ahigher possibility of realization. Global organization not only creates a conciliatory gesture between North and South Korea, but also become a great potential to produce profitable economic revenue as a future industry in the Korean peninsula. As the remarkable precedent, Brussels is the capital city of Belgium, which has 29 Global organizations. Those global organizations branch out diverse auxiliary enterprises and markets with large scale capacities. Total economic revenue from its industry is 11 billion dollar (14% of GDP), and the number of its employees are 92,000 (8% of population).

Conclusion

The future scenario constructed with the potential of North Korea industries is the way that we can define the coexistence of the Korean Peninsula. The economic improvement through advancing the existing industries and injecting new industries will make North Korea take a more positive and attractive position in the world. The above mentioned exemplary cases for each industry helps North Korea to step up to the next level in terms of industrial development. The economic profits do not mean merely the best result for the future scenario of North Korea. As much as evaluating the actual profits from the new economic activities, we need to keep our eyes on the process, and the moment of change in North Korea.

북한의 미래산업

박종호

―

박종호는 PRAUD에서 건축 디자이너이자 도시 연구원이다. 그는 현재 "북한 도시 읽기"의 관련 연구작업에서 북한 주요 도시와 건축물의 유형분석을 담당하고 있으며, 2014 베니스 비엔날레 한국관과 베를린 DNA에 이와 관련된 연구자료 전시작업에 참여하였다. 그는 로드아일랜드 스쿨 오브 디자인 (RISD)에서 건축 학사를 수료했고 그의 졸업작품 "Trace of old protective wall in Seoul"을 발표하였다. 또한 그는 도시 인프라의 경계현상을 통한 건축적 복원 방법론에 대한 연구를 진행중에 있다.

서론

북한의 산업개발은 한반도의 균형적인 발전에 있어서 매우 시급한 과제이다. 한반도는 이상적으로는 통일을 염원하지만 한편으로는 현재 상태의 균형이 깨질 것이라는 두려움 때문에 선뜻 통일에 대해 강한 목소리를 내지 않고 있다. 이러한 근본적인 모순현상을 해소하고 궁극적으로는 상생의 통일을 이루기 위해서는 북한이 실질적으로 얼마만큼의 경제성장을 이루어야 하는지에 대한 제안과 북한의 각 주요도시들의 산업 특성화를 통해 구체적인 산업 개발 계획들을 논의할 필요성이 있다. 북한의 불안한 정치적 상황은 확연히 드러난 현실이고 북한이 한 단계 도약하기 위해서 반드시 해결해야 할 고질적인 문제이지만, 본 글에서는 그 동안 주목하지 않았던 북한의 잠재적인 산업들의 개발과 그에 따른 경제적 효과를 중심으로 미래 시나리오를 이야기하려 한다.

기존 산업의 개발

첫 번째로 기존의 2차 산업의 기반들을 더 높은 차원의 산업으로 성장시키는 것이다. 장기적인 계획을 통해 점차적으로 기존의 산업 기반시설을 확장하고 더욱 넓은 산업시장과의 접촉을 통해서 상당한 경제적 가치를 창출할 수 있을 것이다. 이러한 측면에서 본 연구는 북한의 기존 산업으로부터 산업 경쟁력과 잠재적 성장을 키울 수 있는 응용 가능한 산업들의 여러 유형을 제안하는데 도움을 주었다. 그 유형은 다음과 같다.

- 섬유 / 패션 산업
- 의료 관광 산업
- 농경학 산업

북한의 구성시나 강계시는 60년 역사의 섬유산업을 주요 산업으로 하는 도시다. 현대화된 산업 기반시설과 자본주의 시장을 도입한다면 이 두 도시는 기존의 섬유산업을 기반으로 패션산업과 같은 응용 가능한 산업을 통해 성장이 가능할 것으로 보인다. 이러한 잠재력을 구체화하는 방법은 세계도시들의 성공 사례들을 기반으로 전략적인 계획을 고안하는 것이다. 리옹의 TECHTERA 프로젝트는 섬유산업의 국가 경쟁력 단체로서 섬유산업의 번영을 유지하고 연구, 교육, 그리고 사업을 어우르는 넓은 영역의 확장을 통해 창의적인 기여를 이루고 있다. 또한 밀란의 패션산업은 섬유산업에서 한 단계 더 나아가 다양한 서비스 및 이벤트와 디자이너의 육성을 통해 세련된 도시의 이미지를 성공적으로 이룬 사례라고 평가되고 있다. 이처럼 기존 산업을 창의적인 영역조합 및 확장을 통해 더 높은 수준의 산업으로 이끌고 한편으로는 해외 투자를 유도할 수 있는 응용 가능한 산업을 발전시켜 세련된 도시 이미지를 만들 수 있다면 구성과 강계는 시장 경제력을 갖춘 도시로 성장할 수 있을 것이다.

함흥은 북한에서 두 번째로 규모가 큰 도시로 의료 및 보건 관련 연구시설과 교육시설에서 성장 잠재력을 보이고 있다. 교육시설 기반은 산업성장에서도 큰 연결고리를 갖고 있다. 보스턴은 미국에서 가장 먼저 대학기관이 생긴 도시로서 교육산업을 바탕으로 바이오 테크놀로지, IT 테크놀로지, 등을 세계적인 수준으로 끌어올린 도시로 평가되고 있다. 이처럼 함흥 또한 기존의 잘 갖추어진 의료 연구 및 교육시설이 의료산업의 성장으로 연결시킬 수 있는 발판이 될 수 있으며 궁극적으로는 쿠알라룸푸르처럼 의료관광산업으로까지 확장시킬 수 있다. 쿠알라룸푸르의 의료관광 산업은 97년 아시아 금융위기 이후 시작되었다. 현재 동아시아 및 유럽으로부터 많은 관광객들을 끌어들이고 있으며 약 6백만 달러의 경제효과를 내고 있다.

농업은 북한 전반적으로 가장 많은 비중을 차지하는 산업이지만 생계유지 수단의 기능에 한정되어있다고 할 수 있다. 북한의 많은 도시 중에 사리원은 논경지 비율을 가장 큰 도시다. (전체 행정구역의 72%를 차지한다.) 산업발달의 측면에서 보면 이러한 논경지 비율은 다양한 형태로 산업발전에 활용될 수 있다. 캄피나스는 브라질 10대 도시이자 성공적인 '농경학 산업'의 사례도시이다. 산업 기반 요소로서는 EMBRAPA (Agriculture Farming Enterprise), IAC(Agronomy Institute), ITAL(Food Technology)가 있다. 그리고 '농경학 산업'에 대한 경제수익은 브라질 GDP의 25%를 차지한다. 사리원도 농업과 경영학이란 두 가지 개념을 접목시켜 생계유지에서 기술연구와 개발을 통해 투자를 창출하여 경제적 효과를 얻는 도시로 성장할 수 있다.

새로운 산업의 주입

둘째로 기존에 없던 새로운 산업을 도입하여 고도의 도시성장을 도모하는 것이다. 북한의 도시들은 주요 몇몇 도시들 이외에 특화된 산업이 결핍된 도시들이 많다. 비교적 규모가 있는 산업을 갖고 있는 도시들 또한 세계 선진 도시들의 산업들과 비교해 그 수준이 매우 미약하다. 이러한 상황을 기존의 산업을 개선시키는 노력 외에 새로운 산업을 한 도시에 주입하여 무에서 유를 창조하는 시나리오를 예상해볼 수 있다.

- 카지노 산업
- 테마 공원 / 휴양 산업
- 국제 기구 산업

카지노 산업은 매우 끌리는 산업이다. 라스베가스와 마카오는 카지노 산업의 주입을 통해서 큰 경제적 효과를 보인 주목할 만한 사례 도시들이다. 카지노 산업을 통해 도시가 만들어졌다 해도 과언이 아닌 도시들을 본보기로 해주나 안주와 같은 북한 도시에 카지노 산업을 주입하는 계획도 고려해 볼 수 있다. 또는 올란도의 테마 공원 산업과 칸쿤의 레저관광산업도 매우 매력적인 산업으로 판단 되어진다.

칸쿤의 관광산업을 예로 들자면, 북한의 도시 원산이 가장 적절한 도시로 볼 수 있다. 원산은 규모가 있고 역사적으로 오래된 항만산업을 운영 중이다. 하지만 기존의 항만산업이 기반이 된 지역 이외에도 아직 개발 잠재력을 갖고 있는 넓은 해안면을 소유하고 있다. 특히 동남쪽 해안면은 칸쿤의 관광 요충지의 지형과 매우 흡사하여 레저관광산업으로 손색없는 지역이라고 볼 수 있다. 레저 관광 외에도 의료 관광, 축제 관광과 같은 다양한 형태의 관광 산업을 도입한다면 이 또한 기존에 갖고 있던 북한도시들의 부정적인 이미지를 청산하고 고도의 경제성장을 도모하는데 원동력이 될 수 있다고 본다.

DMZ 세계평화공원과 국제기구 유치는 현 정부가 검토중인 사항이니만큼 실현 가능성이 높다고 할 수 있다. 국제기구유치는 남북 화해 분위기 조성과 안보비용 절감이란 이점뿐만 아니라 큰 경제적 수익을 창출할 수 있는 미래 산업의 하나라고 볼 수 있다. 이처럼 DMZ는 북한의 새로운 산업이라기보다 한반도 공동의 미래산업으로서 논해야 할 항목이다. 사례로 브뤼셀은 벨기에의 수도이자 29국제기구를 유치하는 도시이다. 국제기구들은 다양한 보조 산업들과 큰 산업 규모를 바탕으로 한 시장을 형성하는 효과를 가져왔다. 또한 이에 따른 경제수익은 1억 1천만 달러에 이른다.

결론

북한 산업의 잠재성을 기반으로 한 미래 시나리오는 상생의 한반도를 실현하기 위한 수단이다. 기존 산업의 응용과 새로운 산업의 주입을 통한 북한의 경제 성장은 세계가 북한을 좀더 긍정적이고 매력적인 대상으로 바라볼 수 있는 계기가 될 것이다. 위에 언급한 각 산업에 대한 사례들은 북한이 산업발달 측면에서 다음 단계로 도약하는데 도움을 주는 예들이다. 그러나 북한의 미래 시나리오에 대한 궁극적인 목표를 경제적인 숫자로 설정하는데 그쳐서는 안 된다고 생각한다. 정확한 수익을 평가하는 것만큼이나 중요한 것은 북한의 새로운 경제활동을 통해 변화되는 순간과 그 과정을 주시해야 할 것이다.

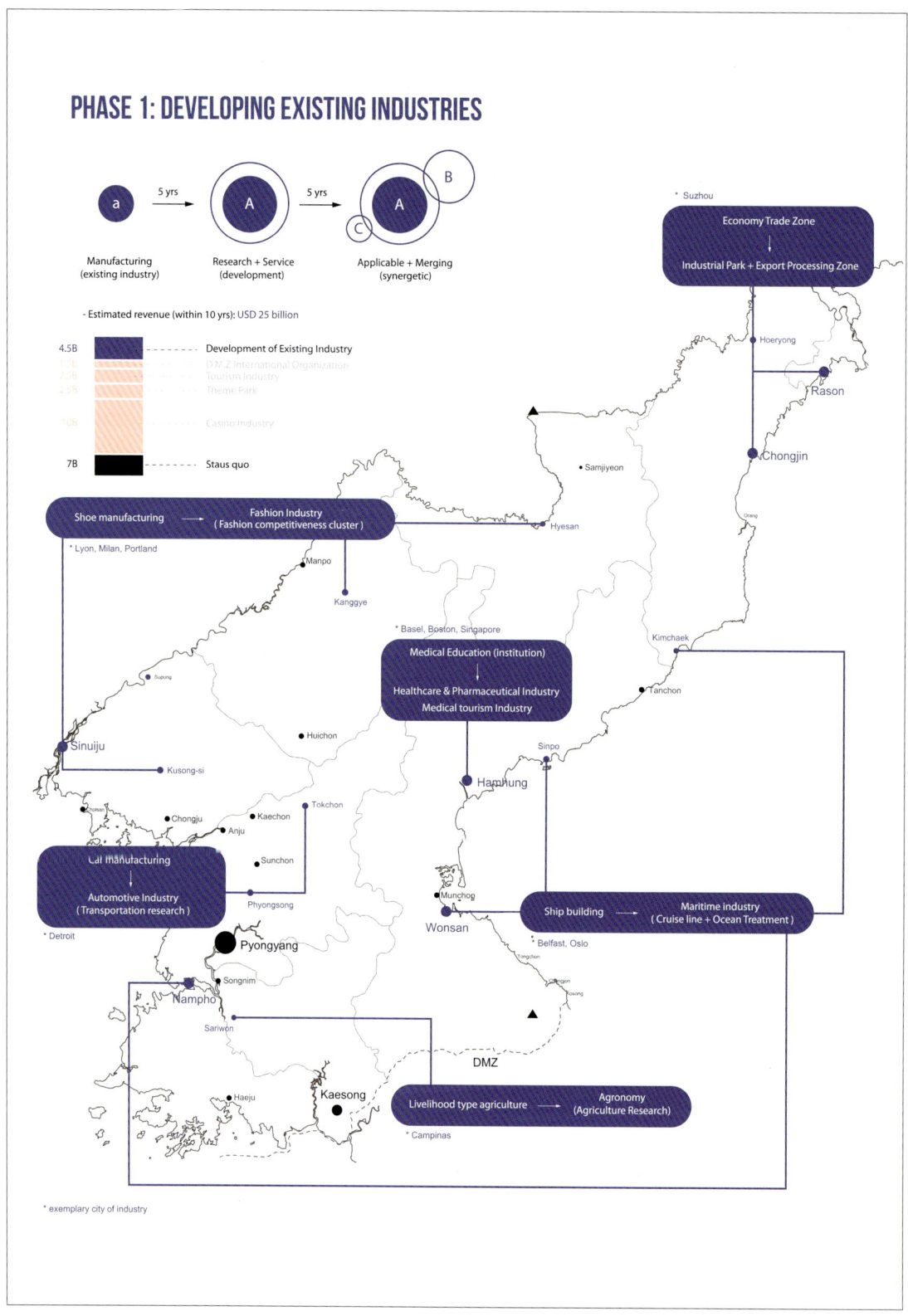

Future Industries of North Korea | Chong Ho Park

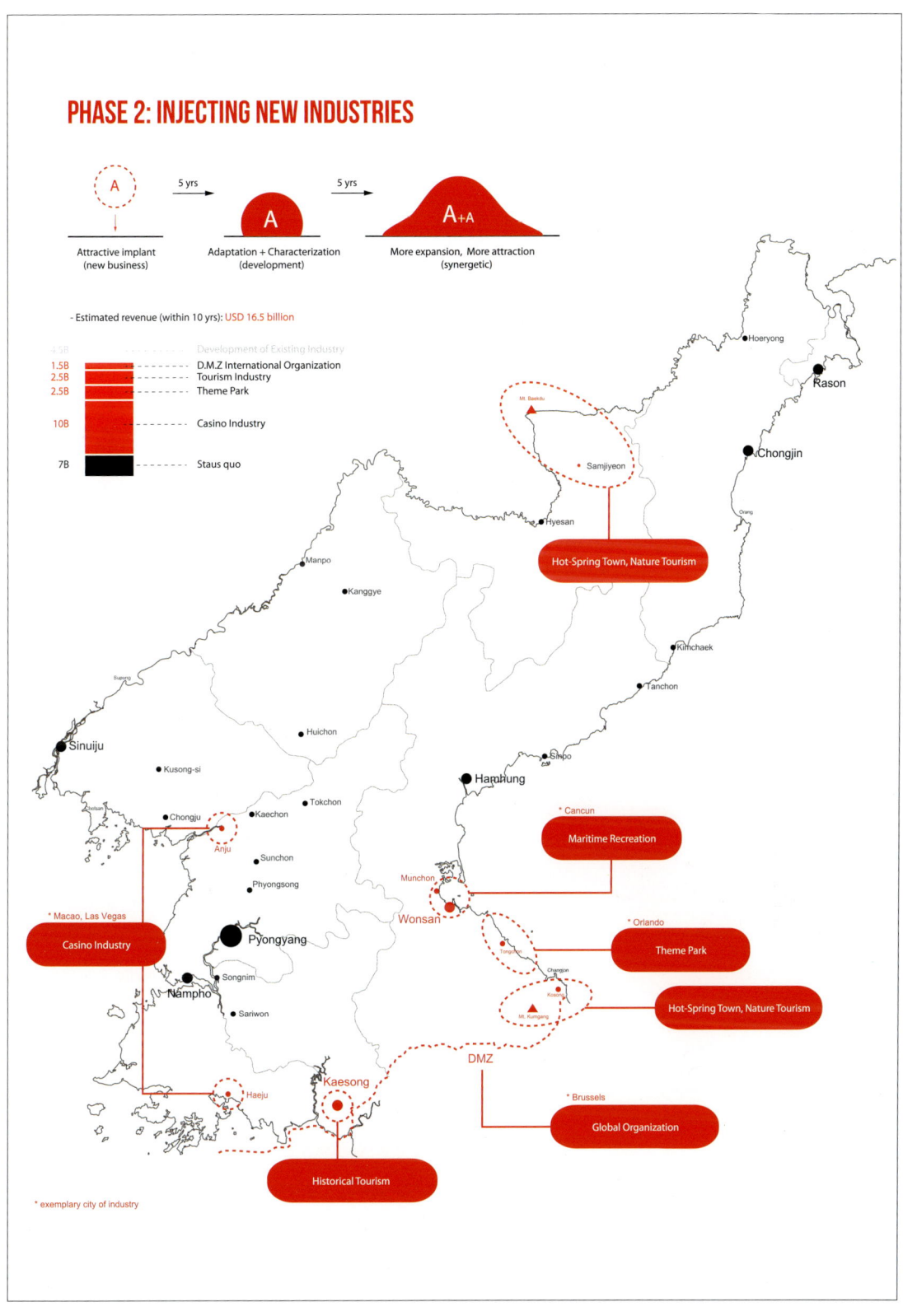

RESILIENT SPATIAL SCENARIOS FOR THE NORTH AND SOUTH KOREAN TRANSBOUNDARY ZONE

Yehre Suh

—

Yehre Suh is the Principal of Office of Urban Terrains and is an Adjunct Professor of Architecture at City College of New York and a Visiting Assistant Professor at the Pratt Institute. She received a B.F.A. and M.F.A. from Seoul National University and a M.Arch. from Harvard Graduate School of Design. Her work investigates the socio-political agency of architecture and its potentials as resilient mechanisms of negotiation and mitigation.
Currently she is working on the project "Tactical Territories," a web platform that focuses on mapping and analysis of parallel urbanisms and its spatial products of Transboundary Zones. In fall 2011, she directed the "Parallel Utopias" as an Options Studio at Cornell University, College of Architecture, Arts and Planning, Department of Architecture, where the Korean transboundary spatial scenarios were developed.
The project received the 2008 Graham Foundation Grant and the 2010 Rotch Foundation Studio Grant.
Saleem H. Ali and Kyong Park were Advisory Critics to the studio. Project Investigators are Burcu Bicer, Michael Cabrera, David Chessrown, Caroline Corbett, Patricia Echeverria, Aura Maria Jaramillo, Christine Kim, Yihua Li, Tansy Mak, Denise Pereira, Aiheidan Rouzi, Alexander Smith, Jeremy Tan.

In the past 60 years, there have been significant efforts and advancements made in economic, cultural, agricultural collaborations and exchanges between North and South Korea. But the extreme political, military fluctuation between the two countries have been problematic for a sustainable maintenance of ongoing collaborations as well as future initiatives. The intent of this article is to identify natural and artificial ecological systems as a means to develop and construct sustainable spatial strategies that are resilient to the extremities of the political climate. By integrating flexible ecological systems to initiate productive collaborations that are based on tourism, agricultural production, scientific research, environmental conservation, and sustainable integration of regional communities, we can envision a transboundary scenario that is sustainable and resilient through the various extremities of the political, military environment.

Agency[1] of Spatial Scenarios

The intent of the article is to explore the possibility of architecture as an agency of negotiation in transboundary conflict territories through the mechanisms of environmental as well as socio-political ecologies.

There is an increase of literature and interest in environmental diplomacy in transboundary conflict zones relative to the field of environmental studies, international governance policies and environmental NGOs.[2] But the field of environmental design that incorporates architecture, landscape architecture and urban design have not yet had much traction in these discussions. In the discourse of transboundary protection areas and collaborative

North and South Korean Collaborative Han River Ecological Research Park (Image by Alexander Smith, David Chessrown, Yehre Suh)

special economic, industrial zones, the typology of globally manufactured spatial products[3] dominate, while site specificity and design remains an afterthought to the process of collaboration and negotiation that structures the policy, governance and management systems. Although peace parks as symbolic destinations can produce attractive scenic developments[4], the process of design as a means of collaboration and negotiation has far more to offer than typical recreational programs.

Through alternative spatial scenarios along the North and South Korean border zones, the projects included in this chapter attempts to demonstrate how spatial scenarios can become an integral part of the collaborative process where spatial opportunities and resilient systems can be designed to operate for development and conservation purposes, while at the same time creating resilient environments that can persevere through military and political extremities. As Hilary Cunningham has stated, "a focus on an ecology-border nexus might expand understandings of and approaches to political borders and their permeable aspects."[5] Transboundary conflicts always contain heightened sensitivity to territorial concerns which entails environmental, ecological conditions that expands the geopolitical border into permeable zones of flux. The field of architecture, landscape architecture and urban design, which deals with the specificities and opportunities of spatial, environmental, territorial, ecological opportunities, can become critical agencies in the pursuit of resilient diplomacy.

The Dilemma of the Korean DMZ and the Necessity of Resilient Spatial Strategies

Korea's Demilitarized Zone(DMZ) is a biodiverse ecological preserve by default, a rich ecological habitat fraught with visible and invisible military, political tension. It is a catch 22 where the biodiversity of a no-man's land oasis can exist only due to the triple layer barbed wire fencing, military surveillance equipments, camouflaged tanks, missile launchers and the incessant patrol by heavily geared soldiers. Sectors of the government and environmental groups have been eager to convert the bio-diverse DMZ and its buffer territory, the Civilian Control Zone(CCZ), into an ecological preservation/conservation zone. But the issue of preservation vs. development of the DMZ and the CCZ remains a contested topic. In Sept. 2011, as part of a long effort to maintain the biodiversity of the DMZ, South Korea's Ministry of Environment unilaterally submitted an application to UNESCO for the designation of 435km2 in the southern part of the DMZ below the Military Demarcation Line, as well as 2,979km2 in the privately controlled areas, as a Biosphere Reserve.[6] But the application was denied by the UNESCO Commission in July 2012. The official reason stated by the Commission was that the research, education buffer zone in the Cheorwon area was insufficient. Although not specified officially, it is also argued by the critics that the application was rejected because it did not have official approval from the UN Command[7], which officially has jurisdiction over the southern half of the DMZ, as well as not having official approval from the North Korean government. Also the local community of Cheorwon poses as a problem due to their reluctance towards preservation zones as prohibiting land development and its economic opportunities.[8]

In 1997, the South Korean government (Republic of Korea, ROK) revised the Natural Environment Conservation Law to include an amendment that specifies that starting from the time the territorial control is ceded to ROK, the DMZ will become a Nature Protection Zone, where no development will be allowed for 2 years.[9] But environmentalists are raising concerns that the 2 years is a very short time to strategize and implement sustainable conservation strategies. Without a long term plan, the 2 year phase will result in de-regularization plans of the DMZ and the adjoining CCZ which will spur highly competitive real estate speculations and development. Especially without an official commitment from North Korea.[10] concerns regarding conservation, development and jurisdiction are overlaid with the indeterminacy and uncertainty of the future, which have been stalling discussions on further possibilities of the current transboundary territories. Much unilateral speculations on post unification scenarios exist but the current conditions at the border region is considered a stalemate and is not thought of having potentials for possibilities of the present.

However, in order to plan for a constructive future, we need to develop flexible alternatives that can respond to various options for the future rather than one specific scenario. Under the current circumstances, sustainable preservation and development path should be pursued through possible spatial opportunities. That exist in between the language of jurisdiction, treaty and political rhetorics, and this will provide a new mechanism of legal capacity that can picture flexible scenarios depending on divergent political and environmental situations.

Opportunity for Flexible Spatial Strategy

With North and South Korea in a state of indeterminate parallelism, it is imperative that we envision sustainable futures and possible alternatives that are not dependent on particular futures but is focused on opportunities of the present that are flexible and adaptable for all impending futures. It is critical that we start the process of sustainable conservation and development today through spatial opportunities available currently. Architecture, through its ability to project resilient spatial interventions that can create sustainable possibilities for diverse ecological scenarios, has the potential to provide spatial strategies of interventions that can co-exist within the jurisdictional possibilities and beyond by cultivating new routes for possible collaborations through the seemingly conflicting environment of extreme political rhetoric and fluctuations.

The idea of resiliency can be referenced to C.S. Holling, who talks about biological resilience of species and its habitats. "Resilience determines the persistence of relationships within a system and is a measure of the ability of these systems to absorb changes of state variables, driving variables, and parameters, and still persist."[11] He points out that "(a) management approach based on resilience... would emphasize the need to keep options open, the need to view events in a regional rather than a local context, and the need to emphasize heterogeneity. Flowing from this would be not the presumption of sufficient knowledge, but the recognition of our ignorance; not the assumption that future events are expected, but that they will be unexpected."[12] In the social-ecology systems study, Holling's idea of ecological resilience was translated into the analysis of environmental conservation and its relationship to societal systems as 'robustness', which initiated more interest in thinking about environmental conservation as means to a sustainable resilient social system rather than just the protection of the environment. "(R)ather than asking how society can better "manage" ecological resources, we ought to be asking "what makes social-ecological systems(SES) robust?"[13]

In the new age of risk society, focus shifts from the production of newness to the maintenance of indeterminacy. If modernization had been a history of revolutions in scientific and technological discoveries, innovations, advancements for an industrial society, the current post industrial society is, according to Ulrich Beck, a risk society that is focused on the consequences of new technologies and developments. "Risk management may be defined as a systematic way of dealing with hazards and insecurities induced and introduced by modernization itself".[14] Risk societies of the contemporary world require reflexive and therefore resilient strategies to maintain and manage the risks of modernization.

Korean Border Typologies and the Open Texture of Language

In the Koreas, three border typologies existed since the 1953 Korean Armistice Agreement. What is not discussed is the discrepancy between what was defined on paper and what exists in reality. The border that was defined by the Armistice have been constantly adjusted by the topographical, natural, ecological forces of the sites. This produces and contains many "inbetween" spaces between language and reality.

The dilemma that exist between the desire to define and fix permanent borders and boundaries vs. the nonstatic ecological systems that cannot be contained can be explained through the 'open texture of language'[15]. "Whichever device, precedent or legistration, is chosen for the communication of standards of behavior, these, however smoothly they work over the great mass of ordinary cases, will at some point where their application is in question, prove indeterminate; they will have what has been termed an open texture."[16] This is best exemplified in river properties and river borders where the legal definition of the line as boundary is difficult to maintain in space and time due to the natural transformations of the topography and land formation as a result of water movements.[17] Due to the open texture of language, text and map agreements of border zones inherently contain ambiguous territories that exist between paper and reality. Spatially, the gaps that exist between the abstract and legal notations of the border sites with the realities on the ground become important opportunities. The dynamic nature of natural and artificial environments defy static definitions of territory and properties and this is where we can find diverse possibilities of interpretation and intervention for resilient spatial scenarios. <Image 1, 2, 3>

The following scenarios are speculative spatial proposals that attempt to use space as a means to navigate inbetween the "lines" of the map and reality. It utilizes human and non-human actors that are part of the political, economic, regional, environmental eco-system of the cito to propose spatial products that are resilient and sustainable to the divergent gradients of the political atmosphere. The projects had been developed in the fall of 2011 with the Cornell University Department of Architecture students.

Scenario 1: DMZ villages Kijong-dong and Taesung-dong / Agro-Tourism Zone

The project explores the possibility of the neutral territories within the DMZ. The villages of Kijong-dong and Taesung-dong are the only two civilian occupied villages allowed to exist within the DMZ per the Armistice. The project attempts to expand

Resilient Soatial Scenarios for the North and South Korean Transboundary Zone | Yehre Suh

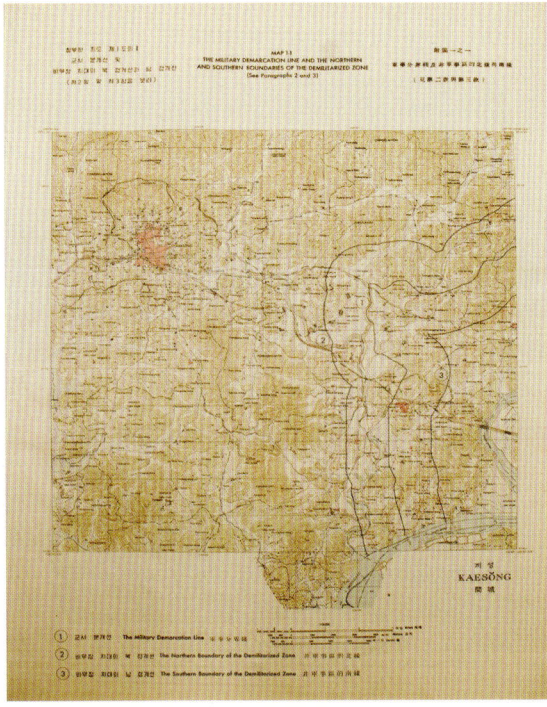

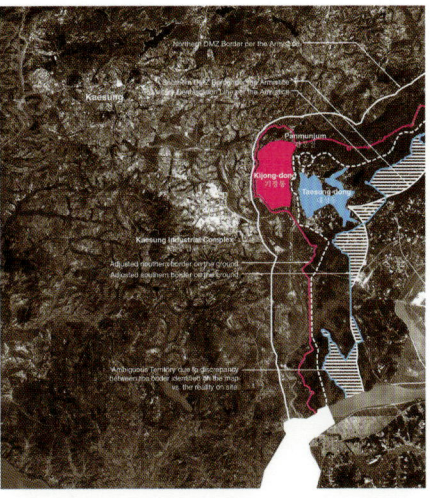

Image 1. The original Map 1 of the Korean Armistice Agreement Map Volume 2 (July 27, 1953); North and South borders of the DMZ and the Military Demarcation Line. The borderlines according to the Korean Armistice Agreement documents are shown in white, while the actual border fence locations of both sides are shown in red and blue. The inbetween space that exists between the lines of the documents vs. the lines in real space, are immanent with resilient spatial potentials (Image by Yehre Suh).

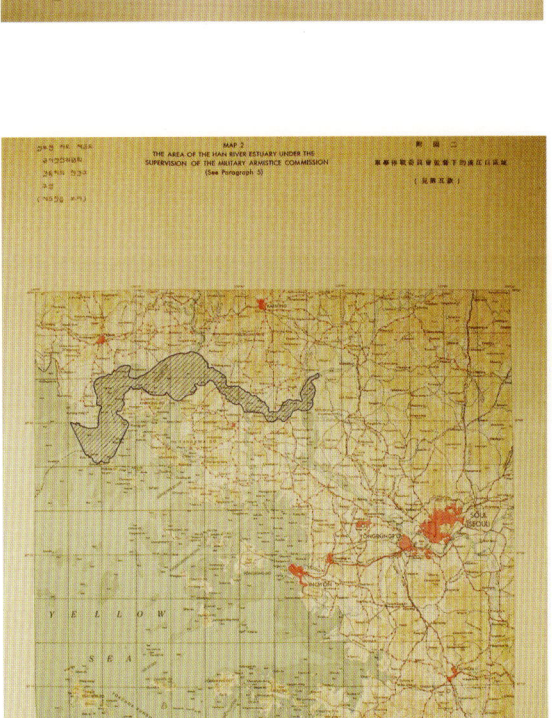

Image 2. The original Map 2 of the Korean Armistice Agreement Map Volume 2 (July 27, 1953); The Area of the Han River Estuary Under the Supervision of the Military Armistice Commission. White shows the area that is identified as a neutral zone accessible by both parties, and the black striped area shows the land area that appears and dissappears everyday according to the tides (Image by Yehre Suh).

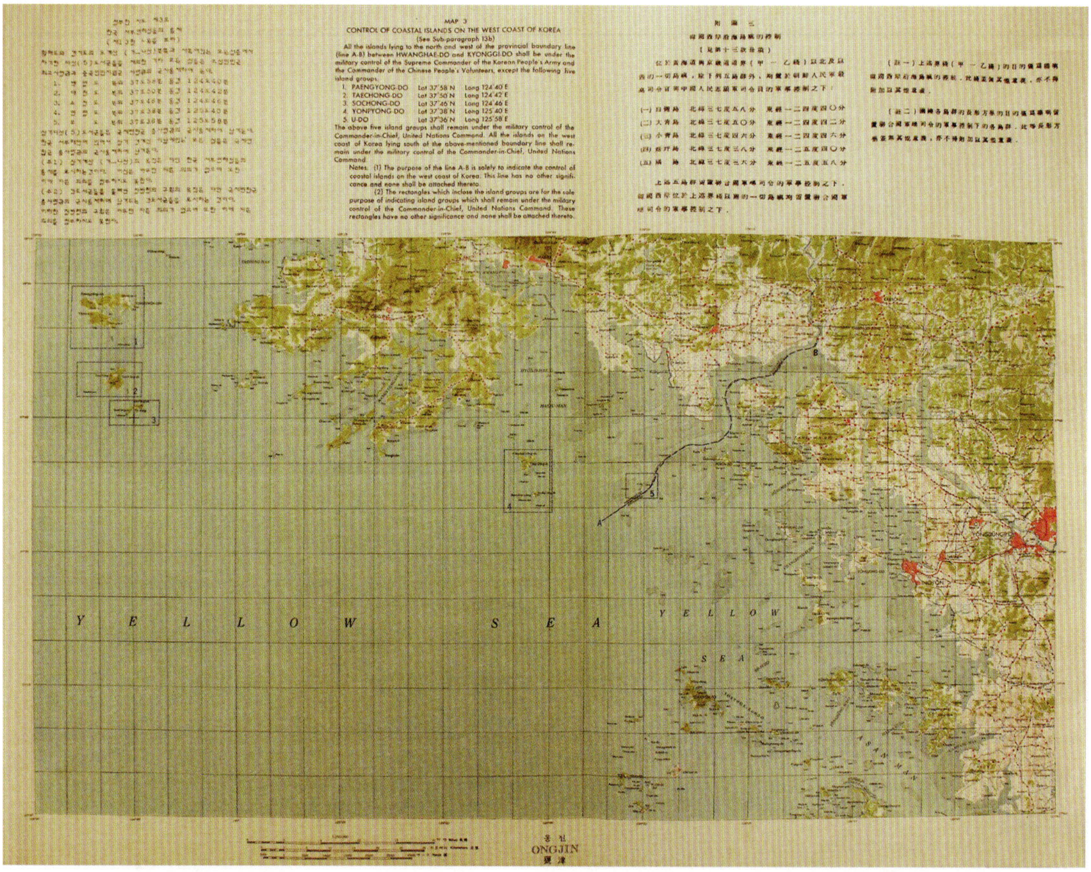

Future Scenarios

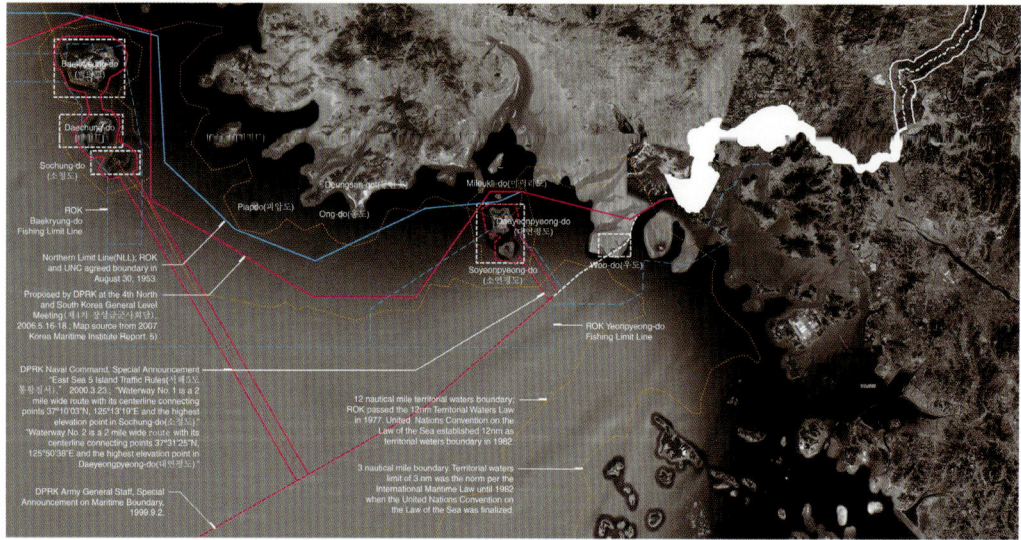

Image 3. The original Map 3 of the Korean Armistice Agreement Map Volume 2 (July 27, 1953); Coastal Islands on the West Coast of Korea. Per the Armistice, the map that defines the border at the five islands of the West Sea allows for multiple interpretations. This results in the North and South Koreas arguing for different maritime borders. The image on the left shows the compilation of the various boundaries argued for by both sides over the past 60 years. White are the notations defined by the Armistice. In red are the lines argued by the North and in blue are the lines argued by the South (Image by Yehre Suh).

the current stagnant separatist border condition into an integrative, education, production oriented collaborative agricultural landscape. Under the governance of an international food and agriculture focused NGO, such as the International Fund for Agricultural Development(IFAD), that is supported in funding by organizations such as the United Nations Development Programme(UNDP), the two villages are to be independently developed into agrotourism sites focused on agricultural education, production and exchange between the North and South Korean villagers with controlled tourist access of the site. The scenario speculates on how the agricultural cycle becomes an integrative mechanism of the political cycle, and how landscape and topography becomes the key organizer of the various natural and artificial actors of the site. Operational strategies of the scenarios are as follows.

One. The agricultural intervention promotes local biodiversity and sustainable farming by merging agricultural systems with existing ecological conditions. The topography of the rice fields are manipulated to establish a sustainable water supply system that is resilient to flooding while diverse crops will be introduced to enable various farming cycles to exist that would create a heterogenious environment that is resistant to environmental and political extremeties.

Two. The farmland is to allow for exchange of agricultural knowledge and technology between the two sides. During peace times, the farmland will act as sites of agricultural collaboration. During periods of tension, the topography of the site allows for a divided yet proximate environment where learning can happen through visual connections between the fields. The southern farmland can function as showcase sites for the north where the farming knowhow can be displayed without actual physical interaction.

Three. Military observation towers will be located at set intervals to allow for surveillance by both armies. The villagers and tourists will be controlled topographically, where landform will operate in section to create physical divisions through elevational changes, while at the same time maintaining visual connections between the two sides.

Four. As political showcases, the villages have leverage to demand federal funding for the town's infrastructure and agricultural, economic production. The political competitiveness of the two States will provide support for advancing agricultural techniques and supply for equipment and materials. As propaganda, exhibition sites, the villages become valuable tourist destinations.

Five. During politically tense periods, the Zone might shutdown and the land might not be accessible for indeterminate periods. The project proposes a way to establish heterogenious crop production cycles to work with the unforeseeable political atmospheres by allowing the land to rest during the conflict periods, allowing the soil to replenish its nutrients naturally.

The scenario speculates on how the agricultural cycle becomes an integrative mechanism of the political cycle and how landscape becomes the key organizer of the various natural and artificial actors of site. It considers not only connection between the process of cultivation, management and harvest of crops and the existing water body, but also possibility of using it as touristic features. Although Kijong-dong and Taesung-dong exists for political propaganda purposes, this project proposes a spatial possibility for growing eco-friendly crops and exchange of experimental agriculture technology under the lubric of propaganda. It is a scenario that allows more exchange between farmers through topographic site planning, increases possibilities for tourism, and yet keeps the overall military surveillance system active. It proposes a territory that develops continuous exchange in agriculture and production facilities by syncing the political cycle with the ecological cycle. <Image 4, 5, 6>

Scenario 2: Han River Estuary / Agro-Science Zone

In the second scenario we approach the second border type along the Han River Estuary. The project utilizes the width of the river identified as the neutral border zone, which as a condominium is, on paper, a co-habitable zone by both North and South Korea. But the current waterfront along both sides of the river are heavily guarded by the military and no one is allowed access into the river. But two times a day the tides reveal a land mass of about 30km2 in the middle of the river that potentially can become co-habitable.[18] The project proposes to utilize the temporal tidal flats to implement air and water pollution monitoring systems through clam and rice farming. The scenario speculates on an international environmental NGO whose objective is to progress scientific research on the ecological habitats and pollution levels of the region as a means to progress scientific research and test agricultural exchange governance systems. The operational strategies of the scenario are as follows.

One. Clam farms will be installed into the tidal land as a cooperative economic development for the south and north residents. The area will only be accessible during low tide two times a day. During non-conflict periods both sides can access the area for cooperative clam farming. During periods of conflict, both sides will take turns accessing the area. Rice fields on both sides of the river will be administered as special test sites where collaborative education and management will study sustainable organic agriculture techniques and technologies. The area's rice will be branded as "Peace Rice" where the collaborative production will be marketed as a brand opportunity. Tourist zones can be set up in the CCZ nearby to market and sell the clam and rice produced from the area.

Two. Environmental monitoring devices will be installed and administered by both sides as test case projects. The clam farms are installed with buoyant pollutant monitoring devices which will monitor the water pollution. Pollution from agriculture pesticide runoff and industrial and chemical discharges from the nearby urban areas will be monitored. Rice fields on both sides of the border are installed with air balloons with air quality monitoring devices. The devices will also allow for a continued ecological survey of the inaccessible river and can be operational with minimal maintenance irrespective of the political climate.

Three. The project can be utilized as a test case of sustainable governance for scientific purposes. The two sides will have to integrate the regional community with environmental researchers and scientists to establish an experimental model of gover-

Resilient Soatial Scenarios for the North and South Korean Transboundary Zone | Yehre Suh

Image 4. INTEGRATE INTO EXISTING TOUR NETWORK

Scenario 1: Agrological Landscape / Existing Landscape of Propaganda
North and South Korea both already utilizes the military and ecological environment adjacent to the DMZ for tourism purposes.
(Images by Denise Pereira, Tansy Mak)

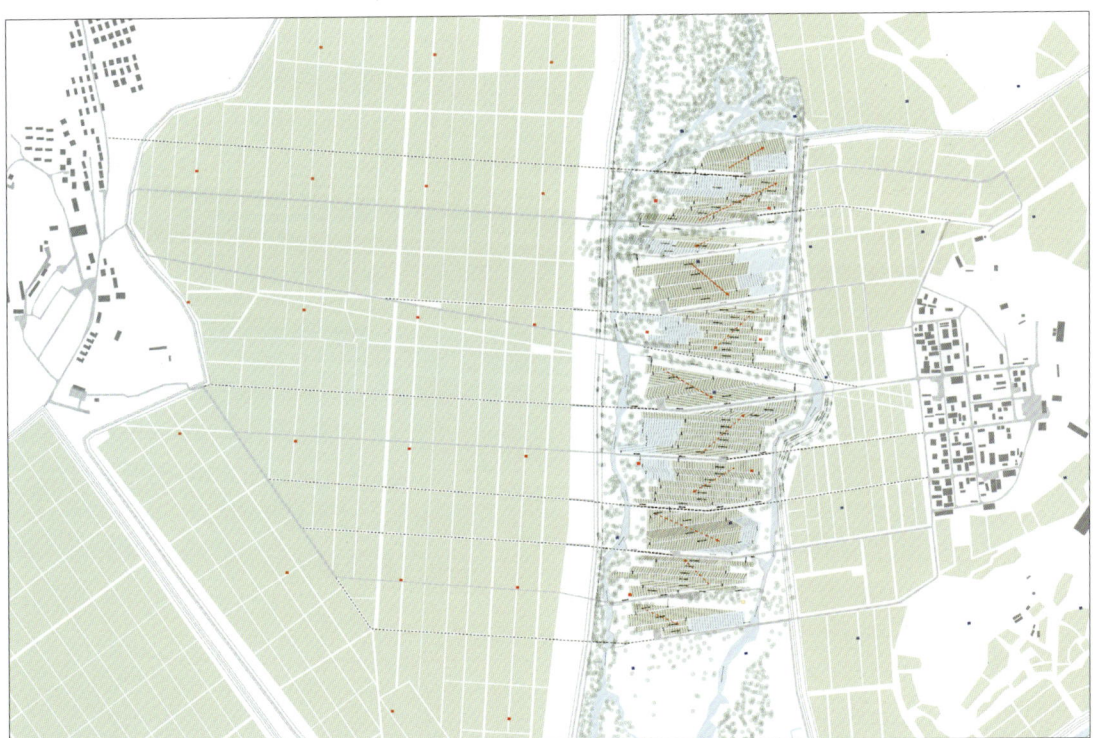

Image 5. Scenario 1: Agrological Landscape
The topographic specificity of the site inbetween Taesung-dong and Kijong-dong is used to create a collaborative agricultural zone. The landform is manipulated to control the water canals for the agricultural fields which enhances the ecological resiliency as well as productivity for propaganda purposes
(Image by Aura Maria Jaramillo, Yihua Li, Patricia Echeverria).

SCENARIO 1: AGRO-LOGICAL LANDSCAPE
Topographic Separation and Cooperation

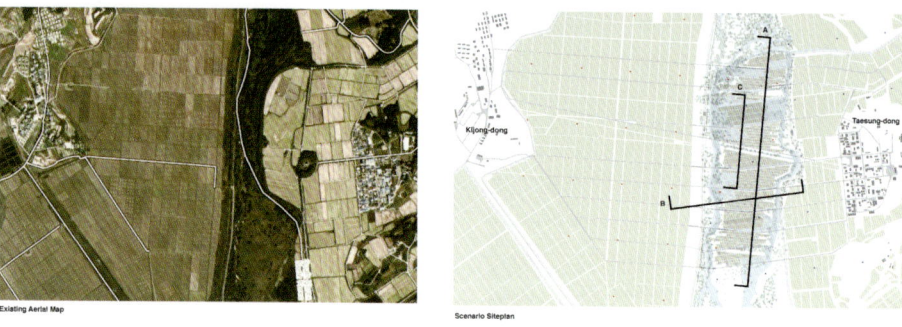

Existing Aerial Map

Scenario Siteplan

Scenario 1: Agrological Landscape
Aerial map of Taesung-dong and Kijong-dong and site plan of proposed site. (Image by Aura Maria Jaramillo, Yihua Li, Patricia Echeverria)

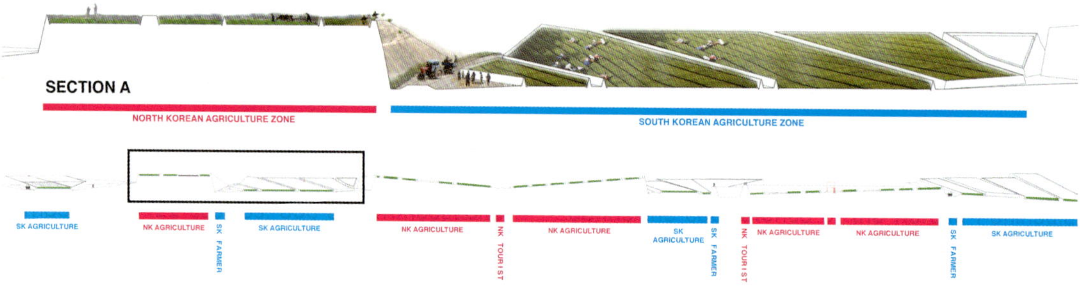

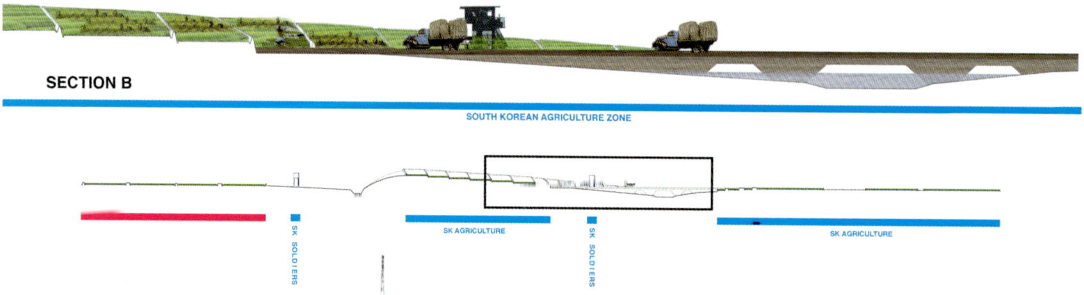

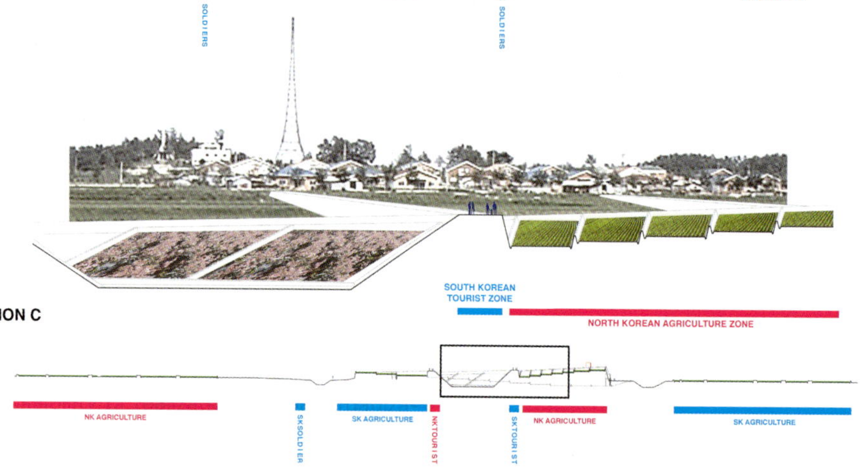

Image 6. Scenario 1: Agrological Landscape
Topographic Separation and Collaboration. The topographic specificity of the site inbetween Taesung-dong and Kijong-dong is used to create a collaborative agricultural zone. The landform is manipulated to control the water canals for the agricultural fields which enhances the ecological resiliency as well as productivity for propaganda purposes. (Image by Aura Maria Jaramillo,Yihua Li, Patricia Echeverria)

nance for the zone. It follows the model of special economic zones but requires integration of regional interests under the rubric of scientific research.

Four. Militarily the tide cycle provides a mechanism of control which minimizes the need for extreme security. The entry points in and out of the river can be easily controlled while at the same time providing potential work, market zones for clam processing.

Five. The area can be completely shutdown in times of heightened conflict. But the monitoring devices will still be operational and with its field of LED lights become a landscape installation which can attract tourists to nearby accessible tourist zones, irrespective of the neutral zone's shutdown. Agricultural productivity and environmental management are both critical issues of the region. By utilizing site specific issues and opportunities of spatial intervention, the project is able to envision a scenario where the daily and seasonal cycles of the tidal lands and its ecological system provides a common ground for political, social, economic interaction and how common agendas for economic production and scientific research can initiate ecological conservation. <Image 7, 8>

Scenario 3: West Sea 5 Islands and Yeonpyeong Island / Aquaculture-Tourism Zone

The third site is situated to the north of Yeonpyeong Island. It is a site fraught with minor and

Image 7. Scenario 2: Residual Fields
Landscape of agricultural production and environmental monitoring. Tidal clam farm and special agricultural zone along the Han River. The site plan shows the layout of the environmental monitoring system devices. (Image by Christine Kim, Caroline Corbett)

Future Scenarios 550

Image 8. Scenario 2: Residual Fields
From the top: Air pollution monitoring devices in the agriculture fields. Clam farm accessible during low tide periods. Monitoring devices turn into a site lighting installation. (Images by Christine Kim, Caroline Corbett)

Through its network system, the fisheries will create an unofficial maritime border which will block access of Chinese fishing boats while delineating separate access zones for South and North Korean fishing boats.

Based on political climates and natural ecological cycles, maritime boundaries in the West Sea are in a constant mode of expansion and contraction. In such a state of continuous flux, the mobile islands function as political, military and ecological monitors of the sea. They allow for shared occupation of the disputed areas during the high fishing seasons, while monitoring sustainable fishing practices. During times of conflict they will function as a neutral third party to create buffer zones in the open waters to police and mitigate the tension. <Image 9, 10, 11>

For a Resilient Future

In the Koreas, ecological conservation and economic development have become important tools of transboundary collaboration, but are questionable regarding its resilience to the political climate. In order to progress dialogue and development inspite of the political atmosphere, it is important to establish resilient strategies that can persist and are beneficial through periods of collaboration as well as conflict. We have to view transboundary territories, not as static military conflict sites, conservation areas or economic, tourism zones, but as experimental territories that can transform social, cultural and political boundaries. For this reason, we need to integrate the creative abilities of architects, landscape architects and planners in their ability to integrate natural and artificial ecologies of the site through the manipulation of space, as a means to re-envision social, political environments that are resilient to the extremeties of transboundary territories. As an investigation into the possibilities of environmental design's political agency and its potential strategies of operation, the spatial scenarios proposed in this project actively engages the geopolitical to envision the transboundary zone not as a means of territorial separation but of productive integration and constructive cooperation.

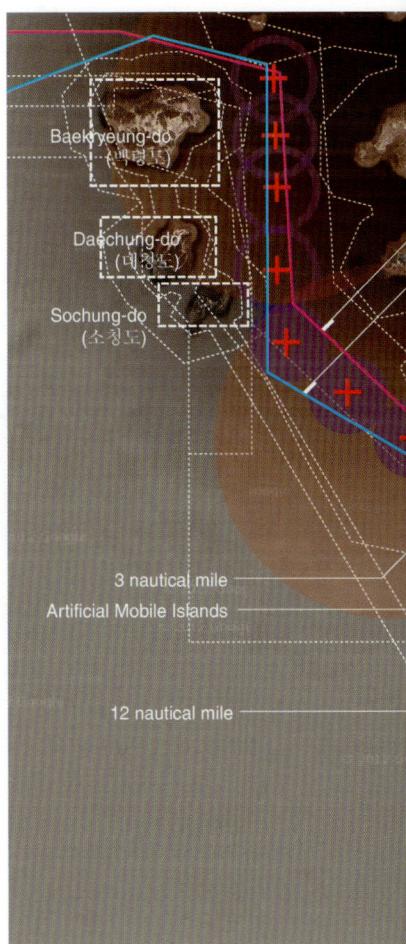

major military clashes due to the ambiguity of the maritime border definition in the Armistice. What is of interest is that as a result of the latest maritime border boundaries argued by both parties, approximately 24km2 neutral zone that is neither claimed by North nor South Korea exists north of the Yeonpyeong Islands.[19] The project takes the opportunity of the neutral maritime territory to propose a series of artificial floating islands as a special aquaculture peace tourism zone. Virtual citizens[20] of Korea from around the world will fund and support the project. And it will operate as an independent third party sovereignty called "Korea" under the guidance of a non-profit organization that maintains the maritime territories.[21] The operation strategies of the scenario are as follows.

One. The islands will operate and be managed by an international non-profit organization or NGO with support from the virtual citizens of "Korea". The islands will function as the core infrastructure for sustainable aquaculture fish farming as well as for fishing tourism. During peace times, North and South Korean local fish farmers will collaborate on the setup and maintenance of the aquaculture systems beyond the neutral zone to ensure sustainable operations in the respective territories of the open sea. During times of conflict, the aquaculture systems can be collected into the neutral zone and operate at a smaller scale. North and South Korean tourists can visit the neutral zone during peace times and international tourists can even travel directly from the Incheon International Airport without requiring a visa entry. During military conflict the zone will be closed off to North and South Korean citizens but will remain open to international tourists.

Two. The artificial islands are to mitigate military tension in the area by providing third party patrol of the region. The islands are operated as a third party sovereignty to act as a neutralizing body in the open waters.[22] During peace times, the mobile islands will patrol the West Sea as a neutral police to keep illegal Chinese fishing boats out of the territories.[23] The neutral policing of the area will reduce minor conflicts between military and fishing boats that often occur due to heavy fogs and heavy ship traffic in the area. In case a conflict arises in the open waters, the artificial islands will spread out along the conflict area and exercise its 12nm territorial waters as a buffer zone to separate the two sides.

Three. The conflict area is a rich habitat for blue crabs which are highly prized species in the region. But due to overfishing by the Chinese fishing boats, there is great urgency to establish conservation strategies for the region's maritime habitat. Sustainable aquaculture systems will help with fishing production while protecting the natural habitat. A sustainable aquaculture practice will be enhanced through governance to ensure the problems associated with management of aquaculture fisheries are mitigated.

Four. The islands and its aquaculture system will be resilient to the political climate through its mobility. The islands will mainly occupy and utilize the neutral zone while being mobile along the disputed waters. The aquaculture system will also be able to contract into the neutral territories during times of conflict while expanding out into the northern and southern seas in times of peace. The fishery will also perform unofficially as a maritime border that can control access into the area.

Future Scenarios

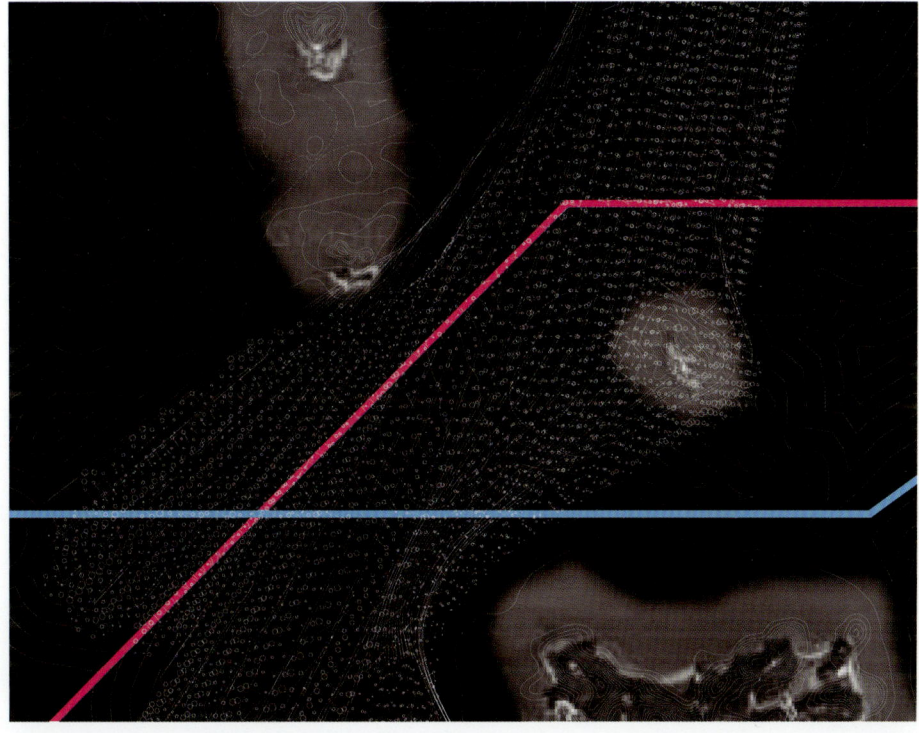

Image 10. Scenario 3: Adaptive Territory
A sustainable and flexible aquaculture farming zone can be established in the neutral maritime territories. The aquaculture systems installed in the open waters will act as a barrier to prevent Chinese fishing boats entering into the area, while at the same time create separate fishing zones for the North and South fishing community (Image by Michael Cabrera, Jeremy Tan, Yehre Suh).

Resilient Soatial Scenarios for the North and South Korean Transboundary Zone | Yehre Suh

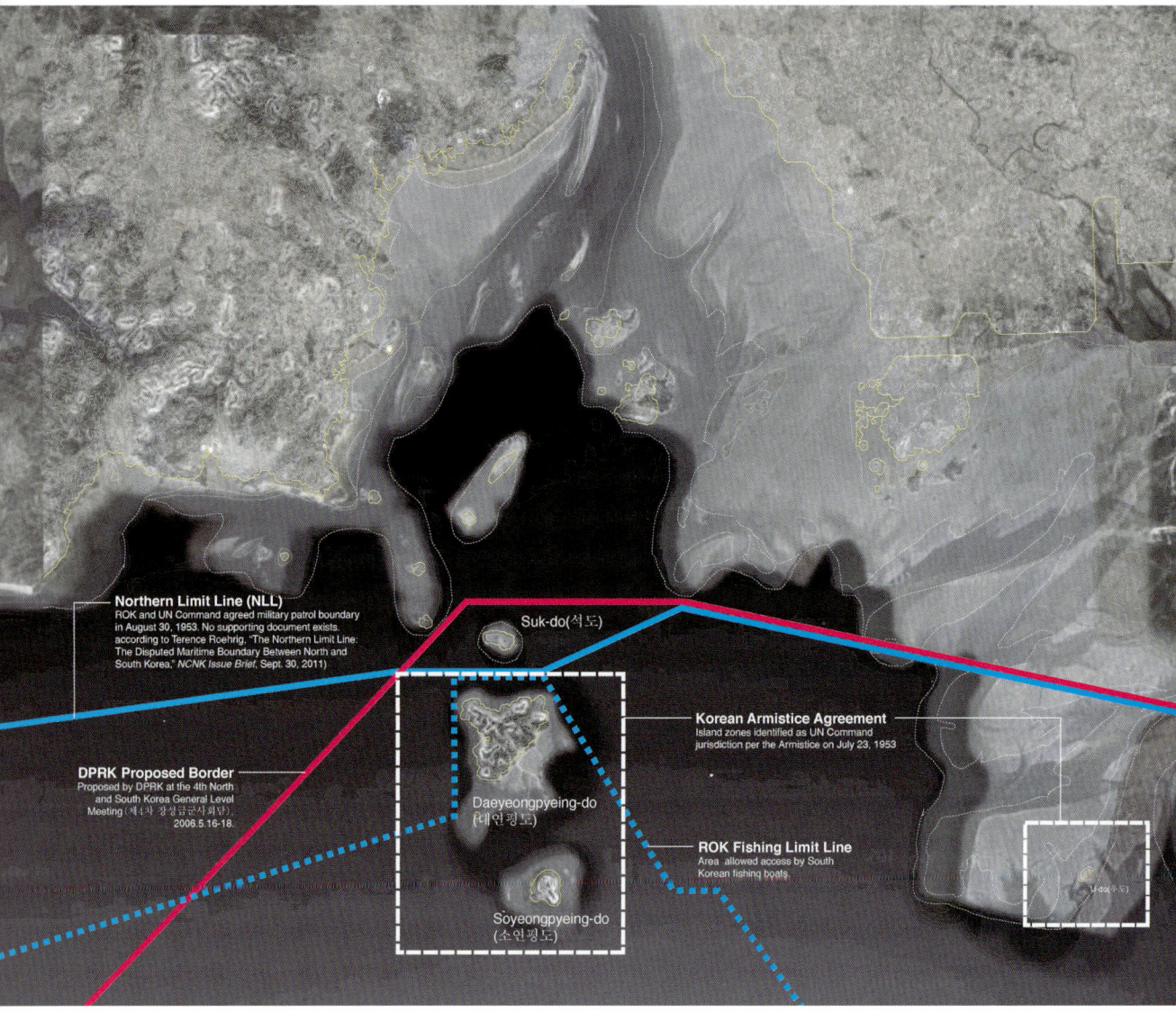

Image 9. Scenario 3: Adaptive Territory
According to the latest maritime boundaries argued by South and North Korea, there is a neutral zone, immediately north of Daeyeonpyeong-do, that remains unclaimed by both parties. (Image by Michael Cabrera, Jeremy Tan, Yehre Suh)

Resilient Soatial Scenarios for the North and South Korean Transboundary Zone | Yehre Suh

Image 11. Scenario 3: Adaptive Territory
During periods of non-tension, the mobile artificial islands will monitor the five islands in the West Sea for maritime biodiversity and species habitat preservation and oversee the collaborative aquaculture farming zone. During periods of military, political tension, the mobile islands will announce the five island areas as a demilitarized non-access zone and will function as a neutral third party that maintains a buffer between the North and South armies.
(Image by Bicer Burcu, Aiheidan Rouci, Yehre Suh)

남북접경지역의
탄력적 공간 시나리오

서예례

—

서예례는 Office of Urban Terrains의 실장으로 뉴욕시립대학의
겸임 교수이자, 프랫 인스티튜트의 객원 조교수이다.
서울대학교에서 B.F.A.와 M.F.A.를 수여하고 하버드 디자인
대학원(Harvard Graduate School of Design)에서
M.Arch.를 수여하였다. 디자인 연구 작업을 통해
공간전략 생산 주체로서 건축의 사회, 정치적 행위능력의
가능성을 물색한다. 현재는 접경지역의 병행적 도시개발과
공간제품을 연구하는 웹 플랫폼 "Tactical Territories"를
진행하고 있다. 남북한 접경지역 공간 시나리오를 탐구한
"Parallel Utopias" 프로젝트는 2011년 가을 코넬 대학교
건축학과(Cornell University, College of Architecture,
Art and Planning, Department of Architecture), 옵션 스튜디오를
통해 진행되었다. 프로젝트는 2008년 그라함 파운데이션 그랜트와
2010년 로치 파운데이션 그랜트를 수여하였다.
살림 알리(Saleem H. Ali)와 박경(Kyong Park)이 스튜디오
고문 크리틱으로 참여하였으며, 프로젝트 참여 학생은 다음과 같다.
Burcu Bicer, Michael Cabrera, David Chessrown,
Caroline Corbett, Patricia Echeverria, Aura Maria Jaramillo,
Christine Kim, Yihua Li, Tansy Mak, Denise Pereira,
Aiheidan Rouzi, Alexander Smith, Jeremy Tan.

지난 60년간 남북한 사이에 수많은 경제적, 문화적, 농경적 협력, 교류 사업이 공식적, 비공식적으로 이루어져 왔다. 하지만 양극을 오가는 정치적, 군사적 대치 관계로 인하여 이러한 작업의 지속 가능한 관계 유지가 매우 어려운 상황이다. 본 작업의 목적은 자연적, 인공적 생태 시스템을 통해 정치적 환경의 극단적 상황에 탄력적이면서도 지속 가능한 공간 전략의 가능성을 제시하는 데 있다. 유연한 생태 시스템을 기반으로 한 환경 보전, 관광, 농경 산업, 과학 기술 연구, 그리고 지역 경제의 지속 가능한 발전을 도모하는 생산적 교류와 협력 가능성을 연구함으로써, 극도의 정치적, 군사적 환경을 넘어설 수 있는 지속 가능하면서도 탄력 있는 접경지역 공간 시나리오를 구상하고자 한다.

공간 시나리오의 행위능력(agency)[1]

본 글은 접경갈등지역의 정치적, 군사적 협상에 있어 환경, 사회, 정치적 생태 시스템의 메커니즘을 기반으로 한 건축 시나리오의 행위능력 가능성을 타진한다.

접경지역 갈등 해소 방안으로서의 환경외교가 환경연구, 국제 거버넌스, 환경 NGO 관련인들의 관심을 끌고 있지만[2], 이 논의에서 환경디자인을 다루는 건축, 조경건축, 도시설계 분야의 관여는 거의 전무한 상태이다. 접경지역을 위주로 생성되고 있는 생태보전구역, 특수경제구역, 특수공업단지, 특수관광지구 등의 환경 공간개발 유형은 글로벌 공간제품(spatial products)[3]이 되어 대거 배출되고 있으며, 이는 전 세계 시장을 대상으로 신 자유주의 경제에 따른 접경지역 협력, 교류 사업들을 통해 도입, 확장되고 있다. 하지만 국제 시장구조를 따르는 권력구조의 산물로서의 공간제품 유형은 효율성, 경제성, 정치적 선전을 중심으로 계획되기 때문에 지속 가능한 지역개발, 지역 기반시설 확충, 탄력적 관리와 운영 측면에서 매우 제한적일 수 밖에 없다. 환경보전, 정화를 목적으로 하는 평화공원과 같이 관광객 유치를 위해 환경디자인이 적용될 수도 있겠지만[4], 자연적, 인공적 공간의 정치적, 사회적 가능성을 타진하는 환경디자인은 지속 가능한 탄력적 시스템을 구상함으로써, 외교협상의 확장적 메커니즘으로 기능할 수 있을 것이다.

따라서 본 글은 공간제품 대신 환경디자인을 통한 공간 시나리오의 창출을 주장한다. 거버넌스 체계, 정책, 구조, 기능 등에 대한 대화 이후 그 틀에 맞는 공간제품을 설치하기 보다는 지역의 공간적 가능성에 대한 대화를 매개로 한 협력구조 계획을 제시한다. 힐러리 커닝햄(Hilary Cunningham)은, "생태-국경적 이해를 통해 정치적 국경의 투과적 가능성을 확장할 수 있을 것"[5]이라고 했다." 접경지역 갈등은 영토에 대한 고도의 예민성을 내재하고 있기 때문에 특정 지역의 공간적, 환경적, 영토적, 생태적 가능성을 타진하는 공간 시나리오는 탄력적 외교 창출을 위한 강한 행위능력을 지니고 있다.

한국 비무장지대(DMZ)의 교착상태

한국의 DMZ는 의도하지 않은 가운데 다양한 생태환경을 형성하게 되었지만, 이는 보이지 않는 군사적, 정치적 긴장감과 함께 공존하는 풍요롭고도 다양한 생태서식지이다. 무인지대 오아시스로 현존하는 이 지역의 풍부한 생물 다양성은 세 겹의 철조망, 군사 감시 시설, 위장 탱크와 미사일 기지, 그리고 끊임없는 군인들의 순찰 덕분에 지속될 수 있는 자연 생태계이기에 군사적, 정치적 생태계와 밀접한 관계를 형성하고 있다. 생물 다양성이 풍부한 DMZ와 민간인 통제지역(민통선, CCZ)의 생태계를 보전하기 위해 정부와 환경 단체들은 많은 노력을 기울이고 있다. 하지만 이 지역의 보전, 혹은 개발의 문제에 대한 다양한 의견들이 산재한다. 지난 십여 년간 남한 정부는 DMZ를 UNESCO 생물권 보전지역(Biosphere Reserve)으로 지정받기 위해 노력했으며, 지난 2011년 9월 환경부는, 군사경계선(Military Demarcation Line, MDL) 남쪽 435㎢의 DMZ 구역과 2,979㎢의 민통선 지역을 UNESCO 생물권 보전지역으로 신청했다.[6] 하지만 2012년 7월 UNESCO는 철원지역에 관련 규약이 요구하는 완충, 또는 전이지역이 갖춰지지 않아 지정 결정을 유보했다. 일부 환경단체들은 DMZ 남쪽 지역의 관할권을 쥐고 있는 유엔사령부[7]와 북한의 동의 부재, 그리고 생태보전으로 인한 지역개발 제한을 우려하는 철원 지역주민들과 지주들의 지원 부족을 그 이유로 들고 있다.[8]

1997년 남한정부는 DMZ 지역의 관할권이 대한민국 정부로 인계되는 순간부터 2년간 개발이 금지된다는 사항을 자연환경보전법에 추가했다.[9] 하지만 DMZ의 지속 가능한 생태보전을 확정할 수 있는 정책을 책정하기에 2년은 매우 짧은 기간이다. 뚜렷한 장기대책 없이 관할권 이전이 이루어진다면 DMZ와 민통선 지역의 규제가 채 풀리기도 전 부동산 투자와 개발이 난무한 지역이 되기 십상이기 때문이다. 환경부와 국제, 국내 환경단체들은 DMZ를 위한 생태보호, 보전 계획들을 제안하고 있지만 유엔사령부 관할지역이라는 이유로 아직 정책 제안에 머물고 있다. 또한, 북한을 제외하고 이루어진 생태보전 정책이라는 한계가 있기도 하다.[10] 민통선 지역에 관해서는 기존의 국가, 환경 NGO 단체들의 보전, 개발 정책들은 지속 가능한 지역 경제개발에 대한 고려가 부족하다는 지적을 받고 있기는 하지만, 지역주민들과 민간사업들의 경제개발에 대한 관심은 무조건적 시장경제 유입으로 인한 지역의 생태환경 파괴의 위험을 동반하고 있다. 접경지역의 보전, 개발, 관할권 문제는 미래의 불확실성과 맞물려 현재의 가능성을 지체시키고 있으며, 통일 후 시나리오들이 단독적으로 존재하기는 하지만 현재의 국경 지역은 정치적 교착상태로 인식되고 있으며, 현재의 잠재력과 가능성을 생각하기 어려운 지역이 되어버렸다.

그러나 생산적 미래를 위해서는 불분명한 병행적 상황에도 불구하고, 특정한 미래가 아닌 여러 미래에 대치할 수 있는 유연한 생산적 대안들을 추구해야 할 것이다. 현재의 상황속에서 가능한 공간적 기회들을 통해 지속 가능한 보전 및 개발 과정을 시작해야 한다. 공간 시나리오를 통해 우리는 관할권, 협정, 정치적 수사법의 언어 아래 존재하는 공간적 기회들을 발견할 수 있으며, 이는 정치적 긴장 상황에 따라 유연한 시나리오들을 상상할 수 있는 새로운 행위능력 메커니즘을 제공한다.
DMZ와 인근 민통선 지역 개발에 대한 지속적인 관심으로 인하여 그간 보존되었던 다양한 동식물 생태계의 변화가 임박하다. 비환경친화적인 개발을 제지함과 동시에 독특한 생태환경의 보존, 그리고 인근 지역의 지속 가능한 생산적 개발을 위해서는, 특정한 미래가 아닌 여러 미래를 예상할 수 있는 탄력적 공간 시나리오들을 추구해야 할 것이다.

탄력적 공간전략의 기회

두 한국의 병행적 공존은 군사적, 정치적 환경의 극한 속에 탄력적이며 적응 가능한 공간적 상황을 필요로 한다. 이처럼 유동적인 상황에 적응하기 위해서는 변형적이고 탄력적인 생태 시스템을 적용한 공간 전략이 필요하며, 이는 환경디자인을 통해 정치적, 사회적, 경제적 시나리오를 협상할 기회를 제공한다.

생태적 탄력성(resilience)의 개념은 생물체와 그 서식지의 탄력적 관계를 연구한 C.S. 홀링(C.S. Holling)으로부터 기원한다. "탄력성은 시스템 내 관계의 지속성을 결정하고, 변이 가능성과 변수들의 변화를 흡수하면서도 지속할 수 있는 시스템 기능의 측정이다."[11] 그는 "탄력성에 기반을 둔 관리 방법은 다양한 옵션을 열어두고, 특정 지역보다는 지역 전반의 상태를 접수해야 하며, 종 다양성을 중시해야 한다. 이는 적합한 지식의 보유보다는 무지를 인지하는 과정이며, 미래의 사태들을 예측하려고 하기 보다는 예측할 수 없다고 추정하는 방법이다."[12] 홀링의 생태적 탄력성 개념은 사회생태시스템(social ecological system) 연구에 있어 환경보전과 이의 사회적 영향을 설명하기 위해 '건장함(robustness)'으로 전환되어 설명된다. 이는 환경보전이 단지 자연의 보호만을 위한 개념이 아닌 지속 가능한 탄력적 사회 구성 시스템으로 이해하기 위해 형성되었다. "사회가 생태자원을 어떻게 효과적으로 '관리'할 수 있는 가를 묻기보다는 사회 생태시스템을 어떻게 건장하게 만들 수 있는가를 질문해야 한다."[13] 현대의 위험사회(risk society)에서는 새로움의 창출보다는 예측 불가능한 상황의 관리를 더 중요시한다. 울리히 벡(Ulrich Beck)은 근대화가 공업사회를 위한 과학 기술의 발견, 혁신, 발전의 진취적 혁명의 역사였다면, 현재 공업화 이후의 사회는 새로운 기술과 발전의 결과를 다루는 위험사회라고 말한다. "위기관리는 근대화에 의해 창출, 발전된 위험과 불안을 다루는 시스템이라 할 수 있다."[14] 벡은 현대사회의 위기를 관리하기 위해 위험사회는 반사적 근대화(reflexive modernity)를 필요로 한다고 말한다. 따라서 반사적, 그리고 탄력적 공간 시나리오는 위기에 대처하기 위한 근대사회의 주 메커니즘이라 할 수 있을 것이다.

건축, 조경건축, 도시설계를 아우르는 환경디자인은 사회적·문화적·정치적 생태 시스템의 통합적 적용을 통해 자연적, 인공적 환경을 조정 및 창출하는 분야이다. 따라서 자연적, 인공적, 그리고 사회적, 정치적 생태 시스템의 디자인을 포괄하는 환경디자인은 공간적 전략을 통해 탄력적 시나리오를 제안할 수 있는 주요 메커니즘이 될 수 있다.

본 글에 제시된 공간 시나리오들은 자연적, 인공적 생태 시스템의 정책적 즉각성을 배경으로 국가 차원에서뿐만 아니라 민간인 차원에서의 경제적, 과학적, 농경적, 교육적 교류와 생산의 가능성을 타진한다. 프로젝트들의 주목적은 현존하는 권력구조를 기반으로 현실적이지만 현실을 넘어설 수 있는 해석의 가능성이 농후한 변이적 공간 시나리오들을 제안하는 데에 있다.

한국의 국경유형과 언어의 열린 구조
(open texture of language)[15]

1953년 7월 27일의 정전협정에 따라 지난 60년간 세 가지 유형의 경계가 남북한 사이에 존재해 왔다. 하지만 정전협정 때문에 규정된 경계와 실제 현실상의 경계 사이에는 매우 큰 오차가 존재해왔다. 협정 언어 상의 경계는 사실상 각 지역의 지형적, 자연적, 생태적 환경으로 인하여 끊임없이 조정됐으며, 이로인해 언어와 현실의 불일치로 인한 사이 공간들이 존재한다.

영토의 경계를 규정하려는 토지소유법과 고정될 수 없는 생태 시스템 사이의 딜레마를 법적 맥락에서는 '언어의 열린 구조'라 일컫는다. "행동기준을 설명하기 위해 선택된 기구, 사례, 혹은 정책이 대부분의 일반적 상황들에 적용될 수는 있겠지만 어느 순간 그 행동기준의 적용이 불분명하고 그 적용이 문제가 되는 경우를 우리는 열린 구조(open texture)라 정의할 수 있다."[16] 언어와 지도의 표기법을 사용하여 정의될 밖에 없는 국경의 경우, 언어의 열린 구조로 인하여 생성되는 모호한 공백이 존재한다. 끊임없이 변화하는 강의 소유권과 그 경계를 규정하고자 하는 법률언어의 한계에서 드러나듯이,[17] 자연현상으로 인해 변화하는 지형의 공간적, 시간적 유동적 상태는 탄력적 공간 시나리오의 가능성을 소유한다. 본 연구는 바로 이러한 사이 공간의 가능성을 이용한 탄력적 공간 시나리오들을 타진해 보고자 한다. 〈그림 1, 2, 3〉

다음 공간 시나리오들은 지도상의 "선"과 땅 위의 현실 사이를 항해하기 위해 공간을 활용하는 추측적 공간 프로포절들이다. 정치환경의 다양한 수위에 탄력적이고 지속가능할 수 있는 공간 가능성들을 제안하기 위해 정치적, 경제적, 지역적, 환경적 생태시스템의 인간, 그리고 비인간 행위자들을 사용한다. 이는 2011년 가을 코넬대학교 건축학과 학생들과 진행한 내용이다.

공간 시나리오 1: DMZ의 기정동과 대성동, 농경-관광지구 / Agro-Logical Landscape

Agro-Logical Landscape 프로젝트는 지역의 농경업에 기반을 둔 통합적 생산, 교육 개발사업을 통해 현재 침체, 석화되어 있는 중립 경계지역의 활성화를 구상한다. 국제, 혹은 지역 농경업 NGO의 관리하에 국제 기구의 재정적 지원을 받음으로써, 두 마을을 농경 관광지역으로 개발하여 남북 농경업 교육과 교류, 그리고 관광객 유치를 목적으로 한다. 공간 시나리오의 전략은 다음과 같다.

첫째, 기존의 수자원과 생태환경을 보완하는 농경 사업을 통해 지역의 생물 다양성을 확립할 수 있는 지속 가능한 농경업을 지원한다. 논두렁과 이를 연결하는 수로의 지형적 조건을 활용하여 홍수와 같은 자연재해에 대응할 수 있는 지속 가능한 배수 시스템을 도입하고, 다양한 수확 사이클을 도모함으로써 다양한 재배작물을 적용하고 환경적 재해에 대응할 수 있는 농업 사이클을 제안한다.

둘째, 양측간의 농경 지식과 기술 교류를 도모한다. 교류가 원활한 경우 양측 농민들은 군의 감시하에 공동 관리 구역 내에서 직접적인 협력작업을 진행할 수 있다. 농지의 지형이 단면적으로 분리되어 있지만 시각적으로 연결되어 있기 때문에, 정치적 갈등이 고조된 상황에서는 협력, 교류가 시범적 차원에서 이루어질 수 있다. 실질적인 만남이 없더라도 양측 농지에서의 작업이 시각적 시범장으로 이용될 수 있다.

셋째, 군 초소가 농지 전체에 일정 간격을 두고 설치되어 양측 군의 감시가 원활하게 이루어질 수 있도록 한다. 주민과 관광객들은 시각적으로 연결되어 있지만, 지형적 분리와 고도의 차이로 인해 실제 움직임이 통제될 수 있다.

넷째, 두 마을은 상대편을 향한 정치적 선전도구로 정부의 특별 지원을 받으며, 이는 두 마을의 상호교류를 위한 기반시설 확충의 계기로 활용될 수 있다. 두 마을 사이에 존재하는 정치적 경쟁 심리는 양측 논밭의 생산력을 높이기 위한 지역개발 메커니즘으로 작용할 수 있다. 생산력을 높이기 위해 농경업 기술 도입과 시설물 확충을 위한 정부의 지원을 높일 수 있고, 국제 관광객 유치를 위해 양측 주민들의 시범 교류장으로 활용될 수 있다.

다섯째, 정치적 갈등이 고조된 상황에서 관광 프로그램과 농경업 교류사업이 중단될 수 있으며, 농지 출입 또한 제한될 수 있다. 현재로서는 쌀 재배만이 이루어지고 있지만 가능할 수 없는 정치적 상황과 이에 따른 농경지 관리의 제한을 대비하여 다양한 농작물 재배를 계획한다.

본 프로젝트는 한편으로 상호협력적 생산에 기반을 둔 농작물 생산과 농업기술 관련 교류를 장려하면서도 다른 한편으로는 이를 관광 프로그램과 연관할 수 있는 상호협력적 외부 자본 유치를 목적으로 한다. 농작물 재배, 관리, 수확 과정을 기존 수로 시스템의 생태적 특성과 연관시키면서도 이를 관광 용도로 개발할 가능성을 함께 고려하는 프로젝트이다. 기정동과 대성동은 남북한의 정치 선전 도구로 지금까지 존재해 왔지만, 본 프로젝트는 정치적 선전도구라는 명목하에 환경친화적 농작물 재배와 실험적 농업 기술의 교류가 가능한 공간의 가능성을 제안한다. 지형적 배치를 통해 지역 농민들의 협력적 교류의 기회를 확장하면서도 관광자원으로서의 가능성, 그리고 총체적인 군사적 감시 시스템 유지가 가능할 수 있는 시나리오이다. 농작물의 생태 사이클을 정치 사이클과 연관시킴으로써 정치 선전도구로서만 존재하기보다는 생산적 기초시설 확립과 지속적인 농경 관련 교류가 가능할 수 있는 지형을 제안한다. 〈그림 4, 5, 6〉

공간 시나리오 2: 한강하류, 농경-과학 지구 / Residual Fields

두 번째 시나리오는 한강 하류의 경계 유형 가능성을 탐색한다. 한강 하구는 세계에서 가장 높은 수위 차를 가진 강 중 하나로, 한강 하구 전반의 수심이 얕으며, 밀물 썰물로 인하여 드러나는 광대한 갯벌이 특징적이다. 정전협정에 따르자면 한강 하구지역은 남북공유지역이 된다. 하지만 현재 한강 강변은 세 겹의 철조망이 양강변에 설치되어있는 출입금지지역이다. 하지만 이 지역은 썰물 때 하루 두 번 약 30㎢ 규모의 갯벌이 드러나며, 조수 차로 인하여 일시적으로 존재하는 이 땅은 협정 문서에 의하면 남북한의 공유 영토가 된다.[18] 따라서 본 프로젝트는 일시적인 갯벌 지역과 그 인근 지역의 조개 밭과 농경지를 활용한 수질, 공기오염 감시 시스템을 구상하며, 이를 위해 국제 NGO 환경, 농업 진흥단체 관할 하에 지역의 환경오염 수준을 감시하는 과학 기구를 통한 거버넌스 구조를 제안한다. 공간 시나리오 전략은 다음과 같다.

첫째, 남북 경제협력지구로 지정된 갯벌에는 조개 양식장이 설치된다. 갯벌은 하루 두 번 썰물 시간대에만 출입이 가능한 지역으로, 평화 시기에는 남북주민 모두 조개 양식장의 공동 출입이 가능하지만, 갈등이 고조된 상황에서는 썰물 스케줄에 따라 양측이 번갈아 가며 관리할 수 있게 된다. 한강 양변을 따라 위치한 농경지는 특수 실험지구로 유기농법과 기술이 시범적으로 사용된다. 이 특수 지역에서 협력적 생산을 통해 수확된 쌀은 "평화의 쌀"로 브랜딩되어 시장에 판매된다. 남한 민통선 인접지역에 특수시장이 설립되어 지역에서 생산된 조개와 쌀을 판매할 수 있는 관광지역이 형성된다.

둘째, 본 프로젝트는 환경오염 감리를 수행한다. 갯벌 내 조개 양식장에는 수면에 부유하며 수질을 감시할 수 있는 관측기구들이 설치되어 양측 과학자들에 의해 관리된다. 인근 농경지에서 배출되는 농약, 살충제, 임진강을 통해 유입되는 개성공업단지의 유축물 그리고 한강을 통해 하구로 배출되는 도시오염 물질들을 감시하는 기구로 작용한다. 강변 인근 지역의 농경지에는 풍선에 부착된 공기 오염 감시기구들이 일정 간격으로 설치된다. 이는 국제 농경업 진흥단체를 통해 주도되는 실험적인 경제, 생산, 환경 통치구조의 설정을 전제로 하고 있으며, 농작지와 환경오염 관측시설들은 UNESCO와 같은 중립적 환경단체 연구원들의 주관 아래 남북 지역주민 대표들과 함께 설치, 관리되는 시나리오이다. 농업 생산력과 이의 경제성을 위한 환경오염 감시는 대도시에 인접한 지역의 큰 관건으로 남북한 양측의 자원관리 문제이기도 하다. 이는 또한 정치적 환경을 불문하고 최소의 관리를 통해 출입 통제 지역의 생태환경을 관리할 수 있는 시스템이기도 하다.

셋째, 과학연구를 위한 지속 가능한 거버넌스의 시범 사례가 된다. 양측 주민들과 환경연구자, 과학자들을 연계시킬 수 있는 지역의 관리체제를 형성한다. 특수경제 지역의 성격을 지니고는 있지만 과학연구를 명목으로 환경친화적인 지역 경제개발을 도모할 수 있다.

넷째, 조수간만의 차로 인해 자연적으로 제한된 갯벌 출입은 군사적 감시 필요를 극소화한다. 강의 출입은 극도로 제한되면서도 조개 밭의 경제성, 생산적 가능성을 극대화할 수 있다. 정치적 갈등이 고조되었을 때 한강 출입이 중단될 수도 있지만, 환경오염 관측기구들은 여전히 작동할 것이다.

다섯, 조개양식장과 논경지에 설치된 오염관측기구들에 부착된 LED 조명은 한강 하구를 뒤덮는 대형 조명설치예술로 작용할 것이며, 따라서 인근 접근 가능지역의 관광객 증가 요인이 될 수 있을 것이다.

이 프로젝트는 조수의 주기와 연관되어있는 생태시스템의 연계를 통해 지역 특수성에 기반을 둔 공간개발을 목적으로 한다. 이는 해당 지역의 정치적, 사회적, 경제적 교류의 장을 마련함으로써, 환경오염관리를 통한 경제력 향상에 대한 관심이 지역 생태보전을 주도하는 시나리오를 제시한다. 〈그림 7, 8〉

공간 시나리오 3: 서해5도, 대연평도 지역, 해양양식-관광 지구 / Adaptive Territory

세 번째 경계 유형은 서해 5도를 둘러싼 서해연안 접경지역으로, 최근 남북의 주장에 따른 해양경계선을 비교했을 때, 남북한 양측의 경계선을 비껴간 약 24 km²의 중립지역이 대연평도 북쪽으로 존재한다.[19] 2005년 남한은 이를 해양평화공원으로 제안했으며, 2007년 남북정상회담을 통해 양측은 '서해평화협력지대'를 설정하기로 협약했다. 하지만 현재 이의 구체적 내용은 남북군사회담에서 지체된 상태이다.

Adaptive Territory 프로젝트는 이 중립지역을 기반으로 이동 가능한 인공섬의 도입을 통해 특수 해양양식업 평화관광지구 설립을 제안한다. 본 시나리오는 비영리조직의 관할하에 인터넷을 통해 세계적으로 분포되어 있는 '가상시민(Virtual Citizen)'[20]들의 재정적 지원을 기반으로 설립된 "코리아(Korea)"라 불리는 중립적 주권국을 제안한다.[21] 공간 시나리오의 전략은 다음과 같다.

첫째, 인공 섬들은 국제 비영리조직에 의해 운영되며, "통합한국"의 가상 시민들의 재정지원으로 운영된다. 섬들은 환경친화적인 해양양식업과 관광업을 위한 기반시설로 작동하면서, 평화시기에는 남북한 인근 어민들이 협력하여 환경친화적 양식업을 진행한다. 필요에 따라 중립지역을 중심으로 남북 관할 영해 내에 양식장이 따로 설치, 운영될 수 있다. 분쟁시 양식장들은 중립지역 내로 철수되어 최소 규모로 운영된다. 평화 시기 양측의 관광객은 중립 지역 안에 배정된 구역들을 방문할 수 있으며, 외국 관광객은 인천국제공항을 통해 비자 없이도 방문이 가능하다. 정치적 갈등이 고조된 시기에는 남북 관광객의 출입은 통제되지만, 외국인 관광객에게는 출입이 허용된다.

둘째, 인공섬들은 군사적 갈등을 최소화시키기 위해 국제해양법에 근거한 주권국의 영해권리를 사용하며 서해연안 접경지역을 감시한다.[22] 평화시기에는 불법 중국 어선들을 감시하고 남북한 군의 충돌을 방지한다.[23] 분쟁 시에는 인공 섬들이 서해연안 접경지역에 일정 간격으로 분포되어 12 해상 마일 영해를 선포함으로써 양측을 분리하는 비무장지대를 형성한다.

셋째, 서해연안 접경지역은 고수입 수산물인 꽃게의 주 서식지이다. 하지만 중국과 남북 어선들의 남획으로 인하여 해양서식지 보전정책이 시급한 상황이다. 환경친화적인 해양양식업을 통해 지역 어민의 수산업을 지원하고 생태서식지 파괴를 방지한다.

넷째, 인공섬들과 양식시설의 유동성은 군사적, 정치적 환경에 탄력적일 수 있는 유연성을 제공한다. 인공섬의 기반시설들은 중립지역을 중심으로 활동할 것이지만, 분쟁방지를 위해 서해 5도 지역을 시찰할 수 있는 유동성을 지닌다. 양식장 시설 또한 분쟁 시 중립지역으로 회수될 것이며, 평화적 시기에는 생산성 확대를 위해 인근 영해로 확장될 것이다. 확장된 양식장은 불법 어선의 영해 침범 방지장치로도 작용할 것이며, 연계 시스템을 통해 중국 어선들의 출입을 제한하는 한편 남북 어선의 출입 구역을 관리할 수 있다.

서해연안 접경지역은 정치적 상황과 자연 생태계의 주기에 따라 극도로 확장, 혹은 감축되는 공간이다. 이렇듯 지속해서 모호한 공간 속에 존재하는 인공섬들은 이 지역의 평화적 공존을 위해 정치적, 군사적, 그리고 환경적 감시기구의 임무를 수행한다. 꽃게 계절 동안은 문제 지역을 시간제로 나누어 남북 어선들이 동일하게 어업을 진행할 수 있도록 하며, 불법 중국어선들을 제어하는 동시에 어류남획을 관리함으로써 환경친화적 어업을 관리하는 기능 또한 수행한다. 군사 분쟁 시 중립국의 권한으로 남북 양측 사이에 완충 지역을 확립하여 군사적 긴장을 완화하고 더 큰 돌발사태를 방지하는 기능을 수행한다. 〈그림 9, 10, 11〉

탄력적 미래를 위하여

공간은 접경지역의 중요한 매개체로 작용한다. 공간을 다루는 환경디자인은 영토적, 지형학적, 생태적으로 복잡다단한 상황들을 분석하는데 매우 활용적인 도구로써, 지속 가능하면서도 친환경적인 생산적 개입 가능성을 타진할 수 있는 중요한 행위 능력을 지닌다. 지금까지 한국에서는 생태보전 문제와 지역개발을 통한 경제적 이윤창출이 대화와 협력의 주 메커니즘으로 작용하였으나, 탄력성이 부족하다는 취약점이 있다. 따라서 기존 공간제품 유형들을 비판적으로 분석하고 이를 기반으로 정치적 상황에 탄력적일 수 있는 공간 시나리오 전략들을 구상해야 할 것이다. 이를 위해 NGO, 정부, 환경정책, 생태학, 환경보전단체 관련자들뿐만 아니라, 건축가, 조경가, 도시계획가들 또한 활발한 행위능력의 주체가 되어야 한다. 국경을 단지 군사분쟁지역, 생태보전지역, 아니면 경제, 관광개발 가능지역만으로 생각하기보다는, 물질적 경계를 뛰어넘어 사회적, 문화적, 그리고 정치적 사고의 경계를 바꿀 수 있는 실험적 공간으로 생각하기 위해서는 공간을 다루는 환경디자이너들의 상상력과 이들의 관여가 필요하다. 본 글에 포함된 공간 시나리오들은 공간의 사회적, 정치적 역할과 이의 가능성을 탐색하고자 하였으며, 공간의 탄력성을 활용함으로써 경계선이 영토의 분리를 위한 도구가 아닌 생산적 통합과 협동의 공간으로 생각해야 할 것이다.

References

Alam, Undala Z., "Questioning the Water Wars Rationale: A Case Study of the Indus Waters Treaty," The Geographical Journal, Vol. 168, No. 4, Dec. 2002.

Ali, Saleem H., ed., Peace Parks: Conservation and Conflict Resolution, Cambridge: MIT Press, 2007.

Anderied, John M., Janssen, Marco A., and Ostrom, Elinor, "A Framework to Analyze the Robustness of Social-ecological Systems from an Institutional Perspective, Ecology and Society, Volume 8, Issue 1: 18, 2004

Beck, Ulrich, Risk Society: Towards a New Modernity, trans. Ritter, Mark, London: Sage Publications, 1992.

Barquet, Karina, Lujala, Päivi and Rød, Jan Ketil, "Transboundary Conservation and Militarized Interstate Disputes," paper presented at the Climate Change and Security Conference, Trondheim, Norway, June 21-24, 2010.

Bridger, Jessica, "Kijong-dong – Potemkin Landscape," Topos, December 20, 2011. Available at ⟨http://www.toposmagazine.com/blog/kijong-dong-potemkin-landscape.html⟩

Carlson, J.M. and Doyle, John, "Complexity and Robustness," PNAS (Procceedings of the National Academy of Sciences), Vol. 99, Suppl. 1, Feb 19, 2002.

Donaldson, John W., "Paradox of the Moving Boundary: Legal Heredity of River Accretion and Avulsion," Water Alternatives, Volume 4, Issue 2.

Duffy, Rosaleen, "Peace Parks and Global Politics: The Paradoxes and Challenges of Global Governance," ed. Saleem H. Ali, Peace Parks: Conservation and Conflict Resolution, Cambridge: MIT Press, 2007.

Easterling, Keller, "Zone: The Spatial Softwares of Extrastatecraft," Places, June 11, 2012. Available at ⟨http://places.designobserver.com/feature/zone-the-spatial-softwares-of-extrastatecraft/34528/⟩

Haas, Peter, Saving the Mediterranean: The Politics of International Environmental Cooperation, New York: Columbia University Press, 1990.

Haas, Peter M., "Epistemic Communities and International Policy Coordination," International Organization, Vol. 46, No. 1, Winter, published by MIT Press, 1992.

Hart, H.L.A., The Concept of Law, New York: Oxford University Press, 1961.

Holling, C.S., "Resilience and Stability of Ecological Systems," Annual Review of Ecology and Systematics, Volume 4, 1973.

"Land Use Terminology Dictionary," published by the Republic of Korea Ministry of Land, Transport and Maritime Affairs, January 2011. Available at ⟨http://luris.mltm.go.kr/web/luris.pdf⟩

Laux, Maria Fariello, "The Potential for Environmental Contributions to Peace," Transboundary Environmental Negotiation: New Approaches to Global Cooperation, eds. Lawrence Susskind, William Moomaw, and Kevin Gallagher, New York: John Wiley & Sons, 2002.

Mackelworth, Peter, "Peace Parks and Transboundary Initiatives: Implications for Marine Conservation and Spatial Planning," Conservation Letters, Volume 5, Issue 2, April 2012.

Querol, Maria, "Rethinking International Rivers and Lakes as Boundaries," Water Resources and International Law, eds. Salman, Salman M.A. and Boisson de Chazournes, Laurence, publication by Hague Academy of International Law, Leiden/Boston: Martinus Nijhoff Publishers, 2005.

Rayfuse, Rosemary and Crawford, Emily, "Climate Change, Sovereignty and Statehood," Legal Studies Research, No. 11/59, University of Sydney Law School, Sept. 2011. Available at ⟨http://www.ilsa.org/jessup/jessup13/Climate%20Change,%20Sovereignty%20and%20Statehood.pdf⟩

Salman, Salman M.A. and Boisson de Chazournes, Laurence, eds., International Watercourses: Enhancing Cooperation and Managing Conflict, World Bank Technical Paper No. 414, The World Bank, Washington D.C., 1998.

Steinberg, Theodore, Slide Mountain: Or, The Folly of Owning Nature, Berkeley: Univ. of California Press, 1995.

Susskind, Lawrence and Islam, Shafiqul, "Water Diplomacy: Creating Value and Building Trust in Transboundary Water Negotiations," Science & Diplomacy, August 22, 2012.

Tartir, Alaa, "Jericho Agro-Industrial Park: A Corridor of Peace or Perpetuation of Occupation?" Position Paper published by Bisan Center for Research and Development, December 2012. Available at ⟨http://en.bisan.org/content/jericho-agro-industrial-park-corridor-peace-or-perpetuation-occupation⟩

Watkins, Kevin, et. al., "Beyond Scarcity: Power, Poverty and the Global Water Crisis, Human Development" report published by the UNDP, 2006. Available at ⟨http://hdr.undp.org/en/media/HDR06-complete.pdf⟩

Weale, Albert, The New Politics of Pollution, Manchester: Manchester University Press, 1991.

"United Nations Convention on the Law of the Non-navigational Uses of International Watercourses," adopted by the General Assembly of the United Nations, May 21, 1997. Available at ⟨http://untreaty.un.org/ilc/texts/instruments/english/conventions/8_3_1997.pdf⟩

"United Nations Convention on the Law of the Sea," December 10, 1982. Available at ⟨http://www.un.org/Depts/los/convention_agreements/texts/unclos/unclos_e.pdf⟩

남정호, 육근형, 이구성, 김종덕, "서해연안 해양평화공원 지정 및 관리 방안 연구(III)," 한국해양수산개발원 보고서, 2007.

박삼옥, 허우긍, 박기호, 박수진, 북한 산업개발 및 남북협력방안: 지리적 접근, 서울대학교 출판부, 2006.

전재경, "DMZ 보전을 위한 법/제도적 방안," DMZ 생물권보전지역 추진 원칙과 과제, 유네스코 한국위원회 주최 토론회 발표, 2009년 10월 17일.

정전협정, Korean Armistice Agreement, July 27, 1953; Treaties and Other International Agreements Series #2782; General Records of the United States

Government; Record Group 11; National Archives.

최희정, "서해연안 접경지역의 이용 현황 및 남북 협력관리 방향," 월간해양수산, 통권 252호, 2005년 9월..

DMZ 생물권보전지역 신청서, 환경부, 문화재청, 산림청, 경기도, 강원도 공동 제작, 2011년 9월.

1 'Agency' is used relative to Bruno Latour's Actor Network Theory.

2 Ali, S.H., ed., 2007. Peace Parks: Conservation and Conflict Resolution. Cambridge: MIT Press.

3 Easterling, K., "Zone: The Spatial Softwares of Extrastatecraft," Places, June 11, 2012. Available at ⟨http://places.designobserver.com/feature/zone-the-spatial-softwares-of-extrastatecraft/34528/⟩

4 Jordan River Peace Park is a successful precedent of collaboration between regional NGOs, scientists and engineers that created a Peace Park that integrates ideas of ecological conservation for the Jordan River. The Friends of the Earth Middle East, the central NGO represented by Israeli, Jordanian and Syrian environemntalists, created a foundation of collaboration, which involved faculty and students from Yale University Architecture Department in New Haven, U.S.A. and the Bezalel Academy of Arts and Design, Jerusalem, together with Jordanian, Palestinian and Israeli architects for design workshops for the design of the Peace Park. "The goal of the event is to develop ideas on how to recreate a wetland from the dry lake bed into a bird sanctuary, convert the old power station into a visitors center, the old workers' homes into eco-lodges and renovate the bridges so they can be used again." Jordan River Peace Park is not included as a precedent in this paper due to it being a post conflict initiative; Ashkenazi, E., "Israeli, Jordanian architects plan peace park in Naharayim ," Haaretz, May 14, 2008. Available at ⟨http://www.haaretz.com/news/israeli-jordanian-architects-plan-peace-park-in-naharayim-1.245799⟩

5 Cunningham, H., 2012. "Permeabilities, Ecology and Geopolitical Boundaries," A Companion to Border Studies, eds. T. M. Wilson and H. Donnan, Chichester, UK: John Wiley & Sons, Ltd., 371–386.

6 Kim, J., "Seoul to seek UNESCO Biosphere Reserve status for DMZ," The Hankyoreh, July 4, 2012. Available at ⟨http://www.hani.co.kr/arti/english_edition/e_international/540913.html⟩

7 The current UN Command (United Nations Command Security Battalion – Joint Security Area, UNCSB-JSA) is a U.S. Army lead joint entity with ROK soldiers. It is no longer under the United Nations's supervision.

8 Mok, J., "UNESCO denies designation of DMZ as Biosphere Reserve," The Kyunghyang Shinmun, July 13, 2012. Available at ⟨http://english.khan.co.kr/khan_art_view.html?artid=201207131046497&code=710100⟩

9 ROK Ministry of Environment, Natural Environment Protection Law, 1997 revisions, Rule No. 2–13.

10 Jaekyong, J., 2009. "The Legal, Policy Procedures for the Conservation of the DMZ," Objectives and Priorities for the Ecological Conservation Zone at the DMZ, UNESCO Korean Committee organized Conference, October 17th.

11 Holling, C.S., 1973. "Resilience and Stability of Ecological Systems," Annual Review of Ecology and Systematics, Volume 4, 17.

12 In the engineering and computation field, Holling's Ecological Resilience is defined as "management of systematic characteristics despite partial or environmental changes"; Carlson, J.M. and Doyle, J., 2002. "Complexity and Robustness," PNAS (Procceedings of the National Academy of Sciences), Vol. 99, Suppl. 1, Feb 19, 2539.

13 Anderied, J.M., Janssen, M.A., and Ostrom, E., 2004. "A Framework to Analyze the Robustness of Social-ecological Systems from an Institutional Perspective," Ecology and Society, 9(1): 18. Available at ⟨http://www.ecologyandsociety.org/vol9/iss1/art18/⟩

14 Beck, U., 1992. Risk Society: Towards a New Modernity, London: Sage Publications, 21.

15 Hart, H.L.A., 1961. The Concept of Law, New York: Oxford University Press, 127–128.

16 Hart, The Concept of Law, 127–128.

17 Steinberg, T., 1995. Slide Mountain: Or, The Folly of Owning Nature, Berkeley: Univ. of California Press.

18 In 2008 past president Lee Myung-bak proposed the Nadeul Island Project as part of his presidential campaign initiative.; Choi, K., "North and South work together to establish North East Asia's commerce center," Monthly Chosun, July, 2008, in Korean. ⟨http://monthly.chosun.com/client/news/viw.asp?nNewsNumb=200807100021&ctcd=&cpage=1⟩

19 Nam, J., Yook, K., Lee, G., and Kim, J., 2007. "Toward Establishing the Marine Peace Park: In the Western Transboundary Coastal Area of the Korean Peninsula," Korean Maritime Insititute Summary Report, Korean version, Appendix 23, 297.

20 The concept of 'Virtual Citizenship' is most prominently exercised by the organization Virtual Citizen of Israel (http://israelforever.org/vci/) which promotes support for the cause of Israel by signing up as an unofficial citizen.

21 The Maritime Peace Park(MPP) Report issued by the Korean Maritime Institute between 2005-2007 had already organized and facilitated an international advisory group composed of multiple institutions and initiatives, including UNESCO, IUCN, the GEF Yellow Sea Large Marine Ecosystem Project, and the UNEP Northwest Pacific Action Plan.; Nam, J., et. al., 2007. "Toward Establishing the Marine Peace Park: In the Western Transboundary Coastal Area of the Korean Peninsula," English version, 45.

22 Sydell, L., 2012. "Don't Like The Government? Make Your Own, On International Waters," NPR, Dec. 17, 2012. Available at ⟨http://www.npr.org/blogs/alltechconsidered/2012/12/17/166887292/dont-like-the-government-make-your-own-on-international-waters⟩

23 Hancocks, P., 2011. "South Korea: Chinese fisherman kill coast guard member," CNN, Dec. 12, 2011. Available at ⟨http://www.cnn.com/2011/12/12/world/asia/south-korea-china-stabbing⟩

1 행위능력(agency)는 브루노 라투어(Bruno Latour)의 행위자-연결망 이론(actor network theory)적 측면에서 사용되며, 이는 인간과 비인간 , 자연과 사회 행위자의 동등한 행위 역량을 의미한다.

2 Ali, S.H., ed., 2007. Peace Parks: Conservation and Conflict Resolution, Cambridge: MIT Press.

3 Easterling, K., 2012. "Zone: The Spatial Softwares of Extrastatecraft," Places, June 11. 〈http://places.designobserver.com/feature/zone-the-spatial-softwares-of-extrastatecraft/34528/〉

4 조르단 강 평화공원(Jordan River Peace Park)는 지역 NGO들과 과학자, 엔지니어들의 협력을 통해 조르단 강의 환경보전을 위해 현실화된 성공적 평화공원의 사례이다. 이스라엘, 조르단, 그리고 시리아의 환경인들을 통해 형성된 Friends of the Earth Middle East은 미국 예일대학교 건축과, 예루살렘의 베자렐 예술 디자인 아카데미(Bezalel Academy of Arts and Design)의 학생들과 교수진, 그리고 이스라엘, 조르단, 시리아의 건축가들의 협력을 통해 평화공원 디자인을 위한 워샵을 진행하였다. "본 이벤트의 목적은 마른 강바닥을 습지로 전환시킬 수 있는 조류 서식지 형성, 노화된 발전소를 방문객 센터로, 오래된 노동자 주택을 생태거처로 바꾸고, 낡은 다리를 재활용하는 공간적 아이디어 창출에 있다." 본 사례는 군사 갈등 완화 이후 이루어진 프로젝트이기에 본 글에 포함되지 않았다;
Ashkenazi, E., "Israeli, Jordanian architects plan peace park in Naharayim ," Haaretz, May 14, 2008. 〈http://www.haaretz.com/news/israeli-jordanian-architects-plan-peace-park-in-naharayim-1.245799〉

5 Cunningham, H., 2012. "Permeabilities, Ecology and Geopolitical Boundaries," A Companion to Border Studies, eds. T. M. Wilson and H. Donnan, Chichester, UK: John Wiley & Sons, Ltd., 371-386.

6 Kim, J., "Seoul to seek UNESCO Biosphere Reserve status for DMZ," The Hankyoreh, July 4, 2012. Available at 〈http://www.hani.co.kr/arti/english_edition/e_international/540913.html〉

7 현 유엔사령부(UN Command: United Nations Command Security Battalion - Joint Security Area, UNCSB-JSA)는 미군 주도로 대한민국 군인을 포함한 부대이다. 한국전쟁 중 UN 협력국들을 대표하여 정전협상을 돕기위해 1952년 5월 5일 힝ㅁㅍㅣ이 푠루ㅁ에 배치된 부내이나. 유엔사냥부는 현새 미국방부 관할 하에 있다. 〈http://8tharmy.korea.army.mil/jsa/〉

8 Mok, J., "UNESCO denies designation of DMZ as Biosphere Reserve," The Kyunghyang Shinmun, July 13, 2012. 〈http://english.khan.co.kr/khan_art_view.html?artid=201207131046497&code=710100〉

9 자연환경보전법, 제2조 제13호

10 전재경, 2009. "DMZ 보전을 위한 법/제도적 방안," DMZ 생물권보전지역 추진 원칙과 과제, 유네스코 한국위원회 주최 토론회 발표, 10월 17일.

11 Holling, C.S., 1973. "Resilience and Stability of Ecological Systems," Annual Review of Ecology and Systematics, Volume 4, 17.

12 홀링의 생태론적 탄력성을 엔지니어링과 컴퓨데이션 분야에서는 "부분, 혹은 환경적 변동에도 불구하고 원하는 시스템적 특성의 관리"로 규정한다; Carlson, J.M. and Doyle, J., 2002. "Complexity and Robustness," PNAS (Procceedings of the National Academy of Sciences), Vol. 99, Suppl. 1, Feb 19, 2539.

13 Anderied, J.M., Janssen, M.A., and Ostrom, E., 2004. "A Framework to Analyze the Robustness of Social-ecological Systems from an Institutional Perspective," Ecology and Society, 9(1): 18. 〈http://www.ecologyandsociety.org/vol9/iss1/art18/〉

14 Beck, U., 1992. Risk Society: Towards a New Modernity, London: Sage Publications, 21.

15 Hart, H.L.A., 1961. The Concept of Law, New York: Oxford University Press, 127-128.

16 Hart, The Concept of Law, 127-128.

17 Steinberg, T., 1995. Slide Mountain: Or, The Folly of Owning Nature, Berkeley: Univ. of California Press

18 이명박이 대선 공략사업으로 2008년 발표한 나들섬 프로젝트는 한강하구의 저수심 지역의 청추초로 불리는 곳에 2020년까지 13년간 2조 6000억원을 투입하여 총면적 30km2를 복토, 인구 20만명 규모의 남북한 협동 국제 비즈니스 신도시를 건설한다는 프로젝트이다. 이 프로젝트는 환경 그룹들의 극한 반대로 대선정책에서 사라지게 되었다. 월간조선, 2008년 7월;
〈http://monthly.chosun.com/client/news/viw.asp?nNewsNumb=200807100021&ctcd=&cpage=1〉

19 남정호, 육근형, 이구성, 김종덕, 2007. "서해연안 해양평화공원 지정 및 관리 방안 연구(III)," 한국해양수산개발원 보고서, 부록 23, 297.

20 '가상시민(virtual citizenship)'의 개념은 이스라엘을 지원하는 국제 비영리 단체 Israel Forever의 사례를 참고한다. 〈http://israelforever.org/vci〉

21 한국해양수산개발원에 의해 2005-2007년 준비된 서해연안 해양평화공원을 위한 보고서는 국제적, 지역적 제3조직의 관여를 추천한다. 이를 위해 UNESCO, IUCN, 그리고 GEF Yellow Sea Large Marine Ecosystem Project, 그리고 UNEP Northwest Pacific Action Plan 등의 기구들의 자문단을 구상, 제시하고 있다; Nam, J., et. al., 2007. "Toward Establishing the Marine Peace Park: In the Western Transboundary Coastal Area of the Korean Peninsula," English version, 45.

22 Sydell, L., 2012. "Don't Like The Government? Make Your Own, On International Waters," NPR, Dec. 17, 2012. 〈http://www.npr.org/blogs/alltechconsidered/2012/12/17/166887292/dont-like-the-government-make-your-own-on-international-waters〉

23 Hancocks, P., 2011. "South Korea: Chinese fisherman kill coast guard member," CNN, Dec. 12, 2011. 〈http://www.cnn.com/2011/12/12/world/asia/south-korea-china-stabbing〉

A CONSTRUCT THE KOREAS (NEVER) MADE TOGETHER: DECONSTRUCTING THE DMZ FOR THE IMAGINARY

Dongsei Kim

—

Dongsei Kim is a registered architect and urbanist. He is an adjunct assistant professor at Columbia University, GSAPP and principal of axu studio. He received his MDesS with distinction from Harvard University, MsAUD from Columbia University, and a B.Arch (Hons) from Victoria University of Wellington. Dongsei's research focuses on how extreme border conditions and their territories can inform fundamental spatial negotiation processes such as "inclusion and exclusion," and how "us and them" are defined in urbanism. He has practiced in New York, Wellington, and Seoul. He has also extensively taught architecture and urbanism with leading universities in Australia, Canada, New Zealand, US, and Korea.

"… Since the world of nations is made by men, it is inside their minds that its principles should be sought. - Giambattista Vico, Principles of a New Science, 1759" (qtd. Koolhaas 1994, 9)

Like the obscure North Korea behind the veil, the infamous Korean Demilitarized Zone (DMZ) is frequently misunderstood. Equally, the DMZ is a dynamic entity that mutates over time, contradictory to its common perception of being a fixed fortified border. By consciously deconstructing the DMZ, it might be emancipated from dominating hegemonic perceptions that reveal its alternative futures.

One of the most ironic aspects of this terrifying military infrastructure is that since the Armistice Agreement was signed in 1953 — despite the DMZ being a stereotypical symbol of extreme conflicts — both Koreas consciously, subconsciously, and collaboratively constructed the DMZ together into their national identity and territory. Here, by construct I am referring not only to both the physical and symbolic constructs, but also the processes of constructing one's identities through such. These processes successfully enabled and contributed to the current identity of both Koreas to be constructed over time. In that respect, the physical and symbolic construction of the DMZ through the processes of including 'us,' and excluding 'them,' was an inevitable imperative for both Koreas in building their respective national identities, particularly in their post-colonial modernization efforts.

It must be recognized that the DMZ was constructed over the last sixty years with North and South Korea playing a role as the protagonist and the antagonist at the same time in their own tragedy. During the sixty years of its construction and operation, scores of spatial negotiations have occurred, some more visible than others. In order to further understand the DMZ's full potentials, we need to excavate some of these spatial negotiations through mapping, thus visualizing them, rendering new interpretations of these perpetuating conditions. These new interpretations then become essential knowledge, instrument, and medium to transcend the persisting sixty-year-old dichotomy and schism; thus allowing one to imagine a renewed productive future for the DMZ.

This deconstructed mapping of the DMZ renders new forward-looking descriptions of the DMZ at the start of the twenty-first century, acknowledging its nineteenth and twentieth century past. First, the 38th parallel north line inscribed on the drawing, reveals the traces of the region's expanding imperial forces in the late nineteenth century. Here the conventional cartographic projection is literally rotated 180 degrees, flipped upside-down. This destabilization of the conventional relationship of the North and South establishes a new foundation for a new perspective to emerge that initiate a deconstruction process, while maintaining the binary confrontation of the two Koreas.

This process then uncovers the realities of the DMZ, how it is used, transgressed, mutated, thickened, expanded, contingent on the lenses they are perceived over time. For example, the DMZ is marked as a thicker zone on both sides, depicting the degree of military controls over these territories dictated by its propinquity to the DMZ and their security measures. Others include multiple lines that visualize the mutating DMZ instigated by economic, ecological, and political processes that seamlessly flow through it, despite the man-made DMZ acting as a barrier. They vividly remind us of how the fences are futile in fending these processes and the absurdity of such installations.

"There are three basic levels of comprehending physical phenomena: first, the exploration of pure physical facts; second, the psychological impact on our inner-self; and third, the imaginative discovery and reconstruction of phenomena in order to conceptualize them." (Ungers 1982, 8)

This mapping exercise is not merely about what the DMZ is, and how it operates, but how the perception of the DMZ impacts the larger political milieu, and ultimately how it has been, and can be politically exploited for maintaining the dominant hegemonic powers at the local and global scale. The DMZ is arguably a Pandora's box full of concealed desires, memories, control, and secret realities of political power, and its hegemonic gluttony. This mapping exercise uncovers, and critically questions the complexities and contradictions of whom the DMZ was designed for, and whom in reality it serves.

Using new paradigms that leap beyond the limits of existing conventions, this de-constructed mapping process starts to construct alternative realities, opening up new potentials and visionary imaginations for the DMZ.

Future Scenarios

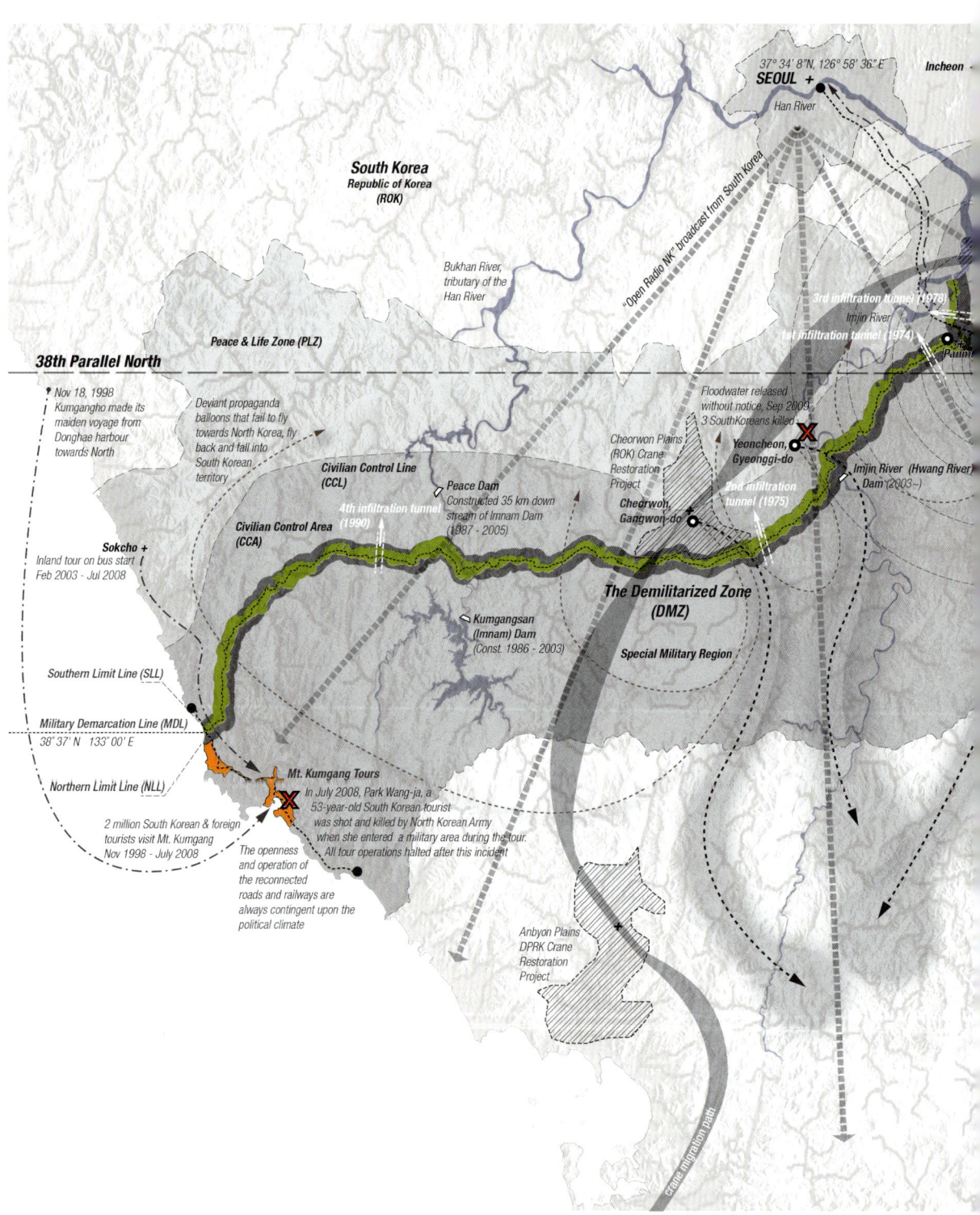

A Construct the Koreas (never) Made Together: Deconstructing the DMZ for the Imaginary | Dongsei Kim

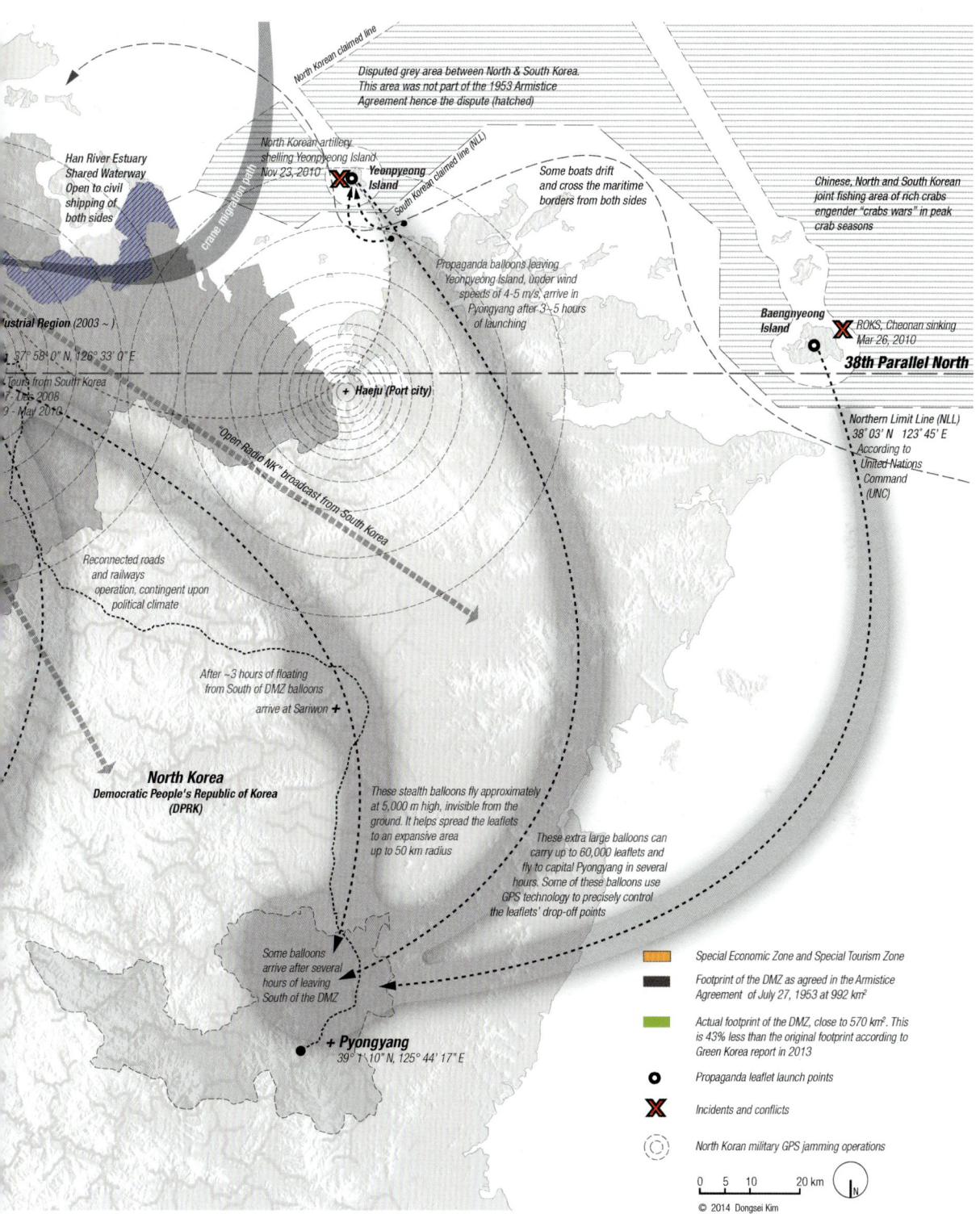

The deconstructing of the Korean Demilitarized Zone (DMZ) © 2013 Dongsei Kim.

남북한이 함께 만든(만들지 않은) 구축물: 상상을 위한 비무장지대의 해체

김동세

―

김동세는 건축가이자 어바니스트(Urbanist)이며, 미국 컬럼비아 대학 겸임 조교수이고 axu studio 소장이다. 그는 하버드 대학교에서 디자인 석사 최우수 학위로 졸업을 하였으며, 컬럼비아 대학에서 도시설계 건축학 석사를, 뉴질랜드 웰링턴의 빅토리아 대학에서 건축학 학사를 취득하였다. 그의 연구는 극단적인 경계부와 그들의 영역이 어떻게 "포용과 배제"와 같은 근본적인 공간적 타협과정에 영향을 미칠 수 있는지, 그리고 "우리와 그들"이 어바니즘에서 어떻게 정의되는지 주목하고 있다. 그는 뉴욕과 웰링턴, 그리고 서울에서 실무를 익혔으며, 호주, 캐나다, 뉴질랜드, 미국, 한국 등 여러 국가의 유수대학에서 강의를 하였다.

"세계의 국가들은 사람에 의해 만들어졌기 때문에, 모색해야 할 그들의 원리는 그들의 생각 속에 있다."-지암바티스타 비코, Principles of a New Science, 1759"(qtd. Koolhaas 1994, 9)

북한이 베일에 쌓여 잘 알려져 있지 않듯이, 오명을 입은 한반도 비무장지대 또한 빈번히 제대로 이해 받지 못하고 있다. 동시에 비무장지대는 시간이 흐르면서 변형하는 동적인 독립체이며 이것은 흔히 알려진 고정되고 보안된 국경이라는 인식에 상반된다. 따라서 비무장지대를 의식적으로 해체해 본다면 지배적인 패권 의식에서 비무장지대를 해방시키고 대안적인 미래를 드러낼 수 있을 것이다.

이 끔찍한 군사시설의 가장 아이러니한 사실 중 하나는 비무장지대가 극도의 갈등의 고정관념적인 상징이라 할지라도 정전협정이 체결된 1953년부터 남북한은 의식적으로, 무의식적으로 그리고 공동으로 이 비무장지대를 국가의 정체성과 영역으로 함께 구축되어졌다는 것이다. 여기서 구축이라 함은 물리적이고 상징적인 구축뿐만이 아니라 그런 과정을 통한 정체성의 구축을 나타낸다. 이러한 과정들 속에서 비무장지대는 시간의 흐름과 함께 현재 남북한의 정체성을 건설 가능하게 하는데 성공적으로 기여 했다. 이러한 점에 있어서 '우리'를 포함하고 '그들'을 제외하는 과정을 통한 비무장지대의 물리적, 상징적 건설은 특히 식민지 이후 근대화 노력에 있어 남북한 각각의 국가 정체성을 확립을 위해 필연적으로 긴요한 일이었다.

지난 60년 간 남한과 북한이 그들 각자의 비극 속에서 주인공과 적대자를 동시에 연기하며 비무장지대를 건설했다는 것을 인지해야 한다. 이 60년 간의 건설과 운용과정에서 여러 번의 공간 협상이 발생했다. 비무장지대의 모든 잠재력을 조금 더 깊이 이해하기 위해서 우리는 이 공간 협상들을 맵핑 (mapping; 지도 제작)으로 형상화하고 지속되는 현상들에 새로운 해석을 부여할 필요가 있다. 이러한 새로운 해석은 지난 60년 간의 지속된 양분과 분립을 초월 가능하게하는 필수적인 지식, 기구, 수단이 되며 비무장지대의 새로운 생산적인 미래를 상상할 수 있도록 해준다.

비무장지대의 해체적 맵핑은 19세기와 20세기의 과거를 인지하며, 21세기 초기에 선 비무장지대의 새로운 진보적 서술을 보여준다. 첫째, 지도의 북위 38선은 19세기 후반 팽창하던 이 지역의 제국 세력의 흔적을 나타낸다. 이 맵핑에서 일반적인 지도의 투시는 말 그대로 180도 회전되어 위 아래가 거꾸로 뒤집혀있다. 이러한 남과 북의 일반적 통념의 관계 불안정화는 현존하는 남북한의 대립구도에서 새로운 관점의 출현 토대를 마련함과 동시에 해체 과정을 개시한다.

이 맵핑 과정은 비무장지대가 시간의 흐름과 보는 관점에 따라서 어떻게 현실 속에서 실질적으로 사용되고, 침범되고, 변형되고, 두터워지고, 팽창하는지를 보여준다. 예를 들어, 이 맵핑에서 비무장지대는 남한과 북한 양측에서 더 넓은 구역으로 표시되는데 이것은 남북한이 비무장지대의 근접한 지역을 어떠한 방법으로 군사적 통제를 하고 있는지를 시각화 한 것이다. 이 맵핑에서 다른 선들은, 사람이 만든 이 비무장지대가 장벽으로서 작용하고 있음에도 불구하고 그것을 넘나들며 흐르는 경제적, 생태적, 정치적 흐름들이 비무장지대를 어떻게 변형시키는지를 시각화 한다. 이 시각화 작업은 장벽들이 이러한 유동적인 흐름들을 막는데 소용이 없고, 터무니 없는 장치들이라는 점을 생생하게 상기시킨다.

"물리적 현상을 이해하는 데는 세 가지 단계가 있다: 첫째, 순수한 물리적 사실의 탐구; 둘째, 우리 내면에 미치는 심리적 영향; 그리고 셋째로 개념화하기 위한 상상적 발견과 현상의 재건이다." (Ungers 1982, 8)

이 맵핑은 단순히 비무장지대란 무엇인지, 어떻게 작용하는지에 관한 시도가 아니라 비무장지대가 더 큰 정치적 환경에 어떠한 영향을 미치는지, 궁극적으로 어떻게 정치적으로 그 지역 그리고 국제적 스케일에서 지배적인 패권을 유지하기 위한 수단으로 이용당할 수 있는지에 관한 것이다. 비무장지대는 감춰진 야망, 기억, 지배, 그리고 정치 권력의 비밀스러운 현실과 그 패권의 욕심으로 가득찬 판도라의 상자로 볼 수 있다. 이 맵핑의 시도를 통해 비무장지대가 누구를 위해 설계되었고 실제로 누구를 위하여 존재하는지에 대한 복합성과 모순을 비판적으로 질문한다.

이 해체적 맵핑 과정은 기존 통념들의 한계를 뛰어넘는 새로운 패러다임을 사용함으로써 비무장지대의 대안적 현실을 구축함과 동시에 새로운 가능성과 상상력을 열어준다.

References

Epilogue: A Non-Design Manifesto for the DMZ:
The South Korean President Park wants a Peace Park in the DMZ. It should be more than a mere Peace Park

The DMZ should be first deconstructed and deeply understood, not prematurely "designed"

The DMZ should be about "to design the conditions" rather than "to condition the design" (Borrowing from Bernard Tschumi's Architecture and Disjuncture, 6)

The DMZ should learn from Marcel Duchamp's "Fountain-Urinal," from the sprit of objet trouvé and detournement

No single individual nor single organization should dictate what the DMZ should be, it should be the conduit for the collective imagination, space of dialogic and agonism

The DMZ should be productive. It should produce food, energy, waste, economy, culture, value, vision, and more

The DMZ should be "more and more, more is more" (Borrowing from Rem Koolhaas)

The DMZ should question the hegemony: power, control and greed

The "DMZ MUST BECOM [sic] A TIGER FARM. 1. TO ATTRACT JAPANESE TOURISTS. 2. TO KEEP ECOLOGY HEAVEN 3. TO EAT UP INVADORS. [sic]" (Borrowing from Nam June Paik, Project DMZ, 1998)

What is the most important thing in the DMZ? It is the people, it is the people, it is the people. (Borrowing from a New Zealand Maori proverb)

Crabb, Cathleen. 1988. "Project DMZ." Vol. 3. New York: Storefront for Art + Architecture.

Koolhaas, Rem. 1994. "Delirious New York : A Retroactive Manifesto for Manhattan." New ed. New York: Monacelli Press.

Kim, Dongsei. 2011. "Demilitarized Zone: Redrawing the Border between North and South Korea Beyond Tourism." 3rd Edition. Cambridge, MA: Blurb.

Kim, Dongsei. 2013. "Borders as Urbanism: Redrawing the Demilitarized Zone (DMZ) between Democratic People's Republic of Korea and Republic of Korea." "Landscape Architecture Frontiers." Vol.1 (2) April. 150-157.

Tschumi, Bernard. 1996. "Architecture and Disjunction." Cambridge, MA: MIT Press.

Ungers, O. M. 1982. "Morphologie City Metaphors." Köln: Verlag der Buchhandlung Walther König.

DAEDONG RIVER PARK

Sunggoo Yang

Team: Doeon Kim, Heebum Kim

—

Sung Goo Yang is pricipal of New York based practice 'Ether Ship'. He received his M.Arch from the Harvard University GSD. His work span encompasses wide spectrum; from urban design to fashion runways, writings and digital artwork —all expressing his interest in the interplay among image, form and cognition. His works include UIA grand prize winning for the Celebration of Cities, 1st prize winning for the Busan Film Factory and more. He was an honored recipient of Merit Award at Boston Sociey of Architects for Unbuilt Design Awards, Next Generation Design Leader by Korean Government, Venora Marmomacc Stone Architecture Design Award, and New York Young Architects award by NY Architectural League. His works have been featured at numeous international jounals such as L'Arca, Surface, Vogue, Dazed, and he has exhibited in places such as Venice Biennale, MIT museum, Plateau Art Gallery Seoul, and Gwangju Biennale.

Mr. Dohee Goo is a scientist researching the future energy at one of the marine research centers on the seaside of Daedong River bank. Everyday, he takes the train from his home in Pyungyang to nearby Daedong Riverside Park, then transfers to the Trans Daedong River Tram to get to the Research Center. Post his morning research, Dohee again takes the tram – providing underwater scenery to get to the Riverside Park for his daily lunch with his colleagues. Unlike the seaside, water level on the river side is more stabilized and serene – ideal for various activities and facilities to be arranged. One can easily find an aquarium, scuba diving facilities, theaters and galleries around here. While these facilities draw many people on weekends, there are also great restaurants and cafes by the riverside where people working nearby come to enjoy lunch time. On the weekends, activities such as festivals, rowing competitions, triathlon, and musical performances take place on stage built over the water. Due to various seasonal programs offered, Daedong Riverside has been attracting thousands of visitors – making it one of the most popular public place in North Korea. Solar panels, algae, and underwater turbines generate electricity for the park, and only electric cars are used at this park – providing the best kind of environment for the area. Working within this dynamic area, Dohee can enjoy dinner with his family by the riverside post his afternoon work and heads home.

대동강 공원

양성구

팀: 김도언, 김희범

—

양성구는 뉴욕을 기반으로 하고 있는 설계사무소 "에테르쉽" 대표이다. 그는 하바드 대학교에서 건축학 석사학위를 취득하였으며, 그의 작업은 어반 디자인(Urban Design)에서부터 패션 런웨이, 에세이와 디지털 아트웍(Digital Art Work) 등 폭 넓은 스펙트럼을 다루고 있으며, 이들 작업은 모두 이미지와 형태 그리고 인식의 상호작용에 관한 그의 관심을 반영하고 있다. 그의 작품은 UIA 공모전 대상 수상작인 "Celebration of Cities"와 "부산 영화 공작소" 1등 수상작 외 다수이며, 보스톤 건축가협회(Boston Society of Architects) 주관 Merit Award, 문화관광부 주관 차세대 디자이너 상, Venora Marmomacc Stone Architecture Design Award와 뉴욕 건축가 연맹 주관 뉴욕 젊은 건축가 상 등을 수상한 경력이 있다. 그의 작품은 L' Arca, Surface, Vogue, Dazed 등 전세계 다양한 잡지에 게재되었으며, 베니스 비엔날레, MIT 박물관, 플라토 아트 갤러리 서울, 광주 비엔날레 등에서 전시되었다.

구도희씨는 대동강물공원 바다 면에 구축되어있는 바다 생태 연구소에서 미래 에너지를 연구하는 과학자이다. 그는 매일 평양에서 전철을 타고 근처에 와서 다시 물 공원 전용 트램을 타고 연구소로 출근한다. 오전 근무를 마친 구 씨는 점심을 먹으러 동료들과 함께 전기 트램을 타고 수중풍경을 지나 강 쪽에 있는 공원시설로 이동한다. 바다 쪽과 달리 강 쪽은 수면이 조절되어서 안정돼 있고, 다양한 레저 문화시설이 있다. 수족관, 수중레저 강습소, 공연장 등이 있고 평일에도 많은 방문객으로 붐비지만, 좋은 식당들과 카페들도 많아 구씨 같은 연구인들이 점심시간에 자주 애용한다. 주말이 되면 각종 페스티벌은 물론 조정경기도 열리고, 강물 위 공연, 음식축제, 철인3종경기 등으로 수만 명의 방문객들로 북적대고, 계절에 따른 다양한 프로그램들로 평양 인근지역에서 가장 인기 있는 도심 공공시설로 평가되고 있다. 시설에 설치된 태양전지판은 물론 수중터빈, 알지 등으로 필요한 전기를 모두 이곳에서 생산하고, 공원 내부에서만 사용되는 전기차로 인해 환경도 매우 쾌적하다. 구 씨는 오후 근무를 마치고 다시 수중에 있는 식당에서 가족들과 저녁을 먹고 집으로 퇴근한다.

Future Scenarios

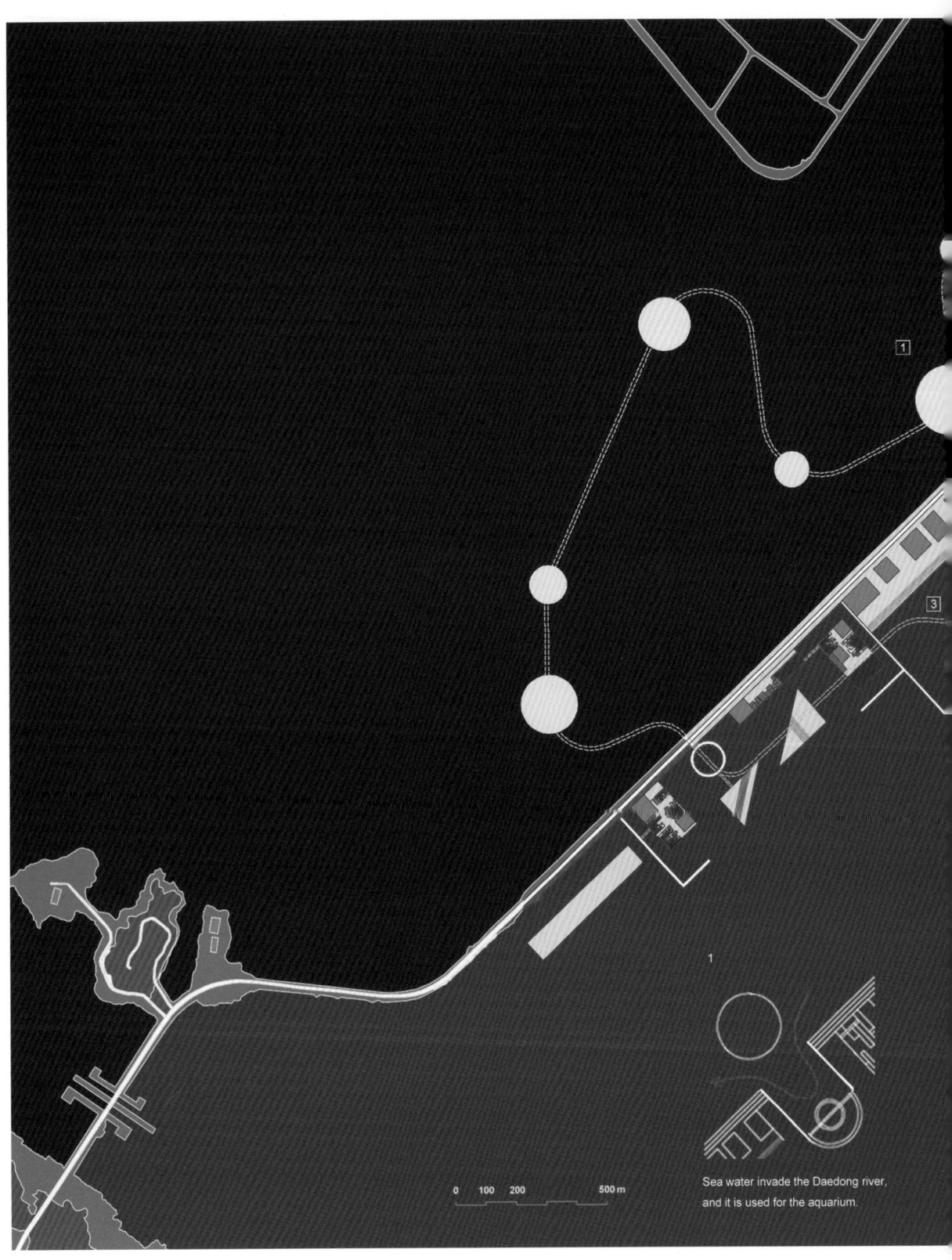

Daedong River Park | Sunggoo Yang

near river path is used for rowing sports.

The tram get around on the park, you can go aquarium, and concert hall from the underwater tram path.

You can experience the diving training. The linear deck is used for the anchorage.

The rectangular geometry provides the pool leisure space, and the river entered in the deck makes it.

Future Scenarios

576

Daedong River Park | Sunggoo Yang

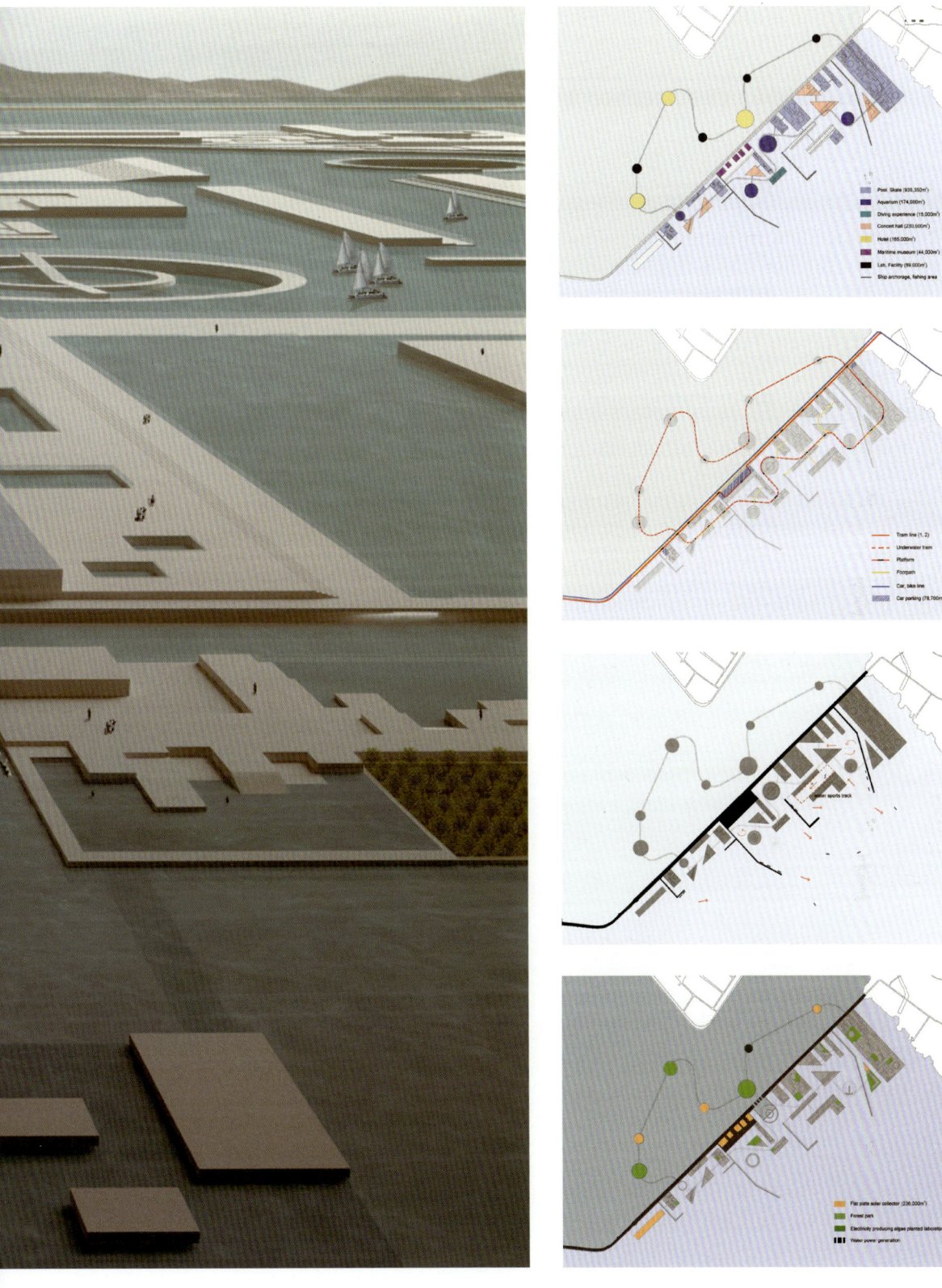

Future Scenarios

the underwater tram, bike, footpath and the platform

concert hall, stand for the water sports and performance

the floated deck ; pool, aquarium, diving hole

the ship anchorage, fishing area

the sea water penetration, aquarium

Sea   Bank   River

Daedong River Park | Sunggoo Yang

BORDER CONTROL PROPOSAL FOR SLOW INTEGRATION

Hye-Young Chung

—

Hye-Young Chung is currently practicing as Senior Lead Designer and Project Architect at Toshiko Mori Architect. She has practiced professionally with leading architecture and design offices in New York, Boston, and Seoul, and has taught and lectured at Harvard University Graduate School of Design, Princeton University School of Architecture, and Columbia University. Her academic pursuits focus on projects that define the boundaries of architectural discourse and typologies through disjunctive contexts.
Hyeyoung earned a Bachelor of Arts in Architecture and Digital Design from Columbia University, and a Master of Architecture from Harvard University Graduate School of Design.

This project aims to address the interstitial space between two political contexts and two political eras. The site is located at the Demilitarized Zone on the Korean peninsula, between two states still technically at war. The political moment is the present one, where efforts for inter-Korean relationships have been made in varying capacity, after being separated for nearly fifty years.

North Korea has been dubbed an unpredictable, dangerous, rogue state with very few allies and a long list of powerful enemies, due to its extreme isolation, human rights violations, and constant nuclear threats. South Korea, in close military allegiance with the United States, has tried different techniques in dealing with the North - from disengagement to trade embargoes, to present-day efforts in economic assistance and engagement.

The efforts made for this level of engagement with North Korea is an extension of the highly controversial Sunshine Policy. Despite the political controversy surrounding these policies, the outcome is that for the first time since the Korean War treaty of 1953, holes have been created in the stringently fortified line of the Demilitarized Zone, and access to North Korea, although highly isolated and tightly chaperoned, has been granted to South Koreans.

However, these areas unavoidably succumb to the political ebbs and flows of the Korean peninsula. When the North declares nuclear tests, the promise that these areas held for reunification become painful reminders that they can be terminated in a split-second, shutting down the long and arduous paths towards building those areas. The question is how to ensure that the process of interrelationship continues while maintaining a stance that befits a time of political uncertainty. What pieces of infrastructure will be used to maintain secure separate states, while slowly opening up the flow of information during what may be the beginnings of a slow process of reunification?

Towards Reunification

The Need For Borders
The South Korean government fears a hasty reunification process because of the effects that it may have on a strong, although young and fragile economy. If reunification happens as fast as it did in Germany (a matter of months according to some, 2 hours according to others) at least 20 million impoverished inhabitants of North Korea will storm South Korean borders. Solely driven by the fear of this ominous threat, the South Korean government has adopted policies to slow down North Korea's collapse. These policies, collectively dubbed the Sunshine Policy, are highly controversial due to the opacity of the funding's distribution once it reaches North Korea.

Two major projects arose out of the Sunshine Policy, the Kaesong Industrial Complex and the Kumgangsan Resort. Dubbed as joint projects, most of the funding was provided by Hyundai-Asan, a South Korean private company. These two projects represent a very specific and unique relationship between nation-states that have drifted apart economically, politically, and culturally, but are tied together by blood.

Inlets and outlets to and from these centers are carefully controlled by military and policy infrastructure. As the number of employees and visitors increase into these free zones from both North and South Korea, more security infrastructure will be necessary to slow down the integration process from both sides. This includes border checkpoints and other physical barriers.

Order Of U/Hetero-Topias

Kumgangsan And Kaesong
The two holes in the DMZ were created, as stated by former advisor to the President, Jung In-Mun, to spur economic homogeneity between the North and the South, so that in the advent of reunification, less tension will occur between the two states.[1] I would like to argue that although this statement is rather Utopian in and of itself, these two Heterotopian projects, Kumgangsan and Kaesong, actually claim larger Utopian ideals involving national identity, brotherly love, and the idea that "blood runs thicker than water."

As stated before, fear of a sudden and chaotic reunification is ultimately driving inter-Korean policies. As Martin Marty states, fear of chaos, or the want for order, are the driving forces behind Utopian ideals, "Behind many analyses of utopia...is the recognition that at their heart is some version of a search for order."[2]

Thus, a large majority of utopian projects are generated as negative critical visualizations of its corresponding chaotic context. The Kaesong and Kumgangsan projects idealistically try to show the continuing bond between the two nations, based on nationalism and sense of identity. The aim for these Heterotopian places is to create a system of orderly reunification for the Korean peninsula.

Heterotopias, by definition, are real places that hold the smoke and mirrors that Utopian ideals rely on. Thus, Heterotopias are, by necessity, separated from the chaos of the real situation.

The real situation on the Korean peninsula is that South Korea and North Korea are still technically at war. The 2002 naval battle that killed 35 North and South Korean sailors is testament to the volatile political situation. Furthermore, the ongoing nuclear debate with North Korea heightens daily, as it continues to test its nuclear capacity. In the meantime, construction doggedly continues at Kaesong and Kumgangsan. Isolated from the realities of the ongoing war between North and South Korea and the fastly intensifying debate with the United States, a masquerade is played out where policies and politics are forgotten and South Koreans play out their dreams of economic equality and brotherhood.

Industrial Utopias

Orderly Resolutions
Out of the two Heterotopian projects, the Kaesong Industrial Complex can be looked at as a typological offshoot of Utopian thought. It falls into a direct lineage of Industrial Utopias. In an effort to deal with new technologies of industrialization in the 18th and 19th centuries, architects grappled with the idea of labor efficiency in industrial colonies. As the primary goal of these industrial cities was to produce more goods, efficient lifestyles for the laborers came under great scrutiny. Living habits of the laborers became synonymous with industrial output.

One of the most famous built industrial utopia is Claude Nicolas Ledoux's Chaux Saltworks (1774), where Ledoux's design principles had "...to conform to the needs and conveniences of a productive factory where the utilization of time offers a first economy."[3] Worker's individual houses and garden plots radiate out from a central area of production, representing not only an efficient system for salt production, but also the subservience of lifestyle to the industrial city. The plan reflected the rigid ordering of men, materials, time, and end product.[4]

As cited by Gillian Darley in her seminal book on the Factory, Anthony Vidler explains that Ledoux manages to join the interests of art with those of government,[5] by architecturally creating a social order that reflects industrial production. However, what really happened in the end is that due to faulty infrastructure, namely that of poor plumbing, the Royal Saltworks never fully reached its production goals, and Ledoux continued to build his ideal production city, but only on paper.

The Industrial City is a co-relation between social order and industrial production. The insistence on the particulars of the social order, leading to a grand master vision, is what makes these projects particularly useful when comparing them to the Kaesong Industrial Project.

The questions of collective space versus individual space, transparency/opacity of hierarchy, and an educational component for the social order of the laborers are all lessons gained from 18th and 19th century industrial towns to apply to the project at Kaesong.

Precedents Of Inter-Separation

Thickening The Borders

Although the political situation of North America is radically different from the one in Korea, an example can be made of the United States' border system, which exemplifies the transferral of economic and political policies to physical built infrastructure. Large-scale developments of the physical infrastructure at America's borders began with NAFTA, reflecting shifting tides in economic relationships between the US and its neighbors.[6] In essence, greater economic mobility between the countries required more physical boundaries.

New levels of security have been installed post-9-11 as the Department of Homeland Security poured billions of dollars into building and hardening the edge of the United States. At the same time that these policies harden the edges, projects committed to softening those same borders are being developed to allow for economic permeability. These include the borders around Tijuana and San Ysidro. Many of these "softer" border projects rely on the THICKENING of the border by incorporating different programs into the edge condition. This condition is reminiscent of Rem Koolhaas's Involuntary Prisoners project, which thickened the cut line between Londoners with program. Industrial development zones, or maquiladora, are examples of thickened areas lining the US-Mexico border. These cities are precedents for the Kaesong Industrial Complex.

The thickening of the border requires that the site is injected with additional program to camouflage the true nature of the border station.

Goals of the Border Station at Kaesong

By negotiating that which divides and controls access to countries - the fence, and the border station - with the thickening of that border with industrial program, an attempt at increased interaction, the goal of this project is to create a place that can be a stepping stone towards increased, mediated interaction between the two nations, whilst engaging the reality of the Korean situation.

The integration of the border station and the education complex into one project solves logistical issues of providing daily training for laborers, all of whom commute to the complex and go through a checking process. By integrating the checkpoint and the educational facility, it will necessitate that a part of the check-in and check-out process will be an educational component teaching basic factory training to North Korean employees.

The integration of the border station (dividing infrastructure) and the education complex (exchanges of connections) also shows that there is a desire to mediate the integration between the two Koreas.

    -Controlling access: Visual and Physical
    -Infrastructure: Border Station - Separation of two communities
    -Architecture: Education/Recreation - Joining of two communities
    -Infrastructure + Architecture = controlled separation and joining

The border station has set rules and forms. The educational complex negotiates the border station

- it finds the poche of the border station, such as residual voids the road layout creates, and occupies those voids, connecting the poche of the border station into a single volume.

The border station and educational complex consistently negotiate each other. The structured poche of the border station informs the organization of the school, such as the entry points and vertical circulation. Whereas the programmatic needs of the school, such as the dimensions of classrooms and relationships between individual classrooms, push and pull the infrastructure.

A thin, continuous exhibition space winds through the educational complex and will be visually accessible to all within the complex, including those in their car or bus waiting to get checked through. It acts as the showcase of the school, demonstrating the utopian dream of the two nations working and learning together. This is the distilled space of exchange of ideas and products.

The classrooms line one side of the exhibition space. The classrooms range in dimension drastically - from auto repair classes, requiring large garage-style spaces – to smaller, conventional classrooms. The classrooms shift in visual accessibility – from total transparency to opacity. Accordingly, the classrooms will take on different functions. Not only will these be places of exchange, with South Koreans as instructors (in the beginning), but will also be places for group gatherings – spaces which are currently lacking for North Korean laborers.

A larger gathering space will be the soccer field that dominates the roof. This seemingly neutral space will provide a place for joint sports tournaments, but also a place for large-scale performances, such as the Mass Games of North Korea, and a place for general assembly.

These three types of assembly spaces – the continuous exhibition hall, the classrooms, and the soccer field – define a myriad of opportunities for interaction between the two communities. These may be stated as hierarchical (classroom), neutral (soccer field/exhibition), or separative (meeting rooms). However, these differing definitions for relationships within the complex will aim to create mediated, thoughtful, and controlled interaction between the two differing nation-states.

국경 통제
느린 통합에 대한 제안

정혜영

—

정혜영은 현재 토시코 모리 건축 설계사무소의 시니어 디자이너이자 프로젝트 아키텍트(architect)이다. 그녀는 뉴욕, 보스턴, 서울 등에서 유수의 설계사무소에서 실무 경험을 쌓았으며, 하버드 대학교 디자인 대학, 프린스턴 건축과, 컬럼비아 대학에서 가르친 경험이 있다. 그녀의 연구는 이분법적인 컨텍스트를 통해 건축적 담론과 유형의 경계를 설정하는 프로젝트에 초점이 맞추어져 있다. 그녀는 컬럼비아 대학에서 예술학 학사를 취득하였으며, 하버드 대학에서 건축학 석사학위를 받았다.

이 프로젝트는 두 정치적인 맥락과 시대 사이의 공간을 다루는 데에 목적이 있다. 그 공간은 아직 엄밀히 말해 휴전 중인 두 국가 사이, 한반도의 비무장지대에 위치한다. 거의 50년 동안 분단된 후, 남북의 관계 개선에 대한 노력은 다양한 방면으로 해온 시점이 현재 정치적인 시점이라고 할 수 있다.

북한은 극단적인 고립, 인권박해, 그리고 지속적인 핵무기 위협으로 매우 소수의 동맹국과 수많은 막강한 적대국들 사이에서 예상할 수 없고 위험하고 거친 국가라 불리고 있다. 미국과 군사적 동맹 관계에 있는 남한은 통상금지에 대한 해약에서부터 경제적 지원과 관계유지를 위한 현재의 노력까지 북한을 대하는데 있어 이전과 다른 전략들을 시도해 오고있다.

북한과 이 정도 차원의 관계를 만들어낸 노력들은 대단히 논란의 소지가 많았던 햇볕정책의 연장이다. 이러한 정책들에 대한 정치적인 논란에도 불구하고 이에 따른 결과로는 1953년 남북전정협정 이후 처음으로 비무장지역 군사분계선에 땅굴이 만들어졌고 결국 고립되고 밀접하게 동반되는 북한과의 접촉이 남한에게 주어졌다.

그러나 이 지역은 한반도의 정치적 변화에 불가피하게 굴복한다. 북한이 핵무기 실험을 선포했을 때 통일에 대한 약속에는 한 순간에 파괴될 수 있으며 국경지역을 통합의 장소로 구축해 나가기 위한 멀고도 험한 길을 끊어버릴 수 있다는 고통스러운 암시가 내포되어 있다. 문제는 정치적인 불안정성의 시기에 걸맞는 입장을 유지하면서 어떻게 상호관계 절차를 지속해 나갈것인가 이다. 어떤 부분의 사회 기반시설이 통일의 서행적인 절차에 시작점이 될 수도 있는 시기동안 정보의 흐름을 천천히 열면서 분리된 두 국가의 안보를 유지할 수 있을 것인가?

통일을 대하여

국경의 필요성
통일은 튼튼한 경제를 바탕으로 이루어졌을 때 그 효과를 볼 수 있기 때문에 북한의 미성숙되고 불안정한 경제적 상황에도 불구하고 남한 정부에서는 성급하게 통일 절차를 논하는 것을 두려워한다. 만약 독일이 이루었던 것처럼 통일이 빠르게 이루어진다면 (어떤 사람들에 의하면 한 달 혹은 2시간 안에) 적어도 2천만의 북한 빈민들이 남한 국경에 들이닥칠 것이다. 이러한 불길한 위협의 두려움 때문에 남한 정부는 북한의 몰락을 서행시키기 위한 정책을 채택했다. 종합적으로 햇볕정책이라고 불리는 이 정책은 북한이 받는 재정적 분배의 불투명성 때문에 매우 논란이 되었다.

햇볕정책 중에 두개의 주요 사업은 개성공단과 금강산 리조트 사업이다. 합동 사업으로 불리어 지는 이 사업은 남한의 사기업인 현대 아산으로부터 대부분의 재정지원을 받았다. 이 두 사업은 경제적·정치적·문화적으로 떨어져 있지만 같은 혈연관계에 있는 두 국가 사이의 매우 구체적이고 독특한 관계를 보여준다.

이 사업의 중심의 입출구는 군사적이고 정책적인 기반에 의해서 조심스럽게 통제된다. 남북으로부터 자유로운 지역의 고용인과 방문자 수가 증가함에 따라 양측의 통합절차를 서행시키기 위해 더욱 보안적인 기반시설이 필요할 것이다. 이것은 국경 검문소와 다른 물리적 경계들을 포함한다.

ORDER OF U/HETERO TOPIA

금강산과 개성
문정인 전 대통령 고문에 의하면 남북한의 경제적인 통합을 형성하고 그로 인해 두 국가 사이의 긴장감을 완화하기 위해 DMZ에 두 개의 통로가 만들어졌다고 한다. 이 두 heteropian 프로젝트인 금강산과 개성 사업은 실질적으로 국가 정체성, 형제사랑 그리고 '피는 물보다 진하다'는 생각을 아우르는, 더 큰 유토피안의 이상을 표명한다.

이전에도 언급했듯이 갑작스럽고 혼란의 통일에 대한 두려움이 남북간의 정책을 궁극적으로 이끌고 있다. "Behind many analyses of utopia…is the recognition that at their heart is some version of a search for order."라는 Martin Marty의 말에 따르면, 혼란의 두려움 또는 질서의 필요는 유토피안의 이상에 원동력이다.

그러므로 혼란의 배경에 부합하는 부정적인 시각화에 따라 대규모의 유토피안 사업이 만들어졌다. 개성과 금강산 사업은 이상주의적으로 두 국가의 지속적인 결속을 보여주기 위해 노력했다. Heterotopian 지역을 위한 목표는 한반도의 질서 있는 통일을 위한 정책을 만드는 것이다.

정의하자면, heterotopias 는 유토피안의 이상이 의존하는 연기와 겨울을 갖고 있는 실질적인 장소이다. 그러므로 heteropias 는 필요에 따라 실질적 상황의 혼란으로부터 분리되어진다.

엄밀히 말해 한반도의 실질적 상황은 남북한이 여전히 전쟁 중이라는 것이다. 2002년 35명의 남북한 선원들의 목숨을 앗아간 연평도 해전은 불안한 정치 상황의 증거이다. 더 나아가 북한이 지속적으로 핵실험을 진행하면서 현재 진행 중인 핵무기 논쟁은 하루하루 고조되고 있다. 이 상황에도 개성과 금강산에서는 공사가 완강하게 진행 중이다.
남북한 사이 진행중인 전쟁의 현실과 미국과 강화되고 있는 논의를 외면할 뿐 아니라 정책과 정치를 잊고 남한 사람들은 경제적인 공등과 형제애를 꿈꾸고 있다.

산업 유토피아

질서 있는 해결
두 Heterotopian 사업 중 개성공단은 유토피안 사상의 유형적인 부분으로 볼 수 있다. 이는 Industrial Utopias의 직접적인 계보에 들어간다. 18세기와 19세기 새로운 산업화 유형을 다루는 노력 속에서 건축가들은 산업 식민지 국가들의 노동 효율성에 대한 생각들로 씨름하였다. 산업도시의 궁극적인 목표가 더 많은 생산품을 생산하는 것이듯 노동자들의 효율적인 생활 방식을 세심히 살펴보게 되었다. 노동자들의 삶의 습관은 산업의 결과물과 같다고 볼 수 있다.

가장 유명한 산업 유토피아 중 하나는 Nicolas Ledoux's Chaux Saltworks(1774)이다. Ledoux의 설계원칙은 "...to conform to the needs and conveniences of a productive factory where the utilization of time offers a first economy."이며, 노동자 개개인의 주거 공간과 정원 공간은 생산의 중심지역으

로 뻗어있다. 소금 생산의 효율적인 구조 뿐만 아니라 산업도시에 생활방식의 종속을 나타내고 있다. 계획 도는 사람, 자재, 시간, 그리고 최종 생산품의 엄격한 질서를 반영한다.

Gillian Darley의 the Factory라는 책의 내용을 인용하자면 Anthony Vidler는 Ledoux가 산업 생산을 반영한 사회적 질서를 건축적으로 만들면서 예술적 관심을 정부의 관심과 결합하였다고 설명했다. 그러나 실질적으로 일어난 결과는 잘못된 기반시설, 즉 부실한 수도시설 등으로 인하여 왕립 제염소가 생산의 목표를 완전히 이루지 못했고 Ledoux가 지속적으로 그의 이상을 설계해 나갔지만 그것은 오로지 이론적으로만 이었다.

The Industrial City가 사회적 질서와 산업 생산력의 상호관계이다. 중대한 비전을 이끄는 사회적 질서의 세부사항에 대한 고집은 개성공단 사업과 비교했을 때 이러한 사업들을 특히 유용하게 만든다.

노동자의 사회질서를 위한 전체적 공간과 개인적 공간, 위계질서의 투명성 및 불투명성, 그리고 교육 구성요소에 대한 문제들은 18세기와 19세기 산업 지역으로부터 개성공단에서 이르기까지 얻어온 모든 교훈들일 것이다.

상호 분리의 사례들

<u>국경지역을 농화시키는 것</u>
비록 북아메리카의 정치적인 상황이 한국의 상황과 현저히 다르다 할지라도 경제적 정치적인 정책에서 물리적으로 건설된 기반시설로의 이전을 예증하는 미국의 국경 시스템의 한가지 예가 존재한다. 미국의 국경에서 물리적 기반시설의 큰 규모 개발이 미국과 접경국들 사이의 경제적 관계에 있어서 변화의 흐름을 반영하는 NAFTA와 함께 시작 되었다. 본질적으로 큰 규모의 국가간 경제 유동성은 더 많은 물리적 경계를 필요로 한다.

미 국토 안보국에서 미국의 경계를 강화하고 구축하는 데에 수십억 달러의 돈을 투자하면서 9.11 테러 이후 새로운 차원의 보안이 확립되었다. 이러한 정책들이 경계선을 강화하는 동시에 같은 국경지역을 경화하는 프로젝트들도 경제적 침투성을 감안하여 개발되고 있다. 이는 티화나와 산 이스드로 주위 접경지역을 포함한다. 많은 '더 부드러운' 국경 계획들은 경계선 상태에 따른 다른 프로그램들을 접목시킴으로써 국경 강화라는 부제에 의존한다. 이는 프로그램과 함께 런던 시민들사이 절선을 강화하는 렘쿨하스의Involuntary Prisoners project를 연상시킨다. 산업개발구역 또는 maquiladora는 미국과 멕시코 국경 지역을 강화시킨 예다. 이러한 도시들은 개성공단을 위한 사례들이다.

국경지역 강화는 본래 국경 역의 성질을 감추기 위해 그 지역에 부과적인 프로그램들을 주입하는 것이 필요하다.

개성 국경역의 목표들
국경 울타리와 국경 역과 같이 국가의 출입을 관리하는 지역에 산업적인 프로그램과 국경지역 강화에 대한 협상과 함께 이 사업의 목표는 한국의 현실을 고려하는 동시에 증가되고 중화되고 있는 두 나라의 상호 교류를 향해 한발 내딛을 수 있는 장소를 만드는 것이다.

국경 역과 교육시설을 하나의 프로젝트로 결합하는 것은 검문소를 통과하고 교육시설을 통학하게 될 노동자들에게 일일 교육을 제공하는 논리적인 이슈를 해결할 수 있다. 검문소와 교육시설을 접목시킴으로써 출입 관리 부분이 북한 노동자들에게 기본적인 공업 지도를 제공하는 교육적인 구성요소가 될 필요가 있다.

국경 역과 교육시설의 결합은 또한 한반도의 결합을 이루려는 욕구를 보여준다.

- 접근 관리: 시각적 그리고 물리적
- 기반시설: 국경 역 – 두 공동체의 분리
- 건축물: 교육/여가 – 두 공동체의 결합
- 기반시설 + 건축물 = 관리된 분리와 결합

국경 역은 그 규칙과 형태를 갖고 있다. 교육 시설은 국경 역을 중재한다. 도로 배치에 따라 생긴 주거공간과 그 공간을 채움, 국경 역의 poche를 하나의 몸체로 연결시키는 것처럼 말이다.

국경 역과 교육 시설은 지속적으로 서로 협상한다. 국경 역의 구조화된 poche는 입구와 수직 이동경로와 같은 학교의 구성을 알려준다. 교실의 크기와 각 교실과의 관계와 같은 학교의 공간 기획의 필요가 사회기반시설을 끌어들이거나 밀어내기도 한다.

가늘고 지속적인 전시 공간은 교육 시설을 통하고 시각적으로 시설 안에 모든 지역에 접근 가능하다. 함께 배우고 일하는 두 국가의 유토피안의 꿈을 보여주는 학교의 열린 공간 역할을 한다. 이것은 생각과 생산품을 교류하는 정화된 공간이다.

교실들은 전시 공간의 한 측면에 나열된다. 교실들은 큰 정비공간을 필요로 하는 자동 수리 교실에서부터 작은 크기의 평범한 교실까지 다양한 크기들로 구성되어있다. 교실들은 전체적으로 투명함으로부터 불투명함에 이르는 시각적인 접근성에 변화를 주고 있다. 따라서, 각 교실들은 다른 기능들을 갖게 될 것이다. 이는 남한과의 지도인력 교류의 장소가 될 뿐만 아니라 북한 노동자들에게 부족한 단체 모임의 장소가 될 것이다.

넓은 집합장소는 지붕을 두르고 있는 축구 경기장이 될 것이다. 보기와 같이 이러한 중립적인 공간은 합동 스포츠 토너먼트의 장소가 될 뿐만 아니라 북한의 집단 경기와 같은 큰 스케일의 행위 장소, 그리고 집회 공간으로써의 역할을 할 것이다.

이 세가지 유형의 집회 공간 (지속적인 전시 공간, 교실, 축구 경기장)은 두 공동체의 수많은 교류의 기회들로 정의된다. 이는 위계 질서적(교실)이고, 중립적(축구 경기장/전시공간)이며 혹은 독립성(집회공간)으로 이야기될 것이다. 그러나 complex 안에서의 관계에 대한 다른 정의들이 두 다른 국가 사이의 중재적이고 사려 깊고 통제된 교류를 목표로 할 것이다.

References

1 Welcome to North Korea. dir. Peter Tetteroo, Video, KRO Dutch Television, 2001.
2 Martin E. Marty, Visions of Utopia, (New York: Oxford University Press, 2003)
3 Gillian Darley, Factory (Hong Kong: Reaktion Books Ltd, 2003) 51.
4 Darley 48
5 Darley 45.
6 Holtzman, Anna. "Frontline Design." Architecture. Oct 2005, p 51.

Future Scenarios

Programming Utopia - Kaesong Border Station

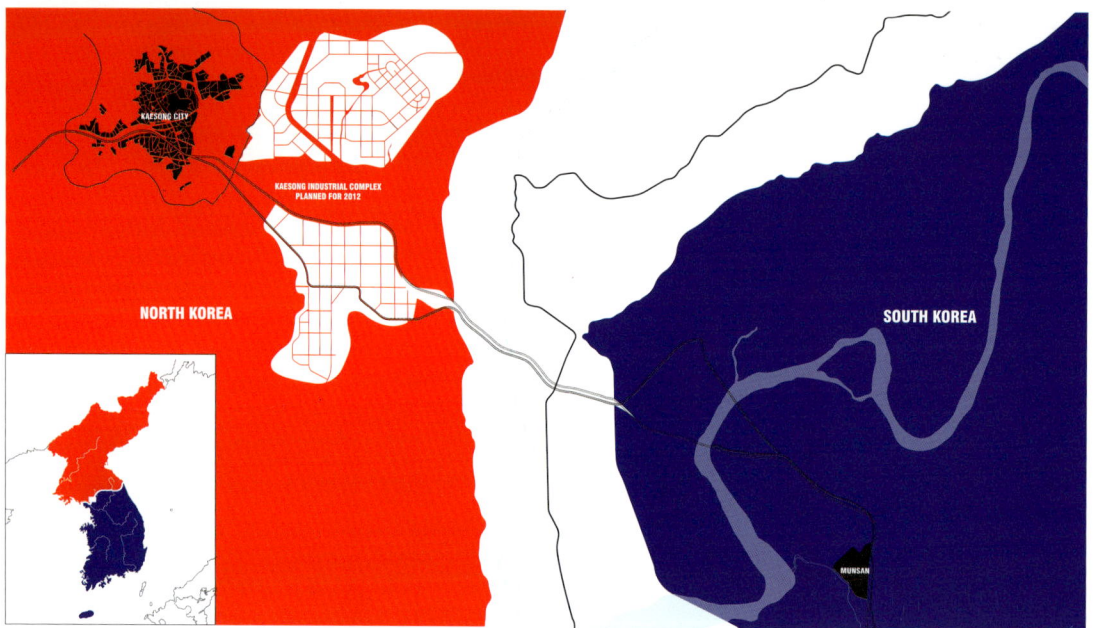

Site - Kaesong Industrial Complex

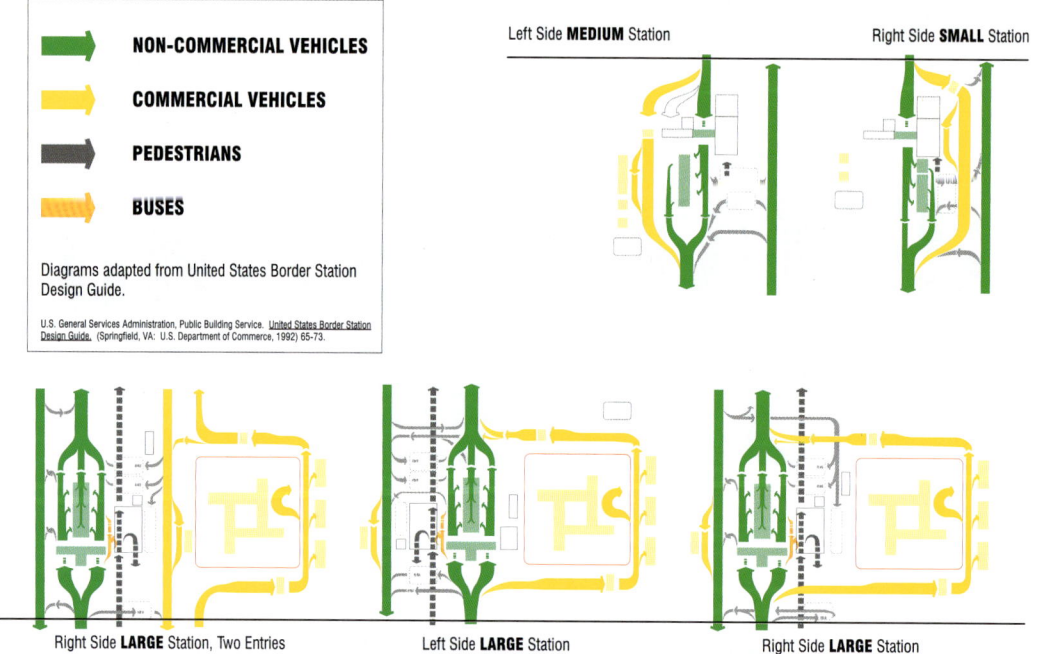

Precedent Study - US Border Station

Border Control Proposal For Slow Integration | Hye-Young Chung

PRECEDENTS OF INTER-SEPARATION
THICKENING THE BORDERS

Although the political situation of North America is radically different from the one in Korea, an example can be made of the United States' border system, which exemplifies the transferral of economic and political policies to physical built infrastructure. Large-scale developments of the physical infrastructure at America's borders began with NAFTA, reflecting shifting tides in economic relationships between the US and its neighbors.1 In essence, greater economic mobility between the countries required more physical boundaries.

New levels of security have been installed post-9-11 as the Department of Homeland Security poured billions of dollars into building and hardening the edge of the United States. At the same time that these policies harden the edges, projects committed to softening those same borders are being developed to allow for economic permeability. These include the borders around Tijuana and San Ysidro.

Many of these "softer" border projects rely on the THICKENING of the border by incorporating different programs into the edge condition. This condition is reminiscent of Rem Koolhaas's Involuntary Prisoners project, which thickened the cut line between Londoners with program. Industrial development zones, or maquiladora, are examples of thickened areas lining the US-Mexico border. These cities are precedents for the Kaesong Industrial Complex.

The thickening of the border requires that the site is injected with additional program to camouflage the true nature of the border station.

상호 분리의 사례들
국경지역의 농화

비록 북아메리카의 정치적인 상황이 한국의 상황과 현저히 다르다 할지라도 경제적 정치적인 정책에서 물리적으로 건설된 기반시설로의 이전을 예증하는 미국의 국경 시스템의 한가지 예가 존재한다. 미국의 국경에서 물리적 기반시설의 큰 규모 개발이 미국과 접경국들사이의 경제적 관계에 있어서 변화의 흐름을 반영하는 NAFTA와 함께 시작 되었다. 본질적으로 큰 규모의 국가간 경제 유동성은 더 많은 물리적 경계를 필요로 한다.

미 국토 안보국에서 미국의 경계를 강화하고 구축하는데 수십억 달러의 돈을 투자하면서 새로운 차원의 보안이 9.11 테러 이후 확립되었다. 이러한 정책들이 경계선을 강화하는 동시에 같은 국경지역을 경화하는 프로젝트들도 경제적 침투성을 감안하여 개발되고 있다. 이는 티화나와 산 이스드로 주위 접경지역을 포함한다.

많은 '더 부드러운' 국경 계획들은 경계선 상태에 따른 다른 프로그램들을 접목시킴으로써 국경 강화라는 부제에 의존한다. 이는 프로그램과 함께 런던 시민들사이 절선을 강화하는 렘쿨하스의 Involuntary Prisoners project를 연상시킨다. 산업개발구역 또는 maquiladora는 미국과 멕시코 국경 지역을 강화시킨 예다. 이러한 도시들은 개성공단을 위한 사례들이다.

국경지역 강화는 본래 국경역의 성질을 감추기위해 그 지역에 부과적인 프로그램들을 주입하는 것이 필요하다.

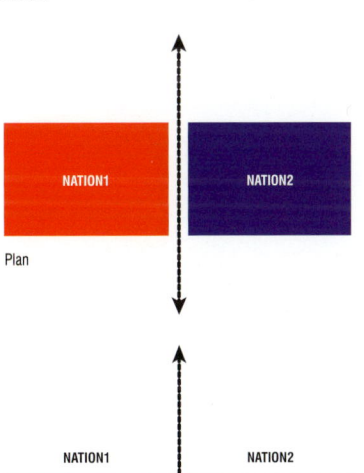

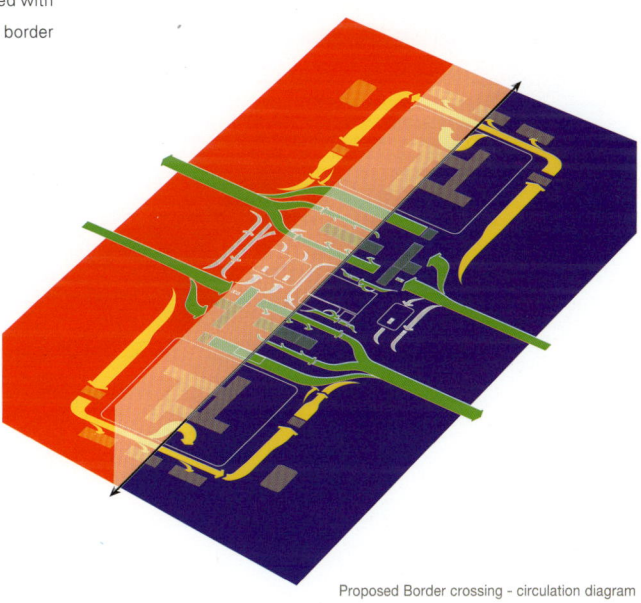

Proposed Border crossing - circulation diagram

Future Scenarios

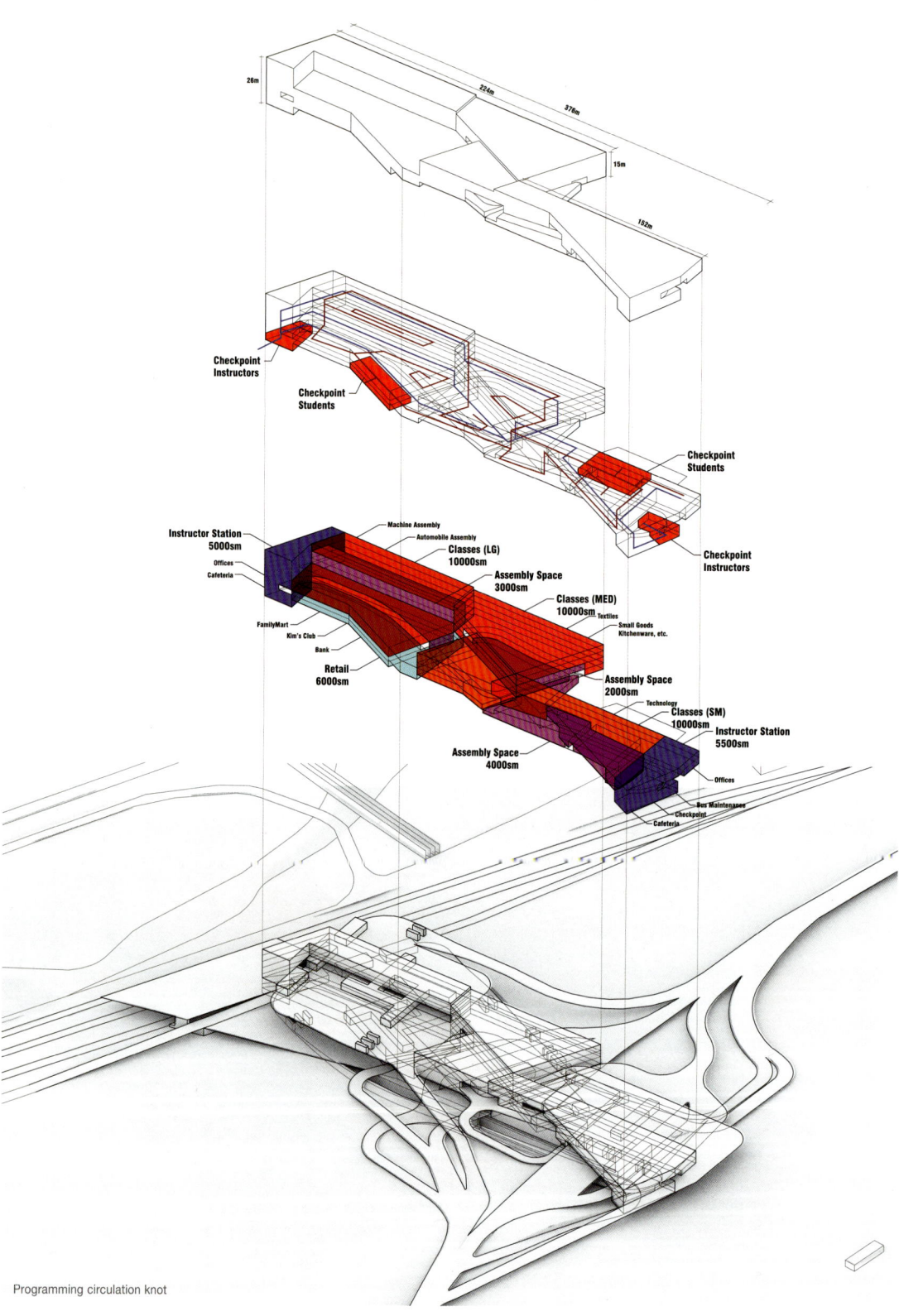

Programming circulation knot

Border Control Proposal For Slow Integration | Hye-Young Chung

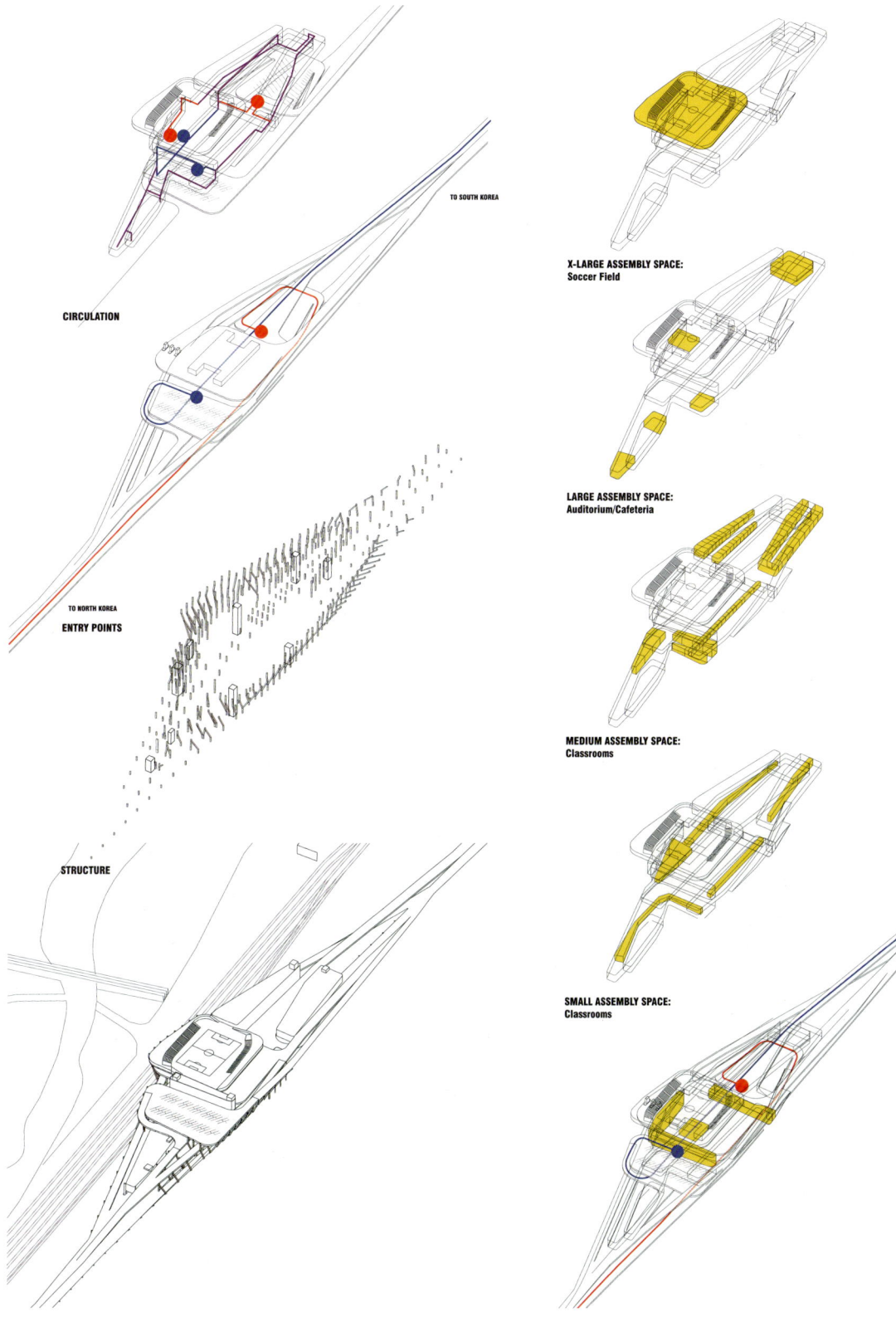

Future Scenarios

STRUCTURAL MEMBRANE NEGOTIATING INFRASTRUCTURE AND PROGRAM

By negotiating that which divides and controls access to countries - the fence, and the border station - with the thickening of that border with industrial program, an attempt at increased interaction, the goal of this project is to create a place that can be a stepping stone towards increased, mediated interaction between the two nations, whilst engaging the reality of the Korean situation.

The integration of the border station and the education complex into one project solves logistical issues of providing daily training for laborers, all of whom commute to the complex and go through a checking process. By integrating the checkpoint and the educational facility, it will necessitate that a part of the check-in and check-out process will be an educational component teaching basic factory training to North Korean employees.

국경 울타리와 국경역과 같이 국가의 출입을 관리하는 지역에 산업적인 프로그램과 함께 국경지역을 강화에 대한 협상과 함께 이 사업의 목표는 한국의 현실을 고려하는 동시에 증가되고 중화되고 있는 두 나라의 상호 교류를 향해 한발 내딧을 수 있는 장소를 만드는 것이다.

국경역과 교육시설을 하나의 프로젝트로 결합하는 것은 검문소를 통과하고 교육시설을 통학하게될 노동자들에게 일일 교육을 제공하는 논리적인 이슈를 해결할 수 있다. 검문소와 교육시설을 접목시킴으로써 출입 관리 부분이 북한 노동자들에게 기본적인 공업 지도를 제공하는 교육적인 구성요소가 될 필요가 있다.

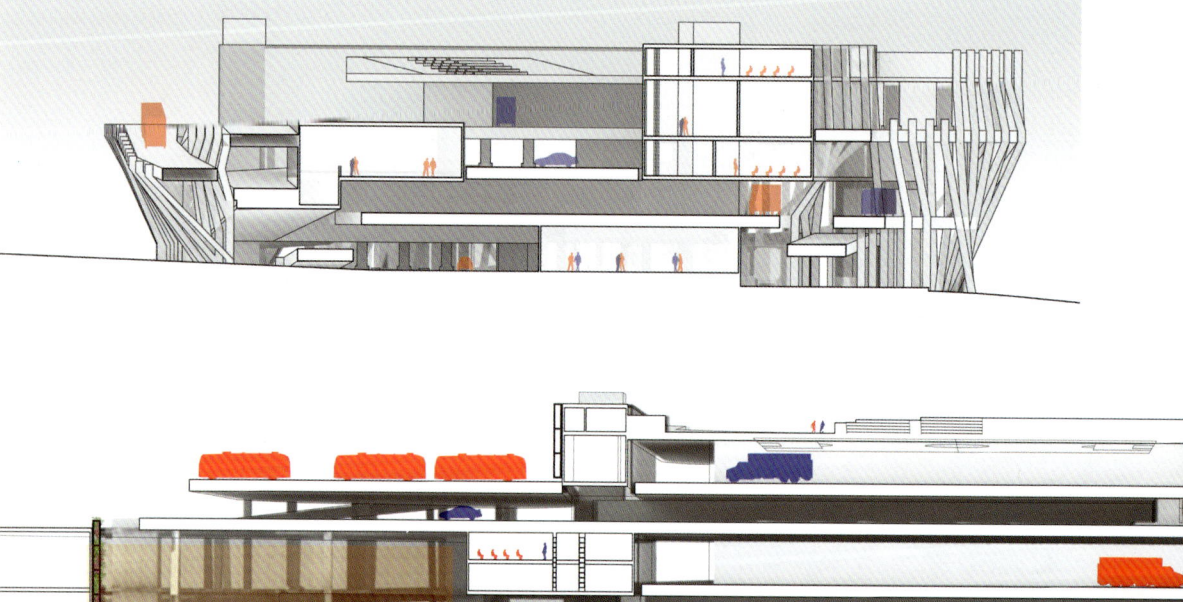

Weaving program into circulation infrastucture

Border Control Proposal For Slow Integration | Hye-Young Chung

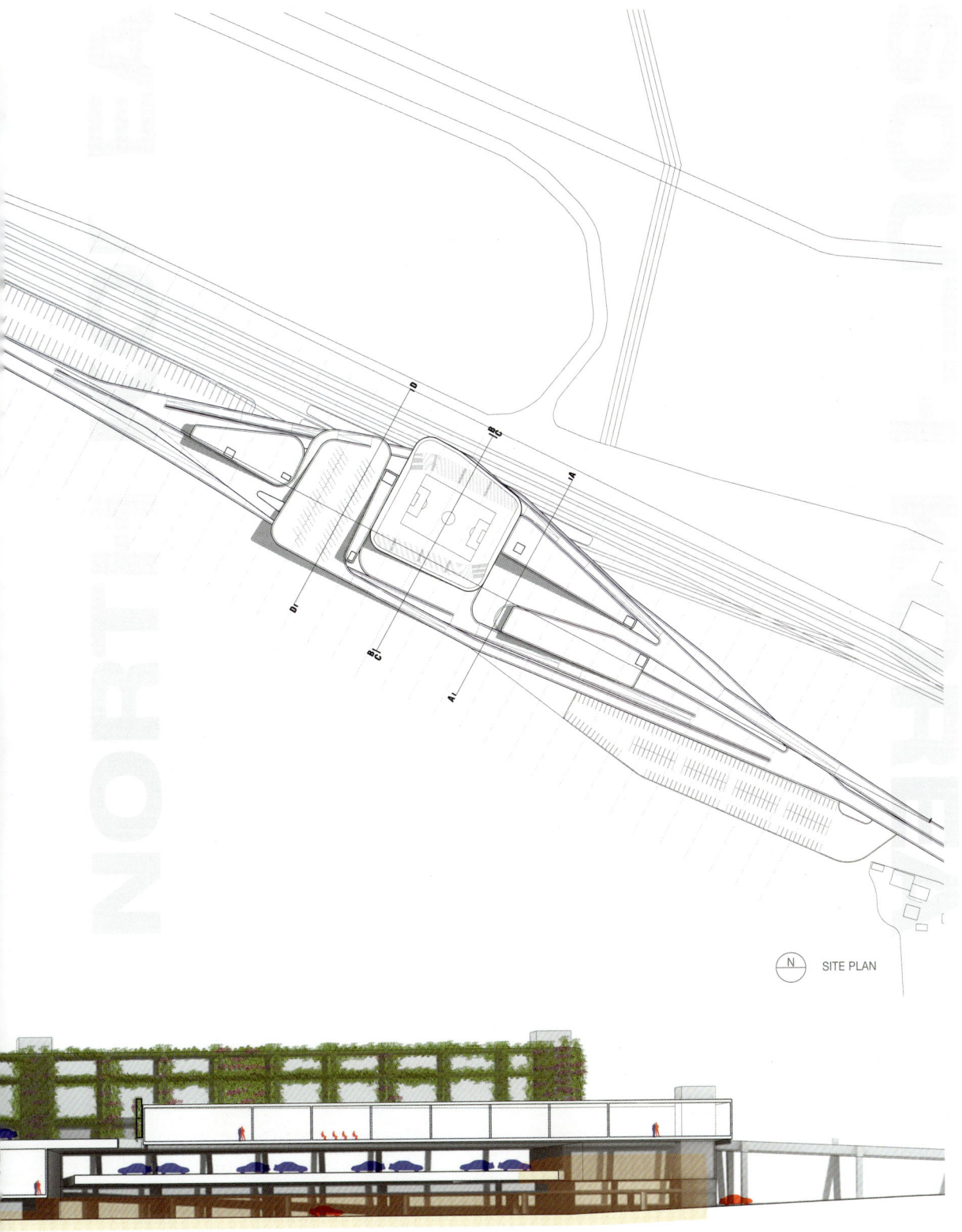

SITE PLAN

LIVING IN THE BORDERLESS : APPLICATION OF SOCIAL MEDIA AS RADICAL URBAN DESIGN TACTICS IN NORTH AND SOUTH KOREA

Sejin Rubella Jo & Soobin Lee

—

Sejin Rubella Jo is an architect and urban designer. She is a visiting instructor at P.I. Art in New York teaching an urbanism class, Faking the City and a researcher working on nonprofit projects in Asia Initiatives Organization. She received her MSAUD from Columbia University, and a B.Arch from Chonnam National University in Korea. Her research projects she currently undertaking is about the development of public city system investigating the link between virtual and physical architecture. Sejin has practiced a wide range of the application of communicative technology and the idea of space info graphics in New York, Korea, Ghana and India.

Soobin Lee is currently working as a research intern at AURI, Architecture and Urban Research Institute in Korea. She is currently researching on how architecture meets the street in the historic context of urban design. She graduated MSAUD program at Graduate School of Architecture, Planning, and Preservation at Columbia University and Bachelor of science in architectural engineering at Kyungpook National University. With ceaseless interest in a relationship between North and South Korea, she has been kept researching on the way to create more democratic interacting methodology between two Korea's spatial communication.

Theme

We start from the question, "What if we could compose the new type of urban design tools that would unite divided people and disparate social standards?" A new media landscape developed by Social Network System has brought cultural, economic, and even political shifts in the 21st century. These changes now have transformed citizens' relationships to physical places and social infrastructures. However, media propaganda also makes paradoxical relations between a liberated public realm and oppressive architectural environments. The aim of this project is to determine how new media technologies can be used in city systems in more democratic architectural surroundings. This project is also premised on the convictions that urban environments with public discourse can help social and economic development and a mediated opening-up of North Korea might be facilitated by using architecture and technology to create shared social spaces between South and North Korea.

Research Background & Problems

Even though North Korea remains distrustful of the world (including even its best ally, China), the country is fortunate to have at least one neighbor that shares its language, history, and ancient culture: South Korea. It's also fortunate in that there are many South Koreans who have a compelling interest in welcoming the citizens of North Korea to a greater participation in the global economy. South Korea is a global leader in information technology, and has a participatory open society as a consequence; however, there are no consistent communication policies or systems connecting North and South Korea. For example, The Kaesong Industrial Complex, located in North Korea, is the most successful co-developing area and has provided the longest communication methodologies between the two Koreas. However, its consistency of operation has always fluctuated depending on political conditions in the two countries.

As mentioned above, we recognize the problems in relation with the absence of communication between the two Koreas, which can be outlined in this brief background.

- The absence of communication tools continues the division between the two Koreas, while a revolutionary moment occurs in networked global society.
- Physically divided, the two Koreas grow further apart in ideology.
- The ideological hostilities invade cyberspace and further divide the people.
- Online and off, propaganda destroys any shared public realm and maintains the political status quo of both North and South Korea.

The Democratic People's Republic of Korea has long suffered the consequences of its political and economic isolation. To survive, the "Hermit Kingdom" must open up economically and socially. The idea is that because North Korea needs to access the entrepreneurial and cultural energies of the South, it must undertake a mediated, closely monitored opening-up; it will be able to do so through a social network of Internet hubs connected exclusively to the South and city systems that will be built in the urban public centers of both North and South Korea. Despite our war and continuing hostilities, many of us look upon participating in some type of reconciliation as our patriotic duty. Another motivation among South Koreans could be entrepreneurial; the North represents a wide-open market. Finally, curiosity about the Hermit Kingdom is the driving force behind its market industries.

Yet North Korea has perhaps more compelling reasons to consider this proposal than South Korea does: The incompetent management of North Korea's economy has resulted in widespread starvation; in 2011, a joint UN survey estimated that over six million North Koreans urgently needed international food assistance to avoid hunger-related death. Nevertheless, the North Korean government's attempts at suppressing its citizenry's knowledge of the outside world have failed; North Koreans learn anyway through their consumption of black-market electronic gadgets and DVDs smuggled from China. Most North Koreans know that life is different beyond borders, and if the Communist Party wishes to remain in power, they must recognize the advantages of opening-up and incorporating some free-market strategies as The Chinese Communist Party has already shown.

Motivating Questions

This project studies the wide range of applications of SNS (Social Network System), which could be used as a communicative technology and a public service program in North and South Korea. We seek to find the inspiration of civic identity in polarized and deteriorated urban environments by exploring possible public network systems in physical and virtual spaces with motivating questions as follows:

-What is the framework of a new media landscape in order to facilitate a win-win relationship for both North and South Korea? The answer to this question would somehow accommodate the different political and economic expectations of the two countries.

- What kind of urban network systems and services based on citizenry empowerment could function as fundamental and sustainable urban design tool to contribute to the architectural environment?

- What type of collaborative democracy would emerge that reflects both cultures, local finances, civil societies, and public identities?

- How can a social network system be organized to stimulate space flexibility beyond the limitations of the virtual and actual territories? Could it offer the entire community a way to share and embrace the differences between the two countries and practice the notion of social empathy in everyday experience?

Summary of Research

To join the private and public spaces of North and South Korea, we will create urban systems that incorporate social media and appropriate architectural interfaces. Although the web access will be carefully monitored and strictly focused on communication between the North and South, the project will recognize the expansion of perception of the urban space, prioritize spatial designs that focus on the relationships of public urban nodes, and experiment with multiple functions (financial, cultural, social, environmental, and institutional) of social media and communicative technologies applied to four public interfaces (market, subway station, street, and plaza) in Pyongyang and Seoul.

Understanding this political complexity posed by the disparate social and physical structures on both sides, this project consists of three main bodies formulated by time frames with themes:

1) PAST: Before the Division: Seeking the justification for this project and possible users and clients (social science and geopolitical approaches); Comparative Research

- Relationships between Korea and other Southeast Asian countries through their geopolitical and economic positions in history

- Research on the transformation of public spaces depending on different social realms in North and South Korea

2) PRESENT: The Cold War Confrontation: Analysis of existing fragmented and vulnerable networks in the two Koreas and finding shared opportunities of cultural and socioeconomic elements and architectural environments where those elements could be implemented (technological and urban design approaches)

- Development of civic interactions of networked public communication

- Research on Internet based e-commerce networks

- Case studies of projects and architecture focusing on public interfaces; theories of digital evolution

3) FUTURE: Maintaining the Mediated-opening of the North: Discovery of entrepreneurial, cultural, and social opportunities which will be brought about in urban nodes of both sides (urban growth modeling approaches)

- This part explore what has happened so far and how it might provide lessons for future policy between North and South Korea and offer directions for establishing regulations for both individuals and societies to coexist in the 21st century. We introduce four figures in this book. The first one is about the development of Social progress in South Korea in PRESENT part, and the other figures are the photo montages of market, street, and plaza in FUTRE part.

Ethical issues & Applicability

This project hopes to make society move forward from fence-mending to establishing substantive city systems that could cope effectively with different kinds of political and economic tensions in the future of global society. Further developed methodologies will also define the meanings and roles of technology and social media implemented in specific conditions, such as psychologically and financially impoverished societies or war-stricken and politically divided states.

Future Scenarios

경계 없는 곳에서 살다
: 남북한 도시 디자인 전략으로서 소셜 미디어의 활용방안

조세진 & 이수빈

—

조세진은 건축가이며 어반 디자이너(Urban Designer)이다.
그녀는 뉴욕 P.lArt 에 출강하며 Faking the City 라는
어바니즘(Urbanism) 수업을 가르치고 있으며,
Asia Initiatives Organization에서 연구원으로 일하고 있다.
그녀는 전남대학교에서 건축학을 전공하고 컬럼비아대학교에서
도시설계 석사학위를 받았다. 현재 그녀가 진행하고 있는
연구 프로젝트는 가상공간과 물리적 건축환경의 연계를 통한
공공 도시스템의 발전이다. 그녀는 뉴욕, 한국, 가나, 인도 등에서
공간 정보와 통신기술의 적용을 이용한 다양한 건축프로젝트를
참여하고 있다.

이수빈은 현재 건축도시공간 연구소 아우리에서
연구인턴으로 일하고 있다. 건축도시공간 연구소(auri)에서
연구인턴으로 일하며 도시 설계의 역사적 맥락 속에서
건축물과 가로 공간의 변화에 관한 연구를 진행중이다.
그녀는 경북대학교 건축공학과를 졸업하고
컬럼비아대학교에서 도시설계 석사학위를 받았다.
그녀는 남북관계에 대한 꾸준한 관심과 연구를 바탕으로
공간의 소통을 통한 남북한 교류의 방법론에 대하여
연구를 지속해오고 있다.

주제

이 프로젝트는 "분단된 민족과 서로 다른 사회적 이념. 관점을 통합할 수 있는 새로운 형태의 도시 디자인 활용방안을 생각해본다면?"이라는 의문에서 시작하게 되었다. 21세기의 새로운 소통 시스템인 소셜 네트워크 시스템(Social Network System)에 의해 생겨난 새로운 미디어 경관은 우리 세대의 문화적, 경제적, 심지어 정치적 변화까지 가져왔다. 이러한 변화들은 이제 도시의 물리적 공간의 형태뿐만 아니라 시민들의 사회적 관계 또한 변화 시키고 있다. 반면, 미디어의 발전과 함께 등장한 정치적 미디어 프로파간다는 변화하는 자유로운 공공 장소성에 대비되어 억압적인 건축 환경의 역설적 관계를 구축한다. 이 프로젝트의 목적은 시민들이 만들어가는 민주적인 건축 환경을 구축하기 위해 새로운 미디어 기술이 도시 시스템 속에서 어떻게 사용될 수 있는지를 보여주고자 함이다. 또한 이 프로젝트는 자유로운 대중담론이 가능한 도시환경(대중의 소통이 자유로이 일어나며 그것을 반영할 수 있는 건축적 환경)이 사회적, 경제적 발전을 도모할 수 있으며, 나아가 남북한이 갖고 있는 건축환경과 정보기술을 적절히 활용하면서 서로가 소통-공유할 수 있는 사회적 공간을 구축하게 된다면 북한 개방정책의 발전 가능성 또한 보여줄 수 있다는 신념을 전제로 한다.

배경과 쟁점

이 시대의 북한은 세계 속에서 이미 신뢰를 잃어 버린 나라로 남아있음에도 불구하고 그들에게는 같은 언어와 역사, 오랜 문화를 공유하는 적어도 하나의 이웃 나라인 대한민국이 있다. 그리고 이 대한민국에는 북한주민들이 글로벌 경제에 참여하는 것에 대하여 큰 관심을 갖고 환영하는 사람들이 많다는 것 또한 사실이며 다행이라 할만 한 일이다. 우리나라는 세계적인 IT 주도국이며 관련한 공간 정보, 네트워크 기술발전과 함께 참여적 개방 사회로 변모해왔다. 하지만 남북한 사이에서 지속적으로 이루어진 변변한 남북대화 정책이나 제도는 없었다고 볼 수 있다. 그 중 그나마 가장 성공적이었던 남북한 공동개발 구역인 개성공단을 살펴볼 수 있지만 이 또한 지속적인 운영은 되지 못하고 두 나라 간의 정치적 환경에 따라 그 운영은 좌지우지 되어온 것이 사실이다.

앞에서 말한 바와 같이 우리는 남북한 사이 소통의 부재로 인한 문제점들이 존재한다는 사실을 알게 되었다. 다음으로는 이 프로젝트에 임하게 된 간략한 배경설명과 함께 이 연구의 진정성을 소개하고자 한다.

　　-소셜 네트워크를 통한 혁신적 사건들이 글로벌 사회를 이어주는 동안 소통 매개의 부재는 두 나라간의 분단을 지속시켰다. 물리적으로 분단된 남북한 사회는 서로 다른 문화적·사회적 이념과 함께 더욱 멀어지고 있다.
　　-이 이념적 적대감은 사이버 공간을 통하여 대중들을 더욱 분열시켰다
　　-온라인과 오프라인에서 미디어를 통한 정치적 선전은 대중들의 공공 공간을 파괴하고 남북 간의 정치적 대치상황 또한 지속시켰다.

조선민주주의인민공화국은(북한의 정식명칭) 정치적·경제적 고립으로 인해 오랜 시간동안 고통을 겪어왔다. 이 "은자의 왕국"이 살아남기 위해서는 사회적·경제적 개방을 도모해야만 한다. 북한은 남한으로부터 기업적·문화적 성장동력을 받을 필요성과 가능성이 있으므로, 두 나라의 중재된, 그리고 면밀히 관찰된 개방의 과정을 거쳐야 한다. 이 프로젝트에서는 남한과 독점적으로 연결된 인터넷 허브(hub)를 통한 소셜 네트워크 시스템이 하나의 도시시스템으로 발전될 수 있는지를 살펴보고 이렇게 구축된 몇몇의 퍼블릭 스페이스(public space)를 디자인 해봄으로써 연구 가능성을 실현시켜 보고자 한다. 전쟁과 계속되는 대치상황으로 인한 적대감에도 불구하고, 많은 대한민국 국민들은 다양한 방법의 남북한 화해와 소통에 참여하길 기다리고 있다. 이와 같은 애국심의 일환으로서의 동기 이외에도 북한은 개방 시장의 기업적 측면에서 큰 관심을 갖고 볼 수 있다. 마지막으로 이 은자의 나라(은둔국가)에 대한 호기심 자체만가지고도 시장 사업의 원동력이 될 것이다.

하지만, 북한은 남한보다 이 제안을 심사숙고해야 할 강력한 이유가 있다. 그것은 바로 북한 경제의 무능력한 경영은 북한 전역의 기아 현상을 초래했다는 것인데, 2011년 UN 합동조사에 의하면, 6백만 명 이상의 북한주민들이 기아로 인한 사망을 벗어나기 위한 국제원조가 필요하다고 밝혀졌다. 더욱이, 일반 시민들의 외부 세상에 관한 정보를 억제하려는 북한 정부의 시도는 실패로 돌아가고 있으며 북한 정부 또한 중국을 통해 밀수되는 전자기기와 DVD등의 소비가 북한과 중국의 암거래시장 이루어지고 있다는 것을 이미 인지하고 있다. 대부분의 북한 주민들은 분단 선을 넘어 존재하는 삶이 다르다는 것을 알고 있으며 북한 정부 또한 그들의 공산체제를 유지하기 위해서는 개방사회의 이점과 병합된 자유시장 체제의 이익들을 인지하고 그 전략들을 수용하여야만 한다.

동기부여를 위한 질문들

이 프로젝트는 기본적으로 남북한 소통수단 뿐만 아니라 공공서비스 프로그램으로서 이용될 수 있는 소셜네트워크 시스템의 광범위한 기술적용에 대한 연구이다. 나아가 아래의 질문들과 함께 물리적 공간과 가상공간에서 적용될수 있는 공공 네트워크 시스템의 적용 가능성을 탐색해보고 분단으로 인해 양극화된 도시환경 속의 시민정체성에 대해 고찰해볼 수 있는 디자인 영감을 찾아보고자 한다.

　　-남한과 북한간의 원원 관계를 가져올 수 있는 새로운 미디어 경관 구조는 무엇일까? 이 질문에 대한 답은 두 나라의 이질적인 정치상황과 경제구조를 모두 수용하는 방법일 것이다.
　　-건축적 환경 발전에 이바지하기 위해서 시민역량제고(on citizenry empowerment)에 바탕을 둔, 근본적이고 지속 가능한 도시설계 도구로서 이용되어지는 도시 네트워크 시스템이나 서비스들은 어떤 것이 있을까?
　　-두 나라의 문화, 지역경제, 시민사회 그리고 공공의 정체성을 반영할수 있는 협의적 민주주의의 형태는 어떻게 나타날 수 있을까?
　　-가상과 현실 영역의 한계를 벗어나 유연한 공간영역을 만들기 위한 소셜네트워크 시스템은 어떻게 구성될 수 있을까? 이 시스템이 두 나라간의 차이를 수용하는 통합된 하나의 공동체를 만들어내고 이 공동의 장소안에서 시민들이 서로 다름을 인정하면서 그들의 일상 생활 속에서 활용 가능한 도시시스템으로서 발전될 수 있을까?

연구 요약

남북한 도시의 (사적인 혹은 공공의) 공간을 연결하기 위하여 소셜 미디어와 건축적 인터페이스를 통합하는 도시 시스템을 제안한다. 비록 웹상의 내용이 어느 정도 검열이 됨을 전제로 하고 디자인 방향이 남북한의 소통에 집중이 되었더라도 다양한 소셜 미디어의 기능(경제적, 문화적, 사회적, 환경적, 교육적 기능)을 평양과 서울의 4개의의 공공 공간(시장, 지하철역, 거리, 광장)에 적용해보면서 도시공간의 확대가능성과 공공공간의 절점들간의 관계에 대해 연구해보고자 한다.

이 프로젝트는 양 국가의 서로 다른 사회적·물리적 구조에서 나타나는 정치적 복잡성의 이해를 돕고자 한정된 시간의 틀과 주제를 가지고 세 가지의 본문으로 나뉘어져 있다.

1)과거(분단이전): 이 프로젝트의 정당성을 찾아 보고 잠재적 사용자와 고객을 찾아본다.(비교분석방법의 접근)
　　－남북한과 동남아시아 국가 간의 관계를 역사를 통한 지정학적, 경제적 위치를 살펴봄으로써 연구.
　　－남북한의 서로 다른 사회적 영역과 함께 발달된 건축적 공공공간의 변화 연구

2)현재(남북 냉전의 대치상황): 기존의 분열되고 위태로운 두 나라 사이 관계망에 대한 분석을 해보고 두 나라 사이의 공유할 수 있는 문화적·사회경제적 유사들이 변한 가능성에 대하여 이들이 실현될 수 있는 건축 환경을 디자인해봄으로써 연구해본다.
　　－공공 통신네트워크를 통한 시민 간의 상호협력의 발전
　　－인터넷 네트워크를 통한 전자 상거래 연구
　　－디지털 진화와 관련한 공공 인터페이스 구축을 연구한 건축 프로젝트 사례조사

3)미래(북한의 중재된 개방 지속): 도시 성장 모델링 접근을 통하여 본 남북한의 도시 결절 점에서 이루어질 기업, 문화, 사회적 차원의 기회를 찾아본다.
　　－이 미래부분 연구에서는 현재까지 어떠한 사건들이 있어 왔는지를 알아보고 이를 통해 남북한의 정책들을 살펴본다. 또한 21세기에 개인과 사회 모두가 공존하기 위한 가이드라인(guideline)을 확립하기 위하여 미래의 남북한 소통정책 방향성을 모색해 보고자 한다. 우리는 이책에서 소개될 4가지의 그래픽을 통해 이러한 개념을 도식화해 보았다. 첫 번째는 '현재' 연구와 관련하여 "소셜 네트워크를 통한 남한의 사회적 발전상"에 관련한 다이어그램이고, 나머지 3개의 도판은 '미래' 연구와 관련해 시장, 거리, 광장에서 이루어지는 미래의 남북한 소통의 연구가 어떻게 실현되는지를 보여주는 아이디어 콜라주이다.

윤리적 쟁점과 적용가능성

이 프로젝트를 통하여 서로 다른 사회가 단순한 관계 회복을 시도하는 방법에서 벗어나 정치적, 경제적 긴장을 능동적으로 완화시킬 수 있는 지속 가능한 도시 시스템을 구축함으로써 우리 사회가 한 발 더 앞으로 전진할 수 있기를 바란다. 앞으로의 연구 방향으로는 IT기술과 소셜 미디어의 적용 가능성에 대한 연구가 이루어지면서 다양하고 발전된 디자인 방안들이 고안될 것이고 이 방안들은 사회심리적으로나 경제적으로 불안한 사회 안에서, 전쟁의 타격을 받은 지역, 그리고 정치적으로 분열된 특정 상황들을 중심으로 하여 그 연구방향과 가능성이 탐구될 것이다.

Future Scenarios

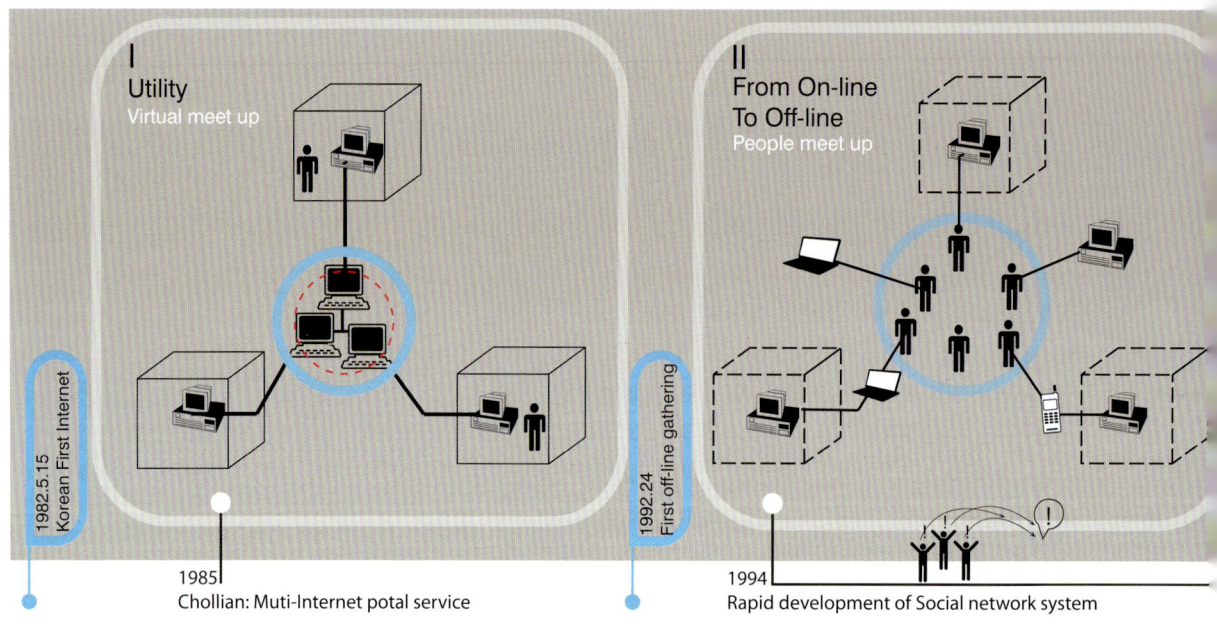

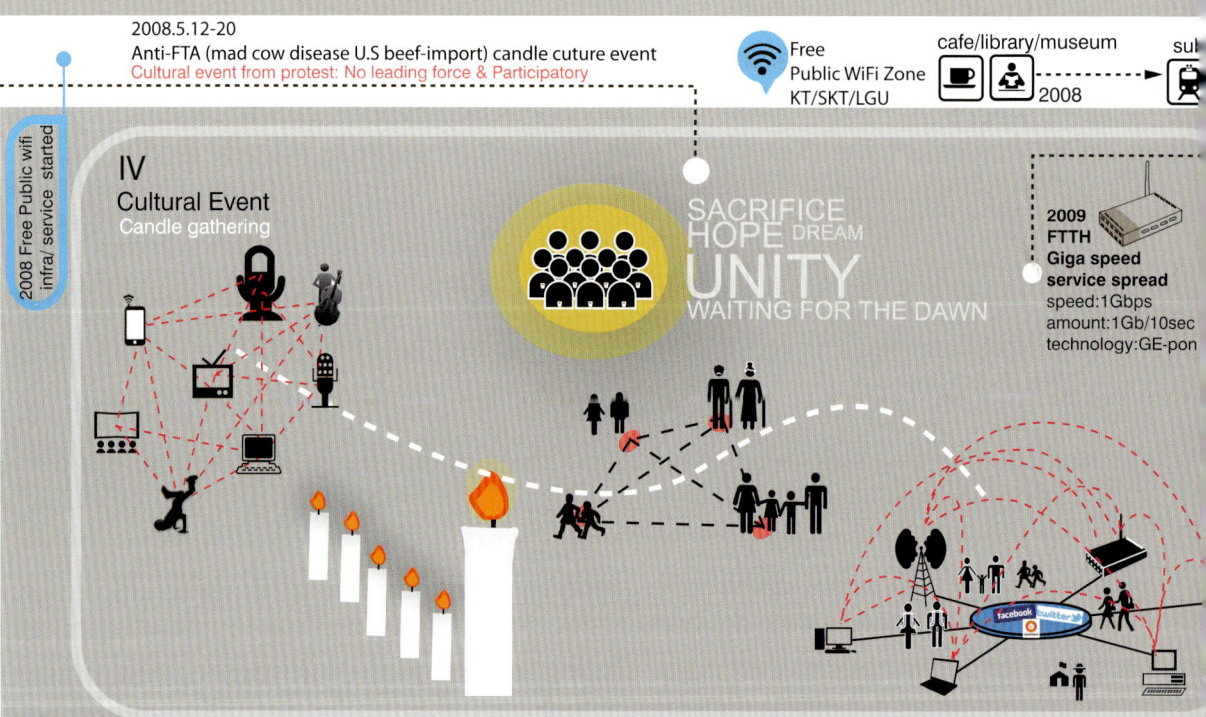

Timeline_ Development & Characteristics of Forming Society with SNS
- How online community comes out to Offline?
- Progress of social and Internet infra structure development.

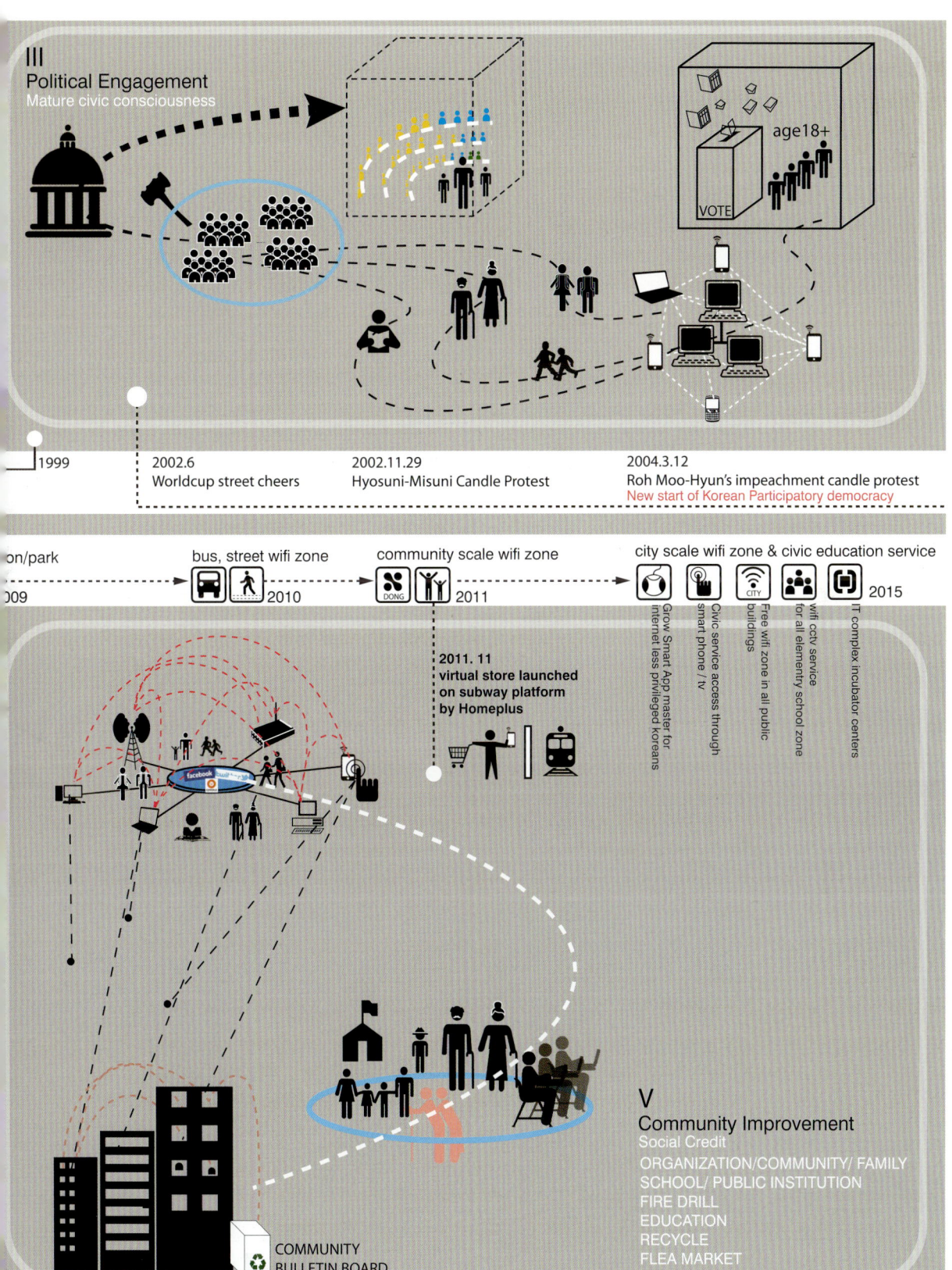

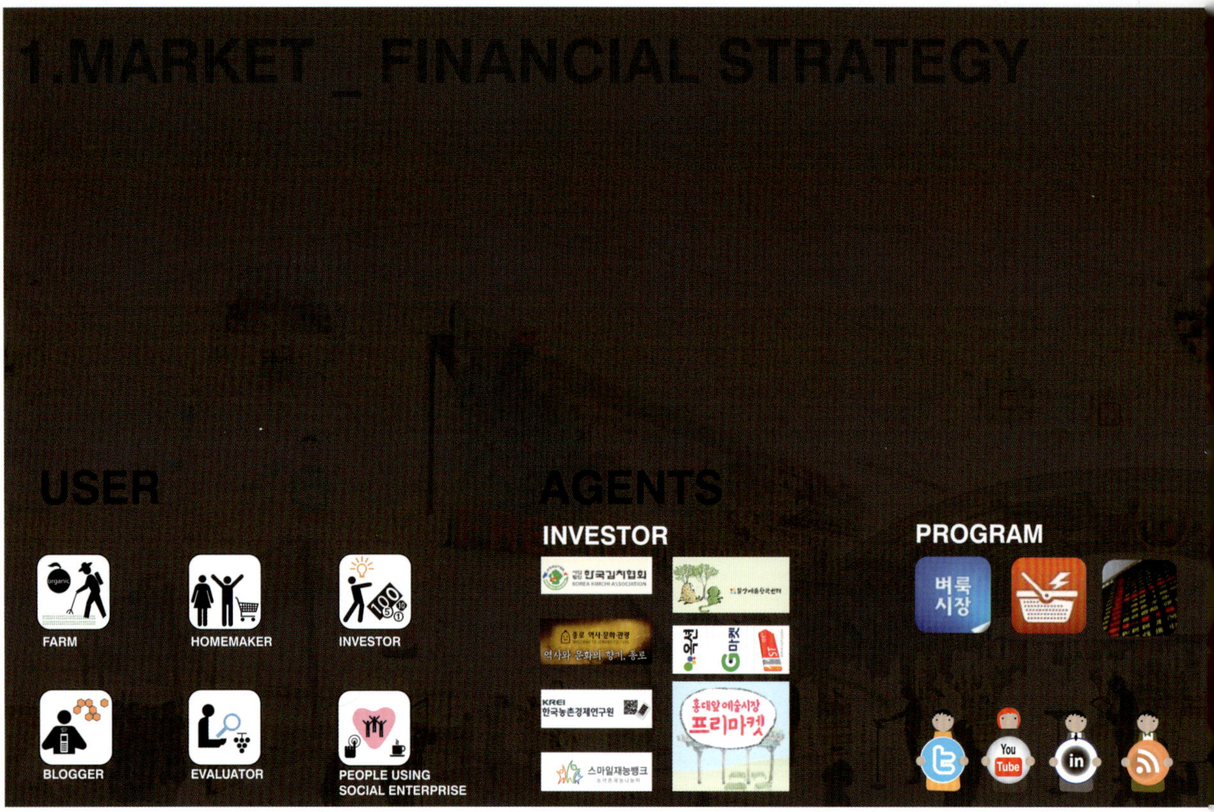
1.MARKET _ FINANCIAL STRATEGY
USER
AGENTS
INVESTOR
PROGRAM
FARM
HOMEMAKER
INVESTOR
BLOGGER
EVALUATOR
PEOPLE USING
SOCIAL ENTERPRISE
한국김치협회
KREI
한국농촌경제연구원
스마일재능뱅크
홍대앞 예술시장
프리마켓
벼룩
시장
You
Tube
in

PUBLIC NODE 1: MARKET **PUBLIC U-Commerce AUCTION in PyungYang & Seoul**

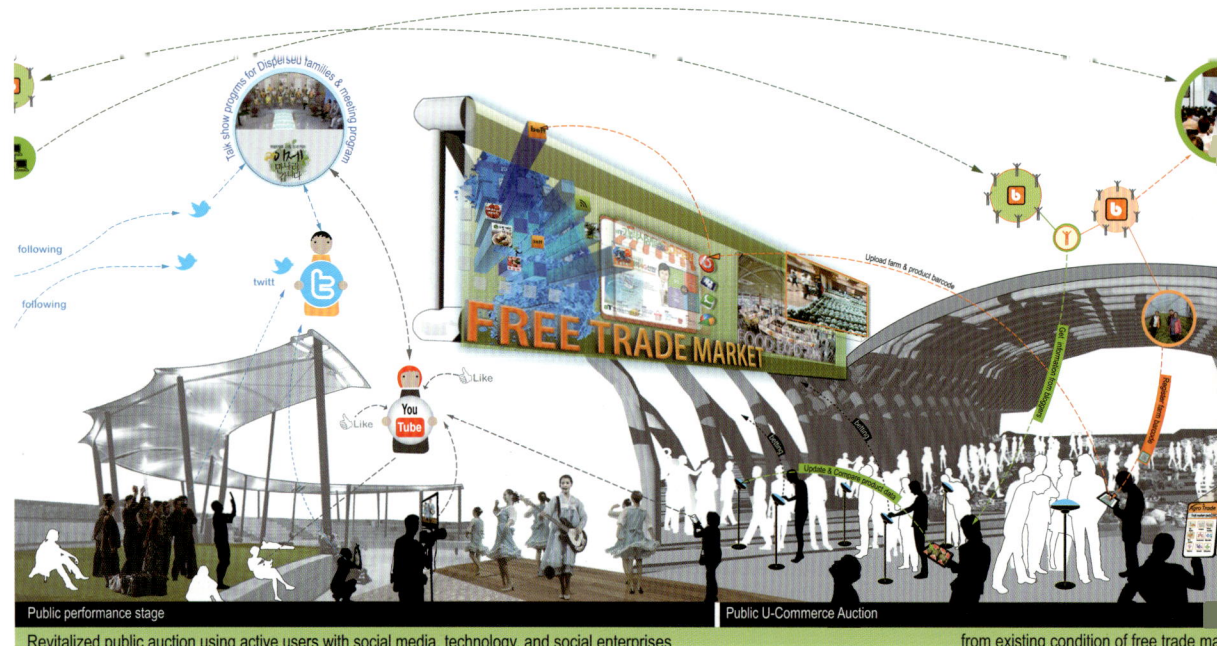

Talk show programs for Dispersed families & meeting program
following
following
twitt
Like
Like
You
Tube
FREE TRADE MARKET
Upload farm & product barcode
Get information from bloggers
Register farm barcode
Update & Compare product data
betting
betting
Public performance stage
Public U-Commerce Auction
Revitalized public auction using active users with social media, technology, and social enterprises
from existing condition of free trade ma

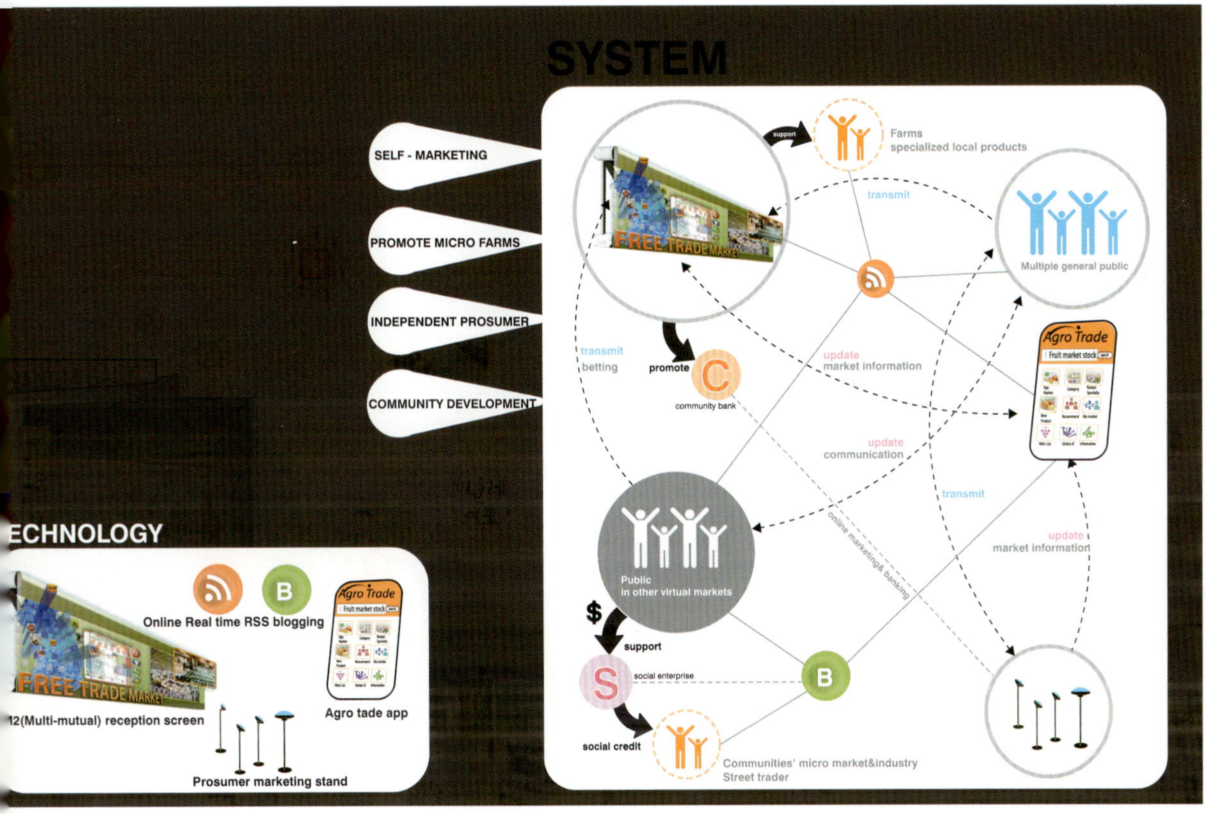
SYSTEM
SELF - MARKETING
PROMOTE MICRO FARMS
INDEPENDENT PROSUMER
COMMUNITY DEVELOPMENT
ECHNOLOGY
Online Real time RSS blogging
Agro Trade
Agro tade app
12(Multi-mutual) reception screen
Prosumer marketing stand
support
Farms
specialized local products
transmit
Multiple general public
transmit
betting
promote
community bank
update
market information
update
communication
transmit
update
market information
online marketing& banking
Public
in other virtual markets
support
social enterprise
social credit
Communities' micro market&industry
Street trader

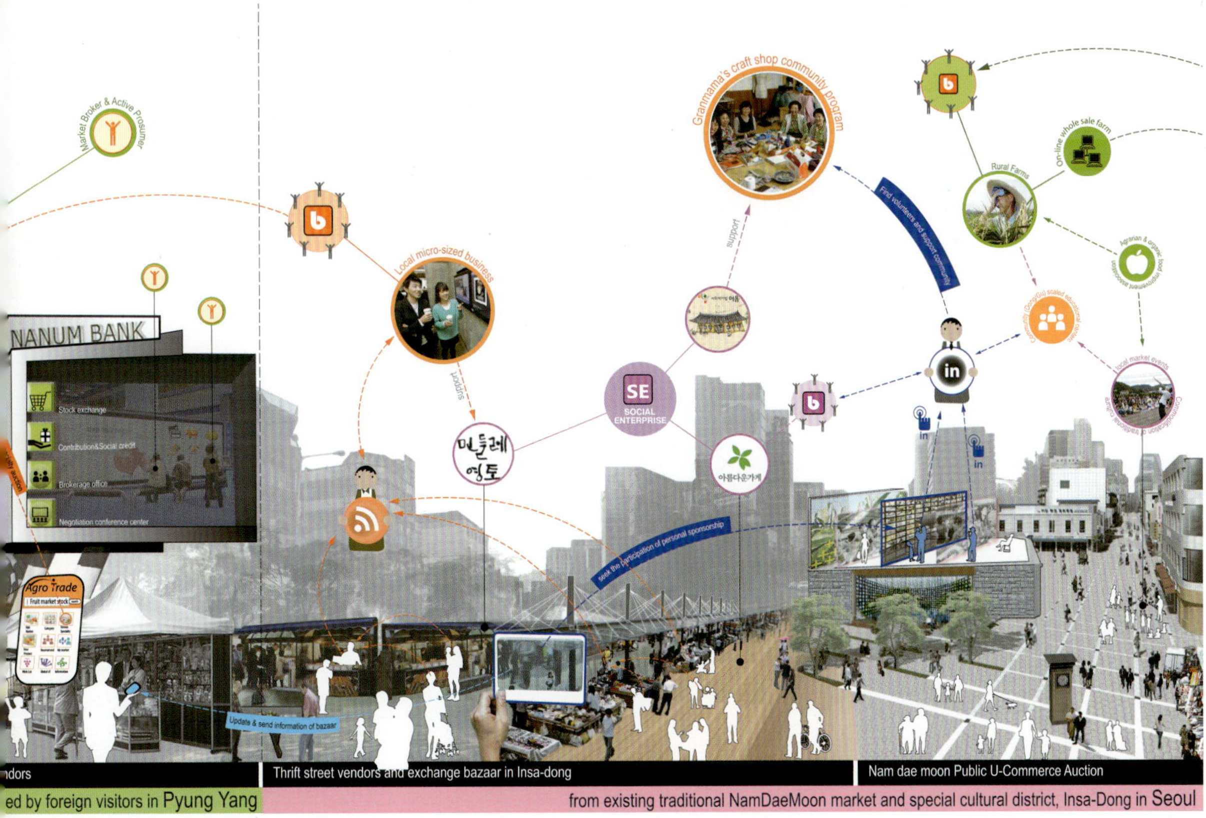
Market Broker & Active Prosumer
NANUM BANK
Stock exchange
Contribution&Social credit
Brokerage office
Negotiation conference center
Local micro-sized business
support
Granmama's craft shop community program
support
Find volunteers and support community
Rural Farms
On-line whole sale farm
SE
SOCIAL ENTERPRISE
아름다운가게
seek the participation of personal sponsorship
Update & send information of bazaar
ndors
Thrift street vendors and exchange bazaar in Insa-dong
Nam dae moon Public U-Commerce Auction
ed by foreign visitors in Pyung Yang
from existing traditional NamDaeMoon market and special cultural district, Insa-Dong in Seoul

Future Scenarios

■ User / Program   ■ Agents

■ Public Node _ Street

   MEDIA Wall_Spontaneous interaction between **PyungYang** & **Seoul**

Street screen will be connected automatically with the SNS services to provide more information of the site, monuments, different cultures shown on the screen by smart phone, tablet pc and etc. By using the these devices, the screen will be act as a gateway to the other city which will allow North and South Koreans to follow each other

- **Public Node _ Plaza**
  MEDIA FOG_INSTANT MESSAGES & EVENT between PyungYang & Seoul

People send their un-filtered(semi-filtered), instant, and desirable text messages to plazas. This makes the cultural and language gap between South and North Korea narrowed or closed in further time period. Before unification, this systme could be semi filtered to be so safe and exact meanings people have. And after unification any sized plazas and squares can be implemented by events and shared communication such as performing flash mobs, concerts, cheering events and educational lectures.

THE MEMORY PALACE: ARCHITECTURE AS A MNEMONIC DEVICE

Jungon Kim

—

Jungon Kim is a graduate of the Master of Architecture program at Harvard GSD. He has earned his undergraduate degree of B.S. in Engineering from Seoul National University. His Master's thesis focuses on the memory that is strongly linked to the concepts of space and imagery. He pursues architectural space in Pyongyang that serve as a remedy for today's tendency of personal and social amnesia.

Memory, both personal and collective, is strongly linked to the concepts of space and imagery. Thus, architectural space and the image that it provides can serve as a remedy for today's tendency of personal and social amnesia.

Argument

The argument starts with stating the relevance of the topic of memory in today's world. With the advent of the information age, acquiring information has become as easy as a tap of a finger. However, the ubiquity, convenience and the speed of accessing information has led our whole generation to experience symptoms of amnesia, where people do not, and therefore, cannot memorize things anymore due to the fact that we can always look it up again.

So then why do we even need to memorize things anymore? Especially in a world where we can access information whenever, and wherever we want to? On the issue of the importance of memorizing, Quintus Miller states, "We interpret the perceptions we gain through our senses on the basis of what we remember. The experiences that steadily accumulate throughout our lives give us the means to decode what we perceive and put it into a larger context." (Miller, 2012). A similar perspective comes from Joshua Foer, the 2006 US memory championship champion, where he says, "Our memories are not storehouses [...] memories are always with us, always shaping how we move through the world and how we perceive it, how we make judgments." (Foer, 2012). The society's critique on the current personal memory loss can also be easily seen through numerous publications and merchandize regarding memorization improvement. The desperate or even frantic public reaction towards memory loss indicates that there is a value in memorizing even in the information era.

The idea of relating memory with space and images goes way back in history. Before the invention of print, practitioners of the ancient art of memory developed elaborate teaching and learning systems based on imaginary spaces furnished with mental reminders. Ancient Roman orators for example, in memorizing their long passages of speeches would deliberately link striking images that would remind themselves of parts of the speech with a certain space that they are familiar with. Later, on delivering their speeches, they would imagine walking through the space, furnished with the mental reminders to help them recall the speech without forgetting the content or the order (Yates, 1966). The so-called "Memory palace" system lead to the designing of actual spaces such as the Memory Theatre. Designed by the Italian philosopher Giulio Camillo in the 16th C., the sole purpose of the theatre was to help memorize. Records do not show how exactly this Memory Theatre operated, but by standing on the stage and gazing at the different images placed on the seating, the person would imprint certain memories onto the images and somehow by doing this, the person's ability to memorize will improve drastically (Yates, 1966).

This system of enhancing one's memory through a technique of impressing 'places' and 'images' on memory is still used nowadays. 2011 US memory champion Nelson Dellis used the memory palace technique to memorize the random order of a deck of cards in only 63 seconds (Simpson, 2012). Joshua Foer, in his book "Moonwalking with Einstein", also explains how this particular technique of memorizing helped him to win the 2006 US memory championship (Foer, 2011). To sum up, the essence of the memory palace method consists of a certain idiosyncratic spatial configuration that has a striking image projected onto it that serves as a mental reminder.

Memories however, are not only formed within an individual. French Philosopher Maurice Halbwachs argues that memories are reconstructed under the influence of the society. As a "totality of thoughts", collective memory is a memory formed in relation to its context which leads to sharing of a memory in the same context (Halbwachs, 1992). A collective memory is also strongly linked to a sense of place and image. A certain space or place within a society, like a structure of the city, can serve as a memory palace of the collective memory of the society. Rossi says that "One can say that the city itself is the collective memory for its people, and like the memory it is associated with objects and places. The city is the locus of the collective memory."(Rossi, 1982). A recent project by the Swiss artist Corinne Vionnet shows a good example of how places in the city can be a locus of collective memory. From online sharing sites she sources her material of hundreds of similar snapshots of landmarks and overlays them as transparent images. The results are slightly blurred, but recognizable images of the landmarks of the top snap shot locations around the world. The images evoke a sense of a collective memory. They quite literally illustrate this idea of hundreds of people sharing the same experience. In this case it is having to see the same thing, or more precise having taking almost the same picture.

Collective memories can also be affected by the information and media technology. Huyssen argues that "Both personal and social memory today are affected by an emerging new structure of temporality generated by the quickening pace of material life on the one hand and by the acceleration of media images and information on the other."(Huyssen, 1995). Another factor that accelerates the loss of collective memory is the rapid pace of ruthless development that happens around the world. Traditional structures passed down over centuries are so effortlessly demolished to make room for new crystalline cities. In the process, people are robbed of their past which gave them a foothold as a society and as individuals. The rapid change of city scenery also affects the development of collective memory. Where the fate of the city's built environment is determined by the market system, the society's collective memory is at stake. A lack of permanence is also lack of memory. Moreover, the loss of collective memory is problematic because it can affect the historical view of a certain nation or even threaten the identity of a nation. Cities like Berlin that are charged with historic sites constantly struggles between the dilemma between historic preservation, national identity, and development. 50 years after the Japanese Colonial era, the South Korean government decided to demolish the iconic Japanese General Government building. Live broadcasting the explosive demolition almost as if it's a national celebration, the event could have been a historical milestone in the nation's history, but the effectiveness or the validity of such decision is yet on debate.

Site

The chosen site is Pyongyang, the capital of North Korea in the premise of the scenario where Korea is re-united. Pyongyang is the only city of North Korea which the country officially exposes to international media. Almost like a showcase city, Pyongyang is filled with monuments and iconic architecture that are purposefully built to show off the superiority of Socialism and the glorification of their dictating leader. In case of a unified Korea, Pyongyang will be an interesting testing ground for an architectural intervention that deals with the many different aspects regarding the issues of memory, may it be remembering, forgetting and reproducing of it.

The specimen site chosen within Pyongyang is the Kim Il Sung Square. Named after the first leader of North Korea, who is also the Grand Father of the current Kim Jung Un, this site is located in the heart of Pyongyang and is a place where many political and symbolic activities of North Korea takes place. The idea of the architectural intervention is to build an inhabitable wall to demarcate the area by wrapping around the square. The project can be discussed largely in two different aspects of memory which is the Collective Memory, and the Personal Memory.

Collective Memory

The building is a view port that frames the vista of the city, becoming a focal point of all the city's icons and vignettes. As a spectator of the city, the building highlights the importance of the existing city, its landscape and imagery and brings it together to a culminating point. In a way, it becomes an archive of the city's scenery.

The building itself by its monumental scale also becomes an icon within the city. It's new presence within the city could become a symbolic mark for the new memories that will start accumulating within the Pyongyang of a new unified Korea. As an anchor point for the city's collective memory, the building's presence should endure the ephemerality of today's physical environment that is instigated by the rapid pace of development. For this matter, the building achieves permanence of its physicality by embracing and, in a way, using its temporal condition.

Japanese shrines for example, are rebuilt every 20 years in order to maintain it-self fresh and new. The actual physicality of the architecture might not be more than 20 years old, but through the process, the presence of the building can last for thousands of years (Hvass, 1998). Also, through this process, the act of rebuilding itself is celebrated and becomes a ritual. This ritual does not only address the issue of preservation, but also a sense of collective memory. Likewise, the proposed building takes on a system where it disassembles and moves on to reassemble at a different site every 25 years. In a time span of a generation, the building might be in a different location with different proportions but yet remains as an anchor point for the city and its people's collective memory.

To make this possible, the building is designed as an assembly of certain numbers of different units. Through the way in which different units connect to each other, the building's interior forms differently, may it be circulation, wall formation etc.. By the fact that the building's spatial configuration can change by the way it assembles, the process of building up the building is highlighted and becomes celebrated.

The building also can instigate and reproduce new collective memories. The monumentality of its presence could activate the site to be occupied with different activities from what it originally was used to be. New types of activities that happens on the site will to start to imbue new social memories on the area.

Personal Memory

For the retaining of personal memory, the building refers back to the method of the memory palace, where one walks through spaces that are furnished with imprinted imagery. With a simple unit of one stairway and walls the unit is rotated and mirrored to create ten different units with an exception of one unit with only a stairway and one with no elements. Four of these units combined create one room with up to four different stairways and wall combinations.

The execution of this combination creates an array of possible room configuration. Each possessing idiosyncratic spatial configuration which consist of walls and stairs. In comprehending each room, a mnemonic technique called the "major system" is adopted, which is a system used to aid in memorizing numbers. The system works by converting numbers into consonant sounds, then into words by adding vowels. The system works on the principle that images can be remembered more easily than numbers. For instance, in memorizing the number "3.1415927" also known as Pi, it could be understood as "MTR, TL, PNK" and then converted to "MeTeoR TaiL PiNK". Then the person will imagine a meteor with a pink tail to remember the number (Wikipedia contributors, 2013).

The major system can be used to understand the 10 different units that compose each room of the building, where the user can walk into a room and immediately convert the configuration of the space into a word, and in turn, an image. Architectural components are now understood in terms of semiotics. This ties back to the early explanation of the memory palace system, where a certain space is used to project an image. In this case, the image can be generated by the space itself. The physical actuality of the space becomes synthesized with the projected imagery. The user of the building will move room after room, implanting images onto each room and eventually composing a narrative or a story which consists of each image. The process of memorizing each room is significant not only because it is a training session for the brain to memorize information more effectively, but also because it is a symbolic event that highlights the lost value of the act of memorizing. Moreover, after memorizing and eventually being familiar with the structure of the rooms, the individual can then start projecting his/her own memories and utilize the space as a personal memory palace.

Finally, by actually taking the stairs, one will ascend to an exterior space where the building frames certain vignettes of the city. The person can now project the image generated from the interior of the building onto the city scenery. This is the point where the collective memory and the personal memory blurs its boundaries where the city scenery is used as a backdrop to project a personal memory.

기억의 장소:
연상기호 장치로서의 건축

김중곤

―

김중곤은 하버드 대학교에서 건축학 석사학위를 취득하였으며, 서울대학교에서 지역시스템 공학 학사를 받았다. 그의 석사논문은 공간과 형상화의 개념과 연계된 기억에 초점을 맞추고 있다. 그의 프로젝트는 오늘날 개인과 사회의 기억상실화 되는 현상의 치유법으로 평양의 건축적 공간을 제안하고 있다.

개인 기억, 집단 기억을 비롯한 기억 전반은 공간, 이미지와 매우 밀접한 관계가 있다. 따라서 건축 공간과 그 건축이 생성하는 이미지(전경)는 현대의 만연한 개인적, 사회적 기억 상실에 대한 보완책을 제시할 수 있다.

배경

논의의 발단은 기억이라는 주제와 현대 사회와의 연관성에서부터 시작한다. 정보화 사회의 도래와 함께 정보에 대한 접근은 인류 문명사의 그 어느 때보다 쉽고 편리해졌다. 초고속 인터넷 망, 스마트 폰 등과 같은 문명의 이기(利器)의 힘을 빌어, 손가락 까딱 한 번이면 필요한 정보를 언제, 어디서든 접할 수 있는 것이 현대 사회이다. 그러나 이러한 정보 접근성의 편리함으로 인해 우리는 더는 정보를 기억하지 않아도 되고, 이 때문에 기억하는 능력을 잃는 지경에 이르렀다. 언제나 정보를 다시 찾아볼 수 있다는 생각 때문에 현대 인류는 전부 일종의 기억 상실증을 앓게 된 것이다.

그렇다면 우리가 이제는 정보를 기억할 필요가 있긴 한 걸까? 현대와 같이 우리가 원하는 때와 장소에서 항상 정보를 접할 수 있는 시대에 정보를 기억한다는 것이 의미가 있을까? 이러한 이슈에 대해 건축가 Quintus Miller는 "우리는 우리가 기억하고 있는 것들을 기반으로 우리가 지각하는 세상에 대한 이해를 수립한다. 우리가 꾸준히 경험하고 기억한 것들의 집적체는 우리가 새롭게 경험하는 것들을 이해하고 그것을 더 큰 그림에서 바라볼 수 있게 해준다." 라고 한다. 2006년 전미(全美) 기억력 대회(US Memory Championship) 우승자 Joshua Foer 또한 비슷한 의견이다. 그는 "우리의 기억은 단순히 정보 저장고가 아니다. … (중략) … 기억은 우리와 항상 함께 있으면서, 우리가 세상을 어떻게 지각하고 이해하는지, 어떤 판단을 내리는지를 결정한다."라고 했다. 현대 사회의 기억력 감퇴에 대한 불안감은 매년 쏟아져 나오는 기억력 향상 관련 서적들만 봐도 알 수 있다. 이러한 대중의 기억력에 대한 절박한 심정은 현대와 같은 정보화 시대에도 기억하는 것에 대한 가치가 중요하다는 것을 시사한다.

기억하는 것과 공간/이미지를 연관시키는 개념은 역사적으로 꽤 오래되었다. 인쇄술이 발명되기 이전, 학자들은 상상의 공간과 그 공간을 채우는 가상의 이미지를 통해 정보를 기억하는 구체적인 기술들을 개발하기도 하였다. 일례로 고대 로마 시대의 웅변가들은 긴 내용의 연설문을 기억하기 위해 그들이 익숙한 공간에다 연설문 각 부분의 내용이 떠오르게끔 하는 강력한 이미지들을 투영시키는 방법을 이용하였다. 이후, 그들은 웅변함과 동시에 머릿속으로 그 공간을 가상으로 걸어 다니는 상상을 하여, 각 공간에 투영된 이미지들을 마주침과 동시에 연설문의 각 내용이 차례대로 기억나게끔 하였다(Yates, 1966). 소위 "기억의 궁전 (Memory Palace)"이라 불리는 기술은 이후 실제 건축 공간을 설계하는데도 이용되었는데, 16세기 이탈리아의 철학가인 Giulio Camillo는 당시 "기억의 극장 (Memory Theatre)"을 설계해 전 유럽에 반향을 불러일으킨 바 있다고 기록되어있다. 기억의 극장은 오로지 기억을 잘하기 위한 용도로 제작되었는데, 구체적인 원리를 설명하는 문서는 남아있지 않지만, 극장에 입장한 사람이 무대 위에 서서 관객석에 비치된 다양한 형상과 이미지들을 바라보며 기억력을 향상하는 방법을 이용했다고 알려졌다(Yates, 1966).

이렇듯, 특정 공간 안에 특정 이미지를 투영시켜 기억을 돕는 기술은 오늘날에도 여전히 사용되고 있다. 2011년 전미(全美) 기억력 대회(US Memory Championship) 우승자 Nelson Dellis는 앞서 설명한 기억의 궁전법을 이용하여 랜덤하게 섞인 카드 한 데크를 단 63초 만에 외우기도 했다. Joshua Foer 또한 그의 저서 "Moonwalking with Einstein"에서 그가 어떻게 기억의 궁전법을 통해 2006년 기억력 대회의 우승자가 되었는지 기술하고 있다. 요약하자면 기억의 궁전법은 결국 "특정한 공간"안에, 기억을 연상시키는 "특정한 이미지"를 투영시킴으로써 작동한다. 그러나 기억은 단지 개인의 범위 내에서만 구성되는 것은 아니다. 프랑스의 철학가 Maurice Halbwachs의 이론을 빌리면, 기억은 사회의 영향으로 재구성되기도 한다. 소위 "집단 기억"이라는 개념으로서, 같은 환경 내의 사람들은 같은 기억을 공유하기도 한다. 집단 기억 또한 공간과 이미지라는 개념과 밀접한 연관이 있다. 도시구조와 같은 사회 차원의 공간이나 장소는 집단 기억을 위한 기억의 궁전이 될 수 있다. 이탈리아 건축가이자 건축 이론가인 Aldo Rossi는 "도시 그 자체가 시민을 위한 집단 기억이 될 수 있다. 그리고 개인 기억과 마찬가지로 그 기억은 사물과 장소와 연관되어 있다. 도시는 집단 기억의 저장소이다."라고 한다. 스위스의 미술가 Corinne Vionnet의 최근작은 도시의 장소가 어떻게 집단 기억의 저장소가 될 수 있는지 잘 보여준다. 그는 온라인 공유 사이트를 통해 얻은 도시 내의 같은 랜드마크를 찍은 수백 장의 서로 다른 사진을 겹쳐 놓았다. 그 결과 나오는 사진 속의 형상은 살짝 흐릿하긴 하지만 명백히 그것이 세계의 어떤 랜드마크를 나타내는지 알아볼 수 있게 한다. 이는 각각의 사진들이 서로 같은 장소에서 비슷한 각도와 거리에서 촬영되었다는 것을 암시한다. 수많은 사진이 겹쳐진 특이한 형상의 이미지를 보고 있자면 각각의 사진들을 촬영한 사람들의 집단 기억을 보고 있는 것과 같은 느낌이 든다. 시간은 각자 다르겠지만, 그들은 모두 같은 공간에서 같은 건축적 이미지를 보고 같은 경험을 공유한 것이다.

개인의 기억과 마찬가지로 집단 기억 또한 현대 사회의 미디어와 정보화로 인해 영향을 받는다. 독일의 학자 Andreas Huyssen은 "개인의 기억뿐 아니라 집단의 기억 또한 현대 사회의 빠르게 소비되는 이미지와 정보, 빨라진 생활 리듬과 그로 인한 일회성, 순간성 등에 영향을 받는다."라고 한다. 집단 기억의 상실을 가속화 하는 또 다른 요소는 전 세계에서 일어나고 있는 급속하고 무자비한 도시개발이다. 수 세기를 거쳐 계승되어 온 전통적인 도시 구조는 새롭고 현대적인 도시를 개발한다는 핑계로 너무나도 쉽게 파괴되어버린다. 이 과정에서 그 도시의 시민들은 그들의 집단적인, 그리고 개인적인 생활 터전이었던 과거를 잔인하게 도둑맞는다. 급격한 도시 전경의 변화 또한 집단 기억의 형성을 저해킨다. 시장 경제 논리에 의해 빠른 속도로 진행되는 도시 개발은 그 도시의 전경을 기억의 저장소로 삼았던 시민들의 집단 기억을 말살해 버린다. 지속성이 없다는 것은 결국 기억이 없다는 것과 같은 의미이기 때문이다. 더구나 이러한 집단 기억의 부재는 국가의 역사관, 그리고 근본적인 국가관까지 위협할 수 있기 때문에 큰 문제가 될 수 있다. 독일의 베를린과 같이 역사적으로 의미 있고 중요한 공간들이 가득한 도시들은 끊임없이 역사적 보존, 국가 정체성, 그리고 도시 개발이라는 가치들 사이에서 갈등한다. 우리나라 정부는 일제 강점기를 겪은 지 약 50년 후인 1993년, 일제 통치의 상징적인 건물 중 하나인 조선 총독부 청사를 철거하기로 하였다. 우리나라 역사에 있어서 상징적이고 의미 있는 사건이었기에 마치 나라의 축제처럼 조선 총독부 청사를 폭파하는 장면을 전국적으로 생중계하기도 하였으나, 그 결정이 과연 옳았던 것인가에 대해서는 지금까지도 여전히 의견이 분분하다.

부지

프로젝트의 부지는 통일된 한국이라는 전제하에서의 평양이다. 평양은 북한 정부에서 유일하게 공식적으로 대외적인 미디어를 통해 공개하고 있는 도시이다. 마치 북한의 거대한 모델 하우스와 같은 평양에는 그들의 사상과 지도자에 대한 찬양을 위해 의도적으로 설치된 수 없이 많은 상징물과 건축물이 즐비하다. 평양은 시민들의 개인적인 기억의 장임은 물론이거니와 특히, 특정한 집단 기억으로 가득 차 있는 기억의 저장소이다. 만약 한국이 통일된다면, 평양이라는 도시공간은 기억의 여러 측면, 즉, 기억함, 망각함, 재생산함 등의 여러 담론을 건축과 도시설계적인 시각으로 논해 볼 수 있는 흥미로운 시험대가 될 수 있을 것이다.

평양 내에서도 프로젝트의 부지로 선정된 곳은 대동강 변에 위치한 김일성 광장이다. 평양의 심장부에 위치한 김일성 광장은 북한의 수많은 상징적, 정치적 행사들이 거행되는 중요한 장소이다. 프로젝트의 개괄적인 개념은 김일성 광장에 사람이 들어갈 수 있는 크기의 벽 구조(inhabitable wall structure)를 둘러치는 것이다. 이 프로젝트는 집단 기억과 개인 기억이라는 두 가지 방향에서 논의할 수 있다.

집단 기억

제안하는 프로젝트의 건축물은 평양의 도시 전경들을 담아내는 전망대가 되어, 도시의 상징적 랜드마크와 장소들의 이미지가 집중되는 중심점이 된다. 도시의 관망자로서 이 건축물은 기존 도시 구조와 자연경관 등의 중요성을 강조하고 도시의 전반적인 전경을 보존한다.

또한, 이 건물은 그 기념비적인 규모로 인해 그 자체로 도시의 상징물이 된다. 도시의 새로운 상징으로서 이 프로젝트는 통일 한국의 평양에 새롭게 재생산될 기억들을 머금을 저장고가 되는 것이다. 따라서 도시의 집단 기억의 기준점으로서 이 건축물은 도시 개발로 인한 건축 환경의 급격한 변화를 견뎌야 할 것이다. 이를 위해 이 건물은 오히려 건축물의 물리적인 순간성을 이용하여 그 영구성을 달성한다.

일본의 신사(神社)는 그 물리적 건축물의 보존을 위해서 20년마다 같은 자리에 같은 재료로 그 건물을 똑같이 다시 짓는다. 때문에, 실제적인 건물의 수명은 20년이 채 안 되었을지라도, 그 건물의 개념적 존재는 수천 년을 이어갈 수 있을 것이다. 또한, 이 과정을 통해, 건물을 다시 짓는 이러한 행위는 그 자체로 하나의 의식이자 풍습으로 승화된다. 이러한 의식은 건축물의 역사적 보존이라는 측면을 넘어, 집단 기억의 보존이라는 개념에서 큰 의미가 있다. 이 프로젝트 또한 25년마다 해체되어서 다른 부지에 새롭게 조립되는 시스템을 차용한다. 한 세대의 시간이 흐름에 따라 건물은 도시 내의 다른 위치에 때로는 다른 비율로 건축되면서 계속해서 도시와 그 시민의 집단 기억의 기준점으로서 남아 있을 것이다.

이를 위해 이 건물은 서로 다른 몇 개의 유닛을 조합하여 건축하는 시스템으로 디자인된다. 각각의 유닛이 서로 간에 조합되는 방식에 따라 건물의 벽 구조, 동선 등의 내부 구조는 다르게 형성된다. 유닛이 조합되는 형태에 따라 건물의 공간적 구성이 달라지고, 이로 인해 건물의 건축 과정의 중요도가 더욱 강조되고, 그 자체가 하나의 의식이 된다.

또한, 이 프로젝트는 새로운 집단 기억을 촉발, 재생산하는 기능을 가진다. 건물의 상징적인 존재감으로 인해, 이 건물이 둘러친 김일성 광장은 원래의 용도, 성격과는 다른 행사 및 행위가 활성화될 것이고, 이로 말미암아 새로운 사회적·집단적 기억의 장이 될 수 있을 것이다.

개인 기억

개인 기억의 보존을 위해 이 건물은 이미지를 투영시킨 건축 공간을 걸어 다니는 기억의 궁전법을 이용한다. 하나의 계단과 벽체 일부로 구성된 기본 단위를 회전시키고 반전시켜 열 개의 서로 다른 유닛을 만든다. 이 열 개의 유닛 중 네 개를 결합하면 하나의 방이 되며, 그로 인해 이 방은 최대 4개의 서로 다른 계단과 각기 다른 형태의 벽 구조를 가지게 된다.

이러한 원리로 방을 구성하게 되면 그 경우의 수로 인해 수많은 방의 조합이 생겨나며, 각각의 방은 고유의 계단 구조와 벽 구조를 가진다. 각각의 방을 이해하는 데에 있어 기억의 기술 중 하나인 "Mnemonic Major System(기억 메이저 시스템)"을 차용한다. 메이저 시스템은 숫자를 기억하기 쉽게 위해 고안된 기억의 기술 중 하나인데, 숫자를 로마 알파벳의 자음으로 인식하고 사이사이에 자유롭게 모음을 끼워 넣어 전체 숫자를 친숙한 낱말로 변환시키는 원리를 가진다. 기본적으로 우리의 지각이 숫자보다는 이미지를 기억하는데 더 효과적이라는 것에 착안한 기억 체계이다. 예를 들어, "파이"로 불리는 무리수 "3.1415927"을 기억할 때, 그 숫자들을 "MTR, TL, PNK"로 인식하고, 이어 모음을 자유롭게 조합하여 "MeTeoR TaiL PiNK(유성 꼬리 분홍색)"이라고 변환할 수 있다. 따라서 파이를 기억하려는 사람은 곧바로 분홍색 꼬리를 가진 유성의 이미지를 떠올리며, 숫자를 기억할 수 있다. 프로젝트 부지가 한국에 있다는 점을 유의하여 필자는 로마 알파벳으로 구성된 메이저 시스템을 한글로도 바꾸어 생각해 보았는데, 예를 들어 위의 3.1415927과 같은 경우 한글 자음 "ㅁㄷㄹ, ㅌㅇ, ㅍㄴㄱ"으로 인식할 수 있고, 모음과 조합하면 "모델 땅 판교"등과 같이 낱말을 꾸밀 수 있다.

위의 메이저 시스템을 이 프로젝트에 이용하면, 열 개의 서로 다른 유닛을 0부터 9까지의 숫자로 볼 수 있고 결국, 방의 구조를 읽어내면 그것을 특정 낱말, 그리고 이미지로 변환할 수 있게 된다. 말하자면 이는 건축의 요소가 기호학적으로 해석될 수 있다는 것이다. 결국 이 원리를 이용하면 방 안에 들어서서 방을 둘러보고는 특정한 이미지를 떠올릴 수 있게 되는 것인데, 이는 앞서 설명한 기억의 궁전법을 적용할 수 있는 조건을 마련해 준다. 특히 이 같은 경우에는 경험자가 공간에 투영시킬 임의의 이미지를 생각할 필요 없이 공간 자체로부터 이미지가 생성되는 것이다. 따라서 물리적인 건축 공간은 그 공간의 해석을 통해 생성된 낱말의 가상적 이미지와 결합하게 되며, 이 건물의 내부를 걸으며 방과 방을 차례대로 통과하는 건물의 경험자는 각각의 방마다 새로운 이미지를 투영시키며 마치 하나의 이야기를 만들어 내듯 공간 구조를 순서대로 기억할 수 있는 것이다. 공간을 기억하는 이러한 과정은, 기억을 효과적으로 할 수 있도록 개개인의 머리를 훈련시키는 측면 뿐 아니라 기억하는 행위 자체의 중요성을 환기시켜주는 상징적인 행위로서의 의의를 가진다. 이 뿐 아니라, 건물 내의 공간을 기억해 그 공간이 익숙해지고 난 뒤에는, 각자의 개인적인 기억을 투영시킬 수 있는 개인 기억의 저장소로고 사용할 수 있을 것이다.

마지막으로, 각 방을 구성하는 계단을 실제로 타고 올라가면, 경험자는 전체의 건물이 도시를 전망하는 외부공간에 도달하게 되는데, 이때 경험자는 건물 내부에서 생성시킨 이미지를 도시 전경을 바라보며 그곳에 투영시킬 수 있게 된다. 그리고 도시의 전경은 개인 기억을 투영시키는 배경이 되며, 이 순간 개인 기억과 집단 기억의 경계가 허물어지게 된다.

Future Scenarios

The Memory Palace: Architecture as a Mnemonic Device | Jungon Kim

Future Scenarios

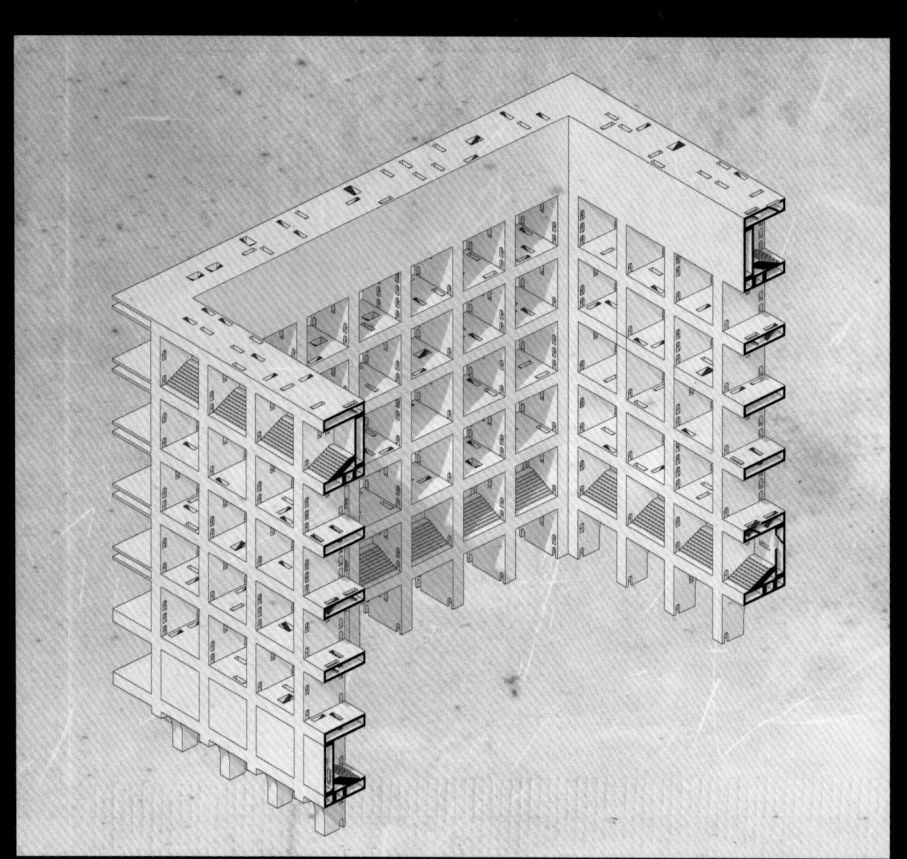

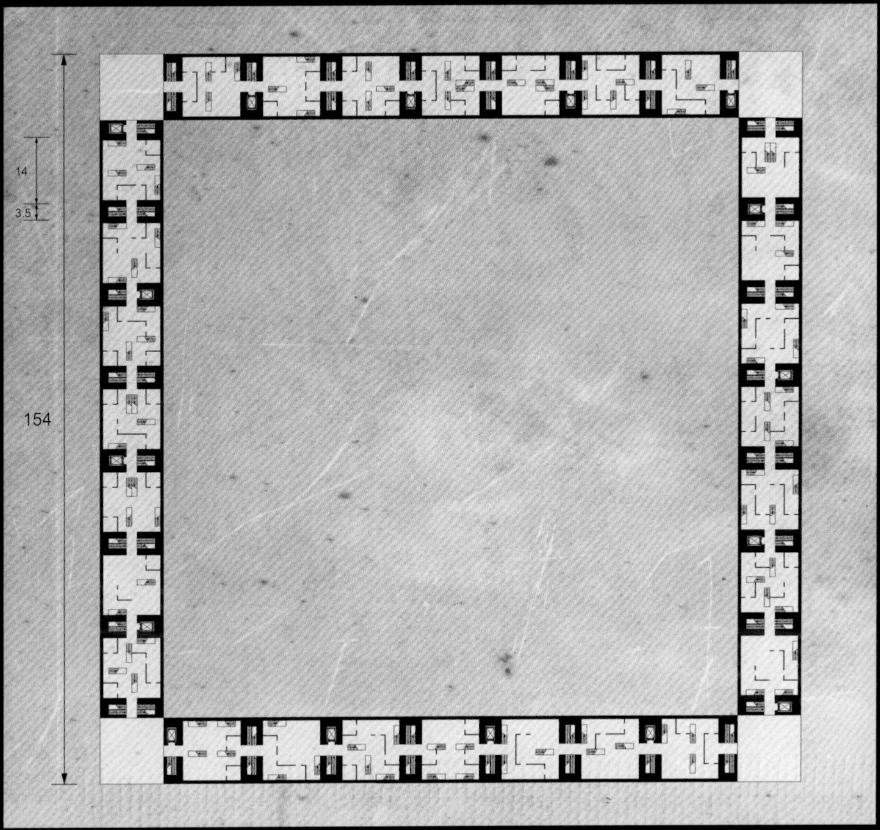

The Memory Palace: Architecture as a Mnemonic Device | Jungon Kim

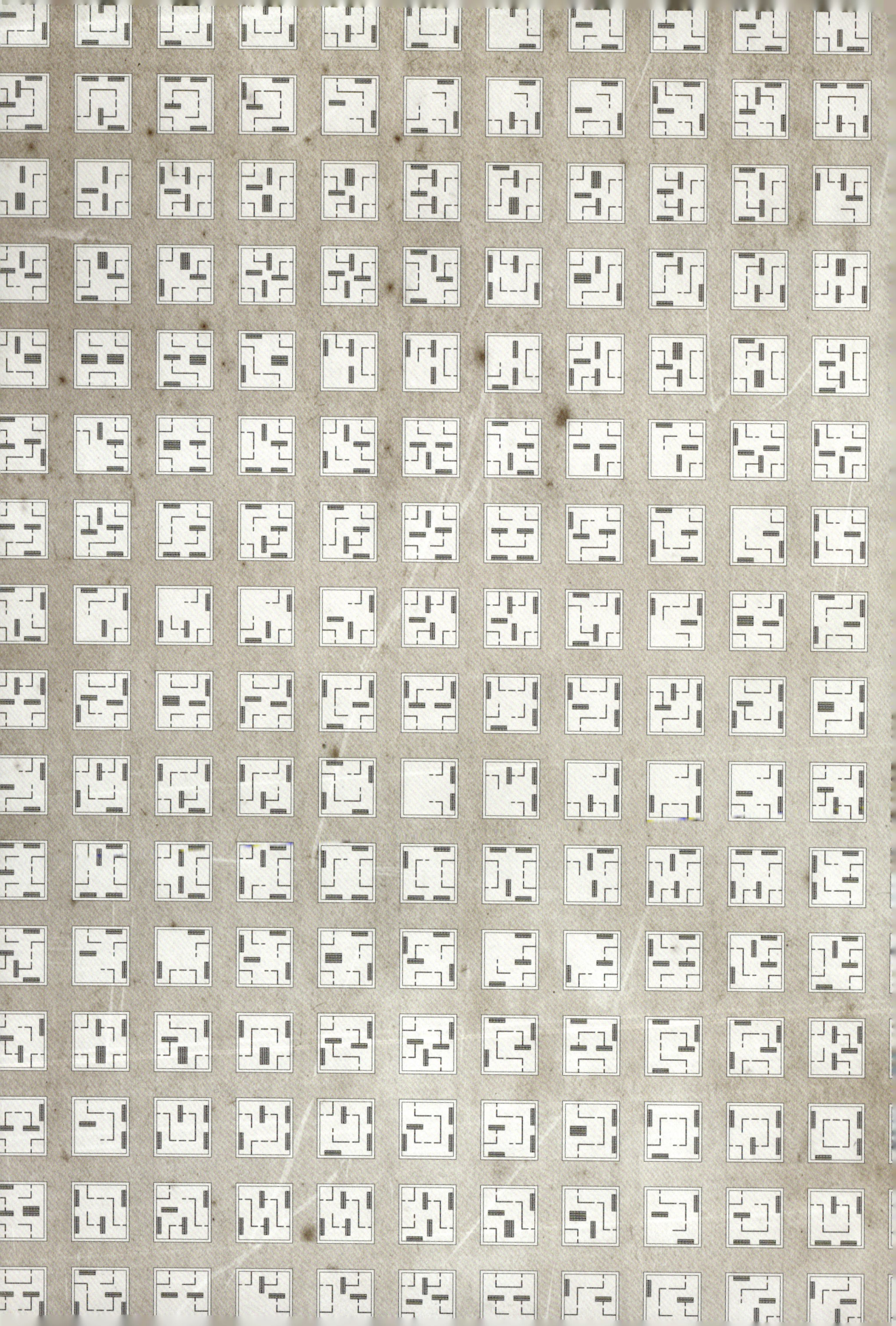

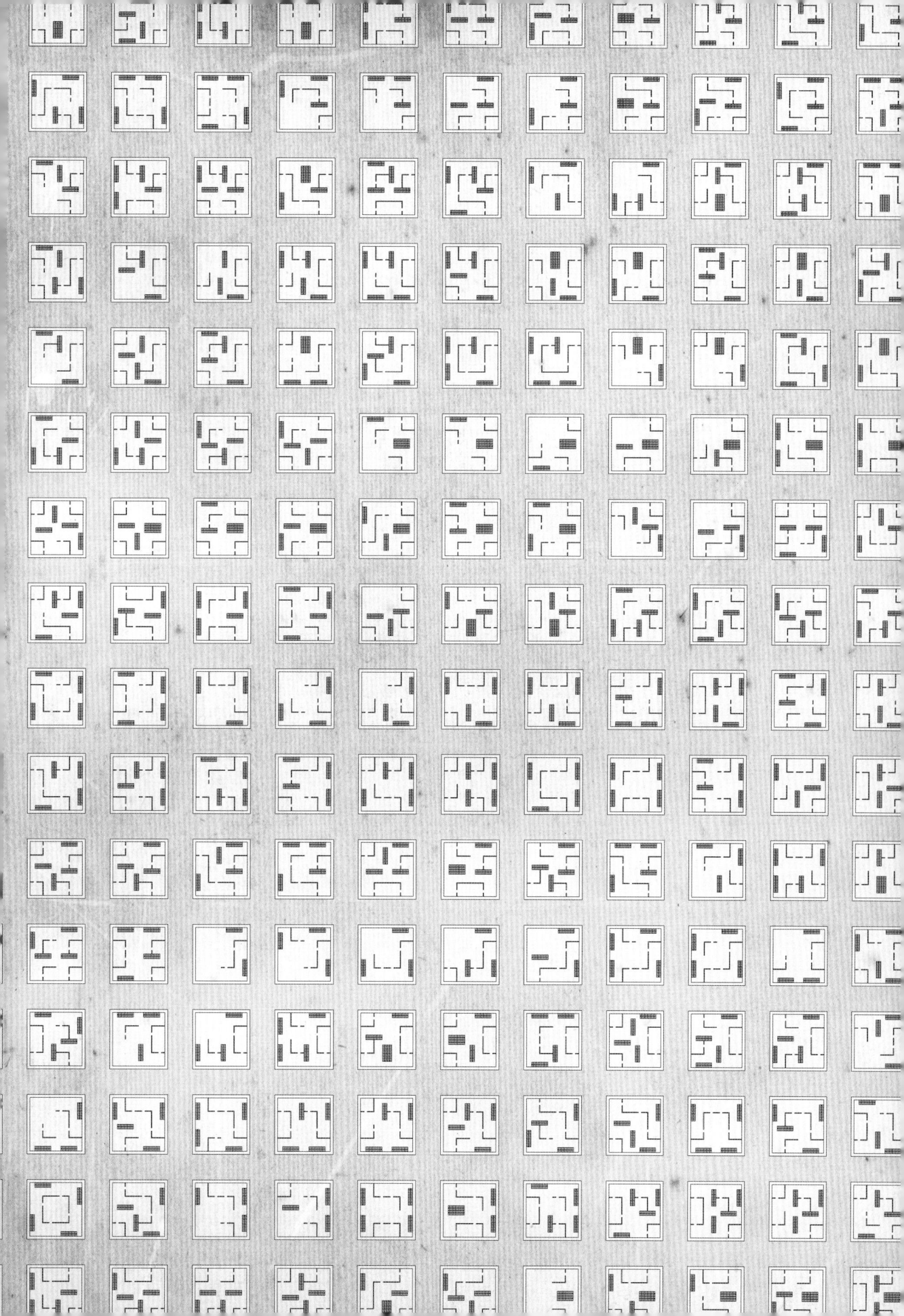

References

Benjamin, Walter. One-Way Street and Other Writings. London: NLB, 1979.

Boyer, M. Christine. The City of Collective Memory: Its Historical Imagery and Architectural Entertainments. Cambridge, MA: The MIT Press, 1994.

de Certeau, Michel. The Practice of Everyday Life. Los Angeles, CA: University of California Press, 1984.

da Costa Meyer, Esther. "The Place of Place in Memory". Spatial Recall: Memory in architecture and landscape. ed. Marc Treib. New York, NY: Routledge, 2009.

Eco, U. "Architecture and Memory". Via number 8, 1986.

Foer, Joshua. Moonwalking with Einstein. New York, NY: The Penguin Press, 2011.

Foucault, M. "Different Spaces". In Aesthetics, Method, and Epistemology. J.D. Faubion (Ed.). New York, NY: The New Press, 1998.

Fried, M. "Grieving for a Lost Home", in The Urban Condition: People and Policy in the Metropolis Ed. L J Duhl, New York, NY: Basic Books), 1963.

Halbwachs, Maurice. On Collective Memory. Chicago, IL: University of Chicago Press, 1992.

Hebbert, Michael. "The Street as Locus of Collective Memory," Environment and Planning D: Society and Space, Volume 23, 2005.

Huyssen, Andreas. Twilight Memories: Marking Time in a Culture of Amnesia. New York, NY: Routledge, 1995.

Hvass, Svend M., Ise – Japan's Ise Shrines – Ancient yet New. Copenhagen. Aristo Publishing, 1998.

Jacoby, Russell. Social Amnesia. Boston, MA: Beacon Press, 1975.

Kansteiner, W. "Finding Meaning in Memory: A Methodological Critique of Collective Memory Studies". History and Theory. Vol.41, No.2, 2002.

Lowenthal, David. The Heritage Crusade and the Spoils of History. England: Cambridge University Press, 1997.

Lyndon, Donlyn and Moore, Charles W., Chambers for a Memory Palace. Cambridge, MA: The MIT Press, 1994.

Lyndon, Donlyn. "The Place Memory". Spatial Recall: Memory in architecture and landscape. ed. Marc Treib. New York, NY: Routledge, 2009.

Nora, Pierre. Realms of Memory. New York, NY: Columbia University Press, 1996.

Otero-Pailos, Jorge. "Mnemonic Value and Historic Preservation". Spatial Recall: Memory in architecture and landscape. ed. Marc Treib. New York, NY: Routledge, 2009.

Pallasmaa, Juhani. "Space, Place, Memory, and Imagination: The Temporal Dimension of Existential Space". Spatial Recall: Memory in architecture and landscape. ed. Marc Treib. New York, NY: Routledge, 2009.

Rossi, Aldo. The Architecture of the City. Cambridge, MA: The MIT Press, 1982.

Rowe, Colin and Koetter, Fred. Collage City. Cambridge, MA: The MIT Press, 1978.

Sak, Segah. Memory and Place: From Ancient Individual Memory to Cyberspace as Contemporary Collective Memory. Bilkent University, Turkey, 2012.

Sheridan, M. P., "Jacopo Ragone and his Rules for Artificial Memory". Manuscripta. St. Louis, MO: St. Louis University Press, 1960.

Šik, Miroslav. And Now the Ensemble!. Zürich : Lars Müller, 2012.

Simpson, Adam. "The Art of Memory." National Geographic March 2012.

Sparrow, Betsy. "Google Effects on Memory: Cognitive Consequences of Having Information ar our Fingertips". Science, Vol.333, 2011.

Treib, Marc. "Yes, Now I Remember: An Introduction". Spatial Recall: Memory in architecture and landscape. ed. Marc Treib. New York, NY: Routledge, 2009.
Whitehead, Anne. Memory. New York, NY: Routledge, 2009.

Wikipedia contributors, "Mnemonic major system," Wikipedia, The Free Encyclopedia. http://en.wikipedia.org/wiki/Mnemonic_major_system (accessed May 8, 2013).

Yates, Frances A., The Art of Memory. Chicago, IL: University of Chicago Press, 1966.

Interview Source

Foer, Joshua and Cooke, Ed. "How Memory Works." (conversation, Serpentine Gallery for "Memory Marathon") 2012.

Image Source

Vionnet, Corinne . "Tiananmen Square." Photo Opportunities 2005-2013 ⟨http://i.huffpost.com/gadgets/slideshows/17596/slide_17596_244603_huge.jpg⟩
Yates, Frances. "Memory Theatre by Giulio Camillo," The Art of Memory (Chicago IL: The University of Chicago Press, 1966), 144. Fig.1.

NEW MICRO-DISTRICT

PRAUD (Dongwoo Yim + Rafael Luna)

—

Boston and Seoul based architectural design and research firm PRAUD was founded by Rafael Luna and Dongwoo Yim in 2010. They have been continuously developing contemporary architectural language "Topology & Typology" through competition projects, studio seminars and realized projects. This is an effort to develop the language of "contemporarism" that breaks the envelop of "Modernism." Meanwhile, their urban researches focus on the interplay between urban transformation and hybrid architectural typologies, and they develop their own research methodology through research and publications, such as "Pyongyang, and Pyongyang After," "I Want to be METROPOLITAN," and "North Korean Atlas." Their projects have been exhibited in various countries including Museum of Modern Art in New York, Parsons the New School for Design, and Venice Biennale, and they have lectured at many institutions such as Harvard University, Parsons the New School for Design, Dartmouth College, Freie Universität Berlin, Boston Society of Archiects, Seoul National University and Youngchoo Forum amongst others.

The aim of this project is to reevaluate how a micro-district, which is the primary urban residential system in Pyongyang, can be transformed when North Korea transitions to a market-economy and housing has to respond to new social and cultural demands.

The Micro-district is the key concept for structuring residential blocks in socialist cities. Similar to Pery's Neighborhood Unit theory, the micro-district is composed with residential units, service facilities and schools, so that a district can work as a basic unit for living. However, the unique factor of the Micro-District, compare to the neighborhood unit theory, is that it also has 'production' facilities within a unit, such as work shops, light factories and manufacturing facilities. The purpose of it is to have the shortest distance between living and working space as well as to have a full sustaining unit that not only consumes products, but also produces them. Therefore, the spatial ownership of a resident in a micro-district is not limited to the residential unit, it also includes the ownership of the working space.

This is a very important concept when we have to foresee how those micro-districts in North Korean cities will transform when they adopt a market-economy system because the "live-work" or the "consumption-production" relationship in a living area is the character of how people in Pyongyang have lived, and how the city has developed its built environment. Thus, to give the identity to the city, it is worth to keep the basic concept even when they have to be transformed in the near future.

The project should start by subdividing a mega-block micro-district into individual lots. As there is no concept of ownership of land, there is no subdivisions of lots in Pyongyang. When subdividing, each lot should be composed with current residential and production facilities to keep the concept of live and work in micro-district, instead of dividing the lot by programs. Hence, each lot, in the new micro-district, will have residential and office space. In the new era, as more white collar occupations are needed and manufacturing businesses are less welcome in residential area, offices are introduced as the replacement of production facilities. Also, new programs such as retails and commercial spaces, which used to emerge in few times in the socialist period, are introduced on the ground level to vibrate urban activities on the street. These facilities are mainly for the residents in the micro-district, but they become the sharing facilities attracting people from other areas as well.

In short, while it responds to new demands in the new era, the new micro-district keeps the concept of previous micro-districts in a way that it creates a independent neighborhood unit that is composed with residential spaces, work spaces, schools, clinics, amenities and retails. This is somewhat similar to the mixed-use development in capitalist countries, but different in the sense that instead of finding the most efficient way of using land by mixing programs, it creates an urban unit system that can sustain without being dependent on certain parts of the city. Therefore, it can realize a new spatial equality in a city because there is a less uneven distributions of urban programs, such as schools, amenities, and retails.

뉴 마이크로 디스트릭트

PRAUD (임동우 + 라파엘 루나)

—

서울과 보스톤을 기반으로 하고 있는 건축설계 및 도시연구 사무소 프라우드PRAUD는 건축가 임동우와 라파엘 루나가 2010년 공동 설립하였다. 프라우드의 건축작업은 공모전, 스튜디오, 실현 작품을 통하여 "토폴로지&타이폴로지"라고 하는 현대 건축언어를 디벨롭해나아가고 있다. 이는 모더니즘에서 벗어난 컨템포러리즘을 추구하고자 하는 건축적 노력이다. 또한 이들의 리서치는 도시의 변화와 건축 타이폴로지의 상호관계에 초점을 맞추며 여러 방법론들을 다양한 리서치와 출판 등을 통하여 개발하고 있다. 그들의 작업은 뉴욕 모마, 뉴욕 파슨스 대학, 베니스 비엔날레 등에서 전시된 바 있으며, 하바드 대학, 파슨스 대학, 다트머스 대학, 베를린 자유대학, 보스톤 건축가협회, 서울대학교, 영추포럼 등에서 강연된바 있다.

이 프로젝트는 북한이 새로운 시장경제 시스템을 도입하면서 평양의 주요 주거시설인 마이크로 디스트릭트 (주택소구역계획)가 어떻게 새로운 주민들의 요구와 사회의 요구, 문화적인 요구를 수용하며 바뀔 것인가를 제안하고 있다.

마이크로 디스트릭트는 사회주의 도시에서 주거시설을 구성하는 가장 기본적인 원리이다. 자본주의 도시에서 페리의 근린주구 이론과 같이, 마이크로 디스트릭트에서도 주거시설과 서비스 시설, 학교 등과 같은 프로그램들이 공존한다. 그러나 근린주구 이론과 구별되는 마이크로 디스트릭트만의 특징은 작업장이나 제조공장과 같은 '생산시설'이 함께 공존한다는 점이다. 이는 직장과 주거를 근접한 거리에 두기 위함과 동시에, 주거시설이 소비만 하는 영역이 아니라 생산을 하기도 하는 영역으로 설정함으로써 자생적인 유닛을 만들기 위함이다. 따라서 이 마이크로 디스트릭트 내에서의 개인의 공간 점유는 단순히 주거영역에만 해당하는 것이 아니라 작업장과 같은 생산영역도 포함하는 것이다.

이는 북한의 도시들이 시장경제 체제를 받아들이기 시작하는 시점에 마이크로 디스트릭트가 어떻게 변화할 것인지 예측해볼 때 매우 중요한 요소이다. 왜냐하면 이 직주근접의 원리, 혹은 생산과 소비영역의 공존은 평양 시민들이 그동안 살아온 방식이기 때문이며, 평양 구축환경의 특징이기 때문이다. 그러므로 이 도시의 전체성을 살리기 위해서는 새로운 시대에 새로운 주거시스템이 도입되더라도 이러한 개념을 지키는 것이 중요하다.

이 프로젝트는 기존의 마이크로 디스트릭트가 있는 메가 블록 (mega block)의 필지를 구획하는 것에서부터 시작한다. 평양에는 토지소유에 대한 개념이 없으므로, 필지의 구획 역시 존재하지 않는다. 새로운 필지를 구획할 때에는 프로그램 별로 필지를 구획하기보다는, 마이크로 디스트릭트의 직주근접의 개념을 유지하기 위해 주거시설과 생산시설을 함께 하나의 필지에 구획하도록 한다. 따라서 새로운 마이크로 디스트릭트에서의 각 필지에는 주거와 사무공간이 들어가게 된다. 시장경제 체제에서는 화이트칼라 직종이 더 많이 생겨나고, 주거시설과 맞붙어 있는 생산시설은 환영 받지 못하기 때문에 기존의 생산시설을 대체하는 프로그램으로서 사무영역이 제안되었다. 또한, 사회주의 국가에서는 쉽게 찾아보기 힘든 상업시설들을 가로 레벨에 제안함으로써 도시에 활력을 주고자 한다. 이들은 기본적으로는 같은 블록 안에 있는 주민들을 위한 시설이지만, 나아가 도시의 시설로서 다른 지역의 주민들과 공유되기도 한다.

결론적으로, 새로운 마이크로 디스트릭트는 새로운 시대의 새로운 요구사항을 반영함과 동시에 주거와 업무, 교육, 의료, 서비스, 상업 기능의 공존을 통해 기존 마이크로 디스트릭트가 추구하고자 했던 개념을 유지한다. 이는 자본주의 사회에서의 주상복합 등과 같은 복합시설 개발과 일면 유사점을 갖는다. 하지만 새로운 마이크로 디스트릭트의 가장 큰 특징은 단순히 효율적인 토지사용을 위해 프로그램들을 혼합하는 것이 아니라, 도시에서 다른 지역에 의존하지 않고도 어느 정도 독립적인 자생 단위를 만드는 방안으로 프로그램들을 혼합하여 제안한다. 그러므로 이는 도시에서의 공간 평등을 이룰 수 있는 한 방안이 된다. 학교, 상업, 기타 서비스 시설 등의 불균형한 분포로 인해 발생하는 도시 공간상의 위계를 최소화할 수 있기 때문이다.

Future Scenarios

SITE

The site is on the East side of Daedong River where it was mostly developed in the 1960s as part of the reconstruction from the Korean War in the 1950s. As it was one of the first areas that was recovered, it followed the 1953 Master Plan for Pyongyang, planned by Kim Jung Hee. Therefore, the site has a very well developed micro-district system with block housing type.

One of the reasons to have mid-rise and linear type housing at the periphery of a block is to have a perspectival effect of the street scape. The linear type housing gives horizontality in perspective so that it can highlight high-rise towers. As there is no concept of land value, Pyongyang could develop street scape based on the perception of pedestrian, and it is the basic logic of their urban design.

Therefore, in the new micro-district, it is also important to keep the horizontality and verticality within the district, not only for the balance between mid and high rise buildings, but also for the perception of pedestrian experiences.

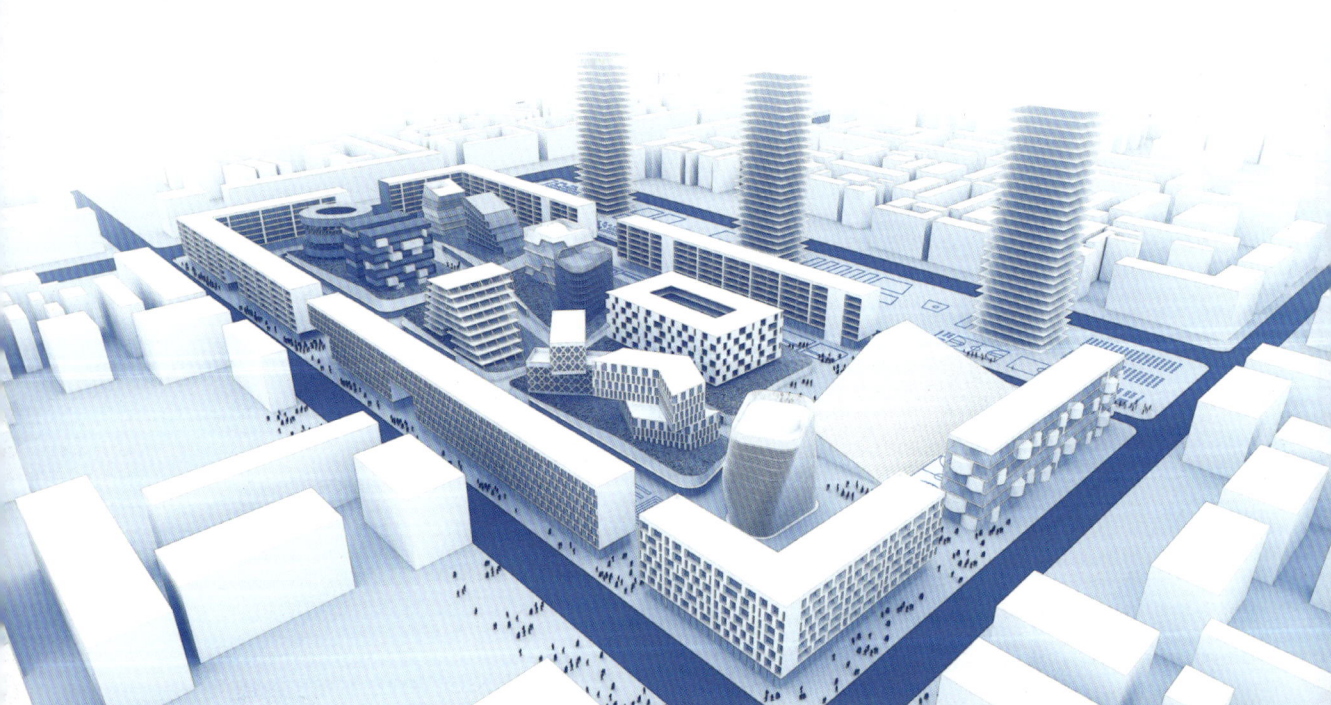

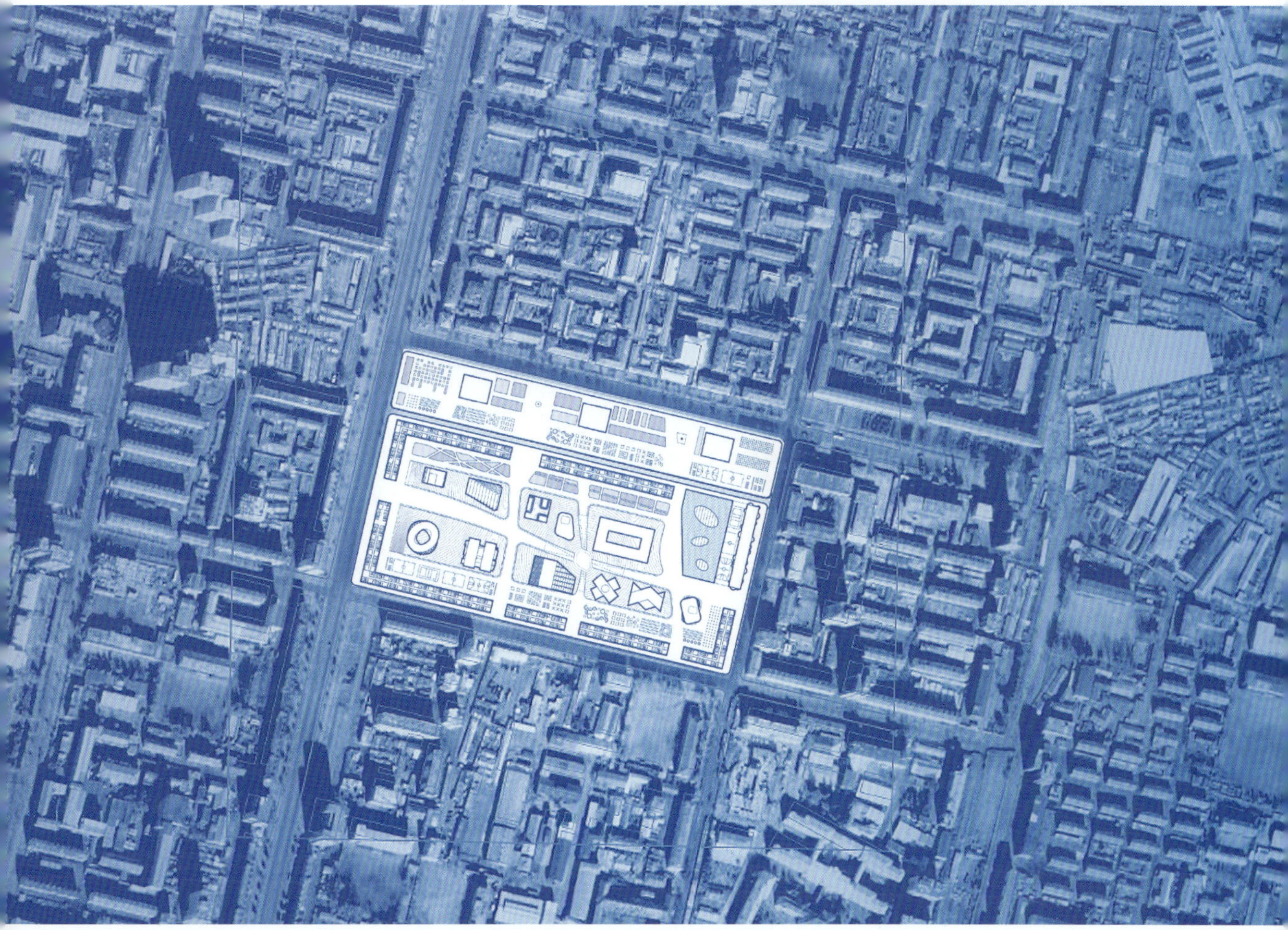

New Micro-District | PRAUD

Future Scenarios

COMPONENTS

1. Housing
The massing for Housing forms the perimeter of the block delineating the urban fabric and enclosing the district mixed programming.

2. Retail
The first retail component is at street level holding the housing mass.
A second retail component is in the form of Retail podiums that mark internal streets inside the micro-district. These podiums hold the commercial buildings on top.

3. Office
Office buildings sit on top the retail podiums, each individual from the other.

4. Factory
The micro-district allows for local manufacturing.

5. Cultural
Cultural facilities building.

6. Recreational Center
Entertainment programming like theatres or sports complex can be hybridized with the educational building.

7. Educational
School is integrated as a building fabric mass.

8. Hotel
With increase in the tourism industry, the micro district can incorporate hotels in order to maintain a diversity of occupants.

9. Highrise
Mixed use programs for density.

10. Landscape
Open parks are integrated with the highrise buildings to create space for the masses. (The Symbolic Space)

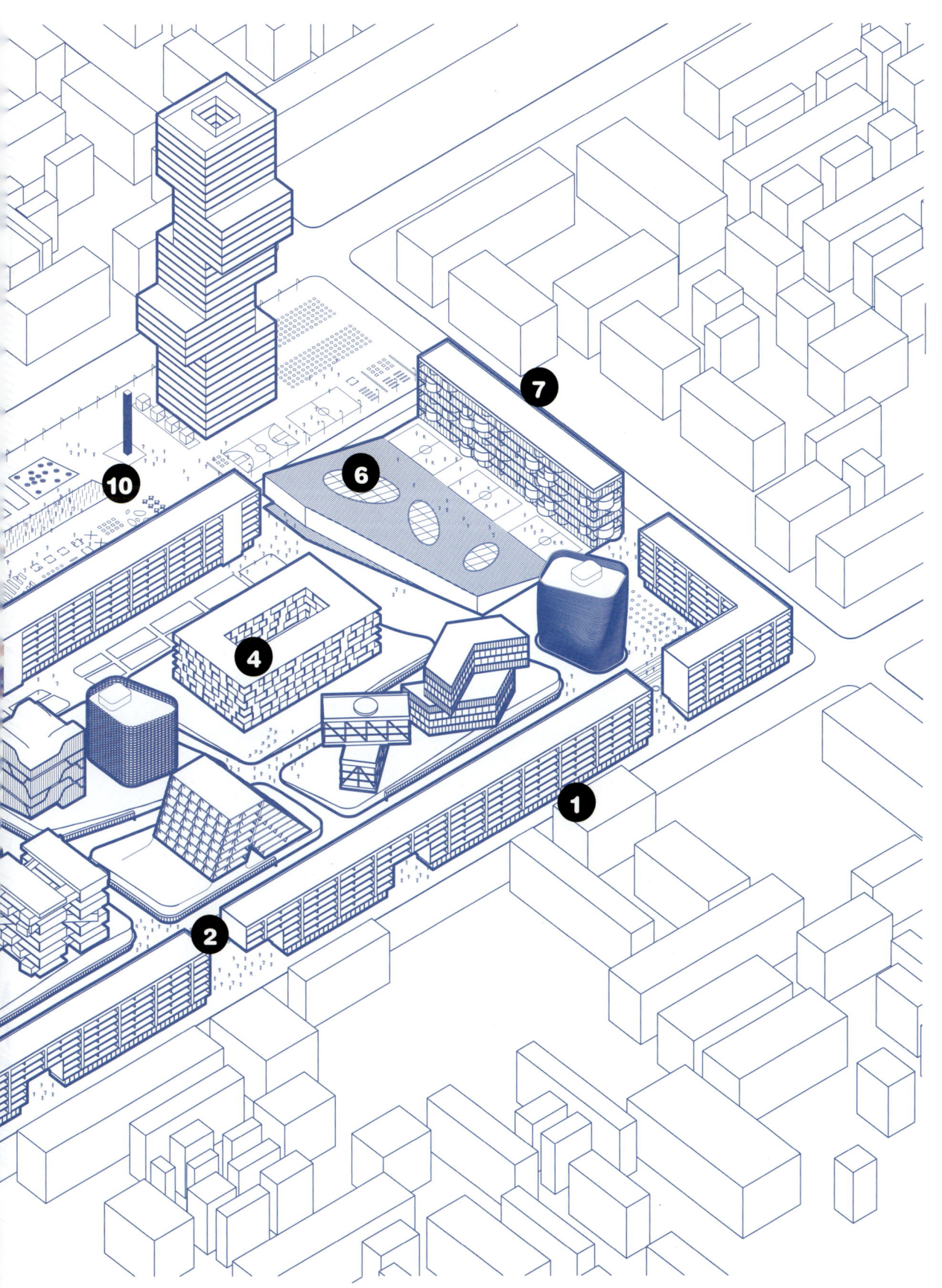

PERIMETER

Following the logic of existing micro-district, the perimeter of the new micro-district is demarcated by a line of housing buildings that follow design parameters of height and density, but allow for individual expression per building. This creates a block facade with diversity language while maintaining a legible urban fabric. Housing is raised above retail at street level.
It is in a way block housing type, but still has porosity that allows public access to the inner side of the micro-district block.

Future Scenarios 638

HOUSING

The housing buildings should allow for flexibility within the family unit. This means that a system is required that could adapt between single room dwellings to three room family dwellings. This can be achieved by having a grid of load bearing walls and service cores.

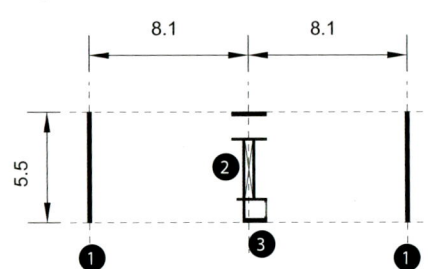

1. Load Bearing Walls
2. Service Core
3. Kimchi Closet

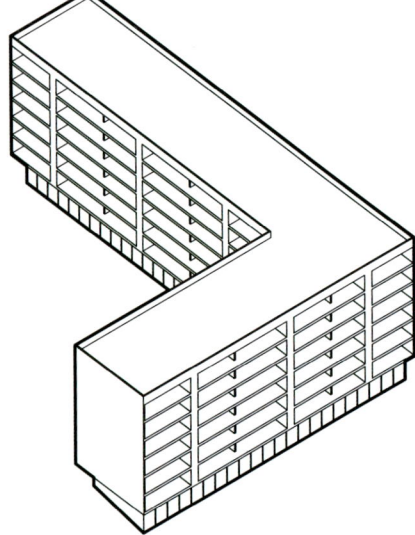

Axon of Housing System

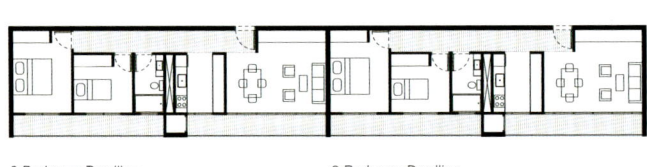

2 Bedroom Dwelling   2 Bedroom Dwelling

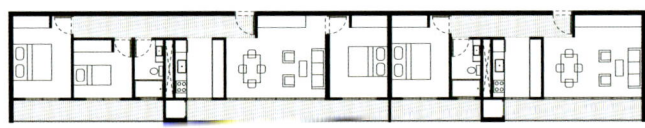

3 Bedroom Dwelling   1 Bedroom Dwelling

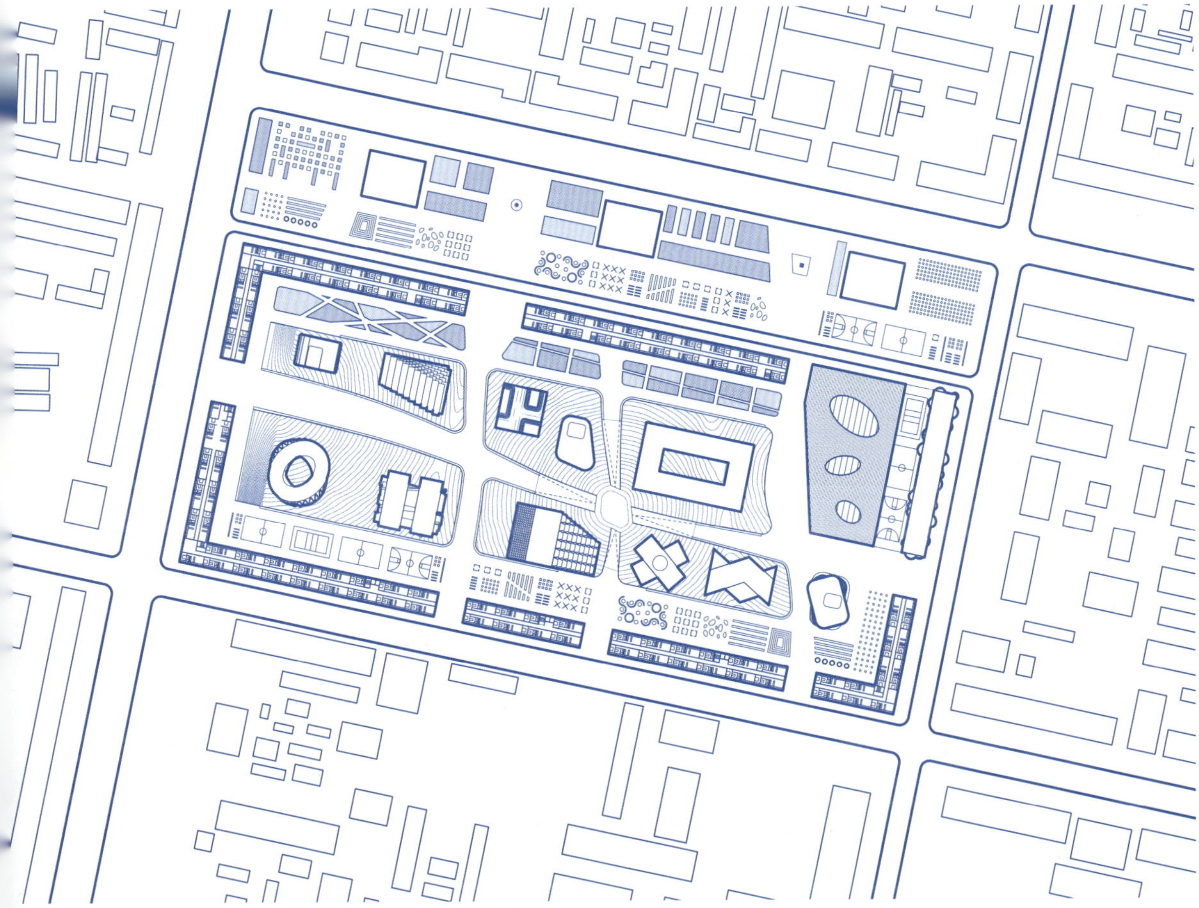

New Micro-District | PRAUD

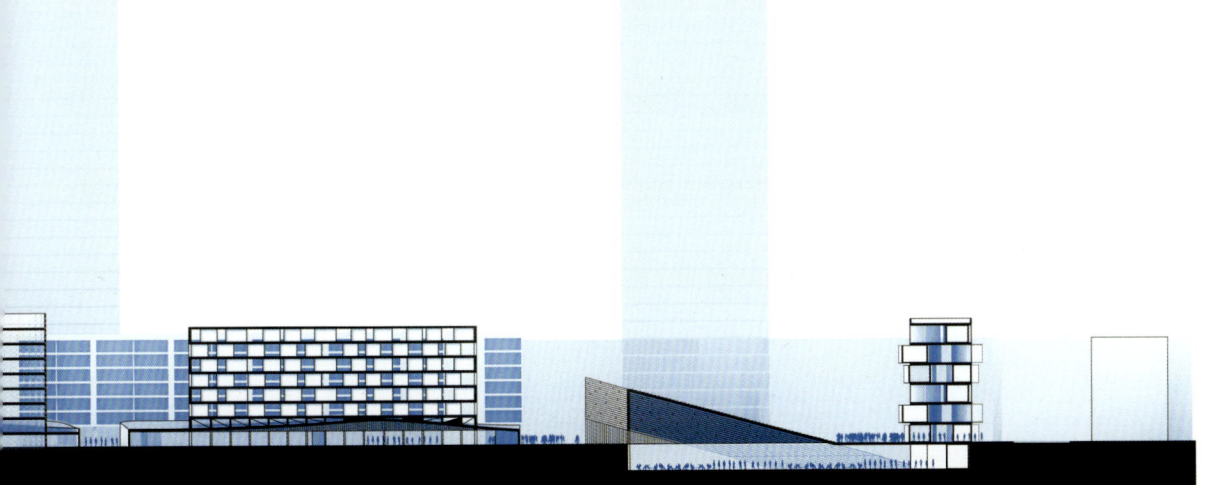

Scale = 1 : 4,000

INNER STREETS

The purpose of the micro-district is to create self-contained neighborhoods that provide all the neccesary amenities. To reevaluate this concept in a capitalist market, the inner part of the block will have to contain a diversity of typologies that provides not only the amenities like, pharmacies, schools, playgrounds, and groceries but also market

based rentable space for offices. Typologies like museums, hospitals, factories, recreational centers, can be distributed between different micro-districts. The inner streets should have a sense of urbanity and diversity with a pedestrian friendly appeal.

Future Scenarios   642

BUILDING TYPOLOGIES

Some of the building typologies presented in this scenario are a cross reference between market rate space and amenities. High-rise buildings are used as density boosters with no predetermined use. Buildings like the School/ Recreatinal Center porvide local facilities for the residents.
Market oriented real estate provides opportunities for the micro-districts to grow as clusters for startups, or existing businesses.

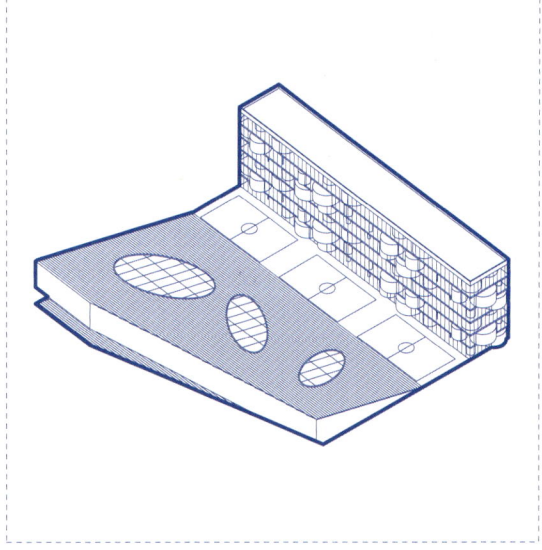

School and Recreational Center

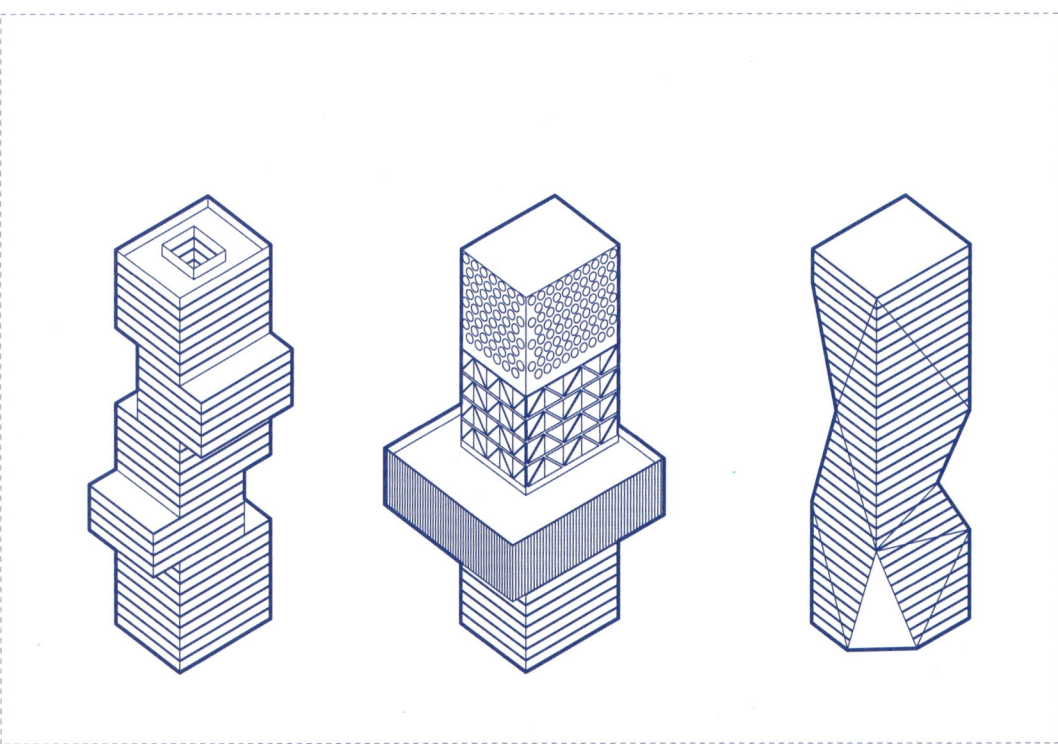

Highrise - Mixed Use

New Micro-District | PRAUD

1. Factory Building
2. Office
3. Office
4. Office
5. Lab
6. Hotel
7. Office
8. Office
9. Office
10. Office
11. Museum/ Cultural Center

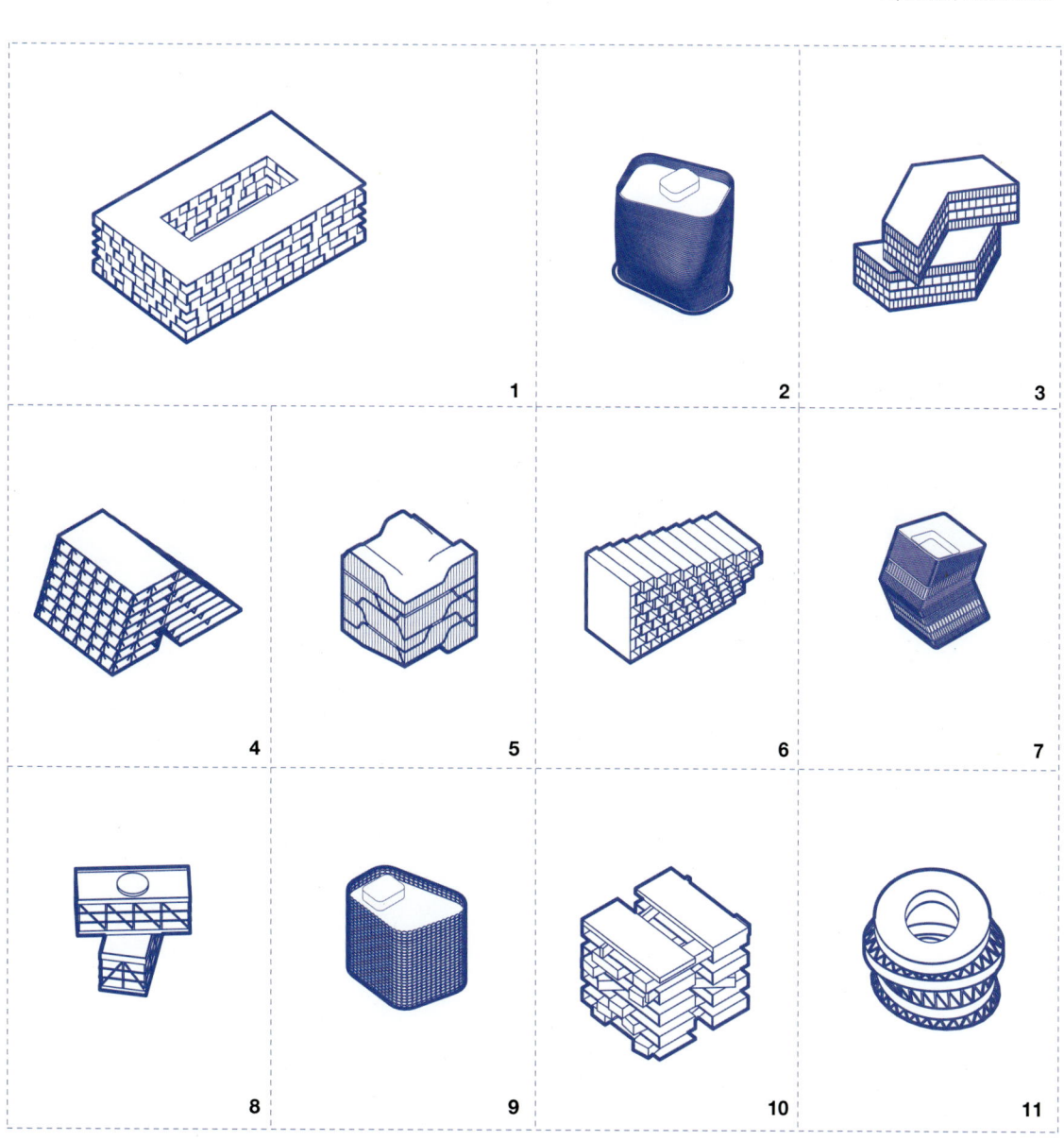

INDEX   **Contributing Authors**

C	Calvin Chua	page. 512
	Chong Ho Park	page. 530
D	David Matthew	page. 54
	Dongsei Kim	page. 104 · 522 · 566
	Dongwoo Yim	page. 8 · 192 · 404 · 502
	Doojin Hwang	page. 482
E	Eunhee Cho	page. 82
G	Gianluca Spezza	page. 34
H	Hye-Young Chung	page. 580
J	Jungon Kim	page. 610
P	PRAUD (Dongwoo Yim + Rafael Luna)	page. 628
R	Rafael Luna	page. 490
	Rainer Dormels	page. 20
S	Sangjun Lee	page. 70
	Sejin Rubella Jo & Soobin Lee	page. 596
	Seoyoung Kim	page. 60
	Sunggoo Yang	page. 572
Y	Yehre Suh	page. 538
	Yunha Lee	page. 384

Title